THE SHORT OXFORD HISTORY
OF THE MODERN WORLD

General Editor: J. M. ROBERTS

THE SHORT OXFORD HISTORY OF THE MODERN WORLD

General Editor: J. M. ROBERTS

THE CRISIS OF PARLIAMENTS: ENGLISH HISTORY 1509–1660
Conrad Russell

EMPIRE TO WELFARE STATE: ENGLISH HISTORY 1906–1985
Third Edition
T. O. Lloyd

THE OLD EUROPEAN ORDER 1660–1800
William Doyle

ENDURANCE AND ENDEAVOUR: RUSSIAN HISTORY 1812–1986
Third Edition
J. N. Westwood

THE LIMITS OF LIBERTY: AMERICAN HISTORY 1607–1980
Maldwyn A. Jones

THE BRITISH EMPIRE 1558–1983
T. O. Lloyd

MODERN INDIA: THE ORIGINS OF AN ASIAN DEMOCRACY
Judith M. Brown

BARRICADES AND BORDERS: EUROPE 1800–1914
Robert Gildea

REBELLIONS AND REVOLUTIONS: CHINA FROM THE 1800S TO THE 1980S
Jack Gray

BRITISH HISTORY 1815–1906
Norman McCord

THE EUROPEAN DYNASTIC STATES
1494–1660

—

RICHARD BONNEY

OXFORD UNIVERSITY PRESS
1991

Oxford University Press, Walton Street, Oxford OX2 6DP

Oxford New York Toronto
Delhi Bombay Calcutta Madras Karachi
Petaling Jaya Singapore Hong Kong Tokyo
Nairobi Dar es Salaam Cape Town
Melbourne Auckland
and associated companies in
Berlin Ibadan

Oxford is a trade mark of Oxford University Press

Published in the United States
by Oxford University Press, New York

British Library Cataloguing in Publication Data
(data available)

Library of Congress Cataloging in Publication Data
Bonney, Richard.
The European dynastic states, 1494-1660/Richard Bonney.
(The Short Oxford history of the modern world)
Includes bibliographical references and index.
1. Europe—History—1492-1648. I. Title. II. Series.
D228.B66 1991 940.2—dc20 91-60
ISBN 0-19-873022-5 (hardback)
ISBN 0-19-873023-3 (pbk.)

Typeset by Cotswold Typesetting Ltd, Cheltenham
Printed in Great Britain by
Bookcraft (Bath) Ltd
Midsomer Norton, Avon

GENERAL EDITOR'S PREFACE

BOTH in Great Britain and in the United States, the idea that students may wish—and may even be expected—to study the history of parts of the world other than their own has steadily gained ground in the last decade. In part this is a reflection of changing social and political concerns: we are coming to realize that we live in one world, and believe we ought therefore to know more about parts of it hitherto neglected, or comparatively neglected, by historians bred in the western tradition of scientific history. In part, too, it reflects changes in the available source-material. Whatever its origin, though, the impulse is beginning to make its mark in schools and colleges. They now need books about Latin America, Africa, or Asia on the scale and at the level of those which in the past introduced their students to European or English history. This is one of the considerations which has shaped the design of this series, which will include such books, as well as others on more familiar and traditional areas of study.

In addition, up-to-date scholarship in English and European history, too, must be made available to each generation of students. Consequently, this series is tripartite. Four volumes in it are devoted to modern European history, in which the British Isles are treated as a part of European society as a whole. A second group of four volumes is more specialized, being confined to English history. The third, larger group contains introductory volumes, covering fairly long periods, about areas and countries which are only now beginning to be studied by others than specialists. Some of these will be defined regionally—the projected volume on Latin America, for example. Those on the United States and Russia, on the other hand, limit themselves to a single legal entity as, in a rather different sense, does another on the British Empire and Commonwealth. In each case, the books in this stream are distinguished by being about a big and important topic for which good, up-to-date introductory manuals are not yet easily available.

The unity which binds these books together, although they will have different levels of details and scope, is that they are all about the 'modern world' referred to in the title of the series. This does not mean that the chronological limitations of each book are the same. Conventionally, histories of different countries line up all their runners at approximately the same starting-gate and get them off together, whether in 1400, 1500, 1600, or any other dramatic, convenient, or merely 'significant' moment. This series follows a different scheme. The latest era of world history is here defined not chronologically but thematically. It is the era in which the fundamental institutions of modern European society first take shape and then spread round the world.

Some institutions of European origin are now so widespread that we too readily take them for granted—the sovereign national state, for example. Yet even in Europe it is only a recent innovation and in many parts of the world the national state did not appear until after 1945. Formally representative political systems (whether real or fictitious) are another of Europe's institutional exports to the world, and there are economic systems, too (such as capitalism). So are European ideologies, such as Marxist communism or Christianity. In all these instances (and many others could be cited), we have examples of the process by which European gradually became World civilization. Sometimes this has seeded new examples of developed 'Western' societies; sometimes it has led to striking disruptions of traditional and eventually to altogether new institutions and cultural forms. The process, however it ends, defines an era by making a break with the past, but does so at different times in different countries: defensible dates could be about 1500 in west European history, about 1800 in the case of Russia, and even later in the history of China. These mark epochs in the history of different countries and regions in which can be discerned the beginnings of processes which eventually tie them into the single world in which we live.

Besides registering different historical rhythms, the books in *The Short Oxford History of the Modern World* do not all have the same pattern. Differences in their structure are required to bring out differences of national and regional life. But each volume expresses a deliberate effort to incorporate the research and thinking which has recently changed the conventional shape of historical writing. The core of a good history must be the provision of the essential information which is necessary to the exercise of historical imagination and judgement. But ideas about what information is essential have been changing recently, for example because of a new emphasis on society and its structure at the expense of the traditional political narrative. Historians and their public—which includes examiners—have begun to think that it may be more revealing to study, say, the growth of cities in nineteenth-century England and its repercussions, than, say, the party struggle. This is only one example of the recent rediscovery of the old idea that history is more than past politics. Many of the authors in this series are young scholars who, because of their own research interests, are familiar with what is going on at the frontier of current historical work. They and their colleagues will seek to absorb into their accounts the research conclusions expressed in the flood of social, cultural, demographic, and other recent monographs.

General books have long sought to reduce to manageable thinking such detailed scholarship, but the recent crumbling of the boundaries which delimited and the landmarks which guided historical work has made this all the more desirable. The conventional separation of English and European history is now an encumbrance to understanding some of the processes in which this country was as much involved as any Continental state (industrialization, for instance). Different views are now taken, too, of certain traditionally important dates. 1917, for example, or 1941, can easily be defended as more significant breaks in the continuity of European history than 1914 or 1939. In some places, old guidelines seem almost to have disappeared altogether as new evidence has been made available and research has addressed itself to old evidence in new ways. Other changes are demanded by changing perspectives. More fundamentally, the need for new general accounts reflects a basic truism about history: that it is theoretically boundless, a continuing debate, and that historians in each generation re-map and re-divide its subject-matter in accordance with their interests and the demands of their society.

This series tried to provide a new map. It is bound to be provisional; that is of the nature of general history. But that is reconcilable with scholarly standards and imaginative presentation. Only by combining those qualities can it provide the authoritative guidance which each generation of readers needs if it is to pick its way through the flood of specialized studies now pouring from what has become one of our major cultural industries.

J.M.R.

PREFACE

THE choice of the title *The European Dynastic States* may at first appear rather odd and even antiquated for a history of early modern Europe. The risk is that it seems to impose an old-fashioned approach on the complex interaction of economic, social, cultural and governmental change in the key historical period analysed here. No such implication is intended. While not all early modern European states were truly dynastic within the definition given in this book, the sense of dynasty was of enormous importance everywhere. Even republican regimes such as Venice or the United Provinces acknowledged this, albeit tacitly, by drawing up specific rules precluding the emergence of a ruling family. At Venice, this led to the institution of a figurehead chief of state (the Doge) and, in the United Provinces, to an attempt in 1654 to exclude on a permanent basis members of the house of Orange from any right to rule in the state. Although these two states appeared to have secured their 'freedom' by avoiding princely rule, there was always a danger of reversion. Almost everywhere else in Europe, ruling dynasties were in place by 1660 if not by 1494, enjoying greater or lesser power in accordance with the prevailing rules of succession, the governmental system and the cultural values both of the dynasty and its subjects.

Even the term 'state' in the early modern period is very hard to interpret. Where did the state begin and where did it end, in terms of political realities, given the absence of a clear distinction between what was 'public' and what was 'private'? When does the 'modern' state emerge as a permanent, impersonal, coercive power which stands apart from the private concerns of a ruling dynasty? There are no simple answers to these questions. Indeed, the year 1989–90 in which this book was completed might seem the worst possible date to attempt an answer, since it also saw the launching of a four-year scientific programme on the origins of the modern state under the auspices of the European Science Foundation. Seven teams of European scholars have been set the task of considering the themes of war and competition between state systems; economic systems and state finance; the legal instruments of power; ruling classes and agents of the state; representation, resistance and sense of community; the individual in political theory and practice; and iconography, propaganda and legitimation. The mass of interpretation and documentation that will be published in 1993 would, no doubt, have changed the final shape and content of this book had it been available in 1989. Certainly, the scholarly community as a whole will not be able to disregard the findings of this joint enterprise: it will no longer be sufficient for comparative European history, based on original research, to be done by one historian in the traditional way.

Yet collective research is neither easy to launch nor to bring to fruition. There are some, indeed, who would argue that it is inherently unsatisfactory and that the lonely furrow of the solo historian is the prerequisite of good scholarship. No such claim is made by the present author, who is only too aware that this book inevitably suffers from some of the limitations of evidence and vision which are the consequences of a one-man effort. It is also a book conceived as part of a series, to parallel Conrad Russell's study of English history in the period, *The Crisis of Parliaments*, and to precede William Doyle's study of European history in a later period, *The Old European Order.* It is hoped that the interpretation offered by the book, based on twenty years of teaching early modern European history and on the insights provided by detailed research into the governing structure of France, will provide a useful perspective on a number of European themes of significance in the period between 1494 and 1660. Much of it results from a reflection on the writings of others. Never before has there been so much historical output of such high quality; the intellectual debt owed to the historians of early modern Europe in the author's own generation is obvious. The author also generously acknowledges the assistance of colleagues in several universities who have read draft sections of the book, and answered specific questions of detail. Because the historiography of European history is continually evolving, in one sense this study can never be finished: but at some point a book must appear, and the departure of the author abroad for two years' intensive study on other projects has concentrated the mind wonderfully. It remains only to thank my wife Margaret for her painstaking work on the maps; to thank her and my parents for their patient reading and rereading of the text and to dedicate the book to my daughters, Katherine and Sarah Bonney.

Richard Bonney

Paris
January 1990

CONTENTS

Lists of Maps and Tables   xiv

Chronology   xv

Lists of the Main European Rulers   xxxi

1. Religious Divisions in Early Modern Europe   I

   1.1 The False Dawn: Attempts at Reform within a United
     Catholic Church   2

   1.2 The Lutheran Message and Its Opponents, 1517–1546   15

   1.3 The Spread of the Early Reformation   29

   1.4 Calvin and the Spread of 'Reformed Protestantism'   43

   1.5 The Counter-Reformation   56

PART ONE
THE DEVELOPMENT OF THE EUROPEAN DYNASTIC STATES

2. Europe in the Age of the Italian Wars, 1494–1559   79

   2.1 The Expansion of France, 1494–1515   80

   2.2 The Opponents of French Expansion: Ferdinand of
     Aragon and Maximilian of Habsburg   88

   2.3 The Reign of Francis I of France, 1515–1547   99

   2.4 The Ascendancy of Charles V   109

   2.5 The Last Phase of the Valois–Habsburg Struggle   124

3. Europe in the Age of the Wars of Religion, 1559–1618   131

   3.1 The Reign of Philip II   131

   3.2 The Civil Wars in the Low Countries   145

   3.3 The French Wars of Religion   163

   3.4 The New Threat to Peace, 1598–1618   179

4. The Struggle for European Hegemony, 1618–1660   188

   4.1 The Thirty Years' War: the Holy Roman Empire and the
     Austrian Habsburg Hereditary Lands, 1618–1648   188

   4.2 The Conflict between the Dutch Republic and Spain,
     1621–1648   203

   4.3 The Survival of Spanish Habsburg Power, 1598–1665   214

   4.4 The Resurgence of France, 1610–1661   224

5. The Outsiders of Europe — 242

   5.1 Denmark and Sweden: the Struggle for Baltic Supremacy — 243

   5.2 Poland-Lithuania and Sweden: Imperial Conflict and Dynastic Struggle — 256

   5.3 Muscovy and Poland-Lithuania: the Attempted 'Gathering of the Russian Lands' — 272

   5.4 Ottoman Supremacy in South-East Europe and the Middle East — 285

PART TWO

THE STRUCTURE OF THE EUROPEAN DYNASTIC STATES

6. The Rise of European Absolutism — 305

   6.1 European Political Thought — 306

   6.2 The Ruler and His Parliaments — 316

   6.3 Royal Administration — 330

   6.4 The State and Military Revolution — 345

   6.5 The State and Financial Revolution — 352

7. Population and Social Structure — 361

   7.1 The People of Europe — 363

   7.2 Agrarian Society — 375

   7.3 Agrarian Rebellion — 387

   7.4 Urban Society — 397

   7.5 Urban Revolt — 407

8. The European Economy — 417

   8.1 The 'Tyranny of Gold and Silver' — 418

   8.2 The European Price Revolution — 424

   8.3 Merchant Banking and the Mechanisms of International Payments — 429

   8.4 The Struggle for European Commercial Primacy in the Old World and the New — 438

   8.5 Constraints on the Growth of Capitalism — 454

9. Court, Culture and Community — 474

   9.1 The Nature and Development of Court Patronage — 474

   9.2 The Iconography and Propaganda of Power — 486

   9.3 Popular Literature and Folk Custom — 494

   9.4 The New Crime of Witchcraft — 502

9.5 The Rise of European Rationalism   512

10. Conclusion: the European Dynastic States   524

Maps   532

Sources for Quotations   542

Guide to Further Reading   572

Index   599

MAPS

1. The Holy Roman Empire   532
2. The Austrian Habsburg Lands   533
3. The French Provinces   534
4. The Italian Peninsula during the Italian Wars   535
5. The Iberian Peninsula   536
6. The Low Countries   537
7. The Baltic   538
8. Poland-Lithuania   539
9. Muscovy   540
10. The Ottoman Lands   541

TABLES

7.1 Population estimates for certain European countries (millions)   365
7.2 Number of towns with a population of over 10,000 inhabitants   398
7.3 Total urban population in towns of over 10,000 inhabitants
   (in thousands)   398
7.4 Percentage of the total population resident in towns of over
   10,000 inhabitants   398
8.1 Index numbers of inflation in 1601–1620   425
8.2 Index numbers of certain selected grain products   426
8.3 Selected comparison between the grain index and general
   commodity index (in index numbers)   427
8.4 Selected comparison of 'real wages' (in index numbers)   427

CHRONOLOGY

1494 Charles VIII of France invades Italy. Overthrow of the Medici and re-establishment of the Florentine Republic. Treaty of Tordesillas between Portugal and Spain partitions the New World into rival empires.

1495 Kingdom of Naples surrenders to Charles VIII. Formation of a Holy League against France under Pope Alexander VI and withdrawal of Charles VIII from Italy. Establishment of the Imperial 'circles' or defence groupings in the Empire; abortive scheme to establish a universal tax (the Common Penny) in the Empire.

1496 Refusal of Polish nobility to renew union with Lithuania.

1497 Death of Don Juan, heir to the Castilian throne: prospects of a female succession on the death of Isabella.

1498 Execution of Savonarola at Florence on grounds of heresy.

1499 Louis XII of France invades Milan. Outbreak of war between Venice and the Ottoman Turks. Swiss Confederation defeats the forces of the Swabian League.

1500 Treaty between Louis XII and Ferdinand of Aragon to partition the kingdom of Naples. Ivan III of Muscovy attacks Lithuania.

1501 Establishment of the Safavid state in Persia by Shah Isma'il I. Charter of Mielnik, confirming the inalienable right of the Polish nobleman to resist the king if he acted 'tyrannically'.

1502 Conclusion of war between Venice and the Ottoman Turks.

1503 Spanish victories over the French in the kingdom of Naples. Truce between Muscovy and Lithuania.

1504 French troops evacuate the kingdom of Naples. War of the Bavarian succession (or Landshut war): defeat of the Wittelsbach forces by the Swabian League.

1505 Louis XII purchases the investiture of the duchy of Milan from the Emperor Maximilian I. Statute of *Nihil novi* in Poland, by which the Chamber of Deputies representing the nobility ensures a veto on royal legislation.

1506 Invasion of Hungary by Maximilian of Habsburg to force his family's contingent rights of succession.

1507 Vasilii III of Muscovy attacks Lithuania.

1508 Formation of the League of Cambrai against Venice.

1509 Crushing French victory over Venice at Agnadello and occupation of most of Venetian territory.

1510 Portuguese capture Goa in India.

1511   Louis XII summons a church council to Pisa in the hope of deposing Pope
        Julius II. Outbreak of the Ottoman war of succession.

1512   Formation of a Holy League against France under Pope Julius II and
        French withdrawal from Italy. Fall of the republic and restoration of the
        Medici dynasty in Florence. The Pope summons the Fifth Lateran Council,
        which meets until 1517. Conquest of Upper Navarre by Ferdinand of
        Aragon.

1513   Swiss defeat a French attempt to reconquer the duchy of Milan.

1514   Capture of Smolensk by Muscovy. Selim I commands the Ottoman army in
        a decisive victory over the Shah of Persia at Chaldiran. Peasant uprising in
        Hungary.

1515   Francis I of France invades Milan, and wins a crushing victory over the
        Swiss at Marignano. Congress of Vienna, at which a dual dynastic union
        between the houses of Habsburg and Jagiellon is agreed.

1516   Francis I's victory in Italy consolidated by an agreement with the Papacy
        (the Concordat of Bologna). Ottoman army under Selim I invades Syria,
        captures Damascus and occupies Palestine. Capture of Algiers by the
        corsair captain Hayreddin (Khair ad-Din) Barbarossa. Habsburg succes-
        sion in Castile proclaimed by Charles of Ghent.

1517   Selim I commands the Ottoman army in a decisive victory over Mamluk
        Egypt. Luther publishes his ninety-five theses against indulgences. Peace of
        Cambrai between France, the Emperor and Castile.

1518   *Cortes* of Castile asks Charles to remain in the kingdom until an heir is
        born. Luther refuses to recant his views.

1519   Election of Charles (V) as King of the Romans (Emperor-elect).

1520   Luther excommunicated by Pope Leo X. Outbreak of the revolt of the
        Comuneros in Castile. The Swedish nobility under Gustavus Vasa rebel
        against Christian II of Denmark and Sweden; severe repression by
        Christian ('bloodbath of Stockholm'). Meeting between Francis I and
        Henry VIII at the Field of Cloth of Gold. Swabian League sells the
        occupied duchy of Württemberg to Charles V.

1521   Luther declared a notorious heretic at the diet of Worms. Ottoman army
        under Süleyman I captures Belgrade. Defeat of the Comunero revolt at
        Villalar. Charles V creates a separate Austrian inheritance for his brother
        Ferdinand, who is also appointed regent in the Holy Roman Empire.
        Habsburg–Papal army recaptures Milan from France.

1522   Complete collapse of the French position in Italy. Ottoman army under
        Süleyman I captures Rhodes. Truce in the war between Muscovy and
        Lithuania.

1523   Abortive revolt of the Constable of Bourbon in France. Henry VIII of
        England invades northern France. Christian II of Denmark deposed by the
        Danish nobility; ending of the Union of Kalmar with Sweden, and election
        of Gustav Vasa as king of Sweden. Defeat of the Franconian knights led by

Franz von Sickingen and Ulrich von Hutten (end of the so-called Knights' War in Germany).

1524 Outbreak of the German Peasants' War. Conversion of Philip of Hesse to Lutheranism. Francis I of France invades Italy and besieges Pavia in winter. Ottomans suppress an abortive rebellion in Egypt.

1525 Main peasant armies in Germany crushed by the Swabian League. Imperial army defeats and captures Francis I at Pavia: collapse of the French position in Italy. Albrecht von Hohenzollern secularizes the Grand Order of the Teutonic Knights (their lands become the Polish vassal state of East Prussia). Abortive revolt of the Janissaries against Süleyman I.

1526 Francis I forced to make concessions to Charles V in order to secure his release from captivity; repudiates the agreement (the Treaty of Madrid) on his return to France. Crushing victory of Ottoman army under Süleyman I at Mohácz; Louis II of Hungary killed in battle; Ottomans occupy Buda. Ferdinand of Habsburg asserts his claim to the kingdoms of Bohemia and Hungary. Adult rebaptism made a capital offence at Zurich. Ferdinand of Habsburg announces a liberal interpretation of the Edict of Worms. Outbreak of the sacramentarian controversy between Luther and Zwingli.

1527 Sack of Rome by unpaid Imperial troops. Imprisonment of Pope Clement VII. Medici expelled from Florence and republic declared. French invasion of Italy. Ferdinand of Habsburg crowned king of Hungary. Death of Machiavelli: *The Prince* and *The Discourses* unpublished in his lifetime.

1528 Genoa transfers allegiance from France to the Imperial side in the Italian wars. Süleyman I accepts John Zápolyai (the anti-Habsburg candidate for the Hungarian succession) as his vassal.

1529 Ottoman army under Süleyman I recaptures Buda and besieges (but fails to take) Vienna. Peace of Cambrai confirms Charles V's possession of Naples and restores the Sforza dynasty as rulers of Milan. 'Protestation' at the diet of Speyer gives Protestantism its name. Adult rebaptism made a capital offence in the Holy Roman Empire. Conference between Lutherans and Zwinglians at Marburg fails to resolve their differences over the Eucharist.

1530 Charles V crowned Emperor at Bologna by Pope Clement VII. Confession of Augsburg (known as the *invariata*) presented by the Lutherans to Charles V. Formation of the Lutheran League of Schmalkalden as a defensive association. End of the last Florentine Republic and restoration of the Medici dynasty.

1531 Zwingli killed at the battle of Kappel between the Protestant and Catholic Swiss cantons. Election of Ferdinand of Habsburg as King of the Romans and thus heir to Charles V. Attempted invasion of Norway and Sweden by Christian II.

1532 Ottoman invasion of Hungary. 'Religious peace' of Nuremberg, by which the Lutherans pledge military support to the Habsburgs and promise to recognize Ferdinand as King of the Romans in return for a truce in Germany until a general council of the church can be summoned.

1533 Ottoman–Habsburg truce in Hungary; Ottoman invasion of Persia. Outbreak of civil war in Denmark on the death of Frederick I.

1534 Restoration of duke Ulrich of Württemberg by the forces of the League of Schmalkalden. Establishment of the Anabaptist 'kingdom' at Münster. Parliament in England enacts the Act of Supremacy. Ottoman army under Süleyman I captures Tabriz and Baghdad in Persia.

1535 Suppression of the Anabaptist 'kingdom' at Münster. Defeat of Lübeck by the forces of Denmark, Sweden and East Prussia. Death of Francesco Sforza of Milan without male heir threatens to reopen the Italian wars. Charles V captures Tunis.

1536 First edition of Calvin's *Institution* or *Institutes*. Establishment of the Reformation at Geneva and subsequent arrival of Calvin there. Concord between Lutherans and Bucer's followers in the south German cities. Christian III wins the Danish war of succession. Establishment of Swedish Lutheran church. Probable signing of a Franco-Ottoman commercial treaty. French occupation of the duchy of Savoy; Imperial invasion of Provence.

1537 Establishment of Danish Lutheran church. Report of the Papal reform commission. French occupation of Piedmont. 'Confederation' movement in Poland.

1538 Truce in the war between France and the Emperor. Calvin and Farel expelled from Geneva. Agreement between Ferdinand and John Zápolyai over the Hungarian succession. Holy League (Pope, Venice and the Emperor) against the Turks in the Mediterranean. Ottomans capture Aden.

1539 Revolt of Ghent against Charles V. Capitulation of Sigismund I of Poland to the 'confederation' movement. Ottomans proclaim suzerainty over Basra.

1540 Charles V 'invests' his son Philip with the duchy of Milan. Ferdinand of Habsburg occupies Pest and besieges Buda to enforce his claim to the whole of the Hungarian succession. Collapse of the Holy League against the Turks in the Mediterranean. Revised Lutheran Confession of Augsburg (*variata*). Foundation of the Jesuit order by Pope Paul III.

1541 Failure of attempts at religious compromise between Catholics and Lutherans at the Colloquy of Regensburg. Charles V apparently consents to further Lutheran expansion in Germany. Return of Calvin to Geneva: imposes the Ecclesiastical Ordinances. Ignatius Loyola first general of the Jesuit order. Failure of Charles V's expedition to Algiers. Süleyman I invades Hungary and annexes the province of Buda.

1542 Pope Paul III summons the Council of Trent. Re-establishment of the Roman Inquisition. Outbreak of war between Francis I and the Emperor; Charles V also involved in war over the duchy of Guelders. Schmalkaldic League attacks duchy of Brunswick-Wolfenbüttel. Peasant rebellion in Sweden led by Nils Dacke.

1543 Victory of Charles V in the war over the duchy of Guelders: annexed as the province of Gelderland. Sorbonne in France publishes its first index of prohibited books. Publication of Copernicus's *On the revolutions of the heavenly spheres.*

1544 Anglo-Imperial invasion of France. Peace of Crépy-en-Laonnais between Charles V and Francis I.

1545 Opening of the Council of Trent. Spanish Inquisition issues an index of prohibited books. Truce between Charles V and Süleyman I.

1546 Death of Luther. Outbreak of the war of the Schmalkaldic League. The Palatinate becomes a Lutheran state. Anglo-French peace treaty signed at Ardres. Basra taken under full Ottoman control.

1547 Crushing victory of Charles V over the Schmalkaldic League at Mühlberg. Transfer of the Council of Trent to Bologna in the Papal States. Coronation of Ivan IV of Muscovy and end of boyar rule during the royal minority. Ferdinand I pays tribute to Süleyman I for his possession of Royal Hungary.

1548 Charles V imposes his own religious settlement for Germany (the Interim of Augsburg). Establishment of the 'Burgundian circle'. Publication of Loyola's *Spiritual Exercises.* Ottoman war with Persia: Süleyman I captures Tabriz.

1549 Swiss confession of faith (*Consensus Tigurinus*), a religious agreement between Calvin and Bullinger. St Francis Xavier arrives in Japan. Burgundian Netherlands recognizes Philip of Habsburg as heir to Charles V. Henri II of France declares war on England.

1550 First formation of a Lutheran league in Germany against the Interim of Augsburg. Anglo-French peace treaty. Repressive 'edict of blood' issued in the Netherlands by Charles V.

1551 Habsburg family agreement over the partition of Charles V's territories ('Augsburg family compact'). Maurice of Saxony joins the League of Torgau against the Interim of Augsburg. Alliance between the German Lutheran princes and Henri II of France at Lochau. Council of Trent reconvenes. Ottomans capture Tripoli.

1552 Henri II of France occupies Metz, Toul and Verdun. Successful rebellion of the German Lutheran princes under Maurice of Saxony: Truce of Passau signed by Ferdinand of Habsburg. War between Ferdinand and Süleyman I over Transylvania. Ivan IV conquers the khanate of Kazan'.

1553 Failure of Charles V's siege of Metz. Corsica occupied by the French.

1554 Failure of Wyatt's rebellion against the marriage of Mary Tudor to Philip of Habsburg. Charles V makes Philip king of Naples. Ottoman war with Persia.

1555 Peace of Augsburg between Catholics and Lutherans in Germany. Abdication of Charles V as ruler in the Low Countries. Peace of Amasya ends Süleyman I's wars with Persia. Ottomans capture Bougie.

1556 Abdication of Charles V from his Spanish lands, from Franch-Comté and as Emperor. Franco-Papal war against Philip II of Spain: last French invasion of Italy in sixteenth century. Süleyman I restores John Sigismund Zápolyai as his vassal in Transylvania. Outbreak of civil war in Livonia. Death of Ignatius Loyola.

1557   First debt-rescheduling ('bankruptcy') of Philip II. Pope Paul IV forced to make peace with Philip II. Crushing Spanish victory over the French at St- Quentin.

1558   French recover Calais from the English. Henri II abandons his alliance with the German Lutheran princes. Ivan IV of Muscovy occupies Estonia: beginning of the Livonian war. Outbreak of the Ottoman war of succession. Beza's (Calvinist) Confession of Faith issued.

1559   Peace of Cateau-Cambrésis ends the Italian wars. End of French occupation of Savoy. Unexpected death of Henri II. French debt rescheduling (collapse of the *grand parti* of Lyon). Index of Prohibited Books published by Pope Paul IV. Publication of the definitive edition of Calvin's *Institution* or *Institutes*. French (Calvinist) Confession of Faith.

1560   Failure of the Huguenot Conspiracy of Amboise in France. Death of Philip Melanchthon. Triumph of Calvinism at Zurich (effective end of Zwinglianism).

1561   Failure of the attempted compromise between Catholics and Calvinists in France (the Colloquy of Poissy). Philip II transfers his capital to Madrid. Erik XIV of Sweden accepts the fealty of Reval in Estonia. Grand Order of the Livonian Knights secularized: Livonia becomes a fief of Sigismund II of Poland. Netherlands (Calvinist) Confession of Faith. Frederick of the Palatinate converts to Calvinism.

1562   Failure of the Edict of Toleration in France (January Edict or Edict of St-Germain): outbreak of the first war of religion. Treaty between Condé and Elizabeth I of England. Last session of the Council of Trent opens.

1563   Assassination of the duc de Guise. End of the first war of religion in France (Edict of Amboise). Frederick II of Denmark declares war on Sweden: Lübeck and Poland ally with Denmark. Ending of the Council of Trent.

1564   Cardinal Granvelle ousted from power in the Netherlands. Peace between Sweden and Muscovy. Defection of prince Kurbskii from Muscovy to Lithuania: commencement of repression in Muscovy. Outbreak of war between Ottomans and Austrian Habsburgs. Pope Pius IV confirms the decrees of the Council of Trent. Pope reissues a more moderate Index of Prohibited Books. Death of Calvin.

1565   Philip II refuses religious concessions in the Netherlands ('letters from the Segovia woods'). Ivan IV establishes a 'state within the state' (*oprichnina*) in Muscovy.

1566   'Compromise' or league of nobility calling for religious concessions in the Netherlands; iconoclastic rioting follows; William of Orange goes into exile. Death of Süleyman I on his thirteenth campaign (seventh in Hungary). Carlo Borromeo accedes to the archbishopric of Milan.

1567   First rebellion in the Netherlands; duke of Alba sent from Spain to suppress it; establishment of the Council of Troubles. Outbreak of the second war of religion in France. Swedish invasion of Norway. Failure of the conspiracy against Ivan IV of Muscovy.

1568   Failure of the exiles' invasion of the Low Countries in support of the rebellion. End of the second war of religion in France (Edict of Longjumeau) and outbreak of the third. Arrest and death of Don Carlos, heir of Philip II. Outbreak of the Morisco rising in Granada. Successful rebellion of John, younger brother of Erik XIV of Sweden. Ottoman conquest of the Yemen.

1569   Deposition of Erik XIV of Sweden and election of John as king. Eviction of the Hafsid dynasty of Tunis by the Ottomans. Death of Condé after the battle of Jarnac. Union of Lublin establishes the Commonwealth (*Rzeczpospolita*) of Poland-Lithuania.

1570   End of the third war of religion in France: Edict of St-Germain allows the Huguenots four fortress towns. Ottoman capture of Cyprus. Peace of Stettin ends the War of the North on disastrous terms for Sweden. Establishment of the Polish Reformed Church (Consensus Sando-miriensis). Sack of Novgorod in Muscovy by the forces of the *oprichnina*.

1571   Formation of the Holy League (Papacy, Venice and Spain) against the Ottomans in the Mediterranean. Don John of Austria crushes the Ottoman fleet at Lepanto. Sack of Moscow by the Tatars. Systematization of the French and Dutch Calvinist confessions of faith at the synods of La Rochelle and Emden.

1572   Assassination of Coligny and St Bartholomew's Day massacres in France: beginning of the fourth war of religion. Henri of Navarre and Henri of Condé forced to abjure. Invasion of the Sea Beggars in Holland; William of Orange recognized as stadholder in much of Holland, Zeeland and Utrecht. Extinction of Jagiellon dynasty in Poland on the death of Sigismund II.

1573   Withdrawal of Venice from the Holy League against the Ottomans in the Mediterranean. Arrival of Requesens as governor-general in the Netherlands. Ending of fourth war of religion in France (Peace of La Rochelle or Edict of Boulogne). Election of Henri of Valois as king of Poland.

1574   Fifth war of religion begins in France, with Huguenots led by Henri of Condé. Coronation of Henri of Valois as king of Poland; after 118 days, he departs for France as Henri III. Ottoman reconquest of Tunis.

1575   Second debt rescheduling ('bankruptcy') of Philip II. Failure of the Breda peace conference in the Netherlands. Revolt of Alençon in France: Catholic Malcontents ally with the Huguenots. Deposition of Henri of Valois as king of Poland. Establishment of a second *oprichnina* in Muscovy in all but name. Death of Bullinger. (Reformed) Bohemian Confession of Faith.

1576   Death of Requesens and interregnum of governor-generalship in the Low Countries. Sack of Antwerp by the mutinous Spanish army of the Low

Countries ('Spanish fury'). Pacification of Ghent in the Low Countries. Henri of Navarre escapes from arrest and joins rebellion of Huguenots. Peace of Monsieur in France ends rebellion of Catholic Malcontents under Alençon. Concessions to Huguenots in the Edict of Beaulieu end the fifth war of religion but provoke the formation of the first Catholic League. Coronation of Stefan Bátory as king of Poland after victory in civil war. Collapse of Safavid Persia following the death of Shah Tahmasp. Publication of Jean Bodin's *Six Bookes of the Commonweale*.

1577 Don John of Austria imposes the Perpetual Edict in the Netherlands. States General deposes Don John of Austria as governor-general and invites Matthias of Habsburg to take the post. Sixth war of religion in France begins and ends (Peace of Bergerac and Edict of Poitiers). Muscovite army under Ivan IV overruns all Livonia except for Riga and Reval. Stefan Bátory makes peace with Danzig in order to concentrate on war with Muscovy.

1578 Don John of Austria and Alexander Farnese (the future duke of Parma) defeat the rebellious Dutch forces at Gembloux. Amsterdam joins the revolt. Death of Don John (replaced by Parma as governor-general). Death of Sebastian of Portugal on crusade in Morocco: unleashes Portuguese succession crisis. Murad III launches Ottoman invasion of Persia. Ottoman truce with Philip II.

1579 Formation of the rival unions of Utrecht and Arras in the Low Countries. Edict of proscription against William of Orange. Stefan Bátory of Poland declares war on Muscovy and captures Polotsk. Philip II arrests Antonio Pérez and ends council faction in Castile. Seventh war of religion in France ended by the Treaty of Nérac.

1580 Spanish army under Alba invades Portugal to secure Philip II's succession. Eighth war of religion in France ended by the Treaty of Fleix. Retirement of Beza as Moderator of Geneva's Company of Pastors. Publication of the Lutheran *Book of Concord*, which settles religious disputes since the death of Luther.

1581 Philip II receives homage from the Portuguese *Cortes* as king of Portugal. William of Orange publishes his *Apology*. Renunciation of Philip II's sovereignty (Act of Dismissal) by the States General of the Low Countries, who appoint the duc d'Anjou. Swedes capture Ivangorod.

1582 Ten year Russo-Polish truce concluded at Yam Zapolski. Muscovite occupation of Siberia. Pope Gregory XIII introduces the new (or Gregorian) calendar.

1583 Failure of duc d'Anjou to seize control at Antwerp ('French fury'). Bavarian and Spanish troops invade the electorate of Cologne. Swedish truce with Muscovy.

1584 Assassination of William of Orange. Capitulation of Bruges and Ghent to Parma. Death of the duc d'Anjou and formation of the Catholic League in France. Treaty of Joinville between Philip II of Spain and the duc de Guise. Death of Ivan IV and regency of Boris Godunov in Muscovy.

1585 Brussels and Antwerp capitulate to Parma. Elizabeth I pledges support to the Dutch rebellion (Treaty of Nonsuch): Leicester appointed lieutenant-general. Rebellion of the Catholic League in France: Henri III capitulates in the Treaty of Nemours. Navarre and Condé excluded from the French succession by bull of Pope Sixtus V. Navarre begins the ninth war of religion in France, which lasts until 1596–8.

1586 Philip II begins plans for an armada against England. Leicester accepts the title of 'absolute governor and general' in the Netherlands; later returns to England. Disputed Polish succession following the death of Stefan Bátory.

1587 Elizabeth I orders the execution of Mary Queen of Scots. Drake attacks Cadiz. Discontent in the Netherlands at Leicester's rule: recalled to England. Election of Sigismund III as king of Poland.

1588 Failure of the Spanish Armada against England. Day of the Barricades in Paris: Henri III and his court forced to leave the capital and to capitulate to the League in the 'edict of union'. Savoy invades the French-held marquisate of Saluzzo. Assassination of the Guises on the orders of Henri III. Sigismund III forced to accept the Third Lithuanian Statute. Deposition of Mohummad Khudabanda in Persia and accession of Shah Abbas I. Molina publishes his views on free will.

1589 Alliance in France between Henri III and Henri of Navarre. Assassination of Henri III and (disputed) accession of Navarre as Henri IV.

1590 Maurice of Nassau captures Breda. States General of the Netherlands declares itself sovereign. Death of 'Charles X' of the League: need to find a Catholic alternative to Henri IV. Parma invades France to relieve the siege of Paris. Ottoman–Persian peace treaty.

1591 Philip II suppresses the revolt of Aragon. Purge organized by League radicals at Paris and Toulouse. Rudolf II refuses to pay tribute to the Ottomans for Royal Hungary. Death of Prince Dimitrii, Ivan IV's son, in Muscovy.

1592 Death of John III opens the Swedish succession crisis. Parma relieves the Anglo-French siege of Rouen; Parma later dies in the Netherlands. Pope Clement VIII issues a revised text of the Latin Vulgate Bible.

1593 Failure of the Estates General of the League to elect a Catholic alternative to Henri IV. Henri IV abjures Calvinism. Murad III decides on an Ottoman war against Rudolf II over Hungary (beginning of the Thirteen Years' War). Duke Charles proclaimed the acting ruler ('leading personage') in Sweden.

1594 Lyon, Rouen and Paris surrender to Henri IV. Coronation of Henri IV at Chartres. *Parlement* of Paris orders the Jesuits to leave France after Jean Châtel's assassination attempt on Henri IV. Maurice of Nassau recovers Groningen. Coronation of Sigismund III as king of Sweden; later departs for Poland. Rebellion of Wallachia, Moldavia and Transylvania against the Ottomans.

1595 Henri IV declares war on Spain. Pope Clement VIII recognizes the validity of Henri IV's abjuration. Bloody accession of Sultan Mehmed III.

1596 Submission of the Catholic League magnates to Henri IV. Archduke Albert arrives in the Spanish Netherlands as governor-general. Second unsuccessful Spanish Armada against England. Sultan Mehmed III leads Ottoman forces to victory at Mezö-Keresztes in Hungary. Outbreak of two rebellions in the Ottoman lands: the *jelali* movement in Anatolia and rebellion in Wallachia led by Mihai Viteazul. Ferdinand of Styria accedes as ruler of Inner Austria. Formation of the Uniate church in Lithuania. Revised Papal Index of Prohibited Books.

1597 Huguenots fail to assist Henri IV in the siege of Amiens, captured by the Spaniards. Third unsuccessful Spanish Armada against England.

1598 Edict of Nantes ends wars of religion in France. Peace of Vervins between France and Spain. Death of Philip II of Spain. Failure of Sigismund III's invasion of Sweden. Boris Godunov elected Tsar of Muscovy: beginning of the 'Time of Troubles'.

1599 Deposition of Sigismund by the Swedish diet (*riksdag*). Henri IV obtains annulment of his marriage to Marguerite of Valois so that he can marry Marie de Médici the following year.

1600 Henri IV declares war on Savoy over its retention of the marquisate of Saluzzo. Charles IX orders the execution of prominent aristocratic opponents in Sweden, and attacks Polish Livonia.

1601 Treaty of Lyon between France and Savoy. Spanish landing in Ireland. End of rebellion in Wallachia.

1602 Formation of the Dutch East India Company.

1603 Collapse of the Swedish position in Livonia. Polish government recognizes the claim of (False) Dimitrii I. Recall of the Jesuits to France. Ottoman law of fratricide not applied on accession of Ahmed I. Shah Abbas I launches Persian war against the Ottomans.

1604 Treaty between England and Spain, ending the war begun in 1585. Revolt of István Bocskai in Hungary. Jacobus Arminius presents his theses on predestination. Establishment of the *droit annuel* (*paulette*) in France. Charles IX accepts the title of king in Sweden. Rebellion of False Dimitrii I in Muscovy.

1605 Dutch siege of Malacca. Death of Boris Godunov; False Dimitrii I crowned as Tsar. Victory of Bocskai's revolt in Hungary. Death of Beza.

1606 Peace of Zsitva-Török between Rudolf II and the Ottoman Turks. Vasilii Shuiskii mounts a successful coup against False Dimitrii I and is crowned Tsar in his place. Revolt of Ivan Bolotnikov comes close to capturing Moscow. 'Confederation movement' (*rokosz*) of Sandomierz against Sigismund III of Poland. Pope Paul V places Venice under Interdict.

1607 Archduke Albert authorizes a cease-fire with the Dutch. Maximilian I of Bavaria seizes the free city of Donauwörth. Amnesty for the Confederation of Sandomierz in Poland. Suppression of Bolotnikov's rising in Muscovy. Pope Paul V removes the Interdict placed on Venice.

1608 Signature of Franco-Dutch and Anglo-Dutch defensive leagues. Rudolf II forced to relinquish control of Austria, Moravia and Hungary to Matthias I. Unsuccessful siege of Moscow by 'False Dimitrii II'.

1609 Twelve Years' Truce between Spain and the United Provinces. Rudolf II grants Letter of Majesty to Bohemian Protestants: Calvinists allowed rights of worship. Foundation of the Bank of Amsterdam. Cleves–Jülich succession crisis. Formation of the rival Protestant Union and Catholic League in Germany. Alliance between Muscovy and Sweden. Death of Arminius.

1610 Assassination of Henri IV of France and minority of Louis XIII. Swedish–Muscovite forces destroyed by the Polish army at Klushino; deposition of Vasilii Shuiskii in a boyar coup. End of the *jelali* movement in Anatolia against the Ottomans. Counter-Remonstrant movement in the Dutch Republic against Arminianism.

1611 Matthias I crowned king of Bohemia after deposition of Rudolf II. Christian IV of Denmark attacks Sweden. Death of Charles IX; nobility impose an accession charter on Gustavus Adolphus. Polish army captures Smolensk.

1612 'Second national host' forces surrender of Polish garrison in Moscow. Matthias I crowned Emperor. Axel Oxenstierna becomes Chancellor of Sweden.

1613 Peace of Knäred between Denmark and Sweden on disastrous terms for the latter. Elector John Sigismund of Brandenburg becomes a Calvinist; the majority of the population remain Lutheran. Michael Romanov elected as Tsar of Muscovy. Catholic missionaries barred from Japan.

1614 Treaty of Xanten provides for a provisional partition of the Cleves–Jülich succession. Defence pact between the Dutch and Sweden.

1615 War between Ferdinand of Styria and Venice over the *Uskoks*. French assembly of the clergy accepts the decrees of the Council of Trent; crown does not.

1616 England withdraws its garrisons from the Netherlands.

1617 Assassination of Concini on the orders of Louis XIII of France. Ferdinand of Styria elected king of Bohemia. Oñate agreement between Ferdinand and Philip III of Spain. Sweden concludes the Peace of Stolbova on advantageous terms with Muscovy. Swedish invasion of Livonia.

1618 Arrest of Cardinal Khlesl by Ferdinand of Styria. Ferdinand elected king of Hungary, but outbreak of the Bohemian rebellion against him ('Defenestration of Prague'). Truces in the war between Poland and Sweden and between Poland and Muscovy. Treaty between Ottomans and Persia ends war begun in 1603. First deposition of Sultan Mustafa I; accession of 'Osman II. Meeting of the Synod of Dort.

1619 Bohemian estates depose Ferdinand as king and elect Frederick V of the Palatinate. Count Matthias Thurn attempts to capture Vienna for the rebel forces. Bethlen Gábor occupies Royal Hungary. Ferdinand elected as Emperor Ferdinand II. Synod of Dort condemns Arminianism; Oldenbarnevelt executed.

1620   Truce between the Protestant Union and the Catholic League in Germany. Bohemian rebellion crushed at the battle of the White Mountain by a joint Bavarian–Imperial army. Saxony occupies Lusatia. Spanish invasion of the Lower Palatinate and the Valtelline. Rebellion of the queen mother in France. War between Poland and the Ottoman Turks: siege of Chocim by the Turks.

1621   Renewal of war between Spain and the Dutch Republic. Collapse of the Protestant Union in Germany. Revolt of the Huguenots in France. Resumption of the Swedish war against Poland: Gustavus Adolphus captures Riga. End of Polish war with the Turks.

1622   Peace of Montpellier between Louis XIII and the Huguenots. Dutch capture Jülich. Failure of Spínola's siege of Bergen-op-Zoom. Olivares becomes chief minister of Philip IV of Spain. Assassination of Sultan 'Osman II; restoration of Mustafa I. Revolt of Abaza Mehmed in Erzerum against Ottoman rule.

1623   Frederick V of the Palatinate deprived of his lands: his electoral title is transferred to Maximilian of Bavaria. Failure of Anglo-Spanish marriage alliance negotiations. French alliance with Venice and Savoy against Spanish ambitions in the Valtelline. Second deposition of Sultan Mustafa I; minority of Murad IV. Shah Abbas I reopens Persian war against the Ottomans: seizes Baghdad.

1624   France goes to war with Spain over the Valtelline. Cardinal de Richelieu becomes chief minister of Louis XIII. Dutch capture Bahía, the capital of Brazil.

1625   Spínola captures Breda from the Dutch. Huguenot rebellion against Louis XIII. General alliance of The Hague against Imperial gains in Germany: intervention of Christian IV of Denmark in the Thirty Years' War. Philip IV announces the Union of Arms scheme. Gustavus Adolphus captures Livonia. Dutch evicted from Bahía. Cossack revolt.

1626   Christian IV of Denmark defeated by Tilly at Lutter. Richelieu obtains peace with the Huguenots and with Spain over the Valtelline. Gustavus Adolphus invades East Prussia.

1627   Ferdinand II imposes a new constitution on Bohemia. War between England and France: English invasion of the Ile de Ré off south-west France in support of a Huguenot rebellion. Death of Vincenzo II Gonzaga: crisis over the Mantuan succession.

1628   Imperial grant of much of the Palatinate to Maximilian of Bavaria. Wallenstein acquires Mecklenburg and is appointed Imperial Admiral: besieges Stralsund. Fall of La Rochelle to Louis XIII. Dutch under Piet Heyn capture the Spanish treasure fleet at Matanzas Bay. End of revolt of Abaza Mehmed in Erzerum against Ottoman rule.

1629   Ferdinand II imposes the Edict of Restitution in Germany: opposed by Pope Urban VIII. Christian IV of Denmark withdraws from the Thirty Years' War on favourable terms at the Peace of Lübeck. First French invasion of Savoy and Montferrat. Peace of Alais ends the revolt of the Huguenots. Truce of Altmark between Sweden and Poland.

1630   Gustavus Adolphus invades Germany. Dismissal of Wallenstein as Imperial generalissimo. Franco-Dutch subsidy treaty. French capture the strategic fortress of Pinerolo in Italy; refuse to ratify the Peace of Regensburg with the Emperor; Richelieu survives a domestic political crisis on the Day of Dupes. Dutch capture Pernambuco in northern Brazil. Cossack revolt.

1631   French treaty with Maximilian of Bavaria and subsidy treaty with Sweden. Rebellion of Gaston d'Orléans in France. Peace treaty between France and Spain at Cherasco ends the Mantuan war. Decisive victory of Gustavus Adolphus over Tilly at Breitenfeld. Sack of Magdeburg. John George of Saxony captures Prague. Wallenstein recalled to Imperial service.

1632   Gustavus Adolphus occupies Munich. Wallenstein recaptures Prague. Death of Gustavus at the inconclusive battle of Lützen. Dutch military gains against Spain in the Low Countries' war. Gaston d'Orléans invades France; Louis XIII occupies Lorraine. Muscovite attack on Poland in the succession crisis following the death of Sigismund III. Ruthless repression by Sultan Murad IV on his accession to personal rule.

1633   Formation of the (Protestant) League of Heilbronn in Germany under Oxenstierna's directorship. Beginnings of French occupation of Alsace. Galileo's views condemned by the Catholic church as heretical.

1634   Murder of Wallenstein on the orders of Ferdinand II. Crushing defeat of the Swedish army at Nördlingen by the combined Spanish–Imperial forces: collapse of the Heilbronn League. Renewal of the Franco-Dutch subsidy alliance. Imposition of French administration in Lorraine. Peace between Poland and Muscovy signed at Polianovka: Ladislas abandons his claim to the Tsardom. Form of Government established in Sweden: constitutional arrangements for Christina's minority.

1635   French declaration of war on Spain: failure of the Franco-Dutch invasion of the Spanish Netherlands. Habsburg-dominated peace imposed on Germany (the Peace of Prague). Truce of Stuhmdorf between Poland and Sweden. Commencement of three years of Cossack revolts. Ottomans recapture Tabriz.

1636   Spanish invasion of France reaches Corbie in the north and Dijon in the east. Swedish victory at Wittstock.

1637   Unsuccessful Spanish invasion of southern France from Catalonia. Dutch recapture Breda. Christian IV of Denmark destroys the Polish fleet.

1638   Capture of Breisach by Bernard of Saxe-Weimar. Capture of Baghdad by Sultan Murad IV. Death of Cornelius Jansen(ius).

1639   Failure of Spanish armadas to recover Brazil and to defeat Dutch naval power in Europe: Tromp defeats the second fleet at the battle of the Downs. Peace of Zuhab concludes Ottoman–Persian war begun in 1623.

1640   Rebellion of Catalonia and secession of Portugal from the union with

Castile: John IV crowned king of Portugal. Dutch treaty with Sweden. Posthumous publication of Jansen's *Augustinius*.

1641 Declaration of the Catalan republic and subsequent transfer of sovereignty to Louis XIII. Franco-Portuguese treaty and Dutch-Portuguese truce. Renewal of the Franco-Swedish alliance. Duc de Soissons, supported by Spain, invades France. Dutch capture Malacca, the centre of the spice trade, and also Luanda in Angola.

1642 Swedish victory at the second battle of Breitenfeld. French capture Perpignan. Death of Richelieu.

1643 Dismissal of Olivares as chief minister of Philip IV. French victory over Spanish army at Rocroi. Death of Louis XIII; minority of Louis XIV; Mazarin becomes chief minister. Opening of the Westphalian peace negotiations. Swedish invasion of Denmark. Pope Urban VIII condemns some of Jansen's propositions (bull *In eminenti*).

1644 Philip IV swears to uphold the Catalan constitution. Torstennson defeats an Imperial army sent to support Denmark at Jüterborg. Majority of Christina of Sweden.

1645 Torstensson defeats the Bavarian–Imperialist army at Jankau. Peace of Brömsebro between Sweden and Denmark, on terms favourable to Sweden. Franco-Danish alliance. Outbreak of the Ottoman war with Venice. Rising of the Portuguese settlers in Dutch Brazil.

1646 Anti-French riots at the Hague on news of the proposed Franco-Spanish marriage alliance.

1647 Cease-fire between Spain and the Dutch Republic. Philip IV appoints Don Luis de Haro as chief minister; Spanish debt rescheduling ('bankruptcy'). Insurrections at Palermo and Naples; proclamation of a Neapolitan republic under the protection of France. Dutch treaty with Denmark.

1648 Peace of Münster signed between Spain and the Dutch Republic. Franco-Swedish victory at Zusmarshausen in Bavaria. Outbreak of the Fronde in France: French debt rescheduling ('bankruptcy'). French victory over the Spaniards at Lens. Peace of Westphalia ends the Thirty Years' War. Ending of the revolt of Naples. Outbreak of the Cossack revolt led by Bogdan Chmielnicki. Deposition and murder of Sultan Ibrahim I; minority of Mehmed IV. Portuguese settlers evict the Dutch from Angola.

1649 Execution of Charles I of England. Peace of Rueil ends Fronde of the Parisian office-holders. Second Dutch treaty with Denmark. Charles Gustavus recognized as Christina's heir in Sweden. John Casimir of Poland amnesties the Cossack revolt. New law code in Muscovy consolidates the enserfment of the peasantry.

1650 Mazarin arrests three princes of the blood (Condé, Conty and Longueville) most closely associated with the Frondeur opposition. Attempted coup by William II of Orange against Amsterdam; negated by his sudden death. Attack on noble privileges at the Swedish *riksdag*.

1651 Mazarin releases the three princes; departs to the electorate of Cologne in exile; declaration of Louis XIV's majority; rebellion of Condé; Mazarin invades France in support of the crown at the end of the year. Chmielnicki accepts the overlordship of the Ottoman sultan, but the Polish forces defeat the Cossacks and impose an interim peace. Hobbes's *Leviathan* published.

1652 Second exile of Mazarin and end of the Fronde at Paris. Castilian army captures Barcelona: end of the Catalan rebellion. Outbreak of the first Anglo-Dutch war. Cossacks repudiate the peace treaty with the Polish government and resolve on war in alliance with Muscovy.

1653 Mazarin returns to Paris as chief minister; Bordeaux, the last bastion of the Fronde, capitulates to the royal army. Spanish debt rescheduling ('bankruptcy'). Christina of Sweden attacks Bremen. Johan de Witt becomes councillor pensionary to the states of Holland. Pope Innocent X issues the bull *Cum occasione*, condemning five propositions attributed to Jansen.

1654 End of Anglo-Dutch war on advantageous terms for England. England declares war on Spain. Abdication of Christina of Sweden and accession of Charles X. Tsar Alexis accepts the decision of the Cossacks at Pereiaslaval to transfer their allegiance to Muscovy. Outbreak of Thirteen Years' War between Muscovy and Poland: Muscovite capture of Smolensk. Portuguese settlers finally evict the Dutch from Brazil.

1655 English fleet captures Jamaica. First Anglo-French treaty. Charles X leads Swedish invasion of Poland.

1656 Spanish victory over France at Valenciennes. Anglo-Swedish trade treaty. Swedish alliance with Brandenburg; subsequently Sweden and allies propose a partition of Poland. Truce between Poland and Muscovy: Muscovy attacks Swedish Livonia. Köprülü Mehmed Pasha appointed grand vizier by Sultan Mehmed IV.

1657 Anglo-French military alliance against Spain. Frederick III of Denmark launches attack on Sweden; Swedish army transferred from Poland and captures Frederiksodde. John Casimir of Poland concedes sovereignty over ducal Prussia to Frederick William of Brandenburg by the Treaty of Wehlau. Dutch war with Portugal. Death of the Cossack leader, Bogdan Chmielnicki. Blaise Pascal publishes his *Provincial Letters* in support of Jansenist views.

1658 Anglo-French victory over Spain at the battle of the Dunes. Portuguese victory over Castile at Elvas. Charles X of Sweden imposes the Treaty of Roskilde on Denmark; launches a surprise attack on Denmark later in the year. Cossack splinter group signs Treaty of Hadziac with Poland.

1659 Peace of the Pyrenees between France and Spain. Dutch assist defence of Copenhagen and De Ruyter defeats Swedish navy at Nyborg. Rival Cossack group signs new treaty with the Tsar. Truce signed between Sweden and Muscovy. Polish victory over Muscovy at Sosnówka.

1660 Marriage of Louis XIV and María Teresa seals Franco-Spanish peace treaty of previous year. Sudden death of Charles X weakens Swedish military power: treaties of Copenhagen and Oliva end the wars with Denmark and Poland. Polish victory over Muscovy at Cudnów. Restoration of Charles II in England.

LISTS OF THE MAIN EUROPEAN RULERS

Holy Roman Emperors (Habsburg Dynasty)

Maximilian I, 1493–1519

Charles V (grandson), 1519–56 (abdication)

Ferdinand I (brother), 1556/8–64

Maximilian II (son), 1564–76

Rudolf II (son), 1576–1612

Matthias I (brother), 1612–19

Ferdinand II (cousin), 1619–37

Ferdinand III (son), 1637–57

Leopold I (son), 1657/8–1705

Kings of Castile and Aragon (Trastamara and Habsburg Dynasties)

Isabella and Ferdinand, 1474/9–1504/16

[Juana (daughter) and Philip I of Habsburg in Castile, 1506]

Carlos I (grandson, later Emperor Charles V), 1516–56

Philip II (son), 1556–98

Philip III (son), 1598–1621

Philip IV (son), 1621–65

Kings of Denmark (Oldenburg Dynasty)

Hans, king of Denmark and Sweden, 1481–1513

Christian II, king of Denmark and Sweden (son), 1513–23

Frederick I (uncle), 1523–33

Interregnum, 1533–4

Christian III (son), 1534–59

Frederick II (son), 1559–88

Christian IV (son), 1588–1648

Frederick III (son), 1648–70

Kings of England (Tudor and Stuart Dynasties)

Henry VII, 1485–1509

Henry VIII (son), 1509–47

Edward VI (son), 1547–53

[Jane, 1553 (usurper)]

Mary I (half-sister of Edward VI), 1553–8 (with Philip of Habsburg, 1554–8)

Elizabeth I (half-sister), 1558–1603

James I (Stuart, James VI of Scotland), 1603–25

Charles I (son), 1625–49

Commonwealth 1649–60 [Oliver Cromwell, Lord Protector, 1653–8; Richard Cromwell, Lord Protector, 1658–9]

Charles II (son of Charles I), 1660–85

Kings of France (Valois and Bourbon Dynasties)

Charles VIII, 1483–98

Louis XII (cousin), 1498–1515

Francis I (cousin), 1515–47

Henri II (son), 1547–59

Francis II (son), 1559–60

Charles IX (brother), 1560–74

Henri III (brother), 1574–89

Henri IV (house of Bourbon), 1589–1610

Louis XIII (son), 1610–43

Louis XIV (son), 1643–1715

Kings of Poland (Jagiellon and Vasa Dynasties)

Jan Olbracht, 1492–1501

Alexander (brother), 1501–6

Sigismund (Zygmunt) I (brother), 1506–48

Sigismund II (son), 1548–72

Interregnum, 1572–3

Henri de Valois, 1573–5

Interregnum, 1575–6

Stefan Bátory of Transylvania, 1576–86

Interregnum 1586–7

Sigismund III (house of Vasa), 1587–1632

Ladislas IV (son), 1632–48

Interregnum, 1648

John Casimir (Jan Kazimierz, brother), 1648–68 (abdication)

Kings of Sweden (Vasa Dynasty)

Gustavus I Vasa, 1523–60

Erik XIV (son), 1560–9

John III (brother), 1569–92

Sigismund I (son), 1592–1600

Charles IX (uncle), 1600/4–11

Gustavus Adolphus (son), 1611–32

Christina (daughter), 1632–54 (abdication)

Charles X (cousin), 1654–60

Charles XI (son), 1660–97

Stadholders and Captains-General of the United Provinces after the Revolt (Orange–Nassau Dynasty)

William I ('the Silent'), 1572–84

Maurice of Nassau (son), 1584–1625

Frederick Henry (brother), 1625–47

William II (son), 1647–50

Period without stadholder, 1650–72

William III (son), 1672–1702

Sultans of the Ottoman Empire (Osmanli or Ottoman Dynasty)

Bayezid II, 1481–1512

Selim I (son), 1512–20

Süleyman I (son), 1520–66

Selim II (son), 1566–74

Murad III (son), 1574–95

Mehmed III (son), 1595–1603

Ahmed I (son), 1603–17

Mustafa I (brother), 1617–18, 1622–3

'Osman II (nephew), 1618–22

Murad IV (brother), 1623–40

Ibrahim I (brother), 1640–8

Mehmed IV (son), 1648–87

Tsars of Muscovy (Dynasties of Riúrik, Godunov and Romanov)

Ivan III, 1462–1505

Vasilii III (son), 1505–33

Ivan IV (son), 1533–84

Fedor I (son), 1584–98

Boris Godunov (brother-in-law), 1598–1605

Fedor II Godunov (son), 1605

[False Dimitrii I (pretender), 1605–6]
Vasilii Shuiskii, 1606–10
Interregnum, 1610–13
Michael Fedorovich Romanov, 1613–45
Alexis I (son), 1645–76

Popes

Alexander VI (Borgia), 1492–1503
Pius III (Piccolimini), 1503
Julius II (della Rovere), 1503–13
Leo X (de' Medici), 1513–21
Adrian VI (Dedel), 1522–3
Clement VII (de' Medici), 1523–34
Paul III (Farnese), 1534–49
Julius III (del Monte), 1550–5
Marcellus II (Cervini), 1555
Paul IV (Caraffa), 1555–9
Pius IV (de' Medici), 1559–65
Pius V (Ghislieri), 1566–72
Gregory XIII (Buoncompagno), 1572–85
Sixtus V (Felice Peretti), 1585–90
Urban VII (Castagna), 1590
Gregory XIV (Sfondrati), 1590–1
Innocent IX (Facchinetti), 1591
Clement VIII (Aldobrandini), 1592–1605
Leo XI (de' Medici), 1605
Paul V (Borghese), 1605–21
Gregory XV (Ludovisi), 1621–3
Urban VIII (Barberini), 1623–44
Innocent X (Pamfili), 1644–55
Alexander VII (Chigi), 1655–67

1

RELIGIOUS DIVISIONS IN EARLY MODERN EUROPE

'ONE faith, one law, one king'.[1] The French adage had been taken for granted in the Middle Ages, but its first constituent at least ceased to be universally applicable in the sixteenth century. Before the Reformation, Catholicism had been regarded as the 'true' faith, the certainty of which would be reinforced by further philosophical enquiry. The Reformation dashed these earlier assumptions. Most contemporaries considered that 'innovation in religion' was a cause of sedition in states and that diversity of religious belief was objectionable in theory and unworkable in practice. In twentieth-century secular society it is difficult to comprehend a Europe in which men and women were prepared to die for specific religious beliefs, or to understand that issues such as the capacity for sin and the certainty of salvation were, if not the only, certainly the chief, preoccupations of informed men and women. Few literate and articulate people in early modern Europe were agnostics or sceptics. The rise of sceptical thought was closely linked to knowledge of ancient Greek philosophy; the key texts of this tradition were printed in translation only after 1562. Even then, scepticism was used in religious argument only to demonstrate the greater validity of one religious creed over others. Before 1655 no one attempted to argue that the Scriptures were anything other than an objective and accurate historical account, or to suggest that they needed to be subjected to the same analysis and scrutiny as other historical documents. The entire Reformation debate took place in the context of the totally literal acceptance of the Scriptures.

It was also a debate confined largely to the elite. At the lower levels of society before the Reformation, few people knew in detail what they were meant to believe. This is not to say that people did not adhere closely to the doctrines of the church; rather, there was much popular superstition and folk culture among the lower ranks of the believers. The idiosyncrasies of popular or local religion were of concern to both Protestant and Catholic reformers. Even after religious divisions became final, with the formal rejection of Protestant doctrine at the Council of Trent (1545–63), Protestant and Catholic clergy alike were unable to overcome the extraordinary tenacity of popular resistance to imposed doctrines and observances. To that extent, both movements may be said to have failed in their reforming purpose.

1.1 The False Dawn: Attempts at Reform within a United Catholic Church

In theory, the church of the Middle Ages was a hierarchy. Power descended from the Pope, via the college of cardinals, to archbishops and bishops in their dioceses. The bishop gave the lead to his secular clergy, the parish priests, whose foremost duties were to administer the sacraments and to provide moral supervision and guidance to the laity. The structure was, in reality, much more complex, because in some areas lay patrons and monastic foundations rather than bishops had strong proprietary interests over the church and its clergy. Benefices were personal property which could be transferred, bought or sold like any landholding. There had also been conflict between the secular and regular clergy (who were themselves divided into the monastic and mendicant orders). Parochial priests had not been expected to preach regularly in the earlier Middle Ages, but by the fifteenth century there was an increasing demand for a preaching and teaching ministry, fuelled to a large extent by the friars. To compound the problems of the church, there were disputes within the regular clergy—between, for example, the rival orders of Franciscans and Dominicans, and within these orders between the Observants (or 'observers' of the original simplicity of the rule) and Conventuals (those who accepted 'interpretations' and mitigations of the rule).

Thus, despite first appearances, the later medieval church was not a monolith. For this reason, though some churchmen advocated change, no single scheme of reform ever commanded universal approval, nor did any one church leader emerge to carry it through. The Papacy was greatly preoccupied with the risk of schism following from the divisions between the great dynastic rulers of Europe and the intensification of secular control over the church. Successive Popes bartered away their power to princes in return for recognition of their theoretical pre-eminence. The 'Catholic monarchs' of Spain, Ferdinand and Isabella, for example had, in practice, appointed bishops, and this right was conferred in perpetuity on Charles V and his successors by his former tutor, Pope Adrian VI, in 1523. Leo X's Concordat with Francis I in 1516 left 620 preferments to the French crown. Yet the Pope retained greater authority in Germany, thanks to its political fragmentation, than in any other European country except Italy itself, and this has an important bearing on the background to the Reformation. Successive meetings of the Imperial diet (the representative institution of the Holy Roman Empire) had enumerated the grievances (*gravamina*) of the German 'nation' against the Papacy. The diet of Worms in 1521 represented the climax of such grievances, some of which sought to break completely with Papal and clerical power in the Empire. However, the same diet which produced this spectacular state- ment of grievances also condemned Martin Luther—the earliest and most important critic of the Papacy—as 'a manifest and obstinate heretic'.² Though the deficiencies of the Papacy and the existence of abuses in the church were clearly important aspects of the problem, they do not fully explain the origins of the Reformation in Germany.

1.1.1 *The Deficiencies of the Papacy before the Council of Trent*

The Pope was both the spiritual head of western Christendom and the secular ruler of the Papal States, which occupied a key strategic area in central Italy. Inevitably, the Pope sought to further the dynastic objectives of his family and office in his relations with foreign powers; wise were the rulers who recognized this policy of self-interest and turned it to their advantage. A foolish French king (Louis XII in 1511–12), out of control of the Italian situation, summoned a council of the church in an attempt to depose Pope Julius II for simony, an attempt which failed. A more sensible king (Francis I in 1515–16), who had been victorious in Italy, sought to accommodate Leo X with a Concordat, even at the price of some domestic difficulty. With the exception of Alexander VI (1492–1503) and Adrian VI (1522–3), all the Popes between 1494 and 1660 were Italians, reflecting the Italian domination of the college of cardinals, which increased with the passing of time. In 1500 there were 21 Italians among 35 cardinals in all; by 1598 Italy provided 46 out of 57. The electoral conclaves provided opportunities for foreign powers to influence the result and for unscrupulous cardinals to sell votes. The Pope depended on cardinals for his election, but once elected he owed them nothing, and could promote the interests of his own family. For the most part, the Renaissance Popes were worldly men: they defended the celibacy of the priesthood, yet at least four of them acknowledged children of their own. The Valencian Rodrigo Borgia (Pope Alexander VI) promoted the cause of his son Cesare in the Romagna. Leo X reinstated his family, the Medici, as rulers of Florence, and made his nephew Lorenzo de' Medici duke of Urbino. The diplomatic mistakes of Clement VII, another Medici Pope, were the main reason for his family's expulsion from Florence in 1527; his subsequent diplomatic success brought them back to power three years later.

Although successive Popes were preoccupied with the promotion of their own family interests, Papal policy was somewhat unpredictable because Rome lacked the continuity provided by a single dynasty. Popes were elected autocrats, whose average reign between 1492 and 1667 lasted less than eight years. Yet despite shifts in alliance, successive Popes were committed to the overriding principle that a strong territorial state in Italy was necessary for the independence of the spiritual head of western Christendom. Apart from looking after his family, an individual Pope usually had three aims: to increase the revenues of the church (both payments to Rome from other European countries and money raised within the Papal States); to strengthen Papal 'absolutism' in terms of an effective, autocratic administration with a subservient college of cardinals and tame nobility; and above all, to regain territorial control throughout the Papal States. In the Romagna and Ancona, former mercenary captains such as the Malatesta at Rimini, the Baglioni at Perugia and the Bentivoglio at Bologna—though supposedly Papal 'vicars'—had established their own ruling dynasties and practical independence. Successive Popes sought to bring such semi-autonomous states back under Papal control.

Such worldly considerations weighed far more with the Papacy than religious reform. The Popes were first and foremost great princes, primarily concerned with temporal power. The reconstitution of the Papal States, the glorification of Rome by ambitious building schemes, and the growth of Papal bureaucracy led to vast expenditure which had to be matched by income. Preoccupation with finance undoubtedly hindered the cause of religious reform. The rebuilding of St Peter's at Rome after 1506 necessitated the sale of Papal indulgences (the remission of so many days in purgatory for sinners, usually amounting to a significant number of years in total) on an unprecedented scale, though even so they produced less than a fifth of all Papal revenues. It was this abuse of the power to grant indulgences which provoked Martin Luther, the Wittenberg professor of biblical theology, to write his ninety-five theses against indulgences, and, it is thought, to nail them to the door of the local castle church in 1517, an event traditionally taken to herald the beginning of the Lutheran revolt. If (as some historians maintain) Luther did not actually nail the theses to the church door, this would suggest that even as late as 1517 he still sought reform within the established church. The incident might never have occurred had the Renaissance Popes acted with more moderation.

From 1460 until about 1536 there existed no relatively independent, reform-minded party within the Curia (the Papal court) to influence the Pope. Since the Pope would not act on his own initiative in religious reforms, only a general council of the church could set them in motion. In the later Middle Ages, some councils (particularly that at Basel in 1433–7) had attempted to strip Popes of their spiritual power and financial resources. The Papal counter-attack had been energetic: the bull *Execrabilis* (1460) denounced men 'imbued with a spirit of rebellion'[3] who claimed a right of appeal from the Pope to a future council of the church. Not only would this right give a licence to sin, but it would also overturn the ecclesiastical hierarchy; accordingly, it was condemned. In 1511–12, Louis XII summoned a church council to Pisa in the hope of deposing Julius II; the Pope condemned it as illegitimate, calling it a *conciliabulum*, not a council. He restated the terms of the bull *Execrabilis*, and summoned the Fifth Lateran Council (1512–17) as a counter-measure.

The Fifth Lateran Council was a missed opportunity for reform. True, it discussed disciplinary reform, but with only one exception (the issue of the immortality of the soul) it failed to consider doctrinal questions which, even if only implicitly, might be said to lie behind practical abuses in clerical and religious life. It was strongly Italian in character, rather than representative of the whole of Catholic Europe. It was as concerned with politics as its counterpart at Pisa had been, declaring Louis XII's throne forfeited to his arch-rival Henry VIII. The debates were held without any real sense of urgency, and the acts of the council were not published until July 1521 (a year after the appearance of Luther's three great manifestos to the German nation). It was generally accepted that only the Pope had the right to 'convoke, transfer and dissolve councils',[4] but the right was not exercised until 1542. The body then called by Pope Paul III came to be known as the Council of Trent, and only began work in December 1545. By then it was far too late. Religious divisions had become entrenched and there was no return to one universal church.

Yet before the Council of Trent, disciplinary matters always ranked high on the agenda for reform drawn up by critics of the Catholic church. The Papacy was blamed for ecclesiastical abuses even where it could not influence the conduct of a national church. However, in Germany and Italy, where the Papacy retained much of its power and could have exercised real authority over the clergy, its influence was not used effectively. Clerical absenteeism was a prime target for reform. The Council of Trent later reaffirmed the principle that the bishop should reside in his diocese and travel round it every year to check on the residence and performance of the parish priests. Yet as late as 1560, more than 70 out of about 250 Italian bishops resided in Rome rather than in their appointed sees. Absenteeism might also be encouraged by pluralism (the holding of several benefices at the same time), which occurred quite frequently in the Holy Roman Empire, where eight or so archbishops and over forty bishops were territorial princes usually elected by their cathedral chapters.

Johann Tetzel was the agent of one such pluralist in 1517, and the man who precipitated Luther's outburst against the sale of Papal indulgences. He was in charge of sales in the archbishopric of Mainz, where Cardinal Albrecht von Hohenzollern had been appointed to the electorate and archbishopric in 1515 at the uncanonical age of 25 (according to canon law, he should have been 30). Albrecht had also acquired the bishoprics of Halberstadt and Magdeburg along the way, which had left him with a debt of 34,000 ducats. Half the proceeds from the sale of the Papal indulgences in his archbishopric were meant to go to Rome, and half to Albrecht and his creditors, the banking house known as the Fuggers of Augsburg. Such simony led to financial pressures, both on the Papacy and the prelates, and could intensify ecclesiastical abuses. But the sale of indulgences was not in itself unpopular: many pious laymen in Germany bought indulgences between 1476 and 1509, just as they embellished churches and endowed preacherships and private masses. Nevertheless, there was an important distinction between the sale of indulgences and its commercial exploitation to help finance pluralism, which was one of the foremost abuses of the church; Luther correctly pointed out that it was difficult 'even for the most learned theologians, to extol to the people at the same time the bounty of indulgences and the need for true contrition'.[5]

After the Council of Trent, the holding of more than one bishopric became generally much less frequent, but the French crown extended rather than limited the practice (called the *commende*) of granting abbeys or other benefices which would normally have been held by regular clergy to secular clergy or even laymen; these individuals, who were not professed members of a religious order, were thus not technically competent to hold them. In the 1630s, Henri of Guise held seven benefices, yielding an annual income of nearly 300,000 *livres*, which made him the most richly endowed ecclesiastic in France. By 1642, Cardinal de Richelieu's benefices provided him with about the same income. Cardinals needed several benefices to provide sufficient income to sustain their 'dignity' as princes of the church, yet even Richelieu's appetite was less voracious than that of his successor as chief minister, Cardinal Mazarin, who held twenty-one abbeys by the time of his death in 1661 and drew one-third of his 2 million *livres* a year in income from this source.

At lower levels in the church, local studies have tended to show an uneven pattern of ecclesiastical abuses before the Reformation. Clerical indiscipline was probably worst in the conservative countryside. On the other hand, in the diocese of Strasbourg, the number of specific clerical abuses (for example, keeping a 'concubine' in defiance of the rule of celibacy, involvement in an act of violence, or instances of alleged non-residence) may actually have declined just before the Reformation. But pluralism was an economic necessity for most priests, since there were too many clerics in relation to the available wealth of the local diocese, and this wealth was not distributed evenly. Once the principle of residence was broken, it was impossible to prevent the spread of abuses. Nevertheless, in Germany, economic oppression by ecclesiastical landowners, and judicial oppression by ecclesiastical courts, seem to have aroused anti-clericalism as least as much as the corruption of a clergy failing in its pastoral duties. The difficulties of the Catholic church arising from the uneven distribution of clerical incomes and the inadequacy of pastoral and theological training remained long after the Council of Trent had ended its sessions. For example, there were still Venetian priests in the later sixteenth century who did not confess or say the offices and Mass regularly (leaving aside the more glaring offences such as sexual misdemeanours and gambling). Bearing in mind the significant number of secular priests and male and female members of the religious orders—some 3 per cent of the population of Venice, and a still higher proportion elsewhere—such general indiscipline was probably inevitable.

1.1.2 *The Champions of Reform: Bishops and Regular Clergy*

Despite the reluctance of the Papacy to tackle ecclesiastical abuses, there were some earlier attempts at reform from within the church, although they ran the risk of being identified with heresy. The late medieval Papacy seems to have won its struggle against heresy, leaving Catholicism virtually unchallenged in western Christendom. The exceptions were Bohemia (where Hussitism had taken over in the 1420s and persisted), southern England (where Lollardy survived sporadically) and Dauphiné and Provence in France (where the Waldensian heresy had taken root), but these movements did little to prepare the way for Luther's new doctrines. Some Catholic reformers did not escape censure. At Florence, the Dominican preacher Savonarola was burnt for heresy in 1498. His message that this was the 'time of the reformation of the church'[6] (and of the city of Florence) was found to have contained 'new doctrines';[7] he was condemned as a schismatic. Some of the German preachers ran into trouble, too, notably Johann Ruchrath von Wesel, the cathedral preacher at Worms, who was deprived of his post in 1477 and forced to recant two years later. Luther was later to say that Wesel 'ruled the university of Erfurt by his books and it was out of these that I studied for my master's degree'.[8] Yet would-be reformers were not all crypto-heretics: some of the most vehement critics of ecclesiastical shortcomings preached orthodox doctrine. Johann Geiler von Kaiserberg, the cathedral preacher at Strasbourg in the years 1478–1510, railed against abuses, but also warned the laity against vernacular Bibles and justified the issuing of Papal indulgences.

The bishops of Strasbourg showed little zeal for reform, and incurred the censure of reformers such as Geiler, but there were a few exceptions. One or two reforming bishops could be found in most European states.

Among the numerous Italian bishops, Gian Matteo Giberti of Verona stands out as a prototype of the reforming bishop later sought by the Council of Trent. Similarly influential was the bishop of Carpentras in Provence, Jacopo Sadoleto, who resided in his diocese from 1527. Towering above them, however, because of the importance of his position as primate of Castile, was Jiménez de Cisneros, archbishop of Toledo. Cisneros was high chancellor of Castile, and actively involved in politics after 1504. His monastic reorganization, and patronage of the Polyglot Bible project, were a vivid testimony that the involvement of churchmen in affairs of state need not mean a neglect of reform. Yet before the 1540s reforming bishops were relatively few. Much depended on chance, particularly where appointments rested with the secular power. In the case of Cisnernos, Queen Isabella had appointed him to Toledo because he had been her personal confessor; her husband, Ferdinand, would have preferred Alfonso, his bastard, who was already archbishop of Zaragoza and was not distinguished by any reforming zeal.

There were also reformers among the regular clergy. The old orders of Dominicans and Augustinians showed a surprising resilience in the sixteenth century, and continued a healthy recruitment rate, despite the conversion of some individual members to the Reformation, and in the case of the Augustinians, the dubious distinction of having had Luther as one of their number. More recently founded orders were able to respond more easily to the changing spiritual requirements of the laity; for example, mixed groups of laity and clergy developed, which were devoted to acts of practical charity. In the Netherlands, there were the Brethren of the Common Life, one strand of the Modern Devotion (*devotio moderna*), whose members included clerics and laymen acting under a common rule but free to pursue their different vocations. Similar groups came into existence in Italy under the title of Oratories of Divine Love, first at Genoa (1500), then Rome (1517) and elsewhere. The reform sentiments of the Italian oratories inspired the new religious orders of Camaldolesi (1510–12), Theatines (1524), Capuchins (1528), Somaschi (1532), Barnabites (1533) and Ursulines (1535). The Theatines were a group of pastoral priests living together under monastic vows, founded by four members of the Roman Oratory of Divine Love, chief of whom were Gaetano da Thiene (St Cajetan) and Gian Pietro Caraffa (later Pope Paul IV). Since their aim was to live the apostolic priestly life as perfectly as possible, Theatines who became bishops tended to bring reform to their dioceses. The Capuchins' chequered early career survived the abjuration of their fourth vicar-general, Bernardino Ochino, in 1541, but they later became the most popular of the orders in the Catholic church because of their saintliness in treating the poor and the sick, especially in time of epidemics.

It is difficult to see what was shared by reforming bishops and like-minded regular clergy in their approach to religious reform. The single most pervasive influence on both groups seems to have been the writings of St Augustine, which became much better known in the fifteenth century (and not only to Luther and Staupitz, his spiritual mentor, as some historians have implied). St Augustine's influence was also important on Luther's contemporaries, men such as Gasparo Contarini, Reginald Pole and Girolamo Seripando, who were to remain Catholics. Furthermore, the Augustine tradition remained strong in the Catholic church after the Council of Trent had ended its sessions. The increased influence of St Augustine seems to have had an important bearing on the development of late medieval scholastic theology, but there was no decisive change in the *practice* of the Catholic religion. Although the Protestant reformers later denounced the manner in which the faith had been practised, and in particular the alleged burden of confession, the confessors themselves were instructed to root out suspicion and discomfort and implant love and tenderness among the faithful. The late medieval church was not an inquisitorial regime: confession was expected to be more frequent than communion, but Christians were asked to confess when appropriate and necessary—sometimes this was interpreted very laxly, on average only once a year in fifteenth-century Flanders, for example. It was recognized that confession could be too frequent as well as too irregular; Johann Eck seems to have reflected the general emphasis of late medieval confessional practice when he warned that a brooding and anxious search for the sins of the laity led only to individual suffering.

1.1.3 *Erasmus and Christian Humanism*

The early humanists of the fourteenth and fifteenth centuries had been interested above all in Latin and Greek literature and had sought to draw moral lessons from its works. Humanism had developed most pre-cociously in Italy; its early diffusion can to a considerable extent be linked to knowledge acquired by visitors travelling to Italy, and to the culture spread by the humanists (mostly secondary figures) who settled abroad. The apogee of humanist activity was the period between 1480 and 1530, when groups of scholars were active in most of the main European countries. Humanism had become in essence the study of the humanities (*studia humanitatis*), an approach to learning that stressed literary and moral rather than philosophical training. The foundation of humanist culture was rhetoric, oratory, and the related disciplines of linguistic study (chiefly Latin grammar), poetry, history and moral philosophy. The chosen target of the humanists was the scholasticism practised in the universities, which emphasized speculative thought, and above all, logic.

Scholastic theology was important at the universities, but it was second to logic and was heavily influenced by it. Biblical studies received little emphasis, and could be avoided almost completely by a study of Peter Lombard's _Sentences_ (_c._1050). Indeed, there is some evidence in the form of complaints to the government of ducal Saxony that at Leipzig in the first decade of the sixteenth century, lectures on theology were few and far between; one student claimed he would need 'the years of Methuselah' to complete his degree requirements.⁹ Late medieval scholasticism is frequently given the label 'nominalism' by historians: nominalism taught that 'universals', that is, abstract concepts, were mere names and had no real substance. Disciples of the 'modern' school of scholasticism (_via moderna_) rejected the position of Aquinas and others that 'universals' had any existence outside the mind; for this reason they were frequently referred to as the nominalist school (_via nominalium_). Today, such distinctions may appear sterile, even superficial, made as they were within an intellectual framework which was destined to be overtaken by curriculum reform in the universities. Such reforms were in turn influenced by humanism, yet there is a danger in slavishly following humanist propaganda and denouncing late medieval scholasticism. To do so minimizes the intellectual achievement of a fifteenth-century nominalist theologian such as Gabriel Biel, a significant figure in his own right but neglected today because he was not a 'precursor' of the Reformation; it also ignores the role played by some of the 'scholastics' themselves (including Luther) in encouraging the humanists to improve the instruction of grammar and rhetoric in Germany.

The title 'prince of humanists' was conferred not on a German, but on a Netherlander, Desiderius Erasmus of Rotterdam (1466/9?–1536). He began his career as an Augustinian monk at Steyn in 1488–93; but in 1493 he was given permission to leave the monastery in order to accompany the bishop of Cambrai to Rome. In the event, the bishop never went to the Eternal City, nor did Erasmus return to the monastery. Instead, he devoted himself to scholarship, as he put it, 'to serve some useful purpose through my efforts'; he had the dual aim of contributing 'to learning and to true piety'. He helped to disseminate Augustinian teaching through his edition of St Augustine's works in ten folio volumes, published in 1529. It was a tribute to the pervasive influence of Augustinianism that the greatest scholar in northern Europe should have undertaken such a task, but Erasmus was not much in sympathy with the saint. He found St Augustine too dogmatic; his own inclinations turned to Christian humanism, which was an attempt to reconcile Platonic philosophy with Christian theology— its fullest early expression was in the work of Marsilio Ficino and his Florentine Academy founded in 1462. Erasmus wanted to preserve what was best in the spirit of antiquity while resisting fanatical intolerance and promoting sound common sense and philosophic moderation. He studied Greek and wrote in Latin, but failed to learn Hebrew. He advocated the study of these three languages as an aid to uncovering the meaning of Christ's teachings; he was instrumental in the founding of a Trilingual College at Louvain in 1517. He wanted 'the simplicity and purity of Christ' to 'penetrate deeply into the minds of men; and this I think can best be brought to pass if with the help provided by the three languages we can exercise our minds in the actual sources'.

Erasmus' *Handbook* (literally, *Dagger*) *of the Christian Soldier* (*Enchiridion Militis Christiani*), which appeared in Latin in 1503, became the most popular summary of Christian humanism, and went into many editions and translations in his lifetime. In it, Erasmus depicted 'the pattern of the Christian life'[10] to provide a guide to practical piety and undogmatic morality. This pedagogic intention was carried over into his Latin *Colloquies*, published in their definitive form in 1533, although most of them had appeared in the years 1523–8. Rather different in content was his *Praise of Folly* (1511), which contained a blatant attack on Pope Julius II. The tone was relatively serene, but the criticism was serious: the church stood accused of failing to provide spiritual leadership. Nevertheless, Erasmus remained loyal to the established church and in 1516 he tactfully dedicated his Latin New Testament to Pope Leo X. As late as 1517, at the time of Luther's stand against Papal indulgences, Erasmus looked forward to a time when his 'philosophy of Christ',[11] an intense religious enthusiasm based on biblical scholarship, would dispel what he considered to be superstition and the empty ceremony of the late medieval church. In his *Instruction of a Christian Prince* (1516) he had summarized his position with a rhetorical question and answer: 'Who is truly Christian? Not he who is baptized or anointed, or who attends church. It is rather the man who has embraced Christ in his innermost feelings of his heart, and who emulates Him by pious deeds.'

Erasmus later incurred the wrath of the church because he made private criticism public without authorization from the Papacy, but his pre-eminence among the scholars of northern Europe ensured that he was not persecuted in his own lifetime. Nevertheless, certain of his theological views (particularly on the sacrament of the Eucharist, or the Mass, where initially he thought, as did the Protestant theologian Oecolompadius, that it was essentially a commemorative service) and his satirical attacks on conventional piety (especially the professional religiosity of monks and friars) brought him dangerously close to a charge of heresy. In Italy, traditionally minded ecclesiastics closely identified him with Luther, and considered Erasmus' fulminations against the trappings of religion to be the essence of the Reformation. However, Erasmus lacked formal theological training and was in the last resort always prepared to submit to the authority of the church—he did not finally reject Oecolampadius' view of the Eucharist on theological grounds but because it was 'opposed to the consensus of the church'; 'the authority of the church', he said, 'bound him' on the issue.[12] Elector Frederick of Saxony said of Erasmus that 'you never know where you are with him'.[13] This ambivalence was recognized by Luther in 1516–17, when he cast doubt on Erasmus' soundness as a theologian and noted that 'human considerations weigh more with Erasmus than the divine'.[14] It was a cruel comment, for there was nothing unworthy about Erasmus' vision of revitalizing the church from within. Nor should he be seen as mealy-mouthed: on the contrary, when he felt a strong commitment to an issue, Erasmus could write almost as vitriolically as Luther himself. He summed up his approach in a letter written in 1529: 'I did not wish that scholastic theology should be abolished, but that it should be purer and more serious ... Never have I condemned the constitutions and rites of the Church, nor taught that they were to be condemned; but I have given preference to the precepts of God; I have shown the progression from ceremonies to better things; and if by the negligence of man anything foreign to them has crept in, I have indicated how such might be corrected, a thing which the Church has often done.'

Erasmus typified the humanists' disinclination to pursue doctrinal questions to the point of confrontation with the ecclesiastical hierarchy. The difference between the humanists and the early Protestant reformers can be neatly summarized in their interpretations of the so-called 'Reformation scripture principle', which served in the 1520s to undermine the authority of church history and tradition. A humanist of the older generation, such as Erasmus, translated the phrase *sola scriptura* as 'not without scripture' and used the slogan as ammunition against an excessive reliance on church tradition. Though at first Luther did not disown the church, he thought it needed fundamental reform: 'you [Papists] have fallen away from us, that is the ancient church, and have set up a new church against the ancient one', he declared.[15] For Luther, the church was not an established hierarchy headed by the Pope so much as the 'gathering of all Christians upon earth' united by baptism: the church was 'a high, deep, hidden thing, which one may neither perceive nor see, but must grasp only by faith through baptism, sacrament and [the] word'.[16]

It was not inevitable that Luther and Erasmus would cross swords and make public the dividing line between Christian humanism and evangelical reform. However, in 1523 Pope Adrian VI asked Erasmus to refute what had emerged as the central aspect of Luther's teaching, that good works were irrelevant to salvation: Luther had asserted that 'the person of the man [must] be good or bad before he can do either a good or a bad work ...'[17] Bowing to the authority of the church hierarchy, Erasmus reluctantly issued a pamphlet *On the Freedom of the Will* the following year. Luther's reaction was predictable and violent. In *The Bondage of the Will* (1525), he declared Erasmus' view of free will 'a downright lie'.[18] The break between the two men was now final and it was never to be healed. The prince of the humanists had turned from a passive supporter to a passive opponent of the Reformation: he was now prepared to denounce Luther's 'arrogant, imprudent, seditious temperament' which threw 'all things sacred and profane into chaos'. Nevertheless, Luther's intransigence could not hide the fact that Erasmus had influenced a whole generation of scholars—Zwingli, Bucer, Melanchthon and Oecolampadius, to name only the most important—who only later turned to evangelical reform and broke with Catholicism. Moreover, Erasmus' views on education were shared by many of those later called 'Protestants' and formed a tradition of optimism about human capabilities within the Reformation. 'There is no branch of learning for which the human mind is not receptive', he averred, but added the proviso 'as long as we do not fail to supply instruction and practice'.[19] The influence of Erasmus' views on education, combined with the notoriety given by Paul IV's prohibition of his writings in 1559, had the effect of rehabilitating him posthumously in the eyes of Protestants.

Although his influence was pervasive, Erasmus did not control the separate humanist developments in Spain, France and Germany. The spread of humanism to Spain was marked by work on the Polyglot Bible in Castile; but Cisneros' concern to defend the orthodoxy of the translation infuriated the leading Spanish humanist Antonio of Lebrixa (known as Nebrija), who refused to associate himself with its publication. Erasmus' writings were not translated into Spanish until the years 1522–5. Nor did humanists escape prosecution in Spain. When Juan de Valdés published his *Dialogue of Christian Doctrine* in 1529, a form of catechism influenced by Erasmus, the Inquisition moved in quickly. Valdés was obliged to flee to Italy, and was subsequently convicted of heresy. His works were prohibited in Spain, and during the absence of Charles V from Castile between 1529 and 1533, the Inquisition prosecuted other humanists, associating in the public mind the teachings of Erasmus with the heresies of Luther. After an initial period of tolerance, the French school of humanism was also attacked, though by the Sorbonne rather than the Inquisition. The central humanist figure in France was Jacques Lefèvre d'Étaples, a mathematician, a grammarian and a philosopher, who had arrived at a mystical approach to Scripture by his own route; his translations of biblical texts are known to have influenced Luther. Guillaume Briçonnet, bishop of Meaux, gave Lefèvre support and encouragement after 1518 and Marguerite of Valois, the king's sister, was a correspondent of the bishop and a disciple of Lefèvre in the years 1521–4. Thereafter, Lefèvre's influence waned as the climate changed to one of persecution and increasingly rigid orthodoxy in France; he was even accused of Lutheranism, though the charge failed to stick.

The German humanists were less united around a central figure than their French or Spanish counterparts. One of them, Johannes Reuchlin, was perhaps the leading Christian authority on Hebrew learning. He was systematically slandered by a Moravian ex-Jew, Joseph (renamed Johann) Pfefferkorn, who led a campaign to suppress all Hebrew writings within the Empire. Reuchlin published a rebuttal of Pfefferkorn's writings entitled the *Eye Mirror* (*Augenspiegel*, 1511) and a subsequent *Defence against His False Accusers of Cologne* (1513). Though these publications were condemned by the universities of Cologne and Paris, the attempt to silence him failed when he received a sentence in his favour from the bishop of Speyer in 1514. Reuchlin's own priority was to defend his reputation rather than the goals and ideals of humanism; he did not attack scholastic theology in general, but reserved his criticisms for the handful of his opponents in the University of Cologne. Yet the attack on him was later interpreted as an outright assault on humanist learning. Both Reuchlin's supporters and opponents used Erasmus' name for their own purposes, although the leading Christian humanist was characteristically equivocal: he thought it 'calamitous to carry on warfare with a sordid and disreputable foe' such as Pfefferkorn; he professed to see no connection between the cause of 'good letters' and the Reuchlin affair.[20] As long as the New Testament was preserved, he would have preferred to see the Old Testament abolished rather than that 'the peace of Christendom should be broken for the sake of the books of the Jews'.[21]

The Reuchlin affair gave German humanism a more assertive and strident tone than elsewhere. Other German humanists did not view it with Erasmus' equanimity. A prominent Imperial knight, Ulrich von Hutten, defended Reuchlin in *Letters of Obscure Men* (1517), which went much further than Erasmus had done in criticizing the Pope (in this case, Leo X), and he appealed to the Emperor to reform the church. There is little doubt that humanists in Germany welcomed Luther's stand against the church hierarchy in 1517–20 because they considered him to be applying humanist principles to the study of Scripture. Yet although Luther encouraged Reuchlin, and drew upon the translations and commentaries of Erasmus and Lefèvre d'Étaples, he was by training not a humanist but a scholastic theologian. He was, however, of a reforming bent, a 'modern' rather than an 'ancient' in the terminology of the university environment in which he worked at Wittenberg, and he was a leading proponent of the reforming statutes introduced by that university in 1518. These statutes established humanist studies there and founded lectureships in Greek and Hebrew: the first professor of Greek was Philip Melanchthon, who was to become Luther's faithful subordinate and one of the leaders of his cause after his death. There was some truth in the view of hard-line Catholics that Christian humanism paved the way for the Lutheran revolt: Erasmus himself admitted that he seemed 'to have taught what Luther teaches, only not so savagely and without paradoxes and enigmas'.[22] Christian humanism had heightened the religious expectations of the laity, placed great emphasis on vernacular scriptures (particularly the epistles of St Paul), and condemned a religion of outward observance. The very swift diffusion of Lutheran and other evangelical ideas in the years 1520–5 arose from an ideological confusion in Germany to which the humanists had contributed more than their fair share.

1.2   The Lutheran Message and Its Opponents, 1517–1546

Many pages have been written about the early career of Martin Luther (1483–1546) before he became involved in the controversy over indulgences in 1517. Most accounts are highly speculative, particularly with regard to the influence of his father and his spiritual crisis in the years 1513–15. What is known for certain is that he passed the years 1509–17 in intensive study and preaching, as did many other worthy clerics. Only two facts indisputably separate Luther from his contemporaries and render his career of unique historical importance. The first is that as a result of his studies he arrived at theological opinions which were truly original, most notably, the doctrine of justification by faith alone. The second is that having developed these new views, Luther refused to keep them to himself. He confronted the church establishment with them in 1518–20. At each stage in the controversy, moreover, Luther not only failed to recant, but set about publicizing his cause. In 1517, he nailed his theses to the church door at Wittenberg in the medieval style of disputation; the following year, he refused to bow to the opinions of the Papal legate, the Dominican Cardinal Cajetan. In June 1520, Pope Leo X condemned Luther's writings and excommunicated him in the bull *Exsurge domine*. The bull condemned forty-one Lutheran propositions as a 'poisonous virus'[23] and defended the concept of purgatory, which Luther had rejected in his theses against indulgences. Whether or not Luther had of his own volition left the Catholic church, from June 1520 he was forced out of it, and the definitive bull of excommunication, *Decet*, was issued in January 1521.

It was crucial to the history of the Reformation that Luther was not silenced, as John Hus had been (by burning). Luther had a powerful, if an unexpected, protector. Elector Frederick the Wise of (Ernestine) Saxony was a paragon of late medieval piety. If he ever read Luther's ninety-five theses against indulgences, he would have had some qualms about offering his support, chiefly since he himself had accumulated Papal indulgences for 127,799 years in purgatory. But politics rather than religious belief governed the elector's behaviour. He was a political opponent of Cardinal Albrecht von Hohenzollern, and had banned Johann Tetzel from selling indulgences in his lands. He had another, financial, motive: he wanted to keep Saxon money at home. There was to be no competition with his local shrine, and no money leaving the duchy for Rome. Frederick also wanted to protect the reputation of the University of Wittenberg, which he had founded in 1502, and whose most famous professor—Martin Luther, appointed in 1512—stood condemned by the Papacy. Finally, as with all the princes of the Holy Roman Empire, he wanted to maintain his independence from the Emperor. At first, the elector was in a strong position. He won the first ballot in the Imperial election of 1519, and his refusal of the office—presumably because he lacked the resources to sustain it—had allowed the electors to agree on Charles V.

When Frederick demanded that no action be taken against Luther without hearing his case, the new Emperor could scarcely refuse. The Papal nuncio failed to stop Luther appearing before the Imperial diet at Worms with the Emperor's personal safeguard. Luther gained notoriety for his cause, and the Papacy suffered a disastrous loss of prestige. Once again, Luther failed to recant 'for it is neither safe nor right to act against one's conscience'.[24] Though Luther was declared a notorious heretic in May 1521, and placed under the ban of the Empire, he was allowed to leave Worms without any action being taken against him. The elector of Saxony initially placed him under protective custody in Wartburg castle. During the remainder of his life, until his death in 1546, Luther continued to enjoy the protection of the electors of Saxony. For nearly twenty-five years he was able to publicize his cause from the relative safety of electoral Saxony.

1.2.1 *The Teaching of Martin Luther*

Stated simply, the originality of Martin Luther's teaching lay in reasserting the link between theological disputation in the universities and the ordinary Christian's experience of contemplation (they had tended to go their separate ways in the later Middle Ages), in undermining the mediatory role of the clergy, and in reducing the number of sacraments from seven to two. This led to the reorganization of Christian behaviour along radically different lines from those advocated by the Catholic church. Between 1517 and his death, Luther was an extraordinarily prolific writer. It comes therefore as something of a surprise to discover that in all his multifarious writings and sermons, Luther never set out any formal theological system. The so-called 'Confession of Augsburg' of

1530, the document to which electoral Saxony and most of the reformed German princes and towns eventually subscribed, was in fact written by his protégé, Philip Melanchthon. The failure to systematize his thought arose in part from the developing religious controversy in which Luther found himself embroiled, and which to a large extent he had precipitated: he had no time for theorizing as long as it was necessary to denounce the opinions of others, or to defend his own views from counter-attack.

Consequently, Luther's views tended to evolve gradually. Nonetheless, it is possible to document a starting-point from which his teaching proceeded naturally: his meditations on Romans i.17, when he was preparing lectures in 1515–16 ('for therein is the righteousness of God revealed from faith to faith: as it is written, The just shall live by faith'). In 1545 Luther described the outcome of these meditations in dramatic terms: 'I felt myself to be born anew', he stated, 'and to enter through open gates into Paradise itself.'[25] And the reason was quite clear. Luther interpreted the term 'righteousness of God' in the biblical text to mean that 'the merciful God justified us by faith'.[26] This in essence was the origin of his doctrine of justification by faith alone, that man attained salvation simply because of his strength of faith, irrespective of his sinful nature or his performance of good works: 'as the soul needs the word [of God] alone for life and justification', Luther wrote, 'so it is justified by faith alone, and not by any works'.[27] Justification by faith had been a traditional Catholic teaching, which was prominent in the writings of St Augustine. But Luther took the doctrine to its extreme, arguing that man could attain salvation although he remained a sinner. This interpretation, when it was fully understood, deeply shocked traditional scholastic theologians, who argued that only a soul purified by love could become united with God and thus attain salvation. Luther's debt to the German mystical tradition, and to his mentor and predecessor in the chair of theology at Wittenberg, Johann von Staupitz, had been considerable, as the Augustinian background to his teaching and the intensity of his viewpoint showed, but he left both far behind when he reached this original conclusion.

In traditional Catholic teaching there were seven sacraments, namely baptism, confirmation, marriage, penance, the Mass (Eucharist), the last rites (extreme unction) and the conferring of priesthood (ordination). The original Augustinian doctrine of justification by faith had been considerably weakened by the sacrament of penance. A decision of the Fourth Lateran Council (1215) required every Christian to confess his sins at least once a year (it is doubtful if the practice was more regular in the fifteenth century) and to do penance for them. Those who had confessed their sins and had received the sacrament of penance were deemed after death to spend only a short time in purgatory to expiate their unforgiven venial sins before attaining salvation. Traditional church doctrine taught that the church itself had the power to remit the penalty for confessed sins because it had an accumulated 'treasury of merits' resulting from the 'keys of the church' being conferred on St Peter;[28] from this idea in turn developed the practice of issuing indulgences, the sale of remissions from time spent in purgatory, which reached its fullest extent after 1476.

Luther's concept of justification by faith alone removed the necessity for both penance and indulgences: a man's faith brought about forgiveness of his sins unconditionally. Luther stated categorically that the church could not remit the divine punishment of sin, and that the merits of Christ and the saints could not be disposed of by the Pope. Luther denounced those manuals of advice to confessors which tried to 'frighten people'.[29] This was not to say that Luther rejected altogether the necessity of doing penance. Throughout his lifetime, Luther underwent confession to a colleague, Bugenhagen, but he argued that this 'most salutary sacrament of penance' had become 'nothing but sheer tyranny' in the hands of the church.[30] The reformers' view of the sacrament of penance in the late Middle Ages was that it amounted to what might be termed a form of social control, with an ascetic sexual morality propounded in the manuals for confessors. Luther and the other reformers rebelled against this, assuaging the doubts and fears of the laity, exalting the status of matrimony (though not as a sacrament), and denying the necessity for clerical celibacy (all the Wittenberg reformers had married by 1525, the year in which Luther married).

The effect of Luther's attack on the concept of purgatory and the sacrament of penance was to undermine the mediatory role of the clergy. In his tract entitled *The Babylonian Captivity of the Church* (1520), Luther denounced ordination as 'the root of the terrible domination of the clergy over the laity' because it set them apart from the laity as a superior class.[31] Instead he proposed a concept which he called the 'universal priesthood of all believers': 'We who have all been baptised', he argued, 'are all uniformly priests in virtue of that very fact. The only addition received by priests is the office of preaching, and even this [is] with our consent . . .'[32] This did not imply that there would not be Lutheran pastors in electoral Saxony, just as there had been Catholic priests before the Reformation. They would be married, however, and their principal role would be to serve the laity, not to exercise discipline through control of the sacraments. Luther saw the role of the laity as being enhanced at the expense of the clergy. He envisaged the householder studying the Bible at home 'mornings and evenings, with his wife, children and servants, so as to make Christians of them, not only memorizing and reciting, but asking what each article means and how they understand it'.[33] Luther completed his own translation of the New Testament by 1522, and of the Old Testament by 1534. His translation of the Bible enjoyed a phenomenal success, a success which led directly to the standardization of the German language. He also determined that the Protestant catechism should include the Ten Commandments, the Apostles' Creed, the Lord's Prayer and the sacraments, and he exhorted the laity to practise it regularly 'so that it will become a natural thing to us . . . a distinguishing sign which no one can remove . . .'[34]

In the 1520s Luther and the other reformers had hopes of converting the laity by preaching and catechism practice, but these were not realized, despite the rapid spread of Protestantism. The tenacious resistance of local religious practice against imposed doctrine was one reason; the inner contradictions of the Lutheran programme were another. It has been seen that Luther and Erasmus differed radically on the issue of free will. Erasmus advised preachers 'not [to] tell the multitude that everything man does ends in sin'. In certain cases this was true, he thought, 'but unlearned persons are bound to interpret it in a way that does them no good'.[35] Luther, however, denied that good works could of themselves lead man towards salvation ('good works do not make . . . a good man, but a good man performs good works')[36] and Melanchthon expressed the Lutheran teaching when he stated that 'the beginning of the Christian life is to be frightened deep in our heart of the wrath of God and of our own sin'.[37] In practice this draconian view of man's depravity was somewhat moderated, but the overall impression of this teaching is that the moral burden on the individual was merely shifted from the sacrament of penance to the problem of belief itself. If men were 'evil through and through',[38] how could they act as 'bishops in their own homes'[39] inculcating the new doctrines? A contemporary reformer at Zurich, Huldrych Zwingli (1484–1531), denied any causal link between original sin and personal guilt. But Lutherans did not accept his reasoning on this, nor on many other matters. In the Confession of Augsburg it was stated categorically that 'because of Adam's fall, all men . . . are conceived and born in sin'.[40]

Before 1525, Luther hoped that the Reformation would develop naturally and peacefully among the laity without being imposed from above by the secular power or from below by any pressure group in society. In March 1522, on his return to the pulpit after his period in protective custody at the Wartburg castle, Luther disowned violent change and advocated 'win[ning] the hearts of the people'.[41] He could have 'led Germany into great bloodshed', so much so that the 'Emperor himself would have been in danger'. But he called such a course of action 'a fool's game'.[42] This view was in accord with the attitude of the elector Frederick the Wise, who made it clear that the Reformation was to proceed without 'division, tumult and trouble'.[43] It did so in Saxony, and by the time of the elector's death in May 1525, the Mass had been abolished in Wittenberg and the elector received the Lutheran Eucharist on his deathbed.

Frederick's successor, his younger brother, John the Steadfast, was far more committed to the evangelical cause, so much so that Luther called him 'God's faithful instrument'.[44] The new elector appointed a committee of visitation which was empowered after June 1527 to deprive of their livings clergy who did not conform to Lutheran beliefs. In March 1528, Melanchthon drew up instructions for the visitors, with a vigorous preface by Luther, and these provided the basis for subsequent Protestant territorial and municipal visitations.

In one of the few really effective pieces of counter-propaganda to Lutheranism, the *Great Lutheran Fool* (1522), Thomas Murner had argued that the Reformation would cause a social revolution: 'Christian [i.e. Protestant] faith frees us from all earthly authority. Before there ever was an emperor, king, or prince, we were all born free in our baptism'; 'to turn the world upside down—that is to bring the gospel into its own!', he contended.[45] Luther regarded these as serious allegations, which had to be refuted. In the same year he stated that he was opposed to 'those who rise in insurrection, no matter how just their cause'.[46] The Knights' War of 1522–3 was a potential disaster for Luther. The leaders of the revolt, Franz von Sickingen and Ulrich von Hutten, had been early supporters of the Reformation and had protected evangelical preachers in their lands. They misjudged their strength, attacked the elector of Trier for reasons of their own ambition (see chapter 6.3.2), and were defeated at Landstuhl in May 1523, where Sickingen was killed. Luther naturally felt it essential to dissociate his movement from an abortive rebellion. In a treatise on *Secular Authority: To what extent it should be obeyed* (1523), he drew the distinction between inward faith, which is immune from coercion, and outward obedience to the secular power. 'These two kingdoms must be sharply distinguished, and both be permitted to remain', Luther wrote, 'the one to produce piety, the other to bring about external peace and prevent evil deeds; neither is sufficient in the world without the other.'[47]

The Peasants' War of 1524–6 proved to be a much greater danger than the Knights' War, because behind it there lay the unintended influence of Luther's treatise *On the Liberty of a Christian Man* (1520). Luther had asserted in it that 'a Christian is a perfectly free lord of all, subject to none'—but later in the same sentence he moderated this statement, which could be taken out of context to imply a political challenge to rulers, by the comment that a Christian was also a 'perfectly dutiful servant of all, subject of all'.[48] Nevertheless, the rebellious peasants looked to Luther, Melanchthon and Frederick the Wise as possible mediators between themselves and the opposing forces of the Swabian League, a league of princes, towns and lesser nobility in south-west Germany, but they looked in vain (see chapter 7.3.3). It is very doubtful whether Luther would ever have responded favourably to the peasant demands, but his strong opposition was assured when he discovered that one of his arch-rivals since 1522, Thomas Müntzer, who had been expelled from electoral Saxony, was preaching to the Thuringian peasants in messianic and millenarian words. Using Daniel vii.26 as his text, Müntzer contended that if the princes did not fight against the godless in God's name, then the sword should be taken from them. Those who opposed the righteous might be slain without any mercy, just as Hezekiah destroyed the priests of Baal. Müntzer's message was that 'lords and princes as they now present themselves are not Christians' and that the time had come 'for bloodshed to fall upon this impenitent and unbelieving world'.[49] To Luther, Müntzer was simply the 'arch-devil of Mühlhausen', and in his tract *Against the Murderous and Thieving Hordes of Peasants* (May 1525), he thundered that nothing was 'more poisonous, obnoxious and devilish than a rebellious man'.[50] In the same month, one of the main peasant armies was crushed at Frankenhausen. Müntzer was captured, tortured and allegedly recanted before execution. Melanchthon pointed to the terrible lessons in his *Horrible History and Judgement of God upon Thomas Müntzer* published later in the year. Had Müntzer's views prevailed, the propertied classes would have stampeded into allegiance with Rome. The high hopes of 1520–5, that the movement for evangelical reform would find its main support among the worthy peasantry acting as lay preachers, were dashed. In Luther's words, 'Müntzer spoiled it all.'[51]

1.2.2 *The Radical Challenge: Millenarianism and Anabaptism*

The idea of the Apocalypse, that the world was coming to an end and the Day of Judgement was at hand for all mankind, was inherent in the early Reformation as it had been in the early Christian church. Luther was firmly convinced by 1520 that Antichrist had established his headquarters at Rome and that the world was nearing the final phase announced in the book of Revelation. He did not see himself as a reformer, but as a preacher of the gospel in a period of prayer and repentance preceding the second coming of Christ. He was responsible for the congregation of the faithful in 'these last days' and he believed that true reformation could only be brought about by God, and not on this earth. In 1530, when he dedicated his translation of the book of Daniel to the young prince John Frederick of Saxony, he commented that 'the world is running faster and faster, hastening towards its end, so that I often have the strong impression that the Last Day may break before we have turned the Holy Scriptures into German!'[52] (Luther did not complete his translation of the Bible until 1534). 'This is the time we have to be prepared to live dangerously', Luther remarked; the kingdom of Christ was near, but in the meantime the Devil was loose in the world. The previous year he had expounded the story of

Gog Magog in the book of Ezekiel: 'for Scripture prophesies to us two terrible tyrants, who on the eve of the Last Day will lay waste and destroy Christendom—the one spiritually and with false and poisonous teaching and worship, that is the Pope with all his Popery—the other with his sword in a bodily and outward fashion . . . and that is the Turk'.[53]

Yet Luther was no chiliast, no believer in the doctrine of the millennium, that Christ would reign in bodily presence on earth for a thousand years. He made no specific prediction as to when the end of the world would come, unlike Hans Wolff and Melchior Hoffman, who both predicted in the same year (1526) that it would end in 1533. Nor did Luther believe in a revolutionary transformation of society brought about by the rule of a theocracy; on the contrary, he preferred secular to clerical power. In his view, a 'strict hard, temporal government' was necessary so that 'peace may not perish, and trade and society may not be utterly destroyed . . . Let no one think that the world can be ruled without blood; the sword of the ruler must be red and bloody; for the world will and must be evil, and the sword is God's rod and vengeance upon it.'[54]

Luther's drastic elimination of five of the seven Catholic sacraments meant that the remaining two—baptism and the Eucharist—assumed unprecedented importance in the reformist movement. The reformers began to disagree among themselves on the interpretation to be placed on them, and to the Wittenberg reformer, it seemed that his leadership was being challenged on all sides by 'fanatics' (*Schwärmer*). Even the moderate Erasmus commented that 'now every Tom, Dick and Harry claims credence, who testifies that he has the Spirit of the gospel'.[55] Another renegade from electoral Saxony, Andreas von Karlstadt, came to have a profoundly disturbing influence on the Reformation by abandoning the sacrament of baptism altogether after he left Wittenberg. Karlstadt refused to baptize infants in his parish at Orlamünde in 1523. Other reformers advocated the rebaptizing of adults. The first recorded instance of this occurred on 21 January 1525 at Zurich, when Conrad Grebel, who was certainly influenced by the views of both Karlstadt and Müntzer, baptized George Blaurock, a married ex-priest from a peasant family near Chur. From this procedure of adult baptism developed the term Anabaptist (although it was not one used by the radicals themselves, and it is a loose description for a collection of differing views held by a variety of men and women). Lutheranism advocated infant baptism, which was the rule in the Catholic church, for it held that though baptism might be involuntary for the child, the community at large believed for him: in this sense it was a sacrament. Whatever the disagreements between Luther, Zwingli, Oecolampadius and Calvin, they were united in defence of infant baptism, albeit from different standpoints. The leading opponent of the Anabaptists was Zwingli, who in the years 1525–7 produced four great tracts defending infant baptism. 'Among these early Anabaptists', Zwingli commented, 'I have seen ... nothing but ... saturnine melancholic characteristics, obstinacy and perversity, with, at the same time, a measureless thirst for fame ...'.[56] Adult rebaptism was first made a capital offence at Zurich in March 1526; it became a capital offence in the whole of the Holy Roman Empire in January 1528, a decision which was reinforced in April 1529.

The radicals argued that infant baptism lacked clear biblical foundation and made the beginning of religious life impersonal and involuntary. They only wanted to baptize people who were old enough to choose freely for themselves the Christian way of life, in imitation of Christ's baptism by John the Baptist. One of the early Anabaptist theologians, Balthasar Hubmaier, argued in his treatises *On the Christian Baptism of Believers* (1525) and *On Infant Baptism* (1527) that an 'inward baptism of the Spirit' must precede the 'outward' form of baptism ('an outward pledge to live a new life according to Christ's word'), without which it was mere hypocrisy: 'woe to those who practise hypocrisy in such matters'.[57] Later Anabaptist theologians, such as Menno Simons in his *Foundation of the Christian Life* (1539), reversed the position of earlier thinkers such as Hubmaier and denied all sacramental character to baptism and the Eucharist: for Simons, adult baptism was only an external sign of obedience and a good conscience.

The structure and organization of the church was also turned upside down by the radicals. The earlier radicals argued that the church was no more than separate, independent units of believers meeting together, not a hierarchy with a definite structure headed by the clergy: each local church was a legitimate 'believing congregation'. Furthermore, they had un-orthodox, and contemporaries thought, dangerous views on the organiza-tion of society. They avoided the normal obligations of citizens, such as military service to defend the state, and the refusal of many of them to take oaths aroused grave fears among the magisterial reformers: 'take away the oath', Zwingli insisted, 'and public order is dissolved'.[58] The radicals wanted the 'free faith' of pacifist communities separated from the secular world, not Lutheran 'state religion'. The true Christian lived 'without external or worldly defences'; he must shun the world, for it was the kingdom of darkness; true citizenship was in heaven not earth: Christ and Belial had nothing in common.[59]

One of the earliest statements of their beliefs was the Schleitheim Con-fession of faith drawn up in February 1527 by Michael Sattler and possibly William Reublin. In this, the only ecclesiastical control they recognized was the use of the 'ban' (by which was meant excommunica-tion). The public should, they thought, refuse to take oaths to uphold the secular power. It is doubtful whether the Schleitheim Confession represented a complete view of the opinions of even one group of radicals in 1527; they certainly did not agree with other radicals who were termed 'certain false brethren among us'.[60] The man who almost single-handedly transplanted Anabaptism into northern Europe, Melchior Hoffman, rejected both of the central tenets of faith in the Schleitheim Confession. He accepted that the secular authority had no place in the realm of faith, at least in normal circumstances. On the other hand, the secular power was legitimate: such sins of weakness and ignorance that a Christian ruler committed in the course of his work did not threaten his salvation, since Christ atoned for them on the cross; even an executioner was a servant of God if he used the axe to enforce justice. Moreover, Hoffman rejected the idea of free congregations without a sense of hierarchy or church structure; instead, they were to be controlled by 'prophets', who were in turn subject to 'apostolic messengers' such as himself.[61] His primary concern was to establish a rival theological position to Luther's (accordingly, the Wittenberg reformer formulated a detailed rebuttal of Hoffman's views in 1527). Unlike Luther, Hoffman and the other radicals refused to attribute Adam's sin to his descendants; man was not therefore bonded to sin—he echoed Erasmus' viewpoint in the debate with Luther over free will, that despite the fall of Adam man was still enlightened by reason. In Hoffman's view, God was 'no respecter of persons ... and has brought [every man] true enlightenment and knowledge, and placed his will again in his own hands ...'.[62] Hoffman abhorred the resort to violence, as Luther did. But he saw that a climate of persecution had advantages for his sect. The true Christian, in his view, should be prepared to face persecution and martyrdom until the Lord ushered in his kingdom with his second coming. Hoffman's rejection of many of the tenets of the Schleitheim Confession suggests that conflicts within the theology of the radicals and the absence of an agreed form of church organization probably prevented Anabaptism becoming a unified mass movement—this despite one historian's description of it as the Protestantism of the poor.

Hoffman was imprisoned at Strasbourg while on his travels in 1533, but his disciple Jan Matthijsz assumed the role of apostolic messenger and announced the second coming of Christ. Matthijsz accepted three of Hoffman's key radical ideas, that the godless must be destroyed before the Last Judgement, that a new theocracy would come to rule over the earth, and that the apostolic messengers would be invulnerable and invincible. These events would usher in the second coming of Christ. However, Matthijsz went further than Hoffman in two key respects: he regarded all religious and secular authorities as tyrannical enemies of the new kingdom of God and thus in need of destruction. Moreover, the holy congregation of the last days (that is, the radical Anabaptist community) should itself take up the sword to secure this—an idea which Hoffman rejected until the end of his life. Matthijsz's millenarian views were propagated in East Friesland, particularly at Emden, in the years 1530–3. In January 1534, he sent representatives to the bishopric of Münster, where the Lutherans were poised to seize control, and they began to rebaptize adults. One of these representatives was Jan Beukelsz ('John of Leyden'), the infamous leader of the later revolt, who had been rebaptized by Matthijsz. Almost immediately, the Lutheran party in the city mistakenly allied with the radical Anabaptists against Münster's bishop, who had blockaded the city. These circumstances allowed the Anabaptists to emerge as the dominant force in municipal elections which were held in February 1534 in an atmosphere of fear and intimidation. Hardly had the Anabaptists been established in power than they began to dismantle the whole of the city's constitutional structure. The isolation and siege of their so-called 'New Jerusalem' had already started.

From the early days of the siege, pamphlets were produced which outlined the ideals and aspirations of the radicals rather than the actual conditions within the city of Münster. After Jan Matthijsz was killed in April 1534, in a foolhardy attempt to disperse the besieging army, John of Leyden established a ruthless theocratic rule. He was king; Münster was his Israel. The citizens were referred to as 'Israelites', and they were governed by Twelve Elders of the Tribes. The death penalty was used freely. All this was bad enough, but what stunned public opinion throughout Europe—and killed Anabaptism as a mass movement, even assuming it had a realistic chance of success in the 1530s—were the twin practices of holding all goods in common and polygamy (even Hoffman condemned the latter practice as 'whoremongering'). The siege lasted over a year, but in the end, the conquest of the New Jerusalem was made possible by betrayal from within, and in June 1535 the city was taken and put to the sword. John of Leyden, who during the siege had taken fifteen wives, was captured, tortured and executed.

Adult rebaptism had been made compulsory at Münster in February 1534, and polygamy was introduced in July 1534 on the pretext that the Old Testament had called for the faithful 'to be fruitful and multiply'. The aim had been to reach the figure of 144,000 inhabitants as quickly as possible, since this had an eschatalogical significance. Thus the family, as it had been known before the Anabaptist regime, was abolished. What had been private was to be made communal: doors were to be kept open to demonstrate that living space, along with food, clothing and wealth, were to be shared by all. It is clear that the Catholic patricians who had ruled Münster before the Anabaptist rising stood to lose everything from these changes; for the upper classes, the restoration of Catholicism and family prosperity were viewed as synonymous. Yet it would be misleading to see the Anabaptist revolt as resting exclusively on lower-class support.

Following the capture of the city, the prince bishop abolished the guilds in June 1535, thus identifying the union of seventeen craft guilds (*Gesamtgilde*) as the instigator of the trouble. In fact, in 1533 the traditional leadership of the guilds seems to have favoured the Lutheran position, but it was swept aside by more radical guildsmen the following year. The millenarian kingdom they sought was a Christian republic with male supremacy. Women had traditionally been excluded from guild membership and from office-holding at Münster, as elsewhere in Europe, and were subordinated in the Anabaptist kingdom to their polygamous husbands: their road to salvation lay through the mediation of rebaptized adult males with God. This did not meet with universal approval: some women at least had strongly opposed the installation of an Anabaptist regime which undermined their social and religious independence. There were many more women Anabaptists than males at Münster, it is true, but this is explained by the city's demographic structure: polygamy served a practical purpose, since it placed the large number of surplus women (spinsters, widows, young servant girls, and so on) firmly under patriarchal authority.

It was characteristic of the hostile attitude of the Lutheran princes that even the usually tolerant Philip of Hesse sent representatives to interrogate John of Leyden, with the aim of establishing a link between him and Hoffman, who was still imprisoned at Strasbourg. The sects had to regroup in August 1536 at Bocholt under the more moderate leadership of David Joris, who rejected both resistance to the secular authority and polygamy. The decisive leadership in a pacifist direction came later with Menno Simons, who became an Anabaptist only in January 1536—the month of Leyden's execution. There were disagreements between Joris and Simons, but after 1544 the Mennonites recognized the need for a more rigid church structure and a more formalized relationship between the individual and the religious community. Menno Simons rejected the Münster experiment in the clearest terms: 'I have never seen Münster, nor have I ever been in their fellowship. I trust that by the grace of God I shall never eat or drink with such . . . unless they truly repent.' Nevertheless, by 1536, the excesses of the kingdom of Münster had killed off the hopes of a successful radical Reformation along Anabaptist lines. In the longer term, it was Calvinism, not Anabaptism, which was to exploit best the radical sentiments left unsatisfied by Lutheran orthodoxy. On the other hand, success was not guaranteed: there remained significant numbers of Anabaptists in the Low Countries, and it is not surprising that Calvinists were particularly vehement in their denunciation of the 'vile and murderous poison' of the 'Münsterites'. As late as 1544, Calvin wrote a tract *Against the Anabaptists*, in which he argued that 'it is easy to see that these wretched feather-brained individuals tend only in one direction, which is to put all to disorder and have all goods in common such that whoever can seize the most will be praised. They may deny any such intention now. But if one removes all the laws and arbitrators from the world, as they intend and strictly demand, what will result except an unrestrained brigandage?'[63]

1.2.3 *The Eucharistic Controversy*

A second area of controversy among the reformers centred on the sacrament of the Eucharist. The biblical text at the heart of the Eucharistic debate was Christ's comment on the bread and wine at the last supper, reported by both St Matthew and St Mark: 'Take, eat; this is my body which is given for you' and 'drink ye all of it, for this is my blood of the new testament, which is shed for many for the remission of sins'. The Roman Catholic teaching of the Mass was established at the Fourth Lateran Council of 1215 and confirmed at the Council of Trent in 1551–2. The flesh, blood, soul and divinity of Christ was taken to be present at the Mass 'really and substantially'. Through consecration of the bread and wine there came about a real conversion of the substances into the flesh and blood of Christ, so that only their appearances (or 'accidents') persisted.

Luther denounced the Catholic doctrine of 'transubstantiation' in *The Babylonian Captivity of the Church* (1520) as 'a human invention ... not supported by Scripture or reason'.[64] The early fathers of the church did not use the term and 'for over 1200 years the church remained orthodox' until the Fourth Lateran Council. Luther insisted that since Christ also said 'drink ye all of it, for this is my blood ...', there was no biblical justification for the Catholic practice of refusing the cup to the laity. The sacrament of the Eucharist or Holy Communion should therefore be received in both kinds, the bread and the wine. Furthermore, Luther denied the church's teaching that the Eucharist was a sacrifice, namely that each time a participant took the bread he literally partook of the body of the sacrificed Christ. He did not, however, maintain (as did the Zwinglians, and later the Calvinists) that the Eucharist was a simple commemorative service, and his teaching on this point is usually (though inaccurately) termed 'consubstantiation'. He believed that the body and blood of Christ coexisted with the bread and wine after it had been consecrated. Luther illustrated this by the analogy of the iron put into the fire, whereby both fire and iron united in the red-hot iron, and yet each continued essentially unchanged. The Confession of Augsburg of 1530 (known as the *invariata*) confirmed his view that 'the body and blood of Christ are really present ... our churches reject those who teach otherwise'.[65]

However, Luther's doctrine was not to be easily supported with biblical texts and it was not readily accepted by all the reformers. Though he had not been prepared to challenge the authority of the church, Erasmus had viewed the Eucharist simply as a commemorative service and other reformers followed this line. It seems that Andreas Karlstadt was the first to teach it, after he was forced out of Wittenberg in 1522. Luther warned the reformers at Strasbourg against Karlstadt, but he seems to have been influential among the south German and Swiss reformers. The Hollander Cornelisz Hoen wrote a short treatise on the Eucharist at some date before 1524, which was published at Zurich in 1525 and is known to have influenced Zwingli. In it, he argued that 'is' in Christ's words 'this is my body' really meant 'signifies'. Johannes Oecolampadius at Basel followed this view, as did Zwingli at Zurich, who recalled that the Greek term *Eucharist* meant thanksgiving, which gave the sacrament a radically different purpose from that of a sacrifice. In August 1525, Zwingli issued the first of six tracts which inaugurated the so-called 'sacramentarian' controversy, a fierce pamphlet war between himself and Luther which lasted from 1526–8. With typical venom, Luther refuted his rivals. In July 1525, he denounced the views of Karlstadt and Zwingli on the Eucharist as 'worse doctrines than those of the [Catholic] propagandists'. In March 1527, he issued a pamphlet entitled *That these words of Christ 'this is my body', etc., still stand firm against the fanatics.*[66]

These differences could not be easily settled and were to have repercussions both inside and outside Germany. The Lutheran princes wanted a doctrinal agreement among the reformers to ease the way to a political union. Despite the pressing need for compromise, the Marburg conference between Lutherans and Zwinglians, summoned by Philip of Hesse in October 1529, ended in disagreement. Personal animosities played a part. Luther thought Zwingli an 'insolent Swiss', whose teachings were 'seven times more dangerous than when he was a Papist . . .'[67] Zwingli in turn denounced Luther's 'countless inconsistencies, absurdities and follies which he babbles out like water lapping on the shore . . .'[68] The debates were undoubtedly heated, and the crucial final article simply noted that 'we have not agreed at this moment whether the true body and blood of Christ be corporally present in the bread and wine . . .'[69] However, the Confession of Augsburg of the following year left the issue in no doubt, and represented a victory for the Lutheran interpretation. But it was not accepted by Zwingli, who drew up his own Confession of Faith (*Fidei ratio*), or by Martin Bucer and Wolfgang Capito of Strasbourg who compiled a rival document known as the Tetrapolitan Confession. Zwingli was pursuing his own military crusade against the Catholic cantons, which led to his death on the battlefield of Kappel in October 1531. After this, Zurich was not in a position to defend Strasbourg or any of the other south German cities against the wrath of the Emperor Charles V. Only electoral Saxony, Hesse and the other Lutheran princes could provide this protection, and they formed the Schmalkaldic League in December 1530 precisely to do this. However, the price of this protection, and of accession to the League, was a heavy one: acceptance of the Confession of Augsburg. Martin Bucer subscribed to this document in 1532 and led a movement of reconciliation (in fact, capitulation) to the Wittenberg reformers that ended with the Concord of 1536.

There were further attempts to break the deadlock between Lutheranism and Zwinglianism, which had resulted in the Swiss churches remaining outside the Confession of Augsburg. In the revised Confession of 1540, known as the *variata*, to which Melanchthon, Bucer and the young Frenchman, Jean Calvin, appended their names, the form of words was changed so that the Lutheran churches taught that with 'the bread and wine the very body and blood of Christ are truly *offered* [instead of "present"] to those who eat the Lord's Supper'.[70] Calvin himself made the Eucharist the central article of faith, but while he criticized Zwingli's position, his own view was equivocal. He rejected Lutheran teaching on the Eucharist as formulated in the Confession of Augsburg of 1530 (the *invariata*), which led him into a heated polemic with the Lutheran Joachim Westphal of Hamburg after 1552. He was also prepared to join with Zurich under the leadership of Heinrich Bullinger in 1549 in a common confession of faith known as the *Consensus Tigurinus*. Yet this document should not be quoted as evidence for Calvin's theological views, as his Lutheran critics tried to do; it represented the extreme limit to which Calvin was prepared to go in the cause of political unity with Zurich. To Calvin the bread and wine were both 'visible signs', a concession to the Zwinglian view, and 'instruments' by which 'the substance is ... given us in its reality',[71] which was close to Luther's teaching. The interpretation of the Eucharist remained a source of contention not merely between Lutherans and Calvinists, but among Lutherans themselves until 1580. What is certain, however, is that all Protestants (including the radicals, who tended to take a more extreme view than Zwingli) rejected transubstantiation and the notion of the sacrifice. The Catholic defence of this doctrine, and the Protestant rejection of 'idolatrous Masses', were crucial reasons for the failure of the Colloquy of Regensburg in April–May 1541, when there was a belated attempt at theological compromise between Catholics and Lutherans (see chapter 1.5.1).

1.3 The Spread of the Early Reformation

Despite the crucial importance of Luther's theological originality, it is essential to recognize that the early Reformation was diverse and had many leaders. It was by no means inevitable that Lutheranism would become the dominant force within the German Reformation; nor was it certain that the movement for reform would itself succeed in the sense of winning a permanent and guaranteed place in the constitution of the Holy Roman Empire. It is possible to see a contrast between the early years of the Reformation, particularly the 1520s, when it was seemingly so successful, and the period after 1540 when it gradually lost its vigour. Some historians have argued that the impact of the Reformation was destined to be of a temporary nature only, since it harnessed short-term social and political aspirations during the 1520s but thereafter resigned itself to becoming purely an intellectual movement, whose existence was guaranteed by a political party—the Schmalkaldic League and its successors.

1.3.1 *The Failure of Catholic Containment in the Empire*

Luther deliberately courted political controversy as part of his strategy for spreading his teaching. In 1520, he addressed the Catholic princes directly in his *Appeal to the Christian Nobility of the German Nation*, written in the vernacular, in which he adroitly listed a range of grievances they felt in their relations with Rome. Many German emperors, Luther claimed, had been 'shamelessly trodden under foot and oppressed by the Popes' and he feared the 'same experience under our noble Emperor Charles'.[72] However, by his Imperial coronation oath at Aachen in October 1520, Charles V had sworn to 'keep and advance' the Catholic faith, to protect the church and show due obedience to the Pope.[73] At the diet of Worms in May 1521, Charles placed Luther under the ban of the Empire and declared him a notorious heretic. The Emperor lectured the assembled princes to do their duty as good Christians. He told them he would 'risk his kingdoms, lordships, friends, body, life and soul' to prevent the spread of heresy. He recalled that previous Emperors, kings of Spain, archdukes of Austria and dukes of Burgundy had all died true sons of the church.[74] To ensure that the ban was known and enforced throughout the Empire, Charles V issued it simultaneously in May 1521 in German and Latin versions for circulation in Germany, and Dutch and French versions to apply to the Netherlands. Charles meant what he said, and where he enjoyed real authority—in the Netherlands and in Spain—the heresy laws were vigorously enforced. By 1525, preachers in the Netherlands were forbidden to so much as mention Luther in their public sermons, even in condemnation, for fear that this would draw people's attention to the reformer of whom they might 'neither [have] thought nor heard' before.[75] Similarly, gatherings to read and discuss the Bible were prohibited, and vernacular editions of the Scriptures thought suspect were burnt. More important still, after 1523 the public authorities in the Netherlands were prepared to burn heretics—though before the Anabaptist scare of 1535, proceedings for heresy were rare, and were far outnumbered by cases of vagabondage, robbery and violence.

The contrast with Germany could not be more complete. Charles V was absent in Spain and then Italy in the years 1522–30. His presence in Germany would have made some difference to the course of the Reformation there, as the fears aroused by his return in 1530–1 indicate. Nevertheless, even if the Emperor had devoted all his attention to the Lutheran problem in Germany, it is difficult to believe that he would have made much headway. The evangelical movement was able to develop in comparative security because of the practical political independence enjoyed by princes and free cities under the Imperial constitution. Luther's books were printed and sold openly in contempt of the Edict of Worms. His cause was championed in municipal councils as well as in public debates staged to ascertain the preferences of burghers and leading citizens. The Imperial diet made a fatal error in February 1523 when it ordered that henceforth the clergy should preach 'only the holy gospel in accordance with the writings approved and accepted by the holy Christian church'.[76] The intention was to safeguard the Catholic interpretation of Scripture. In practice, this decision gave the evangelical preachers a free hand, since they claimed that all they said had biblical authority. The introduction of the Reformation into cities such as Zurich, Strasbourg, Constance and Nuremberg was preceded by lively theological disputations.

The princes were less susceptible than the municipal oligarchies to pressure from below to give evangelical preachers a pulpit, and there were relatively few conversions among them before 1526. Electoral Saxony was a special case because of Luther's residence at Wittenberg. Philip of Hesse was converted initially by Melanchthon in 1524, and within four years he was an articulate spokesman for the Reformation, capable of arguing points of doctrine with Luther and Zwingli. There is no question about the sincerity of his conversion. Speaking about it to his mother in 1525, Philip stated that 'if anyone can prove to me out of the Word of God that I am wrong, then I will gladly follow him'; but if not, he would 'gladly suffer [harm] for the sake of God . . .'[77] The conversion of princes was sincere; but undoubtedly it was also in their financial interests. The secularization of church property was an attraction; monasteries and nunneries were dissolved in Hesse in 1526–7, for example, and the revenues went partly into Philip's coffers and partly towards the cost of founding Marburg University. The revenues from church lands rose as a proportion of Philip's total net revenues from 20 per cent in 1532 to 30 per cent in 1565. In April 1525 the Teutonic Order in Prussia (one of the last crusading orders of the Middle Ages) was dissolved and the Reformation was introduced there. The last Grand Master, Albrecht von Hohenzollern, became the first duke of Prussia with an established revenue from the secularization of church property. But the most extensive seizure of church property occurred in Württemberg, where it had amounted to a third of the landed wealth of the country and double the landholdings of the duke himself: within two years of reconquering his duchy in 1534 (see chapter 2.4.3), duke Ulrich confiscated all monastic property and at least half of the 1,200 benefices held by the secular clergy. Although the church revenues were administered in a separate fund from those of the state after Ulrich's death in 1550, elsewhere in Germany—at least in those principalities where the estates or representative institutions were weak—the immediate financial benefit of secularization went to the prince, and on a larger scale than has sometimes been thought.

Even as late as 1525, such political and financial consequences still lay in the future. Had the Catholic princes formed an effective alliance to attack the Lutherans at an early stage, the progress of the Reformation in Germany might have been seriously impeded. The staunchly Catholic duke George of (Albertine) Saxony summoned a meeting of Catholic princes to Dessau in June 1525 with the aim of defending the church against the teachings of Luther. This threat in turn prompted John the Steadfast, the new elector of (Ernestine) Saxony, and Philip of Hesse to found a rival evangelical grouping. However, in July 1526 Charles V announced his willingness to negotiate with the Pope over the summoning of a general council of the church to discuss ecclesiastical (and perhaps doctrinal) reform, which defused the situation in Germany. At the Imperial diet of Speyer the following month, his brother Ferdinand made the hopelessly optimistic promise of a general council within eighteen months. In the meantime, the Edict of Worms would be implemented 'as each . . . thought right before God and his Imperial majesty'.[78] The Speyer declaration provided a temporary guarantee of security to the Lutherans and maintained the status quo regarding their possession of secularized church lands. In the next three years, the reformed faith continued to make progress, but without any commensurate increase in political effectiveness or organization. When Ferdinand revoked the guarantee at the second diet of Speyer in April 1529, six princes and fourteen Imperial cities 'protested', giving 'Protestantism' its name. Ironically, this same diet saw Protestants and Catholics in complete agreement that rebaptism was an heretical crime and capital offence. They were united against the Anabaptists, which explains the severity of the persecution against this radical sect.

By the end of 1529, the Habsburg position in Europe appeared stronger. A Turkish siege of Vienna had failed and a peace settlement had temporarily ended Charles V's involvement in the Italian wars (see chapter 2.3.3). The scene was set for the Emperor's return to Germany and his decisive intervention in the course of the Reformation. In June 1530 seven princes, together with the representatives of Nuremberg and Reutlingen, presented the Emperor with the Confession of Augsburg, compiled by Melanchthon. In October, Charles rejected the document, and the following month the Imperial diet set the deadline of April 1531 for the return of Lutherans to the Catholic fold. The threat of force was backed up by an attempt to use the supreme Imperial court (*Reichskammergericht*) to enforce the Edict of Worms by judicial means. The Augsburg ultimatum had the effect of concentrating the minds of the Lutheran princes. Before October 1530, John of Saxony had rejected Hesse's argument that attack was the best form of defence and that it was lawful to resist the Emperor. Now a fully-fledged theory of resistance was developed by the reformers. Luther reversed his earlier opinion that the Emperor could not be opposed. Instead, if war broke out, those who opposed 'murderers and bloodthirsty Papists' would be acting in self-defence against unjust force.[79] A more daring ideology went hand in hand with greater doctrinal unity among the reformers; the Lutherans organized themselves more effectively in a new political association, called the League of Schmalkalden, which gradually increased its membership in the 1530s. All of this ultimately led to war with Charles V in 1546–7.

1.3.2 *The Diffusion of the Reformation in Germany*

The historian can only surmise how instrumental were such issues as the medieval doctrine of penance, or the failure of the church to develop a convincing lay piety, in leading individuals to break with the established church. It can rarely have been an easy decision. Apart from the fear of the legal consequences of dissent—execution and the confiscation of the family property of the heretic in the Netherlands, where the Edict of Worms was enforced—individuals had become part of the Catholic church through baptism. Avoidance of confession and the Mass might be interpreted as the first move towards breaking with the Catholic church. Private Bible reading and attendance at evangelical sermons were a further step towards schism. Families might become divided in choosing their form of religious observance. It is impossible to prove that the German public rapidly attained an accurate grasp of Luther's doctrine of justification by faith alone, leaving aside his still more difficult concept of the Eucharist. But the enormous popularity of his writings suggests that the essentials of his message found a receptive audience.

The advent of printing cannot be said to have caused the Reformation.

But it was a powerful instrument in Luther's hand; in his own words, it was 'God's highest and extremest act of grace, whereby the business of the gospel is driven forward'.[80] Probably half the literature which was printed before 1500 (which has been estimated at 10 million books throughout Europe) was religious in character. Both the educated laity and the clergy bought religious books, including Bibles in the vernacular, theological summaries, manuals, breviaries, books of sermons, scholastic and patristic texts. Many of Luther's early writings were in Latin, which in principle posed no linguistic problem to the educated classes; indeed, the relatively undeveloped state of the native languages in France and Germany might have created a greater barrier to communication for the sophisticated theologian used to working in Latin.

Yet Latin was clearly an obstacle to the spread of Reformation ideas among a wider cross-section of society. In Italy, for example, it is thought that less than 5 per cent of the population (including a good number of the clergy) in the sixteenth century could read Latin sufficiently well to be able to understand a book written by Luther or Zwingli. Translations were thus of crucial importance, as Lefèvre d'Étaples had seen, when he promoted his New Testament 'so that the simpler members of the body of Jesus Christ, having it in their language, could be as certain of evangelical truth as those who had it in Latin'.[81] At first, Luther intended his translation of the New Testament to be placed in the hands of the public at large. He said of St John's Gospel and St Paul's Epistle to the Romans that 'every Christian should read these first and foremost and by means of daily reading make them as common and ordinary to himself as his daily bread'.[82] Yet in the last edition of his German New Testament in 1546, the references to laymen reading the Gospel were dropped. Luther's experience in dealing with the radicals had convinced him of the need for expert guidance in the interpretation of the Bible: 'nowadays everyone thinks he is a master of Scripture, and every Tom, Dick and Harry imagines he understands the Bible and knows it inside out'.[83] He commented that his theological works were not destined for the common man, but 'for the theologian and the bishop, so that they may be well educated and thus capable of preaching holy doctrine'.[84] But in contrast, the purpose of his two German catechisms of 1529 was to bridge the gap with the laity. 'The catechism is the layman's Bible', Luther remarked, for 'it contains the whole of what every Christian must know of Christian doctrine.'[85]

Vernacular Bibles were relatively expensive: Luther's Bible cost the equivalent of three weeks' labour for a mason or carpenter in Saxony. The price was sufficiently high that the 200,000 or so German Bibles published in the sixteenth century (perhaps equivalent to one Bible for every seventy people) were probably intended primarily for the Lutheran clergy. In

Denmark and Sweden, the Bible was produced in translation exclusively for distribution to the parishes: the Swedish New Testament of 1526, for example, was financed by a subscription imposed on all the parish clergy of Sweden and Finland. In contrast, the 200,000 or so vernacular Bibles and New Testaments published in the Low Countries between 1520 and 1566, equivalent to one Bible for every twenty-five Flemish speakers, were so numerous that they can only have been purchased by the population at large. Literacy levels and the degree of urbanization were higher in the Low Countries than elsewhere, which helps explain this phenomenon.

Printing had an importance even for the illiterate. It should not be assumed that reading was a private, individual pursuit: on the contrary, it is thought that perhaps most of the reading in the sixteenth century (particularly in the vernacular) was done aloud to an audience. As a result, the modern distinction between the written word and the medium of preaching was more blurred in the Reformation. Zwingli, making no allowances to his audience, wrote either in Latin or in a 'shaggy, tangled German which makes you sweat before you understand it' (according to Luther),[86] but Luther, recognizing the need to bring his message to the people as simply as possible, wrote comprehensible German laced with homely metaphors. Powerful visual images produced by woodcuts reinforced the theological message. Zwingli, Calvin and the Anabaptists disapproved of images as superstitious, but Luther recognized the importance of illustration for 'the children and simple folk, who are more easily moved by pictures and images to recall divine history than through mere words or doctrines'.[87] The Lutheran sacraments of infant baptism and the Eucharist were thus given a pictorial form, which distinguished them from Anabaptism or Zwinglianism. At a later date (by 1554 at Regensburg) the Lutheran catechism was condensed for the illiterate into nine pictures. 'Without images, we can neither think nor understand anything', Luther wrote.[88]

Luther was not only a superb polemicist himself. He also attracted the support of fifty or so lesser writers, and about 630 different pamphlets (*Flugschriften*) poured from the presses in the 1520s, especially in the early years of the decade. These pamphlets were usually printed in quarto size and of a length of about eight to twelve pages. The emergence of important centres of printing at Wittenberg and later at Geneva, as a result of the literary output of the resident theologians (Luther and Calvin) and their supporters, demonstrates that the Reformation had significant consequences for the development of printing. In May 1521, Charles V prohibited the sale, reading, possession, copying, printing, preaching and 'protection' of Lutheran writings. Yet the profits were so immense that printers were prepared to take the risk of contravening Imperial law. In general, cities had to enjoy political and religious security to publish Protestant pamphlet propaganda. There were no French, Dutch or English equivalents to the *Flugschriften* in the early German Reformation. In the other European countries, Protestant literature was clandestine, and thus tended to be in octavo size, which was more easily hidden; it was also usually published anonymously, since the publishers had to work in great secrecy. It is significant that printers were most active in the Imperial cities of Cologne, Nuremberg, Strasbourg, Frankfurt-am-Main and Augsburg; the fairs at Frankfurt-am-Main became the main distribution point. Within the Swiss Confederation, Basel was another important printing centre. Without the political autonomy of such cities, it is unlikely that early Reformation propaganda could have been spread as rapidly or as far afield. Strasbourg in the late 1520s and early 1530s allowed a variety of views, including Anabaptist ones, to be published. The importance of political repression is evident from the fate of Protestant book production at Antwerp during the last decade of Charles V's rule. The city had been a centre for the printing of vernacular Bibles, but an Index in the form of an ordinance (*placard*) of Charles V in 1546 accused the printers of corrupting the words of the gospel and 'added unsound prefaces, summaries, tables and annotations'.[89] From this time on, it was no longer safe to print Protestant books.

It is probable that Luther's works represented one-third of the total number of German books sold in the years 1518–25, which is a measure of his success as a communicator. His New Testament, which was translated into German in just eleven weeks, was published in great secrecy to avoid theft or the counterfeiting of his work. The unauthorized versions greatly exceeded the number of Wittenberg imprints, and Luther denounced the rapid reprinting of his works for commercial gain. He introduced two special insignia, one a lamb with a chalice and cross, the other a rose with a cross flanked by the initials ML to prove 'that these books have passed through my hands, because false impressions and corrupt versions now abound'.[90] Luther's published output was (to paraphrase his own expression) an 'act of grace' manifested primarily in the German language, which helps explain why—with the exception of the Baltic states—Lutheranism came chiefly to be confined to the Holy Roman Empire. During his lifetime, 682 publications of Luther's works appeared in a total of 3,897 editions. The 3,110 German editions made up almost 80 per cent of the entire corpus, with another 628 editions (or about 16 per cent) in Latin. Only 155 editions, or 4 per cent of the total of Luther's works, appeared in translation and these were spread across ten contemporary European languages. Two of the most important works of Luther—the *Appeal to the Christian Nobility of the German Nation* and *The Babylonian Captivity of the Church*, both written in 1520—each went into only one foreign language. *On the Liberty of a Christian Man*, also of the same year, was much more successful, with five editions in five languages, but was less important for an understanding of Luther's doctrine. Some of the translations came very late—the only surviving contemporary translation of Luther into Spanish was published as late as 1540. Of course, Luther was read all over Europe already by 1520 by humanists, the 'friends of Latin'; but his foreign readership tended to be socially exclusive as a consequence of the limited availability of translations. Only in German could one gain a fully rounded impression of Luther's thought. Royal censorship silenced Luther in most of the European monarchies. It was inevitable that Lutheranism would largely be confined to Germany as a result.

Despite the phenomenal success of Reformation pamphleteering, Luther's views might not have been put into effect had it not been for his association with the University of Wittenberg, which had been founded in 1502, just fifteen years before the controversy over indulgences. The German universities were noted for producing preachers who were appointed to serve in the Imperial cities and the many small towns which could provide substantial audiences. Not all preachers became Protestants, but many did, and their sermons were often the decisive stage in the spread of the Reformation in Germany. The real work of conversion was carried out by preaching, reading the Bible and catechism practice—in other words, orally. The great majority of these preachers were younger than Luther and were directly or indirectly his students, or the students of other great reformers. They preached in the vernacular, their chief task being to 'administer the pulpit with diligence'.[91] Often trial sermons were held before a candidate recommended by a university was appointed to his position. It comes as no surprise that the two greatest reformers of the sixteenth century, Luther and Calvin, were also its most formidable preachers. But however influential were the sermons of Luther, it was his disciples who made the impact in the lesser towns: men such as Lang at Erfurt, Link at Altenburg, Brenz at Schwäbisch Hall, Myconius at Gotha, Amsdorf at Magdeburg and Osiander at Nuremberg. Over a third of 176 evangelical preachers active in Germany between 1520 and 1560 had studied at the University of Wittenberg and thus had fallen to a greater or lesser extent under Luther's influence. In one sense the entire quarrel about penance and confession, and free will and justification was a gigantic preaching competition, with the Jesuits later responding to the Protestant challenge by emphasizing the importance of Catholic preaching. However, sometimes sermons were disastrously counter-productive. At Allstedt in July 1524, Thomas Müntzer preached before the future elector John of Saxony and his son, taking as his subject the book of Daniel. Rulers would be overthrown, he warned, unless they used their swords on behalf of the godly people. The sermon resulted in

Müntzer's having to flee from electoral Saxony. More usually, however, preachers were shrewd tacticians, careful to match their views to changes in public opinion, even earning the title 'ambidextrous'[92] because they tried to please all men.

1.3.3   *The Failure of the Early Reformation in the Swiss Confederation*

Although the early Swiss Reformation is always associated with the name of Huldrych Zwingli at Zurich, the Swiss movement (as with the German) should be seen as a diversity. Nevertheless, Zwingli's was the dominant personality in its first years. He had served as a parish priest in 1506–18, first at Glarus and then at Einsiedeln, during which time he had become involved in biblical study in Greek, chiefly under the influence of Erasmus. Zwingli's reputation as a preacher rose to such an extent that in 1519 he was given a pulpit at Zurich. He announced his intentions forcefully in his first sermon, when he stated that 'he would expound the holy gospel of Matthew completely in accordance with divine truth and not with human interpretations'.[93] He denounced the arrival of an indulgence-preacher in the same year, but contrary to his later assertion, there is little evidence that before 1522 his preaching was other than orthodox. In that year, however, he attacked both obligatory Lenten fasting and clerical celibacy (he married secretly, probably in 1523, but did not make this known until the following year). By January 1523, Zwingli was called upon to defend himself against criticism of his evangelical preaching, which he did by submitting sixty-seven theses for public debate. The Zurich city council decided as a result of this debate to require evangelical preaching of all its clerics ('nothing but what can be proved by the holy gospel and the pure and holy scriptures').[94] Later in that year, Zwingli arrived at his interpretation of the sacrament of the Eucharist, which he clearly differentiated from the Catholic Mass ('whereas it is a testament, guarantee or bond, and also a remembrance, they have called it a sacrament or sacrifice').[95] It was not until 1524–5 that Zwingli's view was refined into one of opposition to the Lutheran intepretation of the Eucharist.

In purely theological terms, the most important development of Zwingli's thought was the idea of the covenant between God and his elect. In his *Reply to Hubmaier* (November 1525), Zwingli argued that the New Testament was a renewal of God's covenant with Abraham made in Genesis xvii.1–2 ('I am the Almighty God; walk before me, and be thou perfect. And I will make my covenant between me and thee, and will multiply thee exceedingly'). However, whereas for Abraham the sign of the covenant had been circumcision, for Christians this had become baptism. What was not clear in Zwingli's thought was whether this covenant imposed dual obligations on both man and God or simply acted as a unilateral promise of God to his elect. Zwingli's words seem to imply the former: 'this is the pact of God with man: that He himself should be our God; that we should walk with integrity according to His will'.[96] However, the idea of a dual covenant was developed much more fully in 1528 by Heinrich Bullinger, who argued that man's faith was an explicit condition of the covenant: man's duty was 'to adhere firmly to the one God through faith and to walk in innocence of life for His pleasure'.[97] Whereas Zwingli had used the idea of the covenant primarily to defend his view of the sacraments, and did not thoroughly integrate it into his system of theology, it became a central doctrine for Bullinger in his forty-three-year rule as Zwingli's successor at Zurich (December 1531–September 1575). Bullinger's was the longest unbroken tenure of any prominent first-generation reformer and guaranteed the survival of the Zwinglian Reformation at Zurich until the city finally went Calvinist—that is, when a teaching of predestination to which Bullinger himself did not subscribe was accepted by the city in 1560.

For personal and political, as well as doctrinal, reasons Zwingli always stressed his independence from Luther—but it was not until the summer of 1523 that Zwingli arrived at his most distinctive individual contribution to the Reformation, the idea of a state church which for security and unity of direction should be a function of an evangelical government as at Zurich. In his view church and state were inseparable. It followed that the best Christian made the best magistrate. Part of the reason for his vigorous denunciation of the Anabaptists was that they turned their backs on the machinery of the state: they claimed, he said, that 'their heretical church ... needs no sword, for it is within the perfection of Christ ... The Catabaptists [i.e. Anabaptists] have no citizenship here, no church in which they may live and watch ... but, like wolves that lie in wait in the forests, seizing their prey and fleeing, they cause destruction and then escape.'[98] Zwingli's was thus a theology with an important political dimension: it was calculated to appeal to the south German cities as well as to the Swiss Confederation; indeed, he warned them that 'one should not trust the friendship of tyrants' (meaning Charles V) and that 'under the guise of religion the free cities will lose their liberties'.[99] The appeal of Zwinglianism was greatest at Strasbourg and Constance in the late 1520s, and it was more important than Lutheranism in almost all of the other leading south German cities at this date. Zwingli wanted to turn this latent support into a more tangible anti-Habsburg alliance; he obtained a treaty with Constance in 1527 and another with Strasbourg and Philip of Hesse in November 1530. For a brief moment in the history of the Empire, with the formation of the Christian Civic Union of February 1529 comprising Zurich, Berne, Basel, St Gall, Biel, Strasbourg, Mühlhausen and Schaffhausen, it seemed that the south German towns might 'turn Swiss' as a guarantee both of the new religion and their traditional privileges.

There were two main reasons why this did not happen. The first lay with the development of Lutheranism as a political party under princely leadership—the Schmalkaldic League (see chapter 2.4.3)—that was considerably more powerful than an alliance of towns under the leadership of Zurich. The second was Zwingli's failure to extend his reformation within the Swiss Confederation itself. He had an alliance with Berne after 1528, which was indispensable for Zurich's independence. But whereas Berne wanted to avoid forcible conversions, Zwingli argued in 1531 that the two cities must join forces to dominate the Swiss Confederation: 'if the states are completely in agreement they will be in the Confederation like two oxen drawing a cart and pulling on one yoke . . .'[100] Thus Zwingli plunged the two cities into the disastrous second Kappel war which led to his own death in battle and ended in the capitulation of Zurich and Berne in November 1531. It is true that the Reformation survived unscathed there, as indeed it did at Basel and Schaffhausen: the four cantons which had freely chosen evangelical reform were not to be forced to abandon it, although they could revert to the old faith if a majority of the population favoured this. However, henceforth the Catholic cantons of Uri, Schwyz and Unterwalden, as well as the cities of Lucerne, Zug, Fribourg and Solothurn and their territories were not to be allowed to change their religious allegiance; special arrangements for religious parity were made in the rural cantons of Glarus and Appenzell: the Swiss Reformation was thus end-stopped, with only a minority of four of the thirteen cantons having declared for Protestantism. Since Zwingli had envisaged nothing less than the evangelization of the whole Swiss Confederation, the treaty has to be viewed as a posthumous defeat. However, in 1531 the survival of the Swiss Confederation itself was placed above religious considerations: hard-line Catholic opinion considered that the Catholic cantons should have utilized their victory and eradicated all heresy within the Confederation, but they wisely recognized that they lacked sufficient force to subjugate Zurich and its allies. At no time did a significant Reformation movement take root in Lucerne, the leading Catholic city, and elsewhere too the adherents of the new faith were in a distinct minority. Traditional rivalry between Lucerne and Zurich and between Fribourg and Berne also accounted in part for the different political and religious standpoints which were adopted.

1.3.4 *Consolidation within the Lutheran Movement*

The failure of Zwinglian expansion in the 1530s left Lutheranism with the initiative. Four west European kingdoms—Denmark, Sweden, England and France—were, to a greater or lesser degree, influenced by the Reformation. Of these, only Denmark joined the Schmalkaldic League.

Francis I made overtures to join in an alliance in 1535–6, but he was rebuffed on the grounds that his domestic religious policy was intolerant. Furthermore, the League thought that Francis wished to embroil it in a general war with Charles V. It was in Scandinavia that the Lutheran Reformation made its greatest impact outside Germany. The Danish Church Ordinance of 1537, approved by Luther and closely supervised by his emissary Bugenhagen, established a Danish reformed church during the reign of Christian III. Similarly, the synod at Uppsala in 1536 established a Swedish reformed church during the reign of Gustavus Vasa. Its progress was helped by the archbishop of Uppsala after 1531, Laurentius Petri, who had studied at Wittenberg and had been influenced by Melanchthon. In contrast, the Reformation made only hesitant progress in England under Henry VIII, the king's religious policy being arbitrary in character and inconsistent in practice. Whereas Lutheran pastors influenced policy in the Scandinavian kingdoms, in England this did not happen. Robert Barnes, a close political associate of Thomas Cromwell who had visited Luther at Wittenberg and closely followed his views, was executed in July 1540 shortly after his mentor. There was an abrupt swing to Protestantism under Edward VI (1547–53), but the Second Prayer Book of 1552 showed that Zwinglian influence was uppermost in the mind of its principal author, Thomas Cranmer, archbishop of Canterbury. At least 20,000 Prayer Books were published and distributed throughout the kingdom, and there was a serious attempt to destroy the old liturgical texts. The Catholic reaction under Mary (1553–8) was too brief to undo the earlier Protestant propaganda effort.

Lutheranism was no more successful in France than it had been in England. While Francis I's religious policy was no model of consistency, it was less subject to the whims of the monarch than was Henry VIII's. In the 1520s, the French king had tried to make a distinction between Lutheran heresy and Catholic reform—a difficult task, in which he was opposed both by the Sorbonne and the *Parlement* of Paris. However, in 1534 the king's policy was gravely undermined by the publication and dissemination in several French towns of so-called 'placards' or broadsheets entitled 'true articles on the horrible, great and insupportable abuses of the Papal Mass'.[101] The author, a fairly obscure pastor at Neuchâtel called Antoine Marcourt, favoured the Zwinglian view of the Eucharist. It is clear, however, that although this publication was important in provoking an official lurch towards the persecution of heresy, it did not indicate a shift towards Zwinglianism within the French reform movement itself. For example, there is no evidence that Antoine Marcourt's placards were posted in Rouen or anywhere else in Normandy; yet this was the only province north of the river Loire to be significantly affected by the early Reformation. It is true that sometimes 'sacramentarian' replaced the epithet 'Lutheran' in accusations of heresy; but any assessment of the impact of the main reformers on popular religious belief in France remains problematic for the historian.

Until the mid-1550s, it seems that the French Reformation was an even more diverse movement than its German and Swiss counterparts. No works of Luther were translated into French before 1525, as far as is known, while Zwingli's writings on the Mass were never translated. Several early French tracts, such as Guillaume Farel's *Summary and Brief Declaration* (1525), were closer to a Zwinglian than a Lutheran viewpoint. Anabaptism seems to have made next to no headway in the French-speaking world, doubtless because very little of its religious literature was translated from the German or Dutch. The religious labels seem to have confused contemporaries: the royal prosecutor at Moulins in 1540 talked of 'heresies and sects' in the plural and of 'those suspected of belonging to the Lutheran and other sects'.[102] It is hardly surprising that there was no unified reform movement in France in view of the mounting severity of the persecution, which forced its most important theologians, including Farel and Calvin himself, into exile (see chapter 1.4.2).

The advance of Lutheranism slowed down in the 1540s. In Germany itself, the Lutheran missionary effort became diverted into arid theological disputation with Bullinger, Zwingli's successor at Zurich and a fierce controversialist in his own right. The Reformation had been received with enthusiasm in the German cities initially, but this gradually waned as the ruling oligarchies sought to evade domination by a vigorous Lutheran clergy. At Strasbourg, for example, the laity refused to be dictated to by clerics seeking to impose a Lutheran orthodoxy. Townsmen saw doctrinal issues as inherently complex and politically divisive. Carl Meig of Strasbourg said of the Tetrapolitan Confession in 1534: 'I hope that, as a layman, I won't be trapped into something I don't understand and then forced to confess and believe it.'[103] The secular rulers of Strasbourg stressed a simple Bible-based religion, combined with ethical values; with the exception of a figure such as Jacob Sturm, who tried to encourage his colleagues to study the Tetrapolitan Confession for a full week prior to voting on it, they tried to steer clear of precise theological positions. Not until 1598 did the Lutheran clergy obtain a church ordinance which enshrined its view of the past, namely that the city had adhered to the Confession of Augsburg since 1531 (and not to the Tetrapolitan Confession of 1530) and that it was the clergy, and not the ruling city council, which made religious policy. The posthumous triumph of Lutheran orthodoxy would have surprised Martin Bucer. In 1530, the Tetrapolitan Confession had been presented to Charles V not as the opinions of its authors, Bucer and Wolfgang Capito, but as those of the city's ruling council. In changed circumstances, Bucer had been forced to resign from his presidency of the church assembly in 1549 because the city magistrates felt obliged to placate Charles V.

Shortly after Luther's death in February 1546, the Schmalkaldic League was defeated by the army of Charles V, and in 1548 the Emperor was in a position to impose his own solution, the Interim of Augsburg, on certain principalities and twenty-eight free cities (see chapter 2.4.3). Not until 1552 were the Lutheran princes able to mount a successful rebellion against the Interim, and it was as late as September 1555 that their delegates negotiated a peace at Augsburg which deliberately excluded their new rivals, the Calvinists, from the privileges Lutherans were to enjoy henceforth in Germany. As the German Lutheran princes became increasingly concerned to maintain the *status quo*, their theologians became more intolerant of the threat, real or imagined, of subversion by 'crypto-Calvinists'. There were at least four disputes among the Lutheran theologians, which had not been settled by the time of Melanchthon's death in 1560. The debate within Lutheranism itself led to a proliferation in the number of catechisms. It was not until 1580, precisely fifty years after the Augsburg Confession was presented to Charles V and rejected, that the *Book of Concord* settled the debates between Lutherans. It is scarcely surprising, therefore, that Calvinism, a more united movement, was to reap the main harvest that Luther had sown.

1.4 Calvin and the Spread of 'Reformed Protestantism'

Jean Calvin (1509–64) was twelve years younger than Melanchthon, Luther's faithful subordinate and successor. He thus belonged quite clearly to the second generation of the Reformation. Born at Noyon in France, Calvin was a lawyer, a Christian humanist, and one of the best Latin scholars of the sixteenth century, who wrote in an elegant French prose style—a style more akin, in fact, to Lefèvre d'Étaples than to Luther. He did not become an evangelical before 1529–30, or possibly as late as 1533–4, and his career seems to have followed a clearly defined path from scholasticism via humanism to an outright Lutheran position, though he did not have any sudden 'conversion' comparable to Luther, nor did he arrive at a position independently of Luther, in the manner of Zwingli.

Calvin saw his task primarily as that of defending 'evangelical truth' against its enemies, chiefly Catholics and Anabaptists. Successive Popes, he thought, had fabricated new doctrines as a result of their ignorance of Scripture. 'What a deep night of errors men were immersed in for several ages!', he exclaimed on one occasion. And on another, he remarked, 'all we have attempted to do has been to renew that ancient form of the church'.[104] Calvin therefore saw his work as a restoration of religion, literally a *re*formation. 'We remain unworthy', he wrote, '. . . until there is harmony and unanimity in religion, till God is purely worshipped by all, and all the world is reformed.'[105] He seems to have held Luther in great respect, despite their theological disagreements, but Martin Bucer was the single most decisive influence on his life, particularly during his residence at Strasbourg in 1538–41. Bucer's last work, *On the Kingdom of Christ* (1551), which was published in the year of his death, summed up the work of a lifetime: Bucer advocated a Christian commonwealth in which the ecclesiastical and civil authorities acting together would make the rule of Christ a social reality, a theme which can be traced in Calvin's philosophy. Zwingli and his successor at Zurich, Bullinger, were of less importance to Calvin, although superficially an agreement Calvin reached with Bullinger on the Eucharist in 1549 (the *Consensus Tigurinus*) gives the appearance of much common ground between the two. Calvin's achievement was to elaborate, in his great work, the *Institution* (or *Institutes*) *of the Christian Religion*, 'almost the whole sum of piety and whatever it is necessary to know in the doctrine of salvation'.[106] He also established at Geneva a working model of his idea of the reformed church, which was to inspire Protestants in other countries. Finally, though this had not been his original intention, he arrived at an independent and distinct theological position, which came about largely in polemics with other Protestant theologians.

1.4.1 *Calvin's Mature Theology: Predestination*

Calvin was the greatest biblical commentator of the sixteenth century. His knowledge of Hebrew and his humanist training enabled him to read widely and deeply for the preparation of both his commentaries and his sermons: it is thought that he preached more than 4,000 sermons after his return to Geneva in 1541. He took his preaching ministry extremely seriously, believing that effective preaching required 'a combination of right understanding of Scripture' and 'a special gift for explaining it'. Those insufficiently in touch with ordinary people, who kept 'their knowledge shut up within themselves' ought, in his view, not to preach at all. Good preaching was like the application of good medicine to a patient: 'it is necessary to adapt the medicine to those who need it'. Above all, the preacher must communicate his enthusiasm to his audience: 'doctrine without zeal is . . . a sword in the hand of a lunatic, or lies cold and useless, or serves a perverse ostentation'.[107]

   Yet it is not for his preaching but for one published work, the *Institution* (that is to say, 'instruction' in religion), that Calvin is chiefly remembered. It first appeared in print in 1536, only to be considerably revised in 1539 and 1543; finally, it was enlarged into its definitive Latin and French versions in 1559–60. Calvin is known for his doctrine of predestination, yet although perhaps implicit in the text there was no reference to it in the 1536 edition of the *Institution*, and only a brief mention in the 1539 version. Calvin probably already held the view, since his catechism of 1537 mentioned predestination, but he largely took it for granted. It was only the conflict with Lutherans and anti-predestinarians such as Jérôme Bolsec in 1551 and with the Catholic Pighius in 1552 (Calvin wrote a tract *Concerning the Eternal Predestination of God* in that year) that made an elaboration of the doctrine necessary and gave mature Calvinism its theological distinctiveness in the 1559–60 versions of the *Institution*.

Calvin's central belief was the essentially Lutheran view that man is justified by faith alone. While good works might be of some value, salvation resulted from a man's faith, not his deeds: the best human work, Calvin thought 'is still always spotted and corrupted with some impurity of the flesh and has, so to speak, some dregs mixed with it'. No deed, even of the saints, 'does not deserve shame'. Adam's fall affected us all: even the youngest child bore the 'hidden seed' of Adam and thus 'all of us are subject, by the same inward and secret spiritual impulse, to every moral ill'. Man's 'nature is so perverse that he cannot be roused, driven, or led except to evil'. It is true that Calvin conceded that 'one sees still even in the most wicked and reprobate that there is some impression of the image of God', but without a recognition of man's total depravity one 'knows nothing of original sin'.[108] All the early reformers had accepted some measure of predestination, but it was Calvin who made this a crucially important issue in the 1550s, indeed calling it 'the principal article of the Christian religion'. He defined predestination as 'God's awful decree, by which he determined ... what ... become[s of] each man. For all are not created in equal condition; rather eternal life is fore-ordained to some, eternal damnation to others.' Whereas justification by faith alone emphasized God's mercy, predestination stressed his power. In Calvin's words, God was 'moved to mercy for no other reason but that he wills to be merciful'.[109] God determined those whom he chose as his 'elect', and those whom he rejected as 'reprobate' on just grounds, but ones which were not necessarily intelligible to man: this concept of simultaneous election and reprobation is usually called the double decree of predestination.

Not all reformers were prepared to accept it: for example, Bullinger preached single predestination, that election included potentially all men, and that as many as believed were chosen by God. 'Because some do not believe and perish', Bullinger concluded, 'we do not cast the blame back on God and His predestination, but on the man himself who spurns the grace of God and rejects the heavenly gifts.'[110] This remained Bullinger's position throughout his long career, although he found it increasingly difficult to find supporters to maintain it against Calvinists. For Calvin's opponent Bolsec, the double decree of predestination represented God as an unprincipled tyrant, in effect the author of sin. It was this doctrine more than anything else which brought about a unification of the Lutheran factions by 1580. They all agreed in the *Book of Concord* that predestination removed 'all consolation ... from the gospel and the use of the sacraments ...'[111] Indeed, the designation 'Calvinists' seems to have been first applied by their German Lutheran critics of predestination, such as Joachim Westphal, in an attempt to stigmatize the Swiss reformed faith as a foreign influence in Germany (1552);[112] it was also taken up by Protestants in Basel who were opposed to the death penalty for Servetus in 1553. Calvin himself was alarmed at the use of the term by his opponents.

The Lutheran criticism of predestination as undermining the effect of the sacraments had to be taken seriously. Calvin placed particular stress on frequent Communion, celebrated in a reverent and godly manner, as a means of spiritual renewal: 'from the physical things set forth in the sacrament, we are led to spiritual things by a kind of analogy. Thus, when bread is given as a symbol of Christ's body, we must at once grasp this comparison: as bread nourishes, sustains, and keeps the life of our body, so Christ's body is the only food to invigorate and enliven our soul.'[113] Indeed, he criticized Catholicism as redefined at the Council of Trent for failing to reassure men of salvation during their lifetime. Calvin was in favour of weekly Communion, but agreed to celebrate the Eucharist only once a month in view of the 'infirmity of the people'. He viewed predestination quite differently from his critics. He accepted that it was 'terrible' that 'only a small number, out of an incalculable multitude, should obtain salvation'.[114] Nevertheless, he believed that predestination was taught in the Bible: St Paul had declared to the Ephesians that God 'hath chosen us in him before the foundation of the world, that we should be holy and without blame before him in love. Having predestined us unto the adoption of children by Jesus Christ to himself, according to the good pleasure of his will' (Ephesians i.4–5). Predestination was therefore true, necessary and, moreover, beneficial in its consequences.

Somewhat paradoxically, Calvin regarded predestination as a 'comforting doctrine', a 'confirmation' of faith, bringing 'freedom from worry about the future'.[115] The elect might 'not be immune from toil and care', but the consciousness of their calling provided them with an inner security. The elect still needed their own personal qualities—'the life of the godly ought to be tempered with frugality and sobriety, so that ... throughout its course a sort of perpetual fasting may appear'[116]—and they had to face the challenge of the reprobate, 'born sons of wrath', who were at war with God, the power of Satan himself, and the struggle to repress personal sin: 'the principal combat we must wage is against ourselves and against our vices . . .'[117] Holiness was not achieved rapidly 'in one moment or one day or one year; but through continual and sometimes even slow advances, God wipes out in his elect the corruptions of the flesh, cleanses them of guilt, and consecrates them to himself as temples, renewing all their minds to true purity, that they may repent all their lives and know that this warfare will end only at death'.[118] The history of Israel, the chosen nation of the Old Testament, provided a 'mirror' for the elect in Calvin's own time, though its lessons were chiefly negative: God would punish the sins of the elect just as he had punished those of Israel if their example was followed. Whereas it was the whim of fortune which acted as the determining force in the world in Machiavellian thought (see chapter 6.1.1), for Calvin God's providence 'rules over the smallest details in the governance of the human race and the whole world . . .'[119]

Instead of Bullinger's bilateral covenant between man and God, Calvin argued that there had merely been a one-sided agreement between God and His elect thoughout the ages: 'let us preserve faith, love, obedience as agreed on by us; he on his side will be faithful to us.'[120] The elect had faith simply because they were the elect; the reprobate could never attain it. Of course, the believer had a responsibility to live according to the moral law that was written into his heart by the Holy Spirit: 'each individual has his own kind of living assigned to him by the Lord as a sort of sentry post, so that he may not heedlessly wander about throughout life . . . It is enough if we know that the Lord's calling is in everything the beginning and foundation of well-doing.'[121] Calvin thought 'the whole life of man a ruinous labyrinth of wanderings until he has been converted to Christ'. The reprobate were not rejected because of their actions, however, but because of God's will: he cited the text 'Jacob have I loved, but Esau have I hated' (Romans ix.13).[122]

1.4.2 *Calvin's Career at Geneva and the Influence of Calvinist Church Discipline*

Calvin's first refuge from French persecution in 1534–6 was Basel, where the first edition of the *Institution* appeared in print. Some five months after its publication, he arrived in Geneva, a city of little importance compared with Strasbourg (at least until 1548) or even Zurich; and one which to a certain degree was dependent politically on Berne until 1556. Since 1519, the city had been rent by factions, for and against an alliance with (and probable subjection to) the duke of Savoy. The party opposing the duke were bound by an oath (*Eidgenossen*) and were thus known as *Eugenos*—the probable derivation of the French term 'Huguenot' for a member of the reformed faith.[123] The threat from Savoy was removed from 1536 to 1559 with the French expulsion of duke Charles III from his lands. In May 1536, the Genevan general assembly had sworn to 'live henceforth according to the Law of the Gospel and the Word of God, and . . . to abolish . . . all Papal abuses'.[124] Calvin remained at Geneva for nearly two years; in the first instance attempting to supervise reforms with Guillaume Farel, a colleague twenty years his senior, and to force all inhabitants to subscribe to the Genevan Confession of Faith of November 1536, by which the municipal council had laid down the broad manner of reformed worship. There was popular opposition to this, and Calvin correctly perceived that the council was not supporting his endeavours: he referred to them in a sermon as 'a council of the devil'. In April 1538, both Calvin and Farel were dismissed by the pro-Berne city council, which was relieved to get rid of them.

Farel went to Neuchâtel, where he established himself permanently. Calvin was summoned by Bucer and Wolfgang Capito to Strasbourg, a fateful decision because it brought him under the influence of their theology: of Bucer he said, 'no one in our time has been more precise and diligent in interpreting Scripture than he'.[125] Through his personal contacts with Bucer, Calvin's theological views on predestination and the Eucharist attained a new clarity and precision, while the French congregation at Strasbourg henceforth became the model for all the French churches which Calvin hoped to establish. In September 1541, after changes in the composition of the city council, Calvin was restored to power in Geneva, but he made his return (which was reluctant) conditional on their acceptance of his catechism and the establishment of what constituted in his mind proper ecclesiastical discipline.

It has been argued that the implementation of Calvin's reforms at Geneva amounted to a revolution, with fundamental changes in political organization, social structure and the control of property, and above all in the imposition of a new religious ethic; seldom were the changes brought about by the Reformation as abrupt or as far-reaching as at Geneva. His Ecclesiastical Ordinances of November 1541 provided for pastors who would meet weekly for study of the Scriptures: apart from one Italian, all the pastors nominated by the Company of Pastors and appointed by the town council in sixteenth-century Geneva were French refugees. Inevitably the Company of Pastors would serve not only as a local ministry but also as a missionary enterprise for France itself. There were also to be doctors to instruct believers in true doctrine and to expel errors; elders, laymen nominated and appointed by the government, were to be responsible for the machinery of discipline; finally, deacons would care for the poor and the needy. The Ordinances were also greatly concerned with discipline. The elders and pastors of the Consistory court were to meet every Thursday to discuss church disorders and remedial action. In the last resort, an offender could be forbidden to attend the Eucharist and could be reported to the civil authority ('let him be cut off from the Church and denounced to the magistrate').[126]

At Zurich, where Calvinism did not triumph until the 1560s, disciplinary authority rested entirely with the civil power; moreover, Bullinger had denied the scriptural justification for excommunication—he asserted that it defeated the purpose of the Eucharist, which was to give sinners an opportunity to render thanks to the Lord. In contrast, Calvin denied unreprentant sinners admission to the Eucharist lest their presence profane the solemn event. All those who intended to participate in Communion were expected to intimate their decision beforehand to Calvin. It was the duty of the civil magistrates to back up the decisions of the Consistory and to 'remove superstitions and put an end to all wicked idolatry, to advance the kingdom of Christ and maintain purity of doctrine, to purify scandals and cleanse the filth that corrupts piety . . .'[127] 'The Lord', Calvin asserted, 'cannot endure excess, and it is absolutely necessary that it be severely punished.' He thought it characteristic of the godless always to 'run to extremes'.[128] Thus he set great store by excommunication as 'a holy and lawful discipline taken from the word of God'. The formula of excommunication at Geneva was thus particularly wide, encompassing 'all idolaters, blasphemers, despisers of God, heretics, and all who form sects apart to break the unity of the Church, all perjurers, all who are rebellious to parents and to their superiors, all who are seditious, mutinous, quarrelsome, injurious, all adulterers, fornicators, thieves, misers, ravishers of women, drunkards, gluttons, and all who lead a scandalous life . . .'[129] Geneva was to become the model community: 'if we allow debauched persons and ruffians to bring in their corrupt ways and introduce more evil than we already have, if we permit the profligate and corrupt to come here to practise their lewdness, will we not necessarily become debauched and totally corrupt with them?'[130]

Calvin spent fifteen years in a struggle to maintain religious and moral discipline at Geneva. When he met opponents, he confronted them with all the penalties at his disposal. Sebastian Castellio was forced out of Geneva in 1544 because he denied the divine inspiration of the Song of Songs. In 1551, Jérôme Bolsec denounced Calvin's doctrine of predestination and after a theological disputation was forced to leave the city. Most notorious of all, Michael Servetus was arrested in 1553 and prosecuted in the civil courts on four charges of heresy including Anabaptism and anti-Trinitarianism. He was found guilty and burnt, though Calvin sought to mitigate the sentence to one of beheading. Despite these spectacular illustrations of Calvin's intolerance of opposition, however, it was not until 1555 that the last faction opposing Calvin within the city council was overthrown, and that the council finally confirmed the powers of the Consistory to excommunicate—powers which the reformer had always seen as crucial to its disciplinary functions. Calvin's intolerance is largely explained by his fear of dissenting views which, acting as a 'powerful poison', would flow 'insidiously into our minds' and corrupt the whole of life.[131] In his view, error could do far more damage than military might, and for this reason he favoured the death penalty for heretics.

1.4.3   *Calvinist Theology and Church Discipline after Calvin*

Because Calvin's *Institution* developed into such a long and complex work, no Calvinist church—neither Geneva after Calvin's death in 1564, nor any other national church—accepted it as their Confession of Faith. Instead, each Calvinist church drew up its own organizational document. Calvin did not view such developments as a threat to his own authority, for he did not consider that the organization outlined in the *Institution* was the only one possible, or even the best. Calvin talked indiscriminately of bishops, presbyters, elders and pastors. He stressed the need for ideological unity, but he regarded Geneva merely as an exemplar, no more than what any evangelical church ought to be, rather than the only possible structure. Probably as a result of Bucer's formative influence on him, Calvin always regarded the church as a local community, identifying it with a congregation in a specific town or village. 'Each church' was, in his view, 'free to establish whatever form of organization is suitable and useful for itself, for God has prescribed nothing specific about this'.[132] Since Calvinism was compatible with any political form of government, there would necessarily be varied forms of church organization to suit each one.

The document which was to enjoy the greatest success in influencing the separate Calvinist communities was the Confession of Faith drawn up in September 1558 by Theodore Beza, who was to become Calvin's successor at Geneva. This went through thirty editions in different languages in the years 1560–95. Beza served as Moderator of Geneva's Company of Pastors from Calvin's death until 1580, when he retired from the post. (He did not die until 1605.) Under Beza's influence, and presidency at the Synod of La Rochelle in 1571, there was an attempt to systematize the various national Calvinist Confessions of Faith. These attempts at uniformity continued after Beza's death, for example at the Synod of Dort in 1618–19. Beza's form of Calvinist church discipline is usually taken to be synonymous with Presbyterian organization—in the Calvinist structure, power descended from national synods via consistories (or synods of a region) to local colloquies. This pattern was adopted early on in France (see chapters 3.3.1 and 3.3.5) and was generalized to other European states such as the Netherlands and East Friesland by a decision of the synod of Emden in 1571. Detailed implementation of the Presbyterian model was often relatively late: it was not until 1601 that an edict of elector Frederick IV implemented the scheme in detail in the Rhine Palatinate, the leading Calvinist state in Germany.

In comparison with Lutheranism, Calvinism enjoyed a relative doctrinal unity in the first two generations of its missionary effort. Calvinists also projected their views within an international context in a way that the later followers of Luther did not. Beza's view of church organization seems to have been less flexible than Calvin's: he emphasized Presbyterianism initially in response to the challenge posed in France by Jean Morély, who favoured a greater role for the laity in church government and more autonomy for local congregations. The French national synod at Orléans in April 1562 condemned Morély's 'wicked doctrine . . . [tending] to the confusion and dissipation of the church'.[133] Beza later defended Presbyterianism successfully against the attacks of Thomas Lüber (better known as Erastus), who championed the rights of the secular state over the church in the Rhine Palatinate in the years 1568–70. In England, however, Beza took a more cautious approach to the controversy over church organization in the clash between John Whitgift, Master of Trinity College, Cambridge, and later archbishop of Canterbury, a supporter of episcopacy, and Thomas Cartwright, an advocate of Presbyterianism, at about the same time. Whitgift was doctrinally a Calvinist, and argued that 'if M. Calvin were alive and understood the state of our church and controversy truly, I verily believe that he would utterly condemn your [Cartwright's] doings . . .'[134] Whitgift's view prevailed in England until the civil war, though there was a strong Puritan minority who did not accept the hierarchy of the church.

Beza took a stricter view of Calvinist church organization than Calvin himself, and he also emphasized the distinctive aspects of Calvin's theology, especially on the double decree of predestination, while minimizing other humanist aspects of his thought which had linked him with Erasmus. The harshness of this doctrine explains later attempts to moderate its impact, which were associated with the Dutch reformed minister Jacobus Arminius (1559–1609), who had been trained at Geneva. In 1604, he presented his theses on predestination in which he rejected Calvin's view of 'limited atonement', the idea that Christ's death was for the sake of the elect only. Instead, he believed that Christ died for all believers and not only the elect. It was within man's capacity to achieve salvation, though not all men would succeed. Predestination remained in the sense that God had foreknowledge of an individual's capacity for belief and perseverance. Those who were damned were 'eternal unbelievers . . . by their own fault';[135] if sinners repented and believed, they too could become the elect of God. Arminius' views were contested by his contemporary, Franciscus Gomarus, and condemned by the Synod of Dort held in 1618–19. However, Arminianism made some progress among the elite in England and the Netherlands at the expense of Calvinist orthodoxy in the 1620s and 1630s.

1.4.4 *The Spread of 'Reformed Protestantism' in Europe*

Though Calvin never lost hope that his version of reformed Protestantism would be introduced into Catholic countries as a result of the conversion of rulers, the reality was that the spread of the reformed faith was imperilled by a vigorous Catholic repression that had already been mounted against the Lutheran and Zwinglian challenge. For those who remained in France, Nicodemism must have seemed an attractive option. Just as Nicodemus had come to Christ under cover of night to attest his faith, a faith which survived the crucifixion (John iii and xix.39), so might Protestants avoid the ordeal of persecution by hiding overt signs of their commitment which might bring about the ruin of their movement. By the 1540s, Calvin felt he had to take up his pen against 'libertines', 'Nicodemites' and other 'semi-Christians' in France. In a letter to Luther in January 1545, Calvin denounced such persons who 'continue to defile themselves with the sacrilegious worship of the Papists'.[136] Yet he was living in safety at Geneva; the evangelicals at Paris and elsewhere had to endure both persecution at home and simultaneous criticism from Geneva and they appealed to Strasbourg to intercede for them with the leading opponent of compromise, if need be via the good offices of Luther and Melanchthon. Despite Calvin's overt hostility to the Nicodemites, he sounded a cautious note to the nascent Calvinist congregations in France in recognition of their difficulties; writing to them in July 1547, he commented: 'I am sure that it would be much better if all those who desire to know God should assemble together so that each one acted as a kind of clarion call to the others. And yet it is much better to have travelled half the way, as you have, than not to have set out at all.'[137] He exhorted the French congregations to put the wicked to confusion by their good lives and example. Commenting to Bullinger on the Edict of Châteaubriant of June 1551, which intensified the persecution in France, Calvin remarked that Geneva was named more than ten times in the text, 'always with a mark of infamy attached to it', and that 'the sword is whetted for our throats'.[138] Three years later, he was nevertheless exhorting an unnamed French congregation that they 'must have a certain and settled community constituted as a church' though a public confession of faith was dangerous because of the climate of persecution: 'under these circumstances, it is quite sufficient that the little flock should assemble in secret'.[139]

It was not until about 1554 that Calvin began to offer firm advice to the

French congregations on how to 'gather' a church. 'We must take the moderate line', he argued on another occasion; no minister should desert his post 'out of fear, or treacherously betray his flock, or give an example of cowardice; and yet no one should rashly throw himself away'. However, he conceded that it might sometimes better serve the church for the pastor to leave and so calm the fury of its enemies. Later, as the civil war in France drew nearer, Calvin insisted that ministers 'must continue on their course', whether confronted by exile or burning.[140] Calvinist conversions took place on a massive scale after Henri II's death in 1559, when it seemed that the royal policy of persecution might be coming to an end: by that year there were probably a million French Huguenots, a fifteenth of the population and by far the largest Calvinist congregation in Europe (see chapter 3.3.1). By this date, Geneva could not keep up with the demand for pastors: the Genevan Company of Pastors sent out only eighty-eight pastors to France in the years 1555–62, but the number of churches was estimated in 1562 at 1,785.

The proportion of committed Calvinists in Holland twenty years later was higher, some 6 or 10 per cent of the population, but the proportion was lower in the other provinces of what was to become the Dutch Republic. The early Reformation in the Low Countries was a result of the spread of Luther's works, but in the 1530s Lutheranism had gradually given way to the twin influences of Anabaptism and a hybrid reformed Protestantism imported from Emden, Strasbourg and Zurich. In comparison with France, there was much less dependence on Calvin's Geneva in the Low Countries in the 1550s: only a dozen of the eighty-four preachers active there in the years before 1566, when iconoclastic rioting erupted and the course of the Dutch Reformation changed to one of open revolt (see chapter 3.2.2), were trained in Geneva or had ties with that city. By the time of Calvin's death two years earlier, only four of his works had appeared in Dutch: the Dutch evangelicals were clearly dependent on their knowledge of Latin and French for access to Calvin's works. The Anabaptist threat placed the Dutch Calvinist church on its mettle from the outset: in 1561, the Netherlands Confession of Faith stressed the acceptance of ecclesiastical discipline as a true mark of the church, while civil magistrates were given the responsibility of uprooting idolatry and false religion 'so that the kingdom of Antichrist may be overthrown and the kingdom of Christ Jesus advanced'.[141] The Dutch reformed church adhered to Calvin's principle that admission to the Eucharist was to be carefully supervised. Those outside the congregation could be admitted to hear sermons, but only those who had placed themselves 'under the sweet yoke of our chief shepherd Jesus Christ',[142] and lived their lives accordingly, were regarded as members of the congregation—inevitably, they formed a distinct minority in the population.

If Geneva played a relatively minor role in the development of Calvinism in the Netherlands, the same was true within the German principalities. German Calvinists looked to Heidelberg University as their chief source of inspiration, while the Academy at Strasbourg also played a vital role in the 1560s and 1570s, eventually being displaced by the Academy at Herborn after its foundation in 1584. The spread of Calvinism in the Empire was affected by a number of considerations which were unique to Germany. German Lutheranism had by 1580 become introverted and defensive, as the *Book of Concord*'s denunciation of the Calvinist view of predestination as 'false, horrifying and blasphemous' shows.[140] The Lutheran theologians always rejected any attempts at compromise with their Protestant opponents. There was already a strong tradition of reformed Protestantism on the Zwinglian and Bucerian model in the south German cities. The imposition of the Interim of Augsburg in 1548, after Charles V's victory over the Schmalkaldic League (see chapter 2.4.3), had an unsettling effect comparable to the Marian reaction in England: the Palatinate experienced six changes of religion in thirty-nine years. Nevertheless, Lutheranism ultimately gained a settled place in the Imperial constitution as a result of the Peace of Augsburg in 1555: technically, all Calvinist gains thereafter could be regarded as infringements of the Peace of Augsburg. The Calvinists argued that they had subscribed to the Confession of Augsburg—at least to the 1540 version, the *variata* (see chapter 1.2.3)—and were therefore protected by the religious peace. Furthermore, the splits within Lutheranism offered the Calvinists the prospect of making gains by slow attrition at the expense of the established Protestant religion. Nevertheless, the Calvinist 'second Reformation' in Germany was not the result of spontaneous popular pressure from below, but was led by princes; it often met with popular rejection, most notably in Brandenburg, where after 1613 a Calvinist elector ruled over a largely Lutheran population. Such a compromise emerged only where effective and united resistance was possible by means of strong representative institutions or semi-independent cities which supported the Lutheran position.

The princely leadership of the Calvinist Reformation fell to the Rhine Palatinate, initially a Lutheran latecomer—it did not convert to Lutheranism until 1546. Elector Frederick III agonized whether to convert to Calvinism in the years 1559–61 and then, after he had made his decision in the affirmative, sought in the Heidelberg Catechism to impose unity and uniformity against Lutheran and Anabaptist penetration. His successor, Frederick IV, declared the maintenance of churches and schools in the Palatinate to be 'the foremost part of our rule as elector and the basis of all temporal and heavenly welfare'.[144] In the Low Countries, the main issue was excommunication; in contrast, the German Calvinists emphasized the breaking of bread at the Eucharist, which symbolized for them the denial of the Real Presence in the sacraments. In political terms, the Calvinists were determined, if possible, to strengthen state authority in order to impose the Reformation from above, while abroad they greatly exceeded their real strength in support of what they saw as the international Protestant cause. The small state of Nassau-Dillenburg came close to bankruptcy because of its contributions to the Netherlands revolt (see chapter 3.2.2): its duke, John VI, a brother of William of Orange, converted to Calvinism in 1572–4. However, the leading force in German Calvinism was the Palatinate. John Casimir intervened in both France (on two occasions) and the Netherlands (respectively in 1567–8, 1575–6 and 1578–9). When he became co-regent of the Palatinate in 1583, he had to tread cautiously because Lutherans were appointed to the other co-regencies: however, in 1591 he sent Christian of Anhalt to aid Henri IV's cause in France. It was Christian who became the dominant (and disastrous) influence on Calvinist fortunes after the death of John Casimir in 1592, which led ultimately to the elector Frederick V's fatal acceptance of the Bohemian crown (see chapters 3.4.4 and 4.1.1).

Calvinism also spread to east central Europe, Bohemia, Poland and, above all, Hungary. The efforts of Geneva were concentrated after 1555 on Poland, where a reformed church was established in 1570 by an agreement known as the *Consensus Sandomiriensis* (named after the town of Sandomierz). At least a tenth of the Polish nobility was sympathetic to Calvinism by the end of the sixteenth century, although conversions among townsmen and the peasantry were fewer. The movement reached its peak in the years 1606–7, when there was an abortive revolt, the *rokosz* of Sandomierz, which was directed against arbitrary royal powers and Jesuit influence (see chapter 5.2.4). While some of its leaders were Calvinists, the revolt itself lacked any specific religious affiliation. Gradually the revolt's aims came to appear ignoble and unpatriotic, and Calvinist support declined drastically in numerical terms during the course of the seventeenth century. In Bohemia, Calvinism had even less success than in Poland. The Bohemian Confession of 1575 linked the Protestant faiths around a theology which was mainly Lutheran in emphasis. Not until 1609 was the open profession of Calvinism allowed and Calvinists were a tiny minority (see chapters 3.4.4 and 4.1.1). Only in Hungary did Calvinism really make a lasting impact among the states of central Europe. It was no thanks to Geneva that it did so: in 1592, Beza knew of no one in Hungary to whom he could appeal for funds to assist his beleaguered city. No Hungarian had ever met or corresponded with Calvin. But Zurich had been in contact with Hungary after 1549, and it was upon Bullinger's theology that the Magyar Péter Méliusz drew above all in his confession produced ten years later. The quasi-Calvinist church in Hungary would probably not have survived without powerful backing from the (Catholic) prince (*voivode*) of Transylvania and future king of Poland, Stefan Bátory. Then, a war (1593–1606) between Royal Hungary and the Ottoman Turks (see chapter 5.4.3) gave Calvinism the opportunity to make further progress: István Bocskai used his revolt to become the first reformed *voivode* of Transylvania, and won constitutional concessions for Calvinists elsewhere in Hungary. To contemporaries, Bocskai appeared as the deliverer against tyranny promised by Calvin: an alliance with the Ottomans (called 'Calvino-Turcism' by the Englishmen Rainolds and Gifford in 1597) seemed the best hope of securing the future of Calvinism in both Bohemia and Hungary. Under Bocskai's successor Bethlen Gábor (1613–29), Calvinism became the established ecclesiastical party in Transylvania, and the *voivode* was able to concentrate on an ambitious foreign policy in the Protestant cause.

Calvinism made such progress in Europe in the second half of the sixteenth century—not merely in the states surveyed, but also in England and Scotland—that it seemed to some contemporaries an international movement, co-ordinated from Geneva, with God on its side. Whether or not it received the support of the Deity, it is clear from the analysis of the separate histories of European Calvinism that the dependence on Geneva was much less than it has sometimes been argued. Geneva's influence was greatest in the development of French Calvinism, much less in that of the Dutch, and paled into relative insignificance in Germany and eastern Europe. Similarly, the emergence of a Calvinist theory of resistance in the 1570s (see chapter 6.1.2) was of only marginal importance. Calvinism never became a 'revolutionary party', since it was a conservative movement, with an aristocratic form of organization—in 1571 Beza referred to 'the aristocratic principle of the consistory'.[145] Where Calvinism prospered, it was not usually because of a successful revolt but as a consequence of the peaceful conversion of political leaders: by princes themselves, or by a substantial proportion of the nobility. When support from the nobility faded away, as in France in the 1620s and Poland by the mid-seventeenth century, the future of the Calvinist congregations was thrown into jeopardy.

1.5 The Counter-Reformation

Luther had precipitated the disintegration of the Catholic church as it had been known in the Middle Ages. Not only did he establish a distinctive theology and defend it by a successful revolt against the Papacy, but he also forced a reappraisal, a gathering of forces, a renewal of Catholicism which endured until modern times. At first the Papacy had procrastinated, preferring not to confront the Lutheran challenge on all matters of doctrine. Catholic resurgence required a definitive restatement of traditional doctrine, a new spirituality, and new forms of organization to counter the success of the reformers. By 1563, and the last session of the Council of Trent, there had been achievements in all three areas, but the Catholic church was still on the defensive. A century later, it was clear that although Catholicism had survived relatively unscathed in southern Europe, much of the north had been lost irrevocably to Protestantism.

1.5.1 *The Catholic Church in Confusion before the Council of Trent*

There was a marked change in the attitude of the Papacy towards reform during the pontificate of Paul III (1534–49). He was less concerned with dynastic interests and Italian conflicts than his predecessor, Clement VII, had been, and his policy was one of both repression and reform. He saw that the Protestant reformers posed a severe threat to the future of the Catholic church and recognized the need for a doctrinal response. Among his early appointments to the cardinalate were the Catholic reformers Gasparo Contarini, Jacopo Sadoleto and Reginald Pole. They, and other more conservative cardinals, were made members of a special commission of reform which reported to Paul III in March 1537 (the *Consilium . . . de Emendanda Ecclesia*). Their report condemned abuses in the church and talked about 'innumerable scandals and . . . contempt for holy orders'.[149] Hardly surprisingly, Luther used it as propaganda for his own cause, republishing it with his own sarcastic comments. Paul III's response was more constructive. In May 1542, he resurrected the idea of a general council of the church.

The council which came to be called the Council of Trent met in 1545, twenty-five years after Luther's great manifestos. Yet during the intervening period, the church had not ignored the challenge of the Protestants. Part of the reason for the apparent delay was that the church saw the need to re-examine those fundamental Catholic dogmas which had been criticized or reinterpreted by the reformers. Clearly a response had to be found to the Lutheran emphasis on justification by faith alone. Could the revolution brought about by the evangelical reformers be absorbed by Catholic tradition? Or were the discontinuities too radical, and the system of Papal control too inflexible, for this to happen? These were questions addressed by conferences of Catholics and reformers held between 1530 and 1541 in Germany, ending with a meeting known as the Colloquy of Regensburg in that year, and as late as 1561 in France, with the meeting known as the Colloquy of Poissy. Such issues were also the original reason for summoning the Council of Trent. By January 1546, however, Luther had commented that 'the remedy comes too late, it will not achieve its purpose'. Later in the same year, Melanchthon issued 'reasons why ... the alleged Council of Trent should not be attended nor submitted to' by Protestants. The Schmalkaldic League agreed that it was not the 'free Christian council in German lands' they had been led to expect.[150] The Venetian (Catholic) historian Paolo Sarpi largely confirmed their verdict: 'this council, which pious men desired and procured to reunite the church', he wrote, '... made the split a permanent one and the parties to it irreconcilable'.[151]

Yet this had not been the intention of a number of devout and sincere Catholics, such as Cardinal Gasparo Contarini, the Papal envoy to the Regensburg colloquy of 1541. Contarini was one member of a reform group, known as the *spirituali*, which had emerged at Rome in the 1530s. This group also included other men who went on to hold high office in the church, such as Cortese, Pole and later Morone and Seripando; the great artist Michelangelo had close affinities with it. It is misleading to view this group simply as the spirtual heirs of Erasmus. Because they were cardinals, they enjoyed political influence which he never had; in some cases (notably Pole and Seripando) they took a firm line when they came across obvious manifestations of heresy. Their 'Italian evangelism', however, was more akin to Luther than Erasmus in its pessimism about human nature and its emphasis upon the supremacy of faith. In this period, the distinction between those who remained within the Catholic church and those who became Protestants hinged, to a considerable extent, on their attitudes to the church, on its nature and in particular on its right to pronounce on doctrine, not on the doctrines themselves. Indeed, doctrinal views seem to have been relatively fluid. Reginald Pole's attitude to the Eucharist was almost indentical to Luther's, the difference being that he chose to keep his views to himself, and then to submit to the later definition provided by the Council of Trent.

Contarini, and no doubt other Catholics of his persuasion, believed that the Protestant schism had been caused by the evangelicals' misunderstanding of Catholicism. Once this misunderstanding had been overcome by an appreciation of 'real' Catholicism there would, in Contarini's view, be a reconciliation of the reformers with Rome. Contarini may have known something of Lutheran theology, but was himself guilty of a serious misunderstanding. He underestimated the fundamental Protestant rejection of the Papacy and of the Catholic sacraments, and so his attempt at mediation met with failure. The result of the deliberations in 1541, the Catholic *Book of Regensburg*, which was largely the work of the theologian Johannes Gropper, was not accepted by the Lutherans, who presented counter-articles—though surprisingly, a number of Lutherans, and even the young Jean Calvin, initially agreed with its wording on the doctrine of justification by faith. This interpretation is sometimes termed 'double justification' (*duplex justitia*: it should not be confused with Calvin's concept of a double decree of predestination). It argued that man was justified both by an alien or imputed righteousness, in other words his faith (as Luther taught) and by an inherent righteousness partly of his own creation, his capacity for good (as the medieval church had traditionally taught). Though Contarini wrote a tract on the doctrine in 1541, it is unlikely that it would have been accepted by the reformers in the long term even had the cardinal not died the following year. Both Luther and Pope Paul III rejected this compromise doctrine, as did the Council of Trent in 1547. It was not a doctrine of central importance even to Contarini, who remained a staunch Catholic and defender of the Papacy.

What became clear after 1541, however, was that Paul III was alarmed less by Contarini's failure to reach full agreement with the Lutherans at Regensburg than at the degree of success he had achieved. The Pope rejected Contarini's brand of evangelical Catholicism, and his vote of no confidence meant the defeat of the legate's party in Italy, and the abandonment of any Italian-led Catholic ecumenical initiative. Part of the explanation for the Pope taking fright at this stage was that the new party in control at Rome comprised the 'rejectionists', those who rejected any compromise with the reformers, and were headed by Cardinal Gian Pietro Caraffa (the future Pope Paul IV). The death of the influential Spanish humanist Juan de Valdés in 1541, the defection to Protestantism of his disciples Ochino and Vermigli, and the death of Contarini in 1542, decimated the *spirituali*. The Pope swung from a policy of reform to one of repression, and an old and well-tried institution was revived. In July 1542, the Papal bull *Licet ab initio* re-established the Roman Inquisition with Caraffa in charge of its operations. All appointments of inquisitors as well as the overall direction of the Inquisition were to come from Rome, and the tribunal was empowered to proceed, independently of clerical and secular jurisdiction, against anyone, regardless of rank. Caraffa's first priority was to preserve the faith throughout Italy. The *spirituali* were among the principal targets. When a leading member of the movement, Vittoria Colonna, died in 1547 in a Roman convent, even Cardinal Pole refused to act as executor of her will, for fear of exciting the interest of the Inquisition. Pole himself did not escape punishment; he was excommunicated in 1558 by Caraffa, the new Pope Paul IV.

The crackdown on heresy did not occur throughout Italy at the same pace. Venice was obliged to establish her own Inquisition in 1547, with three lay deputies as participants, but though the Pope was 'superintendant and overseer' of this tribunal, in practice it could act with a measure of independence unless its chief inquisitor consciously promoted Rome's policies, as did Felice Peretti in 1557–9. After 1560, the Venetian inquisitors were appointed by the Pope, who could threaten to replace them if they were insufficiently vigorous in repressing heresy. By the time of Pius V's pontificate (1566–72), if not before, Rome was clearly being regarded by the Venetian Inquisition as the source for authoritative judgements. In reality, it was also difficult to distinguish the policies of the Roman Inquisition from those of the Papacy itself. Paul III's policies thus gained acceptance under later Popes. The threat of the Reformation spreading to even the Italian heartlands of the Papacy had proved too great for Paul III, a potentially reforming Pope: the *spirituali* came to be seen as nascent heretics, just as the Erasmians had been in Spain. Any hint of religious compromise at the Council of Trent was therefore ruled out from the start.

1.5.2 *The Council of Trent, 1545–1563*

At first, it seemed that circumstances were working against the Council of Trent achieving anything at all. It was not just that the Council met so many years after religious opinions had become polarized. It was also very closely related to the general political situation on which its chances of success hinged. It met at Trent(o) in north Italy in 1545–6, but was transferred by the Pope to Bologna in the Papal States in 1547–9; this provoked the fury of the Emperor Charles V, since it could no longer be regarded as meeting nominally within the jurisdiction of the Empire. It met twice later at Trent, in 1551–2 and 1562–3, reflecting acceptance of the Emperor's viewpoint on location if on nothing else. The various national delegations were at loggerheads for much of the Council's deliberations. Leaving aside the French opposition to its existence (which persisted until the last session), and the Spanish opposition to its hurried conclusion, the views of the Pope and the Emperor about it could not have been more divergent. For Paul III, what was needed first and foremost was a doctrinal reply to the reformers; church reforms were very much a secondary interest. The Emperor Charles V, in contrast, wanted to see the Council reforming the church 'so as to shut the mouth of the Protestants'.[146] In the Interim of Augsburg (1548), imposed by Charles V on Germany after the Schmalkaldic war (see chapter 2.4.3), he was prepared to attempt a theological compromise by offering the Lutherans clerical marriage and Communion in both kinds in return for their acceptance of the other traditional Catholic doctrines. His brother and successor, the Emperor Ferdinand I, shared this approach. The Interim proved too much for the Papacy to accept, and it could have led to a schism, had Pope Julius III not reconvened the general council at Trent in May 1551, and had the 'Imperial interim religion' not proved unacceptable to Lutherans.

Yet despite such an unpromising political and religious background, the

Council of Trent did have at least one notable and enduring success. It reunited European Catholics and so defeated the possible creation of independent French or German national Catholic churches. From the first, the Council determined to proceed on Catholic doctrine and church reform simultaneously, but to take a conservative position on doctrinal issues, specifically rejecting Protestant views where necessary. Attendance was generally poor. At no stage were more than 237 votes cast (there were 250 bishops in Italy alone), and most of the crucial decisions were taken by less than 72 members. As with the Fifth Lateran Council (1512–17), the Council of Trent was overwhelmingly Italian in character. Among the 270 bishops attending at one time or another, 187 were Italians, 31 were Spaniards, 26 were French, and only 2 were German. Of the 255 ecclesiastics who signed the final Acts, 189 were Italian. This clear predominance prompts a comment on the attitudes and aspirations of the representatives from the Italian peninsula. It was perhaps best summed up by Pietro Bertrano, the bishop of Fano, who said of the Council in 1547, 'if it will not help those already lost to the Church, it will at least help those still in danger of becoming lost'.[147] The motives of the Italian prelates were pastoral and practical: they wanted to secure a doctrinal definition that could be understood by their flock in Italy, where heresy was making significant inroads in the course of the 1540s. In one of his sermons at Venice, Bernardino Ochino, the general of the Capuchin Order who later defected to Protestantism, asserted that 'almost everyone has his own set of beliefs. Articles, sects, heresies, faiths, and religions have so multiplied that everyone wishes to treat faith after his own manner. Similarly, insofar as works are concerned, everything is up in the air, with so many precepts, decrees, decretals, sanctions, rules, statutes, human traditions, rites, ceremonies, and ways of living that we risk losing our heads.'[148] Once he had abandoned Catholicism, Ochino hoped that Venice would become 'the door' through which the Reformation would enter Italy. Even leading members of the Papal entourage were concerned about the spread of Protestantism: in 1546 Cardinal Jacopo Sadoleto complained to the Venetian ambassador that the city was infected with the 'Lutheran plague'. The presence of a permanent colony of German merchants, many of them Lutherans, certainly made the importation of heresy relatively easy, and it has been suggested that evangelical ideas found widespread support, not merely among upper-class *spirituali* but among the skilled trades and professions, such as lawyers, doctors, notaries, printers, apothecaries, and so on. It was a more restricted audience socially for the Reformation in comparison with Germany or France, but enough to arouse deep fears among the Italian prelates assembled at Trent. Repression forced the evangelical community to become Nicodemites, the term Calvin had used so disparagingly of the French Protestant community in the face of persecution; but to halt the trend altogether, a definitive doctrinal restatement was needed.

The Pope and the Italian bishops consequently acted in unity, and by voting in a block, they had their way on all the most crucial issues, and on one of supreme importance: that each session continued the work of the last, and did not reopen issues which had been previously settled. The views of the Germans and the French went almost by default. The universal church had visibly collapsed in Germany with the signing of the Peace of Augsburg in September 1555, which had given legal recognition to Lutheranism in the Empire. In June 1562, the new Emperor, Ferdinand I, presented a request to the Council that the particular circumstances of Germany be taken into account, but this met with no response from the Italian contingent. In November 1562, a French delegation led by the cardinal of Lorraine arrived at Trent, pledged to support Gallican church privileges—but the delegation was weakened morally by the outbreak of the first war of religion in France. When the Italian predominance in the Council was effectively challenged, it was by the Spanish contingent in the crisis over ecclesiastical residence which blew up in 1562–3. This debate almost turned into one on the ultimate control of the church: the Council was brought to a hurried conclusion by fears of the death of Pius IV and the spectre of a claim by the Council (instead of the conclave of cardinals) to elect his successor. In the event, Pius IV recovered his health and confirmed the decrees of the Council in January 1564. He appointed a special congregation of cardinals to ensure the enforcement of these decrees. Henceforth, the Papacy was to be the sole source of doctrinal interpretation and the judge of disputes arising from the implementation of the disciplinary decrees.

The position of the Protestant reformers had been confronted in 1545–7, when in its first decision, the Council rejected the evangelical reformers' emphasis on scriptural authority for all matters to do with doctrine and maintained that the tradition of the church, the so-called 'uninterrupted succession' (*continua successione*), was an equal source of authority. A second decision reaffirmed the validity of the Latin Vulgate Bible. In the debates, it was pointed out that Luther had frequently revised his own translations of the Bible, and that 'if this liberty were given to everyone, Christians would soon have no idea what to believe'.[152] (On the other hand, as Calvin commented, the risk was that 'Scripture should signify . . . whatever dreaming monks might choose'.)[153] The decision at Trent did not preclude any subsequent revisions of the Latin Vulgate Bible, whose insufficiency the Protestant reformers had demonstrated convincingly, and indeed Clement VIII issued a revised text in 1592: but the delay in this revision is significant. The Council also responded positively to further Protestant criticism by obliging bishops and priests to preach on biblical texts. However, it rejected Luther's concept of man's bondage to sin. Instead, the Council regarded man as merely 'inclined to evil' with a 'diminished' capacity of free will.

This paved the way for what was to prove the decisive decree on justification by faith, issued in January 1547. Girolamo Seripando presented the views of the late Cardinal Contarini and of the *spirituali* concerning 'double justification'. However, this doctrine was vigorously resisted by the Jesuit Diego Laínez, a staunch defender of the Papacy throughout the Council. Laínez regarded 'double justification' as prejudicial to the traditional Catholic emphasis on grace and merit and a denial of the concept of purgatory. The Council eventually arrived at a formula that 'no one can be certain of his being in a state of grace with a certitude of faith that cannot be subject to error'.[154] This 'holy, Catholic doctrine of justification' was a rejection of the Lutheran position, as Melanchthon lamented. It did not prevent subsequent Catholic debate on the subject, as the history of Jansenism was to show; but at Trent it led to the undermining of predestination, the reassertion of the value of good works and (in later sessions) the reaffirmation of purgatory and the use of indulgences, although 'all evil gains' from their sale were condemned.

Other traditional Catholic doctrines were restated in the later sessions of the Council, too, particularly as a result of the influence of conservative Spanish theologians such as Laínez. Penance and extreme unction (the last rites) were redefined in an orthodox Catholic manner. The sacrificial character of the Mass was stressed; it was to be celebrated in Latin and without offering the chalice to the laity. On all these matters, the Protestant view was rejected. A much more controversial issue for the Council was the sacrament of ordination (the conferring of priesthood), which had also been denied by the Protestants. The Council reaffirmed the bishop's authority in his diocese as the 'delegate of the Apostolic See', who was responsible for the task of reform. But the influence of the reformers' criticisms is to be seen in the decision that the bishop was to reside in his diocese, and to travel round it every year to check on the residence and performance of the parish priests.

Trent did not solve two fundamental problems of the church: the accumulation of benefices by individuals and the question of authority to appoint bishops, whether lay or Papal. Where, as in France and Spain, the king retained the right to nominate bishops subject to certain conditions, and the Pope merely ratified the appointment by issuing a bull approving the candidate, then any reform depended entirely on the attitude of the secular power. There were 14 archbishops and 105 bishops in France at the end of the sixteenth century. It took a long time, twenty-five or thirty years, to renew the French episcopate in entirety, and certain royal appointments proved to be less distinguished than others. Progress in improving the quality of the bishops was inevitably slow. Furthermore, the wars of religion in France had strengthened lay control over ecclesiastical appointments and the rights of the laity to enjoy ecclesiastical revenues, which they were unwilling to surrender to the representatives of a reforming Papacy. At the lower levels of the clergy, the great innovation of Trent was a decree for the establishment of diocesan seminaries for the training of secular clergy. But here again implementation was very hesitant. The reason for delays was chiefly financial: bishops were supposed to contribute part of their revenues for the purpose, but they were not always able (or willing) to afford the burden. They were authorized to tax their clergy for the rest, but this was unpopular and led to disputes. Thus though the first French seminary was established at Reims in 1567 by its archbishop, the cardinal of Lorraine, there were relatively few in the kingdom before 1640. Seminaries were still being established in the eighteenth century.

1.5.3 *Papal Policy and the Implementation of the Decrees of the Council of Trent*

Given its circumstances, the Council of Trent was brought to a very successful conclusion; but it could easily have been abortive. Between 1552 and 1562 all work at Trent was suspended, largely as a result of Franco-Imperial (and subsequently Franco-Spanish) hostilities. Four Popes died between 1549 and 1559. Pope Paul IV (1555–9), who was both autocratic and repressive in his attitudes, was violently opposed to the Council and refused to reconvene it during his pontificate. It is an over-simplification to talk of a transition from a Renaissance to a Counter-Reformation Papacy in these years, yet there was clearly a change in Papal attitudes. Though Pius IV, Paul IV's successor, was responsible for the concluding success of the Council, he practised nepotism in the tradition of the Renaissance Popes. The difference was that his nephew, Carlo Borromeo, who had been raised to the cardinalate at the age of 22 and to the archbishopric of Milan at 25 (five years below the normal age set by the Council of Trent), proved to be the outstanding example of a Counter-Reformation reforming prelate.

The success of the Reformation had a disastrous impact on the Papal finances, resulting in an increased dependence on the Papal States for at least three-quarters of the total Papal revenue. It was thus essential that the Pope strengthened his absolute control over his territorial state: this was enhanced in a key respect by Pius V's establishment of a new office in 1566, called the superintendent of the ecclesiastical state, which was held invariably by the Papal nephew (*cardinale nipote*). This became an indispensable arm of the Papacy both in ensuring efficient administration and in curtailing the claims of the college of cardinals; it also set a precedent for the secular monarchies of western Europe as the prototype of what was to become the office of chief minister. Although nepotism had been condemned by the last session of the Council of Trent in 1563, it continued to flourish for a further 150 years until its abolition in 1692: in the view of Pius V and his successors, only the ties of blood ensured the loyalty of the superintendent of the ecclesiastical state. Because he was a cardinal, the Papal nephew could not marry and found an independent dynasty to challenge the Papacy. His office was, moreover, revocable and automatically fell vacant on the death of the Pope.

The term Counter-Reformation, although coined long after the event,[155] has attracted the connotations of great spiritual and intellectual contraction, and narrow bigotry. In some ways these are justified, for there was a hardening of attitudes of the Counter-Reformation Popes, which is best seen in the reintroduction of the Papal Inquisition and the establishment of the Index of Prohibited Books. In 1559, Paul IV withdrew the moderate Index which had been issued by Julius III five years earlier, and published a much sterner list which condemned the entire works of about 550 authors (including Machiavelli, Rabelais and Erasmus), nearly twice the number listed previously, as well as encompassing many more titles. The new Index specifically condemned nearly sixty editions of the Bible published in the vernacular. The effectiveness of the Index and the Inquisition is demonstrated by the fact that whereas in the 1520s ninety-two works by Erasmus were published in Italy, none were published in the 1560s. Erasmus' anti-clericalism and championship of the spiritual independence of the laity were increasingly viewed as incompatible with the ideals of the Counter-Reformation. Even the moderate Index of Pius IV, issued in 1564, banned six of Erasmus' works and required the expurgation of all his other theological writings. A new Index was issued in 1596, adding authors and titles published since the earlier one.

Yet the impact of the Papal Index was slight in some of the more important Catholic countries. In France the same anti-Papal sentiment— known as the defence of 'Gallican liberties'—which was to prevent the reception of the decrees of the Council of Trent also stopped the application of the Papal Index. The Sorbonne had published its first index of prohibited books in 1543, but this and its subsequent revisions do not seem to have been enforced effectively; nor were the royal edicts of 1563, 1566 and 1571, which prohibited the printing of books which did not bear royal permission and the seal of the chancellor. Effective royal censorship did not emerge until the 1630s, or even the 1650s, in France.

Spanish censorship was much more effective, because the crown placed it firmly under the control of the Inquisition, which issued its own Index in 1545, with later revisions in 1551 and 1559. Subsequently, in 1584, the inquisitor-general Gaspar de Quiroga issued a more liberal Expurgatory Index, which, for example, allowed Erasmus' works to be published with substantial excisions. Moreover, Spain attempted to seal itself off from the uncontrolled entry of foreign (and Protestant) ideas; in 1559, Philip II prohibited Spaniards from studying abroad without his permission, even in Catholic countries. Philip II's support for the Spanish Inquisition was notorious: 'I shall always favour and assist the affairs of the Inquisition', he wrote in 1574. He was reluctant to interfere with its practices and sought— not always successfully—to extend its jurisdiction to the other European states under his control. In 1509, 1524, 1547 and 1564, the kingdom of Naples had successfully opposed the introduction of an Inquisition. Philip II proposed a strengthening of the Papal Inquisition in Milan in 1563: the fact that the king was sponsoring the change made it seem that it was intended to introduce a Milanese version of the Spanish Inquisition and this was resisted. There were similar fears in the Low Countries, which explain the increasing hostility of the great nobles to Philip's religious policy (see chapter 3.2.1).

Philip II was the only leading Catholic ruler (leaving aside the kings of Portugal and Poland) to accept the decrees of the Council of Trent immediately, in July 1564, provided that his royal rights were 'in no way infringed'.[156] But Papal power, as opposed to royal authority, within the Iberian peninsula was severely restricted, and there were a number of conflicts between the two, most notably over the imprisonment by the king of Bartolomé de Carranza, archbishop of Toledo and primate of Spain, and the sequestration of his revenues (1559–76). Carranza had occupied his archbishopric for less than a year when he was accused by the Inquisition of Protestantism: the hard line taken by the Spanish Inquisition against heresy is often attributed to Dominican influence. Certainly, the Dominicans were behind the attempt by the Inquisition to limit Jesuit autonomy in Spain, particularly in the years 1587–93. Outside Philip's kingdom, however, the Papacy was able to redress the balance of power. In his capacity as duke of Milan, Philip II encountered grave difficulties with its zealous reforming archbishop, Carlo Borromeo (the nephew of Pius IV), who excommunicated the governor on three occasions. Carlo's cousin and successor, Federico Borromeo, similarly excommunicated a later governor twice. Clearly the interests of a reforming Counter-Reformation prelate were not always easy to reconcile with those of the secular power. It should be noted, however, that Pius IV was a Milanese who vainly hoped for the expulsion of the Spaniards from his native Lombardy: it was no surprise that he supported the archbishop against the Spanish king. However, Philip II and successive Popes found it prudent to limit the impact of these disputes to the immediate locality in the interests of general co-operation in the Catholic cause.

In contrast, the kings of France never formally accepted the decrees of the Council of Trent. Henri III (1574–89), a devout Catholic, refused to do so, and his resolve was stiffened by the opposition of the rebel faction of the Catholic League, which called for acceptance of the decrees (see chapter 3.3.4). After his death, the national representative institution, the Estates General, which was summoned in 1593 by the leaders of the League, and dominated by its supporters, accepted the decrees except where there was a conflict with 'Gallican liberties'. But the decision of this meeting was not regarded as binding by Henri IV, who after his abjuration in 1593 reigned for seventeen years without summoning the Estates General and consequently without accepting the decrees of Trent. In July 1615, the French assembly of the clergy declared that they accepted the decrees; but again the monarchy, this time in the person of the young Louis XIII, distanced itself from the clergy. The persistence of Gallican liberties helps explain why the French Counter-Reformation was so long delayed: it had scarcely been achieved by 1650. The trauma of the French religious wars, and in particular the dominance of the Catholic League, meant that the French bishops were much less docile and compliant than they had been in the reign of Francis I—or would be later, under Louis XIV. The French church was not amenable to leadership by any single individual, certainly not by Richelieu or Mazarin. Prominent figures such as La Rochefoucauld could emerge who were both anti-Gallican and pro-Jesuit—indeed, the early leadership of the French Counter-Reformation rested with such individuals, who had often supported the Catholic League, rather than with the docile 'king's men' among the bishops.

In Germany, full acceptance of the decrees of the Council of Trent was ruled out by the legal recognition of Lutheranism at the Peace of Augsburg of 1555, which had been denounced by Pope Paul IV. It has been estimated that by 1570 about seven-tenths of the population of Germany were Protestants. Lutherans exercised the predominant influence in the national representative institution, the Imperial diet. In northern Germany only three secular princes (Cleves, Grubenhagen and Brunswick-Wolfenbüttel) and one Imperial city (Aachen) remained Catholic. Even in the Austrian homelands, Catholic observance had lapsed. If the traditional Catholic edifice remained, it was not particularly because the ruling dynasty supported it—Maximilian II (1564–76) declared himself 'neither a Catholic nor a Protestant, but a Christian'[157]— but rather that no single Protestant group had the strength or organization to replace it.

Potentially, however, southern Germany was vulnerable to the Counter-Reformation. After 1564 Bavaria was a strictly Catholic country whose duke exercised a control of the church such as Philip II enjoyed in Spain. By 1580, Lutheranism elsewhere in southern Germany was relatively weak. There were three Catholic electorates on which the Catholic church could base an offensive—Mainz, Trier and Cologne. Cologne defected to Protestantism in the years 1580-3, but was forcibly brought back into the Catholic fold as a result of Bavarian intervention. Further to the west, the duchy of Lorraine and the southern (or later, Spanish) Netherlands were great centres of the Counter-Reformation. Pope Gregory XIII (1572-85) took an active interest in winning back as much of Germany as possible for Catholicism. He established the *Congregatio Germanica*, a permanent committee of cardinals to handle the 'German question'. He appointed able Papal nuncios to the Empire, while at Rome the Jesuits trained German priests and imbued them with an ultramontane (that is, Papalist) spirit which they carried back to their German parishes.

In some respects, Papal policy showed greater resolve in the years after the ending of the Council of Trent than in the preceding period, and some of the Popes were remarkable men. The Spanish ambassador at Rome commented that Pope Pius V (1566-72) did not acknowledge consider-ations of human prudence or reasons of state in his policy; he was the architect of the Holy League against the Ottoman Turks. Gregory XIII was particulary active in German affairs, but he also published a code of canon law in 1582, which reinforced Papal control over the post-Tridentine church. Perhaps the most outstanding of the Counter-Reformation Popes was Sixtus V (1585-90), a vigorous defender of the church's independ-ence, who was zealous in his attitude to heresy; he was also an en-lightened town planner for Rome, in terms of both its social requirements and its monuments (see chapter 9.1.3). Spanish influence on the Papacy was thereafter in the ascendant until a diplomatic volte-face of Clement VIII in 1595 freed the Papacy from Habsburg tutelage.

In the seventeenth century, the Papacy gradually lost influence as a consequence of its failure to recognize the validity of the Peace of Augsburg signed with Lutherans in the Empire in 1555, or successive agreements signed by French kings with the Huguenots to bring to an end the various wars of religion in the later sixteenth century. Even the Edict of Restitution of 1629, a measure which strengthened Catholicism in Germany by restoring a number of territories formerly held by Prot-estants (see chapter 4.1.2), was not recognized by Urban VIII (1623-44) 'either in words or deeds' since it might implicitly acknowledge the validity of the Peace of Augsburg, which the Papacy still disputed. The desire not to split the anti-Protestant camp had led Urban VIII to attempt at all costs to prevent war between France and Spain in 1635 as the 'ruin of Catholicism'.[158] Innocent X (1644-55) could only protest when a settle-ment, the Peace of Westphalia, ended a long period of war in Germany in November 1648 with the legal recognition of Protestant, including Calvinist, territorial churches. He complained that the Emperor had ceded lands of the church to heretics in perpetuity, granting them freedom of worship and a permanent voice in the election of the Emperor. He declared that the peace treaty contravened canon law and all previous councils of the church and concordats. But he protested in vain. The secular powers had the initiative in the political settlements affecting the religious balance in Europe and the Pope could no longer influence the course of European power politics.

1.5.4 *Catholic Reform: the New Orders and a New Spirituality*

One of the more positive results of the Counter-Reformation was the impetus for reform among the higher clergy. Cardinal Reginald Pole had argued in 1546 that 'we ourselves are largely responsible for the misfortune that has occurred'—that is, for the rise of heresy, and the collapse of Christian morality—'because we have failed to cultivate the field 'that was entrusted to us. We are like salt that has lost its savour. Unless we do penance, God will not speak to us.'[159] The Council of Trent had accordingly announced in 1547 its wish to 'apply itself to restore ecclesiastical discipline, which has entirely collapsed, and to amend the depraved conduct of the clergy and Christian people'. 'There is nothing which more continuously instructs others unto piety, and reverence for God', ran one of its decrees, 'than the life and example of those who have dedicated themselves to the divine ministry.'[160] Carlo Borromeo, archbishop of Milan, was an outstanding example of such a reforming prelate. He was concerned to give a practical application to the Counter-Reformation throughout his archdiocese. When he acceded to it in 1566, he was its first resident archbishop for eighty years. He implemented several of the decrees of the Council of Trent, for example founding no less than three seminaries for his vast diocese. As apostolic visitor of other sees outside Spanish Lombardy, he was able to spread his own high standards of ecclesiastical life beyond the confines of his diocese. Borromeo's diocesan officials and canons of the cathedral chapter in turn became bishops elsewhere in Italy and exported his ideas. It is nevertheless important to recognize that Carlo Borromeo—who was later canonized—was a prelate of unusual energy, ability and determination who remained in high esteem at Rome because of his earlier work in the Papal Curia. Few were so talented or were able to take advantage of such a favourable set of circumstances to bring about reform.

Although the Counter-Reformation can only be understood as a diverse movement, it is above all the Society of Jesus (better known as the Jesuits) which came to dominate it, and in many ways to personify it. Jesuits crossed national and cultural boundaries while maintaining a unified missionary endeavour. Their canonical beginning dated from September

1540, when Pope Paul III issued the bull *Regimini militantis ecclesiae*. The founder of this order, and its elected general from Lent 1541 until his death, was a Basque gentleman soldier, Don Inigo Lopez de Loyola (St Ignatius, 1491–1556). Though older than Calvin, Loyola was, like him, a second-generation reformer—albeit a Catholic one. (In fact they had both been educated at the Collège de Montaigu in 1528.) But whereas Calvin sought to systematize his theological teaching in one compendium, Loyola's *Spiritual Exercises* (1548) were basically only a series of jottings recording his spiritual experiences in the 1520s. They became, however, the permanent spiritual inspiration of the society Loyola formed, and influential among other Catholics, too; they were used as the basic tool for conversion by the Jesuits.

The first five vicars-general of the Society, spanning the years 1541–1615, were all subjects of the king of Spain, and the first three were Spaniards. Historians have sometimes assumed too readily that the Jesuits were thus tame supporters of Philip II and the Spanish Habsburg cause in Europe. Such a view misunderstands the attitude of the king, who disliked the Jesuits because of their political independence and ultramontane—that is, pro-Papal—viewpoint, and tried to prevent the Papacy from conferring further privileges upon an order which was far from amenable to control by the Spanish crown and its Inquisition. Cardinal Silíceo, archbishop of Toledo, went further and even called them heretics and tried to have the *Spiritual Exercises* condemned by the Inquisition. He disliked the Jesuits because they did not subscribe to his rabid anti-semitism: at least one of the founder-members of the Society—Laínez—was of Jewish extraction. Nevertheless, while this distrust or outright opposition might slow down the progress of the Jesuits in the Spanish kingdoms, it did not halt it. There were 1,440 Jesuits in the Spanish kingdoms by 1580 and the union with Portugal in that year added power-fully to their number. The tendency to regard the Jesuits as the lackeys of Philip II also mistakes the cosmopolitan character of the order at its inception. Of the ten founder-members, there were two Basques and three Castilians, but also two Portuguese, two Frenchmen and two Savoyards (significantly, there were no Italians). A convincing case can be argued for an initial French rather than Spanish influence through the early Jesuit links with the University of Paris and Loyola's adherence to the Parisian system of teaching. However, the vicar-general of the order was always cautious in his dealings with all the Catholic rulers and he was most careful to avoid aligning his order openly in their rivalries.

From the point of view of the great dynastic rulers, one of the principal objections to the Jesuits penetrating their states was that they had taken an oath of allegiance to the Papacy. The bull of foundation specified that they were 'fighting for God in faithful obedience to our most holy lord, the

Pope'.[161] However, there was clearly a dichotomy between a duty to the Pope and a willingness to serve the dynastic ruler as spiritual counsellor or court confessor. Loyola did not want Jesuits to seek such positions, but he certainly believed that the post, when offered, should not be refused. Jesuits, in his view, must work to convert to the Jesuit persuasion 'persons of considerable importance'; their primary task was not to save their own souls, but 'the souls of other people'.[162] It is possible to see a degree of inner contradiction within the movement, as Jesuits became confessors of the great secular rulers; they were, after all, supposed to be the shock-troops of the Counter-Reformation and unswerving supporters of Papal supremacy. Not all fulfilled this role. On the other hand, two prominent Jesuits—the Spaniard Juan de Mariana (in *The King and the Education of the King*, 1599) and the Tuscan Cardinal St Roberto Bellarmino (in *The Supreme Pontiff*, 1610)—fulfilled it with a vengeance, to the extent of justifying tyrannicide and the power of the Papacy to depose the secular ruler. It was because the Jesuits were suspected of holding such views that they were expelled from certain Catholic countries at moments of crisis—from France in the years 1594–1603 following Jean Châtel's assassination attempt on the recently converted Henri IV; and from Venice in the years 1606–7, after Paul V had placed the republic under interdict.

Nor did all Popes regard the Jesuits with favour, despite their oath of allegiance. The Jesuits were basically anti-monastic and anti-mendicant—hence their sympathy with Erasmus' criticisms and his educational programme—and Popes who had been trained in the other orders (Paul IV was a Theatine, Pius V a Dominican and Sixtus V a Franciscan) viewed them with suspicion. The death of Loyola in 1556 plunged the movement into deep crisis, because Nicholas de Bobadilla, one of its founders, argued the rights of the 'founder-fathers' to lead the movement, rather than appoint a vicar-general for life. Moreover, Bobadilla had the ear of Paul IV, who muttered darkly: 'what one Pope has done another Pope can undo'.[163] There was an embarrassing two-year interregnum (1556–8) until Paul IV confirmed the Jesuits' privileges and allowed the appointment of Laínez as vicar-general for life. But none of the Popes attempted to enforce Paul III's original limitation on the size of the movement to sixty, which had been lifted in 1544. There were 2,000 members by the time of Loyola's death in 1556; 3,500 by the death of Laínez in 1565. By this time there were also 130 Jesuit colleges, seminaries and schools. By 1615, there were over 13,000 Jesuits of all grades distributed among 13 administrative areas or 'provinces'. The rise in the number of Jesuits was less dramatic in the seventeenth century: by 1679, there were some 17,600 of them in 35 provinces.

From the start, the Jesuits had interpreted very liberally their original Papal instructions to propagate the faith by public preaching and teaching.

It had been intended that they should travel 'to the Turks, or any other infidels, even those living in the region called India, or to the heretics, schismatics or unbelievers of whatever kind'.[164] St Francis Xavier set an example of Jesuit missionary work overseas by his journey round east Africa to the far east. When he arrived in Japan in 1549, he commented that 'this land is full of idolatries and enemies of Christ'; he nevertheless conceded on another occasion that 'if something is not offensive to God it seems preferable not to change it'.[165] It may be argued that the Catholic church gained some compensation for its losses in Protestant Europe by conversions overseas—although in Japan, persecution was unleashed against the Catholic community in 1613 (and missionaries were not permitted to visit that country again until 1865). Even where such a violent response did not occur, there were two main dangers in the missionary effort. One was that Catholicism would be perceived as the religion of the colonial conqueror: the Tupinamba tribe of Brazil thought that 'the God of the Christians does good for the Christians but not for us'.[166] The other was that, in an attempt to overcome resistance to conversion, the Jesuits came to compromises with non-Christian cultures that would have been refused to the followers of Luther and Calvin in the Old World.

Moreover, the Jesuits' work overseas could be regarded as a diversion of effort: the heretics nearer home posed a more serious threat to the Catholic church than the local religions of the Indians, Filipinos, Chinese, Japanese and indigenous peoples of Latin America. Thus the Jesuits also travelled extensively in continental Europe and they were crucial in the battle against the spread of Protestantism. St Peter Canisius, who travelled more than 6,000 miles, was the most successful of the Jesuit agents in the reconquest of southern Germany and central Europe for Catholicism. He began preaching at Ingolstadt in Bavaria in 1549 and then in the early 1550s founded a college at Vienna as a spiritual base for the Jesuits in the Austrian Habsburg lands and as a teaching establishment promoting the Catholic cause. From Austria he moved on to Bohemia where he carried on the same work at Prague, visiting that city on five occasions in the space of just four years (1555–8). Canisius' educational work, while defensive in character, was comparable to that of the Protestants in its objectives and methods. For example, he published catechisms in Latin, Dutch and German (1555, 1557, 1558 and 1566) of varying length and complexity for pupils at different stages of achievement. His was not an original mind, but originality was not what was needed at such a time. It was precisely in such basic pastoral activity that Catholicism had shown itself so deficient when Luther rebelled against the established church. Nevertheless, the success of Catholic pastoral activity should not be exaggerated; it met the same intractable problem of 'popular religion' as did its Lutheran or Calvinist opponents. One French bishop told the great Counter-Reformation reformer St Vincent de Paul in 1651: 'there is the greatest ignorance among the people; in truth, the greater part of those called Catholics are Catholics only in name, because their fathers were Catholics before them, and not because they know what it means to be a Catholic'.[167] It was a devastating verdict of nearly a century's pastoral effort after the Council of Trent, but one which, on the whole, has been endorsed by local regional studies.

1.5.5 *Old Debates Renewed: Jansenists against Jesuits*

The Council of Trent provided broad definitions of Catholic doctrine to meet the challenge of the Protestant reformers. But it did not, and could not, prevent the continuance of doctrinal debate within Catholicism after its sessions had ended. These debates have a familiar ring about them. The Jesuits were accused by the Jansenists, Catholic rigorists who followed the teaching of Cornelius Jansen(ius) (1585–1638), of laxity, a similar charge to that levelled by Luther against the medieval church. In turn, the Jansenists were accused of crypto-Calvinism because of their views on predestination. All this proves that the issues of salvation and predestination were far from settled at Trent. This continuing debate added to the diversity, and to some extent the vigour, of the Counter-Reformation. Since the Papacy remained the guardian of Catholic theological orthodoxy, and the ultimate source of authority and leadership in the church, this debate did not have quite the same paralysing effect as did, for example, the disputes within Lutheranism after the death of Luther.

Within Catholicism, the leading proponent of the moderate, optimistic, view of salvation was the Jesuit Luis de Molina, whose *Concordance of Free Will with the Gifts of Grace . . .* was published at Lisbon in 1588. Molina admitted that man was incapable of avoiding venial sin, but however sinful his nature, he believed that man still possessed, through God's grace, the opportunity of attaining salvation. Molina accepted that there was divine foreknowledge of future contingent events on earth and thus a form of predestination which he defined as 'God's most high and inscrutable comprehension of every free will'. However, predestination included God's assistance to men by 'grace' which enabled them to merit salvation; without such saving 'grace', indeed, the reprobate could not attain salvation. The Jesuits were not inclined to follow Molina's views entirely, and to some extent successive vicars-general dissociated themselves from them in 1613 and 1616; but there is no doubt that Molinism was highly influential despite some official misgivings among the Jesuit leadership. This new teaching aroused furious opposition (particularly from the Dominicans), and a special congregation or assembly held at

Rome between 1598 and 1607 debated the whole issue. Pope Paul V tried to defuse the quarrel by prohibiting both parties from using the terms 'error' or 'heresy', but the dispute continued. Urban VIII had to repeat the same prohibition in 1625.

Apart from the Dominican opposition, Molinism faced equally formidable opponents in the University of Louvain in the Spanish Netherlands. This university was the stronghold of Baianism, a sort of proto-Jansenism. One of its professors, Michel Baius (1513–89), had been profoundly influenced by the writings of St Augustine and taught—or so his critics asserted—that man cannot by his own free will do good works without God's assistance or 'grace'. These views were condemned by Popes Pius V in 1567 and Gregory XIII in 1579. However, Baius' teaching reappeared in the more influential work of Cornelius Jansen. He, too, had been educated at Louvain and served there as a professor from 1630 to 1636, when he was appointed bishop of Ypres. His great work, significantly titled *Augustinius*, was published posthumously in 1640, despite Jesuit opposition. Jansen defined the Pelagian heresy within the early Christian church as a series of errors concerning the nature of sin and good works. He implicitly condemned the Jesuits as 'semi-Pelagians', denied the efficacy of good works and asserted a rigid form of predestination while distancing himself from Calvin's position. Whether or not it was a misrepresentation of St Augustine's teaching, or heretical on certain points as the Jesuits maintained, the *Augustinius* was never condemned in entirety but only censured and prohibited. However, Jansen's deterministic view of divine intervention, the limitations he set on Christ's redemptive work, and his repetition of certain ideas of Baius which had already been condemned were all censured in Pope Urban VIII's bull *In eminenti* of June 1643.

Events were to prove that Jansenism could not be easily suppressed. It spread rapidly in France in the 1640s and 1650s as a result of the influence of prominent supporters. From 1614 Jansen had been in correspondence with Jean Duvergier de Huranne, abbot of St Cyran in France, who shared most of his views. St Cyran was arrested on Richelieu's orders in 1638, the cardinal and chief minister of the king of France commenting that 'many misfortunes and disorders would have been remedied if Luther and Calvin had been arrested once they began their dogmatizing'.[168] Apart from this religious motive, St Cyran's arrest had political overtones. His correspondence with Jansen had become a political liability after the outbreak of Franco-Spanish hostilities in 1635, for Jansen had written a Habsburg propaganda-piece called *Mars gallicus*. St Cyran was not released until 1643, the year of his death. Thereafter, the French government always suspected Jansenists of being potential rebels, and this view was only reinforced by the civil struggles after 1648 (see chapter 4.4.3).

The government concluded (erroneously) that 'the principal instigators of the rebellion in Paris were the persons attached to the view of this Flemish bishop (Jansen), sworn enemy of the (French) monarchy'.[169]

But by the mid-1640s, French Jansenism had found a formidable ally in the person of Antoine Arnauld, who came from one of the leading families of the French *noblesse de robe* (see chapter 6.3.3), and whose grandfather had led the campaign for the expulsion of the Jesuits in 1594. Antoine Arnauld's tracts *Concerning Frequent Communion* (1643) and *Apology for M. Jansenius* (1644) became best-sellers. Pope Innocent X tried to end the doctrinal controversy by issuing the bull *Cum occasione* in 1653, condemning five propositions attributed to Jansen. The French government followed up this measure by trying to impose a formulary of faith on the clergy in 1656–7, a document which embodied the Papal condemnation. To counter the pressure from the hierarchy of both church and state, Arnauld and his collaborator Pierre Nicole distinguished between what they called the 'question of law' (*droit*), by which they meant whether or not a doctrine was heretical in the view of the church, and the 'question of fact' (*fait*), whether or not the heretical opinion attributed to a certain author was actually expressed in the given book (in this case, in Jansen's *Augustinius*). Arnauld and Nicole maintained that the church was infallible in matters of doctrine, but not in matters of fact, where there was liability to human error. The great French philosopher and satirist Blaise Pascal publicized the view in his *Provincial Letters* (1657), where he argued that for the church to insist that Jansen was the author of heretical opinions was as futile as to condemn Galileo for his approach to cosmology (which of course it had done in 1633: see chapter 9.5.3).

There is truth in the rather facile remark made by some contemporaries that Jansenists were 'simply Catholics who do not like the Jesuits',[170] for it was difficult to find a Jansenist who took a favourable view of the Jesuits. (Conversely, the opposition of Jesuits and other critics created the Jansenist movement as an independent entity.) Dislike of the Jesuits led to an elitist moral rigorism among Jansenists. In its earlier doctrinal form, this rigorism denied the application of divine saving grace to all but a few, and in its later pastoral form, it centred on the attempt of bishops to establish a purified popular religion that was not dissimilar in practice from the model reforms of Charles Borromeo in his archdiocese of Milan. It was thus difficult for Jansenism to become a religious movement with a broad appeal within Catholicism. It remained an austere and minority belief among the laity with few prominent clerical supporters. With some justice, Jansenists have been called 'Catholic Puritans'. But their concerns were the preoccupation of nearly all reformers, Catholic or Protestant, in early modern Europe. And those concerns, despite some sophistry, required a spirit of free enquiry that had been suppressed in the early stages of the Counter-Reformation but which was to form an integral part of the eighteenth-century Enlightenment.

The Reformation had posed questions that the late medieval church had preferred not to face. The Catholic church failed to respond, in the vain hope that Christian unity and Papal supremacy could somehow be maintained, and that Luther and the other reformers would lose their appeal in the fullness of time. Such hopes proved to be illusory. The challenge was posed so vigorously by Luther and later by Calvin that a break with Rome was inevitable. It remains unhealed to the present day and has been a decisive influence on European cultural, and to some extent political, development. After the break, the Catholic church regathered its forces and the Papacy reimposed its leadership on what was left of Catholic Europe. Fundamental questions still remained to be answered within Catholicism, however, which explains the scale and duration of the Jansenist controversy in the seventeenth and eighteenth centuries. In the meantime, the split between Reformation and Counter-Reformation ideologies had become a pervasive new influence on the relations between rulers and their subjects, and to a more limited extent on the international relations between the dynastic rulers of Europe. The new religious divisions are thus the key to an understanding of the character of the age.

PART ONE

THE DEVELOPMENT OF THE EUROPEAN DYNASTIC STATES

2

EUROPE IN THE AGE OF THE ITALIAN WARS, 1494–1559

IN his most famous work, *The Prince*, Machiavelli offered advice on 'how a ruler should act concerning military matters'. 'A ruler', he said, 'should have no other objective and no other concern, nor occupy himself with anything else except war and its methods and practices, for this pertains only to those who rule.' Machiavelli thought it 'evident that if rulers concern themselves more with the refinements of life than with military matters, they lose power'; proficiency in war was 'what enables one to gain power'.[1] Such opinions were not unique to the Florentine political theorist, nor were they confined to the Italian peninsula. Henry VIII was advised that all princes had a natural urge to extend their lands irrespective of the cost, and that a monarch who did not do so was thought to lack 'the noble courage and spirit of all the others'[2]—a potentially fatal weakness. Kings were thus not truly regal if they lost their honour and status: in Philip II's words, 'the dignity and reputation of princes is of no less importance to them than their states'.[3]

War nevertheless had to be proved 'just' in order to be legitimate, and three reasons satisfied this condition. The conflict could simply be declared just or holy by the Pope; or the war was deemed necesssary in the defence of 'patrimony'—landed possessions which had been usurped by another ruler or which were under attack; or war was permissible if its primary aim was to secure a firm peace. Each of these categories was open to debate, disagreement and abuse. The idea of a Christian crusade against Islam was still a reality in early modern Europe, and indeed the Papacy pronounced crusades or Holy Leagues against the Turk at the Fifth Lateran Council in 1513, and later in 1535, 1538, 1560, 1570, 1572 and 1578. The moral authority of the Papacy was gravely undermined, however, by its participation in the Italian wars—which automatically conferred the epithet of 'holy' on whichever league of princes the Pope chose to support at a given moment. As for war in defence of patrimony, since dynastic rights were considered to be perpetual and inalienable, Valois claims to Naples and Milan and Habsburg claims to Burgundy were difficult, if not impossible, to negotiate away in a peace treaty. If one of the legitimate aims of warfare was to secure a firm peace, then the outcome of the war had to be one which was not only likely to satisfy the dynastic interests of the rulers but which would meet some more general object-ive—perhaps parity for the main west European monarchies, the supremacy of, say, France over Spain, or the hegemony of one dynasty (the Empire of Charles V). Certainly each of the rival powers accused the other of seeking domination during the Italian wars: Henri II warned the English that Philip II would not 'forget to follow his father's [Charles V's] teachings, that is, to seize all the states he enters on the pretence of helping them'.[4] The prize was Italian predominance, initially the kingdom of Naples rather than Milan (although it was recognized that the acquisition of Milan might become necessary to guard the possession of southern Italy). The Imperial Grand Chancellor Gattinara called Italy 'the true seat and sceptre to dominate the whole world',[5] and there is no doubt that the political fragmentation of Italy into relatively weak principalities in the later Middle Ages, and its advanced cultural and economic development, served as twin attractions to the expansionist monarchies of western Europe.

2.1   The Expansion of France, 1494–1515

The French claims to Naples and Milan are frequently dismissed by historians as simply legal pretexts for political adventurism. They had lain dormant for much of the fifteenth century. Yet the tenacity with which the Valois kings asserted their rights up to 1559, even when they had really lost their cause by 1530, suggests that these claims were not viewed lightly by contemporaries. Even with the consolidation of Habsburg power in Italy after 1559, the possible revival of French claims as a bargaining-counter remained a real threat. The all-important theme underlying the events of this period was the pursuit of a ruler's inherited rights, rights which may have had no practical application but which were ideologically sacrosanct. The French claim to Naples dated from 1435–42, when the Angevin candidate had been defeated in the war of the Neapolitan suc-cession. It was kept alive after Charles III, the last Angevin count of Provence, died in 1481 and bequeathed all his lands and titles to the king of France: among these titles was one to the kingdom of Naples. In 1494, it was asserted by Charles VIII. The Milanese claim had a longer ancestry. In 1387, the ruling duke of Milan had married his daughter Valentina Visconti to a French duke, with the provision that Valentina was to inherit Milan should the ruling dynasty die out. The last Visconti duke died in 1447, but French rights were not asserted until 1495 by Charles VIII's uncle, Louis d'Orléans. They assumed momentous significance three years later when Louis succeeded to the throne as Louis XII. These dual claims meant that the French king was in effect seeking to bring under his dominion both north and south Italy, and thus to become the arbiter of the whole peninsula. It can be argued that Charles VIII was not motivated entirely by personal ambition: he had hoped to use Naples as the base for a crusade against the Turks. But his successor, Louis XII, had no such plans and seems to have been motivated exclusively by secular considerations.

2.1.1 *The Achievements of the Valois Dynasty*

These rights to Naples and Milan might have been championed earlier but for the Hundred Years' War and the Burgundian threat to France, which preoccupied the French monarchy for much of the fifteenth century. However, one of the most surprising results of the Hundred Years' War with the Lancastrian kings of England was the strengthening of the Valois dynasty. In particular, changes in finance and the army introduced by Charles VII (who reigned from 1422 to 1461, but whose succession was imperilled at least until 1435) were of the greatest importance for the future. He imposed permanent taxes in areas without provincial estates (*pays d'élections*) after 1439 and established a standing army after 1445. Both the amount of taxes and the size of the army could be increased with the passing of time, so that by 1494 it is probably true to say that the king of France had the biggest army and the largest revenue of any European monarch, although both tended to fluctuate. The burden of taxation was spread inequitably and was borne almost exclusively by the peasants; but there were many taxpayers and the increased burden of taxation was tolerable in the most populous European country of the day. The French population may even have doubled between 1450 and 1560; there were already perhaps 16 million inhabitants around 1500 (see table 7.1). The French king was in principle one of the richest monarchs in Europe, at least until he fought a long war or established an expensive system of administration.

Although parts of the kingdom had been devastated in the Hundred Years' War, the countryside was prosperous, for except in border areas such as Picardy and Provence, little fighting took place within the kingdom after 1450. The king took less interest in agriculture than in manufactures and commerce; but by maintaining internal peace he allowed the peasant to get on with his work. The booming population was a great stimulus to agricultural production; this was achieved less by improved farming techniques than by land clearance and reclamation. In the period of agricultural reconstruction before 1520, there were no great famines and the French peasants were more prosperous than they had ever been—or were likely to be in the future once the long-term effects of the rise in prices and the demographic growth of the sixteenth century had made their impact. By about 1520, population growth was tending to outstrip the rise in agricultural production, and grain shortages began to follow in the 1530s and 1540s.

The independence and wealth of the provincial princes had always posed something of a problem to the French monarchy, and had acted as a curb on the development of its power. The princes could not easily be bypassed by royal policy, and the king could only hope for a degree of natural wastage through lack of male heirs. Yet during the reign of Louis XI this potentially factious class disappeared. This was attributable more to good fortune than to the superior political wisdom of the Valois kings. Some princes, like the count of Provence in 1481, bequeathed their lands and titles to the king of France. Had he been less generous, there would have been a war of succession in Provence, as there was to be in Burgundy between 1477 and 1482 and in Brittany in 1487–91. The Burgundian episode was highly unsatisfactory to the French king. Mary of Burgundy defied her father's wishes and obstinately married Maximilian of Habsburg. She arranged that he should inherit all her titles, thus fore-stalling the possibility of a French succession to the complete Burgundian inheritance. Louis XI made the serious tactical error of resorting to force rather than relying on a combination of bribery and diplomacy. This brought a short-term advantage, since in 1477 he seized the provinces of Burgundy in the east and Artois in the north. But it also carried a long-term cost, the permanent alienation of Mary and her heirs. It is true that the war was ended in 1482 with a marriage alliance between France and Burgundy: Louis's son Charles was betrothed to Mary's daughter Margaret (who was only 2; Charles was only 12). Margaret and her dowry—the provinces of Artois and Franche-Comté—were immediately handed into French custody until the marriage took place.

But the Burgundian crisis was not to be solved so easily. Charles VIII (1483–98) inherited another succession problem in Brittany, and the traditional solution—a marriage alliance to avert war—could only be employed to solve one crisis. Charles could not marry both heiresses. Despite the 1482 treaty with Burgundy, Charles in the end chose to marry Anne of Brittany, hoping to pacify Maximilian of Habsburg by returning Artois and Franche-Comté with the repudiated fiancée. Charles's interest had already turned to Italy, and he hoped to secure his northern frontier by this gesture of reconciliation. But such hopes were vain as long as the French retained the province of Burgundy. In any case, Maximilian had his own, conflicting, territorial objectives in Italy. The house of Burgundy increased its political and physical strength when a marriage alliance in 1496 enabled Maximilian's son, Philip the Fair (duke of Burgundy, 1494–

1506), to combine the Low Countries with Castile in the year of his death. Philip and his son Charles, better known as the Emperor Charles V, had ambitions to regain the full Burgundian patrimony: Burgundy, then, was a long-term problem for the Valois dynasty which was exacerbated by Louis XI's use of force where diplomacy should have prevailed.

The French king had more success in Brittany, and the key was the marriage bed, coupled with shrewd diplomacy. Charles VIII's marriage to Anne of Brittany was not only complicated by his previous betrothal to the Burgundian heiress, but also by Anne's previous marriage by proxy to Maximilian of Habsburg in 1490. But Charles did not let this seemingly insurmountable obstacle stand in his way. His actions were drastic; he besieged Rennes in 1491 and married the Breton heiress himself. Anne continued to be the linchpin of French diplomacy during the reign of Charles's successor, his uncle Louis XII, who equalled his predecessor's matrimonial efforts by divorcing his first wife to marry the late king's widow. Anne's death in 1514 permitted Francis, the heir to the throne, to marry her daughter. Such politic marriages were the key to ensuring Brittany's continued loyalty to the crown. The French king retained his hold on the duchy by successive marriage alliances, and administered the duchy through his wife's rights until 1532, when it was permanently incorporated into the kingdom.

Yet it was not royal marriages alone that kept Brittany at peace. A skilful handling of the internal politics of the province contributed to the Valois success here as in other newly acquired territories. Provincial estates (or representative institutions) and local law courts emerged unscathed from the change of ruler in Normandy in 1450, Burgundy in 1477, Provence in 1481 and Brittany in 1491, but new institutions were also established. The first governors of Brittany, Burgundy, Guyenne and Provence (and the Bourbonnais and Auvergne after 1523) all assumed the political functions performed by the last counts or dukes. From 1504 until the end of the *ancien régime*, governors were in post in virtually all the important provinces. These were men recruited from the princes of the blood and the high nobility, especially the king's favourites, and they enjoyed enormous political and military power. But unlike the previous counts and dukes, in theory at least they could be dismissed at will by the king. Yet they could not, and did not, destroy provincial autonomy even if they kept it in bounds. Political stability under the Valois, and the gradual strengthening of provincial government, provided the necessary guarantee of civil peace required for the long task of agricultural improvement, which was itself the main reason for the return of prosperity. Nearly a generation of civil peace at home, disturbed only momentarily by disorders during the minority of Charles VIII, also made possible French intervention in Italy.

2.1.2 *Valois Success and Failure in Italy to 1515*

Although Charles VIII made Naples his first target, and had spent over a year in preparations for the invasion, it still came as a surprise to the 'Italians' in 1494. By February 1495, the French army was victorious; the Neapolitan army had been outmanœuvred in the Romagna, disaffection in the kingdom was rife, and thus Charles VIII won his objective with scarcely a shot fired in anger. Why did this kingdom fall so quickly and so easily to conquerors from such a distant country? Naples had, after all, a secure dynasty. When the king, Ferrante I, died in January 1494 his son, Alfonso, should have succeeded him; he in turn had two sons, Ferrante (II) and Federigo. There was no succession crisis to help the French as there had been in Brittany and Burgundy. But Naples was surrounded by potentially hostile states; each sought to defend its autonomy rather than unite with others against the invader. The French king was able to trade on these rivalries and internal tensions by first forming an alliance with Ludovico Sforza, the regent of Milan, who gave the French army passage across his territories. Florence underwent a political revolution at the approach of the French army, expelling the ineffective Piero de' Medici, and establishing a new republican regime which was, in all but name, a French vassal until 1512. The French army moved through northern Italy unhindered by the Florentines or by Pope Alexander VI, who was frightened into granting it free passage. Lack of a national identity and the inability to unite against a common enemy were obvious weaknesses which benefited the Valois kings.

It is sometimes said that the initial French success was a consequence of superior technology. The French artillery was drawn by horses and could move swiftly so that the Neapolitans found it difficult to take appropriate defensive measures. These weapons continued to play an important role until more effective fortification (the so-called 'angle bastion', a reinforced turret projecting from the fortification) was developed in Italy. Yet the French artillery was scarcely needed. The French had an excellent cavalry force of some 12,400 men, but their weakness was the lack of native infantry, which made them dependent on Swiss or German mercenaries. In 1495, Charles VIII's agents at Turin recruited 12,000 Swiss for the king's service, and the Swiss adhered to the French alliance until 1509. The French king had about 18,000 infantry at the time of the invasion, and his total army of 30,000 combatants was the largest seen for many centuries in western Europe. Sheer size, tactical audacity and a unified command achieved the victory by February 1495.

However, winning a new kingdom was one thing; to keep it was more difficult. Charles's very success united powerful enemies against him, among them Pope Alexander VI, the Emperor Maximilian, Ferdinand of

Aragon, Milan and Venice. The Pope's opposition was a vital rallying-point for Charles's opponents: Pope Alexander VI, the Valencian Rodrigo Borgia, stood by his Spanish loyalties and refused to 'invest' Charles VIII with the kingdom of Naples, despite the offer of 150,000 ducats and an annual tribute. Papal support provided the opposition with the justification of a religious motive, and within a month of Charles's arrival at Naples his opponents had formed an alliance called the Holy League or League of Venice. The weakness of the French position was now revealed. They had only a tiny navy, which made an alliance with the Genoese essential for logistical support. Even this combined fleet could not compete with Venetian and Spanish naval power. The army's overland supply routes were long, and could be severed at any time by disaffected Italian states. Charles VIII was obliged to withdraw before his army was completely cut off, brushing aside the League's Italian mercenaries at Fornovo in July 1495. So ended the Valois' first brief sortie into Italy, but not the monarchy's ambitions. A second invasion was planned, and only the death of the king in 1498 prevented it.

Charles's successor, Louis XII, wanted to win not only Naples but also Milan. Taking the more logical first step, from a geographical and military point of view, he mounted an invasion of northern Italy in 1499–1500. Again, the French were remarkably successful, occupying Genoa in 1499 and later that year attacking Milan itself. Disunity was again the undoing of France's enemies. The League of Venice had broken up as soon as Charles VIII had been forced to retreat, and some of its former members were quick to transfer their allegiance to the other side. Venice itself was one of the last Italian states to form an alliance with the French, but was in no position to hold out independently. Florence was already a French ally: obsessed with a fear of Venetian 'imperialism', she had earlier tried to bribe the Ottoman Turks to attack the Venetian empire in 1497. Venice was therefore embroiled between 1499 and 1502 in a costly war against the Turks, which ended in a significant defeat for her in the eastern Mediterranean.

Even more remarkable was Alexander VI's volte-face. He could not prevent a French invasion, and therefore sought to exploit French military ascendancy for the Papal objective of expelling the former mercenary captains or Papal 'vicars' from their independent states in the Romagna and Ancona. Ludovico Sforza of Milan tried to redress the balance by persuading Sultan Bayezid II that a successful French invasion would merely be a prelude to a crusade against the Ottoman empire (this indeed had been Charles VIII's intention when invading Naples in 1495). Elsewhere, however, the forces gathered against Milan were too powerful. They combined with a disaffected Milanese nobility, who believed that the French king would free them from taxation and other onerous burdens they had suffered under the previous Sforza dynasty. This belief encouraged them to flock to the French cause, and helped bring about the fall of Milan. The new conquest was altogether more feasible for the Valois to maintain because it was closer to home, and the French had guaranteed their lines of communication by their occupation of Genoa, which remained in the Valois camp until 1528. Louis XII held his new duchy for thirteen years (1500–12).

Conceivably, he might have held Milan longer had he not pushed for his second objective, the kingdom of Naples. Louis knew from Charles VIII's difficulties that allies were needed to ensure success, and he also learnt from the Burgundian crisis that diplomacy might succeed where force could not. He induced Ferdinand of Aragon to enter into a secret treaty in November 1500 to partition Naples on the pretext that Federigo, its current ruler, was plotting to 'call the Turk into Europe'.⁶ Unaware of this secret agreement, Federigo allowed Spanish troops under the 'great captain' Gonzalo de Córdoba to land in his kingdom to help in the defence against the French. When he discovered the truth, he threw himself on the mercy of Louis XII, who, in another far-sighted stroke of diplomacy, treated him generously and compensated him with the duchy of Anjou. By 1502, the French held the northern half of the kingdom, including the capital, while Ferdinand held Apulia and Calabria in the south.

The outcome of the partition was entirely predictable: rivalry and jealousy between the two powers turned into open war. As Machiavelli, the great political theorist of the Renaissance, so clearly saw, 'if France could have attacked Naples with her own forces she should have done so. If not, she should not have divided it.' Louis XII, in his view, simply succeeded in bringing into the Italian peninsula a 'rival to whom the ambitious and the discontented might have recourse'.⁷ The partition scheme was in any case unworkable, since it failed to take account of the fact that the most important revenue for the government in Naples came from the tolls levied on migrant flocks of sheep: almost by definition, shepherds and their flocks would acknowledge no political boundary established in Paris or Valladolid. The failure of the Neapolitan scheme was always cited subsequently as an explanation for the inherently unsatisfactory nature of any partition of a state between victor powers. Disputes between France and Aragon broke out in 1502–3. Here Louis XII, for all his army's military experience and successes, met his match in a Spanish force which was well trained, and had superior tactics and organization. The outcome of the war was settled by Córdoba's two victories in April and December 1503. The French evacuated Naples on New Year's Day 1504. This was the first of a long line of distinguished Spanish feats of arms in the sixteenth and seventeenth centuries. The military organization achieved by Córdoba in the Italian wars provided the basis for further developments in the Spanish army after 1534, particularly the larger new units called *tercios*. These successes in Naples greatly increased the possibility of Spanish military intervention in north Italy.

Although in military terms the French invasions had been little short of disastrous for the Italian states, they had been advantageous for some. The Papacy under Alexander VI had largely succeeded in evicting the Papal vicars from the Romagna and Ancona. Venice, too, had tried to use the French alliance for its own purpose; once it had a truce with the Turks it showed its true colours, which were to oppose the Pope and restore the vicars. This was achieved after the death of Alexander VI in August 1503. No Papal retaliation was possible during the brief pontificate of Pius III, and it took Julius II until 1506 to defeat the vicars, again with the help of the French alliance. This episode serves to illustrate the more limited role played by the French in Italy in the later part of Louis XII's reign. No longer were they able to mount full-scale invasions of southern Italy, but they were used by other ambitious powers to assist in military campaigns, and thanks to their retention of Milan they held the upper hand in the affairs of north Italy.

In December 1508, the French joined the most unholy of alliances in the Italian wars, the League of Cambrai. Its origins lay in Venice's independent action against the Emperor Maximilian, who had been defeated by Venetian forces when he attempted to assert suzerainty over Genoa and Milan. Following this victory, Venice had annexed the Habsburg territories of Gorizia, Trieste and Istria. The League of Cambrai was formed between Julius II, France, the Emperor, Ferdinand of Aragon and certain lesser states such as Mantua and Ferrara—a remarkable, if short-lived, diplomatic realignment to oppose Venice. Sir Charles Oman, the military historian of the period, wrote fifty years ago of the League that 'it is hard to understand how the other members of that iniquitous conspiracy were induced to join in a plan of robbery by which the best spoils of Venice were to go to France'.[8] In April 1509, the French army crossed the Alps under the personal command of Louis XII, passed through Milan and then on to the Venetian terra firma. The French won a crushing victory at Agnadello in May 1509. Almost all the Venetian territory in mainland Italy was occupied following this catastrophe. But the war was not over, and the republic was able to prolong hostilities for two years, until the League of Cambrai collapsed.

In the years following the war with Venice, France once again became the object of attack as the Papacy completed yet another shift of allegiance. In 1510, it pursued a new objective in attempting to subjugate the duchy of Ferrara, which relied on France to maintain a precarious independence within the Papal States. Pope Julius II was able to marshal support quite rapidly, and formed a new league against the French comprising Ferdinand of Aragon, the Emperor Maximilian, Henry VIII of England, and the Swiss who had fallen out with their paymaster, Louis XII, in 1509. Again, as so often in the past, the French won some remarkable early victories, this time under their 23-year-old commander, Gaston de Foix. He routed the Spanish and Papal forces in Lombardy; crushed the Venetians; and then besieged Ravenna in the Romagna, hoping to defeat the Spanish–Papal army which was attempting to relieve the city. The French were victorious by April 1512, but Gaston was killed outside Ravenna, and this proved to be the turning-point of French fortunes. Within a month, the Swiss invaded Milan and rapidly installed Ludovico Sforza's elder son Maximilian as duke. The French were forced to evacuate the duchy in June. At the end of August, the approach of the Holy League army undermined the Florentine republic, which almost alone among the Italian states had allied with France: the Medici family was restored as its ruling dynasty. Louis XII attempted to reconquer Milan the following year; but the Swiss mercenaries, defending (as well as oppressing) the duchy, routed the French at Novara in June 1513, and then swept into Burgundy and laid siege to Dijon. They only withdrew after La Trémouille, the local commander, signed a humiliating treaty which Louis XII subsequently refused to ratify. The French had been driven out of Italy, although Louis refused to give up French claims there and was planning a further invasion at the time of his death in 1515.

2.2 The Opponents of French Expansion: Ferdinand of Aragon and Maximilian of Habsburg

French successes in Italy in the last decade of the fifteenth century had significantly changed the balance of power in Europe. If the Valois monarchy was not to be allowed to retain its hold on Naples and Milan, then inevitably one of the other European dynasties would have to be drawn into Italy's affairs. For reasons of historical tradition, the two most obvious challengers were likely to be the Emperor and the king of Aragon. The Aragonese achievements in Italy were in stark contrast with those of the Habsburg Emperor Maximilian I, whose army failed to make any significant gains in north Italy. Financial difficulties and lack of support at home prevented him from taking advantage of French weakness in 1512–13. Habsburg power alone was not sufficient to expel the French from northern Italy. A dynastic union with the Aragonese, achieved by Maximilian's grandson Charles V in 1516–19, on the other hand, was to prove a greater threat to the Valois. A new expanded Empire, with far larger resources of men, equipment and money, was to emerge by 1530 as victor of thirty-six years of warfare in Italy.

2.2.1 *The Achievement of the Catholic Monarchs*

Ferdinand (Fernando) of Aragon had conquered Naples by 1504. This victory was not threatened in his lifetime and proved permanent. In alliance with the Papacy, Ferdinand intervened in north Italy; it was largely a Spanish army which brought about the collapse of the Florentine republic in 1512. The rise of the Aragonese Trastámara dynasty to supremacy in southern Italy by the beginning of the sixteenth century was based on success at home. Peace and good government there allowed Ferdinand to turn his attention to the wider world of European politics. His domestic achievements were founded on a dynastic union with Castile and were shared with his wife Isabella (Isabel), whom he had married in 1469, before either of them had attained power in their respective kingdoms. Isabella became queen of Castile in 1474 and Ferdinand king of Aragon five years later. The union of the crowns was depicted by the American historian Merriman seventy years ago as 'a most unequal partnership, in which the western realm, by the natural course of events, was inevitably bound to assume by far the most important role'.[9]

This inequality had several aspects. Castile was a larger country with a higher population than Aragon—there were perhaps 5 million Castilians as against less than a million Aragonese. Consequently, there were more Castilian than Aragonese taxpayers. They were taxed much more effectively, too. A tax on all goods sold in the kingdom (*alcabala*) had been levied since the 1390s without the consent of the representative institution (*Cortes*) of Castile. Permanent taxation and a weak representative institution enabled Isabella to increase tax revenue in Castile from 73 million *maravedís* on her accession in 1474 to nearly 318 million on her death in 1504 (equivalent to over 847,000 ducats), which seems impressive. Yet the *maravedí* had been debased progressively in the fifteenth century: in real terms, the revenue of 1474 was worth only 60 per cent of that in 1429; in 1504 it had increased by only 40 per cent since 1429. Nonetheless, the main economic difference between the two kingdoms lay elsewhere. Whereas the trading empire of Catalonia, the dynamic sector of the Aragonese economy in the later Middle Ages, was in decline by the time of the union, the Castilian economy was still developing—a consequence of the expanding frontier to the south as the Islamic kingdom of Granada was subdued in the years 1484–92. When this southern expansion came to an end, a whole new world was opened up for the Castilians: exploitation of the American discoveries after 1492 was made a Castilian monopoly. These long-term economic advantages were to give Castile the decisive superiority in the union.

Yet such economic preponderance was to a large extent counter-balanced by the personality and leadership qualities of the king of

Aragon. To Machiavelli, Ferdinand of Aragon was 'a new prince, because from being a weak king he has risen to being, for fame and glory, the first king of Christendom'.[10] In the short term, specific checks were placed on the power of Ferdinand by the marriage contract. Isabella's consent was necessary for the preferment of any foreigner (that is, Aragonese) in Castile. However, the long-term purpose of this dynastic union, which had been negotiated by John II of Aragon, was that the resources and man-power of Castile should be deployed to fulfil Aragonese objectives. In the political sphere, these aims were diametrically opposed to Castilian policy. Castile was traditionally pro-French, while Aragon was hostile to Valois ambitions because of two long-running grievances. In 1462, Louis XI had intervened in the Catalan revolt to seize Roussillon and Cerdagne from John II. These territories were not restored to Aragon until January 1493, when Charles VIII hoped that their restitution would forestall Ferdinand's intervention in Italian affairs. The second dispute concerned the independent kingdom of Navarre: it had been ruled by John II in the years 1425–69, but it had passed subsequently to the d'Albret dynasty. Ferdinand never lost the Aragonese ambition to regain this kingdom, which he did in 1512, although the territory was partitioned. Above all, John II and Ferdinand hoped to re-establish the dynastic state of Alfonso V, who had ruled over Aragon, the Balearic Islands, Sardinia, Sicily and Naples before the partition on his death in 1457. For all of these objectives, the resources of Castile were of critical importance.

Ferdinand's marriage contract imposed another specific curb on his political ambitions. He was bound to support the Castilian objective of conquering the kingdom of Granada, then under Islamic rule. Ferdinand fought in all the campaigns, which ended successfully in 1492. The Papacy had supported the war with remarkably generous grants of indulgences to help finance the *reconquista* and as a reward (and an inducement to join an anti-French alliance) Pope Alexander VI bestowed on Ferdinand and Isabella the title of 'Catholic Monarchs' in 1494. Ferdinand wanted to continue his successful war on Islam with a crusade in north Africa; there were some minor expeditions, but Ferdinand was dissuaded by his council from an all-out offensive. There seems little reason to suppose, however, that the kingdom of Aragon contributed greatly towards the cost of the *reconquista*. The meetings of the three *Cortes* of Aragon (Aragon, Valencia and Catalonia) were less frequent than those of Castile, and so too were the grants of taxes. It followed that the army used before 1504, in Italy as well as in southern Spain, was predominantly a Castilian army, commanded by a Castilian—Gonzalo de Córdoba, the 'great captain'—and financed by Castilian taxpayers. This army was battle-hardened in the campaigns against Islam. Furthermore, the 'great captain' had reorganized it on the model of the Swiss pikemen and the Italian harquebusiers. This combination of experience in war and advanced military techniques helped Ferdinand's later campaigns in Italy in no small measure, and gave his army a reputation second to none. In spite of its successes, there were also unresolved political tensions behind Ferdinand's victorious foreign policy. Castile had helped pay for the Italian war: the first 'expedition to Naples' in 1495 cost Castile 88 million *maravedís*, the second in 1500–4 cost 366 million or nearly a million ducats. Consequently, Isabella's son-in-law, Philip the Fair, claimed Naples as a Castilian possession when the union of the crowns was dissolved on her death in 1504. Ferdinand had no intention of seeing his lifetime's ambition thwarted, and he removed Córdoba from the position of viceroy of Naples because as a Castilian his loyalties might be suspect.

For all the economic and financial power of Castile, Aragonese influence had a formative and decisive effect on its internal politics in at least two ways. The first was during the prolonged succession crisis in Castile. Despite Isabella's considerable achievements, the Castilian nobles had not been quelled during her reign. After her death in 1504, they were prepared to reassert their position, given a favourable opportunity. The natural heiress in Castile was Isabella's daughter, Juana, who married Philip of Habsburg, duke of Burgundy, in 1496. They produced two sons, Charles and Ferdinand, born respectively in 1500 and 1503, and thus the succession should have been secure. Isabella had suspected her daughter of mental instability when she drew up her will, and added a codicil to the effect that if Juana went abroad, or was unable to govern, her father Ferdinand was to be recalled to Castile as 'governor and administrator'. At the time of Isabella's death, Philip and Juana were in Burgundy. Had they chosen to remain there, perhaps Ferdinand would have been acceptable as their regent in Castile, but two factors militated against this solution. One was Ferdinand's second marriage in 1505 to Germaine de Foix, made to improve his claim to Navarre, an alliance that infuriated the Castilians. The second was Philip's own ambition to rule Castile. Ferdinand's diplomatic *faux pas* handed him a golden opportunity to acquire the kingdom. Juana and her Habsburg consort landed in Castile in April 1506, and the nobility rallied to their cause. In June, Ferdinand surrendered the kingdom to his 'most beloved children' and withdrew to Aragon.

June 1506 was a Habsburg *coup d'état*: Philip I was no longer consort but a king in his own right. His unexpected death in September 1506 reversed the situation and probably pushed Juana into insanity. Three years later, she retreated to Tordesillas, taking the corpse of her husband with her, and there she spent the rest of her miserable life. In the meantime, the regency council, under the presidency of Cisneros, invited Ferdinand back into the kingdom. In the years 1507–10, he consolidated his control and he remained the administrator of Castile on behalf of his insane daughter until his death in 1516. In Aragon, Ferdinand's rule was not disputed, and arguably it was Aragon, not Castile, which saved the union of the crowns. It was a close-run affair: had the son of Ferdinand's second marriage survived childbirth, a separate Trastámara dynasty would have held Naples as part of a reconstituted Aragonese empire, while Castile would have pursued its own, possibly hostile, direction as part of the Habsburg inheritance. But Ferdinand had to look to his grand-children to safeguard the future of the dynastic union he had done so much to create. He had no love for his grandson Charles, whom he apparently never saw, for Charles was born in Ghent and remained in Burgundy in his youth. In contrast, the Infante Ferdinand (Fernando) was born in Castile, where he lived until Charles arrived there in 1517. Consequently, in 1512, Ferdinand of Aragon's first will favoured the younger Habsburg prince, the Infante Ferdinand. This will was later retracted, and Ferdinand made Charles his heir in Aragon, and regent on behalf of his mother in Castile (Juana lived on until 1555). Thus in 1516, Charles of Ghent (later Charles V) inherited Naples as well as the other Spanish possessions, and so united two great European dynastic states, the Burgundian lands and the kingdoms of Castile and Aragon.

A second way in which Aragon proved influential within Castilian developments was in the strength of its institutional traditions. The key elements of government in the Aragonese empire were confederation and local government through viceroyalties. The title of viceroy had been used occasionally in Castile during Henry IV's reign (1454–74), but it was under Ferdinand that the office became an established institution in the crown of Aragon. Both Charles V and Philip II built on this model; Charles increased the number of viceroys to nine. There were viceroys in Aragon, Catalonia, Valencia, Navarre, Sardinia, Sicily and Naples at the beginning of his reign; he added Mexico ('New Spain') in 1535 and Peru ('New Castile') in 1544. Confederation, rather than annexation, remained the rule. Although Castile annexed Granada outright in 1492, it was an Islamic possession and thus no precedent was set for the future. At his accession, Ferdinand had sworn before the Aragonese, Catalan and Valencian *Cortes* to observe and respect their privileges and laws. In 1515 Upper Navarre was allowed to retain its autonomous institutions and privileges when it was transferred to the crown of Castile, because Ferdinand followed the Catalan–Aragonese pattern of confederation.

2.2.2 *Maximilian I of Habsburg: the Imperial Constitution*

The striking successes of the Aragonese crown, both at home and in Italy, contrast markedly with the record of Ferdinand's contemporary, the Emperor Maximilian. Maximilian (1493–1519) attempted to mount several conflicting dynastic schemes at the same time without calculating realistically the prospects of success or the cost of incorporating so many heterogeneous territories into his empire. Again, Machiavelli's comments are apt; he said that an Italian alliance with Maximilian brought 'a name [rather] than protection' while in Germany the Emperor was an arbitrator with 'no power to enforce his will'. The imbalance between the political potential of Germany and its actual political achievement was, in Machiavelli's view, the result of a defective constitution.[11] How fair this judgement was can only be assessed by an examination of the complex Imperial constitution.

Since 1356, when the 'Golden Bull' (the fundamental constitutional law of the Holy Roman Empire) was promulgated, a college of seven electors (or electoral princes) had been given the task of choosing its rulers. The electoral college held the Empire together: the German nation did not divide into separate states as did northern Italy, even though it was extra-ordinarily fragmented. Moreover, the college could be made to work in the interests of one dynasty: between 1438 and Napoleon's abrupt dis-mantling of the Imperial constitution in 1806 a Habsburg was elected on all but one occasion. But there was no inevitability about the outcome of an election, and it could lead to an unseemly auction, as in 1519 over the election of Charles V. The electors could impose conditions on the successful candidate and in that year they made the election of Charles V dependent on his acceptance of a 'capitulation'—a charter of privileges which became the first in a series which continued as long as the Empire lasted. These 'capitulations' bolstered the power of the electors, who were regarded as guardians of the Imperial constitution and 'pillars and bulwarks of the Empire'.[12] Without the consent of the electors, no diet (or representative institution) could be summoned nor tax imposed. Charles V's 'capitulation' confirmed that the electors had a free choice in appointing his successor, and the Emperor undertook not to fight a war or contract foreign alliances without their consent.

Furthermore, the Imperial constitution's provision for an elective monarchy impeded any right of succession by inheritance. A sensible Emperor therefore sought to establish the rights of his family during his lifetime. Maximilian was elected King of the Romans—or Emperor-designate—in 1486, within the lifetime of his father. Charles V's brother Ferdinand was elected King of the Romans in 1531, and four similar elections during the lifetime of the Emperor took place in 1562, 1575, 1636 and 1653. Technically, the electors could do no more than appoint a King of the Romans; a Papal coronation was required before the title of Emperor could be assumed. The Emperor Frederick III, for example, was crowned by the Pope in 1452, but despite all his efforts, including the assumption of the title 'Emperor-elect' in 1508, Maximilian was not crowned by the Pope. Charles V's coronation by Clement VII at Bologna in 1530 was the last Papal coronation under the old *Reich*.

The Golden Bull had also prevented appeals from electoral to Imperial courts. This electoral privilege was soon extended to other principalities and to the sixty-six or so free cities (self-governing towns which owed allegiance to the Emperor but which were independent, in practice, of his authority within the Empire). Nevertheless, the Emperor could still intervene in the affairs of the princes if it could be shown that they had denied justice in their courts, or had contravened the laws of the Empire. The Imperial ban (*Reichsacht*) was rarely issued because it required legitimate cause and an army of enforcement, but in 1504 Maximilian successfully issued the Imperial ban over the contested Bavarian succession against Ruprecht, the son of the Elector Palatine. Thanks to the Swabian League, Maximilian defeated him in the war of the Bavarian succession (or Landshut war). 'The king's power in the Empire is so great', reported the Venetian ambassador after Maximilian's victory, 'that no one dares any longer to oppose him.'[13]

The collective importance of the electors at times other than at the Imperial elections can be exaggerated. They lacked any clear identity of interest, and they had their own dynastic preoccupations, especially to avoid the threat of partition—this was always a serious risk, because there was no law of primogeniture applying to the Empire as a whole. Although the four Rhinelanders in the college (the three archbishops of Mainz, Cologne and Trier and the Count Palatine) could sometimes act together, their numerical preponderance did not accurately reflect the real balance of forces in late medieval Germany. Since the prince bishops could not establish their own dynasties, ecclesiastical electorates could not easily develop consistent policies. Nevertheless, Mainz under Berthold von Henneberg played a crucial role as chief spokesman for Imperial reform in the years 1484–1504. The senior secular elector was the king of Bohemia, but the Hussite rebellion of the 1420s, and the subsequent establishment of a new Bohemian dynasty under George Podebrad and the Jagiellons, had increased the gulf between Bohemia and Germany. Berthold von Henneberg complained in 1497 that 'the king of Bohemia is, and should be, an elector of the Empire; but what aid or comfort does he lend to the realm?'[14] The Wittelsbach rulers of the Rhine Palatinate thus became the most influential of the secular electors. They avoided partitioning their lands since few of their younger sons lived beyond infancy, and they could usually count on French support for their general dynastic objectives.

Other electors were not able to present such a united front, as the Wettin rulers of Saxony demonstrated. In 1485, the Ernestine branch of the family assumed the electoral title and resided at Wittenberg; while the

Albertine branch, deprived of the electorate, and contesting possession of the rich bishoprics of Magdeburg and Halberstadt, nursed bitter resentments which broke into the open when duke Maurice attacked his cousin the elector at the time of the Schmalkaldic war (see chapter 2.4.3). Although the lands of the elector of Brandenburg were not formally partitioned, they were fragmented with the establishment of collateral lines of the same dynasty: until 1640 Brandenburg was the weakest of the secular electors. More significantly, some important interests in the Empire had no voice at all in the electoral college. This was true of the Habsburgs between 1439 and 1526, after which Bohemia fell once more to their dynasty (though they had worked closely with the Jagiellon dynasty from 1515) and of the Wittelsbachs in Bavaria until the seventeenth century.

The relative weakness of the electoral princes did not make the Emperor stronger; the result was that strong territorial principalities had not filled the vacuum left by a weak central monarchy when Maximilian came to the throne. Self-help thus became unusually important in the German constitution, one of whose distinctive features was the formation of numerous types of leagues between towns, knights, princes and other nobles. One of the earliest and most important had been the Hanseatic League, an economic league of well over a hundred Baltic, North Sea and inland towns under the leadership of Lübeck. Since these towns were dispersed geographically, they did not establish territorial links or strong common institutions; but they enforced a common code of commercial law and co-ordinated their foreign policy. By 1400, they had reached their peak, and they entered into a long decline in the face of commercial rivalry from Burgundy and the ambitions of the Scandinavian and Polish kings (see chapters 5.1.1 and 8.4.1). A second important league was the Swiss Confederation, which had gradually grown in size after the initial union of three cantons in 1291. The Swiss sought the path of association to counter the territorial ambitions of their Habsburg neighbour and would-be lord. Once the Habsburgs were safely ensconced on the Imperial throne, the relationship between the Swiss and the Empire was inevitably strained. Nevertheless, they sought privileges rather than separation and in 1499 successfully defended their independence against the Swabian League. Maximilian accepted Swiss autonomy as a fact of life, and in 1508, when bargaining for Swiss troops, he emancipated the Confederation from the jurisdiction of the Imperial courts, though it remained formally part of the Empire until 1648. This decision, and an alliance with the French in 1516, gave the Swiss autonomy and neutrality from the German conflicts.

Neither the Hanseatic League nor the Swiss Confederation proved of much assistance to the Emperor—but the Swabian League did. It was formed by the princes, towns and lesser nobility of south-west Germany in 1488 to counter the threat from the Swiss and the Wittelsbach dukes of Bavaria. With a military force of some 1,200 cavalry and 12,000 infantry, the League's army was more than a match for the Wittelsbachs in 1504. When in 1519 duke Ulrich of Württemberg appropriated the free city of Reutlingen, which was surrounded by his territories, the Swabian League took immediate counter-measures. Its forces conquered the duchy, and the following year it was sold to the Habsburgs, who thus acquired a valuable geographical link between their possessions in Austria and the Tyrol and those on the Upper Rhine and in Alsace. For a time, it seemed that the Swabian League might help Maximilian, and later Charles V, establish an effective monarchy in southern Germany based on an alliance with the towns. The alternative, it was thought by contemporaries, was that the towns' fear that the local princes were attempting to undermine their political autonomy would drive them into an alliance with the Swiss Confederation. The Swabian League was still able to take concerted action in 1525, when it crushed the rebel forces in the Peasants' War, but by 1534 it had ceased to exist because of religious differences.

The ultimate demise of the Swabian League should not be allowed to obscure its positive contribution under Maximilian's rule. It helped to maintain peace in the Empire (if necessary through recourse to war) and it gave momentum to the reform of Imperial institutions. The idea of establishing 'circles' (*Kreise*) or groupings for defence throughout the Empire came from the successful Swabian military alliance. Six circles were established in 1495, and the number was extended to ten in 1512. (No Bohemian circle was established and the Burgundian circle only reached its definitive form in 1548.) But it was difficult for these circles to repeat the military or political successes of the Swabian League: they were effective only where there was a pre-existing identity of interests between their members or a powerful regional or outside threat. The Turks invaded Austria, but there was no serious external military threat to Germany between the Hussite wars of the 1430s and the Thirty Years' War: such a threat might have helped forge princely consent to a stronger monarchy, as it had done in France and Castile. No Imperial standing army came into existence, because no Imperial tax was established on a permanent basis. The scheme to levy a Common Penny, suggested in 1495, proved abortive. Instead, a traditional and obsolete list (the *Matrikel*) was employed to determine the men and money owed by each territory of the Empire. The rate could be halved or doubled by the Imperial diet (*Reichstag*, the representative institution of the Empire which met to pass laws and vote taxes), but the proportion of tax that each territory was committed to pay remained fixed.

Although this antiquated tax system could be made to work when there was sufficient political support for the Emperor in the diet, Maximilian did not usually enjoy sufficient prestige for a generous grant. He was always short of funds, and had to summon the Imperial diet on fifteen occasions between 1495 and 1518 to ask for more money. Furthermore, the diet tended to impose unacceptable conditions on any grant since its members did not support Maximilian's dynastic objectives. For his part, the Emperor would not allow the electors or the diet to control the new Imperial institutions (the 'circles', the supreme Imperial court and the governing council). After much wrangling, the supreme Imperial court (*Reichskammergericht*) was allowed to survive because it proved an ineffective instrument for electoral control. Thus the geographical centre of Maximilian's empire was a mass of competing institutions and individuals, each pulling against the other to maintain its independence or survival at the expense of the Emperor. There was no strong central power, and no one grouping to which Maximilian could look for consistent support.

2.2.3 *The Habsburg Homelands and Maximilian's Dynastic Objectives*

The Habsburgs' Austrian homelands (*Erblande*) did not form a unified state. They were fragmented geographically and the family's archducal powers were relatively weak in comparison with those of the representative institutions (estates) there. Neither the Habsburg estates nor the Imperial diet were happy about paying for Maximilian's foreign adventures. Nevertheless, while always insufficient and heavily mortgaged, Maximilian's revenues from his Austrian lands during the period of his later Italian wars (1508–17) were approximately ten times the value of the grants voted by the Imperial diet. In an attempt to raise more money, Maximilian had sought the Burgundian alliance in 1477: he had wanted to divert the ducal revenues towards the more general objectives of Habsburg policy (at that time, the defence of the Austrian homelands from attack by Matthias Corvinus of Hungary). This attempt failed. After 1482, his regency in Burgundy was fiercely contested, matters coming to a head in 1488 when for a time Maximilian was held prisoner in Bruges. The following year, he retreated to the Empire to lick his wounds, leaving Albert of Saxony as his lieutenant in Burgundy. After 1494, Maximilian's son, Philip the Fair, exercised the authority (and enjoyed the revenues) of duke of Burgundy: he had been accepted by the Burgundians as their 'natural prince'. Despite the failure of his rule in the Low Countries, Maximilian returned to the Empire full of Burgundian ideas and obsessed by the Valois legacy. Henceforth Austrians called his central administration the 'Netherlandish government'.[15]

Faced with severe financial difficulties and limited revenues at home, Maximilian was forced to borrow from financiers such as Jacob Fugger of

Augsburg, pledging in advance the revenues of his patrimonial lands. Yet this was not enough. He had no alternative, if he wished to pursue his dynastic ambitions, but to expand his empire and enlarge the potential pool of taxpayers. 'I am not a king of money', Maximilian said on one occasion, 'but I wish to reign over the people and those who have the money; every king fights his enemies with men and money; a warlike regime and reputation count for far more than does money.'[16] In 1438–9, Albert II of Habsburg had briefly ruled both the patrimonial lands and the kingdoms of Bohemia and Hungary, although the Habsburg rule in the latter was short-lived. After Albert's death these states went their different ways under separate dynasties. Although Frederick III adopted the bold motto 'the house of Austria is universal ruler',[17] a motto often interpreted as a proclamation of Habsburg dynastic ambitions, he failed to regain either Bohemia or Hungary. Maximilian revived Habsburg claims to Hungary when, after the death of Matthias Corvinus in 1490, he went to war. The following year, however, he was forced to accept Ladislas Jagiellon as king of both Hungary and Bohemia, though a residual claim of the Habsburgs was recognized. The prospect of a German (Habsburg) succession was anathema to a strong section of the Hungarian nobility led by John Zápolyai, and in 1505 the Hungarian diet declared a foreigner incapable of succeeding to the throne. Maximilian and Ladislas replied with a proposal for a double Habsburg–Jagiellon marriage, and in 1506 the Emperor again invaded Hungary to force acceptance of his family's contingent rights of succession. It took him ten years to subdue Zápolyai's party, but the two betrothals took place at Vienna in 1515. Maximilian was conditionally betrothed to the 12-year-old Anne of Hungary on behalf of his grandson, the Infante Ferdinand (who was in Castile). Louis Jagiellon, Ladislas's son, was betrothed to Maximilian's granddaughter Mary. He in turn was adopted by Maximilian as his son and the whole event was immortalized by Bernhard Strigel in a Habsburg family portrait which also depicted the deceased Mary of Burgundy and Philip of Habsburg.

   Maximilian is usually praised for having secured, through diplomatic and military pressure, the probable succession of his family to the Bohemian and Hungarian kingdoms, but this relative success was offset by complete disaster in Italy. In 1496 he besieged, but failed to capture, the Florentine port of Leghorn (Livorno). In 1508 he was soundly defeated by the Venetian Republic; even after he had joined the League of Cambrai, his siege of Padua ended in failure. When the collapse of French power in northern Italy offered an unprecedented opportunity in 1512–13, Maximilian was too weak to exploit it. He was unable to contest Francis I's recapture of Milan in 1515, because his unpaid troops mutinied as soon as they entered the duchy. The Emperor's territorial gains in 1516 after eight years of war fell far short of his original ambition of conquering

Lombardy and Venetia, and making it the financial base for a revived empire. Italy was nevertheless his obsession. The idea of 'forcing his way to Rome' to obtain a Papal coronation (which was never achieved) was a powerful motive in his policy. It remained for his grandson Charles to restore fully the prestige of the Emperor in Italian and general European politics. First, however, Maximilian had to secure Charles's election in the face of stiff opposition from Francis I of France. In this, the last act of his reign, he was successful.

2.3   The Reign of Francis I of France, 1515–1547

Francis I was 20 at the time of his accession to the French throne on New Year's Day 1515. He could have brought about a change in the foreign policy pursued by Charles VIII and Louis XII. Instead of draining his resources and destroying his people in foreign wars which 'by some mischance [might] end in naught', he could have stayed at home, making the kingdom 'as prosperous and flourishing as possible', loving his subjects, being revered by them and ruling them 'gently'. Such advice was proferred to the English king by Sir Thomas More in 1516; but even in *Utopia* More expected no 'very favourable' response.[18] No one in the French kingdom suggested such a course of action to Francis I in 1515. Indeed, there were legitimate French rights to be championed: if he lacked them in his own right as king, Francis claimed them by virtue of his wife, Claude of Brittany, whom he had married in 1514; she formally ceded her rights to him in June 1515. There were also grave defeats to be avenged, foremost among them the recent humiliation in Italy. The reconquest of Milan was given first priority in Francis's foreign policy.

2.3.1   *Francis I and the Reconquest of Milan, 1515–1521*

Francis was not short of commanders anxious to rectify previous disasters in Italy. He needed few preparations, since he inherited the invasion plan made by Louis XII shortly before his death. The finances for the war were arranged, ironically enough, by borrowing from the Italian bankers at Lyon. The strengths of the army lay, as always, in its artillery and cavalry, which were second to none. The weak link was a lack of infantry, which had to be hired. Some 23,000 German infantry replaced the treacherous Swiss, who were still defending Maximilian Sforza of Milan. To complete his preparations, Francis accumulated an assortment of diplomatic alliances: Genoa was prepared to revert to its former French allegiance in return for local concessions, while Venice as always wanted French assistance against the Emperor Maximilian.

On the advice of the experienced Marshal Trivulzio, Francis chose to invade Italy by the Col de Larche, a pass which was rarely used and poorly defended. After a two-day battle at Marignano in September 1515, which resulted in severe losses on both sides, Francis was victorious. Milan capitulated the following day, but Sforza held out in its citadel until early October. He then accepted a generous pension and permanent residence in France, where he died in 1530. Francis sensibly chose not to rely on military might, but sought to consolidate his position by alliances with the Pope and the Swiss, both of whom had backed the wrong horse. In November 1515, he negotiated a provisional agreement with the Swiss which was ratified as a 'permanent peace' the following year on French payment of a war indemnity. Although this was only a defensive alliance, it was better than none at all. When the king met the Pope in December 1515, he found the price for Papal support a heavy one: abrogation of the restrictions on Papal power in France imposed by a unilateral declaration of the rights of the 'Gallican' church known as the Pragmatic Sanction of Bourges (1438). It is true that on occasions French kings had waived the Sanction in favour of a Concordat with the Pope; but France was the hotbed of conciliarism. The new agreement with the Pope signed by Francis, the Concordat of Bologna, was desperately unpopular in France and was ratified by the *Parlement* of Paris in March 1518 only 'on the repeatedly made behest and command of our lord the king'.[19]

Francis I returned to France in January 1516, leaving the Constable of Bourbon as lieutenant-general in Milan. International events created an uneasy peace until 1520, which facilitated the installation of a French regime in Milan. The death of Ferdinand of Aragon left Charles of Ghent preoccupied with his Spanish inheritance; and then the death of Maximilian further embroiled Charles in a protracted Imperial election. However, separate meetings between the three most powerful rulers of Europe in 1520—Henry VIII of England, Francis I and the new Emperor Charles V—made it clear that there was no prospect of long-term Habsburg acquiescence in the gains of the Valois king. Francis and Charles were 'not at peace', observed the Venetian ambassador; 'they adapt themselves to circumstances, but hate each other very cordially'.[20] All that was needed was an excuse to resume hostilities. Early in 1521, Francis I foolishly provoked a war by proxy when Robert de la Marck, lord of Sedan, invaded Luxembourg (a Habsburg possession) on his behalf, and André de Foix took advantage of the revolt of the Comuneros in Castile to invade Spanish Navarre on behalf of the house of Albret. Both adventures collapsed, and to make matters worse, Pope Leo X in May 1521 suddenly recognized the need for Imperial help in the suppression of Lutheranism in Germany, and threw in his lot with Charles V.

Faced with war on several fronts, Francis drew back from confrontation with the Emperor, and at the Calais conference in the summer of 1521 under Cardinal Wolsey's chairmanship, Chancellor Duprat, representing the Valois king, was instructed to settle all outstanding disputes with the Habsburgs peaceably. However, the Imperial representative at the conference, Chancellor Gattinara, was not to be pacified so easily. Arguing that France had broken the peace, Gattinara demanded the entire Burgundian inheritance (part of which was held by France) as well as Milan, Genoa and Asti for the Habsburgs. Duprat replied that this was not an offer of peace but a declaration of war, and so it was. Even while the Calais conference was proceeding, hostilities commenced. In November 1521, Prospero Colonna breached Milan's defences at the head of the joint Habsburg–Papal forces.

The pattern of past French campaigns in Italy, with early victories quickly followed by defeat, was repeated. After the fall of Milan, the French were expelled from other cities of the duchy. Francis I replied by hiring 16,000 Swiss mercenaries, and would doubtless have left for Italy himself had he not feared a possible English invasion of his kingdom. But the defeat of Lautrec, the French general, at La Bicocca in April 1522 (brought about by the recklessness of his discontented Swiss mercenaries) sealed the outcome of the campaign. By the end of May 1522, when Genoa capitulated, Francis I had lost virtually all he had held in Italy. In July 1522, Henry VIII joined the alliance against him. Pope Leo X had died in December 1521, but this did not greatly help the French cause because his successor, Adrian VI, was Charles V's old tutor and former regent in Castile. Shortly before his death, Adrian abandoned neutrality in favour of an alliance with the Emperor. Yet even now, in the face of overwhelming odds, the French king would not give up his claims in Italy. In August 1523, Francis was ready to attempt the reconquest of Milan, and indeed a French army under Bonnivet crossed the Alps in the late summer, but was chased back ignominiously by the Imperial forces. The king himself was prevented from leading the latest campaign personally because he faced a rebellion at home by the Constable of Bourbon. However, it is doubtful whether the outcome of the 1523 invasion would have been any more successful had Francis himself taken to the field.

2.3.2 *Pavia and the Revived Burgundian Threat*

The Constable of Bourbon, who was the senior figure in the army, had been appointed to his office within a fortnight of Francis's accession to the throne. His lands comprised three duchies, seven counties, two viscounties and seven lordships—an unusually compact block of territory in central France, whose capital, Moulins, was one of the kingdom's great fortresses. Leaving aside the fact that he had not been the French commander in Milan, he had a twofold grievance against Francis. The death of his wife in April 1521 led to a protracted lawsuit during which Francis I and his mother helped themselves to part of the inheritance. The more serious issue, however, was the remarriage of the Constable, who had been offered the hand of one of the Emperor Charles V's sisters. Francis could not be expected to agree to such an alliance, and, indeed, he had hoped to prevent the Constable from remarrying at all, thus averting the possibility of his producing a male heir. Many people felt that the Constable had been unfairly treated, but rebellion against an autocratic and powerful king such as Francis—which the Constable originally planned to coincide with the king's invasion of Italy—was an extremely risky venture. Bourbon had expected more than a thousand nobles to rally to his standard. He had relied on his own military contingent (*compagnie d'ordonnance*) and three others to declare for him; his large estates and extensive patronage had seemed to offer a broadly based support. In fact, he was badly let down even by nobles who had originally encouraged him. The nobility had less cause for discontent than any other social group in France, because it was least affected by the king's financial exactions and had the most to gain from his Italian ventures. The aggressive foreign policy of a strong king was expected to yield results: the nobles were thus fairly united in the search for spoils of war. Later, military defeats would breed discontent and recrimination; the king's patronage policies would spread faction; the incursion of a dangerous new ideology—Calvinism— would harden divisions between noblemen and would make them more receptive to the blandishments of Philip II of Spain. It was not surprising that Bourbon's rebellion collapsed and he had to flee abroad, where he served as an Imperial commander and in June 1524, at Turin, swore allegiance to Henry VIII of England as 'king of France'. Invading the Midi, he entered Aix in August and assumed the title of count of Provence; but by September, with the failure of the siege of Marseille, this military threat was over: Bourbon was retreating along the Mediterranean coast, with Montmorency giving chase. The Bourbon demesne was forfeited to the French crown because of the Constable's treason.

Bourbon's insurrection and an English invasion in 1523 delayed Francis's Italian expedition, as did the virtual bankruptcy of the French crown. An investigation into the royal finances in 1522–3 was followed by two significant administrative reforms, one of which was designed to increase financial accountability, the other to increase revenue. Before 1523 several treasurers handled royal expenditure. After that date, there was only one treasurer (*trésorier de l'Épargne*), and thus the king was in a better position to know how much cash was at his disposal for emergencies. Revenues were increased after 1522 by the public sale of annuities (see chapter 6.5.2), the first time that this had happened in France. These *rentes de l'hôtel de ville* were theoretically guaranteed by the Paris municipality, but in practice the king could default on his obligation to pay interest to the bond-holders. Whether these financial reforms would have been sufficient to sustain a prolonged Italian offensive is doubtful; but in the short term they provided Francis with the means to pursue his Italian ambitions.

He planned a second invasion of Italy, declaring boldly in November 1524 'I want nothing less than the entire state of Milan and the kingdom of Naples.'[21] As a further encouragement, if any was needed, the Imperial army had retreated to Pavia, leaving Milan almost defenceless. Most of the duchy was quickly overrun, but the ease of his conquest led Francis to make two fatal mistakes: the division of his forces (he sent 6,000 men under the duke of Albany to conquer the kingdom of Naples) and a winter siege of Pavia, which immobilized the French army for four months in the open in appalling conditions. When the Imperial forces struck back in late February, the Spanish musketeers (harquebusiers) proved their worth. The Valois king was lucky to survive the biggest slaughter of the French nobility since Agincourt. Francis himself was captured: 'all that is left to me', he wrote to his mother, who was acting as regent in France, 'is my honour and my life, which is safe.'[22] The king remained in captivity at Madrid until March 1526.

Yet the victors failed to capitalize on this complete military victory. They could not agree on a united policy against France. The English hoped for the partitioning of that country: 'not an hour is to be lost', an ecstatic Henry VIII wrote to Charles V after Pavia. The Valois line should be 'abolished, removed and [made] utterly extinct' in his view; doubtless to be replaced by the Tudors.[23] Fortunately for France, and its regent Louise of Savoy, the Emperor responded with moderation, mindful, no doubt, of Henry VIII's inactivity in 1521–2, when the Emperor had wanted an invasion of northern France; Henry's invasion, when it did occur in 1523, brought no permanent gains. A joint invasion in 1525 would have been particularly serious for the French monarchy. However, Henry lacked the financial resources for intervention because of the failure of a special levy called the 'Amicable Grant', and the unreliability of the English army had been revealed in the mutinies during the previous campaign. The Emperor might have chosen to invade the French-held province of Burgundy to regain the patrimony lost by his predecessors in 1477. Some of the inhabitants still regarded him as their lawful ruler, and he would have received a measure of support. However, he had his own financial problems and even before Pavia he had recognized the need to bring the war to a swift conclusion. With the Valois king captured, a new campaign seemed to him to be unnecessary—a serious miscalculation, because it assumed that Francis would be able, or willing, to grant enduring concessions that would satisfy the Emperor. These concessions were succinctly enumerated by Gattinara. There could be no lasting peace, he declared, without the renunciation of all Valois claims in Italy and the restitution of the French-held province of Burgundy to the Empire. But the Imperial side was too exhausted to seize the territory, and the French regency government refused to give it up. The stalemate could only be broken by Francis I ceding the territory voluntarily. This he was naturally reluctant to do, and on two occasions he secretly nullified in advance any document signing away Burgundy. Crucially, while the haggling continued, there was no rebellion in France. The king's subjects appeared to accept the verdict of the *Parlement* of Paris that the nation's misfortunes were a divine retribution and not the fault of their ruler.

Gattinara believed that either Charles V should have kept Francis locked up, or have released him unconditionally in the hope of winning his friendship. He feared that the king would repudiate any treaty signed under duress once he regained his freedom, and that the Habsburgs would be left with a worthless piece of paper and useless hostages. The Emperor did not accept this advice, and preferred to think that Francis could be trusted. The captive king signed a treaty at Madrid in January 1526, renouncing his claims to Italy and the French province of Burgundy as well as suzerainty over Flanders and Artois. He then returned to France, leaving two of his sons as surety for his good faith. Events were to prove Gattinara right. In May 1526, Francis offered a cash ransom for Burgundy, but declared that he could not consider alienating part of his demesne. The estates of Burgundy agreed with the verdict of the king's council that the Treaty of Madrid was 'contrary to all reason and equity'. In the same month, Francis formed the League of Cognac with the Medici Pope Clement VII, Venice, Florence and Francesco Sforza of Milan (with Henry VIII as its 'protector', since the English king had failed to extract the advantages he sought from the Imperial alliance) to put diplomatic pressure on the Emperor to rescind the Treaty of Madrid. Pavia had been a wasted opportunity, and Charles V's chance of regaining the entire Burgundian inheritance was lost for ever.

2.3.3 *The Failure of the League of Cognac and the Occupation of Savoy, 1526–1538*

Francis had hoped to use the League of Cognac as more than a diplomatic counter in his ambition to recover Italian territory. He hoped that the combined military might of its members would force Charles V to make concessions, but the League's forces in Italy were no match for the Habsburg contingents. The first crack in the alliance came in March 1527, when the Medici Pope, Clement VII, was forced by Charles to sign an eight months' truce. This, however, came too late to prevent the sack of

Rome by the unpaid troops of the Constable of Bourbon, who, now fighting as an Imperial commander, was killed while scaling the city wall. The Pope was now a prisoner of the Habsburgs. His family was expelled from Florence in May 1527 and the republican regime that was established showed its hostility to the Medici by declaring the Pope a common debtor to the sum of 212,658 florins. Francis pressed on with his latest Italian campaign notwithstanding faltering allies, and again there were dramatic French victories. Lautrec's army overran all of Lombardy, except Milan, in August 1527. Andrea Doria, a great Genoese naval captain then in exile, entered French service and captured Genoa. Lautrec invaded the kingdom of Naples and by the summer of 1528 its capital seemed about to fall to the French. However, an outbreak of cholera or plague decimated Lautrec's army, Andrea Doria changed sides, and yet again the Imperial forces regained Genoa and relieved Naples. Once more the tide had turned against the French and their retreat was as rapid as their earlier advance. After a French attempt to recapture Genoa had met with disaster in June 1529, Clement VII declared he had 'quite made up [his] mind to become an Imperialist' and signed the Treaty of Barcelona with Charles V.[24] This provided for the restoration of Medici rule in Florence in return for the Emperor being crowned by the Pope.

Francis I could not hold out much longer against the defeat which was inevitable. Peace negotiations began at Cambrai in July and a settlement was reached in August 1529. Francis I appeared to renounce all his Italian claims; he handed over the towns of Hesdin, Arras, Lille and Tournai and surrendered suzerainty over Flanders and Artois. The Emperor graciously accepted an indemnity of 2 million gold *écus* (1.2 million in a lump sum) rather than the French province of Burgundy. Francis, true to form, deserted his Italian allies (except, of course, the Pope, who had deserted him first) and ransomed his sons, obtaining their release by July 1530. He married Eleanor, the sister of his arch-enemy the Emperor, in the same month. His perfidy at Madrid was thus to some extent rewarded at Cambrai, for he had, above all, retained the province of Burgundy. From the Emperor's point of view, peace in Italy, reinforced by a Habsburg-controlled league in December 1529, enabled him to be crowned by the Pope at Bologna in February 1530. This was an all-important legitimization of his title by the highest spiritual authority, which he hoped would add weight to his attempt to settle the religious divisions in Germany.

However, despite all outward appearances to the contrary, Francis I had no intention of abandoning Milan to the Emperor. The Peace of Cambrai merely provided him with a breathing-space to replenish his treasury, rebuild his forces and consolidate his alliances. One possibility was an alliance with the German Protestant princes, although he did not pursue it

with great consistency or enthusiasm. He was somewhat hampered by his
policy of Protestant persecution within France, although never being
short of diplomatic excuses, he claimed in his manifesto to the Imperial
princes and cities, dated February 1535, that the persecution was political,
not religious. Further, he tried scaremongering by stating that if the
friendship between Germans and Frenchmen were destroyed, nothing
would stop the Emperor building a universal monarchy on the ruins of
German liberties. The Schmalkaldic League of German Lutheran princes
and cities was not impressed (see chapter 1.3.4), and in December it
refused to admit the Valois king to their association. Another possibility
for Francis was an alliance with Henry VIII, but the Tudor king's breach
with Rome complicated relations, particularly since Francis had already
committed himself to a third policy, that of a *rapprochement* with the Pope
at the expense of the Emperor. A Medici marriage for the king's second
son, Henri, was contracted in October 1533, but its purpose was
frustrated the following September by the death of Clement VII: the secret
undertakings of Papal support for the reconquest of Milan were thus
rendered null and void. As Francis's attempted Papal alliance weakened,
so he tried to counter Habsburg power by increasing his contacts with the
Ottoman Turks. A commercial treaty with the Turks was signed in
February 1536, but Francis did not take advantage of the chance to co-
ordinate a Franco-Ottoman offensive in Italy the following year. Nevertheless, his alliance with the Turks was valuable; they promised him both
land and sea assistance (which materialized in the war of 1542–4), and in
return he gave Barbarossa's corsairs important tactical support and a port
of refuge on the mainland. Indeed, for eight months in 1544 Toulon was
occupied by the Turks who converted it into a Moslem colony in the most
Christian kingdom.

The whole Milanese issue was reopened in November 1535 by the death
of Francesco Sforza without a male heir. Francis at once proposed that the
duchy be given to his own second son, Henri, whereupon Charles V
rejected the suggestion out of hand. The prince was too close to the
French throne; indeed, he was to become the heir apparent after the death
of the dauphin Francis in August 1536. In February 1536, Francis I
invaded the duchy of Savoy, whose duke, Charles III, was the Emperor's
brother-in-law and ally. Francis claimed that the action was taken in self-
defence. In reality, the invasion was a straightforward ploy to secure
territory as a bargaining-counter for Milan. By May 1536, a state of unde-
clared war existed in north Italy, and in July the Emperor invaded Provence, co-ordinating his attack with an invasion of northern France by
Henry of Nassau, who laid siege to (but failed to capture) Péronne. Aix fell
to the Emperor, but he could not overcome the resistance of Marseille.
Francis's commander, Montmorency, employed a 'scorched earth' policy

in Lower Provence; with 7,000 or 8,000 men dead from famine or dysentery (including Leyva, the Emperor's principal general) Charles V had no alternative but to withdraw. In 1537, the French army went on the offensive, occupying Thérouanne in the north, and overrunning Piedmont. Nevertheless, by the time a truce was signed in January 1538, both sides had run out of money. Francis lacked the means to pursue the Emperor into Italy beyond Piedmont and defeat him decisively. The Emperor had been able to invade France on two fronts, from the north and the south-east, but he lacked the resources to overcome a cautiously conducted defensive campaign when his own lines of communication were fully stretched.

2.3.4 *The Triumph of Faction and the Failure of Conciliation, 1538–1547*

After July 1538, when the two monarchs met at Aigues-Mortes in Languedoc to sign a truce, there was a Franco-Imperial entente, at least on paper, for the next four years. Montmorency's star was in the ascendant for the earlier part of this period as a result of his successful campaign in Provence in 1536. He was promoted to Constable in February 1538 and he controlled French foreign policy until April 1540, when relations with the Emperor took a turn for the worse. Montmorency was a firm believer in the possibility of entente during the lives of the two monarchs, even if this left the issue of Milan unresolved. As a step towards regaining Milan by diplomatic means, Francis offered Charles free passage through France in 1539–40, when the Emperor needed to reach the Netherlands quickly to suppress a revolt at Ghent. Charles accepted this offer, but by June 1540 the talks over Milan had collapsed: in October, the Emperor 'invested' his son Philip with the duchy. Montmorency's enemies at court, chiefly admiral Chabot and the duchesse d'Étampes, the king's mistress, seized on this failure of diplomacy to bring about his fall from royal favour. Montmorency retired from court in June 1541, never to return during Francis's reign.

With Montmorency in disgrace, the faction-fighting at court and within the council became really serious. Admiral Chabot was arrested and prosecuted for treason. The charges did not stick, and Chancellor Poyet, who had helped bring him to trial, was in turn arrested, prosecuted and imprisoned. Poyet's fall in August 1542 and Chabot's death in June 1543 left the king with advisers of lesser stature. His failing health and the lack of affection between him and the heir to the throne, his second son Henri (and their respective mistresses) were serious problems. Further, the rift between the dauphin and his younger brother Charles, which had widened after 1541, was potentially disastrous: Henri remained loyal to the disgraced Montmorency, but Charles became the darling of the duchesse d'Étampes, the Constable's implacable foe.

These harmful intrigues at court were reflected in French foreign policy, which, after Montmorency's policy of entente had been discredited, turned again in an anti-Habsburg direction. From July 1541, Francis's intention may have been to declare war on the Emperor. He waited a year before doing so, in the meantime forming an alliance with Denmark and Sweden (see chapter 5.1.2). The French forces were split as his sons separately laid siege to Luxembourg and Perpignan. This war on two fronts went badly for the French, and the conflict was extended when there was an Anglo-Imperial declaration of war in June 1543. Though the French won a useful victory at Cerisole in Piedmont in April 1544, the Anglo-Imperial invasion of northern France that year necessitated the recall of the French troops and a defensive strategy. Fortunately for the king, Henry VIII was more intent on capturing territory around Calais (specifically Boulogne, which he took in September 1544) than on marching on Paris. He, it seems, had at last learnt that the Hundred Years' War was over and that there could be no repetition of the 1523 campaign, which had attempted deep incursions into France. The impetus of the Imperial invasion was broken by a fruitless forty-one-day siege of St-Dizier. Disgusted at Henry VIII's tactics, the Emperor abandoned his march on Paris in September 1544, and signed the Treaty of Crépy-en-Laonnais. Henry VIII fought on alone despite the threat of French counter-invasion until he made peace at Ardres in June 1546.

As with all other attempts at Franco-Imperial entente, the Peace of Crépy remained a dead letter. The chief beneficiary, Charles d'Orléans, the king's younger son, who would have married one of the Habsburg princesses with a dowry comprising either the Netherlands and Franche-Comté or alternatively Milan, died in September 1545. Had Orléans lived, Francis I would have returned Savoy and Piedmont, and Charles V would have renounced his claim to French Burgundy. The dauphin Henri never forgave the Cardinal de Tournon, who had negotiated the peace, for it appeared to advance his brother's prospects at the expense of his own. Not only would Henri have lost his rights in Italy, he would have seen Charles d'Orléans established in an apanage—a temporary fief created for the younger son of a king—comprising four French duchies. Henri complained formally against this proposal in December 1544. A change in French foreign policy became evident immediately on Charles's death. The French dropped the idea of a compromise settlement with the Emperor, but the government and court were sharply divided on the wisdom of a new war against the Habsburgs. Effective intervention in 1546–7 was ruled out by the king's insolvency. The war of 1542–6 had cost 23 million *livres* and necessitated both administrative reform and a desperate search for money from sales of crown lands, new offices and above all from loans—loans contracted at 16 per cent interest from Italian, Swiss and German bankers at Lyon. By 1547, the king owed his bankers virtually a year's income, and he was in no position to take to the field against the Emperor. Thus Francis I failed in his lifelong bid to extend his dominion beyond the Alps. He held on to Savoy and Piedmont, but these were not the territories he really wanted. Yet he had been a consistent and extraordinarily frustrating opponent for Charles V. He did not, indeed could not, defeat the Emperor: but he could prevent him from achieving success in his own right. It is no accident that the Emperor's greatest military victory—the battle of Mühlberg in Germany—came a month after Francis's death.

2.4 The Ascendancy of Charles V

For convenience historians talk of the 'empire' of Charles V, but when contemporaries used a collective name for his dominions they used the word 'monarchy', as in 1519 when the Imperial Grand Chancellor Gattinara remarked that 'God has set you on the path towards a world monarchy.'[25] Charles gathered his 'monarchy' or 'empire' over a period of about fifteen years (1515–30). The first stage was to claim the Burgundian lands, which he inherited from his father, Philip the Fair, who died in 1506. Charles was declared of age to rule as duke in 1515. Next, the Aragonese inheritance came to Charles in 1516 after the death of his grandfather on the maternal side, Ferdinand, together with the regency of Castile on behalf of his (supposedly insane) mother. The Holy Roman Empire—the last stage in the process of inheritance—came in 1519: after a disputed election, he succeeded Maximilian, his grandfather on the paternal side. However, Charles continued to add to the territories in his possession throughout his life, even as late as 1543, when he acquired Gelderland. As a result of his territorial acquisitions, particularly Milan, Charles acquired an unenviable reputation as an aggressive and acquisitive ruler who ignored the demands both of morality and dynastic rights when it suited him.

The central fact concerning Charles V's inheritance in the years 1516–19 was that it came about almost wholly by accident rather than by design. Neither Ferdinand of Aragon nor Maximilian of Habsburg had wanted or expected Charles to inherit all the lands of the four patrimonies (the possessions respectively of the Austrian Habsburg, Burgundian Valois–Habsburg, Castilian Trastámara and Aragonese Trastámara dynasties in the fifteenth century). Both rulers had wanted the Infante Fernando, Charles V's brother Ferdinand, to succeed to their own patrimony exclusively. But these schemes were irreconcilable, and a partition arrangement imposed by the grandparents was thought unworkable. The brothers had thus been left to agree to a mutually satisfactory partition so as to avoid the risk of warfare between them. Charles, indeed, made some concessions to Ferdinand in 1520–1, but these were less than his brother had hoped for, and the threat of a further, more far-reaching partition hung over Charles's 'monarchy' for the rest of the reign, while both brothers pursued their separate dynastic policies which were to some extent mutually contradictory. In the last resort, Charles was not prepared to countenance partition until the 1550s, when circumstances left him with no real choice.

2.4.1 *Securing a Dispersed Inheritance, 1515–1530*

Of all his inherited territories, the Castilian succession proved perhaps the most problematic to Charles. Cisneros, the president of the council of regency, advised Charles to accept the regency, since the young prince had no right to proclaim himself king in the lifetime of his mother. Yet this was precisely what he did, at Brussels in March 1516 on the advice of his grandfather, the Emperor Maximilian. Cisneros reluctantly acquiesced in a second Habsburg *coup d'état* in Castile, though it was not until October 1517 that the 17-year-old Carlos I saw his new realm. The years 1517–20 were a period of conspicuous and overbearing Burgundian presence in Castile. Charles was not popular with his subjects: he was too inexperienced, he spoke no Castilian, and above all he was not their 'natural lord'. They would have preferred his younger brother, Ferdinand, who had been brought up in the country. In 1518, the *Cortes* of Castile requested that Charles learn their language as soon as possible, that he marry, and until the birth of his son his brother should remain in the kingdom. Charles paid no heed to their requests, and fearing an aristocratic rebellion he packed off his brother, the Infante Ferdinand, first to Burgundy and later to Germany.

Charles's high-handed behaviour in Castile stemmed from his ambition to succeed Maximilian as Emperor. He needed the title of king of Castile to impress the German electors, who alone determined the Imperial succession. Charles's election as King of the Romans (Emperor-elect) in June 1519 created new fears in Castile that could not easily be allayed. In September, the *Cortes* extracted from him the promise that 'the placing of the title of Emperor before that of king of Spain was in no way to be understood as prejudicing the liberty and exemptions of these kingdoms'.[26] The fact remained that the Castilian aristocracy feared the prospect of subordination to the grand designs of Habsburg dynasticism, while the towns were particularly sensitive to the fiscal implications of Charles's policy. When Charles left for Germany in May 1520, it was popularly supposed that he would never return. Riots against taxation broke out almost immediately, and they became a significant rebellion because Charles made the mistake of leaving a Burgundian—Adrian of Utrecht—as regent.

At the end of August 1520, the military chiefs of the rebellion went to Tordesillas, where they presented their grievances to Juana the Mad. By mid-September, the queen had agreed to occupy herself with affairs of state; and the rebels, who had now organized themselves as a Holy League (*Santa Junta*), renounced their allegiance to Charles; they also refused to recognize him as Emperor or to pay for his foreign policy. The revolt drew its strength initially from the Castilian towns—and was therefore known as the revolt of the Comuneros after the municipal council or 'commune' (*comunidad*) established by Toledo at the beginning of the revolt. This example was followed by other towns and came to be regarded as one of its distinctive features. However, not all the important towns joined the League. The rebels wanted to remodel the constitution so that it became a confederation of free towns with the *Cortes* elevated in importance to become the main institution of the state. They wanted to abolish the permanent sales tax (*alcabala*); to reduce the status of the king to that of a low-paid pensioner of the legislature; and to elevate the role of the *Cortes* so that it participated in the really important decisions of state. The rebels were thus the proponents of a traditional, xenophobic Castilian regionalism against an innovative, cosmopolitan Habsburg family enterprise. Had the rebellion succeeded (and it was difficult for the Emperor because it coincided with another serious rebellion in Valencia, the Germanía, and French intervention in Navarre), the fortunes of the Habsburgs and thus the course of European history would have been very different.

The revolt of the Comuneros collapsed after its defeat at Villalar in April 1521 (see chapter 7.5.4). The victory was not won by Charles, however, who was still in Germany, but by the Castilian nobles whose military contingents were essential (in the absence of mercenaries) to act against the urban militia controlled by the rebels. The nobles had previously exploited the weakness of the government to obtain political concessions, most notably the appointment of two Castilians—the Constable and Admiral of Castile—as joint regents with Adrian of Utrecht after September 1520. In the end, they suppressed the rebellion less out of enthusiasm for the king than from fear of a peasant uprising. They expected Charles to feel grateful to them on his return from Germany in July 1522, and to grant them the political power and financial compensation they demanded for their services. Once he had won, however, the king gave away little: the compensation was not as much as the nobles had hoped for, and they were denied political power. Despite this perfunctory treatment, further unrest in Castile was avoided by Charles's presence in the country from 1522 to 1529. He made it the military and financial base for his war on France and his seizure of Milan, and he left only when it was clear that he had won, that he would be crowned Emperor by the Pope, and that he could proceed safely to Germany. This period of residence allayed Castilian fears. It is true that when he married Isabella of Portugal in 1526, he did not consult the *Cortes*. But she bore his son Philip the following year, and he could leave an Iberian regent and a Castilian heir to conceal his absenteeism after 1529 and to soften the fact that Castilian revenues had been placed firmly at the disposal of his family's wider European interests.

The financing of Charles's dynastic ambitions was always somewhat problematic. In the Aragonese kingdoms, the three *Cortes*, usually meeting at Monzón, successfully defended their liberties and refused to vote significant amounts of taxation. Charles did not always get his way even in Castile. He negotiated with the *Cortes* three times in the years 1523–5. The conclusion, which was reached after Pavia, was a fifteen-year moratorium on increases in indirect taxes and a return to the pre-1518 system of collection, which had been controlled by the *Cortes*. This compromise with the towns was further extended in 1539, when taxes were again pegged until 1556. This proved to be a considerable bargain in an age of rising prices. It is true that the *Cortes* supported Charles's foreign policy in the Mediterranean (though not in Germany or on the Austrian frontier), and voted large grants of taxes (*servicios*) throughout his reign. However, the effect of this increase in direct taxation was more than offset by the decline of indirect taxation in real terms. The Castilian economy continued to prosper, but the monarchy headed towards bankruptcy. Revenues had reached only about one million ducats per annum by 1540, when Charles told his brother that he could not be 'sustained except by my kingdoms of Spain'.[27] They continued to increase after this date as the silver mines of Mexico and Peru began to yield their profits to the crown. At no stage in Charles's reign, however, did receipts from the New World reach an average of a million ducats per annum.

The burden of taxation to finance Charles's foreign policy did not rest on Castile alone. Burgundy also contributed a significant amount, which was voted by the provincial states at irregular intervals, and the considerable fluctuations in these grants provided some guarantee of its privileges. In 1534 a defensive union of the Burgundian provinces—the formation of a 'circle' comparable to those elsewhere in the Empire—was proposed by Charles V's regent: the provinces would have made regular financial contributions and have provided a standing army; but the States General rejected the idea. 'If we accept the project', they argued, 'we shall undoubtedly be more united, but we shall be dealt with in the manner of

France'—that is, lose our liberties.[28] Charles continued his expansionist foreign policy, by attempting to bring some of the neighbouring duchies and principalities under his control as ruler of the Netherlands: the 'seventeen provinces' of the Netherlands were his political creation. Tournai was annexed in 1521, Friesland in 1523–4, Utrecht and Overijssel in 1528, Groningen, the Ommelanden and Drenthe in 1536 and the duchy of Guelders (which was renamed Gelderland) in 1543. Finally, the long-awaited Burgundian 'circle' was established in 1548, in the aftermath of Charles's great victory over the Schmalkaldic League in Germany. Thereafter, the Netherlands were only nominally a part of the Holy Roman Empire.

However, the north-eastern provinces of the Low Countries were never ruled effectively by Charles, and this played into the hands of his enemies, especially the Valois king and his ally from 1492 to 1538, Charles of Egmont, duke of Guelders. Charles V never fully defeated Egmont, but he was more successful with the duke's Lutheran successor, William of Cleves, who was forced to abandon both the new religion and his claim to the duchy of Guelders in 1543. Nevertheless, the struggle was a close-run affair: as late as 1542 the opposing army under Maarten van Rossem ('Black Martin') attacked Antwerp and captured Luxembourg. It was not until 1549 that Charles persuaded the separate provinces that after his death they should all obey the same ruler (his son Philip) and the same central institutions. As late as the reign of Philip, moreover, the loyalty of the 'newly conquered territories' to the Habsburg dynasty was suspect; and they neither were, nor wished to be, represented at meetings of the States General, the central representative institution.

The cost of Imperial foreign policy was borne by different territories at different times—not as a result of any clear geographical distribution of responsibilities but according to their presumed fiscal capacity, and above all the ease with which taxes could be levied. There was no general balance sheet for Charles's dominions. Instead, each territory administered its own finances, the most important finance councils being those of Castile (which was reformed in 1523) and Burgundy (reformed in 1531). It is doubtful whether the Italian states were ever more than self-financing (they were not even that in the 1520s). The archducal lands and the Tyrol, with both their revenues and their debts, were transferred to Ferdinand, Charles's younger brother. The financial votes of the Imperial diet continued to be derisory. In 1546 Granvelle—one of Charles's ministers— thought the Empire (i.e. Germany) 'not [worth] a penny, nothing but anxiety and vexation'.[29] This left Burgundy and the Spanish kingdoms, primarily Castile, as Charles's main source of revenue, by default. Despite having access to revenues which must have seemed colossal to Henry VIII of England, Charles lived a hand-to-mouth existence. The Tudor king financed his wars by debasing the coinage. Charles paid for his military campaigns by mortgaging the royal demesne to secure loans from financiers. One of the great achievements of Ferdinand and Isabella had been the appropriation between 1487 and 1499 of the grand masterships of the three wealthy military orders of Calatrava, Alcántara and Santiago, together with their vast lands. In 1524, Charles V mortgaged them to the Fuggers of Augsburg as security for loans, and except for a few years when the contract went to other financiers, this family held the lease for more than a century.

The government in the Low Countries borrowed on Charles's behalf in the Antwerp money market: loans rose from half a million Flemish pounds in 1520 to about 7 million in 1555. Through this sum was impressive, nearly four times as much money was borrowed at the Castilian fairs at Medina del Campo: German, Flemish and Spanish financiers lent Charles almost 29 million ducats between 1520 and 1556 on the expectation of Castilian revenues. Both the scale of borrowing and the interest charges increased in the course of the reign. In the years 1520–32, Charles borrowed less than half a million ducats a year on average, and paid a rate of interest of rather more than 17 per cent. In the last five years of his reign (1552–6) he borrowed nearly 2 million ducats a year and paid a rate of interest of nearly 50 per cent! Charles's reign thus ended in financial catastrophe.

2.4.2 *The Peripatetic Ruler, His Regents and Advisers*

Apart from his seven years in Spain in 1522–9, Charles spent little time in any single part of his empire. In his abdication speech in October 1555 at Brussels, the Emperor stressed the burden imposed by six journeys to Spain, nine to Germany, seven to Italy and ten to the Low Countries, apart from others elsewhere.[30] 'You cannot be everywhere', he told his son Philip in 1548, '... the best way is to hold your kingdoms together by making use of your children.'[31] Charles used Philip as his regent in Spain in 1543–8 and again in 1551–4. His daughter Juana was regent there when Philip was in the Low Countries in 1554–9. But since Charles married relatively late in his reign, his children were of little use to him before 1543. He thus had to employ more distant members of his family. In the Netherlands his first regent was his aunt, Margaret of Austria (1519–30), who had been regent earlier, in 1509–15, during his minority. After her death, Charles appointed his sister, Mary of Hungary (1531–55). Both were extremely capable. In the Holy Roman Empire after 1521, his brother Ferdinand was regent (*Staathalter*) and effective president of the Imperial governing council (*Reichsregiment*). Charles recognized the need for a strong representative in Germany, and fears that the Infante Philip might not outlive his father coupled with an earlier promise to his brother induced him to support the election of Ferdinand as King of the Romans in 1531—a fateful decision, because it prejudiced the Infante's rights to the Imperial title.

The delegation of authority to members of Charles's family carried risks, though with his aunt, his sister and his children these risks were limited to opposition on matters of policy. But his ambitious brother Ferdinand, who had been thwarted of greater prizes such as the Imperial title in 1519, could, and did, establish a rival dynasty with its own objectives in central Europe and the Empire. He married five years earlier than Charles, and his son Maximilian was born the same year as Philip (1527). In 1520–1, Charles had abdicated control over the Austrian archducal lands to his brother, and in 1526 Ferdinand asserted his claim to the kingdoms of Bohemia and Hungary. In Bohemia he was successful, but his rule in Hungary was contested. For obvious reasons, the defence of the eastern frontier against the Turks was a much higher priority with Ferdinand than it was with his brother, who was fully preoccupied with countering the Valois in western Europe and the Ottomans in the western Mediterranean. The difference in emphasis would not have mattered had Hungary brought Ferdinand resources in men and money commensurate with his new responsibilities, but it did not, and he had to turn to the Empire for assistance. Lutheran princes such as Philip of Hesse and John, elector of Saxony, were quick to exploit the opportunity. Their support for Ferdinand's Hungarian campaigns was conditional on a tacit acceptance of their faith and the secularization of church lands in their principalities. Once Ferdinand was King of the Romans, the conflicting policies within the Habsburg dynasty became more pronounced.

Charles inherited from his father a Burgundian court and Burgundian advisers. From 1508 until his death in 1521, the most important adviser was Chièvres, whose policy was to contain but not confront the power of the Valois king. Charles's personal Chancellor, Mercurino Arborio di Gattinara, rose to power under Chièvres and was the most important councillor after 1521. As a Piedmontese, he was well informed about Italian affairs, and was violently anti-French. Even before his death in 1530, however, his influence had begun to wane (as he himself protested) in favour of royal secretaries such as Los Cobos and Granvelle. The change in Imperial policy in 1521 in anti-French direction may in part be explained by the rising influence of Gattinara; but it is misleading to view it simply in these terms. Until Charles's power was secure in Castile, and he had been crowned at Aachen in October 1520, it made very little sense to attempt to challenge the Valois king. Charles's policy was bedevilled by conflicting family and territorial interests, but he was very much his own man after the death of Chièvres: for example, his advisers were prepared to negotiate with the French over the future of Milan, but it is very doubtful if the Emperor himself was prepared to see the duchy lost to his dynasty. In some areas, such as Burgundy, the upper nobility were consulted as a matter of course on high policy; in other areas, such as Castile and the Empire, they were not. Charles kept a measure of control over the local councils by issuing instructions to the regents and his nine viceroys, but inevitably personal and peripatetic government imposed endless delays and allowed each of the Habsburg lands considerable autonomy.

Charles advised his son in 1548 to 'find good viceroys ... [who] will not overstep their instructions'.[32] Trusted viceroys tended to be left in office for a long time: the able Pedro de Toledo, for example, stayed twenty-one years in Naples (1532–53). Most viceroys were great Castilian nobles, but under Charles there was as yet no Castilian monopoly. Ferrante Gonzaga, an Italian, was viceroy of Sicily and governor of Milan; Charles de Lannoy, a Burgundian, served as viceroy of Naples. In 1526, Charles V's lieutenant-general in Italy and head of the Imperial army was a great French prince—the Constable of Bourbon. Origins mattered less than loyalty to the dynasty—the proven loyalty of the Burgundian nobles who occupied the eleven provincial governorships ('stadholderates') was the reason they enjoyed almost viceregal powers.

One of the weaknesses of Charles's approach to government was that frequent absences abroad made it difficult to keep a check on his officials. The Emperor's most important councillors received great favours, but in return they were intensely loyal to their master. There was relatively little faction, certainly in comparison with his son's reign, and no rebellion on the scale of that of the Constable of Bourbon in France. But there were abuses. Francisco de los Cobos was the most important secretary in Castile between 1523 and his death in 1547. But he was also greedy, and used his position to become one of the richest men in the kingdom by the time of his death. Yet the councillors' rewards were small when compared with the profits made by the Imperial financiers who, admittedly, ran much greater risks. Between 1511 and 1527, the Fuggers of Augsburg, the greatest of Maximilian's and Charles's financiers, received a return on capital of 927 per cent, an average of over 54 per cent per annum. At the nadir of Imperial fortunes in 1552, Anton Fugger was still prepared to lend the Emperor 400,000 ducats. The risk was over-involvement in the Habsburg family finances and catastrophic losses in the inevitable bankruptcy declared by Philip II in 1557.

2.4.3 *The Rise and Fall of the Schmalkaldic League, 1531–1547*

Imperial policy in the years 1521–9 was directed towards countering French influence in Italy; in the 1530s, towards the Ottoman threat to the western Mediterranean (a successful campaign against Tunis in 1535 was offset by a disastrous one against Algiers in 1541); in 1543 it concentrated on the war over the duchy of Guelders; and finally in the years 1546–52 on the intractable religious problems in Germany. The problems of governing a dispersed inheritance were only too clear, as Charles fought an active foreign policy on all these fronts. Furthermore, he had a resolute and powerful enemy in Francis I, against whom he had to defend his empire in numerous wars. Constant military campaigns were mounted against a background of rising prices, which led eventually to bankruptcy. Charles, distracted by his many problems, postponed some decisions which could not safely be delayed, in order to deal with what seemed more pressing problems. This led to a fatal inaction in German affairs before 1546.

The League of Schmalkalden was yet another German alliance of those who shared common interests and relied on their own resources rather than those of their Emperor (see chapters 1.3.1 and 2.2.2). Religious differences within the Empire lay behind the League's formation in December 1530, and its leaders were drawn from Lutheran princes, particularly Hesse and the elector of Saxony. Two northern free cities, Magdeburg and Bremen, were in the alliance from the start. They were joined by eight southern towns the following year, including four (Strasbourg, Constance, Memmingen and Lindau) which had accepted Bucer's rival document to Melanchthon's Confession of Augsburg. Zurich, and the close supporters of Zwingli, were absent from the alliance; and at no stage did the Schmalkaldic League represent all the Protestant princes and cities. The cities were less effective in the League because they thought only in terms of defence and the overwhelming need to avoid being crushed separately. The princes were far more aggressive and had at their disposal more money and troops than the cities. As the ally and supporter of the deposed Lutheran duke Ulrich of Württemberg, Philip of Hesse was awaiting a favourable moment to attack the Habsburgs. This came in 1534, when Ulrich's restoration was instigated by Hesse with the help of French subsidies: Württemberg became a Lutheran state, and a member of the League; and Ferdinand, now King of the Romans, lost this strategically important territory. Ferdinand's lack of commitment to regaining Württemberg could not be a greater contrast to Charles's attitude to Milan. Charles had been prepared to fight for a whole generation to regain and keep Milan. Ferdinand, however, was preoccupied with his dynastic interests in Hungary, and the perennial problem of Turkish pressure on the eastern frontier, and he was fearful at the prospect of French intervention in Imperial affairs. This accounts for his signing of the 'religious peace' of Nuremberg in July 1532, under which the Lutherans promised to support the Emperor Charles and to recognize Ferdinand as King of the Romans in return for a truce in Germany until a general council of the church could be summoned. Hesse's actions in 1534 broke the truce, but because Ferdinand failed to respond, new adherents were encouraged to join the League.

After negotiating in vain with the Pope for the summoning of a general council of the church, and drawing up a theological compromise embodied in the *Book of Regensburg* which was accepted by neither side, in July 1541 the Emperor appeared to remove all restrictions on the expansion of Lutheranism in Germany, provided this took place without 'forcibly entic[ing] away or tak[ing] under their protection the subjects of any Catholic state'.[33] The declaration was clearly ambiguous, and the Schmalkaldic League had reason to suspect the Emperor of duplicity because he was trying to arrange private treaties with individual Lutheran princes; in short, he was attempting to divide and rule. This deep suspicion explains why the League broke the truce in 1542 and attacked the duchy of Brunswick-Wolfenbüttel, the last bulwark of Catholicism in northern Germany. The attack was successful, because Charles was embroiled in a new war with the French over Milan and the duchy of Guelders, and Ferdinand still had his troubles in Hungary. The situation changed completely in 1544–5, with the signing of peace with France, a truce with the Turks and the opening of a general council of the church at Trent in December 1545.

Luther died in February 1546. Calvin noted that God sometimes removed good men from the world in order to spare them from the disasters with which he intended to punish their contemporaries. Thus it was, in his view, that Luther had been 'snatched from the world' shortly before Germany was affected by calamitous wars.[34] The Emperor Charles V described his feelings to his sister, Mary of Hungary, after the decision was taken in June 1546 to attack the Schmalkaldic League: 'if we failed to intervene now, all the Estates of Germany would be in danger of breaking with the faith . . . After considering this and considering it again, I decided to embark on war against Hesse and Saxony as transgressors of the peace against the duke of Brunswick and his territory. And although this pretext will not long disguise the fact that it is a matter of religion, yet it serves for the present to divide the renegades.'[35] Pope Paul III was asked to join in an alliance to force the Schmalkaldic League to send representatives to the Council of Trent. He promised Charles an army and a subsidy to fight the League, and announced that the purpose of their alliance was to extirpate heresy in Germany. Cardinal del Monte, the future Pope Julius III, advised Paul III that it was permissible to 'proclaim a crusade against the heretics with the same indulgences and privileges that are granted for the recovery of the Holy Land';[36] instead, in July 1546, the Pope regarded the conflict as a religious war, but not a crusade—and he sent his grandson as commander of the Papal army for the war against the Lutherans.

The members of the Schmalkaldic League, too, were in no doubt that they wanted a preventive war: without the recourse to force, they argued, the 'pure doctrine of the gospel, of our true Christian religion, and the Augsburg Confession' were in danger of suppression.[37] Only the Emperor held back from calling it a war of religion. The views he revealed to his sister were kept private; as far as his public pronouncements were concerned, the crimes committed by the Schmalkaldic League amounted to a 'breach of the public peace'; the purpose of the war was to maintain the integrity of the Empire, in effect against treasonable activity.[38] In alliance with the duke of Bavaria and the Lutheran Maurice of Albertine Saxony, Charles placed Hesse and the elector of Saxony under the ban of the Empire in July 1546. The Schmalkaldic League mobilized its army first and it was almost certainly able to marshal larger forces than the Emperor; however, what it gained in size it lost though disunity and indecision. The crucial victory at Mühlberg went to the Emperor in April 1547, when the elector of Saxony was captured. Hesse surrendered the following June and the war was over.

Charles V's victory over the League seemed absolute, but it had to be converted into a permanent religious and constitutional settlement for the Empire. At the 'armed' diet of Augsburg (so called because the Emperor's forces were still mobilized) in 1547-8, these problems were discussed by the assembled electors, princes and representatives of the cities. For the first time in his reign Charles held the initiative in Germany, but he still failed to get all his own way. He wanted to revive and extend the idea of the Swabian League, creating a German standing army under Imperial control. The opposition to this was overwhelming. Even Catholic Bavaria vetoed the idea and the elector of Brandenburg declared that the Empire would be 'reduced to servitude'. The scheme collapsed. This failure was, however, offset by an agreement to reform the Imperial tribunal (*Reichskammergericht*), ensuring that appointments would be made which were more acceptable to the Emperor and judicial decisions taken which were more in line with Imperial policy.

Both issues were overshadowed by Charles's attempted solution to the religious problem, the so-called Interim of Augsburg of June 1548 (termed an interim settlement 'until the general council could be held'). The 'Imperial interim religion' was not accepted by a still formally united Christendom. The commission which determined the religious settlement was appointed by the Emperor, not the Pope. Though it produced a Catholic text, it tried to accommodate the Lutherans; there was to be no restitution of church property confiscated by the Protestants. The difficulty with the Interim was that it came twenty years too late: by 1548 doctrinal reconciliation was impossible, and the Interim was rejected by Catholics and Lutherans alike. The Lutheran faith was more resilient than

Charles V had foreseen. Even the imprisoned original leaders of the Schmalkaldic League refused to abjure. John Frederick of Saxony acquiesced in the loss of his lands and electoral title, but stood firm in his faith. Philip of Hesse apologized for his actions but remained adamant and imprisoned, despite guarantees made by his son-in-law, Maurice of Saxony, the new elector, a Lutheran who had fought for the Emperor. A new league of Lutheran princes, seeking to attack the Emperor and defeat the Interim, was inevitable and it was formed in 1551–2. What made the new league so dangerous for the Empire, however, was the revival of French power under Henri II.

At first, the rebellion against the Interim was limited to the free city of Magdeburg. By the time the city had been brought to submission (November 1551), a new Protestant league had formed. Its earliest members, in February 1550, were Küstrin, Mecklenburg and Prussia. Maurice of Saxony correctly saw himself as a possible target for attack by them: he was, after all, a Lutheran who had allied with the Emperor and had thus gained significant benefits. With astonishing skill and duplicity, he reversed his allegiance, achieving personal leadership of the new league and extending its membership. He formed an alliance with France, attacked the Emperor and negotiated with his brother the King of the Romans. In May 1551 at Torgau, Maurice joined the league whose objectives now were the release of Philip of Hesse, the revocation of the Interim and opposition to a strong Imperial authority (and implicitly to Philip II's succession) which was called 'beastly, insufferable and ever-lasting servitude as in Spain'.[39]

What gave further substance to the propaganda of the Lutheran princes was the fear of a Habsburg hereditary monarchy that had been aroused by the discussions between the 'Spanish' and 'Austrian' branches of the dynasty at Augsburg in the winter of 1550–1. After six months of wrangling, a compromise known as the Augsburg family compact was reached in March 1551. Charles accepted that Ferdinand would succeed him as Emperor; but Ferdinand was required to support Charles's son Philip as his successor; Philip in turn was required to support Maximilian (Ferdinand's son) as his successor. Some historians call the arrangement an Imperial diktat, and relations between Charles and Ferdinand were never repaired after this meeting. The 'settlement' presupposed a remarkable degree of co-operation between the two branches of the Habsburg family, whose interests diverged; it also tied the hands of the electors in three successive Imperial elections. It thus contravened Charles's election 'capitulation', and in any case it would prove impossible to fulfil, since by 1556 three electors were Lutherans.

In May 1552, Maurice stormed the Ehrenberg pass, and Charles V and his court were forced to flee across the Brenner pass to Villach in

Carinthia: it was the most humiliating event of his life. The volte-face of Maurice was crucial to the success of the Lutheran rebellion. He alone had a significant army (ostensibly for the siege of Magdeburg) which could be used against the Emperor. Charles V would not negotiate with him in person, but Ferdinand had no such scruples. At Passau in June 1552 a truce was reached. Ferdinand wanted an agreement in order to receive further German assistance for a new campaign in Hungary, where the Turks had resumed the offensive. The Emperor was prepared to accept a temporary settlement that did not imply permanent acceptance of the religious divisions in Germany and left him free to counter-attack Henri II. He believed that he could both pacify the Empire and recover his lost reputation by besieging Metz: his advisers were dumbfounded at the risk, given the lateness of the campaigning season and the strength of the city's fortifications. The siege was a disastrous failure.

The revolt of the Lutheran princes in 1552, and the lifting of the siege of Metz (which had been captured by Henri II: see chapter 2.5.1) on New Year's Day 1553, together broke Charles's spirit. Twice in his life—in 1525 and 1547—he had triumphed over his enemies. Twice his enemies had reorganized themselves to rob him of the permanent settlement he sought. The second defeat was much the greater. By 1553 the Emperor, though only as old as the century, was prematurely aged and for much of the year he was reduced to a state of mental collapse verging on breakdown. His sister, Mary of Hungary, kept some semblance of government going during these months. In the rare moments when he attended to government business, what Charles feared above all were religious concessions and the partition of his inheritance. For all practical purposes, he abandoned Germany to its fate, leaving Ferdinand as King of the Romans to sort out the ambiguities of his concessions to the Protestants. Charles acknowledged that the Interim of Augsburg had been a mistake and that it should be abandoned. But he was not prepared to go to a new Imperial diet in person to settle the problem, nor was he willing to be a party to any settlement by which 'our true, ancient, Christian and Catholic religion might be offended, injured, weakened or disgraced'.[40] Charles's attitude made sense in terms of his commitment to the Catholic Empire (*corpus christianum*) of the Middle Ages: the permanent recognition of two religions would destroy this ideal. His brother Ferdinand's attitude was more realistic, however. He naturally sought to retrieve something for his dynasty now that it was clear that the Augsburg family compact of 1551 was a dead letter. Ferdinand did not regard the treaty with the Lutheran princes, which was concluded in September 1555 at Augsburg, as a 'peace of eternal duration' as did Augustus I, the elector of Saxony after 1553. To Ferdinand, the peace was simply another provisional arrangement; the religious issue would be settled by the Council of Trent. As always,

Ferdinand wanted military assistance against the Turks in Hungary. Nevertheless, news of the Peace of Augsburg led Charles V to begin the long process of abdication and the partitioning of his inheritance.

2.4.4 *Charles V: Abdication and Partition of the Inheritance*

Although Charles V had decided to extricate himself from German affairs, he was determined to secure what he could for his son. By the summer of 1553, he thought an English marriage alliance could advance Habsburg interests against the French, and, equally and perhaps more urgently, could strengthen Philip's hand in his rivalry with Ferdinand and his son Maximilian. Ferdinand could have argued that he and his sons were in a much better position to defend the Netherlands against the French, and had a superior claim to the inheritance: but in 1549 Charles had had his son accepted as his heir by all the Burgundian provinces. The Tudor marriage, which was made possible with the accession of the Catholic Mary in 1553, offered the chance of reconstituting the traditional Anglo-Burgundian and Anglo-Spanish alliances. Mary sought Philip's support for her plans for a Catholic restoration in England and naturally wanted an heir. The Emperor and his son saw England as a compensation for the loss of the Empire, and wanted to gain credit from a successful Catholic restoration. Even if the marriage were to fail dynastically, and Mary were to die quite soon, there were crucial short-term gains to be made. Indeed, Philip's growing authority was clear by 1553–4. He had been 'invested' three times with the duchy of Milan (1540, 1546 and 1549) and was its ruler in practice from 1552. This territory, together with the kingdom of Naples, was handed over by his father to give Philip the title of king at the time of his marriage in July 1554.

When he visited England, Philip distributed pensions liberally, tried to make himself popular by learning a few words of English, and exercised an active, though discreet, influence on domestic affairs through those councillors in whom he had confidence. Philip was determined to rule in England, and married Mary for no other purpose, though the Emperor had agreed to limitations on his son's power in the marriage contract of January 1554. In fact, Philip secretly disavowed the terms of the marriage contract, probably for two main reasons. He regarded the clause excluding England from participating in the war between the Emperor and Henri II as detrimental to Habsburg interests: it was precisely to involve England in the war that the marriage had been negotiated. Castilian sentiment was also very much against the succession arrangements, which amounted to disinheriting the Infante Don Carlos (born to Philip in 1545 from his first marriage to Maria of Portugal, who died that year) from the Netherlands and Franche-Comté in favour of any heir from the Habsburg–Tudor marriage. (This was, however, in line with the condition attached to Philip's recognition as Charles V's heir in the Low Countries in 1548-9, that the Low Countries would be separated from the Trastámara inheritance, and given to Philip's second child.) Moreover, an English rebellion could have destroyed the marriage project, or even cost the queen her throne (as was proved when Wyatt raised a force of 3,000 men in Kent in 1554 for the 'avoidance of strangers'). There was a justifiable fear that England would fall into 'the like servitude that Naples, Milan and the king's other dominions be in . . .':[41] the duke of Alba for one boasted that Philip II would become 'the most absolute' monarch the English had ever known.[42] The English alliance of 1554-8 was thus more tenuous and less decisive than Charles V had intended. In July 1555, before the Emperor began his process of abdication, it became clear that Mary Tudor's pregnancy was an illusion—the crucial flaw in the English alliance was that Philip was to have no rights in the kingdom after Mary's death unless she bore him a child, when the guardianship of the realm would devolve upon him. Nevertheless, in June 1557, Philip II's dire financial position forced him to appeal to his English subjects who accepted their obligations to him in his war with France. Thus one of the provisions of the marriage treaty was disregarded.

Despite such uncertainties in the succession, the Emperor had done the best he could for his son. Contemporaries were taken aback by Charles's abdication, for while the sixteenth century had witnessed depositions, no ruler had voluntarily renounced power: Pope Julius III thought it 'the strangest thing ever to happen'.[43] There is an evident symbolism in Charles's successive abdications which were made in the order that he had acquired his lands. Burgundy was renounced to Philip in October 1555 (Franche-Comté came later in April 1556, but only because of a technicality: its truce with France would have been shattered had the abdication taken place earlier). Then the Spanish kingdoms in the Old World and the New were handed over to Philip in January 1556 in three different documents, reflecting the confederative nature of the Spanish monarchy. Finally, Charles rid himself of the Holy Roman Empire in September 1556. His abdication had been postponed at the urgent request of Ferdinand himself, who was disturbed at the prospect of an early Imperial election, and it was not accepted by the electors (who duly elected Ferdinand) until February 1558. There remained the dilemma of the Imperial 'vicariate' in Italy, which had been promised to Philip in the Augsburg family compact of 1551. Charles confirmed this grant of the vicariate at the time of his Spanish abdications. When in July 1558 Philip sought confirmation from the new Emperor, his uncle Ferdinand I refused on the grounds that 'inconveniences, troubles and tumults within the Empire might follow' and that Philip would need to reside in Italy.[44]

In a sense this refusal reflected the traditional rivalry for influence in Italy between the Emperor and the king of Aragon. The Habsburgs were now two separate dynasties whose interests diverged. The split was evident in 1551, and it had hardened by the time of Charles V's death in retirement at the monastery of Yuste in Castile in September 1558. The separation of Habsburg interests was to have momentous consequences. Leaving aside the claims of the Valois 'most Christian King', there were now three contenders for the championship of one ideology. Revived Papal claims to temporal dominion were matched by two Habsburg monarchies; each was to contend for the secular leadership of the Counter-Reformation.

2.5   The Last Phase of the Valois–Habsburg Struggle

The collapse of Charles V's power inside Germany has already been considered. It is now necessary to disentangle the threads of external intervention which had done so much to undermine his triumph over the Lutheran princes. Here the unsettling factor in international relations had been the accession of Henri II of France in 1547. Contrary to Charles V's expectations, Henri proved to be a much more formidable opponent than Francis I had been in his later years. Moreover, the French king had an implacable hatred of the Emperor resulting from his experience as a hostage in Spain (1526–30) after Francis I had broken the terms of the Treaty of Madrid. Not only did Henri II negotiate a much more effective network of alliances than Francis I had been able to do; he was also encouraged to press home the attack on the scattered possessions of the Spanish Habsburgs because of the uncertainties and weaknesses revealed in the transfer of power to Philip II. A further round of fighting in Italy was made inevitable by the election of a violently anti-Habsburg Pope, Paul IV, who claimed that Charles V had 'prompted heresy in order to crush the Papacy and make himself master of Rome, that is to say, master of Italy and the world'.[45] Notwithstanding these new opportunities, had Henri II not possessed sufficient vigour and skill he would have been unable to exploit them, and the new consensus of historians is that he has been underrated as a ruler, at least in terms of his foreign policy.

2.5.1   *The Palace Revolution and the 'March on the Rhine', 1547–1552*

The palace intrigues which had marred the last years of the reign of Francis I and had led to the lack of a coherent foreign policy continued unabated after his death in March 1547. There was the expected change of faces at the French Court. Henri II relegated the old mistress, the duchesse d'Étampes, to her country residence and forced her to disgorge some of the jewels she had obtained from the king. Constable Montmorency was restored to all his offices and given the chief role in the government, where he witnessed the disgrace of his rivals (d'Annebault and Cardinal de Tournon). Though he was a mere baron, he was elevated to the status of duke and peer in July 1551. However, Montmorency did not have everything his own way. The new royal mistress, Diane de Poitiers (subsequently duchesse de Valentinois), was twenty-one years older than the young king—he was only 27 on his accession—and she was as determined as her predecessor to control royal patronage. She it was who brought the immensely ambitious Guises into government as a counter-weight to the Constable's influence: within a few months of the start of the reign, Charles de Lorraine had become a cardinal and François d'Aumale a duke. The factionalism that had been rife under Francis I became all-consuming in the reign of his son.

Francis had left him a troubled inheritance, and one of Henri's immediate problems was to settle the war with England which had been rumbling on since 1544. Boulogne was due to be bought back from the English in 1554, but Montmorency instilled in Henri II from his accession that, as a matter of honour, it had to be retaken by force. This was a striking change in tone from a man who had advocated entente during the previous regime. Events played into the French hands with the death of Henry VIII in January 1547. The English 'protector', Somerset, launched an all-out offensive on Scotland, in an attempt to unite the two kingdoms; and indeed he won a spectacular victory at Pinkie in September. But he failed to gain the close alliance of the Emperor to defend himself from a French counter-attack. In June 1548, 6,000 French troops were landed successfully at Leith. The Scots decided that France was a less dangerous ally than England, and that a French marriage for the infant Mary Queen of Scots was preferable to an alliance with Edward VI. Mary was taken to France, where she was later married to the dauphin Francis. The whole policy was a triumph for the Guises, whose sister, Mary of Lorraine, was appointed regent in Scotland. By 1553, Scotland had become a virtual French province, which was an unexpected bonus for the French monarchy. With the Scots queen safely in France, Henri II could declare war on England in August 1549 and besiege Boulogne. However, the shifting balance of power in England, with the fall of Somerset and the rise of the Duke of Northumberland, led to a reversal of its foreign policy. From the start, Northumberland's aim was peace with the French at any price, and this was achieved by March 1550, when the French victory in Scotland was tacitly accepted and Boulogne was redeemed for 400,000 *écus*, half the indemnity promised to Henry VIII four years earlier. The Emperor stood on the sidelines in the Anglo-French struggle, because he was concerned for the safety of Mary Tudor under the rule of her

Protestant half-brother, Edward VI, and alarmed at the extreme lurch which England had taken towards Protestantism under Northumberland. Furthermore, Charles had problems of his own to settle in Germany.

The new peace with England allowed Henri II to turn his undivided attention to a much more formidable opponent. The Emperor Charles V had been pursuing a repressive campaign against the Lutheran princes, confident of French neutrality as long as the Anglo-French conflict continued. But opposition was gathering in the form of a new Protestant league in Germany, the League of Torgau, which opposed the Interim of Augsburg and resisted Charles's attempt to establish a stronger Imperial authority. At Lochau in October 1551, the Lutheran princes agreed to bring the king of France into the alliance since in return he offered protection for German 'freedom', a subsidy to the rebels and a diversionary war against the Emperor. Though the League included only one elector (Maurice of Saxony), it declared that in future it would have no Emperor who was not a good friend of France; were Henri II disposed to accept the title 'we would be more pleased with him than any other man'.[46] In return for French support, the League backed French claims to Flanders, Artois and Franche-Comté. The Valois king was to attack the three French-speaking free cities (Metz, Toul and Verdun) and could retain them after the peace provided 'jurisdiction [was] reserved to the Holy Empire'. Henri II, acting with a decisiveness his father had lacked on this issue, ratified the agreement in January 1552. War broke out two months later; in April French troops occupied Toul and Metz, and they were in occupation of Verdun by June. Henri II declared himself 'protector' of duke Charles III of Lorraine, who was removed to the Valois court, and French rule was established in his duchy. Henri II's 'march on the Rhine' was carefully coordinated with the rebellion of the Lutheran princes and the elector Maurice's attack on the Imperial position in the Tyrol. Consequently, the Emperor was in no position to counter-attack the Valois king until the end of the year, when he failed to capture Metz after a three-month siege. The Emperor's severe financial difficulties forced him to abandon the siege on New Year's Day 1553. Thereafter, the war became a stalemate, though this was not recognized until the Truce of Vaucelles, negotiated between an Emperor who wished to abdicate and a somewhat war-weary French king in February 1556. The French gains were nevertheless to prove irreversible: the defeat of Charles V in Germany, and the acquisition of Metz, Toul and Verdun, constitute Henri II's main political achievements.

2.5.2 *The Last War and the Peace of Cateau-Cambrésis*

Charles V had already abdicated from his Burgundian and Spanish lands in favour of his son, Philip II, before the Truce of Vaucelles. The Imperial side hoped that it would give Philip a crucial breathing-space to take over the reins of government. But any chance of peace was shattered by a new factor, the temporal ambitions of Pope Paul IV. Though 79 at the time of his accession in May 1555, Paul IV was a man of astonishing energy. He could remember the time when Italy was free from 'those heretics, schismatics, cursed of God, a race of Jews and Moors, the dregs of the world'—free, that is, from the Spaniards.[47] Both the French and the Spaniards were 'barbarians' in his eyes; but, by appealing to their sense of inherited territorial rights, the Pope could use the French to eject the Spaniards from his Neapolitan homeland. Paul IV's pontificate also brought a return to Papal nepotism and dynastic ambitions: within a fortnight of his own promotion, he had elevated his nephew Carlo Caraffa to the cardinalate. The cardinal was dispatched to France in June 1556, ostensibly to convert the truce into a firm peace; in fact he had secret instructions to shatter the truce and reconstitute a firm Valois–Papal alliance. The French king had used the truce to gain new loans from his Italian and German bankers, and buoyed up with new resources, and with this new incentive, he mounted another Italian campaign. This was the last French adventure in Italy until the end of the century. François, duke of Guise, crossed the Alps with 13,200 French troops in December 1556, but instead of attacking Milan, as might have been expected, he marched to Rome. Thence, after much time-wasting, he invaded Naples at Paul IV's request in early April 1557. The campaign went badly, and in August Guise withdrew to the northern front on the king's orders. Paul IV was now defenceless, and he had no alternative but to make peace with Philip II in September. With Pius IV's elevation to the Papacy in 1559, Papal–Imperial relations took a turn for the better; from then until 1595 there was a *modus vivendi* with Philip II, even if there were intermittent conflicts and differences of approach on some issues. The Papacy had finally come to terms with what had now become Spanish predominance in Italy.

The serious fighting between France and Spain was on the northern front, but before it could begin, Philip had to raise money to avert financial catastrophe. On New Year's Day 1557, he had defaulted on his debts, most of which were inherited from his father's excessive borrowing during the war of 1552–6. In June, the king offered to convert high-interest short-term loans into low-interest long-term annuities (*asientos* into *juros*). This rescheduling of debts, and particularly the subsequent agreements with individual financiers, gave Philip one last chance for a military victory, and he took it: he ordered an invasion of France from the north under the command of the exiled duke Emmanuel-Philibert of Savoy. The gamble paid off, for the result, in August 1557, was the greatest French military catastrophe since Pavia. At St-Quentin, the two French commanders, Marshal St-André and Montmorency (and the Constable's two nephews, Coligny and d'Andelot), were captured. French losses were so enormous that an entirely new army had to be formed, with Guise's contingent from Italy as its nucleus. Yet with this untried remnant, Guise managed to take Calais from the English in January 1558 after a siege of only eight days, thus somewhat redressing the military balance. Philip was accused of failing to assist his English subjects, and when in February he tried to persuade a reluctant English government to recapture Calais, he met with no success. Fortunately for the Habsburg cause, the French invasion of the Spanish Netherlands failed disastrously at Gravelines the following July, which may have helped Philip to decide that Calais was, after all, dispensable. However, the recovery of Calais, after a period of English occupation which had lasted since 1360, combined with the earlier acquisitions of Metz, Toul and Verdun, suggest that the reign of Henri II, for all its relatively short duration and its legacy of political collapse at home, should not be dismissed too readily as being a failure. Rather it was a transitional period which, had the reign lasted longer, carried with it the potentiality for a stronger and more aggressive monarchy in France.

By 1558, there was a noticeable change in French policy. Henri II was beginning to have grave doubts about the wisdom of continuing the war, even assuming he had the resources to do so. The spread of Calvinism in France convinced him of the need to 'settle [his] foreign affairs' in order to exterminate heresy (he had abandoned the alliance of the German Lutheran princes for this reason in May 1558). Once they had ransomed themselves, Montmorency and St-André used their influence on the king to work towards peace with Spain. Formal discussions began in October 1558, and two peace treaties were signed in April 1559 at Cateau-Cambrésis. The first treaty marked an acknowledgement that the English had lost Calais, although the French undertook either to return it (which was unlikely) or to pay compensation after eight years. The second treaty was much more important. Its territorial arrangements were overwhelmingly favourable to Spain. Metz, Toul and Verdun were transferred to France; but the French could not have full sovereignty over these towns without the Emperor's consent, and he did not give this until 1648. The French withdrew all their claims to Milan and Naples and the French armies which had occupied Savoy and Piedmont since 1536 were withdrawn. Emmanuel-Philibert I ('Iron Head'), who had served Philip II loyally as governor-general in the Netherlands, deservedly regained his duchy of Savoy as a result of his victory at St-Quentin. He never forgot his dependence on Spain, despite Henri II's insistence that he marry his sister, Marguerite of Valois. The French king retained the marquisate of Saluzzo and five fortresses in Piedmont; but by 1574 all the fortresses had been returned to Savoy, and a later duke of Savoy exploited French internal weakness during the wars of religion to occupy the defenceless marquisate in 1588. Other territorial adjustments included the return of Corsica, which had been under French occupation since 1553, to the republic of Genoa: the island later rebelled unsuccessfully against this change of rule. Spanish occupation of Upper Navarre in 1512 was confirmed, as was the acquisition of Siena in 1557 by Cosimo de' Medici.

To some extent, the balance in the territorial arrangements was supposed to be rectified by two marriage settlements favouring France. The first, the marriage of Henri II's sister to the restored duke of Savoy, failed to achieve its purpose, since she transferred her loyalty to her new husband. The second, Philip II's marriage to Elizabeth of Valois, was more significant for French interests. If it held out few prospects of a Valois succession to the Spanish territories, it at least prevented the possibility of an Anglo-Spanish alliance formed by Philip marrying Elizabeth I of England. (She had in fact refused to marry him when he offered to renew this alliance on her accession in 1558.) This, together, with real French control in Scotland in 1559, appeared to offset Charles V's achievement five years earlier in securing Philip's marriage to Mary Tudor: the new marriage alliance, unlike the first one, could not serve to defend Burgundy against a hostile France. However, Elizabeth's coup in Scotland in 1559–60 dramatically altered the balance, because it resulted in the withdrawal of French troops and Mary Stuart's renunciation of her claims to the English throne. England was then able to play a more independent role in international affairs—assisted by a neutral Philip II until 1570—as signified by the treaty of 1562 with the rebellious French Huguenots, by which the English hoped primarily to regain Calais.

Whatever judgement one forms on the treaties of Cateau-Cambrésis— and opinion in France generally regarded them as a defeat—all calculations were thrown to the winds by the totally unexpected death of Henri II in a jousting accident during the double wedding festivities of July 1559 which followed the peace. The French crown went bankrupt. The Lyon 'great contract' (*grand parti*) had been a personal agreement between the king and his bankers, and the new government had little choice but to default on its obligations. Worse still, the king left four under-age sons; none of them was able to produce a legitimate male heir. Philip II was able to meddle in French domestic affairs as early as March 1561, and he could manipulate the court factions because there was no king of age, or only a feeble king, to stand up to him. Serious though the factions had become in the last years of Henri II, dramatic and irreversible though the spread of Calvinism had been, the French king had previously enjoyed unrivalled power in his kingdom. A weak and divided France during the thirty-six years of official peace between France and Spain after the Treaty of Cateau-Cambrésis was signed in 1559, made possible Spanish preponderance in the affairs of western Europe in the later sixteenth century.

The long period of warfare in Italy between 1494 and 1559 has not always received the attention which it merits: the Venetian ambassador at Philip II's court, Soriano, confirmed that as a result of the Peace of Cateau-Cambrésis, there were only three significant powers—France, Spain and the Ottoman Turks. Deprived of the revenues of Spain and the Netherlands, the Holy Roman Empire seemed to have been eclipsed. The preoccupation of the western European monarchs after 1494 with their own dynastic rivalries and with the struggle for the spoils of Italy had allowed the Ottoman Turks to consolidate a powerful state chiefly by conquest. They not only actively sought western allies but encouraged dissident groups such as the Moriscos in Valencia and Aragon who might work to their advantage. The Ottoman state had exploited the opportunities arising from the complex events which had taken place in the west during the Italian wars (see chapter 5.4.2). Charles V might claim in his dotage that he had spent 'a lifetime fighting heretics';[48] and there is no doubt that earlier in his rule he had wanted to launch a crusade against Islam—a 'general peace' to permit an expedition against the Turks was specified in Charles V's dictated Peace of Madrid, which was imposed on Francis I in 1526. The reality, however, was that Charles V had spent his lifetime opposing the ambitions of France. Peace in the west had been the *sine qua non* for decisive action against the Turks, but the suggestion of the cardinals of the church in 1517, that the princes of Christendom form a 'brotherhood of the holy crusade', had never materialized, despite much propaganda for crusading endeavour and even some discussion of possible action in the years 1517–20. The anti-Turkish crusades amounted merely to Papal grants of crusade indulgences, taxes and privileges to Catholic states such as Austria, Castile, Venice and Poland, and the organization of naval leagues of Christian powers. The *respublica christiana* of the Middle Ages had been dealt a death blow by the Valois–Habsburg rivalry and the emergence of new Protestant states in western Europe. Whereas in 1559 Philip II succeeded in bringing a long war with France to an end, he felt unable—because of the risk of damage to his reputation should he sue for peace—to reach an agreement with the Ottoman Turks in the same year. This was a grave mistake, which put him on the defensive in the Mediterranean in the 1560s, and weakened his ability to protect his other territories. Yet the war against the Turks should not be viewed as a crusade: secular considerations were to prevail in the age of Philip II as they had done in the previous sixty years.

3

EUROPE IN THE AGE OF THE WARS OF RELIGION, 1559–1618

THE war of 1562–3 in France was probably the first to be given openly the description of a 'war of religion', though (as has already been seen) the war of 1546–7 in Germany was a war of religion in fact, if not in name. Thereafter, there were to be many European wars which might be described by this label. Yet, it may be doubted whether there has ever been an age in which religious issues alone, without additional political, social or economic forces, caused wars or even crusades. Europe in the second half of the sixteenth century exemplifies this. Historians have professed to see the beginnings of radical religious parties in France and the Low Countries during this period, and 'the ideological upsurge of the international Protestant community' in the 1570s or thereabouts.[1] The age generated its own powerful legends. Protestants imagined a great Catholic conspiracy, beginning with the meetings of the Council of Trent and extending to the 'interview' at Bayonne in 1565 between the French queen mother, Catherine de Medici, and the duke of Alba, representing Philip II of Spain. There, it was claimed, a plot had been formed to massacre the Protestants which came to its barbarous fruition in the St Bartholomew's Day massacres in France in 1572. In fact, there was no Catholic conspiracy and the Bayonne meeting decided nothing of importance. The massacres of 1572 were chiefly a product of the volatile French domestic situation, not part of an international intrigue. Protestant states found it difficult to sink their political, economic and religious rivalries in a common ideological cause. There was much propaganda, but little practical co-operation: the separate political and religious rebellions of the later sixteenth century never became a single, generalized war of religion.

3.1 The Reign of Philip II

After 1559, Spanish policy was basically conservative, seeking to defend the settlement of Cateau-Cambrésis. The Venetian ambassador commented in the year of the treaty that Philip's aim was 'not to wage war so that he can add to his kingdoms, but to wage peace so that he can keep the lands he has'.[2] This remark stands out in stark contrast with the later 'black legend' which attributed to Philip II the desire to undermine his subjects' liberties, impose versions of the Spanish Inquisition throughout his lands, and proceed with a general offensive against Protestant states. In his earlier years, Philip II was reasonably flexible in his attitudes, and timid in the adoption of policies. He had no preconceived plan to alter the traditional order of society and government in his lands, though he had a determination to combat heresy. The king boasted to Pius V in 1566 that 'rather than suffer the least damage to religion and the service of God' he would 'lose all [his] states and a hundred lives' if he had them, for he neither proposed nor desired to be 'the ruler of heretics'.[3] But he had no intention of embarking on a general crusade against Protestantism in northern Europe. Instead, he hoped to concentrate his resources against Islam in the Mediterranean. He had inherited his father's narrow orthodoxy and his former tutor was Cardinal Silíceo, who as archbishop of Toledo had pressed the king to ratify the laws of purity of blood (*limpieza de sangre*). These laws made pure Christian ancestry an essential condition for all appointments to offices, initially in the church, but later in the state. They were designed to exclude those of Moorish or Jewish blood from holding office. The same policy of intolerance governed the treatment of heretics in the Iberian peninsula. Philip presided in person at five ceremonial burnings of heretics (*autos de fé*), the first immediately on his return to Spain from the Low Countries in 1559.

Though equally fervent in his religion, Philip II ruled his lands in a way quite different from that of the father he had so much admired. Charles V had been a peripatetic emperor. Philip II was a sedentary king. After 1561, when he changed his capital from Valladolid to Madrid, he never set foot outside the Iberian peninsula and rarely left Castile. He later rationalized his reluctance to govern in the manner of his father: 'travelling about one's kingdom is neither useful nor decent', he wrote to his son.[4] If Philip died from fatigue, it originated from reading state papers, not from travel. In the earlier part of his rule, it was not inevitable that he would become 'hispanocentric' in outlook; he was certainly intending to return to the Netherlands as late as 1567. Yet, circumstances and political miscalculation combined to prevent his return to the Low Countries, an omission which later assumed grave political importance. In the sixteenth century, a king's subjects expected to see him and assumed that he would speak their language. Had Philip heeded Charles V's advice to learn languages, perhaps some of his difficulties with his subjects might have been avoided. But Philip was fluent only in Castilian, and when he tried to deliver his father's abdication speech in French at Brussels in October 1555, he stuttered to a standstill.

Philip was not inexperienced. He had been regent in Spain as early as

1543, and in the 1550s he had shown a ruthless determination to build up his own power, and to oppose Charles V's wishes if necessary. But he tended to procrastinate. One cause of indecision was a prolonged crisis over the succession. Philip married four times and had eight children who survived birth, of whom four reached maturity. His heir until 1568 was Don Carlos, the son of his first marriage, but in that year Philip had him arrested and the young prince died in captivity. Philip informed Pius V that 'it ha[d] been God's will that the prince should have such great and numerous defects, partly mental, partly due to his physical condition' that made him 'utterly lacking . . . in the qualifications necessary for ruling'.[5] In effect, Philip barred Don Carlos from the succession for insanity. However, this left a terrible void in the dynasty, and in the same year his third wife died. His last marriage, contracted in November 1570, was to Anne of Austria, the daughter of his cousin, the Emperor Maximilian II. She bore him four sons and one daughter, and of these children the future Philip III grew to maturity as the king's heir. Not until the 1590s, however, could Philip II consider the succession assured. The semi-permanent threat which hung over it and the psychological impact of successive personal tragedies should not be underestimated.

3.1.1 *Philip's System of Government*

'A prince who rules many and diverse realms must have councillors from all of them.'[6] This was the view of Furió Ceriol in his treatise, *The Council and Councillors of the Prince*, published in 1559. Furió wanted Philip to surround himself with experts, who were knowledgeable in languages and history, and to improve and extend the conciliar system. Philip actually had a more restricted range of advisers than his father, who had surrounded himself with a cosmopolitan entourage whose Erasmian attitudes were not shared by the Emperor himself. Philip certainly extended the conciliar system. His Council of Italy, which existed in embryonic form after 1554, had a clear organization and an independent status within five years. It was established to sever the Aragonese control of Naples and Sicily and to help the king distribute offices in the three Italian lands (the other being the duchy of Milan). He also established councils for Portugal in 1582 and Flanders in 1588. But the king did not implement Furió's central proposal, that the outlying regions of his empire should be clearly represented in the personnel of the councils. Instead, Castilians came to dominate the government. Most of the members of the councils resident in Castile were Castilians; so too were most of the viceroys and governors of the various lands; in addition, about one-third of the appointments to the viceroys' councils in Italy were Castilian. The Castilian attitude was clearly imperialistic: 'these Italians', it was said, 'though they are not

Indians, have to be treated as such, so that they understand that we are in charge of them and not they in charge of us.'

There was much more flexibility within the Spanish Habsburg system of government than has usually been allowed. The formal divisions between the numerous councils could be blurred; the king could ask for the advice of ministers although the question under discussion was not part of their normal business. The initiative in formulating and implementing policy lay with the king, who in any case chose his councillors. However, there were three basic weaknesses in the practical workings of Philip's system of government. The first was the inevitable delay posed by the size of the inheritance and the number of governing institutions which received Philip's personal scrutiny. In 1587, towards the height of the Armada scare, the English comforted themselves with the 'nature of the Spaniard', which they thought to be 'slow in all his actions'. In support of this view, they quoted the aphorism of Don Pedro de Toledo, viceroy of Naples under Charles V. He is alleged to have said that 'if death had to come from Spain, he would live a long time'.[8] The second problem was how to exercise control over the viceroys and governors in the various lands, men who were subject to local political pressures and their own ambitions. The barons of Sicily made this island a graveyard for the reputations and careers of several of its viceroys. Unsuccessful viceroys were recalled from both the Netherlands and Naples. In Milan, the problems faced by the governors were less acute (since they exercised the former ducal powers— under the Sforza dukes there was no parliament and the duke had accepted no limitations on his authority), and none were recalled by Philip II.

The third structural weakness in Philip's system of government out-weighed the other two in importance. The royal court and councils were riddled with faction; the development of factions evolved with the impact of personal quarrels and under pressure of events. It was impossible to remain neutral, at least until 1579, since the system dictated that without allegiance there would be no career advancement. A risk of governmental paralysis could arise when the strength of the factions varied between Castile and the outlying regions. Between 1560 and 1564, for example, Granvelle dominated the government of the Netherlands, but his political patron in Castile was the duke of Alba who was virtually in disgrace. The councils in Castile were at this time controlled by Granvelle's enemies, the faction led by 'king Gómez', Ruy Gómez de Silva, prince of Eboli, Philip II's favourite after Alba's fall from grace and the most important influence on policy until 1565. Shifts in the balance between the factions in Castile had a quite disproportionate impact on the development of policy elsewhere, especially in the Netherlands. There, the magnates extracted concessions from the regent and her advisers in 1564, only to find that they were disavowed by the king and his Castilian advisers the following year. Some historians have argued that the factions were so powerful that they prevented the development of an overall Spanish Habsburg policy. Instead, individual ministers and factions subscribed to their own, often mutually irreconcilable, policy objectives.

Conditions were worst in the early years of Philip's reign, when the rivalries between the Eboli and Alba factions were at their height. The prince of Eboli died in 1573, although this did not bring rivalries to an end because the duke of Alba outlived him by nine years. Officially, the rivalry between these two factions, which plagued the first thirteen years of Philip's reign, was ended with the abrupt arrest in July 1579 of Eboli's widow and Antonio Pérez, the king's secretary, who were accused of treasonable activities. In practical terms, it is very doubtful if Philip eliminated faction from his government entirely, but after this date, his administration took on a more settled character. Granvelle was brought in to head the government, but lest he should become too powerful, his appointment was balanced by that of Juan de Zúñiga in 1583; both men died in 1586. Juan de Idiáquez was the heir to Granvelle's thinking, and dealt with foreign affairs after his death. His influence was countered by Christóbal de Moura, who specialized in financial questions, and by Diego de Chinchón, who concentrated on the affairs of Aragon and Italy. From 1585 until 1593 they formed a committee called the Committee of the Night (*Junta de Noche*) to sift through incoming reports before supper, so that the king could see their recommendations the same night. The link between the various regimes was Mateo Vázquez de Leca, who held the office of king's secretary from 1573 until his death in 1592: he specialized in Castilian affairs, but he was also secretary to the Inquisition and the king's personal chaplain, and he often drafted Philip's answers to the Committee of the Night. After Vázquez's death, the king was forced to alter his administrative arrangements yet again, establishing a Governing Committee (*Junta Grande*) with new personnel, including the archduke Albert of Austria, and Philip, the heir to the throne and future Philip III. These changes of advisers clearly had significant effects on policy; but their impact was less after 1579, once Philip had made a determined stand against the factions.

3.1.2 *Finance and Spanish Habsburg Priorities*

Whether or not it can be argued that Philip II's method of defending his dispersed inheritance amounted to a clear-cut system, rather than a response to events, he certainly kept more or less permanently mobilized armies of colossal size for the times. Between 60,000 and 80,000 men were under arms in the Low Countries in the 1570s, some 125,000 men in all of his empire in 1598. Philip II was the richest king in western Europe, and his income grew steadily from his accession until 1580 when it remained level in real terms, as a consequence of the rapid inflation of the last decades of the sixteenth century. The American silver that flooded into Seville in the 1580s and 1590s made up for this shortfall. The crown received only 12.5 million ducats from this source in the first twenty years of Philip's reign. It received 52 million in the last twenty-five years. By 1596 it was possible to budget in the expectation of receiving on average 3 million ducats annually in American silver, nearly four times as much as in 1577. But a note of caution must be struck about such impressive figures. The shipments did not arrive at convenient, predictable intervals. Between 1580 and 1598 the annual shipment exceeded 10 million ducats in four years (1583, 1585, 1595 and 1596); in other years, however, the annual shipment might fall well below the average for the decade. In 1582, 1586 and 1590 there were shipments of less than 3 million ducats; in 1594 and 1597 there were no shipments at all. Financial planning was thus extremely difficult, even assuming that the king attempted to match expenditure to income, which of course he did not. Philip was plagued by financial problems and rescheduled his debts (or went 'bankrupt') three times, in 1557, 1575 and 1596. He inherited a total debt of nearly 30 million ducats; by 1575 it had reached 60 million; by 1598 it was in the region of 100 million. The bankruptcy of 1575 led directly to a mutiny of the unpaid foreign troops in the army of Flanders the following year; this in turn encouraged the seventeen provinces of the Netherlands to attempt co-operation to obtain the expulsion of Philip's mutinous troops.

Philip's financial difficulties graphically illustrate the point that he did not possess sufficient resources to fight a number of enemies, foreign and domestic, at the same time. In this respect, at least, his policy was limited to one of expediency. But some historians have argued that even if the king lacked an overall political plan he must at least have had a set of priorities which determined the allocation of his inadequate resources at any given moment. These priorities have been seen as the fear of a resurgent France, particularly with the threatened Protestant Bourbon succession after 1584; the defence of Spain and the Italian possessions against the maritime threat posed by the Ottoman Turks; and finally, the suppression of heresy, and later rebellion, in the Low Countries. But how could the relative importance of Mediterranean security to Spain be balanced against the war in the Low Countries in any real sense? Philip's advisers might be divided in their opinions, but to the king each of these concerns was important. It is by no means clear that policies could have been ordered according to the resources available for technical reasons; it is virtually certain that the king did not determine them in this way. Policies were formulated first, resources allocated afterwards. A misguided logic encouraged Philip II to increase his political commitments in Europe after 1580; the application of this policy was facilitated by the growth in imports of American silver. The king determined this policy, and the council of finance often had no idea where its money was going; similarly, the council of war had no idea when or if money was due to arrive. Presiding over this chaotic structure was the king who admitted on different occasions his 'ignorance as to financial affairs' and that he had never 'been able to get this business of loans and interests into [his] head'.[9]

3.1.3 The War in the Mediterranean

The most immediate danger faced by the king in the 1560s came from the Ottoman Turks. In the western Mediterranean, it was thought that they might co-ordinate a naval offensive with a Morisco rising within Spain itself. In the first two decades of the sixteenth century, Spain had extended its sphere of influence to a number of north African ports: Peñón de Velez (1507), Oran (1509), Algiers, Tripoli and Bougie (all in 1510) were among the lesser-known conquests of Ferdinand of Aragon in what was essentially a less important theatre of war than Italy. Charles V had not succeeded in retaining control of all of these outposts: one of his most dedicated opponents had been Hayreddin Barbarossa, the governor of Algeria for the Ottoman Turks in the years 1518–34 and their admiral in the western Mediterranean from 1534 until his death in 1546. Charles V had tried to neutralize the threat from Barbarossa's corsair state in Algeria by restoring the Hafsid (Sa'di) dynasty to rule over Tunis after his victory there in 1535. Although they continued to hold Tunis until they were evicted by the Ottomans in 1569, the Hafsids were squeezed out by the Ottoman–corsair advance: in 1551 Tripoli was captured, and Bougie fell in 1555. At this point, Oran remained the only Spanish outpost in north Africa, and the Spanish coastline itself was threatened by the Ottoman advance. The regency government in Spain under Philip's sister Juana ordered a campaign for 'the recovery of Bougie and the conquest of Algiers' despite the opposition of the king, who was absent in the Low Countries.[10] He did not see the urgency or the seriousness of the Ottoman–corsair threat, since he was far removed from the Mediterranean theatre of war and wholly preoccupied with the struggle against France. In the event, the regency government's spectacular act of disobedience met with disaster in August 1558.

Philip might have been able to secure a truce with the Ottomans in 1559, but he spurned this opportunity as likely to lead to 'great loss of our authority' and foolishly attacked Djerba the following year. This resulted in a catastrophic loss of 27 Spanish galleys and 10,000 men. Thereafter, the king had to deploy most of his resources to the continuation of the

Mediterranean war, and to the expensive and slow process of building up a galley fleet. Between 1562 and 1577, the Spanish fleet increased from 55 galleys to 102. It was of great importance that during the first part of this galley construction programme the Ottomans did not assume the offensive; and when they did so in 1570, they did not attack Philip's territories, but captured Cyprus, previously held by Venice. Nor did the Turkish fleet directly assist the Morisco community in Spain, although the Moriscos were regarded as an Ottoman 'fifth column' by the Spanish government. In his last instructions to his son in 1556, Charles V had advised the expulsion of the Moriscos from Spain. Philip did not proceed as far as his father had wished, but the repressive royal policy enforced by Cardinal Espinosa resulted in a serious, though ultimately unsuccessful, revolt of the Moriscos of Granada in 1568–70 (see chapter 7.3.1). Although some 4,000 Turkish or Barbary troops served with the rebel forces of 25,000 men, the rebels were not acting on the orders of the Ottoman government.

Under the auspices of a crusading Pope, Pius V, a Holy League between Spain, the Papacy and Venice was signed in May 1571 to counter the Islamic threat in the Mediterranean. Venice had wished to avoid a league comparable to that signed with Charles V in 1538, which had been viewed subsequently as a betrayal of Venetian interests. Philip had also been deeply suspicious, but the financing of the war was arranged to Spain's satisfaction and in October 1571 Don John of Austria commanded the forces of the joint Christian fleet in the crushing (but ultimately indecisive) victory at Lepanto. The allies lost 12 galleys, the Ottomans 117. The Turks began immediate naval reconstruction, and so this victory led to no permanent adjustment in the balance of forces in the Mediterranean. The death of Pius V in May 1572 robbed the alliance of any political victory and in March 1573 Venice withdrew from the League, exhausted financially and without having recovered Cyprus. When the Turks resumed the offensive in 1574 and captured Tunis, Philip II's impending bankruptcy prevented a counter-attack. Ottoman naval supremacy in the eastern Mediterranean had not been destroyed by Lepanto but, fortunately for Philip, the Turks lacked the resources to wage war in Persia and in the western Mediterranean simultaneously. From 1578, when they invaded Persia, an informal suspension of arms was agreed and this was converted into a permanent truce two years later. It endured because the Ottomans were distracted by long wars, first against Persia and then against the Austrian Habsburgs (see chapter 5.4.3), while to the west, their control over their Tunisian and Algerian fiefs began to slip: as direct Ottoman administration in north Africa weakened, so the prospects of a renewed Turkish offensive in the western Mediterranean faded. Accordingly, Philip II secured the defence of the Iberian coastline almost by default. His successors in the seventeenth century in turn benefited from the internal disorders of the Ottoman state: the truce endured because neither party was strong enough to be certain of making gains by breaking it. As the two great powers allowed their naval preparedness to be run down, so independent corsairs filled the vacuum, and terrorized the Mediterranean during what became a permanent Spanish–Ottoman disengagement.

3.1.4 *The Acquisition of Portugal*

The disengagement in the Mediterranean occurred at a crucial moment, for it enabled Philip to intervene in the Portuguese succession crisis. In August 1578, king Sebastian of Portugal, his nephew, was killed at the battle of Alcazar-el-Kebir, while leading a suicidal campaign against the Sultan of Morocco. Sebastian left no direct heir. He was succeeded by his uncle, Cardinal Henry; but the new king, who was 63 at his accession, was gravely ill, and since he was bound by the vows of celibacy he could not secure his dynasty by providing a son even at this late stage. A native Portuguese family, the house of Braganza, had several claimants to the throne on the extinction of this dynasty—while another claimant, the illegitimate Dom Antonio, the prior of Crato, worked in exile from 1581 until his death in 1595 to oppose the Spanish succession. Crucially, however, Cardinal Henry favoured the Jesuits, who threw in their lot with Philip II and supported his claim. When Cardinal Henry died in February 1580, the issue was still not settled, and a war of succession inevitably resulted. The prior of Crato was proclaimed king at Lisbon in June 1580, but in the same month a Spanish army under the duke of Alba invaded Portugal. Within four months all resistance was crushed and what was later called the 'sixty years of captivity' began. At the *Cortes* of Thomar in April 1581, King Philip I of Portugal (as he styled himself) received the homage of the country's representative institution and swore to uphold the liberties of the kingdom. He promised never to summon the *Cortes* outside Portugal and to establish a council to advise him on Portuguese affairs. The viceroy would be a native Portuguese or a member of the ruling dynasty.

For a period of over two years (1581–3) Philip II remained at Lisbon, while Granvelle was left to run the administration in Madrid. After March 1583, however, the king returned to Castile, much to the chagrin of the Portuguese. Some historians have argued that by this action Philip lost an historic opportunity to rule the Hispanic world from the shores of the Atlantic. Among his advisers, Granvelle certainly suggested Lisbon as Philip's capital—though the idea came in 1586, not 1581, and by then Granvelle's influence was on the decline. The acquisition of Portugal was an enormous accretion of power to Philip. He gained a million new subjects, a long Atlantic seaboard, and he nearly doubled the size of his ocean-going fleet. The balance within Philip's territories had changed, and what was needed was a realistic assessment of the different character of the Habsburg monarchy after 1580. No such reappraisal took place. Philip viewed his inheritance chiefly in dynastic terms. He accepted the Portuguese crown as part of his confederation of territories, the union being comparable in his mind to that of 1479 between Castile and Aragon. The Aragonese tradition prevented radical departures: Lisbon did not become the new capital because it would have represented a break with this tradition. Equally important, it was too far removed from the centres of potential unrest in Philip's kingdoms, particularly Aragon and Valencia with their Morisco populations and their strong regional autonomy.

3.1.5   *The Failure of the Spanish Armada*

The sudden extension of Philip's power naturally provoked alarm, especially in England. Plans for an 'enterprise of England' had been mooted from the time of Elizabeth I's excommunication in 1570, but without any sense of urgency. The early expeditions of Drake and other privateers in the Spanish Indies had been an irritation, but not a direct act of war, and Spanish losses were not excessive. The total cost of defence in the Caribbean between 1535 and 1585 was about 5 million ducats, a real bargain: the crown received 38 million ducats in silver shipments from the New World in the same period. However, the Treaty of Nonsuch of August 1585, by which Elizabeth pledged her support to the rebellion in the Low Countries, completely altered the picture (see chapter 3.2.5). The activities of Drake and his fellow adventurers after September 1585 were on a much larger scale, and the Caribbean defences had to be reorganized to meet the challenge—successfully, in the short term, since the finances were available to Philip; more silver, not less, arrived in Spain in the 1590s. The king's advisers perceived that victory in the Low Countries would not be achieved without eliminating English support for the rebellion.

The objective of an Armada, plans for which were drawn up in the course of 1586, was 'no less the security of the Indies than the recovery of the Netherlands',[11] reflecting the twin concerns of Spanish foreign policy at this time. After the execution of Mary Queen of Scots in February 1587, Philip also wanted to press his own distant claim to the English throne; though in return for financial assistance from the Papacy he was prepared to forgo his rights in favour of his daughter, the Infanta Isabella Clara Eugenia. It is doubtful if the king believed that a successful invasion by an Armada followed by the establishment of a pro-Spanish regime, preferably with Isabella as queen, would ever come to pass. The English Catholics had not mounted an effective rising in the first thirty years of

Elizabeth's reign and proved their loyalty when, in 1588, they rallied to the Tudor dynasty. Even if the Spanish invasion was successful, it was unlikely that the English Catholics would take up arms against the queen. A much more probable outcome for Philip was that territorial gains could be made in England, which had no coherent strategy to resist an invasion had it materialized and inadequate defences to resist the portable heavy cannon carried by the Armada. These acquisitions could then have been used as a bargaining counter to force a change of policy on the existing English regime. There were various possibilities open for negotiation: toleration of Catholicism in England; an end to the English raids on the West Indies; abrogation of the Treaty of Nonsuch (see chapter 3.2.5) and the transfer of the port of Flushing to Habsburg control; perhaps payment of a war indemnity. Any military gains of a successful Armada might thus have been negotiated away by Philip, but it seems probable that the risks and the costs of the venture outweighed any such political advantages. It might have made more sense to concentrate on an invasion of Ireland, where the English officials confidently expected a general insurrection to coincide with the arrival of the Armada in the Channel.

First, there had to be a naval victory. Philip II did not underestimate English seapower and thought overwhelming Spanish force would be necessary to secure a victory. The Armada was the largest fleet that had ever put to sea in the English Channel—10 squadrons of 130 ships in all, of which only about 23 were so-called 'front-line' galleons or galleasses; but it was still considerably outnumbered by the English fleet of 197 ships, which were mostly much smaller—there were only about 20 'front-line' English warships. It was essential, moreover, that the Armada force should succeed in picking up 18,000 men in the Low Countries, part of the powerful land army commanded by the duke of Parma (see chapter 3.2.4) before attempting an invasion: this, as Parma had warned Philip II, proved to be the Armada's undoing. From the outset, the Armada plans were bedevilled with problems. The king had hoped for an Armada of 150 ships, totalling 77,250 tons, and an invasion force from the Low Countries of 55,000 men: it proved impossible to assemble either force on such a scale. Admiral Santa Cruz's original estimate of the cost, 3.8 million ducats, proved to be hopelessly optimistic, the real cost being in the order of 10 million ducats. Then, in February 1588, at a crucial stage in the preparations, Santa Cruz died. His replacement, the duke of Medina Sidonia, was no seaman, though he could be relied on to take expert advice from naval and military experts. He had administrative capacity, both in organizing the departure of the Armada and commanding the convoy once it was at sea. The preparations were delayed by Drake's attack on Cadiz in April 1587, but at the end of May 1588 the 'Invincible' Armada (so called because of its size, not its proven ability) set sail from

Lisbon. By the end of July, as it sighted the English coast, it now comprised 125 ships (five having dropped out on the way) carrying 19,000 seamen and 8,000 soldiers; on board there were 2,431 guns with 123,790 rounds of ammunition.

The transhipment of the landing force in the Low Countries to the Armada itself was extremely hazardous, since Parma, the governor-general in the Low Countries, lacked a deep-water port capable of taking the Spanish galleons. Sir Walter Raleigh later commented: 'to invade by sea upon a perilous coast, being neither in possession of any port, nor succoured by any party, may better fit a prince presuming on his fortune than enriched with understanding.'[12] Had Parma moved out of Dunkirk—as the king suggested in contradictory instructions in December 1587 which Parma refused to carry out and subsequently denounced—his fleet of landing craft would have been destroyed by the Dutch rebels: 'these vessels cannot run the gauntlet of warships', he exclaimed in June 1588, 'they cannot even withstand large waves!'[13] In the event, Parma's three attempts to make contact with the Armada led to nothing. The Armada sailed on regardless, having been scattered by an attack of English fire-ships and running before the prevailing wind. The English fleet was better gunned than the Spanish: the Armada carried only 138 guns of 16-pounder calibre and upwards, and of these the 12 or so largest were siege pieces and unsuited to shipboard use. The corresponding English figure was 251, many of them 18-pounders. Because of the inefficient design of their gun-carriages, the Spaniards were unable to fire their guns frequently enough, and thus did not expend all their shot, except among the lighter calibres. Some of the Spanish guns were poorly cast; they were not of a uniform calibre and the Spanish gunners may have had difficulty in finding shot of the right calibre for the guns on deck! Thus the English were able to inflict serious damage on the Spanish fighting ships off Gravelines, 'discharging our broadsides of ordnance double for their single', as one contemporary put it;[14] but in the end it was the weather rather than the English navy which defeated the Armada. The galleons mostly survived the Atlantic storms but many of the other ships did not; they were wrecked all round the coast of Scotland and Ireland as a result of severe storms. The Spanish commanders and seamen showed considerable courage and endurance: but their strategy and tactics were defective.

Philip II was dismayed by the news of the disaster: only 60 of the 125 ships that sighted England returned; perhaps 15,000 men were lost. He wrote to his chaplain and secretary Mateo Vázquez in despair: 'unless some remedy is found . . . very soon we shall find ourselves in such a state that we shall wish that we had never been born . . . we shall have to witness, quicker than anyone thinks, what we so much fear, if God does not return to fight for His cause.' Philip regarded the defeat of the Armada as a punishment for the nation's sins, and confessed that he would rather die than 'see so much ill fortune and disgrace'.[15] However, he recovered his equilibrium by November 1588, and continued to regard England as a significant security threat which required a decisive response: 'I was moved to undertake the Armada campaign for the service of Our Lord, the defence of His Cause, and the advantage of these realms. And I still feel the same now, and greatly desire that our efforts should achieve what has become all the more necessary because of what has happened.'[16] The council confirmed the policy of war with England, and Philip sent two further abortive fleets against England, in 1596 and 1597, both of which were dispersed by storms. When the Spaniards finally effected a landing, it was in Ireland under Philip III, in 1601, after Philip II's death and it came too late to bolster Tyrone's Catholic rebellion. The risk of the Armada had always been that failure would strengthen the resolve of the parties Philip was seeking to destroy. The Dutch recognized that they had little to fear from a sea-borne invasion, and their primary objective henceforth was to strengthen their landward defences to the south and east. The English were encouraged to attack the Spanish empire: between 1589 and 1591, 235 English ships raided the Spanish colonies in America (although as a result of improved defences the raids gradually became unprofitable). Spanish inability to assist the Irish rebellion in the last four years of Philip II's reign was an accurate reflection of the shift in fortunes that had occurred since the ill-fated Armada of 1588.

3.1.6 *The Aragonese Revolt*

It is said that Queen Isabella had wanted the pretext of a rebellion to conquer the kingdom of Aragon and remove its privileges. She never had the opportunity to put this objective into practice before her death in 1504, nor did her grandson, Charles V. Charles had warned his son that he would find Aragon more difficult to govern than Castile 'because of the nature of its privileges and constitutions, and because its lawlessness, no less prevalent than elsewhere, is more difficult to investigate and punish'. On another occasion, the Emperor commented that 'the Aragonese are more passionate and more easily roused than any other people'.[17] Relations with the eastern kingdom had begun in an atmosphere of crisis at the beginning of the reign. While Philip was in the Low Countries, his sister Juana had been given ultimate authority for Aragonese as well as Castilian affairs: her power had been disregarded by the Aragonese because of her residence in Castile. Worse still, the 'regent of Castile' as he was called, the duke of Francavila, who had been appointed by Juana to govern Aragon, had been forced to flee the eastern kingdom in the summer of 1556: there had been protests at a Castilian being sent to rule the kingdom of Aragon, but Francavila had also made himself extremely unpopular by taking a firm line in eliminating banditry. The king himself failed to obtain recognition as ruler of Aragon while he remained absent abroad, and in January 1559 an illegal meeting of the general *Cortes* of Aragon was summoned by the nobility. What could have developed into a rebellion came to nothing, but Philip did not receive full acknowledgement as king until he visited the kingdom and swore to uphold its privileges (*fueros*) in 1563. Thereafter, Aragon seemed to remain outwardly calm until 1588, when Philip decided to appoint another Castilian, the marquis of Almenara, as effective viceroy, thus apparently ending his agreement to the privilege that all offices in the kingdom were to be held by Aragonese. Almenara ran into such difficulties that he had to return to Castile to obtain increased powers. News that these powers had been granted brought the inhabitants of Zaragoza to fever-pitch.

At this moment, the king's relations with his Aragonese subjects were complicated by the escape of the disgraced former king's secretary, Antonio Pérez, from captivity in Madrid, where he had been held since his arrest for treason in 1579 (see chapter 3.1.1). In April 1590, he fled to Aragon and placed himself under the protection of the Justicia, a judicial official who, since 1348, had been recognized as the interpreter of the laws of the land. The office had become hereditary in the Lanuza family and had been held by Juan IV de Lanuza since 1554. Though generally royalist in his inclinations, Lanuza was obliged by his office to preserve Aragonese privileges. Pérez thus availed himself of the traditional Aragonese privilege of *manifestación*, by which a man threatened by royal officials had the right to protection by the Justicia, who would keep him in his own prison until sentence was pronounced. Benevolent impartiality towards Pérez was not what Philip II had in mind, however, and in May 1591 the prisoner was transferred on the king's orders to the custody of the Inquisition in the expectation that swift justice would be meted out. However, this act of royal vindictiveness sparked off a riot in Zaragoza, during which Almenara was fatally wounded. Pérez was freed after a second riot in September and by November he was intriguing with Henri IV to secure a French invasion of Aragon. Philip II determined to suppress the rebellion before further damage could be done. An army of 12,000 men under the command of Alonso de Vargas was dispatched into Aragon at the end of October. The rebel forces under the new Justicia, Juan V de Lanuza, were no match for the Castilian contingents. Since Aragonese privileges were temporarily in abeyance, Philip had Lanuza beheaded in the market-place of Zaragoza in December 1591. A French-backed invasion in February 1592 was put down with relative ease, and Pérez spent the rest of his life as an exile in France.

Philip II may have been an absolute ruler in theory, and the most powerful ruler in Christendom. He was not, however, an absolute ruler in practice in his eastern kingdoms such as Aragon. He remained loyal to Spanish contractualist theory, that 'the community was not created for the prince, but rather that the prince was created for the sake of the community'.[18] The power of the Inquisition was reaffirmed, since to call into question the Holy Office was to undermine the monarchy itself: an imposing *auto de fé* was held at Zaragoza in October 1592. Yet the modifications to the privileges (*fueros*) of Aragon after its rebellion were moderate. The office of Justicia was no longer independent of royal power; the king could have him removed if he desired. The selection of his subordinate officials was placed more effectively under royal control. There were also changes in the voting rules of the Aragonese representative institution, the *Cortes*, and the king was given a temporary right to appoint non-Aragonese viceroys (until the next session of the *Cortes*, which was held after Philip II's death). None of the Spanish Habsburg kings enjoyed absolute power in Aragon, Valencia and Catalonia, however: when the privileges of Aragon were abolished in 1707, it was under the new Bourbon dynasty. Even in Castile, the traditional bastion of his power, Philip II experienced greater political difficulties in the 1590s than hitherto. From 1593 until the end of his reign, he was locked in a struggle with the *Cortes* of Castile over the issue of the renewal and reform of an extraordinary subsidy (*millones*), a tax agreement first voted in 1590 to offset the financial disaster of the Armada. In November 1598, just under two months after his father's death, Philip III dissolved the *Cortes* without reaching agreement on this vital issue. There was no open political discontent in Castile: but there was a pressing need for retrenchment and reform in the new reign to restore the fortunes of the Spanish Habsburg monarchy.

3.2 The Civil Wars in the Low Countries

One of the primary causes of the decline in Spanish power and influence in Europe was the protracted civil war in the Low Countries. There was nothing inevitable about the revolt of the Netherlands, as it is usually called. At the time of Charles V's abdication in 1555, the Habsburg political system in the Netherlands was not as near to dissolution as is sometimes claimed. It is true that the cost of the war against France had proved (and would continue to prove until 1559) a heavy burden on the taxpayers in the Netherlands. However, after 1559 peace with the French held out the prospect of a gradual reduction in taxation, thus removing the financial grievance. Philip II suffered the disadvantage of being viewed as a Castilian and not the 'natural prince' of Burgundy. There was great resentment against his Castilian entourage, which numbered well over a thousand people, but in this respect the departure of the court to the Iberian peninsula in 1559 was a blessed relief. The Netherlanders were not 'natural' rebels. On the contrary, the Burgundian nobles had served Charles V loyally in his wars. The Emperor's maxim had been that 'there were no people in the world, who, governed mildly (*paternellement*), were more docile to the wishes of their prince than those of the Low Countries . . .' But the Emperor had added the cautionary note that no people hated servitude more than they.[19] Responsibility for the troubles in the Netherlands rests squarely on the shoulders of Philip, his advisers in the Low Countries and Castile, and the mistaken (and often contradictory) policies they pursued.

3.2.1 *The Collapse of Margaret of Parma's Government, 1559–1566*

When Philip left the Netherlands in 1559, he established his half-sister, Margaret, duchess of Parma, as governor-general. She was inexperienced and relied on her inner council, following the model established by Charles V in 1531. This council was a triumvirate; its members were Granvelle, who in essence was chief minister; Viglius, the president of the privy council, a supporter of Granvelle who handled government patronage; and Berlaymont, the president of the council of finance. The great nobles were limited to participating in the council of state but they were ambitious for power and resented the small role they had been allocated. After Philip's departure, two prominent Burgundian nobles, Orange and Egmont, had taken precedence in the council of state. However, with Granvelle's elevation to the cardinalate in May 1561 they were demoted. Orange's sense of personal humiliation cannot be underestimated. He had never enjoyed Philip's confidence as he had that of Charles V. Yet he was by far the richest and most influential magnate in the Low Countries, and Philip's provincial governor (*stadhouder*) in Holland, Zeeland and Utrecht; he was also an independent prince in his own right—the principality of Orange was a small enclave in southern France. The estrangement between Philip and Orange was reinforced by the latter's marriage in 1561 to Anne of Saxony, a Lutheran. Egmont was Philip's stadholder in Flanders, and second only to Alba as a successful military leader in the king's service. Less rich and less talented than Orange, Egmont was nevertheless one of the first among the upper nobility to question Philip's religious policies. As early as 1559, he feared that the Spanish Inquisition might be introduced into the Low Countries. Granvelle was oblivious to the depth of the personal animosity he had aroused, and which resulted in a formal complaint about him to Philip II from Orange and Egmont in July 1561. Granvelle claimed that the great nobles simply wanted offices and rewards to cope with the debts they had amassed as a result of expensive life-styles and costs incurred during the French wars. He favoured discharging their debts and granting them offices, but at a safe distance from the Netherlands: Orange, he thought, 'would not serve badly [as viceroy] in Sicily, for he would then be far from Germany and perhaps live with greater contentment'.[20] Granvelle completely failed to see that the nobles wanted to secure his dismissal in order to revert to the political system of Charles V and that in the meantime Orange and Egmont in particular would indulge in furious competition for control of the leading towns of the Netherlands. By 1564, it was they, and not Granvelle, who were in the ascendancy: Viglius admitted in October of that year that 'the authority of the governors, with the connivance of Her Highness [that is, Margaret of Parma], increases so much that everyone seeks to please them or at least not to displease them'.[21]

The discontent of the great nobles was focused on Philip's decision, in 1559–61, to divide the existing four bishoprics in the Netherlands into eighteen in order to combat heresy more effectively. Granvelle was accused of being the evil genius behind the scheme. It is not difficult to see why: he was elevated to the cardinalate, appointed archbishop of Mechelen, and (unknown to Pius IV and against his wishes) primate of the Netherlands. However, though Granvelle was involved in the implementation of the plan, he did not originate it; such ideas went back to the Valois dukes and had been contemplated since the 1520s. Philip simply obtained the necessary Papal concessions for a useful reform. However, the scheme was politically disastrous. Orange and Egmont protested to Philip in July 1561 that they had not been consulted. Moreover, since the new bishops were to be skilled theologians they would not be drawn automatically from the younger sons of the nobility, as had been the case with such appointments in the past. Furthermore, the ranks of the clergy—and thus it was assumed, at least in the short term, the influence of the government—in the states of the provinces, the local representative institutions, would be increased by the new appointments. In Brabant, the appointment of three bishop-abbots would have disturbed the balance of power between clergy, nobles and the representatives of the towns. Above all, the scheme for the bishoprics reinforced the fear of the imposition of an inquisition akin to the Spanish Inquisition, a fear which was already prevalent in the Low Countries. Each bishop was in effect an inquisitor in his diocese; more bishops meant more inquisitors.

Philip found this fear difficult to understand because, in his view, the religious repression in the Low Countries was already 'more merciless' than the Inquisition in Castile. The Emperor Charles V's narrow religious orthodoxy had been reflected in the passing of a series of heresy laws in the Netherlands, culminating in the draconian so-called 'edict of blood' in May 1550. These laws covered practically every conceivable heresy offence, and between 1523 and 1566 about 1,300 heretics were executed in the Low Countries. Many of those sentenced under Charles V were Anabaptists, drawn from the lower social classes. Under Philip II, the repression shifted southwards to the heart of the Low Countries, and the executions began to include those of well-to-do Calvinists. For this reason, Philip's religious policy was considered far more of a threat than his father's. What struck contemporaries most were the disproportionate penalties written into laws 'of blood rather than ink',[22] in particular the equation of the crime of contravening the heresy laws with treason, and the consequent confiscation of property as well as the execution of offenders. To a relatively tolerant society that had one of the most advanced economies in Europe, this policy seemed to present a generalized threat to property. Had the heresy laws been enforced to the letter, the government would have collapsed much earlier because of its unpopularity. Nevertheless, the king's attitude on religious matters was totally inflexible.

By March 1563, the pressure from Orange, Egmont and Hoorne for the dismissal of Granvelle had become intense, and in August, following the withdrawal of these nobles from the council of state, Margaret of Parma lent her support to their request. Philip distrusted Granvelle in any case, because of his political dependence on the duke of Alba who at this moment was in disgrace and absent from the Spanish government. Thus the Eboli faction at Madrid got its way: Margaret of Parma handed Philip the perfect excuse for disposing of Granvelle. In March 1564, the cardinal was ordered to leave Brussels. He never returned. The nobles thought they had won and they re-entered the council of state. Viglius and Berlaymont were still there, attempting to hold the line after Granvelle's departure, but even Viglius fell under Philip II's suspicion as being too lenient in his approach to heresy prosecutions. The nobles determined to press home their advantage and to obtain the king's approval for a relaxation in the heresy laws. To this end, they dispatched Egmont to Madrid to plead their case, and he returned to the Netherlands convinced of an imminent change in royal policy. In July 1565, Margaret wrote to Philip in support of the nobles' demands for political predominance, religious toleration and the convocation of the States General to remedy urgent financial problems. The reply was slow to arrive, but Philip's 'letters from the Segovia woods' shocked even Margaret, who showed them to the council of state. 'As for the Inquisition', Philip wrote, 'it is my intention that it should be carried out ... this is nothing new, because this was always done in the days of the late Emperor my lord and father.' The king dismissed the fear of public disturbances, and requested Margaret to 'do all that is necessary and not to agree to any different policy'. The time was not opportune for any shift in direction in the Netherlands. The heresy laws should therefore be enforced: the king blamed the spread of heresy on 'the negligence, leniency and duplicity of the judges . . .'[23] Since Egmont had argued that executions simply made martyrs, the king was prepared to have them carried out in secret. Egmont had been on a fool's errand. The nobles were infuriated.

Almost immediately a group sympathetic to Protestantism met secretly to draw up a petition, the 'compromise' or league of the nobility. The 'compromise' was a protest against the heresy laws and it called for opposition to the Inquisition 'in whatever shape, open or covert, under whatever disguise or mask it may assume . . .'[24] It was drafted by Calvinists, but it aimed at a wider audience. About 400 lesser nobles signed it, but while the majority of the great nobles refused to sign, they also neglected to enforce the heresy laws in their provinces. A prominent supporter of the campaign was Hendrik van Brederode, who had connections with the Rhineland aristocracy and dominated the province of Utrecht. In April 1566, at the head of 400 armed and uniformed members of the league—contemptuously termed 'beggars' (*gueux*) by Berlaymont, the president of the council of finance, an epithet which the rebels appropriated for themselves—Brederode presented a petition to Margaret. This called for the mitigation of the heresy laws and a meeting of the States General to prevent 'open revolt and universal rebellion bringing ruin to all the provinces . . .'[25] In the face of this opposition, Margaret virtually surrendered control to the council of state, and requested Philip to make these concessions. The king refused a meeting of the States General point blank and offered only minimal concessions. This left the government hopelessly ill-prepared to meet the challenge of anarchy and rebellion.

3.2.2 *The Abortive Rebellions, the Duke of Alba and the Council of Troubles, 1567–1572*

At the time of the collapse of government in the Netherlands in 1566, anti-clericalism seems to have been widespread, but there were far fewer conversions to Protestantism than in France at the same date. Nevertheless, open-air Protestant services began in Flanders and Hainault in May and spread to the outskirts of Antwerp by mid-June. The 'hedge-preachers' who led the services were not particularly numerous; nor were they exclusively Calvinists or dispatched from Geneva: at this date, a number of confessions were competing in the Netherlands, and Anabaptists retained a significant following (see chapter 1.4.4). In general, the hedge-preachers were men of fairly humble origins who lacked theo-logical training, but made up in zeal for what they lacked in education. By August, events had proceeded a stage further with the destruction of the Catholic images in the churches at Antwerp. This was not the first incident in the 'iconoclastic fury' (*beeldenstormen*), and in some ways it was untypical because its indiscriminate destruction was not repeated else-where. The riots were considerably less violent than those in France; in some cases, the iconoclastic mob was paid for by the local pastor or consistory and the vandalism was carried out by manual workers anxious for a daily wage. At The Hague, the images were removed by paid men 'without causing a commotion'.[26] News of events at Antwerp led to the removal of images from the churches in other great towns, such as at Amsterdam, Delft, The Hague, Ghent and Leiden in the same month. These riots were not simply a reaction to the high grain prices in 1565–6. Prices were less severe than in the crisis of 1521–2 and were already beginning to fall before the outbreak of the riots. In any case, the mobs attacked churches and religious houses, not the property of grain merchants or grain-hoarders. Popular fear of the Inquisition, the weakness of the government at Brussels, above all the absence of Philip II and the apparent impasse of royal policy, all served to encourage religious riot. Protestant pastors were under no illusions about the likely response of Philip II to these riots. 'After he hears of these outrages', one preacher declared, the king would 'come with his Spaniards and smite the people from the land . . . and deliver them into slavery, as Nebuchadnezzar did to the children of Israel.'[27]

The great nobles were caught unawares by the widespread discontent which was revealed by the iconoclastic fury, and they adopted differing political and religious stances which ultimately proved fatal to their general aim of returning to the golden days of Charles V's reign. Louis of Nassau, the brother of William of Orange, tried in vain to raise a mercenary army in Germany. When the first revolt came, it was a damp squib. Calvinists seized power in two southern towns, Tournai and Valenciennes, in the expectation that the great nobles of the Low Countries would lend them military and political support. But they did not. William of Orange had already resigned all his offices and he sought refuge in his younger brother's principality of Nassau-Dillenburg in Germany, where he was joined by other prominent exiles such as Culemborg and Hoogstraten: this small state became a key financial supporter of the exiled rebel leaders after 1566. Brederode joined in the revolt from his lordship of Vianen in the north, it is true; but he was unable to link up with the two rebel towns in the south, which surrendered to the government in the early months of 1567. In late April, Brederode was forced to flee to Emden, and Vianen capitulated within a week. With the death of Brederode in February 1568, Orange was the undisputed leader of the exiles. In that year he made plans for an invasion of the Low Countries on several fronts, but each of the invasion attempts failed.

There were several circumstances which militated against the success of any of these rebellions in 1567–8. Though Orange and his four brothers pursued with determination their 'just and necessary quarrel with the king of Spain',[28] there was no general rebellion by the nobility of the Low Countries, despite widespread discontent. Orange's standing was insufficient to inspire it: not until the Spanish 'fury' of 1576 did the nobility begin to question their allegiance to the Habsburgs. The religious basis for a rebellion did not exist. Few people approved of Philip's policy of persecution of heretics; but though there were large numbers of Calvinists in the south—far more than in the north until the 1580s—their support could not be mobilized effectively and at this time they were deeply divided on the whole question of the legitimacy of resistance to divinely ordained authority. Orange also failed in his attempt to secure a general alliance of Calvinists and Lutherans against Philip's policy. Moreover, the foreign alliances on which any invasion plan depended came to nothing. Elector Augustus of Saxony was set on a policy of non-intervention, and the other German princes followed his example. Though an alliance with the French Huguenots existed from August 1568, this led to few tangible benefits for the rebels in the Low Countries. Orange invaded France in the support of the Calvinist cause in November 1568. Later on, in 1571, he established closer relations with the Huguenot leaders, but the massacre of St Bartholomew the following year shattered his hopes of a French invasion led by Coligny, the Huguenot leader.

Philip's council at Madrid was split on what course to adopt, first in the circumstances of the iconoclastic rioting in 1566 and subsequently in the face of the civil rebellions in 1567–8. There was no certainty that the duke of Alba would be appointed as governor-general of the Netherlands: he was, in fact, the third choice, after the dukes of Parma and Savoy had refused the unenviable command. In the debates at Madrid in the summer and autumn of 1566 Alba did not argue for a policy of punishment and repression (such as his own was to become). Rather, he recalled Charles V's journey to Ghent in 1539 to suppress the rebellion in that town. Philip II must do his duty and visit the Low Countries, distributing pardons and honours as his father had done. All the general would do was to precede the king and punish the ringleaders. However, the faction rivalries at Madrid were so serious that Alba's mission was undermined from the outset. His departure was delayed for six months; his army was reduced to nearly one-sixth of its original size; and control over its financing was handed to the rival Eboli faction! Alba felt cheated of the king's support and this led to his obsession with 'victory' in the Low Countries, through which he hoped to improve his position at the Spanish court. This turned what might have been a reasonable response to a limited rebellion into a catastrophic regime of terror, symbolized by the history of the Council of Troubles, set up five days after Alba's arrival in Brussels in September 1567. Originally intended as a court sitting in the presence of Philip II for the purpose of confiscating the estates of rebel nobles and merchants, it became known as the Council of Blood. Alba's signature authenticated its acts, and between 1567 and 1573 the tribunal condemned thousands of individuals, of whom a significant proportion were executed or banished. Alba was particularly ruthless with the nobility. The political privileges of the knights of the Golden Fleece, who had provided most of the stadholders, were removed in 1567, which enabled him to prosecute certain knights for treason. In September 1567, Egmont and Hoorne were arrested and in June the following year they were executed in the Brussels market place. The executions caused a sensation and alienated the upper nobility from Philip II for over a decade. The king fully revealed his own ruthlessness by holding another prominent rebel, Montigny, imprisoned at Madrid and having him strangled in secret in October 1570.

The persecution policy remained unpopular, as was the governor-general's determination to implement in full the establishment of the new bishoprics. Alba had been empowered to override constitutional limitations provided by provincial privileges. A secret memorandum, perhaps written by Granvelle, advised him 'to make all the states into one kingdom with Brussels its capital'.[29] The king thought it necessary to 'arrange for . . . a fixed, certain and permanent revenue from those provinces for their own maintenance and defence'.[30] The size of the military establishment obliged Alba in March 1569 to seek approval from the provincial states for three new taxes, only one of which (the Hundredth Penny) was put into operation. Collection of the other two unpopular taxes was deferred because Alba was able to make his army self-financing in 1570–1. None the less, with the new threat posed by Orange's invasion in 1572, Philip II insisted on the implementation of the most unpopular tax, the Tenth Penny, a levy of 10 per cent on the price of all moveables and exports. In March 1572, Alba tried to force collection of the tax in Brussels by using detachments of troops, but a tax strike was supported by the provincial states of Hainault, Artois, Flanders and Brabant, which sent deputies to Philip II to protest against taxation without consent. In the northern provinces, the urban patricians (*vroedschappen*) refused to appoint collectors of the Tenth Penny; subsequently their resistance was stiffened by the knowledge that with a threatened invasion from France, Alba lacked the troops to force the levy.

Thousands of refugees fled from Alba's regime of persecution and established Calvinist communities in exile at such disparate places as

Aachen, Emden, Wesel, London and Norwich. There was also a militant minority of privateers who had been hired by Louis of Nassau to assist his invasion in 1568, and who operated under letters of marque issued by William of Orange as a sovereign prince. Orange took his share of the profits and harnessed the energies of a piratical rabble. Their leader, William, baron of Lumey and count of la Marck, was a minor nobleman, a ruthless ruffian committed to avenging the death of Egmont, his kinsman. In March 1572, he requested the use of Dover for his fleet, because his so-called Sea Beggars (*Watergeuzen*) lacked a port in the Low Countries. Elizabeth I, anxious to avoid complicating her relations with Philip II still further (she had seized the Duke of Alba's payships three years earlier), ordered his fleet to leave the English ports. On All Fools' Day 1572, Lumey captured The Brill (Den Briel). Meeting little resistance, because Alba's forces were in the south to counter a possible French invasion, the Sea Beggars established themselves in about fifty towns in the north within the next few months. The rising in the north spread rapidly following the news of Count Louis of Nassau's capture of Mons in late May 1572. Although Alba retook it at the end of September, the Sea Beggars had by then made their main gains.

3.2.3　*The Secession of the Northern Provinces, 1572–1579*

The Sea Beggars were not numerous—only 600 or so had captured The Brill—and they rarely took the northern towns by force of arms. For the most part, the towns capitulated, and the attitude of the urban militia was usually decisive in determining whether or not the Sea Beggars would be admitted. At Gouda, it took only one militiaman opening the gates to fifty or sixty Beggars for the town to be lost to the government: his colleagues would not fire on him. Once the Beggars had gained entry, any agreements they had made with the townspeople to respect their civic privileges and to allow Catholics to worship freely were broken. The fanatical hatred of everything savouring of Popery nurtured by years of exile from Alba's regime was too deeply ingrained: Lumey was responsible for devastating the churches at Haarlem, Leiden, Gouda and Schoonhoven. One contemporary thought the Beggars 'without religion';[31] certainly they did not distinguish themselves as the early leaders of the Calvinist church. In January 1573, Orange was forced to dismiss Lumey as lieutenant to placate the states of Holland.

Orange had expected that the great resentment at Alba's rule would ensure him a more favourable response among the nobility of the Low Countries in 1572 than he had met four years earlier. Yet he was still not regarded as 'father of the fatherland'[32] by those whose support he considered essential. At a meeting of the states of Holland in July 1572, he was recognized as stadholder in Holland, Zeeland and Utrecht, although Philip had his own, loyal, stadholder there already—the count of Bossu. The states thus lent credence to Orange's argument that his (and theirs) was only a temporary suspension of obedience to the lawful sovereign; it was Alba whose government was unconstitutional and thus rebellious. Lacking the support of enough nobles, Orange took refuge in Holland in October 1572; prolonged resistance to Alba's armies seemed unlikely. He thus became leader in a 'domestic war' between the states of Holland and Zeeland and those of the 'obedient' provinces. He was also leader in a civil war within Holland and Zeeland: Amsterdam held out for the government until 1578. The rebels were fighting a war with a common purpose, 'freedom of conscience', which they said had been denied by Philip II and Alba. In fact, they in turn operated an intolerant religious policy: the provisional toleration edict in Holland applied only to non-Catholics; public service of the Mass was proscribed after Easter 1573 for fear that it would lead to rioting; committed Catholics were suspected as traitors to the cause. Though the Calvinist church was not particularly powerful' or well supported by 1573 (indeed, in many rural areas the only Calvinist in the community was the minister), Orange became a Calvinist; however, his political and religious outlook remained quite different from that of the reformed church—he was a *politique* rather than a zealot. His motivation remained obscure to contemporaries, since he himself did not explain it; after his death critics accused him of deviousness and hypocrisy. Thus it was that an articulate man was bestowed with the misleading epithet 'the Silent'.

Commenting on the prospects of the revolt in 1572, the French ambassador thought that 'since the people of Holland are not warlike and lack spirit, there is not a town which will not surrender when the duke's army approaches'.[33] This might well have happened but for a fatal mis-calculation by Alba. Three towns—Mechelen, Zutphen and Naarden—surrendered to him in 1572, of which only one (Zutphen) had actually resisted his army. Yet the inhabitants of all three places were massacred, as were 2,000 or so inhabitants of Haarlem, which submitted to Alba after an eight-month siege in July 1573. After this date there were few Dutch surrenders (though later some foreign mercenary captains betrayed their towns); and Orange's insistence on large-scale flooding of the dykes obliged the Spaniards to break off the sieges of Alkmaar and Leiden. Although Orange was unable to prevent the recapture of Zierikzee in June 1576, he ensured that its resistance had been so protracted that it placed an intolerable burden on Habsburg resources in the Low Countries.

Nevertheless, the prospects for the revolt in the north looked bleak, and from 1576 plans for closer co-operation between the provinces were

afoot. The primary aim was to conclude a military alliance with predominantly Catholic Gelderland, which with its four large rivers would act
as Holland's bulwark. However, the states of the Catholic provinces in the
north resisted these plans for religious reasons until May 1578, when
Orange had his younger brother, John of Nassau-Dillenburg, appointed as
stadholder of Gelderland. Nassau was a much stricter Calvinist than his
elder brother and his missionary spirit was placed at the service of
provincial union; he deliberately sided with those he termed 'co-religionists and true patriots' and adopted unconstitutional methods to deal with
opposition from the Catholic states of Gelderland, which protested at his
'exorbitant novelties'.[34] The Union of Utrecht of January 1579 was the
outcome of his negotiations. Initially, it was the union of three and not
seven provinces. Holland and Zeeland signed freely, while Utrecht joined
only after strong pressure. Orange hesitated at the prospect of an aggressive Protestant league and did not join the 'closer union' until May or June
1579. Nor was the alliance exclusively northern in character: certain towns
of Flanders (notably Ghent), and three of Brabant (Antwerp, Breda and
Lier) belonged to it until they fell to the Spanish army. Nor did the alliance
provide a permanent constitution: of the twenty-six clauses in the Union
of Utrecht, more than half were never put into practice. None the less, it
was the first step along the road to the 'act of dismissal' of July 1581 by
which the States General, meeting at The Hague, transferred allegiance
from Philip II to the duke of Anjou.[35] It seems more than a coincidence
that five of the seven provinces forming the permanent 'closer union' of
Utrecht were territories recently incorporated by Charles V: their ties with
Brussels had never been close, and they had not wanted to be represented
in the southern-dominated States General.

3.2.4   *The Rebellion of the Southern Provinces, 1576–1585*

The failure of repression necessitated the recall of Alba and the appointment of a new governor-general for the Low Countries. However, his first
successor, Medina Celi, lacked sufficient military skill to meet the
challenge of the 1572 rebellion, and Alba continued to act as governor-
general in 1572–3. A replacement was found for Medina, but ten months
elapsed between the appointment of Don Luis de Requesens and his
arrival at Brussels in November 1573, despite the urgency of the military
situation. Requesens favoured negotiation with the rebels, and on his
initiative a conference was arranged at Breda in February 1575. Philip II
knew that the financial weakness of the Spanish government could only
encourage the rebels: 'they are fully aware of it', he wrote as early as July
1574, 'and for that reason they are in no mood for a settlement.'[36] The

royal bankruptcy of September 1575 had been contemplated for over a year, but delayed because of its catastrophic implications on Habsburg policy in the Low Countries: without the regular transfer of funds from Spain, the troops could not be paid. Thus the opposition to Philip came not only from the Dutch but also from his own troops, who mutinied because they were unpaid. Not until the late spring of 1578 was Philip once more able to use bankers to transmit funds to the Netherlands. Alba had shot the ringleaders of the mutiny of the Spanish veterans at Haarlem in 1573, but this did not stop troops rebelling at Antwerp in April 1574. Requesens informed Philip that even if the Dutch 'loved us as sons . . . all the Spanish mutinies would be enough to make us loathed'.[37] He was in despair at the rapid collapse of the 'whole military machine' and the situation was made more desperate by his death in March 1576 without an obvious successor.

At this point, Philip II should have sent a new governor-general promptly to the Netherlands. But almost eight months elapsed; not until early November did Don John of Austria arrive at Luxembourg. By that time the situation was so out of hand that he was in no position to leave his place of safety to negotiate with potential enemies at Brussels. At first, a nine-man council of state took over the government after the death of Requesens. But the army lacked a military leader; after the capture of Zierikzee, it mutinied and sacked Aalst in late July 1576. The council of state panicked and in three successive edicts outlawed the mutineers. Deprived of a safe refuge, they replied by sacking Antwerp in early November, the most destructive event in what came to be known as the 'Spanish fury'. Meanwhile, in early September, the council of state had been arrested by troops under the command of William of Hoorne, lord of Hèze, acting on behalf of the States of Brabant. Immediately after this coup, on the initiative of the states of Brabant and Hainault, the States General was summoned to Brussels. This was the first time since 1477 that the national representative institution had been called without the approval of the ruler. Since 1559, it had been convened only twice and had met only briefly: in 1576–7 it was to become the central organ of government. Special arrangements were made to ensure the co-operation of William of Orange and the experienced troops of Holland and Zeeland in dislodging the mutineers from the southern provinces. The intention of the southerners was to redirect government along traditional lines—the States General was to be 'composed in the same manner' as under Charles V—and to strengthen Catholicism. Once the crisis was over, the southern provinces were prepared to come to terms with Philip II and Don John of Austria. The historian Geyl called the Pacification of Ghent of November 1576 the 'entire fatherland (that is, the 'seventeen provinces') in revolt'[38] but on this occasion there was not even rudimentary co-operation between the seventeen provinces that had formed the Emperor's Burgundian state, for the Pacification was welcomed only in Holland, Zeeland and Brabant.

Don John had no intention of accepting the Pacification of Ghent in its entirety, and renegotiated the religious clauses with the States General in February 1577 (the Perpetual Edict or 'priests' peace'). However, the governor-general continued to be denied real power at Brussels, and, in frustration, left the capital and captured the castle of Namur in July. His apparent aggressive intent alienated the Walloon nobility. In a second act of rebellion, following upon its assumption of the control of the government in order to expel the mutineers in 1576, the States General deposed Don John as governor-general and invited the Emperor's younger brother, the archduke Matthias of Habsburg, a future Emperor but at this date an incompetent youth of 20, to take up the post. It thus hoped to prevent an open breach with Philip II, since Matthias was his cousin. The invitation may also have been a ploy of the duke of Aerschot, who wanted to counteract the growing authority of William of Orange. Tension between the two men became acute when the States General, acting under pressure from the mob at Brussels, appointed Orange to the exceptional position of 'provisional governor' (*ruwaard*) of Brabant, while at the same time making Aerschot governor of neighbouring Flanders. Aerschot went to Ghent to oppose Orange's appointment, but the Orangist party in that city, led by François de la Kéthulle, lord of Ryhove, and Jan van Hembyze, seized control at the end of October 1577, arrested Aerschot and the leading politicians of Flanders, and established a Calvinist regime in Ghent. In the short term, Orange's prestige was increased. He magnanimously secured the release of Aerschot and the other prominent citizens who had been arrested at Ghent after opposing his influence in Flanders. The States General agreed to interpret the Pacification of Ghent in the widest sense and in January 1578 it recognized Orange as permanent governor of Brabant and lieutenant-governor to Matthias. The 'states party'—the supporters of the rebellious States General—had never seemed stronger. Yet in the same month, its army was crushed at Gembloux by a smaller force commanded by Don John and Alexander Farnese (subsequently prince of Parma). By mid-February 1578, Orange, Matthias and the entire States General had to evacuate Brussels for the relative security of Antwerp.

The radical towns in the south, primarily Ghent—but at one time, Bruges, Ypres, Oudenarde and Courtrai were also affected—blamed the disaster of Gembloux on the States General's incompetence and the defeatism of the Catholic Walloon nobility. Peter Dathenus, the Calvinist minister officiating at Ghent after September 1578, stated that it was 'precisely the men in command . . . who have always been servants, friends and companions of the Spaniards'.[39] Another Calvinist preacher, Herman Moded, proclaimed that Catholics were lucky to escape the burnings suffered by Protestants in former times. Persecution of Catholics and iconoclasm were the order of the day at Ghent, although Orange visited the city twice (in December 1578 and August 1579) to expel the radical preachers and restore order. Worse still, the extremists at Ghent called in John Casimir, son of the elector of the Rhine Palatinate, a strict Calvinist whose troops further alienated the local Catholic nobility who were used to running their own affairs. Not all Calvinists were equally fanatical: but there were enough zealots to convince the Catholic majority in the south that Orange's objective of 'religious peace' was a violation of the Pacification of Ghent.

The Habsburg cause was thus presented with a favourable opportunity to exploit the divisions in the Low Countries by the time of Don John of Austria's death in October 1578. Parma was an obvious successor as governor-general: he was popular with the troops; he was already present in the Low Countries; and he had sufficient self-confidence to appeal to the Walloon provinces to return to allegiance to Philip II and defend the Catholic religion. He offered to preserve their privileges as in the time of Charles V; he also promised an amnesty to rebels who laid down their arms, and to withdraw Spanish troops from loyal provinces. At first the response was confused. By the end of October 1578 there was a Catholic Malcontent movement, led by the baron of Montigny, which used disbanded troops of the rebellious States General to capture Menin and cut off supplies to the Calvinist dictatorships at Ghent and Arras. But to strengthen their position, the Malcontents threw in their lot with a union of Catholic Walloon provinces which had originally been instigated by the states of Hainault. Gradually, by January 1579, this was broadened into the Union of Arras, which inaugurated serious negotiations with Parma. By May there was a definitive agreement, ratified by Philip II in September 1579.

Parma considered some of the terms of the Treaty of Arras exorbitant and it was never implemented in full. (He would have had to retire as governor-general within six months under the revised terms of the treaty, which would have proved fatal to the cause of Philip II.) Parma considered clause five the most damaging concession: this required the withdrawal of foreign troops within six weeks and prohibited their return unless there was a foreign war. It was not until February 1582 that he had this clause revoked by a special assembly of the 'reconciled states' (*États réconciliés*), and in the meantime his military effort was hindered. However, he used his diplomatic skills to good effect. He disclaimed a policy of severity (*rigueur*); instead, his would be a regime of goodwill (*bienveillance*).[40] This was not to be confused with weakness. In cases of treason—the abandonment of allegiance to Philip II after an earlier reconciliation—there were still executions. In November 1580, Parma had Hèze executed for such an offence. However, unlike Alba, Parma did not confiscate the wealth of the offending family. Instead, he awarded the traitor's property and titles to loyal members of the same family. In the case of Hèze, the property was transferred to his sister, who was countess of Egmont: the move thus helped secure the loyalty of Philip, count of Egmont. Parma was astute, because part of the impetus to the rebellion in 1576 had come from the heirs of Egmont, Hoorne and Montigny, who sought to avenge the executions under Alba and to obtain restoration of their confiscated estates. Eventually all the great nobles, with the exception of the house of Orange-Nassau, returned to allegiance to Philip II. Because of Orange's intransigence, an edict of proscription was drawn up against him in November 1579, and a price placed on his head. Parma delayed the publication of this edict until the following June. Though in one respect it was a mistake—the ban encouraged Orange to write his famous *Apology*, one of the most effective propaganda pieces of the entire rebellion—the condemnation of Orange as the 'sole leader, author and promoter of the troubles of our state'[41] emphasized the return of the upper nobility to their traditional allegiance. The lesser nobility followed their example.

Parma secured the support of the Catholic nobility because he offered them not only rewards, but also satisfaction for their more general political objectives. They were not interested in the States General, which in their mind was linked with rebellion. What they wanted was power in the council of state, which they continued to enjoy on a reduced scale until 1632 (when it was forfeited as a result of an attempted aristocratic conspiracy). They also wanted power in the local states or representative institutions. There was no obvious alternative to Parma's leadership of the Catholic nobility. Matthias, the rival governor-general appointed by the States General, left the Low Countries to deserved obloquy in June 1581, but Anjou—Orange's proposed successor for Matthias's role, with extended powers—did not arrive until February 1582. Once installed in his various titles (as replacement to Philip II, but without the title of sovereign), Anjou quickly perceived that the responsibility for any military failure rested with him, yet he enjoyed no compensating political control. In January 1583, 3,600 French mercenaries attempted to seize power at Antwerp, but were chased out of the city after losing nearly half their men in the fighting. The 'French fury' succeeded in only three towns (Dunkirk, Dixmude and Termonde) but totally discredited Anjou, who left the Netherlands for good in June 1583 and died in July the following year. It revived traditional hostility to French power and destroyed Orange's attempt to rally the Catholic nobility of the southern provinces: his policy in the south was at an end well before his assassination in July

1584. Martyrdom gained Orange a posthumous reputation he had not
enjoyed in his last years.

After August 1582, Parma had an army of 60,000 men; and the towns of
Flanders and Brabant began to fall steadily to the Spanish cause. The
Calvinist minority in Ghent was embroiled in faction-fighting, and in
October 1583 Hembyze and Dathenus returned from exile in the
Palatinate to begin a new persecution of Catholics. Disgusted at Orange's
policy of supporting Anjou, Hembyze entered into negotiations with
Parma, but he was arrested and executed in August 1584 after news of
Orange's assassination had reached the city. The two most radical towns,
Bruges and Ghent, capitulated respectively in May and September 1584.
Parma was moderate in the terms he offered, because he wanted to use
Ghent as the blockade point on the river Scheldt in his siege of Antwerp.
In March 1585, Brussels capitulated, and the following August Antwerp
followed suit: Parma's crowning triumph had been achieved in thirteen
months' siege.

3.2.5 *The Hardening of the Territorial Boundaries*

One of the chief difficulties in attempting to analyse the causes, development and consequences of the Dutch revolt is that it occurred in a
territory that was only in the early stages of becoming a state. It has
already been observed that Charles V's 'newly conquered territories'
ended up in the Union of Utrecht: the ties of allegiance to Brussels and the
Habsburg dynasty were extremely weak, in part because of the absence of
a powerful local nobility. On the other hand, the town of Groningen,
which defected from the 'states party' in 1580, was resolutely Catholic and
disliked the idea of union with The Hague. It submitted only under
pressure from the army of Maurice of Nassau in 1594. It wanted to pursue
its own interests in peace, and this was the objective of many of the
provinces: Groningen considered that an alliance with Brunswick in the
1590s might have proved more to its interests than incorporation into the
Dutch Republic. The topography of the region did not help in the development of the state: the lines of the great rivers, for example, did not in the
themselves determine the shape of the United Provinces. East Friesland
might have been incorporated into the union, but in the end its links with
the Empire proved too strong. The fortunes of war contributed to the
fluidity of the territorial boundaries: as late as 1600, the political leaders
of the Dutch Republic thought that some or all of the southern provinces
might have been reconquered. Conversely, after the fall of Antwerp in
1585, a Spanish minister, Idiáquez, predicted that Parma would 'finish the
war of the Low Countries in a short time'.[42] Most foreign commentators,
too, expected resistance to Spanish rule to collapse after the assassination

of William of Orange. Defeatism was rife in Holland after the fall of
Antwerp; and Gouda pressed for a resumption of negotiations with Philip
II. What proved in the long term to be the distinctive features of the
rebellion in the north, the gradual development of a republican political
theory and religious toleration (except for Catholics), were precisely the
elements which contemporaries thought would induce collapse. In 1598
Henri IV talked of 'the miracle of Holland'; but he also considered that
'under a prince all difficulties could be resisted better than under the
government of the States [General]'.[43]

The Dutch rebels had also thought princely leadership of their revolt to
be the answer in the aftermath of Orange's assassination. Notwithstanding
the failure of the Anjou experiment, Henri III of France was offered
sovereignty over the rebel provinces, but in February 1585 he refused to
support the Netherlands, realizing that it meant open war against Spain.
The Dutch then turned to England. The same offer was made to Elizabeth
I on the same conditions. The queen declined, even refusing a protector-
ship, which was more humiliating to the rebels. The Dutch negotiators
then requested 'some lord of quality to become leader and director . . .
because matters had run into disorder' since Orange's death.[44] The upshot
was the Treaty of Nonsuch, the preliminary terms of which were signed
shortly after the fall of Antwerp to Parma in August 1585. Robert Dudley,
Earl of Leicester, was to act as Elizabeth's lieutenant-general. Five
thousand infantry and a thousand cavalry were to serve temporarily at the
queen's expense, but the queen's generosity was to be repaid within five
years of a peace treaty. The strategically vital ports of Flushing and The
Brill were to remain in English hands and their garrisons of 1,400 men to
be provided and paid for by the English. (They were withdrawn by James I
for financial reasons in 1616.) There was a fundamental conflict between
the queen and the earl over the purpose of the expedition. Elizabeth I
remained committed to a negotiated settlement with Parma that would
take account of 'Burgundian liberties' and provide a degree of religious
toleration. For Leicester, however, the expedition had a missionary
purpose: he was to be a Puritan Parma for the northern provinces, and to
the fury of the queen, in January 1586 he accepted the title of 'absolute
governor and general'.[45] A fundamental misunderstanding arose from this.
Because the word 'absolute' was used, Leicester seems to have believed
that his power was unlimited; the Dutch simply meant that his appointment was neither temporary nor provisional.

It was subsequently said of Leicester's appointment that 'it had been
better bestowed upon a meaner man of more skill'.[46] Already his political
talents in England had been proved mediocre, and he lacked the necessary
acumen in dealing with the Dutch. At first he relied on a longstanding
supporter of the English alliance, Paulus Buys, who had served as

advocate (*advocaet*) to the states of Holland during Orange's ascendancy (1572–84). Leicester chose as his closest advisers religious refugees from the south, men deeply distrusted in Holland. Subsequently, Leicester made his base in the province of Utrecht, which was pursuing policies hostile to the new advocate of Holland, Johan van Oldenbarnevelt. In April 1586, Leicester insisted on the blockade of the river Scheldt to cut off the town of Antwerp, now under Spanish control. This policy led to discontent among those whose trading interests with Antwerp were affected. The governor returned to England in 1586–7, and it became impractical for the Dutch to wait for Leicester's personal decisions. In any case, the Dutch were anxious to run their own affairs, not least because the English had not proved reliable military allies. During Leicester's absence, Deventer was betrayed to the Spanish by Sir William Stanley and the fortifications of Zutphen also fell, thanks to the actions of Yorke, another English officer. Oldenbarnevelt declared that 'we were never so deceived by the French as by the English'.[47] When Leicester returned in 1587, discontent with English rule had become irreversible. Had he succeeded in his attempt to arrest Oldenbarnevelt and Maurice of Nassau in September, the country might have been plunged into civil war. However, he failed, and he was recalled to England in December. There was a delay in appointing his successor, Willoughby, who never enjoyed the same authority. The capture of Breda from the Spanish by Maurice of Nassau in March 1590 was the first success in the war for ten years and a landmark in the history of the Dutch Republic. The English governorship had been no help to the Dutch. It was clear that they could manage without it, and so in July 1590, the issue of sovereignty was settled for good when the States General declared themselves 'the sovereign institution of the country' with 'no overlord except the deputies of the provincial states themselves'.[48]

By 1590, the Dutch were managing their own affairs, despite the provisions of the Treaty of Nonsuch and the appointment of Willoughby as governor-general. This was a considerable achievement for Oldenbarnevelt, but also attested to the disastrous experience of Leicester's rule. It made Parma's attempted reconquest more difficult, but in any case the Spanish advance slowed down in the late 1580s for quite separate reasons. For one thing, Parma's attention was distracted by fruitless support for the Armada against England and the Catholic League in France. The Spanish advisers of Philip II recognized that 'the attempt to conquer the rebellious provinces by force is to speak of a war without end';[49] war on two fronts was an impossibility. Secondly, though Parma's conciliatory policy towards the southern towns pacified the region, it allowed the free migration of Protestants with their goods to the north. The amnesty of Antwerp lasted four years (1585–9) and 40,000 Protestants left for the north in these years, mostly going to Amsterdam and Middelburg. By 1622, it was estimated that 33 per cent of the population of Amsterdam were immigrants, while the proportions were higher elsewhere, reaching 51 per cent at Haarlem and 67 per cent at Leiden. Their contribution to the Calvinist congregations and to the economic 'miracle' of the northern provinces was immense (see chapter 8.4.4). Over half of the 320 principal depositors in the Bank of Amsterdam in the first two years after it had been founded (1609–11) came from the south. Parma's policy thus indirectly assisted the economic success of the rebellion. A third reason for Parma's failure is that in 1585 and again in 1589 Philip II ruled out 'freedom of conscience or religious peace or anything like it'.[50] The governor-general was unable to offer the political or religious concessions necessary to induce the rebels to make peace, and for this reason he ultimately failed.

Parma's death in December 1592 led to a paralysis in the Spanish military command in 1593–5, made worse by substantial mutinies in the army. At the same time, Maurice of Nassau, Orange's second son, captain-general of the rebels and after 1590 elected stadholder in five provinces (two more than his father), led a series of campaigns resulting in the capture of all the Spanish outposts north of the river Maas. Groningen fell to a siege in July 1594, when the Spanish mutineers refused to march to its relief. Not until the arrival of Philip II's nephew, the archduke Albert, as his representative in the Netherlands in 1596, was there once more a clear military strategy; but he had the additional concern of an open war with France. Though he captured Calais and Ardres in 1596 and Amiens the following year, he was unable to sustain the offensive because of Philip's third bankruptcy. Even with the conclusion of the Franco-Spanish peace in 1598 (see chapter 3.3.5), the mutinies in the Habsburg army in the Low Countries continued almost as annual events until 1606, and they crippled the Spanish military effort. The war thus became a stalemate, though after the withdrawal of England from the war against Spain in 1604 there was a serious reappraisal of policy within the 'rebel' Dutch Republic. The military effort was now shouldered by the Dutch alone, which placed a much greater financial burden on the seven provinces. Nor could the continuation of a French subsidy be taken for granted. What was needed was a political initiative to break the thirty-year conflict between the provinces of the north and south (see chapter 3.4.1).

3.3 The French Wars of Religion

France's weakness after 1559 proved momentous. It enabled Philip II to pursue policies in the Low Countries after 1567 that he would not have dared contemplate in normal circumstances for fear of French retaliation. Although in a technical sense French foreign policy existed in these years, there was little substance to French diplomatic manœuvres since the king could not undertake a foreign war. It is a measure of the emasculation of French foreign policy that both Lorraine and Savoy were left free not only to pursue their own policies (and in the case of Savoy to annexe the French-held marquisate of Saluzzo in 1588), but to dabble in French domestic politics. Paradoxically, the very weakness of the monarchy increased the attractions of a French alliance to the Dutch rebels. At least until 1572, France had the most numerous, and in some respects the most influential, Calvinist church community in Europe. Since they had already confronted the moral, theological and political issues of rebellion such as preoccupied the Dutch, French political theorists exercised a formative influence on radical thought in the Netherlands. Yet whereas in Holland and Zeeland the new religion had gained ground steadily, after initial successes in France, it ultimately encountered such violent resistance that it found itself reduced in most of the realm to the status of a small and politically timid minority.

3.3.1 *The Origins of the French Religious Wars, 1559–1562*

The roots of the French Reformation were diverse. Many of its intellectual origins were to be found among French exiles at Lausanne, Strasbourg and Geneva, driven out of the country by persecution under Francis I and Henri II. In April 1559, Henri II went in person to the *Parlement* of Paris to root out heresy in the most important lawcourt of the land. There, he heard Anne du Bourg, the son of a Chancellor of France, proclaim that 'he had read some of Calvin, but not Luther' and declare it improper for the king 'to make laws concerning religious affairs'.[51] To the king, this was arrogant heresy, which suggested that the legal profession was being subverted by Calvinism. Anne du Bourg was arrested and executed the following December. In fact, Calvinism never dominated the *Parlement*, though in the 1550s, lawyers provided a number of converts to Calvinism, as did the upper nobility. Their first national synod was held illegally in France in 1559. The difficulty of their position was that the Calvinists embodied in their confession of faith an oath to obey the king; yet the king was a Catholic obliged by his coronation oath to extirpate heresy in his kingdom. However, not until 1560–1 was the Calvinist movement politicized. Nor was the term 'Huguenot', almost certainly of Swiss origin (see chapter 1.4.2), used widely before this date as being synonymous with a French Calvinist. Estimates vary greatly, but it is probable that by 1559 there were a million Huguenots, roughly one-fifteenth of the population. In 1562, Coligny claimed that there were 2,150 Protestant churches and 3 million Huguenots, but he may well have been exaggerating their strength in order to impress the regent.

Francis II was 15 at the time of his accession in July 1559, which meant that he was too young to rule in person. The control of government was in the hands of his uncles, the Guises—François, duke of Guise, and Charles of Guise, cardinal of Lorraine. Their policy is not easy to disentangle, since the advancement of the house of Lorraine went hand in hand with their support for Catholicism. Francis II was married to Mary Queen of Scots, the niece of the Guises. On the advice of his uncles, the king continued to issue repressive edicts against his Protestant subjects. The conspiracy of Amboise in the early months of 1560, a plot organized by a lesser nobleman—Jean du Barry, seigneur de la Renaudie—aimed at capturing the court for the Huguenot party and eliminating the influence of the Guise family. The weakness of the conspiracy was that support was confined to the discontented lesser nobility; it lacked firm backing from either Geneva or the great nobility in France. The first prince of the blood, Antoine of Bourbon, king of Navarre, was nominally a Calvinist, but he proved a broken reed to the Protestant cause well before his death in October 1562. His younger brother, Louis I of Bourbon, prince of Condé, was both more dynamic and more committed, but lacked Navarre's social pre-eminence. It was subsequently claimed that Condé had authorized the conspiracy of Amboise. Whatever the truth of the matter, Condé was arrested by the Guises, condemned, and might well have been executed but for the sudden death of Francis II in early December 1560. This resulted in a palace revolution. The Guises lost their predominance; since Charles IX was legally a minor, his mother, Catherine de Medici, became regent, with Navarre as lieutenant-general of the kingdom. One of the first acts of the new regime was to reprieve Condé, who returned to the council of state in March 1561.

Catherine de Medici was a remarkable woman. She was the grand-daughter of the man to whom Machiavelli had dedicated *The Prince*, and she was predisposed to place the interests of the crown above the concern for religious unity. She was both tolerant and devious. She and the Chancellor, Michel de l'Hôpital, were in agreement that the policy of repression had failed and that one of the primary causes of disturbance in the kingdom was the persecution of the Huguenots. The logic of this assessment led them to seek measures of church reform and limited toleration. To this end, a national synod (*colloque* or colloquy) was summoned to Poissy in September 1561. This alarmed Catholic zealots and the Papacy: Laínez, the Jesuit vicar-general, was dispatched to the synod with the express intention of destroying its ecumenical atmosphere. On the other hand, a hard-line Catholic such as the cardinal of Lorraine was apparently prepared to work towards religious compromise, which seems to be an admission that the monarchy itself would be threatened if the position of bishops was undermined and if Calvinist church discipline was imposed. A committee of five members of each faith produced a compromise formula which was rejected by the Sorbonne as 'not only insufficient, but captious and heretical'.[52] Even without such intransigence at home, the reconvening of the Council of Trent meant that the problem of implementing the compromise would have remained. The failure of the synod at Poissy confronted the government with the choice of enforcing the laws against heresy or of granting an edict of toleration. An assembly of notables was summoned to Saint-Germain, where the Chancellor proposed, and the majority accepted, such an edict in January 1562.

Order was breaking down in the French towns before the January edict transformed the position of the Huguenots by providing a restricted legal recognition of Protestant rights of worship. Protestant preaching in the towns by day or night was expressly prohibited, but meetings at which the faithful gathered without firearms were permitted outside town walls. In many of its clauses, the edict was staunchly Catholic in tone; but even so, the government was too weak to enforce its more tolerant clauses in the localities. At the beginning of March, the duke of Guise and his retainers came across a prayer meeting held illegally inside the town of Vassy near the duke's estate at Joinville. About thirty Huguenots were killed in the ensuing 'massacre'. When the Calvinists failed to obtain redress from the crown, hostilities commenced in April. Condé denounced the attempt of the Guises to 'place ... the queen in captivity' and to 'dispose of the kingdom at their own pleasure'. The third national synod of the reformed church, meeting at Orléans, declared Condé 'protector and defender of the house and crown of France' and enabled him to mobilize an army of some 6,000 infantry and 2,000 cavalry.[53] The Guises replied with a request to Charles IX 'neither [to] approve nor suffer in his kingdom any diversity of religion'[54]—in other words, to revoke the January edict. The Huguenot struggle for recognition had become crucially linked with a struggle for power between two opposing factions in the nobility.

3.3.2 *The First Civil War and the Apogee of Huguenot Power*

The power of the Huguenots reached its apogee during the first civil war and its aftermath. However, the weaknesses in the movement soon became all too apparent. The January edict may have deluded many new converts into believing that their cause was about to triumph, and perhaps that the younger brothers of Charles IX, or even the king himself, might abjure Catholicism when they came of age. But control of the large cities was the key to governing the country, and in them Calvinism was especially weak. The Parisian Huguenots, who, for the most part had had to meet in secret until the late 1550s, were few, although they could muster significant congregations in the rue Saint-Jacques and at the Pré-aux-Clercs. In Rouen, the second city of France, the Huguenots comprised at most 21 per cent of the population. In Lyon, the third largest city, about a third of the citizens were Calvinists, of whom the majority had been born outside the town. During the first civil war, the Huguenot minority seized control in Rouen in mid-April 1562; but its dominance ended with the capture and violent sacking of the city by royal forces in October. In Lyon, the Huguenot minority held sway longer, a full eighteen months in 1562–3. At Toulouse, however, six days of municipal insurrection in May 1562 resulted in a Catholic victory, with 200 Huguenots dead in the street fighting and over 200 executed after the rising. After 1563, it was clear that the Huguenot attempt to gain the large cities and thus to increase their political power had failed. Four years later, a Protestant coup failed at Lyon and persecution of the Calvinists recommenced.

In the eight cities with provincial *Parlements* (Paris, Toulouse, Grenoble, Bordeaux, Dijon, Rouen, Aix and Rennes), the stubborn conservative Catholicism of these institutions (despite the crypto-Calvinist convictions of some of their members, who were gradually eliminated in the 1560s) proved decisive. They opposed not only the attempted Huguenot take-over, but also the royal policy of religious compromise. The Huguenot strongholds remained, by default, small towns well away from the watchful eyes of the local *Parlement*, places such as La Rochelle (the bastion of Calvinism in France from 1568 to 1628), Montauban and Nîmes. Especially after 1572, it was such towns which organized Protestant resistance: commando raids from Nîmes and Montpellier secured control of the Cévennes. The Huguenots fought a war without rules in the Midi, attacking towns on feast-days, living off the countryside and generally settling old scores. The extent to which the new religion penetrated into the countryside was limited, and most rural areas remained nominally Catholic. Since the Huguenots frowned on traditional carnivals, fêtes, feast-days and the communal pleasures of dancing and the tavern, there was little to attract peasant converts wedded to a traditional rural culture. The support of the nobility for Calvinism should certainly not be underestimated, however. The Venetian ambassador, Michieli, commented in 1562 that 'the nobles especially are contaminated [with heresy], notably those below the age of forty'.[55] Though most of the great army commanders and the provincial governors remained Catholic, Condé's manifesto in 1562 was signed by La Rochefoucauld, Rohan, Soubise, Coligny, d'Andelot and 4,000 gentlemen of the best and most ancient houses of France'.[56] In one area of Normandy, the *élection* of Bayeux, 40 per cent of the gentry were Protestant in the 1560s, although this number had fallen to about 13 per cent by 1597. Nevertheless, with the exception of the battle of Dreux in December 1562, the Catholic army nearly always comprised a higher number of cavalry (and thus presumably nobles) than the Huguenots, as well as a larger number of foreign mercenaries.

Why so many nobles joined the Protestant cause in the 1560s must remain largely a matter of conjecture, since few left any record of their motives. The great essayist Montaigne was by nature sceptical of the power of religion over men. 'Let us confess the truth', he wrote, that 'those who take up arms out of pure zeal [for] religion' could hardly make up 'one complete company of *gens d'armes*'.[57] Montaigne's scepticism was echoed over seventy years ago by the historian Romier, who argued that the Huguenot nobility had little understanding of doctrinal Calvinism and that their association with the movement was essentially a means of restoring their own status and wealth. Calvinist propaganda was specifically aimed at the French nobility and it used political rather than doctrinal arguments—as for example in François Hotman's *Letter to the Tiger of France* (1560),[58] a justification of the Conspiracy of Amboise and a sustained attack on the Guises which was written to enlist the support of provincial gentry. The propaganda met with some success, not least because dissatisfaction with royal policy and hostility to the wealth of the church were rife among some sections of the nobility. These views were expressed by the baron de Rochefort, the spokesman of the second estate (the nobles), in an important speech to the Estates General of 1560. He attacked recent ennoblements and maintained that noble privileges were 'as ancient as the monarchy itself'.[59] Rochefort asserted that the scandalous wealth of the church had been acquired at the expense of the nobility, who by ancient privilege had the right to worship as they pleased. Hostility to the church may have been reinforced in some areas by the hope of seizing church lands, an idea put forward by the nobility of Languedoc as early as 1561. A royal minority, following the rule of two strong kings, would naturally create a power vacuum in which the nobility enjoyed a greater degree of independence than in the previous generation. The progress of Calvinism was aided both by a weak monarchy and the royal bankruptcy of 1559, which suddenly deprived provincial governors of their normal supply of pensions and gifts and gravely weakened their clientage network. Some local Calvinist communities may actually have bribed nobles to become their 'protectors' at the precise moment that hard-line Catholic governors felt their authority to be undermined by the regency government's policy of limited toleration.

In the first civil war, the Huguenots failed to win a decisive military advantage, while their negotiating position was gravely compromised by Condé's treaty with England, signed in September 1562. Elizabeth I was too weak to offer the Huguenots any significant military assistance, but

Condé's invitation to France's traditional enemy to intervene in the war appeared treasonable. The iconoclastic riots of the Calvinists, and the excesses of some of their commanders, notably the baron des Adrets, who sacked Lyon at the end of April 1562, alienated potential support. François, duke of Guise, was assassinated in February 1563 by a Huguenot, who declared under torture that Coligny, one of the Huguenot leaders, had authorized his mission. Coligny denied the charge and was acquitted; but he did not conceal his view that the assassination was 'the best thing that could happen to this kingdom and to the church of God'.[60] He was wrong, because vendettas among the upper nobility helped to prolong the civil wars. On the other hand, the elimination of Guise, and the capture of Condé and Montmorency by the opposing armies, paved the way for a truce negotiated by Catherine de Medici in March 1563, the first of the 'edicts of pacification' which terminated each of the nine civil wars. The Edict of Amboise reflected the relatively stronger position of the crown. The nobility gained the right to hold Protestant services in their homes; but for everyone else, services were restricted to the suburbs of one town in each lesser judicial area (*bailliage* or *sénéchaussée*). By resorting to arms, the Huguenots had gained a restriction, not an extension, of their rights; and for this reason alone the truce was unlikely to become a permanent peace.

3.3.3 *From the Peace of Amboise to the St Bartholomew Massacres, 1563–1572*

Catherine de Medici's formal power as regent came to an end in August 1563 with the proclamation of Charles IX's majority. But the king was still a boy of 13 and took little part in affairs of state before 1570. Real power remained with the queen mother, who took her son on a grand tour of France in 1564–5 in the hope of pacifying the kingdom. This culminated in the ill-advised meeting with the duke of Alba at Bayonne in June 1565. According to Alba, the idea was formulated there of eliminating five or six Huguenot leaders. News of this 'interview' aroused Protestant fears of a return to the repressive policies of Henri II and the revocation of the Edict of Amboise. In an attempt to prevent this about-turn in royal policy, the Huguenot leaders tried to seize the queen mother and Charles IX at Meaux in September 1567. The coup misfired, but precipitated a second civil war. Condé was once again the leader of the revolt; his manifesto on this occasion was much more extreme, since he proclaimed the French monarchy to be 'limited from its origins by the authority of the nobility and the communities of the provinces and the great towns of the kingdom'.[61] By October, his negotiating terms had risen to include the free exercise of Calvinism throughout the kingdom, the expulsion of

Catherine's Italian entourage, the abolition of taxes imposed since the reign of Louis XII, and the assigning of four fortresses (*places de sûreté*) for the Huguenots. By March 1568, however, after the failure of his blockade of Paris, and the withdrawal of German mercenaries under the Calvinist John Casimir of the Palatinate, Condé was prepared to settle for less—the renewal of the Edict of Amboise.

The 'little peace' of Longjumeau only lasted from March to August 1568. Catherine de Medici could not easily forgive the attempted Protestant coup the previous year, and she inclined towards the policy of the cardinal of Lorraine, which was to eliminate the Huguenot leaders. The third civil war began with the attempted arrest of Condé and Coligny, who escaped to the security of La Rochelle in September after a hazardous four-week journey. The war was much more destructive than its two predecessors, and went badly for the Protestants. In March 1569, their army was routed at Jarnac and Condé died afterwards from his wounds. In October, Coligny's forces were defeated at Moncontour. Though the Huguenots were now on the defensive, the negotiations for a new truce were not altogether against their interests, for the Catholic extremists, Henri, duke of Guise, and the cardinal of Lorraine, were in disgrace as a result of a shift in the political balance between the factions at court which probably resulted from Guise's ambition to marry Marguerite, the king's sister. The Treaty of Saint-Germain of August 1570 restored Protestant rights of worship and permitted the fortress towns of La Rochelle, Montauban, Cognac and La Charité to be garrisoned by them for two years. The Huguenots thus gained less extensive privileges than under the edict of 1562, but with a new guarantee of security provided by the *places de sûreté*.

Between August 1570 and August 1572, there was a serious attempt at reconciliation between the crown and the Huguenot leaders. The first authorized national synod was held at La Rochelle in April 1571, the so-called 'synod of the princes'. It was attended by Jeanne d'Albret, queen of Navarre, her son Henri of Navarre, Henri of Bourbon, prince of Condé, Coligny, Louis of Nassau and 'divers other lords and gentlemen' who signed the resulting confessions of faith. The corner-stone of the reconciliation with the crown was the projected marriage between Henri of Navarre, the first prince of the blood, and Marguerite of Valois, Charles IX's sister. This eventually took place in 1572, but it proved an ill-fated union (it was dissolved twenty-seven years later). Coligny returned to court in September 1571 to press the idea of a French invasion of the Netherlands in support of William of Orange. Since the kingdom was in no position to contemplate war with Spain, which would have been the inevitable result of such an action, he became increasingly isolated. A number of Protestant noblemen, including Coligny, had gathered at Paris for the marriage of Navarre on 18 August 1572. On the morning of 22 August, Coligny survived an assassination attempt in which Catherine de Medici and the king's brother, Anjou, the future Henri III, were probably implicated. The following evening, Charles IX ordered the murder of a selected number of Protestant noblemen, including Coligny. The possibility that the revelation of the 22 August plot would compromise members of his family, combined with the advice of the king's council, forced him to accept the proposal to eliminate the Huguenot leaders, a proposal which perhaps originated with the queen mother. There seems little doubt that the king actively supported the massacres once he had given his consent. It was the royal guards, under the command of Anjou (and with the participation of Guise himself) who murdered Coligny. Within four days of the massacre, the king held a special session (*lit de justice*) of the *Parlement* of Paris, where he assumed full responsibility for what had happened, and issued a royal declaration which stated that the events had taken place to prevent a plot instigated by Coligny.

Catholic extremists at court, and in the Parisian municipality, distorted the king's orders into a call for a general massacre, known subsequently as the St Bartholomew massacre. In the provinces, news of events in the capital was all the encouragement the Catholics needed. The massacres were seen by Catholics as a miraculous escape from Protestant tutelage, and indeed miraculous occurrences seemed to follow the events. After almost every conceivable act of bestiality had been inflicted upon Coligny's corpse, Parisians went on 'pilgrimage' to see displayed the last remains of the feared Huguenot leader who, Catholics alleged (in the queen mother's words), had sought to subvert the state and to deprive the king of his throne.[62]

Even by the standard of atrocities in the French wars of religion, the manner and extent of the violence in the following two months was grotesque. Estimates vary greatly, but some historians put the figure for massacred Huguenots as high as 3,000 for Paris and 10,000 for the rest of France. It was certainly a murderous act of revenge for ten years of attempted Huguenot supremacy. The young princes, Navarre and Condé, were forced to abjure to save their lives and they were kept under house arrest. Without clear leadership, the strengths of the Calvinist movement were rapidly dissipated. The sense of despair at the turn in royal policy was evidenced in a series of radical pamphlets justifying the right of resistance to the sovereign and even tyrannicide (see chapter 6.1.2), though it is doubtful whether the majority of the Huguenots rejected monarchical authority as such. Perhaps even more important was the wave of defections from the Protestant cause, which as Beza noted in December 1572, 'has been and continues to be incredible'.[63] Despondency and disillusion, rather than forced conversions, account for the permanent decline in Calvinist support after 1572. All the high hopes of the 1560s were dashed, and many Huguenots must have decided that conformity or emigration was preferable to a dangerous life in the service of a lost cause. The reduced number of committed Huguenots nevertheless remained a formidable political and military obstacle to the French crown in the Midi. There, they resolved 'never [to] trust those who have so often and so treacherously broken faith and the public peace; never [to] disarm as long as the enemy continues to oppose the true faith and those who profess it; and [to] sign no peace treaties that can be used to start massacres'.[64]

3.3.4   *The Reign of Henri III to 1585*

The St Bartholomew massacres precipitated the fourth civil war. Although it was ended by the Truce of La Rochelle in July 1573, Charles IX never regained firm control of his kingdom. His death in May 1574 did not bring about any sudden political or religious compromise. Anjou, proclaimed king Henri III while he was absent in Poland (where he had been elected king the previous year), was a notorious Catholic extremist. One of the paradoxes of Henri III's reign, however, is the contrast between the behaviour of his youth and his policy as king. His religious convictions never wavered, indeed his fervent devotion exceeded that of all other sixteenth-century kings of France. Yet though he founded oratories and confraternities and indulged in self-flagellation, his Catholic subjects did not find his religious commitment reassuring. The single most important reason for the collapse of Henri III's credibility was his failure to mount an effective campaign against the Huguenots, despite increasing the burden of taxation ostensibly for military purposes. He was faced by an alliance of the opposition—the Huguenot party under Condé (who had escaped from prison and after returning to his Calvinist faith became its 'governor-general and protector' during Navarre's imprisonment) and the Catholic Malcontents, the most prominent of whom were Alençon, the king's younger brother, and Montmorency-Damville, the governor of Languedoc. In September 1575, Alençon escaped from court, and mobilized these combined forces, which were soon reinforced by the arrival of German mercenaries again under the leadership of John Casimir of the Palatinate. The opposition was greatly strengthened by Navarre's escape from court in February 1576 and his assumption of the Huguenot leadership.

The Peace of Monsieur of May 1576 reflected the strength of the combined opposition. It was a disastrous capitulation by Henri III. Alençon was renamed duke of Anjou and acquired an apanage in Anjou, Touraine and Berry: had he married and produced a male heir, he would have been in a strong position to found a collateral dynasty to challenge the main Valois line. His Catholic Malcontent supporters were confirmed in their governorships and offices. Condé and Navarre were restored to their respective governorships of Picardy and Guyenne (where some thought that Navarre was actually king, so great was his power). The Huguenot party won eight fortresses and the posthumuous rehabilitation of Coligny and other leaders massacred in 1572. Calvinists were accorded the right to hold royal offices, and their position was safeguarded by the establishment of 'mixed tribunals' (*chambres mi-parties*) in the *Parlements*, containing Protestant as well as Catholic judges. There was little prospect that the terms of the peace would or could be implemented, and indeed the king's motives in accepting them are open to question: by December 1576, he was seeking the advice of the Estates General, meeting at Blois, on the means of establishing one religion in France. But in agreeing to the Peace of Monsieur, the king had not foreseen the strength of Catholic opposition throughout the kingdom to his concessions to the Protestants. The formation of local Catholic leagues and associations under the control of the provincial governors had been commonplace in the 1560s and early 1570s. The League of 1576 was much more extensive, and a greater threat to the monarchy.

It was apparently started by a local nobleman in Picardy, who refused to follow the terms of the Peace of Monsieur and hand over his town of Péronne to Condé, or allow Protestant services to be held there. The members of the League—in reality, an unspecified number of provincial associations—swore, at the peril of eternal damnation, to provide arms and men in the service of their leader, who was doubtless to be Henri, duke of Guise. There was a specious pretence of loyalty to the crown, but the League brought proposals before the Estates General at the end of November 1576, which implied that the monarchy was elective. These proposals were discussed and rejected by the king, who replied by substituting himself as head of the League in a perfunctory six-month war against the Huguenots in 1577. In the following truce, all leagues, including Catholic ones, were prohibited. The king also restricted somewhat the gains made by the Huguenots the preceding year. These measures were not enough to prevent the drift towards anarchy. The growing evidence of extravagance in Henri III's court and the monopoly of patronage and favour gained by his favourites (*mignons*) simply accentuated it. Two of the king's favourites, Joyeuse and d'Épernon, were Catholic, but they incurred the wrath of the French nobility, most notably the Guises, by securing provincial governorships which they regarded as their own property. Indeed, the king may have tried to counterbalance the power of Guise and his supporters by deliberately promoting his favourites: d'Épernon was given Metz, Toul and Verdun to check the pretensions of Guise in Champagne and to restrict his association with his cousin, duke Charles III of Lorraine.

There was a temporary lull in the fighting after 1580, but any hopes of stability or even reform were dashed by the sudden death of Anjou in June 1584, which left the Protestant Henri of Navarre heir presumptive. This was the unambiguous cause for which Guise, who had retired from the court in 1578, had been waiting. It also presented Philip II with a reliable and powerful supporter in France. By the secret Treaty of Joinville, signed at Guise's country residence on the last day of 1584, Philip II undertook to pay a new Catholic League 50,000 crowns a month while it made war in France to extirpate heresy and secure the succession for the cardinal of Bourbon. Since Cardinal Charles of Bourbon was an ageing political nonentity, he would have been under the thumb of Guise; moreover, he would not have been able to produce a legitimate male heir, so that in effect the monarchy would have become elective. The Treaty of Joinville timed a rebellion of the Catholic League for the first week of April 1585. A manifesto, apparently written by the Jesuit Claude Matthieu, was issued at Péronne, denouncing the power of Joyeuse and d'Épernon, demanding the abolition of taxes imposed since Henri III's accession, and calling for the restoration of power to the nobility and the *Parlements*. Early in July 1585, Henri III again capitulated to what he saw as the overwhelming forces of the opposition. By the terms of the Treaty of Nemours, the king not only offered an amnesty to the rebels, but revoked the previous edicts of pacification, prohibited Calvinist worship, abolished the 'mixed tribunals' and withdrew Huguenot rights to the fortified towns. No Protestant was to be eligible for royal offices. Yet Henri III did not concede the crucial point of recognizing the cardinal of Bourbon as heir presumptive. On the contrary, he remained committed to Navarre's abjuration and succession to the throne. This conflict between Henri III and Guise, and the king's continuing opposition to the League, were temporarily obscured by the Papal bull of excommunication issued in September 1585, which sought to exclude Navarre and Condé from the succession. In an uncharacteristically vehement manifesto, issued at the end of November 1585, Navarre denounced the 'tyranny and usurpation' of the Pope and the League and declared a 'perpetual and irreconcilable war' to secure his rights and those of his religion.[65] The French wars of religion had become in addition a war of Bourbon succession and a war against Spanish intervention. This explains why the ninth and final war lasted twelve years, longer than all the others.

3.3.5 *The War of the Bourbon Succession*

The 'war of the three Henris' (Henri III, Guise and Navarre) in 1585–8 proved indecisive. By the end of 1587, the king's prestige had sunk dismally, while the star of Guise and the League was in the ascendant. During the early months of 1588, there was growing agitation in Paris, fanned by the fanatical preaching of the Parisian (Catholic) *curés*, and the formation of a radical grouping known as the Council of Sixteen, possibly manipulated in the Habsburg interest by Mendoza, the Spanish ambassador. (There were never precisely sixteen in the group. The name was acquired from the committees of public security established in each of the sixteen *quartiers* of Paris after the assassination of the Guises in December 1588: see chapter 7.5.2.) In May 1588, Guise defied the king's orders and entered the capital. Barricades were set up in the streets of Paris by the mob, and the king and his Swiss guards were forced to seek refuge at Chartres. The League drew up a new manifesto, and the king agreed to some of its conditions in an 'edict of union [of Catholics]', regarded by the League as a new fundamental law of the kingdom. In addition, Guise was raised to the position of lieutenant-general of the realm, and the Estates General was summoned to meet at Blois in October. Despite the blandishments of Guise to encourage the Estates General to vote a significant sum of taxes for the war against the Huguenots, the outcome was no more than a derisory sum for this purpose. By December, the king's patience was exhausted with what he considered to be Guise's duplicity. On 23 December, Guise was summoned to Henri III's chambers and hacked to death by the royal guards. His brother, Louis of Lorraine, cardinal of Guise, was imprisoned and murdered the following day. Other leaders of the League were rounded up in the purge. To the extent that the coup had been intended to rid Henri III of the Guises, it achieved its purpose. However, if the king had hoped to regain control of his kingdom, the plan misfired badly. The last of the Valois clearly underestimated the prestige of his victims and the power exercised by the numerous oaths of association that had followed the edict of union in July 1588. Most of the towns and lawcourts north of the river Loire sided with the League, while there were more isolated pockets of resistance to the king further south, for example in Toulouse and Marseille. A number of provincial governors sided with the movement, of whom the most important was Charles of Lorraine, duke of Mayenne. Mayenne was Guise's younger brother and had escaped the purge because he had not attended the Estates General at Blois. He was also governor of Burgundy and he became the effective leader of the aristocratic wing of the rebellion, appropriating his brother's title of lieutenant-general of the kingdom.

Virtually all the theorists and supporters of the League argued, after the assassination of the Guises, that tyrannicide was permissible against Henri III, who was deemed 'unworthy not only of the crown, but unworthy of life'.[66] Matters were made worse when the king, in order to blockade Paris, threw in his lot with Navarre at the end of April 1589. Already, early in

January 1589, the Sorbonne had pronounced Henri III deposed; the alliance between the two Henris appeared to justify their fears that the king had connived at an attempted Protestant usurpation of the monarchy. Mayenne's power was used ostensibly to promote the claims of the cardinal of Bourbon to the French throne. Fortunately for the king and Navarre, 'Charles X of the League' remained in captivity until his death in May 1590. But it was hardly surprising that Henri III's deep unpopularity led to his assassination by the Dominican Jacques Clément at the beginning of August. On his deathbed, Henri III recognized Navarre as his heir, though with the proviso that the new king return to Catholicism. The great majority of Catholics, however, opposed Henri IV's accession and followed the lead of the *Parlement* of Paris in recognizing Charles X. Some of Henri III's supporters came to terms with the new king in August 1589, but their numbers remained few before 1593.

For four years, Henri IV was the most famous Protestant prince in Europe, on whom rested the hopes of the Calvinist cause. Yet his position was decidedly weak. Even his Protestant supporters were divided, some fearing that the king would endanger the existence of the Huguenot party to secure his throne. The king thus tried to maintain a delicate balancing act of retaining the loyalty of Protestants while seeking to attract moderate Catholic opinion. He was assisted by loans from abroad, particularly from England, the Dutch rebels, certain German princes and towns, and most of the Swiss cantons. But as the military stalemate in the war against the League became protracted, the foreign allies demanded repayment of their loans and grew less generous in their support. Deprived of foreign loans by 1593, the king had to compromise with his Catholic subjects. By May 1593, during the conference of Suresnes with representatives of the League, Henri agreed to receive instruction in the Catholic faith. The failure of the Estates General of the League to elect a Catholic alternative to Henri IV as king, and the six months' truce commencing at the end of July provided the ideal timing for his abjuration: Henri's symbolic Mass at Saint-Denis preceded the truce by only five days.

With the expiry of the truce at the beginning of 1594, the prospects of a victory for the League receded. Its cause now rested on the argument that the king's conversion was insincere. The Pope alone could determine the validity of the abjuration, and his views—which turned out to be favourable to Henri IV—were not known until November 1595. The League's attitude was incomprehensible to some, and offended the Gallican and patriotic sentiments of many, who argued that the Gallican church was competent to receive the king with or without Papal confirmation. This contrasts with the Gallican position in the 1580s. Then, there had been hostility to the Papal bull excommunicating Henri, but it was difficult for Gallicans to maintain consistent opposition to the League because of their vision of a united Catholic France. War-weariness was a trump card in Henri IV's hand. Nevertheless, his victory would have proved still more difficult had the League not dissipated its strength through its own divisions. The split between the aristocratic leadership and radical groups in the towns was of crucial importance. At both Toulouse and Paris in 1591, the radicals had attempted to purge the conservative leadership in the *Parlements* by using mob violence. This prompted an aristocratic reaction, led by Mayenne, who arrested some of the more prominent radicals, and by 1594 the local military and financial command of the League had disintegrated into faction-fighting, with the oligarchies in the towns and the office-holders ready to transfer their allegiance to the Bourbon claimant in the belief that he was the only candidate likely to secure civil peace and bring about an improvement in their lot. Moreover, from July 1590 the League had become fatally dependent on Spanish military and financial assistance. Twice in 1590–2, Parma's army was ordered by Philip II to invade from the Netherlands, and it helped to save the beleaguered cities of Paris and Rouen. Yet Parma won no great victories for the League, and in 1593 increased Spanish assistance was made contingent on acceptance of the claim of Isabella, Philip's daughter, to the throne through the right of descent from her mother, Elizabeth of Valois. Philip II was determined to exclude the house of Bourbon from the throne of France; and if his daughter's claim failed, he would settle for an alternative (preferably Habsburg) candidate. The Estates General of the League was faced in 1593 with a multiplicity of candidates and proved unable to make a decision. The Infanta's claim was wrecked by the pronouncement of the *Parlement* of Paris that the Salic Law was a fundamental law of the kingdom, a pronouncement which had the effect of supporting Henri IV's succession, since his claim was thought to be based on this law.

There were many reasons why support for the League was beginning to decline by 1594; nevertheless, the king exploited his opportunity with consummate skill, by offering to meet the demands of dissident supporters of the League among the towns and the nobility. By the late spring of 1594, Meaux, Lyon, Paris and Rouen had fallen to him, and further gains were made by the end of the year. The declaration of open war on Spain in mid-January 1595 was a gamble on the willingness of Frenchmen to sink their differences in the common cause: Henri stated that 'one must be either a Frenchman or a Spaniard'.[67] The gamble met with success. Once the Pope pronounced on the validity of Henri's abjuration, Mayenne, Nemours and Joyeuse all made their peace with the king in January 1596. Only the duke of Mercoeur, bolstered by support from Spain, held out in Brittany as the last outpost of the League until March 1598.

It is sometimes claimed that Henri's victory was achieved for him by a moderate Catholic *politique* party, dedicated to preserving the territorial integrity of the French state and the undivided sovereignty of the crown. It is not difficult to find *politiques* who in the circumstances of the 1590s made individual decisions to join the king for such reasons. Yet there was no *politique* party as such, and certainly no middle ground between the Huguenots and the Catholic League. The League won in the sense that it obtained a Catholic king for France. It lost decisively in that no new law of Catholicity was extracted from him. Reluctantly, because as a convert to the Catholic religion, Henri wished to see France united in one faith, he made concessions to his erstwhile Huguenot supporters at Nantes in April and May 1598 which restored many of the privileges revoked in 1585. The edict conveyed rights of worship somewhat broader than those allowed in 1577, with the château of the local Huguenot magnate confirmed as the focus of Protestant worship. Secularized ecclesiastical property was to be returned by the Protestants, who in turn were to be allowed to enter royal, seigneurial and municipal offices. The 'mixed tribunals' to hear Protestant cases were re-established. In addition, there were secret articles which allowed the Huguenots to retain for eight years (a period subsequently extended) all towns and fortresses in their possession in August 1597, and permitted them a religious organization of consistories, synods and colloquies. Two additional documents assigned an annual subsidy to the Huguenots for the upkeep of their garrisons, which amounted on paper to 675,000 *livres* per annum, though it is doubtful whether as much as this was ever paid in a single year. The edict was no guarantee that the king would not change his mind, however. Only the public part of the settlement—the edict itself—was registered in the *Parlements*, and then with the greatest difficulty. At Paris, Henri had to appear before the *Parlement* in January 1599, reminding the office-holders that he had 'established the state' and that they owed their positions to his victory over the League,[68] before they would accept the edict. Nevertheless, the *Parlement* of Rouen resisted the king until 1609. Even with registration, there was no cast-iron security that a subsequent ruler would not modify the supposedly 'perpetual and irrevocable edict' and this is what happened under Louis XIII in 1629.

The settlement of Nantes could not heal divisions in French society which had lasted for forty years. It was not a permanent solution, because it depended on the will of the king, while the majority of Frenchmen remained Catholic and regarded it as a temporary arrangement to secure peace. The Huguenots continued to distrust a king who had abandoned their faith and against whom they had had to rebel in 1597 to secure the concessions ratified subsequently at Nantes. There remained anxiety about the succession: Jean Châtel nearly assassinated the king in 1594;

two years later, a pretender to the throne calling himself François de Valois, who alleged that he was a previously unknown son of Charles IX, had been executed; Henri had no legitimate heir until 1601 and it was not until the birth of the future Louis XIII that the war of the Bourbon succession could with certainty be said to have been won. These difficulties, combined with the fear of a new Protestant rising, may well have induced Henri IV to adopt a cautious foreign policy in the years after 1598: but war-weariness in France meant that peace itself was worth the purchase. Henri did not break the compromise treaty patched up with Spain at Vervins in May 1598.

3.4 The New Threat to Peace, 1598–1618

The cessation of hostilities after the short war between Spain and France in 1595–8 could not mask the real intention of Henri IV. This was to keep the Spanish and Austrian Habsburgs weak, preferably without recourse to open war against them. It may be an exaggeration to claim, as did his finance minister, the duke of Sully, that the king had a 'grand design' to support the Protestant cause in Europe. Sully was a minority voice in the king's council, and the Catholic ministers clearly promoted a policy of coexistence with the Habsburgs. However, the king mobilized three times, against Savoy in 1600–1, against the duke of Bouillon in 1606, and to intervene in the Cleves–Jülich succession crisis in 1609–10. On the first and last occasions, his actions could have resulted in war with Spain. The extent of his commitment to the Protestant cause at the end of his reign will never be clear because he was assassinated in May 1610 before his military plans had been fully revealed. It was an open question, however, whether the most serious international conflict was likely to arise from the latent hostility between France and Spain, or rather from the collapse of Imperial institutions which might draw other international powers into a German conflict, as in 1609–10. The threat to peace within the Empire after 1608 coincided with a prolonged crisis in the Austrian Habsburg hereditary lands, which gravely compromised any chance of an Imperial initiative to ease the growing tension. There was also serious instability in Italy. Two successive governors of Milan fought duke Charles-Emmanuel of Savoy over the future of the Mantuan succession in 1613–17. Venice was embroiled in a war with Ferdinand of Styria in 1615–17 to expel the Greek Orthodox refugees (*Uskoks*) established at Segna, because they had been engaged in acts of piracy on Venetian shipping. On the other hand, one great conflict appeared to have reached a temporary settlement, the struggle between Spain and the Dutch Republic, which had come to involve several European powers.

3.4.1 *Spain, the Dutch Republic and the Conclusion of the Twelve Years' Truce*

Just four days after the Peace of Vervins in May 1598, Philip II agreed to an autonomy plan for the Spanish Netherlands. This provided for the marriage of archduke Albert to Philip's favourite daughter, Isabella. Together, they would run the Spanish Netherlands with some degree of independence in their lifetime, although during wartime emergencies Spanish interests had to predominate. If they died without children, the southern provinces were immediately to revert to Spain. On his own initiative in March 1607, Albert concluded a cease-fire with the Dutch, which contained a conditional recognition of Dutch sovereignty—an enormous concession of principle. The Spanish government was furious, and refused to ratify the terms of the truce, threatening to depose the archduke. However, Albert was supported by Ambrogio Spínola, the great general sent from Spain to supplant him, but who had come to share Albert's view that the costly war was disadvantageous to Spanish Habsburg interests. Another large-scale mutiny among the Spanish troops the previous year had convinced them of the need for peace. Sieges had turned campaigning in the Low Countries into a war of attrition with small prospects of outright victory. Philip III and his chief minister, Lerma, wanted a peace, not a truce. Lerma proposed to barter Dutch political and religious independence for an end to Dutch commercial expansion. The Dutch had proved extremely successful in the Far East, and had besieged Malacca in 1605; they also proposed to form a West India Company to attack Portuguese interests in Brazil, which were controlled by Spain after the union of Portugal with Spain in 1580. Lerma wanted to disengage from the costly conflict in northern Europe in order to concentrate on the Mediterranean, the traditional centre of Spanish foreign policy. As in the 1560s, this policy coincided with a drive against the Moriscos—indeed, the Moriscos were expelled from the Spanish kingdoms on the same day as the signature of the truce with the Dutch.

The Dutch were bitterly divided on what to do in view of the apparent Spanish willingness to compromise. After failing to recover the southern provinces in 1600, a degree of personal bitterness had soured relations between Oldenbarnevelt, the advocate of Holland, and Maurice of Nassau, the captain-general and stadholder in five provinces. Maurice regarded truce negotiations as a stalling tactic by Spain, and one moreover which would reopen the question of sovereignty and thus possible Dutch subjection to Philip III. He was supported by strong commercial interests which favoured war. This party was led by Reynier Pauw, one of the four burgomasters of Amsterdam, representing the West Indies traders, who wanted to form their own company on the model of the East India

Company set up in March 1602. The strength of these commercial interests made it impossible for Oldenbarnevelt to negotiate a permanent peace with Spain, though he managed to defer the establishment of a Dutch West India Company. Even the negotiation of a truce was difficult to achieve; clause nine of the Union of Utrecht had envisaged unanimous decisions in the declaration of war, the conclusion of a truce or a peace, and the imposition of general financial burdens. In practice, three provinces tended to favour war and accept its consequent financial burden (Zeeland, Friesland and Groningen), while another three tended to be more pacific (Utrecht, Gelderland and Overijssel). This left the final decision with Holland, the seventh province, which was politically and economically predominant. Because of its constitution (the towns of Holland had eighteen votes in the provincial states, while the nobility had only one vote), a decision for war or, in the circumstances of 1606–9, a truce, became a conflict between the towns of Holland. In the protracted negotiations, Oldenbarnevelt's view eventually prevailed that a truce was a safer state of affairs than the prosecution of war, and that by the time the truce expired, Spain might well have come to accept the permanent loss of sovereignty over the northern provinces.

Oldenbarnevelt's hand was strengthened by Franco-Dutch and Anglo-Dutch defensive leagues signed in the course of 1608. But he was unable to gain Spanish acceptance of his original suggestion of a twenty-five-year truce. When the bartering commenced, the Dutch had already reduced their proposal to a more realistic one of fifteen years; the Spanish countered with ten years, and the twelve-year truce signed in April 1609 was the compromise the parties reached. The historian Geyl called it an 'astonishing victory' for the United Provinces. The Dutch gave up no territory, nor did they accept the principle of exclusion from Spanish colonial possessions. Yet in return, they gained a temporary cessation of hostilities and *de facto* independence, since Philip III and the 'archdukes' Albert and Isabella considered them 'free lands, provinces and states, against whom they make no claims ...'[69] However, this recognition of Dutch sovereignty was not *de jure*, since it lasted only for the duration of the truce, and there were residual doubts about Spanish intentions once the truce expired in April 1621. In the meantime, the blockade of the river Scheldt continued—as it had done since Leicester's time as governor-general—and Antwerp was doomed to remain in economic decline.

3.4.2 *Arminianism and the Fall of Oldenbarnevelt, 1609–1618*

Maurice of Nassau and his supporters resigned themselves to the truce, since the attempt to undermine it would have split the Dutch Republic. However, the defeat of their policy intensified their personal hostility towards Oldenbarnevelt and the political and religious principles he personified. The truce with Spain permitted the Dutch the luxury of domestic conflict. By 1618, it brought the country to the verge of civil war. The main issue was Oldenbarnevelt's attempt to settle the church disputes in the Netherlands by maintaining the authority of the States General and the states of Holland, while checking the efforts of the orthodox Calvinists, led by Franciscus Gomarus, to brand as heretics those who recognized the validity of the teaching of Jacobus Arminius (see chapter 1.4.3). After the death of Arminius in 1609, his followers, led by Johannes Uyttenbogaert, adopted even more extreme positions in the Remonstrance of January 1610 'for the revision of the confession and the catechism'.[70] Within two months, six theologians had drawn up a Counter-Remonstrance and a lively pamphlet war ensued. To Maurice of Nassau, to be a Remonstrant implied 'going over to Spain'; indeed, one of the Counter-Remonstrant pamphlets was entitled *Furtherance of the Spanish Plan* and specifically criticized the truce. The religious conflict thus became deeply embroiled with the issue of ultimate political control. Maurice subsequently claimed that Oldenbarnevelt had 'been trying to introduce another form of government, which would have destroyed the church and the republic . . .'[71] Maurice secured the summoning of a national synod in June 1617 on the votes of only four provinces in the States General, with Holland, Utrecht and Overijssel in opposition. In July 1618, a committee 'for the common good' was set up to investigate alleged 'sinister practices . . . in direct conflict with the Union [of Utrecht]'.[72] This decision resulted in Oldenbarnevelt's arrest, which flouted Holland's privileges because of his office as advocate to the provincial states, and established the States General as his judges.

The national synod was opened at Dordrecht (Dort) in November 1618. Besides the Dutch churches, nearly all the foreign Calvinist communities were represented, with the exception of the French. From the start, the synod was predisposed to the Counter-Remonstrant position. The trial of Oldenbarnevelt by the civil authorities and the condemnation of Arminianism by the synod proceeded at the same pace. In May 1619, the decrees of the national synod were read out, with the condemnation of the Remonstrants forming an appendix. Three days later, Oldenbarnevelt was found guilty and the death sentence was passed. He complained that his trial had been illegal, that his views had been misrepresented, and above all that the trial had no validity because of the sovereignty of the province of Holland. His complaints were in vain, and within the week Oldenbarnevelt was executed. It is doubtful whether he had committed any offence which merited a death sentence, but he had certainly alienated Maurice and his supporters, who feared that the Remonstrant church community might become the focus of a rebellious political party.

Maurice could not safely leave imprisoned a man who might be restored to power at a later date. When Maurice died in 1625, his younger brother Frederick Henry became captain-general and proved more sympathetic to Arminianism, though it never became a majority faith in the Low Countries.

3.4.3 *Towards a German Conflict: the Cleves–Jülich Succession Crisis, 1609–1614*

The Emperor Ferdinand I and his son Maximilian II, who succeeded to the Imperial title in 1564, had been moderate Catholics. Rudolf II was in many respects the reverse, and his accession in 1576 coincided with a new determination among the Catholics to enforce their interpretation of the contested clauses in the Peace of Augsburg of 1555 at the Imperial diet, where they held a majority. The spread of Calvinism in the Empire and the Austrian hereditary lands had exposed the fragility of that settlement. It acted as a stimulus to a vigorous Catholic counter-offensive, based initially on Bavaria. Gebhard Truchsess von Waldburg, electoral arch-bishop of Cologne, abjured in 1582. Had Cologne become Protestant, the whole Catholic position on the lower Rhine would have been jeopardized and the Protestants would, moreover, have gained a majority in the electoral college. Pope Gregory XIII deposed Truchsess in 1583; Bavarian and Spanish troops thereupon invaded the territory and defeated him. As a result of this action, members of the Wittelsbach family retained the electorate of Cologne from 1583 to 1761. More importantly, much of north-west Germany became secure for Catholicism, because Ernst, the first Wittelsbach archbishop, also held the sees of Liège, Freising, Hildesheim and Münster.

The achievement, however, rested on the recognition that Spain, Bavaria and the Papacy shared common interests. Rudolf II's role had been minimal, and his lack of commitment to the implementation of Catholic policy in Germany was symbolized by his shifting the seat of government from Vienna to Prague after 1583. At the same time, the Imperial institutions were allowed to decay at an alarming rate. After 1588, the annual commission charged with the final revision of sentences of the Imperial chamber court (*Reichskammergericht*) was no longer summoned because the Protestant administrator of the archbishopric of Magdeburg, which had been reformed after 1555, would have sat on it. In 1598 an interim committee of the Imperial diet was given a similar task, but the Protestants withdrew from it within three years.

In the meantime, the Protestants were given conclusive examples of Catholic determination to oppose the secularization of church property after 1552, and to deny Protestant coexistence in the free cities. The restoration of exclusive Catholic rule in Aachen in 1598, where Protestantism had been tolerated since 1581, was based on a decision of the Imperial aulic council (*Reichshofrat*, the personal court of the Emperor) and put into effect by Spanish troops. In 1607, duke Maximilian I of Bavaria seized the free city of Donauwörth, on the basis of another decision of the Imperial aulic council. Although the Lutherans were in the majority, Maximilian nevertheless transformed the city into a Catholic and Wittelsbach possession. At the Imperial diet of Regensburg in 1608, the Protestants demanded the confirmation of the Peace of Augsburg. The Catholic party offered to renew the peace, provided that all church possessions secularized since 1552 were returned. Cases concerning the restitution of property were to be brought before the Imperial aulic council, precisely that court whose jurisdiction was most fiercely contested by the Calvinists because it was under the closest control of the Emperor. At this point, the Rhine Palatinate and the hard-line Calvinist princes withdrew from the Imperial diet, which for forty years ceased to exist as an effective institution.

In 1591 and 1598, there had been the first signs of a revival of interest in a defensive alliance among Calvinist princes. The leading role was taken by the Elector Palatine Frederick IV, whose marriage (he was brother-in-law of Maurice of Nassau and the duke of Bouillon) had brought him into the mainstream of Calvinist politics. In May 1609, a Protestant Union was established, with Frederick as its director and Christian of Anhalt as its lieutenant. The membership was small, and weakened by defections; Saxony and the Lutheran princes of the north-west kept aloof. The most prominent allies were John Frederick of Württemberg and Maurice of Hesse-Cassel, but no other electoral princes joined (John Sigismund of Brandenburg joined in 1614 but seceded three years later). Protestant self-reliance was matched immediately by the formation of a Catholic League, with Maximilian of Bavaria as its linchpin. This League stated frankly that it opposed the secularization of ecclesiastical property since 1552. Despite a budgetary surplus in Bavaria at a time when the financial difficulties of most German princes were increasing, the League remained relatively weak. The three ecclesiastical electors could not command convincing military or political force. Furthermore, Maximilian of Bavaria was determined to prevent the use of the League for Imperial purposes. Thus when the Emperor Matthias I sought admission to the League, and the inclusion of the conservative Lutheran elector John George of Saxony, Maximilian withdrew and set about forming a new league based on a smaller south German confederation. Faced with the prospect of Imperial absolutism, Maximilian preferred Bavarian autonomy, ardent Catholic though he was.

The first trial of strength for the rival unions came almost immediately in 1609 with the death of duke John William of Cleves, Jülich, Mark and Berg, leaving no direct male heir. Under a stronger ruler, his states might have formed a powerful territory on the lower Rhine; but the old duke had been mad, and had also piled up enormous debts. Moreover, foreign armies had marched at will across his lands, and seized its key strategic points. The two main claimants to this territory in 1609 were Lutherans, and in May they agreed to administer the late duke's territories jointly until their rival claims were adjudicated by a group of friendly princes (unnamed, but presumably Protestant). In Jülich, however, this provisional government of the 'possessor princes' proved unacceptable because the majority of the population was Catholic. The Emperor, therefore, established a counter-government under his cousin archduke Leopold, who occupied the fortress of Jülich in late July: this was likely to draw the Dutch Republic into the conflict, because of Jülich's proximity to the Spanish Netherlands and the consequent risk of a Spanish invasion of the Republic via Cleves and Jülich. Conflict seemed inevitable when the fortress was recaptured at the beginning of September by a joint French, Dutch and German Protestant Union army. The outbreak of a general war was only avoided because of Henri IV's assassination in May 1610, and because it was not in the interest of the Spanish government to exploit its possible advantage in Jülich when eleven years of the truce with the Dutch were unexpired. The Emperor Rudolf II and the archduke Leopold were not strong enough on their own to win the war. But Henri IV had ratified a treaty with the Protestant Union in February 1610 which prolonged French involvement in the crisis, and it was not until March 1613 that the French regency government reneged on its commitments.

The conflict was reopened in 1613–14 by changes of religious affiliation. Wolfgang William of Neuburg became a Catholic secretly in July 1613 and then openly in May 1614, when he married the sister of Maximilian of Bavaria. But at Christmas 1613, John Sigismund of Brandenburg had become a Calvinist. The conversion of the two princes dramatically altered the political alignments, driving the Dutch on to the side of the Brandenburg claimant, while the Habsburgs now supported Neuburg. In May 1614, the Dutch reinforced their garrisons at Jülich, while Wolfgang William seized the town of Düsseldorf. In early September, Spínola, the military commander in the Spanish Netherlands, captured Wesel, the leading town of Cleves, with a force of 20,000 men. After the Dutch and the Spanish forces had consolidated their hold on the duchies, an armistice was concluded in October and confirmed in the Treaty of Xanten in November 1614. The treaty envisaged the provisional partition of the inheritance between the two claimants, with Brandenburg receiving Cleves and Mark, and Neuburg receiving the much larger territories of Jülich and Berg. Despite its provisional status, this partition was to endure until the French Revolution, though in the short term it proved extremely unstable. Despite promises to the contrary, Protestant officials were soon dismissed in Jülich and Berg, and Catholics in Cleves and Mark. Neither Spanish nor Dutch troops withdrew. Spínola's base at Wesel was a strategic threat to Gelderland and Overijssel, and indeed in 1621 his troops invaded Jülich, Cleves and Mark. However, at least the sequestration of the inheritance by the Emperor had been avoided, though perhaps more by the efforts of the Dutch than by those of the German Protestant Union.

3.4.4 *Towards a German Conflict: the Crisis in the Austrian Hereditary Lands, 1608–1618*

The Emperor Rudolf II had no direct heir and after 1600 he was in almost permanent conflict with his younger brother, Matthias, the heir presumptive. Matthias was prepared to use the Protestant estates, or representative institutions, of Hungary, Austria and Moravia to further his cause against his brother in 1606–8. In June 1608, after two family conclaves, Rudolf was forced to relinquish control in these territories to the brother he hated and wished to exclude from the succession. To prevent the loss of Bohemia, Rudolf was forced to grant sweeping concessions to the Protestants in the Letter of Majesty of July 1609. Yet even this proved insufficient, and in May 1611 Matthias was crowned king of Bohemia at Prague. All that was left to Rudolf until his death in January 1612 was the title of Emperor. Matthias had unwittingly played the game of Christian of Anhalt and the Protestant Union. Anhalt wanted the Calvinists in the hereditary lands to use the representative institutions to gain control of the government and so obtain full freedom of worship. The restriction of Austrian Habsburg power in the hereditary lands would lead inevitably to the collapse of Imperial power in Germany too, or so Anhalt hoped. Matthias was no longer young when he received the Imperial crown in 1612, and he seemed little concerned with what might happen after his death. His chief adviser, Cardinal Khlesl, was also an old man, though in his prime he had been the champion of the Counter-Reformation in Austria. Once Matthias was Emperor, however, Khlesl's policy was one of inaction, even appeasement, and it led finally to the catastrophe he had hoped to avoid. In July 1618, the archduke Ferdinand of Styria (ruler of one of the Austrian provinces) connived with the Spanish ambassador to have Khlesl arrested and so brought about a *coup d'état* in which he himself came to power; this high-handed action precluded a peaceful solution to the crisis in the Empire and the hereditary lands.

Matthias's death in March 1619 brought the related problems of the Bohemian and Imperial successions to a head, and began the conflict which history has termed the Thirty Years' War. Matthias had no direct heir, and there were two principal claimants. Philip III of Spain, through his mother, Anna of Habsburg, was a grandson of the Emperor Maximilian II. Archduke Ferdinand of Styria was no more than a nephew, but already he held a considerable amount of power in the Empire as ruler of Inner Austria since 1596. He was elected king of Bohemia in 1617 and of Hungary in 1618 after the Spanish had withdrawn their claims through the so-called Oñate agreement. By this solemn treaty in July 1617, Ferdinand paid for Philip III's renunciation of his claims to the Empire by ceding (at least in theory—Spain was prevented from reaping the full fruits of her diplomatic agility) Alsace, Finale Liguria and Piombino to Spain, in recognition that a male heir of Philip III would be preferred to any female children of his own. He also promised to aid Spain in Lombardy whenever asked to do so.

Yet in 1619, the election of a Protestant Emperor was a theoretical possibility. Two days before Ferdinand's election as Emperor, a new candidate had emerged. The Bohemian estates deposed Ferdinand as king and elected Frederick V of the Palatinate to replace him. There was thus temporarily a 4 to 3 Protestant majority in the electoral college, or so it might have seemed. But news of the Bohemian decision did not reach the electoral meeting at Frankfurt in time, and thus Ferdinand, as king of Bohemia, and an elector, was able to vote for himself as Emperor. On the second ballot the voting was unanimous for Ferdinand II, three Protestants having voted for a Habsburg candidate despite their grave reservations. These reservations were well founded: Ferdinand's policy as archduke of Styria was firmly anti-Protestant. He had had a Jesuit education, and he had made a notorious vow to eliminate heresy throughout his territories. Here was an Emperor of a different mould from the tolerant Maximilian II, the idle Rudolf II and the incompetent Matthias. To the Calvinists at least, Ferdinand II's election was to prove a disaster.

4

THE STRUGGLE FOR EUROPEAN
HEGEMONY, 1618–1660

DURING the whole of the seventeenth century there were only six years in which there was no war in some area of Europe; in the first half of the century there was no year of peace at all. Inflation continued at least until 1650 and military spending increased dramatically. Governments were thus forced to tax their subjects more heavily, which raised the level of social and political tension within several European countries, so much so that some historians have perceived, or thought they perceived, a 'general European crisis' in the 1640s. Nevertheless, though many of the problems faced by the European countries may have been comparable in origin, their evolution was different because of the contrasting political and social structures in the different states.

By 1660, a more stable political structure was beginning to emerge in several European countries, and in western Europe, at least, there was a temporary respite from earlier international conflicts. The Thirty Years' War is the name usually given to three struggles: the war in Germany (1618–48), the renewed conflict between Spain and the Dutch Republic (1621–48) and the open war between France and Spain (1635–59). Each of these conflicts had an earlier origin and distinctive features, yet each also overlapped with the others, so that the Thirty Years' War drew in the whole of western Europe. A resurgent France after 1624 ensured that the dominant issue in the western European conflicts would be the struggle for hegemony between the houses of Bourbon and Habsburg.

4.1 The Thirty Years' War: the Holy Roman Empire and the Austrian Habsburg Hereditary Lands, 1618–1648

The election of Ferdinand II as Emperor in August 1619 brought to the fore the religious and political problems which had been festering in the Empire and in the Austrian Habsburg hereditary lands during the previous half-century. The future of the Counter-Reformation in Germany and the autocratic ambitions of the Emperor were interdependent. The spread of Calvinism had paralysed two of the crucial institutions in the Empire, the supreme Imperial court (*Reichskammergericht*) and the

Imperial diet. This left the Emperor himself, the infrequently summoned meetings of electors, and the Imperial aulic council (*Reichshofrat*, the Emperor's personal council) as the only effective institutions through which representations could be made. Much depended on whether or not the electors would be able to act jointly as a check on Ferdinand II and the aulic council, which was largely under his control. In the short term, the Emperor was weak because the disastrously antiquated Imperial constitution denied him permanent taxation and a standing army. Ferdinand II had no army of his own and was dependent on the support of Lutheran Saxony and Catholic Bavaria to defeat his Bohemian rebels. Yet it was clear that even Catholic electors thought the Emperor should not have a standing army when they secured the dismissal of the Imperial generalissimo Wallenstein in 1630. Wallenstein is alleged to have remarked that the electors and princes of the Empire were no longer necessary. In France and Spain there was only one king, and thus Germany should have only one ruler.[1] Such hints of autocratic intentions aroused suspicion among Catholic princes who shared the Emperor's religious objectives. There was an element of truth in the Franco-Swedish propaganda of the 1630s that the Thirty Years' War was not just a religious war but a war for 'the liberties of Germany'.[2]

4.4.1 *The Bohemian Rebellion and the Occupation of the Palatinate, 1618–1623*

Traditionally, the Thirty Years' War is said to have begun with the so-called 'defenestration of Prague' in May 1618. Two hard-line Catholic representatives of Ferdinand II, who had been elected king of Bohemia the previous July by an overwhelming majority, were thrown out of a 70-foot-high window of the Hradschin castle on the order of the so-called 'defensors' led by Count Matthias Thurn. (The 'defensors' were thirty official guardians of Protestant rights, who were to be chosen in equal numbers from among members of all three Bohemian estates.) The pretext for this act of rebellion was the destruction of Protestant churches at Braunau and Klostergrab. Ferdinand had confirmed the Letter of Majesty, it is true, but had he refused to do so a general revolt would have occurred a year earlier. The crucial point was that neither he nor his Catholic supporters were prepared to acknowledge Protestant equality in Bohemia or the rights of the 'defensors'.

Underlying these religious disagreements were two important constitutional issues. Was the kingdom of Bohemia truly elective, or part of the Habsburg patrimonial lands? What was the nature of the rights enjoyed by the dynasty in the kingdom? Bohemia's constitution of 1500 had embodied an oath imposed on individuals to the 'commonwealth of

Bohemia' as well as to the king, making Bohemia an aristocratic republic in all but name. On the other hand, Ferdinand I had asserted in 1549 the principle of hereditary succession by male primogeniture. The eventual outcome—a royalist victory in 1627 which abolished elective monarchy and vested the Bohemian crown in the Habsburg family—could not have been predicted in 1619. In that year, the Bohemian estates deposed Ferdinand, largely because of his religious policies, and elected Frederick V of the Palatinate as their king in a majority decision. The second issue, of less importance to the fate of the revolt but crucial for Germany, was really a question of whether or not Bohemia could still, in the circumstances of 1619, be considered part of the Holy Roman Empire. Frederick V contended that it could not: he was thus wresting the Bohemian crown not from an Emperor but an Austrian archduke. However, the meeting of the electors at Mühlhausen in March 1620 shattered this argument by declaring Bohemia an integral part of the Empire. The logic of this decision was that the Bohemian rebellion might at a later date turn into a German war. Frederick V, in other words, might not only be driven out of Bohemia, which he had usurped in 1619–20, but also be deprived of his lands and titles in the Empire.

The Bohemian revolt spread rapidly with the formation of a national militia in August 1618 to defend the country from a Habsburg army which attempted to invade from Moravia. Twice in 1619 the rebel generalissimo Count Thurn came within an ace of capturing Ferdinand II at Vienna. The prince of Transylvania, Bethlen Gábor, in alliance with the Bohemian rebels, occupied most of Royal Hungary in 1619–20. Moravia, Upper and Lower Silesia and Upper and Lower Austria joined the Bohemian cause. For a short period, it seemed that Christian of Anhalt's dream of a central European confederation against the Catholic dynasty might be fulfilled. But the early success of the rebellion could not hide the fact that Ferdinand II had much more powerful allies than the Bohemians, even if their assistance was not bought cheaply.

The Papacy could be counted on to back the Catholic dynasty. More importantly, Philip III of Spain had said that 'Germany cannot possibly be abandoned'.[3] In May 1620 he authorized an offensive from the Spanish Netherlands on the Lower Palatinate, which would reveal Frederick's lines of communication to be disastrously over-extended. Meanwhile, the Emperor had astutely purchased the support of the two most powerful princes whose territories were adjacent to Bohemia and who might have reason to fear the rise of Frederick of the Palatinate. In October 1619, he gave control over military operations in Bohemia to Maximilian of Bavaria, who was to hold any territory he conquered in pledge against the repayment of his expenses and (by a secret condition) he was to be awarded Frederick's electoral title after the victory was secured. The

Emperor thus obtained the army of the Catholic League for his cause, and in July 1620 Count Tilly, its commander, crossed into Austria which submitted to him the following month. Military operations were then transferred to southern Bohemia. The second alliance was with the Lutheran John George of Saxony in March 1620, who was offered Lusatia as his war indemnity. In October, the elector captured Bautzen, the capital of Lusatia, almost without a blow. From this moment, the Bohemian rebellion was isolated and caught in a pincer movement.

The rout of the Bohemian army by the joint Imperial–Bavarian forces at the battle of the White Mountain (Bílá Hora) in November 1620 proved decisive for two reasons. Frederick's incapacity as a leader was fully revealed by his decision to flee the country, earning him the epithet the 'Winter King'. Whether Prague could have been saved is debatable: there was a strong suspicion that the citizens would deliver Frederick to the Imperial–Bavarian army as the price of their own immunity (as it was, the victorious forces pillaged the city for a week). Apart from the failure of military leadership, however, the Bohemian rebellion had shown itself hopelessly divided along religious, political and social lines. Lutherans refused to co-operate with Calvinists, nobles with townsmen, and Frederick had rapidly eroded by his actions the early support he had enjoyed. Above all, although he was a German prince, he had failed to obtain the assistance of the Protestant Union. At Ulm in July 1620, the French had negotiated a truce between the Union and the Catholic League. This policy reversed the traditional French support for the Protestant princes, though it served temporarily to rescue the Union from the consequences of Frederick's folly in accepting the Bohemian crown: without the truce, the Imperial–Bavarian army would have turned against the Protestant Union and in the circumstances of 1620–1 would certainly have destroyed it. French diplomacy removed the last check on Frederick's enemies, allowing the Emperor to suppress the Bohemian rebellion and turn his attention to the Palatinate. The Spanish king, Philip III, did not wait for the defeat of the Bohemian rebellion, but empowered Spínola to invade the Lower or Rhine Palatinate in June from his base in the Spanish Netherlands. Spínola commenced his campaign in September, and met little resistance apart from the garrisons of English volunteers at Frankenthal and Mannheim. The occupation of the Lower Palatinate had occurred a full four months before the Imperial ban was pronounced against Frederick in January 1621. Worse still for the Protestant cause, Spínola's army brought about the collapse of the Union in May 1621.

At first, the forces of Maximilian of Bavaria had been too heavily involved in the Bohemian war to enforce the Imperial ban in the Upper Palatinate, which was contiguous with Maximilian's lands. However, in September–October 1621, he expelled the forces of the mercenary captain, Ernst von Mansfeld, from the Upper Palatinate. Once Mansfeld moved his troops to the Lower Palatinate, Maximilian felt justified in military intervention there, too. The Catholic forces won the war in 1622–3. In February 1623, Frederick was formally deprived of his lands and electoral title. The electorate was conferred on Maximilian of Bavaria for his lifetime, with the possibility of restoration to Frederick's children on Maximilian's death. Ferdinand II was by this time in debt to Maximilian to the tune of 16–18 million florins; the elector controlled the revenues of Upper Austria and acted as regent until 1628. No one could doubt that Ferdinand meant in the course of time to buy back Upper Austria by ceding the Palatinate to Maximilian; this is what he did in 1628, granting the Upper and part of the Lower Palatinate to Maximilian and his heirs.

Frederick's rejection of Anglo-Spanish terms for the restoration of his German titles, and the failure of the entente between the two countries in 1623, marked the end of his cause. He died in 1632 at the age of 36, having lost virtually all his wealth as well as his lands as a result of miscalculation in 1619. The defeat proved catastrophic for Bohemia. Twenty-seven leaders of the rebellion were executed in June 1621. By the revised form of government of May 1627, Ferdinand declared Bohemia a Catholic state, and subsequently Protestant nobles were given six months' notice to accept the new ruling. The act of conferring nobility came exclusively within the grant of the king, and thus new titles could be given to faithful supporters, such as Albrecht von Waldstein, better known as Wallenstein, who accumulated sixty-six estates, including the county of Friedland, which was elevated to a duchy in June 1625. In Bohemia as a whole, 486 out of the 911 noble estates were confiscated as a result of the rebellion. An elite of magnates, some of them mercenary captains in origin who bought up large estates with a depreciated currency, was established in place of the traditional Bohemian nobility, an elite which owed its loyalty to the dynasty.

4.1.2 *Danish Intervention and the Edict of Restitution, 1625–1629*

The second war which goes to make up the Thirty Years' War bears little relation to the earlier conflict, although it arose from the circumstances following it, particularly the occupation of the southern part of the Lower Saxon Circle—one of the twelve circles established by Maximilian I in 1512 (see chapter 2.2.2)—by the forces of the Catholic League under the command of Count Tilly. Christian IV of Denmark, a Lutheran, was duke of Holstein and thus a prince of the Empire in his own right. He was also the head of the Lower Saxon Circle and aimed directly or indirectly to gain control of the secularized (or Protestant-held) bishoprics in north-west Germany, which were of key strategic importance. Possession of the archbishopric of Bremen alone gave control of the mouths of the Elbe and Weser rivers. For this reason, Imperial policy by 1623 was set on re-Catholicizing eight disputed bishoprics, while Christian IV moved increasingly from a position of neutrality to leadership of a new Protestant Union. An Anglo-Danish alliance was broadened into a general alliance at The Hague in December 1625, whose signatories were the Netherlands, England, Denmark and the dispossessed Frederick of the Palatinate. Crucially for the future success of this alliance, however, France refused to back an 'evangelical union' which failed to include Catholic princes such as Maximilian of Bavaria.

The fighting was to be carried out by Christian of Denmark, Christian of Brunswick and Ernst of Mansfeld, with Bethlen Gábor from Transylvania acting on the eastern front as a diversion. Christian IV was no military genius, and his plans misfired badly. After occupying the bishoprics of Magdeburg and Halberstadt, Wallenstein, the Imperial commander—with an army of 112,000 men under his command by 1627, thanks to his possession of the rich duchy of Friedland—stopped Mansfeld from crossing the river Elbe near Dessau in April 1626. When Christian of Brunswick died two months later, Tilly could concentrate the forces of the Catholic League against Christian of Denmark. In August 1626, he defeated the Danish king at Lutter, which confirmed his occupation of the Lower Saxon Circle and the Westphalian bishoprics of Münster and Osnabrück. With the failure of the allied campaign in Silesia, Moravia and Hungary, after July 1627 Wallenstein was free to turn to the suppression of all remaining opposition in the Lower Saxon Circle. Tilly and the Catholic League were assigned a subsidiary role in the war, and Wallenstein went on to defeat the dukes of Mecklenburg and Pomerania.

Wallenstein held the duchy of Mecklenburg in 1628, with its key strategic ports of Wismar and Rostock, and in April he was given the title of 'general of the whole Imperial armada as well as admiral of the Atlantic and Baltic seas'.[4] (The so-called 'Imperial Armada' was to be a joint Spanish and Austrian force of forty ships, to be divided into two fleets operating in the Baltic and the North Sea with Wismar as its base of operations. After a flurry of activity to set up the Armada in 1628–9, both it and its stores were captured by Gustavus Adolphus in January 1632.) However, he lacked control of Stralsund, a third important Baltic port. This port was a member of the Hanseatic League and in effect a republic: although it was part of the duchy of Pomerania, its duke was not allowed to set foot on its soil without the town council's prior consent. In April 1628, Wallenstein's forces began the siege of Stralsund, an act which forced Sweden and Denmark to sink their traditional rivalries in a three-year treaty which they signed the following month. The treaty was aimed at provisioning the port by sea, a move which thwarted Wallenstein's plans. Though he failed in the siege, Wallenstein nevertheless defeated Christian IV's land army, and the Danish king was forced to sign the Peace of Lübeck in May 1629. Christian IV retained his hereditary lands in Denmark and Norway, but he was forced to renounce his claims to the German bishoprics and any right to intervene in Imperial affairs at a future date.

Wallenstein's success enabled the Emperor to impose his own solution to the religious problems of Germany in the Edict of Restitution of March 1629. Ironically, Ferdinand II did not consult his commander (who opposed the measure), but listened to his Jesuit confessor and close confidant, Lamormaini. The Emperor believed that he could count on the support of the Catholic electors for the edict, because in the last months of 1627 they had requested him to restore all church lands secularized since the Truce of Passau (1552); he had responded favourably in the autumn of 1628. The Edict of Restitution, which was issued the following May, represented the Catholic view that the secularization of church lands since 1552 was illegal and that only those Protestants adhering to the Confession of Augsburg had been included in the provisions of the Peace of 1555. Calvinism was thus proscribed as a religion in the Empire. This led to the enforcement of Catholicism by Imperial commissioners in five bishoprics and about thirty free cities, a considerable achievement for the Emperor. Before 1629 the question was less whether the Emperor had the right to restore church lands, than whether he had the might to enforce a decision favourable to Catholicism. Wallenstein's triumph and the Edict of Restitution completely altered this situation. However, even the Catholic electors expressed doubts about the legality of the edict. They did not oppose the policy enshrined in it (they, of course, wanted the restoration of church lands) but the manner of its pronouncement. In the summer of 1630 they insisted that its provisions should be scrutinized by a subsequent Imperial diet. The conquerors were divided amongst themselves, and an unedifying race between the Habsburg and Wittelsbach dynasties developed to occupy the reconstituted prince bishoprics. The Habsburgs won, with the prizes of Magdeburg, Bremen, Hildesheim and Halberstadt going to archduke Leopold William (who already held two bishoprics), against the less important Osnabrück, Minden and Verden being acquired by the Wittelsbachs.

The electors responded with a show of strength against the military successes of the Emperor. Wallenstein was dismissed as Imperial generalissimo in August 1630. The Catholic electors hated him personally, considering him 'a man of inferior social status' who had questioned their pre-eminence.[5] They also disliked him because, with an army of 150,000 men under his control by 1630, he seemed to them to be the instrument for creating a possible Habsburg autocracy. They refused to elect

Ferdinand II's son as King of the Romans, thus apparently questioning the Habsburg right of succession to the Imperial title. They also secured a reduction in the size of the Imperial army and a method of financing it which was less satisfactory to the Emperor. Tilly was appointed commander of both the Imperial and Catholic League armies, but with the intolerable and unworkable requirement of keeping the two armies separate. At the moment of Imperial triumph, the electors had unwittingly done their best to assist the Swedish invasion, which was already under way. It was four years before the Emperor's position was fully retrieved.

4.1.3 *Swedish Intervention and the Peace of Prague, 1630–1635*

The defeat of Denmark in 1629 did not give Germany any respite from foreign intervention. Swedish involvement in Imperial affairs was inevitable after Christian IV's defeat and the unveiling of Wallenstein's ambitions to establish a Baltic fleet. Temporarily free from a war with Poland (see chapter 5.2.4), the Swedish king, Gustavus Adolphus, landed on the island of Usedom off Pomerania at the end of June 1630 with an army of only 14,000 men. A quick military response from Wallenstein and his army of 95,000 men (or 150,000, according to his optimistic army lists) could have crushed the invasion at its outset. However, Wallenstein was dismissed that August, and without his reputation for military success, the financial and logistical support for the army was missing.

Gustavus Adolphus' subsequent success in Germany was totally unexpected. It was a reflection both of the military genius of the king and the temporary divisions among his opponents. Within less than two years, he had scored a succession of spectacular triumphs, including the defeat of the elector of Bavaria, leader of the Catholic League, which resulted in the Swedish occupation of Munich in May 1632. The poverty of Sweden, a small kingdom of less than a million inhabitants, necessitated that 'war should sustain war'.[6] This meant the occupation of more and more territory to provision the growing army, and the wholesale movement of the troops to lands which had not been devastated already. Practical necessity therefore dictated that the Swedes should adopt a bold military strategy in an age when most commanders were over-cautious. Gustavus Adolphus obtained a subsidy treaty with France in January 1631, and could have gained one earlier had he so wished, but this did not constrain his actions as Cardinal de Richelieu, Louis XIII's chief minister, had hoped. Indeed, after a decisive triumph at Breitenfeld in September 1631, events went almost entirely Gustavus' way. By March of the following year, he was talking of 'clipping the wings of the Imperialists so they shall never fly again',[7] and some of his more radical supporters, such as William V of Hesse-Cassel, wanted to see the total abolition of the ecclesiastical electorates to ensure that there would be a permanent Protestant majority in the electoral college. There was also talk not simply of the abolition of the Edict of Restitution, but of the secularization of all church lands.

Gustavus Adolphus' war aims expanded with his success. His Chancellor, Axel Oxenstierna, recalled that the king had initially aimed only 'to ensure the safety of his kingdom and the Baltic, and to liberate the oppressed lands' in Germany; 'it was no part of his original intention to press on as far as he did . . .'[8] Swedish military policy combined three elements, each of which broadened with their growing power. Firstly, 'satisfaction', which was the 'recompense and debt of gratitude'[9] that Sweden considered its due from the Protestant states which had been freed from the domination of Ferdinand II. The Swedes now considered these states to be a Swedish fief in Germany. Secondly, security against invasion, which meant Swedish acquisition, or control of, certain key Baltic ports such as Stettin. Thirdly, a wider concept of 'security' which implied a return to the *status quo* of 1618. The Emperor would thus have to abandon his claim to exercise real sovereignty in Germany. Gustavus voiced this opinion, with obvious reference to the fate of the elector of the Palatinate and the Mecklenburg dukes: 'while an elector can sit safe as elector in his land, and a duke is duke and has his liberties', he said, 'then we are safe.'[10]

These three aims were not entirely consistent, and the attitude of the two leading Protestant princes was crucial to their fulfilment. George William of Brandenburg, a Calvinist, was Gustavus' brother-in-law; but they had already clashed over the Swedish war with Poland in East Prussia, because it was a fief the elector of Brandenburg held from the king of Poland. Moreover, on the death of duke Bogislaw XIV of Pomerania without a male heir (an event which did not occur until 1637, but was already foreseen in 1630), George William stood to inherit the duchy. From July 1630, however, Gustavus' recognition of these succession rights had been contingent on George William's eventual payment of a war indemnity, while Bogislaw was allowed to retain Pomerania only on draconian terms. In June 1631, Gustavus had forced George William to join his cause by threatening military occupation, but after the king's death the elector had less to fear from a Swedish royal minority. The other key Protestant prince was the Lutheran John George of Saxony. When, before the Swedish invasion, Gustavus had asked for his alliance, he had been rebuffed because of John George's preference for separate negotiations with the Emperor. Gustavus had not obtained John George's support until September 1631, and like that of George William, his alliance was made under duress. At Breitenfeld, the Saxon allies of the Swedes were routed and John George had fled the field. Relations between the king and the elector of Saxony after this blew hot and cold. John George's forces overran Bohemia and captured Prague in November 1631, a move which greatly benefited the Protestant cause, but the elector always refused to join an evangelical league with Sweden and the other Protestant rulers. Without Saxony, such a league could never be permanent.

The Imperial cause was helped by the ending of war in Italy (see chapter 4.2.2), which released troops from Mantua for service in Germany, and by the recall of Wallenstein at the end of 1631. When Gustavus Adolphus attacked Bavaria in March 1632, even Maximilian, Wallenstein's old enemy and rival, was forced to ask for the assistance of the generalissimo whose dismissal he had secured eighteen months earlier. Gustavus' attack on Bavaria was against the wishes of his French allies and contravened a guarantee of neutrality which had been offered to Maximilian and the Catholic League (and accepted) in January 1631. The conquest of Bavaria was achieved with spectacular devastation. But in May 1632, Wallenstein had reoccupied Prague with a force of 70,000 men. In September and October 1632, there were clashes with Wallenstein's forces which, for the first time, did not go the Swedish king's way. Wallenstein captured Leipzig—which virtually knocked Saxony out of the war—and joined the forces of the Catholic League, which were commanded by Pappenheim following the death of Tilly. The battle near the Saxon town of Lützen in November 1632 fought between the joint Catholic forces of Wallenstein and Pappenheim and the Swedish army of Gustavus was a stalemate, though it ensured that the Swedish army would not be cut off from the Baltic coastline. Wallenstein was forced to withdraw to Bohemia. Crucially, however, Gustavus was killed in battle.

With the death of the king, the Swedish position in Germany was transformed overnight. What had seemed a logical extension of foreign policy under a popular and successful ruler seemed foolhardy during the minority of his daughter, Christina. The king had said that 'our basic war aim is security'.[11] The security of Sweden after his death was said by some Swedish councillors to lie in the evacuation of Swedish troops from the Empire, 'to try every means consistent with reputation and safety' to extricate Sweden from 'the German business'.[12] One man, however, refused to concede to the defeatist position. This was Axel Oxenstierna, the remarkable Chancellor of Sweden during Gustavus' lifetime and the custodian of his political inheritance. His first task was to attempt to reduce the Swedish commitment to the German war, by establishing a political and military leadership which placed a greater burden on the German princes themselves. This seemed to have been achieved in the League of Heilbronn of April 1633, of which Oxenstierna was made sole director or leader. However, the events of the following year proved that the League was fatally weakened by the absence of Lutheran Saxony and the wavering support of Calvinist Brandenburg. The arrears of pay of the troops employed by the Heilbronn League were so enormous that they could only be met by conferring on their commanders what was in effect the freedom to plunder. The essential requirement of the Swedish campaign in Germany, that war should sustain war, could no longer be met. Finally, communications were cut between the Swedish-controlled Baltic littoral and such allies in the south as Württemberg and Hesse-Cassel.

By January 1634, Ferdinand II was convinced of Wallenstein's over-weening ambition and profoundly suspicious of him; the following month he had him murdered. The weakness in the Imperial military command revealed by this event was only overcome by co-operation between the Spanish and Austrian branches of the Habsburg family, something un-paralleled since 1620. In September 1634, the Swedes suffered a crushing defeat at Nördlingen from a combined Habsburg army commanded by Cardinal-Infante Fernando (brother of Philip IV) and Ferdinand III, king of Hungary (the Emperor's son and successor). This opened up the whole of southern Germany to the Habsburg forces and led to immediate peace negotiations between the Emperor and John George of Saxony in November, which resulted in the disintegration of the Heilbronn League. A Habsburg-dominated treaty, which refused any concessions to Sweden or its dwindling band of exiled Calvinist princes, was signed in May 1635 at Prague. It repealed the Edict of Restitution, but left the 'ecclesiastical reservation' clause in force, and excluded Calvinists from legal rights under the Imperial constitution. What was being restored in 1635–6 was not the traditional Imperial constitution, but a stronger Catholic Habsburg monarchy. The point was reinforced by the election in December 1636 of Ferdinand III as King of the Romans, ensuring the succession on his father's death the following February. Not only was there no con-cession to Swedish war aims; there was no compensation for the Swedes either. In August 1635 the Swedish army, which was mostly composed of Germans, mutinied because of lack of pay and took Oxenstierna prisoner at Magdeburg. From this date 'contentment of the soldiery' became an overriding Swedish war aim:[13] without it there could be no security for the state, since the troops threatened to invade the Swedish mainland if they did not receive compensation.

4.1.4   *The Franco-Swedish War Effort, 1635–1648*

The French alliance had always been a mixed blessing to Sweden. It was a hindrance to the extent that Louis XIII and Richelieu wanted to sub-ordinate Sweden to the grand designs of Bourbon foreign policy and to shift the burden of the war effort on to the Swedish army in Germany. Oxenstierna refused to ratify the revised Franco-Swedish alliance of April

1635 in the hope of making a separate peace with the Emperor, but the terms were not forthcoming and military weakness forced him in 1638 to commit Sweden not to do so for three years. When the Franco-Swedish alliance was renewed in 1641, Sweden was bound to fight alongside France for the duration of the war in exchange for subsidies at an increased rate. The attempt by Sweden to obtain a separate negotiating position had failed. On the other hand, the subsidies from France provided a crucial influx of funds that enabled Sweden to gain spectacular, if intermittent, military victories: Banér's great victory at Wittstock in September 1636, and Torstensson's at the second battle of Breitenfeld in October 1642 were notable examples. Victories in turn produced further revenues, when, for example, the city of Leipzig bought off a Swedish attack after Breitenfeld. With a fine irony, the Swedish generals made the Habsburg hereditary lands, especially Bohemia and Moravia, their base of operations so that in the later 1640s war really did pay for war. Moreover, in 1643–5, Sweden felt strong enough to indulge in the luxury of a deliberately planned pre-emptive strike against Denmark, securing Halland in south-west Sweden (which Denmark held) in an attempt to remove another part of the Danish presence on the Swedish side of the Sound, and the two German secularized bishoprics of Bremen and Verden which Denmark had coveted. By this date the Swedish empire was no longer being acquired by accident, but for strategic reasons.

The collapse of the Heilbronn League and the defeat and dispersal of the Swedish army in 1634 had necessitated decisive intervention by France to prevent Swedish capitulation. Nevertheless, from the outset Louis XIII and Richelieu planned a 'war by diversion' and minimum Bourbon military commitment in Germany. This strategy assumed that it was the king of Spain, not the Emperor, who was the real threat to European security. If Philip IV's power was decisively weakened, the French believed that the Emperor would no longer make war on, or unacceptable political demands of, his Protestant subjects. The French position was relatively strong, thanks to its passive role in Germany between 1618 and 1635. France came into the conflict fresh, and with an ability unrivalled among the other European states to finance war on several fronts at the same time. Thus in 1635, at the lowest point in the fortunes of the Swedish and Protestant cause in Germany, a powerful new war fund was provided which neither the Emperor nor the king of Spain could match. On the other hand, France lacked experienced commanders and battle-hardened troops. The great French commanders—Harcourt, Condé the younger, Turenne—had either not yet risen through the ranks or else were not given the resources with which to make an impression. The French government lacked expertise in the problem of administering a war effort on several fronts at the same time. To overcome this weakness and to take control over the war effort in southern Germany, it hired the army of Bernard of Saxe-Weimar in the summer of 1635.

One of the few early French successes was Bernard's capture of Breisach, a great fortress commanding the Rhine, in December 1638; even this gain would have proved illusory had not the victor died the following July without a son. France had been committed to allow Bernard to establish his own dynasty in those parts of Alsace that he captured with the aid of Louis XIII's money. His death presented France with all the benefits and few of the dangers of this policy, and it was bitterly resented by Oxenstierna. Nevertheless, without the French army to prevent Spanish intervention in Imperial affairs, Sweden would not have been able to achieve any of its military successes in Germany. Torstensson defeated a Bavarian–Imperialist army at Jankau in Bohemia in March 1645, and the victory at Zusmarshausen in Bavaria in May 1648 was a combined Franco-Swedish effort under the generalship of Wrangel and Turenne. Thereafter, Sweden was in a position to besiege Prague, and Ferdinand III was forced to agree to peace even though it meant deserting his ally, Philip IV of Spain.

4.1.5 *The Peace of Westphalia, 1648*

The separate treaties signed between the Emperor and the estates of the Empire with France at the Catholic city of Münster, and with Sweden at the Protestant city of Osnabrück, at the end of October 1648, had been a long time coming. There had been a proposed meeting in 1641, and the French had dispatched plenipotentiaries in the autumn of 1643. Convinced that the French royal minority would weaken the allied position, Philip IV had then instructed his ambassadors to attempt to stall any settlement apart from with the Dutch. By February 1646, however, it was already clear to the Imperial advisers that Ferdinand III's position was hopeless because the Swedish armies were able to march at will across the Habsburg hereditary lands. Peace was necessary, at almost any price which preserved complete sovereignty for the Emperor in the hereditary lands and Bohemia. With some exceptions—Lower Austria, and especially Silesia and Hungary—the treaties gave the Emperor a free hand in his own territories to re-establish Habsburg dominance, and as a by-product, to suppress Protestantism. Westphalia was the final blow for the Austrian and Bohemian Protestants who had continued to pin their hopes on Swedish military power reversing the disaster of 1620.

The peace clarified the relative positions of the various participants in the Imperial constitution, and removed the pre-eminence of the Habsburg dynasty in Germany. Henceforth, it would be possible to view the Emperor as acting against as well as for the interests of the Empire, which was taken to be synonymous with the 'Imperial estates'—that is to say, the electors, princes and free cities represented in the diet. All princes were accorded 'territorial superiority' (but not sovereignty, an important distinction) 'in matters ecclesiastical as well as political'.[14] All princes gained the right to conclude treaties both between themselves and with foreign powers. A new version of the Heilbronn League was thus perfectly legitimate, provided that it was not directed against the Empire or the Emperor, an obligation easily evaded. The Emperor had to cede to the Imperial diet the right of declaring war and concluding peace within Germany. The chief Imperial institutions were reorganized to include Protestants (including Calvinists) on an equal footing with Catholics. Religious disputes brought before the Imperial diet were no longer to be decided by a majority vote, but by 'amicable agreement' between the two groups. It was largely Swedish pressure which forced these concessions from the Emperor, destroyed the Edict of Restitution and overturned the Peace of Prague. The Protestant administrators of the reformed north German bishoprics were admitted to the diet with full voting rights and 1624 was accepted as the 'standard year', the date which determined the ownership of church lands. (This was a compromise between extreme Protestant and Catholic demands.)

Restitutions to Sweden's allies were based for the most part on the *status quo* before the war began in 1618, but also bore some relationship to their actions during the war years. Saxony retained Lusatia, its gain from the war of 1620, but nothing else, since elector John George had not been reliable. Two staunch allies of Sweden, the rulers of Hesse-Cassel and Württemberg, were restored completely to their lands and titles. Karl Ludwig, the eldest son of Frederick V, was restored to the Lower Palatinate, and an eighth electoral title was created for his benefit. French lobbying enabled Maximilian of Bavaria to retain the electoral title confiscated from Frederick V and possession of the Upper Palatinate. The French also ensured a partial recognition of Frederick William of Brandenburg's claim to Pomerania. In return for the loss of western Pomerania to Sweden, the elector would be compensated by the grant of the secularized bishoprics of Halberstadt and Minden, as well as by the expectation of the archbishopric of Magdeburg on the death of its Saxon administrator (an event which occurred in 1680). The 'great elector' was to devote the rest of his life to the attempt to undo the wrong he felt he had suffered in 1648 by the loss of part of Pomerania to the Swedes.

The most important beneficiaries of the Peace of Westphalia were France and Sweden, yet the French gains were much less than Cardinal Mazarin, the chief minister of the regency government, had hoped for; arguably peace would not have been signed between France and the Empire but for the outbreak of the Fronde. The Emperor confirmed

French possession of Metz, Toul and Verdun, an established fact since 1552, but not hitherto recognized in Imperial law. He also ceded to the French two key fortresses in Alsace, Philippsburg in the north, and Breisach in the south, which commanded the Rhine; but Strasbourg, the most obvious provincial capital, remained a free city within the Empire. France was accorded the 'prefecture' over ten Alsatian towns (known collectively as the *décapole*) by the treaty, without sovereign control. The Sundgau, with its capital of Ensisheim in southern Alsace, was definitively granted to France. These complicated arrangements were accepted by both sides only in order to reach an agreement, but both hoped to reinterpret them once they were in a stronger position. Finally, the French delegates insisted on the Emperor's neutrality in the continuing war between France and Spain (which was not to end until 1659).

At first, Swedish demands on the Emperor and his allies had been so excessive that they prejudiced any hope of settlement. Gradually, however, they were moderated, but Sweden was left with an extremely favourable outcome, and managed to prevent Denmark from making any gains as a result of its earlier participation in the war. Though Sweden only received the western part of Pomerania, this was by far the most important part of the duchy and contained the vital port of Stettin. In return for giving up eastern Pomerania to Brandenburg, Sweden received the secularized bishoprics of Bremen and Verden (the original Danish objectives), and the Mecklenburg ports of Wismar and Warnemünde. The Peace of Westphalia made Sweden a German as well as a Baltic power, with membership of three Imperial circles and permanent representation in the Imperial diet. The risk was that Sweden might become involved in German domestic wrangles, but the outcome was welcomed at home because it was seen as bolstering the dynasty against its Danish and Polish rivals. Sweden was also paid 5 million *riksdalers* for the 'contentment of the soldiery', only a quarter of the original demand, but enough to bring the size of the army down to a peacetime footing, and Queen Christina alienated crown lands to pay off the mercenary captains.

For the historian Wedgwood, the Thirty Years' War was 'the outstanding example in European history of a meaningless conflict'.[15] This verdict, made shortly before the Second World War and subsequent barbarism in the twentieth century, has not stood the test of time. A constitutional and religious conflict of such magnitude can scarcely be termed meaningless; the very dimension of the wars attests to their significance, even if mercenary soldiers (particularly Lutherans) frequently changed sides following the maxim 'it is no matter what master we serve'.[16] Grimmelshausen's *The Adventures of Simplicissimus the German*, which was written in the 1660s, may well have exaggerated the scale of the atrocities and thus have misled subsequent historical opinion. More recent study has tended to diminish the statistical impact of the fighting; the decline of the population in the Holy Roman Empire is now estimated at 20 per cent, although as late as 1962 there was support for the view that the fall in population might have been as high as 30–40 per cent. But this decline in population was not spread evenly across the Empire; the north-west experienced almost no fighting after 1629, and thus suffered little population loss. The war zones of Mecklenburg, Pomerania and Württemberg, in contrast, were heavily involved in the fighting after Swedish intervention in 1630, and lost over half their populations. The calculation of demographic loss is further complicated by the problem of refugees. What appears from the fragmentary statistics to be a permanent population loss may simply have been a temporary displacement of inhabitants who fled the fighting. The inhabitants of villages fled where they could, often to the protection of town walls. Urban areas thus usually maintained reasonably high population levels, the exception being places which experienced spectacular acts of wanton destruction—Magdeburg, for example, lost 96 per cent of its population after the sack of 1631. In general, the war probably simply aggravated pre-existing social and economic problems, particularly the decline of commerce; only a few ports such as Hamburg and Bremen escaped. Other consequences were heavier municipal debt, the collapse of an independent prosperous peasantry in eastern Germany, and the consequent rise of large-scale estate farming.

4.2 The Conflict between the Dutch Republic and Spain, 1621–1648

The war in Germany caught the Spanish government on the horns of a dilemma. In alliance with the Emperor after 1618, the Spaniards were bound to defend his interests, but this alliance was expensive: it was rapidly appreciated that there was a grave risk of Spain 'bearing all the costs of the war, but only the Imperialists deriving the benefit'.[17] Yet to draw back from the alliance would be a grievous loss of prestige, especially since the Spaniards subscribed to a seventeenth-century version of the domino theory; 'after Germany would fall Italy', in the view of Olivares, the chief minister after 1622, 'after Italy, Flanders, then the Indies, Naples and Sicily'.[18] The risk of entering the conflict was the unravelling of the whole complex structure of Spanish Habsburg defence; but the logical policy was one of total commitment, the gradual move from a series of small wars to a general European war.

However, before Spanish intervention in the Empire could be attempted, there was the Dutch Republic to confront. It is usually assumed that when the twelve-year truce with the Dutch expired in April 1621, the

Spaniards were spoiling to resume this war, and optimistic of their chances of reconquering the seven northern provinces. Despite the emergence of more aggressive ministers than Lerma, it is clear that the Spaniards saw virtually no prospect of doing this. Shortly before his death in July 1621, archduke Albert, the governor of the Spanish Netherlands, observed that Philip IV would have to send over 3 million ducats annually to the Low Countries for 'many years, for this will be a long war'.[19] Albert's death without a male heir in itself altered the balance of power, for although his widow, the Infanta Isabella, remained governor-general, sovereignty reverted to Philip IV. The scheme for an autonomous government in the Low Countries was finally at an end, but even before Albert's death, Philip had made the crucial decision to resume the war.

4.2.1   *The Course of the Dutch–Spanish Conflict before the Intervention of France, 1621–1635*

After the expiry of the Spanish–Dutch truce in April 1621, the Spanish government would have settled for a new one on three conditions. The first was that the Dutch allow Catholics free rights of worship; the second condition was that the river Scheldt be opened to navigation; the third, and most important, determined by Philip III shortly before his death at the end of March 1621, was a complete end to Dutch colonial expansion, which had continued unabated during the truce, and was seen as a serious drawback to renewing it. All three were refused. After Oldenbarnevelt's execution in 1619, his successor held the more lowly title of councillor pensionary (*raadpensionaris*; Oldenbarnevelt had been called advocate to the states of Holland). Decisive political power lay with Maurice of Nassau as stadholder of five provinces. His chief concerns were to maintain the unity of the Dutch Republic and to prevent the conversion of what he considered a disastrous truce into a still more disastrous peace. On both counts, he gradually moved towards support for war. Within three months of the expiry of the truce, the Dutch West India Company was established in a declaration of colonial war. Economic warfare followed immediately.

When fighting began in continental Europe late in 1621, the Spaniards concentrated on the Rhineland, and besieged the Dutch garrison in Jülich, which fell in January 1622 after a five-month siege. But this campaign was largely irrelevant to the task of breaking into the Republic's defences. That began in the following season, when the Spanish commander Spínola besieged the Brabant town of Bergen-op-Zoom. His defeat in October 1622 was the first significant setback for the Spanish army that did not result from financial weakness or mutiny. Spínola was largely inactive in 1623, but he besieged the key frontier fortress of Breda the following year.

Breda fell in May 1625, and was to be the greatest Spanish success of the war (and the inspiration of one of Velázquez's masterpieces). Nevertheless, this triumph failed to convince Olivares that laying siege to Dutch towns was other than a waste of men and money. It did not achieve a spectacular breakthrough of the Dutch defences, which was required for a conclusive Spanish victory, while it weakened the Spanish position in Europe by tying up men and resources for many months at a time when Spain was in conflict with France over the Valtelline. After the fall of Breda, the Spanish army in the Low Countries was put on the defensive, and so it remained (with a brief exception in 1629) until 1635. Instead of pursuing military advantage, the Spanish government attempted to defeat the Dutch by economic warfare.

Embargoes had begun in April 1621, but a total river and canal blockade lasted from 1625 until 1629. This had some effect on Dutch commercial prosperity, but also provoked sweeping retaliatory Dutch embargoes in October 1625 which had a catastrophic effect upon supplies to the Spanish army. Given its history of mutiny, this was a threat to the whole Spanish campaign. When the total blockade against the Dutch was lifted in April 1629, it was not because the Spaniards had gained any significant economic victory, but rather the result of urgent pleas from the Brussels government to Madrid arguing that Spanish troops were starved of pay and supplies and in no fit state to fight the Dutch. Nor could blockades in continental Europe prevent the Dutch colonial advance. In May 1624, the Dutch captured Bahía, the capital of Brazil, from the Portuguese settlers, although they were forced to surrender it in May 1625. In September 1628, Piet Heyn, one of their admirals, seized a Spanish treasure fleet worth 20 million florins (the proceeds of which were paid as a dividend to the Dutch West India Company) at Matanzas Bay in Cuba. In February 1630, the province of Pernambuco in northern Brazil, the centre of the colony's sugar production, was captured by a Dutch expeditionary force. Before long, 300 miles of the coast and the hinterland of north-east Brazil was in Dutch hands, and sugar production was largely taken under their control.

Maurice of Nassau had died in 1625, and since then the Dutch under the leadership of Frederick Henry, his brother, were on the advance in continental Europe, too. In 1629, they took Den Bosch ('s Hertogenbosch) and Wesel. Their greatest progress on land during the entire war came in 1632, with the capture of five towns—including three on the river Maas (Maastricht, Venlo and Roermond)—in quick succession. They now held almost all the crossings over the river Maas and the lower Rhine which had been formerly held by Spain. The Dutch issued a manifesto to the southern provinces, calling on the people to throw off the 'heavy and intolerable yoke of the Spaniards', and it seemed for a time that they might insist on excluding Philip IV and the Infanta Isabella from any future truce negotiations and dealing with the south directly as 'free states'.[20] The aristocracy of Flanders had been restless since the end of 1629 and Hendrik van den Bergh openly rebelled against the Spaniards in 1632. Van den Bergh had been appointed commander of the army of Flanders in 1628, but had subsequently been relieved of his post because of incompetence; in the military crisis of 1632 he defected to the Dutch. But there was no general revolt against Spanish rule, even though the high nobility was permanently excluded from the council of state as a result of van den Bergh's rebellion. Frederick Henry's military success was made possible less by political discontent in the Spanish Netherlands than by a crisis in the Habsburg military command. From 1625, the Spanish army in Flanders had been reduced in size by about a third and there were further reductions in 1632 when part of the army was sent to deal with the advance of Gustavus Adolphus against the Rhine Palatinate. It was an army starved of funds, following the loss of the silver fleet to the Dutch in 1628 and Spanish involvement in the Mantuan war, and lacking supplies because of the trade embargoes still in force. From 1627 until 1633, for the first time in the Dutch war against Spain, the forces of the northern provinces were numerically larger and better provisioned than those of the south. This remained the case until the arrival of the Cardinal-Infante Fernando with reinforcements in late 1634.

Truce negotiations between the Dutch and Spanish governments in 1629 and 1632 led to no settlement. The Dutch seemed to be on the verge of a massive victory, so they refused to make substantial territorial concessions, or to contemplate a halt to their colonial advance. The breakdown of authority in the Spanish Netherlands appeared to have gone so far that Philip IV and Olivares believed no acceptable agreement was possible without a revival of Habsburg fortunes. The French nevertheless became alarmed at signs of Dutch war-weariness, and entered into a subsidy treaty with them in June 1630, which was renewed with increased payments in April 1634. Fear of the revival in the Dutch Republic of a party favouring a new truce was one reason for the French declaration of war on Spain in May 1635.

4.2.2 *The Diversion of Spanish Resources: the Valtelline and Mantuan Wars*

The Dutch had been much helped from time to time by the diversion of Spanish troops to Italy in the 1620s. The Valtelline passes (the Valtellina itself and the Val Engadina) between northern Italy and the Swiss Confederation were vital to the Spanish Habsburgs. The Spanish navy's failure to control the English Channel left Spain dependent on the overland route for sending its troops to the Empire or to the Spanish Netherlands. It was about fifty days' march from the duchy of Milan to the Netherlands when the passes were open. The French sought to interrupt this supply route if possible (as Henri IV had attempted in 1601–3) and after 1618 relations between Spain and France deteriorated sharply over the issue. The matter was complicated: the inhabitants of the Valtelline were Catholic, but their overlords, the Grisons (or Grey Leagues), were Protestant. In July 1620, Spanish troops moved into the Valtelline while the local Catholics massacred some 600 Protestants, including their Grison overlords. Civil war resulted in the following year, and the Habsburg forces overran both the Valtelline and the rest of the Grison territory, and stationed 4,000 troops in the valleys. The completeness of this victory forced the French, weak as they were, to take counter-measures. In February 1623, they formed an alliance with Venice and, rather surprisingly, Savoy, to meet the Habsburg challenge. Though the alliance posed no immediate military threat, in view of the potential diplomatic menace, Spain conceded control of the fortresses in the Valtelline passes to the Papacy, leaving Habsburg troops with free passage through the Valtelline.

The reluctant French government was now forced to call the Spanish bluff. An ultimatum demanded that the Papacy hand over the fortresses to the French. The ambassadors of Savoy and Venice were notified of the French intention to put the dormant triple alliance into effect. The decision of the French government to resort to force was taken in mid-July 1624, before the appointment of Richelieu as chief minister, although he was already a member of the council of state. Richelieu's promotion to chief minister in mid-August did not clarify the position: as Richelieu was a cardinal of the church in a predominantly Catholic country, the Valtelline conflict posed an acute dilemma for him, since the natural allies of France (the Grisons) were Protestant. There were powerful voices in the king's council, not least Michel de Marillac, at this time finance minister, who argued that it was against the interests of Catholicism, and the French monarchy, to support the Grisons. Rather, they said, Louis XIII should concentrate on eliminating the Protestant threat at home, not on contracting alliances with Protestant states abroad which were likely to assist, or at least encourage, the Huguenots.

The war went badly for France. The first strategic objective was to cut communications between Genoa and Milan, thus hampering Spanish attempts to defend the Valtelline passes from a French invasion. However, this operation required naval support to be successful, and in 1624–5 France had no navy worth speaking of, being totally dependent on a loan of twenty ships from the Dutch (which did not become available until March 1625 and were in the end diverted to meet the Huguenot threat at La Rochelle). Without its expected naval support, the French strategy in

Italy collapsed. The army under Constable Lesdiguières made little progress, and by the autumn of 1625 Richelieu was under considerable domestic pressure to negotiate a settlement with the Pope and Philip IV. In Richelieu's view, a compromise peace with the Huguenots was desirable so that an undivided French military effort could be mounted in the Valtelline conflict. Richelieu got his way, in so far as a compromise truce was signed with the Huguenots in February 1626. However, there was insufficient domestic support for the continuation of the Valtelline war, and Richelieu's hold on power at this date was far from secure. To the fury of Savoy and Venice, the French negotiated a unilateral peace with the Spaniards at Monzón in March 1626. The outcome of the Valtelline conflict was far from the definitive victory for which Richelieu had hoped. The Papacy refused at first to order the demolition of the fortresses, as had been agreed in the peace, and it was not until 1627 that it complied. The Spaniards were able still to use the passes as they pleased in 1631 and 1633–4. 'Rectification' of the Peace of Monzón became a French war demand in the later Mantuan war, and in the meantime French diplomacy tried to retrieve the situation somewhat by making secret undertakings to its erstwhile allies which contradicted its public treaty with Spain.

The Mantuan succession was another distraction for the Spaniards; their governors in Milan had already involved them in two wars in 1613–17. At the end of December 1627, Vincenzo II Gonzaga, duke of Mantua and marquis of Montferrat, died, leaving no direct male heir. There were various claimants to the succession, but in his last will and testament, the duke had bequeathed all his lands to Charles III Gonzaga, duke of Nevers, who was a subject of the king of France. The succession was of considerable importance to the Spanish government, since the two Gonzaga states were contiguous with the western and eastern frontiers of Milan. Military intervention was not inevitable or altogether necessary, and Olivares would have been wise to counsel prudence to Philip IV. It was most unlikely that Nevers, once installed in his lands, would act simply as a French puppet; or if he did, that he would be able to pose any serious strategic threat to Milan, which was strongly fortified. Olivares accepted that Nevers was the strongest claimant; his only serious drawbacks, as far as the Spaniards were concerned, were his French origins, and the marriage he had arranged between his son and the late duke's niece without first seeking the approval of Philip IV. Nevertheless, the Spanish chief minister allowed his king's military power to become embroiled in an unnecessary war once Gonzalo Fernández de Córdoba, the governor of Milan, moved on his own initiative to partition Montferrat between Spain and Savoy. It was an act of simple opportunism, but one which ran the risk of bringing French armies into Italy to back Nevers's claim. It is true that at first the Spanish military position appeared overwhelming, with a rapid deterioration of Nevers's hold on Montferrat until only the fortress of Casale, itself under siege, remained his. The legal pretext for Spanish intervention also seemed strong, since Mantua and Montferrat were nominally fiefs of the Empire. Ferdinand II, acting in the spirit of the Oñate agreement (see chapter 3.4.4) and in the interests of his Spanish Habsburg relatives, refused to 'invest' Nevers with the fiefs in March 1628. Subsequently, an Imperial army of invasion was sent into Mantua to assist the Spanish cause against Nevers, and it sacked the capital in July 1630.

Olivares clearly misunderstood the logistical difficulties that the Spanish army would face in besieging Casale: it was to cost 10 million ducats and end in failure. He also underestimated the resolution and the capacity of the French to overrun Savoy and invade Montferrat in two successive campaigns in 1629–30. Initially, France was diverted by the war with England (July 1627–April 1629); the English invaded the Ile-de-Ré and so unleashed the last rebellion of the Huguenots (September 1627–June 1629). Had Casale quickly fallen to the Spaniards, the French would have been powerless to prevent a quick Spanish victory in Montferrat. With the fall of La Rochelle at the end of October 1628, however, a French army was freed for service abroad in Nevers's cause. There was little that the French could do to bolster Nevers's position in Mantua, which depended on his own efforts and those of his Venetian allies. Once Savoy was overrun by Louis XIII, duke Charles-Emmanuel was obliged to accord the French army free passage to Casale in Montferrat; this army succeeded in relieving the first siege in March 1629. The French troops captured the strategic fortress of Pinerolo during their second campaign in March 1630, and so their supply lines from Dauphiné to Italy were secured.

Had either invasion failed, Richelieu's position in the king's council would have been undermined. Even so, he was hard pressed by his critics in the summer and early autumn of 1630. The French retention of Pinerolo was of particular concern because it was (correctly) perceived as likely to bring about permanent conflict with the Spaniards. Disagreement within Louis XIII's council was intensified by Richelieu's repudiation of the peace terms signed with the Emperor at Regensburg in October 1630. Richelieu survived the crisis of the Day of Dupes, and with the removal of his critics, his own authority was strengthened (see chapter 4.4.2). Papal mediation brought an end to the war by the two treaties of Cherasco (April and June 1631), but the outcome was the worst possible one for Spain. There was no territorial gain such as had been envisaged in the partition scheme with Savoy. The Emperor recognized Nevers as the legitimate ruler of Mantua and Montferrat, while as a result of secret undertakings with the new (and pro-French) duke Victor-Amadeus of Savoy, the French retained the fortress of Pinerolo, despite an undertaking in the terms of the peace to surrender it. This gave them a permanent capacity to intervene in Italian affairs, something they had not enjoyed before the war.

4.2.3 *The Franco-Dutch War against Spain, 1635–1648*

Neither France nor Spain regarded the outbreak of war in 1635 as more than a small-scale affair (a 'diversion' in contemporary parlance), and certainly neither anticipated its developing into the full-scale struggle for resources over a whole generation. It has recently been argued that although France declared war first, Spain was actually the more belligerent power. On the other hand, it is clear that Spain was primarily concerned with an offensive war against the Dutch and not against France. In the end, the hostile actions of both states made a drift into open war almost inevitable. The French retention of Pinerolo was regarded by Philip IV as a legitimate *casus belli*. Further attempts by the Papacy to prevent a Franco-Spanish war were resisted behind the scenes by the Spaniards, since Urban VIII was regarded as Francophile. In April 1634, the Spanish council of state debated the possibility of declaring war on France, but found that the European coalition necessary to sustain such a war (Spain, the Emperor, Savoy and Lorraine) did not exist, and the declaration was postponed. Instead, the French declared war first, in May 1635, to forestall imminent Spanish aggression, following the arrest at the end of March of the elector of Trier by a column of Spanish soldiers. Already fearing the prospect of Spanish expansion from the Netherlands into the Rhineland, the elector of Trier had placed himself under French protection in December 1631; and the council of state of Louis XIII, discussing his arrest, concluded that 'the king cannot avoid taking up arms to avenge the affront which he has received by the imprisonment of a prince who has been placed under his protection'.[21] Louis XIII was profoundly distrustful of Spanish intentions, and in a secret memorandum to Richelieu in August 1634 he had argued the case for a 'vigorous open war against Spain in order to secure a beneficial general peace'.[22] Only the prospect of the financial burden of a long war had led Richelieu to postpone intervention until it was imperative, following the collapse of Swedish military power after the battle of Nördlingen in September 1634.

The first Franco-Dutch campaign, a combined invasion of the Spanish Netherlands in June 1635, failed. Philip IV and Olivares had high hopes of a Spanish counter-offensive, but the government at Madrid was divided on whether it was preferable to concentrate the war effort on France or the Dutch Republic. The French boundaries were more vulnerable to invasion, and so the decision was taken to concentrate military action there. In 1636, the army of Flanders reached Corbie on the Somme, about

80 miles from Paris. The Spaniards also invaded from Franche-Comté in the east; and had their planned invasion of Catalonia not been deferred until 1637, this triple offensive might have knocked France out of the war. But the Spaniards were unable to repeat their early success. In December 1638, events began to move in favour of the Bourbons: the capture of Breisach by Bernard of Saxe-Weimar, the German mercenary captain in French pay, cut the Rhineland supply route to the Spanish Netherlands. Spain's best prospect of splitting the Franco-Dutch alliance nevertheless appeared to be to force the Dutch, who had been fighting longer, to make a separate peace; but the invasion of France reduced Spanish pressure on them. In October 1637, the Dutch recaptured Breda, the great trophy of Spínola's campaigns in the 1620s, and this ended the Spanish land offensive against them.

The last phase of the war consequently took place at sea. In 1639, two large armadas were dispatched from Spain, one to Brazil to try to halt the Dutch offensive there by recapturing Pernambuco, the other to the Channel to force supplies and men through to the Low Countries and to challenge Dutch maritime supremacy. The attack on Pernambuco failed even to materialize—the attempt to recover Brazil was a fiasco resulting from incompetent admiralship on the part of the count of La Torre. The Dutch retained their hold on Brazil until the rising of the Portuguese settlers in 1645; this rebellion was eventually successful in 1654. Moreover, the Dutch were once more on the advance in the former Portuguese empire. In August 1641, they occupied Luanda, the base of the Angolan slave trade, and threatened to starve Portuguese Brazil of its plantation labour. (Not until 1648 did the settlers evict the Dutch from Angola.) In 1641, the Dutch East India Company finally succeeded in capturing Malacca, the centre of the spice trade. The Spaniards fared no better with the second armada. At the battle of the Downs in September 1639, the Dutch fleet under Admiral Tromp destroyed thirty-two Spanish warships. The Spanish attempt to break the deadlock had failed, and the Dutch were able to pursue land campaigns against them in 1641 and 1644–5. Although a formal cease-fire was not agreed until June 1647, the Dutch were unable to campaign further because of Holland's refusal to provide funds for the war effort.

The collapse of Spanish naval and military pressure on the Dutch coincided with Habsburg reverses on other fronts and the diversion of resources caused by the rebellions of Catalonia and Portugal. The French hoped to use the Catalan revolt as a means of attacking Philip IV in 'his own kingdoms', by invading Aragon and Valencia and cutting Spanish naval communications with Italy. The French had some striking successes on the southern front, notably the capture of Perpignan in September 1642. The death of the Cardinal-Infante Fernando in November 1641 weakened the command structure in the Spanish army of Flanders, but even so a French invasion was repulsed at Honnecourt in May 1642. Almost exactly a year later, the French had their revenge with Condé's great victory at Rocroi in May 1643. Thereafter, the French made steady progress in the Spanish Netherlands, capturing Gravelines in July 1644, ten towns in 1645 (more than the Dutch had taken in two decades of fighting), and Courtrai and Dunkirk the following year.

These rapid successes simply increased Dutch willingness to make peace with Spain, for the risk inherent in the Franco-Dutch alliance was that partition of the Spanish Netherlands would make a resurgent France the neighbour of the Dutch Republic. 'The Frenchman as your friend, not your neighbour' (*Gallicus amicus non vicinus*)[23] was a maxim cited frequently as an explanation of the equivocal attitude of the Dutch to their ally. It was a view carefully exploited by Philip IV's plenipotentiary at the Westphalian peace negotiations, the count of Peñaranda, who was convinced that Spain's interest lay in peace with the Dutch, not with France. He considered the Dutch more reliable, less powerful and lacking the natural rivalry of the French against Spain. If territory had to be ceded to the Dutch in the Spanish Netherlands, this would serve to bolster them against France. Conversely, to make territorial concessions to the French would 'give them the arms and means to make themselves masters of all seventeen provinces'.[24]

4.2.4 *The Peace of Münster (1648) and its Aftermath in the Dutch Republic*

In retrospect, Spanish duplicity in the peace negotiations and their wish to make a separate peace with the Dutch is very evident. In the winter of 1645–6, Spain proposed a marriage settlement between Louis XIV and María Teresa, Philip IV's eldest daughter, giving her part of the Spanish Netherlands as dowry. Cardinal Mazarin, the French chief minister after 1643, had great hopes from this marriage, because there was a strong chance that the Infanta would become Philip IV's heir presumptive. However, the Spaniards never intended to settle on these terms, and Peñaranda cynically arranged the disclosure of the proposed marriage alliance to the Dutch. When the news reached the Dutch Republic in February 1646, there were anti-French riots at The Hague and the states of Holland passed a resolution declaring that 'France, enlarged by possession of the Spanish Netherlands, will be a dangerous neighbour for our country'.[25] Despite the blandishments of the French ambassador, Abel Servien, the Dutch broke their alliance and ended the so-called Eighty Years' War against Spain (1568–1648) by the Treaty of Münster of January 1648.

The treaty was a great victory for the Dutch. Philip IV bound himself and his successors to a perpetual peace with the Dutch, and recognized them as 'free and sovereign states, provinces and lands' upon which he laid no claim.[26] The Republic made territorial gains from the war, keeping slices of Flanders, Brabant (the so-called 'generality') and Limburg which it had conquered, but not Upper Gelderland. Most of the other points at dispute between the Spaniards and the Dutch were settled in favour of the Republic. Dutch Catholics continued to have no rights of worship, and the river Scheldt remained closed, thus landlocking Antwerp. Spain had gone to war to weaken the Dutch Republic politically and economically in the old world and the new. As a result of the conflict, it was Spain that was weakened. Peace was made with the Dutch so that the war could be continued against France and its proxies, the Catalan and Portuguese rebels. The Dutch made only one concession: they promised not to attack the Spanish empire in the new world.

The brunt of the Dutch attack had been directed against the weaker partner in the union of the crowns, Portugal, whose imperial possessions differed in kind from those of Spain: they were isolated trading posts rather than settled communities and thus were more vulnerable (see chapter 8.4.2). The two Portuguese territories which had been settled inland, Angola and Brazil, were successfully defended after 1648. The Dutch largely dominated European trade with Spain itself after 1648 and they were the most important interlopers in Spanish America, especially at Cartagena (near Panama) and Buenos Aires. By 1661, Spain and its empire overseas were dominated economically by foreign capital and products. This had been substantially less true during the war period because Spanish embargoes and controls had hampered Dutch economic expansion. The institution which had made these controls effective was the Seville Admiralty Board (*Almirantazgo*), established in October 1624 with powers cutting across regional privileges (as did those of the Inquisition). After 1649, its zeal for acting against the Dutch was restricted by Philip IV, and it was finally abolished in January 1661.

The circumstances of a 'sweet peace' in 1648 released political tensions in the Dutch Republic comparable with those of the years 1609–19. William II, stadholder since March 1647, the leading member of the Orange dynasty and brother-in-law to the exiled Charles II of England, wanted to harness his cause to the Stuart dynasty and renew the war with Spain. However, Amsterdam's interests conflicted: 'to enjoy the fruits of the . . . peace' required a reduction in the size of the army and its financial burden.[27] At the end of June 1650, William II denounced this attitude, and arrested six deputies of the states of Holland who shared this viewpoint. His cousin, Count William Frederick, was dispatched with an army to take Amsterdam by surprise, but failed. Though two of the most vehement critics of Orangist policy, Andrew and Cornelius Bicker, were forced to resign their posts in Amsterdam's city government, no permanent constitutional change was achieved. After William II's death in November 1650, the opponents of the Orange dynasty were firmly in control, since William left only a widow, Mary Stuart, and an infant son born a week after his death. After a period of transition, Johan de Witt became councillor pensionary to the states of Holland in July 1653, a post which gave him the political leadership of the Dutch Republic until his resignation, and subsequent murder, in August 1672. The exclusion of the infant William III from his father's offices rumbled on as an issue in Dutch domestic politics throughout the 1650s and 1660s. De Witt regarded exclusion as necessary to avoid a repetition of the attempted coup of 1650, and any adverse dynastic commitments following from a marriage alliance made with the Stuarts in 1641. Theorists such as Pieter de la Court in the *Interest of Holland* (1661) went further, equating true freedom with rule without a stadholder, and arguing that the Dutch Republic needed peace for reasons of trade. One consequence of the 1648 treaty was to make the Dutch the neutrals in most of the European conflicts before 1672, but de Witt found absolute neutrality impossible to achieve. He inherited one Anglo-Dutch war (1652–4), and could not prevent two others (1665–7 and 1672–4) (see chapter 8.4.4). After 1661, the Dutch had more to fear from a resurgent France which might seize Brabant and Flanders than from a weakened Spain. Yet the old distrust of Spain lingered on, and de Witt was unwilling to enter a firm alliance with the Spaniards in the years 1661–72 which alone might have served to restrain French ambitions unleashed in the war of 1672.

4.3 The Survival of Spanish Habsburg Power, 1598–1665

There are few livelier historical controversies than the debate about Spanish decline in the seventeenth century. Historians have talked about the 'rise of France' and the 'decline of Spain' as if they were inevitable phenomena. It may be more accurate to term the years before 1656 (and perhaps up to the death of Philip IV in 1665) as years when Spanish power struggled to survive rather than fell into decline. On the other hand, it seems perverse to consign the concept of Spanish decline to the realm of historical mythology, and to argue, as some historians have done, that Spain could not decline because it had never risen to the status of a great economic power. Political decline must be distinguished from economic, though the two are interrelated and political power results in part (as has been seen from the example of the Dutch) from economic power. The contemporary economic writers, the *arbitristas*, were well aware of Spanish decline. Martín González de Cellorigo, writing in 1600, devoted the first chapter of his *Memorial for the Restoration of the Republic* to the theme of 'how our Spain, however fertile and abundant it may be, is subject to the decline [*declinación*] to which all republics are prone'.[28] He thought the kingdom 'finished, the royal treasury exhausted, the subjects ruined and the republic consumed ...' He observed that Spain lacked entrepreneurs, 'people of the middle sort, whom neither wealth nor poverty prevents from pursuing the rightful kind of business ...' He noted the failure of the owners of land in Castile to ensure its efficient exploitation: 'Those who have the means have not the will', he wrote, 'while those who have the will have not the means.'[29] Cellorigo cannot be dismissed as simply an isolated pessimist; his gloom was shared by a range of contemporary writers. Philip III's government failed to match the words of the *arbitristas* with appropriate remedial action.

4.3.1 *Financial and Economic Problems under Philip III*

The opportunity for reform existed during the reign of Philip III, as the government gradually disengaged itself from Philip II's over-ambitious foreign policy in northern Europe. Moreover, Castile could still expect economic and financial benefits from its empire in the new world. Two of the most important sets of statistics which have been used to demonstrate Spain's economic decline in the seventeenth century are those of the tonnage figures for Spanish transatlantic commerce and the monetary values for the imports of bullion from the new world. Both show a dramatic reduction, but also reveal that the high point of Spanish transatlantic trade was reached in 1605, when the total tonnage of sailings to and from the new world exceeded 59,000 *toneladas*. Not until the crisis year of 1640 did the figure fall below 23,000 *toneladas*, although there was a consistent trend towards decline in the intervening period (see chapter 8.4.3). Registered bullion imports appear to have fallen dramatically over a similar period, from an average of over 8 million ducats per annum in the years 1591–5 to less than a million ducats per annum in the years 1656–60. Yet the registration process is known to have ceased to be effective in the seventeenth century. According to the registers, a total of only 4 million ducats were imported in the years 1656–60, whereas the Dutch public gazettes provide evidence of total bullion imports to the Spanish peninsula in the region of 69 million ducats for the period: indeed, the shipment of 1659 was the largest since 1595. Even the official registers show that the annual average of bullion imports still exceeded 7 million ducats per annum towards the end of Philip III's reign (1616–20), though the direct benefit to the crown from such imports was much less— only just over a million ducats per annum at the end of Philip III's reign.

The responsibility for wasting a slender opportunity to reform the

government must rest with Philip III, a nonentity, and his favourite
(*valido*), a man more than twice his age—the duke of Lerma, chief minister
for twenty years in all but name. The new king reformed the councils of
state, war and finance, and summoned them more regularly than his father
had done. But the regime of Philip III and Lerma is remembered best for
two measures of very doubtful benefit to the Spanish kingdoms. The first,
begun in 1599 and continued intermittently until 1626, was the introduction of copper coinage (*vellón*), minted largely from Swedish copper
sold at Amsterdam. The effect of this rapid debasement was to accentuate
price fluctuations and the general inflation of Castilian prices. The second
measure was the expulsion of about 300,000 Moriscos in 1609–10. Nearly
half of the Moriscos lived in the kingdom of Valencia alone, and there
were considerably fewer in all the other Spanish kingdoms, so the proportionate effect of the expulsion was greatest in Valencia. Although
Lerma and his family came from Old Castile, his original title, marquis of
Denia, was Valencian. Denia was an important coastal town only about 90
kilometres south of Valencia itself. It is more than likely that the marquis
of Denia and (after November 1599) duke of Lerma shared the fears of
nobles haunted by the prospect of an Ottoman sea invasion timed to
coincide with a revolt in the Iberian peninsula. Whatever its economic
disadvantages, expulsion was unquestionably popular, not least because
of its supposed security aspect. On the other hand, it was largely irrelevant
to the crucial problems facing the Spanish monarchy, on which, at best,
Lerma postponed decision. At worst, he exacerbated them. His central
preoccupation was to build up his own fortune, which increased from a
modest 8,000 ducats a year in 1598 to over 932,000 ducats a year by 1625,
the year of his death. His primary concern was to monopolize court
patronage, not to direct policy in the councils; Lerma was lavish in
distributing offices, pensions and privileges. For much of the reign up to
1615 he sought to isolate the king from rival advice and influence by
elaborate court progresses around Old Castile. The court itself increased
in size and extravagance during this period. The maintenance of the royal
family alone under Philip III cost Castile about 1.3 million ducats a year,
or over 10 per cent of the budget.

Most serious of all, Lerma allowed the imbalance in the fiscal burden
between Castile and the other kingdoms to grow to unmanageable proportions. Philip III neglected the subjects of his 'dependent' territories, as
the other kingdoms were now regarded: 'the king is Castilian and nothing
else, and that is how he appears to the other kingdoms', it was said.[30] In
1622, the Catalans lamented that in the previous thirty-seven years they
had seen their king and lord only twice. Philip III summoned the *Cortes* of
Catalonia and Valencia only once (respectively in 1599 and 1604) and the
grants of money from them were derisory; he did not summon the *Cortes*

of Aragon at all. In the meantime, Castile was expected to contribute 6.2 million ducats a year to the royal treasury. Not surprisingly, there were difficulties in extracting these revenues even from Castile. There were protracted negotiations in 1603, 1610 and 1619 for an agreement over the levy of the *millones*, the tax on articles of consumption which was supposed to bring in 3 million ducats a year. By the end of Philip III's reign, the crown had relinquished to the Castilian *Cortes* control of this revenue, and thus some measure of its financial autonomy. After Lerma fell from power in 1618, his son and successor, the duke of Uceda, showed no greater energy than his father in tackling the fundamental problems of the Spanish kingdoms. Gradually power was wrested away from Uceda by the faction of Baltasar de Zúñiga, who favoured intervention on the Imperial side in 1618–19, in what were to prove the first campaigns of the Thirty Years' War.

4.3.2 *The Policies of Olivares as Chief Minister, 1622–1643*

When Philip III died in March 1621, he was succeeded by his 16-year-old son, Philip IV, a boy more intelligent than his father (though scarcely worthy of the epithet 'the great' except in terms of the length of time he ruled). The new king brought in new ministers: after the death of Zúñiga in October 1622, real power came to rest with his nephew, the king's child-hood mentor, Gaspar de Guzmán, count (and after January 1625, count-duke) of Olivares, who remained chief minister and favourite until his dismissal in January 1643. He was quite different from most of his predecessors, and provided—in the early years of the reign at least—a counterpoise to the king's irresolution and inexperience. Where Lerma had vacillated and compromised, Olivares was aggressive and inflexible. Not long after he assumed office, the Valtelline problem presented Olivares with the threat of war against France. This brought to a head the rigidity of the constitutional structure at home and the imbalance in the fiscal burden between Castile and the other kingdoms. On Christmas Day 1624, Olivares presented the so-called 'great' memorandum to Philip IV, advising the king secretly to 'plan and work to reduce these kingdoms of which Spain is composed to the style and laws of Castile, with no difference whatsoever . . .'[31] In essence, the scheme was to Castilianize Aragon, Catalonia, Valencia and Portugal; but in return to remove the Castilian monopoly of office. It was doubtful whether access to office would have acted as sufficient inducement to the regions to forgo their privileges at this time: it was not conceded until June 1640, and then not admitted publicly for fear of an adverse reaction in Castile. However, the offer came to seem profoundly unattractive when Olivares's second, short-term plan, the Union of Arms, was announced in the autumn of 1625.

The aim of the Union was to provide a common reserve of 140,000 men of which Castile and the Indies would still contribute the largest contingent (44,000 men); there would be fixed contributions from the other kingdoms (for example, 16,000 men each from Catalonia and Portugal). This raised the age-old Spanish objection to their troops being used for service abroad, an objection which had prevented Catalonia from assisting Flanders and Aragon from supporting the Habsburg cause in Milan. (In fact, Catalonia gave no assistance in foreign wars. When the French invaded the Basque province of Guipúzcoa in 1638, the Aragonese and Valencians assisted Castile in its defence, but the Catalans did not.) To Olivares, this stubborn defence of privilege was more than an irritant; it was incomprehensible. The fiscal burden on Castile was excessive and therefore had to be shared with the other kingdoms. Catalonia he mistakenly thought was a 'rich province, abundant in men and supplies, and the most unburdened of all these kingdoms'.[32] He assumed the population of Catalonia to be over a million when in fact it was under 400,000. Above all, he wanted to make Catalonia the 'place of arms' of the Iberian peninsula, as was the Spanish Netherlands in northern Europe. However, with the Spanish preoccupation in the Mantuan war, the Union of Arms scheme was placed in abeyance. Indeed, by the time of the outbreak of war with France in May 1635, nothing had been achieved within the Iberian peninsula to improve the potential of the Spanish Habsburg war machine.

The financial problems of the monarchy had actually worsened. When Piet Heyn captured the Spanish silver fleet in 1628, Olivares was unable to secure loan contracts from the financiers. The following year, 2 million ducats were expropriated from private individuals at Seville and dispatched to Milan to pay for the Mantuan war. During this period, there was no growth in the imports of Spanish American bullion such as Philip II had enjoyed to pay for his increased expenditure in the 1590s. On the contrary, in the crisis year of 1640 no silver fleet arrived in Castile at all. However, according to the Dutch public gazettes, the total imports of bullion were much higher than the official figures show, which serves to illustrate the twin problems of fraud and faulty record-keeping faced by the Spanish government. It is estimated that there were total receipts of 75.8 million ducats between 1626 and 1630 (as against 29.9 million officially recorded), 60.9 million between 1631 and 1635 (as against 20.5 million) and 62 million between 1636 and 1640 (as against 19.5 million). Even assuming that the problem was one of inaccurate record-keeping rather than deliberate massaging of the receipts, the higher figures did not necessarily help Philip IV, since the king's share was always much lower than that of private individuals. Even so, the Dutch gazettes suggest that in the years 1623–33 at least, the king received substantially more bullion than the official records show.

The bullion from the New World helped the financial crisis somewhat; but it could not remove the crown's financial difficulties altogether. Olivares did try to implement other schemes to relieve the situation, but these were strenuously opposed. The *Cortes* of Castile forced him to abandon the attempted introduction of the salt tax in 1631–2, and yet a further increase of the sales tax (the *millones*) was ruled out. Shortly before the French declaration of war in May 1635, the council of finance found itself committed to total expenditure of 11 million ducats a year compared with 8 million a decade earlier. Olivares's attempt to reform the constitutional and tax structure of the Spanish kingdoms required the preconditions of peace or a victorious war. Force might be necessary to overcome regional objections to such reforms. Moreover, Catalonia's proximity to France made its loyalty suspect. The Catalans were likely to tolerate only a short war resulting in a quick victory. As the objections to Olivares's policies increased, so the minister's tone became more strident. 'The Catalans ought to see more of the world than Catalonia', he exclaimed, 'the devil take the[ir] constitutions.'[33] Not only were Olivares's policies criticized, but also his methods, and there was opposition to his rule within Castile as well as in the outlying kingdoms. His recourse to special committees (juntas), staffed with his own friends and relations and select officials in whom he could place his trust, alienated support and led to a quite unwarranted nostalgia for the tranquil regime of Lerma. The nobles resented the crown's fiscal demands and retired from Madrid to their estates in self-imposed or compulsory exile. In turn, the chief minister became obsessed with the absence of 'leaders' (*cabezas*) among the aristocracy.[34] It was symptomatic of the alienation of the crown and the nobility that in 1641 a plot to turn Andalusia into an independent kingdom on the model of Portugal was revealed. The principal conspirators were two Andalusian nobles, one of whom was found to be Olivares's own cousin, the duke of Medina Sidonia. Unlike their French counterparts, however, the Castilian nobles—and thus the majority of the nobility—remained quiescent, but a much more pliant and circumspect regime was needed to secure their support after the fall of Olivares in 1643.

4.3.3 *The Catalan Revolt, 1640–1652*

The war against France compelled Olivares to billet troops on an already resentful Catalan population. This became the central cause of conflict between Castile and the standing committee of the Catalan *Cortes* which defended the principality's privileges (the *Diputació*). In May 1640, the accumulated resentments of the Catalan peasants burst into the open; they rebelled against the army billeted on the province, and marched on Barcelona. In the following month, the viceroy, the count of Santa

Coloma, was murdered and Olivares was forced to acknowledge the existence of a 'general rebellion, without a leader and without foreign provocation . . .'[35] The protest of the lower ranks of society was followed by a second rebellion, that of the political leaders of Catalonia, the *Diputats*, who argued that their struggle was not with Philip IV, but only with his evil counsellors (by whom they meant chiefly Olivares). A Castilian army was sent to deal with the revolt. The Catalans in response invited the French to invade Catalonia in September 1640, but it was only after the Castilian army massacred some 600 Catalans at Cambrils in mid-December that the *Diputats* resolved to strengthen their ties with France. In mid-January 1641 a Catalan republic was declared, but because of divisions among the Catalan leaders, the scheme proved impracticable and lasted only a week. Later in the same month, following the surrender of Tarragona to the Castilians, the *Diputats* simply transferred sovereignty to Louis XIII 'as in the time of Charlemagne, with a contract to observe our constitutions'.[36] The French rapidly installed their own regime, which was to prove just as distasteful to the Catalans as that of Philip IV.

The French position in Catalonia was always weak because of the nature of the revolt itself. Just as they had refused to contribute towards Olivares's Union of Arms, so the Catalans refused to provide troops for their own defence against Castile. Instead, the French army had to do this, and did so with reasonable success until 1648. The French generals, called viceroys, were instructed to act in a manner similar to that of their Spanish predecessors when Catalonia was under Philip IV's rule. There was a rapid turnover of viceroys which had an unsettling effect on the conduct of government and tended to increase the already serious faction fighting. With the exception of Harcourt's capture of Rosas in May 1645, the early French victories were not followed up after 1643. Instead, the Castilian army recaptured Monzón and Lérida in 1643–4, and Philip IV improved his chances of regaining Catalonia for the Habsburgs by taking a solemn oath at Lérida in July 1644 to observe the Catalan constitution. Between 1646 and 1648 the French were held to a stalemate in Catalonia. When the French crown declared bankruptcy in 1648, and its troops everywhere were forced to live off the land, support for the French cause collapsed in Catalonia. It had become increasingly clear that the French regime operated in favour of a relatively small number of families who benefited from the confiscated estates and offices of Philip IV's supporters. This small circle of support could only have been broadened following upon military success. With the fall of Barcelona to the Castilian army in October 1652, these French supporters were forced to withdraw to Roussillon. Three months later, Philip IV granted a general pardon, and promised to observe all the principality's laws and liberties as they had existed at the time of his accession to the throne. The Catalan revolt was ended, but the Catalan exiles remained the leading protagonists in the struggle of French Roussillon against Philip IV and opposed the frontier established in 1659, by which France acquired Roussillon and Cerdagne but not the rest of Catalonia.

4.3.4 *The War of Portuguese Secession, 1640–1668*

The secession of Portugal, which had formed part of the Spanish Habsburg inheritance since 1580, was of greater European significance than the rebellion of Catalonia. It was not simply because the war lasted much longer, indeed for nearly thirty years. Olivares had rather taken Portugal for granted. 'Portugal must come to our help in Catalonia', he pronounced, '. . . because on the outcome in Catalonia depends our ability to go to the relief of Brazil . . .'[37] He even produced figures to show that the proposed Portuguese assistance in Catalonia would cost less than a quarter of the Castilian assistance to the Portuguese settlers in Brazil. Despite their lack of achievement, the Castilians had done their best to defend the Portuguese empire, especially Brazil, against Dutch attack. Moreover, there had been neither a war fought along the Portuguese frontier nor a large army billeted on the kingdom, both of which Catalonia had suffered. News of the Catalan revolt none the less encouraged the Portuguese to end a union with Castile that no longer held any attractions. Philip III had visited Portugal only once, in 1619, and Philip IV had been there only as prince (on the same occasion) and not at all as king. A small but influential Hispanophile party in Portugal was eliminated by July 1641. The Portuguese Jesuits, who in 1580 had proved a decisive factor in bringing about the union of the crowns, changed sides in 1640 to help end the 'sixty years' captivity' for reasons that have never been fully explained.

The Portuguese rebelled for a number of other reasons which were deeply rooted in the national psychology, and provided the secession with a unity totally lacking in Catalonia. In the summer of 1637 there had been a revolt in the Alentejo, the Algarve and Ribatejo against the tax demands of the civil governor (*corregidor*) of Évora. Olivares was convinced that this was less a hunger riot than an uprising in defence of Portugal's laws and liberties, and royal troops were sent to the area to restore order in January 1638. Support for the old ruling house of Avis remained strong and the national hope of 'Sebastianism' had taken firm root among the population. (There had been several 'false Sebastians' during the later sixteenth century, named after Sebastian I, who was killed in battle in 1578. Legend had it that Sebastian had not been killed in Morocco. At Venice in 1598, a pretender claimed to be him, and subsequently there were rumours that Pope Clement VIII had received Sebastian at Rome. It was said that the Pope had recognized the justice of his claim, and had

ordered Philip III to hand over the kingdom to him on pain of excommunication. Three falsified Papal bulls dating from different pontificates
circulated in Portugal giving credence to these claims.) The Catalans had
no obvious native dynasty, but Portuguese sentiment was able to rally
around the duke of Braganza, who was in nearest collateral line to the
house of Avis (he was the son of John III's daughter Catarina). He was the
leading aristocrat and the greatest landowner in Portugal. In 1639,
Olivares recognized his key role by appointing him 'Governor of the Arms
of Portugal', and charged him with equipping an army under the Union
scheme, a task which worked to the advantage of the secessionists.
Knowing that this army was to be used the following year to suppress the
Catalan revolt, the conspirators had to act with speed. The result was that
Braganza was crowned as John IV of Portugal in mid-December 1640,
with the proviso that he was king only 'until the return of king Sebastian'
(who by then would have been aged 86!).[38]

The new king entered into a treaty with Louis XIII in June 1641. But the
French lacked the naval power to supply sufficient arms, munitions and
grain to sustain a war with Spain and success depended almost entirely on
support from the Dutch. With cynical disregard for the fate of the
Portuguese settlers in Brazil and Angola, John IV signed a ten years' truce
in June 1641, which suspended the Portuguese claim to north-east Brazil.
In return he received significant Dutch military and naval assistance. The
Portuguese rebellion undermined Spanish power much more fundamentally than the Catalan revolt, because it weakened the embargo
against the Dutch, who quickly re-established their control of the European carrying trade. However, the new alliance with the Dutch was
strained by colonial tensions resulting from the rising of the Portugese
settlers in Brazil and Angola, which led to war in 1657–61. In the peace of
1661, the Dutch received an indemnity as well as Portuguese recognition
of their hold on Guinea and their empire in the Far East. But the course of
the Portuguese war on land against Castile was quite different and much
more decisive than the war at sea. They won several important victories, at
Elvas in 1658, at Ameixial in 1663 and at Villaviciosa in 1665, thus making
secession inevitable. However, Philip IV was spared the final humiliation
of conceding Portuguese independence, which occurred in February 1668
under the regency government.

4.3.5 *Don Luis de Haro and the Policy of Conciliation, 1643–1661*

Inevitably Olivares was blamed for the twin disasters of the Catalan revolt
and the Portuguese secession. In January 1643, he asked to retire from
royal service on grounds of ill health: the king commented that he had
'held off granting him this permission because of the void that his

departure [would] create and the loneliness that his absence [would] cause me'.[39] The departure of Olivares at first convinced Philip IV that he must rule his kingdoms personally, 'since our present difficulties require all my personal attention for their remedy'. It was better, he thought, to treat all ministers equally, 'listening to all without favouring one at another's expense'.[40] Philip began to chair meetings of the council of state on a regular basis, but early in 1647 he appointed Olivares's nephew, Luis de Haro, as chief minister: 'it would be quite inappropriate', Philip argued in explaining his decision, for the king 'to go from house to house among [his] ministers and secretaries, checking on their prompt and proper discharge of their duty . . .'[41] The king's resolution to govern personally had thus lasted only four years. The rise to power of Luis de Haro was less flamboyant and inexorable than that of his uncle, Olivares, and it did not go unchallenged. The former viceroy of Naples, Medina de las Torres, enjoyed considerable power and wealth: although excluded from the *Junta de Estado* dominated by Haro, he was the effective chairman of the council of Aragon and after 1654 he also served as president of the council of Italy. Medina's power, and the balancing of the factions by Philip IV, has led one recent historian to assert that Haro never achieved the predominance enjoyed by Lerma and Olivares between 1598 and 1643.

It is also generally considered that Haro governed with more circumspection and more attention to the wishes of the aristocracy than did his uncle. This was both a consequence of the opposition to Olivares during his last years and a response to the clear signs of aristocratic discontent after 1645, which coincided with a wave of popular rebellion. Peasant and urban unrest swept through the south of Spain in the years 1647–52: at Granada in May 1648 the mob chanted 'long live the king and death to the bad government',[42] and eventually the agitation succeeded in securing the replacement of the civil governor (*corregidor*). At Córdoba in May 1652, the rioting was quelled when extra food supplies were found and a general pardon was issued. Oppressive taxation, harvest failures and the general unpopularity of the government seem to have coalesced as general causes of the agitation, although each riot had its individual precipitant. It was thus expedient for the crown to strengthen its ties with the nobility as the best means of preserving peace and stability. Disgruntled nobles were placated by fiscal concessions to their tenants, and encouraged to return to court, some being offered posts in the government following the abolition of some of Olivares's special juntas. (By the time of Olivares's fall there were more than thirty juntas in existence, and another had to be created in order to discuss their abolition.)

At first, Haro's regime continued the disastrous policies of Olivares's last years. The debt rescheduling—or bankruptcy of the crown's financiers—of 1647 was mismanaged, bringing only 10 million ducats to the crown. The official registers show a fall of over 60 per cent in silver remittances from Spanish America to the crown in the years 1646–50. However, the evidence of the Dutch public gazettes reveals that total imports of precious metals were in the region of 62 million ducats— comparable to the figures the gazettes record for the period 1636–40— rather than the 16.5 million in the official registers, with fraud and non-registration accounting for the difference. The Spanish monarchy was the main loser in this, and indeed, there is reason to suppose that its position was worse than the official figures suggest, since the requirements of overseas defence and administration kept an increasing share of the royal treasure in the Indies. The royal share was perhaps only 14 per cent of the total shipment, much lower than the figure of 30 per cent suggested by the official records. The king received only 4.8 million ducats from the record shipment of 1659; private individuals received 29.2 million. The royal portion declined still further in the later seventeenth century, which contributed crucially to the monarchy's weakness.

The spread of discontent in the outlying regions of the Spanish empire was an equally important problem. There were urban insurrections at Palermo in Sicily and at Naples in the summer of 1647. The revolt of Palermo lasted only from May to September 1647, but that of Naples was considerably longer (July 1647–April 1648) and much more serious. Towards the end of October 1647, a republic was proclaimed there under the protection of the king of France. In December, the duke of Guise disembarked to assist the rebellion with the title of 'duke of the republic' and powers comparable to a Dutch stadholder. But the revolt lacked clear aims and co-ordinated leadership and faltered without French military and naval support, which was unavailable because of the financial pressures on the French monarchy. Naples opened its gates to the Spanish army in April 1648 and in the same month a general amnesty was issued (see chapter 7.5.1). There were no further revolts before the death of Luis de Haro in November 1661, although under Philip IV's successor, Carlos II, there were rebellions in Sardinia and Aragon in 1668, and a successful coup in 1677 was based on Aragon. In the short term, Luis de Haro broke free from the financial and military crisis of 1640–3 by shelving Olivares's plans for constitutional reform within the Iberian peninsula and by holding the line. Reform of this type had to wait for the new Bourbon dynasty and the end of the War of the Spanish Succession in 1714.

4.4   The Resurgence of France, 1610–1661

The assassination of Henri IV on 14 May 1610 threw the political system of France into crisis and revealed the limitations of his achievement. From

1598 peace at home and abroad had given Henri's great finance minister, the duc de Sully, an opportunity to establish a budgetary surplus by reducing expenditure and increasing revenues. The great crisis of the siege of Amiens in 1597, following the betrayal of that city to the Spaniards during the brief war of 1595–8 (see chapter 3.3.5), had taught the king and Sully the need for a reserve fund for military contingencies. This in turn could not be established without careful economy during the years of peace. In comparison with the troubled minority of Henri's successor, Louis XIII, the years between 1598 and 1610 therefore appear settled indeed. This impression is nevertheless misleading. Though Henri IV tried to keep his nobles in their place, he could not prevent them from conspiring against him in alliance with the duke of Savoy or the Spanish Habsburgs: Biron did so in 1602, and was executed; the issue of the succession played a crucial part in the d'Entragues conspiracy of 1604; and the conspiracy of the duc de Bouillon lasted effectively from 1602 until 1606. In 1609, Condé (father of the victor of Rocroi), rightly suspecting the king's attraction towards his wife, took her across the border to the safety of the Spanish Netherlands. Henri IV replied in the same way that he had answered Bouillon's challenge three years earlier, by a general mobilization of troops, although the international ramifications of this crisis were potentially much more serious because it coincided with the Cleves–Jülich succession crisis and the king's determination to support the Protestant cause there (see chapter 3.4.3). What made the conspiracies against Henri IV so dangerous were the reservations which strict Catholics had concerning the validity of his divorce in 1599 and the legitimacy of Marie de Medici's children. The Habsburgs naturally encouraged these doubts, since they had not lost their ambition to weaken France by challenging the principle of hereditary succession. Even without this international dimension, however, it was clear that the removal of a strong king who had supported his finance minister's resistance to the excessive demands of the nobility for pensions and rewards would create an opportunity for aristocratic revenge.

4.4.1 *The Reign of Louis XIII to 1624*

It has been argued that public revulsion at Henri IV's assassination was so great that in the long term the monarchy was strengthened: François Ravaillac's knife, it is contended, assisted the growth of the absolute state. Few contemporaries would have agreed with this interpretation. The regent, Marie de Medici, suffered from the disadvantage of trying to govern in a country in which the Salic Law was a fundamental law of the kingdom. She was also inexperienced, and her Habsburg preferences were rather too obvious. At first the government tried to bribe the great nobility with an outpouring of pensions and gifts after the removal of Sully from power in January 1611. By 1614, however, latent aristocratic discontent had become open rebellion, with the initial revolt led appropriately enough by Condé, the first prince of the blood. He resented the attempts of Concino Concini, the Italian favourite of the regent, and his wife, Leonora Galigaï, to exercise a monopoly of patronage. He also objected to the projected marriage of Louis XIII to Anne of Austria, the daughter of Philip III, and was prepared to lead a general rebellion by Catholic Malcontents and Huguenots (rather akin to Alençon's revolt in 1575–6). In his manifesto to discontented magnates, Condé claimed that confusion and disorder were so rife that only a meeting of the Estates General could prevent the collapse of the state. The government responded to Condé's challenge by summoning the Estates General.

Its meeting did not resolve the political crisis even after the royal declaration of the king's majority in October 1614. Many proposals intended to alleviate the situation were made before the Estates General ended its sessions in February 1615 (their last meeting, it was to prove, before 1789). Their practical impact was small, and was insufficient to prevent a second rebellion by Condé in 1615, who claimed that the discussions of the Estates General had not been free and that their proposals had been deliberately ignored. The Spanish marriage project was said to be shameful and a just cause of apprehension on the part of Protestants. This rhetoric secured Condé the Huguenot alliance (November 1615–May 1616). But this rebellion also came to nothing. The government again attempted to buy itself out of trouble by giving the nobles gifts; but the first prince's rewards, and those of his followers, contrasted with the small gains of the Huguenots, who took most of the blame for the revolt. Most important of all, Concini still remained the power behind the throne, and in September 1616 he had Condé arrested. New ministers (including, for six months, the future Cardinal de Richelieu) were appointed, with a more aggressive policy towards the nobility. But the firm stand against the magnates came too late to save Concini. It was now clear that Condé's supporters would not rest until the Italian favourite was removed from power and the first prince released. Condé was not released until October 1619, but a further aristocratic rebellion occurred in the spring of 1617 which ended with the assassination of Concini towards the end of April. The 16-year-old king was a willing participant in the assassination plot, hoping by this means to free himself from the influence of the queen mother, who was placed under house arrest at Blois.

The *coup d'état* brought to power Charles d'Albert, seigneur de Luynes, who reaped the rewards of his bold counsel to the king over the last few months. In 1619, he was raised to the status of duke and peer, and two years later was appointed both Constable of France and Keeper of the

Seals. Two rebellions led by the queen mother, in 1619 and 1620 (the first immortalized on canvas by Rubens), failed to oust Luynes from this ascendancy. Luynes was the French equivalent to Lerma, sharing that Spanish minister's cynical attitude towards the rewards of office. He was reported to have commended, in an unguarded moment, the Spanish policy of expelling the Moriscos. Louis XIII and his favourite distrusted the Huguenots because of their support of Condé's revolt in 1615–16 and suspected (though unproven) involvement in the rebellion of the queen mother in 1620. Instead of demobilizing after signing peace with Marie de Médicis, Louis XIII marched south to restore Catholicism in Béarn and to incorporate this independent state into the kingdom of France. The invasion of Béarn and Basse Navarre was achieved without great difficulty in October. However, this was the lull before the storm, for their full incorporation into France, and the restoration of Catholicism in Béarn, precipitated nine years of intermittent warfare between Louis XIII and the Huguenots.

The French Protestant assembly at La Rochelle in May 1621 divided France and Béarn into eight military units (*cercles*) and decided to appoint a member of the Huguenot upper nobility to head each of them. Luynes regarded this as an act of rebellion against the monarchy, a latter-day Dutch revolt; whereas it was probably a desperate Huguenot measure for self-defence. A royal army was sent to besiege Montauban, one of the leading fortified cities held by the Huguenots. The war went badly for the government, with the failure of a costly three-month siege of the city. On the death of Luynes in December 1621, Louis XIII proclaimed his intention to rule personally, but he lacked sufficient resolve to match his words with deeds. The king's council was divided against itself, with no single personality capable of giving effective leadership in financial affairs or foreign policy. This was reflected in the protracted first rebellion of the Huguenots, which was not settled until October 1622, when they conceded about half their *villes de sûreté* at the Peace of Montpellier.

In February 1624, La Vieuville emerged temporarily as *de facto* chief minister, foreign minister and finance minister. However, in Richelieu's phrase, La Vieuville was like a drunkard who could not walk a step without stumbling.[43] His foreign policy led to a confrontation with Spain in the Valtelline for which France was ill prepared (see chapter 4.2.2). His financial policy was open to the charge of corruption, while his domestic political position remained weak. He needed more powerful backers, and at the end of April 1624, as the price of support from the queen mother and her religious advisers such as Bérulle, La Vieuville was forced to agree to Richelieu's entry into the king's council. Richelieu was quick to seize the opportunity, and asserted the opinion that cardinals had precedence in the king's council over other dignitaries of the crown such as the Chancellor and Constable (and implicitly, the finance minister). Towards mid-August, La Vieuville offered his resignation, but instead of accepting it, Louis XIII had him arrested and appointed Richelieu as chief minister. La Vieuville was subsequently prosecuted and remained in prison for thirteen months until he managed to escape and flee abroad. In popular estimation, these years in exile turned La Vieuville from a corrupt finance minister into a martyr for his opposition to Richelieu. Nevertheless, in the short term La Vieuville largely brought about his own downfall, and this allowed Richelieu his opportunity to seize power. That hold on power remained contested, however, until November 1630.

4.4.2 *The Ministry of Cardinal de Richelieu, 1624–1642*

Richelieu's rise to power has been compared with that of Olivares, who was only two years his junior. Richelieu obtained power by a more indirect method than Olivares, since he was never the king's favourite. Indeed, two of Louis XIII's favourites—François de Baradat in 1626 and Cinq-Mars in 1642—came to pose a direct threat to Richelieu's position and had to be disgraced. Though he was a French cardinal, Richelieu was never the king's confessor. He had to defend himself from this quarter, too, and in 1637 secured the dismissal of the king's confessor, Père Caussin, because he opposed the cardinal's foreign policy. Within two years of his appointment, Richelieu faced an attempted coup at court. In defusing the crisis, he displayed considerable political skills. He recognized the need to attempt a reconciliation with Gaston d'Orléans, the king's younger brother, but probably realized that it would be short-lived: Gaston was a willing participant in most of the conspiracies and rebellions of Richelieu's ministry. Since Gaston was heir presumptive until 1638, he was a powerful rallying-point for discontent in the way that Alençon had been during the reign of Henri III. On the other hand, the chief minister obtained a permanent understanding with Condé, the first prince of the blood and potentially a much more serious rival. This personal and political agreement stood the acid test of the prolonged struggle for power between Richelieu and his critics in the king's council—the queen mother, Bérulle and Marillac—who opposed the cardinal's foreign policy consistently after August 1625.

Most of the arguments against Richelieu's foreign policy in the Valtelline and Mantuan conflicts (see chapter 4.2.2) proceeded either from fear of the risk of a general European war, or from the existence of other priorities, such as the desire for peaceful coexistence with the Habsburgs abroad and the suppression of heresy at home. Though Richelieu won considerable prestige by forcing the surrender of La Rochelle in October 1628 after a siege lasting a year, the Peace of Alais

(June 1629) was open to criticism from the hard-line *dévot* party, who wanted to see the complete elimination of heresy in France. Instead, Richelieu ended nine years of intermittent civil and religious war in France by guaranteeing the Edict of Nantes (see chapter 3.3.5). The peace was a considerable achievement for the cardinal: whereas previous edicts had given the Huguenots 'advantages [which were] prejudicial to the state', that of Alais was an 'edict of grace', an act of clemency on the part of the king.[44] The political and military organization of the Huguenots was destroyed, all Protestant fortifications were to be razed, all cannon melted down and sold, and the Protestant population disarmed. The great Huguenot leader, the duc de Rohan, was sent into exile, though he received reparations and his troops were allowed to serve the French cause in Italy. The success of the war and of the enforcement of the peace is best illustrated by the fact that the Huguenots did not join any of the subsequent rebellions during the ministries of Richelieu and Mazarin.

Disappointment in the *dévot* party at the outcome of the war against the Huguenots combined with exasperation at Richelieu's apparent intransigence in the Mantuan war to force a trial of strength between the chief minister and his critics in November 1630. This crisis has come to be known as the Day of Dupes because on 11 November Marie de Medici and her cabal thought that they had persuaded the king to dismiss Richelieu. They were 'duped' because the king had either made no decision, or misled them, or changed his mind. Thereafter, Richelieu gradually eliminated his opponents. The Seals were removed from Marillac's custody as Keeper of the Seals (that is, acting Chancellor); he was arrested and later died in captivity. His brother, Louis de Marillac, who was serving with the army in Italy, was also arrested and later put on trial and executed. Towards the end of February 1631, the queen mother was placed under house arrest at Compiègne, but she escaped to the Spanish Netherlands in July. She remained in exile until her death five months before that of Richelieu, her former protégé and now arch-enemy. By March 1631, Gaston d'Orléans and his supporters were in open rebellion against the government. The revolt was based on the Orléanais, but it proved a damp squib when only the nobility rallied to his cause. However, there was still considerable sympathy for Gaston's position among the great nobility, who wished to regain the political independence they had enjoyed during the wars of religion: two governors—those of Burgundy and Picardy—facilitated his escape to Lorraine, while a third (the governor of Provence) went into exile to avoid arrest.

Other nobles joined the rebels in Lorraine, where duke Charles IV welcomed them and showed his support by marrying his sister to Gaston. The duke also allowed Imperial troops to occupy two strategically important fortresses, Vic and Moyenvic, as a challenge to the French.

When Gaston invaded France in the summer of 1632, Montmorency, the governor of Languedoc, declared his support. However, this rebellion also failed for reasons similar to the failure of Gaston's revolt the previous year. After the defeat of Gaston's forces at the battle of Castelnaudary in September, Montmorency was placed on trial before the *Parlement* of Toulouse and executed. Negotiations between the government and Gaston proved abortive, and he went into exile again; this time to the Spanish Netherlands, where he remained until October 1634. Richelieu ordered a purge of the lesser nobility who were suspected of complicity in the rebellion. Royal intendants were sent into the provinces in 1632–3 with exceptionally wide powers, in a response to the security crisis. Furthermore, Louis XIII was determined to remove the threat from Lorraine. There were three French invasions in the space of two years (1632–3). Each time the duke submitted, agreed not to assist the Habsburgs or Gaston, and handed over territorial guarantees; each time he went back on his word. Finally in 1634, a French adminstration was installed, and the duke went into permanent exile as a Habsburg general. Except for a brief interlude in 1641, the exile of the duke of Lorraine was to last for twenty-eight years. Gradually in 1633–6, though for different reasons, French administration was installed in parts of Alsace, too. The effect of these measures was to strengthen greatly the north-east border of France.

The collapse of Gaston's rebellion and the elimination of the threat from Lorraine did not bring an end to conspiracy and intrigue against Richelieu's rule. Gaston was implicated in the conspiracy of the comte de Soissons, who mounted his challenge from the independent frontier fortress of Sedan, where the duc de Bouillon had given him refuge in November 1636; Soissons later entered the service of the king of Spain. In July 1641, the comte de Soissons, the duc de Guise and the duc de Bouillon issued a manifesto at Sedan which was directed against Richelieu's foreign policy. They had formed a military alliance with the Habsburgs, who provided an army which routed the king's troops at the battle of La Marfée, but Soissons was killed in the battle and the rebellion collapsed within a month. The duc de Bouillon and Gaston d'Orléans were also heavily implicated in the following year's conspiracy which was led by Cinq-Mars, the king's favourite. In March 1642, Gaston accepted the provisions of a treaty negotiated on his orders at Madrid by which Philip IV agreed to pay a subsidy to the rebels. After the failure of this conspiracy and attempted rebellion in September, Cinq-Mars and another of the conspirators, de Thou, were declared guilty of treason and executed. Bouillon's life was spared in return for his handing over his principality of Sedan to the crown. Gaston's complicity in this conspiracy could not be overlooked, and in December he was deprived of his governorship of Auvergne and debarred from holding public office in France (though these penalties were withdrawn after Richelieu's death).

The Day of Dupes did not bring an end to all criticism and division within the king's council. However, opposition to Richelieu's foreign policy was henceforth firmly identified with conspiracy and rebellion. No minister seriously challenged the view, presented to Louis XIII by Richelieu in the spring of 1632, that Spain, the Emperor and Lorraine were informally allied against France and that a general war was inevitable. The threat posed by domestic conspiracy and faction helped to delay French intervention in the Thirty Years' War, but the military unpreparedness of France and the parlous state of the king's finances also weighed heavily with the king and his chief minister. A rapid increase in royal expenditure was made inevitable by the subsidies paid to the allies, the size of the armies required for open war, and eventually (as revenues failed to keep pace with expenses) by the interest charge on the borrowing requirement. At its highest level in the 1620s, royal expenditure had not exceeded 55 million *livres*. In the crisis year of 1636, when Habsburg forces invaded France from the Low Countries and Franche-Comté, it exceeded 108 million. Every available source of revenue was tapped, including taxes on office-holding (this left a legacy of resentment which became serious once Louis XIII and Richelieu were removed from the helm). Taxes had already been rising in the 1620s; but a significant increase in the chief direct tax (the *taille*) in the years 1635–48 (estimated in some provinces to have trebled), provoked a wave of peasant rebellion. All forms of taxation were anticipated systematically during Louis XIII's lifetime; the revenue of the *taille* was spent at least one year before it was collected in 1642. The provincial intendants were charged with supervising the levy of arrears of this tax and suppressing tax rebellion. Finally in August 1642, the assessments of the tax were conferred upon the intendants in the *pays d'élections*, which covered the larger area of France without local representative institutions. As a consequence of Richelieu's foreign policy, though probably against the intentions of the chief minister himself, a new system of provincial administration had been established by 1642. Both in their political role of suppressing revolts, and in their financial role of collecting taxes, the intendants were indispensable, and it is difficult to imagine that the shaky political and financial structure of the French kingdom could have escaped serious upheaval until 1648 without them.

Richelieu died in December 1642 without having achieved a peace settlement that would have allowed a return to more orderly forms of administration and lower levels of taxation. There had been secret negotiations with Philip IV and Olivares, but the Spaniards had no reason to make peace in the early years of the war, when events seemed to be going their way. Then Richelieu in turn lost the incentive to make peace in the *annus mirabilis* of 1640, when the French captured Artois, against the background of the revolt of the Catalans and the secession of Portugal. Historians have tended to exaggerate the success of Richelieu (and perhaps conversely, the failure of Olivares) in the light of these events, but the two revolts were not attributable to French military effort but rather to good fortune. Although the cardinal had been reasonably optimistic about French chances in the war, he had stated candidly that once a war was started 'no one can foresee the end and the outcome'.[45] He was probably ill prepared for such a long conflict. Richelieu had entered office with clear reforming intentions and the plain truth was, as he had perceived in 1630, that there was a severe limit on the ability of a government to implement reform while conducting an active foreign policy. 'One must abandon all thought of convenience, economy and internal reform of the kingdom', Richelieu had told Louis XIII during the Mantuan war.[46] A successful end to the war would have enabled Richelieu (as it would Olivares) to pursue his reforms with leisure. Instead, by the time of his death, they had been shelved. Worse still, there was a dangerous legacy of discontent resulting from his dictatorial policy towards the upper nobility and the fiscal exactions on the rest of society.

In the final months of his reign the king, who for eighteen years had been dominated by Richelieu, reversed some of his policies. Louis XIII rehabilitated Gaston, gave him the title of lieutenant-general of the kingdom and made him president of a regency council which was to govern France after his death. The wisdom of these moves was very doubtful; quite apart from his questionable loyalty, it was not clear that Gaston was up to the task. The king also made the regency council pledge to continue his diplomatic alliances and bring the war to fruition. On his death-bed, in a general amnesty to political offenders, the king pardoned all the rebellious great nobles and all the governors dismissed by Richelieu (with only two exceptions). Many nobles returned from exile, or were otherwise rehabilitated, but Richelieu had proscribed so many of them that all their demands could not possibly be met. The king's death in May 1643 inevitably brought about a period of political instability in France, in part a consequence of the royal minority, in part a reaction to Richelieu's autocratic regime.

4.4.3 *Cardinal Mazarin and the Fronde*

The regency of Anne of Austria was proclaimed officially in the *Parlement* of Paris four days after the king's death, and at the same time the limitations on the regent's powers imposed by the last will and testament of

Louis XIII were removed. Anne of Austria could thus become president of the council instead of Gaston, and she was given those powers of appointment and patronage which her husband had sought to deny her. The delicate checks and balances within Louis's proposed regency council were removed at a stroke. Almost inevitably, her favourite, Cardinal Mazarin, was made chief minister. Two foreigners were therefore in charge of the French kingdom: Anne of Austria was the sister of Philip IV and Mazarin was Italian in origin (he became a naturalized Frenchman only in April 1639). For these reasons, if for no others, it would have been political suicide for them to have signed a peace with Spain that could later be criticized as detrimental to French interests. Yet it was regarded as unusual, even by the ministers themselves, for a regency government to fight a foreign war, and it was questionable whether it could be paid for. What contemporaries wanted was an immediate peace settlement, followed by more orderly administration and the reduction of taxation. The advent of a new reign had raised expectations that were not easy to fulfil: Mazarin was vulnerable to the charge that he continued the war 'to make himself indispensable and as a pretext for levying great sums of money for self-enrichment'.[47]

The accusation carried considerable weight because of unprecedented government borrowing. An enormous military effort had to be sustained on several fronts to convince the Spanish negotiators at Westphalia that the French intended to continue the war if necessary. But to mount such a military effort there had to be a continuous flow of funds which only credit could ensure. D'Hémery, the finance minister, anticipated the revenues of the chief direct tax (the *taille*) even more in advance than his predecessors, a policy which meant that without agreement to new taxes the crown was effectively bankrupt. At the very moment that the government was seeking to enforce the registration of new fiscal measures at the *Parlement* of Paris, the office-holders felt their position threatened and saw little reason to co-operate in measures which appeared to be against their interests (see chapter 6.3.3). Between the middle of May and the end of June 1648, the government tried to prevent a joint meeting of the office-holders from the Parisian sovereign courts because it knew this would lead to criticism of, and opposition to, government policies. However, the financiers refused to make further loans to the government until the struggle between the crown and its office-holders was resolved. The government had no alternative but to capitulate. Delegates from the four Parisian sovereign courts met at the *Chambre Saint-Louis* at the end of June 1648.

They were supposed to be discussing their own grievances, not those of the rest of society, but their meeting was turned into 'an occasion of complaint and general dissatisfaction' with the government.[48] The office-holders were not allowed to say that the king was pursuing an unjust and unnecessary war, for that would have been treasonable: declarations of war and peace were an integral part of the king's sovereignty; but they proposed that the revenues for the war should be cut off. Furthermore, they wanted the crown to abolish the intendants in all but six frontier provinces, and return to peacetime methods of administration in time of war, with the dismantling of the system of war finance that had operated since 1635. The immediate consequence of their twenty-seven proposals was the collapse of government: a debt rescheduling ('bankruptcy') was declared in July 1648. The government appeared to make substantial concessions to its critics with regard to direct taxation and the provincial intendants. However, Mazarin did not accept that these concessions had the authority of 'reforms'. Rather, he regarded them as temporary expedients, aimed at retrieving the loss of political control by the government. A full implementation of the proposals would, in Mazarin's view, have abolished 'the most considerable parts of royal authority'.[49] Thus, the declarations would be annulled retrospectively once the king's authority was no longer undermined by the office-holders. This accounts for the chequered history of the proposals of the *Chambre Saint-Louis*.

The chief minister did not believe that Philip IV of Spain would make peace on terms acceptable to France. The war thus had to be continued, and this required, in Mazarin's view, the reinstatement of the intendants and the restoration of the system of war finance. By September 1648, Mazarin and his ministerial colleagues considered for the first time the possibility of removing the royal court from Paris and using the army to blockade the capital to force the sovereign tribunals, especially the *Parlement*, into submission. After further criticism of the government from the *Parlement*, this is what eventually happened in January 1649. The news of Pride's Purge in England, which set parliament along the path of abolishing the monarchy, may have strengthened the resolve of the government. Mazarin was convinced of the parallel between his own position and that of Strafford in England: once Charles I had sacrificed Strafford, so the argument ran, the monarchy itself did not long survive. Mazarin also wanted to ensure that France did not follow the trend across the Channel where the independent financial powers of the crown had been drastically curtailed by parliament. The *Parlement* of Paris responded to the blockade by declaring Mazarin a 'disturber of the public peace, [an] enemy of the king and his state', and pronouncing the position of chief minister illegal.[50] The Parisian courts were not isolated in their struggle, but had support in the provinces, particularly in Normandy and Provence. Moreover, a motley band of discontented nobles (the most prominent of whom was Conty, the younger brother of Condé, the victor at Rocroi) arrived in the capital, and signed an alliance among themselves pledging general support to the *Parlement* and resolute hostility to Mazarin. It looked as if full-scale civil war would break out in France.

Instead, a truce was patched up between the government and a delegation from the Parisian courts (but it did not include their noble supporters) at Rueil in March 1649. The willingness of the office-holders to compromise within three months of the blockade reveals the weakness of the opposition and the relative strength of the government during the Fronde: the rebellion was retrospectively named this after a children's street game in Paris to diminish its importance in the calmer period of the 1660s. The office-holders were faced with a threat to their position on several fronts—from Mazarin and the other ministers initially; but also from the nobles, from Spain, which sought to exploit the discontent, from the populace at a time of a subsistence crisis, and from the spread of radical ideas (during the Fronde some 5,200 political pamphlets or *Mazarinades* were published: the blockade of Paris brought about the first surge in publications). The conservative office-holders feared radicalism, and their desire for a compromise peace was reinforced by considerations of self-interest.

From the outset of the Fronde, there was no broad consensus in France among the opponents of the government about the course of action to be taken, because their definition of the crisis was made from a series of narrowly sectional viewpoints. Moreover, because office-holders purchased their position and did not stand for election, their prestige in the community could not be tested objectively, and the attitude of landowners as a whole was a matter of mere speculation. The *Parlement* of Paris made some attempt to broaden its attack to include other interests, but its views were not shared, for example, by the *Parlement* of Aix-en-Provence. Each *Parlement* had a clearly defined geographical area (*ressort*) in which its jurisdiction ran without appeal except to the king's council. The effect of this was to fragment the opposition to the crown. Thus when a local *Parlement* took to arms during the Fronde, the outcome of the struggle did not necessarily affect those parts of France outside its jurisdiction and under that of a different *Parlement*. There were really four separate conflicts in 1649 based on the *Parlements* of Paris, Rouen, Aix and Bordeaux. Each had a quite distinctive character, and the proposals of the *Chambre Saint-Louis* did not form a common ground between them. Events in one area proceeded at a different pace from the others. Each provincial settlement was unique. For these reasons, the crown was always likely to win the struggle with any one tribunal in France. Without joint resistance by several *Parlements*, it was always likely that regionalism would lead to an eventual royalist victory.

The power vacuum caused by the conflict between the crown and its office-holders was inevitably filled by the great nobility. Control of appointments to provincial governorships and fortresses within the provinces had been a key element in the power asserted by Richelieu and Mazarin. The Fronde cannot be understood except in terms of an accumulation of aristocratic resentment against the patronage policies of the two chief ministers. Richelieu had dismissed many governors, but he did not undertake a generalized attack on the upper nobility as such, or attempt to undermine the importance of the governorships. Mazarin had tried a policy of reconciliation, but even where an exiled governor was restored, this did not produce the desired effect of political stability. The nature of the threat posed by the provincial governors during the Fronde varied from province to province. In some provinces, such as Normandy in 1649, the authority of a Frondeur governor was instrumental in bringing his province into revolt. In others, such as Guyenne and Provence, royalist governors pursued a vendetta against the local *Parlement* which led to civil war. There were also provinces, such as Picardy, where the Fronde was essentially a struggle for power between two families, one of whom held the governorship, the other having been deprived of it previously by Richelieu. These local conflicts were only partly co-ordinated with the struggle for power at the centre after 1649.

During the blockade of Paris, the two most important princes, Gaston d'Orléans and Condé, had supported Mazarin against the *Parlement* and its noble supporters. One of the great French military commanders, Turenne, had sided with the rebels, but his troops failed to back his planned march on Paris in the spring of 1649; without this assistance, Conty and the other Frondeur nobles were unable to prolong their rebellion. By October 1649, however, Condé had turned from support of Mazarin to open criticism. In effect, Condé wished to substitute himself as chief minister, and it was largely a consequence of his ambition that the Fronde was prolonged. Mazarin responded with an audacious, though misguided, coup: the arrest of three princes (Condé, Conty and Longueville) in January 1650. It was misguided because there were continual revolts by their supporters until the princes were released in February 1651. More seriously, however, for the first time in the Fronde, it threw personal responsibility for the disorders on to the chief minister, and made him vulnerable to any sudden shift in alliances or volte-face by former supporters. This occurred in February 1651, when the *Parlement* of Paris requested the exclusion of cardinals from the king's council, and the regent and Gaston d'Orléans agreed on terms for the release of the princes. Mazarin went personally to Le Havre to secure their release, but fearing arrest and prosecution, he then went straight into exile at Brühl in the electorate of Cologne, where he remained until the end of the year.

Mazarin never intended his exile to be more than a breathing-space, a time to allow the intense passions aroused by his period in office, and especially by the arrest of the princes, to die down. He continued to exercise a secret influence over the conduct of government, particularly through letters sent in code to Anne of Austria, whose support he never lost. Meanwhile, Condé sought to dominate the French government, by ousting Mazarin's supporters from office, thereby hoping to ensure that the chief minister would never be in a position to return from exile. However, Gaston remained suspicious of Condé's motives and failed to lend him support against the regent, or to agree to a postponement of the king's majority. Accordingly, when Louis XIV's majority was declared in September 1651, and a ministerial reshuffle revealed that Mazarin had retained his secret influence on government, Condé's response was to go into revolt, using the province of Guyenne as a power base. In November, the first prince of the blood signed an alliance with Spain. At first, Gaston did not join the rebellion, but neither did he support the government, which appeared likely to collapse in the face of determined resistance. It was such a collapse which Mazarin sought to forestall in the most dramatic incident of his entire career: his return from exile in December 1651 at the head of a force of 6,000 German mercenaries hired from the service of the elector of Brandenburg. At the end of January 1652, Mazarin arrived at Poitiers to join the royal court, which had moved there to escape Gaston's control at Paris, in order to direct the campaign against Condé in Guyenne.

Mazarin's return served as a focus for discontent, and at the end of December 1651, the *Parlement* of Paris pronounced him guilty of treason and placed a price on his head. Gaston openly declared his hand, arguing that the king was not of age to rule personally (which was true), and that he was held in captivity by Mazarin (which was not). Gaston also joined an alliance with Condé towards the end of January 1652. There was serious fighting in 1652, and it is probably true to say that support for the government was at its nadir; certainly it was lower than at any time during the ministries of Richelieu and Mazarin. However, at a fairly stiff price—the compensation of his family for losses they had suffered as a result of previous political opposition—Mazarin was able to secure the desertion of Turenne from the rebel cause: he was appointed general of the royalist army, which was perhaps the single most important military factor in the defeat of the princes. Mazarin remained desperately unpopular, but by the late summer of 1652 it was doubtful whether many feared his continuation in office more than the dictatorship of the princes. Mazarin's second exile in August 1652 was really only a ploy to show that the princes, and not the chief minister, were the real cause of the civil war. Paris capitulated in October 1652, and by February 1653 Mazarin had returned to the capital as chief minister, for better or worse. Gaston made his peace with the government in October 1652, but Condé refused to accept second place to

Mazarin and entered Spanish service, where he remained until 1660. Bordeaux, the last bastion of the Fronde, fell at the beginning of August 1653.

In 1652, opposition to Mazarin's continuance in office had been one of the few common bonds linking together a very diverse and ill-organized group of opponents to the regime. Mazarin had survived, and on his return from his second exile he was a much more confident and determined politician whose purpose was to lead the armies of France in a renewed offensive against Spain. He was not interested in exercising revenge over former opponents, but there were to be no more concessions to his domestic critics. The royal declaration of October 1652 disallowed criticism of the ministers by the *Parlement* of Paris, prohibited its interference in affairs of state and financial questions, and annulled its previous interventions in this area. It was not necessary to revoke each unpalatable item of the proposals of the *Chambre Saint-Louis* that had been enacted subsequently. All that was needed was that the king's intention on a particular issue should be made clear. By the end of 1652, the government had some hope of paying for a foreign war once again, since the limit on expenditure had been removed, the taxes suppressed in 1648 had been restored, and the investigation of the financiers halted. In 1653, the provincial intendants were reintroduced with fiscal powers. There was a rapid escalation in both royal expenditure and taxation, and after 1655 there was also a dramatic increase in royal borrowing. Not much had changed from the pre-Fronde years, it seemed, and, not surprisingly, there was comparable discontent in the provinces. Without the royalist victory over its motley grouping of opponents at home, however, the war against Spain could not have been won, and this was Mazarin's supreme achievement. And without Mazarin's survival, and his introduction of the young king gradually, but progressively, to the process of government in the 1650s, the political education of Louis XIV would have taken a very different form. As the Frondeurs had feared, the guiding principles of Louis's first years of personal rule were to be in most respects a consolidation of Mazarin's policies.

4.4.4   *The Last Phase of the Franco-Spanish War, 1648–1659*

The separate peace made with Spain by the Dutch in January 1648 was regarded with dismay in France. It threw the burden of the war effort entirely on the French kingdom for the first time since 1635 (see chapter 4.2.3). Its initial impact was lessened by Condé's defeat of the Spaniards at Lens in August, and French hopes for a change of opinion in the Dutch Republic were not finally dashed until the death of William II in 1650. The outbreak of the Fronde hampered the French war effort; but after the signing of the Peace of Rueil in March 1649 Mazarin tried to proceed as if nothing had happened, and determined on the siege of Cambrai. This petered out because the French government followed the Spanish into bankruptcy: neither was in a position to mount a decisive offensive. Spanish help to the French aristocratic rebels in the Fronde failed to materialize on the scale promised in three agreements (April and June 1650; November 1651). But by 1650–1 the French position was beginning to crumble on the three different war fronts: Italy, Spain and the Spanish Netherlands. The fortresses of Porto Longone and Piombino in the republic of Genoa, lost to the French in 1646, were retaken by the Spaniards in 1650. The key fortress of Casale in Montferrat, held by the French for the duke of Nevers since 1628 (see chapter 4.2.2), was captured in 1652. In July 1651, the army of Don Juan José de Austria advanced on Barcelona, while naval forces established a blockade. The French were unable to relieve the city, which surrendered in October 1652. Though the Catalan front remained open until 1659, the fall of Barcelona ended the revolt. Even on the northern front, where logistical difficulties were greater, the Spaniards made some striking gains in 1652, with the recapture of Dunkirk and Gravelines in the Spanish Netherlands. Had the Fronde not ended in 1652–3, and had the Spaniards not been forced to declare a further bankruptcy in 1653, a Habsburg victory in the war would not have been out of the question.

The change in Spanish military fortunes was reflected in a hardening of the diplomatic position, as Mazarin found to his cost during secret negotiations with them in the course of the Fronde. Philip IV lost any immediate interest in securing peace. 'Since France is so subject to faction and unrest', the Spanish minister Oñate thought it 'very probable that future events [would] considerably improve our prospects, and persuade the enemy to accept a peace on more equal conditions'.[51] 'More equal conditions' was a Spanish euphemism for a return to the *status quo* before 1635, perhaps even to the position of 1610. Before the Spaniards were prepared to begin serious negotiations they insisted on the return of Lorraine (occupied by the French since 1632) to duke Charles IV; Catalonia to Philip IV; and the halting of French assistance to Portugal. Philip IV was not interested in a just peace, only one that was favourable to Spanish interests, and his confidence in ultimate victory led him to spurn the French offer of a reasonable compromise during the mission of the French secretary of state, Lionne, to Madrid in 1656.

The Castilian victory in Catalonia in 1652 enabled men and money to be transferred to the Portuguese front, but John IV's army halted the Castilian advance the following year. From the autumn of 1653, the French army was once more on the offensive in the Spanish Netherlands, with Mazarin personally supervising the details of war administration from Sedan or La Fère, as can be seen in the general letters he sent back to Paris requesting provisions and funds. Worse still for Philip IV, England declared war on Spain in December 1654: Jamaica was captured by the English fleet in 1655, and in 1655–8 the English severely restricted the silver remittances from Spanish America. Apart from the damage caused by Blake's raids, the bulk of the silver shipments was delayed for security reasons until April 1659, less than two months before a preliminary peace was signed with France. This caused the Spanish monarchy acute financial difficulties. It is true that the English fleet failed to take Hispaniola (Haiti), and Spanish Netherlands privateers from Dunkirk and Ostend attacked the English coastline in reprisal. Cromwell's response, however, was to sign the Treaty of Westminster with France in November 1655. This was followed up by a military alliance in March 1657 which committed the French to provide 20,000 men in the field and to defray half the cost of the English military and naval forces. Before the pact, the French had suffered humiliation at the hands of the Spaniards at Valenciennes in July 1656. After it came into force, a string of victories followed, including the Battle of the Dunes (June 1658) and the recapture of Dunkirk and Gravelines. Already in June 1657, the Spanish council of state had noted that 'all we can ask of the army of Flanders is to harass and delay the designs of the enemy';[52] the Anglo-French advance in the Low Countries, combined with reverses on the Portuguese front, convinced Philip IV that he should sue for peace in September 1658, although it was not until November 1659 that the final settlement was signed.

The Peace of the Pyrenees was less advantageous to Spain than Mazarin's proposed terms of 1656, but it was not the disastrous settlement than would have seemed likely in 1640–3. Territorially, Spanish concessions were relatively insignificant. Along the northern frontier, the French won Artois, Gravelines and (after purchase from the English in 1662) Calais, and territory around three fortresses (Le Quesnoy, Landrecies and Avesnes). On her southern frontier, France gained Roussillon and Cerdagne. The duke of Lorraine was to some extent sacrificed to France for the sake of peace, since he had not proved a reliable Spanish ally. Duke Charles IV was eventually returned to his duchy in 1661, but on complicated terms, including some territorial concessions to France and an oath of fealty to France for the duchy of Bar, with only the duchy of Lorraine held as a fief of the Empire. The French abandoned Portugal to its fate, with a secret article in the Peace of the Pyrenees envisaging that 'the affairs of Portugal shall be placed in the state they were in prior to the [revolt]'.[53] With the death of Cromwell, Mazarin had no need to heed the English, who played no part in the peace of 1659. The obvious consequence was for the abandoned or neglected participants in the previous war to join forces in renewing the 'oldest alliance', the Anglo-Portuguese treaty of June 1661, which was sealed by the marriage of Charles II to Catherine of Braganza. Philip IV made peace with France in 1659 to end a long and debilitating war, and in order to use the undivided resources of Habsburg Spain to end the secession of Portugal. But failure followed. By 1665–8, the impression conveyed by the Peace of the Pyrenees, that Spain had tacitly renounced its ambition to exercise European hegemony, had been reinforced by defeat in Portugal.

The most momentous article of the Peace of the Pyrenees was the fourth. It provided for María Teresa, the eldest daughter of Philip IV, to marry Louis XIV (an event which occurred the following year), renouncing her rights to the Habsburg inheritance 'conditionally upon payment of her dowry of 500,000 gold crowns'.[54] The parlous finances of Philip IV prevented payment of the dowry; but in any case the Spanish king and his chief minister were in agreement that the renunciation was invalid because the rights of succession to the throne could not be altered. The Spanish negotiators were fully aware of the French intention to use the marriage to strengthen an eventual Bourbon claim to the Spanish succession, and the treaty was intentionally ambiguous. For five days in November 1661, María Teresa was indeed heiress presumptive to Philip IV, despite her renunciation the previous year, but the entire inheritance was to go to the sickly Carlos II (as he was to become), who was born the same month. In the last years before his death in September 1665, Philip IV's ambitions were much reduced, but he had no intention of handing the Spanish succession over to France. Not only did he reassure his Austrian Habsburg relatives on this point, he negotiated a marriage alliance between his second daughter, Margarita Teresa, and the Emperor Leopold I. Though it ended a twenty-four-year war, the Peace of the Pyrenees and its associated diplomatic alliances would open up the question of the Spanish succession if Carlos II were to die without a direct heir.

5

THE OUTSIDERS OF EUROPE

IN eastern Europe and around the coastline of the Baltic Sea were huge tracts of land containing a relatively low density of population in comparison with the states of western Europe. Here the fifteenth century had witnessed the decline of three significant medieval states. In the Baltic, the Hanseatic League of commercial cities, with Lübeck as its dominant influence, was clearly waning, opening up the possibility of a Danish (or, subsequently, a Swedish) challenge for the position of supremacy over the Baltic Sea. Given the declining power and influence of the Teutonic Knights in the eastern Baltic, Prussia and Livonia were open to annexation. A dangerous power vacuum was created which in the 1550s it seemed might be filled by Muscovy. Finally, the rule of the Khans of the Golden Horde, based on Sarai on the lower Volga, had collapsed in the fifteenth century. Lithuania had escaped the Mongol conquest; Muscovy was not so fortunate, and the victorious Mongol Khan became its first undisputed personal sovereign. The Mongols had once brought a large part of Asia and the Near East under the rule of a single dynasty, of which Muscovy was a tributary state: but subsequently, the Golden Horde broke up into three distinct Khanates of Kazan', Astrakhan' and the Crimea. Though these three states could still raid at will into Poland-Lithuania or Muscovy, they no longer threatened to bring down the ruling dynasties. Indeed, during the reign of Tsar Ivan III, an event traditionally dated to 1480, Moscow ceased to pay tribute to the Golden Horde or its successor states. In the 1550s, Ivan IV subdued Kazan' and Astrakhan' and carried the war into the Crimea, the first Tsar of Muscovy to do so, though the Crimea was to remain a tributary state of the Ottoman Turks.

These momentous changes of the Middle Ages were followed by equally significant developments in the sixteenth century, largely as a result of the rapid expansion of Ottoman power across the Middle East and the Balkans, and into the Danubian plain. Vienna was besieged by the Turks in 1529. But by far the most crucial event was the collapse and partition of the great medieval kingdom of Hungary. Under Matthias Corvinus, who died in 1490, Hungary had held back the Ottoman advance in a succession of wars. In August 1526, however, the Turks destroyed the Hungarian army at Mohácz. More important still, they killed the last

Jagiellon king of Hungary, Louis II. The kingdom subsequently split into Royal Hungary under the Habsburgs, Transylvania under its own prince (*voivode*) and an Ottoman-controlled province based on Buda. Another branch of the Jagiellon dynasty retained the kingdoms of Poland and Lithuania after 1526. Then, on the death of Sigismund II Augustus in July 1572, it died out altogether. There were thus no dynastic certainties in eastern Europe. Nor were there any settled frontiers, for had there been, the 'gathering of the Russian lands' under Muscovy would not have been possible. This political instability led to significant conflicts in the Baltic and eastern Europe with consequences for the whole of Europe of no less importance than were the more famous conflicts in the west.

5.1 Denmark and Sweden: the Struggle for Baltic Supremacy

Apart from the possession of a fleet and secure ports, there were two main keys to Baltic supremacy: control over the shipping entering from the North Sea, and control over that departing from the main eastern ports (Riga, Königsberg, and above all, Danzig). Dynastic rivalries cut across an economic struggle for supremacy. If Denmark retained control of territory on either side of the (Danish) Sound (Sund), as it did until 1658, then notwithstanding any treaty obligations to Sweden, it was relatively easy for it to levy tolls not merely on neutral shipping, but also upon Swedish ships and goods. The Danes had levied tolls over the traffic passing through the Sound since the early fifteenth century, but had been forced to make important concessions: they granted temporary exemptions to the Hanseatic towns in 1435, to the Dutch in 1544, and periodically to Sweden. Despite these apparent successes by rival powers, Denmark always fought back, and continued to levy tolls at the Sound until 1857. The resulting documentary record provides one of the key sources for the economic historian (see chapter 8.4.4). In addition, Denmark and Sweden were in keen rivalry further east over what were in effect colonies in Estonia and Livonia. Possession of these territories, the great prize they both sought, would block off Muscovy's access to the sea—and thus enable the occupying power to levy tolls on Muscovy's trade with the west through the port of Narva. In the longer term these territories might also be used as a base from which to threaten Polish exports from the port of Danzig.

5.1.1 *Christian II and the End of the Union of Kalmar*

Denmark, Norway and Sweden (Finland constituting part of the Swedish kingdom) had been formally united in the Union of Kalmar of 1397, under the leadership of the Danish ruling dynasty. The Danish kings had been relatively powerless in Sweden, however, because the regents they had appointed after the mid-fifteenth century used their delegated powers to undermine the Danes and to play on traditional rivalry between the two nations. Nevertheless, what changed the whole course of Scandinavian history, resulting in the dissolution of the Union of Kalmar in 1523, was not the actions of the regents but the erratic and arbitrary rule of Christian II (king of Denmark and Sweden, 1513–23), who eventually lost all his kingdoms and spent the last twenty-seven years of his life as the captive of the man who usurped his throne.

Christian II had experience in government, since he had been regent in Norway in his father's lifetime. The aggressive and in some instances ill-considered foreign policy he pursued after 1513 did not reflect any great political abilities. His marriage in 1515 to Isabella, the 14-year-old sister of the future Emperor Charles V, was his most important asset. But his links with Burgundy through this marriage, and an alliance with Vasilii III of Muscovy, made him unacceptable to the Hanseatic League. Christian II confronted the League with a threat to create his own northern trading company; he also infuriated two Hanseatic ports whose interests normally diverged, Lübeck and Danzig, by arbitrarily raising the Danish Sound tolls. He vigorously resisted the attempt of the Swedish regent to pursue an independent policy and break away from the Union of Kalmar: between 1517 and 1520 he invaded Sweden on three occasions. Stockholm surrendered to Christian in September 1520, and the helpless Swedish council (*råd*) was forced to proclaim him hereditary rather than elected monarch. After this triumph, Christian II sought to crush his political opponents in the so-called 'bloodbath of Stockholm' in November 1520. The political disputes between Denmark and Sweden in the fifteenth century had been fairly tame affairs compared with Christian's execution of over 80 individuals for political offences: the future Swedish king Gustav Vasa lost his father, brother-in-law and two uncles in the massacre. Far from halting dissent, this action provoked full-scale rebellion. Gustav Vasa defeated Christian's forces in April 1521 and captured Uppsala in May. Gravely underestimating the danger, the king left for the Low Countries in the summer to meet his brother-in-law, the Emperor, who granted him the fief of Holstein, but refused to help him against Sweden and the Hanseatic League, let alone to confer possession of Lübeck. In the meantime, the Swedish revolt gained momentum. By the end of 1521, Gustav Vasa had been elected regent, and most of the kingdom was in the hands of the insurgents.

The reconquest of Sweden was feasible, but given the support of Lübeck and Danzig which Gustav Vasa enjoyed, it would be very difficult. Lübeck assisted both the Swedish and the later Danish rebellions in order to break the Union of Kalmar and to gain more favourable privileges from a weakened Denmark. The subsequent actions of Christian II's admiral and commander, Sören Norby, in a privateering war on Lübeck's commerce with the Baltic towns simply confirmed its attitude (though Norby was eventually defeated in August 1526). In March 1523, the Swedish rebellion was dramatically helped by a *coup d'état* of the Danish nobles, who had been alienated by Christian's legislation promoting the interests of the peasants and burghers. The nobles elected as their king Frederick of Holstein, Christian II's uncle. Frederick claimed that his nephew had tried to deprive him of his inheritance by procuring the Imperial grant of the duchy of Holstein, and won over the conditional support of Lübeck to his cause. At first, Christian sought to defend Copenhagen, but in mid-April 1523, he fled with his wife and children to Burgundy. Copenhagen only fell to the rebels the following January, but the king's departure ensured the success of the rebellion. From June 1523 there were two usurpers on the Scandinavian thrones, Frederick I of Denmark, and Gustav Eriksson Vasa of Sweden. Both had been elected by their respective nobilities. Though Frederick I retained a claim to the Swedish crown, both thrones were weakened by the threat of a counter-revolution sponsored by Christian II in exile. Consequently, relations between the two kingdoms were better than at any time since the previous century. Until his death in April 1533, Frederick I was more concerned with defending his position than asserting his residual claim to the Swedish throne. The tolerant attitude of both kings towards Lutheranism, and a common approach to fleecing the church (which may have been influenced by the Prussian example), also prevented the outbreak of conflict between them.

In exile Christian II remained a disturbing factor in European politics. In February 1530, he agreed to hold his kingdoms, if they were regained, as the Emperor's vassal; and the following June he returned to the Catholic faith he had abjured in 1524 in the hope of receiving Charles V's support for his restoration. Finance and warships were eventually provided, and towards the end of October 1531 Christian landed just south of Arendal on the Norwegian coast. Though he was helped by discontented elements in both Norway and Sweden, his invasion was unsuccessful. Having lost his ships one by one, he accepted Frederick's offer to parley at Copenhagen in July 1532, where he was promptly arrested and imprisoned for the rest of his life, though Frederick was not to enjoy his new-found period of tranquillity for long, for he died in April 1533.

5.1.2 *The Danish War of Succession, 1533–1536*

In normal circumstances, the Danish nobility would have elected as their king Frederick's elder son, Christian III, duke of Holstein, without further ado. But times were not normal. The nobility remained discontented and wanted to exploit the opportunity of an interregnum. The clergy naturally sought to reverse the trend towards the acceptance of the Reformation in the country, and opposed the election of Christian III, a committed Lutheran. Instead, they supported John, a minor and the younger son of the dead king, who was generally thought to be a Catholic. There was also a potential third candidate: under the erratic leadership of Jürgen Wullenweber, Lübeck turned on the Scandinavian kingdoms, declaring the intention of liberating Christian II and restoring him to his thrones. Lübeck's real purpose was to gain control of the Sound and by this means to exclude the Dutch from trading into the Baltic. However, the Hanseatic League was divided on this issue: Danzig, Wismar and Rostock were all favourable to the Dutch.

Copenhagen and Malmö made an alliance with Lübeck, which sent an army to Zeeland under the leadership of Count Christopher of Oldenburg, a distant relative of the Danish royal house. A peasant uprising which was aimed directly at supporting Lübeck's invasion broke out in north Jutland. Already in February 1534 the Danish nobility had been forced by these twin threats to sink its differences with Sweden and join in a treaty of mutual assistance with Gustav Vasa. By July, the nobles had no option but to elect Christian III as their king in order to defend their position. The new king had important brothers-in-law, Gustav Vasa and Albert of Hohenzollern, who came to the assistance of the Danish government. In the course of 1535, Lübeck met military and naval disaster at the hands of Denmark, Sweden and Prussia. In August 1535, a counter-revolution in Lübeck ousted Wullenweber from power. This permitted Christian III to make peace with the city in February 1536, though Gustav Vasa did not sign the treaty until the summer of the following year. Malmö did not capitulate to the Danes until April 1536, and Copenhagen held out until its population was starving in June. But Christian III's German mercenaries proved superior to the resistance, and in October he was able to bolster his position abroad by an alliance with the Lutheran Schmalkaldic League (see chapter 1.3.4). His victory consolidated the Reformation in Denmark. Faced with near-bankruptcy and a hated church which had promoted the civil war and opposed his election, the king tried to cure the first by destroying the second. The bishops were dismissed and ecclesiastical property secularized in an attempt to pay off the royal debts.

Though Sweden was refused admission to the Schmalkaldic League, the Reformation there progressed at a similar speed. By 1540 both countries were firmly Lutheran, as they were to remain, though ironically in the same year they were on the brink of war against each other. In December 1539, a new general tax payable in cash and not in kind was imposed in Sweden for the defence of the country against Denmark 'and against the Schmalkaldic League, which Denmark has incited against us'.[1] Yet in

September 1541, a defensive treaty was signed, which pledged reciprocal protection for all the dominions of both sovereigns; and in January 1542 Sweden followed Denmark into an alliance with France and seemed set on participation in a general European war (see chapter 2.3.4). A Catholic peasant rebellion in Sweden (1542–3) prevented this (see chapter 7.3.1), and exposed the need for a permanent native army. Accordingly in 1544, Sweden became one of the first European countries to establish a standing army, a move which coincided with a general strengthening of monarchical power. Swedish royal supremacy over the church was asserted in that year, and (doubtless influenced by the Danish civil war of 1533–6) the Succession Pact pledged the country to an arrangement unique in Europe: an elective monarchy with provision for male primogeniture. Relations between Denmark and Sweden continued to blow hot and cold, in part because Christian III was prepared to buy out the claims of Christian II's heirs, whereas Gustav Vasa (supported by the Swedish diet (*riksdag*) of 1547) was not. While the entente cooled, however, war was avoided during the reigns of Christian III and Gustav Vasa.

5.1.3 *The Seven Years' War of the North, 1563–1570, and the Deposition of Erik XIV*

Erik XIV, Gustav Vasa's son and the first Swedish king to succeed as hereditary monarch, accepted the fealty of the Hanseatic town of Reval in June 1561. In June the following year he notified Denmark and the Hanseatic League of his intention to use force against the port of Narva, a Hanseatic town recently absorbed by Muscovy. A Swedish attempt to acquire provinces in the eastern Baltic was a challenge which the Danish king was bound to answer. In April 1563, Frederick II, Christian III's son, overcame the objections of his council and declared war on Sweden. In June, Lübeck joined the Danish cause; four months later, so did Poland. The Seven Years' War of the North became for Sweden a war for survival as a Baltic power. Within a month, the only Swedish port of any importance on the western coast, Älvsborg, surrendered to Denmark. However, Sweden fought back in 1564, temporarily capturing Trondheim. In 1565 Varberg in Halland on the south-west peninsula was captured by the Swedes, and in 1567 much of southern Norway, including Oslo, was overrun. The military advance was assisted by the rise of naval power: after 1565 the Swedish navy dominated the Baltic.

Thereafter, the war became a stalemate; though with the paralysis of government following Erik's collapse into insanity in the second half of 1567, stalemate turned again into Swedish military disaster. Erik had quarrelled with one of his younger brothers, John, at the beginning of the reign, and its full consequences now became apparent. John had married Katarina Jagiellonka of Poland in October 1562, at a time when Sweden and Poland were on the verge of war. At Erik's prompting, the Swedish diet declared John guilty of treason in June 1563; the following August he was captured in Estonia and subsequently he and his wife were imprisoned in Sweden for four years. When the latent discontent of the Swedish nobles with Erik's rule burst into the open in the rebellion of midsummer 1568, John was its natural leader. At the end of September, John entered Stockholm, took over the government and called the *riksdag* to pronounce a sentence of deposition on Erik (January 1569). John's younger brother, duke Charles, signified his willingness to accept him as king, and John III was duly elected.

The Swedish rebellion of 1568 weakened the hereditary principle, since it modified the arrangements of 1544, although subsequent decisions of the council and diet confirmed the succession in John's line. Erik had been an arbitrary and erratic ruler: he had ruthlessly eliminated the remnants of the Sture family, who had provided the regent in the first two decades of the sixteenth century; his high court had acted as a court martial during the war, punishing nobles who defaulted on their obligations to provide knight service; finally, during his insanity, he had married a girl of peasant origins. To some extent, the rebels of 1568 had acted in defence of the law; they had certainly preserved their own interests. Yet while the deposed Erik XIV languished in captivity for nine years until his death in February 1577, there were at least seven conspiracies against John III, most of which aimed at Erik's restoration. Ironically, duke Charles, who had been one of the first to criticize Erik, attracted many of that king's former servants into his entourage and was involved in various conspiracies. Charles's holding of the independent duchy of Södermanland enabled him to feud with his elder brother John for the next twenty years with impunity.

John III's accession swiftly broke up the coalition against Sweden. Frederick II was accused of aiming at a *dominium maris Baltici* by Sigismund Augustus, king of Poland, in a phrase which was to become celebrated. Hostilities against Sweden in Livonia ground to a halt when Poland refused to support the Danish cause. In any case, John III wanted peace with Denmark. In the winter of 1567–8 Danish troops had thrust into eastern Sweden; a combined Danish–Lübeck fleet bombarded Reval in July 1569; and Sweden lost one of its few wartime gains, the important fortress of Varberg, the following November. The resulting Peace of Stettin in November 1570 appeared a disaster for Sweden. In the eastern Baltic, Estonia seemed to have been lost to Denmark, since Frederick II's younger brother, duke Magnus, the governor of Estonia, had entered into a treaty with Ivan IV of Muscovy. The Narva trade with Muscovy was to be free to all nations, and thus the Swedish attempt to control it had come to nothing (except that John III continued to harry the trade route for the next eleven years). Lübeck's privileges were restored, almost to the extent of 1523. Älvsborg had to be redeemed by Sweden at a heavy price, which was not paid off until 1578. The Danish reconquest of Sweden had been thwarted: but the Danish pretension to the Swedish throne, while formally renounced, remained only in abeyance. On the other front, the Swedish war with Muscovy continued, with truces, until 1595. But events took a new and dramatic turn in 1576 when the Muscovite armies devastated Frederick II's corner of Livonia. Two years later, duke Magnus fled from Russian service. In the 1580s, Frederick II abandoned his rights in Livonia to Poland and in Estonia to Sweden. The dispute between Denmark and Sweden in the eastern Baltic was over.

5.1.4 *The War of Kalmar, 1611–1613, and Gustavus Adolphus*

From 1588 Denmark had a new king, Christian IV, who did not come of age until 1596. The minority reinforced the power of the Danish nobility, which claimed to be 'so impoverished' that it could not afford the burden of another war.[2] Once he came of age, however, Christian IV was keen to go to war with Sweden, in the hope of escaping the tutelage of his nobles at home. He resurrected the idea of the Union of Kalmar, which he was prepared to impose on Sweden, exploiting the opportunity presented by Swedish intervention in Muscovy (see chapter 5.3.3). In April 1611, he attacked Sweden on two fronts, in the south-west and the south-east, and the subsequent two-year War of Kalmar went badly for Sweden. The fortresses of Älvsborg in the south-west and Kalmar in the south-east surrendered to the Danes, respectively in August 1611 and the spring of 1612. The miscalculations and intransigence of Charles IX of Sweden had done nothing to avert this war. (Charles had mounted a coup against Sigismund, John III's son, in the late 1590s and had succeeded him as effective ruler in 1600 (see chapter 5.2.3).) To make matters worse, Charles IX died as Sweden faced military collapse. In the accession charter imposed on the 17-year-old Gustav Adolf (Gustavus Adolphus) in December 1611, the Swedish nobles avenged the autocratic treatment they had suffered at the hands of Charles IX.

The young king was in no position to fight a war on two fronts with an incompetent navy and an inadequate army. Peace was made at Knäred in January 1613, on terms even more onerous for Sweden than in 1570. Sweden renounced any claim to territory on the Arctic Ocean coast and had to allow Danish ships to trade freely to the ports of Livonia and Courland, the most important being Riga. Most significantly, however, Denmark was to retain Älvsborg (Sweden's only North Sea port) until a huge ransom had been paid: one million *riksdalers* was such a large sum that there seemed little prospect of it being paid within the stipulated time (though with Dutch assistance it was discharged in 1619). The Dutch had intervened to secure the Peace of Knäred in order to protect their commercial interests in the Baltic (see chapter 8.4.4) and entered into a fifteen-year defence pact with Sweden at The Hague in 1614. The Danish claim to Baltic hegemony was undermined by this agreement, which was the first occasion that the term *dominium maris Baltici* appeared in a Swedish official document. It was now clear that the Dutch Republic would not countenance Danish control of the Baltic: Oldenbarnevelt sought to project himself as a protector of Hanseatic interests (a complete reversal of the situation a century earlier) and pronounced that 'we will help the Swedes against everyone'.[3] The Peace of Knäred was thus a Pyrrhic victory for Denmark. It had alienated the Dutch Republic; Sweden had not renounced its expansionist drive, but after making an advantageous peace with Muscovy in 1617, it resumed the offensive against Poland in 1621; while never again would Denmark find so favourable an opportunity to limit Swedish ambitions.

Gustavus Adolphus' victories in Livonia in the 1620s and his subsequent invasion of Polish Prussia (see chapter 5.2.4), remote and obscure as they might seem to the states of western Europe, clearly announced the emergence of Sweden as a military power on a new scale. A further dimension was added to the existing causes of friction in the years 1625–9 by the disastrous failure of Christian IV's leadership of the evangelical union in Germany (see chapter 4.1.2). At the Peace of Lübeck in 1629, he abandoned his leadership of the Protestant party in Germany on astonishingly moderate terms given the extent of his military collapse. Defeat left Christian greatly weakened: he retained the revenue from the Sound dues, but at a time of depression in the Baltic trade. The agricultural-based economy of Denmark was also unable to generate an economic boom which could help to pay off his debts. In contrast, the Swedish income from copper and its arms industry was buoyant, and in the years 1629–35 Sweden also drew revenue from tolls on the Prussian coastal areas. Control of the Pomeranian coast after 1630 enabled Sweden to levy tolls there too. Some of Gustavus' advisers argued that it might be expedient to fight a 'war for German liberties' in Denmark rather than in Pomerania and Mecklenburg, because it would have the advantage of preventing Denmark from profiting from Swedish military disaster or exhaustion. This course of action was not adopted. But with the death of Gustavus at Lützen in 1632, and the collapse of Swedish military authority in Germany in 1634–6, it might have been preferable to have adopted a different strategy for intervention in Germany, or not to have intervened at all.

5.1.5 *Oxenstierna and the Peace of Brömsebro, 1643–1645*

Christian IV, though in desperate financial straits after his defeats in Germany, was prepared to provoke a new attack on Sweden. Oxenstierna, the Swedish Chancellor, told the council (*råd*) in 1639 that Denmark had 'repeatedly chucked us under the chin to see whether our teeth sat firm in our head'.[4] Danish pretensions to Baltic hegemony persisted. In 1637, Christian IV had destroyed the Polish fleet in the Baltic without a declaration of war. He altered the Sound dues eight times between 1629 and 1639, thus incurring the wrath of the Dutch, who entered into a new treaty with Sweden in 1640 to preserve freedom of trade in the Baltic. Christian IV also deliberately encouraged sedition in Sweden: he aided the escape of the Swedish queen mother to Copenhagen, which created a potential focus for opponents of the regency (Gustavus had called her 'a person of no judgement' and excluded her from government).[5] He also intervened in the affairs of north Germany in 1641–2, threatening to side with the Emperor if the Swedes proved obdurate in the forthcoming peace negotiations. Finally, he had tried to subject the free city of Hamburg (an important member of the Hanseatic League) to Danish control by blockading the mouth of the river Elbe in the spring of 1643. Oxenstierna's patience was exhausted and, with the tacit consent of the Dutch, the great Swedish general Torstensson was sent in September to attack Jutland without a declaration of war.

The war of 1643–5 thus came about on the initiative of Sweden, not Denmark, and military and naval success was commensurate with the element of surprise. An Imperial army sent towards Holstein in support of the Danes in the summer of 1644 was destroyed by Torstennson at Jüterborg. The Danish navy was defeated at Femern in the same year. Despite these successes, however, after the majority of Christina was declared in September 1644 Swedish policy took a new turn, seeking peace rather than territorial aggrandizement. The Danish war was popular in Sweden and there had even been hopes of annexing Denmark; but Sweden's effort in Germany had lost the support of the nobles and the Swedish govenment was ready to sue for peace. Peace with Denmark came first. For those who took a hawkish view of foreign policy, the Peace of Brömsebro of August 1645 was inevitably unsatisfactory. Nevertheless, compared with the treaties of 1570 or 1613, it benefited Sweden both politically and territorially. In the north, Christian IV had to give up the Norwegian provinces of Jämtland and Härjedalen (both of which lay on the Swedish side of the mountains), together with the islands of Gotland and Ösel in the Baltic. The secularized bishoprics of Bremen and Verden, which had been the property of Christian's second son, Frederick (later Frederick III), were left under Swedish occupation, confirmed later at the

Peace of Westphalia of 1648. These gains were felt by contemporaries to form 'a bridle for the Jute',[6] that is, to make Danish intervention in Germany extremely difficult. In addition, Sweden was granted exemption from Sound dues for Swedish ships departing from all ports in her possession. As a guarantee of this exemption, Denmark was to hand over Halland, the territory south of Älvsborg, for thirty years. This began the process by which Sweden gained her natural frontiers, the permanent achievement of Charles X; but its more immediate importance was that it ensured the Sound was no longer controlled by a single power. The Swedish gains from the Peace of Westphalia in 1648 (see chapter 4.1.5) were regarded as a bulwark against Denmark, giving Sweden direct access to the market for German mercenaries. Oxenstierna commented on the most important gain, Swedish Pomerania, that it was 'a rope round the king of Denmark's neck'.[7]

The blows struck by Sweden against Denmark successively in 1645 and 1648 appear to some historians to have been terminal, and to mark 'the death of Denmark as a major European power'.[8] In fact, the future was to show that Danish retaliation was always a possibility. Sweden's allies did not wish to substitute a Swedish for a Danish hegemony. Mazarin had not enjoyed the sight of Oxenstierna using French subsidies to attack Denmark, with whom, therefore, in November 1645, France signed a six-year alliance. Even more serious for Sweden was the noticeable cooling of Dutch friendship, and the Republic signed treaties with Denmark in February 1647 and September 1649. On the second occasion, the Dutch bound themselves to pay 140,000 *riksdalers* a year in return for exemption from Sound dues. This proved a real bargain for Denmark, and the Dutch cancelled the arrangement in 1653. But the Dutch treaty appeared to protect Denmark against further Swedish attack, and growing Dutch naval superiority in the Baltic was to hamper the ambitions of Charles X.

5.1.6 *Charles X and the Resolution of the Struggle with Denmark, 1657–1660*

Peace in the Baltic was for a while secure because of the internal politics of Denmark and Sweden. In the last year of his reign (1647–8), Christian IV of Denmark had to accept tight aristocratic control of every aspect of government; when he died in February 1648 the nobles spent months bargaining with his second son, Frederick, before they agreed to elect him as their king. At first, Frederick III was very much the pawn of his brothers-in-law, one of whom, Hannibal Sehested, had held considerable power as regent in Norway. In Sweden, social discontent was greatly intensified by massive alienations of crown lands after 1648, which partly resulted from a change of fiscal policy and partly from Christina's rewards to the swarm of officers returning from the war in Germany. The situation was made worse by her decision in 1649 not to marry, which led ultimately to her abdication and conversion to Catholicism. The Swedish council opposed her wish to stand down, but the queen had her way and Charles Gustavus (the future Charles X, Christina's cousin) was recognized as her heir in 1649. To guarantee the succession, it was still necessary to secure his recognition by the estates (*riksdag*) as hereditary prince, and this was given in August 1650 at the Stockholm diet. In the penultimate year of her reign, in 1653, Christina showed her independence in foreign policy by attacking Bremen, which had resisted her attempts to destroy its status as a fief of the Empire, without consulting either the council or the diet. In May 1652, she secretly notified the Pope of her intentions to become a Catholic, to renounce the throne and to take up residence in Rome. This move, accepted by the Pope in November, was bound to alienate her subjects and she abdicated in June 1654. She attended Mass for the first time on Christmas Eve 1654, while in exile at Brussels.

The accession of Charles X marks a new era in Swedish history. In August 1654, Chancellor Axel Oxenstierna died at the age of 71: he had held the office ever since 1612. He was succeeded by his son Erik, who had been governor of Estonia, and was thus preoccupied with the affairs of the eastern Baltic. The idea of a pre-emptive war against Denmark to secure further gains while that country was still weak was debated in December 1654, but Charles X saw the Muscovite threat as more pressing (see chapter 5.2.5). The Russian capture of Smolensk (September 1654) appeared to threaten the Polish coastlands, and thus control of the trade from the eastern Baltic. War with Denmark might still prove necessary, for if Charles X succeeded in conquering the Polish fief of East Prussia, Denmark might feel driven to attack him before he overran the whole Baltic littoral; and, if he failed, Denmark would not let slip the chance of recovering the territorial losses of 1645. Charles tried to protect himself by the Whitelocke treaty of 1654 with the Cromwellian Protectorate (which was expanded into a trade treaty in July 1656). But Cromwell would not be drawn into a Baltic war against the Dutch, who would inevitably side with Denmark. He clearly regarded Charles's attack on Prussia, which involved a siege of Danzig, as provocative to the Dutch: was not Danzig, he pointed out, 'their bread-basket'?[9] Indeed, the Dutch sent a fleet of forty-two ships to thwart the Swedish blockade of Danzig. But they, too, were cautious about full-scale war. In December 1657, a resolution of the states of Holland (confirmed by the States General in February 1658) recommended a settlement between Sweden and Denmark on the terms of 1645—which meant that the Dutch might be willing to defend Denmark but not to support Danish expansionism.

By their support of his policies, the Dutch unwittingly pushed Frederick

III of Denmark into measures which made war inevitable. Throughout the first half of 1657, Frederick was steadily preparing for the attack on Sweden which he eventually launched in June. He put his forces into a state of military preparedness, and levied mercenaries in the expectation of being able to attack Sweden with the backing of a Habsburg alliance; the Emperor held off, but it seems that the war went ahead as the only means of paying for these troops. Frederick thus coerced his council into agreeing to the invasion of the duchy of Holstein-Gottorp, which belonged to duke Frederick, the father-in-law of Charles X, and which threatened the Swedish overland route to Bremen. The Danish attack might well have been successful, leading to a peace even more advantageous to the Danes than that of 1613. But the generalship of Charles X and the exceptionally hard winter of 1657–8 prevented a Danish military victory. Charles had pressed on from his initial invasion of Prussia deep into Poland. Within six months, he transferred his army from Poland via Pomerania to the gates of Copenhagen. After the fall of Fredriksodde to the Swedes in late October 1657, Charles was in the ascendancy. He wanted the peace of 1645 confirmed and made additional demands in the dictated Treaty of Roskilde at the end of February 1658. The acquisition of Halland was now made definitive, and to this was added three other Danish provinces, Skåne and Blekinge (the southern provinces of the Swedish peninsula adjoining the Sound) and Bohuslän (the south-western province on the Swedish peninsula). The district of Trondheim in Norway and the island of Bornholm in the Baltic were also ceded, but these were returned in 1660. In addition, Charles demanded half the Sound dues for Sweden and the power to close the Sound to any future Dutch fleet which might be sent to impede his military objectives. This final provocative demand ensured that a Dutch fleet would be sent to assist the Danish cause the following year.

This dictated peace was of short duration. Charles X could not demobilize, because he was still at war with Poland and Brandenburg. As in the reign of Gustavus Adolphus, it was still thought that the only safe road to peace lay though continued war. Even if he had been able to secure a definitive settlement with Denmark, Charles made it clear to Cromwell that he intended to attack Brandenburg. The Danes wanted to temper the draconian terms of the Roskilde treaty before ratifying it; Charles wanted to emphasize them, as he made clear to his council in late July. Charles asked the *råd* 'whether, if God gave us good fortune, Denmark should not be reduced to the position of a province of Sweden?'[10] In this event, Charles would wear the Swedish crown, not the Danish, and thus Denmark would be reduced to an inferior status. The Danes would be allowed to retain their own laws, but the form of government would be as in Sweden. The Danish royal family would be imprisoned; the Danish aristocracy dispersed and deported; the city of Copenhagen would be razed to the ground. This was a new Union of Kalmar, with Sweden in the driving seat and Charles X quite as autocratic a ruler as Christian II had been in 1520. Indeed, it was subsequently said of Charles X's rule in Sweden that 'he always, in fact, did whatever he pleased, and since throughout his reign he had the country under arms, he was able to do so with impunity, though it never happened that he actually overstepped the law'.[11]

It was with these great Scandinavian ambitions that Charles launched a surprise attack on Denmark in August 1658, an attack made easier because his troops had never evacuated the country from the earlier war. Its most significant effort was the land and sea blockade of Copenhagen, but the capital held firm for its sovereign until Dutch assistance arrived in the form of a fleet of thirty-five ships. In the course of 1659, Charles's grip on Denmark began to falter. In February, France and England pledged themselves to restore the terms of Roskilde, with modifications in favour of the Dutch. Charles refused such offers of mediation but he suffered a naval defeat at the hands of the Dutch, under the command of de Ruyter, at Nyborg in late November. The sudden illness and death of the Swedish king in February 1660, leaving debts of over 10 million *riksdalers* from his wars, made agreement easier. The Swedish regency government was prepared to settle for a modification of the terms of Roskilde, and this was agreed at the Treaty of Copenhagen in late May and early June 1660. The four former Danish provinces transferred under the terms of Roskilde were now finally part of Sweden, but the clauses excluding foreign warships from the Baltic were excised from the new treaty.

The Peace of Copenhagen ended for forty years the dynastic struggle between the houses of Oldenburg and Vasa. Sweden had achieved its 'natural frontiers' under Charles X and the four Danish provinces acquired in 1658–60 were gradually assimilated into Sweden. The maritime powers (England and the Dutch) had done much better in 1660 than 1658, since an unchallenged Swedish predominance in the Sound would have been as onerous as the former supremacy of Denmark. Above all, the Oldenburg hopes of resurrecting the dynastic union were dead. Swedish and Danish history clearly began to diverge. Though Frederick III and his advisers were chiefly responsible, the aristocratic council was universally blamed in 1660 for launching the disastrous attack on Sweden. Burghers and clergy were in agreement that the mismanagement of affairs since Christian IV's death could only be rectified by making royal authority hereditary and not elective. This was agreed by all three estates in October 1660. Thereafter the old council and the estates disappeared. Hannibal Sehested was appointed treasurer; he dominated the government and introduced reforms on the Swedish model. By an act of bankruptcy, the king's debts were largely removed. That such a nonentity of a king and such a disastrous war should have this favourable outcome was indeed remarkable (see chapter 6.5.4).

The contrast with Sweden was even more striking. There, the death of Charles X left a royal minority until 1672, since Charles XI was only 4 at his accession. There was an abrupt shift of power back to the nobility rather in the manner of 1611 and 1634. The Addition to the Form of Government confirmed the succession arrangements of 1649–50 and decided on triennial diets during the king's minority. But it was a divided aristocracy that ruled, with a less able Chancellor in Magnus de la Gardie than either of the Oxenstiernas, and a dispute between the regents and the council in the 1660s (with the regents representing the royal prerogative). The surprising consequence was that the strongest power in the Baltic in the 1650s, Sweden, was rapidly weakened. In 1675, a relatively small military defeat by the Prussians at Fehrbellin assumed the proportions of a national disaster and paved the way for the autocracy of Charles XI.

5.2 Poland-Lithuania and Sweden: Imperial Conflict and Dynastic Struggle

Certain similarities between Sweden and Poland are immediately obvious. Both were dual states, Poland and Lithuania forming first a personal, and then a constitutional union, just as Sweden and Finland had done. Both societies were dominated by a powerful class of noble families who derived their wealth from their large estates, though the Swedish nobility showed more readiness than the Polish to make sacrifices and waive privileges in the name of patriotism. In both countries the institutions bolstering noble power were relatively strong and the monarchy was weak, although its historic development in the two countries was diametrically opposed. In Sweden in 1523 the monarchy was purely elective, but by 1660 the Vasa kings were 'elected' hereditary monarchs. Until 1572, the Jagiellon kings of Poland were elected monarchs with a tendency towards hereditary succession, but three interregna in 1572, 1576 and 1587 fatally weakened the crown and enshrined the elective principle. The Polish Vasa dynasty was unable to reverse this trend between 1587 and 1668.

Yet the contrasts between the two countries were far more significant than any similarities. Though both were large (especially after Sweden's acquisition of a Baltic empire and some former Danish provinces), Poland-Lithuania was much the more extensive country, amounting to some 435,000 square miles in 1492 and some 386,000 square miles in 1634. It was in fact the largest territorial unit in Europe, slightly bigger than *European* Muscovy and nearly twice the size of France. In terms of population, even in the mid-seventeenth century, Finland and Sweden did not have many more than a million inhabitants between them, while the population of Poland-Lithuania was much greater: one (probably exaggerated) estimate puts it at 11 million, which would have given it the fourth highest population after France, Muscovy and the Holy Roman Empire. Religion was another great difference. With the exception of (Greek Orthodox) Swedish Ingria, acquired in 1617, Sweden enjoyed the rare blessing in Europe of total religious unity. John III (1568–92) flirted with Catholicism for a time, but the Counter-Reformation made little or no headway against the Lutheran monopoly in Sweden. In contrast, Poland-Lithuania remained a confessionally mixed society. Protestantism, and especially Calvinism, made considerable progress, but there were significant Jewish minorities in Poland and Orthodox ones in Lithuania. Even after the Counter-Reformation had made its full impact by 1660, scarcely half the population were Catholics. Religious diversity necessitated tolerance to a degree unprecedented elsewhere in Europe. As the Confederation of Warsaw of January 1573 stated, 'we who differ in religion will keep the peace among ourselves . . .'[12]

The contrasting geographical positions of Sweden and Poland affected their economic structures. The Baltic frontier of Sweden and Finland, which was already long, was greatly extended in 1617 with the acquisition of Karelia and Ingria (or Ingermanland), which guarded Muscovite access to the gulf of Finland. Sweden's Baltic empire was based on naval power; in the words of Axel Oxenstierna, 'if our fleet has the upper hand, then we are masters of the Baltic'.[13] Poland had no navy. When Ladislas IV tried to build one in 1637, it was promptly destroyed by Denmark. Poland was essentially landlocked, with the coast making up only 6 per cent of its frontier, although this 6 per cent was vital, because it gave the country its outlet to the Baltic through the great port of Danzig in Royal or West Prussia. The importance of Danzig was highlighted by the privileges granted to it in 1466, and confirmed subsequently, by which it enjoyed self-government and grew to be five times the size of the royal capital in Warsaw. It handled three-quarters of Poland's total foreign trade, which was predominantly the grain sent in barges down the river Vistula from the Polish hinterland for export. Sweden had no such entrepôt and had an interest in incorporating some Baltic ports within its expanding coastline. But Poland, too, was looking for alternative ports to counterbalance the threat posed by other states: hence the attraction of Livonia to both Sweden and Poland after the 1560s. It contained the prizes of Riga and Pernau and was contiguous with Estonia and its ports of Reval and Narva.

5.2.1 *The Growth of Polish Noble Independence, 1492–1572*

Poland was ruled by the Jagiellon dynasty, founded in the late fourteenth century by a king whose principal achievement had been to halt the advance of the Teutonic Knights of Prussia at the battle of Grunwald (or Tanneberg) in 1410. His grandson, the great Casimir (Kazimierz) IV, ruled both Poland and Lithuania, but on his death in 1492 this state was partitioned between his second and third sons (his eldest son was already king of Bohemia and Hungary). In spite of this partition, by the end of the fifteenth century the Jagiellons seemed more powerful than the Habsburgs, their nearest rivals geographically and in terms of prestige. There were some evident weaknesses, however. The first was that the election of Casimir's second son, Jan Olbracht, as king of Poland in 1492 had undermined the principle of male primogeniture. The second was that the dynastic tie between Poland and Lithuania had been loosened. In Lithuania, the nobles (boyars or warriors) had been more dependent on the ruler than were their Polish counterparts. Historically, they had owed the grand duke personal homage and unlimited military service in return for their land. Nevertheless, Casimir's third son, Alexander, had accepted an accession charter which gave the council of nobility greater power than it had ever had under his father. Further concessions were made by Sigismund, his younger brother, who came to the throne in 1506.

The Jagiellon dynasty possessed a clearer right to hereditary succession in Lithuania than it did in Poland. When the Lithuanians made an offer to renew the union with Poland in 1496, it was rejected by the Polish nobles (*szlachta*) on the grounds that it would limit their right of free election. With the death of Jan Olbracht in June 1501, power in Poland devolved on to the former councillors of Casimir IV, who sought to bolster their position by agreeing to the election of the least able of the Jagiellons, Alexander, grand duke of Lithuania, as king of Poland under very onerous conditions. This action deprived the Jagiellons of their right of hereditary succession in Lithuania, since the election of the Polish king and the Lithuanian grand duke were henceforth declared to be a single joint election. The Polish nobles continued to maintain that their choice was free, irrespective of the late king's plans for his family. This Polish arrangement, enshrined in the Charter of Mielnik, also confirmed the inalienable right of the Polish nobleman to resist the king if he acted tyrannically, a right which would later be formalized in what were called 'confederation movements' (*rokosz*). Finally, the council arrogated supreme power to itself as a ruling senate, with the king acting as its president; the senators were subject only to their peers, which constrained the pretensions of the nobility in general and created a deep-seated grievance among the lesser nobility.

After his Polish coronation in December 1501, Alexander left for Lithuania to fight against Muscovy, without having confirmed or revoked the Charter of Mielnik; he did not return to Poland until the end of 1503 after a truce with Muscovy had been concluded. The senate had proved unable to organize the defence of the country against Tatar attack in the absence of the king, largely because the nobles had refused to pay their taxes. The *szlachta* had already tasted the fruits of success at the diet of 1496, where in return for voting taxes for Jan Olbracht's disastrous expedition against the Ottoman Turks, they had received extensive privileges, in particular a monopoly of landholding: townsmen were forbidden landed possessions 'because they have no place in the ranks of a general levy'.[14] On Alexander's return from Lithuania, the *szlachta* had its revenge on the great lords of the senate who had sought to exclude them from power in the government. At the end of May 1505, the Polish diet passed the statute of *Nihil novi*, which meant that the council could not henceforth force any of its decisions on the king without the support of the Chamber of Deputies in the diet, which represented the *szlachta*. This statute enshrined noble independence in sixteenth-century Poland and limited the power of the monarchy. The crown was further weakened in the same year when the captains-general (*starostas*) of the provinces were given life tenure of their offices: the king was thus unable to strengthen his authority over the provinces by disposing of uncooperative or ineffective *starostas* and replacing them with his own appointees.

In December 1506, Sigismund (Zygmunt) I succeeded his elder brother as king of Poland and grand duke of Lithuania by joint election. The new king recognized the need for military and financial reform; but the earlier decisions of the diet had ossified the constitution and paralysed government. What the nobles demanded was the 'execution'—that is, implementation—of existing laws, not constitutional reform which might threaten their privileges. Yet, without reform, it was difficult for the king to fight a successful war. Poland was in no position to assist the Hungarians against the Ottoman advance in 1526 (see chapter 5.4.2): Sigismund I proposed his candidature to the vacant throne after Mohácz, but he was unable to enforce it because he lacked sufficient resources in men and money. Thwarted in Bohemia and Hungary, Sigismund I was determined to preserve the succession in Poland, and at the diet of 1530 he had his 10-year-old son (the future Sigismund II Augustus) elected as his successor. He was to be the only Polish king in the sixteenth century to have his son elected in his lifetime. But the *szlachta* soon realized their folly. In 1537 a general mobilization against Moldavia was diverted from its original purpose and a 'confederation' (*rokosz*) proclaimed near Lwów. By 1539, Sigismund I was forced to concede to the principal demands of the opposition, notably that he would not issue any new laws and that he would accept that the election of his son in 1530 had technically been illegal. Sigismund's son would become the next king, but after Sigismund II's death the new king would be elected by free vote; all that had been secured by Sigismund I, therefore, was the accession of Sigismund II, which occurred in April 1548, without a second election.

During his father's lifetime, Sigismund II had gained considerable experience in government by ruling for nearly twenty years at Vilna as grand duke of Lithuania. For the next fifteen years, despite becoming king of Poland, Sigismund II did not favour a closer union between the two states. Given his father's difficulties in 1537–9, the Jagiellon dynasty appeared to be more secure in Lithuania than in Poland; and in any case the Lithuanian nobles (boyars) for the most part opposed closer ties with the kingdom. Yet since Lithuania on its own was not strong enough to counter the Muscovite threat which was always present, and the boyars resented the increasing burden of taxation and military service which was necessary to maintain the security of the duchy, greater unity was desirable—if only to share these burdens. But Lithuanian victories against Muscovy strengthened the party which opposed any union with Poland; defeats had the reverse effect. In February 1564, however, Sigismund finally decided to transfer his hereditary rights in Lithuania to the crown of Poland. He prepared the way for union by a series of measures passed in the grand duchy between 1559 and 1566 which made it more akin to Poland in its administrative structure. A powerful separatist party remained in Lithuania, led by Jan Chodkiewicz, who threatened rebellion rather than be 'handed over to the Polish crown by hereditary will, to the slavery and shame of their children', but union was gradually forged by a commitment to parity, 'freeman with free, equals with equal'.[15] It is sometimes asserted that the king agreed to the measure because there was no alternative, since his third marriage had failed to produce an heir and the Jagiellon dynasty was sure to die out. In fact, Sigismund II did not give up hope of securing the dynastic inheritance until 1571; if he could not produce an heir himself, he wished to secure the succession for one of his nephews, such as John Sigismund Zápolyai, prince of Transylvania. Only on Zápolyai's death in March 1571 did the king recognize that his dynasty had come to an end and thus he promoted the candidature of Henri of Valois, who eventually succeeded him, in order to prevent the election of a Habsburg candidate.

The Union of Lublin (July 1569) drew Poland and Lithuania together as one Commonwealth or Republic (*Rzeczpospolita*), with the same elected king, a joint representative institution (*Sejm*) and in principle (though not in practice) a common currency. This measure, 'in which the two states and the two nations have joined and merged into a single nation and a single state',[16] was a unique document in early modern European history. In the earlier empire of Charles V, no component territory had voluntarily renounced rights to another, as did Lithuania to Poland in 1569. But the Union of Lublin was still limited in scope: the Lithuanians were to keep their own laws, their own administration, their own army and the titles of their princely families. There was no consensus on electoral procedure (though this was settled in January 1573, some five months after Sigismund II's death). Nor was there a central treasury or agreement on judicial reform. Indeed, Sigismund III had to make concessions to his Lithuanian magnates before they would accept him as their grand duke. In 1588, he was forced to accept the Third Lithuanian Statute, which stipulated that all laws contrary to it, including several clauses of the Union of Lublin, were invalid. In Poland, the Third Lithuanian Statute was thought by the nobles to be unconstitutional. In Lithuania, the Union of Lublin was still seen almost twenty years later as an act of duress which had violated the separate sovereignty of the grand duchy. But since both documents remained in force until the end of the eighteenth century, it is difficult to see, as some historians have claimed, a process of 'ever-closer fusion of the two states' after 1569.[17]

5.2.2 *The Polish-Lithuanian Acquisition and Defence of Livonia, 1561–1582*

Since 1466, when they had forced the Teutonic Knights into vassal status, the Poles had argued about whether to reach an entente with the Teutonic Knights, or to expel them and annexe their territories. The so-called 'order-state' (*Ordenstaat*) of the Teutonic Knights was founded on monastic vows, and had as its original purpose the aim of crusading against the (then pagan) Lithuanians. The conversion of Jagiellio to Catholicism had deprived the Teutonic Knights of their original purpose, while the progress of the Reformation brought about their military collapse through religious disunity. Yet their state, which included the port of Königsberg, was of key strategic importance to Poland-Lithuania, both in terms of defence (that is to say, the need to avoid it falling under the control of a hostile power) and in order to expand the Polish Baltic littoral. In 1525, Albrecht von Hohenzollern secularized the Grand Order of the Teutonic Knights and paid homage to Sigismund I for his new dukedom. After this first act of homage in April 1525, Albrecht remained a loyal subject and an active participant in Polish affairs; but Sigismund I missed the opportunity of gaining real influence over the affairs of East Prussia, where the house of Hohenzollern, not Jagiellon, still ruled. Matters were made worse in 1562, when in order to gain the support of Brandenburg and to counter Habsburg opposition to the enforcement of Polish objectives in Livonia, Sigismund II recognized the rights of the Hohenzollerns in Brandenburg to succeed in East Prussia should their cousin Albrecht's direct line die out. This occurred in 1618: it was a heavy long-term price to pay for short-term diplomatic support, because the duchy of East Prussia would otherwise have reverted to the Polish crown at this date.

Further to the east, contiguous with the gulf of Riga, were the territories of the other crusading order, the Grand Order of the Livonian Knights of the Sword. By the 1550s, the Reformation was making rapid headway there, too. Because of the divisions among the Knights, it was feared that the Livonian state would collapse, resulting in a power vacuum that might be filled by Muscovy. Hence, Sigismund II tried to secure union with Livonia as early as 1552, but the formation of a defence pact was then postponed by Sigismund's wish not to appear the aggressor; by the paralysis of the Order during the civil war of 1556–7 (largely between pro- and anti-Lithuanian factions); and then by the insistence of its Grand Master (the pro-Polish Gotthard von Kettler) that any treaty should be with Poland and Lithuania and not with Lithuania alone. In 1558, Ivan IV of Muscovy precipitated events, taking Narva and Dorpat and capturing the whole of eastern Estonia except Reval (see chapter 5.3.2): the strategic threat to the north of Livonia was now acute. Though Gotthard von Kettler hurriedly signed a treaty with Lithuania, the grand duchy proved unable to defend Livonia without help from Poland. But Poland was at that moment bound by a truce with Ivan IV, and Polish troops did not join the war until the following year. Sigismund II was now in an extremely strong position to take control of Livonia, helped by divisions among the Livonian Knights, and by the rapid military collapse of the Order. He avoided repeating the mistake his father had made in 1525. The original proposal for union mooted in 1552 had been to create a vassal Livonian duchy; but in a treaty of November 1561, which brought about the secularization of the Livonian Knights, sovereignty passed to Sigismund II personally. No native dynasty was established: the former Grand Master, Kettler, was made duke of Courland and Simigalia; but this dukedom incorporated only the western part of the state south of Riga. Elsewhere, he was only the king's lord lieutenant, and then only until 1566, when this office was occupied by a Lithuanian. Rights over the duchy of Courland remained with Sigismund II until he turned them over to the Polish-Lithuanian Commonwealth in 1569.

The ducal rights had yet to be secured by the fortunes of war, for conflict with Muscovy remained an active threat. Even if Sigismund's appropriation of these rights was vindicated on the battlefield, there remained the question of a residual imperial overlordship. From November 1561, Sigismund was not only confronting Ivan IV in Livonia, but also opposing the objectives of Erik XIV of Sweden in Estonia (see chapter 5.1.3). Erik wanted an alliance with Ivan IV against Denmark and Poland, under the terms of which each gave the other a free hand in Livonia. However, Erik obtained no recognition of any of his claims from

Ivan IV until May 1564, when they were limited to Reval, Pernau, Karkus and Weissenstein. In return, he was forced to acknowledge Ivan's claims to the rest of Livonia and to promise not to interfere with Muscovite trade through the port of Narva. It was impossible for a Swedish king to be friends simultaneously with Muscovy and Poland because of the latter's Baltic ambitions. Erik XIV had chosen Muscovy, but it had brought Sweden few gains; his supplanter, John III, veered towards friendship with Poland without entering into a firm alliance. Once Sigismund II had most of Livonia under his control, he saw little profit in prolonging the struggle. Lithuania was exhausted financially; the Union of Lublin needed to be consolidated; and uppermost in Sigismund's mind remained the question of the succession, a question which remained unsettled at the time of his death in June 1572. The consequent paralysis of the Polish government ruled out all question of renewing the war.

After prolonged negotiations, the Polish succession crisis was resolved with the election of Henri of Valois as king in May 1573 by an estimated 40,000 noble electors. However, the interregnum continued in practice, for Henri did not leave France until December and was not crowned until February 1574. The Polish nobles forced him to concede the so-called 'Henrician articles', which formed a fixed contract for subsequent reigns. These articles provided for the calling of a diet every two years; they prevented the king from naming his successor or marrying without the consent of the diet (thus ensuring the nobility's right to elect their king freely in the future); and insisted on the right of the diet to approve declarations of war, mobilization and taxation. The principle of religious toleration which had been enshrined in the Confederation of Warsaw of the previous year was also included (much to the Catholic Henri's chagrin), as was the rule of 1501 releasing the king's subjects from their oath of obedience if he should fail to carry out his coronation oath. 'French fanaticism',[18] as the Poles called it, was thus firmly excluded, though had Henri taken the trouble to investigate it, he would have found his constitutional position far from hopeless. As Giovanni Botero observed in 1592, almost certainly commenting on Henri's successor, Stefan (István) Bátory, 'the king has as much power as his skill and understanding can give him'.[19] Henri was indolent and preoccupied with events elsewhere, and no wonder, for with the death of his elder brother, Charles IX, at the end of May 1574, he succeeded to the throne of France. Amazingly, the Polish electors never seem to have considered this possibility seriously. Henri clearly intended to retain both crowns, but when he left to claim his French kingdom in the middle of June 1574, after a reign of 118 days, he never returned to Poland.

The weakness of elective monarchy became evident in the chaos following Henri's precipitate departure for France. The absent king was deposed by the diet in May 1575 but there was no immediately obvious successor. In the autumn, the Tatars launched a raid on Poland which was the largest in its history: the kingdom practically collapsed under this invasion and the internal threat of civil war which followed the disputed election. The electoral meeting in November resembled a different kind of battlefield. The two main candidates were the Emperor Maximilian II and Stefan Bátory, prince of Transylvania. Maximilian's electoral campaign lacked resolution and victory went to the more seasoned campaigner. Bátory entered Cracow in March 1576, and had himself crowned. He fulfilled the condition of his election by marrying Anna Jagiellonka, the late king's sister and the last of the Jagiellons. This did not resolve the internal tensions in the kingdom; Danzig refused to renounce its support for the Habsburg candidate, whereupon Bátory besieged it until December 1577 when he was forced to make peace with a city whose landward defences had proved invulnerable. During his election campaign, Bátory had promised action 'for the defence of Christendom', and said that he had not come to Poland to be a mere painted monarch.[20] By this, he meant that he intended to fight Muscovy, not the Turks, whose suzerainty over Transylvania he had long accepted.

Ivan IV struck first. In 1577, taking advantage of Bátory's war with Danzig, he overran all Livonia except Riga and Reval. Lesser men would not have recovered from this shattering blow, but Bátory was a brave commander, an astute politician and a skilful administrator. Lacking money, he was unable to assemble an army for the war with Muscovy until June 1579, when he formally declared war and recaptured Polotsk at the end of August. While greatly concerned about the strategic threat to Livonia, Bátory did not want to defend the duchy by mounting a pro- longed siege campaign which would not have much direct effect upon Ivan IV. Instead, he tried to drive a wedge between Livonia and Muscovy, thus over-extending the latter's lines of communication and making Livonia an unattractive conquest to support. In this policy he was largely successful, capturing the fortified town of Velikie Luki on the river Lovat in September 1580 and then besieging Pskov from August 1581 until February the following year. Sweden had refused to sign a treaty with Poland over Livonia, preferring instead to profit from the Russo-Polish war in order to seize the fruits of victory from Poland. Swedish advances in Ingria and Estonia, where Pontus de la Gardie captured Narva and Weissenstein, combined with Bátory's strategy to force Ivan IV to sue for peace. A ten-year Russo-Polish truce was concluded at Yam Zapolski in mid-January 1582, and it marked a severe defeat for Muscovy. The whole of Livonia was abandoned to the Polish-Lithuanian Commonwealth, and with it the Muscovite plan for direct access to the Baltic—a plan which had to wait for its fulfilment until the reign of Peter the Great. Twenty-four years of Muscovite occupation of Dorpat came to an end, and certain territories to the east of the river Dvina (Polotsk, Velizh and Ushviata) were also handed over to Lithuania. Bátory left Sweden to make its own terms with Ivan IV, and John III prudently concluded two three-year truces in 1583 and 1586.

5.2.3 The Election of Sigismund III and His Deposition in Sweden, 1587–1599

Faced by the need to find an ally against Muscovy, John III had earlier intervened in the Polish elections of 1572–3 and 1575. His assets were his Jagiellon wife and his ability to speak Polish; but he lacked ready money to squander on electioneering and so his bid for the Polish kingdom had been unsuccessful. After the death of Stefan Bátory without a direct heir in December 1586, the prospect of a personal union between the two crowns became much brighter. The widowed queen Anna set her heart on securing the election of John III's son Sigismund, whom she had already made her heir. As the son of a Jagiellon, a Roman Catholic and a Polish-speaker, Sigismund seemed almost a native candidate. Nevertheless, there was another candidate, the archduke Maximilian of Habsburg. The result of the election held in August 1587 was disputed by the loser, Maximilian, who invaded Poland but failed to capture Cracow. Bátory's party, energetically led by Chancellor Jan Zamoyski, controlled the government and army, and stood firm for Sigismund. However, Zamoyski rapidly formed a low opinion of Sigismund, calling him 'our dumb phantom imported from Sweden',[21] and the reign got off to a poor start. John III only allowed Sigismund to leave Sweden after his acceptance of the Statute of Kalmar in September 1587. This provided safeguards against Polish interference in the internal affairs of Sweden and declared Estonia to be a Swedish province. To secure his election as king of Poland, Sigismund's agents had promised on his behalf that Estonia would be transferred to Poland. The two policies were irreconcilable, and stored up trouble for Sigismund. But a more obvious problem was Sigismund's Habsburg marriage in May 1592, which did nothing to heal the divisions in Polish society. His former enemies rallied to him; his erstwhile supporters, led by Zamoyski, opposed the Habsburg alliance, suspecting it formed part of a longer-term plan for the king to sell his crown to a Habsburg candidate so that he could return to his native Sweden. But some compromise between the factions became necessary after the death of John III of Sweden in November 1592. At the diet of May 1593, Sigismund was granted permission to leave for Sweden, and Zamoyski was left to run the country in his absence.

In Sweden, Sigismund's uncle Charles had been the effective ruler in the years 1590–2 and in January 1593 he was proclaimed the 'leading personage' of the realm.[22] Together with the council of state (*råd*), Charles summoned a church council to Uppsala, which reaffirmed the country's commitment to Lutheranism and stated that Catholics should be persecuted. By March 1593, it became a precondition of Sigismund's coronation that he should agree to this policy. Thus the religious settlement was linked to a constitutional issue, and Sigismund was forced to consent to the first accession charter in Swedish history which had been imposed on an hereditary monarch. He was eventually crowned in 1594, but he had to promise to rule Sweden 'with the advice of Charles and the *råd*'.[23] Declarations of war and peace, and diplomatic alliances and all other important matters were not to be taken except with 'the unanimous unconstrained free will of all the estates'.[24] Not surprisingly, he lamented that 'under the cloak of religion much was demanded of us that touched our royal majesty too nearly'.[25] He accused his opponents of borrowing Polish political ideas, particularly with regard to the requirement of unanimity. This criticism was applied particularly to Erik Sparre, whose *Postulata Nobilium* was published in 1594 and was viewed as a definitive statement of Swedish aristocratic constitutionalism. (An earlier treatise by the same author in 1582 in fact suggested the influence of writers such as Duplessis-Mornay, Hotman and Buchanan: see chapter 6.1.2.) Sparre thought that 'if elective monarchs, who are transient, give good privileges, hereditary monarchs whose line is permanent, should give better ones'.[26] Even Charles, for all his conspiring against his nephew, considered such claims excessive. Although Sigismund was prepared to recognize Charles and the council as joint regents during his absence, he was determined to circumscribe their power by appointing castle commanders with pro-Catholic tendencies; and he tried to keep the prerogative of summoning the Swedish diet to himself by condemning Charles's attempts to do so as unlawful. After Sigismund left Sweden for Poland in August 1594, Charles nevertheless summoned two diets, in 1595 and 1597, and proceeded to evict Sigismund's commanders (with the exception of the governor of Finland who controlled an army of 5,000 men which held firm for the king).

Only in 1598 did the Polish diet appreciate that the union of the crowns was in danger because of the growing entrenchment of Charles's power in Sweden. They then voted troops and money on a sufficient scale for Sigismund to mount an invasion of Sweden. Towards the end of July, Sigismund's armada put to sea. Kalmar was captured without great difficulty; and had he moved on to Stockholm without delay, Sigismund might have won the civil war. Instead, he turned aside to less important conquests, and as the weeks passed, Sigismund's initial advantage was dissipated. Charles was able to turn a truce signed in September 1598 to his advantage. His leading noble opponents were handed over to him and Sigismund set sail ignominiously for Danzig in October, never to see Sweden again. The Swedish diet of July 1599 deposed him, but was prepared to vest the succession in his 3-year-old son, Ladislas, provided that he was sent over to Sweden to be educated as a Lutheran under Charles's tutelage, a condition to which the Polish king was never likely to agree. However, as Charles tightened his grip on power, five of his aristocratic opponents, including Erik Sparre, were executed in March 1600. In the same month, Sigismund's line was barred from the Swedish throne. In 1604, Charles IX accepted the title of 'Sweden's ruling lord and king', having delivered Sweden 'from Popish bonds, and foreign yoke and thraldom'.[27] He had won the civil war comprehensively, and the succession was vested in his son Gustav Adolf the following year.

5.2.4 *Livonia: the Centre of the Vasa Dynastic Struggle, 1600–1629*

By June 1600, Charles IX knew that the Polish diet would not help Sigismund recover Sweden and Estonia. Consequently, his attack on Livonia in August can only be classed as naked aggression. Initially, Sweden had the better of the fighting because the Polish army was not under arms, but when it was mobilized it proved greatly superior to the Swedish army which, by the summer of 1603, held only the environs of Reval and Narva. A further military disaster near Weissenstein in September 1604 forced Charles once more to take to the field himself, but his siege of Riga exactly a year later ended in disaster, and he returned to Sweden without any gains. If the Polish political situation had been less volatile, Estonia as well as Livonia would no doubt have been permanently annexed to Poland. Instead, the war became a desultory series of sieges and truces, merged into the larger question of the struggle for ascendancy in Muscovy.

Even after securing Livonia, Sigismund III was no nearer recovering Sweden. In 1605, there were fresh rumours that he was prepared to resign the Polish throne, this time in favour of his son Ladislas, in order to invade Sweden with Habsburg assistance. Chancellor Zamoyski reacted by threatening to deport the king to Sweden if he failed to pay attention to the wishes of the Polish nobility. But Zamoyski's death in June 1605 removed restraints on both the king and his opponents. Sigismund entered into his second Habsburg marriage in December without the consent of the diet, and the following March he announced that he intended to invade Sweden. He also wanted to establish a standing army, permanent taxation and majority voting within the diet. At this point, Michael Zebrzydowski, the Palatine of Cracow, declared a 'confederation' (*rokosz*) in support of the privileges of the nobility (*szlachta*), and he obtained over 50,000 signatures for a 67-point act of remonstrance. The rebellion, for that is what the confederation of Sandomierz turned into in effect, was dispersed in July 1607 only because the two most important military commanders, Chodkiewicz and Zólkiewski, stood firm for the king. But an amnesty was proclaimed because of the strength of the opposition, and at the diet of 1609 the king had to abandon all hope of constitutional reform.

When Charles IX of Sweden died in October 1611, he was succeeded by his eldest son, Gustav II Adolf (Gustavus Adolphus), who was only sixteen. Despite his youth and inexperience, Gustavus was declared a fully empowered king at the diet at the end of the year. Meanwhile, Sigismund had refused to give up his claim to the Swedish throne; hostilities became inevitable, though first Gustavus had to settle his wars with Denmark and Muscovy (see chapters 5.1.4 and 5.3.3). After they came to an end, the struggle with Poland in Livonia was resumed in July 1617, when Gustavus captured the ports of Dünamünde and Pernau. A truce then followed in 1618–20, but when Poland was preoccupied with the Ottoman siege of Chocim (see chapter 5.4.3), Gustavus again attacked Livonia, this time capturing Riga in September 1621. This set Sweden on the way to the conquest of the whole of Livonia in 1625 and a greatly enlarged Baltic empire. A firm peace with Poland, however, meant the renunciation of Sigismund's claims to Sweden; to achieve this, the Swedish king was prepared to renounce his recent conquests. He was willing to sign a truce as early as 1622, and indeed Livonia only became a Swedish province in 1625–6. But the truce brought lasting peace no nearer, and so Gustavus transferred his armies to East Prussia in 1626, with the idea of blocking the export of Polish grain from the Vistula delta. His hope was that the Polish *szlachta* would compel their king to come to terms in the face of this economic embargo. The Swedish armies operated in Royal Prussia, too, occupying all the coastal towns except for Danzig. Despite the military and political pressure, the duke of Prussia remained loyal to Sigismund (although he was Gustavus' brother-in-law), as did the Polish nobles.

By 1629, the mounting cost of the war had made Sweden dependent on the revenue from tolls at the ports of Livonia and Prussia. A greater—and possibly more costly—struggle in Germany also seemed imminent. Already in 1627 a committee of the Swedish *riksdag* had concluded that the Emperor was involved in an 'open conspiracy' to deprive Sweden 'of all trade and navigation and (which is worst of all) of the sovereignty of the Baltic, which from time immemorial has been attached and appertained to the Swedish crown'.[28] Sigismund III was receiving Habsburg help, and Christian IV's intervention in Germany had collapsed. It seemed unlikely that a firm peace with Poland could be achieved speedily, and in any case

Gustavus had lost interest in it. But war in Prussia could not be continued beyond 1629 because the country had been so devastated that it could no longer support the armies of Sweden and Poland (let alone Wallenstein's too). A truce, rather than a peace treaty, offered a number of advantages. It would enable Gustavus to continue to levy tolls upon the Prussian coastal areas legally, and this in turn would provide the funds for a German expedition in 1630. All this was in the French interest, and French diplomacy secured the Truce of Altmark in September 1629, which enabled Gustavus to levy tolls at Memel, Pillau and Elbing for six years; by a supplementary treaty he was allowed a share of the tolls at Danzig, too, although he had not conquered it. Thus a war that had lasted nearly thirty years was ended on a temporary basis, and on terms very much to Sweden's advantage, since most of the Baltic ports from the rivers Neva to Pregolia were in Swedish hands. Sigismund III had not renounced his claim to the Swedish throne, it is true; but he had failed to regain his hereditary kingdom. He had lost Livonia for good and he was a broken man by his death in April 1632.

Gustavus Adolphus' death later in the same year and the minority of Christina encouraged the new Polish king, Ladislas IV, to think he might regain the Swedish throne peacefully. But the Swedish regents scrupulously safeguarded the prerogatives and interests of the crown; any attempt to negotiate with the Polish king was made a political offence; and the constitutional arrangements during Christina's minority were settled in the Form of Government of July 1634. Ladislas IV seemed to have lost his opportunity. Yet the collapse of Swedish military power in Germany, and the expiry of the Truce of Altmark in 1635, still offered him possibilities. Ladislas wanted to reconquer Estonia and Livonia as his hereditary provinces, but the Polish nobility were not prepared to countenance such a strengthening of royal power which might have been regarded as a potential threat to their liberty. The most they would agree to was a war in Prussia to drive the Swedes from the mouths of the Vistula, Pregolia and Niemen, and to remove the tolls on grain exports. Axel Oxenstierna was prepared to leave the German war 'to the Germans . . . and apply all the country's resources to the Polish war', since that was Christina's 'private, direct concern . . .'[29] But the regents did not share his priorities, and in panic they concluded a new truce between Poland and Sweden at Stuhmdorf in September 1635. By the terms of this truce, Ladislas IV's claim to the Swedish throne only remained in abeyance, while the Swedes abandoned their key strategic positions in Prussia and gave up their crucial revenues from the tolls. Oxenstierna thought that after this truce, Sweden was not half the nation she had been before. What he meant was that the regents had paid a heavy financial price for extending the truce for a further twenty-six years until 1661. Oxenstierna was not to know that Ladislas would relinquish his rights to levy tolls at Danzig and the other Prussian ports after 1636. The Swedish loss was therefore not converted into a Polish gain.

5.2.5   Charles X and the 'Deluge', 1654–1660

The Truce of Stuhmdorf between Poland and Sweden held without great difficulties until 1655, when it still had five years to run. Sweden was preoccupied first with the struggle in Germany and then in settling the succession issue once Christina's decisions not to marry and to abdicate were made known. Ladislas IV died in May 1648 and his brother John Casimir (Jan Kazimierz) was elected king of Poland and Lithuania in November. But since the previous year the Commonwealth of Poland and Lithuania had been thrown into turmoil by the Cossack revolt led by Bogdan Chmielnicki (see chapter 5.3.4). Events gradually moved to a crisis, and in January 1654 the general assembly (*rada*) of the Cossacks agreed at Pereiaslaval 'to be under the mighty arm of the Orthodox Eastern Tsar [and] to die in our pious faith, rather than to fall under the rule of a pagan, an enemy of Christ' (that is, the Catholic John Casimir).[30] The forces of Tsar Alexis invaded Poland-Lithuania on two fronts. The new Swedish king, Charles X, saw Muscovy rather than Denmark or Poland as the real threat, for he feared that Muscovy might acquire the Polish coastlands. An alliance with Poland seemed desirable, but before this could come about Poland would have to confirm the cession of Livonia and relinquish the Vasa claim to the Swedish crown.

In the meantime, with the Truce of Stuhmdorf due to expire in 1661, Charles X thought a satisfactory alliance was unlikely to be achieved and so he took a more aggressive line. Without regaining the Prussian tolls, how would Sweden pay for a mercenary army for its defence? Even if there were an alliance with Poland, would there not be a need for security against a Polish change of sides? Charles aimed at the subjection of Courland, the occupation of Royal Prussia, and the control of ducal East Prussia by compelling the elector of Brandenburg to hold it as a fief of the Swedish crown. In the council (*råd*) debates of December 1654, the acquisition of Prussia was seen as a bastion for Swedish Livonia. It was thought 'no bad thing if we could get hold of Danzig';[31] but economic motives were secondary to strategic concerns when Charles X launched his onslaught on Poland. The Swedish king was also influenced by the views of the exiled vice-chancellor of Poland, who in July 1655 had signed in Sweden a capitulation by which West Poland recognized Charles X's protectorate. In October, the Radziwill family in Lithuania negotiated an agreement with Charles by which they carved out a principality for themselves on condition of a Swedish–Lithuanian union. Their principal fear was the loss of Lithuania in the face of a Muscovite advance: earlier in 1655, after the capture of Vilna, Tsar Alexis had begun to style himself 'grand duke of Lithuania, Byelorussia and Podolia'.

The initial Swedish invasion in July 1655 was made from Riga with an army of only 17,000 men. Charles himself arrived with a second army from Swedish Pomerania at the end of August and took Warsaw without a fight in September. When Cracow was taken in October, John Casimir had to seek refuge in Silesia. In four months, Charles X had reduced all Poland except Lwów, Royal Prussia and the Ruthenian territories in the south (which were in revolt: see chapter 5.3.4). When Charles invaded Royal Prussia, only Danzig remained loyal to John Casimir; it was blockaded by the Swedish army. In January 1656, Frederick William of Brandenburg allied with Sweden and accepted ducal Prussia in fief from Charles X. The Swedes were to be given privileged trading rights with the ports of Memel and Pillau, together with half the revenues from their tolls. Sweden and Brandenburg, together with György II Rákóczi of Transylvania and Bogislaw Radziwill of Lithuania, were prepared to preside over a partition of Poland (the so-called compact of Radnoth, drawn up in December 1656). It seems that Chmielnicki and the Cossacks were prepared to concur in this arrangement, but John Casimir had other ideas. He promised Tsar Alexis the succession to the Polish throne (a meaningless gesture, since the diet would never elect Alexis unless he abjured his Orthodoxy) in order to obtain a temporary respite on the eastern front; in fact, Alexis provided rather more than that, by invading Swedish Livonia. An important alliance was formed by John Casimir in May 1657 with another significant European power. The Austrian Habsburgs had viewed with deep concern the extension of Swedish power to Cracow, and thus Leopold I was prepared to ally with the Poles. Finally, in June 1657 Frederick III of Denmark launched a crucial diversionary campaign against Sweden (see chapter 5.1.6).

As a result of these diplomatic realignments, the fortunes of the two sides in Poland fluctuated wildly. In the summer of 1656, John Casimir had recaptured Warsaw, only to lose it the following month to the combined armies of Brandenburg and Sweden, despite greatly superior Polish forces. Nevertheless, the Swedish army had to evacuate the capital again because an anti-Swedish rising in West Poland threatened its line of communications; it later retook Warsaw with Rákóczi's assistance in June 1657, in what proved to be the last occupation of the Polish capital. Once Charles X learnt that Denmark had opened a second front against him in the west, the Swedish forces were transferred to Denmark via Pomerania, and the cause of John Casimir was quickly re-established. The Habsburg army took Cracow at the end of August and Rákóczi was forced to withdraw to Transylvania and pay a war indemnity. But the Habsburg alliance was to prove a hindrance to John Casimir. He was poised to attack Frederick William of Brandenburg, but since Leopold I required the elector's vote in the forthcoming Imperial election he cautioned moderation. John Casimir thus had to concede the Treaty of Wehlau in September 1657, by which Frederick William and the Hohenzollern dynasty received sovereignty over ducal Prussia, a treaty subsequently viewed in Poland as one of doubtful validity because it had been exacted under duress. In February 1658, before Leopold's election, a triple alliance of the Emperor, Poland and Brandenburg was formed against Sweden, though the allies wasted almost a year before they took the offensive. In the meantime, Charles X had defeated Denmark, and by the time the Polish general Stefan Czarniecki attacked the Swedish army from Danish bases in Jutland, the moment of greatest advantage had passed.

It was now clear that Sweden's ability to intervene in Polish affairs had ended, and with the death of Charles X the regents were strongly in favour of peace with both Denmark and Poland. The Peace of Oliva concluded in May 1660 ended a sixty-year conflict within the Vasa family. John Casimir at last formally relinquished the claim of his family to the Swedish throne, although he kept the title of king of Sweden during his lifetime. (The issue was to pass into irrelevance once he resigned as king of Poland in August 1668, thus ending the Polish line of Vasa rulers.) The war had brought no profit to Sweden, and the Muscovite threat remained as real in 1667 as it had been in 1654. On the other hand, Poland had surrendered its sovereignty over ducal East Prussia and was ruined economically: the population of Warsaw had fallen from 18,000 in 1655 to 6,000 in 1659 and the Commonwealth as a whole lost perhaps one-quarter of its subjects, eliminating at a stroke the natural increase of the previous century. In Royal Prussia, the population loss during the war was as high as 60 per cent. The decline of the Vistula trade after 1648 coincided with the collapse of the power and prosperity of the Commonwealth. Once the confidence of foreign merchants was shaken, as it had been in the 1650s when the Dutch had offered record prices for grain in Danzig but had been unable to fill their ships, it could not easily be re-established. Sweden should have been forced to concede Livonia to the Poles or at least to pay a war indemnity to offset the devastation of the country which its aggression had brought about, but Poland was now too weak to insist on such niceties. All its energies were redirected to the war against Muscovy.

5.3 Muscovy and Poland-Lithuania: the Attempted 'Gathering of the Russian Lands'

The primacy of the dual state of Poland-Lithuania in late sixteenth-century eastern Europe did not go unchallenged. A new force appeared, resulting from the phenomenal growth of Muscovy and the pretension of its grand prince of the Riúrik (and after 1613 of the Romanov) dynasty to rule over all 'the Russian lands'. This change occurred in less than a century; at the accession of Ivan III in 1462, there were only 168,000 square miles in Muscovy, making it insignificant in geographical terms in comparison with the kingdom of Casimir IV of Poland. When Ivan's son, Vasilii III, died in 1533, however, the Muscovite lands extended to more than a million square miles, forming a state which far exceeded the size of Sigismund I's territory. By the end of the sixteenth century, with the colonization of Siberia, this total had more than doubled, and continued to expand in the course of the seventeenth century.

Although both states were large, this similarity was far outweighed by the differences between Muscovy and Poland-Lithuania. To begin with, limitations on the peasants' right of free movement seem to have occurred in Poland a full century earlier than in Muscovy. Moreover, whereas in Poland the few remaining fiefs were converted in the course of the sixteenth century into hereditary property owing no direct military service to the rulers, the reverse process occurred in Muscovy, where fiefs became the norm rather than the exception by the 1570s. The political rights of the Muscovite nobility were insignificant in comparison with their Polish counterparts, and there was no parallel to the entrenched position enjoyed by the *szlachta* in the Polish diet. It is possible that the Muscovite Assembly of the Land (*zemskii sobor*), a representative assembly on the Polish model, was introduced in the hope of attracting west Russian nobles from Lithuania into the Muscovite orbit. However, it was only summoned twice in Ivan IV's reign and it was not until the first half of the seventeenth century that it assumed importance. After 1653, when the Polish diet was gaining greater authority than ever before, the Assembly of the Land in Muscovy was not summoned at all. Only briefly (during the 'Time of Troubles') did the Muscovite nobility ever exercise that most precious 'freedom' enjoyed by the Polish *szlachta*, the right of electing their kings. The Muscovite rulers' opinion of this practice was clear. Ivan IV had addressed Sigismund II as 'brother' because he was an hereditary monarch. But he refused to call Sigismund's successor, Stefan Bátory, 'brother' because he had been elected to office. After the Muscovite magnate (boyar) prince Kurbskii defected to Lithuania in 1564, he entered into the spirit of the Polish constitution with relish. Contrasting the tyranny of Ivan IV with the rule of his predecessors, Kurbskii claimed that Ivan III had taken 'frequent counsel with his wise and bold advisers' in the manner of the Polish king.[32] Ivan IV retorted that Russian autocracy was an inheritance from his forefathers: the Muscovite grand princes 'from the beginning have ruled the[ir] dominions, and not the boyars and ... grandees'.[33]

There was an equally important religious difference. Russia had received its Christianity from Byzantium, not from the west, and it had rejected the union between the Greek and Latin churches at Florence in 1439. A *de facto* independent church had been established in Russia from 1448, but its status was only accepted by the other Orthodox churches in 1589. Had it not been for religious differences, the Commonwealth of Poland-Lithuania might well have absorbed most of the Russian population. Fear of persecution by the Catholics was an important factor inducing Orthodox nobles to defect from Lithuania to Muscovy in the fifteenth century. In the next century, it seemed that Poland might fall to the Reformation, thus driving a new wedge between the two states. After the threat from Calvinism appeared to have subsided, part of the Polish-Lithuanian Commonwealth near the Russian border was still pursuing a distinctive religious path which straddled the Orthodox and Catholic churches: in October 1596, a section of the Orthodox hierarchy based in Lithuanian territory formed the Uniate church, Orthodox in ritual but subject to Rome's control. The Uniates were regarded in Muscovy as heretics. The Orthodox church in Lithuania revived under the leadership of Peter Mohyla after 1632; however, he did not rule out the possibility of a union of the churches, a view which was still anathema to Moscow. The development of religious practice in Lithuania demonstrates that there was no Polish-Lithuanian parallel to the Orthodox monopoly in Muscovy, no single church to provide an ideology comparable with that of the Tsar who called himself 'emperor and lord of Orthodox Christians in the entire universe', the successor of the Byzantine emperor, ruling in Moscow, 'the third Rome'.[34]

5.3.1 *The Achievements of Ivan III, 'the Great'*

The stability and vigour of the Riúrik dynasty played a crucial part in the rise of Muscovy: over nearly two centuries between the accession of Vasilii I in 1389 and the death of Ivan IV in 1584, Muscovy had only five rulers. Among these, by far the most important was Ivan III, who reigned for forty-three years (1462–1505). His reign decisively ended the so-called 'apanage' period: this was a time when each generation of the royal family had presumed a right to divide up political power as a form of partible inheritance. After 1485, the younger brothers had to acknowledge Ivan III as 'lord of all Russia', and by the end of his reign virtually all the apanages had been confiscated. Ivan ruthlessly eliminated rival states and principalities such as Yaroslavl' (1463), Rostov (1474), Novgorod (1478) and Tver' (1485). In the apanage period, the nobility had been free to pursue an independent line, because they could choose which prince they wanted to serve, a right known as that of departure (*ot'ezd*). Once Moscow had conquered all of Russia and there were no more independent apanage princes left to whom to transfer one's loyalty, the boyars lost this freedom of choice and they soon found that they had few rights left at all.

Before the reign of Ivan III there was no central direction of the Muscovite army; each prince had his own court and private army. Nor was there a concept of a broader loyalty to the Muscovite grand prince. Ivan established a national army, with its own chancellery and social hierarchy (*mestnichestvo*). It remained a traditional force, based on cavalry, and it was not a standing army; the success of mobilization could hinge on the state of the harvest at the moment of summons. Nevertheless, in the reign of Ivan III it was a powerful weapon: Novgorod's forces were much larger, but they were essentially defensive and no match for those of Moscow. Ivan III may have been an uninspiring general, but he was rarely defeated. Tension between Muscovy and Lithuania was not reduced, as the Lithuanians had hoped, by a dynastic alliance in 1495, when Ivan III's daughter Elena was married to Alexander of Lithuania. Ivan still insisted on using the title 'sovereign of all Russia' instead of the perfectly acceptable and historically accurate 'grand prince of Muscovy'.[35] This pretension, together with Ivan's willingness to receive the Lithuanian defector Prince Bel'sky in contravention of the 1494 treaty, was the real cause of war, rather than Ivan's ostensible desire to protect Orthodoxy in Lithuania.

In May 1500, he launched a triple attack. The early military advantage went to Ivan, but it was offset by the intervention of the Livonian Knights on the side of Lithuania the following year. In 1502, Ivan failed to take Smolensk after a three-month siege and agreed a six-year truce. Though he had captured neither Kiev nor Smolensk, a substantial part of Lithuanian territory, including Chernigov and Putivl', had been acquired. Ivan remained unwilling to sign a peace treaty until what he considered to be 'all the Russian land' had been surrendered by Lithuania. For his part, Alexander of Lithuania insisted on the return of Muscovy's conquests. It is not surprising that war resumed after the death of the original protagonists. Vasilii III attacked Lithuania in April 1507, and at the peace concluded the following year Sigismund I recognized most of Ivan III's conquests. The peace was broken by Muscovy in December 1512; and after two attempts, Vasilii captured Smolensk in July 1514. This fortress, which guarded the upper Dnieper and was the cultural and economic gateway to the west and south, remained in Russian hands until 1611. However, it proved to be the last permanent Muscovite gain in the west for nearly a century-and-a-half, and a truce was concluded in September 1522 which continued until the end of 1533. There was no significant territorial adjustment between the two states until the Livonian war.

5.3.2   *The Disasters of Ivan IV, 'the Dread'*

From the death of Vasilii III in 1533 until Ivan IV's coronation as 'Tsar of all Russia' in 1547, the boyars filled the power vacuum during the royal minority in Muscovy, to disastrous effect. The intrigues, corruption and general misrule during his minority coloured Ivan IV's attitude to the boyars: he claimed that they 'sought power for themselves' and that after the death of his mother, Elena, in February 1538 they had 'ruled as despots over the Tsardom'.[36] His distrust was increased by the events of 1553, when he fell seriously ill and demanded from the boyars an oath of loyalty to his infant son, Dimitrii. At first, several of the boyars refused, preferring prince Vladimir of Staritsa, Ivan's cousin and a king who would have been of age to rule. In 1567, there was further trouble, when a conspiracy led by Ivan Chelyadnin-Fedorov sought to kidnap Ivan on military campaign and hand him over to Sigismund II of Poland. Once again, prince Vladimir was designated as Ivan's successor by certain of the conspirators and was a party to the plot. When the conspiracy was discovered, Vladimir confessed all he knew to the Tsar in an effort to save his neck; but he was too obvious a rallying-point for discontent and Ivan had him executed in 1569. Ivan had several good reasons for viewing the boyars with suspicion, but his distrust nevertheless developed into a mania after his early advisers Alexei Adashev and the priest Sylvester were disgraced in 1560, and prince Kurbskii defected to Lithuania four years later. The execution of 'traitors' began in earnest in 1564; Kurbskii's propaganda projected them as 'martyrs' for boyar privileges. Kurbskii had good reason to feel bitter, for after his defection Ivan had murdered his wife, son and mother. The leading contemporary apologist for Ivan's ruthlessness, Ivan Peresvetov, may have infected the Tsar with some of his own admiration for the Ottoman Sultan and his Janissaries, which was reflected in a cruelty regarded by almost every contemporary western observer as more extreme than anything they had ever seen.

After 1565, Muscovy was a realm of fear. The setbacks in the Livonian war forced Ivan to seek more autocratic powers to deal with princely opposition to the war effort, including if necessary the right to confiscate boyar property. His own isolation was increased by the creation of a 'separate estate' (*oprichnina*) with a 'court for himself and for his entire household'.[37] The lands of Muscovy were divided between Ivan's own patrimony and the rest of the kingdom (*zemshchina*), which was administered by the boyars, led by prince Ivan Bel'skii and prince Ivan Mstislavskii. The German mercenary, Heinrich von Staden, who was employed by Ivan, claimed that he and the other *oprichniks* had 'used all kinds of machinations . . . against the men of the *zemshchina*, all in order to obtain money and goods from them'.[38] Kurbskii called the *oprichniks* 'children of darkness ... hundreds and thousands of times worse than hangmen'.[39] No consistent plan appears to have been formulated for the *oprichnina*, which seems to have passed through several different phases; it is thus difficult to assess its political function. Russian historians have challenged the view that the purpose of the experiment was to substitute a nobility holding fiefs in return for specific services to the Tsar for the boyars and their free (allodial) holdings. But the original area of the *oprichnina* was largely confined to lands held by this form of service tenure without hereditary princely estates, so relatively few confiscations of boyar property were necessary.

Nevertheless, the boyars feared that the *oprichnina* would be extended into boyar lands, and this later happened, though not quite in the way they had expected. Some blurring of the two parts of the state occurred when, for example, members of the *zemshchina* were recruited into Ivan's army whenever the Tsar turned against leading *oprichniks* such as Alexei Basamov. Above all, the *oprichnina* seems to have had the role of punishing those suspected of treasonable dealings with Poland-Lithuania. Novgorod was sacked for this reason in 1570. There is reason to believe that the *oprichnina* would have attacked Moscow, too, but for the fact that an invading force of Tatars from the south got there first in 1571. Their sack of Moscow revealed the extent to which Ivan's military power had been weakened by the division of his kingdom. The *oprichnina* was abolished the following year in the face of the external military threat, and a combined Muscovite army defeated the Tatars. But once the immediate crisis had passed, Ivan reverted to his old ways, and in 1575–6 a second *oprichnina* was established in all but name.

The internal chaos resulting from Ivan's domestic policies was accentuated by the strain of a long period of foreign war which Ivan IV had instigated. In 1503, Ivan III had compelled the Livonian Knights to make a humiliating peace, under the terms of which their possession of Dorpat (formerly part of the early Kievan state) was confirmed only on payment of an annual tribute. In 1554, this treaty came up for renewal, and Ivan IV insisted not only that the tribute continue to be paid for fifteen years but also that the past fifty years' arrears be paid off. When the Knights failed to comply, the long Livonian war broke out. In January 1558, the Muscovite army overran the territory for the first time; Narva fell in May, Dorpat in July, Marienburg in 1560 and Polotsk in 1561. All Livonia seemed at risk. Kurbskii, indeed, argued that it would have fallen to Muscovy had Ivan IV pursued a wiser and less tyrannical policy: 'had he listened to us he might have had the whole land of Livonia under him . . .'[40]

In reality, Ivan's policy seems to have overestimated the ability of Muscovy to retain this long seaboard without a navy. Moreover, the Muscovite army had been raised to meet an earlier Tatar threat and was thus basically a cavalry force. The Livonian war showed that in a set-piece battle the Muscovite army was no match for either the Polish or Swedish armies (see chapter 5.2.2). The point was proved by the Swedish capture of Ivangorod on the river Narva in 1581. It had been the first of a new type of rectangular fortress named after the Tsar, and it was not permanently regained by Muscovy until 1704. The truces of 1582–3, respectively with Poland and Sweden, marked a complete reversal for Muscovy, since Ivan was obliged to cede Livonia to the former and Estonia to the latter. Yet if Ivan's policy of expansion westward met with defeat, it is important to remember his successes in the east. He conquered Kazan' in 1552 and Astrakhan' four years later, thus removing the last check on Muscovy's eastward expansion. With the government's approval, the Stroganov clan commissioned a Cossack general, Ermak, to advance eastward into the valley of the river Ob. His victories caused the downfall of the Tatar kingdom of Kutchum, and by 1582 western Siberia was Muscovite. Ivan IV became the first 'Tsar and great prince of all Rus'.[41] The failure of expansion to the west was thus almost exactly paralleled by its achievement in the east.

5.3.3   *The 'Time of Troubles', 1598–1618*

On Ivan's death in March 1584, he was succeeded by his feeble son, Fedor. Though a few of Ivan's most prominent councillors (notably the *oprichnik* Bogdan Belskii) lost office, most remained in power. This was true of Boris Godunov, Fedor's brother-in-law, guardian, and the effective regent of Muscovy from 1584 to 1598. Boris was both able and ambitious, but his reputation—and thus his ability to govern the country effectively— suffered greatly from the death of prince Dimitrii, Ivan's son by his seventh wife, in May 1591. Dimitrii's death seems to have been purely accidental, resulting from a self-inflicted wound to the throat during an epileptic seizure, but it was enough to start a rumour that Dimitrii had been murdered on Boris's orders as part of a plan to establish the Godunov dynasty after Fedor's death. This rumour was to haunt Boris and intensified the already grave problems of government inherited from Ivan IV's reign. In 1588, sixteen years after the abolition of the *oprichnina*, the English ambassador Giles Fletcher thought that 'this wicked policy and tyrannous practice . . . hath so troubled that country, and filled it so full of grudge and mortal hatred'[42] that a further round of civil war would result. His prediction proved correct when the death of Fedor ended the Riúrik dynasty in January 1598. The Assembly of the Land elected Boris 'sovereign and autocrat of the Tsardom',[43] but an elective Tsardom was almost a contradiction in terms. The inherent instability of the situation worsened when Boris turned on the Romanov clique with whom he had been closely associated, and who had supported his election.

The result was a conspiracy among the nobles to replace Boris as ruler. The Romanovs may well have been behind it, for the first pretender had served in their household. Grigorii Otrep'ev (styling himself the 'true Dimitrii' who had escaped death in 1591) had become a Catholic in Poland and was recognized by the Polish government as the true Tsarevich in 1603. He married Marina Mniszech, daughter of the palatine of Sandomierz: this powerful Catholic Polish family, which had run up substantial debts, thus came to have a financial interest in the advancement of the False Dimitrii's claims. He had an army of 10,000 Cossacks when he marched from Kiev into Muscovy in August 1604. At first he made rapid advances, but then he was forced back to Putivl'. His cause received a new boost with the death of Boris in April 1605 and the subsequent murder of his widow and son. In June 1605, Dimitrii I (as Otrep'ev now called himself) entered Moscow in triumph and was crowned as the true Tsar. But his reign was short-lived, since he neglected either to reward his supporters or to conciliate his opponents. He was murdered in May 1606 in a coup master-minded by Vasilii Shuiskii, a leading boyar, and by other magnates, during which 2,000 or 3,000 Poles and Lithuanians were massacred.

However, Shuiskii's regime was immediately threatened by a rebellion led by Ivan Bolotnikov, a former Ottoman galley slave who had escaped and joined the Cossacks. The argument was now that Tsar (False) Dimitrii had not died in the boyar coup of May 1606, but had miraculously escaped: Marina Mniszech joined her 'husband' in September 1608 apparently with great joy, which seemed to confirm Bolotnikov's claim; but by this date, there were some eight different pretenders claiming to be Dimitrii. Nevertheless, Bolotnikov's was the most serious challenge, and he succeeded temporarily in attracting the support of uprooted, dispossessed princely and boyar families who had been victims of the *oprichnina*. Many of them had been exiled and had scores to settle with the Muscovite ruling group. Bolotnikov's forces came close to capturing Moscow in October 1606, but were forced back to Tula and Kaluga. The noble and peasant wings of the movement proved difficult to reconcile after this military setback, and in October 1607 Shuiskii's forces captured Tula, together with Bolotnikov and 20,000 rebels. Shuiskii instigated a severe repression, but he made the mistake of demobilizing his army and returning to Moscow. A second pretender now established himself with the support of the remnants of Bolotnikov's forces. False Dimitrii II, the 'thief of Tushino', was a pretender of unknown origins. With the support of a consortium of Polish and Lithuanian adventurers, he proclaimed himself Tsar in June 1607 before Shuiskii had succeeded in eliminating

Bolotnikov's threat. His military compaign began in earnest in the spring of 1608, but in June his forces failed to capture Moscow and instead settled down for a long siege. This was a crucial setback, for it allowed Shuiskii to rally his supporters in northern Muscovy, while the pretender's claim was eclipsed by that of Ladislas, the young son of Sigismund III of Poland.

This was not a new claim, for Ladislas's right to the Tsardom had been backed by the Shuiskiis in 1606, before their coup. After Shuiskii's alliance with Sweden in February 1609, under the terms of which a force of 5,000 Swedish troops under Jakob de la Gardie had entered Moscow in March 1610, Ladislas's claim was vigorously supported by Sigismund III. The avowed aim of the Polish campaign, begun in September 1609, was the recapture of Smolensk. However, the Polish commander, Stanislas Zólkiewski, was empowered by the king to act upon a second offer of the Muscovite throne to Ladislas, an offer which had been made by some of False Dimitrii II's former supporters, and to march on Moscow. In June 1610, the Swedish–Muscovite forces were annihilated by Zólkiewski's army at Klushino. In mid-July, Shuiskii was deposed in a boyar coup, and the boyars concluded an agreement with the Polish commander the following month, by which they agreed to elect Ladislas as their Tsar. At this point, Sigismund III's wish to extend Catholic influence, and his own personal ambition, overcame his political sense. He was prepared to allow his son to be brought up in the Orthodox faith; but Sigismund wanted the Tsardom for himself, not for his son, and for the kingdom of Muscovy to be brought within the aegis of the Roman church. Zólkiewski knew that the Muscovites 'would never agree' to this,[44] and he returned to Poland, leaving a strong garrison in Moscow. After a siege lasting a year and half, this Polish garrison was reduced to submission by a heterogeneous force of militia and Cossacks sometimes known as the 'second national host' in October 1612. This 'second national host' established a provisional government and then summoned an Assembly of the Land, which in February 1613 elected Michael Fedorovich Romanov as Tsar, after rejecting any foreign candidate, either Lithuanian or Swedish.

Michael was Fedor Riúrik's second cousin, but he was only sixteen at the time of his election and apparently it was thought that he would be a pliant tool of the new regime. The Romanovs were popular because Michael's grandfather, Nikita Romanov, had been Ivan IV's brother-in-law and one of his most favoured companions; Michael's father, Filaret, had been arrested by Sigismund III for his opposition to the Polish succession and had been held in captivity for eight years. Subsequent Polish intervention in Muscovy proved fruitless but significant territorial concessions were made to Poland by the terms of the Truce of Deulino in December 1618. Ladislas maintained his pretension to the Tsardom until June 1634, but the only tangible Polish gain from the war was the retention of Smolensk, which had been recaptured in June 1611. Muscovy earlier had to make concessions to Sweden at the Peace of Stolbova in March 1617. The loss of Ingria and Karelia to Sweden shut off Muscovy from the Baltic sea, and for the first time Sweden had a strategically defensible frontier in Finland. For the powers which had intervened in Muscovite affairs, the 'Time of Troubles'—a description given to the dynastic and social unrest of the period—had on balance proved beneficial.

On his return from exile in Poland in June 1619, Filaret Romanov was appointed patriarch of all Russia, a position he had been promised by Vasilii Shuiskii in 1606. His years in Poland had given Filaret a burning hatred of that country; and so he used his position as the effective head of government to improve the Tsar's finances and to build up a reserve specifically for launching a war against Poland. His sense of timing was shrewd, for he attacked Smolensk before the expiry of the Truce of Deulino and during the Polish succession crisis following the death of Sigismund III in 1632. However, despite having the advantage of surprise, the Russian army failed to take Smolensk and the war against Poland became a stalemate. Peace was not achieved during his lifetime and after his death in October 1633 the boyars did not share share his priorities. The new government headed by prince Ivan Cherkasskii, a cousin of Tsar Michael, was prepared to confirm the significant territorial concessions made under the terms of the Truce of Deulino as an inducement to Ladislas to renounce his claim to the Muscovite throne; peace was signed at Polianovka in June 1634. The new priority for the Russian government lay in the defence of the southern part of the kingdom. Instead of avenging earlier defeats by Poland, Cherkasskii was concerned to defend Muscovy from the attacks of the Crimean Tatars.

5.3.4 *The Rebellion of the Ukrainian Cossacks and the Thirteen Years' War*

Just under twenty years after the concessions made in the Peace of Polianovka, Muscovy gained an enormous territorial advantage resulting from the defection of Cossacks who had been in service to the Polish Vasa dynasty. This led to the transfer of the Ukraine, subsequently depicted as part of the process of the 'gathering of the Russian lands', although it is important to remember that in 1648, on the eve of the Cossack rebellion, the Ukraine was firmly part of the Polish-Lithuanian Commonwealth. Long oppressed by the Crimean Tatars and poorly defended by the Polish government, it was a region with grievances. The separate Cossack communities which made up the population of the region were by default self-governing; chief among these communities was one forming an outpost in the interior of the steppe known as the Sicz of Zaporoze (from which its members were termed the Zaporozhian Host). The permanent members of the Sicz of Zaporoze probably numbered less than 3,000 until the seventeenth century, though many more joined them if a profitable raid was in the offing. The Orthodox religion was the main requirement for acceptance into the Cossack ranks; but admission to full membership was immediate after a cursory religious test and renunciation of former allegiances and loyalties. Because it was so easy to become a Cossack, their ranks tended to grow, swelled by escaped serfs and former galley slaves of the Ottoman Turks. The Polish government appreciated the danger posed by these independent communities in the Ukraine. It sought to harness their energies by using the Cossacks as a permanent force of mercenary soldiers. They gave good service in the various Polish wars, notably that of 1620–1 against the Turks, but failed to gain the permanent concessions for which they had hoped, namely recognition of noble status comparable to that of the *szlachta* in Poland and an expansion of the numbers of registered Cossacks receiving a pension in return for military service. At the outbreak of a war, the government invariably increased the number of registered Cossacks and the amount of subsidy paid to them; once the war ended, both were reduced.

The Cossacks were unpredictable allies for the Poles; the Polish government was embarrassed by their tendency to turn private quarrels into public wars and by their fierce adherence to Orthodoxy. They had earlier rebelled against the Lithuanian Uniate bishops in 1596, but the revolt had been suppressed. Tension between the Poles and the Cossacks showed itself in the outbreak of sporadic revolts in the seventeenth century (1625, 1630, 1635–8). To defeat these rebellions, the government repeatedly promised to increase the number of registered Cossacks: they rose to 6,000 in 1625 and 8,000 in 1635. After 1638, however, the Polish diet refused to make any further concessions, proclaiming its wish to 'put the idle Cossacks to the plough' and definitively rejecting the idea of incorporating them into the Commonwealth by giving them noble status.[45] For their part, the Cossacks equated the Polish diet's policy with political oppression. From 1638 to 1647, all the ingredients for unrest were present: the register was limited to 6,000 (despite some 60,000 men now claiming Cossack status) and the Uniate church remained in existence although the Cossacks denounced it as infringing the 'rights and freedoms' of 'our Russian nation'.[46]

The Cossack rebellion which broke out in 1648 was the first to assume real international significance. Bogdan Chmielnicki,[47] the military commander of the Cossacks in 1648, was also their first great political leader. Chmielnicki harboured a personal grievance against the Polish nobility because of the seizure of his estate at Subotów. But this alone would not have given him the status of a 'national' leader had he not been able to appeal to the Cossacks' sense of alienation in Polish-Lithuanian society and their wish to defend Orthodoxy. He alleged that Ladislas IV had agreed in 1646 to increase the number of registered Cossacks to 12,000, and to restore 'former privileges and Cossack liberties' if they would help him to attack the Crimean Tatars.[48] However, when this expedition took place in 1647, a force of 26,000 Lithuanians (but not Cossacks) was led by Jarema Wisniowiecki, the governor of Ruthenia, not by Bogdan Chmielnicki, in defiance of the wishes of the king and the diet. Chmielnicki claimed that he had been betrayed; instead of fighting the Tatars, he asked for their assistance against the Lithuanians. Together, Cossacks and Tatars attacked the expedition.

In May 1648, the Cossacks and Tatars won two significant victories, but the death of Ladislas IV and the paralysis of government during the interregnum led to a suspension of hostilities on the Polish side for three months. Chmielnicki supported the election of John Casimir, and sought to come to an agreement with him, but he also opened negotiations with Tsar Alexis in case no compromise could be reached with Poland. It took over a year of negotiations, and a further Cossack victory at Zborów in August 1649, before a compromise emerged. John Casimir proclaimed a general amnesty for the Cossacks, but failed to meet Chmielnicki's original demand, the creation of an autonomous Cossack state in the Ukraine. Instead, he agreed to increase the Cossack list to 40,000; the Union of Brest, which had established the Uniate church, was secretly abrogated; and the Cossacks were to be exempt from the jurisdiction of Polish officials and the Polish nobility. On religious matters, Jesuits, Jews and Catholics were barred from Cossack-held territory, and (although this was not officially sanctioned by John Casimir) the Jews were singled out for particularly harsh treatment. They were hunted down remorselessly in what was probably the greatest single pogrom before Hitler. But another round of fighting was inevitable because of the reprisals of the Polish magnates, led by Wisniowiecki, and Chmielnicki's negotiations with foreign powers (in April 1651 he had accepted the overlordship of the Ottoman Sultan). This time the Cossacks were defeated. The revised peace terms offered by the Polish government at the end of September 1651 halved the Cossack register to 20,000 and confined them to the province of Kiev. The Polish government also insisted on the return of the Jews to Cossack-held territory.

Chmielnicki was powerless to prevent the Cossacks from repudiating this treaty, although he seems to have argued against this policy. In May 1652, the Cossack council resolved to make war on Poland with the help of the Tsar. Yet not until October 1653 was Tsar Alexis advised by the Assembly of the Land at Moscow to receive Chmielnicki and the

Zaporozhian Host as subjects 'for the sake of the Orthodox Christian faith'.[49] In March 1654, the Tsar accepted the decision of the Cossacks at Pereiaslaval (Periaslavl') two months earlier to transfer their allegiance to Muscovy. The significance of this transfer (and indeed the use of the word 'treaty' to describe it) has been greatly debated, and differently interpreted from the viewpoints of Polish, Russian and Ukrainian historians. The contemporary account of the meeting suggests that the Cossacks elected their sovereign from four candidates (John Casimir, the Ottoman Sultan, the Crimean Khan and Tsar Alexis). The subsequent Muscovite royal charter makes the incorporation of the Zaporozhian Host into the Russian state seem conditional on their eternal (rather than conditional) allegiance to the Tsar. The agreement set the Cossack register at 60,000 men (treble the offer from John Casimir in 1651) and confirmed their existing rights and privileges. Since Cossacks served in most of the Muscovite wars of the later seventeenth century and adapted to the military changes that were required, the Periaslavl' agreement proved enduring. However, on the death of Chmielnicki in August 1657, there was no clear successor as Cossack leader and dissension broke out among the Cossacks. One group, headed by Ivan Wyhowski, signed the Treaty of Hadziac with Poland in September 1658, by which an autonomous Ruthenian principality would be linked to the Polish–Lithuanian union (and the Cossack list reduced to 30,000). The rest of the Cossacks subsequently elected Chmielnicki's son, George (Iurii), as their leader and empowered him to sign a new treaty with the Tsar in October 1659, which confirmed the Cossack list at 60,000 men. This group agreed to serve the Tsar wherever he saw fit and not to be 'tempted by any Polish enticements'.[50]

The submission of Bogdan Chmielnicki to the Tsar in 1654 was an open violation of the Polish–Muscovite peace concluded twenty years earlier. Consequently, it led to a new war which was to last for thirteen years (1654–67). The secession of the Ukraine to Muscovy had weakened Poland and at first the war went well for the Muscovite armies. They captured much of the left bank of the upper Dnieper and the western Dvina: the great prize in the first campaign was Smolensk (September 1654), together with thirty-two other towns. In 1655, the Muscovites took Minsk and Vilna, together with much of Byelorussia and the Ukraine. However, the Swedish intervention in Poland in the same year (see chapter 5.2.5) greatly complicated matters, forcing a truce between Tsar Alexis and John Casimir in 1656, which freed the Russian army to attack Swedish Livonia. The Truce of Valiessar signed with Sweden in December 1659 left Alexis with Dorpat, but at the Peace of Kardis in July 1661 the Tsar was forced to renounce all his conquests in Livonia. The withdrawal of Sweden from active participation in the Polish war in 1657 (see chapter

5.1.6) allowed John Casimir to turn his undivided attention to the Russian menace. After part of the Cossack army made peace with Poland the following year, there were two dramatic Polish successes, the victories at Sosnówka and Cudnów, respectively in July 1659 and October 1660.

These catastrophes left Muscovy powerless and deeply in debt. During the war the army had been paid in debased copper coin, but the copper riots in Moscow in July 1662 forced the abandonment of this expedient and with it any hope of financing the war. Nevertheless, although John Casimir was able to harrass the Ukraine, he was not able to mount a significant offensive against Muscovy. The weakness of the Polish-Lithuanian constitution almost inevitably revealed itself at a crucial moment, as it had done frequently in the past, in another of the frequent 'confederation movements' (*rokosz*: see chapter 5.2.1), this time led by Jerzy Lubomirski in 1665–7. In January 1667, faced by the prospect of a Muscovite offensive into what was now a defenceless Lithuania as a result of Lubomirski's revolt, John Casimir was obliged to sign the Truce of Andrusovo with the Russians. This ceded Smolensk, Seversk, Chernigov and Kiev to Muscovy, and divided the Ukraine along the river Dnieper with Muscovy receiving the left bank. These grants were supposed to be a temporary, tactical manoeuvre on the part of the Polish king dictated by his army's preoccupation with civil war. In fact, Muscovy retained Kiev beyond the two-year limit stipulated in the truce, and the territorial concessions proved permanent. Muscovy thus gained greater resources in the struggle for ascendancy in eastern Europe than did its traditional rival, Poland-Lithuania, an advantage which was to be felt in all later confrontations. Ironically, Jerzy Lubomirski, who championed the cause of freedom for the Polish nobility, was no less responsible for this gain than was Bogdan Chmielnicki, the leader of the Zaporozhian Host.

5.4 Ottoman Supremacy in South-East Europe and the Middle East

In the *Six Books of a Commonweal,* first published in 1576 (see chapter 6.1.3), Jean Bodin distinguished between three types of government: monarchical, tyrannical and 'seigneurial'. The characteristic of *la monarchie seigneuriale,* in his view, was that it came into being by conquest of arms and 'the prince is become lord of the goods and persons of his subjects . . . governing them as a master of a family does his slaves'.[51] Bodin added that there were only two such regimes in Europe, one in Turkey, and the other in Muscovy, although they were common in Asia and Africa. In western Europe, he thought, the people would not tolerate this kind of government. The extent to which Muscovy may be regarded as a patrimonial state has already been considered; but the Ottoman realm exceeded Muscovy in the extent of seigneurial monarchy, since the whole arable and pastoral territory of the empire was deemed to be the personal property of the Sultan, with the exception of religious endowments. By 1528 some 87 per cent of Ottoman land was state property (*miri* land), and the revenue of the Ottoman Sultan was about 537 million aspers, equivalent to perhaps 10 million ducats. This was more than twice the revenue enjoyed by the Emperor Charles V and made his contemporary Süleyman I the richest, and hence potentially the most powerful, ruler in Europe. Since the Sultan had an unlimited right to exploit all sources of wealth in the realm as his own imperial possessions, including land, there could be no stable, hereditary nobility because there was no security of property. Thus wealth, power and honour could only be derived from the state, which was militaristic in both ideology and institutions. Shortly before the capture of Constantinople in May 1453, Mehmed II (1451–81) had proclaimed the holy war (*ghaza*) as 'our basic duty'; eight years later he had declared it 'the highway to the paradise of Heaven'.[52] Non-believers were forced to accept Islam or die. However, Jews and Christians could retain their own religion and become the subject of the Moslem ruler provided they paid a special tax.

Whereas they treated Christians with respect and even consideration (lending support to the Reformation in Hungary, for example), the Ottomans showed no mercy to manifestations of Shiite (Shi'i) sectarianism, a fundamentalist view of the Koran, within their dominions. This religious dispute within Islam, which endures to the present day, reached its climax with the propaganda of the Sufi order in the fifteenth century. After Isma'il I became head of the Sufi order, he seized power in Persia and established the rule of his own dynasty and a Shiite state (1501). The Ottomans were orthodox (Sunni) Moslems, and they perceived the new Safavid state as a profound security threat to their eastern borders as well as a challenge to their religious practices. The fervour and single-mindedness of the Ottoman armies owed much to men of Islamic learning who were recruited as teachers in the religious schools (*medreses*) of the learned hierarchy (*ulema*). However, the men who received such education were often former Christians from the Balkans levied through the slave (*devsirme*) system. They thus tended to show rather greater awareness of the problems of the Balkan region than of Iraq and Persia.

It was not degrading to be a slave in the Ottoman state since because most property belonged to the Sultan, the word did not have the same connotations of poverty as it acquired in the west. Slaves could create their own dynasties, for example, and they gained greater status after 1453 when Mehmed II began the practice of appointing his personal slave to the highest office in the land, the grand vizier (*vezir*). Following the Islamic tradition of the Middle Ages, the backbone of the army was provided by slaves recruited through the *devsirme* levy, the so-called 'new troops' or Janissaries (*Yeni-ceris*). The slave army coexisted with a native Islamic military system of warriors (*sipahis*), who drew their subsistance from fiefs (*timars*); these were both lands and fiscal concessions of varying sizes and amounts, and were not heritable. This system worked well until the value of the fiefs was eroded by inflation in the sixteenth century. The educational system also ensured that there was an efficient administration of the law. Though the state was militaristic, it was not arbitrary. Ottoman rule represented a relatively strong and impartial central administration in contrast to the deep social and religious divisions that had permeated the Balkans before the conquest.

5.4.1 *The Ottoman Advance to 1520*

After Mehmed II had destroyed the last bastion of the Byzantine empire and captured Constantinople in May 1453, he renamed it Istanbul and made it the capital of all his lands. He established the basic political, social and administrative traditions which remained fundamental to the later Ottoman state. It was he who laid down the first clear-cut rules organizing the learned hierarchy, which provided the administrators for the state. He appointed Zaganuz Pasha, a slave, as his grand vizier after 1453 and delegated great power to him as the Sultan's 'absolute representative', including control of the army in Istanbul and Europe. Mehmed also established the rule of succession which was to last until 1617. On his accession in 1451, he had an infant brother murdered to prevent any possibility of a rival to the throne; he had fought a pretender at the siege of Constantinople. As a result of these incidents earlier in his reign he therefore issued a law 'for the order of the world'[53] (by which he meant peace in his dominions) that on his accession to the throne, a new Sultan should execute his brothers. This 'law of fratricide' was implemented with vigour and even enthusiasm by his successors: on his accession in 1595, Mehmed III killed off nineteen brothers, and for good measure, twenty sisters as well. The law did not end succession disputes, however. Indeed it made them more likely, since rebellion was the only alternative to execution. Yet the Ottoman state recovered from three great wars of succession (1481–2, 1511–13 and 1558–61), and the law ensured the triumph if not of the ablest or most suitable, at least of a ruthless Sultan.

The great Sultans were dedicated to war, because success enhanced their prestige and secured their control over the army and bureaucracy. Without the kudos of a successful war, it proved difficult for a Sultan, however autocratic, to achieve control of the Ottoman governing system. Mehmed II was known as 'the Conqueror' (*Fatih*) not just for his capture of Constantinople but because he subjugated the entire Balkan region from his existing territory in Rumelia and Bulgaria. Serbia was annexed in 1458–9, the Morea in 1458–60, Bosnia in 1463 and Albania in 1478. Although he was not able to reduce Moldavia and Wallachia completely to vassalage, he mastered the Tatar Khan of the Crimea in 1475, thus providing the Sultans for the next three centuries with a power base to control the Black Sea and a regular supply of fighting men. He also started the first of a series of Ottoman wars with Venice, the chief naval power in the eastern Mediterranean: the war, which lasted from 1463 to 1479, was largely inconclusive, with the exception of the Ottoman acquisition in 1470 of the most important Venetian outpost in the Aegean, the Negropont.

Mehmed's successor, Bayezid II (1481–1512), gained control of the mouths of the rivers Danube and Dniester by capturing Kilia and Akkerman in 1484 and thus was able to regulate Moldavian and Hungarian trade through the Black Sea. However, in Machiavelli's words, Bayezid was 'a man who loved peace more than war' and he preferred to enjoy the 'fruits of his father's labours', in part because until the death of his exiled younger brother Jem in 1495 he faced a disputed succession. He inherited a 'strong kingdom' which could be maintained by 'peaceful methods': but in Machiavelli's view 'the kingdom would have been ruined' had his successor not reversed his policy.[54] Machiavelli seems to have missed the point that Bayezid's military ambition lay with expansion into the Mediterranean and to this end he recruited foreign corsair captains and mounted an ambitious shipbuilding programme. He had contemplated an early resumption of war with Venice: but in 1482 the threat from Jem had forced Bayezid to sign a truce. This war was eventually resumed in July 1499 and brought to a successful conclusion in December 1502. The first war of 1463–79 had revealed the weakness of the Ottoman navy in comparison with Venice; the second war of 1499–1502 demonstrated its dominance in the eastern Mediterranean. Nevertheless, because Bayezid II did not follow the traditional Ottoman policy of land conquest, there was discontent within the army.

Selim I 'the Grim' (*Yavuz*) deposed his father in April 1512, after the Janissaries at Istanbul had rebelled in his support. The pretext of their rebellion was the threat posed to Sunni orthodoxy by the sectarian Safavid state of Persia. In the spring of 1501, Isma'il Safavid had routed the army of the Ak Koyunlu dynasty, entered Tabriz and proclaimed himself Shah Isma'il I, the first ruler of the Safavid dynasty. One of his first actions on his accession was to proclaim the Shiite fundamentalist form of Islam as the religion of the new state, thus clearly differentiating Persia from the

Ottoman empire which might otherwise have tried to incorporate it within its dominions. Bayezid II implored Isma'il to return to orthodox Islam and cease the massacre of Sunni Moslems, but did not otherwise intervene in the internal policies of the Safavid state. Selim was more aggressive, and before he deposed his father he had led raids on Safavid territory from Trebizond, where he was governor. It was therefore clear what his policy would be as Sultan. After extending the law of fratricide to include the murder of his nephews and thus increase his own dynastic security, he concluded an alliance with Mamluk Egypt and Syria and proceeded to march on Persia in April 1514.

The Safavid army proved inferior to that of the Ottomans, and in early September Selim entered Tabriz. This city, which had become the northern capital of the Safavid state, could be captured quite easily by the Ottomans (it was taken by them in 1514, 1534, 1548, 1585 and 1635) but the rest of Azarbayjan, the original centre of the Safavid state, was always a more difficult proposition and was used as a rallying-point by the opponents of Turkish conquest. The disaster of 1514 taught the Safavids to avoid open battle with the Ottomans. They relied instead on a scorched earth policy. Once the Caucasus mountains were crossed, there were no physical barriers to deter or detain the Ottomans in the summer, but the terrain and climate forced them to withdraw each winter. Selim experienced opposition to the continuing war from his Janissaries in 1514–15, but he overcame it by purging the command structure. He established a new province based on Trebizond to which were added his acquisitions of Erzinjan and Baiburd as a springboard for further attacks on the Safavid state. No truce followed the war with Persia of 1514–16, and the Ottomans left the Kurdish chieftains to spread pro-Ottoman and pro-Sunni propaganda. The years following the death of Isma'il in May 1524 were chaotic for the Safavid state. Rival Qizilbash tribes (thousands of whose members had been ruthlessly slaughtered in Anatolia on Selim's orders in 1514) fought for supremacy. Incursions into the respective border regions provided ample reason for a resumption of the conflict by the Ottomans in 1533.

Selim's military aggression was not confined to the east. The Mamluk Sultan of Syria and Egypt correctly guessed that Selim might next attack his territories since there was the strong prospect of a Mamluk–Safavid alliance against Ottoman expansion. Selim, indeed, was convinced that a successful campaign against Persia in the longer term required the elimination of any threat posed by the Mamluks to the south. He marched his army down the valley of the Euphrates and then crossed the plain of Malatia into Mamluk territory. In August 1516, he routed the opposing army near Aleppo, where the last Mamluk Sultan was killed. At the end of the month, Selim reached Damascus, and by the end of the year the

Ottomans occupied Palestine as far as Gaza. This might have been enough for Selim, since his main purpose—to prevent an alliance between Egypt and Persia—had been achieved. However, news of an attempt by the Mamluks to recover Gaza prompted him to cross the Sinai desert in January 1517, to crush the last remnants of the Mamluk army, and to occupy Cairo. In Egypt, the old Mamluk order was allowed to subsist, with its laws, and administration; but the independent fiefs (*timars*) were abolished, since the Ottomans required grain and other provisions from Egypt which the *timar* system would have consumed. In Syria, new fiefs were established along the lines of Ottoman practice elsewhere. Selim profited from the hostility of the local population to the excesses of the last years of Mamluk rule. An attempted revolt in Egypt in 1524 was suppressed, and henceforth Selim's two main acquisitions, Egypt and Syria, yielded about 100 million aspers in revenue out of a total Ottoman revenue of about 530 million. Most of south-western Arabia was conquered, too, except the Yemen (which was left until 1568). Selim thus appropriated the title 'servant and protector of the holy places'[55] following his acquisition of the Hijaz, including Mecca and Medina. Finally, as a result of the conquest, Ottoman overlordship was gradually extended into the Maghreb, starting with Algiers, through an alliance with the corsair Hayreddin (Khair ad-Din) Barbarossa.

5.4.2   *The Apogee of Ottoman Power: the Reign of Süleyman I, 1520–1566*

No other Ottoman prince acceded to the throne with such advantages as those Selim bequeathed to his son Süleyman I 'the law-giver' (*Qanuni*), in September 1520. (His people did not refer to him by the epithet 'the Magnificent' given to him in western Europe.) A lesser prince would have been content to consolidate Selim's achievement by making administrative and legal reforms. Süleyman certainly did this, thus earning his sobriquet; but he also led his army on thirteen great campaigns, spending over ten years in the field and gaining the reputation as one of the greatest of all Ottoman military leaders. From the earliest years of his reign he appreciated the constraints on his foreign policy imposed by Selim's conquests. It was almost impossible to fight simultaneously in east and west because each campaigning season had to begin at Istanbul, and the contingents had to winter in their fiefs, replacing their men and equipment. The overriding need therefore was to alternate between the two theatres of war, keeping his enemies off balance. Although earlier in the reign his primary ambitions were in Europe, he still timed his offensive against the west when the eastern front was quiet. He first captured the gateways to central Europe and the Mediterranean, Belgrade and Rhodes, in August 1521 and December 1522. These were outposts of Christendom which had defied even Mehmed the Conqueror. A revolt of the Janissaries wanting war booty in March 1525 warned the Sultan not to defer a great campaign for too long; the obvious target was the kingdom of Hungary.

Under Louis II Jagiellon, the Hungarian army had been disbanded, and the nobility divided into pro- and anti-Habsburg factions. The opportunity for the Ottomans to establish a client Hungarian state was too good to be missed, and the invasion was well organized. The Hungarian army was crushed at Mohácz at the end of August 1526, where Louis II died in battle. By the second week of September, Süleyman had occupied Buda. As soon as the Sultan retired from the devastated country, factionalism once again became rife in Hungary. John Zápolyai was elected king by a majority of the Hungarian diet and he was crowned at Stuhlweissenburg in November 1526. A minority of the nobles, under the leadership of Istvan Bátory and the dowager queen Mary, summoned a counter-diet which elected Ferdinand I of Habsburg king in December. In September 1527, Ferdinand I defeated Zápolyai at Tokay and had himself crowned at Stuhlweissenburg in November. Although Zápolyai had been overthrown, he refused to give up his claim to the Hungarian throne, and he appealed to Süleyman for recognition in return for payment of tribute. In February 1528 Süleyman accepted Zápolyai as vassal and a second Ottoman invasion began in his support in May 1529. The great Sultan recaptured Buda in September with little trouble and restored Zápolyai to the throne in a campaign which took him to the gates of Vienna in September–October 1529. Ferdinand and his court fled the Austrian capital, but in mid-October Süleyman was forced to raise the siege: the Ottomans had reached the limit of westward expansion from a winter base at Istanbul.

Ferdinand was left in control of so-called Royal Hungary, a narrow band of territory to the west and north of lake Balaton representing no more than 30 per cent of the late medieval Hungarian kingdom (indeed a declining proportion since the Ottoman advance was to continue, reaching its fullest extent only in 1664). Ferdinand tried to extend his possessions by besieging Buda in December 1530, but this only convinced Süleyman of the need for a further campaign. In April 1532, he left Istanbul with a force of 300,000 men and crossed the river Raab into Austria. The siege of Guns delayed his progress for three weeks until the end of August, and the Habsburg army refused to offer a pitched battle. This third Ottoman invasion of Hungary induced Ferdinand to sign a truce with Süleyman in June 1533, by which he recognized the Sultan as his 'father and suzerain', agreed to pay an annual tribute, and abandoned any claim to rule beyond so-called Royal Hungary. This left John Zápolyai as the Ottoman puppet king ruling from Buda. Under the terms of the truce, however, the two kings were entitled to come to a separate agreement between themselves concerning their respective states and sovereignty, subject to Süleyman's ratification. This they did at Várad (Grosswardein) in February 1538. By their agreement, each was to retain his title of king and his current possessions, but on the death of Zápolyai, who was at this time unmarried and childless, his lands would pass to Ferdinand. Süleyman's approval was not sought, and doubtless would not have been given.

Süleyman was unable to give Hungary his full attention at this time, however, for affairs first on the eastern and then on the Mediterranean fronts were diverting him. It was impossible to fight simultaneously at sea and on land. This dictated the timing of Süleyman's war against the first Holy League (the Pope, the Emperor Charles V and Venice) in 1538–40. This offensive, like others in the western Mediterranean in 1542–44 and 1551, occurred when there was a lull in the war with Persia (see chapter 3.1.3). Safavid Persia had recovered from its period of civil war, and after 1533, Shah Tahmasp of Persia was able to continue the aggressive policy of his father against the Ottoman state, including giving encouragement to the Qizilbash tribes to cause trouble in Anatolia. Three wars with the Ottomans were the result (in 1533–5, 1548–9 and 1554–5). The first war began three months after the truce with Ferdinand in Hungary, and Süleyman quickly overran Iraq, capturing Tabriz and Baghdad by the end of 1534. He established the new Ottoman province of Erzerum in the east, placing the Turcoman and Kurdish tribes under closer Ottoman control and attempting to settle the lands of Iraq as new fiefs. Basra fell under Ottoman suzerainty in 1539, but it was only taken under direct control after 1546. This acquisition brought the Ottomans into conflict with Portuguese naval power in the Persian gulf, but despite an energetic campaign by the Ottoman governor of Egypt who was based at Suez, during which Aden was captured in 1538, the Portuguese held on to the straits of Hormuz. After 1554, the Portuguese were largely left to their own devices in the Indian Ocean, which they dominated because of their advanced, ocean-going naval technology. The Peace of Amasya in May 1555, which brought to an end Süleyman's wars with Persia, revealed the respective strengths of the Ottoman and Safavid dynasties. Shah Tahmasp acknowledged the established Ottoman territories (Baghdad, Basra and Iraq, together with most of Kurdistan and western Armenia) and renounced any attempts to mount border raids and spread pro-Shiite propaganda there. For his part, Süleyman abandoned Tabriz, eastern Georgia and Azarbayjan, areas where it was too expensive to retain the garrisons which were needed to hold back the Safavid dynasty. His successors would have been wise not to have altered this balance of power twenty-three years later.

In the later years of his reign, Süleyman consolidated his hold on

Hungary, too. The death of John Zápolyai in July 1540 provoked a crisis of the first magnitude. Shortly before his death, he had married Isabella Jagiellonka of Poland, who bore him a son, John Sigismund Zápolyai. Despite the existence of an heir, Ferdinand sought to enforce the terms of his agreement with Zápolyai in 1538: he occupied Pest, and besieged Buda. György Martinuzzi, the bishop of Várad, who had been the architect of the 1538 agreement and was leading statesman in the Zápolyai party, panicked at the prospect of direct Habsburg rule and called for military assistance from the Ottomans. By August 1541, Süleyman was again encamped at Buda, and this time direct Ottoman control was implanted on that province (*beylerbeylik*). Hungary was divided into three parts, a division which lasted until 1699. The western portion, Royal Hungary, was largely unaffected by the campaign and remained under the rule of Ferdinand of Habsburg. The largest, central portion was transformed into the Ottoman-controlled province of Buda. The somewhat smaller eastern principality of Transylvania was ruled by John Sigismund Zápolyai as a puppet of the Ottomans.

Since the aim of the Zápolyai party all along had been to preserve the territorial integrity of Hungary, the establishment of an Ottoman province deprived it of its political purpose. It seemed to Martinuzzi that a reconciliation with the Habsburgs was the only alternative, and he began negotiations with Ferdinand in 1551. The idea was that John Sigismund should give up the throne in return for territorial compensation in Silesia and that Ferdinand should send an army to protect Transylvania against the Ottomans. But the army of 7,000 men sent to Transylvania was too small for the task, and its commander, Castaldo, committed the fatal mistake of having Martinuzzi assassinated on suspicion of 'treasonable' dealings with the Turks. The assimilation of Transylvania into Habsburg Hungary would not have been easy because of the rapid progress of the Reformation in the principality; it was made impossible by the murder of Martinuzzi. The Ottomans captured Temesvar in south-west Transylvania, which remained under their direct rule. On Süleyman's orders, the Transylvanian diet restored John Sigismund in 1556 as his vassal ruler (*voivode*). If John Sigismund died without heir (as happened in 1571) the Transylvanians were to elect his successor, subject to confirmation of their choice by the Sultan. The pretence of an independent Transylvanian principality was therefore at an end, but it did not stop a desultory war being fought over it between the Habsburgs and Ottomans in the years 1552–62 and 1564–8. The Ottomans had the upper hand throughout the period, as the treaties following the wars reveal. In 1547, Ferdinand agreed to pay annual tribute to the Sultan of 30,000 Hungarian ducats for his possession of Royal Hungary. These terms were repeated in 1562, and also in the treaty of 1568 between Maximilian II and Selim II, but this last treaty also contained territorial adjustments which favoured the Ottomans.

Süleyman's great achievement was to protect his existing empire by acquiring further territories to act as a buffer against his principal adversaries, Safavid Persia and the Austrian Habsburgs. The partition imposed on Hungary, though severely tested in later reigns, was to prove enduring, and the tributary status of Transylvania was roughly parallel to that of Mehmed II's acquisitions—Moldavia (whose tributary status was reaffirmed in 1538) and Wallachia. Süleyman was a great commander, who died in the field in 1566 on his thirteenth campaign (his seventh in Hungary). Because his reign was marked by military success, the Janissaries were for the most part quiescent. From the 1550s, however, the stability of Süleyman's rule had been disturbed by a struggle for power between his sons Selim and Bayezid, which was to lead to civil war. Earlier, in October 1553, Süleyman executed his eldest son, Mustafa, who was suspected of treason. Yet despite these internal troubles, the power struggles that were to disrupt later reigns failed to surface. Undoubtedly one reason was Süleyman's relative loyalty to his grand viziers, three of whom were very able men and held power for nearly half his reign. Piri Mehmed Pasha (grand vizier, 1518–23) had been appointed by Süleyman's father, Selim, and continued in office in the early years of the new reign. Ibrahim Pasha was promoted from relative obscurity in 1523 and was allowed to reform the administration of Egypt the following year after an abortive rebellion. Ibrahim enjoyed great favour, including the right to command the Ottoman army in Iraq in 1536, but he was suddenly executed on Süleyman's orders following the relative failure of the Ottoman campaign that year. The subsequent grand viziers were relatively mediocre, but Sokollu Mehmed Pasha, who was appointed in the penultimate year of Süleyman's reign, served three Sultans with distinction (1565–79).

5.4.3 *The Long Wars and Ottoman Resurgence, 1566–1661*

One of the principal features of Ottoman instability in the years 1579–1617 was the very rapid turnover of grand viziers, who on average survived less than two years in office. This was a consequence of increased court and harem intrigue after Süleyman's death. The first ten Sultans, including Süleyman, were on the whole effective rulers whose success can be marked by the expansion of their empire; their successors were unable to match this, and the era of conquest came virtually to an end. Contemporaries such as Hasan al-Kafi and Koçu Beg, writing respectively in 1596–7 and 1631, talked in terms of decline and tried to analyse the causes. Sir Thomas Roe, the English ambassador in Constantinople, reported in 1622 that 'it is impossible that the empire can endure . . . all the territory . . . is dispeopled [*sic*] for want of justice . . . the revenue is so lessened, that there sufficeth not to pay the soldier, and to maintain the court . . .'[56] But the passing of a remarkably successful era of expansion is not necessarily to be equated with a period of decline. Whatever the difficulties of the Ottoman state, it was not required to make any significant territorial concessions before 1699. It is certainly true that the Sultans who succeeded Süleyman were for the most part an undistinguished group. Selim II (1566–74) was given the epithet 'the sot' (*Sarhos*), which is self-explanatory. He captured Cyprus, which had been under Venetian rule since 1489, but he also suffered the disaster of Lepanto. Murad III (1574–95) was the last of the Sultans to have had some field experience before his accession, having served as a provincial governor under both his father and grandfather. As Sultan, however, he spent most of his time in his harem where he produced some 130 sons. Mehmed III (1595–1603) proved his ruthlessness on his accession with an unparalleled extension of the law of fratricide. He led his army in person to victory at Mezö-Keresztes in Hungary in October 1596.

For a moment it had seemed that the era of Süleyman was to be relived. But the death of Mehmed III in October 1603 produced an unparalleled situation and new dynastic instability. Ahmed I succeeded at the age of 13, and because of his young age the law of fratricide was not applied; nor was it applied systematically thereafter. On Ahmed's death in October 1617, none of his sons was of age; he was succeeded by his brother Mustafa I, who was deposed in February 1618 because he was mad. This brought to power 'Osman II, the eldest son of Ahmed, who was then about fourteen years of age. Rather surprisingly, and probably under the influence of grand vizier Dilawar Pasha, he showed—in Sir Thomas Roe's words—'a brave and well-grounded design . . . of great consequence for the renewing of this decayed empire'.[57] The aim was to raise a new army in the provinces of Asia Minor and Syria which would be powerful enough to allow the Sultan to dispense with the Janissaries, who were now proving unreliable. But before the plan could be brought to fruition, the Janissaries rebelled because of the failure of the war with Poland and the siege of Chocim in particular. 'Osman II was assassinated in May 1622. This led to Mustafa's restoration for a period of fifteen months until his second deposition in September 1623. Another son of Ahmed succeeded, but the new Sultan, Murad IV, was not yet 12 and he did not escape the tutelage of his mother and the court until May 1632.

When Murad IV began his personal rule, he enforced his authority ruthlessly by carrying out some 20,000 executions. He gained a reputation for 'excessive avarice'; what he would not do for prayer, intercession, justice and law he would do for cash, it was said.[58] On Murad's death in February 1640, he was succeeded by his younger brother Ibrahim I, who if not actually mad was eccentric to the point of madness. After 1644, the central government was once more on the verge of collapse and in August 1648 a revolt of the Janissaries and feudal knights (*sipahis*) was followed by Ibrahim's deposition and murder. He was succeeded by his son, the 7-year-old Mehmed IV, who ruled for nearly forty years (1648–87). Further turmoil and political instability followed. When Köprülü Mehmed Pasha was appointed in September 1656, he was the eleventh grand vizier in a reign that had lasted only eight years. However, the crisis of a Venetian blockade of the Dardanelles was the turning-point in the fortunes of the Ottoman empire, for it enabled Köprülü to insist on such autocratic powers that he was able to restore Ottoman fortunes to a considerable extent by the time of his death in October 1661. His power was such that he was able to appoint his son as his successor.

Inferior and erratic leadership after 1566 accounts to some extent for the difficulties experienced by the Ottoman state, but historians are much more inclined to emphasize longer-term social and economic weakness which made decline inevitable. When the era of conquest came to an end, Ottoman revenues were unable to increase further in a period of rapid inflation. This led to the rapid debasement of the asper, so that a revenue that had produced perhaps the equivalent of 10 million ducats under Süleyman I was producing scarcely more than 4 million under Mehmed IV. The finances of the state were poorly administered. Each new accession saw a period of largesse which imposed a crippling burden of debt on the later years of the reign. In the seventeenth century, before the rise of the Köprülü dynasty in 1656, the only period of relative financial stability had been the years of Murad IV's majority and its aftermath (1632–42). Undoubtedly one of the fundamental causes of the growing financial problems of the Ottoman state was the doubling of the number of state pensioners and paid troops between 1563 and 1609, above all the increase in the number of Janissaries after 1574, when they were allowed to enrol their sons into what was becoming an hereditary militia. So frequent and so excessive did their claims become that Sir Thomas Roe felt justified in writing that 'the Turkish emperor is now but the Janissaries' treasurer'.[59] Without such extortion, however, the Janissaries could not have survived, for it is estimated that while the cost of living in the Ottoman empire rose tenfold in the years 1350–1600, official Janissary pay had risen only four times. Increasingly, they supplemented their income by engaging in artisan and small-scale trading activities. New recruits were not needed and in any case could not be paid: consequently the *devsirme* levy of slaves in the Balkan region was abandoned after 1637. The system of *timars* providing a cavalry force also fell into disarray, since the fiefs were too small to enable the knights to finance participation in campaigns. The military ineffectiveness of the *sipahis* was fully revealed in 1596 when some 30,000 abandoned the battlefield at Mezö-Keresztes before the final Ottoman victory and were subsequently dismissed from their holdings in Anatolia. Many fiefs were confiscated by the treasury and farmed out to produce as much revenue as possible, while others were illegally converted into private property by their holders. As a result of these social changes there gradually emerged a powerful group of provincial notables (*ayans*), who often served as revenue farmers and drew economic benefits from the demise of the earlier form of Ottoman administration.

Such social and economic changes might not in themselves have proved disruptive, but they exacerbated social tensions which came to a head in a series of sustained rebellions, notably the bandit (*jelali*) movement in Anatolia (1596–1610), the revolt of Abaza Mehmed in Erzerum (1622–8) and in subsequent revolts in 1647, 1654–5 and 1657–8. The difficulties experienced by the Ottomans in their long wars after 1578 were the chief reason for these rebellions. When the frontiers were expanding, the army was kept content by the prospect of booty or the opportunity to settle the new territories as fiefs. Stable frontiers brought discontent in the army. The unemployed soldiers took to brigandage as a means of livelihood; the prospects for Ottoman victory against Safavid Persia at the end of the sixteenth century were diminished by the need to divert military resources to the suppression of discontent in Anatolia. The Ottoman Sultans were thus hoist by their own petard. Without 'long wars' they could not hope to keep the army content; but there could be no guarantee of launching a successful war, and failure made the problems of government worse.

At first it seemed that the collapse of the Safavid state following the death of Shah Tahmasp in May 1576 offered the Ottomans an opportunity that was too good to be missed. His successor, Isma'il II, was murdered in November 1577, and there was little effective government until the deposition of Mohummad Khudabanda in October 1588. Sultan Murad III decided on war in late 1577, despite the argument of Sokollu Mehmed Pasha, the grand vizier, that 'even if Persia is conquered, its peasantry will not accept becoming subjected to our rule'.[60] The Ottomans nevertheless acquired much of the Caucasus as a result of the Persian war, which lasted thirteen years. At the peace of March 1590, they gained Tabriz, together with most of Azarbayjan and Kurdistan, the territories that Süleyman had abandoned to make peace in 1555. Though he was forced to make such a humiliating peace early in his reign, the new ruler of Persia, Shah Abbas I (1588–1629) was to prove a formidable opponent. Once he had gained firm control in his kingdom, he turned his attention to reconquering the lands lost in 1590.

The war he launched in 1603–18 was timed to take advantage of

Ottoman involvement in the war with the Habsburgs in Hungary and their preoccupation with the *jelali* revolt in Anatolia. In the first five years of the new war, the precarious edifice of Ottoman rule in their new territories collapsed. In 1612, the Ottomans agreed in principle to cede the territorial gains of 1590 and did so in practice in the treaty of September 1618. The border returned to that of 1555, but in 1623 Shah Abbas reopened hostilities by seizing Baghdad and thus threatening Ottoman control of Iraq, which had been secured by Süleyman. Two grand viziers led unsuccessful sieges of Baghdad in 1625–6 and 1630, and the war was not brought to an end until Murad IV captured the city in person in December 1638. The Peace of Zuhab of May 1639 confirmed Süleyman's acquisition of Baghdad, Basra and Iraq (and thus access to the Persian gulf), but left Tabriz, eastern Georgia and Azarbayjan as Safavid territory. This treaty brought about a long period of peace with Persia which lasted until 1726, after the fall of the Safavid dynasty.

Murad III had been unwise to allow the opening of a new phase of warfare with Persia in 1578, and the same criticism could be applied to his decision to renew the war in Hungary in 1593. The chief proponent of war at this time seems to have been the grand vizier, Koja Sinan Pasha, who held the office five times in the period 1580–96, and was the first grand vizier to usurp the authority of the Sultan by taking the Janissaries on campaign. It is true that the Ottomans were incensed by the refusal of the Emperor Rudolf II to pay tribute for Royal Hungary after 1591. The raids of the Greek Orthodox *émigrés* from Serbia and Bosnia (*Uskoks*), who defended the border for the Habsburgs, provided a legitimate pretext for war. Nevertheless, the Ottoman interests would have been best served by limiting the conflict simply to the defence of existing frontiers. The danger of a sustained war was that it might give their tributary principalities of Wallachia, Moldavia and Transylvania cause to rebel, and to ally with the Habsburgs. Such a rebellion occurred in 1594–5, largely as a consequence of the oppressive Ottoman war demands on the tributary states. By 1593, the annual tribute expected from Wallachia had risen nineteen-fold since 1503, sixfold in the case of Moldavia.

Fortunately for Murad III, and his successor Mehmed III, the states were unable to unite against the Ottomans. Mihai Viteazul, *voivode* of Wallachia, tried to force such unity upon them in the years between 1596 and 1601. This attempt failed and the result was Habsburg occupation of the tributary principalities; but the excesses of the army under Giorgio Basta, and the policy of imposing Catholicism in the occupied areas, inevitably led to a reaction in favour of the Ottomans, who had traditionally respected religious sensibilities, particularly in Transylvania. Ahmed I, who succeeded Mehmed III in 1603, found a pliant vassal in István Bocskai, who had formerly served as adviser to the Transylvanian prince Sigismund Bátory, and had thrown in his lot with the Habsburgs in 1595. Though Bocskai had been a supporter of war against the Turks originally, removal from his command in 1598 and confiscation of his estates had alienated him from the Habsburgs. By November 1604, Bocskai's title as *voivode* of Transylvania had been recognized by the Sultan; in April 1605 he evicted Basta's forces from upper Hungary, which shifted the military balance in favour of the Ottomans. Bocskai's *Apology* had served to rally the various Protestant denominations of Transylvania against the threat of Catholic reaction, and he became the first Calvinist prince of Transylvania. However, the achievement was short-lived, because he died shortly afterwards. The Peace of Zsitva-Török of November 1606 was more enduring, since the Habsburg fortresses of Eger in central Hungary and Kanizsa in south-west Hungary were transferred to the Ottomans, though a single cash payment exempted Rudolf II from the humiliating annual 'gift' to the Sultan for his retention of Royal Hungary.

The Thirteen Years' War of 1593–1606 confirmed Ottoman control, direct or indirect, over most of Hungary and successive Emperors honoured the treaty, which was confirmed on five occasions between 1608 and 1642. Indirectly, the Ottomans thus assisted Imperial policy in Germany in a way which invites comparison with the indirect assistance which Süleyman I had lent the Lutheran princes before 1555. Had they backed their Transylvanian vassal, Bethlen Gábor, Bosckai's eventual successor, in his two wars against Ferdinand II, the Emperor's cause would have been much more severely tested in the 1620s and the early history of the Thirty Years' War might have been very different. War with Poland in 1620–1, with Persia in 1623–39 and with Venice in 1645–69 seemed to preclude further Ottoman adventures on the Danubian front. The last war was extremely arduous to the Ottomans, for it involved them in a twenty-two-year siege of Candia (1648–69), though when this fortress fell they were able to wrest Crete from Venetian control. Meanwhile, the Rákóczi dynasty of Transylvanian princes attempted to profit from Ottoman preoccupations elsewhere in Europe by pursuing an independent policy. However, the ambitions of György II Rákóczi in Poland (see chapter 5.2.5), Moldavia and Wallachia brought him into direct conflict with the Ottomans: this led to his deposition by Köprülü Mehmed Pasha in November 1657 and to a succession of disasters which hastened the end of Transylvanian independence. A series of military interventions by the Ottomans exacted an increased annual tribute from Transylvania and installed Mihály I Apafi as *voivode*. Stubborn resistance by Miklós Zrinyi, calling upon Habsburg support, failed to stop the Ottoman advance. Though the forces of Emperor Leopold I won the victory of St Gotthard (Szentgotthárd) in August 1664, his ministers panicked at the prospect of a long war and concluded (unnecessarily, it seemed to some critics) the Peace of Vasvár in September. This transferred Várad (Grosswardein, a town in eastern Hungary) and Neuhäusel (in north-west Hungary) to the Turks in return for a twenty-year truce. This agreement was the main cause of the Wesselényi conspiracy of 1670 by discontented Magyar nobles in Royal Hungary who were frustrated in their ambition to enlarge their estates through new conquests in the province of Buda. Events after 1683 were to demonstrate that the Ottomans were not to be dislodged easily from Hungary, and that the Habsburg dynasty would have difficulty replacing them. For all their domestic problems, the Ottomans were remarkably successful in retaining control of conquered lands.

Whereas the Emperor Charles V had not been powerful enough to destroy pre-existing constitutional arrangements in his conquered territories, the Ottoman Sultans were: they did so in Hungary, in Egypt and in Syria. In two cases, Persia and Hungary, the Ottoman rulers found that they were at the geographical limit of their advance, and respectively in 1639 and 1664 they reached a *modus vivendi* with the rival Safavid and Habsburg dynasties. Only when the Ottomans tried to resume the offensive again in 1683, by once more besieging Vienna, was it discovered that they had overstretched their resources: but they were not evicted from the province of Buda and Transylvania until 1699, and it was not until 1718 that their last foothold in Hungary, the province of Banat, was lost. The gains of Süleyman I had proved remarkably enduring.

One reason for this was the consideration shown by the Ottomans towards their Christian subjects. They could not contemplate making any religious concessions to Shiite Persia, but were prepared to exploit to their own advantage the tensions between Catholics and Protestants in Hungary. Yet apart from the granting of religious autonomy in the Balkans and Hungary there was another reason for the longevity of Ottoman conquest, which resulted from the nature of 'seigneurial monarchy' as Bodin called it, or the patrimonial state as it is usually referred to in modern parlance. Bodin explained: 'the reason why the lordly monarchy is more durable than the royal [as in western Europe], is for that it is more majestical, and that the subjects hold not their lives, goods and liberty [except from] the sovereign prince, who hath by just war conquered them.' In a 'free' monarchy in the west (such as in Denmark, Sweden and Poland), the population would rebel if the king tried to remove their property or other rights. However, in a seigneurial monarchy such as that of the Muscovite Tsar and the Ottoman Sultan, the ruler's subjects became 'humble, abject and [of] . . . servile heart'. The patrimonial state was therefore, in Bodin's view, more stable politically than were the monarchies of western Europe.[61] The history of the *oprichnina* and of the successive revolts of the Janissaries suggest that Bodin may have oversimplified the contrast. On the other hand, the old regime monarchies survived as long in Muscovy and Turkey as almost anywhere else in Europe, and longer than in some states such as France, the kingdom which Bodin had depicted as the exemplar of 'royal' as opposed to a seigneurial monarchy.

PART TWO

THE STRUCTURE OF THE EUROPEAN DYNASTIC STATES

6

THE RISE OF EUROPEAN
ABSOLUTISM

IT has been argued that on at least three occasions in the period 1494–
1660 there was a general European crisis which was characterized by
uprisings in several parts of the Continent. The critical years are said to be
the 1560s, the 1590s and the 1640s, years when political upheavals were
marked in some cases by changes of regime. Contemporary commentators
were struck by certain similarities in the troubles of these years, especially
those of the 1640s. The Dutchman Lieuwe van Aitzema compared the
Naples uprising of 1647 with the Moscow revolt of 1648; the Italian count
Birago Avogadro, drawing upon newspaper reports, published in 1653 a
volume of studies on the uprisings in Catalonia, Portugal, Sicily, England,
France, Naples and Brazil in the previous decade. The troubles of the
1640s have been given a Marxist interpretation; the conjunction of
important political and social upheavals with a fundamental economic
change has been viewed as a decisive moment in the transition from
'feudalism' to capitalism in Europe. However, not only has the original
formulation of the argument been subjected to criticism, but also its
underlying assumption: were economic and social conditions the prime
determinants of political change? There are enough differences between
each episode to defy any search for a common pattern. Certainly there
was political instability in early modern Europe, but this was not new: it
was a frequent feature of public life.

Several modern historians have attempted to analyse the more general
causes of these European crises and some common features have been
perceived, such as for example 'a crisis in the relations between society
and the state'.[1] It has been argued that the growth of government—perhaps
even the rise of absolutist states—combined with other social and
economic developments within society to produce intolerable tensions in
the 1560s, 1590s and 1640s. As evidence for this interpretation, some
historians have cited the development of the idea of the secular state in
political theory, the changing relations of rulers with representative bodies
such as parliaments or estates, the new complexity of royal administration, and the growing military power of states, accompanied by an
increasing fiscal burden. Undoubtedly certain rulers and ministers made

decisive contributions; but the growth of government was such a general phenomenon that it cannot be explained away simply as the work of talented individuals such as Thomas Cromwell in England in the 1530s or Cardinal de Richelieu in France a century later. Fundamental structural changes were at work in the period, and these led to the creation of something akin to the modern state by 1660.

6.1   European Political Thought

The recent scholarly tendency to study ideologies in preference to the isolated texts of great theorists has been beneficial in so far as it has placed the development of political theory within a firm historical context. But a closer examination of the less talented contemporaries of Machiavelli, Bodin and Hobbes has served only to confirm the unique importance of these great writers. Aspects of Machiavelli's work were clearly derivative; but there was neither precedent nor equal for his overall achievement. This judgement seems true also of Bodin and Hobbes in their different ways. All of them were defenders of sovereign power. But there was a rival view among their contemporaries which stressed the constitutional limits on the ruler and raised the possibility of resistance to him if he overstepped them. Thus among the French theorists, Claude de Seyssel, in *The Great Monarchy of France* (written in 1515, but published in 1519), advocated three restraints on the power of the king (religion, justice and established ordinances), while Guillaume Budé, in *The Instruction of the Prince* (1518), did not. These two strands of political thought are often depicted as being in complete opposition, the one an 'absolutist', the other a constitutionalist tradition which was a legacy of the Catholic Middle Ages and was greatly reinforced by the Protestant propaganda of the sixteenth century. But rather than viewing Seyssel as a constitutionalist and Budé as an absolutist, contemporaries would have seen them as writing within the same tradition, one being a moderate, and the other a more extreme, advocate of royal power. Seyssel argued the case for restraint by depicting what the king ought to do in theoretical terms; Budé presented a rhetorical defence of what Francis I actually did in practice.

6.1.1   *Machiavelli's Art of Ruling*

Niccolò Machiavelli (1469–1527) is often regarded as the founder of modern political thought. He was one of the first, and certainly one of the clearest, exponents of the principle of survival as the supreme test in politics. His political writings were based on the experiences of a varied political life. Between 1498 and 1512, he served in the Florentine chancery and was engaged in several diplomatic missions to France, Germany and the Papal States. This career was terminated in November 1512, when he was sacked by the new Medici government which had been restored by the Holy League (see chapter 2.1.2). To some extent, his writings were those of a defeated politician anxious to regain office. But they were also a reflection on past mistakes which had brought about the failure of his cause. He dedicated his writings to members of the Medici family to teach them how to govern properly, as he saw it, and to exhort them not merely to rule over Florence but to 'liberate Italy from the barbarians'.[2] In his retirement Machiavelli wrote *The Art of War* and *The History of Florence* and also the two key works for which he is remembered, *The Prince* and *The Discourses*. Both of the latter were conventional in presentation. *The Prince* was in the long tradition of handbooks for rulers; *The Discourses* were written in the form of commentaries on the classical historian Titus Livy. Yet if the presentation was conventional, the content was not. Machiavelli seems to have delighted in being controversial by overturning traditionally accepted wisdom and defending arguments which were not normally tenable.

Machiavelli's thought proceeded from an intense pessimism about human nature. He thought all men wicked and likely to 'give vent to their malignity . . . when opportunity offers'.[3] What contemporaries would have regarded as traditional princely virtues (liberality, clemency, keeping one's word and so on), Machiavelli dismissed as characteristics which might place the prince at a disadvantage over lesser mortals. In his view, a prince might have to 'act in defiance of good faith, of charity, of kindness, [and] of religion' to 'maintain his state'.[4] In addition, a prince need not necessarily possess 'all the good qualities' of ordinary citizens, but he must nevertheless 'certainly appear to have them',[5] otherwise what were seen as immoral actions might be self-defeating. Machiavelli's conclusion was that it was 'far better to be feared than loved if you cannot be both'.[6] Traditional Christian morality must be discarded 'when the safety of one's country wholly depends on the decision to be taken . . .'[7]

Machiavelli's originality lay not merely in his advocacy of the use of force in the acquisition and retention of political power—for example, he described fortune as a woman to be conquered by force—but also in his characterization of the creative energies required to achieve these ends. He termed these energies *virtù*; but as one would expect, Machiavelli did not equate this with Christian 'virtues'. Indeed, he regarded Christian humility as a positive disadvantage and the cause of the decline in republican values. *Virtù* was defined as statecraft and military skill, or whatever combination of talents were needed in a prince to 'maintain his rule' and 'achieve great things'.[8] Ancient Rome was his model for what

Florence might have been, and perhaps might still become; but the well-being of any society, he thought, depended less on its institutions than on the spirit enlivening them.

The Prince and *The Discourses* remained unpublished during Machiavelli's lifetime, although it seems that manuscript copies circulated quite widely. Within a generation of his death in 1527, however, his views were under attack throughout Catholic and Protestant Europe. The sale of his works was prohibited at Rome in 1549, and his writings were condemned wholesale in Pope Paul IV's Index ten years later. The aftermath of the St Bartholomew massacres saw the publication of the French Calvinist Innocent Gentillet's *Anti-Machiavel* (1576), which enjoyed considerable success as the source-book of anti-Machiavellian propaganda. In this work, Machiavelli was called an 'atheist' who sought to 'establish a tyranny'.[9] The fact that he had stated a clear preference for a republican over a princely regime was forgotten. The myth of the 'murderous Machiavel' had been born.[10]

6.1.2 *Theories of Resistance to Legitimate Authority*

It was no accident that a Calvinist should write one of the most influential treatises against Machiavellianism. Gentillet argued that it was Italian influence on the French government which had unleashed the massacres in France. Protestants did not want to resist the sovereign: they sought peaceful conversion and prayed (usually in vain) for the conversion of princes. Both Luther and Calvin cited the words of St Paul that 'the powers that be are ordained of God' (Romans xiii.1). From this they deduced that the secular power was 'God's representative' and the fundamental purpose of civil society was to uphold the laws of God in the exercise of the true (that is, Lutheran or Calvinist) faith. This scheme did not rule out the possibility that tyrants, too, might be ordained of God to 'punish the wickedness of the people'.[11] Calvin had a more practical reason for discouraging resistance to princes. He was aware of the danger of inciting Catholic repression. He was prepared to accord an individual the right to passive disobedience, especially where obedience to the ruler precluded a prior duty to God; but he never advocated an individual's right to rebel. Only 'magistrates of the people, appointed to restrain the tyranny of kings' had this right, and indeed duty. If such magistrates did not overthrow intolerable governments, they acted impiously towards God and his elect.[12]

Calvin's presentation of the grounds for resistance did not resolve all the practical difficulties of justifying a rebellion. Who were the magistrates and from whom did they, in turn, take their orders? If, as happened in France during the wars of religion, the king and the institutions of the state became linked with the Catholic cause, it was difficult to determine who the 'lesser magistrates' were and what was the nature of their power. On this central point, Calvin was equivocal, although in the period of regency in France (1560–3), he was prepared to allow power to devolve on the Estates General and the princes of the blood. It was left to Calvin's successors to resolve the issue in the completely new context provided by the St Bartholomew massacres in France in 1572. The task of elucidation fell to political writers, who were later given the name 'monarchomachs'.[13] The term literally means 'king-killer' and was first used in 1600. Three of the most important were François Hotman in *Francogallia* (1573); Theodore Beza, who had earlier participated in the Calvinist intrigues before and during the first French civil war in 1562–3, in *The Right of Magistrates . . .* (French edition, 1574); and Philippe du Plessis-Mornay, to whom is usually attributed *The Defence of Liberty against Tyrants* (1579; often called the *Vindiciae* after its Latin title).

These three treatises have a fundamental importance in the history of political thought and the ideological debate during the French wars of religion. It has also been claimed that they provide a crucial stage in the transition from medieval to modern constitutionalism. Hotman's *Francogallia* was drafted as early as 1568 and was approved by the Genevan council under the mistaken impression that it was a purely historical study unlikely to offend the French government. However, the dedication, which was not submitted to the Genevan council, contained an attack on the policy of Louis XI, who, it was alleged, had usurped the liberties of France in the fifteenth century. Although in many respects a tendentious work (Hotman made over 800, often inaccurate, citations, yet referred to no contemporary historical work), the significance of *Francogallia* was that Hotman firmly placed 'the highest administrative authority . . . in the formal public council' which he equated with the French Estates General.[14] This council's area of competence included 'the appointing and deposing of kings'.[15] He took the argument further by concluding that it was not lawful for the king 'to determine anything that affects the condition of the commonwealth as a whole' without the consent of the Estates General.[16] The *Parlements*, on the other hand, he dismissed as a breeding-ground of 'pettifoggery, which we can very truly call the French pox'.[17]

Beza had been in contact with Hotman, but his work went further than *Francogallia*. It was a more concise statement of Calvinist opinion, but when Beza presented the completed draft of *The Right of Magistrates* in July 1573, the Genevan councillors refused to authorize it for publication because they were afraid it would provoke 'troubles and upheavals that would burden this city'.[18] Beza agreed with Hotman on the role of the Estates General, but he recognized that a tyrannical king might prevent it from meeting. In these circumstances, 'lesser magistrates should join together and press for a convocation of estates, while defending themselves against tyranny . . .'[19] Beza defined the lesser magistrates as provincial governors, more generally the nobility, and elected municipal councils supporting the Calvinist cause, whose power emanated not from the ruler but from his sovereignty. Lesser magistrates who acted against a tyrant were in no sense rebels, but were simply performing their sworn duty to God and their country. The practical application of Beza's theories to France meant that the king's violation of the edicts of pacification rendered him guilty of 'flagrant tyranny, to which opposition is permitted . . .'[20] It is not surprising that the Calvinist leadership feared a Catholic backlash from the public statement of such a controversial view.

The Defence of Liberty against Tyrants took the argument a stage further. Obedience to the king was considered to be conditional. If the king neglected God or went over to his enemies (that is to say, failed to support the 'true' or Calvinist religion) he was guilty of 'felony towards God [and] his kingdom is forfeited . . .'[21] Private individuals had no power to act against a tyrant, but estates or lesser magistrates certainly had: 'they are not only permitted but obliged, as part of the duty of their office, and they have no excuse should they fail to act'.[22] It is sometimes said that the *Defence* offered the possibility of single-handed tyrannicide. But while there was an ambiguous phrase regarding those who had 'clearly received an extraordinary calling',[23] private individuals who drew the sword against their king were declared 'seditious, no matter how just their cause may be'.[24] The epithet 'monarchomachs' given to these Huguenot theorists would thus seem an overstatement. Certainly, the Calvinists did have a more radical wing, which was represented by the Scot George Buchanan. In the *Right of the Kingdom in Scotland* (written in 1567 but not published until 1579) he stated that the power to remove a tyrant rested at all times 'not only with the whole body of the people' but 'even with every individual citizen'.[25] Buchanan was a friend and correspondent of Beza and Duplessis-Mornay, but on this crucial issue their views diverged. Huguenot writers flirted with the idea of resistance to the Catholic tyrant in the special circumstances of the 1570s, but there was no permanent commitment to this theory. In the next decade, Hotman acted as a political agent for Henri of Navarre when he claimed the French throne, and in the 1586 edition of *Francogallia* the idea of an active sovereignty vested in the Estates General was virtually removed from the text. The king could not be resisted because it was anticipated that he would be a Calvinist. When Henri IV abjured Calvinism in 1593, Beza considered this a 'great fault', but far from advocating resistance, he counselled the Huguenots to obey their Catholic king.[26]

The two most important Protestant theorists of the next generation were the German Johannes Althusius and the Dutchman Hugo Grotius. Their standpoint was less controversial. In *Politics Methodically Set Forth* (first edition, 1603), Althusius denounced the exercise of absolute power by the ruler, calling it 'wicked and prohibited'.[27] Inspired by the example of the Dutch revolt, Althusius thought 'the spirit of liberty is retained through [the] right of holding assemblies' such as the States General.[28] He also valued certain aspects of the German constitution, claiming that the Imperial election 'capitulations'[29]—the privileges conceded by the Emperor to the electors as the price of his election—were covenants guaranteeing the rights of subjects, who only gave their obedience to him conditionally. He saw the electors as administrators ('ephors') whose task was to prevent the tyranny of the Emperor.[30] Much of this was Calvinist fantasy; it was what Althusius hoped the German constitution would become, not what it actually was. Several of his ideas were refuted by the Arminian Hugo Grotius, whose *Law of War and Peace* (1625) was the first systematic treatise on international law. Grotius rejected the view that supreme power was 'always and without exception' vested in the people.[31] He admitted that at first the people might choose 'what form of government they please' but once the sovereign was established, unconditional obedience was required.[32] 'If that promiscuous right of resistance should be allowed', he argued, 'there would no longer be a state, but a multitude without a union.'[33]

While later Protestant theorists rejected any resistance theory, somewhat ironically a number of Catholic theorists adopted it after Henri of Navarre became the Protestant claimant to the French throne (1584). Two years later, Louis d'Orléans wrote: 'in their *Francogallia*, which is one of the most detestable books ever to see the day ... they cry that it is lawful to choose a king to their desire; tell the heretics that the king of Navarre is not to our desire and that he [should] remain in his Béarn.'[34] Catholic League theorists such as Jean Boucher and Guillaume Rose proceeded further than the Huguenots in justifying tyrannicide. As part of their adherence to scholastic theory, the Jesuits, too, taught the doctrine. They were accused of being 'monarchomachs', as were the theorists of the Catholic League. The Spanish Jesuit Juan de Mariana argued in *The King and the Education of the King* (1599) that tyrannicide might be exercised 'by any private person whatsoever who may wish to come to the aid of the commonwealth'.[35] The assassination of Henri III was 'a detestable spectacle', but served as a reminder to princes that impious actions 'by no means go unpunished'.[36] In his most notorious passage, he spoke of the action of the assassin Jacques Clément as being 'an eternal honour to France, as it seemed to many', a comment which was excised from the second edition in 1605.[37] Given this prevailing attitude in some Jesuit circles, it is scarcely surprising that in December 1594 the *Parlement* of

Paris had demanded the expulsion of the Jesuits from France as 'cor-rupters of youth, disturbers of the public order, enemies of the king and the state'.[38] They were not readmitted until 1603. The *Parlement* condemned the works of three Jesuit authors in 1610 and 1614. Not all Catholic theorists took up such extreme positions, however. A more conventional opinion was expressed by the Gallicized Scots Catholic William Barclay in *The Kingdom and the Royal Power ...* (1600). He considered the tyranny of a legitimate ruler to be a logical impossibility, because the prince was above any human laws by which his acts might be judged.[39]

6.1.3 *Bodin and Legislative Sovereignty*

The reaction against Protestant (and Catholic) resistance theory was particularly strong among political theorists in France. Foremost among these was Jean Bodin (1529/30–96), a French jurist and humanist with a broad range of interests; in an age of academic inhibition, he was a boldly speculative thinker. Though avowedly a Catholic (and a supporter of the Catholic League in the years 1586–94), Bodin's religious views were un-orthodox, not least because he was influenced by Jewish writers. His private meditations, the *Colloquium of the Seven* (1588 or 1593) were not published in his lifetime because they constituted a far-reaching appeal for religious liberty. A moral philosophy pervades his other writings, too. Unlike Machiavelli, Bodin considered that the prince's laws should be 'framed unto the model of the law of God';[40] politics, in other words, was the means to a higher objective and not an end in itself as it had been for the Florentine.

His importance in the development of political theory, however, lies in his definition of absolute power as 'sovereign and perpetual power' and in his equation of this power with the concept of undivided legislative sovereignty.[41] (Bodin understood 'perpetual power' to be an authority which lasted 'for the time of the life of him that hath the power';[42] on the other hand since, for example in France, a new king assumed power immediately on the death of his predecessor, the power of the state, too, was perpetual.)[43] Bodin was less original than is sometimes claimed. The derivation of the term 'absolute power' (*potestas absoluta*) is not to be found in the sixteenth century, or even in the Middle Ages, but in pagan antiquity, in two third-century dicta of the jurist Ulpian. The first is the statement in Justinian's *Digest*, which attributes to Ulpian the sentence 'what has pleased the Emperor has the force of law' (*quod principi placuit legis habet vigorem*).[44] The statement also appears in the *Institutes*, but without this attribution. The remark has been seen as fundamentally important for the development of the idea of sovereignty as derived from

Roman law. A second maxim, also attributed to Ulpian in the *Digest*, 'the prince is freed from—absolved, or above—the laws' (*Princeps legibus solutus est*), is perhaps the forerunner of the term *pouvoir absolu*, the term *absolutus* having become transliterated from *solutus*.[45]

These Roman law maxims had been discussed at length by medieval lawyers, and many theoreticians had sought to give them a 'constitutionalist' gloss. What Bodin did was to reassert the old maxims free from these medieval restraints, providing a much more succinct definition of absolute power than hitherto and, moreover, claiming for it a permanency which had not previously been emphasized. Whereas the medieval king had been viewed as a judge with a number of specific attributes of power—the French theorist Barthelemy Chasseneux had enumerated 208 of them in 1529—Bodin's sovereign was elevated to the position of legislator. Under this mantle all other attributes were subsumed: sovereignty was defined as the power of 'giving laws unto the subjects in general, without their consent'.[46] Although it has been the subject of some controversy among historians, it is generally accepted that Bodin's theory of sovereignty was new in the history of political thought and originated in its developed form in his second important political study, the· *Six Books of a Commonweal* (*République*)—published in 1576, some ten years after his first significant contribution, the *Method for the Easy Comprehension of History*.

Bodin's theory meant that the sovereign exercised a legislative role which was above the civil law. In practice, however, the power of the ruler in France had always been to some extent limited by respect for the fundamental laws of the kingdom and obedience to divine and natural law. If the ruler violated these laws, passive resistance was allowed; for example, a magistrate might resign his office in protest.[47] Despite this tradition, Bodin was not prepared to accept that the people, their magistrates or representative institutions had any right of resistance at all. He implicitly condemned Hotman and Beza as dangerous men who attempted to 'induce ... subjects to rebel against their natural princes, opening the door to a licentious anarchy, which is worse than the harshest tyranny in the world'.[48] Monarchy, in his view, was either absolute and immune from legitimate resistance or it was not true monarchy at all. Surprisingly, however, Bodin insisted on public consent to new taxes, pointing to the example of the Low Countries where fiscal grievances appeared to him to have been a cause of rebellion. Although it was inconsistent with his theory of sovereignty, this right of consent formed a crucial part of Bodin's moral philosophy. 'The property and possession of every man's things' was, he believed, 'reserved to himself'. Natural law allowed the king's subjects to hold property and, by extension, it enshrined their right to consent to taxation.[49]

The extraordinary impact of Bodin's ideas is shown by the fact that he was often quoted by other political writers, although they used his theories to reach quite different conclusions. Later French theorists such as Pierre Grégoire, Charles Loyseau and Cardin Le Bret undermined the internal coherence of Bodin's system by removing his requirement of public consent to taxes. Bodin's arguments became known to a wider European audience through Giovanni Botero's *Reason of State* (1589), which enjoyed considerable success in Italy and Spain. While drawing many examples from Bodin, Botero's advocacy of dissimulation and prudence on the part of the ruler appears to have been more Machiavellian in inspiration.[50] The Flemish philologist Justus Lipsius (Joest Lips) was more obviously critical of Bodin in his most famous works, *Of Constancy in Evil Times* (1584) and *Six Books of Politics* (1589), with his rejection of the assertion that a sovereign was above civil law. Lipsius' main contribution to political thought was as an influential exponent of Renaissance Stoicism, the cult of stoic ethics in the face of adversity. Lipsius thought it better for the subject to 'endure any kind of punishment' meted out by the tyrant rather than to precipitate civil war. But his most striking observation was to equate reason of state with princely prudence. The ruler was permitted to use deceit in moderation if it was in the best interests of his state; only pure treachery, a 'forcible and perfect malice', was condemned.[51]

6.1.4 *Hobbes's* Leviathan

Although Bodin's writings provided extremely fertile ground for contemporary political theorists, his successors were less distinguished men whose work lacked the same impact or originality. It was left to an English political theorist to advance the study by modifying the accepted body of ideas. Thomas Hobbes (1588–1679) was a man with wide interests—in logic, mechanics, optics, politics and jurisprudence. In a period of self-imposed exile in France between 1640 and 1651, Hobbes entered upon the most intellectually fruitful period of his life. He completed the draft of *The Citizen* (*De cive*, 1642) and he wrote the whole of his masterpiece, *Leviathan* (1651). These works grew out of his participation in the circle of scientists and philosophers gathered around the figure of Marin Mersenne. Hobbes spent much of his time in optical experiments and mathematical speculation, and he found support for his idea that 'geometrical' demonstration might be introduced into political science.

The laws of motion were his starting-point. 'Life was but a motion of limbs'; human passions arose from pleasure or aversion, which he took to be 'motions in the head'.[52] Hobbes's aim was to devise a system to contain natural forces which were so powerful that if unregulated they would make 'the life of man solitary, poor, nasty, brutish and short'.[53] In the aphorisms for which *Leviathan* is justly remembered, Hobbes described both the condition and the solution that occurred to him. The state of nature was a state of war, 'that dissolute condition of masterless man, without subjection to laws, and [without] a coercive power to tie their hands from rapine and revenge . . .'[54] The solution was the establishment of the sovereign state for man's protection, 'that great Leviathan . . . that mortal God, to which we owe, under the immortal God, our peace and defence . . .'[55] By this reasoning, Hobbes substituted for Bodin's sovereign or Machiavelli's prince the abstract notion of the sovereign state. The sovereign state's power was 'as great as possibly men can be imagined to make it', unlimited by any civil restraint and subject only to natural law.[56]

In a passage that owes much of its inspiration to Machiavelli, Hobbes allowed no objective moral attributes to regulate the use of the epithets 'good' or 'just'. Instead, he stated explicitly that 'whatsoever is the object of any man's appetite or desire, that is which he for his part calleth good . . .'[57] It therefore followed that no moral attribute could be used to describe the constitution of the state; the state was neither good nor bad, but simply was. Tyranny, in Hobbes's view, was simply a label dreamed up by those who were 'discontented under monarchy'.[58] No law could be unjust, he argued, if it was necessary, since 'the good of the sovereign and the people cannot be separated'.[59] Unlike Bodin, Hobbes was hostile to represent-ative assemblies. It was, he thought, 'an easy thing for men to be deceived by the specious name of liberty'. True liberty was the ability of a man to act where the sovereign had prescribed no rule; generally, 'in the act of our submission consisteth both our obligation and our liberty . . .'[60] Hobbes projected *Leviathan* both as a rationalization of the political *status quo* (in his personal case, submission to the English Republic in 1651), and a justification of monarchy ('that book now fights for kings and for all those who exercise the right of kings', he claimed).[61]

Leviathan received an almost universally hostile reception in England, though not on the Continent. Hobbes was unpopular with royalists for undermining the divine right of kings. His belief in determinism (or 'necessitation', as he called it) led him to deny free will in a famous dispute with bishop John Bramhall, but it was his alleged atheism which most shocked contemporaries. In *The Citizen*, Hobbes called atheism a 'sin of imprudence'; 'the fool hath said in his heart, there is no God'.[62] By his own definition, no man could ever know another's inner belief; anyone forcibly required to confess his belief had the right to say whatever was most likely to clear him of an accusation. Whether Hobbes himself believed in the existence of God will never be known; but it is clear that in his system the church was to be controlled by the state, and the duty of the sovereign was to pronounce upon religious matters. The sovereign had to create a system of rules out of that vacuum, the state of nature: 'what the legislator commands must be held for good, and what he forbids, for evil'.[63] Hobbes did not say that might was right, but that irresistible power justified itself. His view of religion was profoundly offensive to many contemporaries because power, rather than justice or mercy, appeared to be the only divine attribute worthy of esteem.

The political theory of Hobbes as expressed in *Leviathan* might lead one to deduce that by 1651 the modern secular state, or something very near to it, had come into being and was philosophically acceptable to contemporaries. This was far from the case, although there was some contemporary support for Hobbes's position. The theory of the divine right of kings, the power of the ruler being ordained by God, was a more common justification of monarchical power, and proved difficult to supplant. Despite Machiavelli, and perhaps because of the strong reaction to his writings, most contemporaries still assumed that the exercise of power should be guided by Christian morality, not by necessity. Nothing akin to the modern secular state was to be found in practice. Bodin's Commonweal was an harmonious ordering of the body politic in conformity with the laws of God, not an abstract state subject to natural law; his ideas, though modified in subsequent generations, were more influential than were those of Hobbes.

6.2 The Ruler and His Parliaments

Bodin was a deputy to the French Estates General in 1576, the year in which his *Six Books of a Commonweal* was published. He observed that France was 'a pure monarchy, not mingled with the popular power'[64] and noted that the French kings did not summon estates as frequently as the kings of England. However, this did not mean that he supported the abolition of representative institutions. Even French ministers who did not favour such assemblies found they had their uses in times of crisis. The king's subjects did not always receive satisfaction in response to their requests; but Bodin's argument was that their sense of grievance was reduced simply because the king had given them a hearing.[65] One issue which has been much debated by historians is the relative success or failure of different parliaments in the European dynastic states. Attempts to elucidate general principles or theories are open to question. The number of factors which interacted in 'parliamentary history' is so great that each institution has to be viewed in terms of its own relative success or failure. But one thing is clear. At least in the sixteenth century, representative institutions usually prospered in time of war, since many of them met to debate the levy of taxes for military purposes. There the similarities end. Most importantly, the constitution of these assemblies varied widely. Distinctions can be drawn between composite assemblies, one-chamber, two-chamber, three-chamber, even four-chamber and provincial assemblies. Structural differences were bound to affect the capabilities and functions of the assemblies in each country. The parliaments of the European dynastic states were nowhere representative of everyone: the membership of these gatherings was heavily weighted in favour of two main groups, the political classes (those who had landed estates or power in the locality) and those who paid direct taxes. Consequently, their decisions usually reflected the interests of these classes.

6.2.1 *Central Government Power and the Regularity of Sessions*

Bodin had used the evidence of the irregularity of meetings of the French Estates General to support a specific point, that the French monarchy was both strong and 'purely royal' in character, that is to say, not mixed with any aristocratic or democratic forms of government. It is an argument worth exploring in detail for all the European dynastic states, but on the face of it France does not seem to be typical of the rest. A rapid scan of the meetings of other European representative institutions shows a greater frequency of meetings elsewhere. The States General in the Low Countries met on 62 occasions between 1499 and 1576; the *Cortes* of Castile 53 times between 1497 and 1660; there were 41 diets of the Holy Roman Empire between 1492 and 1654; and 46 parliaments in England between 1495 and 1660 (only 45 if the Addled Parliament of 1614 is excluded on the grounds of 'no legislation, no Parliament'; but 84 sessions of parliament produced legislation). Nor should the representative institutions of the states of eastern Europe be overlooked: although only 17 diets were held in Bohemia between 1512 and 1620, the Polish *Sejm* could claim to be the most frequently summoned European assembly, meeting 159 times (almost annually) between 1493 and 1661.

But has Bodin's equation between the frequency of meetings of a representative institution and the relative strength or weakness of the ruling house any validity? As Bodin knew, rulers summoned their assemblies for a variety of reasons other than weakness, including political expediency. Furthermore, one representative institution varied greatly from another in the extent of its power to influence political events and public policy. Behind the generalizations of political theory lie the practical realities of political power in individual European countries which need more detailed examination. The diets of Poland, Hungary and Bohemia were, like the English parliament, bicameral assemblies, the upper house drawn from the magnates, the lower house from the nobility as a whole.

Provincial diets—called 'dietines' (*sejmiki*) in Poland—met more frequently and by the seventeenth century had a greater political impact than
the national assembly. Further east, the Muscovite kingdom had its
Assembly of the Land (*Zemskii Sobor*) which, in its definitive form at the
meeting of 1648–9, was also bicameral. However, its sessions were so
infrequent, and elections were so rarely held, that it can scarcely be
regarded as a representative institution at all. It was not summoned after
1653 and it cannot be considered of any importance in this survey. It is
scarcely surprising that the most autocratic of the east European
monarchies was prepared to tolerate only a weak representative institution.

The Hungarian gentry had been obliged to attend the national diet *en
masse* by the last Jagiellon rulers; the Ottoman-inspired partition of the
kingdom (see chapter 5.4.2) led to a split in this representative unity, even
though Transylvania continued to send observers to the diet of Royal
Hungary until 1659. Under the Habsburgs, personal attendance by all the
gentry was abolished in Royal Hungary. The Hungarian diet was
irregularly summoned but usually well attended and quick to present its
grievances. It was by no means a tame assembly, happy to follow the royal
line. In contrast, the Transylvanian diet met more regularly, but this did
not imply any greater political power than that of the Hungarian diet. It
could elect its ruler (*voivode*), yet it tended to surrender more power to
him. The infrequency of Bohemia's diets has already been noted, but there
were political reasons for this. The general diet was gravely compromised
by its participation in the rebellions of 1547 and 1618–20, and after
Ferdinand II's victory in 1620 (see chapter 4.1.1) it was not summoned
again until 1848. But the element of representative government was
preserved in the provincial diets which formed part of the revised constitution of 1627. Even so, these provincial diets were rarely able to take
an independent line because the clergy had been added as a loyal first
estate, and royal commissioners were given wide control over the
proceedings.

The Polish diet (*Sejm*) was by far the most significant representative
institution in the eastern kingdoms. It achieved its bicameral form in 1493
and rapidly came to exercise a crucial role in restraining the development
of royal power in Poland. It guaranteed noble privileges, most
importantly, the rights of free assembly ('confederation') and of electing
the king. The diet acted as the supreme legislative body and court of
appeal, but by 1660 it was already clear that it suffered from fatal defects
which became increasingly obvious in the late seventeenth and in the
eighteenth centuries. The provincial nobility, represented in its lower
chamber of deputies, had always played a dominant role in the diet. This
was recognized in the statute of *Nihil novi* of 1505, by which the lower

chamber gained a veto on new legislation. Without agreement between the provincial nobility and the magnates of the upper chamber, there could be no enforcement of the law.

The overwhelming need to preserve unity among the nobles in order to avert civil war had led gradually to an exaggerated emphasis on the principle of unanimity, a principle which grew harder to maintain after Lithuania's union with Poland in a commonwealth (*Rzeczpospolita*) in 1569 (see chapter 5.2.1). The logical extension of this principle was the development of the power of veto in Poland. In 1652, a written protest of a Lithuanian deputy led to the dissolution of a meeting of the diet without its passing any legislation. 'I deny' (*veto*) or 'I do not allow it'[66] were words used on fifty-three occasions between 1652 and 1764 to suspend meetings of the Polish diet before any legislation was passed. This *liberum veto* was proclaimed by some Polish nobles as the guarantee that a minority of wise men would be protected from the dictates of a stupid majority. But more perspicacious observers recognized that the hostility between Polish and Lithuanian nobles made the operation of Poland's diet a near impossibility. Not only was it easy to paralyse with the use of the veto, but also its deputies were open to bribery by interested foreign powers. It raised the spectre of a complete breakdown in central representative government and the partition of the commonwealth, a threat which king John Casimir foresaw as early as 1661.

In Germany a similar pattern emerged. The German diet (*Reichstag*) was a tricameral assembly. Its three colleges were filled by the seven electors; numerous territorial princes and bishops; and representatives of the sixty-six or so free cities (*Reichstädte*). The composition of the diet did not necessarily assist the Imperial position, mainly because of the strength of princely representation. In 1495, the Emperor Maximilian I had tried to secure the agreement of the diet to two reforming policies, a standing army and permanent taxation, but his opponents blocked such attempts by appealing to the sentiment of princely independence. The balance of power within the diet was against the Emperor. In 1501–2, at the insistence of his critics, a standing committee of the diet acting as a caretaker government (*Reichsregiment*) was established at Nuremberg. Maximilian strongly opposed this scheme, because he saw that it set a precedent under which Germany could be governed without the Emperor. He managed to kill it off in 1503, though it was resurrected in a diluted form during Charles V's absence from Germany between 1521 and 1530, when the Emperor was represented by a regent, his younger brother Ferdinand. Neither Maximilian nor Charles could put their reforming ideas into practice; nor were they able to bolster their support within the Imperial diet. It was not until after Charles V had defeated the Schmalkaldic League that he felt he could try to strengthen Imperial power (see chapter 2.4.3). Even from his position of strength in 1547–8, however, Charles was unable to move the diet towards reform.

The formal recognition of the religious divisions in the Empire, the Peace of Augsburg (1555), did not advance the Emperor's cause. The mutual suspicion which existed between the religious parties was reflected most clearly in the diet, where the Catholics were in a majority. Meetings were transformed into a congress of diplomatic representatives from the various German principalities and cities, who could not reach any agreement on the interpretation of the Peace of Augsburg, let alone on any new reforming ideas. Each session became more acrimonious than the preceding one. After the diet of 1597–8, the Calvinist elector of the Palatinate and his allies (the so-called 'corresponding princes') refused to contribute towards a subsidy which had been voted through by the Catholic majority. This was tantamount to a denial of the authority of the diet and it coincided with other developments which made civil war inevitable (see chapter 3.4.3).

Between 1613 and 1640 no formal diet was held at all. There were meetings between the Emperor and the electors, but these, too, split along religious lines. Yet although the diet met only once during the Thirty Years' War (in 1640–1), it had not been abolished. The problem was to make it acceptable to the victors in the war and to establish it as an integral part of a revised German constitution. The military successes of the Emperor's opponents secured an agreement on paper in 1648, by which the Emperor transferred to the Imperial diet the right of declaring war and concluding peace within Germany. The Peace of Westphalia envisaged a permanent, indeed an enlarged, role for the diet, with contentious issues settled by 'amicable agreement' between the religious groupings (which now included Calvinists on the Protestant side). Yet only one diet was held in the next decade (in 1653–4) and the permanent diet at Regensburg was not established until 1663. Even then the role of the diet was severely circumscribed because it could not take action on crucial matters such as the levying of taxes or the raising of armies, and if it reached a decision, this could usually be ignored with impunity by the German princes.

The weak, distant Imperial diet, which met so infrequently before 1663, was by default upstaged by the estates (representative institutions) of the German principalities. Most of these were three-chamber assemblies comprising clergy, nobility and townsmen, although as in the Imperial diet, the nobles were usually the dominant class. Some estates were successful in maintaining a balance of power between the classes, but many were swayed by the interests of their princes and consequently lacked any real independence. The infrequency of their meetings can be considered another measure of the weakness of these estates. Some princes, Catholic and Protestant alike, rarely summoned their estates at all. Once Württemberg became Lutheran after the restoration of duke Ulrich in 1534, there were long periods when the estates did not meet—for instance, between 1538 and 1550 or between 1553 and 1565; and they only met once between 1568 and 1593. In Bavaria, the duchy first affected by the Counter-Reformation, there had been thirty-three meetings of the estates between 1508 and 1579, but there were only five under William V (1579–97) and two under Maximilian I (1597–1651), both before the Thirty Years' War. No diet was held between 1612 and 1669, and the latter proved to be the last meeting of the Bavarian estates. Few estates showed the resolve of Saxony, which had the former Chancellor, Dr Nicolaus Crell, executed in 1601 because he had been a Calvinist pursuing auto-cratic policies in a Lutheran state. Even so, the estates of Saxony did not meet for seventeen years between 1640 and 1657.

Despite the considerable financial significance of the secularization of church lands, the progress of the Reformation did not in itself seem to alter the relationship between the German estates and their princes. Only in Brunswick were the estates consulted about introducing the Reforma-tion. In secular matters, too, the prince took the initiative without necessarily wooing his representative assembly. In Hesse and Albertine Saxony, for example, the prince conducted an active foreign policy which required financial assistance from the estates. Relations became strained because the prince had not prepared the ground and won his estates' support. But a show of force by the ruler was usually sufficient to break any resistance. The estates failed in most instances to secure any redress of grievances in exchange for agreeing to princely demands, and most were destined to fulfil a secondary role in the second half of the seven-teenth century.

The Thirty Years' War was the watershed for the estates, a last chance to increase their power in return for political support. Yet they failed to capitalize on this opportunity. The clearest sign of their failure was the levying of taxes by decree of the rulers, which happened, for example, in Bavaria in the 1630s. During the War of the North (1655–60), the Great Elector, who was on the way to becoming one of the leading princely rulers in the Empire, levied taxes by personal decree in Brandenburg, Cleves and Mark. By the end of the war he had gained a standing army and a permanent excise without enlisting the support of the estates. Why were the estates unable to oppose such a policy? Their resistance was undoubtedly hampered because they lacked a theory with which to defend their role in the constitution against the rival power of the prince. Only in ducal East Prussia did such a constitutional theory emerge, due to the special circumstances of Polish suzerainty until 1657. The Prussian estates considered that they possessed privileges which were unalterable and which limited the authority of their ruler, Frederick William. Yet this theory did not protect them in 1662, when the Great Elector arrested his sternest critic in the estates, Hieronymus Roth. Mere political theorizing could not withstand the harsh realities of political practice.

Though historians correctly stress that any representative institution had the potential to achieve influence or even power, it is nevertheless incontrovertible that the French Estates General (composed of clergy, nobility and a third estate of primarily townsmen) failed to realize it. It had an undistinguished pedigree down to 1484, and subsequently it met less frequently than any other representative assembly in contemporary Europe. It did not meet at all between 1484 and 1560. It then met on only five occasions between 1560 and 1615 (in 1560, 1561, 1576, 1588 and 1614–15) and thereafter not again until 1789. It also met illegally once, in 1593, on the summons of the duc de Mayenne, the leader of the Catholic League. Because it met so irregularly, each session has assumed a momentous significance for historians, and each failure to do anything when it did meet has been viewed as a lost opportunity. Its members realized the importance of establishing a regular timetable of meetings. In the 1484 session, they demanded biennial assemblies, but to no avail. At the meeting of 1560, the third estate pressed for sessions to be held every five years, and the demand for a regular summons was made on subsequent occasions. But the seventy-six-year interval between the meetings of 1484 and 1560 suggests that the initiative for reform never lay with the Estates General. Rather, it was the French monarchy which controlled its activities, and the chronology of royal summonses implies that it only met in periods of royal weakness, not periods of strength.

The power of the French monarchy is not the only explanation for the relative failure of the Estates General. Bodin's comments on the weakness of the nobility in the States General of the Netherlands in 1583 are apposite. In his view, the nobles were 'the principal link between the prince and the people in any monarchy'.[67] The failure of the French Estates General in the later sixteenth century can be seen as the failure of the nobility to perform this essential function. The noble estate was hopelessly divided by the spread of the Reformation in France. At the meetings of 1576 and 1588, the Estates General became associated with Catholic religious extremism and criticism of the government, an attitude no doubt fuelled by the frustrations of its political castration. The illegal Estates General of 1593, summoned to elect a Catholic alternative to Henri IV, largely sealed the fate of this national representative institution. Not only did the meeting fail in its main purpose, since it could not agree on a candidate. Worse still, Henri IV won the war with the support of a rival (but non-representative) institution, the *Parlement* of Paris. The three estates again failed to concert their policy (implicitly against the government) at the next and final Estates General of the period, that of 1614–15.

Historians have blamed this lack of unity for the demise of the Estates General in the seventeenth century; but they have exaggerated the degree of tension between the orders which was not in itself sufficient to lead to its failure. Ultimately, the hostility of other institutions in France was just as crucial for its failure, as was its inability to establish a working relationship with the provincial estates, which met much more regularly. More important still was the lack of legislative power in the Estates General and its inability to prevent renewed civil war: quite simply, the institution seemed irrelevant to the problems of the period. When the implementation of reforms was being discussed, for example, it was assemblies of notables, not the Estates General, which were summoned in 1617–18 and 1626–7. Nonetheless, royal policy during the Fronde showed that while the Estates General was in abeyance it had not been abolished. The government could not always rely on the support of the *Parlement* of Paris and other lawcourts. The *Parlement*'s rebellion in 1649 and its uncompromising hostility to Mazarin in 1651–2, led the king to issue two further summonses to the Estates General. Yet his ministers never intended it to meet, correctly believing that the threat to summon an Estates General would be enough to bring the *Parlement* into line. Paradoxically, the very conservativism of absolutism was the best guarantor of representation. In France nothing—certainly no institution—was ever abolished, because to abolish something might be construed as an attack on privilege. Thus, in a great national crisis such as the Fronde or the War of the Spanish Succession, there could be talk of summoning the Estates General, although no meeting in fact took place. It is clear that had the political will been present—or the national emergency more extreme—the national representative institution could have been summoned again.

6.2.2 *Representative Institutions and the Control of Taxation*

The power to approve or to reject grants of money for the support of the monarchy undoubtedly made some countries' representative institutions more powerful than others. This power could be exercised either by the representative institution itself, or by its standing committee which met during the intervals between sessions. The *Cortes* of the Spanish kingdoms provide a striking example of both mechanisms in action, with the standing committees becoming more important in the eastern kingdoms than in Castile because of the relative infrequency with which the full sessions of the representative institutions were held. The general *Cortes* of the crown of Aragon (which represented the kingdoms of Aragon and Valencia and the principality of Catalonia) was summoned to meet at Monzón six times under Charles V, though Philip II called it only twice, in 1563 and 1585. However, a *Cortes* of each constituent part of the Aragonese kingdom sat separately, and in effect the king had to deal with three different institutions which only occasionally met together for convenience. The *Cortes* of Catalonia and Valencia had three estates, the clergy, nobility and towns; those of Aragon had four, with the nobility divided into two estates, the magnates and the lesser nobility (*caballeros*). In practice, the number of times the *Cortes* met did not matter very much, since real political power did not rest with them but with the standing committees of the Aragonese kingdoms. These committees saw their role as guarding against encroachments by the monarchy during the intervals between meetings of the representative institutions, which they did with the utmost vigour. In Catalonia, a dispute between the standing committee (the *Diputació*) and the central government at Madrid over alleged encroachments unleashed the rebellion of 1640 (see chapter 4.3.3).

The *Cortes* of Castile was more amenable to the wishes of its ruler and, perhaps as a result, it was summoned more frequently than the general Aragonese *Cortes*, although there were still long intervals between its meetings. In the Middle Ages it had developed into a tricameral assembly; but the clergy and nobility were summoned only three times by Charles V, and the session of 1538–9 was the last at which they played an active and independent role. Subsequently, the *Cortes* became a unicameral assembly of thirty-six deputies (*procuradores*), two drawn from each of the eighteen towns which enjoyed representation (the number of towns with representation had increased to twenty-three by 1665, with a resulting increase in the number of deputies). However, the power of the *Cortes* was gravely compromised both by its opposition to Charles V's financial measures in 1520 and, even worse, by the participation of most of the towns in the Comunero rebellion of 1520–1 (see chapter 7.5.4). Many of the demands of the rebels were aimed at strengthening the *Cortes*; there were proposals that it should meet triennially, and that its assent to important policy decisions such as the marriage of the king, the appointment of regents and declarations of war should be obligatory. The rebels wanted to abolish the requirement that the *Cortes* should vote a grant of taxes (*servicio*), which instead would become optional, depending on whether there had been full redress of their grievances; moreover, in an age of inflation, they wished to pay indirect taxes pegged at the level of 1494.

Historians used to argue that the power of the *Cortes* was shattered by the defeat of the Comunero rebellion, but this view is not borne out by the subsequent history of the reign. Charles V summoned sixteen sessions of the *Cortes*, of which thirteen were held after the revolt. Furthermore, he reached agreement with them on the level of the indirect taxes and he also allowed a standing committee (*Diputación*) to co-ordinate the levy, neither development suggesting that Charles was dealing with an enfeebled representative institution. His son, Philip II, obtained increases in the indirect taxes in 1561 and he tripled them in 1574; but in 1577, because of political pressure from the *Cortes*, which was in session for nineteen months, the levy had to be reduced from 2.5 to 1.5 million ducats. The enormous cost, and shattering defeat, of the Armada necessitated the raising of new revenues and the levy of a new tax called the *millones*, which the *Cortes* granted in 1590. This tax was in effect an excise such as the nobility had refused to grant in 1538. The temporary nature of the grant of the *millones* left the crown lurching from one conflict with the *Cortes* to another in the seventeenth century. Not only had the king of Castile customarily taken an oath in the *Cortes* to maintain the royal patrimony and to confirm the customs, privileges and liberties of the cities—Philip II, Philip III and Philip IV all did so soon after their accession—but also they had agreed to 'mutual, reciprocal and obligatory' contracts[68] with the *Cortes* which went far beyond petitions of subjects to their king and made the grant of additional taxation conditional on the fulfilment of the contract. In 1642, it was recognized that the *Cortes* had been offered by the crown certain conditions as a 'pact and obligation' and that if these were not honoured then the towns would be freed from contributing to the agreed increases in taxation; on another occasion, it was judged 'very dangerous ... to break with the cities and the ancient custom of these kingdoms'.[69] This was an ascending theory of sovereignty, and a practice of government, which was light years away from Jean Bodin's descending theory, that 'the principal point of sovereign majesty and absolute power ... consist[s] in giving laws unto the subjects in general, without their consent ...'[70]

In each set of negotiations up to 1658, the *Cortes* was able to block unpopular tax reforms and to extract concessions which ensured that it administered the levy through a special commission. As the grant increased, so too did the importance of the commission, and when Philip IV attempted to abolish it in 1648, the *Cortes* defeated him. The amount of taxation under the control of the *Cortes* grew steadily, from about a quarter in 1573, to nearly 40 per cent in 1594; by the 1640s the *Cortes* controlled over half the total amount of taxation and by the 1650s it had responsibility for some 60 per cent. Yet in 1658, the king was able to abolish the commission administering the levy of the *millones* because the power to grant such levies had devolved on the cities. The city councils were in a sense more representative than the *Cortes*, and were easier to deal with. The *Cortes* displayed a singular (and ultimately fatal) failure to resist. It had been the power to administer, not the power to consent to, the *millones* which had given the Castilian *Cortes* its relevance and its *raison d'être*, and after 1665 the crown did not bother to summon it. The queen regent Mariana and her advisers feared that the representative assembly would 'claim some share in government, as happened on other occasions . . .' and thus decided not to call the *Cortes* when it was due in 1667.[71] Far from a weak and compliant *Cortes* being destroyed by an 'absolute' monarchy, the assembly was not summoned because a weak and insecure government could not risk a meeting following upon a recent humiliation abroad in the War of Devolution against Louis XIV. Since the cities were willing to renew the grant of the *millones* without such a meeting, the fate of the Castilian representative assembly was sealed by the cities' decision.

Elsewhere in Europe, the towns remained committed to the continuance of representative institutions. One of the most powerful and enduring representative institutions of Europe was the Swedish *riksdag*, which survived until 1865. It was composed of representatives from four estates, the clergy, nobility, townsmen and, unusually for European assemblies, the peasants. In the early sixteenth century the Swedish *riksdag* had aided the monarchy in establishing the Vasa dynasty and spreading the Reformation throughout Sweden; hence it had considerable political power. Yet as late as 1560 its composition was ill defined and its power over taxation uncertain. It was subject to manipulation by successive rulers, while in the late sixteenth century, under the influence of magnates such as Erik Sparre and Hogenşkilde Bielke, Sweden appeared to be on the way to establishing a Polish-style elective monarchy with the estates acting on the principle of unanimity. Gustavus Adolphus relied on the *riksdag*'s compliance to vote money for his wars, and even if he did not consult them first, the king took care to explain his policy after the decisions had been taken; it was later said that he took their opinion 'less from necessity than with a view to not seeming responsible for any disaster which might ensue'.[72] During the minority of Christina, the power of the *riksdag* grew in a more obvious way. Its monopoly of legislation was admitted. The regents and the governing ministers recognized that the *riksdag*'s consent to new taxes and to conscription was needed (even Oxenstierna considered in 1641 that 'the liberty of the estates . . . consists of a free grant').[73] It made financial grants only for strictly limited periods, thus ensuring that the queen would have to summon it regularly. Oxenstierna was prepared to argue in the last year of his life (1654) that 'the king can make no law, nor alter or repeal any, without the assent of the *riksdag* . . . all sorts of people have their share, either in person or by deputies, in the supreme council of the kingdom by [which alone] those great matters can be done . . .'[74]

In 1650, there was a constitutional crisis. The *riksdag* insisted that its grievances be met before it would grant taxes. Joint meetings were held between three of the estates, to the exclusion of the fourth, the nobility. Majority voting, rather than the unanimity of all four estates, was asserted. This was a far-reaching claim, whose objective was to attack the privileges of the nobility. The other three estates wanted to undermine noble privileges generally and noble wealth in particular, but the nobles appealed to queen Christina. Since she was already contemplating abdication, she chose to support them for her own reasons and the crisis came to nothing. Though its powers were not increased, the *riksdag* emerged unscathed from the crisis in 1650, but a generation later, in 1680, a similar constitutional crisis produced a rather more successful outcome for the other estates and ended with the curtailing of noble privileges exercised through the aristocratic-dominated council (*riksråd*).

In some countries even local representative institutions enjoyed significant fiscal powers. The estates of Languedoc were the most important provincial representative institution in the parts of France known as the 'provinces with estates' (*pays d'états*). They met more regularly, and for longer periods, than any other assembly in the country. Since the fifteenth century, they had also possessed an essential feature of genuine representation: a third estate composed of representatives of the towns that was twice as numerous as the combined estates of the clergy and nobility; voting was by head and not by order. It did not take many defections from the first two estates for the third estate to be left in control of proceedings. The vote of the estates of Languedoc was necessary to raise money for the monarchy, and the way this vote went tended to influence the size of money grants in other provinces such as Brittany, Burgundy and Provence. Thus in some years during the ministries of Richelieu and Mazarin the grants from the estates were derisory or else not forthcoming at all. A variety of political skills was required to control the meetings of the estates of Languedoc (and to a lesser extent, those of Brittany, Burgundy and Provence) which suggests that even in France local representation was more than a charade.

However, the French pattern of representation was uneven: in less than a quarter of the territory ruled by the king of France did provincial estates meet regularly, possess permanent officials, vote taxes for local purposes or prepare lists of grievances (*cahiers*) when they considered that the fiscal demands of the central government were excessive. In origin, all the provincial assemblies were meetings of the three estates, but this had ceased to be true by the early modern period. In Provence, the three estates were not summoned after 1639 and they were replaced by a unicameral Assembly of Communities. In some provinces—Dauphiné after 1628 and Normandy after 1655—the estates ceased to be summoned at all. It is sometimes suggested that Michel de Marillac, the Keeper of the Seals from 1626 to 1630, wanted to abolish the provincial estates altogether, but the evidence is insubstantial. It rests on his attempt to establish financial tribunals called *élections* in Languedoc, Dauphiné, Burgundy and Provence in 1628; but it is by no means clear that he saw the *élections* as replacing the provincial estates. After Marillac's fall from office in 1630 his policy was in any case reversed, and most provinces which already enjoyed a significant degree of representation retained their estates until the end of the *ancien régime.*

6.2.3 *Estates and Federal Constitutions: the Example of the Netherlands*

In the Burgundian lands during the fifteenth and early sixteenth centuries, the central representative institution—the States General—was weak. It was overshadowed by the provincial states because they, not the States General, controlled the levy of taxes. The States General was no more than a meeting of delegates from the provincial states; and the new territories which Charles V won in the north-east were not even represented there. Nevertheless, it met more regularly than any other representative institution in Europe during the reign of Charles V, and in 1534 it showed sufficient resolve to reject his idea of a close defensive union of the Burgundian provinces, a union whose main purpose was to make regular financial contributions and to raise a standing army. Philip II would have preferred not to have summoned the States General at all, but he had to concede regular meetings in the first half of his reign. Then in 1576 it took the initiative and seized power in a *coup d'état* following the death of Requesens, the governor-general, and the mutiny of the Spanish army (see chapter 3.2.4).

The events of September 1576 altered the entire history of the States General, and indeed of representation in the Low Countries. Henceforth associated with rebellion, it would never again be trusted by the government in Madrid. (In 1634, Philip IV said that representative institutions such as the States General were 'pernicious in all times, in all ages, and in all monarchical governments without exception'.)[75] After the southern provinces capitulated to Parma's army of reconquest in the 1580s, the independence of the northern provinces was reflected in the subsequent development of separate representative institutions in the north and the south. Technically, the States General at Antwerp merged with the assembly of the provincial states forming the Union of Utrecht. In the south, any general representation was sporadic after the reconquest; the States General of the Spanish Netherlands met only four times after the revolt, in 1598, 1600, 1612 and 1632, and its influence on the government was insignificant. Although provincial representation remained alive, it was incapable of withstanding the ruler's demands for money, and the presence of a considerable standing army meant that taxation became heavy and arbitrary. For example, in the years 1578–88 the states of Flanders were excluded arbitrarily from the control of the 'aids'—the most important tax, which was levied on movables in one of the richest parts of the Spanish Netherlands—and it was not until the relative decline of Habsburg power in the seventeenth century that it was able once more to assert its position.

In contrast to developments in the south, the States General of what became the United Provinces retained the central position in the constitution which it had acquired in the *coup* of 1576. Twenty-two seats were shared by the seven provinces, and in principle provincial delegates had to reach unanimous decisions. In practice, however, the States General was a congress for the delegates (some of whom were regular attenders over many years, while others were short-term appointments) from semi-autonomous units, the provinces, which jealously guarded their right to make all crucial decisions. The aim of the Union of Utrecht (1579) had been to achieve co-operation between the provinces, while allowing each to retain its separate identity. This balance was difficult to achieve at times of crisis, when the provinces tended to divide according to their perceived self-interest. Minorities were coerced (Zeeland was forced to agree to peace with Spain in 1648 and with Portugal in 1661) and ultimate power remained with the provincial assemblies of the wealthiest provinces. After 1616, the province of Holland paid over 58 per cent of the Republic's annual expenditure. Without its political and economic preponderance (which materialized after the loss of Flanders and Brabant in the 1580s), it is hard to see how this form of government could have been made to work at times when there was no forceful provincial governor (stadholder). During the regime of Johan de Witt, councillor pensionary (*raadpensionaris*) to the States of Holland from 1653 to 1672, Holland's economic predominance gave it control of the Republic's foreign policy.

The Dutch Republic was a unique political phenomenon, but it was not a 'republic' in the sense of resting on an extensive representative system. It has been estimated that as few as 2,000 families participated in the electoral process. Rural areas were represented only in the provinces of Friesland and Groningen. Nor, unlike the estates of the German principalities, was the States General of the United Provinces dominated by the nobility. In Holland, the nobility held only one vote in the states, whereas the towns had eighteen; only in Gelderland, Overijssel and Utrecht did nobility and towns enjoy equal representation. The towns did best out of this system (as they did in Castile) and in Holland and Zeeland especially, they were the dominant political force. Somehow the aims of the Union of Utrecht were achieved, namely that the provinces should 'hold together eternally in all ways and forms as if they were but one province' but that they should do so 'without prejudice to the special and particular privileges, freedoms ... and all other rights of each province and of each town ...'[76]

Elsewhere, there was a general tendency towards fewer sessions of parliaments by 1660—this was true of the States General in the Spanish Netherlands, the *Reichstag*, and the estates in most of the German principalities. In a few countries, such as in France after 1615, and Castile after 1665, representation at a national level had fallen into abeyance. In contrast, the States General was a permanent assembly of deputies sent by the seven provinces of the Dutch Republic. As a form of government based on persuasion, the Dutch model was almost unparalleled, and it is scarcely surprising that it was regarded as the most effective representative institution in early modern Europe. The constitution is sometimes known as the Dutch regent regime: the regents were members both of the municipal councils and the provincial states; they became increasingly self-confident and assertive with the growing economic success of the Dutch Republic. Sir William Temple commented in the reign of Charles II: 'it cannot properly be styled a commonwealth, but is rather a confederacy of seven sovereign provinces united together for their common and mutual defence, without any dependance [*sic*] one upon the other ...'[77]

6.3 Royal Administration

No simple formula can describe the administration of the various European monarchies because of the great complexity of each system and the wide differences between them. For example, England had a parliamentary system of government by the mid-seventeenth century which largely precluded heredity of offices but allowed political parties to develop. France was the complete opposite; it had a strongly monarchical government which had systematized the sale of offices since the reign of Francis I. Political parties, which were considered little more than factions, were frowned on—Jean Bodin thought them 'dangerous and pernicious in every sort of Commonweal'[78]—but could not be prevented. The French system was more common in early modern Europe—but the complexities of the constitutional traditions, and the social and economic structures of the various European states were sufficient to make each regime unique, whether or not the term 'absolutist' is apposite for several of them.

Despite some signs of bureaucratic tendencies in several parts of Europe, the growth of offices and an office-holding class was more advanced in France than in the other European dynastic states in the period. But the French system was not particularly 'modern' in outlook: it was pervaded by patronage and faction, a legacy inherited from the Middle Ages. French patronage relationships have frequently been described as ties of fidelity, with a fundamental emotional bond of loyalty. The client (*créature*) vowed total allegiance to his patron, who in return placed confidence and trust in his client and offered opportunities for advancement and protection. But an examination of the evidence shows that the types of relationship were more varied than this simple pattern suggests. Clients moved on from one patron to another to further their careers. A client, with his patron's consent, might become the client of his patron's patron: thus multiple allegiances became commonplace, and the transfer of allegiance was predictable when the political fortunes of the first or main patron declined. This system could not produce the impartial and non-political civil service which was the ideal of the nineteenth century and, indeed, the concept of bureaucracy itself was unknown in the seventeenth century.

There were, of course, dangers for the crown in dispensing offices as political favours. In sixteenth-century France, great nobles could amass so many offices and such power that they became, in their own localities, more dominant than the monarchy. It was to avoid this build-up of independent regional power that a different class, the local notables—usually office-holders who had been recently ennobled—were deliberately cultivated by the monarchy in the seventeenth century to tame the independence of provincial *Parlements* and estates. The crown and its ministers thus used patronage in the outlying provinces to help achieve political integration. It is difficult to disentangle the ties of patronage, which are by their very nature elusive, but they were the vital force through which the French system of government could operate, not the formal systems of administration with which they existed and which are more easily described.

6.3.1 *Ministerial Decision-Making*

Few European monarchs lived up to Bodin's view of what the absolute ruler's power should be, 'giving laws unto the subjects in general without their consent'.[79] Even in those states such as France, Spain and England which Bodin considered 'truly royal' it is clear that the king's powers could be severely limited by increasing age, decreasing capacity for work and lack of innate ability. Few French kings in this period were as able as Francis I and Henri IV; no later Spanish kings rivalled Charles V and Philip II. It is perhaps fortunate that in most European dynastic states the ruler did not operate alone; he lived within the constraints provided by the constitution and the power of other social or corporate groups. Bodin was correct in grouping together France, Spain and England, for they shared some common characteristics. One was the delegation of power by their rulers to a chief minister in the 1620s, respectively Richelieu, Olivares and

Buckingham. The inability of kings to control the complexities of seventeenth-century government single-handedly made the case for a chief minister persuasive, although the post never became institutionalized. Richelieu and Olivares owed their elevation to their close personal relationships with the monarch, as did their successors, Mazarin and Don Luis de Haro. But there were always strong objections and political drawbacks in delegating such extensive powers to a single subject, which led certain rulers to resume personal control. After about 1660, opposition to the office of chief minister seems to have been in the ascendancy in the west European monarchies, despite the practical advantage of easing the burden of personal responsibility on the monarch. Both Louis XIV and Philip IV after 1661 proved that it was possible for the king to rule without a chief minister. The Emperor Leopold I also ruled without a chief minister after the death of Portia in 1665.

In the period 1620–60, however, chief ministers often succeeded in eclipsing and dismantling the power exercised by other ministers, whose positions were established much earlier. The signs were most obvious in France, where some of the traditional offices of state were in decline in the seventeenth century. The posts of Constable and Admiral were abolished in 1627, early in Richelieu's ministry. French Chancellors had at times been heads of government, notably Cardinal Duprat during Francis I's reign and Michel de l'Hôpital during the regency of Catherine de Medici. However, the disgrace of a Chancellor such as Aligre in 1626 and of his temporary replacement, the Keeper of the Seals—Marillac in 1630—led to a decline in the importance of the Chancellorship. This was to become apparent during the long tenure of Pierre Séguier (1635–72)—particularly after Louis XIV's declaration of personal rule in 1661. Certainly the French Chancellor's power bore no comparison with that of Axel Oxenstierna, the Swedish Chancellor between 1612 and 1654 (see chapters 4.1.3 and 5.1.5).

The great offices in Spain, like those in France, were also suffering a loss of status. Already in 1520, when the Constable and Admiral were made joint regents with Adrian of Utrecht, it was an exceptional delegation of authority by the king which was made to win over the Castilian aristocracy during the revolt of the Comuneros. In 1526, Mercurio Gattinara, Charles V's Chancellor, lost the struggle for influence when his advice about Francis I's untrustworthiness was rejected. He helped to abolish his own office, for, in pique, he refused to affix the seals to the Treaty of Madrid. Consequently, Charles V was forced to perform this task himself, and was heard to mutter that it was the last time he would ever have a Chancellor.[80] There were no more Chancellors after Gattinara's death in 1530. Instead, power was transferred to the two most important secretaries, Nicolas Perrenot, lord of Granvelle, and Francisco de los Cobos. The office of state secretary developed first in Spain, but England and France soon followed: the powers of Thomas Cromwell and Florimond Robertet under their respective monarchs, Henry VIII and Francis I, were soon comparable to their Spanish counterparts.

The transition from secretaryships such as these to full-blown ministries was not a rapid or inevitable process, however. It depended on the constitution of a country, the measure of independence which officials were allowed, and external political pressures on the state. There were twelve royal councils involved in the government of seventeenth-century Spain, a much more rigid governing system than in France. The councils acted with a large measure of autonomy, since the king rarely attended their meetings. Ministerial responsibilities had not developed as fully as in France because of the inflexibility of this conciliar structure and the rigid career pattern, whereby an individual usually proceeded by carefully regulated steps from one level of the hierarchy to the next. Olivares tried to circumvent the councils with special committees or juntas (see chapter 4.3.2), the most important being the so-called *Junta de Ejecución* set up in 1634 to replace the most important royal council, the council of state, as the effective policy-making body. However, the councils sabotaged the work of the juntas and few talented outsiders succeeded in penetrating the charmed circle of officials. The juntas were abolished and the council of state and other councils recovered their full powers after 1643. The growth of Spanish ministerial autonomy was thus abruptly curtailed.

In contrast, ministers and secretaries of state in seventeenth-century France had greater independence of the king's council. The French conciliar structure was less rigid than the Spanish and it was modified significantly in the seventeenth century. A formal council of state (*conseil d'en haut*) came into being by 1643, with its origins in Louis XIII's reign. This met in the presence of the king and issued decrees called *arrêts en commandement*. Other sections of the king's council met without the monarch and issued decrees known as *arrêts simples*. After 1600, the French secretaries of state were in effect office-holders, who bought and sold their positions. However, the post of minister was distinguished from the secretaryships because it could not be bought and sold, but was held by letters patent from the king. Some secretaries of state were never made ministers and consequently they were not called to attend the council of state, while some ministers were appointed before they purchased the office of secretary of state. Thus the rigid and hierarchical career pattern which had developed in Spain did not obtain in France.

Gradually, the remit of French secretaries and ministers became more specialized. In the sixteenth century, responsibility for the French provinces was shared out among the secretaries, and foreign affairs were divided between them on a country-by-country basis. By 1626, the formal division of the French provinces remained, but foreign affairs had been concentrated in the hands of one secretary, and military affairs in the hands of another. Ministerial responsibilities developed more slowly. A war minister was in charge of French intervention in the Thirty Years' War in the 1630s, subject to the guiding influence of Louis XIII and Richelieu. Foreign affairs had been the concern of the chief minister, and it was not until after 1661 that this responsibility developed into a fully-fledged ministerial position in France. The post of superintendent (*surintendant*) of finance had emerged at the time of Sully, and was filled continuously from 1619 to 1661. This official was in an anomalous position, since he was not always a minister, nor was he a secretary of state.

Different arrangements prevailed in Sweden. There, the aristocratic-dominated council (*råd*) had asserted in the fifteenth century that the king should rule 'with the council's counsel' in a form of aristocratic constitutionalism.[81] But the ruling dynasty preferred to rely on secretaries for the purpose of state administration, and in the sixteenth century the nobles campaigned against this policy. By the 1590s, some members of the council were proclaiming that the 'old freedom' of the nobility destroyed by Gustav Vasa should be restored. In March 1600, however, Charles IX had five council members executed, and for the rest of his reign the council's constitutional functions were drastically reduced. The accession of Gustavus Adolphus with full powers to rule during his minority was achieved in 1611 only at the price of an accession charter, and other arrangements, which restored the position of the *råd*, removed the influence of the king's secretaries, and gave the upper aristocracy the political and economic power they had been seeking. These gains were confirmed and extended in the Form of Government of July 1634, issued during Christina's minority, although many of its ideas had been discussed two years earlier by Gustavus Adolphus and Chancellor Oxenstierna. Under the terms of this document, the government of the realm was entrusted to a twenty-five-man council which included the five great officers of state. The detailed administration of the country was to be carried out by five colleges: the supreme courts, the admiralty, the war council, the chancery and the exchequer. Sweden's collegiate system of government was a completely different development from administrative practice in France or Spain, but was to be influential in northern Europe, especially in Russia.

6.3.2 *The Role of the Nobility in Government*

Although the nobility often played a prominent role in many European states in the early modern period, nowhere was it a united class, operating with a common purpose or with shared ideals. The term 'nobility' covered a variety of men with widely disparate resources in money and land, different religious practices and dynastic ambitions; in many countries, too, they split into rival power blocs in opposition to one another. Their interests often worked counter to those of the ruling house and they tended to resist any moves by the ruler to limit or alter their role in the constitution of the state. In eastern Europe, the lack of trained personnel resulted almost inevitably in a government dominated by the nobles. It is probably overstating the case to argue, as one historian has done recently, that the boyars' role in the government of Muscovy was so great during the reign of the allegedly autocratic Ivan IV that the Tsar was not actually in control of the political and administrative structure.[82] This seems incompatible with autocracy, but the boyars certainly formulated policy in the council (*duma*), organized the administration and served as a group in the supreme court. They provided the generals, governors and ambassadors; and their deliberations were particularly important in foreign policy. The *duma* could fluctuate greatly in size, reflecting the relative size of the boyar group, which held a monopoly on appointments to the council. There were twelve or thirteen boyars in Ivan III's *duma* in 1462 but only five or six at the end of his reign in 1505. Vasilii III seems to have left seven trusted boyars in charge of the regency on his death in 1533.

The considerable variations in the size of this important governing group reflects its instability and consequently a lack of long-term security in the Muscovite state. Individuals or whole families could be removed at a stroke by autocratic rulers or by demographic accident: it is striking that only 28 of the 62 families in the pre-1645 council were left in the *duma* by 1668. Although they were not immune to abrupt changes of fortune from above, the boyars seem to have been impervious to assault from below. The growth of a service gentry holding fiefs in the sixteenth century has been observed by historians, but this new social group failed to gain an entry to the *duma*. It was the rise and fall of different factions and family relationships which determined policy, a policy characterized by inconsistency. It is difficult to trace these changing allegiances, since no written record was kept of the *duma*'s sessions and the main evidence for its participation in the legislative process was the formula attached to decrees that 'the Tsar ordered and the boyars affirmed'.[83] But however imperfect was the boyars' role in government, there was no alternative until an educated state service nobility took over the administration of Russia.

In Poland, all nobles were theoretically equal in status; but in practice great differences of power, wealth and social status existed at an early date. Some rulers, notably Ladislas IV, hoped to strengthen the position of the crown by playing on these gradations and building up a royal party among the gentry (*szlachta*), although his scheme to establish a chivalric order in 1637–8 met with little support. The king had the dominant power of patronage in appointments to the sixteen offices of state and to most military positions, which he could use to reward his followers. The *hetman*, the commander of the army, was one such appointment, and by the seventeenth century he exercised considerable influence in foreign policy. But since most of these appointments were made for life, their turnover was very slow; only a few nobles could benefit, and the offices thus became the monopoly of a handful of great families. This fact, perhaps more than any other, tipped the balance against the monarchy in the seventeenth century and in favour of growing magnate power. The Polish rulers were unable to broaden the range of their patronage to take in a wider spectrum of the nobility. This led to unrest, and magnates, including even the *hetman*, demonstrated their independence of the monarchy by rebellion, joining the so-called confederation movements (*rokosz*). The nobility came to dominate political life not only at the centre but also in the local lawcourts and assemblies (*sejmiki*), which grew in importance in the seventeenth century. This magnate domination was based on their extensive landed estates and the build-up of their private armies, both of which the king was powerless to prevent. Nor was he able to open up the nobility by recruiting new men from outside to serve as his officials. Access to the nobility was severely restricted after 1601, because it was dependent on the ratification of the diet. There were few naturalizations of foreigners, and less than 2,000 ennoblements took place between 1569 and 1696, even though noble status was usurped illegally on a widespread scale.

Although aristocratic privilege was less entrenched in Sweden than in Poland, the great noblemen monopolized the most important offices and the same families tended to dominate the council (*råd*) in successive generations. When Gustav Bonde was called to serve in the council in 1727, he was the twentieth member of his family to sit there in unbroken succession. On an earlier occasion, in 1648, when a case between the Oxenstierna and Bielke families came before the council on appeal, it was found that almost all the families represented there were related either to one party, or to the other, or to both, and could not therefore be impartial. The nobility tried to preserve its dominance in the Form of Government of 1634, which stipulated that during the minority of queen Christina there would be no alienations of crown lands, ennoblements or naturalizations of foreigners. But in the ten years following the declaration of her majority in 1644, Christina went on a spree of ennoblement, doubling the number of noble families and sextupling the number of counts and barons. She cynically sold off crown lands and noble titles to droves of army officers, Germans, Dutchmen, Scots and anyone else who could afford them.

The reaction against such an improvident policy quickly set in, but the leadership did not come from the greater nobility. It was the lower estates in the *riksdag* of 1650 who demanded that appointments be made on merit, rather than as rewards to adventurers of the Thirty Years' War. In 1655, the year after Christina's abdication, a partial resumption of crown lands was ordered. Five years later, the Addition to the Form of Government stipulated that appointments be made on merit 'so that no one be excluded on grounds of humble birth, nor advanced solely on the grounds of social standing . . .'[84] No longer did the great nobility have the monopoly of office-holding in the Swedish government. But there had always been a problem with filling the more menial posts. The sale of offices was not practised in Sweden and up to the 1650s the country, like Muscovy, lacked a suitably trained personnel. Thereafter, this educational backwardness seems to have been corrected, but the lower nobility who filled these posts expected to be paid regularly and to gain career advancement through public service. By 1660 the Swedish nobles were calling for a Table of Ranks so that no one 'shall be able to usurp the precedence of another'.[85] When it was adopted in 1680, the Table of Ranks was essentially a victory of the lesser nobility over the upper aristocracy.

The ranks of the nobility were much more clearly distinguished in Germany than elsewhere. One group, the Imperial knights (*Ritterschaft*), held their fiefs directly from the Emperor. But they were vulnerable to the growth of princely power: electors, dukes, landgraves and margraves sought for reasons of self-interest to incorporate such autonomous lordships within their jurisdictions. The *Ritterschaft* formed regional leagues in the later Middle Ages to counteract this trend, and maintain their independence. Even as late as 1522–3, leagues were being formed at Landau in the Rhineland and Schweinfurt in Franconia. The principal social objective of the knights was, however, not to preserve their territorial rights against the princes, but rather to attack the privileges of the cities and the 'mighty ruling men' (*grosse Hansen*) found there. The cities, they claimed, 'harbour under Imperial law and the constitution of the Empire the worst robbers and usurers of the German nation'.[86] One of the noble polemicists, Eberlin von Günzburg, proposed in *The Order of Knights* that the Emperor should appoint nobles to the councils and ambassadorships 'and not allow any Tom, Dick or Harry, any drunks, clerks or financiers to arrange matters of the highest import to the Empire'.[87]

Furthermore, the traditional position occupied by the Imperial knights in the government of states was under attack from below. In the fifteenth century, they had complained about the activities of jurists trained in Roman law who moved from one territory to another for career advancement in the service of the princes. There had been only five German universities in 1400, but there were eighteen by 1520, turning out an ample supply of well-trained graduates to fill the available posts. There was thus little reason for the princes to employ ill-educated knights. In any case, the knights had contradictory aims; they wished to maintain their independence from the princes yet they wanted to be paid for employment in their service. In the larger principalities such as Brandenburg, Bavaria and Saxony, the knights proved feeble opposition. But in Franconia and the Rhineland, where the territorial states were fragmented, knightly resistance was stronger.

In 1522–3, Franz von Sickingen and Ulrich von Hutten launched their misguided attack—known as the Knights' War—on the elector of Trier. Both the leaders were Lutherans, and since Sickingen's castle at Ebernburg was a centre of the Reformation, there clearly was a religious motive (see chapter 1.2.1), but politics were uppermost: the elector of Trier was thought to be a supporter of France. Sickingen had far-fetched dreams of carving out a Franconian duchy for himself. But the knights showed themselves to be hopelessly divided. Two hundred of them turned out to support the bishop of Würzburg against Sickingen. There was no co-operation between the Rhineland and Franconian knights, and both movements were defeated. This military débâcle dashed the prospect of the Imperial knights securing separate representation in the Imperial diet.

Yet they did not suffer a loss of political prestige or independence as a result of their defeat. It would be a mistake to see the majority of the knights of Franconia as cast in the mould of Sickingen and Hutten. Most of them had no radical ideology. They wanted merely to create a political organization which would reinforce their claim to social exclusivity: for them the term 'free knighthood' (*Ritterschaft*) was demeaning, since it carried a connotation of subjection; instead they used the term 'obedient vassalage' (*Lehenleute*).[88] The Imperial diet considered them 'subordinate to no elector, prince or other authority' except the Emperor.[89] In the course of the sixteenth century, this view was given support by the Emperor himself, when he appealed directly to the league of Franconian knights for subsidies to assist his wars against the Turks. Paradoxically, the very independence of the Franconian knights seems to have helped secure their position within both princely councils and the cathedral chapters. The weak and divided secular rulers of Franconia lacked sufficient coercive power to force the knights to recognize their sovereignty within a 'modern' closed state with defined boundaries; in contrast, the Bavarian dukes had succeeded in doing this with their knights as early as 1495. The independence of the Franconian knights was recognized by Emperor Rudolf II in an ordinance (called the *Ritterordnung*) of 1590, and remained sacrosanct until the end of the Holy Roman Empire.

Elsewhere in western Europe, the upper nobility gradually lost its political predominance in the early modern period with the growth of the power of the state. Aristocratic factions had dominated the royal council of Castile for much of the fifteenth century, but after 1480 the great nobles were not allowed to vote on matters of state. The crises of 1504–6 and 1516–22 demonstrated that the power of the nobility had not been extinguished, and the grandees—as they were known from the reign of Charles V—were once again excluded from the council. Thus by default the university-trained jurists (*letrados*), drawn largely from the lesser nobility (*caballeros* or knights), were left in charge of government business. Their rise to political prominence was helped by their exemption from taxation in the later Middle Ages, a privilege confirmed by Charles V in 1547. They came to dominate the sixty or so posts of *corregidor*, the royal officials who controlled administration and justice in the towns. Before the *letrados* gained this monopoly of office, the poor quality of appointments had made the *corregidores* deeply unpopular (which was a contributory factor in the Comunero rebellion: see chapter 7.5.4). This improvement in appointments was only temporary, however. By the seventeenth century, the *corregidores* represented the interests of powerful local families rather than those of the king. Many had dubious connections: the official in Murcia in 1647 protected local bandits from prosecution and actively participated in the lucrative contraband trade with Portugal.

The rise of the educated lesser nobility in sixteenth-century Spain was the result of the ready availability of higher education. The number of universities in Castile had risen from two in the Middle Ages to twenty by 1620; in addition there were thirteen in the kingdom of Aragon. This made Spain one of Europe's best-educated nations, producing graduates in large numbers for jobs which were in short supply. Not only graduates but law professors, too, were regularly recruited into the church and the royal administration. The twenty-four judges (*oidores*) of the *Chancellería* of Valladolid, the oldest, most respected and most important of Castile's royal courts, were required to be *letrados*. Exactly half of the hundred councillors who served Philip IV in the council of Castile (1621–65) were former university professors. Most had come from northern Spain to serve in Madrid and were from families which had been ennobled over at least the previous three generations. Over three-quarters of the councillors had also served for some time in one of the other councils such as the council of finance or council of the Indies. The monopoly of the *letrados* was complete in Philip IV's council of Castile. Jurists were also appointed to the five *Audiencias*, or courts of appeal, but they did not achieve a monopoly of the posts there. At first sight, these appointments would seem to have raised the standard of judicial administration, but more importantly, they opened up office-holding to a wider social spectrum. However, the growing professionalism of the Spanish judicial officials led to a weakening of royal control. The king as chief justiciar had previously appointed frequent visitations to root out judicial corruption; by the seventeenth century, the judicial office-holders were left to their own devices. The result was that, as Olivares observed in a secret memorandum to Philip IV in 1629, justice had fallen into 'almost total abandon'.[90]

Clearly Spain was well on the way to achieving an office-holding nobility. A commentator in the early years of Carlos II's reign (1665–1700) lamented that there were 'offices as if those who occupy them had bought them' and 'dignities made into inheritances or sales'.[91] The crown sold offices in Castile as a ready source of revenue. Between 1621 and 1640, office sales yielded over 90 million ducats, nearly 18 per cent of all revenues. Important parts of royal administration and royal justice were sold off, or made over, to the cities and provinces, and the sale, and especially the heritability, of offices gave the cities a large measure of self-government by the seventeenth century. Direct ennoblement was relatively unimportant because Spanish titles were expensive to purchase and their creation was unpopular. Between 1465 and 1516, almost a thousand individuals, mostly drawn from the larger towns, gained access to the lesser nobility by purchase of offices. But this process of ennoblement was abruptly halted by Charles V, who tried to maintain the exclusivity of the nobility by revoking previous concessions in 1523 and prohibiting any new grants. Only 272 patents of nobility were issued between 1552 and 1700, of which about 250 were sold (see chapter 7.2.1).

6.3.3 *The* noblesse de robe *in France*

The market for offices in Spain was significantly large, but its scale was staggering in France, where venality came to assume outstanding importance. The number of offices in France rose from over 4,000 in 1515 to over 46,000 in 1665; the amount of capital then invested in them was estimated at over 419 million *livres*, equivalent to four or five times the annual revenue of the French monarchy. As a result of ennoblement through office, a significant new class, the *noblesse de robe*, emerged to challenge the political power, if not the social predominance, of the nobility of ancient lineage who followed the career of arms (the *noblesse d'épée*). The latter had dominated the king's council for much of the sixteenth century. The councillors of Francis I and Henri II were princes of the royal blood, dukes and peers, great officers of the kingdom, cardinals and marshals of France. By the second half of the century, although the high nobility retained its majority in the small inner council, it had lost its dominance over the larger councils which dealt with routine administration. As late as 1594, four great nobles including Constable Montmorency-Damville sat on the finance commission of the council. But after 1598, apart from Sully, who was a rather special case because he was a Protestant, the king's council was dominated by the *noblesse de robe*.

It was not simply a matter of the overwhelming numerical strength of the office-holding nobility which pushed the *noblesse d'épée* out of their administrative positions. The factious behaviour of the upper nobility during the wars of religion had resulted in their exclusion; the frequency of aristocratic conspiracy and rebellion in the seventeenth century served only to make this exclusion permanent. When individual great nobles were admitted to the council of state, this was usually during a period of relative royal weakness such as a minority: for example, during the minority of Louis XIV, Gaston and Condé were summoned to the council. In just over fifty-four years of personal rule (1661–1715) Louis XIV appointed only seventeen ministers to his inner council, which never had more than five members at any one time. Of these seventeen appointments, a mere two were drawn from the upper nobility. The offices which remained open to them in the seventeenth century were provincial governorships and military commands (which were purchased) and honorific functions at court. Since virtually none had any legal training, they were unsuited for the relatively sophisticated administrative tasks which had already developed in the seventeenth century. The lesser nobility, or gentry, in the provinces also lacked a legal education and thus they and their sons were also prevented from seeking a career in the administration or the lawcourts. They had to content themselves with the church or the army.

As in seventeenth-century Spain, it was those who had a university education in the law who did best out of the growing bureaucracy of the French state. Lawyers (*robins*) gained a monopoly over the secretaryships of state, in the sections of the king's council dealing with routine administration, in the provincial intendancies established in the 1630s and in the sovereign courts. (The lesser courts were rarely staffed with university-trained jurists.) By the early seventeenth century, remarkable examples of office-holding dynasties had already come into being. The Phélypeaux family provided a succession of nine secretaries of state between 1610 and 1777, though it was exceptional for this type of position. The Nicolay family provided nine first presidents of the *Chambre des Comptes* of Paris in continuous succession from 1506 to 1791.

In France, an office was fully accepted as a piece of private property which could be bought, sold and transmitted in family settlements, just like a plot of land. Already in 1521, Francis I declared that 'most of the offices of the kingdom, of all types, are owned in expectancy'.[92] The historical progression towards this attitude dated from the fifteenth century, when a holder could resign his office to his heir, who held an expectancy (*survivance*). There was no objection from the monarchy to *résignations*, but its concern was first to keep some track of those who were in possession of a particular office, and second, to raise some revenue from it. By 1534 Francis had introduced the notorious '40-day rule', which declared resignations of offices invalid, and subject to forfeiture, unless the owner survived forty days after making the act of resignation. The procedure was difficult to police but obviously inconvenient to the office-holder. The rule occasionaly produced a windfall to the crown by way of forfeiture, but generally any financial benefit to the crown from venality in the sixteenth century arose from the creations of new offices. After 1604, Henry IV and Sully suspended the 40-day rule for office-holders on condition that they paid an annual tax equivalent at the outset of the scheme to one-sixtieth of the value of the office. So arose the notorious annual right or *droit annuel*, also known as the *paulette* after Charles Paulet, the financier who ran the scheme in 1604-5.

The crown regarded the *droit annuel* as a privilege which it was prepared to extend in return for more money. The original grant was first extended to 1618 and then renewed for nine-year periods in 1620, 1630 and 1638. On each occasion, however, the crown extracted forced loans from the office-holders. By 1648 their patience with this policy of exploitation was exhausted: the terms for the renewal of the *droit annuel* proved to be one of the most important factors in the outbreak of the Fronde (see chapter 4.4.3). In the long term, the office-holders won their case, since the crown was forced to concede the *droit annuel* during and after the Fronde on less onerous conditions than originally proposed. There has been much debate as to why the scheme was first introduced in 1604. It may to some extent have had a political purpose, for it removed offices from the clientage network of powerful magnates such as the Guises, who had manipulated the system to build up their following in the Catholic League in the sixteenth century. On the other hand, the political advantages of systematizing the sale of offices in the long term seem slight. The scheme actually increased the independence of office-holders, except when the *droit annuel* was up for renewal, a time which was itself dangerous for the monarchy. The fiscal advantages of the scheme are much more evident. Between 1600 and 1654 some 648 million *livres* were received by the *bureau des parties casuelles*, the special treasury set up to administer revenues from office-holding. This constituted over 28 per cent of ordinary revenue of the crown for the same period. At the peak of the fiscal exploitation of office-holders (which seems to have occurred in the 1620s and 1630s), revenues from this source represented over half the ordinary revenue of the crown.

Historians have frequently stressed the damaging effect of the sale of offices on the French administrative structure. In an effort to increase revenues, one existing office might be divided into two or even three. For example, two chief treasurers (*trésoriers de l'Épargne*) in the 1590s administered the funds of the crown in alternate years. Later, three offices were created out of two, and after 1645, there were four treasurers. Another revenue-raising expedient was time-sharing of offices. Rival groups of office-holders might be created in the same court, each serving for half the year. This was extremely unpopular, and caused the government grave political difficulties when it attempted to introduce this policy in the 1640s at the *Parlements* of Aix-en-Provence and Rouen. The proliferation of offices of no administrative value at the lower level of the office-holding establishment both complicated and weakened the structure of administration in France. After 1583, for example, urban fishmongers were required to buy their businesses, because they had been turned into offices.

The crown received a capital sum from each new office it sold but there was a long-term recurrent cost to be met: the payment of an annual salary to the incumbent. The capital raised from sales is difficult to estimate because it was managed by financiers who took a significant cut from the profits. Moreover, the market in offices, like any property market, might become glutted from time to time, which could cause a shortfall between the theoretical value of the office and the actual price received on sale. The value of all offices in France rose with inflation in the course of the sixteenth century, and some rose much more than the general level of prices. But though the crown obtained entry fees from each new office-holder, it could not benefit from the rise in values. The main beneficiary was the individual who resold his office for a straight profit on the private market: Louis XII was alleged to have said that 'those who purchase office sell retail at a high price what they bought cheaply wholesale'.[93]

Under these circumstances, it was difficult for the French government to make any progress towards reforming the administrative structure. For one thing, to buy out the office-holders the crown would have had to pay inflated valuations which would have been impossible in financial terms. Any attempt to buy them out on reduced values would have been impossible politically. Consequently, few French offices were abolished. They were simply circumvented by the crown, which relied on new institutions to displace and outstrip the old. Yet long after they had ceased to be of service to the state, the old offices lingered on as fossils. Even after the introduction of the provincial intendants in the 1630s, no group of officials was abolished. All that happened was that another layer was added to French bureaucracy, with the intendants supervising financial officials such as the *trésoriers de France* and *élus* who formerly had administered the chief direct tax, the *taille*. The *Parlements* and other sovereign courts felt threatened by 'a new establishment of executive justice in all the provinces of the kingdom' (their description of the intendants);[94] but in the longer term they probably suffered little or no loss of authority since the intendants were prohibited from interfering in the detailed business of the courts (called the *juridiction contentieuse*). Disputes between one court and another had to be settled by the king's council.

The system of office-holding had to be continued for financial and political reasons which had nothing to do with the administrative needs of the crown. It had become an important part of French society. Frenchmen preferred to buy offices rather than to invest in commercial and industrial activities, a fact noted by foreign observers. Sir George Carew, the English ambassador, remarked in 1609 that 'merchants employ their money rather in buying offices than in exercising traffick [that is, trade], because officers' wives go before merchants' wives'.[95] Office in the lesser courts did not ennoble its holder and was consequently less prestigious and less expensive. Most of the important offices in France, however, provided gradual ennoblement over three generations. Before a man could enjoy noble status, it was necessary for his grandfather to have held office for twenty years, or to have died in office, and for his father to have done likewise. This was the case in the sovereign courts, the *Parlements, Cours des Aides* and *Chambres des Comptes*. There were also certain offices which conferred instant personal nobility on their holders and subsequently on their heirs, although twenty years' tenure of office was usually required. In addition, there were ennoblements by letters patent, sold by the crown as a source of revenue but revoked periodically because excessive sales reduced the number of taxpayers paying the *taille*. (Francis I sold at least 153 in his reign. There were a thousand or so ennoblements in the province of Normandy alone between 1550 and 1650.)

In the sixteenth century, oral evidence was accepted as sufficient proof of nobility. A man calling himself *noble homme*, who lived like a noble and was regarded by others as a noble, could enter the ranks of the nobility without difficulty in France. The usurpation of nobility was thus widespread. It cannot be assumed that all office-holding families fulfilled the rules for gradual ennoblement. By the 1660s, when the definition of nobility was made more precise, many such families had undoubtedly achieved it. Written evidence was then required to prove nobility, and paradoxically, the *noblesse de robe* was often in a better position to prove its claim than some families of ancient lineage. Lawyers, after all, kept records. The dates of purchase of offices were usually known from original surviving deeds of title; if not, the records of the court to which the office-holder belonged could be consulted. In contrast, the *noblesse d'épée* rarely had the documentary proof of their titles, which had been held by long usage 'since time immemorial'.

It is sometimes said that the French *noblesse de robe* had ambitions to seek a separate status from the old nobility as a fourth estate of the realm. Indeed, Montaigne said as much in an essay written in 1572. However, although the term *noblesse de robe* was sometimes used by contemporaries (but not by Montaigne) to describe this category of office-holders, it had no juridical status. No fourth estate was established, not least because it is clear that office-holders wanted to be fully assimilated into the ranks of the second estate, the traditional nobility, to which they aspired. Gradually they assumed the characteristics of the older noble class, until by the later eighteenth century the two were almost indistinguishable. It became increasingly difficult to draw any sharp distinction between families whose sons pursued a legal career as against the profession of arms, and indeed both careers might be found in the same family. What would have been unthinkable before 1660 was no longer unusual; the French social hierarchy was more open to newcomers than it might at first appear from the rigid formality of the court.

6.4 The State and Military Revolution

There was probably no year that was entirely peaceful in Europe between 1450 and 1660. Exactly why war was such a permanent feature of life in early modern Europe is a matter of conjecture. Machiavelli considered war the natural activity of princes, while Hobbes thought 'all men that are ambitious of military command are inclined to continue the causes of war, and to stir up trouble and sedition: for there is no honour military but by war . . .'[96] Even the growth of diplomatic activity in Renaissance Europe did not restrict the recourse to war. Indeed, Erasmus considered it a contributory factor: 'among so many treaties and agreements which are now entered into, now rescinded, who can lack a pretext of going to war?', he asked.[97] The nature of the European dynastic state required that rival claims of inheritance be defended through warfare. In the words of one modern historian, 'political Europe was like an estate map, and war was a socially acceptable form of property acquisition'.[98] It was also through systematic warfare, and superior military technology, that western Europe asserted its ascendancy over the rest of the world in the age of expansion (see chapters 8.4.2, 8.4.3 and 8.4.4).

6.4.1 *The Size of Armies and Changes in Military Tactics*

Historians have argued that the period 1560–1660 witnessed a military revolution, which had two main aspects: a series of tactical changes, which had a profound impact upon European warfare; and a new concept of strategy, which envisaged war upon a much broader scale, fought by incomparably larger armies. Leaving aside the very large Ottoman and Muscovite armies (which fought with outmoded technology, by western standards), the French army represents the trend. Charles VIII invaded Italy with a force of 30,540 men in 1494; in 1555 the French army was said to number 50,000 men and by 1635 150,000 men, though the actual figure was significantly lower, perhaps by as much as a half. The total force under the command of the Spanish Habsburgs was thought to be double the size of the French army in 1555 and 1635. The Dutch Republic and Sweden also had sizeable armies of around 50,000 men each in 1635. The Dutch had mobilized 77,000 men at the time of their offensive in 1629.

For the most part, these well-rounded figures were simply those given to the various European kings and their ministers in papers presented by their military strategists. They may have been good paper estimates; but the real army strength in the field was invariably much lower. Statistics of army size in the west European monarchies are bedevilled by high rates of desertion and the abuse of false muster papers, by which commanders corruptly pocketed the pay of fictitious troops. Despite these handicaps, there seems to have been a perceptible increase in the estimated size of armies between the 1530s and 1550s, and then again after the 1570s. To some extent, this reflected the contemporary military requirement for more infantry. More important, perhaps, was the perception that armies were the means to place pressure on entire states—Alba's rule in the Netherlands (1567–73), and the imposition of the Edict of Restitution on large parts of Germany in 1629–30 by the armies of Tilly and Wallenstein, were new political developments which required larger forces to back them up. A further factor was the increasing reliance of armies, particularly in the seventeenth century, on the 'contributions' system—this amounted to a licence to exact cash payments not just from the enemy, but also from neutral or even friendly territory, at well above the rates required for the basic subsistence of the army. These 'contributions' could only be exacted under continuous and heavy military pressure: Wallenstein contended that he could support an army of 50,000 men in Germany by such methods, but not an army of 20,000.

Nevertheless, the active fighting element of these armies invariably formed only a small core of the total number of troops billeted on a state. At Breitenfeld in 1631, 41,000 Swedes and Saxons under Gustavus Adolphus fought Tilly's 31,000 men: but this was a uniquely large-scale fighting force for a single battle before the 1660s. As successive campaigns devastated the theatre of war, it was usual for the numbers of troops to fall, since the alternative was their starvation. The battle of Freiburg was fought in 1644 between armies of about 17,000 men, while Jankau the following year involved Swedish and Imperial forces of only about 15,000 men. These were smaller armies than had fought a hundred years earlier: Charles V had mobilized 50,000 men for the siege of Metz in 1552, while Philip II had raised 45,000 men for the St-Quentin campaign five years later. Even Henry VIII had managed to send over 11,000 troops into France in 1523. There was no sustained increase in the size of armies on the battlefield as distinct from those on campaign before the reign of Louis XIV. Thus in one significant respect it can be argued that there was no military revolution.

Was there a revolution in military tactics? Certainly, there was an increase in firepower. This was clearly discerned in the 1520s, when at La Bicocca in 1522 and Pavia in 1525 respectively the Swiss and the French suffered crushing defeats at the hands of the Spanish harquebusiers, who operated in conjunction with artillery from prepared positions. After the disastrous defeat of the French at Pavia in 1525 there was a noticeable decline in the size of cavalry units in relation to infantry—they rarely exceeded 20 per cent of the total armed force thereafter. Commanders naturally wished to maximize their firepower, and to do this they had to reduce the size of infantry units from 3,000 to between 1,500 and 2,000 men. Without this reduction, the troops at the back of the formation would obstruct one another, and the time taken for successive discharges by each row of soldiers would exceed that required for the first rows to reload. It was dangerous to allow the unit to be extended in long lines, because the musketeers would then be too far away from the protective body of pikemen. The reforms instigated by Maurice of Nassau at the end of the sixteenth century, further reducing the size of infantry units from 1,500 to 500 men, seem to have been too drastic. Gustavus Adolphus was orginally persuaded of the apparent advantages of the small unit, but experience in East Prussia in 1626–9 taught him that such formations were dangerously fragile. As a result, the Swedish army at Breitenfeld in 1631 and Lützen the following year was deployed in larger brigades, which had greater cohesion and striking power, and units of between 1,500 and 2,000 men held their own against the military reformers in the 1630s. Where a decline in these units' strength occurred, it was less the result of conscious military planning than the inability of governments to secure the recruitment and maintainence of full-strength companies.

Though the figures of casualties may be disputed, there can be no doubting, for example, the heavy French losses at Pavia in 1525 and St-Quentin in 1557. On the first occasion, they were at least 2,200 (excluding drownings in the river Ticino), while there were reports of 10,000 and even 14,000 Frenchmen killed. There were fewer deaths on the second occasion—though at least 2,500 French soldiers were killed—but perhaps an even higher number of prisoners was taken. Such disasters were so costly that it is surprising that commanders were prepared to risk their forces in pitched battles. But illness was a much more frequent cause of death than action in battle. Dysentery and the plague wrought more devastation than the musket (though wounds might lead to fatalities weeks or even months after battle). Relatively minor wounds were rendered more dangerous by the absence of permanent military hospitals. The first such establishment, with a staff of 49 and some 330 sickbeds, was at Mechelen in the Low Countries in 1585. This was the sole example in Europe for almost a century. Progress in caring for the wounded was pitifully slow and is symptomatic of the low standing of the military in the eyes of civil society.

The increasing effectiveness of infantry resulted in a predominance of the defensive strategy. On some fronts, such as the Low Countries after 1621, set-piece battles virtually disappeared; protracted sieges took their place. Even before the truce of 1609, battles had been few in relation to the military effort: Nieuwpoort in 1600 and Kallo in 1638 were the last of their kind. The war on this front was characterized more by sieges such as those leading to the fall of Breda to the Spaniards in 1625 and its recapture by the Dutch in 1637. With the exception of the first siege of Breda, the Dutch towns were not starved into submission; rather, the defensive walls were mined. Spínola's siege of Bergen-op-Zoom failed in 1622 because the shafts and emplacements were ineffective. In other theatres of war, however, the garrisons were indeed starved into submission, but the process took so long that a besieging army risked defeat by a relieving column unless it took care to defend itself by means of fortification.

On other war fronts, where there was a less dense network of fortifications, or where there were none at all, relatively rapid and aggressive military progress could be achieved. In eastern Europe, apart from one or two new fortresses such as Smolensk, and the defensive works around certain key ports such as Danzig, there was little evidence of the Italian-influenced angle bastion or *trace italienne* (see chapter 2.1.2). As a result, there were relatively frequent large-scale military combats in the struggle for Livonia before 1630 and in Germany during the Thirty Years' War. Even in Germany, however, generals still tended to fight cautious, defensive campaigns. Strategy tended to be reduced to a crude concern with territorial occupation or at least its denial to the enemy. After his victory at Breitenfeld in 1631, Gustavus Adolphus did not attempt to end the war with a definitive thrust against the Austrian homelands; instead, he sought to expand the 'contributions' levied by his army billeted in the Rhineland. Battles were about the control of territory with supply potential—in the case of Breitenfeld, Gustavus sought to deny Tilly's army the opportunity of using Saxony for 'contributions'. No single military victory, not even those of the Habsburg forces at Nördlingen in 1634, or the French forces at Rocroi in 1643, brought a peace settlement in its wake. Battles were not related to a state's war aims in such a direct way. No state possessed the fighting power to force another to the negotiating table and to accept its peace terms.

6.4.2 *The Organizational Control of Armies*

Why was military pressure such an imprecise instrument of state power in this period? The fundamental reason must be seen to be the administrative and financial inadequacies of the state in wartime. The system of tax collection was geared essentially to peace conditions, which made it impossible to raise large sums of money at the appropriate points in the military calendar—such as spring recruitment, the initial campaign, autumn disbandment and winter quarters. The mechanics of paying an army abroad proved beyond the capacity of most governments, even assuming that they could raise sufficient revenue in the first place. These difficulties were overcome, at least in some measure, by employing military contractors for the purpose. These were the descendants of the mercenary captains (*condottieri*) in the Italian wars, of whose campaigns Machiavelli commented that they were 'commenced without fear, continued without danger, and concluded without loss'.[99] The jibe seems neither accurate nor fair. The methods of the *condottieri* had to be adopted by the French, German, Swiss and Spanish invaders before they could hope to make headway against the Italian states.

Almost all the European rulers followed the practice of employing foreign troops under the command of experienced captains. Dutch and Italian gunners were hired for the English campaign in France in 1523, and companies of handgunners and demi-lances were raised by Flemish and Italian captains trusted by the English government. It was said that for the 1544–5 campaign Henry VIII had hired 'depraved brutish foreign soldiers from all nations under the sun ... Scots, Spaniards, Gascons, Port[uguese], Italians, Albanians, Greeks, Turks, Tatars, Germans, Burgundians [and] Flemings'.[100] This polyglot force was raised for military intervention on a relatively small scale! Really significant armies of occupation required much more substantial mercenary organization: it was Wallenstein's unique logistical genius, and his possession of the rich duchy of Friedland, that enabled an army of 100,000 men to be placed at the service of the Emperor Ferdinand II. On a much smaller scale, the French paid Bernard of Saxe-Weimar 4 million *livres* a year between 1635 and 1639 to enable him to maintain an army of 18,000 men in the field. Foreign troops were recruited systematically in the seventeenth century even in eastern Europe: Tsar Michael Romanov had some 17,400 foreigners in his service in the 1630s, while his son Alexis employed some 60,000 by 1663.

Was there a link between the development of the absolutist state and the employment of a mercenary army? Machiavelli commented on the fate of the Italian communes that 'it is more difficult to bring a republic, armed with its own arms, under the sway of one of its citizens than it is to bring one armed with foreign arms'.[101] At first sight, it seems paradoxical that monarchs concerned with defending their sovereign power should have relied upon armies raised by private contractors who might act with excessive independence. The assassination of Wallenstein in 1634, perhaps on the orders of the Emperor, is a case in point. Louis XIII's treaty with Bernard of Saxe-Weimar is another: had he produced a male heir, Bernard would have established his own dynastic state in Alsace. Only the accident of his death in 1639 left the French king with the benefits, rather than disadvantages, of the alliance and provided the opportunity to assume direct French rule in Alsace. Even Spain, which was the most successful military power in Europe for the longest period of time, did not control royal officials directly after the 1580s. The financial problems under Lerma resulted in the abandonment of direct administration of all branches of military organization after 1618; the Habsburgs never succeeded in permanently regaining it. In purely administrative terms, the Spanish government became less, not more, absolute as a result of its military successes.

The danger was that the fighting commitment of armies might be seriously diminished by reliance on mercenary commanders. Battles seem to have been won and lost on the wings of the fighting forces, enabling the victor to outflank the main body of the enemy. Without the commitment provided by elite forces, embodying a national reputation for which they were prepared to make a far greater sacrifice than their opponents, battles would tend to be bloody but indecisive. The problem with mercenary troops was that if they were unpaid, they would not fight, and the opportunity for a tactical advantage would be lost: the unpaid Swiss in Henri IV's army slowed down his reconquest of France in the 1590s. Mercenaries of the same nationality might appear on both sides with unpredictable consequences for the battle. At Dreux in 1562, the Swiss 'soldiers of the two armies meeting, bullied each other with their pikes lowered without striking a blow', while the German Protestants 'fired, as it were, in the air' rather than kill their co-religionists.[102]

Whereas ordinary soldiers discontented with their lot had no choice but to desert, mutiny was the privilege of elite troops. Two of the greatest military atrocities of the sixteenth century—the sack of Rome in 1527 and that of Antwerp in 1576—were committed by unpaid mercenary armies. There were 46 mutinies in the Spanish army of the Low Countries, 5 in the years 1572-6, 37 in the years 1589-1607. Italians mutinied at Pont-sur-Sambre and Zichem in 1593-4, and were joined by Irish, Walloon,

Burgundian and other discontented comrades. At Zichem, it was said that thirteen different languages were spoken in the camp. Some 480 Italians, 104 Spaniards, 42 Irish and 20 Germans were among the 1,927 men involved in the mutiny at Weert in 1600–2; while at Diest in 1606–7, there were 618 Italians, 191 Germans and 97 Spaniards among the 4,052 men. In each case, Walloons were a dominant force among the rebels. In origin, it seems, the method of mutiny in the Low Countries was perfected by Spaniards and Germans, but it was later copied by other 'nations' in the army of Flanders.

The unreliability of mercenaries meant that arming the domestic population might seem to be preferable. But contemporary opinion was divided on the merits and disadvantages of a native force. Claude de Seyssel argued in 1519 that some mercenaries were necessary so that a native, and potentially revolutionary, infantry would not become too numerous. Justus Lipsius, however, contended that only tyrants had anything to fear from arming the native population; since in his opinion bad government alone led men to rebel, wise rulers had nothing to fear from subjects prepared for military service. Giovanni Botero considered that the republic of Venice and the duchies of Savoy and Tuscany all possessed a domestic militia which had 'never been known to rebel or riot, to loot the countryside, attack towns, fight in the streets, disturb the public peace or do any other harm'. He therefore concluded that 'a ruler should train his subjects in the use of arms'.[103] Though Botero was undoubtedly well informed, he himself admitted the difficulty experienced by the French kings in attempting to establish a native infantry force. The militia of the fifteenth century 'committed so many murders and robberies' that Louis XII employed the Swiss instead; Francis I had reformed the militia in 1534, but this 'dwindled away'; Henri II in turn reformed it in 1556, 'but with little success, owing to its disorderliness and bad administration . . .'[104] Thereafter, the permanent establishment almost disappeared during the wars of religion. Even in the seventeenth century, there was great reluctance among Frenchmen to serve abroad: Richelieu contended that the mere rumour that a unit was to move into Germany could reduce its strength by half overnight. The absence of a large domestic army might thus result not from any fear on the part of the ruler of arming the population, but from the difficulty in recruiting and organizing an army levied in this way. Peasants and the unemployed might well be prepared to join the army as a form of subsistence when the alternative was starvation, but they could not provide a trained and experienced elite army. Mercenary captains who held their subordinate officers together over successive campaigns dealt with this problem at a price: there is not much doubt that the military record of relatively small elite forces deployed against much larger (but less well trained) armies was an impressive one.

6.5   The State and Financial Revolution

Historians and sociologists have stressed the modernizing influence of war on the financial organization of the state. Seventy years ago the German economist Schumpeter argued that the sixteenth century witnessed a transition from a state based on a demesne economy (*Domänenstaat*) to one based on taxing the princes' subjects (*Steuerstaat*). This now seems too simplistic a model, applicable more to the German principalities than, for example, the kingdom of France, where direct taxation had already become permanent in the *pays d'élections* after 1439. Some historians have argued that the term 'finance state' (*Finanzstaat*)—a state dominated by a new financial apparatus, and dependent on the services of merchant bankers and financiers—is more applicable, and have held that this constituted the first stage towards the development of the modern state. Finally, and most recently of all, it has been suggested that certain states experienced a 'financial revolution', with the Habsburg Netherlands under Charles V, and later England after the Glorious Revolution, as the prime candidates. Such a view tends to exaggerate the extent of innovation. In this period most states made relatively little progress in managing their financial affairs.

6.5.1   *The Growth of State Revenue*

The growth of state revenue has been highlighted as one of the direct results of the impact of warfare on the early modern state. It was most marked in sixteenth-century Castile, where it rose from about 847,000 ducats a year on Isabella's death in 1504, to about 2 million a year in 1523 and almost 13 million a year by the end of Philip II's reign in 1598. Thereafter, not only did the annual revenue of the crown of Castile fail to grow, it actually fell in 1608 and 1621, when the figures were respectively 11.5 and 10.5 million ducats a year. In the same period, net French revenues rose from 3.5 million *livres* in 1497 (1.7 million ducats) to 5.2 million *livres* (2.5 million ducats) in 1523 and 15 million (4.5 million ducats) in 1596. Significantly, however, whereas Castilian revenues failed to expand in the seventeenth century, French revenues grew consistently, gross revenue amounting to 20.5 million in 1600 (6.2 million ducats) and reaching nearly 32.8 million *livres* in 1608 (9.9 million ducats) and 42.8 million in 1621 (12.75 million ducats). Moreover, with the declaration of war against Spain in 1635, French revenues continued to expand, averaging some 115 million *livres* a year (35 million ducats), although much of this came from borrowing at very high rates of interest. There are no figures in this period for net French revenues after the costs of the borrowing requirement had been deducted, though one method of calculation would reduce the average income to 56 million *livres* a year (just under 17 million ducats). If increased revenue alone won wars, France should have beaten Spain easily in the war of 1635–59.

In both countries, a distinction was made between those revenues which were classed as ordinary and those considered extraordinary. It was assumed that the king had greater control over the former than the latter, but in many ways the distinction was quite arbitrary: in Botero's words, recourse 'must be had to extraordinary taxes, which then often become ordinary'.[105] The historian is more concerned with the proportion of state revenue provided by direct and indirect taxes, although this is partially concealed by the two classes of revenues. In Spain, among the ordinary revenues the *alcabalas* or sales taxes produced between one million and 2.9 million ducats a year in the period 1559–1621, oscillating between 20 per cent and 30 per cent of total Castilian revenue. Among the extraordinary revenues, the grant of the *Cortes* of Castile, the *servicio*, taken together with the new supplementary tax, the *millones*, rose from 0.4 million ducats to 2.4 million a year in the same period, from about 13 per cent to about 23 per cent of total revenue. The trade taxes—customs duties, border customs levies and taxes on wool exports, which were all ordinary revenues—combined with the mastership (*maestrazgo*) of the three military orders (Santiago, Calatrava and Alcántara, which were extraordinary revenues) produced another growing annual revenue, which rose from 0.69 million to 2.42 million ducats, holding constant at about 23 per cent of total revenue. The 'Three Graces', an extraordinary revenue from ecclesiastical taxes (*Cruzada, subsidio* and *excusado*), yielded an increasing amount, too, rising from 0.3 million ducats to 1.4 million, about 12 or 14 per cent of total revenue. Finally among the significant sources of extraordinary revenue, the Indies provided large sums which oscillated wildly between 0.3 million and 2.6 million ducats, amounting to 12 per cent of total revenue in 1559 and 10.5 per cent in 1621. These proportions conceal the fact that the rate of tax increase varied greatly over the period: taxes tripled in the 1560s and 1570s, but barely kept pace with inflation in the 1580s and 1590s.

Variations in the proportions of total revenue between direct and indirect taxation are more difficult to discern in the other European countries over the same period. In France, we know that quite sharp fluctuations could occur in the relative importance of different revenues over short periods during the first half of the seventeenth century. Thus the chief direct tax, the *taille*, paid by the larger part of France known as

the *pays d'élections*, oscillated between 16 per cent and 60 per cent of
ordinary revenue and 10 per cent and 50 per cent of total revenue in the
period between 1600 and 1654, calculated on the basis of five-year
periods. Similarly, indirect taxes—chiefly levies on the sales of items such
as salt and drink—fluctuated between 18 per cent and 33 per cent of
ordinary revenue, and between 8 per cent and 26 per cent of total revenue,
in the same period. Shifts in ministerial policy accounted in part for these
fluctuations, but taxes were also vulnerable to outside events. Thus,
indirect taxes such as the *gabelle*, the salt tax, were easier to collect in
peacetime than in time of war, when consumption fell. The mainstay of the
French treasury was the *taille*, 'our only certain revenue', as d'Hémery, the
finance minister, called it in 1647.[106] Yet even this tax fell into massive
arrears by 1642 as a result of the rapid increases to help pay for the war
effort.

In an age of inflation, rulers had to increase revenues in the sixteenth
and seventeenth centuries simply to stand still. A fivefold increase in
revenues in the sixteenth century would still barely keep up with rising
military costs (tables 8.1 and 8.2), assuming that one of the main expenses
of keeping an army in the field was feeding it. Wars seem to have varied
greatly in their cost as a proportion of the state's revenue. Some wars, such
as France's invasion of Milan in 1515 (which accounted for 36 per cent of
the kingdom's annual revenue), were relatively cheap; the Spanish war
effort in the Netherlands in the 1590s seems sustainable at some 40 per
cent of revenue; even the French mobilization of 1523, the English
intervention in the Netherlands in 1585, and the Venetian war against
Austria in 1615–17 amounted to only 50 per cent of revenue. These costs
were high enough, bearing in mind that peacetime revenues were normally
fully committed to expenses such as court salaries, building and administrative costs and defence. In other cases, it seems difficult to see how the
war could have been sustained, particularly when it amounted to the
totality of the state's annual revenues—this was the case with Florence's
subsidy to the Holy League against France in 1526, Venice's wars against
the Turks in 1537–40 and 1570–3, and the French war against Charles V
in 1554. Even more disastrous were those wars where the costs escalated
out of all proportion to a state's revenue—Nuremberg's war against
Brandenburg in 1550 was the leading example, where war cost the city 1.5
million *gulden* a year against a revenue of only 170,000. Siena lost its
political independence to Florence in 1555 because it had exhausted itself
financially in war; the greatly increased costs of fortification resulting
from the revolution in military techniques coupled with the impact of
inflation were more than the Sienese exchequer could withstand. Equally
serious, if proportionately less costly, was England's war against France in
1544, where the estimate of war expenditure—£250,000—was already a

problem, since it equalled the annual revenue; however, the estimate
proved hopelessly unrealistic, for the real cost turned out to be nearer
£650,000.

6.5.2 *The Development of a Consolidated Public Debt in Western Europe*

The creation of a public debt large enough to meet interest payments, so
that the state did not default on its obligations, was a remarkably elusive
objective for the west European monarchies of the sixteenth century. The
problem was not a new one and it had been faced first in the Italian
peninsula. Already in 1262, the Venetian Republic had promised lenders
an annual interest of 5 per cent and had specified that certain excises
would be set aside for meeting these interest payments and only then
could they be used for other purposes. This was a relatively precocious
development which was not followed elsewhere in the Italian peninsula,
where on the whole wars were financed by forced rather than voluntary
loans. After 1434, Florence had relied on 'dowry' loans (loans for a
fifteen-year period, on which the accumulated capital and interest
provided a daughter with a handsome dowry), while in the 1530s, Venice
began introducing life annuities. The first long-term debt (*Monte*) was
issued in the Papal States after 1526. By the 1550s, two types of share
(*luoghi*) were issued in the public debt, and were sold as a form of annuity:
one type ceased to be effective on the death of the original lender (who
was regarded as the proprietor of the share capital 'invested'), and it
carried a high rate of interest; a second type of annuity was heritable but
carried a lower rate of interest. Public confidence was secured by Papal
guarantees that shareholders would not suffer a confiscation of their
investment for any reason whatsoever, even in the event of their com-
mitting a crime, whether spiritual or secular.

North of the Alps, life annuities were relied upon relatively frequently
as a financial instrument by the leading cities and provinces of the
Burgundian lands: Ghent, for example, had issued them by the last quarter
of the thirteenth century. Faced with increased taxation and spiralling
costs such as those of fortification, cities in the Low Countries issued life
annuities on a significant scale in the fifteenth century. By the 1530s,
Amsterdam spent in excess of 60 per cent of its annual income on
servicing the interest on these loans; the figures were lower at Dordrecht,
Gouda, Haarlem and Leiden, but in none of these places was the figure
below 40 per cent. In 1515, six cities in Holland, including Amsterdam,
issued heritable annuities at 6.25 per cent interest which were secured
against the ordinary tax levy (*aide ordinaire* or *ordinaris bede*) of the
province. There were another thirteen such issues before 1534, which
resulted in an accumulated interest charge of the equivalent of nearly a

quarter of the gross ordinary tax revenue. The outbreak of the war with France in 1542 led to the establishment of a new excise and land tax payable to the central government and a series of annuities funded from these new revenues, which were collected and disbursed by the provincial representative institutions. As the costs of war continued to rise, so the interest rate payable on annuities had to be increased, from 6.25 per cent in the issues in 1543, to 8.33 per cent in those of the 1550s. At the same time, the regent and her advisers abandoned the custom of the forced buying of annuities: this resulted in an extraordinary increase in voluntary purchase, and a much more effective tapping of urban capital to help fund the debt. Only with the ending of war in 1559 could the process of redeeming these annuities begin: by 1566, the province of Holland, for example, had brought its interest charges to a level well within the combined income from the excise and the land tax. If one of the hallmarks of the modern state is a capacity to carry forward a long-term debt that exceeds its annual income without threat of bankruptcy, then at the provincial level at least, that test of modernity had been achieved in the Netherlands in the 1550s. Indeed, its most recent historian has termed it a 'financial revolution', which was subsequently exported to England only in the 1690s.

Elsewhere, the success in establishing a long-term funded debt was more faltering. In 1522, Francis I introduced heritable annuities at 8.33 per cent throughout the French kingdom, which were secured against the revenues of the municipality of Paris; they were therefore known as *rentes sur l'hôtel de ville*. The interest payments were entrusted to municipal officials from the same social background as the lenders, so that the system was based on a measure of trust, but even so it was used sparingly for the rest of Francis I's reign. Henri II was much more profligate, raising 6.8 million *livres* from such sales in a relatively short reign of twelve years (1547–59), whereas his father had raised only three-quarters of a million from this source in twenty-five years (1522–47). This was as nothing compared to the sales during the period of the wars of religion (25.9 million between 1559 and 1574 alone), and consequently the market became saturated. In Castile, the equivalent financial instrument, the *juros*, increased from a capital value of 5 million ducats in 1515 to 83 million by 1600, much of the growth resulting from the conversion of short-term loans after royal bankruptcies. By the seventeenth century, both of these governments found themselves in difficulties trying to honour interest payments on the funded debt. Between 1629 and 1648, a 5 per cent *juro* gave an effective return of only 2.3 per cent per annum. As the French government was forced both to issue new *rentes* in the 1630s and 1640s and to cut interest payments, it is not surprising the capital value of the investment fell dramatically. By 1641, an annual *rente* of 1,000 *livres* which in 1634 ought to have been worth 14,000 *livres* was selling at a mere 4,000 *livres*, only 28 per cent of its capital value.

6.5.3 *The Reliance on Short-Term Loans*

It seems that by the 1550s, most European monarchs who were engaged in serious warfare could no longer pay for it out of ordinary revenue. They had to borrow in order to sustain the campaigns. In the crisis year of 1552, Charles V's borrowing and the interest payable on his loans both reached record levels. Faced by the invasion of Henri II in alliance with the German Lutheran princes, he had to borrow 3.6 million ducats in Castile, twice as much as in the two previous peak years of 1543 and 1546. This was more than the amount of bullion annually imported from the New World, then averaging 2.36 million ducats a year, though bullion imports in the years 1551–5 paid for the new borrowing (11.8 million as against 8.2 million ducats). However, Charles was also borrowing on the Antwerp money market, where it is estimated that his debts in 1552 stood at another 1.5 million ducats. The crisis of that year enabled the Genoese to assert their dominance as Charles's merchant bankers in Castile, ousting the Germans from their previous monopoly. As the Emperor piled up debts, dwarfing those made by his son in the earlier part of his reign (when allowance is made for inflation), it is scarcely surprising that Henri II of France responded in kind. In 1555, when the Lyon 'great contract' (*grand parti*) was established, Henri's debts stood at 4.6 million *livres*, upon which interest at 16 per cent was guaranteed. By the beginning of 1558, the debts had risen to 12.2 million, and the king was unable to find money to pay the interest, since the revenues allocated for this purpose had been diverted towards the war effort. At his death in 1559, the king owed 16.5 million *livres* (about 7.3 million ducats) at Lyon, the interest on which cost some 3.2 million. The figure was more or less the same as Philip II's debts at the time of his first debt-rescheduling operation in 1557 (7.5 million ducats). Although both France and Spain headed independently into their financial crises, they did so at a similar time and for comparable reasons.

The solution was to reschedule the debt. In the case of the Spanish monarchy, this essentially meant altering the balance between short-term and long-term borrowing, and converting high-interest earning loans (*asientos*) into lower-interest earning bonds (*juros*), usually at 5 per cent interest. After 1557, debt rescheduling became the standard practice in the Spanish monarchy as a technical device to overcome indebtedness. Decrees (*decretos*) suspending or modifying payments were issued in 1560, 1575, 1596, 1607, 1627, 1647, 1652 and 1662. After 1666, this procedure was abandoned by the monarchy, but from the reigns of Philip II to Carlos II there was virtually a separate branch of the treasury dealing with debt conversion. It may seem surprising that merchant bankers were still prepared to lend money to the government given the risk. Yet, usually after protracted negotiations, the bankers were encouraged to proceed by obtaining more favourable terms in a document called the *medio general*: the decree of 1575 led to a settlement just over two years later, while the negotiations begun by the decree of November 1596 were brought to an end in February 1598. In any case, preferential treatment was nearly always meted out to certain important merchant bankers (the Fuggers in 1557–8, 1575 and 1596, and Lorenzo Spínola in 1575, for example), usually those who were prepared to advance new loans (see chapter 8.3.4).

Spanish practice was more systematic than that elsewhere, but the French monarchy similarly rescheduled its debts in 1559, 1598, 1648 and 1661. The policy was less clear-cut, since there was no simple conversion from short-term to long-term borrowing. Nearly 2 million of Henri II's debt was paid off in 1562–3, but at the price of contracting new loans; about 9 million of the short-term debt was still outstanding in 1563–4, and remained so for long after. Outstanding debts in 1598 were considerably higher, while loans revoked in 1648 amounted to about 100 million. The financing of war required credit and brought about a state of perpetual reliance on financiers, whose profits were notorious (see chapter 8.5.1). Financiers were essential to the French monarchy, but the crown was unable to devise a satisfactory system of moderate, guaranteed profits. As a result, absolutism engendered the worst of all possible worlds. It rationalized default on repayment to its creditors in the calling of an extraordinary financial tribunal (*chambre de justice*), most notoriously in 1661. This investigated all financial transactions back to the commencement of the war against Spain in 1635, and ruined some of the more important financiers, whose fortunes had seemed secure only a few months before, by imposing heavy retrospective fines. Absolutism was thus an irresponsible political power whose contractual word was not its bond. High interest rates prevailed, in Colbert's words, because 'the king has no credit . . . people do business with him in the expectation that he will declare bankruptcy'.[107]

6.5.4 *The Diversity of Political and Fiscal Regimes in Early Modern Europe*

There was no single prevailing type of political and fiscal regime in early modern Europe. The 'rise of European absolutism' was a tendency, rather than a uniform development. Relatively few states experienced the sudden change that Denmark underwent in 1660–5, when the estates of 1660 abolished elective monarchy, nullified the act of accession of the ruling king, and placed the making of a new constitution in the hands of

Frederick III. The king's advisers then drew up a document in January 1661, which stated that the king had been accorded absolute power and full authority to decide the order of succession as well as the constitution of the realm; by this instrument, the king's subjects would renounce the rights of criticism and opposition to his rule. The document was circulated throughout Denmark for signature by the representatives of the estates. The king kept a promise to the estates in November 1665 and issued a new constitutional law (*Lex Regia* or *Kongelov*), under the terms of which he swore to maintain the religion of the state (Lutheranism as defined in the Confession of Augsburg); to preserve the realm of Denmark undivided; and to consider the *Lex Regia* as the fundamental law of the realm. Danish absolutism henceforth had something which was unprecedented except in limited monarchies (such as Poland-Lithuania) or republics (such as the United Provinces)—a written constitution.

Denmark should not be taken as the model, for in some absolutist states representative institutions retained their power. In Castile, the power of the *Cortes* actually increased in the first half of the seventeenth century. Here, as in some other states, the crown's need for money guaranteed the survival of representation for a time. Yet in France the monarchy avoided summoning the Estates General after 1614 but managed to increase the fiscal burden on its subjects. The inexorable rise of taxation and royal borrowing in France prompts the question whether a so-called absolute monarchy inevitably, and in all periods, taxed its subjects more heavily than—for example—monarchy limited by parliamentary grant which developed in England. Already in the fifteenth century, Sir John Fortescue had observed that in France—which he called a *dominium regale*—'the king may rule his people by such laws as he makes himself. And therefore he may set upon them such taxes and other impositions as he wishes himself, without their assent.'[108] This he had contrasted with the mixed monarchy of England, which he called a *dominium politicum et regale*. Fortescue was writing in the 1470s, by which time the great significance of the change brought about by Charles VII in 1439 in making the *taille* a permanent tax in the *pays d'élections* was clear for all to see. When the Estates General was summoned in 1468 because of the noble alliance against Louis XI and the threatened loss of Normandy, it discussed matters of high politics but not of royal finance. In the high Middle Ages, the French king had cared little for the consent of his subjects in the imposition of taxes. Thus the divergent paths of England and France in the sixteenth and early seventeenth centuries, with much heavier taxation and public borrowing in the latter than the former, should more properly be seen as a reinforcement of an existing tendency rather than a new development.

But it would be wrong to assume, as English commentators tended to do in the seventeenth century, that the French taxpayers were peculiarly oppressed by their ruler, a 'king of beggars' who had lost their freedom.[109] The French always considered themselves to be free owners of their property, notwithstanding oppressive levels of taxation. François Bernier, for example, a distinguished traveller in the second half of the seventeenth century, contrasted the tyranny (as he saw it) of Moghul India and Ottoman Turkey with the prosperity of France under Louis XIV: 'take away the right of private property in land, and you introduce, as an infallible consequence, tyranny, slavery, injustice, beggary and barbarism . . .', he wrote.[110] Without a political authority, there was no guarantor of family property. France had witnessed the horrors of nearly forty years of intermittent civil war in the late sixteenth century. It is no accident that Bodin's theory of undivided legislative sovereignty had emerged at this time. There had to be a rallying-point, provided by a strong monarchy, to prevent the geographical fragmentation of France and its dismemberment by warring factions. Absolutism can be viewed as a set of arrangements, unique to a particular country, by which the civil power operated to protect private property rights such as those enshrined in public offices and annuities, that had been purchased dearly and whose value could only be guaranteed by the crown. Machiavelli had earlier commented on France that 'people live in security simply because its kings are pledged to observe numerous laws on which the security of all their people depends. It was the intention of the founder of this state that its kings should do as they thought fit in regard to the use of arms and to finance, but that in other respects they should act as the laws required.'[111]

7

POPULATION AND SOCIAL STRUCTURE

THE social structure of early modern Europe, in all its variety and complexity, was a consequence of a mixture of factors: history, prevailing social attitudes and the extent of economic development. 'Structure' is a more helpful term than the term 'class', which tends to imply anachronistic nineteenth-century definitions arising from a market-economy-based interpretation of the period, where the production of material goods and the creation of wealth were dominant. Many older studies, it is true, stressed the decisive role of the middle class in bringing about change in the early modern period, blaming or praising it for such diverse phenomena as the Reformation, the growth of representative institutions and economic expansion. Marxist historical determinism still depicts the revolt of the Netherlands, the English civil war and the French Revolution as 'bourgeois revolutions'. But such concepts are too rigid. Discontented nobles as well as an emergent bourgeoisie played a decisive part in political upheaval, both in the Dutch revolt and the French wars of religion. In most European countries there is little evidence of any consciousness of a dynamic and self-confident middle class, sure of its role and its destiny in society, as was arguably the case with the bourgeoisie in the nineteenth century. The noble ethos, not the values of the middle class, prevailed in early modern Europe. The ambition of the successful entrepreneur was to become a nobleman, not to remain simply a wealthy member of the bourgeoisie. Only in the more advanced economies such as the Dutch Republic and England did so-called 'bourgeois' values prevail in some measure.

Elsewhere in Europe, historians have preferred to describe the social structure in the early modern period less in terms of a class system than of 'orders'. A society of orders is based on social esteem, with rank and honour conferred on particular functions not necessarily related to economic power. 'Everyone knows', it was said at the French Estates General of 1484, 'that the Commonweal is divided into members and estates: the clergy to pray for the others, to counsel, to exhort; the nobility to protect the others by arms; and the people to nourish and sustain the nobles and clergy with payments and produce ...'[1] In the classic three-estate system, fiscal immunity was conferred on those carrying out the functions of prayer and war, which were more highly regarded than the law or trade. Not all the French theorists took the same approach, however. Claude de Seyssel in *The Great Monarchy of France* (1519) distinguished the nobility from middle and lower sections of society within a third estate. But this was untypical. One of the most influential treatises on the society of orders was Charles Loyseau's *Treatise on Orders and Common Ranks* (1610), written nearly a century later. The basic concepts of this work were widely accepted, despite the process of social change, throughout the *ancien régime* in France. Yet the applicability of the concept of a society of orders to other European countries apart from France remains open to question. It would not seem to fit England where the aristocracy and gentry were subject to taxation. Nor was Poland like France, for in the Polish-Lithuanian Commonwealth there were five, not three, estates (*stany*). These were the clergy, nobility, burghers, peasantry and Jews (in Jean Bodin's words, Jewish privileges were 'greater in Polonia and Lithuania than in any other place of the world').[2] In Muscovy, the differences were even greater, since all social groups were dependent on the Tsar, who organized society as his personal patrimony. Instead of estates, Muscovy knew only ranks (*chiny*), such as servants of the Tsar, town taxpayers and country taxpayers.

When the discovery of America brought Europeans into contact with the Amerindians, a mass of literature appeared to explain the differences between peoples in the old world and the new, but few 'anthropological' conclusions of relevance to the European social structure were drawn. There was one exception: Montaigne noted that the Brazilian Indians he had talked to at Rouen had observed the vast disparities of wealth among Europeans. They found it strange, he reported (without further comment), that the poor 'should suffer such injustice and that they did not take the others by the throat or set fire to their houses'.[3] The publication of Sir Thomas More's *Utopia* (1516) helped create a fashion for depicting imaginary societies, but even this genre of writing rarely stimulated plans for drastic changes in contemporary society or government. The prevailing social structure thus seems to have been accepted by the literate and articulate. If men were interested in utopian schemes, it was in the hope that they might produce a formula for creating a harmonious society, not for revolutionizing it. Contemporaries feared anarchy but had no perception of what we would term social revolution. 'Revolution' to them meant circular motion and was largely confined to the context of the rotation (revolutions) of heavenly planets. Contemporaries thought of 'alterations' or 'mutations' in states as being the way forward, not of dramatic change that was consciously willed (as after the French Revolution). Rapid social change was thus feared as giving a licence to anarchy, a fear which had only been reinforced by the terrible experience of the Anabaptist 'kingdom' established at Münster in 1534–5 (see chapter 1.2.2).

7.1 The People of Europe

In modern western society the register of births, marriages and deaths is a fundamental instrument of government. Periodic censuses supplement the routine information gleaned from the registry office. But early modern Europe was in a pre-statistical age, where even the most elementary population figures are a matter of historical controversy. Any modern methods of counting the population were in their infancy in the sixteenth and seventeeth centuries. The requirement of the parish priest to keep registers of baptisms, marriages and deaths dates from 1538 in England and 1539 in France (for baptisms and deaths only). In England, relatively few parish registers survive from before the 1560s or 1570s. In France, while such sources exist for the sixteenth century, they are much more numerous after 1600. In Spain, records of marriages, baptisms and deaths are extant for the second half of the sixteenth century, but their survival is very patchy and the recording of burials was often unsatisfactory. The keeping of such records was, in any case, not part of a general survey of the population. In France, the ordinance of Villers-Cotterêts of August 1539 required registers to be kept: this was not to inaugurate a statistical enquiry but to facilitate the verification of the rights of parties to a lawsuit. Despite the legislation, French record-keeping was far from systematic or accurate. Jean Bodin noted in 1576 that 'the registers are not kept as they ought; this law is ill observed'.[4]

To carry out a census of the population requires a relatively developed administration, which was beyond the capacity of most of the European states. The Italian cities and their successor states were the most sophistic-ated administrators of their populations in this respect. Florence carried out a superb survey (*catasto*) as early as 1427 and others in 1551, 1558, 1622, 1642 and 1672. The Castilian government undertook surveys fairly regularly, too, in 1528–36 (revised in 1541), 1561, 1586, 1591, 1597 and 1646. Of these, the fullest for the sixteenth century was the census of 1591, the purpose of which was to levy equitably a new tax, the *millones*. But in Castile, there was no attempt to establish the total number of inhabitants. Instead of individuals, households (*vecinos*) were counted. To establish the estimated total population, household numbers have to be multiplied by a coefficient (4.5 is usual, but its validity varies from one country to another and from one period to another). This suggests that the population rose from 3.8 million inhabitants in 1528 (856,933 *vecinos*) to 5.9 million inhabitants in 1591 (1,322,292 *vecinos*). It is not certain that any

French census of households or hearths (*feux*) was held in the period, though one had been carried out much earlier, in 1328. There may have been enquiries of sorts in 1636 and 1664, but the first even reasonably reliable one was as late as 1698. For administrative purposes, the French government relied simply on the list of towns and parishes. The Estates General of 1576 was told that there were 27,400 towns and parishes; a government enquiry established that there were 33,226 in 1624 to which a further 2,360 were added as a result of the territorial acquisitions between 1628 and 1662. No reliable population estimate could be provided from such a statistic, however, since the unit of measurement varied from the humblest parish to the largest town. (Nevertheless, a coefficient of around 110 hearths per parish has been suggested, which would give a population of about 17 million in 1624, which seems rather low.) Only in the areas of land tax (*pays de taille réelle*) in the Midi were accurate lists of hearths kept at parish level; these registers (*compoix*) were revised at irregular intervals.

7.1.1 *Population Levels and Family Structure*

The difficulty in estimating population in even the more advanced western European monarchies compels a cautious approach to the attempts to calculate the population for Europe as a whole and its relationship to the world population. It has been suggested that the European population stood at around 70 or 80 million in 1500 (though one estimate puts it as low as 42 million) and then rose to around 100 million by 1660. The world population in about 1650 is estimated at 470 million, but this can be no more than guesswork. Even within Europe itself it is impossible to estimate the population level accurately for large tracts of the European landmass: Bohemia, Hungary and the Balkan area are particularly difficult for the historian. In a period when the population was growing, there were significant differences in the demographic performance of different regions and countries. The population of all the Ottoman lands may have risen from 12 or 13 million in about 1520–30 to 17 or 18 million by 1580, but thereafter the figures are unreliable. The Ottoman lands in Europe are thought to have comprised respectively 5.6 and 8 million out of these totals. There is an estimate of 13 million inhabitants for Muscovy in 1651. The population of the Polish-Lithuanian Commonwealth is thought to have risen from 7.5 million in 1500 to 11 million in 1650, which made it the most populous European state after France and Muscovy. The figures for the other European countries in table 7.1 can be no more than estimates, but they suggest that the population of western Europe rose from nearly 62 million in 1500 to 78 million in 1600, with some decline in the following half-century.

Table 7.1. Population estimates for certain European countries (millions)

	1500	1550	1600	1650
Scandinavia	1.5	1.7	2.0	2.6
England and Wales	2.6	3.2	4.4	5.6
Low Countries	2.35	2.9	3.1	3.9
Germany	12.0	14.0	16.0	12.0
France	16.4	19.0	19.0	20.0
Italy	10.5	11.4	13.1	11.3
Spain	6.8	7.4	8.1	7.1
Austria and Bohemia	3.5	3.6	4.3	4.1
Total western Europe	61.6	70.2	78.0	74.6

Note: For calculations of the urban population see chapter 7.4. Population estimates vary considerably. The total for western Europe includes those countries listed above plus Poland, Portugal, Scotland, Ireland and Switzerland.

Source: J. De Vries, *European Urbanization, 1500–1800* (1984).

In Tudor and Stuart England the annual death-rate fluctuated around 26–29 per 1,000 (twice the modern equivalent), the corresponding birth-rate being about 30–35 (three times the modern equivalent). Mainland European birth- and death-rates always seem to have been above 30 per 1,000. The birth-rate in sixteenth-century Castile and Italy was above 40 per 1,000. In Languedoc and Provence between 1500 and 1560, there was an annual growth rate of the population of one per cent per annum, though the rate fell thereafter. In England infant mortality was high, and the average expectation of life at birth was 35 years or less. Life expectancy was lower still on the Continent, no more than 30 years in some areas, as low as 25 in others. It has now been recognized that the growth of population was regulated by factors other than birth- and death-rates, the age of marriage being seen as of crucial importance since normally older women produce fewer children. The trend towards a later age of first marriage, from 25 to 30 years of age for men, and from 23 to 27 years of age for women, should not be antedated; it seems to have occurred only after 1660 in France, for example. Early marriage was more usual among the upper classes than lower down the social scale, where domestic or agricultural service were recognized means for girls to lay up a dowry. Illegitimacy rates fluctuated somewhat from one period to another and varied according to location. Though the rates were generally low, bastards tended to be conceived by the peasantry during a run of bad harvests when marriage plans were put off; a run of good harvests might result in a boom of weddings. Birth control by *coitus interruptus* was probably not widely practised until the eighteenth century and then only among the upper classes.

The fundamental explanation for the increase in the European population after about 1475 would seem to be plentiful (and early) marriages resulting from the greater security of food supply in a period of good harvests and relatively infrequent plague. But the hypothesis cannot be proved because parish registers were not kept systematically in this period. Nevertheless, it is clear that social pressures were directed towards marriage and securing an heir: marriage was the entry requirement for full membership of society since single men rarely assumed charge of family landholdings. Husbands counselled their wives to remarry should they be bereaved. The importance of dowries and financial considerations in marriage was marked in western Europe even at relatively low levels of society, men sometimes seeking wives whose dowries would enable them to discharge debts, or marrying widows to establish a position in business or on the land.

The density of population over the European mainland varied greatly. The most sparsely populated regions lay east of the river Elbe, the traditional geographical boundary between eastern and western Europe. Even in the more densely populated west, there were great differences. Much of the Low Countries had a density of over 40 inhabitants to the square kilometre, but whereas in Brabant and Hainault the figure may have been higher still, in Friesland and Overijssel it fell to less than 20. In France, it seems, the density of population did not rise above 30, and in Germany it was lower. The Italian states had the highest density in Europe. Only Sardinia had an average of fewer than 30 inhabitants to the square kilometre, but the figure was above 50 around Verona and Vicenza and in the kingdom of Naples; around Padua, it was above 60. Long-term pauperization of the peasantry and seasonal migration for employment often resulted from such high levels of population density.

There were also widely varying units of family structure in Europe, which were largely a consequence of social and economic differences. In Muscovy, and elsewhere in the east, three, sometimes four, generations lived together in large family units; marriage occurred early and there were few servants in the household. In central Europe, family structures were different because houses and plots of land were handed down more securely from one generation to another. The heir lived with his wife and children within the household of the head of the family, for whom special retirement arrangements were made when he became too old to work on the land. Lodgers were often taken in and these subsidiary households enabled otherwise impoverished individuals to subsist. The age of marriage was usually higher than in eastern Europe because of these more settled arrangements. A third pattern is that of north-west Europe, with

so-called small 'nuclear' families, each marriage leading to the creation of
a new household; a relatively late age at marriage was the norm and a
significant number of individuals never married at all. In southern
Europe, large family units were more common than in the north-west,
although the small 'nuclear' family still predominated. For Europe as a
whole, it would seem that the degree of integration of the household was
closely related to the pattern of land inheritance, which varied between
the extremes of unigeniture (the eldest, youngest or simply a chosen son
receiving most of the land) and partible inheritance, which might include
or exclude daughters from the landholding (on variations of peasant
tenure, see chapters 7.2.4 and 7.2.5). The size, nature and timing of dowry
payments also clearly had significant implications for the development of
family structures, while in the absence of property fewer kinship ties
would be expected to develop.

7.1.2   The Recurrence of Pestilence

Most of the general demographic advance of the sixteenth century was, it
seems, no more than the recovery of the population to the level existing
before the Black Death of 1348, the effects of which had persisted in the
low levels of population during the intervening period (c.1350–1470). If,
as seems probable in some areas, the Black Death brought in its wake
mortality rates of over 50 per cent, there was clearly considerable room
for recovery before there could be any real population growth. Indeed,
some historians conclude that despite fluctuations in population levels,
there was no permanently sustained increase between 1320 and 1720. The
recurrence of plague (*Yersinia pestis*) was one of the more important
brakes on the population. A recent study has established that there were
eighteen years of plague in Europe between 1494 and 1660, of which nine
were very serious (1522, 1564, 1580, 1586, 1599, 1604, 1625, 1630 and
1636). The most violent plagues are often the least well known, since
deaths were usually not recorded satisfactorily in the administrative chaos
resulting from the crisis. Even a plague that was less serious for Europe as
a whole might have savage consequences within a particular country. The
plague of 1656–7 produced mortality rates of only 19 per cent at Rome,
but 50 per cent at Naples and 60 per cent at Genoa. Towns which escaped
relatively lightly from one outbreak might succumb more heavily in
another. The mortality rate at Milan was about 18 per cent in 1576–7 but
over 50 per cent in 1630. Venice suffered a mortality rate of 28 per cent in
1575–6 but over 32 per cent in 1630–1.

Communities made vows and offerings to the saints, said prayers,
attended Mass or Communion, and held processions in the hope of

averting such catastrophes. Since there was no clear understanding of the cause of the plague, superstition was rampant. Apart from divine retribution and astrological conjunctions, it was thought that sorcery and even fear of the plague itself caused infection. The best defence against the plague was always recognized to be escape from the infected places and a scrupulous avoidance of victims. Kings, ministers and even whole institutions such as provincial *Parlements* in France would leave the infected locality. As late as 1654, the boyars fled Moscow before the barriers were set up to isolate the contagion. Butchers, bakers, millers and abattoir workers were most likely to come into contact with infected rats and were thus vulnerable, quite apart from those whose vocation was to care for the sick. But whatever his rank in society, no one could be secure from the attack of the disease. The sieur Lefèvre, an office-holder at Dieppe, declared in 1584 that plague measures 'had no great importance since this disease attacks only the riff-raff'.[5] Two days after this pronouncement, he himself was dead.

A heavy burden was placed on local government by the task of recognizing and guarding against the approach of an epidemic, isolating the sick and paying for their support, and controlling the unemployed and disorderly. It was not until after the Fronde that the central government in France took upon itself the task of victualling plague-ridden towns. Because of their tradition of municipal independence, the Italian city states seem to have been better organized at an earlier date: the administration of plague has an important place in the history of government in Italy, notably with respect to the organization of food supplies at a time when tax revenue tended to fall because of the crisis. The quarantine of areas affected by the plague, the burning of 'contaminated' houses and possessions and clothes of plague victims, intensified hardship. The mortality rate in evacuation camps and plague houses was exceptionally high. The co-operation of the medical profession in the treatment of plague victims was often difficult to secure, while burial parties were forcibly recruited in some instances from among the prison population, especially those under sentence of death.

7.1.3 *Population, Food Supply and Subsistence Crises*

Every four or five years a harvest failure affected part of Europe. The timing and extent of the failure varied from country to country. In England between 1494 and 1660, twenty-five harvests were deficient, twelve were bad, while a further four (in 1555, 1556, 1596 and 1661) resulted in dearth. Thirteen crises affected the Parisian area (in 1521–2, 1524–5, 1531–2, 1545–6, 1562–3, 1565–6, 1573–4, 1586–7, 1590–1, 1630–2, 1642–3,

1648–53 and 1660–3). But different localities in France suffered crises at other times, since there was no national grain market. The Dutch experienced at least eight crises in the period, rather fewer than in less developed agricultural regions, but nevertheless they were a serious side-effect of agrarian specialization in the so-called 'golden age'. Four of the Dutch subsistence crises occurred at the same time as those in the Parisian area, and it is clear that the main reason for such harvest failure was climatic. In England, one in four harvests were poor in the second half of the sixteenth century, compared to one in five in the first half. The evidence suggests that in England, in the area around Antwerp, and in Languedoc there were more severe winters, more abundant snowfalls and harder frosts after 1550. The number of late wine harvests also increased, suggesting dull cold springs, and cool damp summers. After 1600, conditions seem to have returned to those of the first half of the sixteenth century. But the history of climate is still in its infancy and the crucial regional variations affecting harvests are difficult to perceive.

Even if the evidence for what has been called a 'little ice age' in the second half of the sixteenth century is as yet inconclusive, it is clear that harvests during this period were rarely ideal. Abnormal weather conditions could thus quickly bring disaster, bearing in mind that harvest yields were low even in normal years. It is difficult to generalize about the quality of the diet of the European peasantry, since this might vary greatly from one locality to another and one harvest to the next. The 33,000 or so inhabitants of Valladolid in mid-sixteenth-century Castile were better fed than their rural counterparts; bread, meat, fish, olive oil and wine provided an estimated daily intake of at least 1,580 calories. But this diet was scarcely adequate and was deficient in vitamin C. By comparison, a rural wage-earner in Languedoc seems to have lived a lordly existence, since he was paid in kind rather than money, which provided a hedge against inflation. It is estimated that he consumed about 4,160 calories a day in 1480 and 4,910 calories a day in 1580. The bread was blacker in the sixteenth century and there was a protein deficiency in most diets: but the average worker was better fed than many people in underdeveloped countries today. Where workers were paid in money and not in kind, impoverishment led to severe malnutrition; there was no defence against inflation, and wage rates collapsed in real terms as grain prices sextupled between 1480 and 1600. In most areas of Europe the population was reasonably well nourished in the first half of the sixteenth century but there was a progressive deterioration in the quality of the diet as population pressure on food resources increased. In areas where the diet was varied and included milk products, chestnuts and fish, the peasants were not necessarily better fed than those who had a greater reliance on bread; but they were less susceptible to subsistence crises. Undernourishment was a considerable factor in the high mortality rates of the seventeenth century.

A subsistence crisis is best defined as an exceptional rise in cereal prices followed by a dramatic increase in deaths (at least double the normal rate) and a fall in the number of births. The average mortality rate in seventeenth-century France was probably between 600,000 and 700,000 a year, on the assumption of a population of between 18 and 20 million and a death-rate of 35 per 1,000. Between 1660 and 1663 France experienced three bad harvests. During the crisis, the mortality rate rose to perhaps one million a year. Taking into account the fall in the birth-rate, there were perhaps between 1 million and 1.5 million fewer inhabitants by 1664. The effects of a subsistence crisis are viewed most clearly in a single locality. At Altopascio, a small parish of about 630 inhabitants in Tuscany, there were four such crises between 1636 and 1660, lasting nine years in all. There were 501 deaths during these years and only 260 births: the population of the parish would thus appear to have been reduced by 241, or over a third. There has been some debate among historical demographers as to whether the increased death-rate or the falling birth-rate was the more important factor regulating the level of the population. Had high death-rates been more important, the crises might have been expected to have hit hardest those areas which were overpopulated. This was not always the case. Though contemporaries called subsistence crises 'mortalities', the decline in the birth-rate, which was less easily observed, seems to have been more crucial. Fewer children were conceived because of amenorrhoea; there was a higher incidence of stillborn births; and there is not much doubt that infants were abandoned to die from exposure because families could not afford to feed extra mouths in time of hardship.

Some areas were relatively well protected from subsistence crises. Valencia imported wheat from Sicily; the Papal States brought in wheat from the Baltic region during the pontificate of Sixtus V (1585–90) and thereafter. Yet specialization of agriculture and the widespread importation of foodstuffs were rare in early modern Europe because of the huge risks of a sudden dearth if the imports failed to arrive as planned. The Low Countries were the exception. There, the rural population concentrated on 'intensive husbandry'; specialized cattle-breeding, commercial crops and horticulture took the place of grain production. By the 1550s, perhaps 14 per cent of the total grain consumption in the Low Countries had to be met by imports from the Baltic region, especially Poland. The proportion was higher a century later: as many as one-third of the 1.5 million inhabitants of the Dutch Republic may have been fed on imported grain. Without a secure source of supply and a merchant marine owned and operated by the Dutch themselves, such dependence on grain imports could not have arisen.

7.1.4 *Responses to Poverty*

The general rise in population in sixteenth-century Europe was reflected in the growth of cities (see chapter 7.4.1). Migration to urban centres was a long-term trend over the century; it was also a short-term trend during periods of famine, and it resulted in a disproportionate growth in the numbers of the urban poor. London in 1594 had twelve times as many beggars as in 1517, although the population of the capital had risen scarcely fourfold. Distinctions need to be drawn between beggary and poverty; definitions of poverty are particularly elusive. The simplest one is the lack of sufficient means for subsistence. At Lyon, a journeyman building worker seeking to support a family of four on his wage alone (without supplementing his income, or his wife also working) would have been able to do so in every year but one between 1475 and 1599. Seventy per cent or less of his wage would have bought the necessary 2.5 kg. of bread a day to feed his family. But a mason's labourer would have found it impossible to support his family in 25 of the years during this same period; a casual labourer in the building trade would have been unable to do this in 74 of the 124 years. The progressive deterioration of wage rates in an age of rising food prices was an important cause of poverty. So too, in the French countryside, was the diminution in the size of peasant land-holdings as a consequence of population pressure. In seventeenth-century Beauvaisis, not far north of Paris, the most common family unit was six people (father, mother, three children and a grandparent). Twelve hectares of land (nearly 30 acres) were needed to feed this unit during a year of plenty; but 27 hectares (nearly 67 acres) were needed in a year of dearth. Only one-tenth of the peasants in the Beauvaisis were able to feed their family in all circumstances because they owned 27 hectares. Many were landless or virtually landless day labourers on paltry or intermittent wages.

Historians draw a further distinction among the poor, distinguishing between the 'structural' and the 'occasional' poor (*pauvres conjoncturels*). The structural poor were those unable to earn a living because of a physical disqualification (what the English poor laws termed the 'impotent poor'), the aged, orphans or impoverished widows. The occasional poor were those temporarily in need of assistance because famine had driven up the price of grain so that they could not afford bread; who were destitute because they were landless labourers; or who lacked income because they were unemployed. The two categories are easy enough to describe as a model, but are much more difficult to distinguish from the surviving statistical evidence.

One section of the second category, the migrant and rootless un-employed, attracted special attention from contemporary legislation.

These beggars were seen as a social danger. They might instigate popular uprisings; they might carry plague; they might even be Anabaptists. Sir Thomas More voiced these fears when he stated in 1527 that beggars acted 'with contempt of God and all good men ... against all laws, rule and governance'.[6] In England it was not until 1576 that people fit and able to work were deemed worthy of help because they were unable to find employment. Before this, the so-called sturdy beggars or vagabonds were to be whipped (after 1530), to endure galley service (after 1545), for a short period (1547–9) to be placed in slavery, and even after 1597 they were to be banished overseas or endure permanent galley service. In France after 1536, vagabonds who refused to leave a town of which they were not native might be sent to the galleys, forced to dig ditches round the town or to clean the filth from the streets. Sturdy beggars could be sent to the galleys at Venice after 1529 and in Castile after 1566. Population pressure alone does not account for the proliferation of legal sanctions against beggars. Many of the laws were the product of specific crises. The Venetian law of 1529 was passed in time of plague and revived in 1545, a year of famine. The Castilian poor law of 1540, which introduced a licensed begging system, followed a disastrous harvest. The desire to prevent a repetition of the food riot at Lyon known as the *grande Rebeyne* (1529) seems to have been uppermost in the minds of reformers establishing the general almonry (*Aumône générale*) in 1531.

Greater municipal intervention in poor relief during such crises has left statistical evidence about those receiving charity. On average, 5 per cent of the population received the weekly food ration (dole) at Lyon between 1534 and 1561. The poor in Toledo were numbered at 11,105 in 1558, equivalent to about 19 per cent of the population. They received a total of 320,000 pounds of free bread in a 60-day period. The previous year a slightly smaller number of the poor were given 960,000 pounds of free bread in a 180-day period. These were impressive amounts of relief and large numbers of poor. But before any definitive conclusions can be reached on contemporary levels of poverty from such evidence, two comments are necessary. Firstly, the proportion of relief distributed among the population seems to have varied greatly from one town to another. This may mean that there were many more needy in one town than in another; but alternatively it may be that different criteria of need were being applied. Secondly, poor relief was a weapon in the religious conflict. In Castile, it reinforced Catholicism, since after 1540 no one could be licensed to beg except by the parish priest and then only after he had confessed and received the (Catholic) Sacrament. This system did not work as well in practice as in theory, since licences could be counterfeited. Thus charity became a form of social control to ensure religious conformity and to win converts, and the figures produced by the administrators are suspect where the community was divided along religious lines. In contrast, poor relief was not used as an instrument to facilitate conversions to Calvinism in the United Provinces. It is true that the reformed church looked after its own poor through the administration of the deacons; but as the acts of the synod of Dordrecht of June 1574 make clear, the young church had neither the resources nor the wish to do so for the community as a whole. Generalized poor relief in the Netherlands remained the responsibility of the churchwardens and overseers of the poor, parish officials who in the early years of the Dutch Revolt were, in all probability, Catholics.

During the sixteenth century, the problem of poverty grew worse. Measures which in one generation had seemed bold innovations were no longer adequate for the scale of the problem. Leaving aside wages policy, the prevention of changes in land usage and the supply of food, measures to deal with poverty seem to have had three general characteristics. The first was to establish systematic provision to replace the sporadic poor relief of the Middle Ages. This was linked with increased secular control of the administration of relief, by the establishment of a general almonry, a common chest or poor-box. Though there were earlier precedents at Nuremberg and Strasbourg, the movement began, it seems, at Ypres in 1525. Such methods in turn influenced the Spanish *émigré* humanist, Juan Luis Vives, whose treatise *On the Relief of the Poor* (*De subventione pauperum*, 1526) argued that poor relief was both a moral obligation of the Christian community and also an expedient measure for those who governed the city in order to avoid sedition. The basic arrangement at Ypres was to prohibit begging, to expel beggars who originated from outside the town and to establish a common fund administered by laymen for the relief of the needy poor. The Mendicant Orders protested against this policy, since they had been deprived of their main source of revenue by the prohibition on begging; they also objected to administration of the fund by laymen. However, in 1531 the Sorbonne declared the Ypres scheme 'pious and salutory'. Lyon established its scheme in the same year, and made it permanent in 1534. Tickets of entitlement to relief were issued to the needy poor. Every Sunday morning, bread and money were distributed to ticket-holders. Poor orphans and foundlings were taken into children's hospitals (quite soon about 300 children were in care), where boys were taught to read and write and girls were taught the skills of the silk trade. Voluntary donations, the principle of Calvin's Geneva, were not always sufficient to pay for such schemes. Lyon moved towards a compulsory levy and Paris instituted a poor tax. A compulsory poor-rate was levied in London from 1547, well before the national parish-rate was established in 1572.

The second general characteristic of sixteenth-century poor relief was the establishment of special beggars' hospitals alongside the consolidation of existing charitable institutions. Toledo, a town of about 60,000 inhabitants, had 27 hospitals in 1576. In addition, there were 143 confraternities, some 20 of which practised open charity as distinct from charity limited to members of the brotherhood. This proliferation of small hospitals was a consequence of historic bequests by lay benefactors, who often laid down stringent conditions against subsequent amalgamation. It was an inefficient system and manifestly inadequate for the growing problem of poverty. A movement to consolidate such hospitals seems to have begun in Italy, where beggars' hospitals were established at Bologna, Brescia, Turin, Modena and Venice in the second half of the sixteenth century. Pope Sixtus V envisaged one for Rome in 1587. The movement spread from Italy to Philip II's lands, and beggars' hospitals were set up at Toledo, Madrid and Barcelona in the early 1580s despite opposition from potential lay benefactors. Most of these hospitals had acute financial problems, so that the movement can be said to have met with only partial success.

The third development was that of confining all the poor considered to be 'idle' in workhouses. The Bridewell in London had served this purpose for sturdy beggars as early as 1552-3, but the Dutch seem to have been the main proponents of 'houses of correction' for the idle poor. A house for men was established at Amsterdam in 1589, another for women in 1596. By 1650 there were a further twenty in the Netherlands. The French began to lock away the poor somewhat later, at Rouen in 1610 and Lyon in 1614. The crown announced its intention of pursuing this policy on a nationwide basis in 1629. But the initiative remained with the towns for a generation until the general hospital (*hôpital général*) was established at Paris in 1656. In June 1662, a royal edict stipulated that comparable institutions should be set up in every town and large village of France 'in order to contain beggars and to instruct them in piety and the Christian religion'.[7] A network of workhouses seemed the best guarantee of social order and this attitude conformed to Counter-Reformation sentiment that the spiritual ministration to the souls of the poor was more important than medical care or charity. (The dead in beggars' hospitals were considered 'cured' if they had confessed, received the last rites and had been properly buried!)

In eastern Europe there were no comparable social responses to poverty, primarily because there was no labour market in the true sense as a result of the generalization of serfdom (see chapter 7.2.5). In Muscovy, the absence of any institutionalized poor relief and the legality of slavery resulted in a phenomenon unique in Europe: an individual could choose to sell himself into slavery. In normal years about one per cent of the population did so, rising to 5 or 10 per cent in times of extraordinary crisis such as the great famine of 1601–3. A law of 1603 stated that starving slaves were to be freed, demonstrating that provision of the means of subsistence was the chief purpose of slavery. In origin, slavery was a contract to borrow money; the slave was to repay the principal of the loan in one year and the interest was to be worked off in labour services. Failure to repay the principal of the debt was common during a famine, and this converted the individual into a full hereditary slave of his creditor. After the 1590s, it became legally impossible to repay the loan and slavery became automatic. A form of dependence was created from which escape to free status became virtually impossible. Thus, until the abolition of slavery in 1723, the numbers of slaves tended to grow until they amounted to about 10 per cent of the Muscovite population. Slavery was the Muscovite alternative to the workhouse in western Europe.

7.2 Agrarian Society

For convenience, historians are apt to distinguish between the rulers and the ruled, and to describe the separate characteristics of peasantry and nobility as though they existed in watertight compartments. This may serve to clarify the issues at times of relative stability, but in a period of rapid social change it is misleading. Recent scholarly controversy has fully revealed the dynamic interrelationship between the prevailing social structure and the pace of economic development in the countryside. There was no immutable law preordaining a free peasantry in western Europe and unfree serfs in the east. But while the detailed nature of the changes, and the reasons for them, are still a matter of debate, historians agree that a continuing and decisive theme in European history is the division in terms of political power, economic organization and social structure which is marked by the line of the river Elbe. East of the river there were large estates, directly administered by the lord and worked by serf labour (*Gutsherrschaft*). West of the river, peasant tenements were leased out by the lord in return for rents (*Grundherrschaft*). Except in a legal sense, serfdom had died out in large areas of western Europe by 1500. There remained a crucial borderland area in Germany, however, where developments were less clear-cut. As the German Peasants' War demonstrated (see chapter 7.3.3), serfdom existed in some of the German states in the form of personal bondage (*Leibeigenschaft*). It was objectionable, even humiliating to the peasants, but it was characterized less by labour services than the extraction by the lord of additional rent in money or kind.

The 'second serfdom' introduced into eastern Europe (so called to distinguish it from the 'first' and earlier serfdom in the medieval west) was a radical innovation. Noble landlords consolidated their position against their tenantry and the outside world by ruling a tightly regulated community. Serfdom was in essence a non-contractual relationship: once fully established, the lord might levy arbitrary exactions and the peasant be denied free movement to escape them. The reasons why this form of serfdom (*Erbuntertänigkeit*) came about in eastern Europe but not in the west defy simple explanation. Up to 1500 economic and social trends in eastern Europe do not seem to have diverged greatly from those in the west. The most obvious distinction between the two areas was that the east was much more thinly populated, with plenty of abandoned land and many deserted tenures (called *puszta* in Hungary and *putoshi* in Muscovy). Labour was at a premium; lords, therefore, had a common interest in binding their remaining tenants to the land. In Prussia in the fifteenth century, ordinances aimed at strengthening the lord's control over his peasants explicitly stated that the shortage of labour was their justification and explanation. Other crucial differences between west and east were the weakness of monarchical power in the east (except in Muscovy), the strength of the nobility, the failure of towns to challenge aristocratic control of the economy and the weak traditions of peasant collective organization. Though the early peasant colonizers of eastern Europe were probably freer than their west European counterparts, passive resistance to the lord's demands at a later date was difficult to achieve because their rights were not entrenched so firmly in village charters (*Weistümer*) and village political institutions. There was also a much clearer link in the east between lordship and the village community. Yet despite these common features, there was greater diversity among the eastern lands than one might expect. The introduction of serfdom was also a slow and gradual process; it was fully achieved only in the seventeenth century.

7.2.1 *Aristocratic Titles*

Any calculation of the number of nobles in early modern Europe depends on contemporary criteria of nobility, which varied somewhat from one country to another. It is thus possible to arrive at rather different estimates. According to one account, nobles constituted 15 per cent of the population in Poland, 10 per cent in Spain and 1 per cent in France. In another, the proportions are reduced respectively to 6.6, 5 and 1 per cent. A much greater precision of terminology is required before such estimates can be deemed reliable. Calculations are further bedevilled by the fact that the European nobility during this period increased at different rates in different countries. The right of the monarch to create new nobles was much more clearly recognized, for example, in France than in Poland. Some monarchs were much more generous than others in creating new titles of ennoblement by sale or otherwise. The record probably rests with Christina of Sweden, but the French kings were profligate in their creations of dukes and peers, in their sales of titles of nobility and above all in their creation of an office-holding nobility. The Spanish kings were more moderate. Even so, the number of great magnates (grandees and titled nobles) in Castile grew from 55 in 1520 to 99 by 1598, 144 by 1621 and 236 by 1665. The assimilation of new nobles into the ranks of the older nobility was rarely easy and was a significant cause of social tension. In Sweden, it led to the demand in 1660 for a Table of Ranks to be drawn up to 'resolve the competitive claims of civil and military office' (see chapter 6.3.2),[8] but this was not done until 1680 (and not in Russia until 1722). No such measure was agreed upon in France, despite the obvious problem of integrating the new nobility of the robe with the traditional nobility of the sword. Instead, the vague definition of nobility was made much more precise in the 1660s. Royal commissioners were empowered to investigate cases of the illegal usurpation of nobility in 1598, 1634 and in the 1660s. When cases of usurpation were proven, a heavy fine was levied and fiscal immunity withdrawn.

The basis of the European aristocracies was privilege; without privilege there could be no true nobility. By respecting or even extending noble privilege, the crown secured noble allegiance. The development of aristocratic business enterprise, usually as a result of specific royal concessions, was greatest in Holstein, Mecklenburg and eastern Europe in general. It was much less noticeable further west. In France, for example, the rule of derogation (*dérogeance*) whereby nobles could lose their status if they committed certain demeaning acts, restricted nobles' economic opportunities. In 1435, Charles VII had refused fiscal exemption for those who sold retail wines on the grounds that 'it is not the business of nobles to be tavern keepers'.[9] Further restrictions followed. In 1560, a royal ordinance prohibited nobles from participation in all forms of trade on penalty of being subjected to taxation. This was renewed in 1579 and was modified (for maritime commerce only) in 1629. In Poland, restrictions operated for the most part in the other direction. After 1633, nobles who occupied themselves with urban pursuits were threatened with the loss of their privileges; but their rural economic activities were already so extensive that they had no need to run the risk of participation in urban enterprise. The growth of aristocratic business interests in eastern Europe generally hindered the development of an independent merchant class in the towns.

Rank and power were crucially interrelated. Power rested with persons of rank. The status of the father usually determined the nobility or otherwise of the hiers. The hereditary principle and the concept of honour both shaped aristocratic assumptions about the place of the nobleman in society. Honour was so highly esteemed that racial myths were formulated to underpin the idea of purity of blood. The aristocracy was deemed to have descended in a direct line from the warlike tribes of the early Middle Ages which had destroyed the Roman empire. In France and Germany, the Franks were heralded as the original nobles; in Spain and Sweden, it was the Goths; in Poland, it was the Sarmartae, and this led to the development of a so-called 'Sarmartian' culture in the seventeenth and eighteenth centuries.

7.2.2 *Noble Privileges in Eastern Europe*

For all the similarities, the actual extent of aristocratic privilege and power varied greatly from one European country to another. In general, privileges were greatest in the east (with the exception of Muscovy), a consequence of the relative weakness of monarchy there. There was an aristocratic monopoly of land purchases, for instance, in Poland after 1496 and in Hungary after 1514. After the Hungarian nobles crushed the great peasant rebellion in that year, István Verböczi's *Tripartitum opus...* (1514) gave the authoritative statement of the constitution, affirming the nobles' independence from the elective monarchy and their supremacy over the peasantry. By the 1540s, significant increases in the size of noble demesnes had taken place in Royal Hungary; this process was further encouraged by a rapid increase in grain prices after 1570 and by government grain purchases for the army during the war against the Turks (1593–1606). Noble land was inalienable, so that large estates, once created, were not subject to fragmentation.

In Poland, the great social and economic differences within the nobility were accentuated before 1589 by the custom of partible inheritance among sons and unmarried daughters. Among the 25,000 or so noble families in Poland there were a large number of 'barefoot *szlachta*', nobles owning very little land who were distinguishable only by their status from rich peasants. At the beginning of the sixteenth century, the average Polish nobleman held no more than two or three properties with serfs; yet by 1650, the pendulum had swung to the other extreme, with a number of great magnates in Poland owning hundreds or even thousands of properties as a result of the introduction of the law of entail in 1589 and the gradual expropriation of peasant landholdings. The average noble estate (*folwark*) doubled in size between 1500 and 1655; the demesne came to represent a quarter of all cultivated land in Poland. After 1588–9, all noble lands were held as allods, free from feudal service to the king, and the law of entail was gradually applied to preserve the great estates.

In Muscovy, partible succession was the norm among the boyars, leading to the fragmentation of large estates, and delaying any increase in the size of the demesne. The establishment of a service nobility under Ivan IV, and its competition with boyar families for peasant labour, was crucial in the enserfment of the peasantry. Ivan IV made the fundamental mistake of granting the service nobility the right to collect rent on their fiefs. This gave the reckless the opportunity to plunder lands which could not legally be transferred to their heirs. On the other hand, it created an attachment to the land among the fief-holders: by the seventeenth century, they became landowners rather than soldiers and sought to raise revenue from the land (thus losing any value as a fighting force).

7.2.3 *Financial Problems of the Nobility in Western Europe*

Against the trend elsewhere in western Europe, there was a significant extension of aristocratic economic power in sixteenth-century Castile. The financial problems of the monarchy led it to sell off to the nobility first the lands belonging to the military orders and then communal lands belonging to the villages. Thus by the seventeenth century most Castilian land was owned by the nobility, and over half of it by only a handful of great families. Some of these noble holdings were huge agglomerations of territory which were virtually independent states. The inequalities of landownership exacerbated social divisions within the Castilian aristocracy which had already been glaringly evident under the Catholic Monarchs. Children of the great magnates intermarried, their parents obtaining dispensations from the laws of consanguinity where necessary. The great discrepancies in wealth between the grandees and the gentry (*caballeros*) were reflected in the size of the dowries commanded by their daughters at the time of marriage, and they were reinforced by the law of entail (*mayorazgo*: this was regularized by legislation passed by the *Cortes* of Toro of 1505). Grandees and other titled nobles had easier access to the monarchy than the gentry, and could obtain the grant of new entails in subsequent generations.

It has sometimes been argued that this law gave the first-born son an interest in the income from his inheritance but no corresponding concern for the capital, which was run down in attempts to extract the maximum amount of ready money from an estate. However, the financial problems of sixteenth-century Castilian nobles seem to have resulted more from the inflexibility of the entailed estate rather than its deliberate abuse by irresponsible heirs. The *mayorazgo* prohibited the sale or mortgage of entailed goods. Unless there was a dramatic rise in income, the nobleman possessing large capital assets might find it difficult to realize his wealth without recourse to borrowing. Noble incomes seem to have kept pace with inflation in the sixteenth century, matching the doubling of prices between 1530 and 1595. Thereafter, they did less well: the cash income of the dukes of Infantado held steady between 1581 and 1636, which meant that their real income fell because of inflation. The value of their seigneurial tithe fell by 9 per cent between 1588 and 1669. The cost of service in the army rose. So too did dowries. Even if the expenses of a nobleman did not rise faster than his income, he had less disposable capital to cover any additional costs that arose. These could not be met out of his regular income as a consequence of the progressive establishment of the entailed estate, a phenomenon which might be termed long-term wealth but short-term penury. Nobles borrowed to cover an immediate financial need such as a dowry payment, only to discover that although their entailed properties were secure from seizure, it was difficult to pay off the debt, despite low rates of interest. By the seventeenth century, great nobles were paying a quarter or even half of their incomes simply to service these debts. The crown intervened to moderate the terms of the debts, protecting great nobles from their creditors: to some extent, this made them dependent politically on the monarchy.

The French monarchy gave no such help to its nobility. It was relatively easy to borrow money in France through annuities (*rentes constituées*), which were guaranteed against property. At any time the borrower could reimburse the capital of the *rente* (though he could never be required to do so), and there were no fixed dates for repayment. Inevitably, because it was easy, borrowing increased. Yet interest rates were high, and crippling debts might be incurred. The French nobility had a real fear of bankruptcy and the consequent loss of their estates at auction, both of which were unknown to their Spanish counterparts. As in Spain, there were great variations of wealth and status among the French nobles. Apart from fiscal exemption, a duke residing at court had virtually nothing in common with a rural gentleman (*hobereau*) in Brittany. Indeed, the latter was scarcely distinguishable, apart from the claim to fiscal exemption, from a more prosperous peasant. Noble estates in France tended to fragment because there was no generalized law of entail. Primogeniture does not seem to have been generally practised even in the area of written law in the Midi, where inheritance arrangements favoured the unilateral settlement on one child. Thus the debts many noble families incurred in the sixteenth century cannot be attributed to the inflexibility of the entailed estate, as they were in Spain. Marriage to a rich heiress was a necessary step to retrieve a shattered fortune. Montaigne commented that 'we do not marry for ourselves, whatever we say; we marry just as much for our posterity, for our family'.[10] The cost of dowries rocketed in France in the sixteeenth and seventeenth centuries. The buoyant dowry market was a source of critical comment from contemporaries, who thought it objectionable that financiers should be able to marry their daughters to the sons of impoverished noblemen.

The financial difficulties of the French nobles might suggest that the income from their estates had failed to keep up with inflation, and that lordship was in disarray. Indeed, the historian Marc Bloch called the period of reconstruction after the Hundred Years' War 'the crisis of seigneurial fortunes'.[11] Some recent local studies have suggested that the noble demesne lost much of its importance during the sixteenth century. In Normandy around 1500, some 80 per cent of the demesnes were smaller than 50 hectares (123.5 acres), with somewhere in the region of 10 or 12 per cent of the cultivated land being demesne, depending on the region. But high grain prices in the sixteenth century presented improved opportunities for demesne farming, which seems to have recovered its importance in some noble estates.

7.2.4 *The Peasantry in Western Europe*

By 1500, the differences in the economic and social status of peasants, and between their tenurial rights in one area and another (or even within the same community) were already very marked. These differences were even more evident by 1660 because of population growth and the price revolution. The two most obvious consequences of these social changes were the pauperization of most (though not all) of the peasants in the west; and the enserfing of most of the peasants in the east. The Swedish example is an unusual but nevertheless interesting case of social change among the peasantry. Essentially there were two categories of peasant. Allodial tenants (*skattebönder*) paid taxes to the crown but neither rent nor dues to a lord. Their position was a particularly favourable one until the 1540s, when a growing burden of royal taxes was imposed on them by the Vasa dynasty. The *landbor*, in contrast, were free tenants who did not own their lands and owed labour services to their immediate overlords. They lacked firm rights of tenure and could be relatively easily evicted from their plots by their lords. But they enjoyed the right of free movement after six or eight years, which would have prevented the imposition of serfdom even had their lords wished to do so. Since he was not subject to royal taxes, the *landbor* was envied by the allodial tenants; many allodial tenants sold their land to change status, thus reducing the size of the available tax base to the monarchy. By the seventeenth century, conditions had changed considerably, and freehold peasants found themselves threatened with degradation, as they were burdened with intolerable labour services and feared eviction without compensation. The freedom of the Swedish yeomen was menaced by the new nobles who had picked up German social attitudes during the Thirty Years' War, and in some cases actually were Germans. At the *riksdag* of 1650 the peasant fourth estate voiced its grievances at the attempted imposition of a 'Livonian slavery'. However the attitude of most Swedish nobles was summed up by the remark of one of them, Gustav Bonde, who commented that 'it is better to milk the cow than to hit it over the head',[12] and in 1652 the estate of the nobility accepted an ordinance fixing the maximum for extraordinary labour services at eighteen days a year.

In northern Castile, though there were many independent peasant free-holders and leaseholders (both were called *labradores*, a term which usually described the ownership of a team of oxen or mules) in the earlier sixteenth century, relatively few were able to benefit from the buoyant market for grain. Many were reduced to the status of day labourers (*jornaleros*), frequently having to migrate to earn a living. Where independent peasants survived unscathed, their position was determined by the nature of their leases. There was no uniform pattern of land tenure. If the leasehold rent was fixed at a relatively low rate at the end of the fifteenth century, the tenant was clearly advantaged in an age of rising prices. Landlords naturally did not view the decline in their real income from such copyhold leases with equanimity. Instead, they sought to hedge against inflation by introducing share-cropping arrangements. In Old Castile and Léon, the terms of the contracts were not particularly draconian: the peasant had to pay the lord one-sixth or one-eighth of the harvest. In Valencia, the terms were harsher, varying from one-sixth to a third of the harvest. There are examples of rents payable by whole villages being reduced, resulting from litigation in the seventeenth century; but such cases seem to have been exceptional. The main defence of the share-croppers was not their capacity for collective protest but the shortage of labour. Thus rents fell in Valencia after the expulsion of the Moriscos in 1609, and remained low during the reign of Philip IV. Spanish share-cropping arrangements seem relatively benign compared to Italy. *Mezzadria*, as it was called, in rural Tuscany left the peasant only half the harvest for subsistence. He thus had to borrow from his employer in times of scarcity, a short-term security which was gained only at the price of long-term indebtedness. The landlord extracted labour services from the peasant to pay off the original debt: these services might be onerous but could not be refused because the alternative was imprisonment for debt. Moreover, there were relatively high rates of dismissal of share-croppers.

If the seigneurial regime in the Spanish kingdoms seems weaker than in rural Tuscany, it nevertheless imposed a heavy burden on the peasants. Although feudal dues were relatively light, representing only a small fraction of the harvest, rents owed to the lord could amount to one-third or even half the harvest. Tithe payments to the church or to a lay impropriator might consume another tenth of the harvest. Moreover, royal taxes on the peasants were increasing, rising to one-tenth of the harvest. The tithe was still heavier than the burden of royal taxes, and evoked some protest; but it was sanctioned by tradition. The royal taxes were hated because they were new (this was particularly true of the *millones*, Philip II's emergency tax to help pay for the Armada). There was a steady rise in taxation between 1570 and 1670, when the burden probably quadrupled. The fiscal burden was more oppressive because there were too few tax-payers (*pecheros*) and too many exemptions. Fernández Navarette, one of the most famous of the proponents of reform (*arbitristas*), argued that it was unjust 'that some should be exempt at the expense of others, and that the whole burden should fall on the weak shoulders of peasants and labourers'.[13] The most that was done to alleviate this situation was a reduction of taxes where appropriate on a local basis. A rural community might easily fall into debt following a few unfavourable harvests. Once this happened, it was very difficult to escape the creditors except by abandoning the village, and rural depopulation became widespread. Padre López Bravo, a commentator at the beginning of Philip IV's reign, noted that 'people abandon the countryside for the towns; the poor become slaves of the rich; and the rich intensify their pursuit of luxury and pleasure'.[14]

In France, comparable burdens of seigneurial dues, rents, tithe and royal taxes fell on the peasants. As in Spain, the dues (*cens*) payable to the immediate lord were light. Many of the contracts between lords and their customary tenants were set down in writing and enforced in the royal courts. Lords sometimes attempted to evict their customary tenants, but as a rule they were unsuccessful. Rents had been stabilized in the period of reconstruction after the Hundred Years' War (*c.*1450–1520), and declined in real terms as prices rose in the sixteenth century. Taxes rose after the Hundred Years' War, but the rate of increase was greater before 1500 than after, when it was reduced in real terms because of inflation. Thus the early years of the sixteenth century were a golden age for the French peasantry, whose position was one of the most advantageous in Europe. Gradually, this advantage was eroded as rents responded in the long term to the peasant demand for land, and as the population rose. Lords could fix higher rents in the seventeenth century, when increases of a third or even a half were sometimes recorded between 1600 and 1660. Taxes also went up, and it has been suggested that the tax burden on a family of four, equivalent to 7 days' output a year in 1547, rose to the equivalent of 14 days' output a year by 1607 and 34 days' output a year by 1675. Variations in fiscal regime, the incidence of taxation and peasant productivity were so great that this sort of calculation cannot be true of all localities. Where the landlord was liable to tax in the areas of land tax (*taille réelle*) in the Midi, rents were higher than in areas of income tax (*taille personnelle*), where the peasant carried the fiscal burden. The total cost to the peasant might thus vary from a fifth to a half of his gross output.

Peasant prosperity in the early sixteenth century carried with it the seeds of a long-term pauperization. The remarkable land registers of the Midi reveal the staggering process of plot subdivision under the impact of demographic growth. At Lespignan in Languedoc, there were 53 middle-ranking peasant proprietors in 1492, but only 34 in 1653. Their share of the land went down from 51 per cent to only 13 per cent. Small-scale peasant proprietors had constituted just under half the total in 1492, but had become the crushing majority (228 out of 262 peasants) by 1653. Elsewhere the evidence is less clear, but there are still indications that the middle-ranking peasants, *laboureurs* who might own a plough and draught animals, were being eliminated. Instead, many peasants were reduced from proprietorship to the status of day labourers (*manouvriers*), hiring themselves out rather than seeking subsistence through direct cultivation. Others became share-croppers on leases which became more rigorous with the passing of time.

7.2.5　*Peasant Tenure in Eastern Europe*

Serfdom was imposed on the countries of eastern Europe at varying speeds and in different ways. In Hungary, labour services had been light in the fifteenth century and the peasants had escaped most forms of personal bondage. Rents in kind, and especially money rents, had been more important than labour services. Even some well-to-do peasants had employed wage labour. Above all, the peasants enjoyed the right of free movement, confirmed at the diet of 1492. Then came the peasant rising of 1514, its savage repression, and the passing by the diet of legislation condemning the peasantry to 'real and perpetual servitude'[15] (see chapter 7.3.1). The new law was not enforced uniformly at first. Prosperous peasants employing wage labour survived and lords still extracted money rents, though rents in kind grew in importance. Gradually, however, communal rights were encroached upon by noble demesnes. Peasants were deprived of their tenements and became share-croppers. After 1548, their lords were entitled to up to 52 days of labour services a year. Another wave of peasant risings (in 1562, 1569–70 and 1571–3) seems to have brought a further intensification of labour services in its wake. During the war against the Turks (1593–1606: see chapter 5.4.3), thousands of Hungarian peasants formed militia bands (*hajduks*) with mutinous soldiers and rebelled to secure personal freedom. The diet responded by banning serf migration in 1608. Thereafter, at least three days' labour services a week were the rule. In practice, the demands of the landlords were without legal limitation; only resistance such as occurred in northern Hungary (in the area of the upper Tisza river) in 1631–2 held back their demands.

In Poland, the royal courts refused to hear appeals from peasants against their lords after 1518. But as late as 1660, perhaps one-third of the peasants in the valley of the river Vistula were free. Further inland, in the principality of Cracow, 70 per cent of all peasants were still free in 1564, 43 per cent in 1660. There were a considerable number of wealthy middle-ranking peasants, some of whom employed wage labour. Yet in Poland, as in Hungary, the position of the peasantry deteriorated as noble demesnes expanded. Whereas 35 per cent of the total peasant labour employed on the estate at Korczyn in Poland had been paid in wages in 1530, only 5 per cent of the total were paid in this way by 1660. The great bulk of labour was supplied by serf bond work, and to a lesser extent by serfs performing ploughing and carting services. Peasant smallholders seem to have been the main recruits for serfdom. Some became serfs voluntarily, by putting their labour at the disposition of their lords, thus guaranteeing that they would retain possession of the family plot which they might otherwise have been obliged to sell. Serfdom in Poland, it seems, was preferable to the state of the landless labourer, whose lot was destitution. Labour services increased as noble incomes began to decline under the impact of inflation. By the seventeenth century, a 16-hectare unit of land owed three days' labour service a week on average. In some areas, treble the legal limit was exacted as labour service. Surprisingly, there were no peasant revolts in Poland against these stringent and inequitable conditions.

There was no homogenous peasantry in Muscovy, and the nature of peasant tenure depended on the type of lordship over the land. The Tsar's 'court lands', his personal patrimony, were uniformly administered and liable to taxation. There was greater diversity on the 'black lands', which were subject to the Tsar not as an individual lord but as ruler of the state. There, the peasants had their own elected officials who until the 1640s distributed the tax burden according to the capacity to pay. On the boyars' estates, the Tsar's writ did not run, although in the reign of Ivan IV they became subject to military service. The *pomest'e* lands, or fiefs, had a stronger tradition of peasant self-government, though this was gradually undermined on the larger fiefs by estate officials. Finally, there were church lands of various types, administered by ecclesiastical law and free from all but intermittent arbitrary taxation.

At first, these variations ensured the survival of a free peasantry. Moreover, unlike the rest of Europe, the population of Muscovy failed to grow in the second half of the sixteenth century. The havoc of the *oprichnina*, the Livonian war and the Time of Troubles (see chapters 5.3.2 and 5.3.3) may even have led to a fall in numbers. Peasants fled areas affected by the troubles, and powerful boyars and monastic landlords, offering them protection and tax privileges, attracted migrants. The *pomeshchiki*, who held small fiefs and were unable to fulfil their military obligations because

of the fall in the numbers of their rent-paying peasants, were at a disadvantage. They demanded greater control over their peasants, and since
the Tsar still needed their military service, he had to accede to their
demands after 1580. At the end of the fifteenth century, peasant movement had been restricted to a period of two weeks in the year, around St
George's Day (26 November). The law code of 1497 required peasants
intent on migration to obtain prior permission from their lord and to make
a graduated so-called 'dwelling payment' to him should they decide to
leave. These arrangements were largely confirmed in the law code of 1550,
suggesting that there had been no perceptible deterioration in peasant
status in the intervening period. Where labour services (*barshchina*)
existed, they seem to have been performed on only one day a week. Dues
in cash or kind (*obrok*) remained the predominant type of peasant
obligation.

   In 1580, the right of peasants to move during the statutory period was
temporarily suspended. The suspension was repeated annually for much
of the period between 1580 and 1603 (which came to be known as the
'forbidden years' as a result) and was made permanent in 1603. This did
not of itself create a servile population, but it was helped by being linked
to the compilation of new land registers, which for the first time provided
tangible evidence of peasant residence. In 1597, landlords were given the
right to reclaim peasants who had left them in the previous five years. In
1607, this right was extended to a fifteen-year retrospective period, but it
was rescinded in the aftermath of the Time of Troubles. The landlord's
right of search reverted to a five-year period; this remained the rule until
1637, when it was increased to nine, and later ten years. The landlords'
request for an unlimited right of search for fugitive serfs was always
rejected by the monarchy until 1649, when it was incorporated in a new
law code. This provided the legal basis for the final enserfment of the
Muscovite peasants, who were henceforth regarded merely as chattels of
their lord. They were forbidden to lodge complaints against him unless
state security was involved, and they were also deprived of their right to
testify in civil disputes. The lord in return was made liable for the payment
of his serfs' taxes to the monarchy. This was the main reason for the
Romanov dynasty's surrender to the aristocracy of almost all its rights
over the peasantry. Yet though the lot of the Russian peasants seems
pretty miserable in terms of legal status, many serfs continued to pay
money rent rather than perform labour services. This gave them the
freedom to engage in small-scale trade and handicrafts, ensuring that they
retained a standard of living higher than mere subsistence levels in all but
crisis years. The basis of commerce in Muscovy was thus widened; trade
was less dependent on urban centres—and consequently less fragile—than
elsewhere in eastern Europe.

7.3 Agrarian Rebellion

The basic unit of European society—in west and east alike—was the village community. Its precise definition and significance differed greatly from one region to another, whether it was a mountainous or lowland area, whether it was land under open cultivation, woodland, marsh, and so on. New villages might be created and others become deserted. Little was absolutely constant at the level of the community. On the other hand, the enduring force of community solidarity is well attested and showed itself at times of rural protest and rebellion. 'State' and 'nation' were abstract concepts which few Europeans understood. There was usually a sense of loyalty to the king personally or to the ruling dynasty. Beyond this, there existed a circumscribed set of local allegiances, sometimes to the lord, sometimes to the priest (though both these ties were subject to strain from time to time), and invariably to the rural community. The elements binding the rural community were usually stronger than those which divided it.

In extreme circumstances, revolt was seen as a right of the community, a response to provocation by those more powerful than itself, and a sort of crude popular justice. It was usually a sense of injustice, real or imagined, which precipitated revolt rather than actual poverty or misery. A relatively small tax increase, for example, might spark off a quite disproportionate response in the populace if the circumstances were right. Rebellion was usually directed against the outsider, the source of innovation imposed against the will of a ferociously traditional rural community. Such innovation might seek to impose a cultural or religious change, to displace one dominant group identity permanently or temporarily by another, or to attempt to change the social and legal order within the local community. It might seek to impose new and intolerable fiscal, tithe or seigneurial burdens on the rural inhabitants—or perhaps attempt to debase their currency, the cause of the revolt in the Swiss Cantons in 1653—thus confiscating their surplus wealth. The more serious revolts were often the result of a combination of such pressures.

7.3.1 *Types of Rural Rebellion*

The leaders of rural revolts in early modern Europe were rarely humble peasants (except perhaps in Hungary in 1514 and Germany in 1524–6). They were more commonly unemployed soldiers, local lords, village priests, rich peasants or the mayors of small towns. Only a few manifestos survive from the rebellions, and these were almost invariably drawn up by members of social groups other than the peasantry. Rebellion was often the response of the better-off peasants whose prosperity was threatened; in such circumstances, the 'leading and richest' parishes often started and co-ordinated the revolt for their own interests, particularly in France. The willingness of rural notables—those who in France were called the 'cocks of the parish' (*coqs de paroisse*)[16]—to participate suggests that class confrontation within the community was rarely a significant factor. The involvement of rural notables was rather an indication of economic and financial inequalities in the countryside. Although the French gentry were personally exempt from the chief direct tax, the *taille*, their peasant farmers and tenants were subject to it. The gentry considered this policy to be unjust, since it amounted to an indirect tax on their own income. They were realistic enough to perceive that they could not expect their peasants to pay simultaneously high rents to themselves and high taxes to the crown. A reduction in taxes would permit existing rents to be paid, and perhaps allow them to be increased. The French lesser nobility thus opposed high taxation and, although they themselves gained nothing directly from this policy, they stood to benefit indirectly if their farmers could afford to pay what they euphemistically called 'a just rent'.[17] Since members of the rural nobility participated in the unrest, it is not surprising that few disturbances resulted in extreme or uncontrollable violence: large-scale fighting, massacres and mutilations were exceptional.

In Sweden, a quite different situation prevailed. There the tax-collector and the lord's bailiff were not competitors for the peasant's resources: the crown and the immediate lord each took a fixed share from the peasant. Consequently, the nobility was under no temptation to incite the peasantry to refuse taxes in the expectation they would be better able to pay rent to their lord. In such circumstances, rural rebellion was very infrequent, with the exception of the revolt of the province of Småland in 1542. This, the most extensive of all peasant uprisings in Swedish history, is a good example of tax rebellion but it was the product of an exceptional set of circumstances; it did not typify the relationship between the crown, landlords and peasants in Sweden. Historians often link it to the intro-duction of the Reformation, and it is true that the peasants wanted a return to the Mass and the restoration of precious objects to the churches. But the main grievances were about the increasing burden of taxation. The revolt was led by Nils Dacke, a peasant, and drew support from cottagers and allodial tenants (*skattebönder*), who paid taxes to the crown but neither rent nor dues to a lord. From 1540, when new land registers were compiled in Sweden, long-neglected tax claims were revived by the crown, which also sought to maximize the yield by redistributing taxes more equitably. Improved enforcement meant that the allodial peasants fell into tax arrears. If they failed to pay their taxes promptly, they were liable to eviction. The list of peasant grievances handed over to the royal troops in

November 1542 makes clear the peasants' resentment at this, as well as at the imposition of illegal seigneurial rents and additional dues such as a levy for the right to pasture pigs in oak forests. They also commented upon the arbitrary conduct of bailiffs and the fact that the wealthy could bribe them and thus avoid eviction.

An obvious example of local resistance to the attempted imposition of cultural and religious orthodoxy is provided by the two revolts in the mountainous area called the Alpujarras in the southern part of the kingdom of Castile (formerly Granada), which occurred in 1499–1500 and 1568–70. The nature of the terrain made possible the defence of a distinctive Islamic culture against an intolerant, Catholicizing central government, but both revolts ended in defeat. In 1502, the defeated Moors had to choose between emigration or conversion. The successors of the Christian Moors who remained, the Moriscos, rebelled in 1568 against the systematic attack undertaken by Cardinal Espinosa on the remaining symbols of their cultural identity such as their language, dress and customs (Islamic prayers, the fast of Ramadan, ritual ablutions and the prohibition of certain foods were the main surviving customs). 'Amongst the Christians we are treated as Moors and despised as Moors', claimed one of their leaders, 'whilst our own Moorish brethren treat us not as Moors but as renegades to the Christians, and neither help nor trust us.'[18] Not surprisingly, murders of Catholic clergy figured prominently in the second Alpujarra uprising. An expensive and gruelling war resulted, and it was not until 1570 that the royal army under Don John of Austria was able to crush the rebellion and forcibly resettle the Moriscos throughout Castile, Aragon and Valencia. Although the Moriscos could no longer rely on geographical or strategic advantages in their cause, in Don John's view, resettlement was not enough to do away with the problem: there would be peace only when the Moriscos had been expelled from the Spanish kingdoms. In 1570, however, Philip II had other priorities. The matter was left to his son, who settled it by forcible expulsions in 1609 (see chapter 4.3.1).

There was clearly a religious aspect to the revolt of the peasants in Austria in 1626. The main focus of hostility was the Bavarian army of occupation, which had been billeted on the country since 1620, when the Austrian estates had linked their cause to that of Bohemia in the movement against Ferdinand II (see chapter 4.1.1). The presence of this army made the attempted restoration of Catholicism by force a possibility. In October 1625, Lutheran peasant proprietors were required to convert to Catholicism by Easter the following year or to emigrate from Austria, suffering severe financial penalties. The leaders of the ensuing revolt were Stefan Fadiger, a tenant farmer of modest means, Christoph Zeller, his brother-in-law, an innkeeper by trade, and Achaz Wiellinger, who aspired to noble status. They sent a set of 138 demands (including that of freedom of conscience) to Ferdinand II in July 1626, claiming loyalty to the Habsburg dynasty over several generations. The demands were rejected. In the subsequent fighting, the Bavarian forces proved superior, though some noblemen assisted the rebellion, and by the spring of 1627, the revolt was suppressed. The imposition of Catholicism was resumed, though a movement of Protestant resistance remained, with the sacraments administered by itinerant lay preachers. Two further revolts, in 1632 and 1636, were on a much smaller scale. The Bavarian army of occupation had by then been withdrawn and these later revolts lacked the unifying focus of opposition it had provided. Wealthy peasants were the main supporters of the revolt of 1626–7; in the later rebellions, the participants were often landless labourers lacking the means or the cohesion to maintain the struggle.

Innovation could go further than the replacement of a particular religious belief. It might displace one dominant ethnic group by another. The attempt of the Polish government to undermine Cossack identity resulted in Chmielnicki's rebellion of 1648–54 (see chapter 5.3.4). The fierce defence of ethnic identity was sometimes linked to religious beliefs when Christian communities perceived themselves under threat from Islam. Two considerable peasant risings in central Europe, in Styria and Carinthia in 1478–9 and in Hungary in 1514, started with this motivation, in crusades against the Turks, but ended in open social conflict with the local nobility who had failed to carry out their crusading obligations. In 1514, the military command had been entrusted by Cardinal Archbishop Tamas Bakocz to György Székely, known as Dózsa, a minor nobleman who had served on previous campaigns. (Dózsa himself was a Szekler, a member of a people which had a tradition of revolt in the sixteenth century.) The nobles did not answer the call to arms, so the cardinal called off the recruiting campaign—but not before the Hungarian plains were aflame with a rebellion by the peasantry, which lasted for six weeks. The peasants, who had paid rent and dues to their lords, felt betrayed by them and were led by Dózsa himself. Franciscan monks provided three of the eight captains of the revolt. Dózsa's manifesto of the summer of 1514 is the only authentic document emanating from the rebellion. It called upon the peasants to fight the 'enemies of the crusade', cowards to whom capital punishment should be meted out,[19] but the social and economic grievances of the Hungarian peasants did not figure in it. The revolt ended in failure, and there was a vicious repression in its aftermath, which saw the beginning of the imposition of serfdom in Hungary.

Peasant revolts were also inspired by attempts to change the social and legal organization of the local community. The revolt against the five 'evil customs' (*malos usos*)[20] in Catalonia in 1484–5—these were two forms of death duty, a fine payable in the case of a wife's adultery, a fine paid if the farm caught fire accidentally, and a fine aimed at restricting the raising of a mortgage—led eventually to their abolition. But the peasant leaders had to pay heavily for their redemption; they were not paid off, in some cases, until 1501. Nevertheless, the Catalan serfs (*remensas*) gained their freedom, albeit at a price, and except for the years 1521–2, 1647–52 and 1688, there were no significant peasant revolts in the Spanish kingdoms. The free Spanish peasants for the most part did not protest against taxation in the manner of their French counterparts.

Unlike comparable revolts in western Europe, the Muscovite risings of 1603 and 1606–7 were followed by severe repression. They did not slow down the speed with which serfdom was being introduced, and were not directed specifically against its imposition. Essentially, these risings were a product of the dynastic uncertainty during the Time of Troubles, and of opposition to Tsar Vasilii Shuiskii at a time when social tension had been exacerbated by famine (1601–3). Furthermore, support for the rebellions came from too wide a social spectrum for them to assume any one specific purpose. The risings were led by slaves, not serfs. The leader in 1603 was a man called Khlopko (*kholop* means a slave); in 1606–7 it was Ivan Bolotnikov. But one or two great boyars also joined the rebellion; so, too, did some disaffected fief-holders bent on dispossessing the boyars. In a country where the towns were relatively unimportant economically, though of some military significance, some fifty towns went over to the rebellion, partly because of the influx of refugees from the famine. Bolotnikov's rebellion probably should not be seen as the first true peasant war in Muscovite history because of the widely different social elements who took part. (The rising of Stepan Razin in 1669–70 has more claim to be the first such peasant war in the country.)

7.3.2 *Peasant Uprisings in France*

There were many rural disturbances in sixteenth-century France. The more important ones were the risings of the Pitauds in south-west France (1548), the *ligue des vilains* in Dauphiné (1579–80), the Gautiers in Normandy (1589), the risings in Brittany (1589–91), the *Bonnets rouges* in Burgundy (1594), and the Tard-Avisés in the Limousin, Périgord and Saintonge (1594–5). The later stages of the French wars of religion show some signs of social antagonism, a consequence of the breakdown of civil order and the resulting oppressive behaviour of local gentry and office-holders. A second period of large-scale disturbances followed French intervention in the Thirty Years' War, when the most famous risings were those in the Angoumois and Saintonge (1636), and those of the Croquants of Périgord (1637), the Va-Nu-Pieds in Lower Normandy (1639) and the

Croquants of the Rouergue (1643). There were no large-scale risings during the Fronde, though small-scale tax rebellion was particularly serious. After the Fronde, further big rebellions in Guyenne in 1655–6 were followed by the risings of the Sabotiers in Sologne (1658), and of the Lustucru in the Boulonnais (1662). None of these rebellions (with the possible exception of the early revolts and the Breton rising of 1675) reveal any profound social antagonisms within the rural communities. The peasants did not criticize their seigneurs, but sought protection—and sometimes, leadership—from them. The most famous example was La Mothe La Forest, a nobleman who led the Croquants in 1637 because he recognized 'the justice of their cause, which he embraced with all his heart'.[21] The absence of any real threat to the social position of the gentry is revealed by the fact that they rarely turned out to suppress rebellion, in profound contrast with the behaviour of the knights in the German Peasants' War. It was usually royal troops, sent by the government from outside the province, which suppressed these revolts.

The few authentic peasant manifestos which survive, for example from the 1636–7 risings, demonstrate the peasants' loyalty to the king, and their acceptance of the myth that he was deceived by evil ministers who failed to inform him of the true state of his kingdom. These evil ministers, who mocked the sufferings of the peasants and levied increased taxes 'under the fine pretext of necessity of state',[22] were not, however, the main focus of hostility. The central and local agents of the fiscal system were seen as the force of oppression. The peasants of Saintonge equated Parisians with tax-contractors (*Parisiens et partisans*), believing they had conspired together to reduce their province to poverty. In their view, many peasants had been forced to give up their land because of the burden of taxation. The ideology of the peasants was simple and is best expressed in slogans of rebellion such as 'long live the king without the *taille*', 'long live the king without the salt tax (*gabelle*)', and 'long live the king, death to the *gabeleurs*'.[23] The main focus for hatred was the financier, called the *gabeleur* or *maltotier*, terms which could vary considerably in their precise application according to local conditions.

The danger of a rebellion spreading outside a single *pays* or province was slight. Each revolt had its own particular causes, each province its distinctive fiscal regime and social structure. The relevance of the slogans of rebellion is explained by the existence of privileged regions of France which paid much less than others in salt tax (*gabelle*). The rumour that the king sought to undermine these privileges (as indeed Francis I had attempted to do in 1542) was sufficient to threaten a general insurrection in the south-west in 1635. Rebellions often began in prosperous parishes which were partially exempt from taxes. In this respect, the large rural insurrections may be linked to the endemic problem of small-scale rioting and resistance to the levy of taxation in seventeenth-century France. Irritating though such revolts undoubtedly were for the crown, they never threatened to bring down the unpopular ministers who were responsible for the objectionable fiscal policies. The main obstacle to the success of an insurrection was the size of the country and the great distances between the locations of the disturbances (for example those in the south-west) from the centre of power at Paris. Unlike Muscovy, there are no instances in early modern France of great armed peasant bands marching on the capital (and even in the Muscovite case, it was a boyar coup, not Bolotnikov's rebellion, which witnessed the occupation of the capital and the downfall of the government: see chapter 5.3.3).

7.3.3 *The Peasants' War in Germany, 1524–1526*

The revolt which began at Stühlingen in the Hegau in June 1524 was the most extensive peasant conflict in early modern Europe. It had been foreshadowed by earlier revolts in Germany and the surrounding area: in the Tyrol in 1478, in the Swiss Confederation in 1489–90 and 1513–15, and in so-called 'Further' Austria in 1499 and 1502. These small-scale insurrections had a variety of motivation. The so-called 'poor Conrad' movement in Württemberg in 1514 was a tax revolt against the oppressive rule of duke Ulrich. The rebellion the following year in Inner Austria saw demands for a return to customary labour services and the reduction of the cost of copyhold renewal and death duties (heriots). The Austrian peasants lamented that priests did their own tithe collection, whereas previously peasants had assessed and collected it themselves. They also complained that the administration of river and forest law had been tightened in the interest of landlords.

The most significant precursor of the Peasants' War seems to have been the so-called 'peasant's laced boot' (*Bundschuh*) movement. Although this term had been used in earlier revolts in the fifteenth century, the radical *Bundschuh* movement comprised four conspiracies in all, in 1493, 1502, 1513 and 1517: the last three were organized by Joss Fritz, a former serf, who took on the role of its itinerant leader (and who necessarily had to go to ground in the periods between the attempted risings). The objectives of the conspirators lacked continuity of purpose, and reflected the varying social and economic conditions in the different regions from which support was drawn in each successive conspiracy. In 1493, they sought the expulsion of the Jews, and the cancellation of existing tolls, excises and the property tax payable to the state; instead of these levies, they were prepared to pay a flat-rate tax. The conspirators of 1502, in contrast, sought to abolish all feudal dues, both ecclesiastical and lay; in addition, the church's wealth was to be expropriated. In 1513, the peasants emphasized their loyalty to the Pope and the Emperor but claimed that they were prepared to fight for divine justice and a moral reform of society: their flag depicted on one side the peasant's laced boot, and on the other the crucified Christ, the Virgin Mary and St John the Baptist, with a peasant kneeling before them; together with the insignia of the Pope and the Emperor, the flag had inscribed on it the words 'Lord, stand by Thy Divine Justice'.[24] Finally, four years later, the conspirators called for the cancellation of all debt and interest charges, and the abolition of all feudal obligations. In none of these risings did Joss Fritz succeed in striking an alliance between his supporters in the countryside and the towns.

This pattern of fragmented regional support repeated itself when the true Peasants' War broke out in 1524–6. By February and March 1525, there were six rebel armies operating in Upper Swabia, though in mid-April the largest of them, estimated at 300,000 men, disbanded without a fight. The Franconian rebels, who took to arms in the middle of March, were defeated in the second week of May, though it was another month before their revolt was finally ended. Rebellion spread rapidly in Thuringia in late April, but the defeat at Frankenhausen in mid-May proved decisive for this army. A few days earlier, rebellion broke out in the Grisons, the archbishopric of Salzburg and the county of Tyrol. It proved the most successful of the movements, and was not defeated until June 1526. There was also a week-long rising in Samland in east Prussia in September 1525, the only rebellion in Germany east of the river Elbe, and it seems to have been quite different from the movements in the south-west. Elsewhere, the formation of separate peasant armies and the lack of experienced commanders were serious shortcomings. So too was the peasant system of military service, by which each village contingent was changed once a month. This ensured that each peasant was able to keep up with the work on his own land, but was obviously detrimental to military discipline and strategy. In contrast, the Samland rising saw the establishment of an army of 2,500 men, but its short duration meant that this fighting force was never really deployed: instead, an armistice was agreed which deferred further action until the return of duke Albrecht, the ruler of the newly secularized Teutonic Knights of Prussia; by the time that he returned, the momentum of resistance had been lost, the peasants could be disarmed, and about fifty peasant leaders were executed.

The diversity of the lands affected by the revolt—in the southern part of the Empire, only the forest cantons of central Switzerland and the duchy of Bavaria were untouched—makes the search for any single unifying cause such as the hated imposition of personal bondage unrealistic. Hostility to serfdom would explain the outbreak of an important rebellion in the Black Forest and Upper Swabia, where the secular and ecclesiastical lords were attempting to tighten the ties of serfdom. It would also account for the absence of trouble in Bavaria, where there was no serfdom. But why then were there later rebellions in Franconia, Thuringia and the Tyrol, where personal bondage scarcely existed? High population density seems to have increased the economic pressures on the peasantry, but it alone was not a clear cause of rebellion in all the lands. It has been suggested that there is a correlation between the incidence of revolt and areas of partible inheritance, which exacerbated land hunger: but again the case of Upper Swabia, which had primogeniture, throws doubt on this theory.

There is a possible correlation between the outbreak of the revolt and areas of relatively advanced economic activity with a tendency towards monoculture. The Peasants' War should not be seen as a revolt of backward rural areas against economic progress centred in the towns. Indeed, the leaders of the rebellion sought to make alliances with the numerous free cities in southern Germany, and their cause was considerably weakened by their inability to do so. Small towns sought neutrality rather than ally with the peasants: a town such as Freiburg, which surrendered to the army of the Black Forest and Breisgau peasantry under the leadership of Hans Müller of Bulgenbach, a commander committed to violent revolutionary insurrection in the name of Christian radicalism, managed to remain aloof from the conflict. At Mühlhausen, the fiery oratory of Thomas Müntzer bridged the gulf between town and country, but this seems an exception to the rule. Usually only unimportant social groups in the towns, such as vineyard workers and gardeners, were sympathetic to the peasants. The revolt often saw prosperous peasants in the vanguard, indeed there was some hostility between the better-off peasants and the cottagers and day-labourers. Former mercenary soldiers, artisans from the towns, Lutheran, and especially Zwinglian lay preachers played a prominent part in the leadership of the movement; serfs were the exception.

By far the most important peasant manifesto was the Twelve Articles of the Swabian Peasants, drawn up in late February 1525. Its joint authors were Christoph Schappeler, a Zwinglian preacher at Memmingen, and Sebastian Lotzer, a journeyman furrier in the same town, who was a Lutheran lay preacher and rose to the post of military secretary of the army of the Upper Swabian peasants. Not surprisingly, they gave the manifesto something of the character of a Reformation tract, containing as it did some 60 biblical references. They also summarized some three hundred lists of peasant grievances and gave them a coherence and general applicability they had not originally possessed. They demanded the free election of ministers by their congregations and the abolition of the irksome smaller tithe on cattle, vegetables and secondary crops. (The high proportion of clerical landlords in the main centres of the revolt suggests that anti-clericalism was a crucial issue.) They condemned personal bondage as 'detestable, seeing that Christ by the shedding of His precious blood has redeemed and bought [i.e. freed] us all . . .'[25] The lords' appropriation of hunting, fishing and forest rights, and their expropriation of communal meadows and arable land were condemned. The arbitrary increase of labour services, and the levying of heriots on widows and orphans were denounced. (Even Lutheran theologians hostile to the Twelve Articles accepted the legitimacy of the demand for the abolition of heriots.) They requested that free tenants should not lose their property as a result of unfair rents and that justice be exercised impartially according to customary law. They concluded boldly that 'if one or more of the articles . . . were not to be [found] in agreement with the Word of God . . . we would abandon them'.[26] The Twelve Articles seemed reasonable in tone, and the significant number of articles concerned with non-servile issues suggests that the manifesto was intended to appeal to free tenant farmers. The latter were seeking to keep control of common land and prevent its alienation to day labourers and landless peasants. Those already in control of the land hoped by these articles to gain access to the woods, fish-ponds and streams and thus improve their economic prospects. Freer access to woodland would, for example, reduce the cost of house construction. To some extent, the German Peasants' War as seen through its propagandists can be seen as motivated by rising expectations.

The Twelve Articles went through twenty-five printed editions in two months, and may have sold as many as 25,000 copies. Despite this widespread diffusion, peasant demands retained regional characteristics. Leaving aside the millenarian visions of Müntzer and Michael Gaismair, it is clear that other ideas competed with the Twelve Articles. There was some support in the fragmented states for the abolition of all lordship in favour of direct and exclusive obedience to the Emperor. In the larger, unitary states, the peasants sought to modify the representative system and secure direct participation as a separate fourth estate. Such inconsistency was matched by a failure of military resolve in the later stages of the war. The territorial fragmentation of Germany and the lack of an Imperial standing army had been decisive in the early successes of the peasants. At first, lesser princes were forced to make concessions. The peasants made considerable progress in Württemberg because duke Ulrich was in exile and the Habsburg-administered duchy was denuded of troops. The Swabian League was weakened by the absence of its seasoned troops on service in Italy. Further north, the government of electoral Saxony was paralysed during the final illness of Frederick the Wise. Had the peasants developed a more effective military union, and had they been clearer about their ultimate political objectives, these short-term advantages might have been put to better effect.

As it was, duke Antoine of Lorraine intervened and won the battle of Saverne in May 1525. After the Habsburg victory at Pavia in Italy, the veterans of the Swabian League were free to return to Germany and quickly re-established the League's military supremacy in south-west Germany. Hesse and Albertine Saxony defeated the Thuringian rebels. Contemporary estimates vary widely, but perhaps 50,000 or even 130,000 peasants were killed in the various battles during the war. The repression in the following months was also severe. Large fines were levied to compensate nobles and ecclesiastics for the destruction of their property. Sometimes a few concessions were made on a local basis: heriots were converted into a less onerous form of property tax, restrictions on marriage outside the lord's jurisdiction were lifted, and so on.

The peasants generally may not have gained great benefits, but they suffered no long-term loss of rights resulting from the disastrous defeat, as is seen from the circumstances of the peasant rising in Upper and Lower Austria in 1594–7. The fiscal burden of the war against the Turks was undoubtedly one cause of this revolt; but the main protest was against an increase in labour services (*robot*) and the timing of the services. The peasants wanted the *robot* reduced to six days a year; the lords demanded twenty-four. In the end, the government imposed a compromise of fourteen. Though some services were levied illegally above this limit, the government decree dashed any prospect of a 'second serfdom' in the Austrian lands comparable to that in eastern Europe. The peasants were not necessarily better off economically, since no limit was placed on the amount of rent payable for commuted labour services (*robotgeld*), which seem to have increased substantially.

7.4 Urban Society

In 1500, between 7 and 8 per cent of people (about 3.4 million) in western Europe lived in 145 urban centres of more than 10,000 inhabitants, most of which were in Italy, France and the Low Countries (see table 7.2). By 1650 this figure rose to about 10 per cent (about 6.2 million) in 197 places. This small increase in the urban population had occurred mainly in the first half of the seventeenth century, at a time when there was little, if any, overall population growth (see table 7.3). The cities were not evenly distributed throughout Europe. In 1500, most European townspeople lived in Mediterranean countries; by 1650 the largest number still lived in Italy, but now France was not far behind (see table 7.4). Urban Europe had come to be based much more on north-west Europe, nearer to the Atlantic Ocean and the North Sea than the Mediterranean, at least in part a reflection of shifting trading patterns.

Table 7.2. Number of towns with a population of over 10,000 inhabitants

	1500	1650
England and Wales	5	8
France	32	44
Germany	23	23
Italy	44	50
Low Countries	23	33
Spain	20	24

Source: De Vries, *European Urbanization,*
p. 29.

Table 7.3. Total urban population in towns
of over 10,000 inhabitants (in thousands)

	1500	1650
England and Wales	80	495
France	688	1,438
Germany	385	528
Italy	1,302	1,577
Low Countries	445	1,018
Spain	414	672

Source: De Vries, *European Urbanization,*
p. 30.

Table 7.4. Percentage of the total population resident in towns of over 10,000
inhabitants

	1500		1650	
	per cent of national total	per cent of European total urban pop.	per cent of national total	per cent of European total urban pop.
England and Wales	3.1	2.3	8.7	8
France	4.2	20	7.2	23.3
Germany	3.2	11.2	4.4	8.5
Italy	12.4	37.8	14.0	25.5
Low Countries	18.9	12.9	26.1	16.5
Spain	6.1	12	9.5	10.9

Source: Calculations based on tables 7.1 and 7.3. The total urban population was
estimated by De Vries at 3,441,000 in 1500 and 6,184,000 in 1650: De Vries, *European
Urbanization,* p. 30.

7.4.1 *Factors in the Success and Failure of Towns*

In Europe in 1500, only Paris, Milan, Venice and Naples (and on the edge of Europe, Istanbul) were cities with more than 100,000 inhabitants. By 1600, London, Rome, Palermo and Lisbon had joined them, and by 1650 two others—Amsterdam and Madrid. Twenty-two cities accounted for over 40 per cent of the total urban growth between 1500 and 1600, either by doubling in size or by adding 30,000 to their population totals. In western Europe in 1500, there were eighteen towns of over 40,000 inhabitants with a total population of under 1.2 million. By 1650, there were thirty-two such towns with a total population of just under 2.5 million. But most of the increase in the towns resulted from a general rise in population, not from the growth of the urban at the expense of the rural sector. Since censuses and tax rolls were on the whole better kept in towns than in the countryside, the documented growth of towns provides some of the firmest evidence for the sixteenth-century population increase which is so difficult to demonstrate from incomplete parish records in the countryside. The total urban population of Holland grew from 140,180 in 1514 to 397,307 in 1622, a rise of almost one per cent per annum. But Holland had already been heavily urbanized at the beginning of the period: the urban population had risen by only 8 per cent (from 51 per cent to 59 per cent). The rate of growth of the towns in Holland varied considerably, with Amsterdam and Leiden growing rapidly, but Haarlem, Delft and Gouda much more slowly. High birth-rates, rather than migration from the countryside, seem to be a decisive factor in Dutch urban growth.

Death-rates were much higher in towns, and often exceeded the birth-rate, particularly in years of crisis. At Nördlingen in Germany, there were 1,982 deaths in 1634 but only 412 births, so that the population of some 8,000 went down by nearly 20 per cent in just one year. In this sense, the demographic position of towns might be unfavourable over a longer period. At Geneva between 1580 and 1679, the total number of births exceeded the total of recorded deaths by only 268 (58,832 births were recorded). At Strasbourg, 30,643 births were recorded between 1600 and 1630, but there were 47,871 deaths in the same period. Without immigration, the population of Strasbourg would have declined by over 17,000 in just one generation. The high death-rate in towns of more than 10,000 inhabitants may mean that immigration was essential not simply for growth but merely to maintain the existing size of towns. As yet, urban historical demography is still in its infancy and there are insufficient examples to prove this argument conclusively. In a town which was in a phase of full expansion, such as Lyon between 1520 and 1563, 60 per cent of the population might be immigrants, though the proportion fell as demographic growth slowed down. Lyon was certainly exceptional, for it drew on a much wider geographical area for immigration than most towns. The disparity of growth rates in towns may indeed be partially explained by the greater ability of some cities to attract immigrants.

The catchment area for migrants was one decisive factor in the success of towns, but commercial competition was equally important, for it could attract migration from one town to another. The urban population was more mobile than that of the countryside: movement from one town to another was far commoner than the momentous first departure from the countryside to the town. Lübeck's population remained static at around 25,000 after 1500: this was a town suffering full economic decline because of commercial competition from the Dutch penetration of the Baltic market. In contrast, Hamburg prospered during the difficulties of the Hanseatic League (though it was itself a member of the League), and particularly after the decline of Antwerp. Its population rose rapidly from 14,000 in 1500 to nearly 50,000 in 1620, making it the leading German town. One of the most striking examples of economic decline halting demographic growth is provided by the Castilian cities. With little or no commerce, and no native merchant dynasties, Valladolid was dependent on the presence of the royal court. The building of the Escorial after 1561, and the transfer of the court to Madrid, proved fatal to its fortunes and demographic growth. The population scarcely grew at all between 1561 (33,000) and 1591 (40,000). Madrid, in contrast, prospered to become the largest city in Spain, with a population of 175,000 by 1630. Its fastest rate of growth was under Philip III (1598–1621), for in 1597 Madrid still had only 65,000 inhabitants, comparable with neighbouring Toledo only 50 miles away, although more than Valladolid. Madrid proved more successful than Toledo in attracting immigrants, because real wages were high and the building boom in the new capital was not matched elsewhere. Increased demands for food led to urban rivalry for inelastic supplies, which resulted in rocketing food prices in most Spanish cities. Madrid was protected from these high prices by government regulation, which diverted food supplies to the capital, keeping prices lower there than at Toledo, despite higher transportation costs. By 1631, Toledo's population had declined to 20,000. The collapse of its textile industry was no doubt the main reason, but the rise in food prices precipitated by the growth of Madrid had pushed up labour costs in this industry which had led to a loss of international competitiveness. Madrid's great period of expansion helped undermine the other Castilian cities: it was a parasite on the surrounding rural and urban economy. By 1650, it was ten times larger than any potential rival among the Castilian cities. However, the increasing burden of taxation after 1575 was arguably even more important than more general economic factors in bringing about the decline of the Castilian towns.

7.4.2   *Towns in Eastern Europe*

Whereas most European countries saw an expansion in the size of towns accompanying the demographic growth of the sixteenth century, the Muscovite towns may actually have declined in size. The population seems to have deserted the towns during the *oprichnina*, the Livonian war and the Time of Troubles. Before the Tatars burnt Moscow in 1571, it was said that there were 40,000 houses, and perhaps 180,000 inhabitants, but any estimate of the overall urban population and its relation to the population of the Muscovite state is guesswork, since towns were defined by legal status, not size. An urban population of 2 per cent is a reasonable hypothesis. The number of towns increased as the boundaries of the state were extended: there were 96 in 1500, 170 by 1600 and 226 by 1650. Even by 1650, there were probably still too few to establish economic dominance over their huge hinterlands. Furthermore, the tendency towards rural self-sufficiency hindered urban development. So too did the relatively primitive means of production and marketing. Unlike western Europe, the Muscovite towns did not produce better goods than the countryside, nor did they produce more at a lower price. Craft guilds, merchant organizations and other institutions of economic self-regulation were all conspicuously absent in Muscovy. Lacking convenient ports, and on the periphery of Europe, the Muscovite towns failed to benefit from the great revival of trade after 1500. The Tsar hindered the free exercise of trade, since its profits were essential to the finances of the state. Ivan III had already made it clear in his treatment of Novgorod in 1478 that merchants and city dwellers would not be allowed independence.

Muscovite towns thus cannot be seen as economic centres. They were either fortified strong-points, like the towns along the Belgorod fortified line constructed between 1636 and 1654, or administrative centres. By the seventeenth century, especially as a result of the law code of 1649, the urban area (*posad*) ceased to refer to the area of taxable state land within the town walls, and came to mean instead those subject to government responsibilities and taxes (*tiaglo*). Within the towns, there were institutions adequate to cope with the relatively simple administrative tasks entrusted to them by the government, but they lacked financial and social power which might have threatened the Tsar's freedom of action. Independent city life did not develop in Muscovy. The cities served the Tsar in the same way as did the service gentry on their fiefs.

In Poland, a comparatively high proportion of the population lived in small towns of less than 10,000 inhabitants—perhaps 20 per cent did so by 1600. These were mainly new towns: nobles founded them to avoid tolls and market dues levied by the longer-established municipalities. At the end of the seventeenth century, 477 out of 741 Polish towns were 'private', dependent on a nobleman who strictly controlled every aspect of their life. The rising political importance of Warsaw, linked to the fortunes of the ruling dynasty, was reflected in its doubling of size from 10,000 in 1550 to 20,000 in 1650. The three royal Prussian ports (Danzig, Elbing and Torun) were unique because of their favourable economic position. Danzig's population more than trebled from 20,000 to 70,000 between 1500 and 1650. The size and wealth of these three towns ensured their political independence—unlike the situation in Poland itself, where the predominance of the *szlachta* led to the subordination of the towns. Manufacturing in the Polish towns was controlled by a rigid guild system, and small-scale production predominated. The generation of urban wealth was further restricted, because in 1565 merchants were forbidden to participate in foreign trade. Although the urban patriciate sought assimilation into the ranks of the nobility as did its counterparts in western Europe, they were hampered because there was no extension of urban landholding into the countryside, a crucial factor in the gentrification of urban society elsewhere. The clergy and nobility in Poland reinforced their grip on urban property by making massive purchases of land which were exempt from town laws and urban taxes. By 1667, only 28 per cent of the area within the town walls of Cracow was owned by the citizens themselves. The political and social passivity of the towns was matched by deepening economic recession. The nobility controlled the institutions of the Polish state and squeezed out any potential threats to their predominance. Danzig rebelled twice to defend its privileges, in 1526 and 1577–8, and almost alone was able to protect its system of government (and the Lutheran religion of its German population) from Catholic royal and aristocratic interference.

7.4.3 *The Political and Social Structure of Towns in Western Europe*

Towns were places of disparate wealth. This was most obvious in the distinction between the property-owning citizens and the property-less mass outside the citizenry. Some of the best evidence comes from the German cities, where in some instances their citizens had to pay property taxes which were self-assessed on oath. The value of such evidence might be viewed with considerable scepticism, were it not that in a town such as Nördlingen, for example, a law of 1528 discouraged under-assessment by empowering the municipal council to purchase property using the tax assessment as the price. The registers of tax assessment thus give the historian probably a fairly accurate picture of the wealth structure in a town. The average tax assessment at Nördlingen in 1579 was 454 florins. But a quarter of the 1,541 'citizens' (that is, heads of households) paid only a minimal tax; three-quarters had assessments of less than 400 florins. The top 2 per cent of the citizens owned a quarter of the wealth; the top 10 per cent owned 60 per cent of the wealth. The rich grew more prosperous between 1579 and 1646, and nine-tenths of the population grew correspondingly poorer. Yet the merchants at Nördlingen between the 1580s and 1620s did rather better than other citizens and grew proportionately richer. It is misleading to talk of successful and unsuccessful occupations, however, because each had its own hierarchy of wealth. The poor wool weaver may have had more in common with the poor shoemaker or tanner than with the richer members of his own craft. In many German towns, there seems to have been a lower citizen group, which would later be termed the petty bourgeoisie (*Kleinbürger*), as distinct from the merchant patricians and proletariat. But there was little collective consciousness among the poorer members of a craft, and the craft system itself precluded a common sense of oppression among citizens who were taxed proportionately more heavily than the rich.

If towns were places of unevenly shared wealth, they were also places dominated by oligarchy, the most famous European example being Venice. The Venetian constitution was frequently commented upon by contemporaries and it was the model to which larger cities which could support a rich patriciate aspired. Venice was seen as uniquely successful because it had achieved unrivalled social and political harmony. The Florentine republics of 1494 and 1527 had not survived the great crises of 1512 and 1530, but the Venetian constitution had withstood episodes such as the War of the League of Cambrai (1509) and the Papal Interdict (1606–7). Natural advantages, wrote Gasparo Contarini in 1523–4, had left Venice 'free and untouched from the violence of an enemy' for 1,100 years. But the chief reason for its survival was 'institutions and laws prudently decreed'.[27] The Venetian constitution was praised because it was a mixed constitution, the Doge representing monarchy, the Senate and Council of Ten aristocracy, and the Great Council 'democracy'. In fact, Venice was an aristocratic republic. The Doge was elected for life, but he was usually elderly (the average age at election of the twenty-three Doges in office between 1400 and 1570 was 72) and his actions were constrained by an election oath (*promissione*). In contrast, the Senate and its inner group, the Council of Ten, represented 300 patricians over the age of 40. The Great Council represented the interests of all legitimate Venetian nobles over the age of 25. Those families who had been members of the nobility in 1297 remained permanently in the patriciate; nobility dated from 1381 in the case of another thirty families, and they too were members of the patriciate as of right. No new entries to the nobility were permitted before 1646, when the costs of the war in Crete against the Turks forced the council to agree to the sale of noble titles for 100,000 ducats each. In 1494, there had been 2,420 noblemen of an age to hold office, but there were only 1,540 by 1652. Venice is thus the earliest and best example of a closed urban nobility. Genoa followed suit some 150 years later. In England, closed oligarchies developed in some towns in the late medieval period, in which, for example, aldermen chose their own replacements: this led to the problem of 'decayed townships' and 'rotten boroughs' which was to require political reform in the nineteenth century.

In Germany, too, some of the free cities came close to achieving a degree of social exclusiveness comparable to that of Venice. In 1516, Christoph Scheurl noted the predominance at Nuremberg of forty-three leading families whose ancestors were already members of the government in the 1220s and 1230s 'and ruled the city': 'we admit no one into our council . . . whose parents and grandparents did not also sit in the council . . .'[28] After the suppression of a rebellion at Nuremberg in 1349, guilds and other craft organizations were abolished and forbidden in perpetuity. The political power of the patricians was thus linked more directly to their economic power than elsewhere in Germany, where the guilds were given a degree of political representation in the greater council of the town. At Nördlingen, for example, twelve guilds each nominated a town councillor, and filled half the places of the twenty-four man council. However, in 1552 Charles V dissolved the guilds and reorganized the council as a self-perpetuating fifteen-man body. Virtually every citizen was eligible for election, but in practice only those with relatives already serving in the council or who had at least a family connection with the city government had any hope of being elected. Membership of the council was limited in practice to the richest one-fifth of the citizens. The fifteen councillors owned between them at least a tenth of the city's wealth, a proportion which rose to 30 per cent by 1646, when the impact of the Thirty Years' War had consolidated the wealth of this elite.

A similar close relationship between certain families and membership of a town's governing body is discernible elsewhere. Most of the ninety Paris city councillors who served between 1535 and 1575 were Parisian by birth. They were men on the make: 31 of the 90 councillors were sons of merchants, but the number of merchants on the city council declined steadily in the course of the sixteenth century. Previous generations had been well on the way to acquiring nobility through the purchase of landed estates, and more than two-fifths of the councillors inherited at least one noble landholding. Marriage was a crucial stage in their advancement. Intermarriage between the families of councillors was so common that only one in eight of the group was not the son, son-in-law or grandson of a man active in city politics. The oligarchic nature of the council seems to have become established in the 1530s, when it became common for one councillor to resign his office to another. At least 43 of the 90 Paris city councillors who have been studied in detail were not elected but were the beneficiaries of resignations. This process was further enhanced after 1581, when Paris city councillors gained the right, enjoyed by royal office-holders in the sovereign courts, to obtain an expectancy on their offices for their sons or other close relatives.

At Lyon, in contrast with Paris, merchants were in the ascendancy. Some 301 merchants acceded to the town council (*consulat*) between 1520 and 1579, but only 82 office-holders and doctors of law did so. Dynasties of merchants had attained a disproportionate position: 121 places on the town council were occupied by members of just 20 of the richest families in the period. Municipal office at Lyon ennobled its holder after 1495, which is early for French towns. Although municipal office in Paris was itself ennobling from 1577, by an edict which retrospectively applied ennoblement from the time of the reign of Henri II, 72 per cent of the new town councillors (*échevins*) between 1594 and 1609 were already noblemen at the time of their election. Toulouse gained this privilege of ennoblement in 1675, but many other towns did not obtain it until later. In the Spanish kingdoms, town councillors bought their offices at a much earlier date. Although in 1494 the sale of municipal offices was prohibited, the practice of resignation was allowed and many offices became heredit-ary. Under Philip II, any restrictions on the sale of municipal offices were removed, with the result that most were bought and sold by the end of his reign. Such sales, and the consequent restriction of office-holding to a small minority, linked with increasingly heavy taxes borne by the Castilian towns, inhibited urban independence and commercial development.

In contrast, where municipal offices were not sold, as in the Dutch Republic, urban wealth and independence could proceed relatively unchecked. Sir William Temple, an acute English observer during the reign of Charles II, commented that Dutch merchant families intermarried with those involved in civic office, and 'thereby introduce[d] their families into the way of government and honour, which consists not here in titles but in public employments'.[29] For Melchior Fokkens, writing his *Description of the Widely Renowned Merchant City of Amsterdam* in 1662, Holland was a promised land, and Amsterdam 'a city that overflows with milk and with cheese'.[30] Such urban panegyrics ignored the fact that even the Dutch Republic witnessed bread riots, at 's Hertogenbosch in 1628 and again in 1662, at Leiden and Gouda in 1630, and at Leiden again in 1638. These events were short-lived, and did not disturb the uninterrupted power enjoyed by the Dutch patriciate from the Middle Ages to the end of the *ancien régime* in 1795. Any 'alterations' or 'changes to the law' (*wets-verzettingen*), which modified the membership of the Amsterdam city council, were exceptional and occurred under the pressure of events, respectively in 1578 (the participation of the city in the Dutch revolt), in 1618 (the fall of Oldenbarnevelt) and in 1672 (the fall of De Witt). Yet

although on the first occasion the Amsterdam civic guard had intervened
to modify the composition of the city council, the States of Holland
resolved three years later, in 1581, that in future no town government in
the province should be permitted to consult the civic guard, the guilds or
any other corporation of citizens about the affairs of the province. The
result, in Temple's words, was 'a sort of oligarchy, and very different from a
popular government':[31] town councillors became in practice free from
interference both from the population at large and (because of the weakness of the federal constitution: see chapter 6.2.3) from the central government. In his pamphlet entitled *A Brief Demonstration* . . ., drawn up in
1587, Francis Vranck, the pensionary of the town of Gouda, denied the
sovereignty both of the people and of the House of Orange. He wrote that
'the government of most of the towns consists of a board of councillors,
chosen from the most prominent citizens . . . Once chosen, the councillors
serve as long as they live and possess burgher rights. When someone dies
or leaves the town, the board chooses a new member from among the citizens to make up their number . . . the citizens accept their decisions as
binding for they have never infringed or opposed these decisions.' Vranck
concluded that the towns were ruled 'absolutely', that is, without interference, by their councils.[32] Hardly surprisingly, Temple concluded that 'a
certain sovereignty', which in his view encompassed 'the power of exercising judicature, levying . . . money, and making war and peace', rested
with the towns in the United Provinces.[33]

In Pieter de la Court's *Interest of Holland* (1661), it was proclaimed that
'Holland now wholly subsists by Traffic (that is, trade)'.[34] In his view, three
principal reasons had brought this about. One was religious toleration,
'the freedom of all sorts of religions differing from the Reformed'. 'Next to
a liberty of serving God', la Court argued, followed 'the liberty of gaining a
livelihood without any dear-bought city-freedom'. Finally, the curtailing of
guild privileges was of crucial importance.[35] At Amsterdam, the status of
citizen (*poorter*) had to be bought, and indeed rose in price from 8 to 12
florins in 1622 and reached 50 florins by 1650. But though such status was
technically required for admission to guilds, and to certain occupations
which included the retail trades, this was not consistently enforced. Many
wholesale occupations were open to non-citizens, as were the industries
not organized in guilds. The ruling patriciate at Amsterdam was actively
involved in trade, whether in the Baltic (especially grain and timber), in
the fisheries (including herring, stockfish and fish-oils), or in shipowning.
The Amsterdam municipality controlled the main financial institutions of
the state, above all the Amsterdam Exchange Bank (*Wisselbank*), which
was founded in 1609. Under Reynier Pauw, and later Andries Bicker, the
Amsterdam municipality proved to be a stout champion of trading
ventures such as the Dutch East and West India Companies. Only after the

fall of the Bicker family following the attempted coup of William II in 1650 (see chapter 4.2.4) were complaints heard that the Amsterdam regents had lost interest in overseas trade and were drawing their money 'from houses, lands and money at interest'.[36] Even relatively small towns in the Netherlands had a strong commitment to trade. At Nijmegen, a town with only about 10,000 inhabitants around 1550, merchants, especially wine merchants, held nearly half of the positions on the town council in the second half of the sixteenth century, even though they accounted for only 4 per cent of the total population.

7.5 Urban Revolt

There were few rural protests in which some townsmen did not participate; the part taken by certain leading citizens of Memmingen in the German Peasants' War is an example. Similarly, agricultural labourers joined in urban disturbances, sometimes mobilized by factions in the town for their own interests, sometimes seeking to dominate the town to rally support for their own cause. But there were also revolts which were predominantly urban in character. Because of the great political importance of cities as centres of wealth and administration, urban unrest tended to assume a greater political significance than rural rebellion. This is evident in the greatest urban insurrection of the period, that of Castile in 1520–1, but it is equally apparent in the Dutch revolt and the French wars of religion. A country which had little violent political upheaval, such as England between the Wars of the Roses and the Civil War, significantly suffered no large-scale urban disturbance.

7.5.1 *Types of Urban Revolt: Food Riots*

Urban insurrections seem to fall into five general categories: food riots, riots against outsiders, riots resulting from faction rivalry, tax riots and large-scale political rebellions. As with rural protest, there was some overlapping: a food riot might develop into a tax riot, and so on. Among the urban revolts which began over food, the *Rebeyne* at Lyon in April 1529, the revolt of Naples in 1585 and that of Palermo in 1647, stand out. The *Rebeyne* was in essence a grain riot involving over a thousand people following the failure of the harvest in the Beauce and Burgundy, the two main areas upon which Lyon was reliant for its food supply. Property was pillaged by the mob looking for grain hoards. Neither artisans nor heretics seem to have played a particularly important part in the rioting; placards posted to denounce grain hoarding were signed collectively by 'the poor' (*le Povre*). Eleven rioters, all manual workers, were executed in the repression which followed, and seventeen were imprisoned, including four bakers and a cleric. A bad harvest was also the immediate cause of the trouble in 1585 at Naples, but there the situation was made much worse by the government authorizing the raising of the price of bread and export flour. One of the city magistrates responsible for this decision was lynched and mutilated. Over 800 people were prosecuted in the brutal repression which followed. Famine preceded the outbreak of rioting at Palermo in May 1647. The revolt was a direct response to the reduction by the city government of the weight of bread from $11\frac{3}{4}$ ounces to 10 ounces. The slogans of the mob, 'long live the king and down with the taxes and the bad government',[37] made it clear that they wanted a general reduction of taxes and not merely the restoration of loaves to their former weight. The viceroy was forced to make concessions, and to suspend the taxes on grain, wine, oil, meat and cheese (the so-called five *gabelles*). Under the leadership of its captain-general, Guiseppi d'Alesi, a former gold-beater, the popular movement sought a further reduction in taxes, greater participation for the guilds in urban government and a reform of legal procedure. The viceroy had d'Alesi and twelve of his supporters murdered, although, unlike contemporary events at Naples, there were relatively few atrocities in this revolt. The failure of guild leadership and the lack of co-operation between Palermo and Messina were crucial to the eventual demise of the movement.

The example of Palermo was a stimulus to a second, near-contemporaneous revolt at Naples, where there were demands for the abolition of taxes on fruit and bread. The viceroy's palace was sacked by the crowd. At first, the violence was largely symbolic, but then it became more systematic under the leadership of Masaniello, a fisherman, and Giulio Genoino, a lawyer who had acted as spokesmen for those wealthy members of the third estate who wanted parity with the nobles in municipal government. A militia force of craftsmen and shopkeepers was mobilized, and attacks were made on the property of leading collaborators with the Spanish administration. An assassination attempt on Masaniello provoked a violent reaction, with ritualized murders, decapitations and mutilations. At the height of his powers as 'captain-general of the people', however, Masaniello was murdered. The mob was enraged both by this and by a drastic reduction in the weight of bread from 24 to 18 ounces. Masaniello's body was carried round the city as if in triumph; he was revered as the 'redeemer' of the people, and his hair was torn out for relics. But his part in the insurrection had been small: only ten days in a revolt which lasted for nine months. The popular militia, which succeeded in maintaining unity and discipline (although it numbered several thousand), was the decisive factor in this organized phase of the revolt. Genoino continued to play a leading part until he clashed with the growing republican party and was banished by popular demand. Although food shortages occurred regularly in early modern Europe, such large-scale urban disturbances related to harvest failures were relatively infrequent. Economic conditions were often worse after the revolt than before. (This was certainly the case at Lyon in 1531, where the price of bread was higher than it had been two years earlier at the time of the *Rebeyne*.) Resentment at alleged maladministration or hoarding of food seems to have inspired the food riots rather than starvation itself.

7.5.2 *Types of Urban Revolt: Riots against Outsiders*

More significant were the numbers of urban riots against outsiders of different categories. They might be suburb dwellers; might hold jurisdiction which was resented (for example, a bishop or seigneur); might be representatives of the judicial, fiscal or military power of the crown; finally, they might simply be foreigners or members of another faith. At Lisbon in April 1506, 2,000 Jews were massacred when plague threatened the city. In relatively pacific London on 'evil May Day' 1517, mobs of apprentices, shopkeepers, artisans and women attacked Italian and French craftsmen and merchants. At Marseille in March 1620, forty-five Algerians and six local inhabitants were killed in a xenophobic riot. Similarly, there were anti-Jewish riots at Frankfurt-am-Main in 1614, when the ghetto was looted and the Jews forced out of the city. The leader of the anti-patrician and anti-Jewish movement, Vincent Fettmilch, was not executed until two years later, when the city councillors who had provided protection to the Jews returned to power. This was an extreme example of the tension between councils and citizens which led to violence in a number of German cities before the outbreak of the Thirty Years' War.

The most notable examples of urban insurrections against perceived outsiders—in reality, members of another faith—are provided by the almost simultaneous risings of the Calvinist cities in Flanders and Brabant in the late 1570s and the Catholic cities of France in the 1580s. Religious struggle incited urban violence. The Calvinist dictatorship at Ghent followed the disastrous defeat of the 'states party' (the supporters of the rebellious States General) at the battle of Gembloux in January 1578 (see chapter 3.2.4). William of Orange's policy of 'religious peace' (*Religions-vrede*) paradoxically intensified religious conflict in towns such as Ghent, where it seemed to work in favour of the Calvinists. Even so, radical preachers such as Peter Dathenus and Herman Moded denounced his moderation, which they linked with a lack of patriotism in the struggle against Spain. In February 1579, there were iconoclastic riots and attacks on Catholics at Ghent: among the popular slogans were 'Antichrist', 'blood of papists' and 'seize the wealth of the rich (*ryckemans goet*)'.[38] The radical Calvinist leadership arbitrarily arrested Catholic priests and citizens to try to impose its will; but such arrests were often followed by the release of the prisoners after a period of time. Though there were fears of a 'peasant war' (*bellum rusticum*)[39] in the surrounding countryside, there was no clear alliance between Ghent Calvinists and the rural communities. Jan van Hembyze, the city leader, talked of making Ghent a 'second Geneva',[40] and in July 1579 required the civil guard to pledge its support for the suppression of Catholicism, the abolition of the Inquisition and the conservation of the town's privileges. At the end of August, however, William of Orange succeeded in forcing the departure of Hembyze for the Palatinate, where he joined Dathenus in exile. In general, the period of Calvinist 'dictatorship' at Ghent seems to have been less violent than comparable events in France during the wars of religion.

The precipitant for the disorders in Paris was Henri III's attempt to restore his political control by introducing professional soldiers into the capital in May 1588. The result was an overwhelming, if short-lived, surge in support for the Catholic League on the Day of the Barricades (see chapter 3.3.5), an event which may in itself have been masterminded by a small group of extremists: contemporary estimates put the figure of Parisians out on the streets during the Day of the Barricades at in excess of 30,000. Catholic violence in the French towns had erupted in three main waves during the wars of religion, in 1562, in 1572 and, to a lesser extent, in 1588–94. By then, the atmosphere had changed considerably since the extreme reaction of the Catholics to the edict of January 1562, which had granted toleration to the Huguenots, and to news of the St Bartholomew massacres ten years later. There were predictions that great disasters would befall the Catholic religion in 1583–4 and 1588–90. On the first occasion, there was a wave of 'white processions' in northern France, gatherings of several thousand men, women and children dressed in white sheeting or cloth, chanting hymns and canticles. The centre of these processional movements was in the Guise heartland of Champagne, and it is likely that the Guises saw them as a way of mobilizing Catholic opinion against Henri III.

Paris was much less affected by outbursts of mass hysteria in 1583–4 than it was in the late 1580s. The processions in the capital between the assassination of the Guises in December 1588 and the first anniversary of the Day of the Barricades in May 1589 were of fundamental importance: thousands of children, again dressed in white, were led by their parish clergy on one occasion; other processions followed, in the words of the contemporary diarist Lestoile, with the participants drawn from 'all the parishes of the capital, all ages, sexes and social conditions; they went two by two through the streets and by the churches, mostly in white shifts and with bare feet even though it was very cold, chanting in great devotion, with burning wax candles in their hands'.[41] Much of this was spontaneous: the role of the parish *curés* was directed less towards arousing such religious demonstrations than sponsoring other forms of extreme propaganda in favour of the League. For League propagandists, 'the particular hand of God'[42] was to be seen in the formation of the Holy Union; for Jean de Caumont, writing in 1587, it was a *Union of Catholics with God and between Themselves*.[43] The atmosphere in the capital was one of eschatological expectation: the second coming of Christ was eagerly anticipated, rather as it had been at Florence in 1494 at the time of Savonarola. The purpose of the Holy Union was 'the conservation of our religion, whose ruin is near at hand'; the 'ruin of Paris' would lead ineluctably to that of the whole kingdom.[44]

Once Henri III had been chased from his capital, and above all once the news spread of his assassination of the Guises, a Catholic dictatorship emerged to protect the faithful in the capital and elsewhere in France from his barbarous tyranny. The influence exerted by the capital over the other French cities was substantial, although under the League a federal structure was intended, and popular support for the League in other French towns took a very different form. The processional movements were less important, while the role of the preachers was greater. At Nantes in the spring of 1589, Jacques Le Bossu used the text of Exodus xxxii.25–9 to justify Mayenne's revolt against Henri III: 'the children of Levi leagued with him and lashed out at those who had changed the religion, although they were often close relatives: and having consecrated their hands in blood, they received benediction.'[45] In the cities in western France there were no institutional revolutions comparable to League innovations such as the councils of the Sixteen in the capital. Nor, for the most part, did other cities witness the violence of 15 November 1591, when three leading members of the Parisian sovereign courts, Barnabé Brisson, the first president of the *Parlement*, and two councillors (Claude Larcher and Jean Tardif), were summarily tried and executed by the radicals in what was consciously intended to be the beginning of a 'St Bartholomew [massacre] of the *Politiques*'.[46] The unfortunate officeholders who were executed were accused of having planned to open the city gates to Henri IV; there is no doubt that Brisson was at most lukewarm in his support of the League. Yet the expected riot against Navarrist supporters in Paris failed to materialize in the aftermath of the executions: in L'Estoile's words, 'this populace of Paris, instead of rising up and seizing arms to cause a riot ... was as silent as if it had been stunned by the blow of a hammer ... being more moved to sadness than to sedition'.[47] The execution of Brisson and his colleagues demonstrated that the Sixteen was no longer moving in step with opinion generally in the capital, and it was the prelude to a gradual collapse in support that led eventually to the capitulation of Paris to Henri IV in March 1594.

7.5.3 *Types of Urban Revolt: Tax Riots*

Such extremes of violent community action, although notorious, were relatively uncommon in towns, where opinion was usually divided. Social and political fragmentation generated faction-fighting, either in the town council, or within a local governing institution (in France, for example, within a provincial sovereign court). The struggles between factions within the oligarchy at Marseille and within the *Parlement* of Aix-en-Provence were largely responsible for the urban revolts in seventeenth-century Provence. Charges of financial mismanagement also played an important part, while election disputes or the suspension of elections could intensify urban rioting. Sometimes the conflicts took the form of struggles between the lower orders and the rich. Trouble at the small town of Romans in Dauphiné in 1580 began in a carnival atmosphere and ended in ten murders; the revolt centred on the craftsmen, who attacked the leading members of the city government, and only one patrician was involved in a subsidiary role. During the Fronde there were popular revolutions at Bordeaux and Angers in 1652, known respectively as the *Ormée* and the *Loricards*, but they were isolated phenomena of short duration. Conflicts resulting from one faction seeking support from the lower orders against a rival faction were more common than confrontations between the rich and the rest.

Tax riots were perhaps the most frequent type of urban disorder, since the privileges of towns were partly fiscal in character. Any attempt by the government to increase the tax burden on new urban wealth was resisted as an encroachment on the sacrosanct town charter. Most smaller French urban disturbances started in this way and were single-grievance movements of short duration. Overwhelmingly, the aim was the defence of the *status quo*. This required little either in the way of a manifesto to justify the rebellion, or of leadership to provide a focus. The immediate cause of rioting was usually self-evident: a forced loan, a tax on the well-to-do, a sales tax, the appropriation by the central government of municipal revenues, and so on. Once the grievance was removed, the rioting ceased. Occasionally, the fiscal threat was more generalized, involving no longer merely a single town, but a number of them in a movement against the central government's encroachment on provincial privilege. The riots at La Rochelle in 1542 and Bordeaux in 1548 fall into this category, forming part of a generalized resistance to the establishment of the salt tax (*gabelle*) in south-west France. So too do the riots in Provence in 1630, 1634, 1649 and 1659, though here the fiscal grievances were different.

Again, the riots at Dijon in 1630, in the Guyenne towns in 1635 and the towns of Normandy in 1639 had a common basis. Doubtless there would have been riots in the Languedoc towns in 1632 had Montmorency's rebellion not been promptly defeated (see chapter 4.4.2). Not surprisingly, the immediate fiscal grievance which posed the threat to provincial privilege was rescinded in all these cases. While this type of urban upheaval was not necessarily the most violent, it presented the greatest challenge to central government.

There were considerable differences between the pace of encroaching state taxation in the various European countries. In France, there were scarcely any urban revolts of significance between 1477 and 1548 (the exceptions are those at Albi in 1491, at Caen in 1514 and at Lyon in 1529, whose causation was strictly local). The menace to urban privileges came after 1550, with the threat to municipal finances posed by the increased fiscal demands of the state during Henri II's war with Philip II and subsequently during the wars of religion. The contrast with the Low Countries is striking: after a series of urban insurrections between 1338 and 1467, the Flemish towns were convulsed by three successive waves of revolt in 1477, 1482–92 and 1537–40. It is no coincidence that taxation trebled in the century before the urban revolts of the 1530s. Where the urban charter had conferred wider privileges of self-government on the townsmen, as was the case with Ghent in 1539, urban resistance to taxation could take the form of an attempted transfer of sovereignty to an apparently more compliant ruler. With the defeat of the revolt by Charles V in February 1540, the privileges of Ghent were solemnly revoked because of this act of treason. The extensive role of the guilds in urban government was undermined; the grand council of the commune was abolished, and town councillors were henceforth to be nominated by the ruler.

Extreme violence was rare. Between 1596 and 1660, it is estimated that there were 264 'insurrectional movements' in sixty or so (mostly small) Provençal towns (out of some 600 communities), but only sixty-nine deaths before 1648. The towns, moreover, became more law-abiding with the passing of time: only three deaths in riots occurred in Provence between 1660 and 1715. A riot such as that at Agen in 1635, where the fury of the mob was such that there were twenty-four victims, including twelve financial office-holders, several of whom were vilely mutilated, was exceptional. At Romans in Dauphiné in 1580, artisans threatened the rich with violence, shouting out that 'within three days Christian flesh will be sold at six *deniers* a pound'.[48] But this threat failed to materialize, and since social tensions in the province were aggravated by a local problem of acute fiscal injustice, no conclusion of more general significance may be accorded to this apparently revolutionary overturning of social values.

The most important urban movements were large-scale political rebellions rather than riots. Florence, which underwent a revolution against the Medici dynasty in 1494 and 1527, experienced no great social conflict as a result, and certainly nothing comparable to the revolt of the Ciompi in 1378. The institutions of the state were modified along republican lines, but little or no social adjustment followed.

7.5.4   The Revolt of the Comuneros of Castile, 1520–1521

The largest urban revolt in early modern Europe was that of the Comuneros in Castile in 1520–1. This was mainly a product of Charles V's misgovernment (see chapter 2.4.1), but it also resulted from the special circumstances in Castile. In the 1470s, Isabella had allied with the Castilian towns against the rebellious great nobility. In the organization known as the Council of the Holy Brotherhood (*Santa Hermandad*) after 1476 the towns were encouraged to act in a league and to form a militia to help maintain public order. But when the Brotherhood was disbanded in 1498, the towns lost their special responsibilities and the crown turned once more to the aristocracy for political and military support. In the meantime, the nobles had begun an offensive to expand their estates at the expense of municipal districts and a number of important towns which later joined the 'commune' (Comunero) movement were threatened. Toledo and Segovia, for example, found that the royal courts provided justice only for the aristocracy. The officials sent to the towns to secure royal political and administrative control (*corregidores*) were unable to halt noble encroachment and were accused of corruption. These officials were forced to flee the towns in the early stages of the Comunero revolt.

The first riots occurred at Toledo, and this town together with three others (Salamanca, Segovia and Toro) formed the first union (*Santa Junta*) at the beginning of August 1520. The number of towns joining the *Junta* rose to thirteen by September, though there were later defections. Most notable among the defections was Burgos in the north, whose economic interests differed from the others, being heavily involved in the wool export trade, whereas the others either had limited economic activities or they were directed towards the south. None of the five Andalusian towns represented in the *Cortes* joined the rebellion. Instead, Seville and Córdoba joined with other towns in the region to form a rival alliance, the League of La Rambla, whose aims were to forestall a Morisco rising in Granada and to prevent by force, if necessary, the extension of the *Junta*'s authority. Nor were the Comuneros able to secure co-operation with the revolutionary alliance (Germanía) of neighbouring Valencia. (This movement seems to have aimed originally at opening up the city councils to representatives of the artisan and merchant classes and to securing local control of the Genoese-dominated grain trade. Later, the Germanía became a crusade for the forced conversion of Valencia's Moriscos.) The original members of the *Santa Junta* developed new electoral procedures and gave the elected delegates control of town policy, whereas previously royal policy as manifested through the actions of the *corregidores* had determined the form and decisions of town government. The towns thus became more radical as the revolt progressed, and by the end of the movement, the council of Valladolid was almost as important as the *Santa Junta* itself.

After September 1520, there were riots in the countryside, too, most notably at Dueñas. Here, the aristocracy, rather than the crown, became to a large extent the focus of rebel hostility. Conversely, the 'preservation of his own and other lord's lands'[49] became the motto not just of the Constable but also of other Castilian magnates anxious to preserve the social order. As the rebellion proceeded, the billeting of troops and fiscal devices such as forced loans alienated former supporters of the rebellion in the towns and among the clergy. There were too many rebel commanders, and they differed on strategy. The initiative was left with the government, which recaptured Tordesillas in December 1520, regaining control of the person of Juana the Mad (who had been captured by the rebels in the previous August), and shattering the myth that she supported (and thus legitimized) the revolt. The royal troops were not particularly numerous or well paid, but there was at least a unified military command. Once the total forces at the disposal of the government were able to join together in February 1521, the crucial victory of Villalar became possible.

The extent of the royalist victory permitted some concessions to be made to rebel demands, notably a more pliant attitude to the *Cortes*, a return to the earlier quota system for collecting indirect taxes and a reorganization of central government. The *corregidores* were restored, but closer attention was paid to the quality of appointments and to the appointees' conduct in office. Repression was mild. Only 293 persons were excluded from the general pardon of 1522, a small number given the scale of the rebellion. Of these about a hundred were later pardoned and only twenty-three were executed. The place of the towns in Castilian society remained secure, so much so that the government channelled patronage to the municipal representatives in the *Cortes*. This in turn had the unfortunate long-term consequence of making them a privileged oligarchy incapable of resisting its fiscal demands.

Great rural and urban insurrections such as the German Peasants' War, the revolt of the Comuneros and the Catholic League in France reveal that rebellion on a significant scale was perfectly possible in early modern Europe. Yet it would be a mistake to read too much into this. Each of these movements was profoundly influenced by unusual circumstances—the absence of Charles V from Germany, and the spread of the Reformation in the case of the Peasants' War; the implantation of a new foreign dynasty with extensive European commitments in the case of the Comuneros; and the assassination of the Guises on the orders of Henri III in the case of the League. Widespread revolt was the product of extraordinary events, not easily replicated. Most revolts, rural or urban, were small-scale and of short duration. Deference was the norm in rural and urban communities. The rule of the seigneur or the patrician was accepted as legitimate and just, and was perceived as a consequence of the divine order: it did not degrade or humiliate the rest of society to leave government and other forms of power and influence in the hands of a few. On the contrary, most peasants and town dwellers felt a profound tie of loyalty to their community, which included the seigneur of the parish or the patricians of the city. The 'rulers' rarely had to impose their authority on the 'ruled', and in any case lacked the police force and bureaucracy to do so. Instead, community and regional loyalties were the cement of society. Community did not mean social equality. There may not have been true 'class' distinctions, at least in the modern understanding of the word, but social gradations between one group and another were maintained by elaborate codes of ritual and precedence and by visible distinctions of dress, which in many states were enforced by the so-called 'sumptuary laws'. Cultural patterns therefore reinforced existing social realities.

8

THE EUROPEAN ECONOMY

ONE of the difficulties faced by the historian of early modern Europe is to describe accurately a society and economy in which backwardness persisted yet where there were important trends towards what might be called modernity, perhaps even capitalism. Precise terminology is not easy to find: for example, are the terms 'pre-industrial' and 'proto-industrial' useful concepts when applied to this period? Recently, some French socio-economic historians, instead of emphasizing change, have substituted the idea of so-called 'immobile history', or 'history that stands still'.[1] They argue that during a long period of what was primarily agrarian history (variously described as 1320–1720, 1450–1720 or 1400–1800), society was imprisoned in its basic economic underdevelopment. This in turn is a revision of the more optimistic viewpoint of the French economic historian Simiand, expressed over fifty years ago, that the sixteenth century was a period of economic expansion (phase A), while the seventeenth century was one of recession (phase B). Such views may contain substantial truths but they are open to three objections. Firstly, the expansion of Simiand's phase A did not occur evenly in all sectors of the economy: agriculture did not prosper throughout Europe in the sixteenth century. Secondly, some economies expanded during Simiand's phase B: the prosperity of the Dutch Republic occurred at a time of general recession. Thirdly, the transition from phase A to phase B did not occur uniformly in Europe at any one fixed date nor was it to be found in all areas of economic activity at the same time. This is particularly true of price levels.

Today it is possible to speak of a world economy in which the economic preponderance of certain giant industrial nations exercises a profound effect on lesser industrial powers and backward non-industrial ones. This world economy is a relatively recent development of the last hundred years or so. Early modern Europe knew no giant industrial nations and no unified world economy. Such industrialization as occurred tended to accentuate the fragmented, regional nature of the economy. There were pockets of modernity and progress in some regions, but inertia and backwardness were the norm in many others. However, it has recently been argued by the American historian Wallerstein that a 'European

world-economy' came into existence in the late fifteenth and early sixteenth century.[2] He calls it this because the geographical areas were linked
economically, as well as by imperial and political ties. In this new
economic structure, merchants could gain greater advantages than they
could hope for within the framework of a single European state. The
discovery and colonization of the New World, and the commercial
exploitation of the Cape route to the Far East, provide the most telling
evidence for this interpretation. Even so, the dimension of imperial
politics remained of decisive importance in this European-dominated
economy: it was the kings of Spain who sought to exploit Mexico and Peru
for their own, European, political reasons. Wallerstein's theory is further
weakened because it is difficult to speak of a world economy; Australasia
was not circumnavigated until the 1640s. The new colonial economies
remained largely undeveloped as consumer societies in their own right
and subservient to the old European states. It is the exploitative
character of the first imperial age which emerges most clearly, not the
emergence of a modern world system.

8.1 The 'Tyranny of Gold and Silver'

Richelieu's maxim that 'gold and silver are the tyrants of the world'[3]
graphically described the reliance of governments in early modern
Europe upon bullion. Sound money, and plenty of it, meant strong
government. A currency prone to debasement or devaluation weakened a
government and could prove fatal in a long war. Monetary strength was a
significant factor in the ultimate victory of France over Spain in the war of
1635–59. Spanish coin flooded into the French kingdom and was reissued
as French coin. Conversely, Spanish greatness in the sixteenth and earlier
seventeenth century rested on its fabulous mining resources in the New
World, which were for a time effectively harnessed to the Habsburg cause.
Sir Benjamin Rudyerd, an English Member of Parliament, declared in
1624 that it was not great territories which made Philip IV powerful but
'his mines ... which minister fuel to feed his vast ambitious desire of
universal monarchy'.[4]

8.1.1 *The Supply of Precious Metals*

The fifteenth century had been one of bullion shortage; some historians
have spoken of a 'great bullion famine'.[5] Between the mid-fourteenth and
the mid-fifteenth centuries, the silver mines of Germany and central
Europe had suffered from low productivity and achieved poor results. The
bullion shortage was accentuated by a permanent balance of payments
deficit with the Levant, brought about by high levels of imports of spices

and luxury products from the Far East. Venice played a commanding role in this trade until the Portuguese developed the Cape route. It had accounted for perhaps three-quarters of the European trade deficit; drawing on the metallic reserves of central Europe and the Baltic, it regularly exported annually one metric ton of gold to the Levant, equivalent to between 10 and 12 metric tons of silver. In comparison, the mint output of the French kingdom was derisory, and depended essentially on recoinage, since France lacked natural resources of precious metals. The maximum annual output in the fifteenth century was 1.8 metric tons for gold coinage and 17.5 metric tons for silver (respectively in 1417 and 1419). The figures for most years were much lower, and the high points of the fifteenth century were, significantly, much lower than those for the fourteenth century.

By the late 1460s, the reduced supply of both gold and silver in Europe led to an increase in the commodity price of bullion. This in turn dictated that new solutions had to be found. New investment in turn encouraged experimentation with new mining methods such as long drainage tunnels (called *adits*) and chain-bucket pumps (called *norias*). The result was that between 1460 and 1530, silver production in Germany and central Europe increased fivefold. European silver production remained higher than imports from the New World until the 1550s, and in central Europe silver remained the predominant medium for commercial transactions, although its importance there was not matched in other parts of Europe. At Venice, both gold and silver were important, while in the Iberian peninsula gold predominated. The severe monetary problems of the Portuguese monarchy in the later Middle Ages had prompted a search for new resources from abroad. Ceuta, the port on the southern shore of the Mediterranean opposite Gibraltar and a terminus of the trans-Sahara gold trade, had been acquired in 1415. After the exploration of the coast of Guinea (the so-called Gold Coast), the castle of São Jorge 'da Mina' was built in 1480 and 'Tibir' gold was imported regularly from Guinea thereafter. These imports never amounted to a great deal; at their apogee between 1500 and 1521, they averaged only 410 kg. a year, and they fell subsequently. Although Portugal's total gold imports were higher, they still amounted to only 700 kg. a year. The Venetians called the king of Portugal the king of gold: but even with the addition of 'Monomotapa' gold from east Africa after the mid-sixteenth century, Portuguese gold was never plentiful. Yet relatively small discoveries or transfers of gold could disrupt its market value disproportionately. It seems that it was the influx first of Portuguese, and later of Castilian, gold which destabilized price trends in the Iberian peninsula. Prices rose later and more slowly elsewhere in Europe.

The discovery of America, and its ruthless exploitation by the Spanish colonizers, transformed the supply of bullion and ended the shortages of the later Middle Ages. According to the official figures of the Spanish government, between 1503 and 1660 a total of some 537 million ducats' worth of treasure was imported from the New World into Spain. Nor did the imports dry up altogether in the later seventeenth century, as was once thought: it is now estimated that about 238 million ducats were imported between 1661 and 1700. Expressed in terms of weight, Spain imported a total of 16,886 metric tons (16.8 million kg.) of silver and 181 metric tons (181,361 kg.) of gold from the New World between 1503 and 1660. Gold alone was imported before 1519, and it remained predominant in the shipments until 1530, rising from 4.9 metric tons in 1503-10 to a peak of 43.6 metric tons in 1551-60. Imports then fell rapidly until 1580, though they regained some of their importance between 1581 and 1600: 19.5 metric tons were imported in the last decade of the sixteenth century. The decline of gold imports was a consistent feature of the first half of the seventeenth century: less than half a metric ton was imported to Spain in the decade 1651-60. Since gold was ten to twelve times more valuable than silver, very large imports of silver were necessary before gold could be displaced as the primary metal. Silver imports already exceeded those of gold in quantity after 1530 but they did not outstrip gold imports in value until after 1560. Moreover, as silver became more abundant, so the value of gold increased. Despite the length of the sea journey, American gold was cheaper to import than African gold: the latter ceased to be of great significance after 1530.

There were virtually no silver imports from the New World before 1530, for the mines of central Europe, which reached their zenith of perhaps 900 metric tons of output in the previous decade, could cope with the demand. But the growth of silver imports was extremely rapid after 1530, rising from a level of 86 metric tons in 1531-40 to 1,118 in 1571-80, and reaching a peak of 2,707 metric tons in 1591-1600. These imports filled the void left by the decline of central European production. They also reflected the discovery and exploitation of rich deposits at Zacatecas and Guanajuato in Mexico, respectively in 1546 and 1548, and Potosí in Peru in 1545. The introduction of the mercury amalgamation process was facilitated by the exploration of mercury deposits at Huancavelica in Peru. Whereas gold is often found in its elemental state, silver occurs in complex compounds: the amalgamation process permitted the exploitation of lower-grade ore from veins which would otherwise have been unprofitable. The large treasure fleets of 1595, 1639 and 1641 brought back the equivalent of two years' total output from Potosí. As some mines became exhausted, others came on stream. Zacatecas produced 6.6 million ducats of silver in 1560-4 but 13.1 in 1620-5, at the height of its activity. In 1630-5, on the eve of the French declaration of war on Spain, it still produced nearly 8.2 million ducats. It was only after 1650 that imports of Spanish silver fell below a million metric tons a decade. The official figures which formed the basis of the calculations of the American historian E. J. Hamilton appear seriously to underestimate the imports in the seventeenth century, and thus any decline after 1600 may be exaggerated.[6] The contemporary Dutch public gazettes published figures of silver imports from Spanish America which were at variance with the official ones; these have been included in the alternative calculations for particular decades (see chapters 4.3.1, 4.3.2 and 4.3.5).[7]

8.1.2 *The Quantity Theory of Money*

New World silver became more important than silver produced in Europe after 1550 because mining output in Germany and central Europe declined in the later sixteenth century. By this date, silver had displaced gold as the dominant metal in currency transactions. Since gold was the more valuable metal, it tended to be the medium for large payments: an increase in the supply of gold might thus be expected to affect chiefly wholesale prices. Silver could discharge relatively small payments: an increase in its supply would affect both retail and wholesale prices. American silver arrived first in Spain, and it is obvious that it must have had some impact on the level of Spanish prices. Exactly what the impact was is difficult to determine, because the royal share of the bullion imports fluctuated sharply from one treasure fleet to the next. Sometimes, the royal share amounted to half the total; on other occasions, it was as low as 12 or 16 per cent. In years when the royal share was low, the effect on Spanish prices was probably greater because more silver remained in circulation in the Iberian peninsula: most of the royal share of bullion left Spain immediately to fund Habsburg international defence commitments. The flow of bullion was in any case uneven because of fluctuations in production and the inevitability of attacks on regular convoys which would have been predictable targets. Periods of bullion shortage were thus interspersed with sudden, dramatic, inflows. Three-quarters of the total bullion imports in the decade 1591–1600 arrived in just three years (1595, 1596 and 1600). But the high imports in these years were not followed by a dramatic increase in Andalusian prices: good harvests in 1600–2 had a depressing effect on grain prices. As far as can be ascertained, price movements seem to have remained autonomous from the level of bullion imports both in Spain and elsewhere in Europe.

Nevertheless, some contemporaries were convinced that there was a connection between the imports of precious metals in the sixteenth century and the European price rise. The link was spotted by Martin de Azpílcueta, a theologian of the University of Salamanca, who noted in his *Resolutory Commentary on Exchange* (1556) that money was scarcer in

France than in Spain, and that goods there were worth less. In Spain, he thought, goods and labour had been cheaper before the discovery of America 'flooded the country with gold and silver'. In his formula, 'money is worth more where and when it is scarce than where and when it is abundant'.[8] This clearly anticipated the so-called quantity theory of money which is usually attributed to Jean Bodin, who formulated it in his *Reply . . . to the Paradoxes of the Seigneur de Malestroit* (1568). Malestroit had argued two years earlier that debasement of the coinage was the cause of French inflation. Bodin had little difficulty in demonstrating that debasement alone could not account for the extent of inflation in France. He maintained instead that the 'main and almost sole' cause of the price rise was 'the abundance of gold and silver'. This, he claimed (incorrectly), was 'the cause no one has touched on until now'.[9] Bodin had the better of the argument with Malestroit. It is calculated that by the 1590s one-third of the percentage change in the cost of goods and services in France was due to the depreciation of money of account (that is, in line with Malestroit's theory), but the remaining two-thirds can be accounted for by causes such as the depreciation of precious metals (that is, Bodin's theory). However, quite different calculations would apply to France and other European countries in different periods of the sixteenth century.

Economic historians have tried to interpret the evidence of bullion imports by applying the equation formulated by the economist Irving Fisher in 1911. He postulated that the quantity of goods exchanged, multiplied by their price, is equal to the volume of money in circulation, multiplied by the number of times the money has changed hands (the so-called 'velocity of circulation'). This equation does not prove that monetary factors are the prime movers in price increases, though it does indeed suggest that the price level is the consequence of the relative movement of the other variables. In fact, even if the Fisher equation (whether in its simple or more sophisticated variants) is accepted, we lack the statistical evidence to apply it to the circumstances of early modern Europe.

It is too often forgotten that bullion imports and mint output levels show only increases in the money stock: they do not tell us anything about the total money stock, which was not measured by contemporaries and can therefore never be known with certainty. Estimates vary greatly: one suggests that the total European money stock in 1500 amounted to an equivalent of 75,000 tons of silver; another, based on the estimate of David Hume in 1752, suggests that it was only 15,000 tons of silver. If we rely on the second estimate, which would seem to be more closely related to the European mining capacity of the Middle Ages, the European stock of precious metals had risen to an equivalent of 37,652 tons of silver by 1660, an increase of about 150 per cent. We are even less well informed about the monetary stock of the separate European countries, with the exception of France, where the total value of coinage issued between 1308 and 1791 is known. Between 1493 and 1660 it was equivalent to 4,133 metric tons of silver. 32.2 million *livres* in coin were issued between 1493 and 1550, 96 million between 1551 and 1610, and the huge figure of 427.3 million between 1611 and 1680. Depending on the rate of renewal of the coin—whether it was at thirty- or sixty-year intervals—the French monetary stock rose from an estimated 25 or 30 million *livres* in 1555 to 60 or 89 million in 1600 and 167 or 201 million in 1650.

Governments managed their finances in monies of account. Monies of account were rarely actual coins; as the monetary specialist Jean Trenchant put it in *Arithmetic* (1561), 'a *franc* or a *livre* is not a coin, but a name which always denotes 20 *sous*'.[10] From time to time, the crown issued a ruling applicable to its lands which fixed the 'course' of money: an increase in the value of a specific coin was a devaluation of the money of account and vice versa. The Spanish monarchy kept its accounts at first in *maravedís*, later in ducats of 375 *maravedís*. The French monarchy accounted first in *écus*, later in *livres tournois*, three of which were officially valued at one *écu*. In practice, it was not easy for governments to control monetary policy. The political and financial difficulties in which the monarchs embroiled themselves had severe monetary consequences. The ransom payable in 1529 for the release of Francis I's sons under the terms of the Peace of Cambrai was equivalent to 3.6 tons of gold, nearly the whole of the total receipts from the New World in the previous decade: for France, which lacked Charles V's monetary resources, the burden of this payment was severe. But as a result of his frequent wars, Charles V's position by the end of his reign was scarcely better: his total debts to foreign financiers roughly approximated the entire receipts from Spanish America during his reign.

Rulers were unable to control the value of money in their lands because as late as 1660 foreign coins still circulated freely as valid currency. Foreign coins were given specific values by the ruler in terms of monies of account: but the mere fact that they were in circulation at all demonstrates that national currencies were not yet firmly established. Money was also an object of merchandise. Coin was exchanged at international centres such as Amsterdam and the so-called 'Besançon' fairs at Piacenza in Italy, where the Genoese dominated exchange dealings. At these centres, the international value of the currency could well differ from its official value within the kingdom: this could lead to the flight of money abroad. Governments made the export of bullion abroad a crime of treason and thus a capital offence: but market forces were more powerful than the coercive power of early modern rulers. The interaction of all these factors makes the 'velocity of circulation' incalculable. Even the 'bi-metallic ratio'—the ratio of gold to silver values—was subject to short-term speculation according to whichever precious metal was rising in price.

There is as yet insufficient evidence on the precise way in which bullion transfers were made between countries, but their significance is nevertheless clearly attested. Spanish bullion was the predominant source for English coin issues under Elizabeth I, no doubt due to the success of English privateering, a favourable balance of trade, and profits made on the difference between the gold–silver ratio in Spain and England. It is clear that all monies of account showed a tendency to devaluation in the sixteenth century, which was an important consequence of inflation. Certain of them lost value much faster than others: the pound sterling did so rapidly, following the debasements under Henry VIII and Edward VI, whereas the florin of the Low Countries lost only 5 per cent of its value in the first half of the sixteenth century, though it lost a further 37 per cent in the second half. Such debasements resulted in a fall in the purchasing power of money. It is estimated that in 1500 the European monetary stock would have bought the equivalent of some 675 million hectolitres of wheat at its purchase price in Spain. By 1600, the increased European monetary stock would have purchased only 225 million hectolitres. The market value of gold and silver had fallen substantially, while the price of wheat had risen dramatically. Much more money was in circulation in Europe by 1660 than ever before, but its value had declined significantly since the beginning of the sixteenth century. This leads us to a consideration of the causes and significance of the European price inflation of the period.

8.2 The European Price Revolution

The basic statistical evidence for the history of prices in early modern Europe is far from perfect; statistical comparison between the prices in one European country and another has barely begun. The simplest procedure for the historian is to list prices as they are found in the archives, but this is not particularly revealing. The average price of a measure (*setier*) of best-quality wheat at Paris, for example, rose from just over one *livre* in 1500, to 4.15 *livres* in 1550, 8.65 *livres* in 1600 and 18 *livres* in 1660. At face value, this seems a staggering price increase; but before an accurate rate of increase can be calculated, we need to know more about the level of prices in the fifteenth century. At Paris, for example, the figure was 0.75 *livres* in 1450; it was already 1.07 *livres* in 1475. We also need information about the relative value of the local money of account: the *livre tournois*, though stable in the sixteenth century compared to other monies of account, nevertheless declined in value in the course of the century. It is also necessary to ascertain what quantities of the product (in this case, wheat) could be purchased for the sum of money—a Parisian *setier* was equivalent to approximately 156 litres in volume or 240 *livres de marc* in weight—before any meaningful comparison can be made with the level of prices elsewhere.

In order to compare prices in Europe at different times, one method chosen by some economic historians is to retain the actual prices of goods in each country, and to calculate the rate of increase in prices by converting these figures into index numbers. This method allows the proportionate increase in one country to be compared with another.[11] For example, if the years 1451–75 are used as the baseline (called index 100), as in the famous Phelps Brown—Hopkins index, the result can be seen in table 8.1. This index provides a perspective on prices in the fifteenth century, but it tends to exaggerate the contrast between very high prices in the sixteenth century and low prices in the fifteenth century. Thus other historians have preferred to take as their baseline a period such as 1565–9, when prices had been on the increase for at least two generations. If the results are averaged for twenty-five-year periods, clear discrepancies in the rate of price increases occur, the rate being higher at Antwerp than Lwów in Poland or at Lyon, with Valencia and Paris lagging some way behind (table 8.2).

Concealed behind the increase in nominal prices, however, is a very considerable difference in the cost of grain from one market to another. This is revealed most clearly when local prices are converted into grams of fine silver. In 1490–9, wheat prices were highest in the Mediterranean area, while those in northern Europe were some 35 per cent lower. Prices in the east were staggeringly low: silver values of 5.5 grams at Cracow and 4.8 grams at Lwów contrast remarkably with the figure of 35.3 grams recorded at Barcelona. With the passing of time, the differences between the price levels in different areas of Europe began to narrow perceptibly, as the rising demand for grain in the west in the later sixteenth century pushed up prices in the east. The rate of price increase was also significantly different from one decade to another during the century. At Florence, the average annual price increase between 1552 and 1560 was

Table 8.1. Index numbers of inflation in 1601–1620 (1451–75 = index 100)

	England	France	Alsace
Food	555	729	517
Industrial products	265	335	294
Builders' wages	200	268	150

Source: E. H. Phelps Brown and S. V. Hopkins, 'Wage-rates and Prices: Evidence for Population Pressure in the Sixteenth Century', *Economica*, new ser., 24 (1957), 298.

Table 8.2. Index numbers of certain selected grain products (1565–9 = index 100)

	Antwerp [rye]	Exeter [average of crops]	Lyon [wheat]	Paris [wheat]	Valencia [wheat]
1475–99	42.1	35.8	36.3	12.4	—
1500–24	39.3	40.1	42.3	23.0	51.9
1525–49	57.9	49.4	66.8	39.5	65.9
1550–74	97.3	106.5	102.4	80.1	101.0
1575–99	218.3	152.5	212.6	168.4	173.1

	Rome [wheat]	Volokolamsk [Muscovy] [rye]	Lwów [Poland] [oats]
1475–99	—	—	—
1500–24	—	—	28.7
1525–49	—	—	44.2
1550–74	87.7	224.3	98.0
1575–99	127.3	154.3	215.8

Source: author's calculations on published figures.

5.2 per cent; but in other periods it was much less (3.3 per cent or 3.1 per cent in 1565–73 and 1590–1600 respectively), while at other times there was a small annual decrease in prices. The Spanish evidence suggests that there was a 2.8 per cent average annual increase in prices from 1501 to 1562, as compared with a 1.3 per cent average annual increase for 1562–1600. The rapid inflation of the first half of the century, with the years 1521–30 seeing the sharpest upward movement of the entire century, was followed (after a sharp upswing between 1561 and 1570) by a slowing down of the inflationary process.

There could be, and were, violent fluctuations in the rate of price increases from one year to the next. Agricultural prices changed according to the season of the year. They varied from region to region and from market to market. Within the same market, prices varied according to the different qualities and quantities of the product being sold. This was particularly true of grain: the Paris statistics demonstrate that wheat, rye and barley prices shared a broadly similar pattern while displaying perceptible differences in detail. It is necessary both to compare the rate of price increase of actual commodities at local markets and to set them against the background of national average prices for each commodity. A comparison of the rate of price increase of grain at local markets with that of other commodities demonstrates that grain almost always rose faster. At Lyon, a cost of living index in which grain is accorded only 50 per cent weighting, the rest being wine, meat, rented accommodation (10 per cent each), clothing and wood for heating (5 per cent each), provides an illustration of this (table 8.3). Real wage rates, that is to say, wages calculated in terms of their buying power in food, also lagged behind the rise in prices (table 8.4).

Table 8.3. Selected comparison between the grain index and general commodity index (in index numbers) (1565–9 = index 100)

	Lyon [wheat]	Lyon ['cost of living']
1525–49	66.8	56.6
1550–74	102.4	91.7
1575–99	212.6	176.8

Source: author's calculations based on R. Gascon, *Grand commerce et vie urbaine au xvie siècle: Lyon et ses marchands* (1971).

Table 8.4. Selected comparison of 'real wages' (in index numbers) (1565–9 = index 100)

	Antwerp mason	Antwerp mason's labourer	Lyon worker
1475–99	92.0	104.1	—
1500–24	101.1	114.6	117.2
1525–49	94.3	97.4	92.4
1550–74	104.0	103.7	92.8
1575–99	88.5	95.3	71.4

Source: author's calculations based on Gascon, *Grand commerce* and H. Van der Wee, *The Growth of the Antwerp Market and the European Economy, Fourteenth–Sixteenth Centuries* (1965).

Clearly, the sixteenth-century price rise resulted in a loss of the wage-earner's purchasing power which made him and his family vulnerable to short-term crises. Though inflation inevitably brought some upward adjustment of wage rates in its wake, the overall picture would seem to confirm one aspect of the 'profit inflation' thesis originally advanced by E. J. Hamilton.[12] In essence, this suggests that capital accumulation was encouraged in the sixteenth century because the rise in the quantity of manufactured goods was greater than any rise in the wages of the work-force. However, the gap between wage rates and the prices of manu-factured goods was less than that between wages and agricultural prices: any increase in profitability, and hence in business and capital investment, was probably lower than might first be expected. The 'profit inflation' thesis has been criticized by those who argue that whereas price inflation was greatest in Spain, and profit inflation (that is, the disparity between price levels and money wages) highest in France, long-term economic growth was in fact greatest in England. The 'profit inflation' thesis is further undermined when the case of the Dutch Republic in the seventeenth century is examined. Dutch wage rates increased until 1640 and remained at relatively high levels thereafter. Thus, it would seem, capital accumulation was rendered more difficult. On the other hand, high wage rates encouraged labour-saving devices in Dutch industry, which also made intensive use of non-human energy resources such as windmills and peat. In one sense, high wages might be seen as an advantage rather than a disadvantage, since they encouraged the introduction of capital-intensive techniques. The adoption of such methods, however, required both an innovatory spirit and the investment to put the ideas into practice.

Generally speaking, one of the main characteristics of the sixteenth-century price rise was that there were no decades when prices were stable, though they were for the five years from 1511 to 1515 in Spain. This is all the more striking when set against the background of a long period of price stability before 1450. The cumulative effect of even a relatively low annual increase in prices over more than a century was to produce a substantially higher level of prices—three or four times higher—by 1660. By the seventeenth century, the rate of price increase was beginning to slow down in most European countries. In Provence, for example, a period of stable prices began in 1594. More generally, the rate of price increase as expressed in silver values had slowed down or stopped altogether by 1600 in southern Europe and by 1630–50 in the north. In terms of nominal prices, however, there was still a rise in some countries, notably in Spain, where inflation followed upon the excessive issue of copper coins.

Causal connections may well exist between the price rise and the great economic and social changes of the sixteenth century; but the historian should beware of attributing simplistic results to what are clearly complex causes. It is too crude to assert, for example, that the price revolution accelerated economic growth and the development of a 'capitalist' economy in the west, while in central Europe and the east it served to strengthen and prolong the feudal system. Many other factors also came into play. Though there was an increase in labour services imposed on the peasants of Brandenburg in the sixteenth century, the rise in prices meant that around 1560 they had to sell fewer bushels of rye to pay their rents than their predecessors had done a century earlier. The new burden of labour services did not cancel out the modest profits of peasant farming. As to the development of capitalism in western Europe, the historian has very little direct evidence in the way of business papers to demonstrate conclusively the thesis of profit inflation.

8.3 Merchant Banking and the Mechanisms of International Payments

Rulers played an increasing part in developing the commercial fortunes of their states in the course of the sixteenth and especially in the seventeenth centuries. Historians tend to call this attitude 'mercantilist', though the concept was not really formulated until the eighteenth century. It was summed up by Voltaire in his aphorism 'it is clear that one country can only gain if another country loses'.[13] During the personal rule of Louis XIV, Colbert had commented that 'everyone . . . agrees that the might and greatness of a state are measured entirely by the quantity of silver it possesses'.[14] Yet the European stock of precious metals was seen as finite. It was thus imperative to do everything possible to restrict the drain of precious metals abroad. The development of French manufactures during the reign of Henri IV was considered to be 'the only way to stop the transportation out of our kingdom of gold and silver to enrich our neighbours'.[15] Trade was viewed by Colbert and other statesmen of the mid-seventeenth century as a peaceful activity but warlike in the aggressiveness with which it was waged. He argued, for example, that Holland should be 'destroyed' by France in a 'money war' destined to keep bullion within the confines of the French kingdom.

Mercantilism was thus a form of national self-defence. The control of economic activity had to be transferred from the local communities to the state since it alone was powerful enough to conduct a bullion war with a rival nation. The conscious quest by the state to improve its economic welfare was a new emphasis in government. Mercantilism helped to overcome religious barriers, for example, by integrating the Jews into the economic life of western Europe after the 1570s. It also led to the development of the national market, although in the period before 1660 it made only slow headway in breaking down internal customs barriers and other restraints on the development of trade within individual states. Despite these handicaps, commerce undoubtedly expanded in the sixteenth and seventeenth centuries, based on various urban centres in different periods. Trade fairs developed there, and out of these fairs grew international money markets, which knew no national barriers. There was, to some extent, a tension between the aims of the state in promoting national self-defence by economic measures (that is, mercantilism) and the merchant banking community, who needed open trading centres where payments could be settled. Only when the great age of these international centres had waned could a full development of mercantilism take place, with states controlling the main economic activities within their borders.

8.3.1   *The Bill of Exchange*

In the period from the thirteenth to the sixteenth century, there was a distinction between abstract monetary accounting units and the mechanism by which payments were made in practice. Each country had its own unit of account; thus the importance of the merchant bankers was that they formed the only link between the abstract accounting units of each state and the practicalities of making payments for trading purposes. Contemporaries made a distinction between commerce, banking and finance; the merchant bankers were involved in more than one of these activities, but their essential role was that of managing the exchange between different units of account at a particular place by means of a technical device known as the 'bill of exchange'. The bill of exchange was an alternative to the exportation of bullion which was frequently prohibited by the rulers of states. At the international fairs, the different accounting units were placed in a formal relationship with one another, and the basis of exchange between them was established by the bankers collectively when setting the rates for each particular fair and by the merchant banker on an individual basis when drawing up his bill of exchange.

In the earlier sixteenth century, this commerce was dominated by Italians, who were organized abroad in 'nations', and were usually exiles from Florence, Lucca, Genoa and (to a lesser extent) Milan. The Strozzi were among the most important of the exiled Florentine families; the Bonvisi dominated the Lucchese exiles until their bankruptcy in 1629. Intermarriage within the exiled 'nations' was the norm, and thus associations of banking families could be renewed following the death or marriage of one of their leading members. The Bonvisi, for example, renewed their associations in more than twenty successive companies in this way between 1505 and 1629; though they were resident at Lyon throughout this period, they concluded no marriage with a Lyonnais family. Gradually, in the course of the sixteenth century the Italians lost their predominance: subsequently, the Spaniards Simon Ruiz and Juan López Gallo, the Fleming Erasmus Schetz, the Englishman Sir Thomas Gresham, and the Fuggers of Augsburg were prominent in the business of bills of exchange.

A distinction was made by contemporaries between different types of exchange which served different purposes, but a bill of exchange had certain fundamental characteristics which were unvarying. At one location, the initiator of the exchange paid a specific sum in one currency (let us say, in Lyon he paid 100 *écus*) to a receiver in another location, who drew his payment in a different currency (say, for example, 37,800 *maravedís* in Seville) via his bankers. Such instruments of exchange were restricted to Latin Christendom: bills of exchange were unknown in Muscovy, the Islamic world and even in Spanish America. They did not circulate freely in the manner of primitive banknotes; on the contrary, a defined contractual relationship was specified within each particular bill. Nevertheless, under the influence of the practice at Antwerp, assignments to third parties containing the clause that the specified sum was 'payable to the bearer'[16] became common. This developed into the so-called 'endorsed' bill of exchange, which greatly extended its transferability and made it potentially an object of commerce: but the practice only became generalized in the course of the seventeenth century. Italian banking practice remained exceptionally conservative, and at Venice in 1652 the endorsed bill of exchange was proscribed.

A network of places where bills of exchange could be honoured came into being. In general, each state had a single (or at least a primary) location for this form of activity. In France, it was Lyon, although Rouen was also of some importance; in the Low Countries, it was Antwerp; in Castile, it was Medina del Campo, although Madrid-Alcalá and Seville were subsidiary centres. Some of the locations permitted exchange throughout the year; others limited them to the season of the fairs, which usually met four times a year. The commerce in bills of exchange rested on a 'merchant arithmetic' which established the rates of exchange for a given location, and quoted what was 'certain' (the rate of exchange in the location itself) against what was 'uncertain' (that prevailing in a different location). It permitted the merchant banker to make a legitimate financial gain on the differences in rates of exchange between currencies and between locations on the basis of past experience and accurate knowledge. Yet the theoretical gain might not always be capable of realization: in 1585, the Bonvisi, acting on behalf of their clients, sent 120,000 *écus* from Lyon to Castile, but could find only 30,000 *écus* there in bills for the return journey to Lyon. Only the so-called bill of exchange 'with recourse' (*con ricorsa*) guaranteed the original lender a high interest charge. Under this arrangement, a predetermined sum of money was successively changed at different fairs and was likely to produce an annual interest of more than 12 per cent. The *ricorsa* was unknown at the Lyon fairs, but it developed rapidly at the Genoese-dominated 'Besançon' fairs. This type of bill disguised a loan contract usually of one year's duration, but it should not be confused with true loan contracts (*asientos*), of which the Genoese were also the masters.

8.3.2 *Antwerp's Greatness*

The rise of Antwerp followed the collapse of the Bruges money market (largely the result of Maximilian I's excessive borrowing requirement), and the transfer of most of the foreign (and especially, Italian) merchant banking communities from one city to the other: by 1516, the Genoese, Florentine and Lucchese communities had all left Bruges for Antwerp, and a significant money market came into place there within two years. The outward sign of Antwerp's commercial supremacy in the sixteenth century was a doubling of its population from 50,000 to 100,000 between 1500 and 1568. The city had seized its advantage initially by becoming the main European outlet for the Portuguese spice trade. The Portuguese needed a distribution network and retail trade in spices: this proved too costly for the Portuguese monarchy to organize directly, because there were delays of a year or eighteen months in obtaining payment. The 'lords of Antwerp', and the foreign merchants there, handled this problem for them. The first Portuguese ship arrived with pepper and cinnamon in 1501; seven years later, king Manuel I founded an Antwerp branch for the sale of his spices, the *Feitoria de Flandres*. In exchange, the Portuguese took on cargoes of central European copper and silver with which they financed subsequent purchases of spices in the Far East. The boom in the market for Portuguese pepper ensured a dramatic growth of the city's fortunes until about 1523. Not even Bruges in its heyday achieved Antwerp's success in dominating, albeit for a short period, almost the entire international commerce in any one commodity. Even at its height, the European spice trade did not reach the capital value of the intra-European grain trade, of which Antwerp itself became an important entrepôt.

At first sight, this domination seems surprising. Antwerp had only a small merchant fleet, and it was not a free city, being subject to the monetary ordinances of the Brussels government. Nevertheless, since 1415 it possessed a well-established system of international fairs; by the 1550s they were held four times a year for six weeks each. These fairs regulated the dates of payments of bills of exchange, and Antwerp seems to have played a crucial role in the development of this instrument of credit. Other financial institutions in the city were advanced: uniquely in the sixteenth century, for example, it possessed its own bankruptcy court. This pioneering financial and commercial role saw Antwerp through the decline in its main trading commodity, for, by the early 1530s, the market for spices had contracted. Lisbon took over Antwerp's role as distributor, and in 1549 the *Feitoria de Flandres* was closed. While trade remained in the doldrums, loans to the ruler were the most profitable way to employ capital, and German financiers, already established in Antwerp because of their participation in the spice trade, made the city the centre of their operations. Economic growth in the Low Countries resumed after 1535, and with the Dutch providing the carrying fleet, Spain began to export wool to Antwerp on an unprecedented scale in return for imports of timber and other products for shipbuilding, plus linen and woollens for its American colonies. The balance of trade came increasingly to favour Antwerp, with the deficit discharged in silver coin and ingots. Nevertheless, for most of the time Charles V's debts at Antwerp rarely exceeded 1 million carolus guilders (about half a million ducats). It was not until the monarchy's financial crisis of 1552 that they reached the staggering figure of 6.7 million carolus guilders and represented a significant proportion of the Low Countries' commercial activity—perhaps equivalent to a third of total imports.

This twenty-year boom came to an abrupt end, however, when Philip II was forced to reschedule his debts in 1557. Although recovery was under way within a few years, trade was largely confined to the cloth industry, linen and tapestry-making. The Antwerp market remained an important one in the late sixteenth century, where bills of exchange could, for the most part, be honoured. But its financial market was redirected towards commercial credit, which was no longer central to the policy of the Spanish Habsburg monarchy. Furthermore, the financial supremacy of the south German merchant bankers was at an end. The rising in Holland in 1572, and the second rescheduling of Philip II's debts three years later (see chapter 3.2.4), broke the back of Antwerp's fortune. From 1577 to 1585, Antwerp was in the rebel camp, and the way was left clear for Genoese predominance, exercised through its control of Habsburg international financial payments. Once Antwerp returned to Philip II's control in 1585, the king made it the centre of his financial operations for the recovery of the rebel provinces in the north: there was thus a marked revival in the city's fortunes, but it, in its turn, was further prejudiced by Philip II's third debt rescheduling in 1596. Although it was no longer of the same importance at the end of the sixteenth century as it had been under Charles V, and despite its lack of stability and reliability, the financial market of Antwerp had made important innovations in the techniques of modern deposit and discount banking which spread throughout western Europe.

8.3.3 *The Lyon Fairs*

Lyon's geographical position, close to what was then the eastern border of France (and thus near to Italy), gave the city its importance in the fifteenth century. Charles VII accorded it three fairs a year in 1446, but after allegations from the merchants of Languedoc that the fairs depleted the monetary stock of the kingdom, the Estates General of 1484 demanded their suppression. Any suspension in trade was only temporary, however, for after 1489 two fairs a year were held at Lyon, and between 1494 and 1562 there were four annually. Italian merchant communities could settle at Lyon without losing their nationality, since foreign merchants were supposedly 'free from all taxes, charges and tributes'.[17] (Only the Genoese were prohibited from trading and banking activities at Lyon for a short time in 1496–9 and 1512–14, and then for a longer period in the years 1528–35 following their abandonment of the French alliance in favour of the Habsburgs. In 1571 and 1576 there were again demands for the exclusion of the Genoese.) Gradually in the course of the sixteenth century, this fiscal exemption was eroded by Francis I and Henri II for short-term financial gain; after 1564 a tax on merchandise entering the city, whether at the time of the fairs or not, was levied on a regular basis and its collection was farmed out to a financier. Consequently there was less reason for foreign merchant bankers to frequent the Lyon fairs.

The fortunes of Lyon as a centre for merchant banking fluctuated in the later sixteenth century. The financial crisis of 1557–9, arising first from Philip II's debt rescheduling and then from the death of Henri II and the rescheduling of the debts of the French monarchy (see chapter 6.5.3), ended the Lyon market's first phase of expansion. A commercial boom after 1559 revived the city's fortunes, and by 1573 it was noted (despite the reduction in the fiscal exemption of foreign merchants) that 'Lyon is the place of exchange which gives the rules to all the other European cities'.[18] There can be little doubt that Lyon had at this time the most extensive commerce in bills of exchange of any city in Europe. Its central location dominated both the north–south axis (for example, exchanges between Florence and Antwerp) and the west–east one (for example, exchanges between Medina del Campo and Florence). But by 1574–5, the Lyon market was once again in financial turmoil as a result of the monetary crisis in the French kingdom. The *livre tournois* as a unit of account had depreciated dramatically and there was a lack of gold coin in circulation. At the same time, the French money for exchange purposes (the *écu de marc*) had lost about 20 per cent of its value in relation to the Italian monies of exchange in the period beween 1562 and 1577: 'six *écus* in France are not worth more than five in most of the countries with which one trades', it was asserted.[19] As a result, there were interminable disputes between Italian merchant bankers and French merchants over the settlement of bills of exchange in gold coin. The monetary devaluation of 1577 in France halted the precipitate decline in the French money of account; and by replacing the *écu de marc* with the *écu au soleil* as the new unit of money for exchange purposes with effect from the fair of August 1575, the trend towards external devaluation was corrected. (The *écu de marc* had been worth 45 *sous* in 1534 and 50 *sous* in 1560, but had subsequently lost its value to the equivalent of 60 *sous*; the value of the new *écu au soleil* had in turn to be fixed at 60 *sous* in 1577.)

Contrary to their intention, these changes resulted in increasing instability in the sophisticated Lyon exchange market. Had it been possible fully to enforce the 1577 monetary regulation, there would have been a deflation; but within a few years, the result was the reverse. There was further inflation, and a growing discrepancy between the unit of account and the real value of money for exchange purposes. The merchant bankers were penalized by a specific clause in the ruling of 1577, which required the settlement of two-thirds of the value of all bills of exchange and other operations at the fairs in gold. The Lyon merchants were already claiming in 1574 that 'the ruin of exchange will shortly follow the ruin of trade',[20] and it was argued in Spain four years later that the Italian merchant bankers 'were the cause of all these novelties'.[21] Lyon went into decline, not just because of the failure of the monetary ruling of 1577, but also as a consequence of the success of the rival 'Besançon' fairs, which allowed the settlement of bills of exchange in silver: the Genoese increasingly dominated the market in bills of exchange as well as in loan contracts. Lyon's decline became permanent after 1589, when the city sided with the Catholic League. There was a further monetary crisis (this time, due to the poor quality of the small coins in circulation), but there was no longer any effective political authority to deal with it. The result was that by the late sixteenth century, three-quarters of the Italian merchant bankers who had established themselves at the city twenty-five years earlier transferred from Lyon to the 'Besançon' fairs.

8.3.4 *The Genoese Payments System*

During the Middle Ages, the republic of Genoa had enjoyed many commercial successes and advantages comparable with Venice, but with two significant omissions: it had not established a mainland empire, and it had not experienced political stability. Fourteen revolutions took place between 1413 and 1453. In 1499 the French occupied the city. Then, in another political upheaval in 1528, the city dramatically changed allegiance and threw in its lot with Charles V. Underlying this volte-face, which dashed French aspirations in northern Italy, was a shrewd perception that the city's long-term economic interests lay in the Habsburg camp: the Genoese knew that they were strong enough to avoid becoming a Spanish colony, but they were too weak to preserve their independence. The Spanish alliance was not entirely unexpected: as early as the fourteenth century, Genoese financiers seeking gold had formed trading relationships in Spain. The loss of trading posts in the Levant as a result of Ottoman conquest, and Venice's domination of the eastern spice trade until the advent of the Portuguese Cape route, led the Genoese to turn increasingly from active maritime commerce to the means of financing it, and from the east to the west. They established a significant presence at

Seville: by 1537 Genoese trade with Spain amounted in value to half the republic's total imports. They also acted as financiers for Columbus' expeditions to America. So-called 'sea loans'—loans to would-be settlers, to merchants hoping to trade with America, and to shipowners fitting out vessels for the transatlantic passage—came to be dominated by the Genoese, with seven bankers alone providing more than half the capital advanced on goods in a six-month period in 1507–8. The Genoese were also prominent slave traders in both the Spanish and Portuguese empires.

The Genoese suffered French reprisals for their change of allegiance in 1528, and they were excluded from the Lyon fairs. This forced them to organize an alternative location for payments and exchange transactions—the so-called 'Besançon' (*Bisenzone*) fairs, which were established for them by Charles V in 1537. A Florentine commented on these fairs in 1581: 'the Genoese have invented a new form of exchange, which they call the Besançon fairs, after their place of origin; one day, they are held in Savoy, the next in Piedmont, then in Lombardy, in the Trentino, at the gates of Genoa, or wherever they so wish; so that we might as well call them Utopia, that is, fairs without a specific location'.[22] After a period when the fairs moved around Franche-Comté, they were eventually established at Piacenza (a possession of the duke of Parma) between 1579 and 1622. At their height, perhaps 200 bankers or their associates attended the annual fairs, settling in the region of 40 million *écus*' worth of business at each. These fairs were a novelty in sixteenth-century Europe, for no commerce other than exchange in bills and money ever took place there.

Furthermore, these fairs made a technical innovation by relying on an *écu de marc* for their money of exchange which (unlike the Lyon *écu*) was not based on the currency of a single state but was an amalgamation of at least five currencies (Castile, Genoa, Venice, Florence and Naples; rates from Antwerp and Lyon were added after 1577). By their use of the *écu de marc*, the Genoese disguised all transactions as international ones, whether they were between two states with different monetary systems or not. The creation of this prototype of the European monetary system was very advantageous to the Genoese, as was their development of what may be viewed as two distinctive (if perverse) monetary instruments, the bill of exchange 'with recourse' (*con ricorsa*), a disguised loan contract, and the *asiento*, a loan contract based on the transfer of coin. The *asiento* continually evolved, and it was a less formal document than the bill of exchange: the sums specified were usually in *écus* or ducats, with a defined exchange rate in *maravedís*. The financier's profit within each *asiento* contract was calculated on the difference between the official value of, for example, the *écu* in Spain and its market rate as defined in the contract itself: Niccoló Grimaldi made a 14.3 per cent gain on his contract for the transfer of a million *escudos* from Spain to Flanders and Milan in May 1558. The *asiento* contract differed from the bill of exchange in that it specified a transfer of money in a single direction at defined dates, with no return. It became the instrument *par excellence* by which the Spanish monarchy financed its international military commitments.

Gradually, during the reign of Charles V, the Genoese market share in the royal loan contracts had increased, so that by the 1550s its merchant bankers were poised to take over from their German counterparts as the single most powerful group of royal financiers. In 1557, they held two-sevenths of the loan contracts of the Spanish monarchy. They were favoured by the crown, and thus well placed to survive the monarchy's need to reschedule its debts in 1557: unlike the German bankers, they were able to offer new loans to Philip II. The Genoese became the most significant group of financiers serving the Spanish Habsburgs, and retained much of their importance even after Philip IV's debt-rescheduling exercise of 1627. They were displaced by the Portuguese who, twenty years later, took the brunt of the losses in yet another repudiation of the royal loans. Thereafter, the Genoese re-emerged as the paramount group. Significantly, none of the Spanish 'bankruptcies' gave any benefit, direct or indirect, to Lyon: rather, the merchant bankers at the 'Besançon' fairs quoted what was 'certain' (the rate of exchange at their fairs) against what was 'uncertain' (the exchange at Lyon), demonstrating that they, not the bankers of Lyon, were the primary financial centre.

At the height of their power, the Genoese dominated a monetary triangle whose points were the fairs of Medina del Campo and those of 'Besançon' and Antwerp. Part of their success rested on the relative fragility of the Spanish money market. Even in their heyday, the fairs of Medina del Campo dealt with only half the volume of business transacted either at the Lyon or the 'Besançon' fairs. Although they had been reasonably prosperous until the 1550s, the Castilian fairs were heavily dependent on the crown: by 1566, half the value of transactions was concerned with royal borrowing, and thus the market was critically affected by Philip II's debt-rescheduling operations. After 1575, loan contracts were negotiated at Madrid, with Medina del Campo acting merely as a clearing-house for what was transacted at the 'Besançon' fairs. When the location of the latter was changed to Novi Ligura (within Genoese territory) after 1622, they became less important, since the Florentine, Milanese and Venetian merchant bankers opposed this decision and boycotted the new site. In part, the decline of the fairs may also have been the result of a fall in the scale of silver shipments from Spanish America. However, the role of the Genoese as financiers for the Habsburgs seems to have remained crucial until Spain made peace with the Dutch Republic in 1648. Subsequently, Spanish silver was transferred north not by abstract bills of exchange but rather in physical bulk, in Dutch ships. After 1659, Spanish military expenditure was redirected towards the attempted reconquest of Portugal, and the prospect of a Genoese recovery was dashed. The 'Besançon' fairs became of purely local Italian significance. By 1660, national money markets had become more important than international ones.

8.4   The Struggle for European Commercial Primacy in the Old World and the New

The years between 1415 and 1550 may with justice be termed an Age of Expansion: they witnessed the spread of the Ottoman empire in the Mediterranean; and the empire-building of Portugal and Spain—and later, of the Netherlands, England and France—in the Atlantic and Pacific. The story of this expansion is one of skill, courage, endurance and achievement on the one hand; and of exploitation, violence, cynicism and human degradation on the other. Trade rivalry was inherent from the 'mercantilist' attitudes of rulers and their advisers; the Age of Expansion led not only to colonization of the New World, but also to an extension overseas of trade rivalries which were intra-European in origin. The chief difference between overseas and European-based trade was not one of goods, which were often similar, but rather of the methods by which business was transacted. Trade with the New World was not settled by means of letters of change, but in precious metals. A world-wide overseas trade came to interpenetrate European trade, so that in the course of the sixteenth century bullion and letters of change gradually became juxtaposed as mechanisms of payment. Notwithstanding the momentous changes which were to lead towards the emergence of something akin to a world economy in the seventeenth century, it is important to remember that within Europe itself few countries possessed even a 'national' economy. In most cases, the markets for goods within the interior of a state were regional. This did not necessarily hinder economic growth, since it ensured diversity of goods and several different types of economic activity within one state; but it shows how extraordinarily fragmented the European economy was when it began to penetrate the world economy.

8.4.1   *Structural Changes in Late Medieval European Commerce*

The economic development of the sixteenth century was made to a considerable extent at the expense of the great powers that had dominated the trade of the later Middle Ages, notably the Hanseatic League and Venice. The peak of Hanseatic prosperity had probably been reached by about 1400; by the 1590s it was in full decline, although the final demise of the

League did not come about until the seventeenth century. Originally a league of over 100 towns, situated on the principal trading routes of northern Europe, the number represented in its diet (*Hansetag*) had dwindled to sixty-three by 1557. An even more dramatic decline occurred in the seventeenth century: only eleven towns were represented in 1628, and a mere nine at the final meeting in 1669. The number of diets also fluctuated greatly, and the end of the League was foreshadowed by the absence of any diet between 1629 and 1669. In part this was a result of the disruption caused by the Thirty Years' War, though to a certain extent its effects were mitigated by Lübeck, Hamburg and Bremen assuming joint direction of common Hanseatic interests.

The decline of the Hanseatic League can be attributed to both political and economic factors. At an early date (1494), the League had been excluded from monopolistic trading rights at Novgorod, while its staple at Bruges was undermined by the rise of Antwerp. In the longer term, the rise of Dutch maritime power in the Baltic carrying trade led to a crucial conflict of interests between towns such as Lübeck, which tried in vain to exclude the Dutch, and towns in Prussia and Livonia, most notably Danzig and Riga, which sought to harness Dutch maritime power for their own commercial advantage. The energetic foreign policy of Lübeck in the 1530s ended in failure, while the Seven Years' War of the North shattered Hanseatic maritime power and made the Livonian towns subject either to Poland or Sweden (see chapter 5.1.3). The Habsburg scheme for a maritime alliance between the Emperor and the principal Baltic towns was rebuffed by the Hansa in the late 1620s as a recipe for further costly wars with the Dutch and the Scandinavian powers.

Above all, the Hansa had flourished in a period of economic consensus in the Middle Ages. It could enjoy prosperity only if all of its members had equal rights and perceived common advantages from the union. The rise in the economic importance of the south German cities challenged the facile assumptions of a unified purpose in the sixteenth century. Danzig was prepared to ally with the merchant financiers of Augsburg, but it was not until 1538 that Lübeck reached an agreement with the Fuggers, the greatest of the Augsburg merchant banking houses, allowing them 'to transport freely and without hindrance all merchandise, including copper, from Danzig and elsewhere, in and through our town, harbour and inshore waters, and to forward it as they wish to Hamburg or elsewhere'.[23] But if the south German cities had been able to challenge the monopoly of the Hanseatic League already, other towns in the north were in an even stronger position to do so. Emden became the home of the Dutch merchant marine in exile during the revolt of the Netherlands. Amsterdam and Hamburg were the twin heirs of Antwerp's greatness after the sixteenth century. Dutch commercial supremacy eventually left the Hansa

lagging behind. In 1668 the town of Wismar summed up the consequences, stating that the League was 'more a shadow than a reality'; there
was, it considered, 'no hope of restoring it to its former prosperity'.[24]

Significant structural changes were also occurring in the Mediterranean.
The obsessive fear of Venetian 'imperialism' among the various Italian
states at the beginning of the sixteenth century was a consequence less of
its political ambitions than of Venice's economic preponderance, which
had been established by the end of the fourteenth century. Doubtless, in
view of its subsequent growth, Genoa would have taken the initiative had
not Venice done so at an earlier date, though the latter was better placed
to exploit the opportunities of trade with the Middle East. The Levant,
indeed, was the life-blood of Venetian trade: when the galleys had sailed
for Syria, the city was for a while drained of bullion. Though Venice
enjoyed more than a century of unchallenged supremacy in the eastern
Mediterranean, from 1378 until 1498, the emergence of the Ottoman
Turks as the main territorial power, and subsequently as the chief naval
force, in the area posed a serious new threat (see chapter 5.4.1). The
Ottomans could have closed off the Levant trade to Venice in 1516–17,
but they chose not to do so, preferring instead to tax the profits on these
trade routes. Nevertheless, Venice was to some extent at their mercy,
which explains the short duration of any wars between them—never more
than three years in the sixteenth century—and the fact that Venice
withdrew from the two Holy Leagues formed to fight the Turks in 1540
and 1573, as soon as it could respectably do so. The twenty-four-year war
for the defence of Crete in the seventeenth century (1645–69) was an
important exception to the tradition of coexistence: for strategic reasons,
the retention of Crete was seen as vital to Venetian commercial interests.

The manufacture of fustian (a mixture of wool and cotton) and silk was
already important in mid-fifteenth-century Venice. Of these two, the
expansion of the woollen industry in the sixteenth century was perhaps
the most spectacular aspect of Venice's development as a manufacturing
centre. Production rose from less than 2,000 cloths a year in 1516 to over
20,000 in 1565 and to a peak of 28,000 in 1602. There was an equally
dramatic decline thereafter, with fewer than 10,000 cloths a year being
manufactured by 1660. This pattern reflects the artificiality of the
industry's growth, which occurred largely by default. In the first half of the
sixteenth century, apart from the trauma of the War of the League of
Cambrai, Venice had enjoyed peace, whereas her neighbours had suffered
devastation during the Italian wars. With the restoration of peace in 1559,
industrial production rose in several Italian towns such as Como,
Bergamo and Florence, so that the Venetian cloth-makers found themselves confronted with a host of competitors: the rate of growth in
production fell. Demand for the Venetian product further faltered in the

seventeenth century because of its high price, a reflection of the excessive labour costs imposed by the powerful craft guilds of spinners, weavers and dyers. Nevertheless, even had the trades not been compulsorily enrolled in guilds, the high urban wages of a great metropolitan centre such as Venice would have placed its drapers at a disadvantage against their competitors. The range of employment opportunities was such that the labour force was in a strong bargaining position, irrespective of the guild structure. High labour costs increasingly made Venetian products uncompetitive, and gradually in the course of the sixteenth century commercial primacy in textiles was surrendered to the interlopers in the eastern Mediterrean, to the English and French. By 1600, the commercial primacy of Venice in the Mediterranean was at an end.

8.4.2 *The First of the New Empires: the Portuguese Empire*

The Portuguese were the first seafaring explorers in the early modern period. After the capture of Ceuta on the north African coast in 1415 (an important Moslem naval base and additionally a terminus for the trans-Sahara gold trade), they made more extensive voyages for fishing, sealing and trading further and further down the west coast of Africa. The task of exploration along the coastline of Guinea (the Gold Coast) was leased by the Portuguese government to Fernão Gomes between 1469 and 1474, and he undertook to cover 100 leagues of coast annually during the period of his lease. The commercial value of the Guinea trade became clear during this period, and instead of renewing the lease after 1474, the Portuguese crown established a royal monopoly. This monopoly was threatened during the war between Portugal and Castile (1475–9), and although the Portuguese were heavily defeated on land, and withdrew all their territorial claims in Castile, the Treaty of Alcaçovas which ended the war confirmed the Portuguese monopoly of fishing, trade and navigation along the west African coast. The Treaty of Tordesillas (1494) was a further diplomatic triumph for the Portuguese, since it reinforced their monopoly over most of the south Atlantic coastline and their control over the only viable commercial route to India. In addition, it was later realized that the Portuguese had accidentally gained the eastern tip of Brazil, which fell within the geographical extent of the territorial arrangements of the treaty, although in 1494 it had not yet been discovered.

The early Portuguese discoveries in Africa were motivated in part by crusading zeal against the Moslems and by the hope of finding a non-Moslem and perhaps Christian ally against Islam ('Prester John'). In addition, there were very important financial considerations. A rapid debasement of the Portuguese coinage had been required to pay for an earlier war against Castile between 1369 and 1379. The result was that by

1383 Portugal had no gold currency and desperately needed a new influx of gold to offset the enormous increase in its value against the debased coinage. The Portuguese knew that Africa had gold, since Ceuta had been frequented by European merchants since the thirteenth century. The establishment of the royal monopoly over the Guinea trade in 1475, and the construction of a royal castle at São Jorge da Mina (El Mina) on the Gold Coast in 1482, led to the effective exploitation of the gold trade of the western Sudan and of the river washings of the Gold Coast itself. There was a steady increase in shipments to the crown, and by 1506 gold from El Mina constituted one-fifth of royal revenues. Subsequent gold finds in east Africa and the East Indies did not significantly alter the balance.

The Portuguese would almost certainly have continued the process of exploration round the Cape of Good Hope, the achievement of Vasco da Gama in 1497–8, whether or not they had suspected that it would open up the spice trade to them. But this gave added impetus to their efforts: once the Cape had been rounded, and the scale of the existing Arab trade in spices fully revealed, it was then merely a question of how to ensure that the Portuguese could stage a take-over. In order to profit fully from their monopoly of the Cape route, they had to destroy the Arab-controlled spice trade. The first step was the establishment of a Portuguese royal factory at the port of Mozambique in 1502. Later, in November 1510, under the leadership of Alfonso de Albuquerque, who was entitled governor of India, Goa was seized. It became the Portuguese headquarters in India. To the west, some attempt was made to dominate the Persian gulf by the seizure of Hormuz in 1515, while to the east, the capture of Malacca in 1511 had provided the Portuguese with the main distribution centre for Indonesian spices, and a naval base to help control the bottle-neck between the Indian Ocean, the Java Sea and the South China Sea. The strategy came from Lisbon, but Albuquerque's energy provided the essential ingredient for implementing it. It was Albuqerque who insisted on the retention of Goa, despite later conquests further to the east, and it was held by the Portuguese until modern times. The success of the policy was staggering: by 1506 over a fifth of Portuguese revenue came from the sale of spices; by 1518–19 almost half. In the second half of the sixteenth century, this income began to wane and it was under serious threat after the formation of the Dutch East India Company in 1602. But by then new sources of revenue had become available.

Brazil was first discovered accidentally by the outward-bound India fleet of Pedro Alvares Cabral in April 1500 (it had unwittingly been assigned to the Portuguese crown by the Treaty of Tordesillas in 1494). The growing fear that the French might settle in this portion of South America ('Antarctic France') eventually necessitated colonization, which began in earnest after 1534. While encouraging the Indians to resist French settlement, the main Portuguese policy was to establish twelve hereditary captaincies to control the Brazilian interior. An experiment on São Tomé, an island off Angola, had shown that slave labour could be used to grow and cut sugar cane: production on the island had increased thirty times between 1530 and 1550. A similar policy was established in Brazil to service the sugar trade: Luanda became the base of the Angola slave trade with Brazil, and about 4,000 slaves a year were exported from west Africa. Since the average life of a slave in Brazil was only about seven years, the slave population there did not grow, but had to be continually replenished. Sugar production rose rapidly. The number of sugar mills increased from 60 in 1570 to 346 by 1629. Exports of sugar rose from 180,000 units (*arrobas*) in 1570 to 2.1 million by 1650. The commercial interdependence of Angola and Brazil meant that a Dutch attack on both in the 1640s posed a serious threat. In origins, the Portugese empire had been little more than a growing shipping lane, whose very long lines of communication had tested the crown's resources in terms of men and ships. It is not surprising that the empire in the East Indies fell prey to the Dutch in the course of the seventeenth century. But in Brazil, the enforced colonization policy and the establishment of hereditary captaincies, of which São Vincente, Pernambuco and Bahía were the most important (the latter administered directly by the crown under a governor-general), offered greater permanency. The Dutch onslaught on these parts of the Portuguese empire was thrown back, first in Angola by 1648, then in Brazil itself some six years later.

8.4.3 *The Spanish Empire in the New World*

Castilian expansionist intentions had been announced as early as 1475, when queen Isabella authorized her subjects to engage in trade with Africa, but the Treaty of Alcaçovas of 1479 dashed these early hopes, by confirming the Portuguese monopoly. A new opportunity did not present itself until 1492–4, with Columbus's epoch-making expeditions to the West Indies. It is significant that Columbus was not a Castilian but a Genoese. It seems that much of the initial impetus for American discovery and colonization came from a small group of Genoese merchants and nobles resident at Seville. Nearly all the most important participants in Spanish overseas expansion were debtors to the Genoese, who used their experience and wealth to issue loans and insurance credits which were a vital aspect of the trade with Spanish America. It was Columbus' genius to find in his first crossing, from the port of Palos on the gulf of Cadiz, the best outward bound and return routes to America. A mining and farming community was established on the island of Hispaniola (Haiti); the

Spaniards then occupied Havana (Cuba) and San Juan (Puerto Rico). The first investigations of the Mexican mainland began in 1506–8, but the men who invaded Mexico came not from Spain directly but from Cuba, and acted on the orders of its governor Velázquez, who appointed Hernan Cortés as his commander in 1519. In just three years, the whole of the Aztec empire was conquered. This remarkable achievement was followed up in the next decade by the conquest of the Inca kingdom of Peru by Pizarro and Almagro. By 1536, the furthest extent of the pre-conquest societies, and with it the natural limit of Spanish expansion, had been reached.

The conquistadors were hungry for land as well as gold. The Spanish kingdoms represented a land mass of only some half-million square kilometres, whereas in the new world, the colonizers had gained an empire of 3 million square kilometres. This enormous area was exploited with considerable ruthlessness and some degree of efficiency. Groups of villages were 'commended' to the care of Spanish colonizers, whose duty was to protect the inhabitants, to appoint and maintain missionary clergy in the villages, and to undertake a share in the military defence of the new viceroyalties (see chapter 2.2.1). This fief (*encomienda*) system was not supposed to result in a transfer of land or jurisdiction to the colonizers, but in practice it did. The Spanish system of pasture farming was transported to America. There was an astonishing increase in the numbers of beef cattle in Spanish America from an estimated 15,000 in 1536 to a million by 1620. The number of sheep was less than that of cattle, but it also rose significantly. The Aztecs and other Indian populations had depended on arable farming, and particularly on maize. The Spanish herdsmen had no respect for the Indians' fields. They were allowed legally to use the stubble for grazing, but their animals overran the Indian crops, thus leading to famine conditions among the indigenous population.

Already in 1550 it had been predicted that 'if cattle are allowed, the Indians will be destroyed'.[25] Recognized grazing places (*estancia*) were granted by the Spanish viceroy as definitive, transmissible property rights to individual colonizers. By the 1560s, these had assumed their final and characteristic shape. A new social and economic unit, the consolidated estate (*hacienda*), had emerged in Spanish America by the seventeeenth century, with a rich territorial aristocracy at the top of the social pyramid and debt-ridden Indian share-croppers at the bottom. Even in mining areas, the consolidated estate was the rule: not only was it useful for mines to be run in conjunction with food-producing *haciendas* because of the large industrial population to be fed, but it was also a way of eliminating mining competition. The pastoral economy was thus geared up to support the expansion in mining production, and the consequent rise in silver remittances to the Old World (see chapter 8.1.1).

The evidence of the Spanish transatlantic trade from Seville shows a period of rapid growth between 1504 and 1550: total shipping, outbound and inbound from the Old World to the New, rose from a mere 300 *toneladas* in 1504 to more than 10,000 by 1520; total tonnage exceeded 20,000 by 1545, and reached a peak of 32,355 *toneladas* in 1550. A sharp depression followed in the 1550s and 1560s: tonnage figures were nearly halved to under 18,000 in 1553, and fell right back to under 8,000 *toneladas* in 1554. By 1565, when the figure rose to nearly 29,000 *toneladas*, the transatlantic trade was experiencing a revival, and rapid growth continued until 1605, when the peak of 59,000 was reached. The trade held up well until 1610, but fell into decline thereafter: from 40,000 *toneladas* in 1615, it was cut right back to under 23,000 by 1640. An analysis of this depression has some bearing on the debate over the nature of the 'general crisis' of the 1640s (see chapter 4.3.1). Some historians have argued that Spanish America, and especially Mexico, was subject to special difficulties after 1620, including greater fiscal pressure from the Spanish monarchy and discontent with the exercise of viceregal power in the years 1620–64. On the other hand, state revenue in Mexico remained steady before 1660, while revenues in Peru reached their zenith in the first half of the seventeenth century: Peru remitted twice as much bullion to Castile as did Mexico in this period. However, the proportion of bullion which was returned to the Old World from the New declined: before 1629, more than half the Mexican state revenue was remitted to Spain; after 1660, the figure was 33 per cent. The Spanish American economy was being reorientated to cope with the defence of the Philippines and the Caribbean. Europe ceased to have the same significance in the New World, while locally produced goods and those imported from the Far East became increasingly important. The Spanish American colonies had been weaned away from the dominant parent power and were beginning to look towards the Pacific for their markets.

8.4.4 *The Rise of the Dutch to World Economic Supremacy*

In one of the earliest and most influential statements of English 'mercantilist' thought, *England's Treasure by Forraign Trade* (published in 1664, but written in 1622), Thomas Mun grasped the significance of the Dutch entrepôt. The Dutch, he wrote, no longer seemed the same as they had been at the time of Habsburg rule. Although their country was small, with little natural resources, 'they can and do likewise serve and sell to other princes, ships, ordnance, cordage, corn, powder, shot and what not, which by their industrious trading they gather from all the quarters of the world: in which courses they are not less injurious to supplant others (especially the English) than they are careful to strengthen themselves'.[26]

In contrast with Venice, which had achieved supremacy only in the Mediterranean, and with the Hansa, which had been dominant only in Baltic, the Dutch were the first to establish a form of world economic hegemony. From the 1550s, Antwerp had been an active entrepôt in its own right rather than a passive depot of goods. But it was not representative of the country as a whole. Nor did that other great city in the Low Countries, Amsterdam, ever achieve complete economic or political dominance over the Dutch Republic as the French economic historian, Fernand Braudel, maintained. It was the Dutch federal state, with its unique political, economic and social forms of organization, which created economic domination throughout the whole known world. Dutch traders came to be the driving force in the part of the globe in which they operated, and their various areas of interest interacted in such a way that the whole was greater than the sum of the parts.

Dutch shipping grew tenfold from 1500 to 1700 and came to dominate the world carrying-trade. By the mid-seventeenth century, the Dutch merchant marine probably totalled 450,000–500,000 tons, three times the tonnage of the English (who had probably 160,000 tons by 1660), and more than the tonnage of England, France, Portugal, Spain and the German states together. The proportion of ships built by the Dutch, though owned by foreigners, was even higher. Efficiency in this key industry was crucial, although not in itself decisive, in the Dutch domination of world commerce. Shipbuilding required considerable resources in good-quality timber. The Baltic area was the main source of timber in the early modern period: the Dutch cornered this trade, since their primacy in the fishing and textile industries ensured that they could offer products for sale that were in demand by the Baltic market. Thus the Dutch could purchase timber more cheaply than their English rivals, and they processed it much more effectively than their competitors, establishing the first modern shipbuilding industry using standardized techniques and, wherever possible, mechanization. Foreign observers, notably Frenchmen sending reports back to Colbert, commented on the Dutch use of wind-powered sawmills, cranes, blocks and tackles, and so on, which increased productivity. These improved techniques were coupled with ship designs greatly superior to those of their rivals. The success of Dutch shipbuilders came from the gradual improvement of inherited and tested designs through small additions and modifications. The cumulative result was a revolutionary design, the long-distance cargo-carrier of the 1590s called the fluyt (*fluit*), a successor of the earlier and smaller flyboat (*vlieboot*). It had a hull design superior to anything on offer in the rest of Europe, its low centre of gravity providing an improved capability for riding out bad weather. Excellent handling qualities helped reduce the size of crews; the Dutch ships tended to have eighteen hands, whereas a foreign crew might be of twenty-six or thirty hands. Expressed in another way, there was usually one Dutch sailor for every 14 tons, compared to one sailor for every 10 tons on foreign vessels. The fluyt of 200 or 400 tons was also a most efficient cargo-carrier, since the size of the hold was large in relation to the rest of the ship. It was of a light pine in construction, except for the hull where heavy oak was needed to withstand exposure to salt water.

Superior design and lower levels of manning in turn brought down operating costs. By the 1580s, the freight costs of Danzig rye resold at Amsterdam added only 20 per cent to the original purchase price. The freight charge to Italy from the Baltic only doubled the original purchase price. Cheaper freight costs meant an increase in shipping, which brought down insurance rates. The Dutch merchants later recalled that during the Twelve Years' Truce with Spain (1609–21), freight charges were reduced through their 'skill and good management': thus they 'swept all nations from the seas, took over nearly all the trade of other lands and served the whole of Europe with [their] ships'.[27] Moreover, in Holland, Zeeland and Friesland the practice of dividing ship-ownership into numerous shares, as small as one-sixty-fourth of the value of the ship, evolved. By this means, ownership of the Dutch fluyts was extended to a wide social spectrum, including timber dealers, shipbuilders, sailmakers, brewers and millers, and so ship-owning and trading interests were spread right across the country.

An efficient shipping industry created the opportunity for increasing Dutch domination in the sixteenth century over the trade in three staple products: salt, wine and fish. By the 1560s, Holland alone possessed a fleet of some 1,800 seagoing ships, of which 500 were based at Amsterdam. At this time, the North Netherlands fishing fleet comprised some 500 herring 'busses' manned by perhaps 7,000 men. The Dutch Great Fishery (*Groote Visscherij*) was established by resolutions of the States of Holland in 1580–2 to supervise the herring trade based on the ports of The Brill, Rotterdam, Schiedam, Delft and Enkhuizen; it helped ensure a uniformly high quality in the curing of fish on board ship and Dutch herring in turn could command a superior price in every market in Europe. But it required a good-quality salt to preserve the flavour, and hence the Dutch sought a convenient market for this product. French salt was geographically the nearest, but had too high a magnesium content; the Dutch favoured Portuguese and Spanish salt from the eastern salt-pans of La Mata and Ibiza, except in the war years when access to this was denied by the embargo imposed by the Spanish government. Zeeland, and especially the towns of Zierikzee and Goes, emerged as the Dutch centre for salt-refining. French wine destined for the ports of the Baltic was an important shipment which required an entrepôt at a convenient intermediate point, since it was ready for export too late in the year to be shipped to the ice-prone waters of the Baltic and the White Sea until the middle of the following year. Low interest rates in the Netherlands enabled Dutch merchants to buy up French wine at a discount and store it before reshipping it north the following season. Middelburg was the official staple for French wine for the entire Netherlands as early as 1523.

Between 1562 and 1657, the Dutch made 113,212 passages eastward and westward into the Baltic, 60 per cent of the total traffic through that waterway. They carried eastward 75 per cent of the total herring, 61 per cent of the total salt, and 35 per cent of the total cloth imported by the Baltic countries. They carried westward 78 per cent of the wheat and 77 per cent of the rye produced by these countries, the latter amounting to seven times the quantity of the former, some 2.8 million *lasts* in total (a *last* is usually taken to be equivalent to 4,000 pounds in weight, although the precise weight would depend on the nature of the commodity being transported). Yet the Dutch presence in the Baltic before the 1590s was less substantial than these figures might suggest. Many of the Dutch ships were very small, while two-thirds of the ships sailing eastward into the Baltic passed the Danish Sound in ballast, that is, without cargo; the remaining third were carrying salt, a bulky commodity but one of low value. Prior to the 1590s, the Dutch ships sailing westward from the Baltic carried grain and timber, the low-priced goods. The high-value Baltic products were still controlled by the merchants of Lübeck, Hamburg and London. The earliest Dutch breakthrough in high-value commerce was not in the Baltic at all, but in the Arctic trade with Muscovy. The English had opened up this commerce first, and the new port of Archangel was founded as a depot for western ships in 1584. After 1600, the Dutch replaced the English as the leading western state trading with Muscovy by this route. The Dutch were able to expand their Baltic trade in spices, sugar and textiles in the late 1590s at the expense of the Hansa; but the merchants of Lübeck still dominated trade with Sweden. The reduction of Dutch freight costs during the Twelve Years' Truce boosted their share of the Baltic trade, which reached its apogee, commanding over 70 per cent of the total after 1614.

This growth of Dutch trade was threatened by the actions of the Danish government in raising the toll at the Sound in 1611–14. The States General demanded that the additional toll be removed 'in accordance with former treaties, usage and precedent' and, in alliance with the Hanseatic League and Sweden, committed itself to the principle of 'free navigation, commerce and traffic in the Baltic and North Sea as well as the estuaries, rivers and waterways feeding into the Baltic and North Sea'.[28] When Christian IV of Denmark was forced to cancel his additional Sound toll, the result was a spectacular boom in Dutch Baltic commerce, which lasted until the

Spanish embargoes imposed in April 1621, and the attacks of Spanish privateers launched from Dunkirk after 1625. The Dutch were excluded from the Iberian market and there was a massive rise in Dutch freight charges. Suddenly, the Hansa towns appeared capable of a revival: in 1622 they were reported as 'flourishing owing to their free and uninterrupted commerce with Spain ...'[29] Additional threats to Dutch primacy in the Baltic came in the late 1620s from (what proved to be) an abortive Habsburg fleet under the command of Wallenstein and a much more dangerous Swedish blockade of Danzig (see chapters 5.1.4 and 5.2.4). Two Danish–Spanish maritime treaties directed against the Dutch were signed in 1632 and 1641, while Christian IV returned to his policy of increasing the Sound tolls in 1638. Fortunately for the Dutch, the Hanseatic towns and the Danes were unable to fill the vacuum left by the exclusion of the Dutch from the Iberian trade, while in 1643–5 an exasperated Sweden attacked Denmark without a declaration of war (see chapter 5.1.5). After sending a fleet through the Sound without paying dues in mid-July 1645, the Dutch obtained directly from Denmark a number of concessions for themselves, including the lowering of the toll. This settlement formed the basis of Dutch maritime supremacy in the Baltic thereafter. The Dutch managed to keep Denmark firmly on their side in the first Anglo-Dutch war (1652–4), when the English were excluded from the Baltic trade. The Swedish–Polish war of 1655–60 reduced the volume of Baltic trade, but the Dutch share of the total remained above 50 per cent. To some extent, the Dutch were able to make up for any shortfall in Polish grain exports by exporting more Russian grain from Archangel. Perhaps most important of all, the Dutch prevented Charles X of Sweden from achieving his ambition of dominating both sides of the Sound and capturing Copenhagen (see chapter 5.1.6). The Dutch Republic had ensured that it achieved a *dominium maris Baltici*, and not Sweden or Denmark.

This example of naked power politics at work to defend Dutch trading interests is paralleled by the history of the United East India Company (the *Verenigde Oost-Indische Compagnie* or VOC). The number of its ships sailing to the Far East rose in each decade of the seventeenth century until the 1680s, and totalled 859 in all from 1602 to 1660. Many of the ships remained in the east to ply the intra-Asiatic trade, so that the number of return voyages was always lower, totalling 432 from 1602 to 1660. Significant quantities of bullion (mostly drawn from Spanish America) were re-exported to Asia by this company, amounting to 53.4 million florins of precious metal between 1602 and 1660. (In addition, significant sums of Japanese gold and silver were drawn into the trade.) Furthermore, between 1650 and 1675 an annual average of half a million florins' worth of goods was exported from the Dutch Republic to Asia.

After 1630, the annual dividends of the company rarely fell below 12.5 per cent. Its spectacular growth suggests the advantages which might accrue to a trading organization, by virtue of its institutional structure, at the expense of Portuguese traders who were constrained by the crown monopoly. Before 1602, the Dutch trading companies in Asia had been partnerships without monopoly rights or a charter from the States General. Competition had reduced profitability and in 1602 these earlier companies were amalgamated into the VOC by charter of the States General. Monopoly and association offered relative security; the company used its monopoly as a guarantee against sudden fluctuations in supply or demand. It was thought that the company would have a lifespan of twenty-one years, but it was intended that the original investment of 6.4 million florins (57 per cent of which was contributed by Amsterdam) would be wound up after only ten years. This did not in fact happen. Shares became the object of negotiation and speculation, and individual investors were able to withdraw their capital. Thus in 1612 the States General decided that the distribution of capital prescribed in the charter should not take place.

The greater availability of capital in comparison with its commercial rivals such as the Portuguese was an important factor in Dutch success in Asian commerce. From the start, the VOC had a close relationship with the Dutch political leadership, on whom it depended for its continued existence. The management rested with an executive committee called the '17 gentlemen' (*Heren XVII*), eight of whom were chosen by Amsterdam and four by Zeeland, which had contributed 20 per cent of the starting capital. The management abandoned peace in 1605, and seized the legendary 'spice islands' of Amboina, Tidora and Ternate (south-east of the Philippines) from the Portuguese: at a stroke, the Dutch created for themselves a near-monopoly in the world's supply of nutmeg, mace and cloves. This was a high-risk strategy, and by 1613 some of the investors protested that the company management had wasted on war an amount equivalent to twice its original capital (that is, 13 million florins). The value of company assets was then said to be under half a million, while considerable sums had been borrowed at interest. The company tried to conceal such information in order to prevent panic among the investors, who were greatly shaken by the fall in the value of VOC shares following news of the Twelve Years' Truce with Spain; but in 1614 an official valuation placed the negotiable assets of the company at 4.3 million florins, excluding the value of the ships, goods in transit, buildings and shipyards. The situation was less disastrous than the critics had alleged. By 1620, negotiable assets had risen to 5 million, while the value of the company's sixty-eight ships was estimated at 10 million. There were, however, debts of 5.6 million. Profits were ploughed back, and dividends were kept low and paid for by borrowing.

The VOC could not consolidate its control over the spice trade of the Indonesian archipelago without also monopolizing the trade in cotton cloth from south-east India, which was the commodity most in demand in the spice-producing areas. Under the aggressive governor-general of the Dutch East Indies, Jan Pieterszon Coen (he held office in 1619–23 and 1625–9), the company expanded its operations in Asia by a deliberate act of policy ('we must have ever more men, ships and money').[30] The executive committee of the VOC made it clear to Coen in 1622 that there were limits to his policy of 'maintaining trade everywhere with power and armed force'.[31] As merchants, the '17 gentlemen' preferred to avoid war if possible; if it proved impossible, war was viewed as an instrument of company policy. The VOC calculated its protection costs rationally and added them to general overheads. Unlike the Portuguese, the Dutch studiously avoided mixing missionary zeal with business, so that from 1640 they were the only European nation permitted to enter and do business in Japan. In contrast, the Chinese preferred to deal with the Portuguese and Spaniards, but in 1624 they were forced to concede to the Dutch a fortified trade factory on Taiwan (Fort Zeelandia), which the Dutch held until 1662. Under Antonio van Diemen's governor-generalship of the Dutch East Indies (1636–45), the policy of sea power to advance the cause of trade continued: Trincomalee in Ceylon was captured in 1639; and Malacca in 1641, after a gruelling blockade. But the greatest successes occurred under his successor, Rykloff van Goens (commander of the Dutch forces in Ceylon and India, 1657–63), who forced the king of Cochin in south-west India to accept the VOC as his 'protector'. Rights formerly enjoyed by the Portuguese were transferred to the Dutch: 'they do intend to make themselves as much the masters of all the pepper countries as now they are of the other spices', commented an English observer.[32] Profits rose faster than the rate of increase in military expenditure: the Dutch more than quadrupled the value of their cinnamon trade in the 1650s.

After several false starts—it had originally been planned in 1607, but was aborted by the Twelve Years' Truce with Spain—the *West-Indische Compagnie* or WIC was eventually established in 1623–4. The Amsterdam chamber of commerce was the location for 43 per cent of the original capital of 6.6 million florins, but much of this was held on behalf of inland cities or even for foreign countries. Although Amsterdam possessed eight out of the nineteen votes on the management committee (*Heren XIX*), its actual contribution to the original capital was in the region of 25 per cent. (Zeeland, which contributed 20 per cent of the original capital, held only four of the votes on the management committee.) The WIC's first trading assault, on Brazil, ended in disastrous failure in 1624–5; but the policy of raiding Spanish and Portuguese vessels was much more successful, culminating in Piet Heyn's capture of the Spanish treasure fleet at Matanzas Bay in Cuba (see chapter 4.2.1). Shares in the WIC reached an all-time high after this event, but plummeted in the 1630s, as it became clear that the company's expenditure far outstripped its income. The expansion in Brazil reached its zenith in the years 1637–44, but it was heavily dependent for its commercial success on the financial backing of the Sephardi Jews at Amsterdam, whose relatives had migrated to Brazil. They were passionately hated by the Catholic Portuguese settlers, who found themselves heavily in debt to Jews for advance purchases of sugar production. With the advent of the truce between Portugal and the Dutch Republic following the secession of Portugal from the union of crowns with Spain, the WIC reduced its military and naval expenditure. This proved fatal to the Dutch cause in Brazil, and when the Catholic Portuguese settlers rebelled, the Dutch and the Jews were forced to withdraw to the forts. The company never recovered from the shattering blow of the loss of Brazil, which undermined the value of its shares. Nevertheless, the peace with Spain in 1648 permitted some Dutch penetration of the markets in the Spanish Caribbean islands which were distant from the main centres of Spanish colonial authority. The mainland of Spanish America proved a more difficult proposition, but the establishment of a base at Curaçao led to the Dutch becoming the principal carriers of the Caribbean trade in the 1660s, which eventually offset the loss of Brazil.

The expansion of the Dutch trade in the East and West Indies was matched by the growth of manufacturing industry at home. At Leiden in the early sixteenth century there had been a prosperous cloth-weaving industry, but under pressure of competition from the south, especially from Hondschoote in Flanders, output had declined to almost nothing by the 1580s. However, the introduction of the 'New Draperies' (bays, says, camelots and fustians, all types of lighter cloths made with worsted yarn spun from combed, long-staple, wool) saved the day for the Dutch industry. The centre of the trade was based again on Leiden, not because of its traditional role in cloth production, but rather the sacking of Hondschoote six times between 1578 and 1582: this had led to the emigration north of skilled Flemish weavers (consequently the population of Leiden rose from 12,016 in 1581 to 26,197 by 1600). Production rose in each decade except for the 1640s, reaching a peak in excess of 130,000 pieces in the 1660s. Such levels of output were always lower than those of England and France, but by the 1640s the Dutch had replaced the English as the leading suppliers of textiles to the Baltic, producing the best cloth in the greatest quantity: from the 1630s, the Dutch cornered in excess of half the market. During the 1630s, moreover, technical improvements took place which gave Leiden fine cloth an improved smoothness of texture (the so-called *lakens*). Although the total number of cloths manufactured declined, the value of the product trebled in twenty-four years from a total of 2.85 million guilders in 1630 to 8.6 million guilders in 1654. The number of workers employed in the industry also rose, and there was a further wave of immigration into the city. The principal markets for Dutch fine cloth were France, Spain and the Ottoman lands in the Levant.

The Dutch rise to world economic supremacy is all the more remarkable in that it occurred at a time when the European economy was entering a period of recession. The peak of bulk grain exports from the Baltic had been reached by 1618; after 1650 these exports were in marked decline. Yet it was not until the peace with Spain in 1648 that the Dutch made their greatest economic advances: English commercial rivalry in the Levant, for example, was almost completely eliminated for a time. The historian Kellenbenz argued that the Dutch Republic never engaged in any form of mercantilism to promote their economic domination. Unlike its main European rivals in the mid-seventeenth century, France and England, it had no need for tariff restrictions on textile imports. In his view, there was no Dutch counterpart to the English Navigation Act of 1651, or Colbert's tariffs of 1662, 1664 and 1669. This view is not wholly convincing. The Dutch had imposed a ban on imports of dyed and dressed cloth and kerseys in 1614, a measure which was principally directed against English commercial competition, and which had remained permanently in place. The English never forgot it, for they believed it to be 'designed to beat down and discourage the manufacture in this realm, and to gaine the same to themselves, which they have in great measure effected . . .'[33] Such official restrictions were exceptional, and in this case arose because the threat posed by English textiles was of unusual significance to Dutch manufactures. In general, the Dutch could avoid introducing punitive measures against their European competitors because after 1648 they enjoyed unrivalled commercial primacy. But their commitment to free trade was only superficial: Hugo Grotius, the theoretician of freedom of the seas, was sent on a delegation to London to argue that the English had no right to participate in the Far Eastern trade which the Dutch had 'conquered' from the Portuguese at great cost in blood and treasure.[34] One consequence of the treaty of 1648 with Spain (see chapter 4.2.4) was that the Dutch were the neutrals in most of the European conflicts before 1672, and there is no doubt that this neutrality was beneficial to their trading interests. Even so, it is undeniable that Dutch economic hegemony was resented, above all by the English and French. Other states—for example, Denmark and Sweden—regarded the Dutch as domineering and presumptuous, but for them the prospect of another state such as England enjoying primacy was worse. The Dutch Republic lacked the manpower and military resources to translate economic primacy into political domination, and for this reason if for no other, the Dutch were always likely to be more acceptable than the English or the French to neutrals such as the Baltic states.

8.5 Constraints on the Growth of Capitalism

This chapter has already stressed the impact of the increasing flow of bullion, the rise in prices and the structural changes in the balance of economic power in Europe (and in the Dutch case, the world), all indicative of the relative modernity of the early modern European economy. Yet this is only a partial and incomplete picture, for there were considerable checks on economic development in the period. The European economy did not take off into self-sustained growth in the sixteenth century in the way that, for example, the English economy did in the later Industrial Revolution. In part this was because of political developments and the inflexibility of the social structure in some European states. There were also ethical and practical constraints which bear consideration in their own right. Finally, there was the long-standing problem of the backwardness of the dominant economic activity in Europe, agriculture, which severely limited the opportunities for growth.

8.5.1 *Catholic and Protestant Attitudes to the Capitalist Ethos*

Few historical questions have so vexed scholars as the relationship between religious conviction and economic and intellectual progress. The Reformation won its greatest successes in northern Europe. Was it coincidental that during the seventeenth century the balance of economic power shifted from the south of Europe to the north—to some extent by 1600, and certainly by 1660? This shift was undoubtedly a consequence of political changes and the ability of the northern, maritime, economies to exploit market opportunities. Protestant England and the Dutch Republic benefited from the economic difficulties of Catholic Spain and the formerly prosperous Italian city states. Yet there is no simple equation between religious affiliation and economic progress. Catholic France was a relatively strong economic power and a decidedly powerful political force by 1660. Some of the German cities declined in economic importance in the period after they had accepted Lutheranism. They had been more prosperous in their Catholic, so-called 'pre-capitalist' days. Nor was economic development always achieved more rapidly in Calvinist states. The activities of members of a 'Calvinist international'[35] have been greatly exaggerated by some historians. They were few in number and their overall significance in the economic development of a state was slight. A man did not have to be a Calvinist, an immigrant and an expelled subject of a Counter-Reformation state to have a good eye for business. Even so, there are telling illustrations of the achievements of such men, above all in creating the economic 'miracle' of the Dutch Republic, and its flourishing culture, in the seventeenth century. Thousands of refugees fled from persecution in the southern (and ultimately, Spanish) Netherlands, bringing with them to the north their capital, expertise and extensive commercial contacts. The culture of the Dutch Republic was greatly enhanced by the influx of schoolmasters, printers, painters and silversmiths from the south. Refugees also revived the economies of several German towns such as Frankfurt, Hamburg and Emden. Large-scale emigration was a minority activity, however, and its effect on the European economy in general was marginal.

For trade and commerce to develop in western Europe (in other words, for there to be 'capital accumulation' or the development of capitalism), a regularized system of credit transactions and interest payments subject to market forces had to exist. Money-lending had to become acceptable in theory as well as in practice, which was a problem for the church. Throughout the Middle Ages, usury had been equated with lending above the rate of 10 per cent. The biblical text (Deuteronomy xxiii.20) had been explicit: 'unto strangers thou mayest lend upon usury; but unto thy brother thou shalt not lend upon usury'. Early councils of the church had condemned usury as incompatible with a Christian life-style and great scholastic theologians had continued this teaching. The man who lent at high rates of interest, the usurer, was a social pariah in the eyes of the medieval church. Luther's hostility to usury, which was a dominant theme throughout his life, was thus uncompromisingly traditional. Until the Peasants' War of 1524–6, Luther was prepared to condemn the taking of interest in any form, and all commercial transactions which resulted in undue profit: 'there is no lending', he wrote, 'except lending without charge, and if a charge is made, it is not a loan'.[36] This view survived into the second generation of the Reformation in modified form. For Calvin, usury was 'eating away at the poor';[37] in his view, the poor should receive interest-free loans. He generally distinguished between 'biting usury', which was taking interest from the defenceless poor, and taking interest on other occasions, which was 'not unlawful, except in so far as it contravenes equity and brotherly union'.[38] The secular power could determine the rate of interest payable on loans: it was perfectly permissible for the lender to reap advantage just as did the borrower. Calvin certainly did not intend that a man might take profits for himself to the injury of his neighbour. A man was not a usurer if he took interest on loans occasionally. It was only by setting up as a money-lender that he could properly be called a usurer. Such a man had no place in the church of God. There was no substantial divergence in theory between the Reformers and the Catholic church on the issue of usury. The Council of Trent condemned usury as theft and its definition was broadened to include 'all that which a man receives beyond the capital he has lent'.[39] This view was endorsed by successive Popes and Counter-Reformation catechisms.

Yet in practice, neither Protestants nor Catholics could avoid recourse to money-lenders if they wished to advance their business dealings or develop their economies; this posed a moral dilemma which had to be explained away. In one of the earliest cases in which Luther resorted to excommunication, a Wittenberg citizen was deemed to have exacted an extortionate price for a house he had sold. For Luther this constituted usury, a heinous moral sin as well as a civil offence. But he regarded traders and merchants, whose trade led them to the temptation of charging an extortionate price, as a necessary evil. As with certain other great tenets of Luther's belief, it is difficult to see consistency throughout his career. During the German Peasants' War, some Lutheran preachers argued that it was unchristian for individuals to give, as well as to take, interest. Against such assertions, Luther stressed that Christians were free to lend money, while the civil authorities could use their coercive power against recalcitrant debtors. He recognized the legitimacy of charging between 4 and 5 per cent interest on loans; he raised this allowable interest rate in 1540 to between 5 and 6 per cent. He also denied individuals the right to ignore usurious contracts into which they had entered freely. Melanchthon, too, recognized the validity of 5 per cent loans, and further argued that the secular power could authorize them; in such cases, the church had no power or right to question their legitimacy. Bucer claimed in 1550 that persons living in England could rightfully claim 10 per cent rates of interest under the law: he thus acknowledged the validity of Henry VIII's act of 1545. At Geneva, rates were much lower. Calvin fixed the maximum rate of interest at 5 per cent in 1547; contravention of this rate resulted in confiscation of the principal plus a fine. As late as 1580, Beza and the College of Pastors opposed the establishment of a bank charging a regular interest rate of 10 per cent. Old attitudes lingered on in Lutheran Germany. As late as 1587, five Lutheran preachers at Regensburg attacked the practice of usury and argued that those who took 5 per cent interest in accordance with civil law were comparable to thieves and murderers. The argument was not accepted by the municipality, and the five firebrands were expelled from the city.

In *England's Treasure by Forraign Trade*, Thomas Mun had grasped the crucial point that low interest rates were essential for trade to prosper: 'Trade decreaseth as usury encreaseth', was his aphorism, 'for they rise and fall together.'[40] It was precisely the low interest rates enjoyed by the Dutch Republic which had helped fuel their economic miracle and drive towards world hegemony. Dutch merchants could borrow at 2.5, 3 or 4 per cent, whereas in England interest rates were double and in France and Germany they were on occasion higher still. Whatever the undoubted economic benefits of low interest rates, there is no doubt that the Dutch allowed market forces to prevail in setting the rate of interest. Yet even in the flourishing economy of the Dutch Republic, the stark expression of a 'capitalist spirit' in a private, entrepreneurial, form was frowned upon by the Reformed church. A distinction was drawn between the activity of private money-lenders (called 'Lombards')[41] and urban commercial banks. The Middelburg Synod of 1581 endorsed public authority lending, but castigated private bankers. Indeed, money-lenders were excluded from Holy Communion in the Dutch Republic until the 1650s. At the synod of Dordrecht in 1574, the town of Delft enquired whether a money-lender might be admitted to the Lord's Supper. The synod replied in the negative: 'Although such a trade is permitted by the magistrates', it was argued, 'it is nevertheless permitted more on account of the hardness and wickedness of man's heart, than on account of God's will.' Besides, 'many hundreds of people would be offended if such a person were admitted'.[42] The Reformers of the sixteenth and early seventeenth centuries lived in a different world from the Protestant 'capitalist' states of the eighteenth century. By that time, the process of economic change had become so complex that it is impossible to make a direct and un-ambiguous connection with the period of the Reformation, or to isolate the religious factor as the single most important element causing a change in economic attitudes.

The dilemma faced by theologians demonstrates that the issue of usury defied a simple response, and helps to explain Catholic France's attitude towards financiers. The capital raised through the Paris money market was essentially provided by the wealthy and privileged social groups, that is to say broadly speaking the nobles, office-holders and rentiers. If there was a threatened royal bankruptcy, contemporaries talked of the ruin of 10,000 families, of whom 'there are a great number of persons of status'.[43] But these families did not wish to be known openly as financiers of the monarchy. Those who had recently attained noble status, or who aspired to it, avoided open participation in financial transactions. This was because the rule of *dérogeance*, by which a nobleman might lose status if he committed a demeaning act, prohibited him from participating directly in business enterprises (see chapter 7.2.1), although he might do so secretly under an assumed name. Strictly speaking, financial activity was not in itself a demeaning act: furthermore, if the service was provided to the king, it was considered honourable.

The dangers of participating openly in financial activity were obvious, however. The unpopularity of royal fiscal policies, and of the agents of those policies, attracted public attention and opprobrium: nobody would wish to be directly associated with them, but any stigma could be avoided if intermediaries were used and secrecy maintained: hence the necessity of financiers as intermediaries. Another obvious danger was that the taking of profit at usurious rates of interest might be viewed as incompatible with the life-style of a nobleman. In December 1648, the archbishop of Paris and the Sorbonne asserted that to lend to the king even at the low rate of 10 per cent was a mortal sin; in fact, many tax contracts carried interest rates of 25 or even 30 per cent. Landed society was patrimonial in outlook: what was gained by the father was handed down to the son with only a few new additions to this inheritance. All that was expected in this rentier mentality was to retain one's patrimony and live off the small but steady income it produced. Rapid capital accumulation was thus regarded by contemporaries as a sin, and in certain circumstances a crime. Secrecy and the use of financiers as intermediaries brought great advantages to the investor. If the financier was regarded as a pariah, a ruthless entrepreneur with an 'insatiable avidity to get rich quick',[44] this served to deflect public attention away from criticism of the privileged few who enjoyed wide social and fiscal privileges and secretly placed their investments with the financier as middleman.

8.5.2 *Changing Attitudes towards Entrepreneurs: the European Jews*

The issue of usury was a crucial touchstone in the attitude of Catholic authorities towards the Jews. In the later Middle Ages, there had already been a hardening of attitudes towards the Jews in several countries which had not expelled them at an earlier date. Expulsions and forced conversions occurred in a number of European states in the fifteenth century. The most famous of these, in scale and presumably in economic significance, was the expulsion of the Jews from the Spanish lands in 1492 by Ferdinand and Isabella, acting under pressure from the Inquisition. It has always been assumed that a massive number of Sephardi (that is, Hispanic) Jews were expelled at that date—perhaps 150,000—and that they took their economic expertise in the woollen-cloth, silk and leather industries, as well as in general commerce, to other states, most notably to the Ottoman lands and to certain Italian states. This exodus is also held to account at least partly for the absence of an entrepreneurial class in Spain by the later sixteenth and earlier seventeenth centuries, a phenomenon reinforced by the expulsion of the Moriscos in 1609. Yet the evidence for the damage wrought by the expulsion is by no means clear-cut. The size of the Jewish community in the Iberian lands in the fifteenth century has not been established beyond reasonable doubt from the extant documents. Tax censuses suggest a much smaller community of perhaps only 15,000 families (or some 70,000 Jews) in Castile on the eve of the exodus, equivalent to 1.6 per cent of the population; there may have been 10,000 Jews in the mainland territories of the crown of Aragon, equivalent to 1.2 per cent of the population there. Furthermore, a six-month period of grace was allowed before the decree of expulsion became effective, during which Christian missionary work would, it was hoped, lead to conversions. It seems likely that some of the Jews remained in Spain and chose the option of conversion which had been offered by the Catholic Monarchs, thus mitigating the economic consequences of the expulsion order. However, contemporary chroniclers were unanimous in the view that most of the Jews left Spain in 1492 or shortly afterwards.

Many of the Spanish Jews who chose exile went at first to Portugal, where they were allowed to exercise their faith until 1497. After this date, the withdrawal of Jewish rights in Portugal was accompanied by forced abjurations in an attempt to prevent emigration. This policy, which was so different from that adopted by the Spanish monarchy, perhaps suggests that the exodus of the Jews from Spain had been more widespread and harmful to the economic interests of the country than some recent historians would have us believe. In Portugal, as in Spain, it seems likely that many Jews chose to convert: until the 1540s there was no Inquisition in Portugal to investigate the validity of such conversions. After the Portuguese Inquisition became an oppressive force in the 1580s, new converts to Catholicism (*conversos* or *Marranos*) came under its scrutiny, leading to further movements of the crypto-Jewish population. Some returned to Spain—where the Inquisition was less intrusive, and where after 1598 Lerma welcomed immigrants (in stark contrast to his attitude to the Moriscos)—while others went to France, Italy, the Low Countries and Hamburg.

Jews were expelled from other European states, including virtually all the German principalities (except Hesse) and the Imperial cities, the Italian states south of Rome, the Low Countries and Provence (except for the Papal enclaves of Avignon and the Comtat Venaissin). The medieval Papacy had tended to protect the Jews in order to discourage Christians from the sin of active usury. In the early sixteenth century, the benevolent attitude of the Papacy is demonstrated by the high interest rates the Jews were allowed to charge: Leo X had permitted them to lend at 60 per cent rates of interest, Paul III at 48 per cent rates. With the accession of the violently anti-Spanish Pope Paul IV in 1555, even the Papacy, the traditional protector of the Jewish community, lurched into hostility: Paul IV's bull *Cum nimis absurdum* ordered the establishment of ghettos for

Jews throughout the Papal States; he was heard to mutter that he would like to burn all the *Marranos*. Pius V was equally hostile, and ordered the expulsion of Jews from Papal territories, with the exception of Rome itself and Ancona, in 1569. This policy was moderated by Sixtus V, but was reintroduced by Clement VIII (with the additional exception of Avignon) in 1593. At Rome, he prohibited Christians from entering Jewish shops or becoming indebted to Jews. Despite such set-backs, the Jews survived, and sometimes prospered in Italy. Pius V reduced the interest rate chargeable by Jews to 12 per cent, but Gregory XIII compromised at 18 per cent, and this remained the rate tolerated by the Papacy for the rest of the sixteenth century. By 1586, 3,500 Jews lived in Rome, forming some 3.5 per cent of the population, while by the end of the century there were at least 279 Jewish banks in 131 places in Italy, and probably many more.

Other Italian states—even the traditionally independent Venetian Republic—were inevitably influenced by the change in attitude of the Papacy. After 1520, the Venetian Jews were allowed to charge 15 per cent interest on pledges and 20 per cent on written bonds in return for payment of an annual tax of 10,000 ducats. But in 1548, while maintaining the level of the annual tax, the Venetian Senate arbitrarily reduced to 12 per cent the maximum interest rate chargeable. In 1556, it was further reduced to 10 per cent, and some Jewish banks failed as a result. Though the rate was raised once more to 12 per cent in 1565, it was probably still uneconomic. In 1571, the Jews were expelled from Venice in the aftermath of the great Christian victory over the Turks at Lepanto. The order was rescinded in 1573, but the Jews were henceforth to lend only to the poor at the same rate of 5 per cent interest as existing Catholic charitable trusts (*Monti di Pieta*) charged. This unusual arrangement lasted for the rest of the period, but it was made tolerable at least before the 1630s by greatly reduced tax demands on the Venetian Jews. From the 1590s onwards, Jews controlled Venetian exports to the Balkans and the Black Sea via Split and Valona. They seem to have used Christians as their agents in this business: 'on Rialto', it was said, 'they send merchandise aboard galleys and ships, and because they cannot do so on their own account, they use the name of a Venetian noble whom they support and who goes everywhere with them . . .'[45] Jewish proposals for loan banks at higher rates of interest failed in the Senate, but the official Jewish banks clearly did not try to eliminate illegal usurious lending at 25 per cent. Buoyed up by the success of their twin activities of pawnbroking and loan-banking, the size of the Jewish community in Venice rose from 0.5 per cent of the population in 1516, when the ghetto was established, to nearly 2.25 per cent by 1642.

The vagaries of the approaches adopted by the Papacy and other Italian states to their Jewish communities contrast markedly with the position of the Austrian Habsburgs, who maintained a consistently favourable policy.

The Emperor had defended the Jews against damaging popular accusations of child kidnapping and ritual murder (the so-called 'blood libels') which were frequently levelled against them by a resentful population. At the diets of Augsburg, Speyer and Regensburg (respectively in 1530, 1544 and 1546), Charles V had confirmed Jewish privileges in the Empire. Yet this was the ruler who had expelled the Sephardi Jews from Naples in 1541. His attitude towards the Ashkenazi community in the Empire is explicable only in terms of the financial support of the German Jewry for his political and military designs: in 1546–7, they were active supporters of the Habsburgs in the war against the Schmalkaldic League. (Given the hostility of the principal reformers, above all Luther, to the Jews, this support is readily explicable.) Ferdinand I was much more hostile to them than was his older brother, and he restricted Jewish privileges in Bohemia (although not in Moravia). But subsequent Emperors reverted to the traditional policy: the privileges granted by Rudolf II in 1577 to the Bohemian Jews were so extensive, and allowed them to participate in such a range of economic activities, that there was a substantial expansion in the community at Prague. The policy was not reversed under Matthias I; indeed, when the anti-Jewish risings occurred at Frankfurt and Worms in 1614, he joined the elector of Mainz in providing troops to reimpose order and restore the property and privileges of the Jewish communities there (see chapter 7.5.2). Faced with the threat posed by the Bohemian rebellion in 1619, Ferdinand II turned to the Jewish community for subsidies and logistical support, and throughout the 1620s their rights were greatly extended both at Prague and Vienna. Jacob Bassevi, who had been ennobled by Matthias in 1614 (the first Jew to be so honoured by the Emperor), controlled the revenues from the Bohemian silver mines and became the second most important financier in the Austrian lands: he was a precursor of the European 'court Jews' of the second half of the seventeenth century. Throughout the Thirty Years' War, with the exception of events at Mantua in 1630 (where the troops were ordered to stop looting the Jewish community), the Imperial army was under orders to protect the Jews when on the offensive. When, as in the 1640s, Imperial fortunes were reversed, the Jews actively supported the Emperor, most notably in the siege of Prague in 1648.

It was not just the Emperor who was convinced of the importance and usefulness of the Jews by the seventeenth century. The Swedish commanders in the Thirty Years' War imposed war contributions on the Jews in the first months after their invasion, but they rapidly perceived the advantages of protecting local Jewish communities, who could provide the cash, food, fodder and horses which were desperately needed. The French commanders in Alsace protected the Jewish communities at Philippsburg and Breisach for similar reasons. Where there was no pressing military consideration, the absolutist ambitions and the growing *raison d'état* philosophy of rulers might suggest that there was an economic advantage to be gained in dealing favourably with the Jews. Henri IV encouraged Jewish emigration to Metz in 1595, while Christian IV of Denmark followed suit for Glückstadt in 1619 and 1630. By the early seventeenth century some of the Spanish economic theoreticians (*arbitristas*), such as Martín González de Cellorigo, were prepared to argue publicly in favour of recalling the Jews for reasons of state, to improve Spain's trading position and state finances. Olivares was certainly prepared to enter into loan contracts with the Portuguese new Christians, some of whom at least were crypto-Jews.

There is thus some evidence that absolutist rulers and their advisers were becoming more enlightened in their dealings with the Jews in the seventeenth century, chiefly for reasons of state power, while representative institutions remained stubbornly conservative: the last meeting of the Estates General before the French Revolution, in 1614–15, manifested a fierce hostility to the Jews. But this is not the whole picture. The Jewish community was most entrenched in two European states whose political development was furthest from absolutism: the United Provinces and the Commonwealth of Poland-Lithuania. The role of the Sephardi Jews in the exploitation of Dutch Brazil in the 1640s (see chapter 8.4.4) was only one aspect of a significant economic presence in the United Provinces which expanded rapidly after the conclusion of peace with Spain in 1648. The Dutch Sephardi were more diversified in their economic interests, and more closely integrated into national economic life, than were the Jews anywhere else in western Europe. One sign of this integration was the extent of their activities on the Amsterdam money market. In the fifteen years from 1646 to 1661, the number of Jewish depositors with the Amsterdam Exchange Bank (*Wisselbank*) rose from 126 to 243; at a time when the total number of depositors was also increasing, this represented a rise from about 7 per cent to 12½ per cent of the total. The keys to Jewish prosperity in the United Provinces were the end of Spanish rule in Portugal in 1640, which opened up new ports to Dutch shipping; and the collapse of Dutch Brazil. Although a financial disaster for some, many Dutch Sephardi returned from the colony with substantial assets which were reinvested at Amsterdam.

In eastern Europe, the great area of diversified Jewish economic activity was in Poland-Lithuania, where the magnates (including Chancellor Zamoyski) encouraged the settlement of German-speaking Ashkenazi Jews. Jews took up leases on noble estates and became essentially the magnates' agents at the eastern terminus of the Baltic–Vistula grain trade. The growth of Jewish communities became so pronounced, and their range of economic activities so far-reaching, that the rebellion led by

Bogdan Chmielnicki in the Ukraine in 1648 represented a fierce Orthodox backlash which unleashed pogroms on a scale not seen since the late Middle Ages (see chapter 5.3.4). But even this setback could not halt the economic progress and numerical strength of the Jewish community of Poland-Lithuania.

8.5.3 *Guilds and the Constraints on Manufacturing Expansion*

In most European towns during the Middle Ages, craft and merchant guilds had been established to help maximize the volume of trade and the consequent benefits to the town and its merchants. They were intended to ensure a satisfactory standard of workmanship, and a fair price, for the product in which the guild specialized, and protection from outside traders. They sought to restrict the number of apprentices a master might keep, the hours he might work and the tools he might use. Their concern was that a good product should be sold at a reasonable price. However, these ideals which dated from the period of the establishment of guilds were gradually lost with the passage of time. Many guilds had become self-interested monopolies which sought to keep prices high by the early modern period. Even the supervision of training through the apprentice system was open to the objection that it provided masters with cheap labour: guilds tended to keep down the wages of unskilled labourers and ensured that relatively few wage-earners were employed. Above all, the guilds restrained capitalist development in the sense that they sought to foster prosperity within the guild system to the benefit of members rather than outsiders. They pursued caution rather than profit; they sought an honest independence, rather than a high income, for the master craftsmen; more significantly, they sought to restrict the scope of commercial competition. Units of production were kept small and the use of out-workers (that is, workers outsider the guild system) by 'capitalists' was strictly controlled. Those who worked within the guild system were subject to a carefully formulated law of contract.

The guilds had played a considerable part in the life and consciousness of town dwellers in the late Middle Ages, promoting ties that were deeper and more extensive than those found in private associations today. Guild membership was a serious matter—guildsmen had a strong sense of the 'honour' of their trade, and they both believed in and enforced high standards of craftsmanship. The sentiment of guild membership was strong: they were often obliged to give each other 'mutual aid' in the form of money as 'brothers' or 'friends'. Craft guilds frequently had their own confraternities, that is to say, a voluntary group within the craft which met together at regular intervals to hear Mass said by the craft's chaplain and to do pious and charitable works in honour of a patron saint: Venice had

119 such *scuole* or confraternities in 1521. These confraternities were concerned with the welfare of members rather than outsiders: the relief of poverty in the craft was more important than its alleviation in society at large. The Venetian evidence from the late Middle Ages suggests that these groups transcended both the rigid ranks of the social hierarchy and the geographical limitation of the parish boundary. They also acted as significant patrons of the visual arts: for example, many of the altars and chapels in Venetian churches were maintained by the trade guilds.

Some towns in the late Middle Ages had seen the guilds exercising a political role, by means of a power-sharing arrangement with the patriciate, often represented in new and old councils respectively, and sometimes along lines laid down by formal constitutional treaty. As late as 1544–5, Clemens Jäger, the city archivist of Augsburg, wrote a *Chronicle of the Weavers' Guild*, which included an extended account of the revolution in 1368 which had established guild rule there; he presented a rhetorical and historical defence of the principles of guild rule in cities. In essence it was justified as promoting a stable constitution since it helped avoid the antipathy between rich and poor. However, a decade later, after the imposition of the Interim of Augsburg by Charles V and the collapse of the Protestant guild party in the city, Jäger wrote a quite different treatise which praised the ancient patriciate of the city, condemned the revolution in 1368 as mob usurpation, and accused the guild regime of gross misconduct.

The impact of the guilds clearly varied from one town to another. As might be expected, they were found generally throughout the Low Countries, one of the most heavily urbanized areas of Europe: in fact, they were more deeply rooted in the south than the north. There, the guilds represented those occupations for which a certain amount of training was required; unskilled tasks were left outside the guild system. Guilds drew their membership from all ranks within the social hierarchy. The survey of the apothecaries' guild at Venice in 1567–8 shows a highly uneven distribution of wealth: less than 5 per cent of the members accounted for nearly half the total capital, while 38 per cent of the members controlled less than 2 per cent of the wealth. A middle group of some 15 per cent of the members controlled roughly the same proportion of capital. In the Low Countries, there might sometimes be a dispute within a trade, between masters and journeymen; but on other occasions, the two elements might combine against a different professional group involved in the manufacture of the same product—for example, fullers against drapers and weavers. Indeed, the history of the guilds in the Low Countries was largely the story of struggles between various craft guilds, tilers against thatchers, carpenters against cabinet-makers, and so on, trying to protect their own livelihoods against related trades rather than a conflict between guilds and patriciate. In the case of some north Italian towns, the original guild structure splintered in order to incorporate workers who had been previously outside these organizations. Supra-guild structures emerged in such cases, sometimes called houses of merchants: these were akin to the original merchant guilds in England, and were large regulatory bodies which co-ordinated and directed all aspects of production, commerce and monetary exchange in cities such as Pavia, Piacenza, Milan, Cremona, Brescia and Verona. These bodies resolved jurisdictional disputes between the guilds, and defined the occupational boundaries of professions.

Doubtless when the demand for goods was increasing, the guilds could take a relatively benign attitude towards the admission of new members or the formation of new associations. On the other hand, when demand was stagnant or declining, they became defensive, seeking to preserve employment for their own members, even to the detriment of other trades within the same community. By the sixteenth century, inheritance came to be one of the main ways, and in some cases the only way, to achieve the status of master in the Low Countries. Between 1510 and 1539, the number of new masters in the brewers' guild at Ghent exactly matched the number of masters' sons (225). Similar trends were apparent among the blacksmiths, carpenters, bricklayers and leather-workers in the same city. This conservative stance was commonplace throughout Europe wherever the guild activity was in decline. This was not, of course, invariably the case. Guild membership seems to have been buoyant at Venice, where a list of the guild of mercers drawn up in 1575 reveals that some 205 members out of the total of 874 had joined as recently as the previous year. The number of mercers' shops increased at Venice from 400 in 1586 to 446 by 1594; although at least 79 shops had gone out of business in the intervening period, they had clearly been speedily replaced. Even in a period of economic decline in the seventeenth century, some guilds, probably representing service industries, prospered against the trend: the number of mercers at Venice increased from 567 in 1595 to 1,747 in 1690.

It is often argued that late medieval craft guilds provided a protective shield behind which merchants and craftsmen could prosper without undue concern for costs, productivity and innovation. The Venetian evidence concerning the guild of mercers suggests that some guilds could expand to cover several trades, with impressive amounts of capital spread among hundreds of small businesses. In 1586, some 400 shops were owned by the 964 members of the guild, at least 250 of these being owned independently, of which some 108 were run by men of humble means. It seems, too, that in great metropolitan centres such as Antwerp, Amsterdam and London—but not Lyon—guilds not only survived in the sixteenth century but prospered, responding to market forces and helping to develop the urban economy. In towns such as Lille and Leiden, where textile manufacturing continued to be based on small commodity production, the medieval guild organization survived into the seventeenth century. Some merchants recognized the value of guilds, which helped share employment opportunities and ran their own benefit schemes for members. Guilds were not units of production or distribution, but units of producers and distributors. They may not have been quite such a constraint on economic development as is sometimes suggested, and it has recently been argued that it was early modern monarchical or princely governments, not town governments or the guilds themselves, which produced rigidity in the guild system. Predictably those guilds which were exempt from taxation or military service did best: thus at Venice, the mercers continued to prosper in the seventeenth century largely because in 1596 they had been exempted from the obligation of personal naval service in the galleys. In contrast, heavy tax demands on other guilds, such as those in the woollen industry, decimated their size and gravely undermined their economic importance. Nevertheless, there is still much to be said for the view that in a trade where two states were competing directly for an international market, the country whose industry retained its old guild structure lost out. The ineffectiveness of the north Italian cotton industry in the face of German competition by 1600 was a result of higher production costs. These higher costs arose from the heavy burden of taxation, the higher wage demands of urban labourers, and guild restrictions which hampered changes in the techniques of production. The obvious way to reduce costs was to employ less skilled rural weavers and to adopt simpler techniques in dyeing and finishing. However, these developments were resolutely opposed by the Italian cotton guilds, which represented the interests of small producers determined to preserve the urban monopoly over production.

8.5.4 *The Backwardness of Agrarian Production*

Conservative attitudes towards the capitalist ethos were certainly important in restricting the growth of the economy, but perhaps the lack of a prosperous rural market for manufactured goods was even more fundamental. It was not just the dominant size of this rural sector that needs to be emphasized (see chapter 7.2.4); it was the inefficiency of agriculture in general which was a constraint on the development of Europe's economy. Agriculture was not, however, untouched by manufacturing activity and in some ways benefited from it. Merchants in the towns provided additional employment to rural artisans: for example, rural weavers were often restricted to the earlier and simpler stages of textile production, or else confined to turning out a range of coarser products such as serges, fustian and linen, while the finishing processes and the manufacture of the more valuable woollens and silks were reserved to skilled urban weavers. This was the 'putting-out' system (called by German historians the *Verlags-wesen* or *Verlaggsystem*, a term derived from the word *Verlger*, a putter-out, that is to say, a merchant who 'puts out' work). This system triumphed, for example, in Nuremberg, where there were no guild restrictions and the merchants put work out to the countryside in order to escape the high labour costs of the city's crafts. Bartolomäus Viatis—a Venetian subject—became one of the richest merchants of his adoptive city of Nuremberg by putting out the manufacture of textiles to country workers in northern Bohemia, Upper Saxony and Silesia. This system must be distinguished from so-called 'proto-industrialization' (what German historians call the *Kaufsystem*), under which independent artisan households worked with their own raw materials and produced a saleable product. In this model, a small farm and the dual occupation of artisan and farmer were crucial to the viability of the enterprise.

Of course, these two models do not represent the full diversity of relationships between the agricultural and industrial sector, but they serve to illustrate the characteristic features of the pre-industrial structure in the rural areas. The *Kaufsystem* seems to have been supported by more fertile and larger agricultural holdings, with a greater seasonality of agricultural work and (perhaps) richer peasants. Where the vine predominated, labour demands were spread more evenly throughout the year, and proto-industry such as the system generated was limited or non-existent. Furthermore, the *Kaufsystem* may have allowed for earlier marriage, and thus more rapid rates of population increase, by freeing marriage from the traditional constraints of inheritance and patriarchal control. Further research is needed, but the Dutch evidence suggests that the population grew most rapidly where rural industry thrived; purely agricultural districts of Holland showed relatively little population growth. The central areas of the Krimpener-Alblasserwaard, where agriculture was the only important source of employment, grew merely from 5,550 to 7,758 inhabitants between 1514 and 1622. However, the riverbank areas, which benefited from shipwharves and brickworks, dikeworks, transportation and other craft activities, grew from 5,700 to 10,309 inhabitants in the same period. Elsewhere, by tending to separate labour from the land, the process may have helped create an industrialized rural workforce before the age of the factory. In economic terms, the *Kaufsystem* seems to have been the older, less developed form of proto-industrialization. The trend in economic development was from *Kaufsystem* to *Verlagssystem*, from small-scale to larger-scale rural production, with greater craft specialization.

Yet this domestic manufacturing was in origin merely an additional activity to supplement a rural family's income. Agriculture was its mainstay, and it was for the most part resolutely traditional. There were relatively few treatises on agricultural methods, though a few were very popular: Olivier de Serres's *Theatre of Agriculture* went through five editions in the seventeenth century after its first publication in France in 1600. But such works did not lead to any technological advances in the methods of cultivation. France was divided into areas of the *charrue*, the plough mounted on wheels chiefly used on the heavier soils of the north, and of the *araire*, the wheel-less plough used mainly on the lighter soils of the Midi. Both types of plough were made of wood; the *araire* tended to be drawn by cattle and sometimes donkeys or mules—all less costly than the horses pulling the *charrues* in northern France. There was a close connection between the choice of draught animal and the type of crop rotation: a biennial system was only suitable where an oat crop was not needed to feed horses. Much of the work was a laborious manual round of chores such as drainage, harrowing, rolling of ploughed land, hoeing and clod breaking, followed up later by hand weeding. A bitter debate between proponents of old methods and the new centred on the question of manuring and soil enrichment. Marling, it was said in France, 'enriches the father but ruins his children';[46] exactly the same was said in England about liming. English techniques were probably well in advance of the French even by the reign of Louis XIV. In France, methods such as ash-spreading (later denounced by Arthur Young) were assumed to be efficacious simply because they were traditional. Green manuring, marling and liming were all considered expensive. Soil improvement was thus dependent on the availability of animal manure, which in turn was affected by the size of herds, the ability to feed the animals, the general fertility of the land and rival claims for the manure produced (particularly from what Colbert thought were the excessive number of vines in France). Some areas had more livestock and thus more manure than others. Some peasants had more animals than others, and those with medium or large holdings had the advantage of being able to pen the sheep and manure the fields directly. Where the subdivision of peasant holdings had reached its fullest extent, the management of sheep runs required strict discipline.

The choice of grain was crucial, for on this all agricultural profits depended. In France, rye crops were sown, especially on poorer soils, and barley where early harvesting was required. Mixed crops, which tended to disappear in areas where farming was geared directly to the market, were considered an insurance against meteorological disaster. Great emphasis was placed on sieving and winnowing in an attempt to save clean and healthy seed for the next season, but in areas of subsistence farming the very seed for sowing might have to be borrowed in crisis years. Even authorities such as Olivier de Serres found it difficult to prescribe how densely the seed should be sown, and any instructions were likely to be only partially fulfilled since the seed was scattered broadcast. When it came to the harvest, the relatively high population density of France meant that the fear of losing grain though the shelling of heads prevented the use of the scythe until the nineteenth century, since it was believed to shake the grain. The sickle was about three times slower in use that the scythe, but it was cheaper to buy since the shorter blade did not have to be imported. More importantly, perhaps, virtually any fit man, woman or child could work with a sickle, while all benefited from the fact that the sickle cut the crop higher. Once gleaning had taken place, the straw was cleared by all under the communal grazing rights (*vaine pâture*). Despite tensions between the employer and his workforce at the time of the harvest, the seigneur tended to respect communal rights, and in the eighteenth century, to oppose attempts to introduce the scythe. Thus even the most limited technological progress was forgone, tradition out-weighing considerations such as time lost and higher wage bills to seasonal workers.

Harvest yields varied widely between countries and within regions. There were more systems of crop rotation than the simple division into biennial and triennial systems, and these coupled with the wide variety of soils complicate any attempt to calculate an average harvest yield even for a single country such as France. In 1600, Olivier de Serres considered a yield of 5 or 6 times the original seed sown to be possible on good lands; in 1707, Vauban thought yields of 10, 12 or even 15 to 1 were possible on some lands, but that the norm, taking into account poor soils, was the relatively low figure of 4.5 to 1. In some French regions, it is possible to calculate variations in the productivity of the land over a period of time. Thus in the Cambrésis, yields varied between 4 and 18 hectolitres to the hectare around 1450; by 1520, there was a partial recovery from agri-cultural depression, and yields had risen to between 10 and 18 hectolitres to the hectare; but towards 1625, they fell again to between 6 and 18. These fluctuations occurred for the most part in the marginal lands, which were badly cultivated during periods of agricultural depression, but which were taken back into full production during periods of prosperity and population growth.

Since there was no real technological breakthrough, any growth in production was dependent on an increase in the numbers of the work-force: the ceiling on cereal production in France seems to have been reached before the Black Death, and was only regained during the reign of Louis XIV; it was not surpassed until the 1830s. The best evidence on this subject is provided by the surviving documentation from the levy of the tithe. The so-called 'great' tithe was levied on basic components of agri-cultural production such as wheat, barley, oats, rye and wine; lesser tithes or green tithes were levied on vegetables and fruit from gardens and orchards. Finally, there were tithes on livestock, commonly known as 'blood tithes'.[47] The tithe could be levied directly by the clergy and its agents. In this case, it was collected every year as the harvest came in, directly from the fields, the threshing-floor, the wine-press, the stables or wherever the crops were stored. Alternatively, the collection of the tithe was leased or 'farmed out' to 'tithe farmers' for one year or several years, in money or kind. Although there were great regional variations in the amount raised from the tithe—from as low as 2.5 per cent to as high as 14 per cent of the harvest yield—where it was levied effectively it reflected trends in agricultural production. There was clear tithe fraud, and some opposition to the levy: but cases of resistance—such as in France in the 1560s—are usually documented, while fraud may be assumed to be a relatively constant factor. But above all, the tithe registers cannot be used with the same confidence as economic indicators throughout Europe. They more reliably reflect the trends in agricultural production in southern (and especially Catholic) Europe; in northern Europe, the tithe was often secularized and converted into dues that were levied arbitrarily, so that they are not an accurate means of measuring production.

The agricultural depression at the end of the Middle Ages led merely to a temporary decline; from 1450 until about 1530 or 1560, depending on the region, there was a relatively rapid recovery, both in the level of population and in agricultural output as measured by the tithe. In the Cambrésis, using the year 1370 as index 100 for the production of cereals (that is to say, corn, oats and barley), the index had recovered to 85 by about 1530. A crisis in agriculture followed, provoked by the passage of troops which damaged or destroyed the crops in the Cambrésis in five of the six years between 1552 and 1557. After the wars had ended and the armies were no longer roaming the countryside, recovery took a long time: there was no growth during the period 1560–1660 and long-term recovery did not begin until after 1660.

By this stage, agricultural depression was a more generalized phenomenon in Europe, characterized by stable grain prices and stagnant production. Grain production reached its peak in Poland around 1560–70, and in Hungary a decade earlier. It declined in Hungary by about 50 per cent between 1570 and 1710, partly because of the long war against the Turks (1593–1606). The decline in Polish production was less severe, amounting to only about 10 per cent in the period 1570–1650, because there was a stimulus provided by the continuing high level of grain exports to the Netherlands. The great fall in Polish production occurred during the Thirteen Years' War against Muscovy (1654–67). In Alsace, however, if tithe evidence is taken as indicative of grain production, the fall in the tithe in the sixteenth century was relatively modest, some 7 per cent, while there was actual growth in the first thirty years of the seventeenth century. It has been argued that Alsace provides a model of what France might have achieved had it not been subjected to the devastation of the wars of religion. However, after 1632, the tithe in Alsace fell to practically nothing as the Thirty Years' War made its impact on the region; and by 1660, although there was a recovery from this very low level, agricultural production was still at less than a half of the pre-war level. The fall in French agricultural production seems to have accelerated in the last quarter of the sixteenth century, when the fighting of the wars of religion (especially the blockades of cities such as Rouen and Paris) was at its most severe. The decline was not uniform throughout the kingdom; it was at its lowest in the area around Paris, the richest grain production region, although even it here it amounted to a fall of about 25 per cent in production. In Auvergne and Languedoc it was higher, at around 35 per cent; while in Burgundy, there was a devastating decline in excess of 40 per cent. Recovery followed the restoration of peace, and had occurred in most regions by 1630. There was a further recession after this date, which coincided with the political disturbances of the Fronde (1648–53) although this varied greatly according to the region: it was most marked in northern France, where there was a fall in production by about a quarter in the Paris region; the Midi, however, was largely unaffected by this recession. The Spanish evidence from the Basque country, Murcia and Galicia also suggests decline in the first third of the seventeenth century.

Tithe evidence, however open to criticism, suggests that agricultural production in most areas of early modern Europe was volatile. It was insufficiently sustained over a long period of time to permit the emergence of a consistently high rural demand for products, which (subject to the pressure of taxation) in turn might have acted as a stimulus to manufacturing production. Only one area, the Low Countries, was the exception to this rule. There, agricultural productivity maintained its high level during the European depression of the fourteenth and fifteenth centuries. Intensification of farming was encouraged both by the growth in urban demand and increased urban investment in the countryside. There was a recession of sorts during the last two-thirds of the fifteenth century, but by the sixteenth century a further increase in production, under the influence of population growth, was well under way. In some areas, such as Louvain, yields of rye, barley and oats were respectively 11, 32 and 72 per cent higher in the period after 1502 than they had been in the fifteenth century. Yet the pattern of prosperity was not uniform. Certain regions in the south, such as Walloon-Brabant and Hesbaye, did not prosper to the same extent because they were dependent on the monoculture of grain. Elsewhere, higher incomes were obtained from specialization and diversification of crops in response to urban demand. Holland and

Friesland concentrated on dairy products. Groningen, Overijssel and Drenthe specialized more in livestock. In northern and western Brabant and in Flanders, horticulture and hops were widespread. In Flanders and Zeeland, flax-growing helped seasonal unemployment in the rural areas and encouraged the weaving and spinning industries. In contrast with the French experience, the rise in population and consequent subdivision of landholdings did not lead to a pauperization of the peasantry, because living standards remained high as a result of the rise in productivity.

In his *Interest of Holland* (1661), Pieter de la Court thought the encouragement of agriculture of no importance in fostering prosperity in the Dutch Republic. The most recent studies have disagreed with his viewpoint: agriculture, industry, shipping and commerce were all interrelated and provided the basis for the flourishing trade of the Republic. Dutch agriculture was efficient, and thus could supply the raw materials and release the unskilled labour needed for industrial expansion, especially shipping and commerce. Moreover, almost uniquely in early modern Europe, a prosperous farming community provided a market for industrial goods which acted as an additional stimulus to economic growth. An analysis of 640 inventories of farm households in the period 1550–1750 shows steadily increasing levels of wealth among the Dutch peasantry. In the early sixteenth century, dishes had been made of wood, but tin plates became much more usual in rural households in the course of the seventeenth century until they were displaced by porcelain at the end of the century. Copper and tin pails, troughs, churns, cheese presses and kettles were common. The most costly pieces of farm equipment, wagons and boats, became more numerous during this period. Beds were the most expensive item of furniture, and the number of beds in a household was thus an indicator of wealth: the number of beds tended to increase in rural households in the Netherlands during the seventeenth century. Whereas in the sixteenth century textiles of all sorts—bedding, linen and clothing—amounted to over half the total value of a household's movable property excluding livestock, by the seventeenth century this proportion fell. A Dutch farmer might have a dozen shirts, forty bed-sheets, half a dozen tablecloths and a dozen table napkins, yet he still had disposable income for the purchase of luxury items. Clocks, porcelain, mirrors, paintings and books were found increasingly and the more prosperous Dutch farmers also possessed silver and gold buckles, beakers, buttons, spoons and ornaments. Since the textile industry was the largest industrial activity in the early modern Dutch economy, such levels of demand for its products clearly acted as a stimulus to growth.

For a comparison between these levels of prosperity and what one may assume to be closer to the European norm, one has only to turn to France. There, the majority of peasants did not have much furniture, rarely more than one or two beds, a table, one or two benches, one or two three-legged stools, and a chest or two. Whereas in the Netherlands an increasing variety and luxury of furniture can be observed by 1650, with large oak chests becoming more common, for example, dressers or cupboards were unusual in France at this time, although a few cupboards began to appear in well-off households in Normandy towards the end of the century. The French peasant might have a few sheets, but these tended to be kept for ceremonial occasions, and for use as shrouds; for the most part, a few blankets were used. Tablecloths and napkins were rare, and there was no great variety of clothing—a few hempen shirts, a few skirts might be found, but most of the clothes in regular use were cloaks, smocks or aprons. The French peasantry was clearly a poor stimulus to a nascent textile industry. Above all, there was little in the way of disposable income in France after taxes had been paid, and there was next to nothing to invest in agricultural improvements, such as more efficient farm equipment. Per capita levels of taxation were high in the Dutch Republic, too, but far from hindering the commercialization of agriculture, this seems to have helped promote it. Above all, the Dutch inventories show that even when farmers had extensive debt and credit transactions they rarely died in debt, and that the value of their cash holdings at the time of death had risen since the sixteenth century and might exceed 10 per cent of the total value of their movable property. When the value of luxury items is also included, the prosperity of the Dutch farmers is fully revealed, and its effect on the economy becomes clear. Demand for manufactured goods and for services grew in the Dutch Republic until about 1660, and this encouraged industrial expansion. This development did not, and indeed could not, occur elsewhere in Europe, with the exception of England after the mid-seventeenth century.

9

COURT, CULTURE AND COMMUNITY

ONE of the most controversial recent historical debates has revolved around the concepts of elite and popular culture. Some have argued that one of the most profound changes during the early modern period was the emergence of a distinctive, self-confident and increasingly sophisticated élite culture—based at the courts of princes and great clerics, and also within the larger cities—and a growing separation between this and popular culture. Others have contested this view, arguing that what is 'élite' cannot be clearly distinguished from what is 'popular' in any particular range of cultural activities. The town is one of the most favoured testing grounds for such theories. Yet there can be little doubt that there was an increasing sophistication in cultural pursuits during the early modern period. There are no simple explanations as to why this should have happened. Clearly the increased wealth of the élite and their expansion in numbers were one important reason: there were more wealthy patrons of the arts, letters and sciences than ever before. Another contributing factor was the broadening of education—more members of the upper classes of society were better educated than ever before and thus gained a more sophisticated taste for what might be termed humanist culture. Then there was that great stimulant of intellectual and cultural development, the rise of printing: Luther called it 'God's highest and extremest act of grace',[1] and he had an acute awareness of its effectiveness as a mechanism for the transmission of his religious views. But printing had a more general significance as a means of cultural diffusion—without it there could have been a north European humanist movement; but it would have been much restricted, and Erasmus might have remained a figure of purely local importance.

9.1 The Nature and Development of Court Patronage

It would perhaps be an overstatement to say that without patrons there would have been no élite culture; but it is evident that upper-class patronage of artists, musicians, men of letters and men of science played a distinctive part in the development of their work. There may have been some art for art's sake; but a starving artist rarely produces the best work of which he is capable—nor, by definition, can he work for very long. Most great works were produced as a result of a prior request from a patron, who had a significant influence on the finished product. Not surprisingly, the courts of kings and great patrons became the principal artistic and intellectual centres (since they were the wealthiest), which in turn conditioned the geographical spread of cultural development. There was a new trend to justify and eulogize the values of courtly culture—the most famous and influential example was Baldesar Castiglione's *Book of the Courtier* (1528), which was one of the most widely read books of the sixteenth century. There were also (much less frequently read) opponents such as Philibert de Vienne, whose *Philosopher of the Court* was published in 1547. The ostentatious wealth and parasitic inactivity of courtiers might arouse comment, but it could not alter the fact that a succession of courts prospered in the late Renaissance and came to exert a cultural influence out of all proportion to their numerical size.

9.1.1 *The Ottoman Court*

Before we consider the variety of courtly culture which developed in western Europe, we should first recognize that one of the greatest cultural achievements lay not in the west but in the east, at the court of Süleyman the Magnificent at Istanbul (1520–66). His personal appearance, jewellery and robes set him apart from all other rulers and attested to his status as the wealthiest of all contemporary sovereigns; like his predecessors, he and his court openly flouted the sumptuary laws of Moslem tradition which forbade the wearing of silks by men. Magnificent festivities and public ceremonies were an inherent feature of Ottoman society; when the Sultan went on any one of his thirteen great campaigns, he was invariably accompanied by his huntsmen, houndsmen and falconers. The festivities to celebrate the circumcision of his sons outdid all comparable western European occasions in both splendour and firework display. The great victories of Süleyman and his predecessor, Selim I, brought the cultural achievements of other dynasties to Istanbul as booty: once Buda was captured in 1526 (see chapter 5.4.2), Süleyman inherited the most famous of all Matthias Corvinus' foundations, the Bibliotheca Corviniana, and many manuscripts were transferred to the Ottoman collection.

The dynasty was further enriched by tribute and the control of the luxury trades from the Far East—silk from Persia, precious jewels from China via India, amber, ivory and furs from Poland and Muscovy, and so on. Clocks and watches of the highest quality were collected with avidity from the west: Süleyman's interest in astronomy and cosmography was attributed to the influence of his Jewish physician, Moses Hamon. Moreover, the Sultan built on an elaborate scale: the mosque of Selimiye at

Istanbul was brought to completion, there were substantial projects at Mecca and Jerusalem, and above all the great mosque at Istanbul, the Süleymaniye, the work of the architect Sinan, was completed by 1557. It has been calculated that he erected 477 buildings, of which 196 are still standing. Calligraphy, illumination and bookbinding prospered at his court, while Süleyman himself was a considerable poet, writing in Ottoman Turkish and in Persian under the pen name *Muhibbi*, 'the affectionate one'. It is above all in illustration that Süleyman's consciousness of his dynastic position emerges most clearly. The *Selimname* was a versified account in Turkish of the conquests of Selim prepared for Süleyman around 1525: its most striking depiction is of Selim's great victory over the Safavids at Chaldiran. A much greater work of art was the *Süleymanname* prepared in Persian by 1558, which contains superb illlustrations of great events of Süleyman's reign: Belgrade in flames, the siege of Rhodes, above all the great victory at Mohácz, followed by the recurring themes of battles with the Austrians and the Persians and the succession difficulties at home. Some of the iconography—particularly the recruitment of tribute children under the *devsirme* system, the meeting of the ministers of state (*divan*) and the reception of ambassadors—is of considerable historical importance. The *Süleymanname* is one of the masterpieces of sixteenth-century Ottoman art, and has no equivalent in western contemporary tradition.

9.1.2 *The Burgundian and Medici Courts of the Fifteenth Century*

In western Europe, there were few courts that could bear comparison with that of the Ottomans. One notable example was the court of the Valois dukes of Burgundy in the fifteenth century, which outdid in splendour the rival royal courts of Lancastrian and Yorkist England and Valois France. This was essentially a French court, betraying the Valois dukes' origins as French princes based on their original landholdings in what became the province of Burgundy. The ducal court was the centre where all who sought to participate in the prosperity of the dynasty gathered, and until Charles the Bold's death at the battle of Nancy in 1477 it seemed prosperous indeed. The court is perhaps best remembered for the splendour of its musical achievement—the cathedral of Cambrai functioning as a court *conservatoire* where music was nurtured—for its remarkable tapestries, jewellery and precious metalwork, and its still more distinctive school of miniature portraiture: one of its most famous artists, Jan Van Eyck, was a member of duke Philip the Good's household, holding the position of *valet de chambre*. The court of Philip the Fair and Margaret of Austria was an active centre for the production of illustrated music manuscripts. Philip the Fair patronized the artist Hieronymus

Bosch, who produced various works for him including a triptych on his familiar theme of the Last Judgement.

A second great court of the fifteenth century was that of the Medici at Florence, which lasted for sixty years (1434–94). Lorenzo de' Medici recorded with approval the fact that between 1434 and 1471 his family had spent the 'incredible sum' of 633,755 florins on 'buildings [and] charities . . .' which, in his opinion, 'gave great lustre to the state'.[2] In contrast to his grandfather Cosimo, Lorenzo was hampered by a shortage of funds: the great Italian historian of the early sixteenth century, Francesco Guicciardini, remarked that his building activities were nil. However, he patronized the arts to the best of his ability, preferring more unusual fields of artistic activity, such as cameos, mosaics and illuminated manuscripts: indeed the early Medici spent far more money on their collection of antiques and engraved gems than on contemporary paintings. Lorenzo's passion for collecting ancient sculpture and pottery is well documented. Ironically, his reputation for good taste was such that Florentine artists and art treasures became widely dispersed over Italy as a result of his recommendations.

Lorenzo himself was a poet, and the most famous example of his patronage of scholarship was the Florentine academy of Marsilio Ficino: the latter sought to harmonize the teaching of Plato and Aristotle. However, relations between the patron and the man of letters were not always harmonious: Lorenzo declined to finance the printing of Ficino's Latin translation of Plato's works, despite the fact that the principal manuscript used by Ficino had been given to him by Cosimo de' Medici. But Ficino's translation of Plotinus appeared at Lorenzo's expense a few months after the ruler's death in 1492. The expulsion of the Medici from Florence two years later imperilled their role as patrons of the arts: their restoration in 1512 was quickly followed by the installation of two Medici Popes (Leo X, 1513–21, and Clement VII, 1523–34), and the family once more tried to enlist the arts in the service of the dynasty. The second expulsion of the Medici in 1527 provoked a systematic wave of vandalism against precious objects which contained the family coat of arms; even the Medici palace was threatened for a time. A second Medici restoration in 1530 led gradually to the establishment of a more stable Tuscan territorial state under Cosimo I (1537–74) and a further glorification of the dynasty by means of cultural patronage.

9.1.3 *The Papal Court*

Without question, the most important centre of court culture in Italy was that of the Pope himself. Already in the second half of the fifteenth century, Nicholas V and Sixtus IV had secured some of the rarest treasures for the Vatican library, which ensured that it became the greatest collection in the western world. Nicholas V (1447–55) planned a vast new Rome, dominated by the redesigned St Peter's and a new Papal palace, and protected by an invincible Castel Sant' Angelo. He sent for the Florentine architects Rossellino and Alberti, tore down the ancient Roman temples near St Peter's and began to lay the foundations of a new basilica. The much criticized Renaissance Popes who ruled from 1471 to 1521 transformed the city and implemented much of the vision of Nicholas V. Under the Borgia Pope Alexander VI (1492–1503), the Papal court expanded considerably in numbers, and there was a strong Catalan element in the household; but the artists and men of letters were nearly all Italians. Apart from two significant fresco commissions, the work sponsored by Alexander was architectural: he completed some of the projects of Nicholas V and Sixtus IV, pulled down more buildings than he put up, and took the greatest interest in the Castel Sant' Angelo.

Not all the changes occurring at Rome during this time can be attributed to Papal patronage: cardinals were building their own palaces, and resident groups of foreigners were also responsible for building some of the churches. Nevertheless, a dynamic Pope such as Alexander's successor, Julius II, still made the most decisive impact on the culture of his times, on the development of his city and indeed on western civilization: one has only to think of his commissions to Michaelangelo to paint the ceiling of the Sistine Chapel (1508–12), to Raphael to decorate the Papal rooms known as the Stanze (1509–17) and to Bramante for the design of St Peter's itself (1505), to appreciate that Julius was not only the greatest patron of his day but one of the greatest of all time, and that Rome was the artistic centre of the western world. Of course, such creative energies were not always productive of harmony: Michaelangelo left Rome in fury after endless disputes with Julius II over the design of his mausoleum, and in vain the Pope sought his return: 'we for our part are not angry with him, knowing the humours of such men of genius'.

Doubtless Popes Leo X and Clement VII continued and consolidated what Julius II had instigated; but little remains from this period, for in 1527 Rome was sacked by the mutinous Imperial army in an event which, while its cultural importance may have been exaggerated, nevertheless was an important psychological shock to the Papacy and to the Italian states in general. Clement VII, shut up in the Castel Sant' Angelo, was virtually the prisoner of the Emperor Charles V, while many contemporaries saw the event as divine retribution on the corruption and degeneration of His Church. The crisis lasted from May 1527 until February 1528, and some art historians consider it was instrumental in bringing about a new Mannerist style. This seems an overstatement. Clearly, both the pace of building in Rome and Papal patronage of the arts went into decline. However, there was a rapid acceleration once more during the short pontificate of Sixtus V (1585–90), and the longer one of Paul V (1605–21), while under Urban VIII (1623–44)—the longest reign in the early modern period—the Papal court emerged as the most spectacular Baroque court in Europe. Maffeo Barberini (who became Pope Urban VIII) was probably the most sophisticated aesthete to ascend the Papal throne; he was an established patron long before he became Pope. Nevertheless, his protection and patronage of Bernini, and his determination to make this sculptor another Michelangelo by directing him into architecture and painting, were of crucial importance. The relationship between Urban VIII and Bernini was exceptional, since for this artist all court protocol was laid aside. Within three years of his accession, and no doubt mindful of the fate of Julius II's mausoleum, which had been left unfinished by Michaelangelo, the Pope had commissioned his own tomb from Bernini, and it was to become one of the great monuments of St Peter's. The canopy (*baldacchino*) for the high altar of that church, which was designed by Bernini, was as much a glorificaton of the Barberini family as of the church, family emblems (bees) being prominent in the decoration. Other members of the family were equally enthusiastic patrons of the arts: Cardinal Francesco Barberini, the Pope's nephew and Papal Vice-Chancellor from 1632, built the Barberini Palace at the Quattro Fontane, the first of the great Baroque palaces at Rome, where he and his brother Antonio established their courts in 1633. Antonio was a patron of the Jesuit order and he established the first modern theatre at Rome as an addition to the Barberini palace. But the financial burden of all this artistic patronage was considerable. The Papacy was already heavily indebted at the accession of Urban VIII, and while war was the chief reason for a near doubling of the debt in his lifetime, there can be little doubt that the economic cost of his patronage contributed significantly to the increased deficit.

9.1.4 *The Imperial Court*

Compared with the splendours of the court of the Renaissance Popes, that of the Emperor Maximilian at Vienna seems very humble indeed. His most enduring achievement was his patronage of scholars: he founded a college of poetics and mathematics at Vienna under the inspiration of Conrad Celtis. But like his political ambitions, his other cultural pursuits were largely a chimera: a proposed triumphal arch was never actually built, and a series of woodcuts by German artists including Dürer are all that remains of his aspiration. Characteristically, his tomb at Innsbruck— which was to have represented the Emperor kneeling on a sarcophogus surrounded by some 140 statues representing his ancestors, prominent courtiers and so on—was never completed. Lack of financial resources seems to have been crucial to the relative cultural impoverishment of Maximilian I's court. In contrast, Charles V presided over a much richer, albeit peripatetic, court. There were, of course, great deeds of his reign to be depicted, and in 1530, on the advice of the Gonzaga duke of Mantua, Charles found in Titian a court artist of the greatest distinction to record these for posterity. Called the Apelles of his age (after the Greek painter at the time of Alexander the Great), Titian was made count palatine, knight of the Golden Spur and knight of Caesar. He responded with three of the greatest portraits of the sixteenth century: that of the Emperor with his dog in 1532, and the two portraits commissioned after the victory at Mühlberg in 1547. In raising the iconography of Charles V from that of a local German victor to the leader of militant Catholicism, Titian had an accomplice in the Milanese Leone Leoni, the chosen sculptor of the Emperor after 1546: he depicted Charles V at his apogee suppressing the Tumult (*Il Furore*), that is the German Lutheran princes. Significantly, no great court artist recorded Charles's abdication less than ten years later (though it was depicted by Frans Francken II, an artist of lesser stature).

The subsequent partition of the Habsburg inheritance permanently split the two court cultures, Austro-German and Spanish, that were already in place by the 1550s. As a result of Ferdinand's acquisition of Royal Hungary in 1526 (see chapter 5.4.2), the court became increasingly the political and cultural centre for the diverse realms of central Europe: without the court, the Austrian Habsburg state, such as it was, might not have existed. Plurality of languages accompanied a diverse political inheritance, and the Emperors displayed a considerable linguistic proficiency. At least in the sixteenth century, the Habsburg court was cosmopolitan in outlook—Charles V had spent most of his reign outside Germany, but the subsequent Emperors, Ferdinand I and Maximilian II, were constantly travelling. Ferdinand I was less cultured than his paternal grandfather, Maximilian I, but was certainly interested in Hebrew studies and in encouraging Czech culture: for example, in 1554 he facilitated the translation into Czech of Sebastian Münster's encyclopaedia *Cosmographia*. Maximilian II's reign witnessed the climax of orthodox humanism in Austria: his court librarian was Hugo Blotius, a Fleming, while efforts were made to secure the great humanist Justus Lipsius for court service (indeed, he made an extended visit to Vienna). After 1573, Maximilian's herbalist and plant-collector was Clusius, the epitome of a cosmopolitan scholar of the time. The classicist Sambucus was his court historiographer and a proponent of Habsburg authority: his private library was secured by Rudolf II in 1584.

In contrast to his predecessors, Rudolf II was a reclusive intellectual who flouted recent tradition by moving the Imperial court from Vienna and residing at Prague in an ostentatious attempt to recall the great epoch of Charles IV of Luxembourg. Rudolf enticed Tycho Brahe, the great cosmographer, to Prague when he was forced to leave Denmark. Later, Johannes Kepler became court mathematician: he subsequently published the *Rudolfine Tables*, a record of thousands of systematic observations of planetary motions made by Tycho, recorded by Kepler, and used by him to formulate his epoch-making three laws of planetary motion (see chapter 9.5.2). At this period, there was no great distinction made between humanist, man of science and occultist: Maximilian II's court had showed some signs of in the occult, but it was to reach its peak under Rudolf II. It was said that the Emperor was 'interested only in wizards, alchemists, Cabalists and the like'; 'he delights in hearing secrets about things both natural and artificial . . .'[3] This obsession with the occult and the Jewish Cabala became linked with the development of a particular Mannerist style with an emphasis on artistic symbolism. In 1604, the Dutch painter and art critic Karel van Mander called Rudolf 'the greatest art patron in the world at the present time'.[4] The Emperor's court at Prague was renowned for its remarkable collection of great paintings—the works of Dürer and Pieter Breughel were particular favourites—which were mixed up with exotica of all kinds derived both from gifts and purchase. It was also celebrated as a centre for applied arts such as the making of flagons, bowls, dishes and clocks.

Rudolf occupied the Imperial throne from thirty-six years, and there was inevitably some reaction against his more eccentric Mannerist taste after his death in 1612. The court was transferred back to Vienna under Matthias and his successors; both the Prague residence and the upkeep of the collections there were abandoned. The dynasty came increasingly to be linked with strict Counter-Reformation Catholicism and the culture of the Baroque. Leopold I (1657–1705) inherited a remarkable picture gallery from his uncle, Leopold William, who had used his position as governor of the Spanish Netherlands to build up a superb collection of Flemish works, part of which was dispersed on his death in 1662. However, the visual arts played merely a supporting role to the promotion of literature and especially music: in 1636, despite the pressures of war, Ferdinand II kept a staff of eighty musicians, while Ferdinand III and Leopold I were both composers. Court ceremonial was already important under Rudolf II; but it came to assume a more significant place in court entertainment by Leopold's reign, and opera was brought to Vienna by some of the pupils of Monteverdi. As court spectacle grew more lavish, so the Italian influence increased: but until the Turkish threat to Vienna was decisively repulsed in the later seventeenth century (see chapter 5.4.3), and before the rebuilding of the Schönbrunn palace in the eighteenth century, the Austrian Habsburg dynasty lacked a Versailles or an Escorial as a permanent home for these activities.

9.1.5 *The Court of the Spanish Habsburgs*

The partition of the Habsburg inheritance after Charles V's abdication had divorced Spain, Burgundy and the Italian states from the Empire. In Spain, Philip II, like his father, was a great lover of the arts and he inherited from him the services of Titian and Leoni. In 1561, the court and its administration were moved from Valladolid to Madrid, and two years later the king resolved to build a new residence, the Escorial, which occupied him throughout much of his long reign. There he lived for most of the time among Jeronymite monks, just as his father had lived for three years at Yuste after his abdication. After 1569, Philip himself was in charge of the building of this palace, with his architect Juan de Herrera being required to carry out his orders without discussion. The building cost the substantial sum of 5.26 million ducats, an average of 142,000 ducats a year between 1562 and 1598. The geometrical severity of the resulting building was the architectural corollary of rigid Spanish Catholicism. Yet inside the sobre façade there were remarkable riches: the Habsburg family tomb, inaugurated in 1574; the crucifixion by Leone Leoni and his son Pompeio; and great works commissioned from Titian, including 'The allegory of Lepanto' and 'Spain coming to the aid of religion'. However, El Greco's 'St Maurice' was not well received by the king in 1582 and this remained the great Greek artist's sole commission for the Escorial: instead, he worked in Toledo, where he painted great altarpieces for the local churches. After the death of Titian and Leoni, Philip II had to be content with second-rate artists. However, he also acquired great private collections—most notably that of his secretary Pérez through confiscation—and he was able to build up a substantial collection of his own, including several works of Hieronymus Bosch which he particularly appreciated perhaps because, in the words of Philip's librarian at the Escorial, that artist was not content to paint men as they outwardly appeared but as they really were.

Philip III was determined to break with the tradition of his father, and thus with residence at the Escorial: he made an abortive attempt to return the court to Valladolid in the years 1601–6, but after 1606 it was permanently transferred to the grim castle palace of the Alcázar in Madrid. The main façade was modernized by the court architect Juan Gómez de Mora during the reign. It was here that a court of some 1,700 people and a government administration of some 400 people, including members of the councils and secretaries, was based. An elaborate etiquette, introduced by

Charles V on the Burgundian model as early as 1548, prevailed. Under Philip IV this court prospered as a great centre of artistic patronage and it possessed one of the finest collections of paintings in Europe. The chief proponents in this were the king himself and his chief minister, Olivares. Philip II had, in his later years, lacked the services of a great artist; Philip IV and Olivares had at their disposal an artist of genius in Valázquez, who was appointed painter to the king in October 1623. They had a model of the ideal relationship between patron and artist in Rubens, who had been the painter and diplomat of the archdukes Albert and Isabella of the Spanish Netherlands: Rubens visited Madrid in 1628–9 and left a lasting impression on both the king and Velázquez. In 1632, Philip IV decided to build a new palace with a garden 'for recreational purposes'[5] and conferred the supervision of the scheme on Olivares. The chief minister pressed ahead with the plans at great speed, sacrificing the overall design and exterior to the adorning of the interior. The Buen Retiro cost 2.5 million ducats, with an average annual expenditure of 250,000 ducats in the 1630s. The paintings executed by Velázquez for the new palace were that artist's largest single commission, while another great artist, Zurbarán was called from Seville to paint a number of pictures for the Hall of Realms in the palace. Velázquez's portraits of members of the dynasty and depictions of great events of the reign—most notably the surrender of Breda—were intended to demonstrate that Spanish power was being revitalized by Philip IV and his chief minister, while Zurbarán's depiction of the labours of Hercules was meant to be associated in people's minds with the dynasty and its triumphs over religious disharmony. The Buen Retiro was a palace built on the principle of seclusion, designed for private royal diversions; it was also a projection of the personality of the chief minister—after his fall from power in 1643 the project was criticized as one aspect of the reaction to his rule.

9.1.6 *The Court of the Kings of France*

The Italian wars left an enduring influence on the French court. Not only did Italian taste predominate; many of the leading personalities were themselves of Italian extraction, a trend reinforced by the marriage of Catherine de Medici to the future Henri II in 1533. Francis I, according to the sixteenth-century architect Androuet du Cerceau, was 'marvellously addicted to buildings',[6] and his three main architectural achievements—the châteaux of Chambord, Madrid and Fontainebleau—all reveal an Italian influence. Right from the beginning of his reign, Francis I was an avid patron of artists and a dedicated collector of artistic works. He invited Leonardo da Vinci to France in 1516, where the genius died three years later; Andrea del Sarto also came at the invitation of the king; the great sculptor and goldsmith, Benvenuto Cellini, visited the kingdom twice, in 1537 and 1540, and carried out some of his finest works there. The king was also a great patron of letters, founding four regius professorships (*lecteurs royaux*) in 1530, two in Greek and two in Hebrew: the Collège de France claims to originate from this foundation. By the end of his reign, Francis had also created a great library at Fontainebleau; twenty-two years after his death, the library was moved to Paris in 1569, where it became the nucleus of what is today the Bibliothèque Nationale.

Henri II appointed Philibert de L'Orme as royal architect immediately on his accession in 1547, and the rebuilding of the château of Anet for the king's mistress, Diane de Poitiers, resulted in one of the masterpieces of sixteenth-century art, placing classical and Italian influences in a French context. De L'Orme also did a considerable amount of work directly for the king, for example at Chambord. Henri provided pensions for the poets Pierre de Ronsard and Joachim Du Bellay, and revealed an interest in the theatre: the first French tragedy was performed for him at Paris in 1552. It was said of the king that he treated men of letters as well as had his father, 'even if he himself was not as well-lettered'.[7] Of Henri's four sons, Charles IX, despite a brusque exterior, had a deep love of poetry and music and was the patron of the poet Ronsard, while Henri III was the most intellectual: from 1576 to 1584 a 'palace academy' met regularly at the Louvre; after 1584, it was replaced by an oratory at Vincennes, which had a more spiritual purpose. A knowledge of Italian culture was the prerequisite of the courtier in the reign of Henri III. The king welcomed Giordano Bruno to his court when he visited France: at his later trial, the Italian recalled the French king's liberalizing influence on the Sorbonne and contrasted it with the inflexibility of the Italian Inquisition (see chapter 9.5.3).

The new Bourbon dynasty shared none of the cultural interests of the later Valois. Henri IV's central artistic preoccupation was to build fitting monuments to the new dynasty in the capital, such as the Pont Neuf across the Seine. The image of 'Henri the great', a king 'of reason' who had brought peace to his kingdom, was consciously cultivated and contrasted with the religious fanaticism of the League. It was said of his son, Louis XIII, in 1627 that his 'inclination is not directed towards building, and France's finances will certainly not be exhausted by his sumptuous edifices—unless one wishes to reproach him for the miserable château of Versailles, which a mere gentleman would not want to boast of having constructed'.[8] In fact, the understated taste of the Palais Royal, the Palais du Luxembourg, the Versailles lodge and the west wing of the Louvre (often referred to as the 'Louis Treize style') amount to an architectural achievement of some importance despite the studied indifference of the king himself. For a time, the cultural centre of the court was not focused exclusively on the king himself: just as Catherine de Medici had been preoccupied with building schemes during Henri III's reign, so too the chief ministers of Louis XIII and the young Louis XIV, Richelieu and Mazarin, and Foucquet (the finance minister in the 1650s) were great builders, patrons of the arts and collectors. By the 1660s, however, cultural leadership was to be firmly wrested back by the crown: the planning of Versailles was a joint achievement of the king himself and Colbert, his controller-general of finance and superintendent of buildings, with Jules Hardouin-Mansart as architect and André Le Nôtre as designer of the gardens. The location of the king's bedroom at Versailles, only one room away from the Hall of Mirrors, the room used for great state occasions, would not have been acceptable in other countries; but the accessibility of the king was to a large extent negated by an excessive formality at the French court. The entire court was on hand, formally dressed, from the moment of the king's ceremonial awakening until he retired at night. The court was thus rigidly dominated by ceremonial, which served a political function, as the king recalled in his memoirs: 'those who imagine that this is merely a matter of ceremony make a great mistake. The people over whom we reign, who are not able to penetrate matters deeply, base their judgements ordinarily on what they see externally, and it is usually on the basis of precedence and rank that they measure their respect and obedience.'[9]

By the mid-seventeenth century, the French court outdid all the others in Europe in terms of culture and ceremony; its influence was geographically far-reaching and lasted well into the eighteenth century. As a sign of this, one has only to look at the most northerly court in Europe, that of Sweden. The great Swedish victories of the 1640s and 1650s had yielded in booty some of the great art treasures of northern Europe: in 1648 the Swedish army captured Prague, and queen Christina ensured that Rudolf II's art treasures at the Hradschin castle were carefully moved to Stockholm. The Swedish victories in Denmark a decade later ensured that Christian IV's treasures at Kronborg and Frederiksborg were also seized. Such a method of accumulating artistic works inevitably led to an eclectic collection, which reflected the tastes not of the Swedish monarchy but of those who had originally built up the treasures. But if one asks what was the style of the Swedish court itself by the mid-seventeenth century, then clearly the answer was French. Christina corresponded with Pascal, brought Descartes to Stockholm, and employed Sebastian Bourdon as court painter. During the royal minority after 1660, prominent court nobles such as Magnus de la Gardie, Wrangel, Oxenstierna and others, constructed palaces and gardens on the French style. French influence continued and intensified during the personal rule of Charles XI and the reign of Charles XII under the influence of the court architect, Nicodemus Tessin the younger, who sought to equal the French achievement. In the same way that at the beginning of the sixteenth century Italian cultural values had dominated Europe, and the French court in particular, by the 1660s cultural leadership and influence throughout most of Europe had passed to the court of Louis XIV.

9.2   The Iconography and Propaganda of Power

The emergence of distinctive cultures located at different court centres in Europe was a characteristic feature of the intellectual and artistic achievement of the early modern period. Since the court was the principal focus of wealth and influence, it was there that the leading artists, architects, poets and scientists tended to congregate. But court culture was more than a random gathering of such people under the patronage of the wealthy or the powerful. It was consciously developed by the patrons for a political purpose: to enhance the prestige of the ruling dynasty. The early modern state lacked powerful 'modern' instruments of government such as subservient bureaucracies and large police forces; furthermore, it had to live with an antiquated fiscal system which was inadequate for its needs and curbed its growth (see chapter 6.5.1). And yet, despite these handicaps, the state appeared to become stronger during this period: much of this development was an illusion, a confidence trick consciously perpetrated by rulers on their subjects by giving the impression that they possessed great political power by visual (or iconographical) and written (or propagandist) means. The 'rise of European absolutism', the terminology which later historians have attached to this phenomenon, was in part a late sixteenth- and early seventeenth-century creation of the media.

9.2.1   *Manifestations of Power in Monarchical States: the Kingdom of France*

The most significant example of the visual and written presentation of absolute monarchy was provided by the French kingdom, the state with the fewest institutional restraints on royal power and the most influential of the European courts by 1660. André du Chesne in his *Antiquities and Researches into the Grandeur and Majesty of the Kings of France* (1609) considered that four main ceremonials characterized the French monarchy: the coronation; the so-called *lit de justice*, a special session of the *Parlement* under the presidency of the king or a member of the royal family; the royal entry into towns; and the royal funeral ceremony. The coronation was originally the most important of the ceremonies, but it lost much of its significance under the Bourbon dynasty. This resulted firstly

from the long delay of nearly five years in obtaining Henri IV's coronation
(1589–94). Subsequently, three successive royal minorities diminished the
importance of the coronation, since the juridical commencement of the
reign was then dated from the inaugural *lit de justice* and not the coronation itself. The discrepancy between the two dates amounted to only a
few months in Louis XIII's case (in 1610), but it was eleven years for Louis
XIV (the inaugural *lit de justice* was in 1643 but the coronation was not
held until 1654). The Valois monarchs, Louis XII, Francis I and Henri II,
had all been crowned within a few months of their predecessor's death, as
soon as the mourning was completed and the coronation arrangements
could be made.

The delay between the two events was significant because of the
importance attributed by political theorists to the coronation oath taken
by the king: if the country was governed, and the laws administered, for
several years without the coronation oath having been taken, then the oath
had clearly lost much of its constitutional role as a sort of legal contract
between ruler and subjects. The French king pledged himself twice, once
in an oath concerning the bishops and the church, the other in the so-
called 'oath of the kingdom'. The political theorist Bossuet explained the
ceremony in these terms, basing his words on earlier descriptions:
'The prince swears to God ... to maintain the privileges of the Church; to
conserve the Catholic faith which he has received from his predecessors;
to prevent violence [in his kingdom], and to render justice to all his
subjects. This oath is the foundation of civil peace: and God is obliged by
his own self-evident truth to ensure that it is fulfilled, since he is the sole
judge.'[10] After a number of other promises, the new king was obliged to
swear to 'govern and defend' the kingdom with which God had entrusted
him, according to the justice of his predecessors; he swore to 'conserve the
sovereignty, rights and nobilities of the crown of France, without alienating them or transferring them to anyone; and to exterminate ...
according to his power all notable heretics who had been condemned by
the church'.[11] The 'sacred' character of the French monarchy was revealed
by the terms of the oath: 'your kingdom which God has accorded to you
...'[12] According to Bossuet, God had established kings as his ministers to
reign over his people; the person of the king was sacred, and any attack on
him was an act of sacrilege; it followed that a subject must 'obey the prince
as a principle of religion and a matter of conscience'.[13] But an equivalent
responsibility rested on the king: 'kings must respect their own power, and
only use it in the public good'.[14]

The second ceremony described by du Chesne was the *lit de justice*, a
special convocation of the *Parlement* which, with its ceremonial and
speeches, was another occasion for promoting the political purpose of the
French monarchy, and one which became more frequent in the course of

the seventeenth century. The king made forty-seven such visits to the *Parlement* of Paris between 1315 and 1713. After the posthumous publication of Jean du Tillet's *Collection Concerning the Kings of France* (1580), a myth developed about the origins of the *lit de justice*, suggesting that in the Middle Ages it was a medieval political assembly. This was untrue: two innovatory *lits de justice* were held by Francis I in 1527. They were political experiments to deal with the particular circumstances arising from the rebellion of the Constable of Bourbon and the king's refusal to ratify the treaty extracted from him under duress while he was held in captivity at Madrid. The term *lit de justice* had different meanings later, and the assembly was used for different purposes between 1527 and 1673. There were relatively few in the sixteenth century, whereas Louis XIII held twenty (all but three at Paris) in the early seventeenth century. Most of these were designed to secure the registration of fiscal edicts against the opposition of the *Parlements*. In contrast, Louis XIV held only nineteen in his much longer reign, all before 1673. The five dating from his minority (1643–51) had raised constitutional issues. The *lit de justice* of October 1652 was particularly important since it was held at the royal palace of the Louvre, this location serving to humiliate the *Parlement* of Paris at the end of the Fronde.

Louis XIV's inaugural *lit de justice* was not his first public act: he had already officially 'entered' Paris as monarch three days earlier in May 1643. Royal entries into the French capital were ceremonies organized by the *Parlement* of Paris between 1431 and 1515, and then, increasingly, by royal officials from 1515 to 1660. They were relatively frequent in the late Middle Ages and the sixteenth century, when for the most part the monarchy was itinerant: there were at least thirteen 'official' entries into Paris in the sixteenth century but only four in the seventeenth (all before 1661). Royal entries also took place in the great provincial cities, such as Rouen, Lyon and Bordeaux. In 1498, Charles VIII had asserted his right to pardon offenders at the moment of his entry into towns, whether on the first or subsequent entry, because, he said, the right of pardon was one of the 'royal rights and prerogatives which our predecessors and progenitors as kings had traditionally used at the time of their accession and entry into the towns of our kingdom'.[15] The numbers of such pardons are not known.

Traditionally on these occasions the king received gifts from his subjects, which were gradually transformed into unpopular taxes. Despite the fiscal aspects of the accession itself, the royal entry into towns was an important opportunity to display the king to his subjects in an age when monarchical power was essentially personal. The increasing emphasis on the personal authority of the ruler was demonstrated by the way in which the king was presented. At the Paris entry ceremony of 1549, Henri II received the principal magistrates and leaders of the city corporations seated in an armchair of blue velvet. But for Charles IX's entry in 1571, the king was placed in a chair on a dais with two ceremonial staircases: the king's chair was elevated three steps above the stage and covered with a canopy. In 1660, Louis XIV's 'throne or high dais' was eighteen steps high and under a blue pavilion roof scattered with fleurs-de-lys. The mayor of Paris (*prévôt des marchands*) declared that the capital 'could only conceive for Your Majesty thoughts of praise, obedience and affection; it had no wish other than for your glory, no ambition other than for your grandeur'.[16]

By 1660, the French court had ceased to be itinerant, and after 1682 it settled definitively at Versailles. A new ceremonial had to be found to replace the royal entry into towns, one which would permit the king's subjects some illusory contact with their sovereign. The official celebratory Mass, or *Te Deum*, seems to have filled this role in time of war, not least because it had a much more precise message for the political classes. By attending in full ceremony, the chief corporations of the town, including the municipal council and the *Parlement*, demonstrated their loyalty to the dynasty and its foreign policy objectives. Ministers could exploit this opportunity by sending letters patent authorizing these celebratory Masses to be held throughout the kingdom to explain and justify royal policies with the aim of establishing a national consensus which permitted the war to be continued and unpopular taxes to be levied. A second type of *Te Deum* was organized to rally support for the dynasty itself, either because of the happy circumstances of a birth, or the misfortunes of a death, within the circle of the royal family.

The death of leading members of the royal family, and above all of the king himself, had always been the occasion for important ceremonial. After 1422, under English influence, a funeral effigy of the late king was shown to the public for a fixed period before the body was interred; after 1498 the *Parlement* of Paris declared that this effigy represented the 'living king',[17] and one was displayed at each funeral thereafter until 1610. This ceremony illustrated in a vivid manner the king's 'two bodies', one purely human and mortal, the other a royal dignity (*dignitas regia*) which never died. During a period of forty days of mourning, when the new king was not seen publicly, it seemed as if there was an interregnum. Nonetheless, the king's council continued to issue edicts and decrees during the period of mourning. In 1576, Jean Bodin affirmed the new 'absolutist' argument, according to which there was no interregnum as the funeral effigy might seem to indicate: 'For it is an old proverb with us, That the king doth never die, but that so soon as he is dead, the next male of his stock is seized of the kingdom, and in possession thereof before he be crowned . . .'[18] Nevertheless, the idea of the king's two bodies did not entirely disappear, and there remained a tension in France between the dynastic idea of kingship and the view that it was an office which could not be disposed of at the king's pleasure. This dichotomy is summed up by the two most famous remarks attributed to Louis XIV. On the one hand, he is reported to have said in 1655 or thereabouts 'the state is mine' (*l'État c'est à moi*); on the other hand, on his deathbed, Dangeau reported him as saying 'I am departing, but the state will remain' (*Je m'en vais, mais l'État demeurera toujours*).[19]

9.2.2 Manifestations of Power in Republican Regimes: Venice and the Dutch Republic

In the cultures generated by, or associated with, cities, public and private activities interacted within the same buildings and streets; there was also a blending of institutional and individual benefaction, which led to a distinct 'urban' culture. Townsmen of all ranks and wealth attended services at the same churches which were embellished at the expense of the élite (in this sense the leading families who held office or had status in the town). Much of the visual art of the Italian Renaissance was the product of a merger between patrician and communal art—it was produced not just for the benefit of the patron, be he an individual or an institution, but also for the city. In the late medieval period, there was a strong tradition of artists' workshops in the great Italian cities and in those of northern Europe, such as Bruges and Ghent, Cologne and Nuremberg. With their decline in the sixteenth century in both Italy and Germany, it became apparent that the high point of creative activity in the towns was over. Venice was the one city of Italy where the visual arts suffered no decline in this period, and the continued artistic vitality may have been connected with the unique survival of the Venetian city state. The cultural balance shifted to northern Europe in the seventeenth century, and Amsterdam and Paris became the other two paradigms of urban culture; these two cities were the largest centres of population in their states, as was Venice, and they housed the most advanced urban cultures.

By 1600, eighty-six days in the year had some ceremonial importance for the Venetian Republic. Many honoured a saint (St Mark in particular); some recalled important events in the city's history (such as the victory at Lepanto); and others served to display the power of the Doge and other city functionaries. This calendar was much more secular than that of Florence, where all festival days but one were associated with the intercession of a saint; but even at Venice the religious festivals were of prime significance. Saints were venerated there either because their relics were in Venice or because they were accredited with decisive intervention on behalf of the city: St Marina, for instance, was given credit for the recovery of Padua in 1509, and St Roch became the object of official devotion after the plague of 1576, when the prayers offered to him were thought to have helped bring the plague to an end. The Venetians' devotion to the Papacy was symbolized in the carrying of a white candle in processions on feast-days, a tradition associated with Pope Alexander III, who in 1177 was said to have conferred this privilege on the city as a sign of 'noble honour' and of his special affection.[20] Ascension Day linked secular and religious themes together; the Doge was symbolically 'married' to the sea in a ceremonial boat procession around the lagoon, where he dropped a gold ring overboard with the words, 'we espouse thee, O sea, as a sign of true and perpetual dominion'.[21] Thus the Doge reaffirmed his state's right of domination over the trade routes and lands of the eastern Mediterranean. On Palm Sunday, he led a well-organized procession which served to emphasize his political pre-eminence within the community, and on St Mark's principal feast day (25 April), the Doge's procession ritually enacted his lordship over the guilds and other non-noble institutions. However, the Doge was no more than first among equals within the Venetian governing elite. Virtually all his public words, gestures and acts were subject to legal and ceremonial regulation. The senate reserved the right to elect the most important naval official, the captain-general of the sea, but exceptionally the Doge himself conferred the banner of St Mark, the emblem of office, on the man elected. However, the funeral ceremony for the Doge and the ensuing interregnum procedures, which were controlled by the supreme magistrates (*signoria*), served to reassert aristocratic control over the office and forestall any attempt at dynastic succession.

By the end of the sixteenth century, the Doge and the supreme magistrates participated in about sixteen annual processions, a considerable increase in the course of the century, frequently linked with commemorations of victories. On St Vitus' Day (15 June), they gave thanks for the defeat of the Tiepolo conspiracy in 1310, thus attempting to ensure that there would not be future conspiracies; but equally, on St Isidore's Day (16 April), they led a procession to give thanks for the fact that Doge Falier had failed to establish a form of despotism in 1355. The ceremonial calendar of the early modern Venetian state was a mirror of its proverbial political stability which it hoped would endure. Even the procession of Corpus Christi was turned to political advantage. During the crisis of the Interdict in 1606–7, the government expressly commanded in May 1606 that the Corpus Christi procession be held in defiance of the Pope, with floats alluding to the jurisdictional claims of the republic and stressing the separation of ecclesiastical and political authority. Sir Henri Wooton, the English ambassador, observed that the procession had a twofold purpose: 'first, to contain the people in good order with superstition, the foolish band of obedience; second, to let the

Pope know . . . that notwithstanding his interdict, they had friars enough and other clergymen to furnish out the day.'[22]

As for Amsterdam, remarked William Aglionby in 1660, 'Tis commonly said this city is very like Venice. For my part, I believe Amsterdam to be much superior in riches . . .'[23] A crucial difference, he thought, was that prosperity extended right through all ranks of the population. Like the Venetians, the Dutch had recourse to the lion as a symbol of national unity, the *leo belgicus* superimposed on the seventeen undivided provinces, rather than the seven of the north alone. But in contrast with the Venetians, who had developed an historical mythology which supplied a pedigree of immemorial antiquity and continuity, the Dutch had committed themselves irrevocably through the Revolt to a break with their Burgundian past. Tacitus' history of the Batavian rebellion against Rome provided them with suitable historical antecedents; but as with other potent myths, the model was an invention of an ancient past in order to flatter and legitimize the present. The ancient Batavians were depicted as hardy, frugal, industrious, addicted to cleanliness and liberty—and above all, they governed through a periodically convened popular assembly, the precursor of the States General: 'by Dutchmen we mean men who are born and bred under a free government'.[24] The excesses of Alba's regime were retold and embellished in order to create allegiance to the new state: the Dutch were the children of Israel, who in the words of Adriaan Valerius' *Netherlands Anthem of Commemoration* (1626) had 'received succour and favour when stricken by ferocious tyrants'.[25]

The conspicuous wealth of the Dutch Republic was similarly seen as a presumptive sign of membership of God's elect. It was said that Holland was a land, and Amsterdam a city, overflowing with milk and cheese. In their kitchens and parlours the Dutch 'middling sort' were lavishly equipped with expensive pots and pans. The feasts held in honour of some great event, such as the relief of Bergen-op-Zoom in 1622, or the Peace of Münster of 1648, gave the rich opportunities to make donations of vessels in silver or gold which were meant to remind later generations of past magnificence. The church denounced smoking as a sin, but it was confidently said that 'if a Hollander should be bereft of his pipe of tobacco he could not blissfully enter Heaven'.[26] Drinking was also widespread: there were 518 alehouses in Amsterdam alone in 1613, one for every 200 inhabitants. There was a danger, however, that an excess of wealth might result in divine punishment for man's sin; there were many telling biblical examples of this, such as the fate of Solomon's kingdom.

It seems that the Protestant ethic did not restrain consumption to the advantage of capital accumulation. Perhaps this was because the Calvinist church represented only a minority: indeed, in no other country in sixteenth- and seventeenth-century Europe did the dominant church party fail so obviously to impose its views on the population at large as in the Netherlands. The prevalence of prostitution in port cities such as Amsterdam and Rotterdam is a case in point. Nor was Dutch culture socially homogeneous. Poverty and exploitation were significant aspects of Dutch economic life—it was only the rural peasantry, not the urban poor, who formed a proportionately smaller grouping in Dutch society than they did in other countries. Striking visual images such as Jan Steen's 'The burgher of Delft and his daughters' (1655) and Jacob Ochtervelt's 'Street musicians at the door' (1665) contrasted the opulence of the rich with the economic dependence of the poor, and it is an open question whether the patriciate and the urban poor were united in accepting the town hierarchy.

The predominantly urban—or certainly community-based—culture of the Netherlands was the antithesis of French courtly culture in the seventeenth century. There was no place in the federal system of the Dutch Republic for a mannered aristocracy or a leisured court. Yet this is not to say that the Dutch rejected the artistic tradition of painting political leaders or indeed of owning such portraits. In seventeenth-century Delft, a sampling of probate records suggests that one family in four owned a portrait of a member of the House of Orange. In the republican United Provinces, attachment to national heroes was apparently stronger than it was in monarchical France. At Paris during the reign of Louis XIV, similar evidence suggests that ownership of portraits seems to have been largely confined to members of the royal court, usually those who had commissioned them in the first place, and the well-to-do, notably the office-holders and *parlementaires*. At Metz, only one family in sixteen owned a portrait of Louis XIII or Louis XIV. Portraits of the regent, Anne of Austria, and important figures such as Cardinal de Richelieu were rarer still. It was not until the eighteenth century that the portrait became popular and ownership was broadened to all social categories in France. In contrast, a speculative art market existed in the Netherlands in the seventeenth century, in which the authorship of a painting was important for its value, and even relatively modest public officials could identify the styles of specific masters for the purposes of aesthetic judgement and valuation for investment purposes. It has been called 'the first mass consumers' art market in European history': the English visitor William Aglionby commented that 'pictures are very common here, there being scarce an ordinary tradesman whose house is not decorated with them'.[27] Again, this was a sign that fairly advanced cultural values, in particular the appreciation of the visual arts, had spread throughout Dutch urban society. It reflected a wide diffusion of wealth, and suggests that even within a republican regime there was a strong attachment to the dynastic principle as personified in the house of Orange.

9.3 Popular Literature and Folk Custom

It is an over-simplification to define popular culture as the traditions of the non-élite, since there was upper-class participation, especially at local festivals. The crucial difference between élite and popular culture was that whereas the élite could and did take part in what may be termed popular traditions and ceremonial, the people did not participate at all in élite culture. Gradually, the two spheres became more clearly separated and by the later seventeenth century, and in some cases earlier, the upper classes had withdrawn from their participation in popular culture. The search for a monolithic European-wide popular culture is self-defeating. Regional cultures varied widely because of differences in the social structure and physical environment—for example, there were contrasts between the culture of the mountains and the culture of the plains, between farmers and herdsmen, especially shepherds. Above all, there was a crucial divide between urban and rural popular culture. In large towns, ballad-singers and clowns performed regularly, whereas villagers would see them only occasionally. The guild system gave townsmen distinctive identities which were manifested on occasions such as the feast of Corpus Christi. The more sophisticated urban social stratification brought with it a higher degree of cultural differentiation, for example between weavers and shoemakers.

9.3.1 *Popular Literary Sources*

Some idea of the range of popular culture may be obtained from the uneven survival of written sources. Of particular interest is the *Book of the Distaffs* (*Évangiles des quenouilles*) first published at Bruges in about 1475, which went into eight French editions in the sixteenth century. This provides considerable insight into the paradoxes of popular culture, with its lack of clear demarcations between good and evil, life and death, sacred and secular. There is a central preoccupation with the human body, and in particular urine and excrement. Some of this was designed simply to impose a taboo: urinating against the wall of a monastery or a cemetery was said to lead to apoplexy or kidney stones. Other guidance was offered more in hope than certainty: a woman who kept her hands tightly clasped during intercourse was thought to be guaranteed a son. Such folk beliefs could have serious dimensions: Noël du Fail and Montaigne both refer to the contemporary belief in sixteenth-century France that sorcery was used to deny couples the capacity to consummate their marriage, in particular by the mythical ligature (*aiguillette*). Montaigne dismissed these 'impressions of apprehension and fear', while noting that they were frequently 'the

sole topic of conversation'.²⁸ Yet as late as 1622 Pierre de Lancre noted
that 'there is hardly a man who dares to marry except in secret. One finds
oneself bound [that is, made sterile] without knowing by whom and in so
many different ways that the most skilful have no knowledge of how it is
done.'²⁹ The central obsession with the body—particularly its more
grotesque aspects—during the Renaissance is exemplified in Rabelais's
Gargantua and *Pantagruel*, written in the years 1532–42. It can be seen in
the tradition at Bologna of holding anatomical lessons in public during
Carnival 'in order to enable the maskers to participate'.³⁰ The great
Andreas Vesalius held dissections for the benefit of audiences of two
hundred people at Padua in 1540; he recorded that huge crowds attended
his dissections of genital organs. Anatomists needed compliant public
authorities to supply them with a regular flow of corpses, chiefly from
those executed; the executions themselves were of course public spec-
tacles.

Folk belief originated both in oral tradition and in the chap-books or
pedlars' books sold by chapmen and *colporteurs*, so called after the neck-
bag in which they kept their stock of titles. They were not a particularly
numerous group: 45 pedlars were authorized in France in 1611, 50 in 1635
and still only 120 in 1712. These relatively small numbers suggest that the
sales of chap-books had most effect in large and small towns rather than in
the countryside. It was certainly in towns that there was a larger literate
audience, though still small in relation to the size of the urban population.
The French chap-books were bound in blue paper (and hence are referred
to by historians as the *Bibliothèque bleue*) and originated at Troyes in the
beginning of the seventeenth century. Sold for 2 *sous* apiece at a time
when an urban worker's wage was between 15 and 20 *sous* a week, the
chap-books were not particularly expensive. Nevertheless, it should be
noted that the political pamphlets (*Mazarinades*) of the Fronde (1648–53)
sold for less—sometimes half a *sou*—and thereby reached a wider
audience.

The process of mediation is crucial for an understanding of the dissemination of popular culture. At Gerlingen in Württemberg a vinegrower
named Hans Keil started off a story in 1648 that he had been visited by an
angel in his vineyard, who had lamented the sins of the population, taken
Keil's knife and cut six of his vines, which began to bleed. Keil's vision and
accompanying prophecy was published in broadsides and chap-books all
over southern Germany. The authorities considered the prophecy
potentially seditious and in April 1648 took elaborate measures to locate
the chapmen and destroy as many copies of the pamphlet as could be
found. Though the villagers were not prepared to take an oath on the
subject, many of them reported having seen fresh blood flowing from the
stalks of the vines. Yet in fact, Keil confessed that he had made up the

whole story. He was the mediator in the development of popular culture in his village, since he was probably the person who read the most widely: he took bits and pieces from the various pamphlets in his possession, and refashioned them into a pamphlet relevant to the needs of his community—which in his view was to do penance—at the end of the Thirty Years' War. More dangerous, politically and financially, for the government was the dissemination by chapmen of falsified decrees. In seventeenth-century France, many of these circulated, purporting to emanate from the council of state and to grant tax remissions to rural communities.

Much of both rural and urban popular culture is difficult for the historian to trace since it was transmitted orally, or took the form of festivals which were impermanent and left few records. Entertainment was often provided on an itinerant basis, it being easier to change audience than repertoire. Travelling entertainers were frequently regarded as beggars; some were blind. There were also obscure part-time storytellers, musicians, preachers and healers spreading popular traditions. The chief location for their activities varied from one country to another—in France it was the inn (*cabaret*), while in Italy it was more likely to be the town square (*piazza*). Mock sermons were a traditional part of the clown's repertoire, and there were common themes—the triumphant or just ruler, the outlaw (popular only in his own region), the feared outsider (the Turk, Jew or witch). The most important settings were festivals: spontaneous celebrations, weddings and banquets, confraternity or guild festivals, festivals limited to one street or one neighbourhood, church fairs and celebrations of the anniversary of a church dedication, community festivals such as the feast of a patron saint, processions on Rogation Days, burlesque festivals, and finally Carnival. The feast of St Martin was a time when the winter pig—or sometimes an ox—was slaughtered and salted; as late as 1655 the Synod of Utrecht in the Dutch Republic lamented the 'pagan and idolatrous' festivities associated with the cult of St Martin which were celebrated in the precincts of the cathedral.[31]

9.3.2 *Carnival and Charivari*

There were two types of Carnival, those dominated by the upper classes and those which were more popular in inspiration. Under the restored Medici regime in early sixteenth-century Florence, the celebrations of Carnival were more events to which the people came, political pantomines staged and orchestrated by the ruling families, rather than events made by the people themselves. The same was true of Carnival at Toulouse as late as 1624, where the upper classes used the festival as a vehicle for asserting their status and power. The Parisian diarist Pierre de l'Estoile noted in

February 1584 that during the Mardi Gras celebrations, the king and the duc d'Anjou 'went together through the streets of Paris, followed by all their favourites and *mignons*, mounted and masked, disguised as merchants, priests, lawyers, etc., tearing about with loose rein, knocking down people, or beating them with sticks, especially others who were masked. This was because on this day the King wished it to be a royal privilege to go about masked. They went to the fair in Saint-Germain and committed infinite insolences, rioting and disturbing the good people . . .'[32] The main themes of a purely 'popular' Carnival were food, sex and violence, with the world—that is, the social order—turned upside-down. The great contrast was between the excess of Carnival feast-days (*jours gras*) and the self-sacrifice of Lent (*jours maigres*). At Bologna in 1506, and no doubt on many other occasions, a mock battle was held between the armies of Lent and Carnival. Similar scenes took place at Nuremberg from the fourteenth century until 1539, when the influence of the Reformation brought the tradition to a close, while in the Low Countries Pieter Breughel the Elder depicted one such mock battle in a famous painting twenty year later.

Beyond Carnival there was also 'charivari', carnival-type rituals of popular justice accompanied by rough music, usually directed against old men married (usually for the second time) to young women, husbands cuckolded by their wives, domineering women, and so on. In May 1517, forty-two members of the Abbey of Misrule of the rue Mercière in Lyon elected an abbot and other officers, and set up councillors to 'govern' the streets and 'keep peace and amity among the members'.[33] They planned a parade on an ass directed against a well-to-do tanner who had recently been beaten by his wife, 'in order to repress the temerity and audacity of women who beat their husbands and of those who would like to do so . . .'[34] At Lectoure in 1643 charivari (called chalibaly) was described as 'having been observed in this kingdom from time immemorial' and was thought perfectly acceptable provided it was held 'without scandal or evil design'.[35] Charivari was a ritual which had close affinity to the shame punishments meted out officially under certain of the late medieval French customary law codes (the mixture of the penal and the festive was also a feature of Carnival). There were upper-class reservations about charivari, for example that it might lead to sedition, that it might act as a cloak for malicious accusations, and that its leading participants might be base and troublesome members of the community. However, there is some evidence of élite patronage of charivaris, while both Carnival and charivari seem to have served on occasion as instruments of social control: in the words of Claude de Rubys, a Lyon lawyer writing in 1604, 'it is sometimes expedient to allow the people to play the fool and make merry, lest by holding them in with too great a rigour, we put them in despair . . .'[36] Subordinate levels of society could purge their resentments without resorting to revolt or riot, while the lifting of normal taboos and restraints for a short period served to re-emphasize them once that exceptional period had passed. Nevertheless, rebels and rioters sometimes used the ritual and symbol of Carnival to legitimize their actions (see chapter 7.5.3) and Carnival could sometimes turn to political protest, as at Bordeaux in February 1651 when Cardinal Mazarin's effigy was executed and burnt (twice). The connection between Carnival and popular protest nevertheless usually proved counter-productive: the traditional fête held at Béziers was stopped by the urban authorities in 1660–1 because the town had proved a hotbed of discontent in the 1650s.

9.3.3   *The Public Authorities and Popular Culture*

Popular culture was not unchanging or monolithic. The culture of craftsmen and peasants developed spontaneously during the period, and varied from region to region. What one might term inherited items of culture were continually changing shape as new social contexts arose, deriving from modifications to the religious, social and economic structure. It is difficult to separate popular culture from changing concepts of 'person', 'community' and 'lordship' anywhere in Europe (in Germany lordship is referred to as *Herrschaft*, an almost untranslatable term which covers a variety of meanings including authority, domination and the state). The person had, of course, to relate to his community, the village corporation (*Gemeinde*). One form of identification of the social and moral community was attendance at the Catholic Mass or Protestant Eucharist. The refusal to attend Communion might result from quarrels and feuds with neighbours within the village community. In Württemberg, a Lutheran state from 1534, Johannes Brenz, the most influential local reformer, taught that magistrates should punish stubborn, quarrelsome and disobedient persons, no doubt thinking in terms of heretics and Anabaptists. But subsequent interpretation by the ecclesistical visitors widened the teaching to include those who scorned God's Word, or individuals who refused to take the sacraments. On the other hand, they maintained that to partake of the Eucharist in an unworthy state—for example, with an agitated heart, a bad conscience, or while in a state of dispute with one's neighbours—was a form of madness. Those who did not participate were seen as either Anabaptists or subject to the malevolent influence of magic. In 1587, Hans Weiss refused to attend Communion at Neckartailfingen because 'he had envy and hate against the village authorities, who had unfairly reported him to the chief administrative official of the district [*Vogt*] . . .'[37] Weiss was ordered to be imprisoned until he saw the error of his ways. Thus religious institutions were used to buttress political authority in the Württemberg parishes: *Herrschaft* demanded obedience. Individuals were under pressure to reconcile themselves to domination, not just from external sources, but also in their consciences.

Both Catholic and Protestant authorities attacked some aspects of popular culture from the later sixteenth century onwards and attempted to impose a new uniformity among the faithful. Yet the extent of their criticisms should perhaps not be exaggerated. The source material for the historians of popular culture is difficult to evaluate, and the historical techniques for its study are still in their infancy, but it seems fairly clear that there was no generalized attack upon popular culture in the early modern period. Popular customs and traditions were allowed to subsist unless they posed some exceptional threat to the maintenance of order. The culture of the upper classes was also permeated with at least some of the traditions, customs and attitudes of the rest of the population. Relatively isolated cases of criticism are much easier to document than generalized acceptance of popular culture. Already in the 1495 edition of his *Ship of Fools*, the Strasbourg lawyer Sebastian Brant had denounced the 'folly' of Carnival. The following year, shortly before the Florentine Carnival, Savonarola preached a sermon suggesting that 'instead of mad pranks' people should collect alms for the respectable poor. Johan Geiler von Kaiserberg, the cathedral preacher at Strasbourg, denounced excessive eating, drinking, dancing and gaming at church festivals, which he considered 'the ruin of the common people'.[38] Erasmus commented that the Carnival he witnessed at Siena in 1509 was 'unchristian' because it contained 'traces of ancient paganism', while the people over-indulged in licence.[39] Charivari was seen by Catholic reformers as a mockery of the sacrament of matrimony. Protestant theologians tried to draw more precise boundaries between the sacred and secular aspects of marriage, by prohibiting rowdy wedding processions and emphasizing the role of prayer before marriage. For their part, reforming Catholic theologians failed to distinguish between mock baptisms and sacrilege, and likewise between popular sermons and mock sermons. Gian Matteo Giberti, bishop of Verona, condemned preachers who 'tell ridiculous stories and old wives' tales in the manner of buffoons and make their congregation roar with laughter'[40]—in other words, those who aped the mannerisms of popular story-tellers. By the mid-seventeenth century, Jansenist bishops in France such as Pavillon at Alet and Caulet at Pamiers were trying to stamp out fêtes, though with mixed success. The official hostility of some Catholic and Protestant theologians towards important manifestations of popular culture was reinforced by the withdrawal of the urban upper classes from participation in Carnival, while the great urban fêtes and processions of the seventeenth century became tame in comparison with their sixteenth-century forerunners.

Yet we should be wary about attributing too great an influence over popular culture to Catholic and Protestant theologians. Even in the great trauma of the French wars of religion, the role of the Catholic clergy in unleashing popular violence has perhaps been exaggerated. It is true that in 1562 the bishop of Nîmes was said to have encouraged Catholic children to murder Protestants 'following the Lord's word, that his power would be most clearly manifested by innocent persons'.[41] But such murders were not reciprocated by Protestant children, since they did not receive the encouragement and approval of their families to do so. This suggests that the social environment in which the Catholic children operated—the world which 'encouraged the children, approving what they did'[42]—was more important than the role of the extreme Catholic clergy, although undoubtedly at every stage of the wars of religion there were radical priests who were prepared to urge their parishioners on to violence. It is difficult to understand the motivation which led men, women and children to perpetrate what today would be termed crimes of humanity. Perhaps the single most important factor was the belief that the end of the world was at hand and that the second coming of Christ was imminent. These views were not just the common currency of many Catholic, Lutheran and radical (but not Calvinist) theologians; they were propagated in the numerous astrological predictions which were published in almanacs and read avidly at the court, in town and country-side. Above all, they were popularized by Michel Nostradamus, who predicted the coming of civil war in France, and who saw in the conjunction of Saturn and Venus in August 1565 the likely occasion of the second coming of Christ. Linked with these ideas was the realization that the future of Catholicism in France was imperilled by the spread of Protestantism. Catholics therefore had to take to arms and eliminate heretics by direct action: *not* to have murdered Coligny at the beginning of the St Bartholomew massacres would, in such a world-view, have been regarded as a sin. A Catholic riot at Toulouse in mid-February 1563 was attributed to a prediction of Nostradamus, who had stated that the city was in danger of being seized by the Protestants the following day. Printed prophecies induced panic, and panic in turn unleashed collective violence during the French wars of religion. It is an open question whether such extreme and generalized violence would have been possible without the impact of the printed word.

Gradually, out of the collapse of the resistance of the Catholic League to Henri IV a more 'rational', perhaps a more stoical, world-view emerged and one which was less susceptible to astrological predictions and the belief in the second coming of Christ. By the period of the Fronde, the influence of the printed word was even more critical. During the League, and the minority of Louis XIII, several hundred pamphlets a year were published at times of crisis; but in the Fronde, during the three-month siege of Paris in the spring of 1649, a thousand pamphlets were published. This dramatic change in the scale of printed material was fundamental to the circulation of ideas. Each faction had its own literary output, its own authors and printing presses during the Fronde: the Frondeurs of 1649 produced about 1,800 of the total of 5,200 *Mazarinades*; the party of Condé and the princes about 1,950, far outstripping the government contribution of about 600, and those of other political tendencies (a mere 350). The remaining 500 pamphlets showed little clear political affiliation. This was a relatively sophisticated division of political opinion, and one moreover which evolved with events (the output of the Frondeurs was greatest in 1649, while that of the princes was most significant in 1652). All the important political and military events of the Fronde were marked by an outpouring of pamphlets; they included elements of information which today would be known as 'news flashes'. There were both commercial and partisan political reasons for publishing the news as fast as possible. Yet the popular press at the time of the Fronde also influenced events in a direct way and tried to mould public opinion on almost every issue. The return of the king to Paris in August 1649, after the first civil war, was postponed for five months by the violent language of the pamphlets circulating in the capital. Mazarin was advised that 'no one could be so foolhardy as to counsel the return [of the king] when such licence is seen and while disorder continues unchecked at Paris'.[43] Riots at the Luxembourg palace in December 1651 seem to have been provoked by printed handbills, and from the spring of 1652 onwards the princes' party encouraged popular violence in its printed output (including precise times and locations for the rendezvous of the rioters). In the end, there was no St Bartholomew massacre of the Mazarin party, but with language such as 'long live God, long live the king, down with Mazarin, down with the Mazarins, down with the Mazarines, fire on this accursed breed, no quarter, kill, kill, kill, kill' and 'exterminate the Mazarins'[44] this seems to have been more by accident than design on the part of the anti-government forces in 1652. The literature of the Fronde combined vitriolic personal attacks with more general concerns such as the aim of reducing the tax burden on the population as a whole. Information was systematically manipulated to achieve party objectives: defeats were transmuted into victories; riots were scarcely reported at all in goverment-inspired pamphlets; rumours, usually false, were given wide currency; private and public documents were falsified to give credence to false news, and so on. The printed word had become an instrument in the domestic political struggle and a form of psychological warfare in its own right. The audience for this intense form of propaganda must have been much more sophisticated by the mid-seventeenth century than has usually been recognized.

9.4   The New Crime of Witchcraft

The crime of witchcraft did not exist in the earlier Middle Ages. The idea of devils in male and female guise, *incubi* and *succubi*, was certainly prevalent in popular culture; there was also a concept of *maleficium*, the belief that one could harm one's neighbours by occult means. It was only in the later Middle Ages that the idea of an act of unnatural sexual intercourse between the Devil and a male or female (especially the latter) was defined: as a result of this act, humans were thought to acquire magic powers and become semi-demonic beings. This new idea was, it seems, imposed by the upper levels of society, and its general acceptance was perhaps the single most important impetus to the 'great European witch-hunt'. The first really substantial persecution was that of the Waldensian heretics in the Cottian Alps bordering France and Italy. By 1428 the idea that Waldensian heretics made nocturnal flights to the witches' nocturnal meeting or 'sabbat' seems to have been given credence by some orthodox Catholics on a scale sufficient to unleash persecution: for much of the period the standard term to describe witchcraft in this region was *Vauderie*, so named after the Waldensian heresy.

9.4.1   *The Conventional Viewpoint*

The official attitude towards witchcraft is revealed in the manuals of inquisitors, of which the most famous was the *Hammer of Witchcraft* (*Malleus maleficarum*), first published by Jacobus Sprenger and Heinrich Kramer (Henricus Institoris) in 1486. It was subsequently republished in at least thirteen editions up to 1520, and revised in another sixteen between 1574 and 1669. In addition to Germany, for which the text was prepared, there were editions in France, Italy and England. Sprenger and Kramer were experienced witch-hunters: they were responsible for the execution of forty-eight witches in 1486 alone. Part I of the *Malleus* introduced the idea of *incubi* and *succubi*. It attributed the greater number of female witches than male to the fact that 'all witchcraft comes from carnal lust, which is in women insatiable'.[45] Part II presented the pact with the Devil: 'it is common to all ... [witches] to practise carnal copulation with Devils',[46] it asserted boldly, and the various methods of intercourse between *incubi* and witches were enumerated. The supposed powers of witches, the prevention of their procreation, their ability to change men into the shapes of beasts, to enter human bodies without harming them ('prestidigitation'), and to inflict infirmity, 'even leprosy or epilepsy', were all discussed in detail. It was taken for granted that witches who were midwives committed 'most horrid crimes',[47] including killing children or offering them to Devils, and furthermore that witches could injure cattle, raise up hailstorms and tempests and cause lightning to blast both men and beasts. There was some recognition that men and not women might be witches, most notably in a section on the witchcraft of archers. Various remedies were prescribed for those who were affected by different forms of witchcraft. Part III was the most useful part of the manual from the point of view of the inquisitor, itemizing how witnesses were to be examined, how witches were to be arrested, and the points which the judge should consider before consigning the prisoner to torture. If the witch was not induced by terror to confess, then torture was to be continued on the second or third day, but then it was not to be repeated subsequently until there was some indication of its probable success. During the intervals between torture, the witch was never to be left alone, lest the Devil caused her to commit suicide.

Such are the bare outlines of the manual compiled by the two Dominican inquisitors who had acted on a bull of Pope Innocent VIII issued in December 1484, which in itself had lent credence to the existence of *incubi* and *succubi*. Important as was the *Malleus maleficarum*, it was rarely mentioned in sermons and trial records of the period. In general, law courts distinguished between manipulative sorcery—where the evidence of neighbours was sufficient to convict—and diabolism, private or communal meetings with the Devil—where confession was necessary (and hence torture might be needed to secure it). This élite interpretation of witchcraft never merged fully with popular beliefs. In the sources which reveal popular attitudes—for example, in Lorraine, where spontaneous, pre-torture confessions survive—the diabolical pact was a marginal aspect. Witchcraft was depicted in such sources essentially as the power to harm people, animals or the community at large, a power ascribed to specific individuals and carried out by occult means. Witchcraft in England was viewed as positive acts of hostility to the community, rather than relations with the Devil as such. In France, in contrast, almost all the trials assumed an implicit or explicit pact with the Devil. So-called 'white magic', that is to say, faith-healing by 'cunning' men or women, was also much more suspect to the French than to the English courts. On the other hand, catastrophes affecting the local community were rarely attributed to the malevolent influence of witches in France. Plague unleashed witch-hunting mania at Geneva in 1545, 1567–71 and 1615. Hail damage to crops had the same effect in south-west Germany (despite the preaching of Lutheran theologians), and in

Catholic Lorraine. Clearly, the indigenous popular belief in the occult took distinctive forms from one country to another.

Scholarly opinion on the extent of witchcraft was divided in the first decades of the sixteenth century. Erasmus satirized the confusion between heresy and sorcery in his *Praise of Folly*, while the humanist authors of *Letters of Obscure Men* ridiculed witchcraft beliefs. However, within a few years there is little doubt that the prevalent view even among Protestant theologians in Germany was that the diabolical pact between witches and the Devil was indeed possible. In 1522, Luther called witches 'Devil's whores who steal milk, raise storms, ride on goats or broomsticks, lame or maim people, torture babies in their cradles, change things into different shapes . . .'[48] He later condemned lawyers who wanted precise evidence and denied 'open and flagrant proofs of witchcraft';[49] in 1541, he approved of the execution of four witches at Wittenberg. However, one of Luther's followers, Johann Brenz, took a less severe line, arguing that natural disasters arose from God's punishment rather than as a result of human intervention: 'Satan, knowing of a future hailstorm, excites the witch to try to stir up a storm by her incantations . . . witchcraft itself can do nothing.'[50] Reformed Protestantism was just as credulous. Calvin was fightened by the so-called 'plague-spreaders' (*engraisseurs*)[51] at Geneva, who were the victims of several witch-hunts; but only once—in 1545—did he himself ask the city magistrates to investigate a case of witchcraft. The Calvinist Thomas Erastus argued in 1572 that even if witches killed their victims by poisoning rather than by supernatural means they were not madmen or women and deserved death for attempting to use the help of the Devil to harm others.

Jean Bodin's treatise against witchcraft, the *Demonomania of Sorcerers* (*Démonomanie des sorciers*), which was published for the first time in 1580, is often said to be representative of contemporary Catholic opinion. Although one of the great minds of his age, Bodin was credulous in matters of the occult. He considered that witches were guilty of fifteen specific crimes, including denial of God, murdering children before they had been baptised, incest, disinterring the dead, eating human flesh and drinking blood, killing humans by means of poisons and spells, killing cattle, causing famine on the land and infertility in the fields, and having sexual intercourse with the Devil. Just as murderers should be apprehended and punished, witches should be discovered and burned 'so that the wrath and vengeance of God may cease'. Citing the *Malleus maleficarum*, Bodin illustrated his case with evidence from a German town near Constance whose plague did not subside until witchcraft in the region had been destroyed. However, although he greatly feared witches, Bodin was relatively moderate about trial procedure itself. He considered admissible evidence to include three elements: material proof, such as written pacts signed with the Devil; free confession, that is, without torture or the threat of torture; and finally, eyewitness accounts of an act of witchcraft. The last was clearly the most contentious issue, but Bodin considered that traditional jurisprudence had been too strict in this respect. Witchcraft was considered a *crimen exceptum*, a crime distinct from all others: Bodin explained that 'proof of such evil is so obscure and difficult that not one out of a million witches would be accused and punished if regular legal procedure were followed'.[52]

9.4.2 *The Spread of Persecution against Witches*

Exodus xxii.18 enjoined the faithful: 'Thou shalt not suffer a witch to live.' Had this exhortation been followed throughout the Middle Ages, a sudden rise in prosecutions in the early modern period would have been unlikely. But following the relative tolerance of the medieval period, at least until the fifteenth century, the increased numbers of witchcraft trials in the sixteenth century is striking, and explanations have naturally been sought. The influence of the *Malleus maleficarum* has been exaggerated. Witchcraft trials did not start suddenly because of the publication of one particular manual for inquisitors, although the production and dissemination of the various witchcraft manuals may have increased the likelihood of trials: it should be noted that extensive trials took place in Mainz and Bamberg, which were early centres of printing. The manuals reflected a hardening of attitudes and helped spread those attitudes; they did not themselves bring about the change. Nor should the scale of the witch-hunt be exaggerated; it varied greatly from region to region even in sixteenth-century Europe, as did its nature. Witch-hunts against multiple suspects were rare in England: apart from Lancaster in 1612, those in Essex in 1645 and Newcastle in 1648 were the sole instances of multiple charges, which were provoked and sustained by individual witch-hunters. The largest collective execution in England was of nineteen women in Essex in 1645. Recent scholarship has tended to reduce the exaggerated numbers of executions which appeared in contemporary accounts in continental Europe: the *Parlement* of Paris ordered scarcely more than 100 executions of witches between 1565 and 1640, while perhaps another 350 executions were carried out locally within its jurisdiction. The incompleteness of the evidence makes such estimates hazardous: it was sometimes the case that the trial papers were burnt with the witch, to obliterate the memory as well as remove the person of the offender; in other cases, lynch law prevailed. Nevertheless, other parts of Europe certainly average a higher rate of trials and convictions. It is thought that Lorraine, for example, conducted some 3,000 trials in the period 1580–1630, with a conviction rate approaching 90 per cent. Yet Geneva experienced 477 trials and 141 executions between the Reformation and the last recorded trial, a conviction rate of about only 30 per cent. The incidence of capital punishment clearly varied according to region, but even in the worst-affected areas it has been over-dramatized. At Bamberg, the number of executions for the period 1624–31, for example, seems to have been nearer 300 than the 600 previously suggested. The term 'great European witch-hunt' seems to be an exaggeration.

Yet the number of witch trials did increase in the late sixteenth and early seventeenth centuries. This was either because the climate of opinion had changed so that the demand for the persecution of witches had grown, or because it had become easier to obtain a successful prosecution. Prosecutions of witches would not have been allowed to proceed without upper-class approval: the behaviour and motivation of the ruling élite is crucial in explaining the new fashion for witch-hunting. In some cases it may have been used as a form of social control, albeit infrequently. The attitude to witchcraft among the élites was extraordinarily diverse, which helps to account for the different responses of the various European states. A shift in attitudes can be observed commonly in cases where (for example) the court was informed that the old woman accused had been a witch all her life. In the late Middle Ages and the early sixteenth century such accusations may not have led to prosecution, but by the end of the century, the authorities pursued such cases with zeal. The quality of the evidence had not changed, but *maleficium* was seen in a new and more sinister light. Since the crime of witchcraft by definition could not be proven by traditional written evidence, witnesses had to be allowed to make statements without suffering penalties for frivolous or malicious accusations. Such penalties had been commonplace in the Middle Ages: as late as 1451, a man at Strasbourg who had accused a woman of *maleficium* and had failed to prove his case was arrested, tried for calumny and drowned in the river Ill. However, the general law code promulgated by Charles V in the Holy Roman Empire in 1532 (*Constitutio criminalis carolina*) not only imposed the death penalty for witchcraft but shifted the responsibility for proving guilt in such cases from the accuser to the court official, which had the effect of making frivolous or vindictive accusations possible.

Charles V's law code suggests that witch persecution could be encouraged by the action of the state. Although witchcraft legislation was passed in England in 1542 and 1563, previous legal arrangements seem until then to have been found sufficient for dealing with accusations: neither of these acts, which were subsequently repealed (respectively in 1547 and 1604), mentioned the witch's compact with the Devil. In contrast to the Spanish Netherlands and Lorraine, where the authorities in the late sixteenth century encouraged their subjects to prosecute witches in the courts, appellate jurisdiction in France tended to restrain persecution. Panics about witches in France in 1587–8, 1623 and 1643–4 led to a hostile reaction against such trials among judges, who were less influenced by scepticism about witchcraft than by the desire to put a stop to outbreaks of lynching in the localities. Peaks of official persecution, far from pacifying village feeling, seemed to generate higher numbers of illegal killings. As the custodians of law and order, members of the *Parlement* of Paris, and their counterparts in the provincial *Parlements* (and even the *Parlement* of neighbouring Franche-Comté at Dôle), had an interest in restraining local persecution. Special factors prevailed in the *Parlement* of Rouen, and it supported witch-hunting within its jurisdiction longer than most of its counterparts. In Lorraine, by contrast with the French kingdom, the ducal court had little power to restrain witch trials initiated in the local courts. It was not only the cataclysm of the Thirty Years' War and French military occupation which put an end to witch trials there, but also the introduction of a French-style appellate jurisdiction in the 1630s.

It is revealing in the context of appellate jurisdiction to compare the rates of prosecution for witchcraft as against other types of criminal prosecutions. Witchcraft was not numerically the most important type of criminal case heard before the *Parlement* of Paris: in the periods 1572–85 and 1614–26, infanticide cases were more common; death sentences for this offence were more common than for witchcraft. (In numerical terms these two types of case considerably outstripped those concerning bigamy, sodomy and homicide.) The total number of prosecutions in all the different categories tended to rise and fall in roughly the same proportion. This pattern reflects the development towards the criminalization of female offences: after 1556, women were required in France to declare that they were pregnant and to have the birth of their child witnessed. Those who failed to make the appropriate statement of pregnancy and who then gave birth to a stillborn child were deemed culpable of premeditated infanticide. This draconian law places witchcraft cases in their true perspective: a significant proportion of these, unlike infanticide cases, did not result in the death sentence.

In some years, a crisis atmosphere seems to have prevailed and witchcraft cases showed a sharp rise, notably after the St Bartholomew massacres in 1572 and in the months preceding Henri IV's assassination. Generally, however, the attitude of the *Parlement* of Paris towards witchcraft cases was less severe than that of the lesser courts: until 1624, when the matter was settled in its favour by a royal ordinance, the *Parlement* sought in vain to reserve for itself the review of all witchcraft cases carrying the death sentence. In Champagne, it was estimated that in a seven-year period in the 1590s more than 300 executions were carried out by the lesser courts without the *Parlement* of Paris having had the opportunity to review the cases in question. Two local magistrates were removed from their offices and a witch-hunter was sent to the galleys in an attempt to halt what were tantamount to local lynchings. The fact that these lynchings occurred in Champagne, a great bastion of the Catholic League, might indicate a connection between the traumas of the wars of religion and the pattern of witch-hunting: hunting seems to have ceased when the 'true religion' had been established at parish level. A further pattern to emerge from these cases was that over half of those reviewed by the *Parlement* of Paris (565 out of 1,094 cases between 1564 and 1639) concerned allegations of witchcraft against men—at first, this might seem to point to a continuation of the fifteenth-century linkage between heresy (then of the Waldensian kind) and the persecution of male witches. In fact, however, only three of the cases reviewed by the *Parlement* involved Protestants; the rest of the suspects were nominally Catholic, although they were not regarded as such because they had entered into a pact with the Devil.

One perhaps surprising feature of the Inquisition was its concern to preserve correct legal procedures. Contrary to what might be expected, in the Basque witch-hunt of 1609–14 the witch-hunter Pierre de Lancre proved more ruthless in the French province of Labourd than did the Spanish inquisitor Alonso de Salazar in Spanish Navarre and Guipúzcoa. Whereas Lancre was certain that the whole Basque-speaking pays de Labourd was infected by the witch sect, and published witch confessions as 'proof' in his *Description of the Inconstancy of Evil Angels and Demons* (1612), Salazar became convinced that the very process of witch-hunting, not least the atmosphere of hysteria and intimidation it generated, produced so-called confessions which were in fact false. In August 1614, the council of the Inquisition supported Salazar's contention, which in effect marked an end to official witch-hunting in Spain. Two years later, Salazar succeeded in transferring 289 witch cases from Vizcaya to the Inquisition for sentencing; the cases were suspended and the witches absolved. Three hundred witches were hanged in Catalonia in 1616–19, but the Inquisition eventually intervened successfully against local independence to bring the persecution to a halt. Clearly, the same phenomenon was open to quite different interpretations according to the local legal procedures and the witch-hunter's personal viewpoint. It has been established for south-west Germany that Catholic magistrates conducted nearly twice as many witchcraft trials as their Protestant counterparts, and executed over three-and-a-half times the number of victims. However, the example of Salazar in the Basque territories undermines the plausibility of any simple connection between the Counter-Reformation and witch persecution.

The effect of different local legal procedures was also crucial to the rate of successful prosecutions and the severity of convictions. The constant factor was the demand in the rural communities (and some urban ones as well) for the persecution of witches. This could take distinctive forms. Between 1575 and 1620 in Friuli, near Udine in north-eastern Italy, there were unusual cases of so-called witchbeaters (Benandanti), peasants who saw themselves as entrusted to fight those guilty of witchcraft, who aimed to destroy the fertility of the crops or to kill children. The outcome of the battle against evil would decide whether the coming year would be one of plenty or famine. The summons to enlist came to the Benandanti in their sleep, and they underwent their battles in a state of trance, all suggesting that the belief in witches was deeply engrained at the lower levels of society. Elsewhere, the typical accuser may be viewed as someone whose position in local society was endangered, and who was striking back at the suspect in desperation. It has been suggested, for example, that as the traditional sense of communal responsibility declined under the impact of the population and price rises of the late fifteenth and sixteenth centuries, elderly women who were unable to provide for themselves were felt to be a burden which the village was no longer willing to shoulder. Hence they were prime targets for witchcraft allegations. It has also been argued that spinsters and widows increased greatly in number during this period and came to be viewed as an alien and unwelcome element in a society where the patriarchal family still constituted the norm. This rejection of the social misfit, whether male or female and for whatever precise reasons, was the product of a local community undergoing crisis; once the crisis passed, the social misfit might once more be tolerated. In this respect, a distinction needs to be drawn between accusations of witchcraft, which may be explained in terms of the immediate social environment of the witch and the accuser, and prosecutions for witchcraft, where the attitude of the élite played a part. Every community had numerous suspect persons, who in an atmosphere of economic or demographic crisis and mutual suspicion might be accused of witchcraft. Witchcraft was a charge usually levelled against the poor and downtrodden: secret magical powers of revenge were the way in which such individuals were thought to assert themselves against a brutalized existence, usually without any certain proof of witchcraft. Seen in this light, many trials may have been simply a settling of accounts between a majority of the village community and those whom it resented.

9.4.3 *New Attitudes towards Witchcraft*

Almost as suddenly as the trials had begun, the great wave of witch persecution come to an end in the second half of the seventeenth century. There are no simple explanations for this. Certain authorities had always been sceptical as to whether the crime of witchcraft could be proven. In 1526, the Council of the Inquisition in Castile had required inquisitors to proceed with relative scepticism. If, for example, a witch confessed to murdering a child or an adult, they were to ascertain whether the victim died at the time alleged by the witch, if the death might have been from natural causes, and whether there were any marks on the body or any other unusual circumstances concerning the death. They were to find out how the witch entered and left the house, and if this was by an open window or door or whether someone allowed her to enter. If a witch confessed to destroying crops, enquiries were to be made to see if the alleged damage was really inflicted or if the fields had been exposed to inclement weather which was sufficient cause for the loss of the crops. If a witch confessed to summoning up gales or hailstorms, it was to be determined whether these took place at a season when such weather was a normal occurrence. By careful questioning of others living in the same house, the inquisitors were to establish if the witch had left the house on the night in question when she maintained that she had been present at the witches' nocturnal gathering or 'sabbat'. In a further development in 1538, the Council of the Inquisition required inquisitors to instruct priests to explain to the people that damage to crops could be a natural consequence of bad weather and that sometimes it was attributable to divine retribution for human sinfulness. Crop damage occurred everywhere, whether there were witches present or not, and it was therefore undesirable for people to believe that witches were always to blame.

It was against this background of official scepticism that Alonso de Salazar commenced his witch-hunt in the Spanish Basque country in 1609–14 and immediately found himself in difficulties with his two fellow inquisitors, Becerra and Valle. They argued that witches should be equated with heretics and suffer the same punishment, a point which Salazar denied. They also considered that the trial record should contain 'only the final, well-reasoned confessions that agree with what is already known about witchcraft'. Salazar, in contrast, vigorously asserted that the confessions should be written down in full 'with their contradictions and absurdities'.[53] 'It is clear', he wrote in 1613, 'that the witches are not to be believed, and that the judges should not pass sentence on anyone, unless the case can be proven by external and objective evidence sufficient to convince everyone who hears it.'[54] Who, he asked, could accept that a person could fly through the air and travel a hundred leagues in an hour; that a woman could pass through a space not big enough for a fly; that a person could make himself invisible; that he could be in a river or in the sea and not get wet, or that he could be in bed and at the 'sabbat' at the same time? These and other such claims Salazar dismissed as beyond all human reason.

Such appeals to human reason to dismiss hysterical claims were one of the great liberating forces of mankind in the early modern period. The

Cleves physician Johann Weyer had argued in *Concerning the Powers of Demons* (*De praestigiis daemonum*, 1563) that many supposed witches were innocent melancholics and that even the guilty ones were mere tools of Satan, incapable of doing harm by their own activities. Weyer denied that the pact with the Devil existed and considered that punishment for witches should be confined to those who had been proved to be poisoners. His views were more influential than is sometimes thought, and he had a number of articulate disciples in Germany by 1630. In England, he influenced Reginald Scot, who also denied the pact with the Devil in his *Discoverie of Witchcraft* (1584). Nevertheless, it is clear that such views were minority ones during the sixteenth century. Not until the Dutch Cartesian Balthasar Bekker published *The Enchanted World* (*Betoorverde weereld*, 1691) was witchcraft denied in its fundamental aspect, on the grounds that spirit and matter could not influence one another: since the Devil was a spirit, he could not have physical effects in the world.

It matters not whether the appeal to human reason resulted from precise legal procedures concerning admissible evidence, as in the case of Salazar, or from a theoretical scepticism, as in the case of Weyer and Bekker. The important point is that it occurred, though not, it is true, at the same pace in each country or for the same combination of reasons. In France, a series of scandalous cases of hysterical imposture—the most notable example being the so-called 'possession' at the Ursuline convent at Loudun in 1632–4—had created a new scepticism about the occult. Urbain Grandier, the curé at Loudun, had been denounced by the nuns as a witch; he was condemned to death, tortured and executed. But this took place on the orders of a royal commissioner, Laubardemont, who had been sent there by Richelieu to make an example of Grandier in all probability as part of a personal vendetta. Cases of supernatural possession cannot be altogether equated with witchcraft cases, but it should be noted that whereas even the *Parlement* of Paris had been credulous in its acceptance of testimony on witchcraft, Louis XIV, despite persisting in his bigotry towards Protestants and Jansenists, intervened decisively to stop further witchcraft trials in the 1670s. In England, the last execution of a witch (Alice Molland) took place in 1685. There are relatively few examples elsewhere after this date, and in some cases the executions had stopped considerably earlier. The desire to halt the murderous lynch atmosphere that prevailed in the localities during witch-hunts may have appealed increasingly to the custodians of law and order. In some cases, there was also a recognition of the possible fiscal motives for witch-hunting, since according to legal practice in the country concerned, the witch's goods might go to the lord, or to the Inquisition, or to the officials responsible for the trial.

The appeal to human reason, chiefly in practical rather than theoretical terms, seems to have played a decisive role in the decline of witch-hunting. But there are also two important subsidiary influences, which played a crucial part in some areas. The first of these is the possible lessening of social tensions within the village community which had led to witchcraft accusations in the first place, and the gradual impact of urban values on that community. Such imperceptible changes in social attitudes are very difficult to demonstrate, and until more is known about the social context of the trials no firm conclusions can be drawn. A second subsidiary influence on the decline of witchcraft trials was what one might call the state's conquest of the borderlands. Some of the most important trials had occurred in the frontier regions, which were crucial battlegrounds between the rival confessions, between orthodox faith and local folk custom, and between central political power and regional privilege. The Basque area falls into this category; so too does the borderland between France, Franche-Comté, the Swiss Cantons and Savoy; witch persecution in south-western Germany occurred precisely in an area which was territorially fragmented; while the duchy of Lorraine, where Nicolas Rémy attempted to instigate a general witch-hunt between 1576 and 1612 (although he did not succeed: witchcraft scares remained small-scale and local), was both fragmented territorially and subject to a power struggle between France and the Austrian Habsburgs. Some of these borderlands, most obviously the Basque area, were never effectively subdued: animosities between villages of rival confessions arising from the wars of religion, and between the Basque and non-Basque population, were profound and long-lasting. Even in the later seventeenth century, the Basques on the French side of the border were not regarded as politically reliable, but whereas in the previous century they might have been seen as witches, they were subsequently regarded as coin counterfeiters, an offence that was at least capable of objective proof. Witch-hunting usually ceased under the occupation of an alien army or when the 'true' religion had prevailed at parish level. The triumph of orthodox, even 'official' religion, rather than the rise of a more secular society, helped dispense with witch persecution even in the borderlands.

9.5 The Rise of European Rationalism

Witchcraft debates played an important part in the development of European rationalism. The opponents of witch-trials appealed for greater scepticism: it is therefore possible to argue that some long-term benefit for civilization arose from the evil of persecution. Before about 1630 the belief in witchcraft was so all-pervasive that it is surprising that there were any sceptics to doubt the rationality of the case. Such a belief formed part of a world-view in which sin was stressed and where deprivation and misfortune were explained by demonism; witchcraft itself was not seen as an incongruous feature of an otherwise normal world, but rather as an inversion of the normal world, a manifestation of misrule as evident, for example, as 'charivari' was in the actual world. It was closely associated in people's minds with rebellion; a form of spiritual apostasy was thought to take place at the 'sabbat'. The prevalence of this world-view means that it is misleading to contrast the many who accepted the existence of witch-craft with the few who utterly rejected it: there was a middle ground of authors who were familiar with sceptical arguments and who tried to discriminate between what could be accepted and what rejected. What is certain, however, is that the scientific relevance of occult phenomena was taken for granted by almost everyone: people seriously believed that a study of witchcraft would help reveal the true secrets of nature. In this respect, the preoccupation with witchcraft was no different from that with monsters, which were increasingly seen as natural wonders rather than signs of God's wrath, and were thought to provide useful lessons for anatomy, physiology and even embryology.

9.5.1 *The Legacy of Ancient Greece and the New Spirit of Enquiry*

A 'rationalist' in the broadest sense is one who places special emphasis on man's rational capacities and gives particular value to reason and rationalism. In a restricted and technical sense, rationalism may be contrasted with empiricism: whereas empiricists stress that all human knowledge derives essentially from sensory experience, rationalists stress the role played by reason and *a priori* knowledge (for example, a prior belief in God's existence). The arch-empiricist Francis Bacon observed in the seventeenth century that 'empiricists are like ants: they collect and put to use; but rationalists, like spiders, spin threads out of themselves'.[55] Nevertheless, despite Bacon's dictum, the distinction between the two strands of philosophical and scientific enquiry cannot be and never was absolute, least of all in an individual's intellectual career. Even Descartes, who is seen as the pivotal figure in the transition from classical to modern philosophy and in particular as the supreme exponent of a rationalist viewpoint, nevertheless denounced scholastic philosophers for neglecting experiments and 'expecting truth to germinate from their own heads like Minerva from the head of Jupiter'. He stated that he 'knew of no other expedient than to look for further experiments that will give different results, depending on whether one or another explanation is correct'. This was far from a rigid allegiance to *a priori* knowledge as against empiricism: Descartes seems to have advocated initial intuition to con-struct a set of first principles which would then be verified in detail by experimentation.

The rise of European rationalism, which in one sense was no more than the transition from a credulous to a more critical spirit, is one of the great turning-points in western civilization. It was not inevitable, nor was its outcome certain. To modern eyes, it seems incredible that contemporaries in the sixteenth century should have been so dominated by a world-view determined in essence by the writings of the ancient Greeks—Aristotle and Ptolemy on cosmology, and Galen on anatomy. However, St Paul had cautioned (Romans xi.20) 'be not high-minded, but fear', and his condemnation of moral pride became a standard warning against intellectual curiosity. Erasmus had discounted this, arguing that St Paul did not condemn erudition, but sought to restrain mankind from boasting about worldly success; his words, he thought, were addressed to rich people and not to learned men. The Protestant reformers did not follow Erasmus' interpretation. Calvin considered that God 'does not wish us to be too wise'.[56] 'Nothing hinders and prevents us from embracing the promises of God', he argued, 'more than when we ponder what can be done naturally and what is probable.'[57] God's rule was 'not restricted to the order of nature, which he easily changes whenever it seems right'.[58] Indeed, God would be 'driven from his throne' if there was a fixed order of nature. In his view, God 'often deliberately changes the laws of nature so that we may know that what he freely confers is exclusively determined by his will'.[59] The majority view of the purpose of scholarly enquiry was to confirm the findings of the ancients: Galen's collected works were reprinted at Venice in 1525, and even the revolutionary sixteenth-century treatise on anatomy, Vesalius' *De fabrica* (1543), was in many respects a compilation of Galen's writings. The revolutionary aspect of Vesalius' work was the use of anatomical drawings—probably by John Stephen of Calcar—based on dissected human anatomies. Even Vesalius admitted in one passage, however, that one of the drawings had been modified to fit Galen's words, and this adaptation is significant in revealing contemporary reliance on the authority of the ancients.

It was inherent in the gradual process of intellectual search that ultimately, at an unpredictable point in time, conflict with the church would arise. For a 'modern' scientific or rational attitude to emerge, theology, it seemed, would face relegation to a concern with doctrine and morals, thus leaving the high ground of intellectual enquiry to science: instead of being the handmaiden of theology, science had to assert itself. This self-assertion was far from straightforward. Nearly all those we would call scientists in the sixteenth and early seventeenth centuries were religious men. Even the iconoclastic Paracelsus, the founder of modern medical chemistry who lambasted Galen and other authorities, drew no clear line between religion and science or between his religious and his natural philosophy: in his view, religion was not to be banished from the study of medicine. Paracelsus died in 1541, but his influence grew in the closing decades of the sixteenth century up to 1605, when collected editions of his works became widely available. Certain of his opponents, notably Thomas Erastus, took particular exception to his Neoplatonist unification of spiritual and corporeal phenomena.

9.5.2 *The Copernican Revolution*

No scientific figure in the sixteenth century did more to overturn established viewpoints, and in particular to undermine an accepted religious attitude, than the great Bohemian astronomer Nicolaus Copernicus (Mikolaj Kopernik). His celebrated masterpiece, *On the Revolutions of the Heavenly Spheres* (*De revolutionibus orbium coelestium*, 1543), was published on the advice of the cardinal of Capua and the bishop of Culm and dedicated to Pope Paul III. In his introduction Copernicus recognized that he might be condemned by the church, but much of his book was sufficiently mathematical to be readable by no one except a technically proficient astronomer: opposition to his book might have arisen earlier had the presentation been simplified. He asserted the heliostatic principle, that the earth revolves round the sun, in defiance of the geostatic tradition, that the earth remained static at the centre of the universe, as Aristotle had maintained. The geostatic tradition seemed also to rest on an explicit biblical text (Joshua x.13): 'and the sun stood still, and the moon stayed, until the people had avenged themselves upon their enemies'. It was for this specific reason (apart from his general conservatism) that Luther condemned the new heliostatic theory, while Osiander had prefaced the German edition with a comment that it was a mathematical hypothesis which could not be regarded as objective truth.

Not only did it seem to violate Aristotelian physics, not to mention other technical objections which might be levelled against it, but Copernicus' view also appeared contrary to common sense and experience: who had ever *felt* the motion of the earth? Did not one's eyes witness the fact that the heavens revolved around the earth? Thus Copernicus seemed to oppose the rationalism of his age, which was why in the eyes of some of his contemporaries *De revolutionibus* diminished rather than enhanced his reputation. This concept of the annual motion of the earth was Copernicus' chief claim to originality, and it was this which fundamentally condemned his hypothesis not only in the eyes of church— because of its alleged heretical consequences—but also in the view of majority opinion.

Copernicus' masterpiece was published in the year of his death, and the reception of his ideas in the various European countries proceeded at a tortuous pace. On receiving advance notice of Copernicus' revolutionary view of the world, Luther had issued a blanket condemnation: 'the new astronomer wants to prove that the Earth goes round, and not the heavens, the Sun and the Moon . . . But that is the way nowadays; whoever wants to be clever must produce something of his own, which is bound to be best since he has produced it! The fool will turn the whole science of astronomy upside down . . .'[60] Melanchthon commented on the same theme that 'some wise ruler should curb the imprudence of talents'. (One such ruler, the Emperor Charles V, was sent a copy of Copernicus' book by Sebastian Kurz in March 1543 'since your Majesty is a keen mathematician'—but there is no evidence that he took Melanchthon's advice.) Catholic opinion was equally hostile. Bodin quoted Melanchton's refutation of Copernicus.[61] Even the greatest of sixteenth-century sceptics, Montaigne, denounced the implications of Copernicus' world system: 'it is the vanity of this . . . imagination that makes man see himself as the equal of God, endowed with godlike qualities . . .'[62]

Much more plausible to contemporaries, although it did not survive beyond the seventeenth century, was the later argument of Tycho Brahe, a Danish Lutheran who was a firm believer in astrology. From 1576 until 1597 he spent most of his time at Uraniborg castle and the adjacent Stjaerneborg observatory on the islet of Ven in observations of the stars and the solar system. He asserted in his treatise *On the Most Recent Phenomena of the Ethereal World* (1588) that the planets revolved around the sun, while the sun in turn rotated around a fixed earth. This view appeared to preserve the advantages of the Copernican system, without incurring some of its apparently absurd and heretical consequences. Two men undermined Tycho Brahe's compromise: Johannes Kepler, his assistant in the last year of his life (1600–1) at Prague, and Galileo Galilei. To some extent, despite their very different points of view, they worked in tandem. They were both convinced Copernicans, and it was Kepler who as early as 1597 urged Galileo to publish his Copernican arguments. His own achievement in *New Astronomy Studied Through Causes, or Celestial Physics* (*Astronomia nova*, 1609) was to discover new laws of planetary motion, that planets moved in ellipses with the Sun at one focus—one single curve sufficing for each planet. Kepler used analogy freely and consciously in both his mathematical and astronomical works: using the magnet as an example, he argued that both the earth and the sun were large magnets and that every planetary body was magnetic or quasi-magnetic. He denounced Bodin for his figurative comparison between state systems and types of proportion (Bodin had equated democracy with an arithmetical proportion, aristocracy with a geometric one and monarchy with a harmonic form): such comparisons, Kepler argued, were 'only symbolic, not visibly expressed in connection with some solid body, as mathematics requires'. He also condemned the ancient Greek Ptolemy for using comparisons in a poetical and rhetorical way, but he reserved his main polemic for Robert Fludd, a contemporary Englishman. Fludd clearly had an idiosyncratic view of the world, which he set down in the form of illustrations to his *Metaphysical, Physical and Technical History of the Macro and Microcosm* (1617–21). This work contained, for example, a visual depiction of man's faculties, with the world of images mediating between the world of senses and the world of the intellect. In his *Harmonies of the World* (1619), Kepler singled out for particular criticism Fludd's enigmatic writing, his preoccupation with the occult, his preference for ancients over modern writers, and his recourse to pictorial symbolism.

The significance of Kepler's attack lies in its appeal for proof, and its demand for a rational scientific explanation of causation. Kepler was not a 'pure' scientist in a modern sense: he retained a belief that planetary configurations imparted to the individual a lifelong temperamental influence at the moment of birth. On the other hand, he rejected a simple belief in astrological influence on events, and dismissed Pythagoras' theories derived from the study of numbers. Kepler was not a modern scientist in that he saw himself as carrying on a mathematical tradition derived from Plato, Euclid and Ptolemy. For him, religious and philosophical considerations remained paramount: Kepler was a Protestant. Rather, his aim was to provide a fitting philosophical framework for new astronomical discoveries, 'so that I might ascribe the motion of the Sun to the earth itself by physical, or rather metaphysical reasoning, as Copernicus did by mathematical'.[63] It was no purpose of Kepler's that philosophical considerations should be banished completely from the realm of science.

9.5.3 *Galileo and the Conflict with the Church*

Galileo, the second scientist to undermine Tycho Brahe's compromise, was by nature an iconoclast: his criticisms of Aristotle aroused the resentment of his colleagues at the university of Pisa after 1589, where the mathematical tradition was associated with mystical and astrological tendencies. He was thus moved to a mathematics lectureship at Padua in the anti-clerical Venetian state in 1592, where the tradition was more one of technical mathematics. There he plunged himself into the study of mechanics and the construction of his first telescope. His fame spread, and he began to tire of giving public lectures, 'for in these one can lecture only about very elementary matters and there are many people who can do that'. Galileo settled in 1610 in Tuscany (for the same salary he had received in Padua, but with the additional status of the titles of chief mathematician and philosopher to the grand duke). His appointment was conditional on his avoiding utterances which might have a theological implication. For Galileo this was tantamount to denying himself: above all he was publicist and a partisan for the Copernican system. He published new evidence in support of Copernicus in *The Starry Messenger* (1610) and *Letters on Sunspots* (1613), while even his two greatest works, the *Dialogue on the Chief Systems of the World* (1632) and the *Mathematical Discourses and Demonstrations Concerning Two New Sciences* (1638) were sustained polemics on the same theme.

Galileo believed that the science of motion and the appraisal of its results in astronomy were the twin keys to an understanding of the universe. A conclusion might be known before it could be proved: of Pythagoras he said 'the certainty of the conclusion was conducive not a little to the investigating of the demonstration . . .' The theory of motion, which was central to Galileo's preoccupations, was not new: Tartaglia had proclaimed the science of ballistics in 1537 and was the first writer to compute the ranges of cannon by means of tables derived from a theory of dynamics. However, neither Tartaglia nor Leonardo da Vinci before him had been prepared to reject the categorization of Aristotelian dynamics, namely that there were two kinds of motion, natural and violent. No one before Galileo succeeded in arriving at a correct deduction of the relationship between time, velocity and distance, the essence of the law of motion (kinematics). The law of acceleration which resulted from his discoveries in about 1609 was the foundation of dynamics, and in turn it exercised a considerable influence over the evolution of scientific method in the seventeenth century. For Galileo the new mechanics were the foundation of the new cosmology. He ignored the complexities of planetary motion, on which Kepler spent much of his career. Instead, Galileo consciously sought to interpret Copernicus' mathematical model in terms of natural philosophy: the new mechanics were put at the service of Copernican astronomy, even though contemporaries would have been surprised at the discovery that the same mechanical laws were appropriate for celestial and terrestrial motion. The decisive proof for the Copernican system he held to be the tides for 'if the terrestrial globe were immovable, the ebb and flow of the oceans could not occur naturally . . .'; in his analysis of the tides, however, Galileo blatantly disregarded established observations. He was far removed from a modern scientific attitude in one respect at least, namely that approximate knowledge is open to indefinite improvement; instead, he believed that the natural order was perfectly determined and that the object of physics was to make its laws explicit. 'All arguments concerning nature', he wrote, 'are either correct and true or else incorrect and false . . . To pretend that truth is so deeply hidden from us and that it is hard to distinguish it from falsehood is quite preposterous: the truth remains hidden only while we have nothing but false opinions and doubtful speculations; but hardly has truth made its appearance than its light will dispel the dark shadows.'

Galileo tried to draw a distinction between religious knowledge and scientific investigation. In his view, a correct interpretation of the Bible would confirm the basic unity of science and religion. The problem rested with the literal interpretation of Scripture and the text in Joshua x.13: if Joshua had indeed succeeded in bidding the sun to stand still, then the case against Copernicus appeared overwhelming. In general, Galileo rejected the recourse to biblical texts: in scientific discussion the enquiry should proceed from 'sense experiences and necessary demonstrations' rather than from the authority of the Bible. In other words, it was not that the Bible was wrong, but that its true meaning had to be understood. This in turn posed the question of authority: the Catholic church claimed the right, in states which had been subject to the Counter-Reformation, to determine interpretations of Scripture and points of doctrine. Even Galileo submitted himself to the authority of the church, thus apparently admitting the right of the ecclesiastical authorities to pass religious censure upon his arguments. That the church would indeed use such powers had already been demonstrated by the case of Giordano Bruno. He was burnt in 1600 because he was an apostate from a religious order who had taught the plurality of the worlds, that is, that there are other universes similar to our own, inhabited also by immortal souls. This was merely quasi-scientific speculation, in no way comparable with Galileo's work. But in 1615 Tommaso Campanella, who had been imprisoned by the Inquisition in the kingdom of Naples since 1599 for heresy and his advocacy of insurrection, threw his dubious support behind Galileo. This, and a relatively trivial incident at a dinner party that year, in which one of Galileo's supporters—Benedetto Castelli—in his own words 'played the theologian', cast a shadow over Galileo's theories and a period of deliberation commenced within the church.

One of the first responses came from Cardinal Bellarmino, who restated the Aristotelian position in *The Mind's Ascent to God by a Ladder of Created Things* (1615). Without 'true demonstration', he asserted, the Copernican view was a 'a very dangerous thing' which would serve to irritate all theologians and scholastic philosophers; it could 'injure the holy faith by suggesting that the Scriptures are false'. In 1616, the Roman Inquisition declared belief in the reality of the Copernican system to be heresy, and placed *De revolutionibus* on the Index of forbidden books (where it remained until 1822). Following the deaths of Paul V and Bellarmino in 1621, the new Pope, Urban VIII, told Galileo that he was free to write on the respective merits of different 'world systems'—that is, the geostatic and heliostatic theories—but he could not pronounce in favour of one of them unless he had conclusive proof. The Pope made clear his view that such proof was impossible: 'saving the appearances in one way' could not guarantee that God had not 'saved the appearances' in a totally different way.[64] Galileo was told to insert this argument into any future publication. But his *Dialogue on the Two Chief Systems of the World* (1632), which was almost completely sold out in the few months before the Inquisition ordered its seizure, rejected the Papal viewpoint and mercilessly derided the Aristotelian position. It asserted that it was necessary 'to new-mould the brains of men, and make them apt to distinguish truth from falsehood'. In his 'preface to the discerning reader', Galileo refuted the allegation that the Inquisition's equation of belief in the Copernican system with heresy implied that the church did not understand the merits of the Polish astronomer's case. He contended that other considerations resulting from 'piety, religion, the knowledge of Divine Omnipotence, and a consciousness of the limitations of the human mind' had influenced the decision. The grand duke of Tuscany did not withdraw his favour from Galileo, but for political reasons he could not defend him from the Roman Inquisition as the Venetian Republic undoubtedly could and would have done had he chosen to remain there in 1610. Within sixteen months of the publication of the *Dialogue*, Galileo was forced to recant his 'errors and heresies ... contrary to the Holy Church' and to swear in future neither to speak or write 'that which might cause a similar suspicion towards me'.[65] Galileo had already attracted the attention of the Inquisition as a result of the publication in 1623 of his atomistic theory of matter, which appeared to undermine the doctrine of transubstantiation (how could, literally, the Eucharistic wafer be transformed into the body of Christ, while retaining the sense of being bread?). It is possible that this was regarded more seriously than Copernicanism, and that Galileo's trial was stage-managed to preserve the authority of Urban VIII and prevent a greater scandal of heresy in the church. In any event, Galileo's recantation was an important short-term setback for the heliostatic view of the world. There is evidence that some (like Descartes) who were disposed to favour it were impelled either to express their ideas in veiled and guarded terms, or (again like Descartes) to do so from a safe sanctuary. In Descartes's case, this was from the Dutch Republic, where he had arrived earlier in 1628, and where there was no inquisitorial power to bring him to account for his views.

9.5.4 *Cartesian Rationalism*

The logical outcome of the Galilean conflict with the church was for scientists to call for the removal of interference from theologians. Francis Bacon had already declared in *New Logic* (*Novum organum*, 1620) that 'the corruption of philosophy by superstition and an admixture of theology is ... widely spread and does the greatest harm ... Very meet it is therefore that we be sober-minded, and give to faith that only which is faith's.'[66] Bacon's empirical approach made little headway on the Continent. Paris became the centre of scientific enquiry in the 1630s, and meetings of informal groups of scientists preceded the formation of the Royal Academy of Sciences in 1666. In the absence of Descartes, the leading figure in this group was Marin Mersenne, who maintained a vast correspondence while also publishing significant works in his own right between 1644 and 1651 (the last published posthumously: he died in 1648), in which—for example—he corrected one of Galileo's errors and described the motion of descent as a paraboloid. Mersenne was a leading opponent of Fludd and the influence of occult modes of thought in scientific enquiry, and he was equally dismissive of neo-Aristotelian naturalism. Mersenne and his group of followers were involved in research on the physiological and psychological aspects of sensation, and it was with this group that the political philosopher Hobbes associated himself during his exile from England (see chapter 6.1.4).

Yet the key personality in the developing rift between science and religion was not the English exile to France but the French exile to the Netherlands, René Descartes. In his four seminal works, *Discourse on Method* (1637), *Principles of Philosophy* (1644), *Passions of the Spirit* (1649) and *Treatise of Man* (published posthumously in 1664), Descartes offered a new and revolutionary mechanistic philosophy of the universe. Though chiefly remembered today as a philosopher, Descartes was a scientist in his own right: his *Discourse on Method* was composed as an introduction to three scientific essays, while his *Treatise of Man* resulted from protracted study, including almost daily visits to the butchers' shops, and resulting dissections on organs such as eyes, brains, lungs and hearts. He was greatly influenced by the Copernican theory and in his work there were no clear dividing lines between physiology, psychology, general physics and cosmology. For Descartes, occult phenomena were either unreal or had mechanical explanations: 'there are', he wrote, 'no powers in stones and plants that are so mysterious, and no marvels attributed to sympathetic and antipathetic influences that are so astonishing, that they cannot be explained in this way. In short, there is nothing in the whole of nature (nothing, that is, which should be referred to purely corporeal causes, i.e. those devoid of thought and mind) which is incapable of being deductively explained on the basis of these selfsame principles ...'[67] He did not reject the role of religion in science: he claimed that he would retain the religion in which, by the grace of God, he had been brought up. He maintained that the laws of the material universe were established by God, and that mathematical and other 'truths' could not exist without a prior divine authority which implants such knowledge. And yet

Descartes's method of reasoning might lead the enquirer to doubt the very existence of God. In his famous statement 'I am thinking, therefore I exist (*Cogito, ergo sum*)'[68] he accepted as certainty only what was self-evident, and found such self-evident certainty only in his own consciousness. Once he had established his own being, Descartes derived the existence of God from a specific act of his own consciousness, the recognition of a perfection which he did not possess, and which must have proceeded from perfection itself, namely from God.

Descartes asserted that all knowledge of truth was implanted by God, yet his philosophy opened the door to atheism since it made an absolute distinction between mind and matter and did not depend at all upon the revelation of the Scriptures. In the *Principles of Philosophy*, Descartes provided two levels of explanation for the motion of parts of matter. The primary cause 'it seems obvious to me' (*videtur* in the Latin, *il me semble que* in the French, reflecting uncertainty), he wrote, was God.[69] However, after creation, God's role was reduced merely to conserving matter in motion ('God likewise always preserves the same quantity of motion in matter').[70] As for the laws of nature, these were described as nothing more than the laws of motion, 'with the whole visible universe as if it were a machine: I have considered only the various shapes and movements of its parts'.[71] Even in the *Treatise of Man*, he produced a mechanistic model: 'these functions follow from the mere arrangement of the machine's organs every bit as naturally as the movements of a clock or other automaton follow from the arrangement of its counter-weights and wheels'.[72] Where in all this was the soul? Descartes saw the human body as a machine; he thought physics would provide a foundation for morality, rather than vice versa. It is not surprising that Descartes's works were placed on the Index of prohibited books in 1663, although his ideas endured as an authoritative and influential system.

It has been argued that despite his contempt for scholasticism, Descartes sought for himself the authority of a new Aristotle, while the new scientific movement ('Cartesianism', as it was called after him) became ultimately a sterile bulwark against innovation and a philosophical justification for religious orthodoxy. 'It may be doubted', it has been said by the distinguished historian of science A. R. Hall, 'whether the Cartesian philosophy of science ever produced a single useful thought, save in the mind of its originator.'[73] Such a judgement may seem excessively severe, given the intellectual ebullience of the Paris school of scientists gathered initially around the figure of Marin Mersenne and the fact the *Principles of Philosophy* of 1644 inaugurated a mechanistic theory of the universe which was not completely displaced until 1687, with the publication of Newton's *Principia*. Descartes died in

1650, but whatever judgement one forms of the Cartesian world-view, there can be no doubt that his legacy was enduring and that it was the prevailing intellectual viewpoint in the second half of the seventeenth century: the predominant culture was French, and it was in France that Cartesianism made its greatest impact. By 1660, the world itself could never again be viewed in the way that it had been in 1500. The rationalist, even mechanistic, view of the generation of Descartes had come to replace (albeit after a long and tortuous—sometimes even a circuitous—process) the humanist, but relatively credulous, generation of Erasmus. This was the result of a century-and-a-half of intellectual ferment, but it was also a measure of the widening gulf between élite culture and popular culture. As science shook itself free from the twin influences of religion and the occult, and as intellectual debate became widespread in cultivated *salon* society, so what we think of as popular culture increasingly took on its form as 'low' culture without élite participation.

10

CONCLUSION
THE EUROPEAN DYNASTIC STATES

No family has ever attained such greatness and power by means of kinship and matrimonial alliances as the House of Austria ... and because this means of aggrandisement is both just and peaceful it must be considered as secure and lasting above all others ... Only among the French, who hold by some Salic Law of unknown origin (which excludes all women from the Crown of France) is there no possibility of using this system of kinship for increasing the size of a ruler's possessions.

THUS wrote Giovanni Botero in his *Reason of State*, which appeared in 1589.[1] For most of the period 1494–1660, the majority of the European monarchies were not nation states as we understand them today. They were dynastic conglomerations acquired through inheritance, either from father to son or from another relative who produced no direct male heir of his own; through marriage alliances; or (more unusually) from accidental fortunes of war. The union of Castile and Burgundy would not have happened had not Don Juan, the heir to the Castilian throne, died unexpectedly in 1497. The collapse of Burgundy in 1477 on the death of Charles the Bold, the last male Valois duke, strikingly illustrates the problem of holding together such an inheritance. To the modern eye, some of these dynastic states seem very odd indeed, and would appear to have had no future. Their various geographic components seemed too disparate in terms of culture, language and institutions. Often they appeared indefensible because they were separated from each other by large tracts of sea or by intervening hostile states within the land mass of continental Europe; certainly there were formidable logistical difficulties in governing a kingdom such as Alfonso V of Aragon held in the fifteenth century, or above all, Charles V's in the first half of the sixteenth. In some cases, even in western Europe, the geographical boundaries of states were not clearly settled. A general territorial uncertainty hung over eastern Europe after the partition of Hungary; it was exacerbated during the conflicts between Poland and Sweden and between Muscovy and Lithuania; and it was made manifest in the transfer of the Ukraine to Muscovy in 1654.

Unstable boundaries were not the only source of dispute: existing empires and kingdoms could be divided by rulers, while new dynastic states could arise which challenged those already in existence. The division of the inheritance of Charles V in 1555–6 is a well-known example of partition. It is less well known (because the threat was averted) that little more than a decade earlier an anti-Habsburg state might have emerged on the Lower Rhine as a result of marriage alliances, centred on Cleves–Jülich, with dynastic links to Guelders. Ominously for Charles V, it would have acted in alliance with France, had not his victory in the war for the duchy of Guelders (1542–3) dashed the prospect of such a state's emergence. Other dynastic unions overcame a relatively unpromising start. The Habsburgs, for example, survived a number of challenges in the majority of their Burgundian provinces and in the entirety of Castile until the extinction of the dynasty in 1700. The potential for survival or growth of dynastic states even in the sixteenth and seventeenth centuries was greater than it has sometimes appeared to historians.

How could such (apparently) insecurely based kingdoms survive and even develop? One answer might lie in the innate conservatism of their rulers and institutions. A dynastic state was in essence a personal union of territories. In institutional terms, the state was unified only in the person of its prince. Most rulers had enclaves of territory within their states which owed allegiance to another prince, but which might be confiscated as a bargaining counter in time of war. In each component territory, the ruler might boast a different title. If the prince had any sense, he took care not to attempt to abolish the local customs and institutions of his different lands. The 'legitimate' ruler was thus not only the prince with a legal title to rule but, by extension, one who preserved the 'liberties' of his different peoples. Constitutional conservatism on the part of the prince might increase the loyalty of his subjects towards the ruling dynasty. The power of some princes within their territories developed faster than that of others, but all princes had to take care that this process did not take place at a rate unacceptable to what—for want of a better term—we may call the 'political classes' in their lands. This was one reason why, to the modern eye, states were so annoyingly, so inconveniently, slow to develop—why no 'absolute king' in theory enjoyed absolute power in practice. The theoretical power of the king had to be free from restriction to offset the practical limitations on his power. This is why the terms 'absolutism' and 'centralization' should be used with caution in the history of early modern Europe. After all, they were formulated as concepts only during the French Revolution.

Yet there were some unmistakeable signs that the disparate states formed by dynastic ties were becoming more difficult to manage in the course of the sixteenth century. In the Empire, for example, the revolt of the Lutheran princes in 1551–2 unleashed propaganda in favour of

Henri II of France and against the succession of Philip II; it was feared that Philip would introduce a form of rule that would leave Germany servient to Spain. However, in this case, the crisis was resolved by Charles V's decision to abdicate and partition his inheritance. At the end of the century, the Swedish rebellion against Sigismund of Poland clearly demonstrated that a 'foreign' ruler of the wrong religion who did not reside in the country could not hope to retain his throne: but dynastic loyalties remained strong. Even when it deposed Sigismund, the Swedish diet was prepared to vest the succession in his son, Ladislas, provided that he was educated as a Lutheran in Sweden.

Clearly, religious differences played a crucial role in the development of opposition to the idea of the dynastic state. Looking back on the whole course of the Dutch Revolt, Philip Marnix, the leading councillor of William of Orange, considered that the Emperor Charles V had been 'the original cause of all our calamities, since with his absolute power, and without the advice of the estates, he had given orders at Worms for the placards [suppressing heresy] . . .'[2] Religious divisions tended to give birth to opposition groups who looked to foreign rulers for support for their causes. Yet in Germany, where the schism originated, the ruling dynasty and the institutions of the Empire remained largely unchallenged from 1555 until 1618, and survived even the great trauma of the Thirty Years' War. Why should this be? There were always some Protestant princes, such as the elector of Saxony, who in certain circumstances were prepared to throw in their lot with the Catholic Emperor, or whose loyalty to the concept of empire was greater than their desire for a Protestant protector from outside. Catholic princes such as the duke of Bavaria might enter into treaties with other foreign powers. Even in the religious wars in the Low Countries and France, the Protestants were reluctant to break their ties of allegiance to the legitimate sovereign.

The most telling example of this conservatism occurred during the Dutch revolt when the States General negotiated with the duc d'Anjou to secure a ruler *before* they deposed Philip II. The arguments against the dynastic state of Charles V and Philip II were clearly expressed in these negotiations which led to the Treaty of Plessis-lez-Tours (September 1580). Firstly, in a dynastic state the risk was that a ruler might become an absentee, as had Philip II. It might have taken the Dutch twenty years to protest against his absenteeism, but they were not going to repeat the same mistake with Anjou: if he went abroad, he was to leave a governor who was to the satisfaction of the States General. Secondly, the Netherlands was not to be incorporated into the kingdom of France as a result of this alliance with Anjou. This might lead either to an absentee ruler or—'a worse inconvenience'—government by foreigners: the 'ancient hatred' of the Spaniards for the Low Countries, and the experience of rule by the duke of Alba, had taught them that it could never again be tolerated. Anjou's French advisers (with one exception) were to be excluded from participation in the Dutch council of state: 'Frenchmen should hold office in France . . .' Anjou was obliged to take the customary solemn oath before each province (as, indeed, Philip II had done in 1549) as well as a general one before the States General; moreover, he had to observe every clause of the Treaty of Plessis-lez-Tours. Any lapse on his part would free the States General from their oath of obedience and empower them to 'take another prince, or otherwise provide for their affairs, as they found suitable'. Anjou and his advisers argued strongly against the inclusion of this clause, which they thought likely to encourage 'very dangerous rebellions and revolts', and also at the denial of the title of 'sovereign' for Anjou. But they protested in vain. The Dutch negotiators were firm on all points: if to be a 'sovereign' meant enjoying absolute power, they asserted, then this was against their 'laws, customs and privileges'.[3]

A dynastic ruler's legal title to a throne might be contested because of rival interpretations of the law of succession. During the early modern period, the chances of there being an undisputed adult, male succession at any one time were slim. Thus the development of royal or princely power was severely limited. Different European countries had different laws of succession. Some were elective monarchies, duchies or principalities; the majority were not. In France, succession through the female line was barred, as was the right of women to succeed to the throne, although this rule—the so-called Salic Law—was challenged in the later sixteenth century and was not definitively proclaimed as a 'fundamental law' until 1593. In Castile and England, however, there was no similar prohibition on female rulers, and both states had queens of some distinction in the fifteenth and sixteenth centuries. It was possible for a dynastic union to break up because of different succession laws applying in various parts of the state; alternative candidates might succeed in the component territories according to the local custom. When alternative candidates were also of different religious affiliations, the risks of protracted conflict and the collapse of the dynastic state increased proportionately. European history is littered with wars of succession, many of which were fought over key strategic areas for very high stakes.

The German principalities were weakened by the absence of any law of primogeniture applying within the Empire as a whole. The Great Elector Frederick William managed to escape from Polish suzerainty over his duchy of Prussia in 1657; he diminished the power of the estates in his various lands and he established a standing army financed by permanent taxes under electoral control. The rise of Brandenburg-Prussia under the Great Elector has been seen as an inevitable development. Yet at his death in 1688, a lifetime's work might have been thrown away because he was prepared to partition his lands among his four sons. In the long term, the Hohenzollerns were more successful than their German rivals simply because they prevented such partitions and they were more determined to enforce their authority over their united lands. The contrast with Hesse under landgrave Philip could not be more striking. Hesse had played an important role in the first generation of the Reformation, but on Philip's death in 1567 his lands were partitioned between four sons. Although two of these ruling lines died out, the division between Hesse-Cassel and Hesse-Darmstadt became permanent. Their rulers quarrelled over the partition of the other two Hesse principalities, and the dispute was exacerbated by religious differences, since the duke of Hesse-Cassel became a Calvinist in 1605 though his subjects were Lutheran. Other, more important states than Hesse fragmented, as did Bavaria between 1410 and 1505, Saxony between 1485 and 1547, and the Austrian Habsburg lands between 1564 and 1618. Only when the laws of primogeniture were adopted by territories, for example by the Wittelsbachs in 1506 and the Austrian Habsburgs in 1621, could partition and the consequent instability of state boundaries be avoided. It has been argued that Protestant princes tended to cling to the concept of partible inheritance for religious reasons, since the Lutheran family ideal enjoined equal care for all the offspring of a dynasty. It was easier for Catholic rulers to place their children in ecclesiastical benefices, which helped overcome the dangers of partible inheritance; but perhaps it was not until the crisis of the Thirty Years' War and the waning of religious fervour that there was general acceptance of primogeniture among the German princes.

Beyond the complicated influence of the laws of succession, however, lies another fundamental problem, that of ensuring the survival of the dynasty through an adequate supply of heirs. Too few sons, and a ruling dynasty risked extinction; too many sons, and the dynastic state might be dismembered if the ruler came under pressure to divide his lands between his sons, or to establish temporary fiefs (apanages) for them. The sons, in turn, could create new dynasties from their own marriages and in time these new families could challenge the founding dynasty. The struggle between France and Burgundy in the fifteenth century resulted from precisely such a state of affairs, both ruling lines descending from the Valois family. By the 1550s the Habsburgs had a similar problem, with the growth of a new and dangerous rivalry between the 'Spanish' and 'Austrian' branches. A ruler could never be absolutely sure that he had the right number of potential heirs, even when by the law of averages there should have been no problem. For example, Henri II died in 1559 leaving four under-aged sons: but within thirty years all were dead, without having produced a legitimate male heir between them. The Valois dynasty was thus extinguished.

Another great problem for the dynastic state was defence in time of war. European states experienced some difficulty in gearing themselves up to the challenge of war in the early modern period because of rising prices: the costs of government, but more seriously, the costs of armies, rose enormously. Numbers under arms grew dramatically. Taxes had to be increased to meet the spiralling military budget. War stirred up discontent, imposed severe strains on the institutional and administrative capacity of the state, and tested the loyalty of the subjects to their prince. The largest states had the greatest difficulties in organizing and financing their own defence, and could fall an easy prey to their enemies unless some other factors came into play; the Habsburg monarchy, for example, was saved by the imports into Spain of bullion from the New World in the sixteenth century. The greater the extent of the dynastic union, the greater the diversity of its institutions and subjects. A dynastic state was thus ill-equipped to meet the challenge of war because of the absence of common institutions, the lack of a permanent army or a common defence fund. Each component territory argued that it would fight, and perhaps even pay for, its own war but not someone else's—even if they shared the same dynastic ruler. What was needed was an 'absolute' ruler, with the power to overcome regional particularism in an overriding national—or dynastic—emergency: in one such crisis, in 1543, the Emperor Charles V imposed a universal tax in the Netherlands without the consent of the representative institutions on the basis of his 'absolute power'.[4]

There was some progress in the period from 1494 to 1660, with the strengthening of monarchical ambitions and self-confidence, and above all, the growth in the capacity of the state to enforce its will on its subjects. Institutional and fiscal change had only partially been achieved in most of the European states by 1660. In France, for example, the state's fiscal needs had led to a massive change in the social structure of the kingdom through the sale of offices over a period of more than a hundred years. A class of royal officials who owned their offices as private property had been established; they were very numerous in 1660, and their wealth and political influence was incomparably greater than it had been at the beginning of the sixteenth century. Within the limits of a kingdom, the state was able to influence the movement of the economy to a much greater extent in 1660 than at the beginning of the sixteenth century: the instruments of tariff control and fiscal and monetary policy were used in a systematic way in the perceived interests of the 'state' which would not have been possible in 1500. For the first time, economic rivalry between states could assume primacy over the more traditional form of dynastic conflict: the first Anglo-Dutch war of 1652–4, fought between two republics, is a significant precursor of later continental wars in which economic and colonial rivalry were important aspects. States began to use embargoes systematically as an instrument of military policy, with devastating effect for the economy in general and the trade of those states which were singled out as the object of these embargoes in particular. The Spanish trade embargo in the period 1621–47 was largely effective in curbing Dutch trade with the Iberian peninsula. Where, as in the Baltic, the Dutch could use sea-power to protect their trade, the interests of the state took precedence over diplomatic niceties in dealings with, for example, Denmark and Sweden who, on occasion, might threaten Dutch supremacy in the region. The age of 'mercantilism' had already arrived by 1620.

Yet the rise of the modern state was incomplete in 1660. The great wars of Louis XIV's reign would still be infused with a substantial element of dynastic rivalry, in which the older conception of the dynastic state vied with the more modern idea of the impersonal state in which the function of kingship was that of an office. The Allied pamphlets condemned the principle that the state was 'owned' by the ruler, who could dispose of it according to his whim, as Carlos II of Spain was to do in 1700: 'everyone knows', proclaimed one of their most important pamphlets, 'that kingship is an office, an administration, giving kings no proprietary possession'.[5] In 1660, monarchies were still considered to be dynastic states, perhaps even in England, despite the significance of the English Revolution and the return of Charles II to his kingdom on terms set by parliament. Such traditional views might prevail, as in France under Louis XIV, even in circumstances in which they ran contrary to the interests of preserving peace after earlier devastating wars. This suggests the essential conservatism of contemporary political theory. The ideological strengthening of monarchy in the period between 1500 and 1660 was much more significant than any fiscal or institutional development within the state itself. This is illustrated by the striking developments in political theory (see chapter 6.1), in the development of a court culture (see chapter 9.1) and in the ways in which power was presented by visual and propaganda means (see chapter 9.2).

As a result of these developments, the state certainly *seemed* much stronger than ever before, and this illusion was in itself important in helping to increase its power: people were more willing to put up with the encroachment of the state, partly because they felt that they were powerless to prevent it, but more importantly because they were committed to the ideals of dynastic monarchy and to the particular aspirations of rulers as presented in imagery, ceremonial and written propaganda. The techniques of presenting the state's objectives had become much more sophisticated between 1500 and 1660; at the same time the 'audience', the ruler's subjects, had become much better informed as a result of the development of education and printing. For Bossuet, one of the main proponents of the power of Louis XIV, government was a work of 'reason and intelligence' (*un ouvrage de raison et d'intelligence*).[6] Bossuet provided four characteristics of monarchical power: according to him, it was 'sacred'; it was 'paternal'; it was 'absolute, that is to say, independent'; finally it was 'subject to reason' (*soumise à la raison*).[7] None of these first three characteristics was new: monarchy was thought to be divinely ordained as an institution; in France, it was arranged on the principle of male primogeniture; there, the power of the monarch was considered to be absolute, that is, subject to no institutional restraint. But the theory that monarchy had to justify itself by good government, that 'the prince's wisdom made his people happy',[8] that 'wisdom rather than force was the safety of states',[9] while not new, assumed greater significance in an age when the intellectual trend was itself one of rationalism (see chapter 9.5.4).

The idea that government should, and indeed could, be organized on rational lines for rational purposes is perhaps a delusion, but one which seems to have been accepted within the European dynastic states by 1660. That war should no longer be fought chiefly about religious principles might seem to be an enduring legacy of the Peace of Westphalia which ended the Thirty Years' War in 1648. The theory of a European 'states system' in which wars might still be fought, but for limited objectives, with limited consequences (above all, they should pose no threat to the internal structure of the state itself) was also a rational idea which assumed some significance in the aftermath of the great trauma of the Thirty Years' War. A distinction needs to be made in dealings between states of whatever religious denomination, where secular interests prevailed throughout the seventeenth century, and the internal organization of states, where religious considerations were still paramount. Although we may begin to perceive the beginnings of a separation of religion from politics in this new age of rationalism, as Cromwell discovered in the 1650s, this was the slowest of all developments in the early modern state. The dynastic state had been displaced by the idea of kingship as an office and the beginnings of the modern 'impersonal state' long before secular principles assumed primacy over religious ones in the internal ordering of states. The great religious divisions and conflicts of the early modern period had left a deep and enduring impression upon a society struggling to cast off the medieval for the modern world.

Maps

Map 1. The Holy Roman Empire

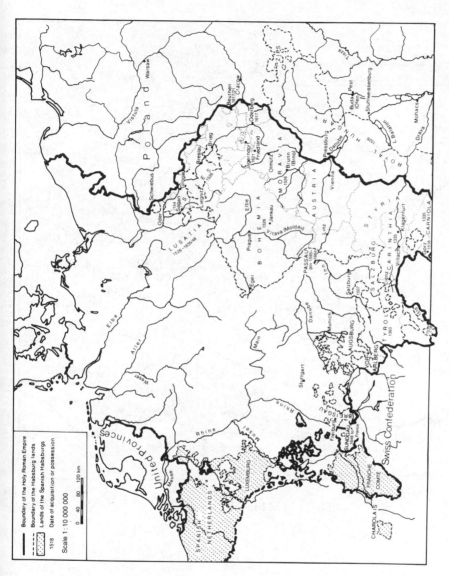

Map 2. The Austrian Habsburg Lands

Maps

Map 3. The French Provinces

Map 4. The Italian Peninsula during the Italian Wars

Map 5.   The Iberian Peninsula

Map 6. The Low Countries

Map 7. The Baltic

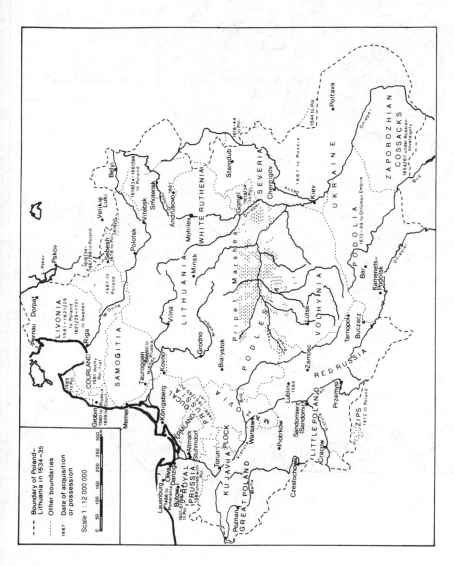

Map 8. Poland–Lithuania

Map 9. Muscovy

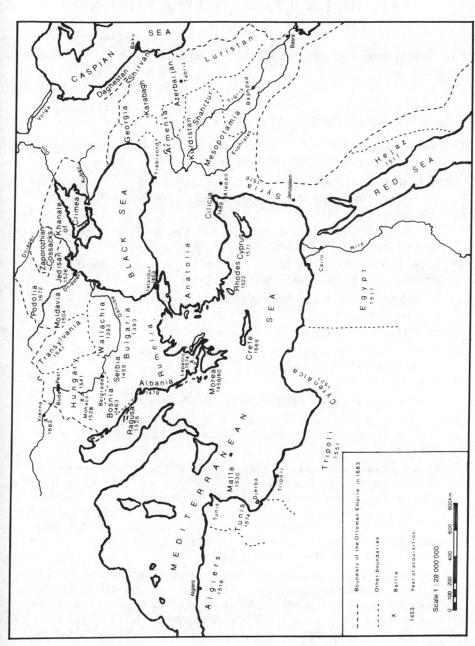

Map 10. The Ottoman Lands

SOURCES FOR QUOTATIONS

Note: In accordance with the conventions for the series, only direct quotations are attributed.

1 Religious Divisions in Early Modern Europe (pp. 1–76)

[The author is indebted to Dr A. C. Duke of the University of Southampton for his comments on this section and for certain of the references which he supplied.]

1. D. R. Kelley, *The Beginning of Ideology: Consciousness and Society in the French Reformation* (1981), pp. 63, 224. P. Zagorin, *Rebels and Rulers, 1500–1660* (1982), i. 140, 148.

2. For the condemnation of Luther: *Martin Luther*, ed. E. G. Rupp and B. Drewery (repr. 1979), pp. 61–2.

3. C. M. D. Crowder, *Unity, Heresy and Reform, 1378–1460: The Conciliar Response to the Grand Schism* (1977), pp. 179–81.

4. F. Oakley, 'Conciliarism at the Fifth Lateran Council?', *Church History*, 41 (1972), 459–61.

5. *Martin Luther*, ed. Rupp and Drewery, p. 21.

6. D. Weinstein, *Savonarola and Florence: Prophecy and Patriotism in the Renaissance* (1970), p. 157.

7. Ibid. 288.

8. E. J. Dempsey-Douglass, *Justification in Late Medieval Preaching* . . . (1966), p. 101 n. 3.

9. J. H. Overfield, *Humanism and Scholasticism in Late Medieval Germany* (1984), p. 49.

10. M. A. Screech, *Ecstasy and the Praise of Folly* (1980), p. 13. 'Do you not know, Christian warrior', Erasmus wrote, 'that you gave yourself completely to Christ when you experienced the mysteries of baptism . . . ? What else does the sign of the cross on the forehead mean, than that you, as long as you live, will serve under his banners?': E. W. Kohls, 'The principal theological thoughts in the *Enchiridion militis Christiani*', *Essays on the Works of Erasmus*, ed. R. L. DeMolen (1978), p. 61.

11. Erasmus defined his *philosophia Christi* in the Exhortation (*Paraclesis*) to readers of his New Testament (1516). 'What else is the philosophy of Christ, which He himself calls a rebirth', he wrote, 'than the restoration of human nature originally well formed? . . . If we seek a model for life, why does another example take precedence for us over that of Christ himself?': *Essays on the Works of Erasmus*, ed. DeMolen, p. 24.

12. B. M. G. Reardon, *Religious Thought in the Reformation* (1981), p. 34.

13. Ibid. 43.

14. Variant translations: S. E. Ozment, *The Age of Reform: An Intellectual and Religious History of Late Medieval and Reformation Europe* (1980), p. 290. L. B. Spitz, *The Religious Renaissance of the German Humanists* (1963), p. 231. Reardon, *Religious Thought in the Reformation*, p. 40.

15. *Luther's Works. XLI. Church and Ministry* (1966), p. 194.

16. E. G. Rupp, *The Righteousness of God: Luther Studies* (repr. 1953), pp. 234–5, 317–18.

17. *Martin Luther*, ed. Rupp and Drewery, p. 53.

18. *Luther and Erasmus: Free Will and Salvation*, ed. E. G. Rupp, P. S. Watson *et al.*, p. 104. Ozment, *The Age of Reform*, p. 298.

19. G. Strauss, *Luther's House of Learning: The Indoctrination of the Young in the German Reformation* (1978), p. 82.

20. Overfield, *Humanism and Scholasticism in Late Medieval Germany*, pp. 284, 287.

21. Ibid. 289.

22. Reardon, *Religious Thought in the Reformation*, p. 40.

23. *Martin Luther*, ed. Rupp and Drewery, pp. 36–40. Inexplicably, the 41st proposition was not reprinted by Rupp and Drewery. Consult *Documents Illustrative of the Continental Reformation*, ed. B. J. Kidd (repr. 1967), p. 78.

24. *Martin Luther*, ed. Rupp and Drewery, p. 60. *New Cambridge Modern History*, ii. 82.

25. Variant translation in E. G. Rupp, *The Righteousness of God: Luther Studies* (repr. 1963), p. 122. *Martin Luther*, ed. Rupp and Drewery, p. 6. Ozment, *The Age of Reform*, p. 230.

26. Ibid.

27. *Martin Luther*, ed. Rupp and Drewery, p. 51.

28. Luther denied the Papal power of the keys and the medieval concept of the 'treasures of the Church' in theses 26 and 56 against indulgences: ibid. 20, 22. He denied the power of the keys more generally in the *Address to the Christian Nobility of the German Nation* and in *The Babylonian Captivity of the Church*: ibid. 44, 49.

29. S. E. Ozment, *The Reformation in the Cities: The Appeal of Protestantism to Sixteenth-Century Germany and Switzerland* (repr. 1980), p. 50. T. N. Tentler, *Sin and Confession on the Eve of the Reformation* (1977), p. 359.

30. Ozment, *The Reformation in the Cities*, p. 51.

31. *Martin Luther: Selections from His Writings . . .*, ed. J. Dillenberger (1961), p. 345.

32. Ibid.

33. Strauss, *Luther's House of Learning: The Indoctrination of the Young in the German Reformation*, pp. 123–4.

34. Ibid. 152–3.

35. Ibid. 211.

36. Reardon, *Religious Thought in the Reformation*, p. 58. *Martin Luther*, ed. Rupp and Drewery, p. 53.

37. Strauss, *Luther's House of Learning: The Indoctrination of the Young in the German Reformation*, p. 212.

38. Ibid. 33.

39. Ibid. 4.

40. Ibid. 95.

41. Ozment, *The Reformation in the Cities*, p. 144.

42. A. G. Dickens, *The German Nation and Martin Luther* (1974), p. 101.

43. Ozment, *The Reformation in the Cities*, p. 141.

44. Strauss, *Luther's House of Learning: The Indoctrination of the Young in the German Reformation*, p. 251.

45. Ozment, *The Reformation in the Cities*, pp. 109–10.

46. Ozment, *The Age of Reform*, p. 282.

47. *Martin Luther: Selections from His Writings* . . ., ed. Dillenberger, p. 371. *Martin Luther*, ed. Rupp and Drewery, p. 109.

48. *Martin Luther: Selections from His Writings* . . ., ed. Dillenberger, p. 53. *Martin Luther*, ed. Rupp and Drewery, p. 50.

49. G. H. Williams, *The Radical Reformation* (1962), p. 76. E. G. Rupp, *Patterns of Reformation* (1969), p. 240.

50. Variant translations in Ozment, *The Age of Reform*, p. 284. H. G. Koenigsberger, 'The Reformation and social revolution', *The Reformation Crisis*, ed. J. Hurstfield (1965), p. 90. *Martin Luther*, ed. Rupp and Drewery, p. 122.

51. Strauss, *Luther's House of Learning: The Indoctrination of the Young in the German Reformation*, p. 300.

52. E. G. Rupp, 'Luther against "the Turk, the Pope and the Devil"', *Seven-Headed Luther* . . ., ed. P. N. Brooks (1983), p. 257.

53. Ibid. 258.

54. B. Nelson, *The Idea of Usury: From Tribal Brotherhood to Universal Otherhood* (2nd edn., 1969), pp. 50–1.

55. *Luther and Erasmus: Free Will and Salvation*, ed. Rupp, Watson *et al.*, p. 45.

56. *Huldrych Zwingli*, ed. G. R. Potter (1978), p. 41.

57. T. Bergsten, *Bulthasar Hubmaier: Anabaptist Theologian and Martyr*, trans. I. J. Barnes and W. R. Estep (1978), pp. 293–4.

58. *Huldrych Zwingli*, ed. Potter, p. 43.

59. *The Reformation: A Narrative History Related by Contemporary Observers and Participants*, ed. H. J. Hillerbrand (1964), p. 237.

60. Ibid. 235–8.

61. K. Deppermann, *Melchior Hoffman: Social Unrest and Apocalyptic Visions in the Age of Reformation*, trans. M. Wren (1987), pp. 80, 251–2, 265.

62. Williams, *The Radical Reformation*, p. 839. Variant translation in Deppermann, *Melchior Hoffman*, p. 225: 'Thus it is the same for everyman, be he Jew, Turk or Christian; he will be judged as a person for what he has done in the light of the knowledge he has, to the extent that he has seen the truth.' Variant translation in *Spiritual and Anabaptist Writers*, ed. G. H. Williams and A. H. Mergal (1957), p. 192: 'For all men are called ... but no one has been elected except for them who have struggled through to victory. And in case of them struggle and conquer, all of them should also be elected by God ... His will rather is that all come to repentance, receive the knowledge of truth, and be saved.'

63. *John Calvin*, ed. G. R. Potter and M. Greengrass (1983), p. 115.

64. *Martin Luther: Selections from His Writings ...*, ed. Dillenberger, p. 267. Reardon, *Religious Thought in the Reformation*, p. 78.

65. *Martin Luther*, ed. Rupp and Drewery, p. 146. For the analogy of the iron in the fire: ibid. 48.

66. Ibid. 132–5.

67. Reardon, *Religious Thought in the Reformation*, p. 109.

68. *Martin Luther*, ed. Rupp and Drewery, p. 138. *Huldrych Zwingli*, ed. Potter, p. 106.

69. Ozment, *The Age of Reform*, p. 337.

70. Reardon, *Religious Thought in the Reformation*, p. 141. F. Wendel, *Calvin: The Origins and Development of His Religious Thought*, trans. P. Mairet (repr. 1965), p. 135.

71. Wendel, *Calvin*, pp. 338–9. T. H. L. Parker, *John Calvin: A Biography* (1975), pp. 43–6, 136–8. Reardon, *Religious Thought in the Reformation*, p. 201.

72. *Martin Luther: Selections from His Writings ...*, ed. Dillenberger, pp. 405–6.

73. J. Lortz, *The Reformation in Germany* (German edn., 1939–40; trans. R. Walls, 1968), i. 309.

74. Ibid. i. 318–19.

75. A. C. Duke, 'The face of popular religious dissent in the Low Countries, 1520–1530', *Journal of Ecclesiastical History*, 26 (1975), 44.

76. Ibid. 62. Ozment, *The Reformation in the Cities*, p. 146.

77. A. O. Hancock, 'Philipp of Hesse's view of the relationship of prince and church', *Church History*, 35 (1966), 162.

78. Variant translations in S. A. Fischer-Galati, *Ottoman Imperialism and*

German Protestantism, 1521–1555 (1959), p. 26; K. Brandi, *Charles V,* trans. C. V. Wedgwood (1939, repr. 1965), p. 246; *New Cambridge Modern History,* ii. 340.

79. Q. Skinner, *The Foundations of Modern Political Thought* (2 vols., 1978), ii. 202. Contrast Luther's earlier view: ibid. ii. 196–7. In 1539, Luther denied that the Empire was an absolute monarchy: W. D. J. Cargill-Thompson, *The Political Thought of Martin Luther* (1984), p. 108.

80. Dickens, *The German Nation and Martin Luther,* p. 109.

81. *La Réforme et le livre: l'Europe de l'imprimé, 1517 vers 1570,* ed. J.-F. Gilmont (1990), p. 481.

82. R. Gawthorp and G. Strauss, 'Protestantism and literacy in early modern Germany', *Past and Present,* 104 (1984), 34.

83. Ibid. 35.

84. *La Réforme et le livre,* ed. Gilmont, p. 487.

85. Gawthorp and Strauss, 'Protestantism and literacy in early modern Germany', p. 35.

86. G. R. Potter, 'Zwingli and Calvin', *The Reformation Crisis,* ed. Hurstfield, p. 33.

87. R. W. Scribner, *For the Sake of Simple Folk: Popular Propaganda for the German Reformation* (1981), frontispiece and p. 244.

88. Ibid. 250.

89. *La Réforme et le livre,* ed. Gilmont, p. 212.

90. Ibid. 62.

91. M. Hannemann, *The Diffusion of the Reformation in South-Western Germany, 1518–34* (1974), p. 150.

92. Ibid. 22.

93. *Huldrych Zwingli,* ed. Potter, p. 15.

94. Variant translations in ibid. 26 and Ozment, *The Reformation in the Cities,* p. 145.

95. *Huldrych Zwingli,* ed. Potter, p. 32.

96. J. W. Baker, *Heinrich Bullinger and the Covenant: The Other Reformed Tradition* (1980), pp. 15–16.

97. Ibid. 17.

98. *Huldrych Zwingli,* ed. Potter, p. 42.

99. Ibid. 126.

100. Ibid. 133.

101. G. Berthoud, *Antoine Marcourt. Réformateur et pamphlétaire: du 'Livre des Marchands' aux placards de 1534* (1973), p. 287.

102. D. J. Nicholls, 'The nature of popular heresy in France, 1520–42', *Historical Journal,* 26 (1983), 274.

103. L. J. Abray, *The People's Reformation: Magistrates, Clergy and Commons in Strasbourg, 1500–98* (1985), p. 178. Idem, 'The laity's religion: Lutheranism in sixteenth-century Strasbourg', *The German People and the Reformation*, ed. R. Po-chia Hsia (1988), pp. 228–9.

104. W. J. Bouwsma, *John Calvin: A Sixteenth-Century Portrait* (1988), p. 84.

105. Ibid. 84, 192.

106. H. Höpfl, *The Christian Polity of John Calvin* (1982), p. 19.

107. Bouwsma, *John Calvin: A Sixteenth-Century Portrait*, pp. 126–7.

108. Ibid. 139–40, 142–3.

109. Ibid. 173. Variant translations in *John Calvin*, ed. G. E. Duffield (1966), p. 103; *Calvin: Institutes of the Christian Religion*, ed. J. T. McNeill (1960), i. xxxiii; *John Calvin*, ed. Potter and Greengrass, p. 30; Reardon, *Religious Thought in the Reformation*, p. 191.

110. Baker, *Heinrich Bullinger and the Covenant: The Other Reformed Tradition*, p. 37.

111. *New Cambridge Modern History*, iii. 83.

112. A. E. McGrath, *The Intellectual Origins of the European Reformation* (1987), p. 6 n. 9.

113. *John Calvin*, ed. Potter and Greengrass, pp. 37–8.

114. Bouwsma, *John Calvin: A Sixteenth-Century Portrait*, p. 173.

115. Höpfl, *The Christian Polity of John Calvin*, p. 233.

116. Bouwsma, *John Calvin: A Sixteenth-Century Portrait*, pp. 89, 181.

117. Ibid. 183.

118. Ibid. 187.

119. Ibid. 169.

120. Ibid. 96.

121. Ibid. 74. *John Calvin*, ed. Potter and Greengrass, p. 32.

122. Bouwsma, *John Calvin: A Sixteenth-Century Portrait*, p. 46.

123. E. W. Monter, *Calvin's Geneva* (1967), pp. 35–44, 66. N. M. Sutherland, *The Huguenot Struggle for Recognition* (1980), pp. 101, 352.

124. *Documents Illustrative of the Continental Reformation*, ed. Kidd, p. 519. Monter, *Calvin's Geneva*, p. 56. *John Calvin*, ed. Potter and Greengrass, p. 48.

125. Bouwsma, *John Calvin: A Sixteenth-Century Portrait*, p. 22.

126. Ibid. 219.

127. Ibid. 211.

128. Ibid. 50.

129. *John Calvin*, ed. Potter and Greengrass, p. 76.

130. Bouwsma, *John Calvin: A Sixteenth-Century Portrait*, p. 218.

131. Ibid. 101.

132. Ibid. 223.

133. R. M. Kingdon, *Geneva and the Consolidation of the French Protestant Movement, 1564–1572* ... (1967), p. 63.

134. *John Calvin*, ed. Duffield, p. 36.

135. C. Bangs, *Arminius: A Study in the Dutch Reformation* (1971), p. 262.

136. Bouwsma, *John Calvin: A Sixteenth-Century Portrait*, p. 216.

137. *John Calvin*, ed. Potter and Greengrass, p. 145.

138. Ibid. 146.

139. Ibid. 152.

140. Bouwsma, *John Calvin: A Sixteenth-Century Portrait*, pp. 221–2.

141. A. C. Duke, 'The Ambivalent Face of Calvinism in the Netherlands, 1561–1618', *International Calvinism, 1541–1715*, ed. M. Prestwich (1985), p. 129.

142. Ibid. 130.

143. *New Cambridge Modern History*, iii. 83.

144. H. J. Cohn, 'The Territorial Princes in Germany's Second Reformation, 1559–1622', *International Calvinism, 1541–1715*, ed. Prestwich, p. 151.

145. M. Prestwich, 'Calvinism in France, 1555–1629', *International Calvinism, 1541–1715*, ed. Prestwich, p. 84.

146. A. G. Dickens, *The Counter-Reformation* (1968), p. 98.

147. H. Jedin, *A History of the Council of Trent* (2 vols., 1957–61), ii. 207, 210–11.

148. P. Sarpi, *History of Benefices and Selections from History of the Council of Trent*, ed. P. Burke (1967), p. 117.

149. Lortz, *The Reformation in Germany*, ii. 305. Jedin, *A History of the Council of Trent*, ii. 159.

150. N. S. Davidson, *The Counter-Reformation* (1987), p. 9.

151. J. Martin, 'Salvation and society in sixteenth-century Venice: popular evangelism in a Renaissance city', *Journal of Modern History*, 60 (1988), 230.

152. Sarpi, *History*, ed. Burke, p. 170.

153. T. W. Casteel, 'Calvin and Trent: Calvin's reaction to the Council of Trent in the context of his conciliar thought', *Harvard Theological Review*, 63 (1970), 105.

154. Jedin, *A History of the Council of Trent*, ii. 297.

155. In 1776, by the Göttingen jurist, Johann Stephan Pütter.

156. J. Delumeau, *Catholicism between Luther and Voltaire* ..., trans. J. Moiser (1977), p. 25.

157. L. W. Spitz, 'Imperialism, particularism and toleration in the Holy Roman Empire', *The Massacre of St Bartholomew: Reappraisals and Documents*, ed. A. Soman (1974), p. 73.

158. A. Leman, *Urbain VIII et la rivalité de la France et de la maison d'Autriche de 1631 à 1635* (1920), pp. 150, 429. R. Bireley, *Religion and Politics in the Age of the Counter-Reformation: Emperor Ferdinand II, William Lamormaini SJ, and the Formulation of Imperial Policy* (1981), p. 82.

159. Davidson, *The Counter-Reformation*, p. 23.

160. Ibid. 25.

161. *The Reformation: A Narrative History Related by Contemporary Observers and Participants*, ed. Hillerbrand, p. 438.

162. A. L. Martin, *Henry III and the Jesuit Politicians* (1973), p. 21. J. Brodrick, *The Origins of the Jesuits* (repr. 1942), p. 95.

163. J. Brodrick, *The Progress of the Jesuits, 1556–79* (1946), p. 20.

164. *The Reformation: A Narrative History Related by Contemporary Observers and Participants*, ed. Hillerbrand, p. 438.

165. Davidson, *The Counter-Reformation*, p. 63.

166. Ibid. 70.

167. Ibid. 37.

168. A. Adam, *Du mysticisme à la révolte. Les jansénistes du xviie siècle* (1968), p. 57.

169. R. M. Golden, *The Godly Rebellion: Parisian Curés and the Religious Fronde, 1652–1662* (1981), p. 130.

170. Ibid. 127.

2 Europe in the Age of the Italian Wars, 1494–1559 (pp. 79–130)

1. N. Machiavelli, *The Prince*, trans. Bull, p. 51.

2. M. J. Rodríguez-Salgado, *The Changing Face of Empire: Charles V, Philip II and Habsburg Authority, 1551–1559* (1988), p. 25.

3. Ibid.

4. Ibid. 33.

5. Ibid. 32 n. 47.

6. G. Mattingly, *Renaissance Diplomacy* (repr. 1965), p. 157.

7. Machiavelli, *The Prince*, trans. Bull, p. 42.

8. C. W. C. Oman, *A History of the Art of War in the Sixteenth Century* (1937), p. 24.

9. R. B. Merriman, *The Rise of the Spanish Empire in the Old World and the New* (4 vols., 1918–34; repr. 1962), i. 84.

10. Machiavelli, *The Prince*, trans. Bull, p. 119.

11. N. Machiavelli, *Discourses*, ed. B. Crick (1970), pp. 304, 336.

12. F. R. H. DuBoulay, *Germany in the Later Middle Ages* (1983), p. 40.

13. T. A. Brady, *Turning Swiss: Cities and Empire, 1450–1550* (1985), p. 79.

14. *Manifestations of Discontent in Germany on the Eve of the Reformation . . .*, ed. G. Strauss (1971), p. 32.

15. T. A. Brady Jr., 'Imperial destinies: a new biography of the Emperor Maximilian I', *Journal of Modern History*, 62 (1990), 309.

16. Ibid. 308.

17. *Austriae est imperare omni universo*, abbreviated to AEIOU.

18. *Utopia: The Complete Works of Sir Thomas More* IV, ed. E. Surtz and J. H. Hexter (1965), p. 91. Also quoted by J. R. Hale, *Renaissance Europe, 1480–1520* (1971), pp. 88–9.

19. R. J. Knecht, 'The Concordat of 1516: a reassessment', *Government in Reformation Europe, 1520–1560*, ed. H. J. Cohn (1971), p. 103.

20. R. J. Knecht, *Francis I* (1982), p. 82.

21. Ibid. 165.

22. Ibid. 172.

23. J. J. Scarisbrick, *Henry VIII* (repr. 1976), p. 185.

24. Knecht, *Francis I*, p. 218.

25. Brandi, *Charles V*, trans. Wedgwood, p. 112. *New Cambridge Modern History*, ii. 301, 308.

26. J. H. Elliott, *Imperial Spain, 1469–1716* (1963), p. 167.

27. Ibid. 200, 206.

28. *New Cambridge Modern History*, ii. 311.

29. Brandi, *Charles V*, trans. Wedgwood, p. 542.

30. Ibid. 633. Merriman, *The Rise of the Spanish Empire in the Old World and the New*, iii. 395.

31. Brandi, *Charles V*, trans. Wedgwood, p. 585.

32. Ibid.

33. Fischer-Galati, *Ottoman Imperialism and German Protestantism, 1521–1555*, p. 82.

34. Bouwsma, *John Calvin*, p. 107.

35. K. Repgen, 'What is a "religious war"?', *Politics and Society in Reformation Europe . . .*, ed. E. I. Kouri and T. Scott (1987), p. 319.

36. Ibid. 323.

37. Ibid. 321.

38. Ibid. 320.

39. G. R. Elton, *Reformation Europe, 1517–1559* (1963), p. 261. Variant translation in Lortz, *The Reformation in Germany*, ii. 311.

40. H. Tüchle, 'The Peace of Augsburg: new order or lull in the fighting?', *Government in Reformation Europe, 1520–1560*, ed. Cohn, p. 147.

41. D. M. Loades, *The Reign of Mary Tudor: Politics, Government and Religion in England, 1553–1558* (1979), p. 244.

42. Rodríguez-Salgado, *The Changing Face of Empire*, p. 98.

43. Ibid. 126.

44. F. Braudel, *The Mediterranean and the Mediterranean World in the Age of Philip II*, trans. S. Reynolds (repr. 1973), ii. 936–7.

45. Rodríguez-Salgado, *The Changing Face of Empire*, p. 147.

46. Lortz, *The Reformation in Germany*, ii. 312.

47. Braudel, *The Mediterranean and the Mediterranean World*, ii. 938.

48. Rodríguez-Salgado, *The Changing Face of Empire*, p. 217.

3 Europe in the Age of the Wars of Religion, 1559–1618 (pp. 131–87)

1. Kelley, *The Beginning of Ideology: Consciousness and Society in the French Reformation*, p. 314.

2. P. Pierson, *Philip II of Spain* (1975), p. 131.

3. H. G. Koenigsberger, 'The statecraft of Philip II', *European Studies Review*, 1 (1971), 11. Pierson, *Philip II of Spain*, p. 167. N. G. Parker, *Philip II* (repr. 1979), p. 53.

4. Parker, *Philip II*, p. 24.

5. J. Lynch, *Spain under the Habsburgs. I. Empire and Absolutism, 1516–1598* (1964), p. 179.

6. J. A. Fernández-Santamaria, *The State, War and Peace: Spanish Political Thought in the Renaissance* (1977), p. 290.

7. H. G. Koenigsberger, *The Practice of Empire: The Government of Sicily under Philip II* (1969), p. 48. *New Cambridge Modern History*, iii. 238.

8. *Calendar of State Papers: Foreign, 1586–8*, ed. S. C. Thomas (1927), xxi pt. i. 453.

9. Parker, *Philip II*, p. 123.

10. Rodríguez-Salgado, *The Changing Face of Empire*, pp. 271, 282.

11. Lynch, *Spain under the Habsburgs*, i. 315.

12. C. Martin and N. G. Parker, *The Spanish Armada* (1988), p. 268.

13. Ibid. 184.

14. Ibid. 207.

15. Ibid. 258.

16. Ibid. 263.

17. Brandi, *Charles V*, trans. Wedgwood, p. 487. Lynch, *Spain under the Habsburgs*, i. 337.

18. Koenigsberger, 'The statecraft of Philip II', p. 3.

19. L. Van der Essen, *Alexandre Farnèse, prince de Parme . . .* (1933–7), ii. 47.

20. H. G. Koenigsberger, 'Orange, Granvelle and Philip II', *Politics and Society in Reformation Europe*, ed. Kouri and Scott, p. 369.

21. Ibid. 366.

22. L.-E. Halkin, *La réforme en Belgique sous Charles Quint* (1957), p. 112.

23. *Texts Concerning the Revolt of the Netherlands*, ed. E. H. Kossmann and A. F. Mellink (1975), p. 55.

24. Ibid. 60. A. C. Duke, 'Salvation by coercion: the controversy surrounding the "inquisition" in the Low Countries', *Reformation Principle and Practice* . . ., ed. P. N. Brooks (1980), p. 137.

25. *Texts Concerning the Revolt of the Netherlands*, ed. Kossmann and Mellink, p. 63.

26. A. C. Duke and D. H. A. Kolff, 'The time of troubles in the county of Holland, 1566–7', *Tijdschrift voor geschiedenis*, 82 (1969), 322.

27. P. M. Crew, *Calvinist Preaching and Iconoclasm in the Netherlands, 1544–1569* (1978), pp. 14–15.

28. K. W. Swart, *William the Silent and the Revolt of the Netherlands* (Historical Association, 1978), p. 15.

29. Lynch, *Spain under the Habsburgs*, i. 280 and ultimately A. L. E. Verheyden, *Le conseil des troubles: liste des condamnés, 1567–1573* (1961), p. 508.

30. N. G. Parker, *The Dutch Revolt* (1977), p. 114.

31. A. C. Duke and R. L. Jones, 'Towards a reformed polity in Holland, 1572–8', *Tijdschrift voor geschiedenis*, 89 (1976), 377.

32. *Texts Concerning the Revolt of the Netherlands*, ed. Kossmann and Mellink, p. 92.

33. Parker, *The Dutch Revolt*, p. 142.

34. J. C. Boogman, 'The union of Utrecht: its genesis and consequences', *Bijdragen en mededelingen betreffende de geschiedenis der Nederlanden*, 94 (1979), 385.

35. 'Edict of the States General . . . by which they declare that the king of Spain has forfeited the sovereignty and government of the . . . Netherlands . . .': *Texts Concerning the Revolt of the Netherlands*, ed. Kossmann and Mellink, p. 216.

36. A. W. Lovett, *Philip II and Mateo Vázquez de Leca: The Government of Spain, 1572–92* (1977), p. 51.

37. A. W. Lovett, 'The governorship of Don Luis de Requesens, 1573–6. A Spanish view', *European Studies Review*, 2 (1972), 194.

38. P. Geyl, *The Revolt of the Netherlands, 1555–1609* (1932), p. 144.

39. *Texts Concerning the Revolt of the Netherlands*, ed. Kossmann and Mellink, p. 158.

40. Van der Essen, *Alexandre Farnèse*, ii. 292.

41. Ibid. ii. 270. For the *Apology*: *Texts Concerning the Revolt of the Netherlands*, ed. Kossmann and Mellink, pp. 211–16. *The Apologie of Prince William of Orange against the Proclamation of the King of Spaine*, ed. H. Wansink (1969).

42. Van der Essen, *Alexandre Farnèse*, v. 1.

43. J. den Tex, *Oldenbarnevelt* (2 vols., 1973), i. 270.

44. *Texts Concerning the Revolt of the Netherlands*, ed. Kossmann and Mellink, p. 45.

45. C. H. Wilson, *Queen Elizabeth and the Revolt of the Netherlands* (1970), p. 92.

46. Ibid. 103.

47. den Tex, *Oldenbarnevelt*, i. 93.

48. Parker, *The Dutch Revolt*, p. 243.

49. Ibid. 223.

50. Loc. cit. N. G. Parker, *The Army of Flanders and the Spanish Road, 1567–1659* (1972), p. 132.

51. Kelley, *The Beginning of Ideology*, pp. 172–3.

52. P.-F. Geisendorf, *Théodore de Bèze* (1949, repr. 1971), p. 164.

53. Skinner, *The Foundations of Modern Political Thought*, ii. 302. J. H. M. Salmon, *Society in Crisis: France in the Sixteenth Century* (1975), pp. 142–3. Geisendorf, p. 205. Kelley, pp. 255, 277.

54. Geisendorf, *Théodore de Bèze*, p. 205.

55. R. J. Knecht, *The French Wars of Religion, 1559–1598* (1989), p. 106.

56. R. M. Kingdon, *Geneva and the Coming of the Wars of Religion in France, 1555–1563* (1956), p. 6.

57. Salmon, *Society in Crisis: France in the Sixteenth Century*, p. 127.

58. F. Hotman, *Le tigre* [1560], ed. C. Read (1970). The tiger was the Cardinal de Lorraine.

59. A. Devyver, *Le sang épuré: les préjugés de race chez les gentilshommes français de l'ancien régime, 1560–1720* (1973), pp. 65–7, 106.

60. J. Shimizu, *Conflict of Loyalties: Politics and Religion in the Career of Gaspard de Coligny, Admiral of France, 1519–1572* (1970), p. 106.

61. Salmon, *Society in Crisis: France in the Sixteenth Century*, p. 170.

62. For the queen mother: D. Crouzet, *Les guerriers de Dieu: la violence au temps des troubles de religion, vers 1525–vers 1610* (1990), ii. 24. For the 'pilgrimage': ibid. ii. 98.

63. P. Benedict, *Rouen during the Wars of Religion* (1981), pp. 123, 138.

64. Knecht, *The French Wars of Religion*, p. 109.

65. Sutherland, *The Huguenot Struggle for Recognition*, p. 281.

66. Benedict, *Rouen during the Wars of Religion*, p. 177.

67. R. J. Bonney, *The King's Debts: Finance and Politics in France, 1589–1661* (1981), p. 45 n. 1.

68. R. É. Mousnier, *The Assassination of Henri IV, 14 May 1610*, trans. R. J. Spencer (1973), p. 365.

69. *The Low Countries in Early Modern Times*, ed. H. H. Rowen (1972), p. 112.

70. den Tex, *Oldenbarnevelt*, ii. 457.

71. Ibid. ii. 681.

72. Ibid. ii. 643.

4 The Struggle for European Hegemony, 1618–1660 (pp. 188–241)

1. H. F. Schwarz, *The Imperial Privy Council in the Seventeenth Century* (1943, repr. 1972), p. 95.

2. *Sweden as a Great Power, 1611–1697: Government, Society, Foreign Policy*, ed. M. Roberts (repr. 1973), p. 146.

3. J. H. Elliott, *The Revolt of the Catalans . . . 1598–1640* (1963), p. 190. J. V. Polišenský, *The Thirty Years' War* (trans. R. J. W. Evans, 1971), p. 123.

4. J. V. Polišenský, *War and Society in Europe, 1618–1648* (1978), p. 139.

5. B. Nischan, 'Brandenburg and the edict of restitution. A study of the impact of the Imperial-Catholic and the Swedish threats on the policies of the electorate of Brandenburg in the years 1628–31' (unpublished University of Pennsylvania Ph.D. thesis, 1971), p. 138.

6. M. Roberts, 'The politicial objectives of Gustavus Adolphus in Germany, 1630–2'; idem, *Essays in Swedish History* (1967), p. 86.

7. Ibid. 97.

8. *Sweden as a Great Power*, ed. Roberts, p. 139.

9. M. Roberts, 'The Swedish dilemma, 1633–41', *The Thirty Years' War*, ed. N. G. Parker (1985), p. 157.

10. Ibid.

11. *Sweden as a Great Power*, ed. Roberts, p. 139.

12. Ibid. 150.

13. Ibid. 153.

14. *New Cambridge Modern History*, iv. 354.

15. C. V. Wedgwood, *The Thirty Years' War* (1938, repr. 1966), p. 526.

16. N. G. Parker, 'The universal soldier', *The Thirty Years' War*, ed. Parker, p. 195.

17. R. A. Stradling, *Europe and the Decline of Spain . . . 1580–1720* (1981), p. 70.

18. Ibid. 72.

19. J. I. Israel, *The Dutch Republic and the Hispanic World, 1606–61* (1982), p. 85.

20. Ibid. 184, 242.

21. Bonney, *The King's Debts: Finance and Politics in France, 1589–1661*, p. 169.

22. Ibid. 168.

23. H. H. Rowen, *John de Witt: Grand Pensionary of Holland, 1625–1672* (1978), p. 26.

24. Israel, *The Dutch Republic and the Hispanic World*, p. 359.

25. N. G. Parker, *Spain and the Netherlands, 1559–1659* (1979), p. 59.

26. *The Low Countries in Early Modern Times*, ed. Rowen, p. 181.

27. H. H. Rowen, 'The revolution that wasn't: the *coup d'état* of 1650 in Holland', *European Studies Review*, 4 (1974), 107; idem, *John de Witt*, p. 31.

28. J. H. Elliott, 'Self-perception and decline in early seventeenth-century Spain', *Past and Present*, 74 (1977), 48; idem, *Spain and Its World, 1500–1700: Selected Essays* (1989), p. 248.

29. *New Cambridge Modern History*, iv. 450. Elliott, *The Revolt of the Catalans*, p. 183.

30. *New Cambridge Modern History*, iv. 438. Elliott, *The Revolt of the Catalans*, p. 153.

31. *New Cambridge Modern History*, iv. 463. Elliott, *The Revolt of the Catalans*, p. 200.

32. Ibid. 360.

33. Ibid. 375, 401.

34. J. H. Elliott, *The Count-Duke of Olivares: The Statesman in an Age of Decline* (1986), pp. 505, 537, 567.

35. Elliott, *The Revolt of the Catalans*, p. 489.

36. Ibid. 522.

37. Ibid. 517.

38. Y.-M. Bercé, *Le roi caché: sauveurs et imposteurs: mythes politiques populaires dans l'Europe moderne* (1990), p. 77.

39. Elliott, *The Count-Duke of Olivares: The Statesman in an Age of Decline*, p. 649. R. A. Stradling, *Philip IV and the Government of Spain, 1621–1665* (1988), p. 254.

40. Stradling, *Philip IV and the Government of Spain, 1621–1665*, p. 249.

41. Ibid. 261.

42. Ibid. 200.

43. Bonney, *The King's Debts: Finance and Politics in France, 1589–1661*, p. 112.

44. R. J. Bonney, *Political Change in France under Richelieu and Mazarin, 1624–1661* (1978), p. 389.

45. Ibid. 37.

46. Bonney, *The King's Debts: Finance and Politics in France, 1589–1661*, p. 152.

47. Bonney, *Political Change in France under Richelieu and Mazarin*, p. 52; idem, *The King's Debts: Finance and Politics in France, 1589–1661*, p. 212; idem, 'Cardinal Mazarin et la question de responsabilité', *La Fronde en questions*, ed. R. Duchêne et P. Ronzeaud (1989), 329–38.

48. Bonney, *The King's Debts: Finance and Politics in France, 1589–1661*, p. 203.

49. Bonney, *Political Change in France under Richelieu and Mazarin*, p. 58; idem, 'The English and French civil wars', *History*, 65 (1980), 370.

50. Bonney, *The King's Debts: Finance and Politics in France, 1589–1661*, p. 212.

51. Stradling, *Europe and the Decline of Spain*, p. 132.

52. Ibid. 126.

53. H. V. Livermore, *A New History of Portugal* (1966), p. 187 (where the term 'revolution' rather than 'revolt' is used).

54. H. H. Rowen, *The King's State: Proprietary Dynasticism in Early Modern France* (1980), pp. 72–3.

5 The Outsiders of Europe (pp. 242–301)

1. M. Roberts, *The Early Vasas* (1968), p. 127.

2. E. L. Petersen, *The Crisis of the Danish Aristocracy, 1580–1660* (1967), p. 11.

3. den Tex, *Oldenbarnevelt*, ii. 491 n. 1.

4. M. Roberts, *The Swedish Imperial Experience, 1560–1718* (1980), p. 7.

5. *Sweden as a Great Power*, ed. Roberts, p. 17.

6. Roberts, *The Swedish Imperial Experience*, p. 7. *New Cambridge Modern History*, iv. 408.

7. Roberts, *The Swedish Imperial Experience*, p. 123.

8. N. G. Parker, *Europe in Crisis, 1598–1648* (1979), p. 288.

9. Roberts, *Essays in Swedish History*, pp. 152, 183 n. 94.

10. *Sweden as a Great Power*, ed. Roberts, pp. 171–2. Roberts, *The Swedish Imperial Experience*, p. 8.

11. *Sweden as a Great Power*, ed. Roberts, p. 60.

12. A. Jobert, *De Luther à Mohila: la Pologne dans la crise de la Chrétienté, 1517–1648* (1974), p. 169. N. Davies, *God's Playground: A History of Poland. I. The Origins to 1795* (1981), p. 160.

13. Roberts, *The Swedish Imperial Experience*, p. 131 n. 2.

14. Cambridge History of Poland. *From the Origins to Sobieski (to 1696)*, ed. W. F. Reddaway *et al.* (1950), p. 260.

15. Davies, *God's Playground: A History of Poland. I. The Origins to 1795*, p. 153.

16. *A Sourcebook for Russian History from Early Times to 1917. I. Early Times to the Late Seventeenth Century*, ed. G. Vernadsky *et al.* (1972), p. 285.

17. Contrast *Cambridge History of Poland*, ed. Reddaway *et al.*, p. 365.

18. Ibid. 371.

19. Davies, *God's Playground: A History of Poland. I. The Origins to 1795*, p. 364.

20. Ibid. 429. *Cambridge History of Poland*, ed. Reddaway *et al.*, p. 380.

21. Davies, *God's Playground: A History of Poland. I. The Origins to 1795*, p. 436.

22. Roberts, *The Early Vasas*, p. 326.

23. Ibid. 342.

24. Ibid. 346.

25. Ibid. 341.

26. Ibid. 348.

27. Ibid. 387–8.

28. M. Roberts, *Gustavus Adolphus: A History of Sweden, 1611–32* (2 vols., 1958), ii. 353.

29. Roberts, *The Swedish Imperial Experience*, p. 13 n. 1. Cf. idem, 'The Swedish dilemma', p. 156.

30. *A Sourcebook for Russian History*, ed. Vernadsky *et al.*, i. 299.

31. *Sweden as a Great Power*, ed. Roberts, p. 169. Roberts, *The Swedish Imperial Experience*, p. 40.

32. *Prince A. M. Kurbsky's History of Ivan IV*, ed. J. L. I. Fennell (1965), p. 89. G. Alef, 'The boyar *duma* in the reign of Ivan III', *Slavonic and East European Review*, 45 (1967), 92.

33. *The Correspondence between Prince A. M. Kurbsky and Tsar Ivan IV of Russia, 1564–1579*, ed. J. L. I. Fennell (1963), p. 27. Alef, 'The boyar *duma* in the reign of Ivan III', p. 94. E. L. Keenan disputed the authenticity of this correspondence in 1971, but the traditional interpretation was reasserted in 1980 by N. Rossing and B. Rønne.

34. R. Pipes, *Russia under the Old Regime* (1974), pp. 73, 233.

35. J. L. I. Fennell, *Ivan the Great of Moscow* (1961), p. 152.

36. I. Grey, *Ivan the Terrible* (1963, repr. 1966), p. 71.

37. *A Sourcebook for Russian History*, ed. Vernadsky *et al.*, i. 144.

38. Ibid. i. 147. H. von Staden, *The Land and Government of Muscovy . . .*, ed. T. Esper (1967), p. 19.

39. *The Correspondence between Prince A. M. Kurbsky and Tsar Ivan IV of Russia*, ed. Fennell, p. 243.

40. *Prince A. M. Kurbsky's History of Ivan IV*, ed. Fennell, p. 149.

41. Pipes, *Russia under the Old Regime*, p. 76.

42. *A Sourcebook for Russian History*, ed. Vernadsky *et al.*, i. 178. *New Cambridge Modern History*, ii. 561.

43. *A Sourcebook for Russian History*, ed. Vernadsky *et al.*, i. 153.

44. Ibid. i. 196.

45. Davies, *God's Playground: A History of Poland*. I. *The Origins to 1795*, p. 446. P. Longworth, *The Cossacks* (1969), p. 195.

46. *A Sourcebook for Russian History*, ed. Vernadsky *et al.*, i. 296. The French commentator, Guillaume de Beauplan, writing in 1650, noted the Cossacks' great love of liberty, 'without which they do not desire to live', but considered them 'a faithless people, treacherous, perfidious, and not to be trusted but upon good security': C. B. O'Brien, *Muscovy and the Ukraine: From the Pereiaslavl Agreement to the Truce of Andrusovo, 1654–1667* (1963), p. 9.

47. The Polish spelling of his name has been preferred, because of the origins of the rebellion; it is spelt Khmel'nyts'kyi in Ukrainian and Khmel'nitskii in Russian.

48. *Cambridge History of Poland*, ed. Reddaway *et al.*, p. 511.

49. *A Sourcebook for Russian History*, ed. Vernadsky *et al.*, i. 299.

50. Ibid. i. 303.

51. J. Bodin, *The Six Bookes of a Commonweale*, ed. K. D. McRae (1962), p. 200.

52. *The Cambridge History of Islam. I. The Central Islamic Lands*, ed. P. M. Holt, A. K. S. Lambton and B. Lewis (1970), p. 295. A. C. Hess, 'The evolution of the Ottoman seaborne empire in the age of the oceanic discoveries, 1453–1525', *American Historical Review*, 75 (1970), 1902.

53. *The Cambridge History of Islam*, ed. Holt, Lambton and Lewis, i. 303. Cf. Botero's comment that 'when a man knows that whoever obtains the throne will put him to death, he considers his own interests and raises an armed force with the assistance of subjects of the country or foreigners': G. Botero, *The Reason of State*, trans. P. J. and D. P. Waley (1956), p. 85.

54. Machiavelli, *Discourses*, ed. Crick, p. 166. *New Cambridge Modern History*, i. 410.

55. *The Cambridge History of Islam*, ed. Holt, Lambton and Lewis, i. 321. S. J. Shaw, *History of the Ottoman Empire and Modern Turkey. I. Empire of the Gazis: The Rise and Decline of the Ottoman Empire, 1280–1808* (1976), p. 85. *New Cambridge Modern History*, i. 417.

56. L. S. Stavrianos, *The Balkans since 1453* (1958), p. 117.

57. *New Cambridge Modern History*, iv. 625.

58. Ibid. iv. 635.

59. Ibid. iv. 626.

60. C. M. Kortpeter, *Ottoman Imperialism during the Reformation: Europe and the Caucasus* (1973), p. 45.

61. Bodin, *The Six Bookes of a Commonweale*, ed. McRae, p. 204.

6 The Rise of European Absolutism (pp. 305–60)

1. H. R. Trevor-Roper, 'The general crisis of the seventeenth century', *Crisis in Europe, 1560–1660*, ed. T. H. Aston (1965), p. 67.

2. Machiavelli, *The Prince*, trans. Bull, p. 133.

3. Machiavelli, *Discourses*, ed. Crick, p. 112. Skinner, *The Foundations of Modern Political Thought*, i. 186.

4. Machiavelli, *The Prince*, trans. Bull, p. 101. Skinner, *The Foundations of Modern Political Thought*, i. 133.

5. Machiavelli, *The Prince*, trans. Bull, p. 100. Skinner, *The Foundations of Modern Political Thought*, i. 132.

6. Machiavelli, *The Prince*, trans. Bull, p. 96. Skinner, *The Foundations of Modern Political Thought*, i. 136.

7. Machiavelli, *Discourses*, ed. Crick, p. 515. Skinner, *The Foundations of Modern Political Thought*, i. 183.

8. R. Price, 'The senses of *virtú* in Machiavelli', *European Studies Review*, 3 (1973), 345. Skinner, *The Foundations of Modern Political Thought*, i. 138.

9. I. Gentillet, *Anti-Machiavel*, ed. C. E. Rathé (1968), pp. 190, 541.

10. Skinner, *The Foundations of Modern Political Thought*, i. 136.

11. Thus both Luther (ibid. ii. 19) and Calvin (ibid. ii. 194).

12. Ibid. ii. 230. Parker, *John Calvin*, pp. 147–8. Cf. H. A. Lloyd, 'Calvin and the duty of guardians to resist', *Journal of Ecclesiastical History*, 32 (1981), 65–7 and the comment by P. Stein, ibid. 69–70.

13. W. Barclay, *The Kingdom and the Royal Power*, trans. G. Moore (1954). Barclay's tract, which was published at Paris in 1600, was directed 'against Buchanan, Brutus, Boucher and other monarchomachs'. In this, he argued (ibid. 145) that 'kings are constituted by God, that kings reign through God . . . God bestows on kings lawfully constituted, whether by divine inspiration or permission [of] the peoples this prerogative of authority, which is superior to all power of the people . . .' Ibid. 268: 'What the monarchomachs say—that the king is subject to the laws, and that he can be forced into an observation of them—that we have already made plain is repugnant to written, divine and human laws.'

14. F. Hotman, *Francogallia*, trans. J. H. M. Salmon and ed. R. E. Giesey (1972), p. 291. *Constitutionalism and Resistance in the Sixteenth Century: Three Treatises by Hotman, Beza and Mornay*, ed. J. H. Franklin (1969), p. 66.

15. Hotman, *Francogallia*, trans. Salmon and ed. Giesey, p. 333. *Constitutionalism and Resistance in the Sixteenth Century*, ed. Franklin, p. 73.

16. Hotman, *Francogallia*, trans. Salmon and ed. Giesey, p. 459. *Constitutionalism and Resistance in the Sixteenth Century*, ed. Franklin, p. 91.

17. Hotman, *Francogallia*, trans. Salmon and ed. Giesey, p. 519.

18. T. de Bèze, *Du droit des magistrats*, ed. R. M. Kingdon (1970), p. 76.

19. Ibid. 53. *Constitutionalism and Resistance in the Sixteenth Century*, ed. Franklin, pp. 129–30.

20. de Bèze, *Du droit des magistrats*, ed. Kingdon, p. 66: 'manifeste Tyrannie'. *Constitutionalism and Resistance in the Sixteenth Century*, ed. Franklin, pp. 134–5.

21. *Constitutionalism and Resistance in the Sixteenth Century*, ed. Franklin, p. 143. Franklin's translation is to be preferred to that in *A Defence of Liberty against Tyrants: A Translation of the* Vindiciae contra tyrannos . . ., ed. H. J. Laski (1924).

22. *Constitutionalism and Resistance in the Sixteenth Century*, ed. Franklin, p. 191.

23. Ibid. 157–8.

24. Ibid. 154–6 (where the kingdom of Münster is cited as one reason why individuals should not have this right), 195, 197.

25. Skinner, *The Foundations of Modern Political Thought*, ii. 343.

26. Geisendorf, *Théodore de Bèze*, pp. 412, 415.

27. J. Althusius, *Politics Methodically Set Forth, and Illustrated with Sacred and Profane Examples* ... (1603), trans. F. S. Carney (1965), p. 117. Althusius denied that 'absolute power, or what is called the plenitude of power, can ... be given to the supreme magistrate': ibid. 116. He specifically attacked Bodin (ibid. 5 and 66—where he refuted his definition of supreme and perpetual power) and William Barclay (ibid. 103–10, 159).

28. Ibid. 181 (where he praised Hotman). In general, he commended the history of the Dutch revolt against Spain, which 'offer[ed] examples of this care and defence by ephors': ibid. 10–11, 101.

29. Ibid. 121–3, where he reprints Charles V's election capitulation, in the form given by Johannes Sleiden (Strasbourg, 1555).

30. Ibid. 187. He mentioned the rights of the electors conceded by the Golden Bull: ibid. 95. The ephors (i.e. electors in Germany) elected the supreme magistrate: ibid. 118.

31. H. Grotius [Hugo de Groot], *De jure belli ac pacis Libri tres*, trans. F. W. Kelsey, 1925, ii. 103. R. Tuck, *Natural Rights Theories: Their Origin and Development* (1979), p. 78.

32. Tuck, *Natural Rights Theories*, pp. 77–8.

33. Ibid. 79.

34. F. J. Baumgartner, *Radical Reactionaries: The Political Thought of the French Catholic League* (1975), p. 72.

35. Skinner, *The Foundations of Modern Political Thought*, ii. 346. G. Lewy, *Constitutionalism and Statecraft during the Golden Age of Spain: A Study of the Politicial Philosophy of Juan de Mariana SJ* (1960), p. 35.

36. Ibid. 69.

37. Ibid. 69 n. 16, 140.

38. Ibid. 139.

39. Barclay, *The Kingdom and the Royal Power*, trans. Moore, p. 145: 'the king is viewed as some power higher and more august than the people's ...' W. F. Church, *Constitutional Thought in Sixteenth-Century France: A Study in the Evolution of Ideas* (1941), p. 333.

40. D. Parker, 'Law, society and the state in the thought of Jean Bodin', *History of Political Thought*, 2 (1981), 270.

41. Bodin, *The Six Bookes of a Commonweale*, ed. McRae, p. 84: 'majesty or sovereignty is the most high, absolute and perpetual power over the citizens and subjects in a Commonweal ...'

42. Ibid. 87. Cf. ibid. 85: 'sovereignty is not limited either in power, charge or time certain'.

43. This was most clearly expressed by Loyseau, Bodin's intellectual successor, in his discussion of the maxim *le mort saisit le vif.* But Loyseau himself cited Bodin's earlier discussion of sovereignty: R. J. Bonney, *L'absolutisme* (1989), p. 38.

44. F. Schulz, 'Bracton on kingship', *English Historical Review*, 60 (1945), 154–5. Schulz commented: 'we cannot reconstruct Ulpian's text with any certainty, but he must have written something like this: *quod principi placuit, legis habet vicem . . .*'

45. Schulz, 'Bracton on kingship', p. 158. Ulpian was talking about a specific *lex*, the *lex Papia*.

46. Bodin, *Les six livres de la république* (1583 edn.), p. 142. Idem, *The Six Bookes of a Commonweale*, ed. McRae, p. 98.

47. Though Bodin was equivocal on this matter, in most instances denying an individual's right to resign office: id., *The Six Bookes of a Commonweale*, ed. McRae, p. 316.

48. Cf. p. 539: 'for the greatest tyranny is nothing so miserable as an anarchy, when there is neither prince nor magistrate, none that obeyeth, neither yet any that commandeth'.

49. Skinner, *The Foundations of Modern Political Thought*, ii. 296–7, 297 n. 1.

50. Botero, *The Reason of State*, ed. Waley, p. xiii (Machiavelli 'bases his reason of state on lack of conscience') and p. 48 (dissimulation is a great aid and Louis XI of France thought it an important part of the art of ruling).

51. G. Oestreich, *Neostoicism and the Early Modern State*, ed. B. Oestreich and H. G. Koenigsberger, trans. D. McLintock (1982), pp. 43–4. J. Lipsius, *Six Bookes of Politickes or Civil Doctrine*, trans. W. Jones (1594) in *The English Experience*, 287 (1970).

52. T. A. Spragens Jr., *The Politics of Motion: The World of Thomas Hobbes* (1973), p. 69.

53. T. Hobbes, *Leviathan*, ed. J. Plamenatz (1962), p. 143.

54. Ibid. 185.

55. Ibid. 176.

56. Ibid. 203.

57. Ibid. 90.

58. Ibid. 186.

59. Ibid. 304–5.

60. Ibid. 208–9, 211.

61. P. King, *The Ideology of Order: A Comparative Analysis of Jean Bodin and Thomas Hobbes* (1974), p. 159. K. V. Thomas, 'The social origins of Hobbes's political thought', *Hobbes Studies*, ed. K. C. Brown (1965), p. 201.

62. T. Hobbes, *The Citizen [De cive]: Philosophical Rudiments concerning government and society* in *Man and citizen*, ed. B. Gert (1972, repr. 1978),

p. 284n. W. B. Glover, 'God and Thomas Hobbes', *Hobbes Studies*, ed. Brown, p. 162.

63. Variant translations in J. W. N. Watkins, *Hobbes's System of Ideas* ... (1965), p. 155. Hobbes, *The Citizen*, ed. Gert, pp. 244–5.

64. Bodin, *The Six Bookes of a Commonweale*, ed. McRae, p. 192.

65. Ibid. 384.

66. L. Konopczyński, *Le Liberum veto: étude sur le développement du principe majoritaire* (1930), p. 196. J. Żmuidzinas, *Commonwealth polono-lithauanien ou l'Union de l'Lublin, 1569* (1978), p. 193. Davies, *God's Playground: A History of Poland. I. The Origins to 1795*, pp. 345–6.

67. C. Griffiths, *Representative Government in Western Europe in the Sixteenth Century* (1968), p. 505.

68. I. A. A. Thompson, 'Crown and *Cortes* in Castile, 1590–1665', *Parliament, Estates and Representation*, 2 (1982), 34.

69. Ibid. 34–5, 42.

70. Bodin, *The Six Bookes of a Commonweale*, ed. McRae, p. 98.

71. I. A. A. Thompson, 'The end of the *Cortes* of Castile', *Parliaments, Estates and Representation*, 4 (1984), 127.

72. A. F. Upton, 'The Swedish *riksdag* and the English parliament in the seventeenth century—some comparisons', *The Swedish Riksdag in an International Perspective*, ed. N. Stjernquist (1989), p. 122.

73. *Sweden as a Great Power*, ed. Roberts, p. 34.

74. H. G. Koenigsberger, '*Riksdag*, parliament and States General in the sixteenth and seventeenth centuries', *The Swedish Riksdag in an International Perspective*, ed. Stjernquist, p. 60.

75. Elliott, *The Count-Duke of Olivares: The Statesman in an Age of Decline*, p. 470.

76. *Texts Concerning the Revolt of the Netherlands*, ed. Kossmann and Mellink, p. 166.

77. Sir William Temple, *Observations upon the United Provinces of the Netherlands*, ed. G. N. Clark (1932), p. 56.

78. Bodin, *The Six Bookes of a Commonweale*, ed. McRae, p. 519; cf. ibid. 540.

79. Ibid. 98.

80. J. M. Headley, *The Emperor and His Chancellor: A Study of the Imperial Chancellery under Gattinara* (1983), p. 57.

81. M. Roberts, 'On aristocratic constitutionalism in Swedish history', idem, *Essays in Swedish History*, p. 16.

82. E. L. Keenan, 'Vita: Ivan Vasil'evich. Terrible czar, 1530–84', *Harvard Magazine* (1978), 49.

83. Pipes, *Russia under the Old Regime*, p. 106.

84. *Sweden as a Great Power*, ed. Roberts, p. 52.

85. Ibid. 116.

86. W. R. Hitchcock, *The Background of the Knights' Revolt, 1522–1523* (1958), p. 25.

87. Ibid. 68.

88. M. J. LeGates, 'The knights and the problems of political organizing in sixteenth-century Germany', *Central European History*, 7 (1974), 133.

89. Ibid. 105.

90. R. L. Kagan, *Lawsuits and Litigants in Castile, 1500–1700* (1981), p. 206.

91. Ibid. 209.

92. R. É. Mousnier, *La vénalité des offices sous Henri IV et Louis XIII* (2nd edn., 1971), p. 46.

93. Botero, *The Reason of State*, ed. Waley, p. 22.

94. Bonney, *Political Change in France under Richelieu and Mazarin, 1624–1661*, p. 33.

95. Sir George Carew, 'A relation of the state of France', *An Historical View of the Negotiations between the Courts of England, France and Brussels*, ed. T. Birch (1749), p. 435.

96. Machiavelli, *The Prince*, trans. Bull, p. 87. Hobbes, *Leviathan*, ed. Plamenatz, pp. 123–4.

97. J. R. Hale, *War and Society in Renaissance Europe, 1450–1620* (1985), p. 36.

98. Ibid. 22.

99. N. G. Parker, 'The military revolution, 1560–1660: a myth?', idem, *Spain and the Netherlands, 1559–1659 . . .* (1979), p. 88.

100. Hale, *War and Society in Renaissance Europe, 1450–1620*, p. 70.

101. Cf. Machiavelli, *The Prince*, ed. Q. Skinner and R. Price (1988), p. 43: 'they are disunited, ambitious and treacherous . . .'

102. Hale, *War and Society in Renaissance Europe, 1450–1620* (1985), pp. 70–1.

103. Ibid. 251.

104. Botero, *The Reason of State*, ed. Waley, pp. 170–1.

105. Ibid. 135.

106. Bonney, *The King's Debts: Finance and Politics in France, 1624–1661*, p. 198.

107. Ibid. 274.

108. Sir John Fortescue, *The Governance of England*, ed. C. Plummer (1885), p. 109.

109. Carew, 'A relation of the state of France', p. 463. Bonney, *The King's Debts: Finance and Politics in France, 1624–1661*, p. 60 n. 3.

110. F. Bernier, *Voyages* (2 vols., 1699), i. 319. Bonney, *L'absolutisme*, p. 68. P. Anderson, *Lineages of the Absolutist State* (repr. 1974), p. 399.

111. Machiavelli, *Discourses*, ed. Crick, p. 157.

7 Population and Social Structure (pp. 361–416)

1. P. S. Lewis, *Later Medieval France: The Polity* (1968), pp. 167–8.

2. Bodin, *The Six Bookes of a Commonweale*, ed. McRae, p. 381.

3. Michel de Montaigne, *Essays*, trans. J. M. Cohen (repr. 1966), p. 119.

4. Bodin, *The Six Bookes of a Commonweale*, ed. McRae, p. 640.

5. J.-N. Biraben, *Les hommes et la peste en France et dans les pays européens et méditerranéens* (2 vols., 1975, 1976), ii. 36.

6. C. Lis and H. Soly, *Poverty and Capitalism in Pre-industrial Europe* (1979), p. 86.

7. Ibid. 122. J.-P. Gutton, *La société et les pauvres: l'exemple de la généralité de Lyon, 1534–1789* (1971), p. 328.

8. *Sweden as a Great Power*, ed. Roberts, p. 116.

9. D. Bitton, *The French Nobility in Crisis, 1560–1640* (1969), p. 65. There was a similar phrasing in an ordinance of Charles VI in 1393: Lewis, *Later Medieval France*, p. 175.

10. D. M. Frame, *Montaigne: A Biography* (1965), p. 91.

11. M. Bloch, *French Rural History: An Essay on Its Basic Characteristics*, trans. J. Sondheimer (1966), p. 112.

12. M. Roberts, 'Queen Christina and the general crisis of the seventeenth century', *Crisis in Europe*, ed. Aston, p. 211.

13. J. Lynch, *Spain under the Habsburgs. II. Spain and America, 1598–1700* (2nd edn., 1981), p. 153.

14. Ibid.

15. *New Cambridge Modern History*, i. 389.

16. Y.-M. Bercé, *Histoire des croquants: étude des soulèvements populaires au xviie siècle dans le sud-ouest de la France* (2 vols., 1974), i. 77.

17. R. J. Bonney, *Society and Government in France under Richelieu and Mazarin, 1624–61* (1988), pp. 174, 182–3.

18. D. Hurtado de Medoza, *The War in Granada* (1674), trans. M. Shuttleworth (1982), p. 48.

19. J. M. Bak, 'Delinquent lords and foresaken serfs: thoughts on war and society during the crisis of feudalism', *Society in Change: Studies in Honor of B. K. Kiraly*, ed. S. B. Vardy (1983), p. 300.

20. R. H. Hilton, *Bond Men Made Free: Medieval Peasant Movements and the English Rising of 1381* (repr. 1977), p. 117.

21. Bercé, *Histoire des croquants*, i. 411–12.

22. Bonney, *Society and Government in France under Richelieu and Mazarin, 1624–61*, p. 208.

23. Ibid. 203. Bercé, *Histoire des croquants*, ii. 590. Zagorin, *Rebels and Rulers, 1500–1660*, i. 225.

24. T. Scott, *Freiburg and the Breisgau: Town–Country Relations in the Age of Reformation and Peasants' War* (1986), p. 179.

25. H. J. Cohn, 'The peasants of Swabia', *The German Peasant War of 1525*, ed. J. M. Bak (1976), p. 15.

26. Ibid. 18.

27. The book was published posthumously: G. Contarini, *The Commonwealth and Government of Venice* (1543), trans. L. Lewkenor (1599), in *The English Experience*, 101 (1969), 5. Cf. W. J. Bouwsma, *Venice and the Defense of Republican Liberty* (1968), pp. 145–53.

28. G. Strauss, *Nuremberg in the Sixteenth Century* (1966), p. 61.

29. Temple, *Observations upon the United Provinces . . .*, ed. Clark, pp. 100–1.

30. S. Schama, *The Embarrassment of Riches: An Interpretation of Dutch Culture in the Golden Age* (repr. 1988), p. 301.

31. Temple, *Observations upon the United Provinces . . .*, ed. Clark, p. 58.

32. *Texts Concerning the Revolt of the Netherlands*, ed. Kossmann and Mellink, pp. 277–8.

33. Temple, *Observations upon the United Provinces . . .*, ed. Clark, p. 57.

34. *The Low Countries in Early Modern Times . . .*, ed. Rowen, p. 205.

35. Ibid. 208–10.

36. H. Kamen, *European Society, 1500–1700* (1984), p. 135.

37. H. G. Koenigsberger, *Estates and Revolutions: Essays in Early Modern European History* (1971), p. 209.

38. T. Wittman, *Les gueux dans les 'bonnes villes' de Flandres, 1577–1584* (1960), p. 277.

39. Ibid. 280.

40. Ibid. 307–8.

41. D. Richet, 'Politique et religion: les processions à Paris en 1589', *La France d'ancien régime: Études réunies en l'honneur de Pierre Goubert*, no ed. (1984), pp. 625–6.

42. R. Descimon, *Qui étaient les seize? Mythes et réalités de la Ligue parisienne, 1585–94* (1983), p. 47.

43. Ibid. 9.

44. D. Crouzet, 'La représentation du temps à l'époque de la Ligue', *Revue historique*, 270 (1983), 369.

45. R. R. Harding, 'Revolution and reform in the Holy League: Angers, Rennes, Nantes', *Journal of Modern History*, 53 (1981), 412.

46. E. Barnavi and R. Descimon, *La Sainte Ligue: le juge et la potence* . . . (1985), p. 24.

47. Ibid. 25. M. Greengrass, 'The Sixteen, radical politics in Paris during the League', *History*, 69 (1984), 435.

48. E. Le Roy Ladurie, *Carnival: A People's Uprising at Romans, 1579–80*, trans. M. Feeney (1980), pp. 179, 208. Author's translation from the French original.

49. J. Pérez, *La révolution des 'Comunidades' des Castille, 1520–1* (1970), p. 472 n. 66.

8 The European Economy (pp. 417–73)

1. E. Le Roy Ladurie, *The Mind and Method of the Historian*, trans. S. and B. Reynolds (1981), pp. 1, 291 n. 1.

2. I. A. Wallerstein, *The Modern World-System: Capitalist Agriculture and the Origins of the European World-Economy in the Sixteenth Century* (1974), p. 15.

3. A.-J. du Plessis, Cardinal de Richelieu [?], *Testament politique*, ed. L. André (1947), p. 428.

4. J. H. Elliott, *The Old World and the New, 1492–1650* (1970), pp. 90–1. Idem, *Spain and Its World, 1500–1700*, p. 22.

5. J. Day, 'The great bullion famine of the fifteenth century', *Past and Present*, 79 (1978).

6. E. J. Hamilton, *American Treasure and the Price Revolution in Spain, 1501–1650* (1934).

7. M. Morineau, *Incroyables gazettes et fabuleux métaux: les retours des trésors américains d'après les gazettes hollandaises, xvie–xviiie siècles* (1984).

8. H. G. Koenigsberger and G.L. Mosse, *Europe in the Sixteenth Century* (1968), p. 26. P. Vilar, *A History of Gold and Money, 1450–1920*, trans. J. White (1976), p. 163.

9. Vilar, *A History of Gold and Money, 1450–1920*, pp. 183–4.

10. M.-T. Boyer-Xambeu, G. Deleplace and L. Gillard, *Monnaie privée et pouvoir des princes: l'économie des relations monétaires à la Renaissance* (1986), p. 9.

11. For an introduction to index numbers, consult R. Floud, *An Introduction to Quantitative Methods for Historians* (1973), pp. 117–19.

12. E. J. Hamilton, 'American treasure and the rise of capitalism, 1500–1700', *Economica*, 9 (1929).

13. F. Braudel, *Civilization and Capitalism, 15th–18th Century. II. The Wheels of Commerce*, trans. S. Reynolds (1982), p. 544.

14. Ibid. 545.

15. Ibid.

16. R. De Roover, *L'évolution de la lettre de change, xive-xviiie siècles* (1953), p. 87. H. Van der Wee, *The Growth of the Antwerp Market and the European Economy, Fourteenth–Sixteenth Centuries* (1963), ii. 344–5.

17. Boyer-Xambeu, Deleplace and Gillard, *Monnaie privée et pouvoir des princes*, p. 147.

18. Ibid. 173.

19. Ibid. 323.

20. R. Gascon, *Grand commerce et vie urbaine au xvie siècle: Lyon et ses marchands* (2 vols., 1971), ii. 671.

21. H. Lapeyre, *Une famille de marchands: les Ruiz . . .* (1955), p. 450.

22. Boyer-Xambeu, Deleplace and Gillard, *Monnaie privée et pouvoir des princes*, p. 165.

23. P. Dollinger, *The German Hansa*, trans. D. S. Ault and S. H. Steinberg (1970), p. 319.

24. Ibid. 368.

25. F. Chevalier, *Land and Society in Colonial Mexico* (1963), p. 94.

26. T. Mun, *England's Treasure by Forraign Trade*, repr. (Oxford, 1933), p. 74. J. I. Israel, *Dutch Primacy in World Trade, 1585–1740* (1989), p. 13.

27. Ibid. 91.

28. Ibid. 95.

29. Ibid. 127.

30. N. J. Steensgaard, 'The Dutch East India Company as an institutional innovation', *Dutch Capitalism and World Capitalism*, ed. M. Aymard (1982), p. 252.

31. Ibid. 255.

32. Israel, *Dutch Primacy in World Trade, 1585–1740*, p. 250.

33. C. Wilson, *England's Apprenticeship, 1603–1763* (repr. 1966), p. 163.

34. Israel, *Dutch Primacy in World Trade, 1585–1740*, pp. 104–5.

35. H. R. Trevor-Roper, *Religion, the Reformation and Social Change . . .* (1967), p. 33.

36. Christ's precept was 'Lend, hoping for nothing again' (Luke vi.35): J. Le Goff, *Time, Work and Culture in the Middle Ages*, trans. A. Goldhammer (1980), p. 61. H. A. Oberman, *Masters of the Reformation: The Emergence of a New Intellectual Climate in Europe* (1981), p. 133. Cf. B. Pullan, *Rich and Poor in Renaissance Venice: The Social Institutions of a Catholic State to 1620* (1971), p. 433.

37. Mun, *England's Treasure by Forraign Trade*, p. 59.

38. B. Nelson, *The Idea of Usury: From Tribal Brotherhood to Universal Otherhood* (2nd edn., 1969), p. 31.

39. A. Biéler, *La pensée économique et sociale de Calvin* (1959), pp. 456–61, 471–3.

40. Nelson, *The Idea of Usury: From Tribal Brotherhood to Universal Otherhood*, p. 79.

41. J. C. Riemersma, *Religious Factors in Early Dutch Capitalism, 1550–1650* (1967), p. 77.

42. The author is grateful to Dr A. C. Duke for a copy of this document.

43. Bonney, *The King's Debts: Finance and Politics in France, 1624–1661*, p. 278.

44. Ibid. 279.

45. B. Pullan, *The Jews of Europe and the Inquisition of Venice, 1550–1670* (1983), p. 178.

46. J. Meuvret, *Le problème des subsistances à l'époque de Louis XIV* (6 vols., 1977, 1987 and 1989), i. 140.

47. E. Le Roy Ladurie and J. Goy, *Tithe and Agrarian History from the Fourteenth to the Nineteenth Centuries*, trans. S. Burke (1982), p. 14.

9 Court, Culture and Community (pp. 474–523)

1. Dickens, *The German Nation and Martin Luther*, p. 109.

2. E. B. Fryde, 'Lorenzo de' Medici: high finance and the patronage of art and learning', *The Courts of Europe: Politics, Patronage and Royalty, 1400–1800*, ed. A. G. Dickens (1977), p. 80.

3. R. J. W. Evans, *Rudolf II and His World: A Study in Intellectual History, 1576–1612* (1973, repr. 1984), p. 196.

4. Ibid. 162.

5. J. Brown and J. H. Elliott, *A Palace for a King: The Buen Retiro and the Court of Philip IV* (1980), p. 57. Cf. J. H. Elliott, 'Philip IV of Spain: prisoner of ceremony', *The Courts of Europe: Politics, Patronage and Royalty, 1400–1800*, ed. Dickens.

6. R. J. Knecht, 'Francis I: prince and patron of the northern Renaissance', *The Courts of Europe: Politics, Patronage and Royalty, 1400–1800*, ed. Dickens, p. 109. Cf. Knecht, *Francis I*, p. 256.

7. F. J. Baumgartner, *Henri II, King of France, 1547–1559* (1988), p. 113.

8. A. L. Moote, *Louis XIII: The Just* (1989), p. 256.

9. Bonney, *L'absolutisme*, p. 46.

10. Bossuet, *Politique tirée des propres paroles de l'Écriture sainte*, ed. Le Brun, p. 266. Bonney, *L'absolutisme*, p. 49.

11. Bossuet, *Politique tirée des propres paroles de l'Écriture sainte*, ed. Le Brun, p. 268. Bonney, *L'absolutisme*, p. 50.

12. Bossuet, *Politique tirée des propres paroles de l'Écriture sainte*, ed. Le Brun, p. 267. Bonney, *L'absolutisme*, p. 50.

13. Bossuet, *Politique tirée des propres paroles de l'Écriture sainte*, ed. Le Brun, p. 67. Bonney, *L'absolutisme*, p. 51.

14. Bossuet, *Politique tirée des propres paroles de l'Écriture sainte*, ed. Le Brun, p. 70. Bonney, *L'absolutisme*, p. 51.

15. L. M. Bryant, *The King and the City in the Parisian Royal Entry Ceremony: Politics, Ritual and Art in the Renaissance* (1986), pp. 25–6. Bonney, *L'absolutisme*, p. 39.

16. Bryant, *The King and the City in the Parisian Royal Entry Ceremony: Politics, Ritual and Art in the Renaissance*, p. 101. Bonney, *L'absolutisme*, p. 40.

17. R. E. Giesey, *Le roi ne meurt jamais* (1987), p. 280. Bonney, *L'absolutisme*, p. 43.

18. Giesey, *Le roi ne meurt jamais*, pp. 270–1. Bonney, *L'absolutisme*, p. 44.

19. H. H. Rowen, *The King's State: Proprietary Dynasticism in Early Modern France* (1980), pp. 70, 76. *Journal du marquis de Dangeau*, ed. E. Soulié and L. Dussieux, (1858), xv. 111 n. 1.

20. E. Muir, *Civic Ritual in Renaissance Venice* (1981), p. 104.

21. Ibid. 122.

22. W. J. Bouwsma, *Venice and the Defense of Republican Liberty: Renaissance Values in the Age of the Counter-Reformation* (1968), p. 390.

23. Schama, *The Embarrassment of Riches: An Interpretation of Dutch Culture in the Golden Age*, pp. 293–4.

24. Ibid. 78, 288.

25. Ibid. 98.

26. Ibid. 198.

27. Ibid. 318.

28. Le Roy Ladurie, *The Mind and Method of the Historian*, trans. Reynolds, p. 87.

29. Ibid.

30. G. Ferrari, 'Public anatomy lessons and the Carnival in Bologna', *Past and Present*, 117 (1987), 52.

31. Schama, *The Embarrassment of Riches: An Interpretation of Dutch Culture in the Golden Age*, p. 183.

32. *The Paris of Henry of Navarre as Seen by Pierre de l'Estoile ...*, ed. N. L. Roelker (1958), p. 99.

33. N. Z. Davis, 'The reasons of misrule: youth groups and charivaris in sixteenth-century France', *Past and Present*, 50 (1971), 64.

34. Ibid. 65.

35. Y.-M. Bercé, *Fête et révolte: des mentalités populaires en France du xviie au xviiie siècle* (1976), p. 43.

36. Davis, 'The reasons of misrule: youth groups and charivaris in sixteenth-century France', p. 41.

37. D. W. Sabean, *Power in the Blood: Popular Culture and Village Discourse in Early Modern Germany* (1984), p. 40.

38. P. Burke, *Popular Culture in Early Modern Europe* (1978, repr. 1983), p. 217.

39. Ibid. 209.

40. Ibid. 211.

41. Crouzet, *Les guerriers de Dieu*, i. 78.

42. Ibid. i. 85.

43. H. Carrier, *La presse de la Fronde, 1648–1653: les Mazarinades. I. La conquête de l'opinion* (1989), pp. 287–8.

44. Ibid. 289, 291.

45. *Malleus Maleficarum: The Hammer of Witchcraft* . . ., trans. M. Summers (repr. 1968), p. 29.

46. Ibid. 55.

47. Ibid. 115, 127.

48. E.W. Monter, *Witchcraft in France and Switzerland: The Borderlands during the Reformation* (1976), p. 31.

49. Ibid.

50. H. C. E. Midelfort, *Witch Hunting in Southwestern Germany, 1562–1684: The Social and Intellectual Foundations* (1972), p. 38.

51. Monter, *Witchcraft in France and Switzerland: The Borderlands during the Reformation*, p. 31. The greatest panic at Geneva was in 1571, seven years after Calvin's death: ibid. 45.

52. Midelfort, *Witch Hunting in Southwestern Germany, 1562–1684: The Social and Intellectual Foundations*, p. 19.

53. G. Henningsen, *The Witches' Advocate: Basque Witchcraft and the Spanish Inquisition, 1609–1614* (1980), p. 353.

54. Ibid. 350.

55. J. Cottingham, *Rationalism* (1984), pp. 7–8.

56. Bouwsma, *John Calvin: A Sixteenth-Century Portrait*, p. 157.

57. Ibid. 164.

58. Ibid.

59. Ibid. 165, 166–7.

60. A. Avantage, *Sun Stand Thou Still* (1949), p. 116.

61. Bodin, *The Six Bookes of a Commonweale*, ed. McRae, p. 455.

62. B. Easlea, *Witch Hunting, Magic and the New Philosophy: An Introduction to the Debates of the Scientific Revolution, 1450–1750* (1980), p 70.

63. B. Vickers, 'Analogy versus identity: the rejection of occult symbolism, 1580–1680', *Occult and Scientific Mentalities in the Renaissance*, ed. Vickers (1984), p. 152. J. V. Field, *Kepler's Geometrical Cosmology* (1988), p. 126.

64. Easlea, *Witch Hunting, Magic and the New Philosophy: An Introduction to the Debates of the Scientific Revolution, 1450–1750*, p. 78.

65. Galileo Galilei, *Dialogue Concerning the Two Chief World Systems—Ptolemaic and Copernican*, trans. S. Drake (1967), p. 6.

66. Easlea, *Witch Hunting, Magic and the New Philosophy: An Introduction to the Debates of the Scientific Revolution, 1450–1750*, p. 86.

67. *The Philosophical Writings of Descartes*, trans. J. Cottingham, R. Stoothoff and D. Murdoch (2 vols., 1984–5), i. 279.

68. *The Philosophical Writings of Descartes*, trans. Cottingham *et al.*, i. 127.

69. Ibid. i. 240.

70. Ibid. Cf. ibid. i. 243.

71. Ibid. i. 279.

72. Ibid. i. 108.

73. A. R. Hall, *The Scientific Revolution, 1500–1800: The Formation of the Modern Scientific Attitude* (1954, 2nd edn., 1962), p. 182.

10 Conclusion: the European Dynastic States (pp. 524–531)

1. Botero, *The Reason of State*, trans. Waley, p. 162.

2. Bonney, *L'absolutisme*, p. 27. Griffiths, *Representative Government in Western Europe in the Sixteenth Century*, p. 497.

3. [Philippe Marnix de Sainte-Aldegonde?], 'Rapport fait au prince d'Orange et aux États Généraux par les ambassadeurs qu'ils avaient envoyés au duc d'Anjou pour lui offrir la souveraineté des Pays-Bas', *Correspondance de Guillaume le Taciturne . . .*, ed. L. P. Gachard (1854), iv. 421–72.

4. J. D. Tracy, *A Financial Revolution in the Habsburg Netherlands: Renten and Renteniers in the County of Holland, 1515–1565* (1985), p. 33.

5. Rowen, *The King's State: Proprietary Dynasticism in Early Modern France*, p. 117.

6. Bossuet, *Politique tirée des propres paroles de l'Écriture sainte*, ed. Le Brun, p. 114. Bonney, *L'absolutisme*, p. 63.

7. Bossuet, *Politique tirée des propres paroles de l'Écriture sainte*, ed. Le Brun, p. 64. Bonney, *L'absolutisme*, p. 50.

8. Bossuet, *Politique tirée des propres paroles de l'Écriture sainte*, ed. Le Brun, p. 119.

9. Ibid. 121.

GUIDE TO FURTHER READING

Note: This guide to further reading, which is arranged according to chapter subsections, is not intended to be exhaustive but an indication of some of the more useful works available in English or French.

There are a number of short volumes which cover part of the period 1494–1660, such as J. R. Hale, *Renaissance Europe, 1480–1520* (repr. 1977); G. R. Elton, *Reformation Europe, 1517–1559* (1963); J. H. Elliott, *Europe Divided, 1559–1598* (repr. 1975); N. G. Parker, *Europe in Crisis, 1598–1648* (1979); and J. W. Stoye, *Europe Unfolding, 1648–1688* (repr. 1976). Also useful is the more detailed *New Cambridge Modern History. I. The Renaissance, 1493–1520*, ed. D. Hay (repr. 1975); *II. The Reformation, 1520–1559*, ed. G. R. Elton (repr. 1976); *III. The Counter-Reformation and Price Revolution, 1559–1610*, ed. R. B. Wernham (repr. 1971); *IV. The Decline of Spain and the Thirty Years' War, 1609–48/59*, ed. J. P. Cooper (1970); *XIII. Companion Volume*, ed. P. Burke (1979); and *XIV. Atlas*, ed. H. C. Darby and H. Fullard (repr. 1978). There is a valuable introductory bibliography published by the Historical Association: *Early Modern European History, c.1492–1789*, ed. H. Dunthorne and H. M. Scott (1983); but the standard bibliographic work of reference is the Historical Association's *Annual Bulletin of Historical Literature*, currently edited (volume 75, 1989) by M. Greengrass.

I RELIGIOUS DIVISIONS IN EARLY MODERN EUROPE

The standard introductory works on the Reformation include A. G. Dickens, *Reformation and Society in Sixteenth-Century Europe* (1966), S. E. Ozment, *The Age of Reform: An Intellectual and Religious History of Late Medieval and Reformation Europe* (1980) and B. M. G. Reardon, *Religious Thought in the Reformation* (1981). There is an interesting long essay by J. A. Bossy, *Christianity in the West, 1400–1700* (1985), which is helpful on pre-Reformation Christianity but tends to minimize the impact of the Reformation. The reverse tradition is exemplified by P. Chaunu, *Église, culture et société: Essais sur Réforme et Contre-Réforme, 1517–1620* (2nd edn., 1984). The immense bibliography on the Reformation is introduced in *Reformation Europe: A Guide to Research*, ed. S. E. Ozment (1982).

1.1 For fifteenth-century grievances in Germany, *Manifestations of Discontent in Germany on the Eve of the Reformation . . .*, ed. G. Strauss (1971). The problems of the Papacy are discussed in C. M. D. Crowder, *Unity, Heresy and Reform, 1378–1460: The Conciliar Response to the Grand Schism* (1977) and F. Oakley, 'Conciliarism at the Fifth Lateran Council?', *Church History*, 41 (1972). Among the individual Popes, much information on Alexander VI and on the Medici Popes may be gleaned respectively from M. E. Mallet, *The Borgias: The Rise and Fall of a Renaissance Dynasty* (1969) and J. N. Stephens,

The Fall of the Florentine Republic, 1512–1530 (1983). For the Waldensian heresy, E. Cameron, *The Reformation of the Heretics: The Waldenses of the Alps, 1480–1580* (1984). In many respects an untypical reformer, Savonarola is given a biography by D. Weinstein, *Savonarola and Florence: Prophecy and Patriotism in the Renaissance* (1970). Geiler, a more conventional figure, is featured in E. J. Dempsey-Douglass, *Justification in Late Medieval Preaching . . .* (1966). The most impressive study of the difficulties of implementing reform in the Empire is F. Rapp, *Réformes et Réformation à Strasbourg: Église et société dans le diocèse de Strasbourg, 1450–1525* (1974), although the issue of anti-clericalism is highlighted in H. J. Cohn, 'Anticlericalism in the German Peasants' War', *P[ast and] P[resent]*, 83 (1979). For late medieval scholasticism the most helpful introduction is J. H. Overfield, *Humanism and Scholasticism in Late Medieval Germany* (1984). There is a useful study of Biel, one of the fifteenth-century nominalists, by H. A. Oberman, *The Harvest of Medieval Theology: Gabriel Biel and Late Medieval Nominalism* (1963). The best way into Erasmus is through his writings. For those with sufficient time and stamina, there is the exemplary University of Toronto *Collected Works*, under a multiple editorship in progress since 1974. The brief collection *Erasmus and His Age: Selected Letters of Desiderius Erasmus*, ed. H. J. Hillerbrand, trans. M. A. Haworth (1970) is more approachable, while his adages are edited as *Erasmus on His Times: A Shortened Version of the 'Adages' of Erasmus*, ed. M. M. Phillips (1967). The publishing history of the *Colloquies* emerges from F. Bierlaire, *Érasme et ses colloques: le livre d'une vie* (1977), while his work as a translator is assessed by E. Rummel, *Erasmus as a Translator of the Classics* (1985). The fullest discussion of *In Praise of Folly* is M. A. Screech, *Ecstasy and the Praise of Folly* (1980). Erasmus as a politician is viewed by J. D. Tracy, *The Politics of Erasmus: A Pacifist Intellectual and His Political Milieu* (1979), while different aspects of his work are explored in *Essays on the Works of Erasmus*, ed. R. L. DeMolen (1978). For Erasmianism in Spain, see J. C. Nieto, *Juan de Valdés and the Origins of the Spanish and Italian Reformation* (1970), while for Germany consult L. B. Spitz, *The Religious Renaissance of the German Humanists* (1963). There is a good chapter on Reuchlin in Overfield, *Humanism and Scholasticism*, while, more generally, there is now a useful collection of essays with the self-explanatory title, *The Impact of Humanism on Western Europe*, ed. A. Goodman and A. Mackay (1989).

1.2 For the intellectual origins of the Reformation, consult *The Reformation in Medieval Perspective*, ed. S. E. Ozment (1971), Ozment, *The Age of Reform* (above) and A. E. McGrath, *The Intellectual Origins of the European Reformation* (1987). Luther's relationship with his mentor is discussed by D. C. Steinmetz, *Luther and Staupitz: An Essay in the Intellectual Origins of the Protestant Reformation* (1980). There are useful chapters on spirituality, including that of Luther, Zwingli, Bullinger, Calvin and the radicals in *Christian Spirituality: High Middle Ages and Reformation*, ed. J. Raitt (1987). The best introduction on Luther is still A. G. Dickens, *The German Nation and Martin Luther* (1974). For hero-worship of Luther, R. W. Scribner,

'Incombustible Luther: the image of the reformer in early modern Germany', *PP*, 110 (1986) reprinted in idem, *Popular Culture and Popular Movements in Reformation Germany* (1987); for the several sides to Luther's personality, see *Seven-Headed Luther*, ed. P. N. Brooks (1983); while for his political thought, W. D. J. Cargill-Thompson, *The Political Thought of Martin Luther* (1984). *Martin Luther*, ed. E. G. Rupp and B. Drewery (repr. 1979), and *Martin Luther: Selections from His Writings*, ed. J. Dillenberger (1961), are useful introductory collections of Luther's writings. The publications of E. G. Rupp remain fundamental on Luther: *The Righteousness of God: Luther Studies* (1947) and *Luther's Progress to the Diet of Worms* (1951, repr. 1964). For the 'fanatics' see also Rupp, *Patterns of Reformation* (1969). An introduction to the Radicals is provided by M. Mullett, *Radical Religious Movements in Early Modern Europe* (1980), but G. H. Williams, *The Radical Reformation* (1962) remains essential for the detail. C. P. Clasen, *Anabaptism: A Social History, 1525–1618* (1972) provides a social study of the Anabaptists; their theology emerges from *The Origins and Characteristics of Anabaptism*, ed. M. Lienhard (1977) and A. L. E. Verheyden, *Anabaptism in Flanders, 1530–1650: A Century of Struggle* (1961). Too few radicals have been studied in depth but K. Deppermann, *Melchior Hoffman: Social Unrest and Apocalyptic Visions in the Age of Reformation*, trans. M. Wren (1987) and T. Bergsten, *Bulthasar Hubmaier: Anabaptist Theologian and Martyr*, trans. I. J. Barnes and W. R. Estep (1978) provide additional details. For Zwingli: G. R. Potter, *Zwingli* (1976) and *Huldrych Zwingli*, ed. idem (1978), a selection from his writings. Zwingli's successor is often forgotten: J. W. Baker, *Heinrich Bullinger and the Covenant: The Other Reformed Tradition* (1980) rescues Bullinger from obscurity.

1.3 There is now a useful collection of essays, *The German People and the Reformation*, ed. R. Po-chia Hsia (1988). A recent introduction to the German Reformation is R. W. Scribner, *The German Reformation* (1986); the same author's *For the Sake of Simple Folk: Popular Propaganda for the German Reformation* (1981) is excellent on Lutheran visual propaganda. Lutheran educational propaganda emerges clearly from G. Strauss, *Luther's House of Learning: The Indoctrination of the Young in the German Reformation* (1978); consult also idem, 'Lutheranism and literacy: a reassessment', *Religion and Society in Early Modern Europe*, ed. K. von Greyerz (1984), idem, 'Success and failure in the German Reformation', *PP*, 67 (1975) and R. Gawthrop and G. Strauss, 'Protestantism and literacy in early modern Germany', *PP*, 104 (1984). The primacy of oral communication is stressed in R. W. Scribner, 'Oral culture and the diffusion of Reformation ideas', *History of European Ideas*, 5 (1984), while for the Reformation and printing there is now a useful collection of essays, *La Réforme et le livre: l'Europe de l'imprimé, 1517–vers 1570*, ed. J.-F. Gilmont (1990). More generally on printing, consult E. Eisenstein, *The Printing Press as an Agent of Change* (1979) and *The Printing Revolution in Early Modern Europe* (1984). Leading Reformation preachers are studied in idem, 'Practice and principle in the German towns: preachers and people', *Reformation Principle and Practice ...*, ed. P. N. Brooks (1980). The

Reformation in the cities can be viewed through two main introductions: B. Moeller, *Imperial Cities and the Reformation* (1972) and S. E. Ozment, *The Reformation in the Cities: The Appeal of Protestantism to Sixteenth-Century Germany and Switzerland* (repr. 1980). A particularly stimulating new interpretation is provided by T. A. Brady, *Turning Swiss: Cities and Empire, 1450–1550* (1985) and idem, 'The common man and the lost Austria in the West: a contribution to the German problem', *Politics and Society in Reformation Europe . . .*, ed. E. I. Kouri and T. Scott (1987). Strasbourg has been particularly well studied: apart from Rapp (above), T. A. Brady, *Ruling Class, Regime and Reformation at Strasbourg, 1520–1555* (1978), and L. J. Abray, *The People's Reformation: Magistrates, Clergy and Commons in Strasbourg, 1500–1598* (1985) show how long it took to establish the Lutheran Reformation in one particularly important city. Other urban studies are G. Strauss, 'Protestant dogma and city government. The case of Nuremberg', *PP*, 36 (1967), R. W. Scribner, 'Civic unity and the Reformation in Erfurt', *PP*, 66 (1975), and idem, 'Why was there no Reformation in Cologne?', *Bulletin of the Institute of Historical Research*, 49 (1976), and an interesting perspective is provided by H. R. Guggisberg, 'The problem of "failure" in the Swiss Reformation: some preliminary reflections', *Politics and Society in Reformation Europe*, ed. Kouri and Scott. The implantation of Lutheran territorial churches is discussed by H. J. Cohn, 'Church property in the German Protestant principalities', ibid. The same volume has an important contribution by B. Moeller, 'Luther in Europe: his works in translation, 1517–46.' There is much less historiography on the princely Reformation. Q. Skinner, *The Foundations of Modern Political Thought. II. The Age of Reformation* (1978), has some interesting pages on how Luther and his followers faced up to the implications of the League of Schmalkalden, while Luther's general attitude to the princes is discussed by M. S. Lausten, 'Lutherus. Luther and the princes', *Seven-Headed Luther*, ed. P. N. Brooks (1983). There is an approach to Philip of Hesse in A. O. Hancock, 'Philip of Hesse's view of the relationship of prince and church', *Church History*, 35 (1966), while princely attitudes in the 1550s are summarized in L. W. Spitz, 'Particularism and peace: Augsburg, 1555', *Church History*, 25 (1956). One of the best guides into the principalities remains F. L. Carsten, *Princes and Parliaments in Germany from the Fifteenth to the Eighteenth Century* (1959). On the difficulties facing Lutheranism outside Germany, A. C. Duke, 'The face of popular religious dissent in the Low Countries, 1520–1530', *Journal of Ecclesiastical History*, 26 (1975) and D. J. Nicholls, 'The nature of popular heresy in France, 1520–1542', *Historical Journal*, 26 (1983).

1.4   There are numerous biographical or semi-biographical treatments of Calvin: T. H. L. Parker, *John Calvin: A Biography* (1975) is particularly useful, while W. J. Bouwsma, *John Calvin: A Sixteenth-Century Portrait* (1988) is more conceptual in approach. *John Calvin*, ed. G. R. Potter and M. Greengrass (1983), provides a useful selection of his writings, although Calvin, *The Institutes of the Christian Religion*, trans. F. L. Battles, ed. J. T. McNeill (1961) remains indispensable. H. Höpfl, *The Christian Polity of John Calvin* (1982) is also valuable, and there is information on Calvin's reforms at Geneva in the collected essays of R. M. Kingdon, *Church and Society in Reformation Europe* (1985). There is still much of interest in F. Wendel, *Calvin: The Origins and Development of His Religious Thought*, trans. P. Mairet (repr. 1965). For Calvin's view of resistance, H. A. Lloyd, 'Calvin and the duty of guardians to resist', *Journal of Ecclesiastical History*, 32 (1981). C. Bangs, *Arminius: A Study in the Dutch Reformation* (1971) is a study of the father of Arminianism. On the spread of Calvinism there is now a very useful collection of essays: *International Calvinism, 1541–1715*, ed. M. Prestwich (1985). In this volume, there are important contributions on Geneva (1541–1605) by G. Lewis, on France (1555–1629) by M. Prestwich, on the Netherlands (1561–1618) by A. C. Duke, on Germany (1559–1622) by H. J. Cohn, and on east central Europe (1540–1700) by R. J. W. Evans. M. Greengrass, *The French Reformation* (Historical Association Studies, 1987) is also a useful overview of the largest Calvinist community.

1.5 Introductions to the Counter-Reformation include A. G. Dickens, *The Counter-Reformation* (1968), M. Mullett, *The Counter-Reformation and the Catholic Reformation in Early Modern Europe* (1984), N. S. Davidson, *The Counter-Reformation* (1987) and, more difficult, A. D. Wright, *The Counter-Reformation: Catholic Europe and the Non-Christian World* (1982). P. Janelle, *The Catholic Reformation* (1949) and H. O. Evenett, *The Spirit of the Counter-Reformation* (1968) still have something to offer, but the new general approach is that of J. Delumeau, *Catholicism between Luther and Voltaire: A New View of the Counter-Reformation* (1977). New lines of enquiry are also explored in detail by P. C. Matheson, *Cardinal Contarini at Regensburg* (1972) and D. Fenlon, *Heresy and Obedience in Tridentine Italy: Cardinal Pole and the Counter-Reformation* (1972). The incomplete translation of the standard study on Trent is H. Jedin, *A History of the Council of Trent* (2 vols., 1957–61), supplemented by idem, *Papal Legate at the Council of Trent: Cardinal Seripando* (1947). That members of the Council were correct to fear the spread of evangelical thinking even into Italy has recently been suggested by J. Martin, 'Salvation and society in sixteenth-century Venice: popular evangelism in a Renaissance city', *Journal of Modern History*, 60 (1988). For censorship, there are studies by P. F. Grendler, *The Roman Inquisition and the Venetian Press* (1977) and A. Soman, 'Press, pulpit and censorship in France before Richelieu', *Proceedings of the American Philosophical Society* (1976). A summary of research developments on the Inquisition is provided by N. G. Parker, 'Some recent work on the Inquisition in Spain and Italy', *Journal of Modern History*, 54 (1982); a fuller one is provided by *The Inquisition in Early Modern Europe: Studies on Sources and Methods*, ed. G. Henningsen and J. Tedeschi (1986). Specialist studies are B. Pullan, *The Jews of Europe and the Inquisition of Venice, 1550–1670* (1983); H. Kamen, *Inquisition and Society in Spain* (1985); N. S. Davidson, 'Rome and the Venetian Inquisition in the sixteenth century', *Journal of Ecclesiastical History*, 39 (1988); and (by way of comparison) A. C. Duke, 'Salvation by coercion: the controversy surrounding the "Inquisition" in the Low Countries', *Reformation Principle and Practice . . .*, ed. P. N. Brooks (1980). The Papal nephew is studied by M. Laurain-

Portemer, 'Monarchie et gouvernement: Mazarin et le modèle romain', *La France et l'Italie au temps de Mazarin* (1985) and elsewhere, while for Papal absolutism generally, J. Delumeau, 'Le progrès de la centralisation dans l'état pontifical au xvie siècle', *Revue historique*, 226 (1961) and, most recently, P. Prodi, *The Papal Prince: One Body and Two Souls: The Papal Monarchy in Early Modern Europe*, trans. S. Haskins (1988). For the Jesuits, there is a new introduction by J. J. Scarisbrick, *The Jesuits and the Catholic Reformation* (Historical Association, 1988), but the standard account remains buried in the pious work of J. Brodrick, *The Origin of the Jesuits* (1940) and idem, *The Progress of the Jesuits* (1947). Two examples of studies on Jesuit politicians are A. Lynn Martin, *Henry III and the Jesuit Politicians* (1973) and R. Bireley, *Religion and Politics in the Age of the Counter-Reformation: Emperor Ferdinand II, William Lamormaini SJ, and the Formulation of Imperial Policy* (1981). A useful introduction to the Jansenists is provided by R. Briggs, 'The Catholic Puritans: Jansenists and rigorists in France', *Puritans and Revolutionaries*, ed. D. Pennington and K. V. Thomas (1978), reprinted in Briggs, *Communities of Belief: Cultural and Social Tension in Early Modern France* (1988): this volume also contains several other important essays on the nature of French Catholicism. The standard brief account of the rise of Jansenism is A. Adam, *Du mysticisme à la révolte: les jansénistes du xviie siècle* (1968), but a penetrating monograph is R. M. Golden, *The Godly Rebellion: Parisian Curés and the Religious Fronde, 1652–1662* (1981). Studies of local religion after Trent include A. N. Galpern, *The Religions of the People in Sixteenth-Century Champagne* (1976) and W. A. Christian, *Local Religion in Sixteenth-Century Spain* (1981).

2 EUROPE IN THE AGE OF THE ITALIAN WARS, 1494–1559

2.1 There is now a useful introduction to the building of the French state: D. Parker, *The Making of French Absolutism* (1983). For the fifteenth-century background to French expansion, P. S. Lewis, *Later Medieval France: The Polity* (1968) and *The Recovery of France in the Fifteenth Century*, ed. idem (1971). There are useful comments on French representative institutions in J. R. Major, *Representative Institutions in Renaissance France, 1421–1559* (1960) and idem, *Representative Government in Early Modern France* (1980). The governors are studied by R. R. Harding, *Anatomy of a Power Elite: The Provincial Governors of Early Modern France* (1978). There is an excellent French study of the reign of Charles VIII: Y. Labande-Mailfert, *Charles VIII et son milieu: La jeunesse au pouvoir* (1975). There is nothing comparable for the reign of Louis XII, although some of the reasons for the success of his Milanese campaign emerge clearly from D. M. Bueno de Mesquita, 'The place of despotism in Italian politics', *Europe in the Late Middle Ages*, ed. J. R. Hale, J. R. Highfield and B. Smalley (repr. 1970). A useful survey of diplomacy during the Italian wars is G. Mattingly, *Renaissance Diplomacy* (1955, repr. 1965). The problem posed by the Papal vicars emerges clearly from C. M. Ady, *The Bentivoglio of Bologna: A Study in Despotism* (1937); P. J. Jones, *The Malatesta of Rimini and the Papal State: A Political History* (1974); and C. F.

Black, 'The Baglioni as tyrants of Perugia, 1488–1540', E[*nglish*] H[*istorical*] R[*eview*], 85 (1970). Of the Popes who responded, Alexander VI and Clement VII have been well studied (above 1.1). The pivotal role of Genoa is briefly discerned in P. Coles, 'The crisis of Renaissance society: Genoa, 1488–1507', *PP*, 11 (1957). Both Florence and Venice have substantial bibliographies in their own right, but introductions are to be found in J. R. Hale, *Florence and the Medici: The Pattern of Control* (1977), *Renaissance Venice*, ed. J. R. Hale (1973) and W. H. McNeill, *Venice, the Hinge of Europe, 1081–1797* (1974).

2.2 Spain before the reign of Charles V (Carlos I) is reasonably well served in English. There are useful introductions by J. H. Elliott, *Imperial Spain, 1469–1716* (1963), A. MacKay, *Spain in the Middle Ages: From Frontier to Empire, 1000–1500* (1977), J. N. Hillgarth, *The Spanish Kingdoms, 1250–1516*. II. *Castilian Hegemony, 1410–1516* (1978) and H. Kamen, *Spain, 1469–1714: A Society of Conflict* (1983). There is still information to be gleaned from R. B. Merriman, *The Rise of the Spanish Empire in the Old World and the New* (4 vols., 1918–34), and the same author's venerable study of representation should not be neglected: 'The *Cortes* of the Spanish kingdoms in the later Middle Ages', *EHR*, 16 (1910–11). There is a worthy collection of essays on *Spain in the Fifteenth Century, 1369–1516*, ed. J. R. L. Highfield (1963), while the same author's study of the nobility is of importance: 'The Catholic kings and the titled nobility of Castile', *Europe in the late Middle Ages*, ed. Hale, Highfield and Smalley (1965). The financial history of the Catholic monarchs has been reappraised by M. A. Ladero Quesada, 'Les finances royales de Castille à la veille des temps modernes', *Annales E.S.C.*, 25 (1970), 775–88. There is a useful introduction to the late medieval Empire by F. R. H. DuBoulay, *Germany in the later Middle Ages* (1983). In English, there is only one, rather feeble, biography of Maximilian I: G. Benecke, *Maximilian I* (1982), but see now the review article of Hermann Wiesflecker's biography in German by T. A. Brady Jr., 'Imperial destinies: a new bibliography of the Emperor Maximilian I', *Journal of Modern History*, 62 (1990). Imperial institutions, and the failure of Imperial reform, have been served rather better in English: H. S. Offler, 'Aspects of government in the late medieval Empire', *Europe in the Late Middle Ages*, ed. Hale, Highfield and Smalley; H. Baron, 'Imperial reform and the Habsburgs, 1486–1504', *American Historical Review*, 44 (1938–9); F. Hartung, 'Imperial reform, 1435–1495 . . .', *Pre-Reformation Germany*, ed. Strauss. See also *The Old Reich: Essays on German Political Institutions, 1495–1806*, ed. J. A. Vann and S. W. Rowan (1974) and *The Holy Roman Empire: A Dictionary Handbook*, ed. J. W. Zophyn (1980). For two German leagues of very different kinds, P. Dollinger, *The German Hansa*, trans. D. S. Ault and S. H. Steinberg (1970) and W. Oechsli, *History of Switzerland, 1499–1914* (1922), although the German origins are left rather obscure in the latter. Maximilian's financial problems emerge from R. H. Ehrenberg, *Capital and Finance in the Age of the Renaissance . . .*, trans. H. M. Lucas (1928) and L. Shick, *Un grand homme d'affaires au début du xvie siècle* (1957).

2.3 Francis I is now comprehensively surveyed in R. J. Knecht's magisterial *Francis I* (1982), but the same author's related publications should not be forgotten: 'Francis I and absolute monarchy', *Historical Association Pamphlet* 72 (1969) and *French Renaissance Monarchy: Francis I and Henri II* (1984). There is also a French biography: J. Jacquart, *François Ier* (1981). The Concordat of Bologna has been studied by R. J. Knecht, 'The Concordat of 1516: a reassessment', *Government in Reformation Europe, 1520–1560*, ed. H. J. Cohn (1971), while the king's religious position is elucidated in idem, 'Francis I, "defender of the faith"?', *Wealth and Power in Tudor England*, ed. E. W. Ives, R. J. Knecht and J. J. Scarisbrick (1978). One of the king's main rivals is studied by J. J. Scarisbrick, *Henry VIII* (repr. 1976). The Tudor king's foreign policy is surveyed by S. J. Gunn, 'The French wars of Henry VIII', *The Origins of War in Early Modern Europe*, ed. J. Black (1987), while the same author has studied one key campaign in more detail: 'The duke of Suffolk's march on Paris in 1523', *EHR*, 101 (1986). For French foreign policy at the end of Francis I's reign: D. L. Potter, 'Foreign policy in the age of the Reformation: French involvement in the Schmalkaldic war, 1544–7', *Historical Journal*, 20 (1977).

2.4 The standard biography of Charles V remains K. Brandi, *Charles V*, trans. C. V. Wedgwood (1939, repr. 1965), but M. Fernandez Alvarez, *Charles V* (1976) is a more recent synthesis. Of value, too, is J. Lynch, *Spain under the Habsburgs. I. Empire and Absolutism, 1516–1598* (1964), while Elliott and Kamen (above, 2.2) remain important as introductions. The article by H. G. Koenigsberger on 'The empire of Charles V' has been reproduced in idem, *The Habsburgs and Europe, 1516–1660* (1971); another of his volumes of essays, *Estates and Revolutions . . .* (1971) is important for an understanding of the period. Gattinara has been studied by J. M. Headley, *The Emperor and His Chancellor: A Study of the Imperial Chancellery under Gattinara* (1983), and los Cobos by H. Keniston, *Francisco de los Cobos: Secretary of the Emperor Charles V* (1960). On the stadholders in the Low Countries, consult P. Rosenfeld, 'The provincial governors of the Netherlands from the minority of Charles V to the revolt', *Government in Reformation Europe, 1520–60*, ed. Cohn. The foreign policy of the Empire is surveyed in S. A. Fischer-Galati, *Ottoman Imperialism and German Protestantism, 1521–1555* (1959), while various aspects of Charles's financial problems are revealed by M. Baelde, 'Financial policy and the evolution of the demesne in the Netherlands under Charles V and Philip II, 1530–60', *Government in Reformation Europe, 1520–60*, ed. Cohn, and F. Braudel, 'Les emprunts de Charles-Quint sur la place d'Anvers', *Charles-Quint et son temps* (1959). The magisterial study of R. Carande, *Carlos V y sus banqueros* (1944–9) has not been translated. Castilian history under Charles V has been fundamentally reappraised by C. R. Henricks, 'Charles V and the *Cortes* of Castile. Politics in Renaissance Spain' (unpub. Ph.D. thesis, Cornell, 1976). Information on the advantages to Philip II of the English alliance may be gleaned from D. M. Loades, *The Reign of Mary Tudor: Politics, Government and Religion in England, 1553–1558* (1979). For the Peace of Augsburg, two studies are particularly useful:

H. Tüchle, 'The Peace of Augsburg: new order or lull in the fighting?', *Government in Reformation Europe*, ed. Cohn, and L. W. Spitz, 'Particularism and peace' (above, 1.3). The same author has studied its aftermath: Spitz, 'Imperialism, particularism and toleration in the Holy Roman Empire', *The Massacre of St. Bartholomew: Reappraisals and Documents*, ed. A. Soman (1974).

2.5 Henri II remains a rather neglected monarch, although there have been recent biographies by I. Cloulas, *Henri II* (1985) and by F. J. Baumgartner, *Henri II, King of France, 1547–1559* (1988). The most detailed survey of foreign policy during the period is provided by the last part of F. Braudel, *The Mediterranean and the Mediterranean World in the Age of Philip II*, trans. S. Reynolds (repr. 1973), now supplemented by Rodríguez-Salgado (see 3.1 below). French foreign policy at the end of Henri II's reign is also considered by C. S. L. Davies, 'England and the French war, 1557–9', *The Mid-Tudor Polity, c.1540–1560*, ed. J. Loach and R. Tittler (1980). For Henri II's financial problems, R. Doucet, 'Le grand parti de Lyon au xvie siècle', *Revue historique*, 171 (1933).

3 EUROPE IN THE AGE OF THE WARS OF RELIGION, 1559–1618

3.1 Apart from the volumes by Lynch, Elliott, Kamen and Koenigsberger cited above (2.2 and 2.5), there is a valuable introduction by H. G. Koenigsberger, 'The statecraft of Philip II', *E[uropean] S[tudies] R[eview]* 1 (1971); the same author has provided a more detailed study of Sicily: idem, *The Practice of Empire: The Government of Sicily under Philip II* (1969). There are two recent biographies, by P. Pierson, *Philip II of Spain* (1975) and by N. G. Parker, *Philip II* (repr. 1979). Parker's collected essays are particularly useful: idem, *Spain and the Netherlands, 1559–1659* (1979). There is also detailed work on one of the secretaries by A. W. Lovett, *Philip II and Mateo Vázquez de Leca: The Government of Spain, 1572–92* (1977); the same author has provided a more general interpretation: idem, *Early Habsburg Spain, 1516–98* (1986). One of the most important detailed studies is I. A. A. Thompson, *War and Government in Habsburg Spain, 1560–1620* (1976), while there is a recent study of the 1550s: M. J. Rodríguez-Salgado, *The Changing Face of Empire: Charles V, Philip II and Habsburg Authority, 1551–1559* (1988). Regrettably, two important theses remain unpublished: P. D. Lagomarsino, 'Court factions and the formulation of Spanish policy towards the Netherlands, 1559–67' (Cambridge, 1973) and C. D. G. Riley, 'The state of Milan in the reign of Philip II of Spain' (Oxford, 1977). Braudel, *The Mediterranean*, (above 2.3) remains indispensable for a general understanding of Philip II's problems. The background to his political attitudes is sketched by B. Hamilton, *Political Thought in Sixteenth-Century Spain* . . . (1963); the most extreme theorist is studied by G. Lewy, *Constitutionalism and Statecraft during the Golden Age of Spain: A Study of the Political Philosophy of Juan de Mariana SJ* (1960). G. Mattingly, *The Defeat of the Spanish Armada* (1959, repr. 1988) is a classic account of the débâcle, but now largely superseded by C. Martin and N. G. Parker, *The Spanish Armada* (1988); consult also S. L. Adams, *The Armada Campaign of 1588* (Historical Association, 1988), J. Fernández-Armesto, *The Spanish*

Armada: The Experience of War in 1588 (1988) and *Armada, 1588–1988: An International Exhibition to Commemorate the Spanish Armada*, ed. M. J. Rodríguez-Salgado *et al.* (1988). There is a more general account of the Spanish Habsburg defence system: P. E. Hoffmann, *The Spanish Crown and the Defense of the Caribbean, 1535–1583: Precedent, Patrimonialism and Royal Parsimony* (1980). For Philip's financial problems, A. Castillo, 'Dette flottante et dette consolidée en Espagne de 1557 à 1600', *Annales E.S.C.*, 18 (1963). For his dealings with one of his representative institutions, C. Jago, 'Philip II and the *Cortes* of 1576', *PP*, 109 (1985).

3.2 The most recent introduction to the civil wars in the Low Countries is N. G. Parker, *The Dutch Revolt* (1977); this draws on much recent research, including the author's own *The Army of Flanders and the Spanish Road, 1567–1659* (1972). There is a brief overview by J. W. Smit, 'The Netherlands revolution', *Preconditions of Revolution in Early Modern Europe*, ed. R. Forster and J. P. Greene (1970) and an interpretation by G. Griffiths, 'The revolutionary character of the revolt of the Netherlands', *Comparative Studies in Society and History*, 2 (1959–60). Despite its great age, H. Pirenne, *Histoire de Belgique. III. 1477–1567* (2nd edn, 1912) and *IV. 1567–1648* (1919) remains one of the best accounts, although also still of interest are P. Geyl, *The Revolt of the Netherlands, 1555–1609* (1932) and the riposte by G. Malengreau, *L'esprit particulariste et la révolution des Pays-Bas au xvie siècle, 1578–84* (1936). For the early conflict between the government and the nobles, H. G. Koenigsberger, 'Orange, Granvelle and Philip II', *Politics and Society in Reformation Europe*, ed. Kouri and Scott. The definitive study of the bishoprics scheme is M. Dierickx, *L'érection des nouveaux diocèses aux Pays-Bas, 1559–1570* (1967). On the Inquisition scare, A. C. Duke, 'Salvation by coercion' (above 1.5); for the persecution under Habsburgs, idem, 'Building heaven in hell's despite: the early history of the Reformation in the towns of the Low Countries', *Britain and the Netherlands*, 7 (1981); for concepts of loyalty, idem, 'From king and country to king or country? Loyalty and treason in the revolt of the Netherlands', *Transactions of the Royal Historical Society*, 32 (1982). These articles are now usefully reprinted with others in A. C. Duke, *Reformation and Revolt in the Low Countries* (1990). The iconoclastic riots of 1566 are studied by Duke and D. H. A. Kolff, 'The time of troubles in the county of Holland, 1566–7', *T[ijdschrift] v[oor] g[eschiedenis]*, 82 (1969) and by P. M. Crew, *Calvinist Preaching and Iconoclasm in the Netherlands, 1544–1569* (1978). The slow progress of Calvinism in Holland is reviewed in A. C. Duke and R. L. Jones, 'Towards a reformed polity in Holland, 1572–8', *TVG*, 89 (1976). The Spanish army and military policy is discussed in the works of Parker (above and 3.1) and by L. Van der Essen, 'Croisade contre les hérétiques ou guerre contre des rebelles? . . .', *Revue d'histoire ecclésiastique*, 51 (1956). There are useful accounts of some of the key personalities by K. W. Swart, *William the Silent and the Revolt of the Netherlands* (Historical Association, 1978); two articles by A. W. Lovett on Requesens in *ESR*, 1 (1971) and 2 (1972) and, most important of all, L. Van der Essen, *Alexandre Farnèse, prince de Parme . . .* (1933–7). The role of the civic militia is studied by J. C. Grayson, 'The civic militia in the county of Holland, 1560–81', *B[ijdragen en] m[ededelingen betreffende de] g[eschiedenis der] N[eder-landen]*, 95 (1980). There are two useful studies on 1576: M. Baelde, 'The Pacification of Ghent in 1576 . . .', *A[cta] H[istoriae] N[eerlandicae]*, ll (1978) and P. Van Peteghem, 'Flanders in 1576: revolutionary or reactionary?', ibid. 12 (1979). Calvinist extremism in the south is somewhat eccentricly surveyed in T. Wittman, *Les gueux dans les 'bonnes villes' de Flandres, 1577–84* (1969). The northern union is studied by J. C. Boogman, 'The union of Utrecht: its genesis and consequences', *BMGN*, 94 (1979). Finally, and of inestimable importance, *Texts Concerning the Revolt of the Netherlands*, ed. E. H. Kossmann and A. F. Mellink (1975): the introduction provides the best survey of the political thought of the revolt.

3.3 Among the introductions to the French wars of religion are R. Briggs, *Early Modern France, 1560–1715* (1977) and J. H. M. Salmon, *Society in Crisis: France in the Sixteenth Century* (1975). More conceptual in approach is H. A. Lloyd, *The State, France and the Sixteenth Century* (1980). The standard account from the Protestant viewpoint is N. M. Sutherland, *The Huguenot Struggle for Recognition* (1980); D. R. Kelley, *The Beginning of Ideology: Consciousness and Society in the French Reformation* (1981) is more original. P. Mack Holt, *The Duke of Anjou and the Politique Struggle during the Wars of Religion* (1986) provides some insights on one of the key individuals; J. Shimizu, *Conflict of Loyalties: Politics and Religion in the Career of Gaspard de Coligny, Admiral of France, 1519–1572* (1970) on another. P. Benedict, *Rouen during the Wars of Religion* (1981) is an excellent local study; much information on Lyon and on religious riot is contained in N. Z. Davis, *Society and Culture in Early Modern France* (1975). Henri III's dealings with the Jesuits is discussed by Lynn Martin (above 1.5), while De Lamar Jensen, *Diplomacy and Dogmatism: Bernardino de Mendoza and the Catholic League* (1964) discusses the intrigues leading to his demise. The whole period of the Catholic League has been opened up in recent years: among the important contributions are R. A. Jackson, 'Elective kingship and *consensus populi . . .*', *Journal of Modern History*, 44 (1972); J. H. M. Salmon, 'The Paris sixteen, 1589–94: the social analysis of a revolutionary movement', ibid. 44 (1972); F. J. Baumgartner, *Radical Reactionaries: The Political Thought of the French Catholic League* (1975); M. Greengrass, 'The sixteen, radical politics in Paris during the League', *History*, 69 (1984); R. Descimon, 'La Ligue à Paris, 1585–1594: une révision', *Annales E.S.C.*, 37 (1982); idem, *Qui étaient les seize? Mythes et réalités de la Ligue parisienne, 1585–1594* (1983); E. Barnavi, *Le parti de Dieu: étude sociale et politique de la Ligue parisienne, 1584–1594* (Louvain, 1980); and Barnavi and Descimon, *La Sainte Ligue, le juge et la potence: l'assassinat du président Brisson, 15 novembre 1591* (1985). A fundamental reappraisal of religious violence is being undertaken by D. Crouzet, 'Recherches sur les processions blanches, 1583–4', *Histoire, économie, société*, 1 (1982); and, above all, consult the same author's remarkable study of *Les guerriers de Dieu: la violence au temps des troubles de religion, vers 1525–vers 1610* (2 vols., 1990). Useful sidelights are thrown on the war of the Bourbon succession by H. A. Lloyd, *The Rouen Campaign, 1590–2: Politics, Warfare and the Early Modern State* (1973), while for the settlement of Nantes, R. É. Mousnier, *The Assassination of Henri IV. 14 May 1610*, trans. R. J. Spencer (1973) is particularly useful.

3.4 J. den Tex, *Oldenbarnevelt* (2 vols., 1973) is the standard biography of the leading figure in the Dutch Republic in the negotiations over the truce and the growing religious controversy. R. J. W. Evans, *Rudolf II and His World: A Study in Intellectual History, 1576–1612* (1973, repr. 1984) is a superb study of the eccentric Habsburg ruler; the same author's *The Making of the Habsburg Monarchy, 1550–1700* (1979) is excellent on the background to the Thirty Years' War. Also useful is C. P. Clasen, *The Palatinate in European History, 1559–1660* (1963), while V.-L. Tapié, *Monarchie et peuples du Danube* (1969) is something of a classic. There is a useful collection of essays entitled *The European Crisis of the 1590s*, ed. P. A. Clark (1985). Most of the other literature arises in the context of the Thirty Years' War (4.1 below).

4 THE STRUGGLE FOR EUROPEAN HEGEMONY, 1618–1660

4.1 *The Thirty Years' War*, ed. N. G. Parker (1985) is the best recent introduction. See also H. G. Koenigsberger, 'The European civil war', idem, *The Habsburgs and Europe, 1516–1660* (1971); G. Pagès, *The Thirty Years' War* (trans. 1971); J. V. Polišenský, *The Thirty Years' War* (trans. R. J. W. Evans, 1971) and S. H. Steinberg, *The Thirty Years' War and the Conflict for European Hegemony, 1600–60* (1966). On imperial policy, Bireley, *Religion and Politics* (above 1.5) and H. F. Schwarz, *The Imperial Privy Council in the Seventeenth Century* (repr. 1972) have something to offer in addition to Evans (above 3.4). Two of the main personalities are studied in G. Mann, *Wallenstein* (1976) and M. Roberts, 'The politicial objectives of Gustavus Adolphus in Germany, 1630–2', idem, *Essays in Swedish History* (1967). There are important contributions on the army in the Thirty Years' War by Redlich and Parrott (below 6.4). The threat of the Edict of Restitution is discussed by B. Nischan, *Brandenburg and the Edict of Restitution* (1979), while the consequences of the war are assessed in G. Benecke, 'The problem of death and destruction in Germany during the Thirty Years' War', *ESR*, 2 (1972).

4.2 There has been recent work of high quality on the renewal of the conflict between the Dutch Republic and Spain: J. I. Israel, 'A conflict of empires: Spain and the Netherlands, 1618–48', *PP*, 76 (1977) and the same author's *The Dutch Republic and the Hispanic World, 1606–61* (1982). Three of his more detailed articles are also particularly helpful: 'The Holland towns and the Dutch–Spanish conflict', *BMGN*, 94 (1979); 'The States General and the strategic regulation of the Dutch river trade, 1621–1636', ibid. 95 (1980); and 'Frederick Henry and the Dutch political factions', *EHR*, 98 (1983). These and other articles are now usefully collected in J. I. Israel, *Empires and Entrepôts: The Dutch, the Spanish Monarchy and the Jews, 1585–1713* (1990). The issue of the intervention of France has been reassessed by R. A. Stradling, 'Olivares and the origins of the Franco-Spanish war, *1627–1635*', *EHR*, 101 (1986) and by D. A. Parrott, 'The causes of the Franco-Spanish war of *1635–59*', *The Origins of War in Early Modern Europe*, ed. J. Black (1987). For the later history of the Dutch Republic: H. H. Rowen, 'The revolution that wasn't: the *coup d'état* of 1650 in Holland', *ESR*, 4 (1974); idem, *John de Witt: Grand Pensionary of Holland, 1625–1672* (1978); and idem, *The Princes of Orange: The Stadholders in the Dutch Republic* (1988).

4.3 Apart from the works by Elliott and Kamen (above 2.2), the survival of Spanish Habsburg power is surveyed by J. Lynch, *Spain under the Habsburgs. II. Spain and America, 1598–1700* (1969) and by R. A. Stradling, *Europe and the Decline of Spain . . . 1580–1720* (1981). There has been some lively debate on the theme of decline: J. H. Elliott, 'The decline of Spain', *PP*, 20 (1961); idem, 'Self-perception and decline in early seventeenth-century Spain', *PP*, 74 (1977) (these articles have now been usefully collected together: idem, *Spain and Its World, 1500–1700: Selected Essays* (1989)); H. Kamen, 'The decline of Spain: a[n] historical myth', ibid. 81 (1978); and a further debate, ibid. 91 (1981); on the same theme, R. A. Stradling, 'Seventeenth-century Spain: decline or survival?' *ESR*, 9 (1979). Lerma's objectives have been reassessed in P. Williams, 'Lerma, Old Castile and the travels of Philip III of Spain', *History*, 73 (1988). The two outstanding books on seventeenth-century Spain are J. H. Elliott, *The Revolt of the Catalans . . . 1598–1640* (1963) and the same author's *The Count-Duke of Olivares: The Statesman in an Age of Decline* (1986); see also idem, *Richelieu and Olivares* (1984) and idem, 'The statecraft of Olivares', *The Diversity of History . . .*, ed. Elliott and H. G. Koenigsberger (1970). There has been a recent revision of Philip IV's reign: see R. A. Stradling, *Philip IV and the Government of Spain, 1621–1665* (1988). There is some additional material on this period in H. Kamen, *Spain in the Later Seventeenth Century, 1665–1700* (1980). A good study of one of the Spanish kingdoms is J. Casey, *The Kingdom of Valencia in the Seventeenth Century* (1979); see also idem, 'Moriscos and the depopulation of Valencia', *PP*, 50 (1971).

4.4 The recovery of France after the wars of religion is surveyed by M. Greengrass, *France in the Age of Henri IV: The Struggle for Stability* (1984). See also D. J. Buisseret, *Henry IV* (1984) and idem, *Sully and the Growth of Centralized Government in France, 1598–1610* (1968). For the regency period, J. M. Hayden, *France and the Estates General of 1614* (1974), while V. L. Tapié, *France in the Age of Louis XIII and Richelieu*, trans. D. McN. Lockie (1974) provides a narrative. A. D. Lublinskaya, *French Absolutism: The Crucial Phase, 1620–9* (1968) and D. Parker, *La Rochelle and the French Monarchy: Conflict and Order in Seventeenth-Century France* (1980) cover the 1620s. W. F. Church, *Richelieu and Reason of State* (1972) is useful for the pamphlet controversies, while O. A. Ranum, *Richelieu and the Councillors of Louis XIII . . . 1635–42* (1963) studies the ministerial clients. R. J. Bonney, 'Absolutism: what's in a name?', *French History*, 1 (1987) surveys the recent literature on the subject, while idem, *Political Change in France under*

Richelieu and Mazarin, 1624–1661 (1978) assesses the impact of central government upon the localities; idem, *The King's Debts: Finance and Politics in France, 1589–1661* (1981) considers the problems of the government in more detail, while idem, *Society and Government in France under Richelieu and Mazarin, 1624–61* (1988) provides documents in translation. Two important local studies are S. Kettering, *Patrons, Brokers and Clients in Seventeenth-Century France* (1986) and W. H. Beik, *Absolutism and Society in Seventeenth-Century France: State Power and Provincial Aristocracy in Languedoc* (1985). For the Fronde: R. É. Mousnier, 'The Fronde', *Preconditions of Revolution in Early Modern Europe*, ed. R. Forster and J. P. Greene (1970); A. L. Moote, *The Revolt of the Judges: The Parlement of Paris and the Fronde, 1643–52* (1971); R. J. Bonney, 'The French civil war, 1649–53', *ESR*, 8 (1978); idem, 'Cardinal Mazarin and the great nobility during the Fronde', *EHR*, 96 (1981); idem, 'Cardinal Mazarin and his critics: the remonstrances of 1652', *Journal of European Studies*, 10 (1980); idem, 'The English and French civil wars', *History*, 65 (1980); and for the aftermath: A. N. Hamscher, *The Parlement of Paris after the Fronde, 1653–1673* (1976). The fundamental study of propaganda and public debate during the Fronde is now H. Carrier, *La presse et la Fronde, 1648–1653. Les Mazarinades: la conquête de l'opinion* (1989).

5 THE OUTSIDERS OF EUROPE

5.1 For the struggle for Baltic supremacy, the reader is indebted to the works of M. Roberts: see especially *The Swedish Imperial Experience, 1560–1718* (1980); also *The Early Vasas* (1968); *Gustavus Adolphus and the Rise of Sweden* (1973); *Sweden as a Great Power, 1611–1697: Government, Society, Foreign Policy* (repr. 1973); and his *Essays in Swedish History* (1967). A more recent interpretation is S. Oakley, 'War in the Baltic', *The Origins of War in Early Modern Europe*, ed J. Black (1987). An economic interpretation is provided by A. Attman, *The Struggle for Baltic Markets: Powers in Conflict, 1558–1618* (1979).

5.2 There are two modern accounts of Poland-Lithuania: N. Davies, *God's Playground: A History of Poland. I. The Origins to 1795* (1981) and A. Zamoyski, *The Polish Way: A Thousand-Year History of the Poles and Their Culture* (1987). For a narrative account: *Cambridge History of Poland: From the Origins to Sobieski (to 1696)*, ed. W. F. Reddaway *et al.* (1950). Details on Poland's religious composition are provided by A. Jobert, *De Luther à Mohila: la Pologne dans la crise de la Chrétienté, 1517–1648* (1974). On constitutional matters, L. Konopczyński, *Le Liberum veto: étude sur le développement du principe majoritaire* (1930) and J. Žmuidzinas, *Commonwealth polono-lithauanien ou l'Union de l'Lublin, 1569* (1978). There is a valuable collection of essays: *A Republic of Nobles: Studies in Polish History to 1864*, ed. J. K. Fedorowicz (1982).

5.3 The best account of Muscovy is R. Pipes, *Russia under the Old Regime* (1974), although R. Hellie, *Enserfment and Military Change in Muscovy* (1971) is fundamental on military organization. The most recent general works are R. O. Crummey, *The Formation of Muscovy, 1304–1614* (1987) and P. Dukes, *The Making of Russian Absolutism, 1613–1801* (1982). Also of assistance are P. Dukes, *A History of Russia* (1974); and G. Vernadsky, *The Tsardom of Moscow, 1547–1682* (1969). For Ivan III: J. L. I. Fennell, *Ivan the Great of Moscow* (1961). For Ivan IV, 'the dread': I. Grey, *Ivan the Terrible* (1963, repr. 1966); R. G. Skrynnikov, *Ivan the Terrible*, trans. H. F. Graham (1981); *Prince A. M. Kurbsky's History of Ivan IV*, trans. J. L. I. Fennell (1965); B. Nørretranders, *The Shaping of Czardom under Ivan Groznyj* (1964, repr. 1971); and finally (a polemic) A. Yanov, *The Origins of Autocracy: Ivan the Terrible in Russian History*, trans. S. Dunn (1981). S. F. Platonov, *The Time of Troubles: A[n] Historical Study of the Internal Crisis and Social Struggle of Sixteenth- and Seventeenth-Century Muscovy*, trans. J. T. Alexander (1970) is an old account (orig. edn., 1923). For the later period, J. T. Fuhrmann, *Tsar Alexis: His Reign and His Russia* (1981). Of interest for the frontier regions are: W. H. McNeill, *Europe's Steppe Frontier, 1500–1800: A Study of the Eastward Movement in Europe* (repr. 1975) and J. L. Wieczynski, *The Russian Frontier: The Impact of Borderlands upon the Course of Early Russian History* (1976). For the Chmielnicki rebellion: F. E. Sysyn, 'Ukrainian–Polish relations in the seventeenth century: the role of national consciousness and national conflict in the Khmelnytsky revolt', *Poland and Ukraine: Past and Present*, ed. P. J. Potichnyj (1980) and C. B. O'Brien, *Muscovy and the Ukraine: From the Pereiaslavl Agreement to the Truce of Andrusovo, 1654–1667* (1963).

5.4   Some of the reasons for Ottoman supremacy in south-east Europe and the Middle East emerge from H. Inalcík, *The Ottoman Empire: The Classical Age, 1300–1600* (1973); P. Wittek, *The Rise of the Ottoman Empire* (1938, repr. 1971); *The Cambridge History of Islam. I. The Central Islamic Lands*, ed. P. M. Holt, A. K. S. Lambton and B. Lewis (1970); S. J. Shaw, *History of the Ottoman Empire and Modern Turkey. I. Empire of the Gazis: The Rise and Decline of the Ottoman Empire, 1280–1808* (1976); and, most recently, *Histoire de l'empire ottoman*, ed. R. Mantran (1989). Detailed studies of particular areas under Ottoman rule include S. J. Shaw, *The Financial and Administrative Development of Ottoman Egypt, 1517–1798* (1962) and B. McGowan, *Economic Life in Ottoman Europe: Taxation, Trade and the Struggle for Land, 1600–1800* (1981). For Ottoman policy towards the east generally, C. M. Kortpeter, *Ottoman Imperialism during the Reformation: Europe and the Caucasus* (1973). Ottoman military matters are studied by H. Inalcík, 'Ottoman methods of conquest', *Studia Islamica*, 2 (1954) and by D. Pipes, *Slave Soldiers and Islam: The Genesis of a Military System* (1981). Perceptions of Ottoman rule are evaluated by B. Lewis, 'Ottoman observers of Ottoman decline', *Islamic Studies*, 1 (1962). On the Balkans: G. Rothenberg, *The Austrian Military Border in Croatia, 1522–1747* (1960) and P. F. Sugar, *South-Eastern Europe under Ottoman Rule, 1354–1804* (1977). For Ottoman Hungary, there are works of vulgarization: L. Makkai, *Histoire de Transylvanie* (1946) and *A History of Hungary*, ed. E. Palményi (1975). The most important research is that of A. C. Hess: 'The battle of Lepanto and its place in

Mediterranean history', *PP*, 57 (1972); 'The Moriscos: an Ottoman fifth column in sixteenth-century Spain', *American Historical Review*, 74 (1968); 'The evolution of the Ottoman seaborne empire in the age of the oceanic discoveries, 1453–1525', ibid. 75 (1970); and idem, *The Forgotten Frontier: A History of the Sixteenth-Century Ibero-African Frontier* (1978). Also of interest is J. H. Pryor, *Geography, Technology and War: Studies in the Maritime History of the Mediterranean* (1988).

6 THE RISE OF EUROPEAN ABSOLUTISM

6.1 The fundamental introduction to European political thought is Q. Skinner, *The Foundations of Modern Political Thought* (2 vols., 1978); see also idem, *Machiavelli* (1981). Both *The Prince* and *The Discourses* are available in translation. Among the profusion of writings on Machiavelli, consult J. R. Hale, *Machiavelli and Renaissance Italy* (1961); F. Gilbert, *Machiavelli and Guicciardini: Politics and History in Sixteenth-Century Florence* (1965); J. G. A. Pocock, *The Machiavellian Moment: Florentine Political Thought and the Atlantic Republican Tradition* (1975); B. Guillemain, *Machiavel: l'antropologie politique* (1977); H. Baron, 'Machiavelli: the republican citizen and author of "The Prince"', *EHR*, 76 (1961); and J. N. Stephens and H. C. Butters, 'New light on Machiavelli', ibid. 97 (1982). A particularly interesting riposte to the Florentine is I. Gentillet, *Anti-Machiavel*, ed. C. E. Rathé (1968). The Protestant theorists are assessed by L. Arenilla, 'Le calvinisme et le droit de résistance à l'état', *Annales E.S.C.*, 22 (1967); J. H. Franklin, 'Constitutionalism in the sixteenth century: the Protestant monarchomachs', *Political Theory and Social Change*, ed. D. Spitz (1967); and R. E. Giesey, 'The monarchomach triumvirs: Hotman, Beza, Mornay', *Bulletin d'humanisme et Renaissance*, 32 (1970). The relevant texts are presented in an abridged form in *Constitutionalism and Resistance in the Sixteenth Century: Three Treatises by Hotman, Beza and Mornay*, ed. J. H. Franklin (1969). Full modern editions of two of them are available: F. Hotman, *Francogallia*, trans. J. H. M. Salmon and ed. R. E. Giesey (1972); T. de Bèze, *Du droit des magistrats*, ed. R. M. Kingdon (1970); for the the third, the translation *A Defence of Liberty against Tyrants* . . ., ed. H. J. Laski (1924) is poor. The career of one of the key theorists is discussed by D. R. Kelley, *François Hotman: A Revolutionary's Ordeal* (1973). Two later successors are available in translation: *The Politics of Johannes Althusius* . . ., trans. F. S. Carney (1965) and H. Grotius, *De jure belli ac pacis* . . ., trans. F. W. Kelsley (1925). For Grotius, consult also R. Tuck, *Natural Rights Theories: Their Origin and Development* (1979). The anti-Monarchomach theorist is also available in translation: W. Barclay, *The Kingdom and the Royal Power*, trans. G. Moore (1954). For Bodin, there is the magisterial edition of Richard Knolles's English translation of 1606: Bodin, *The Six Bookes of a Commonweale*, ed. K. D. McRae (1962). Among the authorities to be consulted, see J. H. Franklin, *Jean Bodin and the Rise of Absolutist Theory* (1973); D. Parker, 'Law, society and the state in the thought of Jean Bodin', *History of Political Thought*, 2 (1981); *Jean Bodin* . . ., ed.

H. Denzer (1973); and above all, the research of P. L. Rose, 'Bodin's universe and its paradoxes . . .', *Politics and Society in Reformation Europe*, ed. E. I. Kouri and T. Scott (1987); idem, 'The *politique* and the prophet. Bodin and the Catholic League, 1589–94', *Historical Journal*, 21 (1978); idem, 'Bodin and the Bourbon succession to the French throne, 1583–94', *Sixteenth-Century Journal*, 9 (1978); idem, *Bodin and the Great God of Nature* (1980). For two Catholic theorists somewhat influenced by Bodin: J. Lipsius, *Sixe Bookes of Politickes or Civil Doctrine*, trans. W. Jones (1594) in *The English Experience*, 287 (1970) and G. Botero, *The Reason of State*, trans. P. J. and D. P. Waley (1956). For Spanish theorists, see 3.1 above. An interesting comparison between Bodin and Hobbes is made by P. King, *The Ideology of Order: A Comparative Analysis of Jean Bodin and Thomas Hobbes* (1974). Among the vast literature on Hobbes, particularly interesting are T. A. Spragens Jr., *The Politics of Motion: The World of Thomas Hobbes* (1973); Q. Skinner, 'History and ideology in the English Revolution', *Historical Journal*, 8 (1965); idem, 'Thomas Hobbes and his disciples in England and France', *Comparative Studies in Society and History*, 8 (1966); and K. V. Thomas, 'The social origins of Hobbes's political thought', *Hobbes Studies*, ed. K. C. Brown (1965).

6.2　There are several introductory works on European parliaments: A. Marongui, *Medieval Parliaments* (1968); A. R. Myers, *European Parliaments before* 1789 (1975); C. Griffiths, *Representative Government in Western Europe in the Sixteenth Century* (1968); H. G. Koenigsberger, *'Dominium Regale' or 'Dominium Politicum et Regale': Monarchies and Parliaments in Early Modern Europe* (1975) and the same author's *Estates and Revolutions . . .* (1971). For France, see the works by Major (above 2.1) and Hayden (above 4.4), and for Germany, Carsten (above 1.3). For Spain, C. Jago, 'Habsburg absolutism and the *Cortes* of Castile', *American Historical Review*, 86 (1981) and idem, 'Philip II and the *Cortes* of Castile', *PP*, 109 (1985); also important are the studies of I. A. A. Thompson, 'Crown and *Cortes* in Castile, 1590–1665', *Parliaments, Estates and Representation*, 2 (1982); idem, 'The end of the Cortes of Castile', *Parliaments, Estates and Representation*, 4 (1984). One of the best studies on Parliament in England is C. S. R. Russell, *Parliaments and English Politics, 1621–9* (1979), while for the Low Countries consult J. Gilissen, 'Les États Généraux en Belgique et aux Pays-Bas sous l'ancien régime', *Recueils de la société Jean Bodin* 24 (1966) and J. Dhont, *Estates or Powers: Essays in the Parliamentary History of the Southern Netherlands from the Twelfth to the Eighteenth Century* (1977). For Sweden, see *The Swedish Riksdag in an International Perspective*, ed. N. Stjernquist (1989); A. F. Upton, 'The *riksdag* of 1680 and the establishment of royal absolutism in Sweden', *EHR*, 102 (1987); and N. Kishakoff-Dumont, 'La royauté et les États en Suède au xviie et xviie siècles, 1639–1772', *Études sur l'histoire des assemblées d'états* (1966). For representation in central and eastern Europe, consult the following works: K. Górski, 'Les débuts de la représentation de la *communitas nobilium* dans les assemblées d'états de l'est européen', *Anciens pays et assemblées d'états*, 47 (1968); V. Vanecek, 'Trois catégories d'assemblées d'états dans la couronne de Bohême du xvie siècle', *Album Helen Maud Cam*,

1 (1960); J. Jedruch, *Constitutions, Elections and Legislatures of Poland, 1493–1977: A Guide to Their History* (1982); and J. L. H. Keep, 'The decline of the *zemsky sobor*', *Slavonic and East European Review*, 36 (1957–8).

6.3 There is a comparative article on the growth of ministerial government: J. Bérenger, 'Pour une enquête européene. Le problème du ministériat au xviie siècle', *Annales E.S.C.*, 29 (1974), while Elliott, *Richelieu and Olivares* (above 4.3) is a useful comparative monograph. For Germany, G. Oestreich, *Neostoicism and the Early Modern State*, ed. B. Oestreich and H. G. Koenigsberger, trans. D. McLintock (1982), while W. R. Hitchcock, *The Background of the Knights' Revolt, 1522–1523* (1958) has information on the knights in Germany. For the *noblesse de robe* in France, see A. L. Moote, 'The French crown versus its judicial and financial officials', *Journal of Modern History*, 34 (1962), but above all R. É. Mousnier, *La vénalité des offices sous Henri IV et Louis XIII* (2nd edn., 1971) and idem, *La plume, la faucille et le marteau: institutions et société en France du moyen âge à la Révolution* (1970). Comparison with Spain is facilitated by R. L. Kagan, *Lawsuits and Litigants in Castile, 1500–1700* (1981), and there is still comparative material worth consulting in K. W. Swart, *Sale of Offices in the Seventeenth Century* (1949).

6.4 The fundamental reappraisal is N. G. Parker, *The Military Revolution: Military Innovation and the Rise of the West, 1500–1800* (1988); also of importance are J. R. Hale, *War and Society in Renaissance Europe, 1450–1620* (1985); A. Corvisier, *Armies and Societies in Europe, 1494–1789*, trans. A. T. Siddall (1979); M. Roberts, 'The military revolution, 1560–1660', repr. in Roberts, *Essays in Swedish History* (1967); N. G. Parker, 'The military revolution, 1560–1660—a myth?', *Journal of Modern History*, 47 (1967), repr. in Parker, *Spain and the Netherlands, 1559–1659* (1979). The ubiquitous mercenaries are surveyed by V. G. Kiernan, 'Foreign mercenaries and absolute monarchy', *PP*, 11 (1957), repr. in *Crisis in Europe, 1560–1660*, ed. T. H. Aston (1965). There are various detailed studies of the army and strategy in different European countries. For Germany, F. Redlich, *The German Military Enterpriser and His Workforce* (1964) and D. A. Parrott, 'Strategy and tactics in the Thirty Years' War: "the military revolution"', *Militärgeschichtliche Mitteilungen*, 18 (1985). For Spain, Thompson (above 3.1); for Italy, M. E. Mallett, *Mercenaries and Their Masters: Warfare in Renaissance Italy* (1974); and idem and J. R. Hale, *The Military Organization of a Renaissance State: Venice c.1400 to 1617* (1984). For France: P. Contamine, *Guerre, état et société à la fin du moyen âge: études sur les armées des rois de France, 1337–1494* (1972); F. Lot, *Recherches sur les effectifs des armées françaises des guerres d'Italie aux guerres de religion, 1494–1562* (1962); and J. A. Lynn, 'Tactical evolution in the French army, 1560–1660', *French Historical Studies*, 14 (1985).

6.5 Still of some importance, despite its great age (it originally appeared in German in 1918), is J. Schumpeter, 'The crisis of the tax state', *International Economic Papers*, 4 (1954). More recently, J. Meyer, *Le poids de l'État* (1983) has a broad canvas, while there are more detailed articles by specialists on various European countries: *Genèse de l'État moderne: prélèvement et redistribution*, ed. J.-P. Genet and M. Le Mené (1987). For the Low Countries: J. D. Tracy, *A Financial Revolution in the Habsburg Netherlands: Renten and Renteniers in the County of Holland, 1515–1565* (1985). For Spain: Ladero Quesada (above 2.2) and Thompson (above 3.1). For France, apart from Bonney (above 4.4), M. Wolfe, *The Fiscal System of Renaissance France* (1972); D. Hickey, *The Coming of French Absolutism: The Struggle for Tax Reform in the Province of Dauphiné, 1540–1640* (1986); and J. B. Collins, *Fiscal Limits of Absolutism: Direct Taxation in Early Seventeenth-Century France* (1988). The salt tax is studied by J.-C. Hocquet, *Le sel et le pouvoir de l'an mil à la Révolution française* (1985) and by idem, *Le roi, le marchand et le sel* (1987).

7 POPULATION AND SOCIAL STRUCTURE

7.1 For consistency, population figures have been taken from De Vries (7.4 below), despite imperfections. An ambitious survey is J. Dupâquier, M. R. Reinhard and A. Armengaud, *Histoire générale de la population mondiale* (1968). France and Spain have been best studied: for Spain, A. Molinié-Bertrand, *Au siècle d'or: l'Espagne et ses hommes. La population du royaume de Castille au xvie siècle* (1985); for France, *Histoire de la population française. II. De la Renaissance à 1789*, ed. J. Dupâquier (1988); idem, *Statistiques démographiques du bassin parisien, 1636–1720* (1977); idem, *La population rural du bassin parisien à l'époque de Louis XIV* (1979); F. Le Brun, 'Les crises démographiques en France au xviie et xviiie siècles', *Annales E.S.C.*, 35 (1980). For family structure, J.-L. Flandrin, *Families in Former Times: Kinship, Household and Sexuality*, trans. R. Southern (1979); M. Mitterauer and R. Sieder, *The European Family: Patriarchy to Partnership from the Middle Ages to the Present* (1982); and R. A. Houlbrooke, *The English Family, 1450–1700* (1984). On the recurrence of pestilence, J.-N. Biraben, *Les hommes et la peste en France et dans les pays européens et méditerranéens* (2 vols., 1975, 1976) is a fundamental contribution. There are detailed studies: C. M. Cipolla, *Cristofano and the Plague: A Study in the History of Public Health in the Age of Galileo* (1973); idem, *Faith, Reason and the Plague: A Tuscan Story of the Seventeenth Century* (1979); and idem, *Fighting the Plague in Seventeenth-Century Italy* (1981). For the evolution of European food consumption, B. Bennassar and J. Goy, 'Contribution à l'histoire de la consommation alimentaire du xvie au xixe siècle', *Annales E.S.C.*, 30 (1975). For poverty in the Middle Ages: M. Mollat, *The Poor in the Middle Ages: An Essay in Social History*, trans. A. Goldhammer (1986). Among the local studies, B. Geremek, *The Margins of Society in Late Medieval Paris*, trans. J. Birrell (1987). For the early modern period, C. Lis and H. Soly, *Poverty and Capitalism in Pre-industrial Europe* (1979) and B. Pullan, 'Catholics and the poor in early modern Europe', *Transactions of the Royal Historical Society*, 5th ser., 26 (1976). Among the detailed studies, for Venice, idem, *Rich and Poor in Renaissance Venice: The Social Institutions of a Catholic State to 1620* (1971); for Lyon, Davis (above 3.3) and J.-P. Gutton, *La société et les pauvres: l'exemple de la généralité de Lyon, 1534–1789* (1971);

for Toledo, L. Martz, *Poverty and Welfare in Habsburg Spain: The Example of Toledo* (1983); while an unusual eastern European response is depicted splendidly by R. Hellie, *Slavery in Russia, 1450–1725* (1982).

7.2 For social structure generally: R. É. Mousnier, *Social Hierarchies: 1450 to the Present*, trans. P. Evans (1973). There has been a recent debate on class structure and the economy: R. Brenner, 'Agrarian class structure and economic development in pre-industrial Europe', *PP*, 70 (1976); debate ibid. 78 and 79 (1978); riposte from Brenner, ibid. 97 (1982); the debate has since been reprinted as *The Brenner Debate: Agrarian Class Structure and Economic Development in Pre-industrial Europe*, ed. T. H. Aston and C. H. E. Philpin (1985). Among the general surveys of the nobility, consult F. Billacois, 'La crise de la noblesse européene, 1550–1650: une mise au point', *Revue d'histoire moderne et contemporaine*, 23 (1976); and M. L. Bush, *Noble Privilege* (1983) and idem, *Rich Noble, Poor Noble* (1988). Among the detailed studies, for Denmark, E. L. Petersen, *The Crisis of the Danish Nobility, 1580–1660* (1967) is thin; in contrast, there is an impressive study of Castile: M.-C. Gerbet, *La noblesse dans le royaume de Castille: étude sur ses structures sociales en Estrémadure, 1454–1516* (1979); also of importance is C. Jago, 'The influence of debt on the relations between crown and aristocracy in seventeenth-century Castile', *Economic History Review*, 26 (1973); H. Nader, 'Noble income in sixteenth-century Castile: the case of the marquises of Mondéjar, 1480–1580', ibid. 30 (1977). For Venice, J. C. Davis, *The Decline of the Venetian Nobility as a Ruling Class* (1962). For the Low Countries, S. Marshall, *The Dutch Gentry, 1500–1650: Family, Faith and Fortune* (1987). The evolution of noble privileges in eastern Europe emerges from the detailed studies: for Hungary, of Z. P. Pach, 'The development of feudal rent in Hungary in the fifteenth century', *Economic History Review*, 29 (1966) and idem, 'Sixteenth-century Hungary: commercial activity and market production by the nobles', *Economy and Society in Early Modern Europe . . .*, ed. P. Burke (1972); and for Poland: J. Topolski, 'La réféodalisation dans l'économie des grands domaines en Europe centrale et orientale', *Studia historiae oeconomicae*, 6 (1971) and idem, 'The manorial serf economy . . .', *Agricultural History*, 48 (1974); regrettably, W. Kula, *An Economic Theory of the Feudal System: Towards a Model of the Polish Economy, 1500–1800* (1976) is impenetrable. For the ethos of the French *noblesse d'épée*, the classic study is A. Devyver, *Le sang épuré: les préjugés de race chez les gentilshommes français de l'ancien régime, 1560–1720* (1973). For the Castilian peasantry: N. Salomon, *La nouvelle Castille à la fin du xvie siècle d'après les Relaciones Topográficas* (1964); D. E. Vassberg, 'The *Tierras Baldías*: community property and public lands in sixteenth-century Castile', *Agricultural History*, 48 (1974); and M. R. Weisser, *The Peasants of the Montes: The Roots of Rural Rebellion in Spain* (1976). A Tuscan contrast is provided by F. McArdle, *Altopascio: A Study in Tuscan Rural Society, 1587–1784* (1978). For France, P. Goubert, *The French Peasantry in the Seventeenth Century*, trans. I. Patterson (1986) and the works cited (below 8.5); for the Low Countries: M. P. Gutmann, *War and Rural Life in the Early Modern Low Countries* (1980). The

Austrian peasantry is studied by H. Rebel, *Peasant Classes: The Bureaucrat-ization of Property and Family Tenure under Early Habsburg Absolutism, 1511–1636* (1983). For the borderland between east and west: W. W. Hagen, 'How mighty the Junkers? Peasant rents and seigneurial profits in sixteenth-century Brandenburg', *PP*, 108 (1985). The general survey of peasant tenure in eastern Europe is J. Blum, 'The rise of serfdom in eastern Europe', *American Historical Review*, 62 (1957); idem, *Lord and Peasant in Russia from the Ninth to the Nineteenth Century* (1961) is a fundamental introduction on the Russian peasantry. Also of importance are R. E. F. Smith, *The Enserfment of the Russian Peasantry* (1968) and idem, *Peasant Farming in Muscovy* (1977). For Hungary, there is the collective volume entitled *Paysannerie française, paysannerie hongroise, xvie–xxe siècles*, ed. B. Köpeczi and E. H. Balázs (1973).

7.3 A general survey of both urban and agrarian rebellion is provided by Y.-M. Bercé, *Revolt and Revolution in Early Modern Europe: An Essay on the History of Political Violence*, trans. J. A. Bergin (1987) and P. Zagorin, *Rebels and Rulers, 1500–1660* (1982). An overview of rural movements in English is R. É. Mousnier, *Peasant Uprisings in Seventeenth-Century France, Russia and China*, trans. B. Pearce (repr. 1971); this was reviewed by M. O. Gateley, A. L. Moote and J. E. Willis Jr, 'Seventeenth-century peasant "furies": some problems of comparative history', *PP*, 51 (1971). For Dósza, J. M. Bak, 'Delinquent lords and foresaken serfs: thoughts on war and society during the crisis of feudalism', *Society in Change: Studies in Honor of B. K. Kiraly*, ed. S. B. Vardy (1983). For peasant uprisings in France, the best brief account is Y.-M. Bercé, *Histoire des croquants* (1986 revision of his much larger work of 1974); also useful is M. Foisil, *La révolte des Nu-Pieds et les révoltes normandes de 1639* (1970); while the Mousnier–Porshnev debate is translated in *France in Crisis, 1620–1675*, ed. P. J. Coveney (1977). For the Peasants' War in Germany, there is a useful survey by T. Scott, 'The Peasants' War: an historiographical review', *Historical Journal*, 22 (1979). The two main collections of articles are *The German Peasant War of 1525*, ed. J. Bak (1976) and *The German Peasant War: New Viewpoints*, ed. R. W. Scribner and G. Benecke (1979). There is also the a general study by P. Blickle, *The Revolution of 1525: The German Peasants' War from a New Perspective*, trans. T. A. Brady and H. C. E. Midelfort (1981). More detailed studies include T. Scott, 'Reformation and Peasants' War in Waldshut and environs: a structural analysis', *Archiv für Reformationsgeschichte*, 69 (1978) and 70 (1979); H. Zins, 'Aspects of the peasant rising in East Prussia in 1525', *Slavonic and East European Review*, 38 (1959); and Cohn (above 1.1).

7.4 The standard account is now J. De Vries, *European Urbanization, 1500–1800* (1984). The growth of Spanish towns has been especially well studied: for Madrid, D. R. Ringrose, *Madrid and the Spanish Economy, 1560–1850* (1983); for Valladolid, B. Bennassar, *Valladolid au siècle d'or: une ville de Castille et sa campagne au xvie siècle* (1967); finally, C. R. Phillips, *Cuidad Real, 1500–1750: Growth, Crisis and Readjustment in the Spanish Economy*

(1979). For Rome, J. Delumeau, *Vie économique et sociale de Rome dans la seconde moitié du xvie siècle* (1959). There is a splendid study of Lyon: R. Gascon, *Grand commerce et vie urbaine au xvie siècle: Lyon et ses marchands* (1971). Towns in eastern Europe are less well served, but see J. M. Hittle, *The Service City: State and Townsmen in Russia, 1600–1800* (1979); and P. Bushkovitch, *The Merchants of Moscow, 1580–1650* (1980). There is an excellent detailed study of the political and social structure of one western European town: C. R. Friedrichs, 'Capitalism, mobility and class formation in the early modern German city', *PP*, 69 (1975) and id., *Urban Society in an Age of War: Nördlingen, 1580–1720* (1979). Also of importance is R. S. DuPlessis and M. C. Howell, 'Reconsidering the early modern urban economy: the cases of Leiden and Lille', *PP*, 94 (1982). Some useful points are made by D. J. Roorda, 'The ruling classes in Holland in the seventeenth century', *Britain and the Netherlands*, ed. J. S. Bromley and E. H. Kossmann, ii (1964).

7.5 Among the various urban rebellions, the most detailed studies concern France: R. Pillorget, *Les mouvements insurrectionnels de Provence entre 1596 et 1715* (1975). Also well studied is the revolt at Naples: R. Villari, 'Masaniello: contemporary and recent interpretations', *PP*, 108 (1985) and P. Burke, 'The Virgin of the Carmine and the revolt of Masaniello', ibid. 99 (1983). For the revolt of the Comuneros of Castile, see especially J. Pérez, *La révolution des 'Comunidades' de Castille, 1520–1* (1970) and S. L. Haliczer, *The Comuneros of Castile: The Forging of a Revolution, 1475–1521* (1981).

8 THE EUROPEAN ECONOMY

The standard work of reference for this subject is the *Cambridge Economic History of Europe. IV. The Economy of Expanding Europe in the Sixteenth and Seventeenth Centuries*, ed. E. E. Rich and C. H. Wilson (1967); and *V. The Economic Organization of Early Modern Europe*, ed. E. E. Rich and C. H. Wilson (1977). A recent extensive synthesis is F. Braudel, *Civilization and Capitalism, 15th–18th Century*, trans. S. Reynolds (3 vols., 1981–4). Some useful statistics are provided by *An Introduction to the Sources of European Economic History, 1500–1800. I. Western Europe*, ed. C. H. Wilson and N. G. Parker (1977) and by N. J. G. Pounds, *An Historical Geography of Europe, 1500–1840* (1979). ·

8.1 A useful introduction on the 'tyranny of gold and silver' is P. Vilar, *A History of Gold and Money, 1450–1920*, trans. J. White (1976). For the late medieval background, H. A. Miskimin, *The Economy of Later Renaissance Europe, 1460–1600* (1977) and J. Day, 'The great bullion famine of the fifteenth century', *PP*, 79 (1978). For the supply of precious metals, the standard account of E. J. Hamilton, *American Treasure and the Price Revolution in Spain, 1501–1650* (1934). These figures have now been revised by M. Morineau, *Incroyables gazettes et fabuleux métaux: les retours des trésors américains d'après les gazettes hollandaises, xvie–xviiie siècles* (1984). The most complete study of the impact of monetary change on the economy is

F. C. Spooner, *The International Economy and Monetary Movements in France, 1493–1725* (1972). For the quantity theory of money, there is a useful discussion in R. B. Outhwaite, *Inflation in Tudor and Stuart England* (1969), while there has been an edition of *La response de Jean Bodin à M. de Malestroit*, 1568, ed. H. Hauser (1932).

8.2 There is a useful collection of essays on the price rise: *Economy and Society in Early Modern Europe: Essays from Annales*, ed. P. Burke (1972). Among the detailed studies for eastern Europe: S. Hoszowski, *Les prix à Lwow, xvie–xviie siècles* (1954) and A. G. Mankov, *Le mouvement des prix dans l'état russe du xvie siècle* (1957). Of particular interest is R. Romano, 'Between the sixteenth and seventeenth centuries: the economic crisis of 1619–22', *The General Crisis of the Seventeenth Century*, ed. N. G. Parker and L. M. Smith (repr. 1985).

8.3 Among the introductions on the struggle for European commercial primacy are I. Wallerstein, *The Modern World-System* (2 vols., 1974, 1980); and Braudel, *Civilization and Capitalism*, especially volume iii. There is a useful collection of essays: *Revisions in Mercantilism*, ed. D. C. Coleman (1969). For the Hanseatic League, see Dollinger (2.2 above); there is no general work on the economic decline of Italy, but a detailed collection of essays is *Crisis and Change in the Venetian Economy in the Sixteenth and Seventeenth Centuries*, ed. B. Pullan (1968). On Antwerp's greatness, the fundamental work is H. Van der Wee, *The Growth of the Antwerp Market and the European Economy, Fourteenth–Sixteenth Centuries* (1965); for Amsterdam, V. Barbour, *Capitalism in Amsterdam in the Seventeenth Century* (1963). The Genoese economy in the fifteenth century is assessed by J. Heers, *Gênes au xve siècle* (1961); the payments system in the late sixteenth century is discussed in the difficult work by J. Gentil da Silva, *Banque et crédit en Italie au xviie siècle* (1969).

8.4 The discoveries and early colonial struggle are surveyed by J. H. Parry, *The Age of Reconnaissance* (repr. 1964) and by G. V. Scammell, *The World Encompassed: The First European Maritime Empires, c.800–1650* (1981). More detailed, for the Portuguese empire, is C. R. Boxer, *The Portuguese Seaborne Empire, 1415–1825* (1969); Portuguese superiority in guns and ships is argued by C. M. Cipolla, *Guns and Sails in the Early Phase of European Expansion, 1400–1700* (1965). The most detailed study is V. Magalhães-Godinho, *L'économie de l'empire portugais au xve et xvie siècles* (1969). For the Portuguese in Brazil: F. Mauro, *Le Portugal et l'Atlantique au xviie siècle, 1570–1670* (1960). For the Spanish empire, there is an introduction by J. H. Parry, *The Spanish Seaborne Empire* (1966), but the fundamental work is H. and P. Chaunu, *Séville et l'Atlantique, 1504–1650* (8 vols., 1955–9). The role of the Genoese has been stressed by R. Pike, *Enterprise and Adventure: The Genoese in Seville and the Opening of the New World* (1966). On the land settlement, F. Chevalier, *Land and Society in Colonial Mexico* (1963) is particularly useful. There has been an excellent study of one of the mining communities: P. J. Bakewell, *Silver Mining and Society in Colonial Mexico: Zacatecas, 1546–1700* (1971). The issue of whether or not the Spanish empire had a general crisis has been the subject of debate: J. I. Israel, 'Mexico and the "general crisis" of the seventeenth century', *PP*, 63 (1974) and idem, *Race, Class and Politics in Colonial Mexico, 1610–1670* (1975); J. J. TePaske and H. S. Klein, 'The seventeenth-century crisis in New Spain: myth or reality?', *PP*, 90 (1981). For the rise of the Dutch empire: C. R. Boxer, *The Dutch Seaborne Empire, 1600–1800* (1965), while *Dutch Capitalism and World Capitalism*, ed. M. Aymard (1982) is a particularly useful collection of essays. Both have now been displaced by the masterly account of J. I. Israel, *Dutch Primacy in World Trade, 1585–1740* (1989). For the Baltic trade, P. Jeannin, 'Les comptes du Sund comme source pour la construction d'indices généraux de l'activité économique en Europe, xvie–xviiie siècle', *Revue historique*, 231 (1964).

8.5 Calvin's objections to usury are well studied by A. Biéler, *La pensée économique et sociale de Calvin* (1959). See also J. C. Riemersma, *Religious Factors in Early Dutch Capitalism, 1550–1650* (1967). For Jansenist hostility to usury: R. Taveneaux, *Jansénisme et prêt à intérêt . . .* (1977). B. Nelson, *The Idea of Usury: From Tribal Brotherhood to Universal Otherhood* (2nd edn., 1969), is an overview. The French financiers have been studied by F. Bayard, *Le monde des financiers au xviie siècle* (1988) and by D. Dessert, *Argent, pouvoir et société au grand siècle* (1984). The expulsion of the Jews from Spain is reassessed by H. Kamen, 'The Mediterranean and the expulsion of Spanish Jews in 1492', *PP*, 119 (1988). For the Jews at Rome: L. Poliakov, *Jewish Bankers and the Holy See, from the Thirteenth to the Seventeenth Century*, trans. M. Kochan (1977). See also Pullan (above 1.5). For the position of the Jews in Europe generally, J. I. Israel, *European Jewry in the Age of Mercantilism, 1550–1750* (1985). On guilds, see R. Mackenny, *Tradesmen and Trades: The World of the Guilds in Venice and Europe, c.1250–c.1650* (1987). Variations on the theme of the backwardness of agrarian production may be discerned from E. Le Roy Ladurie and J. Goy, *Tithe and Agrarian History from the Fourteenth to the Nineteenth Centuries*, trans. S. Burke (1982). For French agriculture, see especially *Histoire de la France rurale. II. L'âge classique des paysans, 1340–1789*, ed. E. Le Roy Ladurie (1975) and idem, *The French Peasantry, 1450–1660*, trans. A. Sheridan (1987). J. Meuvret, *Le problème des subsistances à l'époque de Louis XIV* (6 vols., 1977–89) is fundamental for an understanding of agricultural techniques. For details on Polish agriculture: P. Kriedte, *Peasants, Landlords and Merchant Capitalists: Europe and the World Economy, 1500–1800* (1983). The exceptional progress of Dutch agriculture is surveyed by B. H. Slicher van Bath, 'The rise of intensive husbandry in the Low Countries', *Britain and the Netherlands*, 1 (1960) and by J. de Vries, *The Dutch Rural Economy in the Golden Age, 1500–1700* (1974).

9 COURT, CULTURE AND COMMUNITY

9.1 The best introduction to courtly patronage is *The Courts of Europe: Politics, Patronage and Royalty, 1400–1800*, ed. A. G. Dickens (1977). The marvels of

Ottoman civilization are well documented in J. M. Rogers and R. M. Ward, *Süleyman the Magnificent* (1988) and E. Atil, *Süleymanname: The Illustrated History of Süleyman the Magnificent* (1986). Burgundian civilization is depicted in W. Prevenier and W. Blockmans, *The Burgundian Netherlands* (1986). J. R. Hale introduces Medici culture in *Florence and the Medici: The Pattern of Control* (1977). Certain Habsburg courts are discussed by H. R. Trevor-Roper, *Princes and Artists: Patronage and Ideology at Four Habsburg Courts, 1517–1633* (1976). However, the original work on the Spanish Habsburg court is J. Brown and J. H. Elliott, *A Palace for a King: The Buen Retiro and the Court of Philip IV* (1980), while for the Austrian Habsburgs it is that of Evans, *Rudolf II and His World* (above 3.4).

9.2 The collective urban culture of Venice is well brought out by E. Muir, *Civic Ritual in Renaissance Venice* (1981), although there are many works which provide detailed insights, such as W. J. Bouwsma, *Venice and the Defense of Republican Liberty: Renaissance Values in the Age of the Counter-Reformation* (1968), P. F. Grendler, *The Roman Inquisition and the Venetian Press, 1540–1605* (1977) and Pullan, *Rich and Poor in Renaissance Venice* (above 7.1). There is a useful collection of articles entitled *Renaissance Venice*, ed. Hale (above 2.1), and there are also several general books such as D. S. Chambers, *The Imperial Age of Venice, 1380–1580* (1970), O. Logan, *Culture and Society in Venice, 1470–1790* (1972) and McNeill (above 2.1). Contarini's account was translated: G. Contarino [*sic*], *The Commonwealth and Government of Venice*, trans. L. Lewkenor (1599). Some comparison between Venice and Florence is possible by means of R. C. Trexler, *Public Life in Renaissance Florence* (1980) and of Venice and Amsterdam by means of P. Burke, *Venice and Amsterdam: A Study of Seventeenth-Century Élites* (1974). There has been much praise for S. Schama, *The Embarrassment of Riches: An Interpretation of Dutch Culture in the Golden Age* (repr. 1988). There is nothing comparable for French urban culture, although the most important recent study is A. Pardailhé-Galabrun, *La naissance de l'intime: 3000 foyers parisiens, xviiᵉ–xviiiᵉ siècles* (1988). There is also material in *Histoire de la France urbaine. III. La ville classique de la Renaissance aux Révolutions*, ed. E. Le Roy Ladurie (1981). Among the growing number of urban studies are: K. Norberg, *Rich and Poor in Grenoble, 1600–1814* (1985), Benedict, *Rouen* (above 3.3) and *Cities and Social Change in Early Modern France*, ed. Benedict (1989), and R. A. Schneider, *Public Life in Toulouse, 1463–1789: From Municipal Republic to Cosmopolitan City* (1989). Of particular interest is P. Benedict, 'The ownership of paintings in seventeenth-century Metz', *PP*, 109 (1985).

9.3 For popular culture, there are two useful starting-points in P. Burke, *Popular Culture in Early Modern Europe* (1978, repr. 1983) and (less approachable) R. Muchembled, *Popular Culture and Élite Culture in France, 1400–1750*, trans. L. Cochrane (1985). For Germany, there are some interesting essays in D. W. Sabean, *Power in the Blood: Popular Culture and Village Discourse in Early Modern Germany* (1984). For the historiography, there is a guide in

S. Clark, 'French historians and early modern popular culture', *PP*, 100 (1983). For public interest in anatomy: G. Ferrari, 'Public anatomy lessons and the Carnival in Bologna', *PP*, 117 (1987). For charivari there are stimulating guides in N. Z. Davis, 'The reasons of misrule: youth groups and charivaris in sixteenth-century France', *PP*, 50 (1971); Y.-M. Bercé, *Fête et révolte: des mentalités populaires en France du xviie au xviiie siècle* (1976); and M. Ingram, 'Ridings, rough music and the "reform of popular culture" in early modern England', *PP*, 105 (1984). The tensions between Protestant reformers and popular wedding traditions are revealed by L. Roper, '"Going to church and street": weddings in Reformation Augsburg', *PP*, 106 (1985).

9.4 The most important manual of inquisitors is available in incomplete translation: *Malleus maleficarum: The Hammer of Witchcraft* ..., trans. M. Summers (repr. 1968). On the witches' sabbath, C. Ginzburg, 'Popular cult or inquisitorial stereotype?', *Understanding Popular Culture* ..., ed. S. L. Kaplan (1984). A particularly useful synthesis is C. Larner, '*Crimen exceptum*? The crime of witchcraft in Europe', *Crime and the Law: The Social History of Crime in Western Europe since 1500*, ed. V. A. C. Gattrell, B. Lenman and G. Parker (1980), 49–75, reprinted in Larner, *Witchcraft and Popular Religion: The Politics of Popular Belief* (1984). The subject of witchcraft was revived in recent times by J. Caro Baroja, *The World of the Witches* (trans. N. Glendenning, 1964), and H. R. Trevor-Roper's article, subsequently reprinted in his *The European Witch-Craze of the 16th. and 17th. Centuries and Other Essays* (1969); since this time, general studies on witchcraft now abound, such as N. Cohn, *Europe's Inner Demons: An Enquiry Inspired by the Great Witch-Hunt* (1975) and R. Kieckhefer, *European Witchtrials: Their Foundation in Popular and Learned Culture, 1300–1500* (1976). There are several important studies of witchcraft in different regions: H. C. E. Midelfort, *Witch Hunting in South-Western Germany, 1562–1684: The Social and Intellectual Foundations* (1972); E. W. Monter, *Witchcraft in France and Switzerland: The Borderlands during the Reformation* (1976); A. Soman, 'La sorcellerie devant le Parlement de Paris, 1565–1640', *Annales E.S.C.*, 32 (1977); idem, 'La décriminalisation de la sorcellerie en France', *Histoire, économie et société*, 4 (1985); G. Henningsen, *The Witches' Advocate: Basque Witchcraft and the Spanish Inquisition, 1609–1614* (1980) and the first three chapters of Briggs, *Communities of Belief* (above 1.5), which draw on research into witchcraft in Lorraine. Also of considerable interest are the chapters on witchcraft in Muchembled, *Popular Culture and Élite Culture*; K. V. Thomas, *Religion and the Decline of Magic: Studies in Popular Beliefs in Sixteenth- and Seventeenth-Century England* (repr. 1973); and the article by S. Clark on 'Inversion, misrule and the meaning of witchcraft', *PP*, 87 (1980).

9.5 There are some stimulating suggestions in J. Cottingham, *Rationalism* (1984). The relationship between belief in the occult and scientific enquiry is suggested in S. Clark, 'The scientific status of demonology', *Occult and Scientific Mentalities in the Renaissance*, ed. B. Vickers (1984) and B. Easlea, *Witch Hunting, Magic and the New Philosophy: An Introduction to the*

Debates of the Scientific Revolution, 1450–1750 (1980). For the preoccupation with monsters, K. Park and L. J. Daston, 'Unnatural conceptions: the study of monsters in France and England', *PP*, 92 (1981). On forbidden knowledge, C. Ginzburg, 'High and low: the theme of forbidden knowledge in the sixteenth and seventeenth centuries', *PP*, 73 (1976). There are important contributions on the Fludd–Kepler polemic by E. Rosen and J. V. Field in *Occult and Scientific Mentalities*, ed. Vickers; the same volume also contains a study by W. L. Hine on Mersenne. One of the more challenging interpretations of the scientific revolution is H. G. Koenigsberger, 'Science and religion in early modern Europe', *Political Symbolism in Modern Europe*, ed. S. Drescher *et al.* (1982). Still of great value as an introduction is A. R. Hall, *The Scientific Revolution, 1500–1800: The Formation of the Modern Scientific Attitude* (1954, 2nd edn., 1962). The fullest treatment of Copernicus is T. S. Kuhn, *The Copernican Revolution: Planetary Astronomy in the Development of Western Thought* (1957, repr. 1970). For Kepler, J. V. Field, *Kepler's Geometrical Cosmology* (1988). There are many studies of Galileo, notably W. R. Shea, *Galileo's Intellectual Revolution* (1972); M. A. Finocchiaro, *Galileo and the Art of Reasoning: Rhetorical Foundations of Logic and Scientific Method* (1980); *New Perspectives on Galileo*, ed. R. E. Butts and J. C. Pitt (1978); and M. Clavelin, *The Natural Philosophy of Galileo: Essays on the Origins and Formation of Classical Mechanics*, trans. A. J. Pomerans (1974). For Giordano Bruno, there are two different interpretations: F. A. Yates, *Giordano Bruno and the Hermetic Tradition* (1964) and P.-H. Michel, *The Cosmology of Giordano Bruno*, trans. R. E. W. Maddison (1973). For Descartes, A. Kenny, *Descartes: A Study of His Philosophy* (1968); B. Williams, *Descartes: The Project of Pure Enquiry* (1978); and D. M. Clarke, *Descartes' Philosophy of Science* (1982). Descartes's *Principles of Philosophy* have been translated by V. R. and R. P. Miller (1983) and his *Treatise of Man* by T. S. Hall (1972). For the relationship of science to the state: D. Goodman, *Power and Penury: Government Technology and Science in Philip II's Spain* (1988).

INDEX

[d. = died; r. = *regnabat*]

Aachen 30, 67, 153
  restoration of exclusive Catholic rule
    (1598) 184
Aalst 156
Abbas I, Shah of Persia (r. 1588–1629)
  determined opponent of Ottomans
    297–8
  humiliating peace conceded to Ottomans
    (1590) 297
absolutism 525
  and mercenary armies 350–1
  Bodin's theory 312–13, 360
  Bossuet's theory 530–1
  contrast between property rights under
    absolutism and eastern despotism 360
  established by consent in Denmark
    (1660) 255–6, 358–9
  in Castile 145, 326
  in France 323
Adashev, Alexei, adviser to Ivan IV 276
Aden 292
Admiral:
  in Castile 111, 332
  in France 332
Adrets, baron des, Huguenot commander
  169
Adrian VI (Adrian Dedel, Adrian of
  Utrecht), Regent in Castile (1520–1)
  and Pope (1522–3) 2, 3, 12, 101, 111
advocate (*advocaet*) to the states of
  Holland 162
Aerschot, Philippe de Croy, duke of
  (1526–95), stadholder of Flanders 157
Agen, riot at (1635) 413
Aglionby, William 492, 493
Agnadello, battle of (1509) 87
agnosticism 1
agriculture 466–73
  dominant size and backwardness of
    agricultural sector of economy 466
  evidence of tithe yields 469–71
  harvest yields 469
  manuring and marling 468
  proto-industrialization (*Kaufsystem*) 467
  putting-out system (*Verlaggsystem*) 467
  reliance on sickles 469
  sowing of crops 468–9

types of plough 468
  see also capitalism
Ahmed I, Ottoman sultan (r. 1603–17)
  295, 298
Aigues-Mortes, meeting at 107
Aitzema, Lieuwe van 305
Aix-en-Provence 102, 106, 167, 235, 343,
  412
Akkerman 288
Alais, Peace of (1629) 178, 228–9
Alba, Fernando Alvarez de Toledo, duke of
  (1507–82) 146
  appointed governor-general in the Low
    Countries 151
  defends southern border of Low
    Countries (1572) 152
  disgrace 134, 148
  establishes Council of Troubles 152
  execution of Egmont and Hoorne 152
  instructed to override privileges of Low
    Countries 152, 492
  interview at Bayonne 131, 169
  invades Portugal 139
  levies Tenth Penny 152
  military nature of regime 346
  miscalculates urban resistance in Low
    Countries 154
  recalled from the Low Countries 155
  repression in the Low Countries 152
  role in faction struggles 134, 135
  shoots ringleaders of mutiny 156
  supports Philip II's absolutist ambitions
    123
Albania 288
Albert II, of Habsburg (Holy Roman
  Emperor, 1438–9) 98
Albert of Habsburg (1559–1621), nephew
  of Philip II, archduke and joint ruler of
  the Netherlands (r. 1598–1621) 135,
  180
  governor-general (1596–8) 163
  patronage of Rubens 483
  pessimism about chances of reconquering
    United Provinces 204
  threatened with deposition 180
  and truce with United Provinces 181
Albert, of Saxony, Regent in Burgundy 97
Alberti, Leon Battista (1404–72) 478

Albi, riot at (1491) 413
Albuquerque, Alfonso de, governor of India
    442
alcabala 89, 111–12, 353
Alcaçovas, Treaty of (1479) 441, 443
Alençon, *see* Anjou
Aleppo 289
Alesi, Guiseppi d', captain-general of the
    revolt at Palermo (1647) 408
Alexander, king of Poland (r. 1501–6) 258
  concessions to the nobility on his
    accession 258
  as ruler of Lithuania 275
Alexander VI (Rodrigo Borgia), Pope
    (1492–1503) 3, 84–5, 87, 90
  and Castel Sant'Angelo 478
  son, Cesare Borgia 3
Alexis I, Tsar of Muscovy (r. 1645–76) 349
  claims Lithuania, Byelorussia and
    Podolia 271
  invasion of Livonia 271
  invasion of Poland–Lithuania 270
Alfonso V, king of Aragon 90, 524
Algiers 117, 137, 138
  Ottoman overlordship 290
Aligre, Étienne II d' (1550–1635),
    Chancellor of France 332
Al-Kafi, Hasan, theorist of Ottoman
    decline 294
Alkmaar 154
Almagro, joint conqueror of Peru with
    Pizarro 444
Almenara, marquis of, viceroy in Aragon
    144
almonry, general, for poor relief 372, 373
Alpujarras, mountains in southern Castile
    389
Alsace 96, 187, 230, 350
  French protection to the Jews in 461
  grain production in 470–1
Altopascio 370
Althusius, Johannes, German political
    theorist 311
Altmark, Truce of (1629) 269
Älvsborg, Swedish coastal fortress 247,
    249, 250, 252
Amasya, Peace of (1555) 292
Amboina 450
Amboise, Conspiracy of (1560) 165, 168
Ameixial, battle of (1663) 222
amenorrhoea 370
America, Spanish:
  development of large estates (*haciendas*)
    444
  discovery and conquest of 89, 443–4
  Dutch penetration of the markets of 213,
    452

exploitation of deposits at Potosí in
    Peru 420
exploitation of deposits at Zacatecas and
    Guanajuato in Mexico 420
exports of bullion to the Old World 136,
    140, 215, 218, 223, 420, 421
fief (*encomienda*) system established
    444
grazing places (*estancias*) established
    444
no bills of exchange circulate in Spanish
    America 431
Spanish transtlantic trade 215, 445
see also Mexico; Peru
Amerindians 362
Amicable Grant 103
Amiens, Spanish capture of (1597) 163,
    225
Amsdorf, Nicholas, Lutheran reformer at
    Magdeburg 37
Amsterdam 150, 439, 446
  alehouses at 492
  alterations to the law (*wetsverzettingen*)
    405–6
  attempted purge of city council, by
    William II 213–14
  cost of debt servicing 355
  Exchange Bank (*Wisselbank,* 1609) 163,
    406, 462
  fishing fleet 447
  houses for correction 374
  immigration 163
  involvement of ruling patriciate in trade
    406–7
  loyalty to Philip II until 1578 154, 405
  prostitution at 493
  purchase of status of citizen (*poorter*)
    406
  Sephardi Jewish community at 451, 462
  share capital in East and West India
    Companies 450, 451
  size of population 399
  survival of guild structure at 465
  urban culture at 492–3
Anabaptism 22–7, 42, 53, 498
  declared a capital offence at Zurich 23
  declared a capital offence in the Empire
    23, 32
  fear of 372
  importance in the Low Countries 53,
    149
  persecution in the Low Countries 148
  view of church and civil society 23
  see also baptism; Hoffman; Hubmaier;
    Münster, radical Anabaptist 'kingdom'
    at; Simons
Anatolia 289

Andelot, François de Châtillon, d'
(1521–69), colonel-general of the
French infantry 128, 167
Andrusovo, Truce of (1667) 285
Angers:
Loricards at (1652) 412
angle bastion or *trace italienne* 84, 348
Angola:
Dutch attack on 443
exportation of slave labour force to Brazil
443
rising of Portuguese settlers (1648) 211,
213, 222
Anhalt-Bernburg, Christian I (1568–1630),
prince of 55
encourages Frederick V over Bohemian
rebellion 190
general of the Evangelical Union (1609)
184
seeks to undermine Habsburgs in
hereditary lands 186
Anjou, François de Valois (1556–84), duke
of Alençon and youngest son of
Henri II 497
death leads to succession crisis in France
174
gains allegiance of Dutch rebels (1581)
155, 159, 160
gains apanage (1576) 172–3
leads Malcontent movement in France
(1575–6) 172, 228
Marnix's report on negotiations with
526–7
Anjou, French duchy of 80, 86
Anne of Austria, fourth wife of Philip II
133
Anne of Austria (1601–66), daughter of
Philip III, wife of Louis XIII and regent
of France (r. 1643–51) 226, 493
unlimited regency asserted 232–3
Anne of Brittany, Breton heiress 83
Anne of Hungary, wife of Emperor
Ferdinand I 98
Annebault, Claude d' (d. 1552), admiral of
France 125
anticlericalism 2–3, 6–7, 149, 168
Antonio, *see* Crato
Antwerp 113, 446
affected by blockade of Scheldt 162, 181
amnesty (1585–9) 162–3
capitulation to Parma (1585) 160
climatic change in Antwerp area 369
currency 436
economic decline of 400
evolution of the credit market under
Charles V and Philip II 433, 437

failure of 'French fury' (1583) 159
fairs for bills of exchange to be settled
431, 432, 434
and Hanseatic League 439
iconoclastic fury at 149–50
increase in population 432
influences evolution of bill of exchange
431, 432
joins Union of Utrecht (1579) 155
money market 114, 357
rate of price increase of rye 425, 426
rate of increase of 'real wages' at 427
sack of (1576) 156, 350
spice trade organized at 432
States General withdraws to (1578) 157
survival of guild structure at 465
transfer of foreign banking communities
from Bruges 432
Apanage 108
Apocalypse 21, 500
apostolic messengers 24
Arabia, south-western 290
Aragon, kingdom of:
attitude of Isabella and Charles V
towards 143
Cortes of Aragon 216–17, 324
Cortes of three kingdoms 90, 112, 144,
145, 323–4
expulsion of Sephardi Jews 458–9
fueros 144, 145, 217
Justicia 144, 145
manifestación 144
Moriscos in 130
population 89, 365
prospect of a French invasion 211
rebellions: (1591–2) 144; (1668) 224;
(1677) 224
size of urban population (with Castile)
398
union with Castile preserved 92, 140
unrest in 140
viceroyalties 92
arbitristas, Spanish economic writers 214,
215, 383
Archangel 448, 449
Ardres:
capture of (1596) 163
Peace of (1546) 108
Armada, Spanish, against England:
cost 141, 145
in 1588 134, 140–2
inadequacy of Spanish gunnery 142
later Armadas 143
political objectives 141
size 141
Armenia 292

armies:
  administrative weakness of states 349,
    529
  casualties 347–8
  contractors 349
  contributions system 346, 348
  desertion 346
  evolution in size of 346
  military hospitals 238
  mutinies 350–1
  siege warfare 348
  tactics 347
  see also mercenaries
Arminius, Jacobus (1559–1609) 51, 182
Arnauld, Antoine (1612–94), French
    Jansenist 75
Arras 105, 158
  Treaty of (1579) 158
Artois 82, 104–5, 126, 152
  French capture of (1640) 232
  French retain at Peace of the Pyrenees
    (1659) 240
asientos, loan contracts 127, 431, 436–7
Assembly of the Land (zemskii sobor) 273,
    283, 318
Astrakhan', khanate of 242, 278
Augsburg:
  evolution of guild rule 464
  Peace of (1555) 43, 54, 62, 68, 121–2,
    183, 320
  see also Fugger
Augustinianism, see St Augustine
Australasia 418
Austria 96, 113, 130
  acceptance of primogeniture (1621) 528
  estates 97
  fate of Protestants in, after 1648 200
  house of Austria, see Habsburg dynasty
  labour services (robot) 397
  partition (1564–1618) 528
  peasant rebellion (1594–7) 397
  peasant rebellion (1626) 389–90
  population estimates 365
  rebellion (1620) 190
  succession of Ferdinand I 115
  tradition of peasant revolt 393
autos de fé, ceremonial burnings of heretics
    in Spain 132, 145
Auvergne 83
  agricultural production in 473
Avesnes 240
Avogadro, Birago 305
Azarbayjan 289, 292, 297, 298
Azpílcueta Navarro, Martin de (1491–
    1586), theologian of the university of
    Salamanca and economic
    theorist 421–2

Aztecs 444

Bacon, Francis (1561–1626), viscount of St
    Albans, philosopher 513, 520–1
Baghdad 292 298
Bahía 205 443
Baiburd 289
Baius, Michel (1513–89), Catholic
    theologian 74
Bakocz, Tamas, Cardinal 390
Balaton, lake 291
Baltic, see Dominium Maris Baltici
Bamberg, witchcraft executions at 506
ban, Imperial (Reichsacht) 16, 30, 94, 119,
    191
Banat 300
Banér, Johnan (1596–1641), Swedish
    general 199
banking, merchant 429
  bankers manage exchange by means of
    bill of exchange 430
baptism, infant 17, 18, 22
  Lutheran view 22
  register of baptisms 363
  see also Anabaptism
Bar 240
Baradat, François de (1604–82), favourite
    of Louis XIII 228
Barbarossa, Hayreddin (Khair ad-Din),
    governor of Algeria (r. 1518–34) and
    Ottoman admiral (1534–46) 106, 137,
    290
Barberini dynasty, cultural achievement of
    479
  see also Urban VIII
Barcelona:
  beggars' hospitals 374
  fall of (1652) 220, 239
  treaty of (1529) 105
  wheat price converted into grams of
    silver 426
Barclay, William, Gallicized Scots political
    theorist 312, 560 n. 39
  originator of term 'monarchomach' 309,
    559 n. 13
Barnes, Robert, Lutheran reformer in
    England 41
Basamov, Alexei 277
Basel 28, 39, 40, 46, 47
Basra 292, 298
Bassevi, Jacob, court Jew, first Jew to be
    ennobled by the Emperor 461
Basta, Giorgio, Habsburg general in
    Moldavia, Transylvania, and Wallachia
    298
bastardy 365

Bátory, Stefan (István), opponent of
Ottoman power in Hungary 291
Bátory, Stefan (István), *voivode* of
Transylvania (r. 1571–5), and king of
Poland (r. 1576–86) 56, 273
accepts Ottoman suzerainty of
Transylvania 264
death without a direct heir 265
marries Anna Jagiellonka 264
opposes Muscovy from moment of his
accession in Poland 264
power described by Giovanni Botero
263
strategy for dealing with Muscovy 264
Bautzen 191
Bavaria, duchy and later electorate of 67,
95
acceptance of primogeniture (1506) 528
alliance with Charles V 119
estates of 321
independence of knights undermined
338
partition of duchy (1410–1505) 528
role in Counter-Reformation 183
untouched by German Peasants' War
394, 395
war of succession (or Landshut war) 94
see also Maximilian I of Bavaria
Bayeux 167
Bayezid II, Ottoman sultan (r. 1481–1512)
85, 288
attitude to Safavid Persia 289
deposed by his son, Selim 288
naval building programme 288
war of succession with Jem 288
Bayonne, interview at (1565) 131
Béarn, vicomté de 311
independence suppressed by Louis XIII
227
Beauce 407
Beauvaisis, peasant landholdings in 371
Beg, Koçu, theorist of Ottoman decline 294
beggars (*gueux*):
of 1566 149
of 1572 (*Watergeuzen*) 153
Bekker, Balthasar, Dutch Cartesian 511
Belgorod fortified line 401
Belgrade 290
Bellarmino, Cardinal St. Roberto (1542–
1621), Jesuit political theorist 71
opponent of the Copernican system 519
Bellay, Joachim du (1522–60), poet 484
Belskii, Bogdan 278
Bel'skii, Ivan, prince 276
Benandanti 509
Berg 185, 186
Bergamo 440

Bergen-op-Zoom, siege of (1622) 204, 348,
492
Bergh, Hendrik van den, count (1573–1638)
conspiracy of, in Spanish Netherlands
(1632) 206
Berlaymont, Charles, baron of (1510–78),
president of the council of finance in
the Netherlands 146, 148
Berne 39, 40, 48
Bernier, François (1620–88), French
traveller in the Far East 360
Bernini, Gian Lorenzo (1598–1680),
Baroque architect, painter, and
sculptor 479
Bertrano, Pietro, bishop of Fano 61
Bérulle, Pierre, Cardinal de (1575–1629),
religious adviser of Maria de' Medici
and later critic of Richelieu 227, 228
Besançon fairs (*Bisenzone*), organized by
Genoese 431, 436–8
change location 436
displace the Antwerp money market 433
result from exclusion of Genoese from
Lyon 434, 436
settle bills of exchange in silver 435
utilize an amalgamation of currencies
436
Beukelsz, Jan ('John of Leyden'), radical
Anabaptist leader at Münster 25
Beza, Theodore (Theodore de Bèze,
1519–1605), Moderator of the
Company of Pastors at Geneva and
Calvin's successor 50, 55
on abjuration of Henri IV 310
and Calvinist confessions of faith 50
despair at abjurations in France 171
political theories implicitly condemned
by Bodin 313
and predestination 51
and Presbyterian organization 50–1, 56
The Right of Magistrates (1574) 309–10
on usury 456
see also Arminius
Béziers 498
Bible:
Erasmus' translation of New Testament
11
Luther's translation 18
Luther and private Bible study 18
Polyglot in Castile 8, 13
prohibition on private gatherings to read
Bible 30
study at Universities 10
vernacular editions prohibited 65
vernacular in Germany 34
vernacular in Netherlands 35
Vulgate 62

Bibliothèque bleue 495
Bicker, Andrew, Amsterdam burgomaster
214, 407
Bicker, Cornelius (1592–1654), Amsterdam
burgomaster 214, 407
Biel, Gabriel, nominalist theologian 10
Bielke, Hogenskilde, Swedish magnate 326
family 336
'bi-metallic ratio', ratio of gold to silver
values 423–4
Biron, Charles de Gontaut, duke of (1562–
1602) 225
birth-rate 365, 370, 399
Bishops 2, 5, 63
in France 6, 67
in Germany 5
in Italy 5
Blake, Robert, English admiral 240
Blekinge 254
Blotius, Hugo, court librarian to Maximilian
II 480
Bobadilla, Nicholas de, Jesuit 71
Bocholt 26
Bocskai, István, first Calvinist *voivode* of
Transylvania 56, 298–9
Bodin, Jean (1529/30–96), French political
theorist 306
on causation of European price rise 422
comparison between state systems and
types of proportion condemned by
Kepler 516
condemns heliostatic theory of
Copernicus 516
Demonomania of Sorcerers (1580)
504–5
distinction between monarchical,
tyrannical, and seigneurial monarchy
285
France a pure monarchy 316, 317
king never dies, according to Bodin 489
longevity of seigneurial monarchy 300,
301
need for strong central power to preserve
order 360
on political parties 330
on register of baptisms and deaths 363
on representative institutions 316
Six Books of a Commonweal
(République) (1576) 313
undivided legislative sovereignty and
other ideas 312–14, 325, 331
Bohemia, kingdom of:
diet 318
divisions during rebellion of 1619–20
191
during Thirty Years' war 199

estates depose Ferdinand II (1619) 187,
190
fate of Protestants in, after 1648 200
Habsburg succession (1526) 95, 115
imposition of new constitution by
Ferdinand II (1627) 190, 192
issues in the revolt of 1620 189–90
Ladislas Jagiellon, king 98
land transfer following defeat of 1620
rebellion 192
Letter of Majesty (1609) 186
number of sessions of diet (1512–1620)
317
population estimates 365
under the Jagiellon dynasty 94
Bohemian Confession (1575) 55
Bohuslän 254
Bologna 374, 495, 497
Bolotnikov, Ivan, former galley slave and
leader of insurrection in Muscovy
(1606–7) 279, 391, 393
Bolsec, Jérôme, anti-predestinarian 45, 46,
49
Bonde, Gustav 336, 382
Bonvisi, Lucchese banking family at Lyon
430
Book of Concord (1580) 43, 46, 54
Book of the Distaffs (1475 and
subsequently) 494
*Book of Regensburg (*1541) 58, 118
Bordeaux 167, 235
Carnival at 498
Fronde at 238
Ormée at (1652–3) 412
revolt at (1548) 412
royal entry at 488
Boris Godunov (d. 1605), Tsar of Muscovy
(r. 1598–1605)
anarchy at death 279
effective regent (1584–98) 278
elected Tsar 278–9
Bornholm 254
Borromeo, Carlo, Cardinal and archbishop
of Milan 64, 66, 69, 75
Borromeo, Federico, archbishop of Milan
66
Bosch, Hieronymus (*c.*1450–*c.*1516), artist
at the Burgundian court 476–7, 482
Bosnia 288, 298
Bossu, Maximilien Hennin, count of
(1542–78), stadholder of Holland,
Zeeland, and Utrecht for Philip II after
Orange's resignation 154
Bossuet, Jacques-Bénigne (1627–1704),
theologian and political theorist of the
power of Louis XIV 487, 530–1

Botero, Giovanni (1533–1617), Italian
  political theorist:
  on distinction between ordinary and
    extraordinary revenues 353
  on domestic militias 351
  on the dynastic state 524
  on the power of Polish king 263
  Reason of State (1589) 314
Boucher, Jean, political theorist of the
  Catholic League 311
Bougie 137
Bouillion, Frédéric-Maurice de la Tour
  d'Auvergne, duke of (1605–52), prince
  of Sedan
  rebel against Richelieu 230
Bouillon, Henri de la Tour d'Auvergne,
  duke of (1555–1623), prince of Sedan
  184
  conspiracy (1606) 179, 225
Boulogne 108, 125
Boulonnais:
  peasant rebellion (Lustucru, 1662) 392
Bourbon, Charles III, duc de and Constable
  of France (1490–1527) 100, 101
  Imperial commander 102, 116
  rebellion (1523) 102
  Sack of Rome and death 104–5
Bourbon, Charles, Cardinal de (1523–90,
  'Charles X' of the League) 174, 176
Bourbon dynasty:
  succession in France 136
  succession in Spain 145
  see also Condé; Navarre
Bourbonnais 83
Bourdon, Sebastian (1616–71), painter 485
boyars, in Muscovy 276
  see also Muscovy
Brabant 147, 152, 155, 160, 213, 329, 409
  agricultural production in 471
  and Pacification of Ghent 157
  population density 366
  role of States in coup of 1576 156
Braganza, dynasty of 139
Brahe, Tycho (1546–1601), Danish
  astronomer 481, 516
Bramante, Donato d'Agnolo (1444–1514):
  design for St Peter's 478
Brandenburg, electorate of 54, 95
  elector George William, brother-in-law of
    Gustavus Adolphus 196, 268, 270
  elector John Sigismund 184, 185
  estates of 321
  modest peasant prosperity in 428
  partition of Cleves-Jülich succession 185
  see also Frederick William I
Brant, Sebastian (1457–1521) 499

Braudel, Fernand, economic historian 446
Brazil 72, 180, 222
  chance allocation to Portugal in Treaty of
    Tordesillas 441, 442–3
  Dutch advance in 205, 211, 443, 452
  establishment of sugar industry 443
  hereditary captaincies 443
  importation of slave labour force from
    Angola 443
  rising of Portuguese settlers (1645) 211,
    213
  Sephardi Jewish community in Dutch
    Brazil 452, 462
Breda:
  captured by Maurice of Nassau (1590)
    162
  captured by Spínola (1625) 204–5, 348
  joins Union of Utrecht (1579) 155
  recaptured by Frederick Henry (1637)
    211, 348
Brederode, Hendrik van, lord of Vianen
    (1531–68) 149, 150–1
Breisach, fortress of 200, 202
  Jewish community protected by French
    461
Breisgau 395
Breitenfeld, first battle of (1631) 195, 196,
    346, 347
Breitenfeld, second battle of (1642) 199
Bremen 117, 193, 199, 202, 203, 251, 253,
    254
  and the Hanseatic League 439
Brenz, Johannes (Johann Brentzen),
    Lutheran reformer at Schwäbisch
    Hall 37
  and punishment of dissenting opinions
    498
  on witchcraft 504
Brescia 374
Brethren of the Common Life 8
Breughel, Pieter (c.1525–69) 481, 497
Briçonnet, Guillaume, bishop of Meaux
    13
Brill, The (Den Briel) 153, 161, 447
Brittany:
  estates of 327
  impoverished nobility 380
  incorporation into France 83
  League in 177
  peasant rising of 1675 392
  Valois succession 83
  war of succession 82–3
Brömsebro, Peace of (1645) 251–2
Bruges 157, 431–2, 439
  artists' workshops at 490
  capitulation to Parma (1584) 160

Bruno, Giordano (1548–1600) 484, 519
Brunswick 160
Brunswick-Wolfenbüttel 67
  attacked by Schmalkaldic League 118
  duke Christian (1599–1626), military
    captain 193
Brussels 152, 155, 157, 253
  capitulation to Parma (1585) 160
Bucer, Martin (1490–1551), Reformed
    theologian at Strasbourg 13, 28, 29,
    44, 54, 117
  On the Kingdom of Christ (1551) 44
  on usury 456
Buchanan, George (1506–82), Calvinist
    political theorist 266, 310
Buckingham, George Villiers, duke of
    (1592–1628), favourite of James I and
    Charles I 332
Buda 291, 293, 300
  Ottoman-controlled province of (1541)
    243, 293
Budé, Guillaume (1468–1540), humanist
    and political theorist 306
Buen Retiro, palace of the 483
Buenos Aires 213
Bugenhagen, Johannes (1485–1558),
    Lutheran theologian and confessor to
    Luther 18
  and Danish church ordinance 41
Bulgaria 288
Bullinger, Heinrich, Zwingli's successor at
    Zurich (d. 1575) 29, 39, 42, 44, 49, 52,
    55
  and single predestination 45
Burgos, during Comunero rebellion 414
Burgundy, French province (acquired 1477)
    82, 83, 407
  agricultural production in 471
  estates 104, 327
  governor 229
  Habsburg claims to 79, 103, 105, 108
  invaded 88
  Mayenne governor of 175
  revolt of Bonnets rouges (1594) 391
Burgundy, Valois and later Habsburg, duchy
    of:
  Burgundian liberties 161
  Charles V's abdication 123
  cultural achievement of Valois court
    476–7
  defence against France 129
  threat to France 81
  war of succession 82
  see also Low Countries
Buys, Paulus, advocate to the states of
    Holland (1572–84) 161–2
Byelorussia 271, 284

Cadiz 141, 443
Caen, riot at (1514) 413
Cajetan, Cardinal (Tommaso da Vio) 15
Calais 128, 129, 163, 240
Calvin, Jean (1509–64), French exile and
    reformed theologian at Geneva 22, 29,
    164
  Against the Anabaptists (1544) 26–7
  agreement with Bullinger (1549) 29, 44
  career 43, 48, 70
  and church organization 50, 52–3
  and Council of Trent 62
  denounces Nicodemism 52, 61–2
  and double predestination 45–6
  Ecclesiastical Ordinances (1541) 48
  on erudition 514
  and Eucharist 29, 46, 48, 53
  influence of Bucer 44, 48
  Institution (or *Institutes*) *of the Christian
    Religion* (1st edn., 1536) 44–5
  and justification by faith alone 45, 58–9
  and Luther 44, 118
  political conservatism 308–9
  and preaching 37, 44
  and Reformation 43–4, 76
  and usury 455, 456
  and witchcraft 504
Calvinists/Calvinism:
  'Calvinist International' 454–5
  excluded from Peace of Augsburg 43, 54,
    121, 183, 194, 198
  exiles from the Low Countries 152–3
  first use of term 46
  hostility to Anabaptism 26
  numerical strength in the Low
    Countries 151, 154, 163
  persecution in the Low Countries 148
  recognized in Peace of Westphalia 68,
    201
  relative strength in France and the
    Netherlands 164
  'Second Reformation' in Germany 54
  spread in France 102, 129
  see also Beza; Huguenots
Cambrai:
  Peace of, or Ladies' Peace (1529) 105,
    423
  siege of (1649) 239
Cambrésis, harvest yields in 469, 470
Cambrils, massacre at 220
Campanella, Tommaso (1568–1639),
    philosopher 519
Candia, siege of (1648–69) 299
Canisius, St Peter (1521–97) 72
capitalism:
  debate on concepts of pre- and proto-
    industrialization 417, 467

preference for purchase of office rather than commerce 344
price encouragement to capital accumulation 427-8
religion and the rise of, debate on 454-5
see also agriculture
Capito, Wolfgang, reformed theologian at Strasbourg 28, 48
capitulation, election, in Holy Roman Empire 93, 311
Caraffa, Carlo, nephew of Pope Paul IV 127
Cardinals, college of 3, 65
conclave of 62
Caribbean, Spanish defence of 140, 141
Carlos II (1661-1700), last Habsburg king of Spain (r. 1665-1700) 224, 340, 357, 530
see also Mariana of Austria
Carnival 495, 496, 497, 499
at Romans (1580) 413
Carranza, Bartolomé de, archbishop of Toledo 66
Cartagena 213
Cartwright, Thomas, Presbyterian 51
Casale, fortress in Montferrat 209, 239
Casimir IV (Kazimierz IV), king of Poland and Lithuania (r. 1445-92) 258, 273
Castaldo, Giam Battista, Habsburg commander in Transylvania 293
Castellio, Sebastian 49
Castelnaudary, battle of (1632) 230
Castiglione, Baldessare (1478-1529) 475
Castile:
abandonment of direct administration of army after 1618 350
annuities (*juros*) 356
arbitristas 214, 215, 383
army 86-7, 90, 103, 135-6, 156, 218, 346
birth-rate in 365
bullion imports 136, 215, 218, 224
concessions to financiers (*medio general*) 358
conciliar structure 333
conversion from *asientos* to *juros* 357
Cortes 89, 110, 111, 112, 145, 217, 219, 359
Cortes and Comunero movement 414
council of finance 113, 137
Council of the Holy Brotherhood (*Santa Hermandad*) 414
Council of the Inquisition relatively sceptical on witchcraft 509-10
council of war 137
courts of appeal (*Audiencias*) 339
crusade indulgences 130
currency 436
debts of nobility 380
dowry market 379
dynastic union under Philip the Fair 82-3
evolution of powers of *Cortes* 324-6
fairs for bills of exchange to be settled in 431
fiscal burden 218, 219
fiscal burden on peasantry 382-3
fiscal burden stultifies growth of towns 400
fiscal exemptions 383
fueros, privileges guaranteed by kings of Castile 325
Gothic myth 378
government officials in localities (*corregidores*) 339, 414, 415
growing imbalance between Castile and other territories 216
households (*vecinos*) 363
law of entail (*mayorazgo*) 379
legislation concerning vagrancy 372
lesser nobility (*caballeros*) 339, 379
licences for beggary 372
merchant marine 446
mining resources in New World 418
money of account 423
no equivalent to Salic Law 527
nobility 91, 111, 219, 376
number of sessions of *Cortes* (1497-1660) 317
Olivares's plans to Castilianize the other kingdoms 217
peasant day labourers (*jornaleros*) 382
peasant freeholders and leaseholders (*labradores*) 382
peasant rebellions 223, 391
peasant share-croppers 382
political predominance under Philip II 133-4
population 89, 365
principal market for Dutch textiles 453
procuradores, deputies of towns 324, 326, 415
rate of increase in prices 426
reduction of aristocratic dominance in councils 338-9
regency 111, 325-6
reputation abroad 120
revenues 89, 112, 136, 352-3
revenues anticipated 114
rise of university-trained jurists (*letrados*) 339-40
royal share of bullion imports 421
sale of offices and municipal offices 340, 405

Castile (*cont.*)
  servicios 112, 324, 353
  Seville Admiralty Board (*Almirantazgo*)
    213
  size of urban population (with Aragon)
    398
  standing committee of *Cortes*
    (*Diputación*) 324–5
  suspension of loan contracts (*decretos*)
    357
  tax censuses 363
  taxpayers (*pecheros*) 383
  types of revenue 353
  wool exports to the Low Countries 414,
    432
  see also Charles V; Cisneros; Comuneros;
    Isabella of Castile; Olivares; Philip II;
    Philip III; Philip IV
Catalonia 89, 145, 221, 239
  absentee rule 216
  Catalan republic declared 220
  Corts 216
  Diputació 219, 220, 324
  five evil customs (*malos usos*) 390
  fueros 217, 220
  peasant rebellion (1484–5) 390–1
  political divisions 220
  rebellion (1640) 211, 213, 219–22
  reliance of rebellion in 1640 on French
    support 220, 232
  serfs (*remensas*) 391
  Union of Arms and 218
  viceroyalty 92
  witchcraft in 508
Cateau-Cambrésis, Peace of (1559) 128–9
Catechism:
  Counter-Reformation and 72, 456
  Luther and 19 34
Catherine de' Medici (Catherine de
    Médicis, 1519–89), wife of Henri II,
    and regent of France (r. 1560–3) 106,
    165, 169, 170, 309, 332, 483, 484
  criticism of Italian entourage 169–70
  interview at Bayonne 131
  regency 165
  role in St Bartholomew massacres 171
  secures edict of Amboise (1563) 169
Catholic monarchs 2, 90, 114
  see also Ferdinand of Aragon; Isabella of
    Castile
Caucasus, mountains 289, 297
Caulet, François-Étienne de (1610–1680),
    Jansenist bishop of Pamiers 499
Caumont, Jean, propagandist of the
    Catholic League 411
Caussin, Père Nicolas (1583–1651), Jesuit
    confessor of Louis XIII 228

celibacy, clerical 18, 38
Cellini, Benvenuto (1500–71), sculptor,
    goldsmith, and art historian 484
Celtis, Conrad (1459–1508) 479
Centralization 525
Ceriol, Furió, Spanish political theorist 133
Cerisole, battle of (1544) 108
Ceuta 419, 441, 442
Ceylon 451
Chabot, Philippe (1480–1543), seigneur de
    Brion, Admiral of France 107
Chaldiran, battle of (1514) 289, 476
Chambord, château de 483
Chambre Saint-Louis, meeting of
    representatives of Parisian sovereign
    courts at (1648) 233–4, 235, 238
Chambres mi-parties, mixed tribunals in
    French *Parlements* to hear Protestant
    cases 173, 178
Champagne 173, 410, 507–8
Chancellor:
  in France 227
Charivari 497, 499
Charles I (1600–49), king of England
    (r. 1625–49) 234
Charles II (1630–85), king of England
    (r. 1660–85) 213, 330, 530
Charles II, king of Spain, *see* Carlos II
Charles V (1500–58), Holy Roman
    Emperor (r. 1519–56), duke of
    Burgundy (r. 1506–55); Carlos I, king
    of Castile and Aragon (r. 1516–56),
    etc. 2, 100, 260, 331, 339, 340, 352
  abdication 122–3, 145
  absences from Germany 31
  absences from Spain 13, 110–11, 114
  'absolute power' exercised in the Low
    Countries (1543) 529
  advice to Philip II 114, 116, 132, 138,
    143, 146
  alliance with Christian II of Denmark
    244, 245
  attacks Schmalkaldic League 118
  Augsburg family compact 120
  birth at Ghent 91, 92
  Burgundian patrimony 83, 101, 103, 104
  Castilian resentment at Burgundian court
    110
  contrast between his rule and Ottoman
    practice 300
  contrast between his treatment of
    Ashkenazi and Sephardi Jews 461
  coronation oath at Aachen 30, 115
  and *Cortes* of Castle 110–11, 112, 324–5
  court culture 480, 482–3
  crusading ideal 130
  death at Yuste 124

at diet of Worms 30
election as Emperor contested 16, 99, 110
election capitulation 93, 120
Erasmian entourage 133
flees to Villach 120–1
general law code for the Empire
 (*Constitutio criminalis carolina*) 506
generality of the Low Countries
 established 113, 155, 160, 328
and Genoese 435, 436
holds Pope Clement VII virtual
 prisoner 104–5, 478
and Imperial reform 114, 119, 319–20
imposes Interim of Augsburg 43, 54, 60, 119, 120, 121, 126, 464
imposes Treaty of Madrid (1526) 104, 130, 332
influence on Philip II 132
Italian policy 88, 107, 108, 116
logistical problem of his dynastic state 524
marriage 112
Milanese policy 108, 116
negotiates English marriage for Philip 122–3
north African policy 137
Papal coronation (1530) 94, 105
partition of inheritance 110, 120, 525
political system in the Low Countries 146, 147
proclaims himself king of Castile in
 lifetime of his mother 110
recourse to short-term borrowing 114, 357, 423
regents 111, 114
religious policy in Germany 28–9, 30, 33
revenues 286
seeks general council of Church 32, 60, 118
sent a copy of Copernicus' *On the
 Revolutions of the Heavenly Spheres* 516
siege of Metz 121, 126, 347
suppresses heresy in the Low Countries 30–1, 33, 147–8
suppresses revolt at Ghent (1539–40) 107, 151, 413
travels between his lands 114, 132
uses Castile as base of empire 112
viceroys 92, 116
victory at Pavia (1525) 103
victory at Mühlberg (1547) 109, 119
Charles VII, king of France (r. 1422–61) 81, 359, 377, 433
Charles VIII, king of France (r. 1483–98) 80, 82–3

army under 346
invades Naples 84–5
restores Roussillon and Cerdagne 90
royal entry under 488
Charles IX (1550–74), king of France
 (r. 1560–74) 165, 166, 179
Calvinist hopes for his abjuration 166
cultural interests 484
death 263
loss of authority after St Bartholomew
 massacres 172
majority (1563) 169
participates in affairs of state 169
role in St Bartholomew massacres 171
royal entry under 489
Charles IX (1550–1611), king of Sweden
 (r. 1600/4–11)
coup against Sigismund 249, 266–7
effective ruler of Sweden (1590–3) 266
elected king (1604) 267
hostility to Erik Sparre and aristocratic
 opponents 266, 267, 334
hostility to John III 248
summons *riksdag* during absence of
 Sigismund 266
Sweden faces military collapse at time of
 his death 249
war of aggression in Livonia 267
Charles X (Charles Gustavus, duke of
 Pfalz-Zweibrücken-Kleeburg,
 1622–60), king of Sweden (r. 1654–60)
achieves natural frontiers of Sweden 252, 255
autocratic ambitions 255
cultural pillaging in Denmark 485
debts at death 255
enlargement of ambitions after Treaty of
 Roskilde 254–5
fears Muscovite advance into Poland 253, 270
generalship secures Treaty of Roskilde
 with Denmark 254
recognized as heir to Christina (1649) 253
surprise attack on Denmark (1658) 255
terms for alliance with Poland 270
war aims in 1654 270
withdraws from war in Poland 271, 284
'Charles X of the League', *see* Bourbon,
 Charles, Cardinal de
Charles XI, king of Sweden (r. 1660–97) 256, 485
aristocratic rule during minority 256
Charles de Valois, duke of Burgundy
 (Charles the Bold, d. 1477) 82, 476, 524
Charles de Valois, duc d'Orléans (1522–45),
 third son of Francis I 107–8

Chasseneux, Barthélemy, president of the
Parlement of Aix and political
theorist 313
Châtel, Jean, attempted assassin of Henri
IV (1594) 178
Chelyadnin-Fedorov, Ivan 276
Cherasco, Treates of (1631) 209
Cherkasskii, Ivan, prince, cousin of Tsar
Michael 281
Chernigov 275, 285
chief minister, role of, in seventeenth
century 331-2
Chièvres, Guillaume de Croy, sieur de
(1458-1521), minister of Charles
V 115
Chiliasm 22, 500
China 72, 451
Chinchón, Diego de, secretary to Philip II
135
Chmielnicki, Bogdan (d. 1657), first great
Cossack political leader and head of
Cossack rebellion against Poland 270,
282, 390, 558 n. 47
death 284
grievances 282
hostility to Jews 283, 463
negotiations during revolt 283-4
political consequences of revolt 285
revolt splits after death of Chmielnicki
284
submission to Tsar Alexis (1654) 284
Chmielnicki, George (Iurii):
leads Cossack faction into renewed
alliance with Tsar Alexis 284
Chocim, Ottoman siege of (1620) 268, 295
Chodkiewicz, Charles, Polish general 268
Chodkiewicz, Jan, separatist leader of
Lithuania 260
Christian II, king of Denmark and Sweden
(r. 1513-23) 255
alienates Danish nobility 245
arbitrary and erratic rule 244
bloodbath of Stockholm (1520) 244
invasion of 1531-2 245
rights of succession bought out in
Denmark 247
support of Lübeck for his restoration
246
Christian III, king of Denmark (r. 1534-59)
buys out Christian II's succession rights
247
duke of Holstein 245
establishes Reformation in Denmark 41,
246
wins war of succession (1533-6) 245-6
Christian IV (1577-1648), king of Denmark
(r. 1588-1648) 249

accepts aristocratic control of
government shortly before death 252
blockades the Elbe 251
concessions to the Dutch 252, 449
destroys the Polish fleet 251, 257
encourages Jewish settlement at
Glückstadt 462
forced to sign the Peace of Lübeck
(1629) 194, 195, 250, 268
motives for intervention in Thirty Years'
War 192-3
provocations to Sweden in the 1630s and
1640s 251
raises Sound tolls: (1611-14) 448;
(1630s) 251, 449
seeks foreign war to escape aristocratic
tutelage 249
seeks Imperial alliance 251
treasures pillaged after his death 485
Christian Civic Union (1529) 39
Christina (1626-89), queen of Sweden
(r. 1632-54)
abdication (1654) 253, 337
alienates crown lands 202, 252-3, 336
cultural pillaging abroad and court
culture at home 485
decision to abdicate and convert to
Catholicism 253, 270
ennoblements 336
political significance of minority 197,
334
and *riksdag* 326, 337
seeks peace abroad once of age to rule
251
Christopher of Oldenburg, count 246
Cinq-Mars, Henri Coiffier de Ruzé,
marquis de (1620-42), favourite of
Louis XIII and conspirator against
Richelieu 228
conspiracy and execution (1642) 230
Ciompi, revolt of at Florence (1378) 414
circles, Imperial (*Kreise*) 96, 113, 192
Cisneros, Jiménez de, archbishop of Toledo
and high chancellor of Castile
(1437-1517) 8
president of council of regency in Castile
110
cities, Castilian:
and revolt of the Comuneros 111, 324,
414
cities, European:
definition of citizenship 402-3
growth in size 371, 397-8
migration to, during famine 371
see also guilds; merchants; oligarchy
cities, Imperial 94
desire for autonomy 96

and printing during the Reformation 36
and the Reformation 31, 42, 454
class, applicability of concept of 361
Claude of Brittany, first wife of Francis I 99
Clement VII (Giulio de' Medici), Pope
(1523–34) 94, 104, 477, 478
alliance with Charles V 105
alliance with Francis I 106
and Medici family interests 3, 57, 106
Clement VIII (Ippolito Aldobrandini), Pope
(1592–1605) 62, 68, 221
accepts Henri IV's abjuration 176
and Jews 460
Clément, Jacques, Dominican, assassin of
Henri III 176, 311
Clergy, regular 2, 8
new religious orders 8
satirized by Erasmus 11
Cleves 67, 185, 186
Cleves-Jülich succession crisis (1609–14)
184–6, 225
duke John William 185
partition (1614) 186
climate, change in 369
Coen, Jan Pieterszon (1587–1629),
governor-general of Dutch East
Indies 451
Cognac 170
coitus interruptus 365–6
Colbert, Jean-Baptiste, marquis de
Seignelay (1619–83), intendant of
finance (1661–5) and later
controller-general of finance (1665–83)
of Louis XIV 358, 446
bullionist and mercantilist views 429
directs cultural activities in the reign of
Louis XIV 485
hostility to excessive number of vines in
France 468
hostility to the United Provinces 429
tariff policy against the Dutch 453
Coligny, Gaspard de Châtillon, comte de
(1519–72), admiral of France 128,
167, 170
assassination 171
corpse a subject for pilgrimage by
Catholics 171, 500
exaggerates strength of Calvinism in
France 164–5
justifies assassination of Guise 169
posthumously rehabilitated 173
seeks to invade Low Countries 151, 170
Collège de Montaigu 70
colloquy, *see* Marburg; Poissy; Regensburg
Cologne, electorate of 68, 94
abjuration of Truchsess 183
artists' workshops at city of 490
Mazarin's exile at Brühl 236

Wittelsbach seizure of 183
University of 14
Colonna, Prospero, Imperial
commander 101
Colonna, Vittoria 59
Columbus, Christopher (1451–1506) 443
Committee of the Night (*Junta de Noche*)
135
Common Penny 96
Communion, Holy, *see* Eucharist
Communism, practised at Münster 25
community or village corporation
(*Gemeinde*) 416, 498
Como 440
Compromise, or League of Nobility in the
Low Countries (1566) 149
Comuneros, revolt of, in Castile (1520–1)
100, 111, 407, 415, 416
commune (*comunidad*) 111, 414
Holy League (*Santa Junta*) 111, 414
repression 415
rival League of La Rambla 414
spread of revolt to peasantry 415
Concini, Concino (?–1617), marquis
d'Ancre 226
Concord (1536), between Lutherans and
south German cities 29
Concordat of Bologna (1516) 2, 100
Condé, collateral branch of the Bourbon
dynasty:
Henri I de Bourbon, prince of Condé
(d. 1588) 170, 171, 172, 174
Henri II de Bourbon, prince of Condé
(1588–1646) 225, 226, 228
Louis I de Bourbon, prince of Condé
(1530–69) 165, 167, 168–9, 170
Louis II de Bourbon, prince of Condé
(1621–86) 199, 212, 236, 237, 238,
341, 501
Confession of Augsburg:
defence of, in Schmalkaldic War 119
invariata of 1530 16–17, 19, 27, 28–9,
33, 117
variata of 1540 29, 54
see also Bohemian Confession;
Consensus Sandomiriensis; *Consensus
Tigurinus*; Low Countries: Netherlands
Confession of Faith; Schleitheim
Confession; Tetrapolitan Confession;
Zwingli
confession, auricular 9, 17
Luther and 18
congregationalism 51
conseil d'en haut in France 333
Consensus Sandomiriensis 55
Consensus Tigurinus (Swiss Confession of
Faith, 1549) 29, 44
Consistory at Geneva 49, 56

Constable:
  in Castile 111, 332, 415
  in France 228, 332
Constance 31, 39, 117
Constantinople, *see* Istanbul
Constitution, Imperial 31, 93
Constitutions, written, in Europe 359
Contarini, Gasparo (1483–1542), Cardinal
  9, 57, 59
  double justification 59, 63
  Papal envoy to the Regensburg colloquy
  58
  on Venetian constitution 403
continua successione 62
Conty, Armand de Bourbon, prince de
  (1629–66), younger brother of Condé
  arrest of princes (1650) 236
  Frondeur in 1649 234
Copenhagen 246, 254, 255
  Peace of (1660) 255
Copernicus, Nicolaus (Mikolaj Kopernik,
  1473–1547), Bohemian astronomer
  and discoverer of the heliostatic
  principle 515
  *On the Revolutions of the Heavenly
    Spheres* subsequently condemned by
    the Roman Inquisition 519
copper:
  coinage, in Muscovy 285
  coinage (*vellón*), in Castile 216
  riots in Muscovy (1662) 285
  Swedish copper 216, 250
Corbie, Spanish capture of (1636) 210
Córdoba 223
  during Comunero rebellion 414
Córdoba, Gonzalo de, the 'great captain'
  86, 90
  viceroy of Naples 91
Córdoba, Gonzalo Fernández de (1585–
  1635), governor of Milan 208
coronation, in France 486–7
Corpus Christi, feast of 494
Corsica 129
Cortes, see Aragon; Castile; Portugal
Cortés, Hernan (1485–1547) 444
Corts, see Catalonia
Cossacks 278, 279, 281
  tradition of revolt in seventeenth
  century 282
  see also Chmielnicki, Bogdan, and
  George
Council of Aragon:
  deprived of control over Italian affairs
  133
Council of Flanders 133
council, Imperial aulic (*Reichshofrat*) 184,
  189

council, Imperial governing
  (*Reichsregiment*) 114, 188, 319
Council of Italy 133
Council of Portugal 133
Council of Sixteen, during Catholic League
  in France 175
Council of Trent (1545–63) 1, 5, 9, 46, 57,
  59, 60–4, 69, 118, 166
  attendance at 61
  condemns usury 456
  decision on justification 63
  decision on predestination 63
  dominated by Italians 61
  not all issues settled at Council 73
  Protestant legend 131
  Spanish challenge to Italian dominance
  62
Council of Troubles in the Low Countries
  (1567–73) 152
Councillor Pensionary (*raadpensionaris*) to
  the States of Holland 204
councils of the Church:
  Basel (1433–7) 4
  condemn usury 455
  Lateran, Fifth (1512–17) 5, 61, 79
  Pisa (*Conciliabulum* of 1511–12) 5
  see also Council of Trent
Counter-Reformation 57, 65, 548 n. 155
  in France 67
  in Germany 67–8
  see also Borromeo, Carlo
Counter-Remonstrant party, in the United
  Provinces 182
Courland 249, 262, 270
court, royal:
  cost of, in Castile 216
court, supreme Imperial
  (*Reichskammergericht*) 33, 97, 119
  paralysis by end of sixteenth century 183
Courtrai 157, 212
covenant, *see* elect
Cracow 265, 271, 402
  wheat price converted into grams of
  silver 426
Cranmer, Thomas (1489–1556), archbishop
  of Canterbury 41
Crato, Dom Antonio (1531–95), prior of,
  illegitimate claimant to the Portuguese
  throne 139
Crell, Dr Nicolaus, chancellor of Saxony
  (executed 1601) 321
Crépy-en-Laonnais, treaty of (1544) 108
Crete, war for 299, 403
Crimea, khanate of 242, 283, 284
  tributary state of Ottomans 242, 288
crisis, general European 188, 305
crisis, subsistence 368–9

defined 370
in Muscovy (1601-3) 375, 391
Cromwell, Oliver (1599-1658), Lord
    Protector of England (1653-8) 254
  alliance with Charles X of Sweden 253
  alliance with Mazarin 240
  and religious toleration 531
  views on Swedish threat to Danzig 253
Cromwell, Thomas (1485?-1540), earl of
    Essex 306, 333
crusade 79, 118, 130, 131, 390
Cuba 205, 452
Cudnów, battle of (1660) 285
cuius regio, eius religio:
  rejection of, in Brandenburg 54
Culemborg 150
culture, debate on the concepts of elite and
    popular 474, 494, 523
Curaçao 452
Cyprus 138
Czarniecki, Stefan, Polish general 272

Dacke, Nils, leader of Swedish peasant
    rebellion (1542-3) 247, 388-9
Danube, river 288
Danzig 243, 348, 447
  Charles X fails to capture 271
  Gustavus Adolphus fails to capture 268
  and the Hanseatic League 439
  inflation of grain prices in 1650s 272
  infuriated by Christian II's policy
    regarding Sound tolls 244
  Ladislas IV relinquishes rights of toll at
    270
  opposes election of Stefan Bátory as king
    of Poland 264
  political autonomy and rebellions 257,
    402
  population 257, 402
  supports Swedish rebellion of 1523 244
  threatened by Charles X of Sweden 253
Dathenus, Peter (1531-88), Calvinist
    minister at Ghent 157-8, 160, 409,
    410
Dauphiné 209
  estates of 327, 328
  revolt (*ligue des vilains*, 1579-80) 391
Death, Black (1348) 367, 469
  see also plague
death-rate 365, 370, 399
deaths, register of 363
Décapole, prefecture of ten towns in
    Alsace 202
defenestration of Prague (1618) 189
Defensors, in Bohemia 189
Delft 150, 447
  rate of population growth 399

'demesne state' (*Domänenstaat*) 352
Den Bosch ('s Hertogenbosch) 205
  bread riots (1628) 405
Denmark:
  absolutism established (1660) 255-6,
    358-9
  alliance with France under Francis I 108,
    247
  alliance with Sweden to provision
    Stralsund 193
  alliances with France and United
    Provinces under Christian IV 252
  clergy 246
  early Reformation in 41, 245, 246
  fears Dutch economic supremacy less
    than English or French 453-4
  'free' monarchy within Bodin's definition
    300
  nobility 245-6, 249, 252, 255
  population estimates (with Sweden) 365
  pretension to the Swedish throne 249
  primacy of agricultural sector 250
  satisfactory peace treaties with Sweden:
    (1570) 248-9; (1613) 249-50
  unsatisfactory peace treaties with
    Sweden: (1645) 251-2; (1658) 254;
    (1660) 255
  see also Brömsebro, Peace of; Christian
    II; Christian III; Christian IV; Frederick
    I; Frederick II; Frederick III; Knäred,
    Peace of; Oliva, Peace of; Roskilde,
    Treaty of; Stettin, Peace of; Sound
derogation, rule of (*dérogeance*), in France
    377, 457
Descartes, René (1596-1650), French
    mathematician, scientist and
    philosopher 485, 513, 521-3
  mechanistic model 522
  method of reasoning and the existence of
    God 522
  and occult phenomena 521
  principal publications 521
  works placed on the Index 522
Dessau 32
  battle of (1626) 193
Deulino, Truce of (1618) 280, 281
Devolution, War of (1667-8) 326
Dévot party, in France 207, 229
devotio moderna 8
Diemen, Antonio van (1593-1645),
    governor-general of Dutch East
    Indies 451
Dieppe 368
Diest, mutiny at 351
diet, Imperial (*Reichstag*) 2-3, 67, 96, 183
  Augsburg, diet of (1530) 33, 461
  Augsburg, 'armed' diet of (1547-8) 119

diet, Imperial (*Reichstag*) (*cont.*)
　decision on preaching (1523) 31
　during the Thirty Years' War 320
　evolution of powers 319–20
　number of sessions (1492–1654) 317
　paralysis by beginning of seventeenth
　　century 183–4
　Peace of Westphalia and 201, 320
　Regensburg, diet of (1546) 461
　Regensburg, diet of (1608) 184
　Regensburg, permanent diet of
　　(established 1663) 320
　Speyer, diet of (1526) 32
　Speyer, diet of (1529) 32
　Speyer, diet of (1544) 461
　support for the Imperial knights 338
　Worms, diet of (1521) 3, 16, 30
diet, Polish (*Sejm*) 273
　dietines (*sejmiki*) 318, 336
　evolution of powers of diet 318–19
　liberum veto 319
　number of sessions, (1493–1661) 317
　Statute of *Nihil novi* 259
　under the Union of Lublin 260
Dijon 167
Dilawar Pasha, grand vizier of sultan
　'Osman II 295
Dimitrii, prince, son of Ivan IV 278
　False Dimitrii I (Grigorii Otrep'ev) 279
　False Dimitrii II ('thief of Tushino')
　　279–80
Dixmude 159
Djerba 137
Dnieper, river 284, 285
Dniester, river 288
Doge, at Venice ix, 403, 490, 491
　election oath (*promissione*) 403
　supreme magistrates' attempt to forestall
　　dynastic succession 491
Dominican order 66
Dominium Maris Baltici 248, 250, 449, 453
　number of Dutch Baltic sailings 448
Don Carlos, Infante, first son of Philip II
　122, 133
Donauwörth:
　seized by Maximilian of Bavaria (1607)
　　184
Dordrecht (Dort) 182
　cost of debt servicing 355
　see also Synod of Dort
Doria, Andrea, Genoese naval captain 105
Dorpat 262, 277, 284
　occupied by Muscovy for twenty-four
　　years 264–5
Downs, battle of (1639) 211
dowries 365, 366, 367, 379, 380
　dowry loans 355

Dózsa, György Székely, known as, leader of
　Hungarian revolt (1514) 390
Drake, Sir Francis (1543–96) 140, 141
Drenthe 113
　specializes in livestock 472
Dreux, battle of (1562) 168, 350
du Bourg, Anne, Calvinist martyr 164
du Cerceau, Jacques Androuet (1510?–85),
　architect 483
du Chesne, André (1584–1640), scholar
　486
Dueñas 415
du Fail, Noël, French agronomist and
　folklorist 494
Dünamünde 268
Dunes, battle of (1658) 240
Dunkirk 142, 159, 212, 239, 240
Dupes, Day of, political crisis in France
　(1630) 229
Duplessis-Mornay, Philippe (1549–1623),
　Huguenot political theorist 266
　The Defence of Liberty against Tyrants
　　(1579) 309, 310
Duprat, Antoine (1464–1535), Cardinal and
　Chancellor of France 101, 332
Dürer, Albrecht (1471–1528) 479, 481
Düsseldorf 185
Dutch Republic, *see* United Provinces
du Tillet, Jean, sieur de la Bussière 488
Dvina, river 284
dynastic states, survival and problems of
　524–9
　Bossuet on monarchical power 531
dysentry 348

East Friesland 160
Eboli, Ruy Gómez de Silva, prince of, count
　of Melito ('king Gómez', 1516–73),
　Portuguese noble and favourite of
　Philip II 134–5
　faction of 148 151
Ecclesiastical reservation, interpretation of
　the Peace of Augsburg 198
Eck, Johann (= Johann Maier, 1486/9–
　1543), Catholic theologian and
　polemicist 9
écu au soleil 434
écu de marc 434, 436
Edict of Châteaubriant (1551) 52
Edict of Nantes (1598) 178
Edict of Restitution (1629) 68, 194, 196,
　198, 201
　imposed by military pressure 346
education, general broadening of 474
　see also universities
Edward VI, king of England (r. 1547–53)
　41, 125–6

Eger 299
Egmont, Charles of, duke of Guelders 113
Egmont, Lamoral, count of, prince of Gavre
(1522–68), stadholder in Flanders
146, 147, 148, 153
execution 152
family reconciled by Parma 159
fears Inquisition 146
mission to Madrid 148
Egypt 289, 290, 300
attempted revolt (1524) 290, 294
revenue from Egypt and Syria as a
proportion of total Ottoman revenues
290
see also Selim I
Eidgenossen 47
Elbe, river 193
Elbing 269, 402
Eleanor, of Austria, second wife of Francis
I 105
elect 38, 45, 46, 47, 51
Election, Imperial (1519) 16, 93
Electors (or electoral princes) of the Holy
Roman Empire 93–5
and Edict of Restitution 194
infrequently summoned 189
meeting at Mühlhausen (1620) 190
see also Bohemia; Brandenburg;
Cologne; Mainz; Palatinate; Saxony;
Trier
Elizabeth I (1533–1603), queen of England
(r. 1558–1603) 129
arrests duke of Alba's payships 153
denies port to Sea Beggars 153
rejects sovereignty of United Provinces
161
signs Treaty of Hampton Court with
Condé (1562) 168–9
supports Dutch revolt in Treaty of
Nonsuch (1585) 140, 161
Elizabeth of Valois (1545–68), queen of
Spain, daughter of Henri II and third
wife of Philip II 129, 177
Elvas, battle of (1658) 222
Emden 25, 150, 153, 455
Emperor, Holy Roman 92–4
distinction between Emperor and
'Imperial estates' (1648) 200–1
see also Charles V; Ferdinand I;
Ferdinand II; Ferdinand III; Leopold I;
Mathias I; Maximilian I; Maximilian II;
Rudolf II
Empire, Holy Roman 113, 130
abdication of Charles V 123
army 96, 119, 190–1, 193–4, 194–5, 197,
198, 200
cities (*Reichstädte*) 94, 319

expulsion of Jews 459
fiefs of 122, 209, 240
Frankish myth 378
merchant marine 446
peasant's laced boot (*Bundschuh*)
movement 393–4
Peasants' War 387, 394–7
personal bondage (*Leibeigenschaft*) 375
population density 366
population estimates 365
population loss during Thirty Years' War
202–3
silver mines 418, 419
size of urban population 398
see also Ban; diet, imperial; election;
Electors; Emperor; Habsburg dynasty;
Ritterschaft
England:
absence of Catholic rising against
Elizabeth 140–1
alliance with Sweden under Cromwell 253
attacks on Spanish empire 140, 143, 240
Baltic interests 255
birth-rate in 365
Castilian bullion source for English coin
issues under Elizabeth 424
closed oligarchies 404
contrast with French governing structure
330–1, 359–60
cost of intervention in the Netherlands
(1585) 354
death-rate in 365
debasements under Henry VIII and
Edward VI 424
defensive league with United Provinces
(1608) 181
displaced by Dutch in Levant trade 453
displaces Venice in Levant trade 441
Dutch ban on English cloth imports 453
Dutch displace English as the leading
textile suppliers to Baltic 452–3
early Reformation in 41
English role in Arctic trade with Muscovy
448
expedition to the Ile-de-Ré (1627) 209
fiscal base 362
harvest failures 368, 369
Industrial Revolution 454
influence on French funeral ceremonial
489
interest rate in 457
Irish rebellion against 143
joins the alliance of The Hague (1625)
193
lack of large-scale urban disturbance 407
legislation on beggary and poverty 371,
372

England (*cont.*)
  legislation on usury 456
  legislation on witchcraft 506
  merchant guilds 465
  merchant marine 446
  Navigation Acts 453
  no equivalent to Salic Law 527
  number of sessions of Parliament
    (1495–1660) 317
  resentment at Dutch economic
    hegemony 453
  size of urban population 398
  support for Henri IV 176
  wars with the Dutch: (1652–4) 214, 449;
    (1665–7) 214; (1672–4) 214
  witchcraft in 503, 505, 511
  withdraws from war with Spain (1604)
    163
  see also Charles I; Cromwell; Edward VI;
    Elizabeth I; Henry VIII; James I; Mary
    I; Nonsuch, Treaty of
English Civil War 361
Enkhuizen 447
Ennoblements:
  in Castile 340, 377
  in France 344, 377
  in Poland 336
  in Sweden 336–7, 377
  at Venice 403–4
Entragues, Henriette d' (1579–1633),
    mistress of Henri IV: conspiracy of
    members of her family (1604) 225
entry, royal, in France 488–9
Épernon, Jean-Louis Nogaret de la Valette,
    duc d' (1554–1642), favourite of Henri
    III
  governor of Metz, Toul, and Verdun 173
Erasmus, Desiderius, of Rotterdam
    (1466/9?–1536) 10–15, 523
  attitude to the Reformation 22
  and Carnival 499
  debate with Luther on free will 12–13
    24
  diffusion of his ideas 474
  Enchiridion Militis Christiani (1503) 11
  on erudition 515
  Instruction of a Christian Prince (1516)
    11
  Praise of Folly (1511) 11, 504
  role in the Reuchlin controversy 14
  views on education 13, 71
  writings condemned (1559) 65–6
  on war 345
Erastus, Thomas (Thomas Lüber) 51
  on witchcraft 504
Erblande 97

Erfurt 37
Erik XIV (d. 1577), king of Sweden
    (r. 1560–9):
  colonial policy in Estonia 247, 262–3
  deposition 248
  favours alliance with Muscovy 263
  insanity 247
Ermak, Cossack general 278
Erzerum 292, 297
Erzinjan 289
Escorial, Philip II's palace 400
  cost of building it 482
Espinosa, Diego de, Cardinal (1502–72):
  repressive policy against Moriscos 138,
    389
Estates General, in France:
  evolution of its powers 322–3
  in Huguenot theory 309, 310
  of 1468 359
  of 1484 361, 433
  of 1560 168
  of 1576 173, 322
  of 1588 175, 322
  of 1593 (of League) 67, 177, 322
  of 1614–15 226, 322–3, 462
  see also France, provincial estates
Estonia 243, 248, 257, 264, 267
Étampes, Anne d'Heilly, duchesse d' (1508–
    80), mistress of Francis I 107, 124–5
Eucharist 9, 17, 22, 27–9, 367
  attendance at as identification with
    community 498
  breaking of bread at 54–5
  Erasmus and 11, 28
  Protestant debate over exclusion from
    48–9, 53, 457
  see also Calvin; Luther; Marburg; Mass,
    Catholic; Zwingli
Euphrates, river 289
European 'world-economy' thesis 417–18,
    438
  diversity and fragmentation of European
    economy 438
exchange, bill of 430–1, 438
  with recourse (*con ricorsa*) 431, 436
excommunication:
  at Geneva 49–50
Eyck, Jan Van, artist at Burgundian
    court 476

Fadiger, Stefan, joint leader of peasant
    rebellion in Austria 389
family structure:
  differences in Europe 366–7

Farel, Guillaume (1489–1565), French
    reformed theologian in exile at Geneva
    and later Neuchâtel 42, 48
Federigo, king of Naples 86
Fedor I, last Muscovite Tsar of the Riúrik
    dynasty (r. 1584–98) 278
Fehrbellin, battle of (1675) 256
Feitoria de Flandres, Antwerp branch for
    the sale of Portuguese spices 432
Femern, battle of (1644) 251
Ferdinand I (1503–64), Holy Roman
    Emperor (r. 1556/8–64):
  accepts Ottoman suzerainty for Royal
    Hungary 291, 293
  accession in Austria and the Tyrol 113
  accession in Hungary (1526) 291
  Augsburg family compact 120
  birth 91–2
  dynastic ambitions 115
  elected Emperor (1558) 123
  encouragement of Czech culture 480
  exiled from Castile to forestall rebellion
    110
  King of the Romans (1531) 93, 115
  negotiates agreement of Várad
    (Grosswardein) with Zápolyai 292
  negotiates Peace of Augsburg (1555)
    121–2
  negotiates truce of Passau (1552) 121
  preoccupation with Turkish menace 115
  refuses Philip II Imperial vicariate 123
  Regent in the Empire 32, 114
  religious peace of Nuremberg (1532)
    117–18
  religious policy 60, 62, 183
  restricts Jewish privileges in Bohemia
    461
Ferdinand II (1580–1637), Holy Roman
    Emperor (r. 1619–37) 196
  arrests Cardinal Khlesl (1618) 186
  career before becoming Emperor 179,
    186, 187
  court culture under 481
  election 187, 188
  imposes new constitution in Bohemia
    (1627) 190, 192
  intervenes in Mantuan succession crisis
    209
  loans from Jewish community 461
  reliance on Bavaria and Saxony to defeat
    Bohemia 189
  and revolt of peasants of Austria 389,
    390
  secures renunciation of Philip III's claims
    to Empire 187
  vow to eliminate heresy 187
Ferdinand III (1608–57), Holy Roman
    Emperor (r. 1637–57):
  court culture under 481
  electors refuse to elect him King of the
    Romans (1630) 195
  forced to concede Peace of Westphalia
    200
  King of the Romans (1636) 93, 198
  supports Christian IV against Sweden 251
  wins battle of Nördlingen (1634) 198
Ferdinand IV, King of the Romans (1653)
    94
Ferdinand (Fernando) II, king of Aragon
    (r. 1479–1516) 2, 8, 84–5, 86, 88,
    89–92, 100, 109
  favours succession of Infante Fernando
    92, 109
  foreign policy 91
  marriage contract 90
  north African policy 137
  remarriage 91
  second regency in Castile 91–2
  testament of Isabella 91
Ferdinand (Fernando), Cardinal-Infante
    (1609–41), governor-general of the
    Spanish Netherlands:
  death 211–12
  reinforces Spanish army in Netherlands
    206
  wins battle of Nördlingen (1634) 198
Fernández Navarette, Pedro, *arbitristra* 383
Ferrante I, king of Naples 84
Ferrara 87
Fettmilch, Vincent, leader of anti-Jewish
    movement at Frankfurt-am-Main
    (1614) 409
Ficino, Marsilio (1433–99), founder of
    Florentine Academy 10, 477
Filaret Romanov, patriarch of all Russia
    280, 281
  hatred of Poland 281
Finale Liguria 187
'finance state' (*Finanzstaat*) 352
financial revolution 352
financiers:
  in France 238, 358, 457–8
  see also banking, merchant
Finland 243, 256, 257, 266, 281
Fisher, Irving, economist ('Fisher equation')
    422
Flanders 104, 105, 126, 149, 152, 155,
    160, 213, 329, 409
  flax-growing in 472
  states of 329
Fletcher, Dr Giles (c.1548–1611)
  view on the *oprichnina* quoted 278

Florence:
bankers abroad 430
bills of exchange 434
Carnival at 499
cloth production at 440
cost of war in 1526 354
cultural achievement of Medici court 477
currency 436
foreign policy 104
merchant bankers oppose location of fairs in Genoese territory 437
no social conflict in the wake of political revolution 414
public credit 355
restoration of Medici (1512) 88, 307
revolution of 1494 84, 403, 411
revolution of 1527 105, 403
tax census (*catasto*) 363
and Venice 85
Fludd, Robert, English occultist 517
Flugschriften, see pamphlets
Flushing 141, 161
Foix, André de, seigneur de Lesparre (d. 1548), French commander 100
Foix, Gaston de (d. 1512), French commander 88
Foix, Germaine de (1488–1538), second wife of Ferdinand of Aragon 91
Fokkens, Melchior, panegyrist of Amsterdam 405
Fontainebleau, château de 483, 484
Forest, Black 394, 395
Form of Government (1634), in Sweden 269, 334, 336
Addition to the Form of Government (1660) 256, 337
Fornovo, battle of (1495) 85
Fortescue, Sir John (*c.*1385–*c.*1479) 359
Foucquet, Nicolas, vicomte de Melun and marquis de Belle-Isle (1615–80), finance minister of Louis XIV (1653–61) 485
Francavila, duke of, viceroy of Aragon 143, 144
France 130
agricultural production in 471
alleged oppression of taxpayers 359, 360
alliance with Denmark to counterbalance Sweden 252
annuities (*rentes sur l'hôtel de ville*) 102–3, 356
'Antarctic France' 442–3
appeal of Calvinism to lawyers 164
appeal of Calvinism to nobility 164, 167–8

areas of land tax (*pays de taille réelle*) 364, 383
army 84, 99, 346
attempted establishment of *élections* in *pays d'états* 327–8
bankruptcy of 1648 234
bureau des parties casuelles 342
Calvinist national synods: (1559) 164; (1562) 166; (1571) 170
Calvinist organization in 50–1, 52–3, 102
censorship 65
census of population 364
comparison between prosperous Dutch and poor French peasantry 472–3
conciliar structure 333
contrast with English governing structure 330–1, 359–60
coqs de paroisse 388
coronation oath of king 164
death-rate in 370
declarations of war on Spain 177, 199, 210
decline of aristocratic domination of king's council 340–1
defensive league with United Provinces (1608) 181
depreciation of the *livre tournois* 434–5
difficulty in organizing a native infantry 351
dismay caused by Dutch-Spanish Peace (1648) 238
displaces Venice in Levant trade 441
dowry market 380
droit annuel or *paulette* 342
early Reformation in 41–2, 164
ecclesiastical structure 63
extraordinary financial tribunals (*chambres de justice*) 358
fiscal burden on peasantry 360, 383
Frankish myth 378
French Revolution 361, 462, 525
gains from Peace of Westphalia 201–2
gentry resentment at fiscal burden on their tenant farmers 388
households (*feux*) 364
interest rate on loans in 457, 458
Jansenism in 74–5
lack of foreign policy during wars of religion 164
land tax registers (*compoix*) 364
land tax registers reveal pauperization 384
legislation concerning vagrancy 372
loss of capital value of *rentes* 356–7
merchant marine 446

middle-ranking peasants (*laboureurs*) 384
ministries and secretaryships of state 333–4
monetary devaluation 434–5
money of account 423
myth of evil ministers 392
nobility 102, 340–1, 344–5, 376
nobility during Fronde 235–6
patronage relationships 330–1
pays d'élections 81, 231, 352, 354
peasant day labourers (*manouvriers*) 384
peasant rebellions 231, 388, 391–3
policy of encouraging general hospitals (*hôpitaux généraux*) 374
population density 366
population estimates 365
population and fiscal burden 81
post of finance minister (*surintendant des finances*) 334
principal market for Dutch textiles 453
private borrowing by annuities (*rentes constituées*) 380
provincial estates (areas known as *pays d'états*) 327–8
recoinage in the Middle Ages 419
rents in 383
reputation of liberty abroad 112–13
resentment at Dutch economic hegemony 453
revenues compared with those of Castile 352–3
rise in royal expenditure 231, 238
rule of derogation (*dérogeance*) 377, 457
sale of offices in 340–4
scale of royal borrowing 233, 357, 358
size of noble demesnes 381
size of urban population 398
support for Bavaria 193
types of decree of the council 333
types of revenue 354–5
value of *livre tournois* 424
wars of religion in 62, 166–78
witchcraft in 503, 504, 505, 507–8, 511, 512
see also Charles VII; Charles VIII; Estates General; Francis I; Francis II; Henri II; Louis XI; Louis XII; Louis XIII; Louis XIV; *Parlement* of Paris; *Parlements*, provincial
Franche-Comté 82, 108, 126, 211, 231, 436
Charles V's abdication 123
witchcraft trials in 507, 512
Francis I, king of France (1494–1547, r. 1515–47) 2, 3, 331, 333, 340, 351, 392

alliance with Ottoman Turks 106
captured at Pavia 103
conquers Milan 100, 354
cost of war in 1523 354
court culture under 483–4
creation of *rentes* during reign of 356
dynastic rights 99, 103
financial problems 102–3, 108–9
German princes and 105–6
and *lit de justice* 488
marriages 83, 105
opponent of Charles V 100, 109
policy at accession 99
religious policy 41, 164
repudiates treaty of Madrid (1526) 104
sale of offices under 341–2
theorists on his power 306
see also Clement VII; Leo X
Francis II, king of France (r. 1559–60)
government dominated by Guises 165
married to Mary Queen of Scots 125, 165
Francken, Frans II, artist 480
Franconia:
Imperial knights of 338
Peasants' War in 394, 395
Frankenhausen, battle of (1525) 394
Frankenthal 191
Frankfurt-am-Main 36, 455
anti-Jewish riots (1614) 409, 461
Frederick, duke of Holstein (Frederick I, king of Denmark, r. 1523–33) 245
Frederick II, king of Denmark (r. 1559–88)
accused of seeking Baltic hegemony 248
attacks Sweden (1563) 247
forced to abandon rights in Estonia and Livonia 249
Frederick III, king of Denmark (r. 1648–70)
accepts aristocratic control 252
believes he has Dutch support to attack Sweden 253–4, 271
debts rescheduled 256
first 'absolute' ruler of Denmark 255–6, 358–9
loses Bremen and Verden 251
Frederick III, Holy Roman Emperor (r. 1440–93) 93, 98
Frederick Henry (1584–1647), third son of William of Orange, stadholder and captain general of the United Provinces (1625–47):
military advance under 205, 206
sympathetic to Arminianism 183
Frederick William I of Hohenzollern (1620–88), 'Great Elector' of Brandenburg (r. 1640–88)
hostility to estates 321–2

Frederick William I of Hohenzollern (*cont.*)
  inadequate gains from Peace of
    Westphalia 201
  partitions inheritance at his death 527–8
  supplies Mazarin with mercenaries
    during the Fronde 237
  threatened with attack by Charles X 254
  treaty of Wehlau confers sovereignty over
    ducal Prussia (1657) 272, 527
Frederiksodde 254
Freiburg 395
  battle of (1644) 346
Freising 183
'French fury' (1583) 159
Friesland 113
  East Friesland 25, 50
  favours war 181
  population density in 366
  ship-ownership in 447
Fritz, Joss, leader of the 'peasant's laced
    boot' (*Bundschuh*) movement 393
Friuli 509
Fronde, political upheaval in France
    (1648–53) 233–8
  issue of renewal of *droit annuel* as
    precipitant 233, 342
  opposition of the aristocracy 235–8
  opposition of the *Parlements* 234–5
  propaganda during 500–2
  regional and institutional fragmentation
    of opposition 235
  see also Mazarin
Fugger, banking house of Augsburg 6,
    97–8, 114, 116, 358, 430
  agreement with Lübeck 439
  loan of Anton Fugger (1552) 116
funeral ceremony, royal, in France 489–90

Gabelle, salt tax:
  extension attempted in Castile 219
  in France 354, 392, 412
Gábor, Bethlen, *voivode* of Transylvania
    (1613–29) 56, 190, 193, 299
Gailigaï, Leonora Dori, marquise d'Ancre
    (*c.*1576–1617) 226
Galilei, Galileo (1564–1642), astronomer
    and mathematician 75, 516
  atomistic theory of matter 520
  commitment to the Copernican system
    518
  early career 517
  enunciates the law of motion 518
  forced to recant (1633) 520
  main publications 518
  and religious authority 519

Gallicanism, in France 62, 65, 67, 176
  Pragmatic Sanction of Bourges (1438)
    100
Gama, Vasco da (*c.*1460–1524) 442
Gardie, Jakob de la, Swedish general 280
Gardie, Magnus de la, Chancellor of
    Sweden 256, 485
Gardie, Pontus de la, Swedish general 264
Gaston d'Orléans (1608–60), younger
    brother of Louis XIII:
  aristocratic supporters 229
  conspirator against Richelieu 228
  debarred from office by Richelieu 231
  exile in Lorraine 229
  exile in Spanish Netherlands 230
  joins Condé's rebellion against Mazarin
    (1652) 237
  marries Marguerite de Vaudemont 229
  rebellion (1631) 229
  role in Cinq-Mars conspiracy (1642) 230
  role in Soissons conspiracy 230
  summoned to council during minority of
    Louis XIV 341
  support for Mazarin in first Fronde 236
Gattinara, Mercurino Arborio di (1465–
    1530), Imperial Grand Chancellor 80,
    101, 103–4, 109, 115, 332
Gaza 290
Geiler von Kaysersberg, Johann (1445–
    1510), cathedral preacher at
    Strasbourg 7, 499
Gelderland, acquired by Charles V (1543)
    109, 113
  Catholic province which resists Union of
    Utrecht 155
  favours peace 181
  nobility in 329
  partition 213
  see also Guelders
Gembloux, battle of (1578) 157, 409
Geneva 44, 54, 55, 56, 149, 164
  accepts Reformation (1536) 48
  and Calvinist 'Revolution' 48–9, 52
  Company of Pastors 48, 53
  Consistory 49–50
  population figures at 399
  prudence of municipality regarding
    Huguenot publications 309
  and usury 456
  voluntary donations for poor relief 373
  witchcraft at 503, 505–6
Genoa 85, 86, 99, 101, 105, 129, 207, 239,
    440
  bankers abroad 430
  currency 436
  early commercial success compared with
    Venice 435

Genoese as bankers of Charles V and
  kings of Spain 357, 437
  investment in sea loans and overseas
  exploration 435–6
  plague (1656–7) at 367
  political volte-face and alignment with
  Charles V 435, 436
  see also 'Besançon' fairs
Genoino, Giulio, lawyer and leader of revolt
  at Naples (1647–8) 408
Gentillet, Innocent, Protestant anti-
  Machiavellian propagandist 308
Georgia, eastern 292, 298
Gerlingen 495
Germanía, revolt in Valencia 111, 414, 415
Germany, *see* Empire, Holy Roman
Geyl, Pieter, Dutch historian 156, 181
ghaza, holy war 286
Ghent:
  artists' workshops at 490
  Calvinist dicatorship at (1577–84) 157,
    158, 160, 410
  capitulation to Parma (1584) 160
  faction-fighting at 160
  guilds at 465
  iconoclasm after 1578 158, 409–10
  iconoclastic fury at 150
  joins Union of Utrecht (1579) 155
  life annuities 255
  revolt at (1539–40) 107, 151, 413
Giberti, Gian Matteo, bishop of Verona 8,
  499
Glückstadt 462
Goa 442
Godunov dynasty, *see* Boris Godunov
Goens, Rykloff van (1619–82), commander
  of the Dutch forces in Ceylon and India
  451
Goes 447
gold, search for:
  imports from the New World 420
  'Monomotapa' gold from east Africa 419
  production in Japan 449
  São Jorge 'da Mina' (El Mina) 419, 442
  'Tibir' gold from Guinea 419, 442
Golden Bull (1356) 93
Golden Horde 242
Gomarus, Franciscus (1553–1641), strict
  Calvinist and opponent of Arminius
  51–2, 182
Gomes, Fernão, Portuguese explorer of
  Guinea coastline 441
Gonzaga, Ferrante (1507–57), viceroy of
  Charles V in Sicily and governor of
  Milan 116
González de Cellorigo, Martín, Spanish
  economic writer 214–15, 462

Gotland 251
Gouda 153
  bread riots (1630) 405
  cost of debt servicing 355
  rate of population growth 399
Governing Committee (*Junta Grande*) 135
governors, provincial:
  in France 83, 236
  stadholderates in the Low Countries 116
Granada, Islamic kingdom of 89, 90
  annexed by Castile 92
  city 223
grand parti, Lyon 'great contract' 129, 357,
  434
Grandier, Urbain, curé at Loudun 511
Granvelle, Antoine Perrenot de (1517–86),
  Cardinal, minister of Philip II
  dependence on Alba's faction 134, 148
  favours transfer of government to Lisbon
    139
  hostility to his ascendancy 147
  possible author of Alba's instructions
    152
  primate in the Netherlands 147
  role in government in Castile (1579–86)
    135, 139
  role in government in the Low Countries
    (1559–64) 146, 147, 148
Granvelle, Nicolas Perrenot de, minister of
  Charles V 113, 115, 332
Gravelines 142, 212, 239, 240
Grebel, Conrad, Anabaptist 22
Greco, El (Domenikos Theotokopoulos,
  1541–1614), artist 482
Grégoire, Pierre, French political theorist
  314
Gregory XIII (Buoncompagno), Pope
  (1572–85) 68, 74, 183
  and rate of interest on Jewish lending
    460
Grenoble 167
Gresham, Sir Thomas 430
Grimaldi, Niccolò, loan contractor in the
  service of Philip II 436–7
Grimmelshausen, Hans Jakob Christoffel
  (1621–76), author and soldier 202
Grisons (or Grey Leagues) 207
Groningen 113, 160, 163
  favours war 181
  specializes in livestock 472
Gropper, Johannes, Catholic theologian 58
Grotius (Groot, Hugo de, 1583–1645),
  humanist, jurist, diplomat and political
  theorist 453
  *Law of War and Peace (*1625) 311
Grundherrschaft, peasant tenements leased
  out by the lord in return for rents 375

Grunwald (or Tanneberg), battle of (1410) 258

Guelders, duchy of:
Charles of Egmont, duke 113
war of succession (1543) 117, 118, 525
William of Cleves, duke 113
see also Gelderland

Guicciardini, Francesco (1483–1540) 477

guilds:
general evolution in Europe 463–6
in German cities 404
guild confraternities 463–4
their purpose 463
in towns in the Low Countries 413

Guinea (the so-called Gold Coast) 222, 419

Guipúzcoa 218, 508

Guise, family:
Charles de Lorraine, Cardinal of Lorraine 62, 64, 125, 165, 170
Charles de Lorraine, duke of Mayenne (1554–1611) 175, 176, 177, 322
François de Lorraine, duke of (1519–63) 125, 127, 128 ,165, 166, 169
Henri de Lorraine, Cardinal of Guise 6
Henri de Lorraine, duke of (1550–88) 170, 171, 173, 174, 175, 410
Henri de Lorraine, duke of (1614–64), 'duke of the republic' of Naples 224, 230
Louis de Lorraine, Cardinal of Guise (c.1554–88) 175
Marie de Lorraine, regent in Scotland 125
Philippe-Emmanuel de Lorraine, duke of Mercoeur (1558–1602) 177
propaganda against Guises 168

Guns 291

Günzburg, Eberlin von, polemicist in favour of the Imperial knights 337

Gustavus Adolphus (1594–1632) (Gustaf II Adolf, king of Sweden, r. 1611–32)
accedes to throne at sixteen 268
accession charter imposed at seventeen 249, 334
advance threatened by Spain 206
attacks Poland (1621) 250, 268
captures Imperial Armada 193
considers his wife a person of no judgement 251
death at Lützen 197, 250, 347
decisive victory at Breitenfeld 195, 196, 346, 347
defeats Bavaria and captures Munich 195
discusses Form of Government with Oxenstierna 334
early peace settlements with Denmark and Muscovy 268
invades Pomerania (1630) 195
rights of succession recognized (1605) 267
and *riksdag* 326
signs Truce of Altmark (1629) 269
strategy after Breitenfeld 348
subsidy treaty with France (1631) 195
tactical innovations in army 347
transfers war to Prussia (1626) 250, 268
war aims in Germany 196

Gustavus Eriksson Vasa (Gustaf I, king of Sweden, r. 1523–60) 41
considered to have destroyed 'old freedom' of nobility 334
elected king (1523) 245
elected regent of Sweden (1521) 244
family decimated in bloodbath of Stockholm 244
role in war of Danish succession 246

Gutsherrschaft, large estates administered by lord and worked with serf labour 375

Guyenne 236
base for Condé's rebellion (1651–2) 237
peasant rebellions (1655–6) 392

Haarlem 153, 154, 163
cost of debt servicing at 355
rate of population growth at 399

Habsburg dynasty:
and Edict of Restitution 194
as exemplar of the dynastic state 525
extinction of dynasty in Spain 145, 525
as Holy Roman Emperors 93
and Peace of Westphalia 200
rivalry between two branches of family 124, 528
threat to Swiss 95
see also Emperor, Holy Roman

Hadziac, Treaty of (1658) 284

Hafsid (Sa'di) dynasty 137

Hague, The 150, 160, 212
alliance of (1625) 193

Hainault 149, 152
population density in 366
role of States in the coup of 1576 156

Halberstadt 95, 193, 201

Hall, A. R., historian of science 522

Halland 247
Swedish acquisition of (1645) 199, 252
Swedish acquisition made definitive (1658) 254

Hamburg 203, 251, 439, 455
and the Hanseatic League 439
and Jews 459

merchants control high-value Baltic products 448
population growth 400
Hamilton, Earl J., historian of American treasure imports and the price rise 421
'profit inflation' thesis 427
Hampton Court, Treaty of (1562) 129, 168
Hanseatic League (Hansa) 95, 242, 251, 438–40, 446
conflicts of interests within 439
diet (*Hansetag*) 439
displaced by the Dutch in the Baltic trade 448, 449
gains temporary exemption from Danish Sound tolls 243
hostility to Christian II 244
new rivals in the north 439–40
rise of south German cities 439
Harcourt, Henri de Lorraine, comte d' (1601–66), French commander 199, 220
Hardouin-Mansart, Jules (1646–1708), architect 485
Härjedalen 251
Haro y Zúñiga, Don Luis Méndez de (d. 1661), nephew of Olivares and chief minister of Philip IV 223–4, 332
circumspection 223
harvests:
effect of good harvests on population levels 366
failure of 368–9
Havana (Cuba) 444
'hedge-preachers', in the Low Countries 149–50
Hegau 393
Heidelberg Catechism 54
Heidelberg, University of 54
Heilbronn, League of (1633) 197, 198, 199, 201
Hembyze, Jan van (1513–84), Calvinist leader at Ghent 157, 160, 410
Hémery, Michel Particelle, sieur d' (Particelli d'Émery, 1596–1650), controller-general of finance and later finance minister (*surintendant*) during the minority of Louis XIV 233
Henri II, king of France (1519–59, r. 1547–59) 340, 351
accession and palace revolution 123–4
breaks with German Lutherans 128
captivity at Madrid (1526–30) 104, 105, 124
captures Metz 121, 126
cost of war against Charles V 354
court culture under 484
foreign policy 124, 126

impact of his death 53, 129, 528
intervenes in German affairs 120
Medici marriage 106
negotiates peace with England (1550) 125
offered Imperial title 126, 525–6
propaganda 80
proposed for Milanese succession (1535) 106
recourse to annuities (*rentes sur l'hôtel de ville*) 356
recourse to short-term borrowing 357
recovers Calais 128
religious policy 128, 164
royal entry under 488–9
threat to municipal finances posed by king's fiscal demands 413
Henri III, king of Poland (r. 1573–5) and king of France (r. 1574–89)
assassination 176, 311
assassination of the Guises (1588) 175, 411, 416
capitulation in Edict of Union (1588) 175
capitulation in Peace of Monsieur (1576) 172–3
capitulation in Treaty of Nemours (1585) 174
court culture under 484
deathbed recognition of Navarre's rights 176
deposed as king of Poland (1575) 264
election capitulation in Poland 263
forced to agree to religious toleration in Poland 263
junction with Navarre's army 175–6
and Mardi Gras celebrations (1584) 497
personality 172
refuses to accept decrees of Council of Trent 67
reign of 118 days in Poland 263
rejects sovereignty of United Provinces 161
role in St Bartholomew massacres 171
supporters join Henri IV's cause 176
Henri IV (1553–1610), king of Navarre (r. 1572–1610) and king of France (r. 1589–1610) 144, 170, 331, 350, 411
abjures Protestantism (1593) 176
assassinated 179, 225, 507
assassination attempts on life of 178
court culture under 484
declares war on Spain (1595) 177
doubts about legitimacy of divorce 225
effect of his succession and abjuration on Huguenot political theory 310
escapes from court (1576) 172

Henri IV (*cont.*)
  establishes the *droit annuel* or *paulette*
    342
  excluded from succession by Papal bull
    (1585) 174
  first marriage (1572) 170–1
  forced to abjure Protestantism (1572)
    171
  foreign policy towards Habsburgs 179
  governor of Guyenne (1562–96) 173
  heir presumptive to French throne (1584)
    174
  intervenes in Cleves–Jülich succession
    crisis (1609–10) 179, 185
  as king of reason 500
  political upheaval resulting from
    assassination 224–5
  receives foreign aid during war of
    Bourbon succession 55, 176
  recovers Paris (1594) 177, 412
  refuses to accept decrees of Council of
    Trent 67
  succession difficulties 179
  war against Savoy (1600–1) 179
Henry VIII, king of England (r. 1509–47)
    5, 41, 79, 88, 100, 101, 102, 104, 106,
    108, 113–14, 125, 333
  cost of war in France (1544) 354–5
  hopes to displace Valois dynasty after
    Pavia 103
  size of army in France (1523) 347
Henry, Cardinal and king of Portugal
    (r. 1578–80) 139
Herborn, Calvinist Academy at 54
heresy 3, 7
Herrera, Juan de (1530–97), architect of
    Philip II 482
Herrschaft 498, 499
Hesbaye, agricultural production in 471
Hesse, Philip, landgrave of (r. 1509–67),
    early supporter of the Reformation 26,
    28, 29, 32, 33, 39, 117
  aggressive foreign policy 117
  attacked by Charles V 118
  conversion by Melanchthon 31
  exploits Ferdinand's Turkish problems
    115
  and German Peasants' War 397
  imprisoned 120
  Jews tolerated in Hesse 459
  partitions inheritance at death between
    Cassel and Darmstadt 528
  secularizes church lands 31
Hesse-Cassel 201, 528
  duke Maurice 184
  duke William V 195–6

Heyn, Pieter Pieterszoon, admiral of Dutch
    WIC:
  captures Spanish treasure fleet
    (1628) 205, 218
Hèze, William of Hoorne, lord of
    (1533–80) 156
  execution ordered by Parma 159
Hijaz 290
Hildesheim 183
Hispaniola (Haiti) 240, 443
Hobbes, Thomas (1588–1679), scientist and
    political theorist 306
  contrasts with Machiavelli and Bodin
    315
  Leviathan (1651) 314–16
  The Citizen (1642) 314, 315
  on war 345
Hoen, Cornelisz, humanist scholar and
    theologian 28
Hoffman, Melchior, Anabaptist theologian
    22, 24
Hohenzollern, Albrecht von, first duke of
    East Prussia (1525) 32, 246, 261
  suppresses outbreak of German Peasants'
    War in his lands 394
Hohenzollern, Cardinal Albrecht von 5–6,
    16
Hohenzollern dynasty 261
  see also Frederick William I
Holland, County of 53
  arrest of six deputies of, by William II
    213
  comparative population growth
    according to diversification of
    employment 467
  contribution to budget of United
    Provinces 329
  excise and land tax 356
  freedom of conscience in 154
  hostility to projected Franco-Spanish
    marriage 212
  interest charge on loans 355–6
  joins Union of Utrecht (1579) 155
  Krimpener-Albasserwaard, agricultural
    region in 467
  'miracle' of Holland 161, 163, 455
  opposes trial of Oldenbarnevelt 182
  and Pacification of Ghent 157
  political divisions (1606–9) 181
  rebellion (1572) 154, 156
  refuses to finance continuation of war
    against Spain 211
  ship-ownership in 447
  size of urban population 399
  sovereignty undermined by Maurice of
    Nassau 182

States of 153, 329
States establish the Great Fishery (*Groote Visscherij*) 447
States oppose expansion of France into Spanish Netherlands 212
States reassert terms of treaty of Brömsebro 253
Holstein 244, 254
  aristocratic business enterprise 377
Hondschoote 452
Honnecourt, battle of (1642) 212
Hoogstraten, Anthony Lalaing, count of (c.1530–68) 150
Hoorne, Philippe de Montmorency, count of (1524–68) 152
  family reconciled by Parma 159
Hormuz 442
Host, Second National, in Muscovy 280
Host, Zaprozhian, *see* Chmielnicki, Bogdan, and George
Hotman, François (1524–90), Huguenot political theorist 266
  denounced by theoreticians of the League 311
  Francogallia (1st edn., 1573) 309
  implicitly condemned by Bodin 313
  Le Tigre (1560) 168
  modifications to the 1586 edition of *Francogallia* 310
Hradschin castle 485
Hubmaier, Balthasar (d. 1528), Anabaptist theologian 23
  Zwingli's refutation of 38
Huguenots (French Calvinists) 47, 53, 129, 164
  acquire *villes de sûreté* 170, 227
  alliance with William of Orange 151
  attempt to seize main cities 166–7
  edict of Amboise (1563) 169
  edict of January 1562 166
  manifestos: (1562) 166; (1567) 169
  numerical strength 164–5
  rebellion of 1615–16 226
  rebellion of 1621–2 227
  rebellion of 1625–6 208
  rebellion of 1627–9 209
  peace of Alais (1629) 178, 228–9
  peace of Longjumeau (1568) 170
  peace of St-Germain (1570) 170
  raids of 167
  resistance theory 171
  settlement of Nantes (1598) 178
  social support 168
  truce of La Rochelle (1573) 172
  see also Calvinists/Calvinism; France
humanism 9, 37

Hume, David, eighteenth-century political economist 422
Hundred Years' War 81
Hungary, kingdom of:
  aristocratic monopoly of land purchase 378
  deserted tenures (*puszta*) 376
  extension and intensification of serfdom 384
  grain production in 470
  Ladislas II Jagiellon, king of Bohemia (1471–1516) and Hungary (1490–1516) 98
  noble-dominated constitution affirmed by Verböczi 378
  partition (1526) 243
  peasant revolt led by Dózsa 390
  see also Buda, province of; Hungary, Royal; Matthias Corvinus; Transylvania
Hungary, Royal or Habsburg (after partition in 1526)
  aristocratic estates inalienable 378
  diet of 318
  estates of 186
  extension and intensification of serfdom 384
  invasion by Bethlen Gábor (1619–20) 190
  peasant militia bands (*hajduks*) 384
  peasant uprisings 384
  succession of Ferdinand I 115, 291
  unaffected by creation of Ottman province of Buda (1541) 293
  and war of 1626 193
  war with Turks (1593–1606) 56
Hus, John 15
Hussitism 7, 94
Hutten, Ulrich von (1488–1523), German knight, humanist, and Lutheran polemicist 14, 20, 338, 504

Ibiza 447
Ibrahim I, Ottoman sultan (r. 1640–8)
  his madness and deposition by Janissaries 296
Ibrahim Pasha, grand vizier (r. 1523–36) of Süleyman I 294
iconoclastic riots:
  in the Netherlands (*beeldenstormen*) 53, 150
  in France 169
Idiáquez, Juan de, secretary to Philip II 135, 160
illegitimacy rates 365
Incas 444

Index of Prohibited Books 65
  see also Paul IV
India 451
  see also Goa
Indies, east, collective term for Portuguese
  (and later Spanish and Dutch) empire
  in Far East 442, 450–1
Indies, west, collective term for Spanish
  America 218
  see also Mexico; Peru
Indulgences, Papal 4, 5–6, 7, 11, 18, 38, 63
infant mortality 365
Infantado, dukes of, in Castile 379–80
Ingria (or Ingermanland) 264
  acquired by Sweden (1617) 257
inheritance, rules of:
  as influence on family structure in Europe
  367
Innocent VIII (Giambattista Cibo), Pope
  (1484–92) 503
Innocent X (Giambattista Pamfili), Pope
  (1644–55) 68, 75
  accepts Christina of Sweden's abjuration
  (1652) 253
Innsbruck 479
Inquisition, Roman or Papal 59, 65
  and condemnation of Galileo (1633) 520
Inquisition, Spanish 13, 30, 65–6, 132,
  144, 213, 458
Inquisition, Venetian 59–60
Intendants, in France 230, 231, 234, 238,
  343–4
  circumvent *trésoriers de France* and *élus*
  343
interest, rate of, on loans 114, 448
Interim of Augsburg (1548) 43, 54, 60,
  119, 120, 121, 464
Iraq 292, 298
Isabella (Isabel), queen of Castile
  (r. 1474–1504) 2, 8
  alliance with towns against the great
  nobility 414
  attitude to Aragon 143
  death and dissolution of union with
  Aragon 91
  marriage contract 90
  revenues 89, 352
  troubled succession on death 91
Isabella Clara Eugenia, favourite daughter
  of Philip II, ruler of the Spanish
  Netherlands with archduke Albert
  (1598–1621) and governor-general
  after his death (1621–33) 180, 181,
  204
  dynastic claim to English throne 140
  dynastic claim to French throne 177
  patronage of Rubens 483

and truce with United Provinces 181
Isma'il I, first Shiite Shah of Persia
  (r. 1501–24)
  death 289
  establishes Shiite state (1501) 286, 288
Isma'il II, Shah of Persia (r. 1576–7) 297
Istanbul 287, 288, 295, 476
  base for Ottoman campaigns 290, 291
Italy 80, 124, 454
  birth-rate in 365
  expulsion of Jews from certain states 459
  guild structure a factor in high production
  costs 466
  number of Jewish banks 460
  peasant share-cropping system
  (*Mezzadria*) 382
  plague quarantine measures 368
  population density in 366
  population estimates 365
  size of urban population 398
  see also Florence; Genoa; Milan; Naples;
  Papal States; Venice
Ivan III, Tsar of Muscovy (r. 1462–1505)
  242, 273, 274–5
  duma under 335
  eliminates rival states 274
  ends apanage period 274
  fails to capture Smolensk 275
  marries daughter to Alexander of
  Lithuania 275
  pretensions 275
Ivan IV, Tsar of Muscovy (r. 1533–84) 242
  conquers Siberia 278
  defends autocracy 273
  duma under 335
  forced to abandon Estonia to Sweden
  278
  forced to abandon Livonia to Poland at
  truce of Yam Zapolski (1582) 264, 278
  gains upper hand in his dealings with Erik
  XIV of Sweden 263
  predominance of nobility during minority
  (until 1547) 276
  pretext for launching Livonian war 277
  seizes Estonia (1558) 262
  seizes Livonia (1577) 264
  treaty with Magnus prince of Denmark
  248
  Tsar and great prince of all Rus 278
  unleashes the *oprichnina* 276–7, 278
  use of the term 'brother' to recognize
  hereditary monarchs 273
Ivangorod, fall of (1581) 278

Jäger, Clemens, city archivist of Augsburg
  464

Jagiellon dynasty, late medieval kings of
Hungary, Poland and Bohemia 243,
257-8, 259, 260
  Louis II, last Jagiellon king of Hungary
(d. 1526) 242-3, 291
  marriage alliance with Habsburgs 98
  marriage alliance with Zápolyai dynasty
293
  see also Bohemia; Hungary; Poland
James I, king of England (1566-1625,
r. 1603-25; James VI of Scotland) 161
Jämtland 251
Jan Olbracht, king of Poland (r. 1492-1501)
258
Janissaries, *see* Ottoman state
Jankau, battle of (1645) 200, 346-7
Jansenism 63, 73, 75
  distinction of *droit* and *fait* 75
Jansen(ius), Cornelius (1585-1638), bishop
of Ypres and Catholic rigorist
73-4
Japan 72, 451
Jarnac, battle of (1569) 170
Jesuits (Society of Jesus) 69-70
  as court confessors 71
  in France 71, 228, 311-12
  in Germany 37, 72
  missionary work overseas 72
  numbers 71
  in Poland 55
  role in the Portuguese union with, and
secession, from Spain 139, 221
  in Spain 66, 70
  in Venice 71
Jews:
  benefit from new mercantilist attitudes of
states 429
  converts to Catholicism (*conversos* or
Marranos) 459
  establishment of ghettos 459-60
  expulsions and forced conversions of
Sephardi Jews 458-9
  growing tolerance of rulers in seventeenth
century 461-3
  hostility of the 'peasant's laced boot'
(*Bundschuh*) movement 393
  pogrom at Lisbon (1506) 409
  in Poland 257, 283, 362, 462-3
  rates of interest allowed by Papacy on
Jewish lending 460
  riots against Jews at Frankfurt-am-Main
(1614) 409
  tolerance of successive Emperors to
Ashkenazi Jews 461
  see also Chmielnicki, Bogdan, and
George

John II, king of Aragon 90
John III, king of Sweden (r. 1568/9-92)
  Catholic tendencies 257
  deposes Erik XIV (1569) 248
  imprisonment by Erik XIV (1563) 248
  intervenes in Polish elections 265
  Polish marriage (1562) 248
  seeks friendship with Poland 263
  seeks to exploit Russo-Polish war 264
  seeks to harry Narva trade with Muscovy
249
  truces with Muscovy 265
John IV, duke of Braganza and king of
Portugal (r. 1640-56)
  military success of revolt 239
  treaty with France (1641) 222
  truce with the United Provinces (1641)
222
John of Austria, Don (1547-78), illegitimate
son of Charles V and commander of
Philip II
  appointed governor-general in the Low
Countries (1576) 156
  crushes revolt of Moriscos (1570) 389
  negotiates the Perpetual Edict (1577)
157
  policy in the Low Countries 157-8
  victory at Gembloux (1578) 157, 409
  victory at Lepanto (1571) 138
John Casimir (Jan Kazimierz, 1595-1648),
king of Poland and Lithuania
(r. 1648-68)
  abdication 272
  collapse of his position in Poland
(1655-6) 271
  election after interregnum 270
  forced to sign Truce of Andrusovo
(1667) 285
  negotiates with Chmielnicki 283, 284
  promises Tsar Alexis the Polish
succession and secures truce 271, 284
  recaptures much of Poland (1656) 271
  splits Cossack movement after death of
Chmielnicki 284
Joinville, Guise estate at 166
  secret treaty of (1584) 174
Joris, David, Anabaptist leader 26
Joyeuse, Anne duke of (1561-87), Admiral
of France and favourite of Henri III
173
Joyeuse, Henri, duke of (1567-1608) 177
Juan, Don, Habsburg heir (d. 1497) 524
Juan José de Austria (1629-79), Don,
illegitimate son of Philip IV:
  captures Barcelona 239
  leads *coup d'état* based on Aragon 224

Juana, daughter of Charles V and Regent of
    Charles V and Philip II 114
  policy towards Aragon 143
  policy towards north Africa 137
Juana, 'the Mad', queen of Castile
    (r. 1504–6; d. 1555) 91
  rights ignored by Charles of Ghent 110
  rights recognized during revolt of the
    Comuneros 111, 415
Jülich 185, 186, 204
Julius II (Giuliano della Rovere), Pope
    (1503–13) 3, 11, 87
  one of the greatest art patrons of all time
    478
Julius III (Giovanni Maria del Monte), Pope
    (1550–5) 60, 118
  attitude to Charles V's abdication 123
  Index (1554) 65
Juntas, Olivares's recourse to, in Castile
    219
juros, annuities in Spain 127
justification by faith alone, *see* Luther
Jüterborg, battle of (1644) 251
Jutland 251, 272

Kallo, battle of (1638) 348
Kalmar 249
  Statute of Kalmar (1587) 265
  see also Union of Kalmar
Kaluga 279
Kanizsa 299
Kappel 28, 40
Kardis, Peace of (1661) 284
Karelia:
  acquired by Sweden (1617) 257, 281
Karkus 263
Karlstadt, Andreas Bodenstein von
    (1477–1541), Lutheran and later
    Anabaptist theologian 22, 28
Kazan', khanate of 242, 278
Keil, Hans, visionary in Württemberg
    495–6
Kellenbenz, Hermann, economic historian
    453
Kepler, Johann(es) (1571–1630),
    astronomer 481, 518
  condemns Bodin's comparison between
    state systems and types of proportion
    516
  polemic with Robert Fludd 517
Kettler, Gotthard von, last Grand Master of
    the Livonian Knights, and first duke of
    Courland and Simigalia 262
Khlesl, Melchior, Cardinal, chief minister of
    Emperor Matthias 186

Khlopko 391
Kiev 275, 279, 285
Kilia 288
King of the Romans, Emperor-designate
    93, 110
Kleinbürger, petty bourgeoisie 403
Klushino, battle of (1610) 280
Knäred, Peace of (1613) 249–50
Knights' War (1522–3) 20, 338
Koja Sinan Pasha, grand vizier of Ottoman
    sultans five times (r. 1580–96 with
    interruptions) 298
Königsberg 243, 261
Köprülü Mehmed Pasha, grand vizier
    (r. 1656–61) of Sultan Mehmed IV
    296, 299
Korczyn 385
Kramer, Heinrich, witch-hunter 502
Kreise, see circles, Imperial
Kurbskii, Andrei Mikhailovitch (1528–83),
    prince:
  contends that Muscovite moderation
    would have gained Livonia 277
  criticizes Muscovite autocracy 273
  defects to Lithuania 276
Kurdish tribes 289, 292
  Kurdistan 297
Küstrin 120
Kutchum, Tatar kingdom 278

La Bicocca, battle of (1522) 101, 347
Labourd 508
La Charité 170
la Court, Pieter (1618–85), Leiden textile
    manufacturer and economic and
    political theorist 214
  Interest of Holland (1661) 214, 406, 472
Ladislas IV (Wladislaw, 1595–1648), king of
    Poland (r. 1632–48)
  chivalric order scheme 335
  elected Tsar of Muscovy 280
  renounces claim to Tsardom (1634) 281
  succession rights in Poland 267, 269
  succession rights in Sweden 267, 269,
    526
Laínez, Diego (1512–60), Jesuit
    Vicar-General 63, 70, 71, 165
la Marck, Robert II de, lord of Sedan
    (d. 1536) 100
La Marfée, battle of (1641) 230
La Mata 447
Lamormaini, William, SJ (1570–1648),
    Jesuit confessor of Ferdinand II 194
La Mothe La Forest, noble leader of
    Croquants of Périgord (1637) 392

Lancre, Pierre de, witch-hunter 495, 508
Landrecies 240
Lang, Johannes (d. 1531), Lutheran
    reformer at Erfurt 37
Languedoc:
    agricultural production in 471
    church lands in 168
    climatic change in 369
    diet of population 369
    estates of 327, 328
    merchants oppose the Lyon fairs 433
    population growth 365
Lannoy, Charles de (1482–1527), viceroy
    for Charles V in Naples 116
Lanuza, family of Justicias in Aragon:
    Jean IV 144
    Jean V 144
Larcher, Claude, councillor of the
    Parlement executed by the Catholic
    League at Paris 411
la Renaudie, Jean du Barry, seigneur de,
    organizer of Conspiracy of Amboise
    (1560) 165
La Rochefoucauld, François, comte de,
    Huguenot leader 167
La Rochefoucauld, François de (1558–
    1645), Cardinal 67
La Rochelle 167, 170, 207, 209, 227, 228
    riot at (1542) 412
Laubardemont, Jean de Martin, seigneur de
    (?-1655), intendant under Richelieu
    511
Lausanne 164
La Vieuville, Charles, marquis and later duc
    de (?-1653):
    de facto chief minister of Louis XIII
    227–8
    foreign policy 207
League of Cambrai (1508) 87, 98
League of Cognac (1526) 104
League, Catholic, in France 67, 415, 416
    ascendancy after the assassination of
    Guises 176, 411
    councils dominated by radicals at Paris
    411
    and decrees of Council of Trent 67
    divisions 177
    execution of Brisson and others (1591)
    411
    first formation (1576) 173
    impact of abjuration of Henri IV 176
    intervention of Papacy 174, 176
    pamphlets published during its
    ascendancy 501
    patronage control of Guises and others
    over offices during 342
    political theorists of 311

rebellion of 1585 174
rebellion of 1588 175
role of fanatical preaching 411
treaty with Philip II (1584) 174
League, Catholic, in Germany 184, 190,
    191, 192, 197
League, Holy:
    against the Ottoman Turks (1538–40)
    138, 292, 354
    against the Ottoman Turks (1571–3) 68,
    138
League, Holy, or League of Venice (1495)
    85
League, Holy (*Santa Junta*), during the
    revolt of the Comuneros, *see*
    Comuneros
Le Bossu, Jacques, radical preacher during
    the League at Nantes 411
Le Bret, Cardin, seigneur de Flacourt
    (1558–1655), French jurist and
    councillor of state 314
Lecteurs royaux 484
Lectoure 497
Lefèvre, Jacques, d'Étaples (1450–1536),
    French humanist 13, 14, 34, 43
Leghorn (Livorno) 98
Le Havre 236
Lehenleute, description of Imperial knights
    338
Leicester, Robert Dudley, earl of
    (1533–88):
    'absolute governor and general' in the
    United Provinces (1586) 161
    attempts *coup d'état* against opponents
    162
    bases his power on Utrecht 162
    blockade of Scheldt 162, 181
    lieutenant-general of Elizabeth I (1585)
    161
    recalled 162
Leiden 150, 153, 154, 163
    bread riots (1630, 1638) 405
    cost of debt servicing 355
    rate of population growth 399, 452
    survival of guild structure at 466
    textile industry at 452–3
Leipzig 197, 199
    University of 10
Le Nôtre, André (1613–1700),
    keeper-general of the king's gardens in
    France 485
Lens, battle of (1648) 238
Leo X (Giovanni de' Medici), Pope (1513–
    21) 2, 3, 11, 14, 15, 101, 477, 478
    alliance with Charles V 100
    Concordat of Bologna 100
    and Medici family interests 3

Léon 382
Leonardo da Vinci (1452–1519), artistic
    genius and polymath 483, 518
Leoni, Leone, artist at the court of Charles
    V and Philip II 480
Leopold I (1640–1705), Holy Roman
    Emperor (1658–1705):
  advised against a long war with the Turks
    299–300
  counsels moderation with regard to
    Polish dealings with Brandenburg 272
  court culture under 481
  intervenes in Poland 271, 272
  marries Margarita Teresa, daughter of
    Philip IV 241
  rules without a chief minister after 1665
    332
  see also Vasvár, Peace of
Leopold, archduke, bishop of Passau, etc.
    185
Leopold William, archduke, bishop of
    Passau, etc. (d. 1662), governor-general
    of the Spanish Netherlands (1646–55)
  acquires Magdeburg, Bremen,
    Hildesheim, and Halberstadt 194
  art collection 481
Lepanto, battle of (1571) 138, 295, 460,
    490
Le Quesnoy 240
Lérida 220
Lerma, Francisco Gomez de Sandoval y
    Rojas, marquis de Denia, duke of
    (1553–1625), first minister of Philip III
    (1598–1618) 227, 350
  contrast between attitude to Jews and
    Moriscos 216, 459
  fears Morisco rising 216
  fortune 216
  nostalgia for his regime 219
  patronage policy 216
  seeks peace with United Provinces 180,
    204
  seeks to isolate king from other advice
    216
Lesdiguières, François de Bonne, duc de
    (1543–1626), last Constable of France
    208
Lespignan 384
L'Estoile, Pierre (1546–1611), Parisian
    diarist 411, 496–7
Levant trade 419, 435, 440, 453
L'Hôpital, Michel (1505–73), Chancellor of
    France (1560–73) 165, 166, 332
Liège 183
Lier 155
Lille, survival of guild structure at 466

Limburg 213
Limousin, French province:
  peasant rebellions 391
limpieza de sangre, laws concerning purity
    of blood in Spain 132
Lindau 117
Link, Lutheran reformer at Altenburg 37
Lionne, Hugues de, marquis de Berny
    (1611–71), French minister of state,
    and nephew of Abel Servien 239
Lipsius, Justus (Joest Lips), Flemish
    philologist and political theorist 314,
    351, 480
Lisbon 139, 140, 142
  displaces Antwerp as distributor of
    Portuguese spices 432
  pogrom of Jews (1506) 409
  size of population 399
lit de justice, in France 487–8
Lithuania:
  dependence of nobility on ruler 258
  nobles oppose closer ties with Poland
    260
  Poles reject renewal of union (1496) 258
  wars with Muscovy 258–9, 260
Livonia 242, 243, 248, 249, 257, 284, 348,
    439
  Swedish conquest (1625) 268
Lochau, Treaty of (1551) 126
Lollardy 7
Lombards, private money-lenders 457
Lombardy 436
London:
  Bridewell 374
  compulsory poor-rate 373
  Evil May Day (1517) 409
  merchants control high-value Baltic
    products 448
  number of beggars 371
  receives Dutch exiles 153
Longueville, Henri II d'Orléans, duc de
    (1595–1663) 236
López Bravo, Padre, arbitrista 383
López Gallo, Juan, Spanish banker 430
L'Orme, Philibert de (1505/10–1570) 484
Lorraine, Cardinal of, see Guise
Lorraine, duchy of 68, 164, 210
  duke Antoine 397
  duke Charles III 126, 173
  duke Charles IV (1604–75) 229, 230,
    239, 240
  French regime installed (1634–61) 230
  witchcraft in 503, 504, 505, 506–7, 512
Los Cobos, Francisco de, secretary of
    Charles V in Castile (1523–47) 115,
    116, 332

Lotzer, Sebastian, joint author of Twelve
Articles of the Swabian Peasants
(1525) 395–6
Loudun, 'possession' at Ursuline convent at
511
Louis XI, king of France (r. 1461–83) 82,
83, 90, 359
Louis XII, king of France (r. 1498–1515) 3,
5, 81, 83, 351
conquest of Milan 85–6
defeats Venice 87
evicted from Milan 88
on sale of offices 343
partitions Naples 86
Louis XIII, king of France (1601–43,
r. 1610–43) 198, 493
attacks Béarn (1620) 227
birth 179
court culture under 484, 485
decision to rule personally 227
final crisis with Marie de Medici (1630–1)
229
and *lit de justice* 488
pamphlets published during royal
minority 501
Peace of Alais modifies settlement of
Nantes (1629) 178, 228–9
receives sovereignty of Catalonia 220
regency council arrangements 232
rehabilitates Gaston after Richelieu's
death 231, 232
secret peace negotiations with Spain 231
supports Richelieu on Day of Dupes
(1630) 229
and war by diversion (1634–5) 199, 210
see also Richelieu
Louis XIV (1638–1715), king of France
(r. 1643–1715) 326, 360, 429, 469, 493
army size under 347
attitude to the state 490, 530
council under 341
court culture under 485, 486
halts witchcraft prosecutions 511
influence of Mazarin 238
and *lit de justice* 488
majority declared (1651) 237
royal entry under 489
rules without a chief minister 332
Louise of Savoy (1476–1531), Regent
during the absence of Francis I 103
Louvain, University of 74
Louvre, Palais du 484, 488
Low Countries (seventeen Burgundian
provinces or 'generality' united by
Charles V):
agricultural production in 471

Bodin on origins of revolt in 313
Calvinist criticism of Walloon nobility
157–8
Calvinist organization in 50, 53
chronology of revolt in the Flemish towns
413
currency stability in first half of sixteenth
century 424
defensive union proposed 112–13
dynastic union under Philip the Fair
82–3
enforcement of heresy laws in 30–1, 33,
147
fear of Inquisition 66, 147, 150
finance council in 113
financial paralysis (1575–6) 156
fiscal grievances 145
gains temporary exemption from Danish
Sound tolls 243
generality created by Charles V 113
importance of guilds in cities 464, 465,
466
mutinies of army in 136, 156, 163, 180,
350
Netherlands Confession of Faith (1561)
53
partition envisaged 122–3; after the
partition, *see* Netherlands, Spanish;
United Provinces
Philip II recognized as Charles V's heir in
Low Countries 113, 122
Philip II leaves Low Countries
permanently (1559) 132, 146
population density 366
population estimates 365
possible alienation under Charles V 108
resentment at Philip II's Castilian
entourage 146
rise of 'intensive husbandry' 370
size of army in 135
size of urban population 398
Loyola, Inigo Lopez de (St Ignatius
1491–1556), founder of Jesuit
order 70, 71
Spiritual Exercises (1548) 70
Loyseau, Charles (1564–1627), French
jurist 314, 362
Luanda 211, 443
Lübeck 95, 242, 246
and the Hanseatic League 439
infuriated by Christian II's policy
regarding Sound tolls 244
joins Denmark in the Seven Years' War of
the North (1563–70) 247
merchants control high-value Baltic
products 448

Lübeck (*cont.*)
  Peace of (1629) 194, 250
  population figures and economic decline 400
  supports Swedish rebellion of 1523 244
  see also Wullenweber
Lubomirski, Jerzy, *rokosz* of (1665–7) 285
Lucca:
  bankers abroad 430
Lucerne 40
Lumey, William, count van der Marck, lord of (1542–78), leader of Sea Beggars (1572) 153
  dismissed by William of Orange 153
Lusatia 191, 201
Luther, Martin (1483–1546), foremost Protestant theologian:
  Against the Murderous and Thieving Hordes of Peasants (1525) 21
  Appeal to the Christian Nobility of the German Nation (1520) 30, 36
  and Augustinianism 9
  Babylonian Captivity of the Church (1520) 18, 27, 36
  career 4, 8, 16, 20
  and church 12, 18
  condemned as a heretic (1520–1) 3, 15, 16
  condemns heliostatic theory of Copernicus 515, 516
  and confession 18
  death 118
  denounces Zwingli 28
  editions of his works 36
  equates Papacy with Antichrist 21–2, 57
  and Eucharist 27
  and 'fanatics' 22, 24, 28
  and free will/good works 12–13, 17, 19, 63
  and general council of the Church 57–8
  German prose style 35–6
  and humanism 14, 37
  and infant baptism 22
  influences on Luther: Erasmus 12; Staupitz 9, 17; Wesel 7
  justification by faith alone 15, 17–18, 59
  On the Liberty of a Christian Man (1520) 20, 37
  political conservatism 19–20, 22, 33, 308
  and preaching 37
  priesthood of all believers 18
  and printing 34–7, 474
  and Reformation 21, 76
  refusal to recant 16
  Secular Authority: to what extent it should be obeyed (1523) 20

  theses against indulgences 4, 6, 11, 15
  translation of the Bible 18–19, 21, 34, 62
  and usury 455, 456
  and visual images 35
  on witchcraft 504
Lutherans/Lutheranism:
  in Denmark 41
  divisions after Luther's death 29, 43, 46, 54
  spread within German-speaking lands 37, 42–3
  in Sweden 41
  theological disputes with Bullinger 42
Lützen, battle of (1632) 197, 250, 347
Luxembourg 100, 108, 113, 156
Luxembourg, Palais du 484, 501
Luynes, Charles d'Albert, later duke of (1578–1621), favourite and chief minister of Louis XIII 226–7
Lwów 271
  rate of price increase of oats at 425, 426
  wheat price converted into grams of silver 426
Lyon:
  Carnival at 497
  currency at 436
  decline of fairs in last quarter of sixteenth century 435
  fails to benefit from Habsburg debt rescheduling 437
  fairs for bills of exchange to be settled at 431, 434
  fairs require settlement of bills of exchange in gold coin 434
  fiscal concessions to foreign nationals 434
  food ration (dole) 372
  food riot (*grande Rebeyne*, 1529) 372, 407, 409, 413
  general almonry (*Aumône générale*) 372, 373
  Huguenot seizures of power (1562–3, 1567) 167
  importance of immigration 399–400
  Italian and other foreign bankers at 99, 109, 127
  municipal office ennobling at 405
  rate of price increase of wheat index compared with cost of living index and 'real wages' 426–7
  royal entry in 488
  survival of guild structure at 465
  town falls to Henri IV 177
  town sacked by baron des Adrets (1562) 169
  town sides with the Catholic League 435
  wage rates at 371
  workhouse 374

Maastricht 205
Machiavelli, Niccolò (1469–1527),
  Florentine political theorist and
  statesman 47, 65, 79, 86, 90, 93, 288,
  306
  anti-Machiavellian propaganda 308, 316
  career and principal works 306–8
  on France 360
  on mercenary captains 349
  survival as the supreme test in politics
  306
  virtù 307
  on war 345
Madrid 139, 152, 482, 483
  asientos and bills of exchange at 431, 437
  beggars' hospitals 374
  size of population at 399, 400
Madrid, château de 483
Madrid, Treaty of (1526), *see* Charles V
Magdeburg 95, 117, 120, 121, 193, 201,
  203
  Protestant administrator 183
Magnus, prince of Denmark, governor of
  Estonia 248, 249
Mainz, electorate of 68, 94
  Berthold von Henneberg and Imperial
  reform 94
Malacca 180, 442
Malcontent movement:
  in France 172, 226
  in the Low Countries 158
Malestroit, Jehann Cherruyt, sieur de,
  controversialist on the causation of
  inflation in France 422
*Malleus maleficarum (Hammer of
  Witchcraft*, 1486) 502–3, 505
Malmö 246
Mamluk dynasty, of Egypt and Syria:
  last ruler crushed by Selim I (1516) 289
Mander, Karel van, painter and art critic
  481
Mannheim 191
Mansfeld, Ernst count von, mercenary
  captain 192, 193
Mantua 87, 461
  sacked (1630) 209
  succession crisis 179
  Vincenzo II Gonzaga, last Gonzaga duke
  208
  war of the Mantuan succession 197,
  208–10, 228
  see also Nevers
Marburg:
  conference or colloquy (1529) 28
  University 31
Marcourt, Antoine, reformed pastor at
  Neuchâtel 41

Margaret of Austria, aunt of Charles V and
  regent in the Low Countries (r. 1509–
  15, 1519–30) 114, 476
Marguerite of Valois (Marguerite
  d'Angoulême, 1492–1549), sister of
  Francis I 13
Marguerite of Valois (1553–1616), sister of
  Charles IX and first wife of Henri IV
  170
Maria de' Medici (Marie de Médicis
  (1573–1642), wife of Henri IV and
  regent of France, r. 1610–14) 225
  final crisis with Louis XIII (1630–1) 229
  rebellions of 1619 and 1620 227
  unpopularity of Italian favourites 226
Maria of Portugal, first wife of Philip II
  122
María Teresa (1638–83), eldest daughter of
  Philip IV and wife of Louis XIV
  212, 241
Mariana of Austria, wife of Philip IV and
  regent for Carlos II (1665–75)
  concedes Portuguese independence
  (1668) 222
  fails to summon *Cortes* of Castile (1667)
  326
Mariana, Juan de (1536–1624), Spanish
  Jesuit political theorist 71, 311
Marienburg 277
Marignano, battle of (1515) 100
Marillac, Louis de (1572–1632), Marshal of
  France 229
Marillac, Michel de, seigneur de Fayet
  (1536–1632), French finance minister
  (1624–6) and Keeper of the Seals
  (1626–30)
  arrest (1630) 229, 332
  and attempted establishment of *élections*
  in *pays d'états* 327–8
  opposes Richelieu's foreign policy 207,
  228
Mark 185, 186
Marnix, Philip, seigneur de St Aldegonde
  (1540–98), adviser of William of
  Orange:
  report on negotiations with Anjou 526–7
marriage:
  age at 365, 366
  register of 363
Marseille 102, 106, 175
  xenophobic riot (1620) 409
Martinuzzi, György, bishop of Várad 293
Mary I, queen of England (r. 1553–8) 122,
  123, 129
Mary of Burgundy (1457–82), daughter of
  Charles the Bold and Burgundian
  heiress (r. 1477–82) 82

Mary of Hungary, granddaughter of Maximilian I and sister of Charles V, Regent in the Low Countries (r. 1531– 55) 98, 114, 121
Mary Queen of Scots (Mary Stuart, r. 1542–68, d. 1587) 125, 140
Masaniello, fisherman and leader of revolt at Naples (1647) 408
Mass, Catholic 17, 27, 38, 41, 367
  attendance as identification with community 498
  Inquisition attracted by implications of Galileo's atomistic theory of matter for belief in real presence 520
  reaffirmed at Council of Trent 63
  suspension of Mass in Protestant states 19, 154, 204
  see also Eucharist
Matanzas Bay 205, 452
Matrikel 96
Matthias I (1557–1619), Holy Roman Emperor (r. 1612–19) 187
  conflict with Rudolf II 186
  decline of court culture under 481
  departs from the Netherlands (1581) 159
  inertia as Emperor 186
  invitation to serve as governor general of Netherlands (1577) 157
  protects Jewish communities 461
  seeks admission to Catholic League 184
Matthias Corvinus, king of Hungary (d. 1490) 97, 98, 242
  library 475
Matthieu, Claude, Jesuit 174
Matthijsz, Jan, radical Anabaptist leader at Münster 25
Maurice of Nassau-Orange (1567–1625), second son of William of Orange, captain general of the United Provinces and stadholder of five provinces 184
  captures Breda (1590) 162
  death 183, 205
  holds decisive political power after execution of Oldenbarnevelt 204
  Leicester seeks arrest of 162
  military campaigns 160, 163
  opposition to peace with Spain 180
  supported by West Indies trading interests 180
  supports Counter-Remonstrants 182
  tactical innovations 347
Maximilian I (1459–1519), Holy Roman Emperor (r. 1493–1519) 82, 109
  advises Charles of Ghent to seize Castilian throne 110
  assists election of Charles V 99
  Burgundian policy 97
  court culture under 480–1

Emperor-elect (1508) 93–4
  excessive borrowing of 431
  favours succession of Ferdinand 109
  financial problems 97
  German policy 94
  Hungarian policy 98
  and Imperial reform 96, 97, 319
  Italian policy 84, 87, 88, 98–9
  King of the Romans (1486) 93
  marriage alliance with Jagiellons 98
Maximilian II (1527–76), Holy Roman Emperor (r. 1564–76):
  accepts Ottoman suzerainty for Royal Hungary 293
  birth 115
  court culture under 480
  King of the Romans (1562) 93
  negotiates Spanish marriage for his daughter 133, 187
  religious policy 67, 183, 187
  seeks Polish crown (1575–6) 264
Maximilian I of Bavaria, duke (r. 1597– 1651) and (after 1623) elector:
  assists Ferdinand II against Frederick V 190, 191, 192
  defeated by Gustavus Adolphus (1632) 195
  defeats rising of Austrian peasants 389, 390
  forms Catholic League (1609) 184
  later defeats in Thirty Years' War 200
  marriage alliance with Neubourg 185
  obtains electorate (1623) 192
  obtains Upper Palatinate (1628) 192
  occupies Upper Austria 192, 389
  opposes Habsburg absolutism 184, 189, 194–5
  promised electoral title by Ferdinand II 190
  requests assistance from Wallenstein 197
  retains electoral title and Upper Palatinate after Peace of Westphalia 201
  seizes Donauwörth (1607) 184
  supported by France 193, 197
Maximilian, of Habsburg, archduke:
  candidate in Polish election 265
Mazarin, Jules (Giulio Mazarini, 1602–61), chief minister of Louis XIV (1643–61) 67, 327, 332
  accused of warmongering 233
  alliance with Cromwell 240
  benefices 6
  chief minister through favour of Anne of Austria 233
  controls political education of Louis XIV 238
  criticism of *Parlement* of Paris 234

cultural activities under 485
disappointed by Peace of Westphalia
    201-2
effigy burnt 498
first exile at Brühl (1651) 236
hostility to Swedish misuse of French
    subsidies 252
parallel with Strafford in England 234
political miscalculation in arresting the
    three princes (1650) 236
remains in power after first Fronde 235
resentment at his control of
    governorships 236
returns from exile with German
    mercenaries 237
second exile (1652) a ploy 237
supervises French campaign in Spanish
    Netherlands 239-40
victory over opponents at end of Fronde
    238
see also pamphlets
Meaux:
    attempted Huguenot coup at (1567) 169
    falls to Henri IV 177
Mecca 290
Mechelen 147, 154, 348
Mecklenburg, duchy of 120, 193
    acquired by Wallenstein 193
    aristocratic business enterprise 377
    deposition of dukes 196
    population loss 203
Medici:
    Carnival under the restored dynasty 496
    Cosimo I, grand duke (r. 1537-74) 477
    Cosimo de' Medici 129, 477
    failure of dynasty to defend Galileo 520
    Lorenzo de' Medici 477
    Piero de' Medici 84
    see also Catherine de' Medici; Clement
        VII; Florence; Leo X; Maria de' Medici
Medina 290
Medina Celi, Juan Luis de la Carda, duke of
    (c.1540-75) 155
Medina de Las Torres, Ramiro Núñez de
    Guzmán, duke of, son-in-law of
    Olivares, viceroy of Naples, later
    president of the council of Italy 223
Medina del Campo, fairs or money market
    at 114, 431, 434, 437
Medina Sidonia, Alonso Pérez de Guzmán,
    duke of (1550-1615) 141
Medina Sidonia, Gaspar Pérez de Guzmán,
    duke of:
    conspiracy of (1641) 219
Mehmed II 'the Conqueror', Ottoman sultan
    (r. 1451-81) 286, 287, 288, 291, 294
Mehmed III, Ottoman sultan (r. 1595-
    1603) 298

bloody accession of 287, 295
Mehmed IV, Ottoman sultan (r. 1648-87):
    and Chmielnicki revolt 284
    minority at accession 296
Melanchthon, Philip(p) (1497-1560),
    Lutheran theologian 13, 14-15, 17,
    19, 20, 21, 29, 31, 33, 41, 43, 52, 58,
    63
    condemns heliostatic theory of
        Copernicus 516
Méliusz, Péter, Hungarian reformed
    theologian 55
Memel 269, 271
Memmingen 117
    role in drafting Twelve Articles of the
        Swabian Peasants (1525) 395-6, 407
Mendoza, Bernadino de, Spanish
    ambassador to France 175
Menin 158
mercantilism 429, 530
    first Anglo-Dutch war as precursor of
        wars of economic rivalry 529
    trade embargoes as instrument of
        government policy 205, 529-30
mercenaries:
    German 84, 99, 349, 350
    Italian (*condottieri*) 349
    lack of mercenaries in Castile 111
    political unreliability 350-1
    polyglot force recruited by Henry VIII
        349
    Swiss, *see* Swiss Confederation
merchants 403
Mercoeur, *see* Guise
Mersenne, Marin (1588-1648), French
    scientist and mathematician 314, 521,
    522
Metz 128, 202
    art market at 493
    failure of Charles V's siege of (1552-3)
        121, 126, 347
    Jewish immigration encouraged by Henri
        IV 462
Mexico ('New Spain') 92, 112, 445
Mezö-Keresztes, battle of (1596) 295, 297
Michael Fedorovich Romanov, Tsar of
    Muscovy (r. 1613-45) 280, 349
Michelangelo Buonarroti (1475-1564),
    artistic genius 58
    Sistine Chapel commission 478
Michieli, Venetian ambassador to France
    167
Middelburg 163, 457, 448
mignons, favourites of Henri III 173, 497
Milan:
    archbishopric 64
    bankers abroad 430
    defence of 127

Milan (*cont.*)
  foreign policy before conquest 84, 85
  French conquest: (1499) 85, 87
  French loss of duchy: (1512) 88; (1521)
    101
  French reconquest (1515) 100, 354;
    (1524) 103
  governor partitions Mantuan succession
    with Savoy 208
  Habsburg claims to 101
  Inquisition 66
  merchant bankers oppose location of
    fairs in Genoese territory 437
  Philip II invested with duchy 107, 122
  plague (1576–7, 1630) 367
  political control under Philip II 133, 134
  possible alienation of 108
  reputation 123
  role in Valtelline and Mantuan wars 207,
    208
  size of population 399
  supply base for Spanish Netherlands 207
  Valois dynastic claims to 79, 80, 128
  see also Sforza dynasty
millenarianism 22, 500
millones, tax on commodities in Castile
  145, 217, 219, 325, 353, 383
Minden 194, 201
Minsk 284
Mniszech, Marina, wife of False Dimitri I
  (and II) 279
Moded, Herman, Calvinist minister in Low
  Countries 158, 409
Mohácz, battle of (1526) 242–3, 259, 291,
  476
Mohummad Khudabanda, Shah of Persia
  (deposed 1588) 297
Moldavia, Ottoman tributary state 288,
  294, 298
Molina, Luis de, Jesuit theologian 73
'monarchomachs' 309, 310, 559 n. 13
monarchs, Catholic, *see* Ferdinand; Isabella
  of Castile
Moncontour, battle of (1569) 170
money:
  as an object of merchandise 423
  circulation of foreign coins 423
  estimates of value of European money
    stock 422–3, 424
  monies of account 423
Mons 153
Monsieur, Peace of (1576) 172–3
Montaigne, Michel de (1522–92), essayist:
  on Amerindian attitudes to European
    social structure 362
  condemns heliostatic theory of
    Copernicus 516

  on fourth estate 345
  on the ligature (*aiguillette*) 494–5
  on marriage 380
  on noble support for Calvinism 168
Montauban 167, 170
Montigny, Emmanuel Philibert de Lalaing,
  baron of (1557–90) 158
Montigny, Florence Montmorency, baron of
  (1527–70) 152
  family reconciled by Parma 159
Montmorency, Anne de (1493–1567),
  Constable of France 102, 106–7, 107,
  125, 127–8, 169
  captured at St Quentin (1557) 127–8
  disgrace (1541) 107
  return to favour (1547) 125
  seeks reconciliation with Charles V 107
Montmorency, Henri I de, comte de
  Damville (1534–1614), Constable of
  France after 1593, governor of
  Languedoc 172, 340
Montmorency, Henri II de (1595–1632),
  governor of Languedoc 230
Montpellier 167
Monzón 220
  Treaty of (1626) 208
Moravia 190, 193, 199
More, Sir Thomas (1478–1535), Chancellor
  of England
  and beggars 372
  Utopia (1516) 99, 362
Morea 288
Morély, Jean, French Calvinist and
  congregationalist 51
Moriscos 130, 137, 138, 140, 415
  expulsion (1609) 180, 216, 227, 458
  revolt (1568–70) 138, 389
Moscow 277, 368, 401
Moulins 42, 101
Moura, Christóbal de, secretary to Philip II
  135
Moyenvic 229
Moyhla, Peter, leader of Orthodox church
  in Poland 274
Mstislavskii, Ivan, prince 276
Mühlberg, battle of (1547) 109, 119, 480
Mühlhausen 21, 39, 190, 395
Müller, Hans, of Bulgenbach, peasant
  commander in the German Peasants'
  War 395
Mun, Thomas, author of *England's Treasure
  by Forraign Trade* 445, 456
Münster:
  bishopric 183, 193
  Peace of Westphalia negotiated at 200
  radical Anabaptist 'kingdom' at (1534–5)
    25–6

Treaty of (1648), between Spain and the
  United Provinces 212–13, 492
Münster, Sebastian 480
Müntzer, Thomas (1489–1525), radical
  theologian in German Reformation
  21, 37–8, 395, 396
Murad III, Ottoman sultan (r. 1574–95):
  powers of procreation 295
  unwise to reopen war with Austrian
    Habsburgs 298
  unwise to reopen war with Persia 298
Murad IV, Ottoman sultan (r. 1623–40):
  captures Baghdad in person (1638) 298
  minority until 1632 295
  period of financial stability 296
  ruthlessness 295
Murcia 339
Murner, Thomas, Catholic polemicist 20
Muscovy:
  army no match for Polish or Swedish
    armies 277–8
  attempt to occupy Livonia repulsed
    under Ivan IV 262, 264
  attempted gathering of Russian lands
    243
  boyar domination of government through
    the *duma* 335
  dependence of Tsar on service nobility
    379, 385–6
  deserted tenures (*putoshi*) 376
  Dutch role in Arctic trade with Muscovy
    448
  English role in Arctic trade with Muscovy
    448
  extension and intensification of serfdom
    385–6
  fiefs (*pomest'e*) 273, 385
  growth in size of country 273
  importance of Orthodoxy 274
  labour services (*barshchina*) 386
  lack of navy 277
  landlord's right of search for fugitive
    peasants 386
  limitation on peasants' right of free
    movement 273
  longevity of seigneurial monarchy,
    according to Bodin 300
  no bills of exchange circulate in 431
  nobility in 335
  noble right of departure (*ot'ezd*) 274–5
  oprichnina 276–7, 278, 279, 385, 401
  outmoded technology of army 346
  partible succession the norm on boyar
    estates 378
  patrimonial state 285
  peasant rebellion 391, 393
  population estimate 364

serfdom 374, 385–6
  size of urban population 401
  slavery 374–5
  social hierarchy (*mestnichestvo*) 275
  social ranks (*chiny*) 362
  subjection to government responsibilities
    and taxes (*tiaglo*) 401
  territorial advantage from transfer of
    Ukraine 281
  urban area (*posad*) 401
  use of foreign mercenaries 349
  wars with Lithuania 258–9
  western Baltic states seek to block access
    to Baltic 243, 247
  see also Andrusovo, Truce of;
    Bolotnikov; Boris Godunov; Deulino,
    Truce of; Dimitrii; Ivan III; Ivan IV;
    Kardis, Peace of; Polianovka, Peace of;
    Stolbova, Peace of; Valiessar, Truce of;
    Vasilii III; Vasilii Shuiskii
Mustafa I, Ottoman sultan (r. 1617–18,
    1622–3):
  deposed twice 295
  his madness 295
Myconius (Oswald Geisshüssler), Lutheran
  reformer at Gotha and later at Basel
  37

Naarden 154
Namur 157
Nancy, battle of (1477) 476
Nantes, settlement of (1598) 178
Naples:
  accession of Philip II (1554) 122
  currency 436
  French conquest of: (1494–5) 84–5;
    (1500) 86; (1524) 103; (1528) 105
  French invasion of (1557) 127
  partition of (1500) 86
  plague at (1656–7) 367
  political control under Philip II 133, 134
  population density 366
  proposal to introduce Inquisition 66
  reputation of 123
  revolt of (1585) 408
  revolt of (1647–8) 224, 408–9
  size of population 399
  Valois dynastic claims to 79, 80, 128
  viceroyalty 91, 92
Narva, port of 243, 247, 248–9, 257, 262,
    263, 264, 277
  river 278
Nassau, Louis count of (1538–74) 150,
    153, 170
Nassau-Dillenburg 55, 150
  John VI (1536–1606), duke, stadholder of
    Gelderland 55, 155

Navarre, kingdom of:
  Antoine de Bourbon, king of 165
  Basse Navarre and campaign of 1620 227
  French invasion (1521) 100, 111
  Jeanne d'Albret (1528–72), queen of 170
  partition (1512) 90
  union of Upper Navarre with Castile
    (1515) 92, 129
  viceroyalty in Spanish (Upper) Navarre
    92
  witchcraft in Spanish (Upper) Navarre
    508
  see also Bourbon dynasty; Henri IV, king
    of Navarre and France
Neckartailfingen 498
Negropont 288
Netherlands, see Low Countries; United
  Provinces
Netherlands, Spanish 68, 74
  conspiracy of Hendrik van den Bergh
    206
  council of state 159
  difficulties of army in 206
  Dutch propaganda against Spanish rule
    205–6
  impose economic embargoes against
    Dutch 205
  mutinies of Habsburg army in 350–1
  prospects of partition 212
  reliance on overland supply route from
    Milan 207
  witchcraft in 506–7
Neubourg, Wolfgang William, duke of 185
Neuhäusel 300
Neva, river 269
Nevers, Charles III Gonzaga (d. 1637), duke
  of, French claimant to the succession of
  Mantua and Montferrat 208, 209
Newton, Sir Isaac (1642–1727), scientific
  genius 522
Nicholas V, Pope (1447–55) 477, 478
Nicodemism 52, 61
Nicolay, family of first presidents of
  Chambre des Comptes of Paris 341
Nicole, Pierre (1625–95), French
  Jansenist 75
Niemen, river 269
Nieuwpoort, battle of (1600) 348
Nijmwegen 407
Nîmes 167, 500
nobility:
  in Castile 91, 111, 219, 376
  in France 102, 340–1, 344–5, 376
  in Muscovy 335
  in Poland (*szlachta*) 256, 258, 259, 268,
    273, 335–6, 376, 378

  in Sweden 256, 377
  usurpation of 344, 377
  see also ennoblements
noblesse d'épée 340
noblesse de robe 75, 178, 231, 233, 340–5
nominalism 10
Nonsuch, Treaty of (1585) 140, 141, 161,
  162
Norby, Sören, Danish admiral and privateer
  245
Nördlingen:
  battle of (1634) 198, 210, 348
  guild representation in city government
    before 1552 404
  population loss at 399
  tax assessment on oath 402–3
Normandy 83, 359
  estates of 327
  support for first Fronde (1649) 234, 236
Northumberland, John Dudley, duke of
  (1504?–53), Lord Protector 125, 126
Norwich 153
Nostradamus, Michel, astrologer and
  prophesier 500
Notables, Assemblies of, in France 323
  at St Germain (1562) 166
Novara, battle of (1513) 88
Novgorod 274, 275, 277, 401, 439
Novi Liguria 437
Nuremberg 31, 33, 319
  artists' workshops at 490
  Carnival at 497
  cost of war against Brandenburg (1550)
    354
  poor relief at 373
Nyborg, battle of (1659) 255

Ob, river 278
Ochino, Bernardino (1487–1564),
  vicar-general of Capuchin Order and
  later reformed theologian 8, 59, 61
Ochtervelt, Jacob, Dutch artist 493
Oecolompadius, Johannes (Johann
  Hausschein, d. 1531), Protestant
  reformer at Basel 11, 12, 13, 22, 28
office-holders, in France, see noblesse de
  robe
Oldenbarnevelt, Johan van (1547–1619),
  advocate to the states of Holland
  (1584–1619) 162, 405
  attempts to settle religious disputes 182
  conflict with Maurice of Nassau 180
  defends freedom of navigation in the
    Baltic 250
  negotiates Twelve Years' Truce 181
  trial and execution 182, 204

Oldenburg 255
oligarchy:
 in England 404
 at Nuremberg 404
 at Paris 404–5
 regent regime in the United Provinces
   405–7
 at Venice 403
Oliva, Peace of (1660) 272
Olivares, Gaspar de Guzmán, count–duke
   of (1587–1645), chief minister of Philip
   IV (1622–43) 331, 332
 aggressive attitude towards France
   (1634–5) 210
 attitude to tax rebellion in Portugal
   (1637) 221
 blamed for revolts of 1640 222
 career 217
 contrasts with Richelieu 232
 criticizes cost of siege warfare in
   Netherlands 205
 on decline of justice 340
 denounces Catalonia's defence of
   privilege 218, 219
 domino theory 203
 encourages lending by Portuguese
   crypto-Jews 462
 great memorandum 217
 imposes embargoes in Low Countries
   205
 Junta de Ejecución 333
 laments absence of leaders among
   aristocracy 219
 mistakes in Mantuan succession crisis
   208
 propounds Union of Arms (1625)
   217–18
 recourse to juntas 219, 223, 333
 resignation accepted 222–3
 supervises cultural projects under Philip
   IV 483
Ommelanden 113
Oñate, Beltán Vélez de Guevara, count of
   239
Oñate, Don Iñigo Vélez de Guevara, count
   of, Spanish ambassador to Vienna
   (1617–25):
 agreement with Ferdinand II (1617) 187,
   209
Oprichnina, separate estate in Muscovy
   controlled by Tsar's supporters 276–7,
   279, 301, 385
Oran 137
Orange-Nassau, dynasty of 406
 loyalty to, as indicated by ownership of
   portraits 493

 see also Frederick Henry; John of
   Nassau-Dillenburg; Maurice of Nassau;
   William of Nassau, prince of Orange;
   William II; William III
Oratories of Divine Love 8
Order, Grand, of the Livonian Knights 262,
   275
 civil war of 1556–7 262
 Order secularized (1561) 262
 peace of 1503 277
 see also Livonia
Order, Grand, of the Teutonic Knights
   (*Ordenstaat*) 242, 258, 261
 regulations on tenant rights 376
 see also Prussia, East
orders, Mendicant 2, 373
orders, Military, in Castile 114, 353, 379
orders, society of 361–2
ordination 17, 18, 63
Orléanais 229
Orthodox, Greek, religion:
 as factor in Cossack revolt 270, 282
 importance in Muscovy 274
 in Lithuania 257
 Polish hostility to 271
Ösel 251
Osiander (Andreas Hosemann,
   1498–1552), Lutheran reformer at
   Nuremberg 37
 writes preface to Copernicus' *On the
   Revolutions of the Heavenly Spheres*
   515
Oslo 247
'Osman II, Ottoman sultan (r. 1618–22)
 assassinated by Janissaries 295
 seeks to rule without Janissaries 295
Osnabrück 193, 194
 Peace of Westphalia negotiated at 200
Ostend 240
Ottoman (Osmanli) dynasty:
 law of succession (law of fratricide) 287
 law of succession abrogated (1617) 295
Ottoman state 22, 32–3, 56, 86, 130
 absence of territorial concessions before
   1699 295, 300
 alliance with France 106
 bandit (*Jelali*) movement 297, 298
 contrasted with France by François
   Bernier 360
 debasement of the asper 296
 feudal knights (*sipahis*) 287, 297
 fiefs (*timars*) 290, 296–7
 grand vizier (*vezir*) 287, 294, 295, 296
 harem intrigue 294
 impact on Venetian and other European
   trade with the Levant 435, 440

Ottoman state (*cont.*)
  inflation in the Ottoman state 296
  Janissaries (*Yeni-ceris*) 276, 287, 289,
    291, 294, 295, 296, 298, 301
  learned hierarchy (*ulema*) 286
  longevity of seigneurial monarchy,
    according to Bodin 300
  no bills of exchange circulate in 431
  opposition to Shiite Persia 288–9, 300
  outmoded technology of army 346
  patrimonial state 286
  population estimates 364
  principal market for Dutch textiles 453
  prospects of a crusade against them
    reduced 130
  provinces (*beylerbeyliks*) 293
  receive Sephardi Jews after expulsion
    from Spain 458
  religious autonomy conceded on
    occasion 287, 300
  religious schools (*medreses*) 286
  revenues 286, 296
  revolts (other than of Janissaries) 297
  rise of provincial notables (*ayans*) 297
  slave system (*devsirme*) 286, 296, 476
  state property (*miri* land) 286
  wars with Austrian Habsburgs: (1529–33)
    291; later wars with Charles V 118;
    (1552–62, 1564–8) 293;
    (1593–1606) 56, 138, 298–9
  wars with Persia: (1514–16) 289;
    (1533–5, 1548–9, 1554–5) 292;
    (1578–90) 138, 297;
    (1603–18) 297–8; (1623–39) 298
  war with Poland (1620–1) 282, 295, 299
  wars of succession 287, 294
  wars with Venice: (1463–79) 288;
    (1499–1502) 85, 288; (1538–40) 292;
    (1571–3) 68, 138; (1645–69) 299, 440
  see also Ahmed I; Amasya, Peace of;
    Bayezid II; Ibrahim I; Istanbul;
    Mehmed II; Mehmed III; Mehmed IV;
    Murad IV; Mustafa I; 'Osman II; Selim
    I; Selim II; Süleyman I; Zsitva-Török,
    Peace of
Oudenarde 157
Overijssel 113, 329
  favours peace 181
  opposes trial of Oldenbarnevelt 182
  population density 366
  specializes in livestock 472
Oxenstierna, Axel (1583–1654), Chancellor
  of Sweden (1612–54):
  custodian of Gustavus Adolphus' political
    inheritance 197
  directs League of Heilbronn 197
  family 336

on Gustavus Adolphus' war aims 196
held prisoner at Magdeburg 198
Mazarin critical of misuse of French
  subsidies by 252
on naval power 257
patience with Denmark exhausted
  (1643) 251
refuses to ratify renewed alliance with
  France 198–9
and *riksdag* 326, 332
resents French alliance with Saxe-Weimar
  200
role in the lifetime of Gustavus Adolphus
  334
views on war with Poland 269
Oxenstierna, Eric, Chancellor of Sweden
  485
  governor of Estonia 253

Pacification of Ghent in Low Countries
  (1576) 156–7
Padua:
  population density 366
  public dissections held at 495
Palais Royal 484
Palatinate, Rhine, electorate of 51, 54, 94,
  160
  deprivation of electoral title 196
  Frederick III, elector 54
  Frederick IV, elector 51, 54, 184
  Frederick V, elector, and king of Bohemia
    55, 187, 190, 191, 192, 193
  John Casimir (1543–92), Regent
    (r. 1583–92) 55, 158, 170, 172
  Karl Ludwig, elector, reinstated after
    Peace of Westphalia 201
  leadership of German Calvinism 54,
    190, 320
  occupation of 191–2
Palermo:
  revolt (1647) 224, 408
  size of population 399
pamphlets:
  during the Catholic League in France
    501
  during the Fronde in France
    (*Mazarinades*) 235, 495, 501–2
  in the German Reformation
    (*Flugschriften*) 35–6
Papacy 2, 3–4
  consolidated debt 355
  dynastic interests of Popes 3
  emerges stronger after Council of Trent
    62
  finances of 4, 64
  and Holy war 79

importation of Baltic wheat into Papal
States 370
Index 65
Italian domination of elections of Popes
3
and Jesuits 70–1
loss of influence in secular affairs 68–9
nepotism of 3, 65
Papal Curia 4, 57
Papal vicars 4, 85, 87
political objectives 4
see also Alexander VI; Clement VII;
Innocent X; Julius II; Leo X; Papal
bulls; Paul III; Paul IV; Pius IV; Pius V;
Urban VIII
Papal bulls:
Cum nimis absurdum (1555) 459
Cum occasione (1653) 75
Decet (1521) 15
Execrabilis (1460) 4–5
Exsurge domine (1520) 15
In eminenti (1643) 74
Licet ab initio (1542) 59
Regimini militantis ecclesiae (1540) 70
papal nephew (*cardinale nipote*) 64–5
Pappenheim, Godfrey Henry (d. 1632),
count, Bavarian general 197
Paracelsus (*c.*1493–1541), chemist 514–15
Paris:
barricades established at (1588) 175, 410
blockade of during Fronde 234–5
blockade of during League 471
extremism under Catholic League 177
falls to Henri IV 177, 412
Fronde at 236, 237
Frondeur propaganda and agitation at
501
general hospital (*hôpital général*) 374
growth of oligarchy through resignation
of office 404–5
harvest failures 368–9
Huguenot congregation at 167
mayor (*prévôt des marchands*) 489
measurement of wheat employed at 425
penitential processions following
assassination of Guises 410–11
poor tax 373
rate of increase of price of wheat at 426
relative prices of wheat, rye, and barley
at 426
royal entry at 488
size of population of 399
urban culture at 490, 493
Parlement of Paris 41, 167, 171
declares Mazarin a disturber of the public
peace 234
development of *lit de justice* 488

hostility to the Estates General 322, 333
opposes Concordat of Bologna 100
opposes edict of Nantes (1598–9) 178
opposes Jesuits and Jesuit political
theories 311–12
prohibited from interference in affairs of
state (1652) 238
pronounces in favour of the Salic Law
(1593) 177
recognizes Charles X of the League
(1589) 176
regency of Anne of Austria proclaimed at
(1643) 232
and royal effigy 489
seeks exclusion of Cardinals from
government (1651) 236
and witchcraft 505, 507–8, 511
Parlements, provincial, in France 167, 178,
331
escape plague 368
establishment of *semestres*, or doubling of
functions at 343
factions within and participation in
rioting 412
failure of united opposition during the
Fronde 235
hostility to intendants 343–4
known collectively, with other tribunals,
as sovereign courts until 1665 344
Parliament, in England:
number of sessions (1495–1660) 317
Parliaments, crisis of, in seventeenth
century 330
evolution of their powers in Europe
316–30
Parma, Alexander (Alessandro) Farnese,
duke of (1545–92), nephew of Philip II
and governor-general of the Low
Countries (r. 1578–92) 157, 158, 160,
328, 436
criticizes Armada plans 142
intervenes in France 177
negotiates Treaty of Arras 158
reconquest slows down 162–3
statesmanship 158–9
Parma, Margaret (1522–86), duchess of,
governor-general of the Low Countries
(r. 1559–67), half-sister of Philip II
146, 147, 148, 149
Pascal, Blaise (1623–62), French
philosopher and satirist 75
Passau, truce of (1552) 121, 194
patronage, in France 330–1
Paul III (Alessandro Farnese), Pope
(1534–49) 57, 515
founds Jesuits 69–70, 71
reform commission 57

Paul III, Pope (*cont.*)
    rejects compromise with Lutherans 59,
      60
    summons Council of Trent 5, 57
    and war of Schmalkaldic League 118
Paul IV (Gian Pietro Caraffa), Pope
    (1555–9) 8, 59, 64, 67, 71
    anti-Habsburg policy 124, 127
    desire to liberate Naples 127
    heads Roman Inquisition 59
    hostility to Jews and *Marranos* 459–60
    Index (1559) 13, 65, 308
Paul V (Camillo Borghese), Pope (1605–21)
    71, 74, 479, 519
Paulet, Charles, French financier 342
Pauw, Reynier (1564–1636), burgomaster of
    Amsterdam 180
Pavia, battle of (1525) 103, 112, 127, 347
Pavillon, Nicolas (1597–1677), Jansenist
    bishop of Alet 499
Pays d'élections 81, 231, 352, 354
pedlars 495
    role dissemination of popular culture
    496
Peñaranda, Don Gaspar de Bracamonte,
    count of (d. 1676), Spanish
    plenipotentiary at the Westphalian
    peace negotiations 212
Peñón de Velez 137
Pereiaslaval (Periaslavl'), agreement of
    (1654) 270, 284
Peresvetov, Ivan 276
Pérez, Antonio, secretary to Philip II 482
    arrest (1579) 135
    escape to Aragon (1590) 144
Périgord:
    Croquants (1637) 391
    Tard-Avisés (1594–5) 391
Pernambuco, province of, in Brazil 205,
    211, 443
Pernau 257, 263, 268
Péronne 106, 173, 174
Perpetual Edict (1577) 157
Perpignan 108, 211
Persia:
    creation of Shiite state (1501) 286, 288
    see also Isma'il I
Peru ('New Castile') 92, 112, 445
Pest 293
Petition (1566), in the Low Countries 149
Petri, Laurentius (Lars Petersson), and
    introduction of Swedish Reformation
    41
Pfefferkorn, Johann 14
Phelps Brown, E. H. and Hopkins, S. V,
    historians of European price rise:
    index numbers of inflation 425

Phélypeaux, family of secretaries of state in
    France 341
Philip I, 'the Fair' duke of Burgundy
    (r. 1494–1506), king of Castile
    (r. 1506) 82–3, 91, 97, 109, 476
Philip II, king of Castile and Aragon, etc.
    (1527–98, r. 1556–98) and Philip I of
    Portugal (r. 1581–98) 66, 79, 331
    advisers 133
    Austrian Habsburg marriage 133, 187
    bankruptcies: (1557) 116, 123, 127, 136,
      433, 437; (1575) 136, 138, 155–6, 433;
      (1596) 136, 163, 433
    birth 112
    bishopric scheme in the Low Countries
      147
    black legend 132
    Castilian predominance under 133–4
    and Cateau-Cambrésis 131
    conciliar system 133–4
    contractualist theory 145
    cost of war in the Netherlands in 1590s
      354
    and Council of Trent 66
    court culture under 482
    crushing victory at St Quentin 127–8,
      347
    delays in governmental system 134
    despair at defeat of Armada 142–3
    dynastic attitude 140
    dynastic claims to English throne 140
    and English alliance (1554–8) 123
    English marriage 122
    excludes Don Carlos from succession
      133
    factions at court and in councils 134–5
    financial expertise 137
    fleet in the Mediterranean under 137–8
    foreign policy 102
    French marriage 129, 177
    and iconoclastic riots of 1566 150
    impact of his debt rescheduling
      operations on Antwerp money
      market 433
    and Inquisition 66, 132, 147–9
    insists on levy of Tenth Penny 152
    intervenes in French domestic affairs
      129–30, 174, 177
    invested with duchy of Milan 107, 122
    and Jesuits 70
    king of Naples (1554) 122
    leaves Netherlands permanently (1559)
      132, 146
    letters from the Segovia woods 148–9
    and loss of Calais 128
    opposition to his succession in the
      Empire 120, 525–6

and Papacy 127
policy towards north Africa 137
policy towards Ottoman Turks 130, 136
political priorities 136–7
Portuguese marriage 119
Portuguese succession 139
proficiency in languages 132
propaganda against 80
ratifies Parma's Treaty of Arras 158
recognized as Charles V's heir in Low
    Countries 113, 122
recourse to borrowing 136, 357
refusal to accord States General in Low
    Countries during revolt 149, 328
regencies in Castile 114, 132–3
rejects compromise settlement with
    United Provinces 163
rejects idea of expelling Moriscos 389
removes restrictions on sale of municipal
    offices 405
revenues of 136, 352
responsibility for disorder in the Low
    Countries 146
sedentary rule 132
seeks Imperial vicariate 123
seeks renewal of English alliance 129
succession difficulties 123, 133
Philip III (1578–1621), king of Castile and
    Aragon, etc. (r. 1598–1621) 143
    claim to Imperial title 187
    court culture under 482–3
    intervention in Cleves-Jülich succession
        crisis 185
    lack of reforming achievement 215–16
    and Portugal 221
    role in government under Philip II 135
    seeks peace with United Provinces 180
    supports Ferdinand II against Frederick
        V 190
    and truce with United Provinces 181
    see also Lerma
Philip IV (1605–65), king of Castile and
    Aragon, etc. (r. 1621–65) 217, 332,
    339, 340
    attitude to States General 328
    considers ruling without a chief minister
        223
    court culture under 483
    death 214
    debt rescheduling 223–4, 239, 437
    decision to resume conflict with United
        Provinces 204
    intransigence in Westphalian peace
        negotiations and after regarding France
        200, 239
    mining resources in New World 418
    and Portugal 221

promises to observe privileges of
    Catalonia 220
resumes sovereignty of Spanish
    Netherlands 204
seeks peace with France to continue war
    with Portugal 240, 241
seeks peace with United Provinces to
    continue war with France 212
succession implication of marriages of
    María Teresa and Margarita
    Teresa 241
support to conspiracy and rebellion in
    France 230, 235, 239
    see also Haro; Olivares
Philippines 445, 450
Philippsburg, fortress of 202
    Jewish community protected by French
        461
Piacenza 436
Picardy 81
    governor of 229
Piedmont 107, 128, 436
    see also Savoy
Pighius, Albert, Catholic theologian 45
Pillau 269, 271
Pinerolo, fortress of 209–10
Pinkie, battle of (1547) 125
Piombino 187, 239
Piri Mehmed Pasha, grand vizier (r. 1518–
    23) of two Ottoman sultans 294
Pius III (Francesco Piccolimini), Pope
    (1503) 87
Pius IV (Giovanni Angelo de' Medici), Pope
    (1559–64) 62, 64, 147
    Index (1564) 65
    political ambitions 66
    relations with Spain 127
Pius V (Ghislieri), Pope (1566–72) 60, 68,
    71, 74, 132, 138
    hostility to Jews 460
Pizarro, Francisco (c.1471/5–1541) 444
placards (1534), in France 41
plague (*Yersinia pestis*) 348, 367
    quarantine measures 368
    vulnerable social groups 368
    see also Death, Black
Plessis-lez-Tours, treaty of (1580) 526, 527
pluralism 5, 6, 63, 183, 194
Poissy, Colloquy of (1561) 57, 165
Poitiers, Diane de (1499–1566), duchesse
    de Valentinois 125, 484
Poland, kingdom of, united with Lithuania
    after 1569 in Commonwealth or
    Republic (*Rzeczpospolita*) 242, 260
    acquires Livonia 262–3, 439
    alliance with the Emperor and Denmark
        (1658) 272

Poland (*cont.*)
  Ashkenazi Jewish community in Poland
    257, 283, 362, 462–3
  crusade indulgences 130
  elective monarchy 258, 359
  evolution of monarchical power 256
  extension and intensification of serfdom
    385
  fiefs abolished 273, 378
  fleet destroyed 251, 257
  'free' monarchy within Bodin's definition
    300
  grain exports to the Low Countries 370
  grain production in 470
  growth of aristocratic business interests
    377
  hetman, commander of the army 336
  hostility to Cossacks 282
  interregna: (1572–3) 263; (1632) 281;
    (1648) 283
  intervention in Muscovy 279–80
  introduction of law of entail 378
  limitation on peasants' right of free
    movement 273
  movement for the 'execution' of the laws
    259
  nobility (*szlachta*) 256, 258, 259, 268,
    273, 335–6, 376, 378
  noble monopoly of land purchases 259,
    378
  number of sessions of the *Sejm*
    (1493–1661) 317
  population estimates 257, 364
  private towns dependent on nobles
    401–2
  religious diversity 257
  'Sarmartian' culture 378
  seeks peace with Sweden (1660) to
    continue war with Muscovy 272
  size of average noble estate (*folwark*)
    378
  size of country 256
  size of urban population 401–2
  social structure of estates (*stany*) 362
  statute of *Nihil novi* 259, 318–19
  treaty of Wehlau (1657) regarded as of
    doubtful validity 272
  Uniate church 274, 282, 283
  Union of Lublin (1569) 260–1, 319
  unsatisfactory truce with Muscovy
    (1667) 285
  war against Turks (1620–1) 282, 295
  see also Altmark, Truce of; Andrusovo,
    Truce of; Deulino, Truce of; Oliva,
    Peace of; Polianovka, Peace of; *Rokosz*;
    Warsaw, Confederation of
Pole, Reginald, Cardinal 9, 57, 58, 59, 69

Polianovka, Peace of (1634) 281
politiques, in France 178, 411
Polotsk 264, 265, 277
polygamy, practised at Münster 25, 26
Pomerania 193
  population loss 203
  succession arrangements on death of
    Bogislaw XIV 196
  Swedish western (after 1648) 271
Pont-sur-Sambre, mutiny at 350
population:
  density 366
  estimate for Europe and world 364
  growth of in sixteenth century 81–2
  nutrition of 369–70
Portia (Porcia), John-Ferdinand, count of
    (1615–65), chief minister of Leopold I
    (1657–65) 332
Porto Longone 239
Portugal:
  abandoned by France (1659) 240
  alliance with England (1661) 240–1
  alliance with France (1641) 222, 232,
    239
  capture of straits of Hormuz 292
  Cortes 139
  dominates Indian Ocean in sixteenth
    century 292
  establishment of empire 441–3
  forced conversions of Sephardi Jews 459
  fueros 139, 217
  Habsburg kings absentee rulers 221
  loss of much of Far Eastern trade to
    Dutch 450, 451, 453
  merchant marine 446
  monetary crisis prompts search for new
    source of bullion 419, 441–2
  opening up of the Cape route 419
  rebellion and war of secession
    (1640–68) 211, 213, 221–2
  revenue from gold 442
  revenue from spices 442
  revolt against the governor of Évora
    (1637) 221
  spice trade at Antwerp organized by
    Manuel I 432
  succession crisis 139
  Union of Arms 218
  union with Castile (1580) 139, 180
  see also gold, search for; Sebastian I
poverty, definitions of 371
  poor relief 372–4
Poyet, Guillaume (1473–1548), Chancellor
    of France 107
Prague 183, 191, 197, 200, 481
  Jewish community at 461
  Peace of (1635) 198, 201

preaching 2, 31, 37–8
predestination, *see* Arminius; Beza; Calvin;
  Council of Trent; Jansen(ius); Molina
Pregolia, river 269
Presbyterianism 50
prices:
  beginnings of slow down in rate of price
    increase 428
  comparative prices converted in silver
    values 425
  distinction between nominal and silver
    prices 425, 428
  effect of debasement/devaluation on
    prices 422, 428, 434–5
  of grain in Hungary after 1570 378
  of grain in Netherlands (1565–6) 150
  imports of bullion as a factor in price
    rise 419, 421–2
  rate of increase (nominal values)
    converted into index numbers 426
  of wheat at Paris 424
Pride's Purge (1649), in England 234
primogeniture, law of:
  absence of general law in the Empire 94,
    528
Princeps legibus solutus est 313
printing:
  and the Reformation 33–7
processions:
  during plague 367–8
  'profit inflation' thesis 427
  see also Hamilton, Earl J.
Protestantism, *see* Anabaptism; Calvinism;
  Lutheranism; Zwinglianism
Protestation (1529) 32
Provence 81, 82, 83, 102
  estates of 327, 328
  expulsion of Jews 459
  governor of 229
  population growth 365
  prices 428
  riots 412, 413
  support for first Fronde (1649) 234, 236
Prussia, East 242
  could have reverted to Poland in 1618
    261–2
  intervention of Charles X 253, 270
  intervention of Gustavus Adolphus 195,
    196, 250, 268
  joins League of Torgau 120
  secularization of church property in
    31–2, 261
  to be held as a Swedish fief (1656) 271
  treaty of Wehlau confers sovereignty to
    Frederick William (1657) 272
  see also Frederick William I;
    Hohenzollern, Albrecht von

Prussia, Royal or West 257
  intervention of Charles X 270, 271
  intervention of Gustavus Adolphus 268
  population loss during war of 1654–60
    272
Pskov 264
Purgatory 15, 16, 17, 63
Puritanism 51
Putivl' 275, 279
Pyrenees, Peace of the (1659) 240–1

Qizilbash tribes 289, 292
quod principi placuit legis habet vigorem
  312

Raab, river 291
Rabelais, François (1494–1553), French
  author 65, 495
Råd, aristocratic-dominated council in
  Sweden (and Denmark) 244, 251, 254,
  266, 270, 327, 334, 336
Rada, general assembly of the Cossacks
  270, 284
Radnoth, Compact of (1656) 271
Radziwill, Bogislaw 270, 271
Raleigh, Sir Walter 142
Ranks, Table of:
  in Russia 377
  in Sweden 337, 377
Raphael (Rafaello Sanzio, 1483–1520):
  Stanze commission 478
rationalism, in Europe, rise of 512–23
Ravaillac, François, assassin of Henri IV
  225
Ravenna, battle of (1512) 88
Razin, Stepan, leader of Muscovite peasant
  rebellion 391
rebellions, peasant:
  in Austria 389–90
  in Castile 223, 391
  in Denmark (Jutland, 1534) 246
  in France 231, 388, 391–3
  in Holy Roman Empire 387, 393–7
  in Hungary 384, 387
  in Muscovy 391, 393
  in Sweden (1542–3) 247, 388–9
  in Swiss Confederation 387, 393
  see also War, German Peasants'
reconquista 90
Reformation:
  in Bohemia 55
  in Denmark 41, 245, 246
  in England 41
  in France 41–2, 50, 52–3, 164

Reformation (*cont.*)
  in Holy Roman Empire 42-3, 54-5
  in Hungary 55-6
  in Italy 58, 59-60, 61-2
  in Low Countries 53
  in Poland 55
  in Saxony 20
  in Sweden 41, 245, 246
  see also Bucer; Calvin; Calvinism;
    Luther; Lutheranism; Melanchthon;
    Oecolampadius; Zwingli
Regensburg 35, 456
  Conference or Colloquy of (1541) 29, 57
  Peace of (1630) 209
Reichsacht, see ban, Imperial
Reichshofrat, see council, Imperial aulic
Reichskammergericht, see court, supreme
  Imperial
Reichsregiment, see council, Imperial
  governing
Reichstädte, Imperial cities 94, 319
Reichstag, see diet, Imperial
Reims 64
religion, war of:
  first usage of term 118-19, 131
  see also Huguenots; League, Catholic
Remonstrant party, in the United Provinces
  182
Rémy, Nicolas, witch-hunter in Lorraine
  512
Rennes 167
Rentes de l'hôtel de ville, see annuities
reprobate 47
Requesens y Zúñiga, Luis de (1528-76),
  governor-general of the Low Countries
  (1573-6) 155, 328
resistance theory 308-12
  Calvinist 56
  Lutheran 33
Reuchlin, Johannes (1455-1522), humanist
  and Hebrew scholar 14
Reval 247, 248, 257, 263, 264
revolt, Dutch 149-55, 361
  see also States General; United
    Provinces; William I of Nassau
revolution:
  'bourgeois', Marxist concept of 361
  contemporary concept of 362-3
Rhodes 290
Riga 243, 257, 262, 264, 271, 439
Riksdag, Swedish national representative
  institution 247, 253, 268, 337, 481
  evolution of its powers 326-7
Riksråd, see Råd
Ritterschaft, Imperial knights:
  position of Franconian knights
    guaranteed by ordinance of 1590 338

seek to defend their role in government
    against princes, cities, and
    lawyers 337-8
  see also Knights' War
Robertet, Florimond (d. 1527), French
    secretary of state 333
Roe, Sir Thomas, English ambassador to
    the Ottoman court 295
Rueil, Peace of (1649), during Fronde 239
Reutlingen 33, 96
Richelieu, Armand du Plessis (1585-1642),
    Cardinal de, chief minister of Louis
    XIII (1624-42) 67, 327, 331, 332, 351,
    493
  benefices 6
  control of foreign policy after 1630 231
  cultural activities under 485
  encourages Truce of Altmark (1629) 269
  enters the king's council (1624) 227
  evolution of war ministry under 334
  first ministry (1616-17) 226
  on gold and silver 418
  governmental changes under 231
  hopes of reform dashed 232
  invades Savoy (1629-30) 209
  and Jansenism 74
  policy in Valtelline conflict 207
  postpones French entry into Thirty Years'
    War 210
  protects Bavaria 197
  repudiates Marillac's attempted
    establishment of *élections* in *pays
    d'états* 327-8
  repudiates Peace of Regensburg 209
  resentment at his control of
    governorships 236
  retention of Pinerolo 209-10
  subsidy treaty with Sweden (1631) 195,
    198-9
  survives crisis of Day of Dupes (1630)
    229
  and war by diversion 199
Riúrik dynasty 273, 274
Rochefort, baron de, spokesman of nobility
    at Estates General of 1560 168
Rocroi, battle of (1643) 212, 225, 348
Roermond 205
Rohan, Henri de, duke (1579-1638), leader
    of Huguenot rebellion 229
Rohan, René II de, Protestant nobleman
    167
Rokosz, Polish 'confederation movement' or
    noble rebellion
  enshrined in Charter of Mielnik (1501)
    258, 318, 336
  of Jerzy Lubomirski (1665-7) 285
  of Lwów (1537) 259

of Sandomierz (1606–7) 55, 267–8
Romanov dynasty 273, 279
  dynasty surrenders rights over peasantry
    to aristocracy 386
  Nikita Romanov 280
  *see also*Alexis; Filaret; Michael
    Fedorovich Romanov
Romans, Carnival at (1580) 412, 413
Rome:
  plague (1656–7) 367
  rate of increase in price of wheat at 426
  rebuilding of, under the influence of the
    Papacy 478–9
  sack of (1527) 104–5, 350, 478–9
  size of Jewish community 460
  size of population at 399
Romier, Lucien, historian 168
Ronsard, Pierre de (1525–85), poet 484
Rosas 220
Rose, Guillaume, political theorist of the
  Catholic League 311
Roskilde, Treaty of (1658) 254
Rossem, Maarten van ('Black Martin'),
  mercenary captain 113
Rostock 193
Rostov 274
Rotterdam 447
  prostitution at 493
Rouen 235, 343
  blockade of, during League 471
  fairs for bills of exchange to be settled at
    431
  falls to Henri IV 177
  Huguenot community at 167
  royal entry at 488
  workhouse 374
Rouergue:
  Croquants of (1643) 391–2
Roussillon (and Cerdagne):
  acquired by Louis XI (1462) 90
  acquired by Louis XIV (1659) 221, 240
  restored by Charles VIII (1493) 90
Rubens, Pieter-Paul (1577–1640), diplomat
  and artist at the court of Albert and
  Isabella 227, 483
Rudolf II, (1552–1612, Holy Roman
  Emperor, r. 1576–1612) 187
  conflict with Matthias 186
  court culture 480–1
  and Imperial knights 338
  intervention in Cleves-Jülich succession
    crisis 185
  King of the Romans (1575) 93
  makes Prague his capital 183
  privileges to Bohemia Jews 461
  refuses to pay tribute to Ottomans for
    Royal Hungary 298, 299

religious policy 183
Rudyerd, Sir Benjamin, English Member of
  Parliament 418
Ruiz, Simon, Spanish banker 430
Rumelia 288
Russia, *see* Muscovy
Ruthenia 271
Ruyter, Michael-Adriaanzoon van (1607–
  76), Dutch admiral 255
Ryhove, François de la Kéthulle, lord of
  (*c.*1531–85), Calvinist leader at Ghent
  157
Rzeczpospolita, see Poland

Sacraments 16, 17, 63
Sadoleto, Jacopo, bishop of Carpentras 8,
  57, 61
Safavid dynasty 286, 288, 298
  avoidance of open battle with the
    Ottomans after 1514 289
  see also Persia
St André, Jacques d'Albon, seigneur de,
  Marshal of France 128
St Augustine 9, 10, 17, 74
St Bartholomew massacres (1572) 131,
  151, 172, 308, 309, 500, 501, 507
St Cyran, Jean-Ambroise Duvergier de
  Huranne (1581–1643), abbot of 74
St Dizier 108
St Gotthard (Szentgotthárd), battle of
  (1664) 299
St Martin, feast of 496
St Paul 15, 46, 308
St Peter, and the power of the keys 18
St Peter's, Rome, rebuilding of 4, 478–9
St Quentin, battle of (1557) 127–8, 347
Saintonge, French province 392
Salamanca, during Comunero rebellion
  414
Salazar, Alonso de, Spanish inquisitor 508,
  510
Salic Law 177, 524, 527
Saluzzo (Saluces), marquisate of 128, 129
Samland, rising of (1525) 394
San Juan (Puerto Rico) 444
Sandomierz 55
  Palatine of 279
  rokosz of (1606–7) 55, 267–8
Santa Coloma, Dalmau de Queralt, count
  of, viceroy of Catalonia 219–20
Santa Cruz, marquis of, admiral 141
São Tomé 443
São Vincente 443
Sarai 242
Sardinia 92
  population density of 366
  rebellion of (1668) 224

Sarpi, Fra Paolo (1552–1623), Venetian
historian 58
Sarto, Andrea del (1486–1531) 483
Saverne, battle of (1525) 397
Savonarola, Girolamo (1452–98),
Florentine messianic preacher 7, 411,
499
Savoy 47, 128, 210, 436
annexation of Saluzzo (1588) 164
Charles III, duke 47–8, 106
Charles Emmanuel, duke 179, 209
Emmanuel Philibert (Emanuele
Filiberto) I ('Iron Head'), duke 127,
128
French invasion (1536) 106, 108, 109
French invasions (1629–30) 209
partitions Mantuan succession with
Milan 208
Victor-Amadeus I (1586–1637),
duke 209–10
war with France (1600–1) 179
wars with Milan (1613–17) 179
witchcraft in 512
Saxe-Weimar, Bernard, duke of (1604–39),
mercenary captain 200, 349, 350
captures Breisach (1638) 200, 211
Saxony, ducal (Albertine branch of the
Wettin dynasty) 10, 397
George, duke 32
Saxony, electoral (Ernestine branch of the
Wettin dynasty) 18, 29, 31, 184
Augustus I, elector 121, 151
estates of 321
Frederick III (the Wise, d. 1525), elector
12, 16, 19, 20, 396
John Frederick, elector 21, 118, 119,
120
John George (1585–1656), elector 184,
189, 191, 196–7, 201
John (the Steadfast), elector 20, 32, 33,
37, 115, 117
Maurice, first elector of Albertine branch
of the Wettin dynasty (d. 1553) 95,
119, 120, 121, 126
partition of 1485 94–5, 528
scepticism 1
Schaffhausen 39, 40
Schappeler, Christoph, joint author of
Twelve Articles of the Swabian
Peasants (1525) 395–6
Scheldt, river:
blockade of Antwerp by Leicester 162,
181
blockade of Antwerp by Parma 160
continuation of blockade by the Dutch
181, 204, 213

Schetz, Erasmus, Flemish banker 430
Scheurl, Christoph, historian of Nuremberg
404
Schiedam 447
Schleitheim Confession (1527) 23–4
Schmalkaldic League (League of
Schmalkalden 1530/1–47) 29, 30, 33,
40, 41, 43, 54, 58, 106, 117–19, 246
Schmalkaldic War (War of the League of
Schmalkalden, 1546–7) 95, 113, 119
scholasticism 10
Schoonhoven 153
Scot, Reginald, English sceptic on
witchcraft 511
Scotland 125
English coup in (1559–60) 129
Sebastian I, king of Portugal (r. 1557–78)
139
legend of his immortality ('Sebastianism')
221–2
secularization, of church property during
the Reformation 31–2
Sedan, principality of, incorporated into
France (1642) 230
Segovia, during Comunero rebellion 414
Séguier, Pierre V, seigneur d'Autry
(1577–1672), Chancellor of France
(1635–72) 332
Sehested, Hannibal, regent of Norway and
minister of Frederick III of Denmark
252, 255
Sejm, see diet, Polish
Selim I ('the Grim'), Ottoman sultan
(r. 1512–20):
aggressive attitude to Safavid state before
becoming sultan 289
captures Tabriz (1514) 289
crushes Mamluk Egypt and Syria 289–90
deposes his father, Bayezid II 288
occupies Cairo (1517) 290
Selimname 476
Selim II ('the Sot'), Ottoman sultan
(r. 1566–74) 293, 295
wins war of succession 294
seminaries 64, 69
Serbia 288, 298
serfdom:
decline in western Europe 375
extension in Hungary 384
extension in Muscovy 374, 385–6
extension in Poland 385
personal bondage (*Leibeigenschaft*) in
Germany 375
second serfdom (*Erbuntertänigkeit*) in
eastern Europe 375–6
Seripando, Girolamo, Cardinal 9, 58, 63

Serres, Olivier, seigneur du Pradel
(1539–1619), French agronomist and
author of the *Theatre of Agriculture*
468, 469
Servetus, Michael (Miguel Serveto y Reves,
1511?–53) 46, 49
Servien, Abel (1593–1659), French minister
of war (1630–6), finance minister
(1653–9) and plenipotentiary at the
Westphalian peace negotiations 212
Seven Years' War of the North (1563–70)
247–9
Seversk 285
Seville 443
fairs for bills of exchange to be settled
at 431
Seyssel, Claude de (1450–1520), bishop of
Marseille, French political theorist
306, 351, 362
Sforza dynasty, of Milan:
Francesco Sforza, duke (d. 1535) 104,
106
Ludovico, regent of Milan 84, 85
Maximilian, duke 88, 100
powers enjoyed by dynasty 134
Shiite faith 286, 292
see also Persia; Safavid dynasty
Sicily 92, 147
political control under Philip II 133, 134
rebellion (1647) 224
Sickingen, Franz von, joint leader of
Knights' War (1522–3) 20, 338
Siena 129, 499
loss of independence due to cost of war
354
Sigismund I (Zygmunt), king of Poland
(r. 1506–48) 258
concessions to the nobility on his
accession 258
obtains election of his son as successor
(1530) 259
Sigismund II ('Augustus'), last Jagiellon king
of Poland (r. 1548–72) 243, 247, 248,
273
accession without being re-elected
(1548) 260
gains sovereignty of Livonia (1561) 262
promotes Union of Lublin 260–1
seeks to consolidate Union of Lublin 263
seeks a successor 260
Sigismund III, king of Poland (r. 1587–
1632) and Sweden (Sigismund I,
r. 1592–1600)
alliance with Habsburgs 268
accession charter before coronation in
Sweden (1594) 266

arrests Filaret Romanov 280
death 269
deposed as king of Sweden 267, 526
forced to accept Statute of Kalmar
(1587) 265
forced to concede the Third Lithuanian
Statute (1588) 261
granted permission to leave Poland for
Sweden (1593) 265
heir of Anna Jagiellonka 265
invasion of Sweden fails (1598) 266–7
loss of Livonia to Sweden (1625) 268
Polish diet refuses to countenance a
second invasion of Sweden 267
political miscalculation in Muscovy 280
refuses to abandon claim to Swedish
throne 268, 269
seeks to appoint Catholic fortress
commanders in Sweden 266
two Habsburg marriages 265, 267
Silesia 190, 193, 293
Silíceo, Cardinal archbishop of Toledo 70
and *limpieza de sangre* 132
silver, search for:
dominant medium in currency
transactions by mid-sixteenth
century 421
exploitation of deposits at Potosí in Peru
420
exploitation of deposits at Zacatecas and
Guanajuato in Mexico 420
imports from the New World 420, 421
production in Europe 418–19, 421
production in Japan 449
see also America
Simiand, François, French economic
historian 417
Simons, Menno (1492–1559), Anabaptist
theologian 23, 26
rejection of the 'kingdom' of Münster 26
Sinan, Ottoman architect 476
Sixteen, *see* Council of Sixteen
Sixtus V (Felice Peretti) Pope (1585–90)
68, 71, 479
envisages beggars' hospital 374
excludes Navarre and Condé from French
succession 174
imports Baltic wheat into Papal States
370
moderation towards Jews 460
Skåne 254
slavery:
in Muscovy 374–5
in Ottoman lands 286–7
Småland rising (1542–3) 247, 388–9
Smolensk 275, 281, 348

Smolensk (*cont.*)
  captured by Muscovy: (1512) 275;
    (1654) 253, 284
  recaptured by Poland: (1611) 280–1
  transferred by Truce of Andrusovo to
    Muscovy 285
Södermanland, duchy of 248
Soissons, Louis II de Bourbon, comte de
    (1604–41) 230
Sokollu Mehmed Pasha, grand vizier of
    three Ottoman sultans (r. 1565–79)
    294, 297
Sola scriptura 12
Sologne:
  rebellion of Sabotiers in (1658) 392
Somerset, Edward Seymour, duke of
    (1500–52), Lord Protector 125
Sorbonne, Faculty of theology of the
    University of Paris 13, 14, 41, 65, 70
  pronounces on the almonry scheme at
    Ypres 373
  pronounces deposition of Henri III 176
  rejects formula of Colloquy of Poissy
    166
sorcery:
  and plague 368, 504
  see also witchcraft
Soriano, Venetian ambassador to Spain
    130
Sosnówka, battle of (1659) 285
Soubise, Protestant nobleman 167
Sound (Sund), Danish 199, 243
  Charles X seeks half the value of tolls
    254
  Sweden gains permanent exemption 252
  tolls increased by Christian II 244
  tolls levied by Danish king from fifteenth
    century 243
  United Provinces purchase temporary
    exemption 252
  see also Christian IV
sovereign courts, in France, see *Parlements*
sovereignty:
  of the Baltic 268
  in East Prussia 272
  in the Holy Roman Empire 201
  in the Spanish Netherlands 180, 204
  in the United Provinces 162, 180–1, 213,
    406
Spain 130
  abdication of Charles V 123
  agricultural production in 471
  bullion imports 136, 215, 218, 223
  censorship 65–6
  concept of decline (*declinación*) 214–15
  growing imbalance between Castile and
    other territories 216

and 'profit inflation thesis' 427–8
support for Imperial position in Thirty
    Years' War 203, 206
transatlantic commerce 215
triple invasion of France (1636–7)
    210–11
weakness of navy 206
  see also Aragon; Castile; Catalonia
'Spanish Fury' (1576) 156
Sparre, Erik, aristocratic opponent of
    Charles IX and Swedish political
    theorist 266, 267, 326
spices, trade in 418, 440
  nutmeg, mace, and cloves 442, 450
  pepper 432, 442, 451
Spínola, Ambrogio (1569–1630), marquis of
    Los Balbases, Spanish general
  besieges Bergen-op-Zoom (1622) 204,
    348
  captures Breda (1625) 204–5, 211, 348
  invades Jülich, Cleves, and Mark (1621)
    186, 204
  occupies Lower Palatinate 191
  seizes Wesel 185, 186
  supports truce with Dutch 180
  threatens Gelderland and Overijssel 186
Spínola, Lorenzo, financier of Philip II 358
spirituali 58, 59, 61, 63
Split 460
Sprenger, Jacobus, witch-hunter 502
Staden, Heinrich von, German mercenary
    captain 276
Stadholder (*stadhouder*) in the Low
    Countries 146
starostas, Polish captains-general 259
States General of the Low Countries,
    representative institution of the
    Burgundian provinces 112, 113
  appoints Orange as provisional governor
    of Brabant 157
  coup d'état of 1576 156, 328
  deposes Don John of Austria 157
  invitation to archduke Matthias 157
  negotiations with Don John of Austria
    157
  number of sessions (1499–1576) 317
  after partition (1579), *see* States General
    of the Spanish Netherlands; States
    General of the United Provinces
States General of the Spanish Netherlands:
  diminished role after revolt and partition
    159, 328
States General of the United Provinces:
  Act of Dismissal of Philip II (1581) 155,
    526
  assert principle of free navigation in
    Baltic 448

assert their sovereignty (1590) 162
Batavian culture 492
Bodin on weakness of 322
establish charters for East and West India
   Companies 450, 451–2
gain central position in the constitution
   329–30
Henri IV on weaknesses of 161
judge Oldenbarnevelt (1619) 182
political role in negotiations with Anjou
   526–7
reassert terms of treaty of Brömsebro
   253
'states system', theory of, after Peace of
   Westphalia 531
Staupitz, Johann von 9, 17
Steen, Jan, Dutch artist 493
Stettin 202
   Peace of (1570) 248–9
Stockholm:
   bloodbath of Stockholm (1520) 244
stoicism 314
Stolbova, Peace of (1617) 250, 281
Strafford, Thomas Wentworth, earl of
   (d. 1641) 234
Stralsund, siege of 193–4
Strasbourg (or Strassburg until 1681) 6, 7,
   24, 26, 28, 31, 39, 117, 164, 202
   Academy at 54
   poor relief 373
   population figures 399
Strigel, Bernhard, Habsburg court painter
   98
Strozzi, Florentine banking family 430
Stühlingen 393
Stuhlweissenburg 291
Stuhmdorf, Truce of (1635) 269, 270
Sture family, in Sweden 248
subsistence crisis, *see* crisis, subsistence
Süleyman I ('the law-giver', called in the
   west 'the Magnificent'), Ottoman sultan
   (r. 1520–66):
   achievement 294, 300
   captures Belgrade and Rhodes 290–1
   crushes Jagiellon Hungary at Mohácz
     (1526) 242–3, 259, 291, 476
   cultural achievement at his court 475–6
   executes his eldest son, Mustafa 294
   as law-giver 290
   leads seven campaigns in Hungary 294
   leads thirteen campaigns in person 290
   relative loyalty to grand viziers 294
   Süleymanname 476
Sully, Maximilien de Bethune, baron de
   Rosny, duke of (1559–1641):
   establishes the *droit annuel* or
     paulette 342

finance minister of Henri IV
   (1598–1611) 179, 226, 334, 341
sumptuary laws 416
Sundgau 202
Sunni Moslems 286, 289
Swabia, Upper, in German Peasants' War
   394, 395
Twelve Articles of the Swabian Peasants
   (1525) 395–6
Swabian League 20, 95–6, 119, 396, 397
Sweden:
   acquires Estonia 247–9, 439
   acquires Halland (1645) 199
   acquires Livonia (1625) 268
   acquires western (Swedish) Pomerania
     (1648) 201, 202
   advantageous peace with Muscovy (1617)
     250, 281
   alliance with Denmark to provision
     Stralsund 193
   alliances with France 108, 247
   allodial tenants (*skattebönder*) 381, 388
   aristocratic rebellion (1568) 248
   aristocratic revenge after Charles IX's
     death 249
   army 346
   arrears of army pay subsidized after
     Peace of Westphalia 202
   attacks Poland: (1600) 267; (1621) 250,
     268; (1655) 270–1
   becomes a German power after Peace of
     Westphalia 202, 252
   collegiate system of government
     established 334
   deposition of Sigismund (1599) 267
   disastrous peace of 1570 248–9
   early fiscal measures 246
   early Reformation in 41, 245, 246
   evolution of monarchical power in 256
   fears Dutch economic supremacy less
     than English or French 453–4
   'free' monarchy within Bodin's definition
     300
   free tenants (*landbor*) 381
   gains 'permanent' exemption from Danish
     Sound tolls 252
   gains temporary exemption from Danish
     Sound tolls 243
   Gothic myth 378
   inability to pay for foreign warfare 195
   Lutheran settlement confirmed (1593)
     266
   Lutheran settlement consolidated by
     Charles IX's victory over Sigismund
     267
   mutiny of army 198
   native conscript army 247

Sweden (*cont.*)
  nobility 256, 377
  peasant rebellion (1542–3) 247, 388–9
  peasantry 381–2
  population 195, 256–7
  population estimates (with Denmark)
    365
  pre-emptive war against Denmark
    considered 250; launched (1643–5)
    199, 251; considered again (1654) 253;
    launched (1658) 255
  protection to Jews in the Empire 461
  revenues from tolls on Baltic ports 250
  rise of naval power 247, 251, 257
  satisfactory peace treaties with Denmark:
    (1645) 251–2; (1658) 254; (1660)
    255
  Succession Pact (1544) 247
  unpunished by Poland for Charles X's
    aggression 272
  unsatisfactory peace treaties with
    Denmark: (1570) 248–9; (1613)
    249–50
  war with Muscovy 249
  see also Altmark, Truce of; Brömsebro,
    Peace of; Charles IX; Charles X;
    Charles XI; Christina; Copenhagen,
    Peace of; Erick XIV; Estonia; Form of
    Government; Gustavus Adolphus;
    Gustavus Eriksson Vasa; Ingria; John
    III; Kardis, Peace of; Karelia; Knäred,
    Peace of; Oliva, Peace of; Oxenstierna;
    Råd; *Riksdag*; Roskilde, Peace of;
    Sigismund III; Stettin, Peace of;
    Stolbova, Peace of; Stuhmdorf, Truce
    of; Valiessar, Truce of; Westphalia,
    Peace of
Swiss Confederation 38–40, 95
  central cantons relatively untouched by
    German Peasants' War 394
  pikemen 90
  revolt of 1653 against debased currency
    387
  role of Swiss as mercenaries 84, 88, 99,
    100, 101, 350, 351
  witchcraft in 512
Sylvester, priest, adviser to Ivan IV 276
Synod of Dort (Dordrecht):
    (1574) 373, 457
    (1618–19) 50, 52, 182
Synod of Emden (1571) 50
Synod of La Rochelle (1571) 50, 170
Synod of Utrecht (1655) 496
Syria 289, 290, 300, 440
  see also Selim I
szlachta, nobility in Poland 258, 259, 268,
    273, 282

Tabriz 298
  Ottoman conquests of 289, 292, 297
Tahmasp, Shah of Persia (d. 1576) 292, 297
taille, chief direct tax, in France 231,
    353–4, 388, 392
  anticipated by d'Hémery 233, 354
Taiwan 451
Tardif, Jean, councillor of the *Parlement* of
    Paris, executed by the Catholic League
    411
Tarragona 220
Tartaglia, Niccolò, theoretician of ballistics
    518
Tatars 259, 264, 277, 278, 281, 283, 401
Te Deum, celebratory Mass, in France 489
Temesvar 293
Temple, Sir William, English ambassador
    and political commentator on the
    United Provinces 330, 405, 406
Tenth Penny 152
tercios 87
Termonde 159
Ternate 450
Tessin, Nicodemus, the younger (1654–
    1728), Swedish architect 485
Tetrapolitan Confession 28
Tetzel, Johann 5, 16
Thirteen Years' War (1593–1606) 56, 138,
    198–9
Thomar 139
Thou, François-Auguste de, baron de Meslé
    (1607–42) 230
Thuringia, during German Peasants' War
    395, 397
Thurn, Matthias, count, generalissimo of
    Bohemian rebellion 189, 190
Ticino, river 347
Tidora 450
Tilly, Jean Tserclaes, count of (1559–1632),
    commander of the Catholic League for
    Maximilian of Bavaria 191, 192
  at Breitenfeld 346, 348
  required to keep Catholic League and
    Habsburg armies separate 195
'Time of Troubles' 273, 278–81, 385, 401
  see also Muscovy
Tisza river 384
tithe farmers 470
tithe yields, evidence of 469–71
Titian (Tiziano Vicelli, *c.*1490–1576), artist
    at the court of Charles V and Philip II
    480, 482
Toledo 8
  beggars' hospitals 374
  during revolt of the Comuneros 111, 414
  food ration at 372
  population figures 400

Toledo, Pedro de, viceroy of Charles V in
  Naples (1532–53) 116
  aphorism of 134
Tordesillas 91, 111
  Treaty of (1494) 441
Torgau, Lutheran league of (1552) 43, 120,
  126
Torre, Fernando Mascarenhas, count of,
  Spanish admiral 211
Torstennson, Lennart (1603–51), count of
  Ortala, Swedish general 199, 200, 251
Torun 402
Toul 126, 128, 202
Toulouse:
  Carnival at 496
  Huguenot rebellion at (1562) 167
  municipal office not ennobling until
    1675 405
  Parlement of 167
  riot at attributed to prediction of
    Nostradamus 500
  strength of League at 175, 177
Tournai 105, 113, 150
Tournon, François de (1489–1562),
  Cardinal 108, 125
Transylvania, Ottoman tributary state of
  243, 293, 294, 298, 300
  diet of 318
  voivode Apafi, Mihály I 299
  voivode Bátory, Stefan 56
  voivode Bocskai, István 56
  voivode Gábor, Bethlen (1613–29) 56
  voivode Rákóczi, György II 271, 299
  voivode Zápolyai, John Sigismund 293
Trastámara dynasty 89, 92
  see also Aragon; Castile
Trebizond 289
Trenchant, Jean, writer on monetary
  exchange 423
Trent, Council of, *see* Council of Trent
Trentino 436
Trésorier de l'Épargne, chief Treasurer in
  France 102
  effect of proliferation of offices 342–3
Trier, electorate of 68, 94
  Spanish arrest of elector Philip
    Christopher von Sötern 210
Trincomalee 451
Tripoli 137
Tromp, Maarten Harpetszoon (1597–1653),
  Dutch admiral 211
Trondheim 247, 254
Truchsess von Walburg, Gerhard,
  archbishop of Cologne 183
Tsar, of Muscovy:
  limitation of power according to nature of
    land tenure 385

religious pretension 274
  see also Muscovy
Tula 279
Tunis 117, 137, 138
Turcoman tribes 292
Turenne, Henri de la Tour d'Auvergne,
  vicomte de (1611–75), French
  general 199, 200
  abandons Fronde 237
Turin 374
Turks, Ottoman, *see* Ottoman state
Tuscany 382
Tver' 274
Twelve Years' Truce (1609–21) 181,
  203–4, 447
tyrannicide 71
Tyrol 96, 113, 126
Tyrone, Hugh O'Neill, earl of 143

Uceda, Cristóbal de Sandoval, Rojas y de la
  Cerda, first duke of 217
Ukraine 281, 282, 524
  partition of (1667) 285
  see also Chmielnicki
Ulpian, third-century jurist 312
Uniate church, *see* Poland
Union of Arms (1625), scheme propounded
  by Olivares 217–18
Union of Arras (1579) 158
Union of Kalmar (1397–1523),
  Scandinavian union of the crowns of
  Denmark, Norway, Sweden and
  Finland 243–4, 249, 255
Union of Lublin (1569) 260–1, 319
Union, Protestant, in Germany 184, 185,
  191
Union of Utrecht (1579) 155, 181, 182,
  328, 329
United Provinces 53
  apogee of Baltic trade 448–9
  Arctic trade with Muscovy 448
  army 346
  bread riots in 405
  Calvinist attitude to money-lending in
    457
  Calvinist emigration from southern
    provinces 163
  Calvinist organization of poor relief 373
  colonial advance in Brazil 205
  commercial interests threatened by
    Charles X of Sweden 253, 254, 255,
    449, 530
  commercial prosperity at time of
    European depression 417
  comparison between prosperous Dutch
    and poor French peasantry 472–3

United Provinces (*cont.*)
  concessions obtained from Denmark
    252, 449, 530
  conditional recognition of sovereignty
    (1607) 180
  constitution 181, 329–30
  de facto independence (1609) 181
  defensive leagues with England and
    France (1608) 181
  denial of Catholic rights of worship 154,
    204, 213
  difficulties in Baltic grain supply in
    1650s 272
  dominance of salt, wine, and fish trades
    447–8
  East India Company (VOC, founded
    1602) 180–1, 442, 449–51
  efficiency of shipbuilding industry 446
  emergence of a distinctive culture 455,
    492–3
  evolution of Dutch trade 445–54
  exploit commercial possibilities of peace
    of 1648 213
  fears of partition of Spanish Netherlands
    212
  fifteen-year defence pact with Sweden
    (1614) 250, 448
  harvest failures in 369
  immigration from the south as a factor in
    economic growth 455
  importance of agricultural efficiency for
    the economy in general 472
  impose embargoes in retaliation to
    Spanish embargoes 205
  interest rates in 448, 457
  intervention in Cleves-Jülich succession
    crisis 185
  join the alliance of The Hague (1625)
    193
  manifesto to Spanish Netherlands 205–6
  mercantilist attitude 453–4
  municipal offices not sold in 405
  neutrality in main European conflicts
    after 1648 214, 453
  number of Baltic sailings 448
  political conflict of 1648–50 213–14
  political system after republic established
    329–30
  population estimates (with Spanish
    Netherlands) 365
  protect Hanseatic trading interests in
    seventeenth century 250
  purchase temporary exemption from
    Sound tolls 252
  receive subsidy from France 206
  reduced freight costs 447
  regent regime 330, 405–7
  resistance encouraged by defeat of
    Armada 143
  rise of 'intensive husbandry' 370
  secure Baltic trading interests at Peace of
    Knäred (1613) 250, 448
  Sephardi Jewish community in 451, 462
  ships transport Spanish American silver
    north after 1648 437–8
  size of urban population (with Spanish
    Netherlands) 398
  speculative art market in 493
  superior design of the fluyt 446–7
  territorial gains (1648) 213
  textile industry 452–3
  Vranck on location of sovereignty 406
  wage rates and capital accumulation 428
  war with France (1672–8) 214
  wars with England: (1652–4) 214, 449;
    (1665–7) 214; (1672–4) 214
  West India Company (WIC) 180, 181,
    204, 451–2
  written constitution 359
  see also Amsterdam; Holland; Low
    Countries; Orange-Nassau dynasty;
    Union of Utrecht
Universities 9-10
  in Aragon and Castile 339
  in the Empire 337
  see also Cologne; Heidelberg; Louvain;
    Marburg; Sorbonne (Faculty of
    Theology of University of Paris);
    Wittenberg
Uppsala 244
Urban VIII (Maffeo Barberini), Pope
    (1623–44) 68, 74, 210
  Baroque court culture under 479
  initial tolerance towards the Copernican
    system 519–20
Urbanization, *see* cities, European
Ushviata 265
Uskoks 179, 298
Usury 455–8
Utrecht 113, 149, 329
  base of Leicester's power 162
  favours peace 181
  joins Union of Utrecht (1579) 155
  opposes trial of Oldenbarnevelt 182
  see also Union of Utrecht
Uyttenbogaert, Johannes, leader of
    Remonstrant party 182

Valdés, Juan de (d. 1541) 13, 59
Valencia, kingdom of 145, 211
  Cortes 216, 324
  fueros 217
  importation of wheat from Sicily 370
  Moriscos in 130

peasant sharecroppers in 382
rate of increase in price of wheat in 425,
426
unrest in 140
viceroyalty 92
Valenciennes 150
battle of (1656) 240
Valerius, Adriaan, historian of the United
Provinces 492
Valiessar, Truce of (1659) 284
Valladolid 482
Chancellería 339
diet of population 369
during Comunero rebellion 415
population figures 400
Valois dynasty:
crisis in succession after 1584 174, 528
struggle between French and Burgundian
branches of dynasty in fifteenth century
528
succession problems before 1584 129
see also Anjou; Charles VII; Charles VIII;
Charles IX; Francis I; Francis II; Henri
II; Henri III; Louis XI; Louis XII
Valona 460
Valtelline, passes 206–8, 227, 228
Várad (Grosswardein) 300
Varberg 247, 248
Vargas, Alonso de, Castilian commander
144
Vasa dynasty, in Sweden and Poland 255,
256
Vasilii III, Tsar of Muscovy (r. 1505–33)
273, 275, 276
alliance with Christian II of Denmark
244
attacks Lithuania 275
captures Smolensk (1514) 275
duma under 335
Vasilii Shuiskii, Tsar of Muscovy
(r. 1606–10) 279–80, 281, 391
Vassy, massacre at (1562) 166
Vasvár, Peace of (1664) 300
Vauban, Sébastien Le Prestre, seigneur de
(1633–1707), fortifications specialist
and fiscal reformer 469
Vaucelles, Truce of (1556) 126, 127
Vázquez, Mateo, de Leca, secretary to
Philip II (1573–92) 135, 142
Velázquez, governor of Cuba 444
Velázquez y Silva, Diego Rodriguez de
(1599–1660), great Spanish artist 205,
483
Veliki Luki 264
Velizh 265
venality, *see* Castile, sale of offices; France,
sale of offices

Venice 221, 438, 446
annexation of Gorizia, Trieste, and Istria
87
beggars' hospitals 374
Catholic charitable trusts (*Monti di
Pieta*) 460
closed urban nobility 403–4
constitution 403
cost of war against the Austrian
Habsburgs (1615–17) 354
cost of wars against Turks 354
crusade indulgences 130
currency 436
defeat at Agnadello (1509) in war of
League of Cambrai 87, 403, 440
early recourse to public credit 355
ennoblement at 403–4
evolution of policy towards the Jews at
460
foreign policy 85, 87, 99, 104, 138, 179
guild confraternities (*scuole*) 463–4
guilds 441, 464, 465, 466
heresy at 61
Interdict (1606–7) 71, 403, 491–2
Jewish ghetto established (1516) 460
legislation concerning vagrancy 372
life annuities at 355
merchant bankers oppose location of
fairs in Genoese territory 437
plague (1575–6, 1630–1) 367
role in exporting European silver in
return for spices from Far East 418–19
role in Mantuan conflict 209
role in Valtelline conflict 207–8
size of population 399
structure of municipal councils 403
urban culture at 490–1
wars with Ottoman Turks: (1463–79)
288; (1499–1502) 85, 288;
(1538–40) 292; (1571–3) 68, 138;
(1645–69) 299, 440
woollen industry 440–1
see also Inquisition, Venetian
Venlo 205
Verböczi, István, theoretician of
aristocratic-dominanted constitution in
Hungary 378
Verden 194, 199, 202, 251
Verdun 126, 128, 202
Vermigli, Peter Martyr 59
Verona:
population density 366
Versailles 482, 485, 489
Vervins, Peace of (1598) 163, 179, 180
Vesalius, Andreas (1514–64), anatomist
495, 514
Vianen 150

Viatis, Bartolomäus, merchant of
    Nuremberg and textile manufacturer
    467
Vic 229
Vicenza:
    population density 366
viceroyalties, Spanish system of 92, 116,
    134
Vienna 481
    Jewish community at 461
    siege of (1529) 32–3, 291
    siege of (1683) 300
Vienne, Philibert de 475
Viglius, Johann ab Aytta van Zwichem
    (1507–77), president of the privy
    council in the Netherlands 146, 148
village:
    charters (*Weistümer*) 376
    communal lands, in Castile 379
    community 387
Villalar, battle of (1521) 111, 415
Villaviciosa, battle of (1665) 222
Villers-Cotterêts, edict of (1539) 363
Vilna (Vilnius) 260, 284
Vincent de Paul, St (1581–1660), French
    Catholic reformer 73
Vistula, river 268, 269
    role of Jews in trade 462
    trade in grain 257, 272
Viteazul, Mihai, *voivode* of Wallachia 298
Vives, Juan Luis (1492–1540), Spanish
    émigré humanist 373
Vizcaya 508
Vladimir of Staritsa, prince, rival to Ivan IV
    276
Volokolamsk, Muscovy:
    rate of increase in price of rye at 426
Voltaire, quoted 429
Vranck (Francken), Francis (c.1555–1617),
    pensionary of the town of Gouda, on
    location of sovereignty in the United
    Provinces 406
Vries, Johan de, historian of urban
    population:
    calculations of the urban population in
        Europe 398
    population estimates for certain
        European countries 365
Vulgate, *see* Bible

wage rates 371, 426–8
Waldensian heresy 7, 502
Wallachia, Ottoman tributary state 288,
    294, 298
    see also Viteazul, Mihai

Wallenstein, Albrecht von (Waldstein,
    1579–1634), duke of Friedland,
    Imperial generalissimo 189, 192, 193,
    194, 197, 269
    acquires Mecklenburg 193
    assassination 198, 350
    Imperial admiral 193
    logistical genius 349
Wallerstein, Immanuel, American economic
    historian 417–18
Walloon:
    provinces 158
    troops, in Spanish army: propensity to
        mutiny 350–1
War, German Peasants' (1524–6) 20–1, 96,
    415, 416, 455
    anti-clericalism in 395–6
    defeat and repression 397
    diversity of lands affected 394–5
    failure to secure alliance with towns 395
    influence of Zwinglian preachers 395
    partible inheritance and 395
    political weakness in the Empire a factor
        in early success 396
    regional character of peasant demands
        396
    serfdom and 394–5, 396
    six rebel armies 394
    system of military service 394
    Twelve Articles of the Swabian Peasants
        (1525) 395–6
War of Kalmar (1611–13) 249–50
Warnemünde 202
Warsaw 271
    Confederation of (1573) 257, 263
    population of 257, 272, 402
Wehlau, Treaty of (1657) 272
Weiss, Hans, refusal to attend Communion
    (1587) 498–9
Weissenstein 263, 264
Wesel 153, 185, 186, 205
Wesel, Johann Ruchrath von, cathedral
    preacher at Worms 7
Weser, river 193
Wesselényi conspiracy (1670), in Royal
    Hungary 300
Westminster, Treaty of (1655) 240
Westphal, Joachim, Lutheran polemicist at
    Hamburg 29, 46
Westphalia, Peace of (1648) 68–9, 200–2,
    252, 531
    and role of Imperial diet 201, 320
Wettin dynasty, see Saxony
Weyer, Johann, Cleves physician and
    sceptic on witchcraft 511
White Mountain (Bílá Hora), battle of
    (1620) 191

Whitelocke, Bulstrode, English ambassador
    to Sweden 253
Whitgift, John (1532–1604), Master of
    Trinity College, Cambridge, and later
    archbishop of Canterbury 51
Wiellinger, Achaz, joint leader of peasant
    rebellion in Austria 389
William I of Nassau, prince of Orange
    ('William the Silent', 1533–84),
    stadholder of Holland, Zeeland, and
    Utrecht 146, 147, 148, 170
  advised by Marnix 526
  Apology (1581) 159
  assassination (1584) 159–60
  becomes a Calvinist (1573) 154
  defeatism in United Provinces after his
    death 161
  edict of proscription (1580) 159
  failure of alliance with Anjou 159
  'father of the fatherland' 153
  floods the dykes 154
  hesitates at Union of Utrecht (1579) 155
  invades Low Countries (1572) 152
  leads exiles in Germany 151
  letters of marque to Sea Beggars 153
  objective of religious peace
    (*Religionsvrede*) 158, 409
  provisional governor of Brabant 157
  rebel stadholder of Holland, Zeeland,
    and Utrecht 154
  resigns offices 150
  Saxon/Lutheran marriage 146
  supports States General after *coup d'état*
    of 1576 156
William II of Nassau (1626–50), prince of
    Orange, son of Frederick Henry,
    captain-general and stadholder in the
    United Provinces
  attempted *coup d'état* (1650) 213–14
  brother-in-law of Charles II 213
  favours war with Spain 213, 238
William III of Nassau (1650–1702), prince
    of Orange, posthumous son of William
    II, captain-general and stadholder in
    the United Provinces, and later king of
    England 214
William Frederick of Nassau, count, cousin
    of William II 213
Willoughby, English commander in the
    United Provinces 162
Wismar 193, 202, 440
Wisniowiecki, Jarema, governor of
    Ruthenia 283
witchcraft, crime of 502–12
  Bible and 505
  borderland regions and 512
  changes in social attitudes reduce
    allegations of 512

crimen exceptum 505
  distinction between manipulative sorcery
    and diabolism 503
  incubi and *succubi* 502, 503
  nocturnal meetings with Devil ('sabbats')
    502
  penalties for frivolous or malicious
    accusations reduced 506
  'plague-spreaders' (*engraisseurs*) 504
  'prestidigitation' 503
  rise of scepticism concerning accusations
    of 509–12
  role of score settling in witchcraft
    allegations 509
  witchbeaters (Benandanti) 509
  see also *Malleus maleficarum*; *Parlement*
    of Paris; Salazar
Witt, Johan de (1625–72), councillor
    pensionary to the states of Holland
    (1653–72) 214, 329, 405
Wittelsbach dynasty 95, 183
  and Edict of Restitution 194
  see also Bavaria; Cologne; Palatinate
Wittenberg 28, 29, 504
  University of 14, 16, 37
Wolff, Hans 22
Wolsey, Thomas (*c.*1473–1530), Chancellor
    of England and Cardinal 101
women:
  prosecutions against, for premeditated
    infanticide 507
  widows and unmarried women 509
Wooton, Sir Henry 491
Worms, anti-Jewish riots at (1614) 461
Worms, diet of (1521), *see* diet, Imperial
Worms, edict of (1521) 30, 526
  modification revoked (1529) 32
  modified (1526) 32
  threat to enforce edict in the Empire
    (1530) 33
Wrangel, Carl Gustaf (1613–76), count,
    Swedish general 200, 485
Wullenweber, Jürgen, leader of Lübeck 246
Württemberg, duchy of 201, 495, 496
  acquisition by Habsburgs (1520) 96
  death of duke Ulrich (1550) 32
  duke John Frederick 184
  estates of 321
  expulsion of duke Ulrich (1519) 96
  Lutheran Reformation established 117
  'poor Conrad' movement (1514) 393
  population loss 203
  restoration of duke Ulrich (1534) 117
  secularization of church property in 32
  spread of German Peasants' War in 396
Würzburg, bishop of 338
Wyatt, Sir Thomas (1520?–54) 123
Wyhowski, Ivan, Cossack leader 284

Xanten, Treaty of (1614) 185
Xavier, St Francis (1505–62) 72

Yam Zapolski, Truce of (1582) 264
Yaroslavl' 274
Yemen 290
Ypres 157
  poor relief 373

Zaganuz Pasha, grand vizier of Mehmed II
  287
Zamoyski, Jan (d. 1605), Chancellor of
  Poland 265, 267
  encourages Jewish settlement 462
  opinion of Sigismund III 265
Zápolyai, *voivodes* of Transylvania
  voivode John 98, 291, 293
  voivode John Sigismund 260, 293
  see also Transylvania
Zaporoze, Sicz of (Zaporozhian Host) 282
  see also Chmielnicki, Bogdan and George
Zaragoza 8, 144, 145
Zebrzydowski, Michael, Palatine of Cracow
  and leader of *rokosz* of 1605 267
Zeeland 146, 154
  favours war 181
  flax-growing 472
  joins Union of Utrecht (1579) 155
  opposition to peace treaties of 1648 and
    1661 329
  and Pacification of Ghent 157
  rebellion (1572) 154, 156
  share capital in East and West India
    Companies 450, 451–2
  ship-ownership in 447
Zeller, Christoph, joint leader of peasant
  rebellion in Austria 389
Zemshchina, area of Muscovy not in Tsar's
  'separate estate' 276–7
Zemskii sobor, see Assembly of the Land

Zichem, mutiny at 350, 351
Zierikzee 154, 156, 447
Zólkiewski, Stanislas, Polish general 268,
  280
Zrinyi, Miklós, leader of Transylvanian
  resistance to closer Ottoman rule 299
Zsitva-Török, Peace of (1606) 299
Zúñiga, Baltasar de (1561–1622) 217
Zúñiga, Juan de, secretary to Philip II 135
Zurbarán, Francisco de, artist under Philip
  IV 483
Zurich 22, 23, 28, 31, 38, 39, 55
  accepts Calvinism (1560) 39, 49
  refusal to adhere to Schmalkaldic League
    117
Zusmarshausen, battle of (1648) 200
Zutphen 154
Zwingli, Huldrych (1484–1531), Protestant
  reformer at Zurich:
  and civil society 23
  and Eucharist 28, 38
  and infant baptism 22–3, 39
  and original sin 19
  death 28, 40
  denounces Luther 28
  early career 38
  Fidei ratio (Zwingli's Confession of faith)
    28
  German prose style 35
  influence on Calvin 44
  influences: of Erasmus 13; of Hoen 28
  search for alliance against Charles V 39
  see also Bullinger; Zurich
Zwinglians/Zwinglianism:
  appeal to south German cities 39, 54
  in France 41
  refusal of Zwinglians to adhere to
    Confession of Augsburg 29
  refusal of Zwinglians to adhere to
    Schmalkaldic League 117